U.S.–Soviet
Security Cooperation

U.S.–Soviet Security Cooperation

ACHIEVEMENTS, FAILURES, LESSONS

Edited by
Alexander L. George
Philip J. Farley
Alexander Dallin

New York   Oxford
OXFORD UNIVERSITY PRESS
1988

Oxford University Press

Oxford   New York   Toronto
Delhi   Bombay   Calcutta   Madras   Karachi
Petaling Jaya   Singapore   Hong Kong   Tokyo
Nairobi   Dar es Salaam   Cape Town
Melbourne   Auckland
and associated companies in
Beirut   Berlin   Ibadan   Nicosia

Copyright © 1988 by Oxford University Press, Inc.

Published by Oxford University Press, Inc.,
200 Madison Avenue, New York, New York 10016
Oxford is a registered trademark of Oxford University Press

Library of Congress Cataloging-in-Publication Data

U.S.–Soviet security cooperation.

Includes index.
1. Arms control.   2. United States—Foreign
relations—Soviet Union.   3. Soviet Union—
Foreign relations—United States.   I. George,
Alexander L.   II. Farley, Philip J., 1916–
III. Dallin, Alexander   IV. U.S.–Soviet security
cooperation.
JX1974.U84   1988   327.73047   87-24788
ISBN 0-19-505397-4
ISBN 0-19-505398-2 (pbk.)

2 4 6 8 9 7 5 3 1

Printed in the United States of America
on acid-free paper

To Julie, in celebration of April 20, 1948.

A.L.G.

To Gerard C. Smith, with whom most of this history
is shared experience.

P.J.F.

To those who taught me about Russia and America.

A.D.

Preface

This book provides the first comprehensive and systematic study of the efforts the United States and the Soviet Union have made since World War II to develop and carry out cooperative arrangements to improve their own security and that of other nations. It includes twenty-two case studies of U.S.–Soviet efforts to deal with European security issues, arms control, and regional and international security problems. Each case study has been written by a highly qualified specialist who comes to the task either with relevant experience in international affairs or an academic research background.

The study, initiated in October 1985, was organized and directed by Alexander George, with the assistance of Philip J. Farley and Alexander Dallin. As coeditors of the volume, Dallin was primarily responsible for supervising the case studies that appear in Part Two, Farley for those in Part Three, and George for case studies in Part Four.

When we initiated the project, our aim was to do as good a study as possible in two years' time in order to make the results available on a timely basis to the larger audience of policymakers and scholars who have a special interest in this subject. We hope that our book will stimulate serious discussion, reflection, and additional research on U.S.–Soviet efforts to find ways of cooperating in order to enhance security. In addition, many of the chapters may prove of interest to thoughtful citizens seeking to reach their own judgments as to the feasibility, risk, and potential value of such difficult cooperation.

This new book is a follow-up to the collaborative volume entitled *Managing U.S.–Soviet Rivalry: Problems of Crisis Prevention* (1983), which Alexander George organized and edited. That book triggered a series of meetings and joint research activities (still ongoing) between a group of American specialists and Soviet academicians, sponsored by the International Research and Exchanges Board (IREX) on the subject of avoiding crises. The present book, it is hoped, will also stimulate discussions with Soviet academicians and functionaries on the subject of security cooperation.

We would like to express deep appreciation to our collaborators not merely for their invaluable contributions to the volume but also for the enthusiasm with which they endorsed the importance and timeliness of this study. Each of the case studies they have provided stands on its own and makes a distinctive contribution to understanding the conditions under which security cooperation does or does not take place. In Part Five we have attempted to extract from the twenty-two case studies some broader implications and generalizations about the problems and prospects for U.S.–Soviet security cooperation and to place these observations in a theoretical as well as a policy framework. While the case studies have contributed significantly to what we present in Part Five, the individual authors of these case studies do not bear any responsibility for the analysis presented in Part Five or in the Epilogue.

We also want to thank Professor Raimo Väyrynen (University of Helsinki) and Dr. Harald Müller (Peace Research Institute, Frankfurt) for participating in the authors' conference in May 1986 and for their helpful written commentaries.

We would like to express our appreciation to those who funded the project. Basic support was provided by The Ford Foundation. Supplementary grants were received from The Rockefeller Foundation (for the authors' conference and for participation by Professor Väyrynen and Dr. Müller), The Carnegie Corporation of New York, The Center for International Security and Arms Control (Stanford University), and the Berkeley-Stanford Program on Soviet International Behavior. Alexander George would also like to express his appreciation to the John T. and Catherine T. MacArthur Foundation for its award of a prize fellowship for 1983–88.

We deeply appreciate the enormously helpful administrative services provided by Arlee Ellis, the highly professional editing of the entire manuscript by Rachelle Marshall, the ever-efficient and cheerful typing and secretarial services of Willa Leonard, and the services of Eliska Ryznar, who had the challenging task of preparing the index.

Stanford, Calif.   A.L.G.
July 1987   P.J.F.
         A.D.

Contents

    Philip J. Farley
29 Strategies for Facilitating Cooperation   692
    Alexander L. George

    Epilogue: Perspectives   712
    Appendix   723
    Contributors   727
    Index   735

I

THE STRUCTURE
AND PLAN OF THE STUDY

1

Research Objectives and Methods

The starting point of this study is the hypothesis that the United States and the Soviet Union perceive that they have a strong interest in managing their rivalry in order to control its costs and risks. This shared interest, we believe, is coupled with a more diffuse recognition of two other goals: namely, the desirability of developing over time a more cooperative, orderly, and stable U.S.–Soviet relationship, and regional and global institutions and arrangements that create some additional order in the international system from which the two superpowers benefit at least indirectly. However, although the United States and the Soviet Union may subscribe to these longer-range goals, they have rather amorphous and somewhat divergent conceptions of what the norms, "rules," and modalities of a more cooperative relationship and a better structured international system should be. Awareness of these differences can only have been heightened as a result of the abortive experiment in détente launched by Richard Nixon and Leonid Brezhnev in the early 1970s.[1]

It should be noted that while these several goals do bear some relationship to each other, the objective of managing rivalry to reduce its costs and risks is less ambitious than the goal of developing a more cooperative, orderly, and stable relationship and a better structured international system. Progress in managing rivalry may well contribute to these longer-range, more difficult objectives but it can be pursued more or less independently of them. However, diverging U.S.–Soviet conceptions of longer-range goals can constrain progress in finding ways of managing the rivalry.

RESEARCH OBJECTIVES

The present study focuses primarily on efforts made by the United States and the Soviet Union since World War II to develop cooperative arrangements in security matters. (U.S.–Soviet cooperation in non-security activities, such as trade, and scientific and cultural exchanges, is not included in the study.)

We wish to emphasize at the outset of the study that cooperation is not regarded here as an end in itself; rather, it is a means—and only one means—for achieving improvements in security. There are bound to be serious limits on promoting mutual security solely through formal and tacit U.S.–Soviet agreements (or multilateral agreements in which Moscow and Washington participate). Therefore, the scope of inquiry and the policy agenda need to be broadened to include attention to ways other than cooperative agreements by means of which the two superpowers can improve mutual security.

Alternative forms of cooperation and ways of enhancing mutual security that have been and can be utilized will also be considered in this study. These alternatives include *mutual adjustment* stemming from respect for each other's power and interests; *reciprocal coordination* of unilateral American and Soviet policies and actions in ways that reduce both sides' insecurity; and *unilateral actions* that either side can take without expectation of reciprocity. One side may act in such a way as to (a) contribute directly to its own security without increasing the other side's insecurity, or (b) contribute indirectly to its own security by reducing the other side's insecurity and, therefore, also reducing the pressure it feels to engage in countermoves that may exacerbate competition for arms and influence.

If cooperative agreements are not always possible or necessary for the realization of mutual security benefits, the fact remains that they have played an important, if at times also a controversial, role in the development of U.S.–Soviet relations.

The research objectives of the study are to answer the following questions: what *conditions and circumstances* have led Moscow and Washington on many occasions to seek, and on occasion to achieve, some form of cooperation on security matters? What have been the *obstacles* to cooperation and how were they overcome? What *factors and strategies* have facilitated cooperative efforts? What have been the *problems of implementation;* how well have cooperative arrangements worked out in practice, and why were some agreements effectively implemented and others not?

Our investigation will focus on these questions. If the study can provide useful answers, the results should be helpful in addressing a number of difficult theoretical and policy-relevant questions: how much and what types of cooperation in security matters can one expect from the United States and the Soviet Union? What are the uses and limitations of cooperation in security matters? What alternatives to cooperative agreements exist for enhancing mutual security?

We shall be particularly interested in the *incentives* each superpower has experienced for trying to achieve agreement or mutual adjustment on security matters. How, under what circumstances, and why do incentives for security cooperation emerge? This must be regarded as a central research question because, given the fundamentally competitive, conflictful relationship between the United States and the Soviet Union and their acute mutual distrust, each superpower understandably has a strong preference for relying on its own efforts to assure its security rather than to depend on cooperative arrangements with a powerful, distrusted adversary for this purpose.

RESEARCH STRATEGY

Our research strategy for achieving these objectives is an adaptation of the method of structured, focused comparison of relevant historical cases.[2] This method, utilized with considerable success in previous studies, is designed to produce theory and policy-relevant results from a systematic assessment of historical experience. As investigators are increasingly recognizing,[3] cooperation in security matters is highly context-dependent since it is subject to the interplay of many variables. In the last analysis, whether the United States and the Soviet Union succeed in developing a cooperative arrangement on a particular security matter depends not only on the policies of each superpower but also on the interaction between them, the outcome of which is sensitive to many other factors and, therefore, highly indeterminate.

Accordingly, one cannot expect to develop a robust theory, one that provides sufficient knowledge to permit confident predictions of when Moscow and Washington will succeed or fail in developing security cooperation. As is often the case, explanation of outcomes of this kind is somewhat easier than prediction. But this is not to say that we expected to find a common general explanation either for all cases of successful cooperation, or for all failures. There were some important elements in common for explanations of successful cases and for the failures, and these we attempted to identify. But there were also important differences in the explanations. We found several different paths to successful cooperation, and several different roads to failure.[4]

Twenty-two case studies were commissioned for the study, each by a highly qualified specialist on a particular security issue. Useful analyses of some of these cases already existed. Our task in planning the study was to develop a common approach and a detailed set of general questions to be asked by each author, insofar as these questions were appropriate to his or her case study. The plan for the study was described in a twenty-page prospectus which provided the starting point and framework for all of the case studies. (The most important part of the prospectus, the set of questions developed to guide the case studies, is reproduced in the Appendix.) Additional coordination among the cases was achieved by holding an authors' conference on the basis of the first drafts of the case studies. The reader will note that the case studies in Parts Two, Three, and Four vary considerably in length, largely because some of the cases are of a much more complex nature and require more detailed treatment than others.

Much, though not all, of the experience of the United States and the Soviet Union in attempting to develop security cooperation since World War II has been included in this study. Not all of this experience can be neatly compartmentalized into discrete cases of successful and unsuccessful cooperation. There are instances of partial or incomplete cooperation, and mixed cases that include elements of success and failure. Efforts to deal cooperatively with some security problems continue over a period of years and progress, if it occurs, may be uneven and reversible. Circumstances can change, calling into question the value of a previous agreement. Similarly, the superpowers may "learn" from previous experiences and acquire additional knowledge about complex security matters that alters their interest in, and approach to, cooperating on security matters.[5] In some security-issue areas, such as avoiding nuclear proliferation, U.S.–Soviet cooperation can take on a cumulative character over time. And, finally, there is the possibility of a synergistic effect between specific cooperative agreements and the central over-all U.S.–Soviet relationship, which will receive considerable attention in subsequent chapters.

Security, as the concept is employed in the study, is a complex amalgam of many different issues and problems. We have grouped the rich and varied experience of superpower efforts at security cooperation into three categories. Part Two includes six case studies of efforts (multilateral as well as bilateral) to promote security and stabilization in Europe, beginning with the World War II agreement on the occupation and administration of postwar Germany and including the recently concluded Stockholm conference.

Part Three comprises nine studies of efforts to cooperate on various arms control issues.

Part Four groups together seven studies of efforts to deal with problems of regional security, crisis avoidance, and crisis management.

And, finally, Part Five draws upon the case studies to provide analytical conclusions and lessons in six brief chapters, and the Epilogue provides reflections and perspective on the development of security cooperation.

The individuals we requested to do the twenty-two case studies come from either policy-making or academic research backgrounds. This selection of authors reflects a major objective of the study, namely a desire to *bring theory and practice into closer, more fruitful interaction* in order to improve our understanding of the challenging task of developing, where possible, mutually advantageous security cooperation between the two superpowers. Consistent with this objective, we have planned and implemented the study with a view towards bridging the gap between the academician's more abstract way of studying international relations and the practitioner's more concrete perspective on these matters. We believe that the improvement of both theory and practice requires a two-way interaction between these perspectives, and this we have tried to accomplish in the present study.

The next section of this chapter discusses the different strands of international relations theory that contribute to the study of U.S.–Soviet security cooperation. The general reader who has no interest in theoretical approaches to cooperation can skim through this section or go directly to the case studies in Part Two.

WHAT DOES INTERNATIONAL RELATIONS THEORY OFFER FOR UNDERSTANDING U.S.–SOVIET SECURITY COOPERATION?

At this time, it must be said, international relations theory does not contribute very much for understanding U.S.–Soviet security cooperation. The situation was summarized very aptly by Joseph Nye in a recent assessment of the state of international relations theory in general: "In a domain as complex as international relations, it is not surprising that the power of theories is limited. Generalizations are based on a small series of events which have multiple causes at several levels of analysis. Strategic interaction is inherently indeterminate, and domestic as well as systemic causes must be considered. Realism is the most promising and useful first approximation but it does not take us very far."[6]

Realist Theory

Elaborating on Nye's overall assessment of the limited utility of realist theory we may note, in particular, that it offers little help for understanding U.S.–Soviet security cooperation. If it is true, as realist theory posits, that in the "anarchic" international system in which states exist—that is, a system that lacks a strong central authority capable of establishing and enforcing rules—states are forced to rely ultimately on "self-help" to provide for their security and wellbeing, then why would powerful antagonists such as the Soviet Union and the United States, which seem to have ample resources for "self-help," seriously consider and occasionally enter into cooperative arrangements to enhance their security and wellbeing? It is one of the limitations of realist theory that it does not adequately deal with this apparent paradox. Similarly, if it is true that the two superpowers, like all great powers in the past, compete for relative advantage and greater influence in much of the world, often at each other's expense, then how does one explain the anomaly of their interest in developing cooperation in matters that affect their security?[7]

The common answer to these questions is that the fear of Armageddon drives—or ought to drive—the superpowers, if they are rational, to work out cooperative arrangements to lessen or abolish the danger of thermonuclear war. This is doubtless an important motivation and yet, even if it is regarded as a necessary condition for U.S.–Soviet security cooperation, it is obviously not a sufficient condition. In fact, one may question whether fear of thermonuclear holocaust is indeed a necessary condition for security cooperation given the historical fact that adversarial powers were able to cooperate in security matters in the *prenuclear* era. And, besides, not all U.S.–Soviet security cooperation can be traced to the fear of thermonuclear war. Clearly other incentives also operate.

Regional Integration Theory

There has been, of course, much cooperation among other states in the international system and various theories have been formulated to account for it. For example, regional integration theory was formulated to assist in understanding the development in Western Europe after World War II of a pluralistic security and economic community.[8] And, as Joseph Nye notes,[9] many aspects of integration theory were later utilized for analyzing the emergence of broader international economic interdependence among states in the international system.[10]

However, it has to be expected that cooperation in security affairs between pronounced adversaries such as the United States and the Soviet Union is a particularly difficult enterprise that must be regarded as a special case, one that cannot be adequately explained by theories that were developed to account for regional integration or broader international economic interdependence. We cannot expect that security cooperation among the NATO allies can generate theory that will help us understand the problem of U.S.–Soviet security cooperation. Neither can we expect much of relevance for this purpose from theories that account, however successfully, for the cooperative behavior induced by a hegemonic state in its relations with weaker allies and neutrals.[11]

While all forms of international cooperation no doubt have some elements in common, as general cooperation theory assumes, it is the differences affecting U.S.–Soviet security relations that concern us here.[12] It is for this reason that we believe it more useful to regard U.S.–Soviet security cooperation as a special case that will be better understood by developing a more specific theory.

Game Theory and Cooperation

Recent applications of game theory, and particularly the Prisoners' Dilemma game, have been the source of stimulating ideas for studying how cooperation can develop in mixed-motive situations, where actors experience a mix of shared and conflicting interests. Many years of intensive work by numerous investigators led a few years ago to the publication by Robert Axelrod of *The Evolution of Cooperation*,[13] which offers an experimentally derived "solution" to the Prisoners' Dilemma, namely, the "tit-for-tat" strategy (to be discussed in Chapter 29).

While Axelrod's study offers stimulating ideas of possible relevance to U.S.–Soviet relations, it focuses on the Prisoners' Dilemma *per se* and not on the security dilemma[14] and the more general problem of cooperation in international politics. Efforts to transfer or adapt Axelrod's solution to the Prisoners' Dilemma—namely, the tit-for-tat strategy—encounter the familiar problem of assessing the external validity of a theory developed under simplified, controlled experimental conditions. A number of writers who have warmly praised Axelrod's contribution to the Prisoners' Dilemma literature have nonetheless concluded that it has limited relevance for international politics, which differs from the Prisoners' Dilemma in many fundamental respects.[15] Indeed, in the final chapters of *The Evolution of Cooperation,* Axelrod offered a number of useful suggestions for adapting his work to the study of cooperation in the international arena. And, together with others, he has subsequently pursued this task in more detail.[16]

Also relevant is the work of other political scientists, particularly that of Robert Jervis who has refined the concept of security dilemma and identified variables that exacerbate or alleviate its effects.[17] Jervis' study contains a number of seminal ideas that have stimulated other important work. One of Jervis' general observations is that the greater the gain from defection, and the greater the fear of being exploited, the less likely the chance for cooperation in a Prisoners' Dilemma type of situation. In a situation of this kind one or the other player may attempt to encourage cooperation by seeking to decrease both the potential gains from unilateral defection and the prospective losses from unrequited cooperation. Jervis also suggests that cooperation is more likely when (and if) defensive military technologies are easily distinguishable from offensive weapons systems. In addition, cooperation is more likely when both actors believe that defensive rather than offensive strategies are dominant. These are useful analytical distinctions even though they are not easily applied to the complex structure of contemporary strategic postures and doctrines.

The *World Politics* Study

There is general agreement that game theoretic hypotheses regarding conditions and strategies that favor cooperation must be subjected to intensive examination in relevant historical cases. A major step in this direction was taken a few years ago in a collaborative study published in *World Politics.*[18]

For present purposes we need not describe in detail the complex analytical structure of this study and all of its findings.[19] Kenneth Oye states in the opening essay that the starting point of the *World Politics* study was a "unified analytical structure" composed of three game theoretic structural variables: "mutuality of interest," "shadow of the future," and "number of players."[20] These three variables, derived from games that have been employed to study the problem of cooperation, form the basis for a core theory of three hypotheses that is the starting point for the investigation.[21] According to these three hypotheses (which are stated in probabilistic terms) cooperation is *more likely* (1) if the payoff for defection (noncooperation) for either player is small when the other side cooperates, (2) if the interaction between the players is repeated many times (in which case "the shadow of the future" will encourage players to forego the temptation to obtain short-term gains from defection because to do so would jeopardize achievement of important gains in the future), and (3) if the number of players is low.

We note that each of these three hypotheses states a loose, very general bivariate relationship of a probabilistic type.[22] We refer to these hypotheses as "loose" and very general because they leave unanswered the question as to *why* and *how* the payoff structure, the shadow of the future, and the number of players affect the prospect of cooperation. In other words, each hypothesis needs filling in. Recognizing this, Oye provides for each hypothesis a theoretical specification as to how the structural variable in question might be expected to affect the behavior of the actors in ways that would increase the likelihood of cooperation. The theoretical specifications of why and how each of these three structural variables promotes cooperation are quite plausible (whether they are valid is another matter that requires empirical analysis), and they serve to enrich the three hypotheses and render them more useful for developing explanations for specific instances of cooperation and noncooperation.

Oye also recognizes that there are many situations in which cooperation is not likely to take place despite the presence of one or another of these structural variables. (In other words, the three variables—either separately or together—are not sufficient conditions for cooperation.) Among the reasons for this is that various other factors can operate as *impediments* to cooperation. Among those listed by Oye are such things as ideological and cognitive variables; military and economic doctrines; force structures; domestic factional, organizational, and bureaucratic influences on decision-making; and the ability of actors to distinguish reliably between cooperation and defection by other players. While most of the possible impediments to cooperation Oye lists are already familiar to students and practitioners, his discussion of them enriches the analytical framework he is developing and increases its usefulness for purposes of explanation.

Thus far we have discussed only one of the two objectives of the *World Politics* study, namely the goal of improving the ability to explain the occurrence or nonoccurrence of cooperation in international relations. The other objective of the study is to contribute to a *prescriptive* theory of how actors can promote cooperation if they want to do so. With this second objective in mind Oye adds to his discussion of each of the three structural hypotheses and the impediments a set of provisional prescriptions for strategies players might adopt to increase the likelihood of cooperation. (These strategies include ways of trying to alter payoff structures; lengthening the shadow of the future; reducing the number of players or dealing in some way with the complexities created by multiple players; and ways of improving the efficacy of reciprocity strategies.) The strategies identified are all relevant, although it is not clear how they can be made to work; and they constitute useful though not necessarily novel suggestions for policy-making purposes.

Working with the rich explanatory-prescriptive framework provided in Oye's opening essay, other participants in the study analyze six historical cases, three involving security issues and three having to do with political economy. The case studies serve, in Oye's words, to "provide a limited trial" of the hypotheses and prescriptive propositions contained in the analytic framework he provides for the study.[23]

What are the results of this trial? In the concluding chapter of the study, Robert Axelrod and Robert Keohane are careful not to overstate what was accomplished: the three dimensions—mutuality of interest, shadow of the future, number of players—"help us to understand the success and failure of attempts at cooperation in both military-security and political-economic relations." Since the three dimensions in question are structural variables, Axelrod and Keohane add the appropriate clarification that these dimensions come into play insofar as they "affect the *propensity of actors* to cooperate."[24]

Of particular interest here is the emphasis Axelrod and Keohane place on the need for moving beyond the *structural* form of the hypotheses to empirical analysis of the *decision-making processes* of the actors and the *strategic interaction* between them.[25] The authors of the *World Politics* study recognize that the international system and its workings are much more complex than the simple game structures and simulations which drew attention to the importance of these three structural variables. Axelrod and Keohane note that world politics includes "a rich variety of contexts" that cannot be ignored in studying the phenomenon of cooperation: "issues arise against distinctive backgrounds of past experience; they are linked to other issues being dealt with simultaneously by the same actors; and they are viewed by participants through the prisms of their expectations about the future."[26] Drawing on materials from the case studies, Axelrod and Keohane identify some of these contextual variables and examine their implications for the problem of cooperation. They present useful observations and insights about "multilevel games" and "issue-linkage," the uses and limitations of the principle of reciprocity in strategies for facilitating cooperation, factors that can facilitate application of reciprocity, and ways of attempting to alter the context in which interaction takes place—via meta-strategies and institutions—in order to facilitate cooperation.

What emerges from a close reading of the *World Politics* study that may be of particular interest to specialists in theories of international relations is the extent to which, starting from an austere structural level of analysis, the *World Politics* study was forced to rely more heavily on the decision-making level of analysis. Thus, having started with a game theory framework in which variables of domestic politics, and individual perception and decision making are assumed not to be important, Axelrod and Keohane in their conclusion are struck by the importance of such variables in influencing prospects for cooperation. They acknowledge that the contributors to the study "did not specifically set out to explore the role of perception in decisionmaking, but the importance of perception has kept asserting itself."[27] Again, given the central importance in game theory of the payoff structure, it is one of the important learning experiences of the *World Politics* project that "mutuality of interests is not based simply upon objective factors, but is grounded upon the actors' perceptions of their own interests. Perceptions define interests. Therefore, to understand the degree of mutuality of interests (or to enhance this mutuality) we must understand the process by which interests are perceived and preferences determined."[28]

Another important learning experience of the *World Politics* project is the image that emerged of decision makers as *active* agents, not tightly constrained by objective situational factors of a "game" that has a fixed payoff structure. As Axelrod and Keohane put it: "We also discovered something else: over and over again we observed that the real world actors were not satisfied with simply selecting strategies based upon the situation in which they found themselves. In many cases we saw deliberate efforts to change the very structure of that situation by changing the context in which each of them would be acting."[29]

Finally, the *World Politics* study points to the establishment of international regimes as one very important means of changing the context of interaction so as to facilitate cooperation. Regimes reinforce and institutionalize the reciprocity on which cooperation is based; regimes may help to develop new norms; and they may change the context within which actors operate by changing the structure of their interaction.[30] In agreement with the authors of the *World Politics* project in this respect, we will turn in the next section of this chapter to a discussion of the relevance of regime theory to study of U.S.–Soviet security cooperation. But before doing so we want to point out some lacunae and limitations of the *World Politics* study which we attempt to rectify in our own study.

1. The *World Politics* study fails to recognize a factor that is of central importance for understanding the development of mutual U.S.–Soviet interests in security cooperation. As Chapter 26 emphasizes, incentives for cooperation arise when the United States and/or the Soviet Union realize that they cannot provide adequately for their security through unilateral policies and actions. Awareness that one's security is una-

voidably vulnerable to the adversary's behavior and/or that pursuing security solely through unilateral policies would be too costly and risky creates incentives that may be powerful enough to overcome reluctance to enter into cooperative arrangements.

2. The *World Politics* study implicitly assumes that all instances of successful security cooperation are sufficiently similar so that no differentiation among them is necessary for developing explanatory or prescriptive theory. In our own study (Chapter 26) we have concluded that it is advantageous to develop a typology of security cooperation. We identify different types of cooperative arrangements and argue that cases of successful security cooperation do not all have the same explanation.[31] Failure to recognize this, we believe, will severely limit the further development of explanatory theory and the refinement of prescriptive theory for the study of cooperation.

3. We believe that the practice evident in Oye's opening chapter of formulating hypotheses about the contribution to cooperation made by payoff structures, shadow of the future, and number of players in probabilistic terms should be replaced by efforts to state them in the form of "conditional generalizations."[32] It would be more useful to try to identify the conditions under which a general explanatory hypothesis is true and the conditions under which the opposite may be true rather than to state that cooperation is "more likely" if a factor is present. For example, contrary to the pervasive assumption of the *World Politics* study that a long "shadow of the future" is likely to favor, or almost always favors, the possibility of cooperation, this factor actually plays a much more variable role in U.S.–Soviet relations. When two states regard their relationship as highly conflictful and are distrustful of each other's long-range intentions, as is the case in U.S.–Soviet relations, the shadow of the future may *discourage* one or both from capitalizing on an opportunity for a short-run gain in security from a cooperative agreement out of fear that to do so will hamper its ability to compete effectively in the future. As will be noted in Chapter 27, the shadow of the future tends to be viewed as ominous by the United States and the Soviet Union and as a result, contrary to a major theme of the *World Politics* study, concern for the future may hamper rather than facilitate cooperation. This is not to say that the shadow of the future is not capable of playing a constructive role from time to time in promoting U.S.–Soviet cooperation but its influence is highly variable.

The position the *World Politics* study takes on the relation between number of players and prospects for cooperation is also troublesome. Once again, empirical analysis of U.S.–Soviet experience in security cooperation indicates that sometimes the fact that multiple actors are involved in dealing with a security issue will increase, not decrease (as the *World Politics* study conveys), the possibility of cooperation. Thus, the emergence of U.S.–Soviet détente in the early 1970s was encouraged and in some respects facilitated by our allies, particularly by Charles de Gaulle and later the West German leaders who promoted *Ostpolitik*. U.S. allies and neutral states participating in the Conference on Security and Cooperation in Europe, as John Maresca shows in his chapter in this volume, played an active role in pushing the two superpowers into agreement on some provisions of the Helsinki Accord. And, as Deborah Shapley indicates in her chapter, states other than the United States and the Soviet Union played an important role in the origins and development of the Antarctica regime.

Viewing the task of theory development as that of formulating conditional generalizations in order to capture the variability in the influence such factors have on cooperation is distinctly preferable to stating that the relationship can take only one direction and that this is "likely" on a probabilistic basis.

4. The *World Politics* study does briefly note that cooperation is not always necessary for the realization of mutual interests and that under certain conditions "the
pursuit of self-interest, without regard to the action of others, will automatically lead to
mutual gains . . ."[33] However, the *World Politics* study does not pursue this important
insight in elaborating its theoretical framework or in its conclusions, although the observation is referred to in some of the case studies.[34] Rather, the pervasive underlying
assumption of the *World Politics* study is that cooperation is necessary in order to realize
mutual interests. In our own study we call attention in Chapter 26 to the fact that
unilateral actions the superpowers can and do take, often without expectation of reciprocity,
contribute significantly to mutual security.

5. The *World Politics* study notes that "internal factional, organizational, and bureaucratic dysfunctions" can be important impediments to working out cooperative arrangements.[35] This is referred to as the problem of "control." Once again, however,
these and other well-known domestic constraints on policymakers' ability to explore
cooperative arrangements with other actors receive little attention in the explanatory
efforts of the *World Politics* study[36] and are largely passed over in the set of prescriptions offered for improving the prospects for cooperation. Efforts to explain the role of
domestic constraints on policy making admittedly encounter difficult data problems.
Nonetheless, a number of case studies in the present volume do succeed in illuminating
the role they played, and we strongly emphasize the critical task of dealing with various
domestic factors that top political leaders in the United States and the Soviet Union
must perform in pursuing opportunities for mutually beneficial security cooperation.

6. The *World Politics* study has relatively little to say on another important aspect
of security cooperation, namely the policy maker's task of assessing the risks of agreements and developing unilateral and bilateral ways of making such risks more manageable and, hence, acceptable. This issue is the central focus of many of our own case
studies and is the subject of Chapter 28.

7. In the final chapter of the *World Politics* study, Axelrod and Keohane emphasize the importance of issue-linkage in strategies for achieving cooperation. In this connection, they make brief mention of "contextual" issue-linkage, a term they employ to
refer to cases in which "a given bargain is placed within the context of a more important
long-term relationship in such a way that the long-term relationship affects the outcome
of the particular bargaining process."[37] Following these leads of the *World Politics*
study our own investigation distinguishes different types of issue-linkage and has turned
up a great deal of evidence regarding the role that "contextual" issue-linkage has played
in efforts to promote U.S.–Soviet security cooperation. Going beyond the *World Politics* study we emphasize the critical role played by the state of over-all superpower
relations in promoting or discouraging security cooperation at different times.

These reservations notwithstanding, the *World Politics* essays make a unique contribution to the study of cooperation in the international system. In our own study,
which was initiated before publication of the *World Politics* symposium, we employed
an approach that is not pegged to game-theoretic concepts and, as the questions listed
in the Appendix indicate, our framework is broader and more detailed. In particular,
our approach was influenced by the theoretical-empirical literature on international regimes developed by scholars during the past decade or so.

Regime Theory

As Nye notes, the concept of regime was borrowed from international law and broadened to incorporate the whole range of explicit and implicit norms, rules, and decision-making procedures developed within a given issue-area, which serve to constrain the behavior of participating states and around which their expectations converge.[38] Nye writes: "The fact that most theorizing about international regimes occurred in the area of international political economy had unfortunate effects. For example, the concern with the role of the dominant actor within an N-person game ('hegemonic stability theory') made the theory seem irrelevant to bipolar U.S.–Soviet relations."[39]

The question arises, quite naturally, whether regimes are possible also in the U.S.–Soviet security interface. Most specialists in international relations believe that, given the critical importance attached to security by major actors in the international system, it is inherently more difficult for them to agree on and to develop a viable security regime. Those who have addressed the possibility of achieving U.S.–Soviet cooperation in security matters have sometimes conceptualized the problem in terms of the basic question whether a "security regime" is at all feasible.[40] Some specialists have given a quite pessimistic answer to this question. It has been suggested that such cooperation on security matters as exists or is likely to develop between the two superpowers results more from elementary considerations of prudence than a desire to develop a well-defined, institutionalized security regime based on norms, rules, and procedures around which U.S. and Soviet expectations converge.

Whether or not one agrees with these pessimistic views regarding the feasibility of a U.S.–Soviet security regime—and we do not—it is useful to view the problem of cooperation from the standpoint of regime theory. This enables us to draw on the considerable practical experience that has already accumulated with respect to the creation, maintenance, change, and erosion of regimes in *nonsecurity* aspects of international relations, and on the related theories that attempt to explain such developments.

The concept of "regime" is particularly valuable because it moves discussion and inquiry away from the narrow focus on *moves and strategies* for solving a Prisoners' Dilemma type situation that has preoccupied game theorists. Instead, regime theory shifts attention to the relevance of *agreements that establish principles, procedures, and institutions* for regulating competition as well as facilitating cooperation in specified security sub-issues. The concept of "regime" (in contrast to the concept of a "solution" to the Prisoners' Dilemma) also has the merit of focusing attention on the importance of creating appropriate *institutions* for facilitating cooperative strategies and for implementing cooperative agreements.[41] In contrast, Axelrod's solution to the Prisoners' Dilemma game does not involve the development of institutions or agreed-upon procedures for monitoring and encouraging compliance with the rules and norms the actors have agreed to for purposes of regulating competition and facilitating cooperation.[42] In fact, most game theory "exists" in an institution-free world, a now recognized limitation that is leading to efforts to construct more complex game theories that try to formally model the potential impact of such factors as institutions, enforcement mechanisms, and means of communication between actors.

The present study starts from the premise and expectation that, given the history, nature, and context of the U.S.–Soviet security relationship, a *comprehensive* security regime, one that would deal with all or most aspects of the competition and rivalry affecting the security interface of the two superpowers, is not feasible. At the same time, however, we reject the premise that a security regime is an either-or proposition: that there will either be a comprehensive security regime or none at all, and that viable, useful cooperative security arrangements are not possible unless they are parts of a comprehensive security regime. We believe it is more useful to regard the security dimension of U.S.–Soviet relations as embracing many issues, some of which can be decoupled from each other and become the focus for efforts to contrive mutually acceptable cooperative arrangements. At the same time, since many security issues are related in some way to one other, efforts at cooperation can be mutually reinforcing and contribute to the emergence of an imperfect but valuable security regime.

This perspective enables us to reflect more usefully on the fact that the United States and the Soviet Union have been successful in working out viable, mutually useful arrangements for some of their security problems but not for others. Thus, as this study makes clear, the two superpowers have succeeded in developing regimes, and some quasi- or partial regimes, for some of their specific security interfaces.

How much further Moscow and Washington can go in constructing and strengthening arrangements in the security area is an open question. We must also recognize that circumstances change and, as in the field of international economic relations, existing security agreements and arrangements may erode and disappear. It must be recognized that superpower incentives for developing security regimes tend to be both weak and ambivalent and that formidable difficulties and obstacles stand in the way of developing viable cooperative arrangements. Therefore, one cannot expect anything like a comprehensive U.S.–Soviet security regime to emerge.

Regimes, however, are *not* the only means for achieving significant cooperation and mutual adjustment in security matters. As our study emphasizes, particularly in Chapter 26, much of value has been and can be achieved through less extensive forms of cooperative behavior. Such behavior may include tacit agreements, coordination by the two superpowers of unilateral policies in the absence of any kind of agreement, and the adoption by Moscow and Washington of prudent policies and restrained behavior out of respect for the other superpower's power and interests and not merely because of a shared fear of devastating warfare.

The term "regime" is sometimes applied very loosely to refer to these less well-defined, less structured forms of cooperation and mutual adjustment. This semantical practice causes confusion and should be avoided. But we need to recognize the existence of regime-like arrangements that approximate the concept of regime in some respects. As our case studies illustrate, there are recognizable variations in the scope and clarity of norms and rules, in the adequacy of procedures to implement them, in the degree of institutionalization, and in the degree to which actors comply with regime norms and rules and the extent to which they are enforced. The explicit definition of a well-defined regime is a useful analytical tool, but it should not be applied so rigidly that it prevents us from seeing nuances and variations, partial and quasi-regimes as well as arrangements that fully meet the definition. In the Epilogue we shall return to the question of the extent to which U.S.–Soviet security cooperation has taken the form of regimes.

Notes

1. See Alexander L. George, ed., *Managing U.S.–Soviet Rivalry* (Boulder, Colo.: Westview Press, 1983), especially chapters 2, 5, 6, 13, and 15.

2. The comparison of cases in such a study is "focused" in the sense that not every aspect

of the historical cases is investigated but only those aspects relevant to the research objectives of the study. The comparison of cases is "structured" by the specification of a number of general questions that are asked, insofar as appropriate, in each case, thereby facilitating comparison. These questions reflect the theoretical and policy-relevant variables imbedded in the framework for the study. For a fuller description of the focused, structured method see Alexander L. George, "Case Studies and Theory Development," in P. G. Lauren, ed., *Diplomatic History: New Approaches* (New York: Free Press, 1979); Alexander L. George, "Case Studies and Theory Development," paper presented to the Second Annual Symposium on Information Processing in Organizations, Carnegie-Mellon University, October 15–16, 1982; and Alexander L. George and Timothy J. McKeown, "Case Studies and Theories of Organizational Decisionmaking," in *Advances in Information Processing,* vol. 2 (Greenwich, Conn.: JAI Press), 1985.

3. See, for example, Robert Axelrod and Robert O. Keohane, who conclude the collaborative project on cooperation in which they participated by emphasizing the importance of many contextual variables: "To ignore the effects of context would be to overlook many of the most interesting questions raised by a game-theoretic perspective on the problem of cooperation." Again, "a contextual approach to strategy . . . helps to forge necessary links between game-theoretic arguments and theories about international regimes." Robert Axelrod and Robert O. Keohane, "Achieving Cooperation Under Anarchy: Strategies and Institutions," *World Politics,* vol. 38, no. 1 (October 1985): 226–254.

4. We refer here to what is called "equifinality" in general systems theory (and what John Stuart Mill many years ago called the problem of "plurality of causes")—namely, the fact that for many social phenomena similar outcomes on the dependent variable are often produced by different causal patterns. This phenomenon has important implications that constrain the search for universal explanations and require formulation of conditional generalizations.

5. On the importance of learning see particularly Joseph S. Nye, "Nuclear Learning and U.S.–Soviet Security Regimes," paper delivered to the 1986 annual meeting of the American Political Science Association, Washington, D. C. (revision of September 17, 1986). On the cumulation of "consensual knowledge" on complex security matters that can alter the perception of interest in cooperation, see Ernst Haas, "Why Collaborate? Issue-linkages and International Regimes," *World Politics,* vol. 32, no. 1 (October 1980): 357–405.

6. Nye, "Nuclear Learning," p. 3.

7. Some degree of cooperation may not be anomalous in terms of realist theory but the theory does not explain why cooperation may develop in some issue areas but not others. We need not replace realist theory to explain these occurrences but to do so requires that realist theory be supplemented with additional theories. (I am indebted to Steven Weber for this observation.)

8. See, for example, Karl Deutsch et al., *Political Community and the North Atlantic Area* (Princeton, N.J.: Princeton University Press, 1957); Ernst Haas, *The Uniting of Europe* (Stanford, Calif.: Stanford University Press, 1958); Joseph S. Nye, *Peace in Parts* (Boston: Little, Brown, 1971).

9. Nye, "Nuclear Learning," pp. 5–6.

10. See, for example, Robert O. Keohane and Joseph S. Nye, *Power and Interdependence* (Boston: Little, Brown, 1977). Considerable cooperation in *nonsecurity* areas has also developed between the United States and the Soviet Union. Many agreements of this kind were concluded during the height of the Nixon-Brezhnev era. For a useful account see Nish Jamgotch, ed., *Sectors of Mutual Benefit in U.S.–Soviet Relations* (Durham, N.C.: Duke University Press, 1985).

11. See, for example, Robert O. Keohane, *After Hegemony* (Princeton, N.J.: Princeton University Press, 1984).

12. U.S.–Soviet security relations differ in a number of important respects from relations among members of an alliance such as NATO or relations between a hegemonic state and weaker allies and neutrals. For one thing, the security dilemma is experienced much more acutely in U.S.–Soviet relations, as are the impact of rival hostile ideologies, lack of trust, and language and cultural barriers.

13. *The Evolution of Cooperation* (New York: Basic Books, 1984).

14. The security dilemma and its constraints on cooperation are discussed in Chapter 27.

15. See, for example, Joanne Gowa, "Anarchy, Egoism, and Third Images: The Evolution of Cooperation and International Relations," *International Organization,* vol. 40, no. 1 (Winter 1986): 167–186; Francis A. Beer, "Games and Metaphors," *Journal of Conflict Resolution,* vol. 30, no. 1 (March 1986): 171–191; Deborah Larson, "Crisis Prevention and the Austrian State Treaty," *International Organization,* vol. 41, no. 1 (Winter 1987): 27–61; Robert Jervis, "Cooperation Under Anarchy: Problems and Limitations," draft manuscript, July 1986; Duncan Snidal, "Coordination Versus Prisoners' Dilemma: Implications for International Cooperation and Regimes," *American Political Science Review,* vol. 79, no. 4 (December 1985): 923–942.

16. Axelrod and Keohane, "Achieving Cooperation."

17. See in particular Jervis' "Cooperation Under the Security Dilemma," *World Politics,* vol. 30, no. 2 (January 1978); 167–214.

18. This study, edited by Kenneth A. Oye, is entitled "Cooperation Under Anarchy." It appeared in the issue of *World Politics* (October 1985), cited in footnote 3, and was subsequently published as a book under the same title in 1986 by Princeton University Press.

19. The writing of this section has benefited from discussions with Steven Weber and Jack Levy. They are not responsible, however, for the observations offered here.

20. Kenneth A. Oye, "Explaining Cooperation Under Anarchy: Hypotheses and Strategies," *World Politics,* p. 2.

21. It should be noted that we, not the authors of the study, refer to these three game theoretic concepts as "variables." For reasons not made clear in the *World Politics* study, its authors prefer to refer to them, variously, as "circumstantial dimensions," "situational predispositions," "situational dimensions," "game theoretic dimensions," and "structural conditions." Ibid., pp. 2, 23, 228, 238, 253. Similarly, we, not the authors of the *World Politics* study, refer to the three hypotheses noted here—which play a prominent role in their study—as a "core theory." In fact, these authors (with the exception of Duncan Snidal) carefully refrain from labeling as "theory" either the "unified analytical structure," with which they start their investigation, or the explanatory and prescriptive hypotheses they develop during the course of the study. Snidal refers to "the explanatory power of the empirical elaboration of the theory" in discussing the function of the case studies. Ibid., p. 55.

22. The three variables—mutuality of interest, shadow of the future, and number of players—are stated and dealt with in the study in qualitative terms. How strong each variable must be in order to contribute effectively to cooperation is not indicated. The authors of the *World Politics* study do not say whether they regard any of these three variables as a "necessary" condition for cooperation; presumably all that can be claimed is that the presence of the variable "favors" cooperation. Nor do the authors attempt to hazard a judgment as to the relative importance of the three variables. Clearly, then, to the extent that these three hypotheses form a "core theory" it is not a well-enough developed deductive theory to be capable of generating confident predictions; nor does the *World Politics* study claim to have developed a predictive theory. Rather, the claim is merely that these three hypotheses, together with other variables, help to provide explanations in concrete cases. The authors do not, however, claim to have developed a general explanatory theory.

23. *World Politics,* p. 22. Since the authors of the study do not claim to put forward a theory of cooperation, one cannot say that the case studies are used for theory-testing. Rather, the six cases—evidently a fortuitous selection and not a representative sample—serve to illustrate the relevance and usefulness of some of the concepts, hypotheses, and prescriptions advanced in Oye's opening essay for explaining the outcomes of the six cases examined.

24. *World Politics,* pp. 227, 228.

25. Readers familiar with international relations theory will recognize that, in effect, Axelrod and Keohane appear to be asserting that the further development of cooperation theory requires us to move from the structural level of analysis to the decision-making and interaction

levels—that is, not simply to make assumptions about what goes on in the Black Box of decision making and the Black Box of strategic interaction but, insofar as possible, to study directly the processes of decision making and interaction.

26. *World Politics,* p. 227.

27. Ibid., p. 247.

28. Ibid., p. 229. A similar observation is made about the length of the "shadow of the future" (p. 234).

29. Ibid., pp. 348–9.

30. Ibid., pp. 250–1.

31. In other words, our empirical study of many cases of successful U.S.–Soviet cooperation in security matters indicates, as was noted in footnote 4, that this phenomenon is characterized by what is called "equifinality" in general systems theory. The fact that similar outcomes on a dependent variable are associated with quite different causal patterns reinforces the need (noted in the following paragraph) for the development of "conditional generalizations" in lieu of single causal assertions of a probabilistic character.

32. The need for conditional generalizations is implicitly recognized in the concluding chapter of the *World Politics* study by Axelrod and Keohane.

33. Oye, "Explaining Cooperation," p. 6.

34. See particularly George W. Downs, David M. Rocke, and Randolph M. Siverson, "Arms Races and Cooperation," pp. 118–146. These authors identify several conditions in which unilateral strategies contribute to lessening arms races.

35. Oye, "Explaining Cooperation," p. 16.

36. One exception is the brief treatment of control problems in the chapter by Downs, Rocke, and Siverson. The importance of domestic factors is evident in Stephen Van Evera's discussion of misperceptions that contributed to the failure of the European powers to cooperate in order to avoid World War I. He focuses largely on the extraordinary influence of European professional militaries on civilian opinion and the social stratification of European societies as contributing to some of the misperceptions. ("Why Cooperation Failed in 1914," pp. 95–99.)

37. Axelrod and Keohane, "Achieving Cooperation," p. 241.

38. Nye, "Nuclear Learning," p. 6. Nye cites the generally accepted definition of regimes put forward by Stephen Krasner in his edited volume, *International Regimes* (Ithaca, N.Y.: Cornell University Press, 1983).

39. Nye, "Nuclear Learning," p. 7.

40. See, for example, Charles Lipson, "International Cooperation in Economic and Security Affairs," *World Politics,* vol. 37, no. 1 (October 1984): 1–23.

41. Relevant here is Robert Keohane's concept of regime as an enabling mechanism, one that aids actors in their attempts to design cooperative arrangements by easing information transfer, decreasing transaction costs, and facilitating "enforcement" of agreements *(After Hegemony).*

42. It should be noted that Axelrod, in discussing the broader implications of his experimental study, does begin to relax the sparse assumptions of the institution-free world of his model and calls attention to the potential impact of the development of "social structures." See particularly chapter 8 of *The Evolution of Cooperation.* (I am indebted to Steven Weber for calling this to my attention.)

II

CASE STUDIES: EFFORTS TO PROMOTE STABILIZATION IN EUROPE

2

The World War II Allied Agreement on Occupation and Administration of Postwar Germany

DAVID SCHOENBAUM

"On July 17, 1945, the President of the United States of America, Harry S. Truman, the Chairman of the Council of People's Commissars of the Union of Soviet Socialist Republics, Generalissimo J. V. Stalin, and the Prime Minister of Great Britain, Winston S. Churchill, together with Mr. Clement R. Attlee, met in the Tripartite Conference of Berlin. They were accompanied by the Foreign Secretaries of the three Governments . . . There were nine meetings between July 17 and July 25 . . . The meetings of the Conference were held at the Cecilienhof, near Potsdam. The Conference ended on August 2, 1945." [1]

". . . when the conferees, especially the Americans, having had enough, signed their names and went home," the Potsdam Declaration might have added. By their own accounts, the Americans were both pleased with themselves and exasperated with the results of the conference. [2] As so often, one can only guess how the Russians felt. But Ambassador Averell Harriman's post-victory interview with Stalin at least implies that they had probably not departed smiling. [3] In their respective and quite different ways, both sides were convinced that they were playing from strength. "The Russians need us more than we need them," Truman told Harriman on their first meeting in April 1945. It was unrealistic to expect 100 percent cooperation of the Russians, the new President conceded, but he hoped for 85 percent. For their part, the Russians were convinced that increased postwar exports to the Soviet Union were a matter of "life and death" for the American economy. [4] Yet there was also the matter of the atom bomb, whose successful test Truman had mentioned to Stalin in the course of the Potsdam conference. Stalin "must have been aware," his biographer argues, "of the extent to which the new weapon, abruptly tilting the scales of military power in favor of the United States, was likely to intensify and dramatize the conflict between the allies." [5]

To the extent there was an inter-allied agreement on the occupation and administration of postwar Germany and its allies, it was probably the Potsdam Declaration. *Faute de mieux,* it was understood as such, even by the French, who were excluded from the conference and who understandably refused to regard what was decided there as binding. France aside, the Declaration established "principles" that both sides were to employ as surrogate weaponry in their Cold War for decades afterwards. [6] Yet nothing suggests that the signatories were being coy when they attached the qualification "in

the initial control period'' to their directives on the zonal partition and military government of postwar Germany, and the provisional assignment of both territorial and economic spoils.

The terms of the Declaration represent the fullest confirmation and codification of
existing agreement, partial agreement, and agreement to disagree, before the wartime
alliance itself began to come apart for reasons having only partly to do with Germany.
Neither a peace treaty nor a conscious declaration of Cold War in itself, Potsdam is
probably best seen in retrospect as a benchmark.

In effect, the Declaration ratified the wartime status quo between the allies. In
1943, the allies had agreed, for their respective reasons, on Germany's unconditional
surrender. Before the year was over, they began to discuss its dismemberment and joint
occupation. A legacy of the Moscow foreign ministers' meeting in October and the
Teheran summit a month later, a European Advisory Commission (EAC) of ambassadorial-
level representatives convened in London in January 1944 to address ex officio the
common problems of orderly surrender and military occupation arising from Germany's
capitulation. Before passing into history, the EAC settled on a British formula for zonal
partition and common administration, and agreed on a British formula for the actual
instrument of surrender.

Its handiwork still visible after more than forty years, the EAC turned out to be
among the most significant deliberative bodies of World War II. But this was hardly
intended by its creators, Britain's Foreign Secretary Anthony Eden and the Foreign
Office aside. On the contrary, Americans and Russians were determined to keep it on
the shortest possible leash and to limit genuine advisory initiative as much as they could.
Ambassador John Winant, the American representative, ''had no latitude of operation
himself,'' George Kennan, his political advisor, recalled, ''and small need of a political
advisor to help him.'' Ironically, the major source of friction was an intramural difference between the War Department and the Joint Chiefs of Staff, who instructed the
Americans at the EAC, and the State Department, which didn't. As Kennan saw it, the
effective block was not just the U.S. Army's inability to reach a common position, but
its apparent aversion to political decisions as such. At a loss for help from his superiors
in the State Department, Kennan resolved the deadlock resourcefully but unconvention-
ally by going directly to the President.

Considering the actual postwar map of Germany, and the differences that were to
divide both Europe and the wartime allies within a few years, it was ironic again that
the EAC's most memorable drama was not a squabble between East and West, but
between the British and Americans. Both the British and Americans wanted to occupy
the northwest zone of Germany, including the North Sea ports. In the end, the Americans yielded, leaving the British in Hamburg and the Ruhr, and the Americans in the
south and southwest. The arrangement was ratified pro forma in the EAC. But the
differences again were typically settled at the summit, between President Roosevelt and
Prime Minister Churchill.[7]

With the invasion of France and the rapid advance of allied armies, questions of
what to do with Germany became more urgent, but also more contentious, for both the
Soviet Union and the Western allies. At the Yalta summit in early 1945, conferees both
addressed and fudged the questions of Poland's postwar government and borders, and
of reparations claims, that is, how much of what for whom? Both postwar superpowers
subsequently insisted that the other had made firm commitments. The Americans wanted

and expected free elections in Poland and elsewhere. The Russians wanted and expected material reparations from Germany on a scale so vast as to approximate wartime Lend-Lease. In fact, some major decisions were preempted unilaterally before the allies had even reconvened after Yalta. "I don't like it," Roosevelt's indignant successor told his diary at Potsdam as he acknowledged how the Russians and Poles had already divided Germany "without so much as a by your leave."[8] Other decisions were deferred until a later meeting, in part because of insoluble differences between the conferees, in part because the war itself was far from over. Victory in Europe was still some months and much bitter German resistance away, and there was no reason to believe the Pacific war would be over in the foreseeable future.

In its way, Potsdam recapitulated previous discussions, and amalgamated others. Secretary of State James F. Byrnes was particularly proud of his take-it-or-leave-it proposal, linking reparations, the Polish-German border, and admission of the former German allies to the United Nations.[9] Among the results were dismemberment of Germany at the Western Neisse, rather than the Eastern Neisse as previously favored by the Western allies; an unworkable formula that assured the Russians a fixed percentage of an indeterminate amount of reparations and virtually precluded the economic unity the allies ostensibly intended to maintain; and peace with Italy, Hungary, Romania, and Bulgaria as members of their respective blocs. All of these decisions have had lasting consequences.

But the text itself belies any intention of diplomatic or juridical definitiveness with respect to Germany or very much else. On the one hand, military governors were to exercise supreme authority within their respective zones. On the other, as the text clearly stipulates, "During the occupation Germany shall be treated as a single economic unit"; "So far as practicable, there shall be uniformity of treatment of the German population throughout Germany" and "supreme authority is exercised . . . jointly" by an Allied Control Council "in matters affecting Germany as a whole." Somewhat ironically, considering the city's dramatic history in the years to follow, the text refers to Berlin only as the venue of the Allied Control Council, though both Harriman and Ben Cohen of the American delegation were "distinctly uneasy" about the idea of putting it there, considering the still-unresolved question of Western access to the former, and presumably future, capital.[10]

The text confirmed that Germany would be dismembered de facto. But it also took pains to establish that, pending de jure settlement by the peace conference that would presumably follow, the hitherto German territories east of the Oder-Neisse line were under Soviet or Polish administration only. "For the fourth time I restated my position and explained that territorial cessions had to be made by treaty and ratified by the Senate," Truman told his diary emphatically.[11] "To prepare for eventual peaceful cooperation in international life by Germany," the occupiers committed themselves to disarm, demilitarize, and denazify the country, but also to democratize the population in their custody.

Subsequent headings address reparations, the disposal of the German navy and merchant marine; the future status of Koenigsberg "and the adjacent area"; war criminals; Austria; Poland; the eventual conclusion of peace treaties with Italy, Bulgaria, Romania, Hungary, and Finland, and their admission to the United Nations; trusteeships for Italian overseas territories; revised procedures for allied control commissions that had already become objects of controversy in Romania, Bulgaria, and Hungary; a euphemistically titled provision for "Orderly Transfers of German Populations," and a generic reference to meetings between "the Chiefs of Staff of the three Governments on military matters of common interest."

Yet, revealingly, the subject of the very first subhead is not the victors' relationship to the Germans, let alone to Austria, Italy, or Germany's other wartime allies, but their relationship to one another. Its provision "for the establishment of a Council of Foreign Ministers . . . to continue the necessary preparatory work for the peace settlement" confirms what was virtually self-evident in 1945: that the signatories expected further summits to follow Potsdam just as earlier summits had preceded it, and regarded the postwar occupation and administration of Germany as issues inextricably connected with their broadest hopes and concerns for the postwar world.

In the meantime, the victors proceeded to occupy and administer Germany on their own terms. In fact, it remained a matter of vivid controversy whether these were compatible with the Potsdam accords the Big Three had agreed to jointly, or were even consistent in themselves. But in contrast to Potsdam, the terms of zonal policy could be formidably precise. Though its drastic economic sanctions, proscriptions of contact with the German population, and the like were subsequently written off as counterproductive and unworkable, the original policy guideline for the American zone, more generally known as JCS-1067, is more than twice as long as the Potsdam accords for all of Germany.[12] The impact of zonal, or independent national, policy was also intended to be lasting, particularly in the Soviet zone, where the basic outlines of the later German Democratic Republic could be clearly recognized within a year after the war.[13] Yet after their fashion, both sides continued to comply with Potsdam for years and decades afterwards, and it is widely agreed that it was at least 1947 before Americans basically resolved to reverse their original policies.

WHY THE AGREEMENTS CAN BE SEEN BOTH AS SUCCESS AND FAILURE

Given the already considerable and probably unbridgeable differences in the way the United States and the Soviet Union saw Germany and one another, the arrangements they reached together are perhaps all the more remarkable. Not only are many of them still visible and operative after nearly forty years of Cold War, many have even been ratified post facto by postwar German governments as well as the original authors. Measured by their ostensible goal, the restoration of a kind of radically improved Weimar Republic within truncated borders that the Potsdam accords seem to imply, the arrangements might be considered a failure. But measured against the minimal goal of defeating a common enemy and keeping it defeated, they compare favorably, for example, with the Treaty of Versailles and most other solutions to "the German Question" since at least the 1848 revolutions.

It is, in fact, both humbling and illuminating to realize how the wartime agreements on the postwar occupation and administration of Germany and its former allies continue to defy or evade easy classification—agreements plural, it should be emphasized, since it is virtually impossible to point to any single arrangement, including Potsdam, that was seen at the time as definitive. Were they still alive, it would probably surprise the signatories that what they almost self-evidently regarded as the provisional, improvisatory, and incremental product of wartime contingencies had not only turned into one of those proverbial provisoria that lasted, but had become an almost reassuringly familiar feature in a postwar landscape significantly different from what they presumably had in mind.

Should we regard the arrangements and consequences of the Teheran, Yalta, and Potsdam summits, the 1943 Moscow foreign ministers conference, the EAC, and all the rest, as diplomatic successes or implementational failures, agreements to agree or disagree, evidence of *la force des choses,* or lost opportunities? In one sense or another, the answer to each alternative is both yes and no. Even after forty years, the context, motivation, and general expectations of the wartime agreements on Germany not only challenge our basic assumptions about the origins and premises of the superpower relationship and Cold War, but our very sense of historical effect and cause, political means and ends.

On the one hand, it was relatively easy to reach agreements on occupation, dismemberment, partition, reparations, expulsions, disarmament, democratization, denazification and all the rest, at least in principle, because the negotiating parties were concerned, even eager, to reach them for a variety of contingent and long-term reasons. But the agreements covered a multitude of cracks, and required a lot of paper. Similarly, the obstacles to agreement were quite severe, given the vast differences in national interest, historical experience, and policy-making process that divided the two powers. Yet once made, the agreements were both successfully and unsuccessfully implemented for reasons having to do with Germany, interests of other powers, the relationship between the superpowers per se, and the intrinsic ambiguity of the agreements. It is imaginable that the governments involved might have reached significantly different arrangements. But one can reasonably ask whether the world today would be a better place to live in if they had.

On the other hand, it was not only initially difficult but became progressively harder to reach agreement as the war went on because the imminence of victory required the allies to reach more decisions of greater precision, which in turn could only amplify the inherent differences between them. Yet the obstacles to agreement, while considerable, were not insuperable, since neither the United States nor the Soviet Union had an immediate interest in ending cooperation with the end of the war, and both seem to have favored agreements on Germany, however imperfect, to no agreement at all. The obstacles to agreement lay in the very nature and basic values of the respective states. Agreement on significantly different terms would have required the superpowers to be significantly different countries from what history had actually made them.

THE U.S.–SOVIET RELATIONSHIP
AND AMERICAN PUBLIC OPINION

As might be imagined, many of the basic ambiguities of the agreements on Germany derived from basic ambiguities of the Soviet-American alliance itself. It is hard to recall the alliance without also recalling the metaphorical glass, half-filled and half-empty, or Dr. Johnson's observation about dogs walking on their hind legs: "It is not done well; but you are surprised to find it done at all." [14] As Shakespeare said of greatness, some nations are born allies, some achieve alliances and some have alliances thrust upon them. Only the last describes the Soviet-American relationship in World War II. To a point, the alliance owed its existence to the historical memory of interested Americans including President Roosevelt, who were determined to learn from errors going back to the Wilsonian debacle after World War I, the better to exploit a second chance at genuine postwar cooperation. To a qualified degree, it also owed its existence to Stalin. A believing Marxist-Leninist and a grand master of *realpolitik,* he was a connoisseur of power who recognized the economic and potential military supremacy of the United States before the war began.[15] Stalin is unlikely to have had any taste or capacity for the kind of postwar cooperation that appealed to so many of Roosevelt's constituents. But he clearly saw the United States as a force to propitiate and contend with. In the end, of course, it was neither Roosevelt nor Stalin, but Hitler who created the alliance, and even then only after both the United States and Soviet Union had made elaborate, even frantic, efforts to stay out of the war.

From Washington to Hollywood, American wartime propagandists worked overtime to gainsay the differences between such reluctant allies, and demonstrate the natural affinities of history, temperament, style, and national interest that made the alliance practically inevitable. But in fact, it was nothing of the kind. If Gallup reported in early 1939 that 83 percent of Americans would rather see Russia win in the event of war between Russia and Germany, this only meant that Americans disliked Germany more than Russia. Asked the same summer to name their favorite country, 12 percent said Britain, 7 percent France, 3 percent Germany, but only 1 percent the Soviet Union. Asked to name their least favorite country, 58 percent named Germany, 12 percent Italy and 8 percent the Soviet Union. Asked to name the foreign statesman they liked least, "Both American and French voters named Hitler, Mussolini, and Stalin in that order," Gallup reported even before conclusion of the Hitler-Stalin pact in August. During the winter war with Finland of 1939–40, Americans expressed their support for Finland by a margin of 88–1. On the eve of the German invasion of the Soviet Union, after nearly two years of German-Soviet cooperation, 71 percent of Americans believed that "the Communist party in this country should be forbidden by law," with virtually no difference between high-, middle-, and low-income respondents.[16]

Predictably, American attitudes changed significantly with the German invasion of the Soviet Union. Only days afterward, Americans reported that they favored Russia over Germany by 72–4, with 17 percent reporting no difference and 7 percent no opinion. Income variation seems again to have had little effect on answers, though Catholics, whose support for the Russians was 65–6, lowered the national average. Asked, on the other hand, for their actual assessment of the war, only 22 percent of Americans believed the Russians would eventually win. On the second anniversary of the Hitler-Stalin pact and the German invasion of Poland, Americans nonetheless rejected by 58–34 a separate peace with Germany at Russia's expense, even if Germany should agree to pull out of the other conquered states. By December 1941, with America finally in the war, there was 80–10 support for a "joint war council" of "the United States, Britain, Russia and their allies" to plan common operations against the Axis powers, though "operations" was presumably understood in a military sense only, since a poll in spring 1942 showed a majority of Americans reluctant to consider peace plans until the war was won.[17]

Yet as late as January 1943, fewer than one American in two replied positively to the question "Do you think Russia can be trusted to cooperate with us when the war is over?" Posed repeatedly throughout the war, the question produced impressively consistent results. Trust for the Soviet Union peaked at nearly 70 percent among the college-educated and respondents in business or the professions. But it hovered at around 40 percent among the grade school-educated and manual workers. Only with both Allied and Soviet forces converging on Germany in March 1945 did trust enjoy a positive majority of 55–31. Yet even in the euphoria of victory three months later, positive answers had declined to 45 percent. Perhaps paradoxically, 49 percent of Americans nonetheless favored a postwar defensive alliance with the Soviet Union. In October 1945, they opposed a $6 billion postwar loan to the Soviet Union by a 2–1 margin— though it should be added for perspective that a few months later they also opposed a $4 billion postwar loan to Britain by the same margin. The survey data recall an aphorism of the Viennese publicist Karl Kraus. "She said to herself: Sleep with him, all right. But no intimacy." [18]

HOW EACH SIDE DEFINED
ITS INTERESTS AND OBJECTIVES

In a sense, Germany was what World War II was all about. No war in history, not even the Thirty Years War, the wars of Napoleon or World War I, was more self-evidently fought to determine the future of Germany. This was as true for America, whose earliest war plans [19] put Europe at the head of the strategic table, as it was for the Soviet Union.

Yet for both powers, Germany was only in part an end in itself. Their hopes and plans for Germany were also subsumed in the allies' view of the world and their relationship with one another. Throughout the war, Americans, both private and official, tended to frame Germany within the larger question of a post-isolationist America. But even before America formally entered the war, commitments were measured against the tolerances and expectations of allies and domestic constituencies. They were then accommodated to the actual course of military operations.

Two of the foundations of Soviet-American agreement—and disagreement—on the eventual occupation and administration of Germany were thus established before the wartime alliance itself. Between them, they constituted America's war goals, and an implied challenge to the Soviet Union's. Hortatory and unspecific as it was, the Atlantic Charter of September 1941 was to Roosevelt the necessary condition if Americans were to join the British empire in the war against Hitler.[20] But the Charter's envisaged postwar world of national self-determination, collective security, and equal economic opportunity could also be understood as a signal to the Russians, and a mortgage on future American policy. Soviet territorial claims, particularly on Poland, were in direct and inevitable conflict with the stated goals of the Anglo-American alliance. Since there was no imaginable solution to the Polish problem that did not also affect the Germans of East or West Prussia, Pomerania, Silesia, or Danzig, the resulting differences on the future of Poland embarrassed and preoccupied the Western allies from the beginning of their alliance with the Soviet Union, and compounded the difficulties of a settlement on Germany through the end of the war—and indeed well beyond it.

The other stipulation for a German settlement, and the agreements on joint occupation and administration it would require, was the demand for Germany's unconditional surrender. It was proclaimed unilaterally by Roosevelt at a Casablanca press conference in January 1943, almost a year before Roosevelt and Stalin even met. But it too was a signal to the Russians, who themselves acceded to it only later, that America would stay the course,[21] notwithstanding delays in mounting a second front in Western Europe. Because it implied joint responsibility and presumable cooperation in the postwar government of a Germany defeated and occupied by the victors, the Casablanca declaration effectively bound together both powers, barring a separate peace between Germany and the Soviet Union or a quite extraordinary turn of military fortune that permitted, or required, occupation by only one of the allies. Such a plan, in fact, existed. Known as RANKIN, it foresaw a race for Berlin in the event of sudden German collapse. But its purpose was not to beat the Russians; it was rather to prevent chaos.[22]

In any case, this was all quite hypothetical. In practice, unilateralism was no longer an option. Even in early 1943, with Soviet and German forces locked in the battle for Stalingrad and Anglo-American forces preparing to take the offensive in North Africa, two points were already quite clear and would become clearer as the war progressed. First, the postwar disposition of Germany could no longer be addressed in isolation from other issues. Second, Americans neither could nor wanted to address the occupation and administration of postwar Germany alone.

Despite its profound concern, and almost legendary internal differences, about the role and place of Germany in a postwar settlement, Washington was at least as fervently concerned with the defeat of Japan and a new order in the Pacific, a reluctant America's perennial susceptibility to isolationism, and the country's future global role. Agreement on Germany accordingly became a means to a variety of ends. They ranged from assurance of Soviet support in the Pacific war—"There were many reasons for my going to Potsdam, but the most urgent . . . was to get from Stalin a personal reaffirmation of Russia's entry into the war against Japan," Truman still maintained years later in his memoirs[23]—to concern for Senate ratification of the United Nations and the eventual peace treaty that were finally and definitively to ease America into an active and responsible role in world affairs.

It was a fact of wartime life by 1943 that the Soviet ally was more equal than others if Americans were to win the victory and get the postwar world they wanted. As a result, two hitherto separable issues, the future of Germany and the future of Soviet-American relations, began to merge almost from the first Soviet-American contacts in the aftermath of the German invasion. At the same time, the relative weight of the Anglo-American alliance declined until it could seem to Harriman at Potsdam that Secretary of State Byrnes looked on the discussions "as an argument between Stalin and Churchill, and that he was going to mediate between the two."[24]

HOW AGREEMENT REFLECTED BOTH DISCRETE AND COMPLEMENTARY INTERESTS

Secure for the last time behind two oceans, America could to some degree regard Germany as a discretionary problem. There was little question of physical attack, despite the elaborate fantasies of German naval planners and the desperate improvisations of Wilhelmine diplomacy.[25] As Stalin himself was aware, America could choose whether and when to intervene in Europe. Given the way Americans traditionally viewed human rights, single-power hegemony in Europe, and freedom of the seas, there were perfectly good reasons for Americans to join the anti-German side in two world wars. But it was no accident that extended and embittered national debate preceded both interventions.

It was also no surprise that Russia, as a continental power, should take a different view. For the Russians, irrespective of regime, Germany was an existential problem. Be it as ally or adversary, role model or cautionary example, it was also the object of an exemplary love-hate relationship and an integral part of the continental balance of which Russia too was an inextricable part.

For Soviet policymakers, like their American counterparts, the impact of historical memory could hardly be overestimated. But refracted through the double prism of Russian and Soviet experience, and again through the astigmatic lens of Marxist ideology, memory was a problematic guide. Just as the Wilsonian experience left its marks on Roosevelt, World War I, the Bolshevik revolution, civil war, and foreign interventions could hardly help but have left their marks on Stalin. But abortive speculations in German revolution at the end of World War I, the collapse of Weimar, the rise of Hitler, and disasters in miscalculation from Brest-Litovsk and Rapallo to the Hitler-Stalin pact, left their marks on Soviet policy too.

If the Wilsonian values of the Atlantic Charter were America's closest approximation of war goals, the territorial claims of the Hitler-Stalin pact might be seen as the Soviet equivalent, with further such demands self-confidently delivered on Foreign Minister Vyacheslav Molotov's visit to Berlin in November 1940.[26] Ironically, the Soviet goals survived the fracture of the alliance that occasioned them. Stalin explicitly linked the same claims to the general issue of Anglo-Soviet trust and the formulation of common war goals when he wrote to Churchill in November 1941.[27] They were already on the agenda when Britain's Foreign Minister Eden arrived in Moscow a month later, and Molotov himself delivered them in Washington the following May.[28]

In the abstract, both powers saw their interests as symmetrical, or at least as complementary. For the Soviet Union, as for the United States, the purpose of the war was a postwar order of global and regional security in which Germany would no longer be a threat. Taken at their wartime words, both sides sought vengeance and security. They agreed to preserve the unified Germany that had existed since 1870. But, paradoxically, they also wanted it dismembered or at least rearranged, and possibly under the control of other powers. Roosevelt, for example, spoke regularly of leaving Germany to the Europeans, and had serious doubts as late as Yalta whether Americans could be persuaded to stay on in Europe for even two years after victory. But Stalin too was deeply reluctant to be left holding the bag for Germany without the support of the Western allies. At the same time, there were also plans for a postwar Germany transformed by the occupying powers into a form more congenial to the occupiers, though not necessarily into their literal copy, since it was understood that Germany had a style and history of its own. Communism fit Germany as a saddle fits a cow, Stalin reportedly told Stanislaw Mikolajczyk, the Polish exile premier, in August 1944,[29] and while he presumably told Milovan Djilas with equivalent sincerity that the export of social systems would distinguish World War II from previous wars,[30] this was hardly conclusive evidence of his plans for postwar Germany.

Given the creeds, interests, styles, and historical experience both sides brought with them, any consensus on the meanings of global and regional security, self-determination, or democracy, was a lot to ask. But there was at least a basic, if imperfect, consensus on what was needed to make Germany unthreatening.

The area of agreement was actually fairly substantial, and at least two of the fundamentals were as good as axiomatic to both postwar superpowers. First, they meant to eradicate National Socialism, on grounds that the Nazi regime was evil, but not necessarily identical with Germany, and that Nazi and German might therefore be separable. Second, they intended to liquidate "Greater Germany," the expansive conflation of prewar Germany with Austria, the Sudetenland, and various other border territories that Hitler had assembled between 1938 and 1940 in the name of national self-determination. This meant eventual restoration of Austrian independence after four-power occupation on the German model; reversion of annexed territories of Alsace and Lorraine to France; and Czechoslovakia's recovery of the Sudetenland. By the end of 1943 at the latest, it was also clear that the new Polish frontiers, which so concerned the Russians and which the Western powers could hardly oppose by a military presence of their own, meant new German frontiers as well.

Given the growing certainty of German defeat, and German inability or unwillingness to respond to Soviet peace initiatives, it was also clear that unconditional surrender must lead inexorably to common allied policies on surrender and occupation. It seemed logical, in turn, that an occupation regime would keep the Germans under control until the victors could agree on some more permanent postwar status. Meanwhile the occupiers would presumably see to the post-Nazi transformation, or at least normalization, of the Germans. Reparations were another area of vague consensus. While America had no intrinsic interest in reparations, they obviously mattered a great deal not only to the Russians, but to all occupied Europeans. So Americans had no interest in opposing them per se, despite traumatic memories of what they had led to in the 1920s and 1930s.

There was consensus again on who was to occupy Germany and on at least one large purpose of the occupation. While there might be some question of who should govern postwar France, there was remarkably little resistance to letting France help govern postwar Germany, at least once it was established that the French zone would be created at no cost to the Soviet zone. Though actual procedure remained strikingly unspecific until almost the end of the war, it was also agreed in principle that major war criminals would somehow be prosecuted and, still more vaguely, arraigned and extradited.[31]

In actual practice, this all proved complicated in ways the signatories scarcely imagined. With at least a consensus of declared intent behind them, both sides seemed to expect their arrangements to work out, and determined, in their respective ways, to get along, at least in Germany.

WHAT THE TWO SIDES WANTED
AND WHAT THEY WERE PREPARED TO PAY

Paradoxically, internal differences on both sides might actually have facilitated agreement. In practice, intramural differences buffered direct confrontation between the sides. Concerned lest they squabble openly with their associates and partners, both sides tended in dealing with each other to favor the soft formulation that subsequently led to wrath, but meanwhile saved both from the hazards of precision at the conference table. Not only were both governments internally divided on their actual purposes in Germany, they were also at odds on Europe, the world, and their relationship with one another. As usual, the American differences are more accessible to historical examination. They are, in fact, an anthology, even a walk-in museum, of bureaucratic politics at the highest level. But Soviet behavior both during and after the war leaves little doubt of similar confusions.

On the American side, postwar planning began quite early, and eventually engaged much of the executive branch of government. By early 1942, the War Department was training military administrators, though it was unclear for what. Meanwhile, a top-level State Department task force was already at work on Germany.[32] War and State were subsequently joined by Treasury, whose intermittent but powerful influence on German policy was an American specialty without equivalence in the other allied governments; by the OSS, the wild card of wartime Washington with its ubiquitous connections and its cadre of German-Jewish intellectuals; by various bureaucratic smallfry like the Foreign Economic Administration; and a kaleidoscopic series of interagency committees.[33]

Finally, there was the President, who was the linchpin in the entire process by constitutional mandate. As it happened, Roosevelt was personally as well as institutionally interested in Germany. He liked making foreign policy, knew a little about Germany from personal experience, and had strong, if ambiguous, views about its future. But he also liked to defer decisions while allies, associates, and subordinates worked out and debated alternatives. The result reflected both the President's role and style, his decision and indecision. By the end of the war in Europe, there were at least two significantly different American policies on Germany, respectively embodied in JCS-1067 and the Potsdam accords. Each was eventually carried out concurrently by a new President who sincerely believed he was only executing Roosevelt's intent.[34]

Whatever the shortcomings in the American position and the German settlement it contributed to, it is hard to ascribe them to official disinterest or inattention. The problem lay elsewhere. All the actors had learned from events within their lifetimes. They had, however, learned significantly different things. While Nazis were to be punished and Germany to be decentralized, in the prevailing State Department view, Germans were to be rehabilitated in the long run, because the costs of doing otherwise were too great for Europe and the world. Perhaps most important, given the disaster of post-World War I reparations, the economic confusion they led to, and the orgy of malignant nationalism that followed in the 1930s, the State Department took a dim view of economic sanctions. It pushed hard for economic reconstruction instead, and generally favored German economic recovery—though there was also at least a strong minority position that gave postwar economic priority to France. Both the State Department consensus and the Department's relative bureaucratic weight were perceptible in the Potsdam agreements of 1945, which provided inter alia for a unified German economy and a German central administration.

Under Secretary of State Sumner Welles, who was an unreconstructed hawk and a close personal friend of the President's, was a significant exception to the prevailing consensus. Even after their abortive attempt to kill Hitler in July 1944, Welles still believed the Prussian generals ran Germany. His book on postwar peacemaking, with its proposal for radical dismemberment of Germany, was a bestseller in 1944.[35] But his views ceased to matter very much after his rather abrupt resignation from office in the summer of 1943, and the death of his friend Roosevelt.

On the other hand, it mattered quite a lot in the bureaucratic politics of wartime Washington that Henry Stimson, the secretary of war, shared the State Department position. A man of considerable personal authority and a Republican of strong internationalist sympathies, Stimson was an important figure of domestic consensus in a Democratic administration. As secretary of state himself in the early 1930s, he had also concluded that the relatively punitive peace imposed on Germany in 1919 was unworkable. With victory approaching, Stimson's views weighed heavily against Treasury-supported plans for the "pastoralization" and radical dismemberment of Germany.[36]

Yet even Stimson had an uphill fight against his department's inertia. Notwithstanding the healthy respect of Wall Street Republicans like himself and Assistant Secretary John J. McCloy for the integrity of the international economy, the Army's disposition was to avoid political commitments wherever possible, and simply get on with the war. At the EAC in 1944, the Army not only held out against any practicable plan for the zonal division of Germany, but did everything possible to keep the nonmilitary

Americans in the delegation from agreeing to anyone else's. Insisting that the invasion of Europe was a "purely military" enterprise, Army spokesmen even argued that zonal division should be left to military fortune.[37] With precedents as remote as Cuba, the Philippines, and the postbellum South to guide it, the Army inclined to see the job of military government as the restoration of administrative normality. Ironically, their circumspection only favored the Treasury's quite contrary views. Treasury wanted to wipe out the German economy. The Army wanted to avoid responsibility for running it. Their respective interests led to the legendary sanctions embodied in JCS-1067, issued about two weeks after Roosevelt's death, and thus to a position dramatically different from what the State Department espoused and Truman and Stalin agreed to, scarcely three months later. Yet both Potsdam, with its vision of German economic unity, and JCS-1067, with its unilateral implication of a Carthaginian peace in the U.S. zone, were binding American policy.

In a curious way, the rise and fall and rise again of Treasury policy not only illuminated American choices and processes, but Soviet processes too. Treasury had become a major actor because of its responsibility for printing and distributing occupation currency. But this was no more than a necessary condition. It assumed the actual role it did because its senior officials regarded themselves as the Administration's conscience in matters involving postwar economic cooperation, and because Henry A. Morgenthau, Jr., the secretary of the treasury, was a friend and neighbor of Franklin D. Roosevelt, the President of the United States. Treasury influence on planning for postwar Germany took two forms. One was the so-called Morgenthau plan, which Roosevelt not only adopted for a brief moment in September 1944, but even managed to peddle to the British. The other was allied policy, ratified at the ministerial level but initiated below it, for debauching the German currency.

At one level, the Morgenthau plan reflected the Secretary's campaign against the Army's relatively lenient view of military government. But its deeper sources were a debate on reparations for victims of German conquest already well underway by the summer of 1944 as allied armies approached the German borders, and the institutional conviction of the British Foreign Office that German economic chaos was a good thing for all parties. "What we want from Germany is peace, not reparations," Morgenthau's assistant secretary, Harry Dexter White, argued in August 1944. "If to obtain that objective, it was necessary to reduce Germany to the status of a fifth-rate power, that should be done."[38] To supporters of the Morgenthau plan, the logic was virtually axiomatic: if "pastoralization" was the goal, it followed that the whole German industrial economy could be distributed as reparations, with the British and Russians as the presumable beneficiaries.

The irony was that neither ally saw it this way. Stalin appears to have had nothing good to say about the Morgenthau plan, and it was never accepted as common allied policy. White seems to have believed, in fact, that assurance of a big American postwar loan would increase Soviet support for the Treasury position. His position implies that, far from seeing the Morgenthau plan as good for Soviet interests, the Russians needed incentives to accept it.[39]

The Treasury's decision to issue the Russians a duplicate set of plates for printing occupation currency was another story. It was clear from what they did that the Russians found it hard to decide whether they wanted to operate and tap the German industrial economy, or pack it up and ship it home. But they were as keen for a cheap occupation as any other victor, and the access to Naafis and PXs afforded by a common currency can only have made the idea of postwar inflation more attractive. Since the Russians had been assured of virtually any amount of American military marks anyway, and could plausibly threaten to print their own money in the event American plates were denied, the Army acquiesced in the decision. Whether intended or not, what resulted was a flood of funny money that did as much to drown interzonal cooperation in the occupation and administration of Germany as any of the war's more celebrated decisions. Before the party finally ended in a currency reform that the Russians bitterly contested, it was estimated that the Russians issued at least 78 billion military marks, compared to the Western allies' 10.5 billion.[40]

In many ways, the Soviet dilemmas mirrored those of their allies, just as Soviet policies imply a similar series of improvisations, trade-offs, trial balloons, and bureaucratic compromises. Georgi Malenkov, for example, was believed to favor stripping German industry for economic reasons; Anastas Mikoyan and Andrei Zhdanov to oppose it for both practical and political reasons.[41] Americans, at least, had two plans for the administration of postwar Germany. Marshal Vasilii Sokolovsky's political advisor Sergei Tiulpanov, the number two man in the Soviet military administration, admitted after the war that the Russians, in effect, had not even had one.[42]

After the fact, Soviet policy could be seen to conform impressively to an "Action Program" cooked up on orders from above by a committee of German exile *apparatchiki* in Moscow between October 1944 and their departure for Germany the following February.[43] But German Communists were actually the last resort in a quest for German interlocutors that had begun with Foreign Minister Joachim von Ribbentrop. Had there been any anti-Hitler Nazis to deal with, there might have been a deal with them as late as 1943. In the aftermath of Stalingrad, hopes turned instead to the anti-Nazi right, incorporated in a National Committee for Free Germany, whose leadership consisted heavily and conspicuously of aristocratic military officers. The mandate to be the Russians' Germans seems to have fallen to the German Communists in Moscow only when all else failed. Even then, the Russians seem never to have regarded their plans for the Soviet zone as a binding model for all Germany, or as preemptive of some different arrangement they might reach with their allies.[44]

Like Roosevelt, Stalin was the ultimate arbiter, though, again like Roosevelt, his style could be remarkably opaque. "From what is known today about Stalin's style of decision making, it appears that he seldom made up his mind in advance," Mastny argues, "or if he did, he would not immediately reveal his choices even to his associates."[45] His views on Germany seem as prolix and elusive as Roosevelt's.

Soviet ambivalence seems to have reflected a calculus of priorities in some ways complementary to those of their allies, but in some ways very different. The immediate concern was obviously to prevail and ultimately triumph in a total war with an implacable adversary, whose stated policy was not simply the capitulation, but the annihilation of the Soviet Union.[46] For the Soviet Union as for the United States, definitive decisions on reconstruction, general and regional security, the postwar shape of Germany, Europe and all the rest, had therefore to await the outcome of the war and the defeat of the Germans.

Paradoxically, the challenge of Hitler's war on the Soviet Union led the Russians to consider three different courses. Each was in some degree at odds with the other, but none seems to have been mutually exclusive. The first was a separate peace with Germany—or in any case a more accommodating peace than the unconditional surrender demanded by the Western allies. Whether the intention was cutting losses, hedging bets,

or bringing pressure on the Western allies to step up their own military pace, it continued to figure in Soviet policy until nearly the end of the war. The question of postwar
Germany seems to have turned up for the first time as a common Soviet-American issue
only because of American concern for what might happen if the Germans collapsed
before the Allies arrived in France. When the subject appeared on the agenda of the
foreign ministers meeting in Moscow in October 1943, it was because the State Department wanted to address it. Even then, the Russians responded evasively to a State
Department draft calling for joint occupation, demilitarization, and decentralization of
Germany, territorial revisions, and extradition of war criminals.[47]

The second Soviet course, particularly after June 1941, was obviously alliance with
Britain and the United States. In practice, this meant accommodation of their concerns
with the expectation that the rewards of wartime collaboration, of which Lend-Lease
was a powerful example, might continue after the war was over. From an orthodox
Soviet point of view, the Western allies might be scarcely less hostile to the Soviet
Union than the Germans were. Soviet policy could as plausibly regard them as rivals,
even adversaries, with respect to postwar Germany. Yet they were not merely *real*
powers in the sense of the *Realpolitik* that Soviet diplomacy invariably favored. They
were also likely winners, and Stalin himself acknowledged that their military support
and industrial resources were a matter of existential importance.[48]

The third course all along was seduction, cooptation, pursuit, or outright invention
of East European clients and satellites to assure the security of the Soviet Union against
future aggression. This led inevitably to Soviet designs on their neighbors' sovereignty
and territory. Ironically, these led to conflicts with Germany before June 1941 and the
Western democracies thereafter. Yet the allied accords on the occupation and administration of Germany can be seen as much as a complement to Soviet designs in Eastern
Europe as an alternative to them.

As a general proposition, Americans wanted a global order of collective security,
that is, a United Nations with its Security Council and five permanent members, including the Soviet Union, in which America would finally play the responsible role it had
rejected in 1919. They also wanted all possible help in the continuing war against Japan.
They regarded the Soviet Union as a crucial partner, both during the war and after. In
the President's grand design, they were one of the four global "policemen," whose
respective regional beats added up to the balance of power Roosevelt considered essential to a peaceful postwar order. It was hoped that they would thus make a postwar
United Nations workable, as the prewar League of Nations was not, and so make it
acceptable to a U.S. Senate, whose rejection of Woodrow Wilson's League was both
vivid and formative in Roosevelt's memory. For their part, Soviet leaders wanted postwar
reconstruction aid, a Western hedge or buffer against German recovery, and a regional
sphere of influence that would at least insure them against the isolation and foreign
invasion the Soviet Union had known since 1917 and Russia had known much longer.
Just as the Americans considered the Russians integral to their postwar plans, so was
the United States considered crucial to the Soviet Union's idea of a postwar order.

Germany was where everybody's wishes met. Consistency was largely in the eye
of the beholder. ". . . the Soviet Union was pursuing two contradictory policies at the
same time: a policy of cooperation with the United States and Britain and a policy of
extending its control over the neighboring states of Eastern Europe without challenge
from the United States," Harriman told Truman.[49] He could hardly be aware of a third
policy concurrent with the other two. Even as the war was ending, banners in the Soviet

zone quoting Stalin proclaimed that "Hitlers come and go, but the German people goes on forever." An indigenous Communist *apparat,* that once carried 15 percent of the vote in national elections, was meanwhile bidding hard for German hearts and minds. Yet for the moment at least, each of the three policies was at least as valid as the American odd couple embodied in the Potsdam Declaration and JCS-1067.

Some degree of cooperation was obviously important to both sides, and both were prepared to pay a price. For all the increasing unease about events in Eastern Europe, and an endless succession of Soviet slights and rebuffs in the course of the war, Americans believed in postwar cooperation, notwithstanding the warnings of a Kennan or a Harriman. The military was especially reluctant to risk the wartime alliance, including the promised Soviet intervention against Japan.[50] The Russians were no less anxious about being left alone to exhaust themselves against the Germans.[51] Both sides honored the zonal agreements, once made. RANKIN aside, there was no question of a Western "race for Berlin"[52] or Prague, though postwar anxieties were already mounting. The Western allies also agreed to waive the Geneva and Hague conventions so German prisoners of war could be regarded as potential forced labor.[53]

As subsequent events confirmed, the United States had no intention of going to war over Eastern Europe, let alone the Oder-Neisse territories, just as the Russians had no intention of going to war over Berlin. As always, Western motives and accommodations are easier to map. But there are hints, at least, of meaningful Soviet accommodation. Soviet reticence over Western and American unilateralism in Italy and Japan must surely have been regarded in Moscow as Eastern tit for Western tat, while Stalin's consistently hesitant support for East European Communists, not to mention wartime dissolution of the Comintern, at least inter alia reflected consideration for Western sensibilities.[54]

HOW THE TWO SIDES SAW THE RISKS
OF AGREEMENT AND DISAGREEMENT

There were obvious risks and some less obvious. Ironically, considering Stalin's reservations, there was always an undertone of Western anxiety that the Russians not only meant to communize Germany, but that they might actually succeed.[55] More significantly as the war progressed, there was anxiety about the fate of Eastern Europe and the general direction of Soviet intentions. It was clear early on that the cost of agreement on Germany included the sovereignty of the Baltic republics and dismemberment of East Prussia. Attendant risks included threats to the postwar independence of Eastern Europe, which was a major war goal, and the consequent alienation of Catholic voters in Buffalo, Milwaukee, and Detroit, which was inevitably of concern to a Democratic President.[56] For those who thought about it, including Roosevelt, cooperation with the Russians was a Hobson's choice.[57] But "for the peace of the world," as he told Morgenthau, Roosevelt saw no other alternative.[58]

Yet the choices can hardly have been easier for the Russians. Cooperation with the West on Germany or anything else meant potential exposure to the West, a proverbial source of anxiety since the czars. It also meant at least a degree of dependence on powers that were both militarily and economically superior to the Soviet Union, and inimical to it by definition. Only the West, however, could supply, and deny, the goods and political recognition the Russians most wanted and needed. There was surely less to the brutally automatic suspension of Lend-Lease than met the eye at war's end. But the conspicuous inaction of both the Administration and Congress on a request for $6 billion in postwar credits only rendered more urgent the Soviet need for German industrial reparations. Yet the West persisted in linking these to concessions on Poland, a matter of even greater Soviet concern, while meanwhile denying the Russians direct access to the Ruhr.[59] The linkage only made the Russians less cooperative. It was, as Mastny argues with a nice sense of paradox, as though they had to prove Marx wrong[60] by showing that political consciousness preceded economic being. In the great dialectical scheme of things, economic weakness presumably meant economic dependence, which in turn meant political dependence. So the agreements on Germany as a "single economic unit," with their implied claim on badly needed reparations, also implied an unacceptable Western mortgage on Soviet political independence. Yet at least until the war was over, when it became apparent that the Russians were going to get neither Lend-Lease, nor a U.S. loan, nor direct access to the Ruhr, the Soviet Union, like the United States, seems to have seen no obvious alternative to cooperation.

WHY AND HOW TOP LEADERS ON BOTH SIDES WERE COMMITTED AND ENGAGED

Given both personal interest and the issues at stake, the engagement of top-level leaders was virtually assured in the quest for agreement. Since, directly or indirectly, the future of Germany was what the war was all about, it was axiomatic that agreements affecting it required summit-level decisions. The peculiar role of the U.S. President as both chief executive and commander-in-chief only enhanced the authority of Roosevelt and Truman. Stalin's position as General Secretary of the Soviet Communist Party, which he and his associates alike seemed to view as an extension of the czar's role by other means, also enhanced his authority. Delegated authority invariably led back to the top. Harry Hopkins and Averell Harriman were Roosevelt's personal representatives just as Molotov was Stalin's, and authority in Washington was personalized beyond anything imaginable, save, perhaps, in Moscow. Roosevelt answered in some degree to Congress, to an electorate and public opinion, but never to a cabinet in the parliamentary sense.[61] Stalin effectively answered to no one.

Not everything could be decided at the top, of course. As a result, decisions made short of the summit had consequences top leaders presumably never bargained for—on access to Berlin or the management of occupation currency, for example. Created by the Teheran summit to propose alternatives and options that eventually included the zonal partition of Germany and Berlin, the machinery of joint administration, and the surrender document itself, the EAC was clearly more influential than either Americans or Russians anticipated or intended. Somewhat similarly, the U.S. Treasury continued to play a role in Germany's postwar economy long after its role in Germany's postwar government had ended. But the decisions and indecisions alike were covered and ratified at the summit, and it is not easily imaginable that the allies would have come to other arrangements had Stalin and Roosevelt themselves been present. In contrast to Roosevelt, who took his secretary of the treasury to Quebec to meet Churchill, and his secretary of state nowhere at all to meet Stalin, Truman believed in the State Department as the appropriate organ of foreign policy, and respected the authority of his diplomats. But there was no question in his case where the buck stopped either.

HOW TOP LEADERS ON BOTH SIDES
FACED AND MET DOMESTIC PRESSURES

So far as one can see, both leaders got what they wanted from the folks at home. Roosevelt's feat, especially, was a prodigy of coalition-building at all levels. Support for postwar cooperation with the Russians, and therefore a presidential mandate to negotiate, extended from the Treasury economists, organized liberals, and the CIO, who were the President's most loyal supporters, to the Army, the Wall Street establishment, and large sectors of the Republican party. East European constituents, the Catholic episcopacy, and even skeptical negotiators like Harriman and Kennan suspended their disbelief for the duration. Republicans too responded supportively when polled on the accomplishments of Yalta in March 1945. Among the 70 percent of respondents to a national poll who had heard of the conference, 61 percent, including 52 percent of the previous November's Dewey voters, reported a favorable impression of its accomplishments, compared to only 9 and 12 percent respectively who said they were displeased.[62]

The German agreements reflected domestic pressures, both direct and indirect and so, to some degree, did the rise and fall of the Morgenthau plan. Americans wanted a Carthaginian peace but did not want or intend to pay for it. The deliberate ambiguity of the reparations agreement reflected the same concern. Rightly or not, Americans believed they had paid for German reparations after World War I; they were not about to repeat the error.[63] "Note that nowhere in the Potsdam Protocol is there any provision for the payment of reparations from current production," Byrnes declared emphatically in his memoirs.[64] It is hard to disengage the sequence of effect and cause that link Congressional reservations about a postwar loan to Soviet priorities in Poland and Eastern Europe, Soviet suspicion to American denial of reparations from the Western zones of Germany, and American reparations policy to reciprocal food deliveries from the Soviet zone.

The revealing if ultimately irrelevant squabble between Roosevelt and Churchill over which zone of Germany Americans would occupy was another indicator of domestic pressure. It reflected Roosevelt's conviction that Americans must stay close to the North Sea exits since they were presumably reluctant to stay on in Europe at all. Even the decision to include France in the joint occupation had its domestic component: if Americans were unwilling to mount the watch on the Rhine, somebody else would have to do it.

Given the familiar opacities of Soviet politics, any assessment of domestic opinion as a factor in German, or any other foreign, policy is largely speculation. Soviet positions on Poland, forced labor, and due process for German war criminals, for example, led to friction with the West, and thus might imaginably have been in conflict with Stalin's own preference for open-ended pragmatism. The Red army's legendary brutalization of allied, let alone of enemy, civilians challenged the tolerance even of communist allies.[65] It is at least conceivable that the more conventionally Russian-nationalist, and above all anti-German aspects, of Soviet policy were in some sense acknowledgements of, if not concessions to, national feeling or army sensibilities Stalin felt he had to make.

WHY IT SEEMS UNLIKELY THAT CHANCES
WERE MISSED DUE TO LEADERSHIP

Given the deep ambivalence on both sides, both with respect to Germany and one another, it is hard to see where significant opportunities for mutual accommodation were missed, or how greater engagement or different leadership might have avoided missing them. The Anglo-American invasion of Europe the Russians wanted so badly in 1942 or 1943 might have changed the nature of agreement on Germany in either of two ways. If successful, it might have modified Soviet suspicion that the Western allies were deliberately seeking to weaken the Soviet Union,[66] and led to a military balance in Central, even Eastern, Europe more favorable to the Western powers at war's end. A failure could have led to domestic backlash in the Western democracies, still longer delays in mounting an invasion of France, a military balance in Central, even Western, Europe more favorable to the Soviet Union—or even, if imagination is to frolic unrestrained, first use of atomic weapons against the Germans, not Japan. Any or all of these possibilities would have changed the nature of agreement on the postwar occupation and administration of Germany. But given the military, industrial, and political realities standing between the Anglo-American armies and the Normandy beaches in 1942–43, there is little to gain from such iffy speculation.

Imaginably, a President Byrnes in 1945 might have tried a little harder than Truman, and a President Wallace a little harder than Byrnes, to pursue agreement with the Russians. But as Democratic presidents, both would sooner or later have had to deal with the same concerned constituents, the same Congress and the same indigenously democratic pressures that Truman did from a country upset by Soviet behavior in Eastern Europe, opposed to being made to pay once more for German reparations, and frantic to bring home the troops.

Given the American disposition to get on with the war, get on with the Russians, and get troops home from Europe, it is also hard to see how "a race for Berlin," or a hard line on withdrawal of U.S. troops from their positions in Bohemia and Saxony at war's end, would have made postwar agreement any likelier. Considering the postwar history of Berlin, more specific guarantees of Western access would surely have spared a lot of trouble. But access to the city was rather the evidence of good faith than a cause of it. If the allies were in agreement on the joint occupation of Germany and Berlin, guaranteed access to Berlin presumably followed axiomatically from the general agreement. If, on the other hand, access to Berlin itself required guarantees, then it was presumably because the allies had deeper reservations about Germany and one another. It is therefore hard to imagine that greater precision on Berlin would have advanced more general agreement on Germany. Given the irreconcilable positions on Poland and reparations that existed a priori, it is hard to see how any leaders, but particularly Americans, could have conceded what both sides understood as basic national values and interests without even more radical changes in their respective national equations.

WHY BOTH SIDES FELT SOME SENSE
OF URGENCY—BUT NOT ALWAYS

Like so much else in the diplomacy of World War II, the question of urgency is only another invitation to paradox. Considering that both allies were engaged in history's biggest war to determine Germany's future, it is remarkable how little they managed to say about it, and how reluctantly they actually said it, even at home, let alone in their relations with one another. Of some eight hundred titles on postwar planning, conscientiously abstracted and anthologized by the Library of Congress for presumable official use between the summer of 1943 and the end of 1944, fewer than fifty deal with Germany in even a general sense.[67] But the same reticence can be seen at the highest level. The future of Germany occupies perhaps fifty of eighteen hundred printed pages in the published correspondence of Roosevelt and Churchill. It is scarcely visible at all in Stalin's published correspondence with Roosevelt and Truman.[68] Combined with their actual behavior, the silence confirms a certain sense of urgency—but for summit diplomacy and open options, not agreement per se.

As a wartime rule of thumb, urgency of agreement increased with the likelihood of victory or imminence of defeat, and clearly reflected concern on each side that the other might reconsider its position both on Germany and the alliance per se before the war was won. But the general proposition subsumed a variety of special cases. Some agreement was obviously urgent in 1941–42 if there were to be an alliance at all; that is, both countries had to agree that Germany was a common enemy and that each required the other's support to win the war against the Germans. Urgency obviously receded thereafter until Stalingrad and the collapse of Italy turned thoughts on both sides to the challenges of victory. Allied procrastination over the ''second front'' in France was a famous inhibitor of agreement, especially by the Russians. At the same time, it led to Allied initiatives like the declaration of unconditional surrender, lest the Russians lose faith or interest and seek common cause with the conservative German right incorporated in the National Committee on Free Germany. The imminence of D-Day and the spectacular successes that followed were an incentive to both sides to increase the pace of wartime planning. But the facts of American political life left their marks too. Agreement with Stalin on Poland, for example, which was an integral part of any plan for postwar Germany, was hardly what Roosevelt needed in an election year, and both sides found good reasons to skip a summit altogether between the end of 1943, when they met in Teheran, and early 1945, when they met at Yalta. By the time they met at Potsdam, the fact of German capitulation imposed its own urgency on both sides; on the Russians if they were to get the political recognition and economic benefits they wanted from both Germany and their allies, on the Americans if they were to win Soviet support for the war in the Pacific and the United Nations that most Americans regarded as the chosen vessel of the postwar order. But the agreements at Potsdam themselves confirm that the negotiators were meanwhile prepared to settle for the open-ended status quo post bellum pending further negotiations. Whatever their considerable designs on their respective zones, it is hard to say of the Russians, and virtually impossible to say of the United States, that the division of Germany, at least to the west of the Oder-Neisse line, was consciously regarded as inevitable or desirable until some years later.

HOW LINKAGES AND IMAGES ON BOTH SIDES HELPED LEAD TO BREAKDOWN

To some degree, the breakdown in U.S.–Soviet relations can be ascribed to self-fulfilling expectations, at least on the Russian side. ''It was as if he needed to believe we were betraying him,'' Harriman recalled of Stalin.[69] Considering whom they met and what they knew, it is not remarkable that Americans like Kennan and Harriman, who dealt with the Russians regularly, were consistently more cautious about the future than

Americans further away. Ironically, considering the McCarthyite clichés that followed the war, circumspection came first from the State Department. Meanwhile, senior military leaders like George Marshall and Dwight Eisenhower, and even James Forrestal, the secretary of the navy and first postwar secretary of defense, were in the basically pro-Soviet mainstream of middle-class American opinion. They both wanted and expected cooperation to continue.[70] "He is honest—but smart as hell," Roosevelt's successor told his diary after meeting Stalin at Potsdam. "I liked the little son of a bitch," he added with the implication of betrayal in an unsent letter to Dean Acheson years later.[71] By comparison, Stalin told Djilas that "Churchill will pick your pocket of a kopeck," while Roosevelt "dips in his hand only for bigger coins."[72]

Yet the erosion of the agreements on Germany that followed can be as plausibly ascribed to the efforts to attain or restore them as to unilateral abrogation. In American perspective, loans, grants, reparations deliveries, and so forth were seen as the complement to political accommodation. In Soviet perspective, their delay or denial seems rather to have confirmed an a priori presumption of American bad faith.[73] The Russians saw American distaste for reparations, cancellation of Lend-Lease, delay of the postwar loan request,[74] exclusion of the Soviet Union from direct access to the Ruhr, and suspension of Western reparations deliveries as economic sticks. But from an American perspective they could as reasonably be seen as the extension of carrots by other means, incentives to achieve the administrative and economic unity of Germany—and thereby cut the costs of American military government—that Americans understood as the purpose of Potsdam. Even the Berlin blockade, which so unsurprisingly alarmed the Western powers in 1948, could be seen through Soviet eyes as a drastic—though also abortive, and wildly counterproductive—effort to reverse the Western currency reform that so obviously confirmed the failure of four-power government in Germany, and the end of common hopes for Germany as a "single economic unit."

One can argue that the Cold War between the United States and Soviet Union had already started months, or even years, before Potsdam, as an inevitable consequence of irreconcilable differences between the powers on everything from the postwar government of Poland to the meaning of history or the truths we hold to be self-evident. One can as reasonably argue that it still lay months ahead, or even that it need never have happened at all, had the Russians only been clearer about the extent of their ambitions, and the Americans more forthright about the limits of their toleration. The agreements on Germany, incrementally negotiated between 1943 and 1945, are inconclusive evidence either way. Their breakdown was rather an effect of East-West conflict than its cause.

HOW COMPLIANCE FAILURES WERE BOTH
EFFECT AND CAUSE OF BREAKDOWN

In a sense, the history of implementation is a history of the postwar era. Preservation of a "single economic unit" was obviously a failure, though interzonal trade continued even during the Berlin blockade,[75] and today's East German economy is substantially integrated in the European Community through its West German customers, bankers, and suppliers. The reparations provisions, clearly a crucial key to the viability of all the other agreements,[76] were in bad trouble by early 1946.

"Uniformity of treatment . . . throughout Germany" was hardly attainable either, given the sometimes dramatically different premises that divided not only Americans from Russians, but Americans from Britons, and all three from the French. The Bundeswehr and National People's Army (NVA) reflect the failures of German disarmament—though also its successes, since neither has much in common with the German national army that surrendered to the allies. Berlin became at once the epicenter and barometer of the Cold War.[77] Both the Berlin Agreement of 1971 and the Helsinki Final Act of 1975, which is and will presumably remain the closest approximation of the peace treaty anticipated at Potsdam, ratify a postwar status quo quite different from anything foreseen there, or even at Paris in 1947, where Molotov's defense of German unity contrasted starkly with the standard French communist opposition to German unity in any form.[78]

Self-inflicted or not, there was no way then or since that the "transfer" of ethnic Germans from Poland, Czechoslovakia, and Hungary in 1945–46 could be called "orderly," let alone "humane." The impact of millions of Eastern refugees on Western military governors can hardly be underestimated either.[79] Their pressure on limited food supplies and services was only one more source of American frustration with reparations arrangements that seemed to require much of the Western zones and little of the Russians. In fact, there is strong evidence that Soviet failure to deliver foodstuffs in compensation for deliveries from the West was linked rather to spectacular failures of farm policy in the Soviet zone than to deliberate noncompliance with the Potsdam settlement.[80] But it was not surprising that General Lucius Clay, who was incomparably the most influential figure in American military government, took a different view, and intended or not, the burden on Western military government was the same.

"That the present quadripartite administration of Germany has been a failure from the US standpoint is almost universally acknowledged," Robert Murphy, the senior State Department representative in Germany, declared as early as January 1947. "It was always intended, at least by the US and British, that the Allies should direct and control Germany," he insisted. "It was never envisaged that they should govern, and the present system has proved unequal to this unforeseen task."

In Murphy's view, "the more recalcitrant parties," a rubric that included the French no less than the Russians, were at the same time guilty of "adherence . . . to the letter of written statutes which they claim can only be amended by agreement of all the governments," and perversion "to their own use of the autonomy reserved to the zonal administrations." The result was "separate regimes . . . which daily become more hardened by useage (sic) and established interest and which will be all the more difficult to absorb into a responsible and viable entity."[81]

HOW BOTH SIDES MIGHT SEE
THE AGREEMENTS AS SUCCESSFUL

Yet seen at least by their own lights, the superpowers actually did much of what they came to do. Both Germany and Austria were occupied as planned, and regained their varying degrees of postwar independence, if not in the sense originally intended. Western-style democratization was achieved in the Western zones and Austria, if not in the subsequent German Democratic Republic. But it was always an act of faith to assume that Soviet and American definitions and expectations of democracy coincided anyway. In their respective ways, the occupiers took seriously their mandate to eliminate "excessive concentration of economic power as exemplified . . . by cartels, syndicates, trusts and other monopolistic arrangements," the Americans by antitrust action and industrial codetermination, the Russians by forced socialization. Denazification, like so much else, worked quite differently from what anyone might have imagined. Symbolized by a legendary questionnaire distributed universally in the U.S. zone,[82] American efforts collapsed under the weight of bureaucratic zeal. Soviet efforts took the form of local purges, which encouraged flight to other zones, and cooptation of smaller-fry Nazis by the zonal regime itself or a political subsidiary.[83] But measured by the larger goal of a non-Nazi postwar Germany, it is hard to call denazification a failure, and measured against the common goal of assuring "that Germany never again will threaten her neighbors or the peace of the world," allied policy might even, with all due caution, be called a success.

Placing responsibility for the postwar disappointments is an open-ended exercise. At least from Yalta on, the reparations arrangements are a prime example of how ambiguity was as often intentional as inadvertent, and as frequently a premise of wartime agreement as of postwar friction. Divergent interests clearly emerged after Germany's defeat, though both parties took years to sort out their choices between dividing Germany and reunifying it. Changing circumstances elsewhere, including confrontation in Iran or Greece or changing majorities in Congress, clearly left their marks on the government of postwar Germany. So, of course, did France, which was adamantly opposed to German unity in any form, and dedicated to Germany's political and economic division. Well before the Russians reached conclusions of their own about their German choices, the French had vetoed suprazonal initiatives on economic administration and national party organizations that might conceivably have worked, and so been difficult to reverse.[84]

From a Western perspective, forced socializations and land reforms in the Soviet zone, like the forced amalgamations of the Communist and Social Democratic parties, were a violation of democratic norms and preemption of common allied policy. But from a Soviet perspective, Western occupation policy meant only the intention to restore the undemocratic, pre-Nazi status quo.[85]

Unsurprisingly under the circumstances, further agreement, let alone the envisaged peace treaty, receded as a practical goal, leaving behind the lowest common denominator of wartime consensus: that both sides were prepared to fight for Germany, that neither was prepared to fight the other for it, and that neither could conceive of any Central European order preferable to their own ad hoc arrangements. The traditional "German question," that is, unification of Germany at what price to whom, still surfaced on high-level agenda as late as the Geneva Foreign Ministers meeting of 1959. It commanded at least topical attention, on such issues as Berlin, human rights, and the validity of the postwar borders, in the era of détente. Even today, it still exercises a certain fascination as an object of political speculation.

Yet it was, and remains, hard to imagine any consensus that could lead back to reunification or the open ends of 1945. Leaving aside the years between Bismarck's victories and Hitler's defeat, a more or less unitary German national state has been the exception, not the rule, in European history for reasons having as much to do with the Germans as their neighbors and the victors of World War II. At recurring intervals, each superpower has flirted with the other's German client, and tolerated flirtations with its own. German-German relations have meanwhile yielded a degree of normalization between significantly and increasingly different Germanies, and even different Europes, not easily imaginable in the 1960s, let alone the 1950s. But today's intra-German normality not only challenges and coexists with the Berlin Wall and the old zonal border, with NATO and the Warsaw Pact; in some degree, it depends on them. Improbably compounded of cooperation and confrontation, paradox and purpose, consensus and cross-purpose, intention and inadvertence, superpower agreements on postwar Germany have thus resulted in a security regime *sui generis* that has kept the peace in Europe since World War II.

Notes

1. Report on the Tripartite Conference of Potsdam, Department of State *Bulletin,* vol. XIII, no. 319 (1945), pp. 153–61.

2. Harry S. Truman, *Memoirs,* vol. I (Garden City: Doubleday, 1955–56), pp. 452–55; James F. Byrnes, *Speaking Frankly* (New York and London: Harper, 1947), pp. 85–87.

3. W. Averell Harriman and Elie Abel, *Special Envoy to Churchill and Stalin, 1941–46* (New York: Random House, 1975), pp. 514–15.

4. Ibid., pp. 447–48.

5. Isaac Deutscher, *Stalin* (New York: Oxford University Press, 1967), p. 548.

6. Ernst Deuerlein, ''Auslegung und Vollzug des Potsdamer Abkommens,'' in Ernst Deuerlein et al., *Potsdam und die deutsche Frage* (Cologne: Verlag Wissenschaft und Politik, 1970), pp. 36–92.

7. George F. Kennan, *Memoirs (1925–50)* (Boston: Little, Brown, 1969), pp. 175–197; Lord Strang, *At Home and Abroad* (London: A. Deutsch, 1956), pp. 199–225; Warren F. Kimball, ed., *Churchill and Roosevelt, The Complete Correspondence* (Princeton, N.J.: Princeton University Press, 1984), vol. II, p. 746; John Lewis Gaddis, *The United States and the Origins of the Cold War* (New York: Columbia University Press, 1972), pp. 111 ff.; Paul Hammond, ''Directives for the Wartime Occupation of Germany,'' in Harold Stein, ed., *Civil-Military Decisions* (University, Ala.: University of Alabama Press, 1963), pp. 329ff.

8. Robert H. Ferrell, ed., *Off the Record* (New York: Harper & Row, 1980), p. 58.

9. Byrnes, *Speaking Frankly,* p. 85; Herbert Feis, *Between War and Peace* (Princeton, N.J.: Princeton University Press, 1960), pp. 253 ff.

10. Harriman and Abel, *Special Envoy,* p. 487.

11. Ferrell, *Off the Record,* p. 56.

12. Published as ''Directive to Commander-in-Chief of United States Forces of Occupation Regarding Military Government of Germany,'' Department of State *Bulletin,* vol. XIII, no. 319 (1945), pp. 596–607.

13. Wolfgang Leonhard, *Die Revolution entlaesst ihre Kinder* (Cologne: Kiepenheuer & Witsch, 1955), pp. 324 ff.; Gregory W. Sandford, *From Hitler to Ulbricht* (Princeton, N.J.: Princeton University Press, 1983), passim.

14. *The Oxford Dictionary of Quotations* (Oxford, New York, Toronto, and Melbourne: Oxford University Press, 1979), p. 275.

15. Deutscher, *Stalin,* p. 429.

16. *The Gallup Poll,* vol. 1 (New York: Random House, 1972), pp. 133, 167–68, 197, 285.

17. Ibid., pp. 288–89, 296; Robert Dallek, *Franklin D. Roosevelt and American Foreign Policy* (New York: Oxford University Press, 1979), p. 359.

18. Karl Kraus, *Auswahl aus dem Werk* (Munich: Kosel-Verlag, 1957), p. 14.

19. Kent Greenfield, *American Strategy in World War II* (Baltimore: Johns Hopkins University Press, 1963), passim; Forrest C. Pogue, *George C. Marshall: Ordeal and Hope* (New York: Viking Press, 1966), pp. 19–80.

20. The text can be found in *Foreign Relations of the United States (FRUS) 1941,* vol. I (Washington, D.C.: U.S. Government Printing Office, 1968), pp. 367–69.

21. The transcript of the press conference and subsequent communiqué can be found in

FRUS: Conference at Washington 1941–42 and Casablanca 1943 (Washington, D.C.: U.S. Government Printing Office, 1968), pp. 726–31 and 847.

22. Kimball, *Churchill and Roosevelt,* vol. II, p. 606; Robert E. Sherwood, *Roosevelt and Hopkins,* vol. II (New York: Harper, 1950), pp. 322–23.

23. Truman, *Memoirs,* p. 454.

24. Harriman and Abel, *Special Envoy,* p. 488.

25. Holger Herwig, *The Politics of Frustration* (Boston: Little, Brown, 1976), passim; Barbara Tuchman, *The Zimmermann Telegram* (New York: Viking Press, 1958), passim.

26. George F. Kennan, *Russia and the West* (Boston: Little, Brown, 1961), pp. 315–48; Alan Bullock, *Hitler* (New York: Harper & Row, 1962), pp. 616–21.

27. USSR Commission for the Publication of Diplomatic Documents, *Stalin's Correspondence with Churchill and Attlee, 1941–45,* vol. I (Moscow: Foreign Language Publishing House, 1957), pp. 33, 36.

28. Dallek, *Franklin D. Roosevelt,* pp. 339 ff.; Harriman and Abel, *Special Envoy,* pp. 109–10, 121, 135–7.

29. Deutscher, *Stalin,* p. 537.

30. Milovan Djilas, *Conversations with Stalin* (New York: Harcourt, Brace and World, 1962), p. 90.

31. Bradley F. Smith, *Reaching Judgment at Nuremberg* (New York: Basic Books, 1977), pp. 20–45.

32. Hammond, "Directives For Wartime Occupation," p. 317; Hajo Holborn, *American Military Government* (Washington, D.C.: Infantry Journal Press, 1947), pp. 3 ff.

33. Cf. Hammond, "Directives for Wartime Occupation," pp. 348 ff.; David Rees, *Harry Dexter White* (New York: McCann & Geoghegan, 1973), pp. 173 ff.; Alfons Soellner, *Zur Archaeologie der Demokratie in Deutschland* (Frankfurt am Main: Europäische Verlagsanstalt, 1982), passim.

34. Truman, *Memoirs,* pp. 25–7, 340.

35. Sumner Welles, *The Time for Decision* (Cleveland and New York: Harper, 1945), pp. 336 ff.

36. Henry L. Stimson and McGeorge Bundy, *On Active Service in Peace and War* (New York: Harper, 1948), pp. 566–68.

37. George F. Kennan, *Memoirs,* pp. 164 ff.; John L. Snell, *Dilemma Over Germany* (New Orleans: Hauser Press, 1959), pp. 53 ff.; Gaddis, *The United States and the Origins of the Cold War,* p. 76.

38. Rees, *Harry Dexter White,* p. 248.

39. Vojtech Mastny, *Russia's Road to the Cold War* (New York: Columbia University Press, 1979), pp. 233 ff.; Warren Kimball, *Swords or Plowshares?* (Philadelphia: Lippincott, 1976), pp. 4 ff.; Rees, *Harry Dexter White,* p. 301.

40. Rees, *Harry Dexter White,* pp. 173 ff.; 251 ff.; 485.

41. Mastny, *Russia's Road,* p. 215.

42. Ibid., pp. 280–81.

43. Alexander Fischer, "Antifaschismus und Demokratie," in Deuerlein, *Potsdam,* pp. 23 ff.

44. Mastny, *Russia's Road,* pp. 233 ff.

45. Ibid., p. 213.

46. Alexander Dallin, *German Rule in Russia* (Boulder, Colo.: Westview Press, 1981), pp. 44–59.

47. Tony Sharp, *The Wartime Alliance and the Zonal Division of Germany* (Oxford: Clarendon Press, 1975), p. 3; Mastny, *Russia's Road,* pp. 73 ff., 111 ff., 233 ff.

48. Harriman and Abel, *Special Envoy,* pp. 277 ff., pp. 285 ff.

49. Ibid., p. 447.

50. James McGregor Burns, *Roosevelt: The Soldier of Freedom* (New York: Harcourt Brace Jovanovich, 1970), p. 515, pp. 572 ff.

51. Deutscher, *Stalin*, p. 475.

52. Stephen E. Ambrose, *Eisenhower and Berlin, 1945* (New York: W. W. Norton, 1967), passim; Harriman and Abel, *Special Envoy*, pp. 478 ff.

53. Strang, *At Home*, pp. 209 ff.; Mastny, *Russia's Road*, pp. 150 ff.

54. Deutscher, *Stalin*, pp. 474–75; Mastny, *Russia's Road*, pp. 131 ff., p. 181.

55. David Dallin, "Russia's Plans for Germany," *American Mercury* (October 1944).

56. Burns, *Roosevelt*, p. 152; Dallek, *Franklin D. Roosevelt*, p. 503.

57. Burns, *Roosevelt*, pp. 534–39; Dallek, *Franklin D. Roosevelt*, p. 440.

58. Quoted in Burns, *Roosevelt*, p. 515.

59. Harriman and Abel, *Special Envoy*, pp. 384 ff.; Gaddis, *The United States and the Origins of the Cold War*, pp., 175 ff.

60. Mastny, *Russia's Road*, p. 215.

61. J. M. Lee, *The Churchill Coalition* (Hamden, Conn.: Archon Books, 1980), p. 143.

62. *The Gallup Poll*, p. 492.

63. John E. Backer, *The Decision to Divide Germany* (Durham, N.C.: Duke University Press, 1978), pp. 46 ff.; Charles de Gaulle, *Mémoires de Guerre: Le Salut* (Paris: Librairie Plon, 1959), pp. 465.

64. Byrnes, *Speaking Frankly*, p. 86.

65. Djilas, *Conversations*, pp. 87–88.

66. Burns, *Roosevelt*, pp. 373–4.

67. *Abstracts of Postwar Literature*, 3 vols. (Washington, D.C.: Library of Congress, 1944–45).

68. USSR Commission for the Publication of Diplomatic Documents. *Stalin's Correspondence with Roosevelt and Truman*, vol. II (Moscow: Foreign Language Publishing House, 1957).

69. Harriman and Abel, *Special Envoy*, p. 438.

70. Ibid., pp. 344–46, 502–03.

71. Ferrell, *Off the Record*, pp. 53, 349.

72. Djilas, *Conversations*, p. 61.

73. Harriman and Abel, *Special Envoy*, p. 438.

74. Arthur Schlesinger, Jr., et al., *The Origins of the Cold War* (Waltham, Mass.: and Toronto: Ginn-Blaisdell, 1970), p. 67.

75. J. P. Nettl, *The Eastern Zone and Soviet Policy in Germany*, (London, New York, and Toronto: Oxford University Press, 1951), pp. 228–29.

76. Nettl, *The Eastern Zone*, p. 299; Bruce Kuklick, *American Policy and the Division of Germany* (Ithaca and London: Cornell University Press, 1972), passim.

77. Anne-Marie Le Gloannec, *Un Mur à Berlin* (Brussels: Editions Complexe, 1985), passim.

78. Nettl, *The Eastern Zone*, p. 289.

79. Jean Edward Smith, ed., *The Papers of General Lucius D. Clay* (Bloomington, Ind.; and London: Indiana University Press, 1974), pp. 95, 183–84.

80. Sandford, *From Hitler to Ulbricht*, pp. 104 ff.

81. Robert Murphy, "The Allied Control Authority for Germany," memo submitted to the Secretary of State, January 6, 1947. Copy in James K. Pollock Papers, Bentley Library, University of Michigan.

82. Ernst von Salomon, *Der Fragebogen* (Hamburg: Rowohlt, 1952), passim.

83. Helga A. Welsh, "Die Entnazifizierung der Universitaet Leipzig," *Vierteljahrshefte für Zeitgeschichte*, vol. 2, 1985, pp. 339 ff.

84. Roy Willis, *France, Germany and the New Europe* (London, Oxford and New York: Oxford University Press, 1968), p. 17.

85. Sandford, *From Hitler to Ulbricht*, pp. 185, 229.

3

Negotiations for an Austrian State Treaty

KURT STEINER

The "State Treaty for the Re-establishment of an Independent and Democratic Austria between the USSR, the UK, the USA and France of the one part, and Austria of the other part," was signed at the Belvedere Palace in Vienna on May 15, 1955. It was the result of negotiations over a period of more than eight years.[1] The story of the negotiations among the Allied powers and—after 1954—between them and Austria is one of fits and starts, of periods in which cooperation seemed imminent and periods in which one or the other side engaged in delaying tactics, as dictated by their perceptions of their security interests at a given time. These perceptions were closely related to developments in the Cold War between the United States and the USSR. Statements by the post-Stalin leadership, ostensibly aimed at replacing the Cold War with "peaceful co-existence," were met in the West by demands that the USSR prove its sincerity by deeds, and Western leaders mentioned Soviet agreement to an Austrian treaty as a test of sincerity. The breakthrough came in February 1955, and the treaty was signed three months later.

The basic formula on which agreement was finally reached was that of Austrian neutrality. Although formal consideration of some form of Austrian neutrality was proposed by the USSR at the meeting of the Council of Foreign Ministers (CFM) in Berlin in early 1954, one looks in vain for an articulation of the formula in the text of the treaty. Instead, the manner in which Austria was to assume the status of "permanent neutrality on the Swiss model" was stipulated between an Austrian delegation and the Soviet government in the so-called "Moscow Memorandum" of April 1955, and the Western powers agreed to it when they met in Vienna to sign the treaty.

The negotiations for the Austrian treaty dealt at great length with such issues as boundaries, claims arising out of the war, and the disposition of German assets in Austria. But there was a more basic issue, underlying the negotiations although barely mentioned in their early stages. It concerned the future position of Austria in relation to the two emerging power blocs. It was only by raising and finally solving this issue—in a manner that denied to both sides incorporation of all or part of Austria into their power blocs and removed the country from their territorial competition—that a settlement became possible.

The Austrian settlement was a part of the postwar settlements in Europe. The negotiations started belatedly in 1947 and continued for years. They were strongly affected by the development of the security relationship between the United States and the USSR during this period. For this reason the negotiations cannot be understood simply as attempts to settle the Austrian question itself, but they have to be viewed against the backdrop of events outside Austria and even outside Europe.

With these considerations in mind the present essay does not deal in great detail with the specific issues or with the claims and concessions put forth by the two sides at various times during the negotiations.[2] The focus is rather on the basic issue of Austria's position in relation to the two power blocs, and on the broad international context of the negotiations. The first part sketches the negotiations chronologically within that international context, while the second part analyzes the negotiations and the final settlement with reference to the original objectives of the two sides.

PART I: CHRONOLOGY

FROM GRAND ALLIANCE TO COLD WAR: 1945–47

On November 1, 1943 the governments of the United States, the United Kingdom, and the USSR declared in Moscow that Austria "shall be liberated from German domination," and they affirmed their wish "to see Austria re-established as a free and independent state." This wish was a natural by-product of the plans for the dismemberment of Nazi Germany.[3] But, mindful of the problems of the economic viability of the small Austrian state after the first World War, the Western allies were not convinced that an independent Austria should remain a permanent part of the European postwar order. Churchill in particular preferred the subsequent integration of Austria in some form of a federation of Danubian states, including possibly Bavaria, and such views found some sympathy in Washington.[4] Although it was known that Molotov opposed the creation of a federation, the British idea of Austrian independence as a first stage, to be followed by its association with some larger unit, was cautiously hinted at in the Moscow Declaration, which stated that the establishment of an independent Austria would "open the way for the Austrian people themselves, as well as those neighboring states which will be faced with similar problems, to find that political and economic security which is the only basis for lasting peace."[5]

The first draft of the Moscow Declaration was presented by Great Britain, which generally took the lead in planning for the postwar fate of Austria. The United States considered Europe to be primarily of concern to Britain and the Soviet Union. In a private talk with Archbishop—later Cardinal—Spellman in September 1943, President Franklin Roosevelt gave an affirmative reply to the question whether Austria (together with Hungary and Croatia) would fall under some sort of Russian protectorate.[6]

Washington's lack of interest in Austria was evident when the European Advisory Committee (EAC) in London considered the manner in which a defeated Germany (including Austria) was to be occupied. When it came to the establishment of occupation zones in Austria, there was uncertainty whether the United States would participate in the occupation at all, and if so to what extent. Great Britain proposed at the EAC in January 1944 that Austria be predominantly an American zone. But the United States advocated that "Austria, along with the south German zone, should be under occupation of United Kingdom forces," while the Americans would occupy the northwestern zone of Germany. In September 1944 the Americans agreed to exchange zones in Germany with Britain, but as far as the occupation of Austria was concerned they intended to send only a "token force" to Vienna, the rest of the country to be divided into a British and a Soviet zone. The Soviet government, which apparently saw Britain as its main competitor in the struggle for spheres of influence in Europe, proposed that Austria be occupied jointly by forces of the three powers, and in a note at the end of November 1944, it insisted on the equal participation of the Americans, who should control a zone bordering on the southern zone of Germany. Finally, on December 9, 1944, the United States agreed.[7]

As the war drew to a close, the actual occupation of parts of Austria proceeded apace. Before the war was over, on April 27, 1945, a provisional Austrian government was founded in the Soviet zone with the Socialist Karl Renner as chancellor. For the time being this government was recognized only by the Soviet Union, and the question arose whether its authority should be extended to the Western zones. As in other European matters, it was the role of the United States to mediate between the position of the USSR and that of the United Kingdom, which was opposed to the recognition of the Renner government by the West. The Western allies finally granted recognition on October 20, 1945. The memorandum of the Allied Council, which had been constituted by this time, obligated the Renner government to hold elections before the end of 1945. In view of Western anxieties regarding a communist takeover, expressed later from time to time, it is important to note that in the elections of November 25, 1945, the Communist Party captured only 4 (out of 165) seats in the National Assembly, and that it has never held more than 5 seats since then.

The EAC reached agreements regarding zones, including a fourth zone for France, in early July 1945. It also established—as noted above—a control mechanism for Austria as a whole in the form of an Allied Council. Foreshadowing the negotiations for an Austrian treaty, the Allies agreed at the Potsdam Conference in July and August 1945 that Austria would not have to pay reparations. However, German property in Austria (as well as elsewhere) could be claimed by the occupying powers in their respective zones. The vague formulation of this decision opened the door for protracted wrangling over German assets that became a prominent feature of the negotiations for an Austrian treaty. Another result of the Conference was the institutionalization of the Council of Foreign Ministers (CFM), which was to play an important role in these negotiations.

The focus of this essay on the relationship between the negotiations and the security interests of the United States and the USSR requires a few words about the change in American views on the character of the overall European settlement. Roosevelt opposed the establishment of spheres of influence in principle, as contrary to his vision of "One World" in which the victorious Allies would pursue a common policy. His secretary of state Cordell Hull stated to Congress in November 1943 that in the postwar era "there will no longer be need for spheres of influence . . . or any other special arrangements through which, in the unhappy past, the nations strove to safeguard their security or to promote their interests."[8] Nevertheless, Churchill and Stalin discussed the distribution of British and Soviet spheres of influence in Southeast Europe in Moscow in October 1944. However, their plans became irrelevant because of the de facto situation created by the advance of the Red Army, and the decrease in British and the increase in American power. The position of the United States also changed. Roosevelt's perspective on the intentions of the Soviet Union, which was basic to his "One World" ideals, was abandoned. Divergences about the meaning of the Yalta agreement, the Soviet policy of *faits accomplis,* and the behavior of the Soviet Union and its troops in occupied areas contributed to this change. The USSR was increasingly seen as an aggressive and potentially threatening power. In this atmosphere of growing tensions, the CFM meeting in London in the fall of 1945 at which the Soviet Union presented draft treaties for Romania, Bulgaria, and Hungary, ended in disagreement. Some compromises were reached at the meeting in Moscow in December 1945, but after that meeting, President Harry Truman opposed further concessions, having grown "tired of babying the Soviets." Roosevelt's "Grand Design" of cooperation with the USSR in securing world peace was replaced by a steadfast policy opposing a potentially worldwide Soviet expansionism.[9]

As far as Austria was concerned, the United States pressed in 1946 for an early conclusion of a treaty, preferably simultaneously with the conclusion of the treaties with the Balkan states. One reason for the U.S. eagerness to conclude a treaty at this time was that a treaty with Austria would presumably end the presence of Soviet troops in that country. If so, there would be no need to include in the treaties with Hungary and Romania provisions for the continued presence of Soviet troops in these countries as a communication link with the Soviet troops in Austria.[10] But when the United States proposed to place the Austrian treaty on the agenda of the foreign ministers' meeting in Paris beginning on April 25, 1946, Foreign Minister Vyacheslav Molotov rejected this proposal, arguing that the agenda was already too crowded and that the USSR had not yet received a U.S. draft of the treaty. Such a draft was circulated on May 29 for a discussion at the meeting when it reconvened on June 15.[11] The subject of Austria was briefly discussed on the last day of the meeting (July 12), but Molotov insisted that the treaties with other states (including not only Hungary, Romania and Bulgaria, but also Italy and Finland) would have to be concluded before negotiations on Germany and Austria could begin. The agreement on these treaties in early 1947—including in the case of the treaties with Hungary and Romania provisions for the presence of Soviet troops to protect communication lines during the occupation of Austria—removed this obstacle to a consideration of an Austrian treaty. A negotiating team of special envoys, called the Deputies for Austria, began work in London in January 1947 on the preparation of treaty drafts which were to be submitted to the CFM meeting in Moscow in March of that year.[12]

BEGINNING AND SUSPENSION OF NEGOTIATIONS: JANUARY 1947 TO MAY 1948

The meeting of the Deputies for Austria on January 16, 1947, was the first of a series of meetings of that body that did not end—after a number of lengthy suspensions—until its 260th session on February 9, 1953. Yugoslavia, invited for a hearing as were other members of the war time alliance against Germany, presented territorial and reparations claims against Austria. The Western deputies opposed these claims; the Soviet delegation supported them in a noticeably lukewarm fashion.[13] While the deputies were unable to reach agreement on this and a number of other issues—including that of German assets for which each of the powers presented a proposal—they agreed in 29 meetings between January 16 and February 25, 1947 fully or in part on thirty articles of a draft, covering about one half of the final treaty. The draft was then to be completed at the CFM meeting which began in Moscow on March 10, 1947.[14]

The foreign ministers met at a time of a general hardening of East-West relations. Only two days after the conference started, President Truman declared it to be U.S. policy to support nations that resisted their subjugation through armed minorities or outside pressure. This so-called "Truman Doctrine" was announced in the context of events in Greece and Turkey (where the United States took over a role originally envisioned for the British), but it had a wider, though unspecified, application. Next door to Austria, in Hungary, the Soviet Union supported the communists' tactics of gradually ousting their opponents, which eventually brought the country under communist rule. Similar processes of depriving anti-Soviet leadership elites of their power took place in Poland, Bulgaria and Romania. Witnessing the gradual formation of a Soviet satellite system in Eastern Europe, the United States was no longer inclined to compromises with the USSR in order to achieve the early conclusion of an Austrian treaty. The sticking point in the negotiations was not so much the issue of Yugoslav claims— although it was kept on the agenda by the Soviets—but rather the issue of German assets. It is not clear to what extent the efforts of the Soviet Union to obtain the most favorable economic terms in the treaty were simply motivated by its needs to restore its war-ravaged economy. The Americans, at any rate, saw the Soviet insistence on their terms as part of a larger scheme to gain economic influence in Austria, and ultimately to make Austria a Soviet satellite.[15] On the last day of this unproductive conference, April 24, 1947, Molotov proposed that a four-power Austrian Treaty Commission (ATC) in Vienna should discuss the articles that had not been agreed upon and, especially, the articles regarding German assets. This proposal was accepted.[16]

The Austrian government, which had counted on the Western powers for an early conclusion of the treaty, blamed the inflexible attitude of the United States on the issue of the German assets for the failure to achieve a settlement. Reporting to the National Assembly on May 7, 1947, Foreign Minister Karl Gruber expressed his opinion that this question could have been solved. The policy of the Western powers, he stated, had turned out to be a policy of missed opportunities.[17] According to Gruber's official report on the conference, John Foster Dulles—who served as Republican adviser to George Marshall at the conference—had told him that he could, if necessary, envision an economic union of Western Austria with the Western zones of Germany, and that he was opposed to a prohibition of an *Anschluss* in the treaty for this reason. Gruber considered such a policy, which would lead to a partition of Austria, unacceptable.[18]

Taking note of the Austrians' disappointed expectations, the Joint Chiefs of Staff in a communication to the U.S. high commissioner to Austria, General Geoffrey Keyes, of May 25, 1947 warned that this disappointment must not be allowed ultimately to diminish U.S. influence in Central Europe, stating that the U.S. government, which "continues to regard Austria as of the greatest political and strategic interest," cannot "let this key area fall under exclusive Soviet influence."[19] The ATC began its meeting in May 1947. A proposal in one of the last of its 85 sessions provided the opportunity for a resumption of negotiations. This was the so-called Cherrière plan. It was based on an Austrian initiative, worked out in detail by David Greenberg, an American member of the ATC, and officially presented with the concurrence of the British member by the French High Commissioner General Paul Cherrière. Its essential aim was to convert most of the Soviet claims to German property into claims for delivery of goods out of current Austrian production.[20]

The foreign ministers next met in London between November 25 and December 15, 1947, mainly to discuss the German question, but they did not reach any agreement. On November 27, Cherrière outlined details of his plan regarding German assets in Austria, but only at the end of the conference did Molotov express the Soviet Union's willingness to negotiate for an Austrian treaty on the basis of the Cherrière plan. The

Soviet Union made a counterproposal on January 24, 1948. Although the Soviet demands exceeded those recognized in the Cherrière plan—for example, Austria's payment was to be $200 million instead of $100 million—Austrian officials welcomed the counterproposal as an indication of Soviet willingness to bargain on the German assets issue and to restrict Soviet claims to the oil and shipping industries. As far as the dollar payment—which they hoped could be bargained down to $150 million—was concerned, they felt that "U.S. interest in freeing Austria from Soviet influence and attaching it to western orbit is sufficiently strong so that some way will be found to provide necessary dollars." The British Foreign Office thought it was now possible to reach a genuine solution with the Soviet Union, but it was uncertain "whether U.S. seeks definite solution with Soviets and will work toward that end, or whether (State) Department is convinced no such solution is possible and is only going through motions." In fact, as Marshall informed the embassy in London on February 3, 1948, the State Department remained skeptical about the Soviets' motives in submitting their proposal. He suspected that a Soviet objective was "to shift onus on Western States for failure to obtain treaty." This became a theme, running through many communications thereafter. U.S. minister to Austria John Erhardt in Vienna, commenting on Soviet motives on February 5, acknowledged that the Soviets might aim at shifting the onus. But he also discussed the possibility that "Soviets now actually wish to reach early settlement" and that unfavorable developments in Austria and elsewhere in Europe may have led the Soviets to a major shift in strategy, although not in their long term objective of dominating Austria.[21]

With the Cherrière plan and the Soviet counterproposal on the table, the deputies for Austria met in London 47 times between February 20 and May 6, 1948. The events of the turbulent year of 1948 made this an inauspicious time for successful negotiations between West and East. In Hungary, the communists' political tactics enabled them to take control of the country. In late February, the communists in Czechoslovakia, using extra parliamentary pressures and Soviet support—although without overt intervention—achieved in a formally legal manner a de facto monopoly of power in that country. On the other hand, the relationship between the USSR and Yugoslavia began to show signs of strain, although the extent of this rupture was not yet apparent to the West.

Whatever its motivation, the Soviet Union made concession after concession in London in February and March 1948. The successful accomplishment of communist takeovers in Hungary and Czechoslovakia may have satisfied its immediate security interests and thus played a role in this respect.[22] Britain wanted to use the concessions "to get the best bargain for Austria." The Austrians, while alarmed by the events in Prague and therefore pressing for the build-up of an Austrian defense force with Western aid, still desired an early conclusion of the treaty and with it an end to the occupation.

But for the Americans the real questions were whether or not the conclusion of a treaty, involving the withdrawal of Allied troops, was indeed desirable at this juncture and, if not, how to extricate themselves from the negotiations without assuming the onus for their breakdown. On February 27, 1948, Samuel Reber, the leader of the U.S. delegation in London, raised the first question succinctly in a telegram to Marshall: Was conclusion of a treaty at this time, however desirable from a political and economic point of view as far as Austria was concerned, desirable from a strategic point of view? General Keyes pointed out that the presence of Western occupation forces not only prevented overt acts of aggression against Austria, but also kept intact an unbroken front from Italy through Austria and Germany to the North Sea. Marshall advised the deputies to continue negotiating "but on the basis of US bargaining position greatly hardened by Czech example." On March 7, he informed them that "JCS has given opinion that from military point of view treaty which would involve troop withdrawal is undesirable in light of newest Soviet action." Erhardt felt that a treaty was still desirable politically if certain conditions were guaranteed before troop withdrawals, one of them being that "Austria be brought into full participation with whatever measures of economic and political collaboration may emerge in western Europe during the next few months." In the meantime he opposed a premature evacuation of Western powers because it entailed the hazard of a possible loss of all Austria.[23]

In line with these considerations, the United States looked for an occasion to terminate the negotiations. On the other hand, the USSR appeared eager to reach an agreement. Thus, on March 31, it reduced its demand for a lump sum payment by Austria to $150 million, payable in six years. The State Department felt that this "major concession" made it impossible to break off discussion as far as the issue of German assets was concerned. To recapture the initiative, lost to the Soviets, it was necessary to "make some spectacular counterproposals" on that issue.

On April 5, the British deputy by prearrangement offered some concessions to the Soviets' regarding oil exploration in Austria. The Soviet deputies thereupon surprised their Western counterparts by reducing their claims relating to oil production, exploration, and refining as well as those regarding the assets of the Danube Steamship Company. Reber introduced his report on this development with the statement: "Today we were hit by a flying saucer." He felt that the Soviet move precluded breaking off the meeting on the issue of German assets. What were the Western deputies to do if the Soviets also yielded on other issues? He stated: "We feel the $64 question still remains unanswered, i.e., do you want a treaty in the present situation in Europe? If not what is your advice on best tactics to be employed in breaking off negotiations?"[24]

By this time the Soviets had begun to restrict allied access to Berlin as the first step in the blockade of Berlin. This raised in the minds of U.S. decisionmakers the specter of a blockade also of Vienna, and transport restrictions imposed by the Soviet occupation authorities in Austria increased these fears.[25] The American view now was that the Soviets wanted a quick conclusion of the treaty because their objective of seizing power in Austria could be more effectively pursued after withdrawal of the Western occupation forces. In a cable of April 21, Erhardt recommended that if signing the treaty had become unavoidable, the West should delay ratification and in the meantime "energetically knit Austria into the structure of western European cooperation." Before a Western troop withdrawal Austria's army and police should be strengthened sufficiently to meet emergencies. This should be coupled with a guarantee of assistance from the Western powers to Austria in the event that Austrian sovereignty or independence was threatened.[26]

However, in the end the West found an excuse for suspending the negotiation in a discussion of the Yugoslav claims. When the Soviet deputy, Nikolai Koktomov, indicated that Yugoslavia's legitimate interests included some boundary changes, Reber then stated that "now further discussion seems to be futile," and the deputies adjourned sine die.[27]

While the American negotiators thus achieved their goal of suspending the talks, the British government soon had second thoughts on whether it had been wise to push the Soviets into a corner, thereby stiffening their attitude, and the French had similar concerns. The Austrians, who had vigorously opposed the Yugoslav territorial claims, began to think that the rift between Stalin and Tito gave promise that the Soviets might drop their support for these claims completely. By October 1948 Washington, now buoyant over the success of the Berlin airlift and the weakening of the USSR in the Balkans, was willing to resume the negotiations, but unwilling to take the initiative. With American blessing the Austrians asked the four powers to examine the possibility of a resumption of the negotiations. These notes received a positive response, and a meeting of the deputies in London was scheduled for February 9, 1949. The United States focused, in the meantime, on the creation, equipment and training of an Austrian security force.[28]

THE NEGOTIATIONS ARE RESUMED AND FROZEN: 1949–53

The Deputies for Austria met in London fifty-three times between February and May 1949, but made little progress. The negotiations were continued at the meeting of the CFM in Paris between May 23 and June 20, 1949.

In the meantime the tension between the State Department and the U.S. military establishment increased. General Keyes persistently argued for a continued military occupation of Austria. Thus he stated in a telegram of May 19, 1949, to the Department of the Army that this occupation was no longer related to any military issues of World War II, but instead to "the struggle against Communism and against Soviet aggressive economic and political penetration of Western Europe," adding that "Austria's acceptance of the burden of occupation can be considered as her share in the defeat of Communism." On June 14, 1949, he insisted that it was necessary that a decision "be taken at the top policy level, i.e. the National Security Council" on the answer to the basic question, namely "is military occupation of Austria strategically and/or politically (a) essential or (b) desirable, and if so, to what extent?" The National Security Council met on June 16, but it failed to take any action on a report (NSC 38/1) presented by the new secretary of defense, Louis Johnson. The basic question remained as yet unanswered, and the wrangling between the diplomats and the military continued during and after the Paris Conference.[29]

At Paris the issue of Yugoslavia was laid to rest at the initiative of Soviet Foreign Minister Andrei Vyshinsky (who had replaced Molotov) by inserting an article in the treaty guaranteeing the protection of the rights of the Slovene and Croatian minorities in Austria. Some progress was also achieved on the economic clauses on the basis of a Western working paper. On the last day of the CFM meeting the deputies for Austria were instructed to resume their sessions in order to reach agreement on the treaty as a whole by September 1, 1949. The conclusion of the State Treaty seemed to be at hand.[30] However, the hopes raised by the compromises of Paris were of short duration. While the deputies were able to reduce the number of articles that had not been agreed upon from eighteen to nine, events on the international scene and in Washington led to a collapse of those hopes in the fall of 1949.

Vyshinsky had tried in Paris to secure a return to four power control of Germany— which had collapsed on March 20, 1948, when the Soviets withdrew from the Allied Control Commission—in order to forestall the establishment of the Federal Republic in the Western zones. The Federal Republic was nevertheless established in September 1949, and the German Democratic Republic was established in October. On August 23, 1949, Truman announced that the USSR had exploded an atomic bomb. By September the communists were victorious in China. Under these circumstances the question whether the United States should want an Austrian treaty to be concluded became even more salient. On September 28 Acting Secretary of State James Webb sent a telegram to Secretary Dean Acheson (who was in New York at the United Nations at the time) stating that "appeasement of the Soviets only to get a peace at any price at this time invokes for the US larger and longer range problems which outweigh the benefits of a quick and easy settlement." He added: "Accepting the Russian demands to achieve a quick settlement after the atomic announcement would in our view have more serious general repercussions in Europe than failure to conclude the treaty immediately and would give the Soviets misleading and possibly dangerous impression of our general attitude at this time." When Acheson met the French foreign minister Robert Schuman and the British foreign minister Ernest Bevin in New York, he also stated that it was undesirable to accept the Soviet terms "within two weeks of the atomic explosion in the USSR." Bevin and Schuman, on the other hand, urged an early conclusion of the treaty. But subsequent conferences of the Western foreign ministers with Vyshinsky yielded few results, and the ministers agreed only that the deputies should resume their meetings in New York.[31]

In Washington, problems of coordinating policymaking within the State Department and between the State Department and the military establishment, including the Department of Defense, continued. Francis Williamson, the acting chief of the State Department's Division of Austrian Affairs, reported in a letter to John Erhardt that Secretary of Defense Johnson had taken the position in the NSC that a treaty was not desirable since the Army could not provide the necessary means for assuring Austria's internal security. Aside from citing Johnson's misgivings, Williamson's letter and the reports about the talks of Acheson with Bevin and Schuman mention repeatedly the need to obtain the Senate's consent to the treaty as an important domestic consideration.[32]

The Austrians viewed the American attitude with bitter disappointment. Gruber instructed the Austrian minister in Washington, Dr. Ludwig Kleinwächter, to make it clear that it was erroneous to ascribe the difficulties in concluding the treaty at this time exclusively to Soviet demands, and that Austria considered the policy of prolonging the occupation as directed against her interests. Gruber also prepared a letter of protest to Acheson, appealing to him not to prevent the conclusion of the treaty. When Kleinwächter presented the draft letter to the State Department, he was prevailed upon to withdraw it.[33]

Finally, the disagreement between the State and Defense departments was brought before the President on October 26, 1949. Truman decided that "the treaty should be concluded in order to obtain the withdrawal of Soviet military forces from Austria and to gain the general political advantages which will be derived from this action," but he added that steps should be taken prior to the withdrawal of the occupation forces to establish an adequate Austrian security force.[34]

In the meantime, the deputies had met ten times in New York and had agreed on some additional articles (including some paragraphs of the article on German assets). They continued their meetings beyond the originally envisioned period. In their meeting on November 11, the U.S. deputy announced that the United States would be willing to accept the wording of the Soviet draft on German assets. The Western powers also dropped their insistence on an article regarding compensation to be paid by Austria for the assets of Western oil companies, leaving this issue to bilateral negotiations with Austria.

But while the United States now showed a willingness to make concessions, the Soviets' attitude changed, and they now engaged in dilatory tactics. The Soviet deputy insisted that Soviet claims for reimbursement for their distribution of food—mainly dried peas—to the population in their zone immediately after the war had to be settled by direct negotiations between the Austrian and the Soviet authorities in Austria before agreement on the relevant treaty article was possible. Later he announced that negotiations in Vienna had reached an impasse, and the deputies thereupon decided to adjourn until January 8, 1950, when they would meet again in London. But there, too, the Soviet deputy declared he could not discuss any of the treaty's five remaining articles until the negotiations in Vienna had been concluded.[35]

The meetings dragged on through April 1950. In a meeting on May 4, 1950, the Soviets presented a new condition for the conclusion of the treaty, namely the liquidation of the Anglo-American military base in Trieste, established in contravention to the provisions of the treaty with Italy of 1947.

The explanation for the Soviet shift must again be sought in international developments at the time. The sharpening of the conflict with Tito made it appear advisable for the USSR to keep its troops as close as possible to Yugoslavia. The conclusion of an Austrian treaty would have meant a withdrawal of Soviet troops from neighboring Austria, as well as from Hungary and Romania where, according to the treaties with these countries, Soviet troops were permitted to be stationed as a communication link to the occupation troops in Austria. The demand for liquidation of the Western military and naval presence in Trieste, made at a time when Yugoslavia and the Western powers were drawing closer to each other, was also linked to the rift with Tito. Two articles in *Pravda*—one at the end of February, the other in early May—stated that the Western powers' noncompliance with the provisions of the Italian peace treaty regarding Trieste indicated they might also fail to comply with an Austrian treaty, and instead transform Austria, too, into an "Anglo-American war base."[36]

With the outbreak of the Korean war in June 1950, the number of meetings of the deputies dwindled: there were only three in the second half of that year. Beginning in March 1951 some meetings were held, but they were abortive, and they were broken off on June 21, 1951. In September 1951 the Western foreign ministers met in Washington and decided to make a new effort in the meetings of the deputies to fulfill the long overdue pledge of independence to the Austrian people. On December 28 the United States (which by rotation was to chair the next meeting of the deputies) sent out invitations for a meeting in London on January 21, 1952. Three days before that date the Soviets responded that they would attend only on condition that the question of Trieste and of the "remilitarization" of Austria by the Western powers be discussed. In the end the meeting was postponed indefinitely. There was no meeting of the deputies during the entire year of 1952.[37]

In the meantime the NSC had adopted on May 4, 1950, a report (NSC 38/5) on "Future Courses of U.S. Action with Respect to Austria." The report, which was approved by Truman with some revisions (NSC 38/6) the following day, throws light on U.S. objectives as well as on the U.S. perception of Soviet objectives. The U.S. objective was stated as the conclusion of a treaty "reestablishing an independent and Western-oriented Austria." Such a treaty would prevent "Soviet domination of Austria, which would result in penetration of the East West 'frontier' by a salient extending westward to the Swiss border and permit Soviet control of the principal North-South lines of communication in Central Europe," as well as partition of Austria. Prior to the withdrawal of the occupation troops an adequate security force would have to be created. The major Soviet objective was estimated to be Soviet control of all of Austria, since a Western-oriented Austria would penetrate the East-West frontier by a salient extending eastward to the Hungarian border and would deny the Soviets the Vienna communications center. If the Soviets were unable to achieve their major objective, they would consider partition as a secondary objective, and in terms of capabilities the United States could not prevent the establishment of a rump government in the Eastern zone.

The report mentioned two courses of action that were subsequently followed. One of these recommendations, effectuated in October 1950, concerned the appointment of civilian high commissioners in lieu of the military high commissioners.[38] The other recommendation was to substitute for the treaty that had been discussed up to that time a four-power declaration, which would utilize certain articles of the treaty that had been agreed upon.

The proposed declaration was the origin of what became known as the "short" or "abbreviated" treaty. The British and the French, while skeptical about the idea, went along with it in February when Acheson agreed that the question whether this "short treaty" was an alternative to the longer one, and should be presented to the USSR as such, "should be left blurred."[39]

The short treaty consisted of a preamble and eight articles. Some of the articles followed in general those agreed upon in the negotiations, but Article 6 was a conspicuous departure. It required each of the occupying powers to relinquish to Austria within 90 days all property it held or claimed as German property or war booty. The Soviet Union could hardly have been expected to agree to this. This Article, after all, wiped out all the Soviets had bargained for regarding their economic claims in years of negotiating.

The short treaty was presented to the Soviet Union on March 13, 1952, but their response did not come until August 14, 1952. It rejected the proposal as not in accord with the Potsdam agreement, and asked for its withdrawal. The Western powers thereupon declared their willingness to reinsert certain articles of the long draft, and they proposed a meeting of the deputies in London on September 29 to initial the new draft as amended to meet Soviet objectives. However, the Soviets declared that they would not participate in any discussions until the short treaty was withdrawn.

In October 1952 the U.N. General Assembly passed a resolution, appealing to the four occupying powers to make urgent efforts to reach agreement on an Austrian treaty, and the Western powers issued another invitation for a meeting of the deputies. Two meetings—numbered 259 and 260—were held in London on February 6 and 9, 1953. The new Soviet deputy, Andrei Gromyko, insisted that no substantive discussions could take place until the short treaty was withdrawn, and the meetings were then suspended. They turned out to be the last meetings of the deputies. In response to further invitations the Soviets stated that such meetings did not promise to be successful, and they proposed that instead the Austrian question should be considered "through diplomatic channels by means of an appropriate exchange of opinions."[40]

In following the progress, or lack of it, in the negotiations for an Austrian treaty, I have omitted mentioning a development of some relevance to the future course of these negotiations. On March 10, 1952, while negotiations for a treaty establishing a European Defense Community were drawing to a close, the USSR submitted to the Western powers a detailed proposal for a peace treaty with Germany. It envisioned a reunification of Germany and provided that Germany would obligate itself not to enter any "coalitions or military alliances" directed against any state that had fought against Germany in World War II—a formulation that was to play a role later in regard to the post-occupation status of Austria. After the EDC treaty was signed, but while its ratification was pending (it was not ratified by France), the Soviets continued to press for a solution to the German question based on its proposal.[41]

In this context, informal conversations between a Soviet and an Austrian diplomat in September 1952 are of interest. The Soviet diplomat indicated that the USSR might be willing to pull out of Austria provided that Austria was not subsequently included in the Western defense system. However, his country could not agree to such a pull-out if the United States were allowed to have military bases or troops in Austria, and he suggested twice that "Austria should pursue a policy of neutrality, similar to Sweden or Switzerland." He also thought that Austria should "at long last take an initiative in this question."[42]

After Stalin's death in March 1953, Moscow's new course became apparent on the world scene in a number of steps. At Stalin's funeral on March 8 Premier Georgi Malenkov spoke of the possibilities of peaceful competition between different social systems, and on March 15 he applied this concept specifically to the relations between the United States and the USSR. The Soviets apologized for a fatal collision between a Soviet and a British aircraft over the Soviet zone of Germany, and they loosened traffic blocks around Berlin; after a visit to Moscow, Chinese leaders accepted an American proposal to exchange sick and wounded prisoners in Korea; and the Soviet Union dropped its objections to the nomination of Dag Hammarskjöld to be secretary-general of the United Nations. "We are drowning in a sea of honey," Emmet Hughes, one of President Eisenhower's speech writers, complained.[43]

The Soviets also made conciliatory gestures in Austria. In April 1953, they offered amnesty to Austrian POWs and civilian internees; in June they separated the function of commanding general from that of high commissioner, the latter being a civilian who was then made ambassador to Austria with an invitation to Austria to elevate its representation in Moscow to an embassy; the Soviets relaxed various types of controls, including traffic controls and censorship; and they announced that they would pay their own occupation costs (as the United States had done since 1947).[44]

The Western powers wrestled with the question of an appropriate response to this new Soviet attitude. Churchill was optimistic about the implications of the change in Soviet leadership. In an address to the House of Commons on April 20, 1953, he suggested that an informal summit meeting without fixed agenda be held as a first effort toward reaching an understanding, and in another address on May 11 he spoke of a possible "healthy evolution in Russia." Dulles, on the other hand, doubted that any important results could come out of an informal summit as long as the Soviets promoted a war of aggression in Korea and refused "to restore independence to Austria and withdraw their occupation troops from that small and inoffensive country." The conclusion of an Austrian treaty was repeatedly mentioned as a test of Soviet sincerity. Thus Eisenhower stated in his "Chance for Peace" speech of April 16, 1953, that the conclusion of an armistice in Korea and "the Soviet Union's signature upon an Austrian treaty" would be signs of sincere intent.[45]

The Austrian government, under its new chancellor Julius Raab, now sought to emancipate its diplomacy from its close ties to the Western powers in order to restart the negotiations.[46] A significant Austrian initiative was taken on June 20, 1953, when Foreign Minister Gruber visited Indian Prime Minister Jawaharlal Nehru, then vacationing in Switzerland. His purpose was to explore Soviet perceptions regarding Austria's future status with the help of K. P. S. Menon, the Indian ambassador in Moscow. In a subsequent memorandum, Gruber informed Menon of the possibility of an Austrian declaration, ratified by parliament, to the effect that Austria would not join any military combination. Menon discussed the matter informally with Molotov on June 30, 1953, adding that he personally could envision that a declaration not to enter alliances with one of the power blocs and not to permit them military bases in Austria could be useful. But Molotov only answered: "Such a declaration would certainly be useful, but as you know and as you can see from the case of the long and short treaty draft, declarations can be made and unmade." Thus, the immediate effect of the Austrian initiative was disappointing.[47]

As for the resumption of negotiations, various notes were exchanged between the USSR on the one hand, and the Western powers as well as Austria on the other. On August 17 the Western powers proposed a meeting of the deputies in which they would not introduce for consideration the abbreviated treaty, on the "understanding that there will be no extraneous issues raised." But the Soviets insisted that the abbreviated treaty be withdrawn without conditions. In a note of September 23, 1953, Austria withdrew its support of the abbreviated treaty, and on November 25 the U.S. government declared that "in order to remove any possible misunderstanding" (of the Western note of August 17) it wished "once more" to state that "this draft is withdrawn." On the next day the Soviets, responding to an earlier U.S. note of November 16, expressed their readiness to participate in a meeting of the CFM, and they suggested Berlin as a suitable place for such a meeting. The Soviet proposal was accepted by the Western powers, and the Berlin Conference began on January 25, 1954.[48]

THE AUSTRIAN QUESTION AT THE BERLIN CONFERENCE: FEBRUARY 1954

At the Berlin Conference the Austrian question was linked with the German question, which was uppermost in the minds of the Western as well as the Soviet negotiators. The United States and its allies were determined to rearm the Federal Republic of Germany and to integrate it into a European defense system. In this they had the strong support of German Chancellor Konrad Adenauer and his party. But Stalin's proposal of March 10, 1952, for a unified, neutralized Germany was not without effect on German public opinion. Elsewhere in Europe centrifugal tendencies were strengthened by the Soviet Union's new foreign policy.

As I noted earlier, it was envisioned that Western European military integration, with the participation of a rearmed Germany, would take the form of a European Defense Community (EDC). The treaty to create EDC had been signed in the spring of 1952 between France, the Federal Republic, the Benelux countries, and Italy. In the Federal Republic, Adenauer was able to achieve ratification against strong opposition on March 19, 1952. But ratification in France became increasingly doubtful, and this kept the debate alive also in Germany. The Soviet Union for its part vigorously opposed EDC and the rearmament of Germany, and it did so at length in its note of November 26, 1953, in which it agreed to the CFM meeting in Berlin.

As for Austria, it was expected that the idea of some future neutrality status of the country would be discussed in Berlin. The idea was not new in Austria, but it had become more prominent in 1953 with the Austrian initiative to explore Soviet attitudes toward this issue with the help of India. The United States would have preferred to avoid a discussion of Austrian neutrality for obvious reasons. Would not the example of a neutral and unpartitioned Austria serve as a lure to Germany to follow suit, and strengthen the forces in West Germany that opposed Adenauer's policies favoring integration with the West over unification? The Western powers were particularly apprehensive about the attitude of the Austrian delegation at the Berlin conference because for the first time it was to be an equal participant rather than being present only for a "hearing."[49] Might the Austrians agree to the neutralization of their country in order to avoid partition and achieve an end to the occupation?

To discuss these apprehensions the representatives of the three Western powers met with the Austrian Foreign Minister Leopold Figl three weeks before the beginning of the Berlin conference. Llewellyn Thompson, the U.S. ambassador, stated that the Western powers would reject Soviet proposals involving the neutralization of Austria by means of the state treaty. Figl declared that Austria was also opposed to a neutrality clause in the treaty because it would constitute a limitation of Austrian sovereignty and invite future foreign interventions. Thompson then considered the possibility that the USSR would offer Austria bilateral negotiations regarding a declaration of neutrality. In this case, he stated, the Western powers expected that Austria would immediately contact them. The Austrians agreed and promised not to take any initiative in the question. On January 13 Chancellor Raab and Foreign Minister Figl discussed among themselves what the Austrian delegation should do if the question of neutrality were raised. They decided that in such a case the delegates would refer to the repeated declarations of their government that Austria would not join any military alliance, but would oppose a neutrality clause in the treaty itself unless it was coupled with a guarantee by the four powers.[50]

For the reasons indicated above, the possibility of some neutral status for Austria was also of great concern to the German government. The German government spokesman Felix Eckhardt came to Vienna to discuss these concerns with Figl. He stressed that Austrian neutrality, imposed by the four powers, would be a "dangerous example" for Germany. Figl assured him that Austria would be neutral by its own sovereign decision, or there would be no state treaty.[51]

The discussion on this issue continued behind the scenes in Berlin. On February 7, 1954—five days before negotiations on Austria began—Dulles stated in a confidential conversation with prominent journalists that Austria needed no neutralization since the country would have its own army to guarantee security after the state treaty was concluded. He added that the United States had never tried to persuade Austria to join a military alliance, such as EDC or NATO. But in a talk with Figl and State Secretary Bruno Kreisky he urged them to consider whether declarations that Austria had no intention to join any military alliance did not contain great risks, and he pointed out that belonging to a great alliance was very significant for small states. Dulles, Eden, and French Premier Georges Bidault prevailed upon Figl to postpone a declaration regarding Austria's intention not to join alliances, which he had planned to include in his first statement at the conference on February 12. He delivered it instead on February 13, a day after Molotov had put the USSR's proposal before the conference.[52]

The proposal contained two essential points. One went straight to the issues discussed above; the other dealt with the question of the timing of the withdrawal of troops. As to the first point, Molotov proposed that a new article (Article 4b) be inserted in the existing draft of the treaty. This article obliged Austria "not to enter any coalitions or military alliances, directed against any power that participated with its armed forces in the war against Germany and in the liberation of Austria." Furthermore, Austria was not to permit the installation of foreign military bases on its territory or the use of foreign military advisers or specialists in Austria. This was to be coupled with an obligation of the four powers to observe the provisions of the new article. The formulation of Austria's obligations was, of course, almost a verbatim repetition of a clause in Stalin's proposal of March 10, 1952, regarding Germany.

The Western powers were determined to reject this proposal. Dulles in particular objected to the idea of "imposing neutrality on Austria as a permanent servitude." Such an imposition would mean that Austria would in fact not become a sovereign and independent state. In this connection Dulles made the following statement:

> A neutral status is an honorable status if it is voluntarily chosen by a nation. Switzerland has chosen to be neutral, and as a neutral she has achieved an honorable place in the family of nations. Under the Austrian state treaty as heretofore drafted, Austria would be free to choose for itself to be a neutral state like Switzerland. Certainly the United States would fully respect its choice in this respect as it fully respects the choice of the Swiss Nation.[53]

The Austrians had no doubt about Dulles' real concerns. Thus Figl reported to Vienna on February 15: "The Western powers reject an article regarding prohibition of alliances as incompatible with the sovereignty of a free state. (In reality: prejudice for Germany)."[54] In Vienna there was interest in exploring Molotov's proposal in some detail. Chancellor Raab and Vice Chancellor Adolf Schärf instructed Figl on February 15 that, after consultations with the Western powers, negotiations about the term "coalition," used in Molotov's proposal, might be possible provided that the term did not encompass treaties and organizations of an economic nature. Shortly after the telegram was sent the Western high commissioners visited Raab and Schärf. They declared that their governments considered the article proposed by Molotov unacceptable, and that they hoped the Austrian delegation in Berlin would avoid discussing the article both in bilateral talks with the Soviets and in the conference itself. Thereupon, Raab and Schärf sent another cable to Figl, withdrawing their earlier instructions.

On the last day of the conference Molotov proposed a compromise. He was willing to withdraw the demand that neutral status for Austria be anchored in the treaty in the form of his proposed Article 4b, and to accept instead a unilateral declaration of the Austrian government at the time of the signing of the treaty, which would be annexed to the treaty in the form of a protocol. This was rejected by the Western powers and by Austria.[55]

Molotov's second point concerned the timing of the withdrawal of troops from Austria. He proposed that it should not take place until conclusion of a peace treaty with Germany, rather than within 90 days after the Austrian state treaty had become effective, as previously agreed. The occupation would officially end when the state treaty became valid. Thus the troops remaining in Austria thereafter would not perform any occupation functions. Their presence would be regulated by a special agreement worked out by the four powers with Austrian participation.[56]

While Molotov's proposal of a prohibition of coalitions and alliances was more strongly opposed by the Western powers than by Austria, it was the other way around in regard to his proposal regarding troop withdrawal. The Austrians realized that the proposal would perpetuate the presence of foreign troops. Since ending that presence was the highest priority for the Austrians, they felt they would have to accept the no-alliance clause if Molotov made such an acceptance a condition for dropping the clause regarding the timing of troop withdrawals, and Kreisky so informed Eden. The Western powers, on the other hand, preferred a continued presence of foreign troops—including their own—to the acceptance of a clause prohibiting coalitions and alliances. At the end of the conference Molotov dropped his demand that the troops should remain until the conclusion of a German peace treaty, and he proposed instead that the issue of troop withdrawals be negotiated during the year 1955. An Austrian proposal for a compromise according to which the troops would be withdrawn no later than June 30, 1955, was supported by the Western powers, but rejected by Molotov.[57]

The issue of German assets, so controversial in earlier negotiations, was not prominent at Berlin. In his initial statement on February 12, 1954, Molotov declared that the USSR would accept compensation for German assets in their zone in the form of a delivery of Austrian products instead of U.S. dollars. Dulles offered to agree to the Soviet version of all remaining disputed articles in the existing draft on the condition that the treaty be signed then and there. But since the two main issues raised by Molotov's proposals could not be resolved, the conference ended in failure as far as the Austrian treaty was concerned. The final communiqué stated tersely: "The foreign ministers have had a full exchange of views on the German question, on the problem of European security, and on the Austrian question. They were unable to reach agreement upon these matters."[58]

The failure of the Berlin conference meant that the negotiations were now deadlocked. With the factual demise of the meetings of the deputies on Austria there was no institution for continuing discussions on the treaty. During the last session in Berlin Molotov had proposed the establishment of a commission in Vienna, consisting of the ambassadors of the four powers and the representatives of the Austrian government. But Dulles opposed this proposal as illusory as long as the USSR was not willing to specify a time for the withdrawal of troops.

After the conference, the Austrians searched for ways to keep the state treaty on the international agenda. On July 22, 1954, they officially proposed to the four occupying powers the establishment of a permanent commission, including an Austrian representative. In deference to Dulles's statement in Berlin and in consideration of some harsh measures by the Soviet occupation authorities after the failure of Berlin, they stated that the commission's function would be to discuss questions regarding the alleviation of Austria's present situation, rather than the state treaty itself. The Western powers agreed to the proposal, but the Soviet Union insisted that the commission should deal with the draft of the state treaty and questions relating to its conclusion.[59]

At Berlin the Austrian question was linked to the German question and the issue of EDC. Later, on August 30, 1954, the French Chamber of Deputies rejected the EDC treaty. The Western powers thereupon replaced the concept of a supranational army under EDC by an alternative solution for the problem of integrating West Germany into the Western defense system. The Federal Republic was to be admitted to NATO, a military alliance with separate national armies, including a German army. The Paris treaties, embodying this new concept, were signed on October 25, 1954. Of course, ratification of these treaties was not a foregone conclusion. The Soviet Union, eager to prevent ratification, issued on November 13, 1954, an invitation to a Conference on European Security. It was declined on November 29, 1954, by the Western powers, determined to press on with the ratification of the peace treaties.

As far as Austria was concerned, the USSR feared an extension of NATO to include at least western Austria, and a neutral Austria must have seemed to them preferable to such a prospect. Besides, the example of a neutral Austria might still serve the purpose it was meant to serve in regard to the now defunct EDC, namely to induce some members of NATO to reconsider the need for integrating a rearmed Germany into the alliance, thus throwing into doubt their ratification of the Paris treaties.[60] Beginning in late summer of 1954, lower ranking Soviet diplomats in Vienna started a number of informal conversations with officials of the Austrian Foreign Ministry to indicate Soviet willingness to conduct further negotiations on the treaty and to invite Austrian initiatives. A conversation on October 13—after the demise of EDC, but before the signing of the Paris treaties—brought more concrete suggestions. The Soviet diplomats hinted that the position taken by Molotov in Berlin could be revised. They stated that any proposal that included an effective guarantee that Austria would not join a military alliance or allow foreign military bases could be discussed, and they added that while German rearmament made a guarantee of Austrian neutrality all the more necessary, a solution to the German question was not a precondition for the solution of the Austrian question.[61]

The signing of the Paris treaties signaled the temporary end to such overtures. On December 9, 1954, the Soviet government warned that ratification of the Paris treaties would not only prevent further negotiations on the reunification of Germany, but also "not contribute to an agreement on the Austrian state treaty." A day later Molotov declared that "negotiations on the German as well as the Austrian problem are useless on the basis of the ratification of the Paris agreements." There were other signs of a less friendly Soviet attitude concerning the occupation of Austria. Thus, in December 1954 the Soviet high commissioner demanded that the Allied Council pass a resolution condemning the United States for violating the zonal agreement by stationing its troops in the French zone in order to secure a connection between American units in West Germany and Italy. This, he stated, was part of the aggressive NATO activities that were endangering the unity of Austria.

By the end of 1954 it seemed uncertain whether the Soviets could prevent ratification of the Paris treaties, but the achievement of this Soviet goal was not hopeless in view of the fate of EDC. In West Germany, although considerable opposition continued, ratification of the treaties was not in doubt. On December 30, the Paris treaties were approved by the French Chamber of Deputies by a bare majority. However, approval by the Council of the Republic was still necessary, and at the turn of the year there was a chance that it would not be forthcoming. The German question remained linked to the Austrian question, and the hopes for a state treaty were low as the year 1955 began.[62]

THE FINAL PHASE: FEBRUARY TO MAY 1955

The final phase of the negotiations was characterized by Soviet initiatives that in turn were related to the ascendancy of Nikita Khrushchev. The power struggle between Khrushchev, then first secretary of the Communist Party, and Malenkov, the chairman of the Council of Ministers, found expression in a number of controversies regarding the priorities of consumer goods and heavy industry, as well as over issues of defense and foreign policy. In the end, Khrushchev emerged victorious. He retained his powerful position, but Malenkov was replaced by Bulganin, who had sided with Khrushchev in the power struggle. Molotov, who had also opposed Malenkov, remained foreign minister.

At the session of the Supreme Soviet on February 8, 1955, to which Malenkov tendered his resignation and which approved Khrushchev's nomination of Bulganin as Malenkov's successor, Molotov presented a wide-ranging foreign policy report. In regard to Austria he stated that the Soviet government considered further delay in the conclusion of a treaty unjustified. If appropriate measures to preclude the possibility of a new *Anschluss* were taken by the four powers, a withdrawal of their troops from Austria could be carried out without waiting for the German peace treaty. Molotov repeated his proposal regarding Austria's obligations not to join coalitions and military alliances and not to allow foreign military bases on its territory, adding—as in Berlin— that corresponding obligations would have to be undertaken by the four powers. Finally, he proposed that a four-power conference with Austrian participation be called without delay to examine the German problem as well as the conclusion of an Austrian treaty, stressing once more that in the event of ratification of the Paris treaties (which at that time had still to be approved by the German *Bundestag* and by the French Council of the Republic), a resurgence of West German militarism would create a serious danger of *Anschluss*. Molotov thus continued to link the question of Austria to the German question, although no longer to the conclusion of a German peace treaty.[63]

On February 25, 1955, Molotov discussed the text of his report with Norbert Bischoff, the Austrian ambassador in Moscow. In regard to the linkage between the Austrian and German questions he suggested that an agreement on effective measures to prevent an *Anschluss* in the future would make an end to the occupation possible, and that Austria and the Soviet Union should together search for a solution to this problem. Once an agreement on such a solution was reached, the Soviet Union would invite Austrian Chancellor Raab and others to Moscow. He added that a four-power conference with Austrian participation to discuss his proposals of February 8 would have to be called prior to the ratification of the Paris treaties. Bischoff considered this an unlikely possibility.[64]

The Austrian government was pleased with the tenor of Molotov's statements. It instructed Bischoff to tell Molotov that it was no less interested than the Soviet government in a guarantee against *Anschluss,* but that it considered ''unilateral negotiations with only one occupying power not to be the appropriate means'' to achieve such a guarantee.[65]

Bischoff presented the Austrian government's official response to Molotov's initiatives in the form of a memorandum on March 14. While the Austrian government supported Molotov's call for a conference, provided that it would deal with the Austrian state treaty separately, it suggested that the guarantee against *Anschluss* and the form of the Austrian declaration against foreign military alliances and bases should first be clarified. Bischoff reported to Vienna that Molotov considered purely verbal guarantees not to be helpful, so the problem was how to make the guarantees ''effective.'' He expressed the opinion that the proposed conference did not necessarily have to be convened before ratification of the Paris treaties, and that the Soviets wanted a state treaty and a withdrawal of troops from the Western zones to avoid the creation of a line of partition running through the European continent.[66]

But not all developments occurred at such a formal diplomatic level. Private and informal conversations were used by Soviet and Austrian diplomats to launch trial balloons, sometimes with significant results. At a luncheon, given by Kreisky, to which two Soviet diplomats were invited among others, Kreisky insistently asked the second highest member of the Soviet mission, Sergei Kudriavtsev, about Molotov's ideas regarding guarantees against an *Anschluss*. When Kudriavtsev responded that it was up to Austria to tell the USSR what kind of guarantees it would accept, Kreisky read aloud the declaration, signed at the Congress of Vienna in 1815, recognizing the permanent neutrality of Switzerland, and guaranteeing the integrity and inviolability of Swiss territory. He asked his Soviet guest whether the USSR would consider permanent neutrality after the Swiss model an adequate guarantee against a new *Anschluss*. Kudriavtsev gave a positive answer. Three days later, Chancellor Raab gave a radio address which foreshadowed the solution to the Austrian question that was finally adopted. By referring implicitly to the act of the Congress of Vienna regarding Swiss neutrality, he hinted at the formula of a "permanent neutrality on the Swiss model," and by stating that Austria would be willing to assume its obligations regarding military alliances and foreign bases "in a solemn form," he hinted at the passage of a constitutional law by the Austrian parliament.[67]

The Soviet Union's response to the Austrian memorandum was significant in various respects. Above all, it indicated that the Soviet Union abandoned the linkage between the Austrian and the German questions by agreeing to Austria's proposal of a separate conference devoted only to the Austrian treaty. The note referred again to the increased danger of an *Anschluss,* arising from plans for the militarization of Western Germany (the German *Bundestag* had already approved the Paris treaties at the time, and the French Council of the Republic was to follow suit three days later), and stated that this made it necessary to examine the "problem of the measures to be taken in the future if a direct threat of an *Anschluss* became acute." The latter clause was a gloss over an informal Soviet proposal in the above mentioned private conversation between Kreisky and Kudriavtsev to the effect that under such circumstances the powers could re-occupy Austria, a proposal that was, of course, unacceptable to the Austrians. As for the proposed Austrian declaration, the note significantly referred only to a prohibition of military bases and alliances, dropping the term "coalition" in earlier formulations. Also significantly, the note did not demand that the Austrian prohibition against military bases or alliances be anchored in the treaty itself or in an appendix to it.[68]

When Molotov presented the note to Ambassador Bischoff, he also invited Chancellor Raab and an Austrian delegation to Moscow. In anticipation of this visit the Austrian government called its ambassadors in Moscow, Washington, London, and Paris to Vienna for consultations to discuss the attitude of the Western powers and, particularly, of the United States to this development. Ambassador Gruber reported that the U.S. government (and, in particular, the military) was not happy about the invitation, and that Dulles had stressed that the Austrian delegation to Moscow should use the word "neutrality" as little as possible. Ambassador Bischoff stated again that the USSR wanted to establish a neutrality zone, including Switzerland, Austria, and Yugoslavia, in order to prevent the creation of a transcontinental frontline, running from Lubeck to Trieste.[69]

On March 29, the Austrians accepted the Soviet invitation, and the date for the visit of an Austrian delegation was fixed for April 11, 1955. On April 5, the Western powers presented a joint note to the Austrian government stating that any Soviet proposals promising restoration of the freedom of Austria should be discussed by the ambassadors of the four powers in Vienna and the Austrian government.[70]

The Austrian delegation to Moscow consisted of Raab, Schärf, Figl and Kreisky.

At a dinner given by the delegation on the evening of the first day of negotiations, Premier Nikolai Bulganin indicated that the ratification of the Paris Treaties had not affected the Soviet Union's willingness to conclude the Austrian treaty. In the first session itself Molotov was conciliatory. He declared that the Soviet government was ready to sign a treaty that would fix a term in the near future for troop withdrawals, and that it would stick to the concessions regarding German assets, made in Berlin. The Austrian delegation stated Austria's readiness to declare "in an internationally binding form" that it would not join any military alliances and not permit foreign bases on its territory. Both parties favored a four-power guarantee of Austria's independence.

It did not take long before Molotov became more concrete regarding the form of the Austrian declaration desired by the Soviet Union. When Raab stated that Austria's declaration might be submitted to all powers, Molotov suggested that it would be useful to declare that Austria would adopt a "policy of neutrality," adding that the Soviet Union envisioned for Austria a status like that of Switzerland. The Austrian delegation knew that it had to take a position regarding the use of the term "neutrality," not in some vague ad hoc meaning in which it had occasionally been used heretofore, but in its meaning in international law. In the internal discussions of the delegation the Socialist Vice-Chancellor Schärf preferred a policy of nonalignment or de facto neutrality (such as practiced by Sweden) to a de jure neutrality, while Raab had no hesitation in adopting the latter type. To alleviate Austrian concerns about the reaction of the Western powers to a de jure neutrality, Molotov quoted verbatim the statement of Dulles at Berlin regarding the difference between a neutrality imposed from the outside and a voluntarily accepted neutrality, which Dulles had called an "honorable status." To make it clear that Austrian neutrality was a voluntarily accepted one, the Austrian government should make the declaration in the form of an Austrian initiative after the signing of the treaty. The Austrians realized that "neutrality according to the Swiss model" was the formula on which the conclusion of the treaty hinged. When Raab accepted that formula, it was clear that the basis for the conclusion of the treaty had been laid. There followed some bargaining about economic issues, but agreement on these was reached in a relatively short time.[71]

On April 15, a lengthy memorandum regarding the results of the discussions was signed. The clause on neutrality in the Moscow Memorandum stated that Austria would issue a declaration obligating itself to perpetual neutrality of the Swiss type, and that it would obtain international recognition for this declaration immediately after ratification of the state treaty. There followed a clause regarding a four-power guarantee of the integrity and inviolability of Austrian territory.

In a second part, the USSR declared its readiness to sign the treaty immediately and its agreement to a withdrawal of all occupation troops after the treaty came into force, but not later than December 31, 1955. It stated its willingness to recognize Austria's declaration of neutrality according to the Swiss model, and to participate in the above-mentioned four-power guarantee. The rest of the memorandum dealt mainly with the economic clauses of the treaty.[72]

Four days after the signing of the memorandum the USSR proposed a meeting of the foreign ministers in Vienna. The Western powers insisted, however, that the conference be prepared by a meeting of ambassadors. The ambassadorial conference with Austrian participation began on May 2, and it resulted in some changes in the treaty, most of which favored Austrian interests. In regard to the deadline for troop withdrawals a French compromise was adopted according to which the troops would be withdrawn within 90 days after ratification and "in so far as possible not later than December 31, 1955." [73]

On May 14—the very day on which the foundation was laid for the Warsaw Pact— the foreign ministers met in Vienna. They approved the preparatory work of the ambassadorial conference. On a proposal by Figl the clause in the preamble of the treaty that echoed the statement in the Moscow Declaration of 1943 regarding Austria's responsibility for having participated on the German side in the war was eliminated. Molotov, who presided, read the parts of the Moscow Memorandum related to Austria's neutrality. None of the Western foreign ministers had any objection in principle. On May 15, the signatures were affixed to the treaty in the baroque Belvedere Palace. The foreign ministers stepped out on the balcony, and Figl announced to the assembled, jubilant multitude: "Austria is free." [74]

Austria ratified the treaty on June 14, and with the completion of the entire ratification process on July 27, the 90-day period for troop withdrawals began. On October 25 the last of the occupation troops left Austria. On the next day, the Austrian National Assembly passed the federal constitutional law relating to Austrian neutrality. Article I stated:

> (1) For the purpose of the permanent maintenance of her external independence and for the purpose of the inviolability of her territory Austria of her own free will declares herewith her permanent neutrality, which she is resolved to maintain and defend with all means at her disposal.

> (2) In order to secure these purposes Austria will never in the future accede to any military alliances nor permit the establishment of military bases of foreign states on her territory.

The constitutional law came into force on November 5. On November 14, the Austrian government asked all governments with which it had diplomatic relations to recognize Austria's neutrality. The four signature powers conveyed their recognition in identical notes on December 6, as fifteen other nations had already done by this time. Others followed suit during the next year. Contrary to Switzerland, Austria did not perceive its neutrality as preventing membership in the United Nations. In the preamble to the treaty the allied signatories supported Austria's application to the United Nations, and Austria was admitted to U.N. membership on December 14, 1955. [75]

As noted above, Austria's neutrality is not anchored in the treaty itself. The four powers did not assume any function of guaranteeing the country's independence or neutrality. In these regards, questions have arisen on two occasions since 1955. During his state visit to Austria in 1960, Khrushchev stated that the Soviet Union could not stand idly aside in the event of a violation of Austrian neutrality. The Austrians issued an official reply to the effect that Khrushchev's observations were not in accordance with Austria's policy of neutrality, and that Austria had the sole right of determining when her neutrality was threatened or violated, and was the sole judge of how the threat or violation was to be countered. When Austria's President Rudolph Kirchschläger visited Washington in March 1984, President Reagan referred twice to the United States as a "guarantor of Austrian sovereignty." While this raised eyebrows in Kirchschläger's entourage (which included the foreign minister), and while it was discussed in the Austrian press, no official Austrian response followed in this case. A diplomatic incident involving a violation of Austria's neutrality occurred in 1958. At the time of the Lebanon crisis of that year, U.S. war planes flew over Austria, without Austrian permission, on their way from Germany to the Middle East. Austria protested, and on July 22, 1958 an American apology was tendered together with assurances that Austrian territorial integrity would be respected in the future.[76]

These relatively minor incidents notwithstanding, the solutions found for the Austrian question—the treaty and the declaration of neutrality—have withstood the test of time. No serious compliance issues have arisen, and no side has had second thoughts about the value or viability of the agreed upon solution.

The state treaty is often characterized—as Dulles characterized it in his report to President Eisenhower of May 27, 1955—as marking "the first withdrawal in Europe of Soviet troops from the forward positions they occupied in 1945."[77] This rather obscures a more basic aspect of the treaty. It was the last of the postwar settlements in Europe, the last piece in the giant puzzle, fixing the future positions of the two blocs on the map. Whatever colors one wishes to assign to these positions, Austria's color on the map was not to be either one of them.

PART II: ANALYSIS

INTERNATIONAL CONTEXT

The Austrian state treaty is usually considered a case of a successful cooperative U.S.–USSR arrangement that came as a surprise after eight years of rather fruitless negotiations. The lack of success over these eight years is frequently attributed to the difficulty of the issues that were the substance of the negotiations. However, other causes, related to the general political relationship between the United States and the USSR, were at least equally responsible.

In this relationship three phases can be distinguished in the postwar period. The first phase reflected Roosevelt's thinking in terms of the Great Alliance of World War II. The Moscow Declaration of 1943, which stated the Allied war aims as far as Austria was concerned and implicitly fixed the object of the subsequent negotiations as the reestablishment of an independent Austria, was a product of this period. The United States did not as yet envision for itself an important role in Europe in general, and in Austria in particular. The dispositions regarding that small country were not considered a matter affecting U.S. security, as evidenced by the disinterest in U.S. participation in its occupation.

The second—and longest—phase was that of the Cold War. By early 1946 the optimism about U.S. relations with the USSR was replaced by the view that Soviet expansionism had to be contained. By the spring of 1947 the deputies for Austria had developed a draft for an Austrian treaty, and it was thought that the CFM meeting in Moscow would complete that draft. But that meeting was overshadowed by the pronouncement of the Truman Doctrine two days after the meeting began. Within the policy of containment, Austria was now seen to be "of the greatest political strategic interest" for the United States, a "key area" that could not be allowed "to fall under exclusive Soviet influence."[78] The continued presence of Western occupation troops under the status quo became preferable to the conclusion of a treaty with its consequence of Western troops withdrawals. This attitude hardened after the communist takeover in Czechoslovakia in 1948. Thus the United States sought ways to defect from the negotiations at the meetings of the deputies in London in February and March 1948 without assuming the onus of having torpedoed them, and the USSR's concessions at that meeting became an embarrassment for the Western powers.

The most important issue of the Cold War in Europe was the formation of the blocs of the emerging two superpowers. With the collapse of the four-power arrangements in Germany and the partition of the country into two German states, the issue became focused on the integration of the German states into the bloc structure. When NATO was formed in April 1949, the strategic importance of Austria for the West as a corridor from the Western zones of Germany (soon to become the Federal Republic) across the Alpine region to Italy increased. But other considerations—the explosion of the first Soviet atomic bomb, the establishment of the German Democratic Republic, the communist victory in China, and finally the Korean war—also handicapped cooperation at the conference table. Negotiations on Austria were frozen from the middle of 1950 through 1953.

In 1952 Stalin's abortive proposals for a peace treaty for a unified Germany initiated a subphase of the Cold War. The proposals indicated that the USSR was willing to pay a price to prevent West German remilitarization, which was the keystone for the consolidation of the Western military bloc. The formula of "no alliances, no foreign bases," that originated in Stalin's plan for Germany, was introduced into the negotiations on Austria when they resumed in Berlin at the CFM level in 1954. As Stalin's new course was continued after his death by the troika of the Soviet leadership, there were signs that the United States was willing to cooperate conditionally in lessening international tensions, as evidenced by the Geneva conference regarding Korea and Indochina in 1954. But in regard to Germany, the Western powers did not want to give up the integration of the FRG into a Western defense system—finally achieved by the Paris Treaties of October 1954—in exchange for the country's neutral status. The formula of "no alliances, no foreign military bases" was also unacceptable to them in the case of Austria, because its application to Austria was considered a lure to the FRG to forego integration into the Western defense system in favor of reunification. Thus the Berlin conference led to no agreement.

The third phase was a period of transition from the Cold War to the détente sought by Khrushchev. In the preceding subphase, the signing of an Austrian treaty had been mentioned repeatedly by Western leaders as a test of Soviet sincerity. When the treaty was signed on May 15, 1955, it initiated a course of events that led to the Geneva summit in August 1955 and to a cooling of the tensions between the two blocs. With the treaty, the postwar settlements in Europe were completed by excepting Austria from the process of bloc formation. In short, for reasons that varied over time, the Cold War prevented the conclusion of an Austrian treaty until 1955, and it was only in the context of lessening Cold War tensions that cooperation in a settlement became possible.

The settlement excluded Austria from the competition between East and West. In this settlement both sides gave up their original, albeit publicly not articulated, objectives in Austria in exchange for political stability in the area.

OBJECTIVES

Throughout the long period of negotiations, each side depicted itself as working steadfastly and against the recalcitrance of the other side for the earliest possible implementation of the Moscow Declaration of 1943. In reality, both sides in the Cold War had other, less altruistic objectives than the reestablishment of an independent, democratic

Austria. These objectives do not reveal themselves as long as the negotiations are viewed as attempts to solve disagreements over the specific terms for giving Austria its independence. As a matter of fact, the specific issues that dominated the negotiations for years—Yugoslavian claims, Trieste, "dried pea" debts, and even German assets—had only a slight relevance to the final agreement.[79] Nor do the objectives stand out clearly unless the focus on the final stages of the negotiations—a focus that is rather common in the literature—is broadened to encompass the attitudes displayed by the two sides during the earlier stages. Some of these objectives were publicly denied when perceived and asserted by the other side. This was true particularly of each side's maximum objective, which was to absorb Austria as a whole into its orbit. The volumes on *Foreign Relations of the United States* and other sources reveal a good deal of evidence that Austria's integration into the Western orbit was the goal of American policymakers at various levels. It must suffice here to cite only a few examples out of a greater number. On April 30, 1948, Secretary George C. Marshall expressed the State Department's view that "Austrian security is related to Western security and arrangements for latter should envisage eventual Austrian inclusion." In a meeting of the NSC on May 20, 1948, that dealt with the future role of the United States in the Brussels Pact, Secretary of the Army Kenneth Royall suggested "that any arrangement made should be sufficiently flexible so that Spain, Germany and Austria could later be added." In line with this, President Truman approved a policy statement in July according to which the later adherence "of Spain, Germany and Austria, or the western zones of the last two countries" was to be suggested to the Brussels Pact powers.[80] Later, in July 1948, the U.S. minister to Austria John Erhardt urged that the United States "seize any opportunity to bind Austria more closely, economically, politically and militarily to the Western European Community." In July 1949 a paper prepared by the interdepartmental Foreign Assistance Correlation Committee stated that the equipment of Austrian security forces was "in the opinion of the Department of State and the National Military Establishment, which is shared by the National Security Council and the Joint Chiefs of Staff, the urgent requirement for keeping Austria in the Western orbit after the conclusion of the treaty." In early May 1950, the NSC report on "Future Courses of U.S. Action with Respect to Austria" that was approved in a somewhat revised form by Truman, saw the U.S. objective as the conclusion of a treaty "reestablishing an independent and Western-oriented Austria." While Dulles told journalists at the time of the CFM meeting in Berlin in 1954 that the United States had never tried to persuade Austria to join a military alliance, such as EDC or NATO, he privately urged Austrian Foreign Minister Figl and State Secretary Kreisky to consider the great risks involved in their intended declaration not to join any military alliance, and he stressed the significance of adherence to a great alliance for small states.[81]

Unfortunately, we have no similar documentation for the nonpublic discussions of relevant Soviet decision makers regarding their objectives in Austria. This does not, of course rule out the possibility that their maximum objective was to absorb Austria into the Eastern orbit. The intent to do so in a manner similar to the one used in Eastern European countries was probably quite prominent in their minds in the early stages of the occupation, and the formation and unilateral recognition of the Renner government before an Allied control mechanism was established was probably meant as a step towards its realization.[82] Yet, differences between Austria and the other countries must have made the realization of such a plan appear progressively more difficult. In the first postwar elections in Austria in November 1945 the Communist Party garnered only 5 percent of the vote, as compared with 17 percent in the Hungarian election of the same month and 37 percent in the Czechoslovak elections of May 1946. While the communists had held several important positions in Renner's provisional government, after the election they were given only the unimportant Ministry of Electrification as an obvious sop to the Soviet occupation authorities. The Austrian parties rejected the establishment of a "national front," the preferred vehicle for ultimate communist takeover elsewhere. The Socialist Party in particular rejected the idea of a merger with the communists, such as was to occur in Czechoslovakia and later in East Germany.[83]

On the reasonable premise that Soviet objectives can be deduced from Soviet actions in Austria, some observers point to events that supposedly were communist attempts at a takeover. Sven Allard claims that there were three such attempts between 1947 and 1950. This claim is of doubtful validity as far as the nature of the first two events—both in 1947—is concerned.[84] The third event took place in the fall of 1950, and its character is still the object of controversy. Allard calls it an "attempt at revolution" and Bader and Cronin refer to it as a "Communist putsch." The overt cause was opposition to rumored price and wage arrangements; the communists' goal was certainly to change the trade union leadership in their favor, and the method involved demonstrations, including acts of sabotage and violence, coupled with a call for a general strike. The general strike failed when the Socialist trade unionists turned against its communist instigators. The key question is whether the activities of the Soviet occupation authorities indicated an intent to take over Austria by way of a coup. Unquestionably, in the beginning they gave their tacit support and some indirect assistance to the strikers within their zone. But, as Bader notes, they were "simply not prepared to go the limit." Thus they informed the secretary of the Communist Party that the strike was "inopportune," partly for economic reasons and partly because of the difficult international situation. This hardly supports the thesis that the episode indicates a Soviet objective of using it to take over all of Austria.[85]

Of course, integration of Austria into one or the other orbit would have denied the other side an extension of its territorial influence. Analytically, such a denial could have been a more modest objective, separate from the objective of integration of the country into one of the orbits. The security interests involved are mentioned in the above-mentioned NSC report of spring 1950 (which, however, considered reestablishment of a Western-oriented Austria as the major U.S. objective). It stated that Soviet domination of Austria "would result in penetration of the East-West 'frontier' by a salient extending westward to the Swiss border and permit Soviet control of the principal North-South lines of communication in Central Europe." On the other hand, it pointed out that "Western-oriented Austria would penetrate the East-West frontier by a salient extending eastward to the Hungarian border and permit denial of the Vienna communication center." With these considerations in mind, for some time both sides preferred continuation of the occupation to a treaty that would end the presence of their troops in Austria. Until 1955, neither side was ready to abandon its major objective, and to accept a solution that denied both sides influence over Austria, such as proposed by the Austrian government beginning in 1953.

There was, of course, also the possibility of partitioning the country. Each side accused the other of having partition as a secondary objective in violation of the pledge of reestablishing an independent Austria, contained in the Moscow Declaration of 1943. The NSC report of 1950 opposed partition, but there is evidence in the record that the Western powers at other times considered it as a possible, although not very desirable, solution. As I stated in the first part of this essay, in early 1947 Dulles—then a Republican adviser to Marshall at the CFM meeting in Moscow—envisioned an economic union of western Austria with the western zones of Germany. In February 1948, Erhardt, anticipating that the Soviets might seek a settlement on the basis of partition, considered such a settlement "unnecessary" from the Western point of view, since the North-South corridor could be maintained simply by the continued occupation of western Austria by Allied troops. The Austrian government naturally found both a partition and a continuing occupation of undetermined length equally unacceptable.

It is doubtful whether the Soviet Union seriously considered partition as the basis for a settlement. Certainly they never proposed it or otherwise indicated interest in it during the negotiations. While an integration of the western part of a partitioned Austria into the western zones of Germany was at least feasible in terms of language and political leanings of the population, it is difficult to envision what the Soviet Union could have done with its zone. Aside from the pronounced anticommunism of the population and its political leadership—fed by the behavior of Soviet occupation troops—integration of the German-speaking Austrians into the neighboring states, Czechoslovakia and Hungary, would probably have been a source of perennial frictions. On the other hand, the eastern part of the ministate of Austria as a separate state would have been economically even less viable than was the whole of Austria during the interwar years.[86]

The objective of integrating Austria into one or the other orbit was unobtainable through negotiations (except, perhaps, by some territorial swap which neither party considered because it would have unravelled the postwar settlements). Similarly unobtainable by negotiations was the objective of excluding only one party from influence in the area. Partition of the country could have been obtained easily by either party, but it was an undesirable solution for both.[87] There remained the possibility of denying both sides achievement of the objectives of integration or predominant influence. This was ultimately the solution that was adopted in 1955. Why was this common denominator not found until then?

REASONS FOR THE DELAY OF COOPERATION

One reason was certainly the absence of a feeling of urgency on either side. While the occupation of the country by troops of the increasingly antagonistic power blocs was a potential source of conflict, there was no sense of an impending crisis at any given time. Potential crises were defused at the Allied Council, which continued to operate to the end of the occupation. For example, in the spring of 1948 there were Allied and Austrian fears of a Soviet blockade of Vienna, similar to that imposed on Berlin, and the Soviet authorities did, indeed, institute some restrictions, including the setting up of road blocks, on traffic into Vienna. But, these were discussed in the Allied Council, and when the Western members rejected Soviet demands for modification of the relevant access agreements the Soviet authorities dropped their demands and lifted the restrictions, thus ending the matter. The events in the fall of 1950 could also have led to a crisis. But the Austrian cabinet and the Western powers felt that the intervention of Western troops was neither necessary nor desirable. Allied troops were kept out of sight to avoid clashes, and Soviet troops did not intervene in support of the communist instigators of the strike movement. There were Western recriminations regarding the event in the Allied Council for the next two months, but as Stearman states, these only "served admirably to keep alive a subject which must have been painful to the Soviets and their Communist protégés.''[88]

Another reason for the long delay in reaching the settlement has already been mentioned. The two sides weighed the benefits of concluding a treaty, which would lead to the withdrawal of their troops, against the benefits of a continued status quo, and—for reasons that changed over time—opted for the latter. The U.S. military establishment, in particular, feared that a withdrawal of Western troops would create a strategic vacuum, and it therefore opposed conclusion of a treaty until an effective Austrian security force was in place. At the height of the disagreement between the State and Defense Departments regarding the desirability of a treaty in 1949, Truman's decision in favor of continued negotiations was coupled with the proviso that in the meantime steps be taken to establish such a security force. Earlier, when he had been informed by the State Department that the cost of continuing the U.S. occupation might run as high as $200 million a year, he "thought this not an excessive price to prevent the Russians from extending the Iron Curtain to the western boundaries of Austria."[89] For the Soviet Union, the presence of their occupation troops in Austria was to some extent linked to the ostensible *raison d'être* of their troops in Hungary and Romania which, in accordance with the peace treaties with these countries, were to protect communication lines with the troops in Austria. Under the altered circumstances of 1954, Molotov proposed in Berlin that the troop withdrawal be effectuated only after a peace treaty with Germany. This, he stated, was necessary to avert the dangers of a new *Anschluss* arising from a remilitarized Germany, a shorthand term at the time for the suspected Western objective of integrating Austria into the emerging Western security system. Although the proposal made it clear that the troops of both sides would no longer perform occupation functions, it would nevertheless have meant the continued presence of foreign troops in Austria for an extended and uncertain period.[90]

Third, a settlement was hampered by a deep-seated mutual distrust on both sides. Since U.S. policy makers considered it to be axiomatic that the major Soviet objective was absorption of Austria in the Soviet bloc, it was assumed that Soviet demands as well as Soviet concessions at various times served that objective. In 1947, when the USSR insisted on a high price for the German assets, this was seen as a ploy to gain economic influence in Austria and ultimately turn the country into a Soviet satellite. When the USSR made economic concessions in January 1948 in response to the Cherrière plan, this was considered as a shift in Soviet strategy toward the "pursuit by more indirect means of long-term objective domination of country."

Dulles's distrust of the intentions of the USSR is well known. Molotov was not less distrustful of the intentions of the U.S. leadership. Thus his negotiators argued in May 1950 that Western actions in Trieste in violation of the peace treaty with Italy were evidence of Western untrustworthiness, and Molotov stressed this argument in Berlin in 1954. When he cold-shouldered the Austrian initiative for an Austrian declaration of neutrality in 1953, he cited the Western proposal of a short treaty that abandoned some agreements already reached, as a sign of Western duplicity, which proved that declarations "could be made today and revoked tomorrow."

A fourth, and very important, reason for the delay was the influence of international events on the attitudes of both sides. As shown in the chronological part of this essay, U.S. attitudes toward cooperation with the USSR hardened after the communist takeover in Czechoslovakia in 1948, and after the first test of a Soviet atomic bomb in 1949. Both sides engaged in delaying tactics during the Korean War, which led to a standstill in the negotiations. When negotiations were resumed in 1953, the linkage of the Austrian question with the German question became the main handicap. This linkage increased Soviet interest in concluding an Austrian treaty that recognized Austria's neutrality and could therefore be used as a lure to West Germany, while the West had an interest in preventing a treaty on that basis, because it could potentially endanger the completion of the Paris Pact arrangements.

The West's position was in line with the interests of the FRG government, which injected itself into the negotiations because it feared that the example of a neutral and unpartitioned Austria would strengthen its domestic opposition. It should be noted that the Soviet initiatives that led to a breakthrough in 1955 were also based on considerations of a global character, as I discuss below.

FACTORS FAVORING COOPERATION

The failure of the negotiations during a protracted period can be explained by the above mentioned obstacles to cooperation. What were the forces that worked in favor of such cooperation, and that in the end made it possible?

At times when the United States was reluctant to conclude a treaty, such as in the fall of 1949, its allies, Britain and France, urged concession when they saw an opportunity for a settlement. While Truman in 1949 was willing to ''go it alone'' in preventing a treaty that, as he stated, ''made it impossible for an independent Austria to survive,'' at other times alliance considerations made it necessary to accommodate the views of Britain and France when they diverged from those of U.S. policy makers.[91] Another factor was the pressure of the Austrian government for conclusion of a treaty, provided it did not entail the partition or loss of territory, or the continued presence of foreign troops. For example, the Austrian government was willing to pay a higher economic price for such a treaty than the United States was willing to concede. Its urgings in this direction were unwelcome to U.S. policy makers, and were sometimes disregarded. But there was also the countervailing view that the United States had an interest in maintaining the generally pro-Western and anti-Soviet leanings of the Austrian people and their government, and that this interest dictated some consideration for the Austrian positions. Finally, there was the ineluctable fact that all four powers had committed themselves in the Moscow Declaration of 1943 to reestablish an independent Austria. Each side blamed the other for preventing the redemption of this pledge, and neither side wanted to bear the onus of having torpedoed the negotiations. In this sense concern for Austrian as well as world public opinion worked in favor of some cooperation.

The concern for world public opinion was heightened by the Soviet campaign to lessen Cold-War tensions, especially after Stalin's death. But this concern was counteracted by the need to avoid a level of cooperation that would negatively influence the construction of a Western security system including the FRG. In the spring of 1955 the achievement of such a system was no longer in doubt. There was now a Soviet offer to sign a treaty, worked out in bilateral USSR-Austrian talks in Moscow, and this offer could not easily be disregarded. After all, the willingness of the USSR to conclude a treaty had been repeatedly cited as a test of Soviet sincerity in its efforts toward a thaw in its relations with the Western powers. In addition, the formula of an Austrian neutrality that was not anchored in the treaty itself was difficult for the United States to reject in view of the statements by Dulles at the Berlin Conference, which Molotov quoted with considerable emphasis in his talks with the Austrian delegation in Moscow and again at the final meeting of the CFM preceding the signing of the treaty. In addition, in view of the Moscow Declaration of 1943 it became difficult after ten years to argue for a continuation of the occupation. Even the U.S. military establishment, which had long preferred such a continuation to a treaty providing for troop withdrawals—on the grounds that Western withdrawal would create a military vacuum—was sufficiently reassured by the creation of an Austrian security force to accept the conclusion of a treaty as a calculated risk.

BENEFITS AND COSTS OF THE SETTLEMENT

There were benefits as well as costs involved for both sides in accepting a settlement that required them to give up their maximum objectives of incorporating Austria into their respective orbits in exchange for a denial of that objective to the other side. For the USSR, a strategic benefit of a neutral Austria was the creation of a barrier extending from the Hungarian border to the Swiss-French border, separating the northern from the southern tier of NATO. Considering that the United States had long been intent on maintaining a North-South corridor, agreement to Austrian neutrality involved a considerable cost, but it was now willing to accept that cost. Karl Gruber, who was Austrian ambassador to Washington in 1955, suggested that the new emphasis on nuclear strategy and thus a deemphasis of territorial considerations may have lessened the opposition of the U.S. military establishment, although it was not very happy about giving up the corridor.[92]

Neutrality also meant that the original objective of a "Western-oriented" Austria had to be abandoned or at least redefined and limited. Dulles tried to save whatever he could of this concept. When he presented Gruber with the U.S. note recognizing Austrian neutrality on December 6, 1955, he expressed the hope that Austria would realize that "the only military danger threatening Austria came from the East," that it would take this into account in building its military institutions, and would "not make itself dependent on the potential adversary in armaments and ammunition." Gruber responded that it was already clear that the Austrian army would rely essentially on Western resources.[93] Since the United States assumed that only the Soviet bloc was a military danger to Austria, there may have been some consolation in the fact that Austrian neutrality was to be an armed neutrality, as indicated in the constitutional law of October 26, 1955.

Finally, there were Austrian assurances that neutrality would not change Austria's fundamental ideological democratic orientation. The official commentary accompanying the government's submission of the constitutional law to the National Assembly stressed that neutrality did not impose any limits on the neutral state's internal and foreign policies and, since it did not bind individual citizens, it did not involve any obligation of ideological neutrality.[94]

RISKS OF THE SETTLEMENT FOR THE SOVIET UNION

Austrian neutrality involved certain risks for the USSR. According to the peace treaties with Hungary and Romania, Soviet troops were stationed in these countries "for the maintenance of the lines of communication of the Soviet Army with the Soviet zone of occupation in Austria." This purpose became untenable with the end of the occupation of Austria. It is therefore significant that the Warsaw Pact was concluded on May 14,

1955, the day before the signing of the Austrian treaty. The pact was to serve the USSR as a new legal basis for the presence of its troops in Hungary, Romania and other countries such as Czechoslovakia.[95]

There was also the risk that the example of a neutral Austria could encourage some countries in the Soviet bloc to attempt to take a similar stance. This danger was heightened by stirrings of greater national independence on the one hand, and, on the other, by the very fact that the new course of Soviet foreign policy implied greater acceptability of nonalignment or neutrality elsewhere. A drift within the bloc in these directions would have been disastrous to Soviet power, security, and prestige. This consideration was part of the controversy between Khrushchev and Molotov. Molotov saw a bad precedent in the troop evacuation from Austria necessitated by its neutrality. Khrushchev, on the other hand, stressed that the Austrian settlement concerned a country that was not a "people's democracy," so that it could not serve as a precedent for countries within the socialist camp. Khrushchev prevailed, and by February 8 Molotov had accommodated himself to Khrushchev's views.[96]

The idea that the Austrian settlement could serve as an example for the countries of Eastern Europe, and thus could contribute to a rollback of Soviet power occurred also to Dulles. Two days after signing the treaty he stated in a televised report that the Austrian treaty marked the first time that an area of Europe was liberated by a withdrawal of the Red Army, adding: "It also is going to carry a whole lot of new problems into the satellite area . . . The example of what has happened here, I thought as we saw the cheering, waving crowd, is going to be something contagious, and there are going to be other people who are going to want to be able to cheer and wave their national flags."[97]

SOVIET MOTIVES IN THE SPRING OF 1955

It is sometimes suggested that the Soviet Union intended even in 1955 to use the example of Austrian neutrality to prevent the ratification of the Paris treaties and the incorporation of the FRG into NATO. However, the counterargument that the USSR must have realized at the time of the signing of the Austrian treaty that the entry of the FRG into NATO had become irreversible is more convincing. It is supported by the fact that the ratification of the Paris treaties on May 5, 1955, did not affect Soviet attitudes regarding the Austrian treaty.[98]

Khrushchev had longer range objectives, with a world context in mind. In his controversy with Molotov he had stressed that it was "more important to give a widely visible clear signal of willingness to negotiate, than to cling to military positions of little significance." Later, in 1958, he stated that his objective had been to use Austria as "an object lesson in the principles of peaceful coexistence."[99] To gain acceptance of those principles, the Soviet government made peace with Tito, withdrew from the naval base of Porkkala in Finland and agreed to Finland's joining the Nordic Council, invited Adenauer to Moscow as a first step in the normalization of relations between the USSR and the FRG, and offered to consider disarmament plans involving on-site inspections within the USSR. The campaign for coexistence was also pursued in the underdeveloped world, where Khrushchev and Bulganin enthusiastically welcomed the Bandung conference of Afro-Asian nations.

It is consistent with this broad Soviet objective that Bulganin, referring to the Austrian example at the Warsaw Pact conference, expressed the opinion that "there are quite a number of states, both in Europe and in Asia, which are averse to joining aggressive military blocs,'' and that Molotov at the signing of the Austrian treaty welcomed Austria's position of honest neutrality, adding that ''this position will be supported with satisfaction by other nations of Europe, and not only of Europe.'' [100]

The acceptance of the principle of coexistence by the Western powers was to be symbolized by a summit meeting. The Soviet Union had proposed such a meeting for some time. At least intermittently after 1953, it was supported by Churchill and by various groups in the West. Although Dulles continued to counsel against it, Eisenhower judged the time to be ripe for a summit after the ratification of the Paris agreements and the signing of the Austrian treaty. He hoped that the summit would ''change the spirit that has characterized the intergovernmental relationships of the world during the past ten years.'' When the summit conference took place in Geneva in July 1955 amid high expectations of a new ''Geneva spirit,'' an important Soviet objective seemed to have been attained. [101]

THE AUSTRIAN STATE TREATY: A MODEL?

On the thirtieth anniversary of the signing of the Austrian State Treaty the representatives of the signatory powers assembled at a ceremony in Vienna. Each of them proclaimed the treaty a success and claimed credit for his government for its achievement. Thus Secretary of State George Shultz stated on the eve of the ceremony that the treaty was for the U.S. ''one of the greatest successes of the post-war period,'' that it was a model to be emulated at present, and that it taught the lesson that with patience, steadfastness, decisiveness, and ingenuity peaceful change on the East-West border was possible. At the ceremony itself Foreign Minister Andrei Gromyko saw the treaty as evidence that negotiations, however difficult, could solve the more complicated international problems, and British Foreign Secretary Geoffrey Howe considered the negotiations for the treaty a model, applicable to the present. However, in a symposium held on the occasion of the anniversary, Austria's Foreign Minister Leopold Gratz expressed doubts that the Austrian settlement had the character of a model that could be used in other conflict situations, and he stressed the elements that were specific to that settlement. [102]

The truth is probably somewhere in between. The Austrian settlement has a model character in terms of some generally applicable conditions that were necessary to bring it about. Thus both sides had to come to the conclusion that their conflicting maximum objectives in Austria could not be attained by negotiations and that, on the other hand, the negotiations and the occupation of Austria by both sides could not continue indefinitely. Each side also had to recognize that the attainment of its maximum objectives in this situation was not of vital strategic or economic importance, a recognition that lessened the intensity of the conflict. This factor was related to the small size of the country, which also militated against partition as a possible solution. The fact that neither side had a preponderance of influence or power in the area was an additional factor. Given these circumstances, proposals to remove a neutral Austria from the competition between the two power blocs did not involve any costs that either side considered unacceptably high, including a loss of face or prestige. On the plus side, acceptance of these proposals not only laid the Austrian question to rest after eight years of haggling, but also completed the process of postwar settlements in Europe ten years after World War II had ended. The tradeoff for any costs or risks, incurred by either bloc, was the achievement of political stability in the area, an interest that could be shared by both sides.

But while these conditions may have been necessary for a settlement, they may not have been sufficient to bring it about. As suggested by Gratz, there was indeed also a specific element, namely the Soviet objective at the time to replace the Cold War by an era of peaceful coexistence. Without Khrushchev's pursuit of this objective the final compromise might not have been reached and the treaty might not have been signed in 1955.

Notes

I am grateful to Michael McFaul for his research assistance.

1. The term "State Treaty" rather than "Peace Treaty" was used because Austria, having been absorbed into Germany in 1938, was not considered to have been a belligerent in the Second World War. See Gerald Stourzh, *Geschichte des Staatsvertrages* (Graz: Verlag Styria, 1980), pp. 10–12. (Hereafter cited as Stourzh, *Geschichte*.)

2. The slight relevance of the negotiations to the final agreement is also stressed by Robert L. Ferring, "The Austrian State Treaty of 1955 and the Cold War," *Western Political Quarterly*, vol. 21, no. 4 (December 1968): 651; and by Audrey Kurth Cronin, *Great Power Politics and the Struggle over Austria 1945–1955* (Ithaca, N.Y.: Cornell University Press, 1986), p. 160.

3. As early as December 1941, in conversations with Foreign Secretary Anthony Eden, Stalin proposed the reestablishment of Austria, together with the establishment of a separate Bavaria and the abandonment of German control over the Rhineland. See Anthony Eden, *Memoirs: The Reckoning* (Boston: Houghton Mifflin, 1965), p. 335.

4. A memorandum of the Committee on Postwar Programs (a planning group within the State Department, established in January 1944) of June 8, 1944 referred to the "initial independence of Austria" and recommended that "there be no definite prohibition at the end of the war against a future decision of the Austrian people to effect close economic or political relationships with neighboring states." *Foreign Relations of the United States* (hereafter FR, followed by appropriate year and volume), 1944, volume I, pp. 438–40.

5. For the text of the Moscow Declaration, see FR, 1943, volume I, p. 701. For a discussion of Allied wartime planning regarding Austria, see Fritz Fellner, "Die aussenpolitische und völkerrechtliche Situation Österreichs 1938" in Erika Weinzierl and Felix Skalnik, eds., *Österreich: Die Zweite Republik* (Graz: Böhlau, 1972).

6. Robert I. Gannon, *The Cardinal Spellman Story* (New York: Doubleday, 1962), pp. 223–24.

7. Stourzh, *Geschichte*, pp. 5–8; FR, 1944, I, p. 442; Manfried Rauchensteiner, *Der Sonderfall* (Graz: Styria, 1979), pp. 20–45.

8. Quoted in John Lewis Gaddis, *Russia, the Soviet Union and the United States* (New York: John Wiley, 1978), p. 176.

9. See Harry S Truman, *Memoirs* (Garden City, N.Y.: Doubleday, 1956), vol. I, p. 552; and Wilfried Loth, *Die Teilung der Welt, 1941–1955* (Munich: DTV, 1980), pp. 51–53, 86–118. The reluctance of the United States to accept the principle of agreed-upon spheres of interest is reflected in a discussion of John Erhardt, the U.S. political adviser in Austria, with two members of the U.S. staff at the CFM in London in early 1946. They felt that while it was "likely that the Soviet government would be willing to enter into a sort of understanding as to a division of Europe into spheres of interest, under which Hungary and Rumania would fall in the Soviet sphere, and under which Austria should pass to the Western sphere," the U.S. government "wishes to avoid such a settlement." See FR, 1946, V, p. 284.

10. FR, 1946, pp. 285, 307–309, 326; FR, 1947, II, pp. 158–60; and Stourzh, *Geschichte*, pp. 10 and 12.

11. FR, 1946, V, pp. 336, 342–45. The text of the draft is to be found in Stourzh, *Geschichte,* pp. 217–18.

12. Stourzh, *Geschichte,* pp. 14–15; Eva-Maria Czaky, *Der Weg zur Freiheit und Neutralität* (Vienna: Österreichische Gesellschaft für Aussenpolitik, 1980), p. 3.

13. See FR, 1947, II, p. 133, and Stourzh, *Geschichte,* pp. 32–34. See also the notes exchanged between the USSR and Yugoslavia, as reported in Department of State *Bulletin* (hereafter *Bulletin*), January 8, 1953, p. 809. The Soviet position on the Yugoslav claims provided the United States in May 1948 with an ostensible excuse for suspending the talks, as shown at the end of this section.

14. The deputies resumed their deliberations in Moscow on March 11, 1947. For a resumé of their work in London, see FR 1947, II, pp. 136–37; also Stourzh, *Geschichte,* pp. 31–32.

15. See FR 1947, II, pp. 131, 159, 324–76; also William B. Bader, *Austria Between East and West* (Stanford: Stanford University Press, 1966), pp. 190–91.

16. FR, 1947, II, pp. 374–76, 516–73. A comparison of the draft at the end of the Moscow conference with the final treaty is to be found in Stourzh, *Geschichte,* pp. 241–301.

17. Czaky, *Der Weg,* pp. 140–49.

18. Stourzh, *Geschichte,* p. 41.

19. FR, 1947, II, pp. 1176–78.

20. Stourzh, *Geschichte,* p. 48; Rauchensteiner, *Der Sonderfall,* pp. 217–18.

21. FR, 1948, II, pp. 1448–49 (Soviet proposal) and pp. 1449–62. Among the unfavorable developments in Austria Erhardt mentioned were the increasing unpopularity of the USSR, the continuing insignificance of the Communist Party, and the economic and psychological effects of U.S. aid.

22. Rauchensteiner, *Der Sonderfall,* p. 277.

23. FR, 1948, II, pp. 1468–73.

24. Ibid., pp. 1488–90.

25. Ibid., pp. 1497–98; see also William Lloyd Stearman, *The Soviet Union and the Occupation of Austria* (Bonn: Siegler, 1962), pp. 115–17.

26. FR, 1948, II, pp. 1499–1500.

27. Ibid., p. 1510; see also Stourzh, *Geschichte,* pp. 52–53; Karl Gruber, *Zwischen Befreiung und Freiheit* (Vienna: Ullstein, 1953), p. 196. Gruber states that Koktomov's response may not have been in accordance with his instructions or may not have been translated correctly.

28. FR, 1948, II, pp. 1513; 1949, III, pp. 1237–58; Stourzh, *Geschichte,* p. 54; Rauchensteiner, *Der Sonderfall,* pp. 240, 246.

29. FR, 1949, III, pp. 1284–87.

30. Stourzh, *Geschichte,* pp. 56–57; Cary T. Grayson, *Austria's International Position* (Geneva: Librairie E. Droz, 1953), pp. 146–47, 245–46.

31. FR, 1949, III, pp. 1160–1168, pp. 1120–27, and Cronin, *Great Power Politics,* pp. 80–85. President Truman stated that the United States should not agree to a treaty that made it impossible for an independent Austria to survive even if Schuman and Bevin were willing to do so. He did not think that the cost of preventing an extension of the Iron Curtain to the Western borders of Austria by continuing the American presence there was excessive.

32. FR, 1949, III, pp. 1123, 1128, 1160, 1162, 1164, 1171–72, 1287.

33. Ibid., p. 1172; Stourzh, *Geschichte,* pp. 67–68.

34. FR, 1949, III, pp. 1186–87; Rauchensteiner, *Der Sonderfall,* p. 274. Material regarding U.S. interest in the creation of an Austrian security force is in FR 1949, III, pp. 1236–58. A paper prepared by the (interdepartmental) Foreign Assistance Correlation Committee stated that the State Department, the military establishment, the NSC and the JCS agreed that the equipment of such a force was the "urgent requirement for keeping Austria in the Western orbit after the conclusion of the treaty." (p. 1248)

35. Stourzh, *Geschichte,* pp. 71–74; Rauchensteiner, *Der Sonderfall,* p. 275; Grayson, *Austria's Position,* pp. 148–50. This episode is known as the "Dried Peas Debt."

36. Stourzh, *Geschichte*, pp. 74–75; Grayson, *Austria's Position*, pp. 149–51; Rauchensteiner, *Der Sonderfall*, pp. 275–78.

37. Stourzh, *Geschichte*, p. 76; Grayson, *Austria's Position*, pp. 151–53.

38. FR, 1950, IV, pp. 387–97. The military was successful in inserting into the original NSC report a clause requiring assurance that before Western occupation forces were withdrawn, Austrian security forces would be reasonably adequate to maintain internal security. But they failed in their opposition to the change from a military to a civilian high commissioner.

39. FR, 1952–1954, V, pp. 131–35, 277–79; Cronin, *Great Power Politics*, pp. 15–17.

40. Stourzh, *Geschichte*, pp. 76–81; Grayson, *Austria's Position*, pp. 153–57 and pp. 250–252 for the text of the short treaty; see also Department of State *Bulletin*, June 8, 1950, p. 815. For Soviet views on the short treaty, see *Current Digest of the Soviet Press*, vol. IV (1952), nos. 34, 40.

41. See Loth, *Die Teilung*, pp. 283–88.

42. Gerald Stourzh, "Toward the Settlement of 1955," *Austrian History Yearbook*, vol. 17/18 (1981–82), pp. 177–78; also Alfons Schilcher, *Österreich und die Grossmächte* (Vienna: Geyer Edition, 1980) pp. 154–69.

43. See Deborah W. Larson, "Crisis Prevention and the Austrian State Treaty," paper delivered at the 1985 Annual Meeting of the American Political Science Association, New Orleans, August 29–September 1, 1985, pp. 7–9.

44. Stourzh, *Geschichte*, pp. 82–83; Grayson, *Austria's Position*, pp. 165–67; Larson, *Crisis Prevention*, pp. 12–13; see also David J. Dallin, *Soviet Foreign Policy After Stalin* (Philadelphia: Lippincott, 1961), pp. 128–30.

45. Larson, *Crisis Prevention*, p. 11.

46. Thus in a memorandum to the Soviet government of June 30, 1953 it agreed with the Soviet suggestion of May 25 to replace the meetings of deputies by negotiations, "through diplomatic channels." See Stourzh, *Geschichte*, p. 85; Czaky, *Der Weg*, 292–96; Cronin, *Great Power Politics*, pp. 125–27.

47. Stourzh, *Geschichte*, pp. 86–89, Schilcher, *Österreich*, pp. 178–83. The Austrian initiatives were considered unwelcome by the United States and Britain. Earlier, Erhardt had stressed the "obvious hazards of neutrality policy" after some Socialist leaders in Austria had shown a vague receptivity to such a policy when the idea was raised by the French commander in Austria, General M. E. Béthouart, in a speech that he gave in Paris in May 1948. See, FR, 1948, II, pp. 1401–3; and Stourzh, *Geschichte*, pp. 103–4.

48. See, *Bulletin*, July 27, 1953, p. 107; August 31, 1953, p. 282-83; October 26, 1953, pp. 547–50; December 7, 1953, pp. 785–86; and (for the Soviet note of November 26, 1953) December 21, 1953, pp. 852–54. Regarding the Austrian note of September 23, see Stourzh, *Geschichte*, pp. 89–90.

49. See Czaky, *Der Weg*, pp. 298, 322.

50. Schilcher, *Österreich*, pp. 187–198. The British ambassador discussed the question once more with Figl on January 22, urging him not to state at Berlin that all questions regarding Austria's neutrality would be a matter for a decision of the four powers, because this would be "unnecessary and perhaps dangerous in certain respects (e.g., the future of Germany)." Figl assured him that he would limit himself to a reference to earlier Austrian declarations not to join alliances (ibid., p. 204).

51. Stourzh, *Geschichte*, pp. 117–18. A telegram from the Austrian delegation in Berlin to Vienna indicated some resentment about the negative attitude of the Adenauer government and of the German delegation in Berlin towards the conclusion of an Austrian treaty, which the Germans considered to be of no urgency as long as there was no solution to the German question. See Schilcher, *Österreich*, p. 205.

52. Stourzh, *Geschichte*, pp. 121, and 201–202 (footnote 98); Figl's statement is in Czaky, *Der Weg*, pp. 329–30.

53. Department of State Publication No. 5399, *Foreign Ministers Meeting. Berlin Discus-*

sions January 25–February 18, 1954 (Washington: U.S. Government Printing Office, 1954), p.
190. The statement is surprising in view of Dulles' negative opinion on neutrality, expressed on
other occasions. Thus in a speech on July 9, 1956, Dulles disapproved of "the principle of
neutrality," calling it "an obsolete conception and, except under very exceptional circumstances,
. . . an immoral and short sighted conception." See Stourzh, "Settlement," p. 180 (footnote
13). See also John Foster Dulles, *War and Peace* (New York: Macmillan, 1957), 1957), p. 73,
where Dulles condemns the earlier "groping" of the noncommunist nations in the United Nations
for a neutrality that was based on the erroneous notion that the differences between the United
States and USSR were merely episodes in a great power struggle. Cronin (*Great Power Politics,*
p. 134) states that Dulles's statement in Berlin was in line with the views of President Eisenhower, expressed to him a few days before the conference.

    54. Schilcher, *Österreich,* pp. 206–207. Aside from the concerns articulated by Dulles (re-
garding Austria's sovereignty) and those recognized by Figl (apprehension that Germany might
be pressured to follow Austria's example and adopt neutrality), the Western allies also opposed
restrictions on Austria's freedom of action because they still hoped that Austria would adhere to
the Western alliance, or at least establish close political and possibly military relations with it.
See Sven Allard, *Russia and the Austrian State Treaty* (University Park: Pennsylvania State University Press, 1970), p. 117.

    55. Schilcher, *Österreich,* pp. 207–210; Stourzh, *Geschichte* pp. 123–25.

    56. See Czaky, *Der Weg,* p. 328. According to Molotov the purpose of the proposal was to
prevent attempts at a new *Anschluss.*

    57. Stourzh, *Geschichte,* pp. 124–25; Schilcher, *Österreich,* pp. 211–12; Czaky, *Der Weg,*
pp. 334–45.

    58. Czaky, *Der Weg,* p. 327. The final communiqué can be found in Royal Institute of
International Affairs, *Documents on International Affairs 1954* (London: Oxford University Press,
1957), pp. 78–79 (hereafter cited by title of collection, followed by appropriate year). In his
concluding statement Dulles withdrew his acceptance of the Soviet version of the disputed articles, offered on the assumption that the treaty would be signed in Berlin. See Schilcher, *Österreich,* p. 212.

    59. Schilcher, *Österreich,* pp. 224–25; Czaky, *Der Weg,* pp. 347–50.

    60. See, e.g. David J. Dallin, *Soviet Foreign Policy,* p. 254; J. M. Macintosh, *Strategy and
Tactics of Soviet Foreign Policy* (London: Oxford University Press, 1962) pp. 85–87; Allard,
Russia, pp. 131–51; Cronin, *Great Power Politics,* p. 145.

    61. Schilcher, *Österreich,* pp. 232–35.

    62. Allard, *Russia,* pp. 137–40, 151–52; Stearman, *The Soviet Union,* pp. 147–48.

    63. *Documents on International Affairs 1955,* pp. 217–18, contains relevant excerpts from
Molotov's report.

    64. Schilcher, *Österreich,* pp. 238–40; see also Czaky, *Der Weg,* pp. 351–53.

    65. Schilcher, *Österreich,* pp. 240–41.

    66. Perhaps significantly, the earlier reference to the inappropriateness of unilateral negoti-
ations was omitted in the Austrian memorandum of March 14. See Czaky, *Der Weg,* pp. 353–
54; Schilcher, *Österreich,* pp. 245–49.

    67. Allard, *Russia,* pp. 172–75; Stourzh, *Geschichte,* pp. 134–38; Czaky, *Der Weg,* pp.
355–56.

    68. For the text of the Soviet note, see Czaky, *Der Weg,* pp. 356–57. See also Stourzh,
Geschichte, pp. 138–39.

    69. Schilcher, *Österreich,* pp. 250–276; Stourzh, *Geschichte,* pp. 140–42. The Federal Re-
public, concerned that Western troop withdrawal might threaten German security, sent a parliamentary delegation, led by a general, to Washington to warn of the strategic consequences of a
separation of the northern and southern tiers of NATO by a neutral Austria. See Karl Gruber, *Ein
politisches Leben* (Vienna: Molden, 1975), p. 154.

    70. Czaky, *Der Weg,* pp. 357, 359.

71. Stourzh, *Geschichte*, pp. 142–63; Schilcher, *Österreich*, pp. 276–77; also Allard, *Russia*, pp. 187–89.

72. For the text of the memorandum and the communiqué about the negotiations, see Department of State, *The Austrian State Treaty*, pp. 79–82. See also Czaky, *Der Weg*, pp. 362–66; and Allard, *Russia*, pp. 185–91.

73. Stearman, *The Soviet Union*, pp. 151–53; Stourzh, *Geschichte*, pp. 163–67. See also *Documents on International Affairs 1955*, pp. 224–26.

74. For the text of the treaty, see Department of State, *American Foreign Policy 1950–1955* (Washington, D.C.: U.S. Government Printing Office, 1957), pp. 643–77. Instead of the proposed four-power guarantee the powers only declared in Article 2 that they would respect the independence and territorial integrity of Austria. On this, see Allard, *Russia*, pp. 190, 192–93, 196–97.

75. Stourzh, *Geschichte*, pp. 170–72; Heinrich Siegler, *Austria: Problems and Achievements* (Bonn: Siegler, 1963) pp. 28–33; *Documents on International Affairs 1955*, p. 239.

76. Siegler, *Austria*, pp. 33–66; Stearman, *The Soviet Union*, p. 177; Bundespressedienst, *Österreich-Bericht* (an overview of Austrian newspaper reports and editorials), 35. Jahrgang, No. 51 (March 1, 1984); Thomas D. Schlesinger, *Austrian Neutrality in Postwar Europe* (Vienna: Braumuller, 1972), pp. 121–22.

77. See *American Foreign Policy 1950–1955*, p. 679.

78. Unless indicated by a separate footnote, quotes in this part of the essay are generally based on the text of Part I.

79. Ferring, "The Austrian State Treaty," p. 651.

80. FR, 1948, II, p. 1501; Harry S Truman, *Memoirs* (Garden City, N.Y.: Doubleday, 1956), Vol. II, pp. 245–46.

81. FR, 1948, Vol. II, p. 1408; FR, 1949, III, p. 1248; FR, 1950, Vol. III, p. 387; see also the relevant sections of Part I of this essay and footnotes 39 and 54.

82. On early Soviet objectives, see also Cronin, *Great Power Politics*, pp. 50–51, 111–12.

83. Allard (*Russia*, pp. 97–99) quotes a Soviet diplomat who told him years later: "Only now do we understand that we had already conclusively lost Austria by the election of November 1945." See also Bader, *Austria*, pp. 17–19, 41–54.

84. Allard, *Russia*, pp. 91, 101–104; and regarding one of the events of 1947, Cronin, *Great Power Politics*, pp. 50–52. But see also Karl Gruber, *Ein politisches Leben* (Vienna: Molden, 1975), pp. 93–102; Rauchensteiner, *Der Sonderfall*, pp. 202–06.

85. Bader, *Austria*, p. 181; Cronin, *Great Power Politics*, pp. 108–11; Rauchensteiner, *Der Sonderfall*, pp. 289–297. Gruber relates in *Ein politisches Leben* (p. 102) that Vyshinsky told him in New York a few days after these events that Soviet policy in Austria aimed at the maintenance of the status quo, so that the Austrians had nothing to worry about in regard to the domestic situation.

86. Erhardt discussed the pros and cons of partition from the Soviet point of view in a communication to the Acting Secretary of State of January 10, 1949. He stated that maintaining Eastern Austria as a separate state would be "politically and economically artificial to an embarassing degree," while attaching Eastern Austria to any of its neighbors "would certainly be unwelcome to Czechoslovakia, which would wish neither to take in a new German minority nor to see Hungary enlarged to such a degree." See FR, 1949, Vol. III, pp. 1258–59.

87. The NSC Report 38/5, approved by Truman on May 5, 1950, rejected negotiations for a separate treaty with Austria without Soviet participation (along the lines of peace treaty negotiations with Japan, then under way) as not desirable as it would lead to partition of Austria, if not Soviet domination of all Austria, by failing to secure the withdrawal of Soviet military forces. The report also admitted that the United States "could not prevent the Soviet authorities establishing a rump government in the Eastern zone." The above mentioned events of the fall of 1950 might have presented an opportunity for the USSR to do so, but it chose not to pursue this option.

88. Stearman, *The Soviet Union*, pp. 115–27.

82   *Kurt Steiner*

89. For the quote, see footnote 31.

90. See footnote 56.

91. See footnote 31. On disagreements among the Western powers, see Cronin, *Great Power Politics*, pp. 54–58, 80–85, 96–101. Occasionally the State Department explained its reluctance to accept these views of Britain and France by reference to the need of obtaining the consent of the Senate to the treaty, stressing the negative impact of Soviet actions in the international arena on that body.

92. Stourzh, *Geschichte*, p. 140; Schilcher, *Österreich*, pp. 252–53, 259. Publication of the volume of *Foreign Relations of the United States* for 1955 will throw more light on the internal discussions within the U.S. government in that year. Ambassador Llewellyn Thompson felt that the concern regarding the corridor was groundless because in case of war a Soviet violation of Austrian neutrality would entitle the United States to intervene in defense of the country and to maintain the link at the Brenner pass. See Allard, *Russia*, p. 193.

93. Schilcher, *Österreich*, pp. 344–45.

94. Siegler, *Austria*, p. 39; Czaky, *Der Weg*, p. 436. In the discussions preceding the departure of the Austrian delegation to Moscow, Chancellor Raab stated that Austria would make no concessions regarding its principle of rejection of Bolshevism, and he asked the Austrian ambassadors to the Western powers to reassure them in this regard. See Schilcher, *Österreich*, p. 262.

95. Dallin, *Soviet Foreign Policy*, p. 164.

96. Allard, *Russia*, pp. 216–18; Dallin, *Soviet Foreign Policy*, pp. 230, 250, 254–55; Ferring, "The Austrian State Treaty," pp. 660–61; Larson, *Crisis Prevention*, p. 21; Cronin, *Great Power Politics*, pp. 152–53.

97. Larson, *Crisis Prevention*, pp. 28–29. In the course of the revolt in Hungary in 1956, Premier Imre Nagy did, indeed, pursue a short-lived policy of neutrality. According to Bill Lomax, *Hungary 1956* (New York: St. Martin's Press, 1976) Nagy referred to "the possibility of neutralising Hungary on the Austrian pattern." (p. 65)

98. Bader, *Austria*, pp. 201–202; Stourzh, "Settlement," p. 186. In July 1955 Bulganin stated that the Soviet government did not suggest a West German renunciation of the Paris agreements, and that it was absolutely unrealistic to expect that West Germany resign from this alignment. (Dallin, *Soviet Foreign Policy*, p. 279.)

99. The quotes are from Bruno Kreisky, *Die Herausforderung* (Düsseldorf: Econ, 1963), p. 103; and Bader, *Austria*, p. 208.

100. See, e.g., Dallin, *Soviet Foreign Policy*, pp. 273 and 279; Bader, *Austria*, p. 206. Contrary to some interpretations of Molotov's statement (e.g. Fearing, "The Austrian State Treaty," p. 665), he did not link the solution of the German question to the idea of neutrality. For his statement see Czaky, *Der Weg*, pp. 406–408.

101. The quote is from Townsend Hoopes, *The Devil and John Foster Dulles* (Boston: Little, Brown, 1973), p. 295.

102. In his TV report on the conclusion of the treaty on May 17, 1955, Dulles had already stated that the Soviets' willingness to take their troops out of Austria was "one of those breaks that come if you keep on steadily, keeping the pressure on" (Larson, *Crisis Prevention*, p. 25). About Western claims to have assiduously sought a treaty since 1947, Cronin (*Great Power Politics*) states that they "were not entirely true" and that "the public image—unified Western powers are repeatedly stymied in their earnest quest for Austrian independence—was carefully cultivated but not always accurate." For a recent restatement of the "public image" see Kenneth L. Adelman and Charles A. Sorrels, "Negotiating with Moscow: the Case of Austria," in *The National Interest* (Spring 1986); 61–65. The statements by Shultz and Gratz are in *Österreich-Bericht*, No. 112/1985, those by Gromyko and Howe in the Austrian Foreign Ministry's *Aussenpolitischer Bericht 1985* (Vienna: Manz, 1986), pp. 406–10.

4

Berlin in a Divided Germany: An Evolving International Regime

JONATHAN DEAN

In 1987 a city in Central Europe vigorously celebrated its 750th anniversary, despite the fact that that city, Berlin, no longer exists, at least in agreed East-West terminology. In discussing East-West relations, Western officials do speak of "Berlin," while Soviet officials refer to "Berlin West." Western officials are referring to "Greater Berlin," the capital city of the Third Reich that was divided into four sectors of military occupation at the end of World War II. Soviet officials are referring only to the three Western sectors of Berlin. For them, there is only one Berlin—the capital of the German Democratic Republic (GDR), an area known to Western officials as the "Eastern Sector of Berlin."

These divergent designations reflect the division of Berlin and of Germany itself into two radically different political systems. They also reflect differences in basic legal definition of the Berlin situation. In the Western view, the rights in Berlin of the three Western allies—and of the Soviet Union—are original "rights of conquest" directly derived from their participation in the World II victory over Nazi Germany. In the Soviet view, the rights of France, the United Kingdom, and the United States in the three Western sectors of Berlin are not original rights but secondary rights, derived by agreement from the Soviet Union, which conquered and occupied Berlin at the end of the Second World War.

These East–West differences are and remain so fundamental that the formulators of the Quadripartite Agreement between France, the United Kingdom, the USSR, and the United States, signed in Berlin on September 3, 1971, could agree only on the term "relevant area" as the subject of the agreement on which they had been working for some sixteen months.

Yet when officials of both East and West refer to Berlin's "status," they are referring to the same thing, the ensemble of rules and procedures that has grown up around divided Berlin. These rules and procedures, which prescribe and circumscribe the actions and interactions of representatives of France, the United Kingdom, the United States, the USSR, and of German officials in both parts of the divided city and country, constitute what has been called a security regime.[1] In the international context, a security regime can be seen as a set of rules that allows two or more countries to live more safely with a continuing and dangerous dispute—in this case the division of Berlin— which cannot be fully resolved to the satisfaction of all parties or dealt with by force except at unacceptable cost. It is a more explicit, more deliberate version of what is often called a "modus vivendi."[2] Divided Berlin exists and is governed under such an international regime.

Throughout the forty years of the Berlin regime's existence, there have been repeated East-West differences over it. At least twice—in 1948 with the Berlin blockade, and in 1958–61 when Nikita Khrushchev threatened to make unilateral changes in the status of Berlin—the regime threatened to collapse, and there were real possibilities of East-West conflict. In each case, the Soviet Union retreated from extreme positions and the Berlin regime was reestablished, with modifications.

In fact, the Berlin regime has changed importantly during the past forty years. Its original form was a set of agreed rules by which the four victorious wartime allies governed the former German capital. This arrangement lasted for three years, from June 1945, when the Western allies entered Berlin, to June 1948, when the Soviets blockaded the city. At that time, the Berlin regime underwent fundamental change. Instead of an arrangement for joint administration of a unified city, it became a four-power modus vivendi for administering a divided city in a divided nation. In 1971, the Quadripartite Agreement made a major adjustment that reduced both the risks of the existing regime and the hardships it caused for Berliners. It did so primarily by converting the existing Four-Power regime to a two-tier arrangement, inserting a second tier, a German one, associating the two German states that have emerged on the territory of divided Germany with the operation of the Berlin regime. In essence, though there are differences in the legal status of participants, the Four-Power Berlin regime was converted to a Six-Power regime. At the same time, both East and West accepted constraints on achievement of their ultimate aims with regard to Berlin, the USSR and GDR on their aim of incorporating the Western Sectors in the GDR through increasing GDR control over the access routes, and the Federal Republic by suspending its claim that Berlin was an integral part of the Federal Republic.

This chapter tells the always absorbing, often dramatic story of the Four-Power Berlin regime and of its conversion to a Six-Power regime, a development that can be described either as a succession of regimes or as an evolving single regime. It is the story of the deliberate, cooperative stabilization of a dangerous point of East-West confrontation. This development, although in many respects unique, could, like the SALT agreements, serve as a model for deliberate efforts to insulate specific areas of friction and competition, such as the Persian Gulf, from the daily flow of continuing U.S.–Soviet competition, and establish rules for administering these issues so as to reduce their potentiality for triggering a confrontational crisis. Here we seek to identify the elements that constituted obstacles to this effort and those that made success possible.

THE FIRST BERLIN REGIME

The original structure of the Berlin regime was established by the European Advisory Commission, which started its work in London in January 1944 as a joint commission of the United Kingdom, the United States, and the Soviet Union to coordinate postwar policy in Europe. On September 12, 1944, as World War II still raged in Europe, representatives of the three countries in the Commission signed the Protocol on Zones of Occupation and Administration of the Greater Berlin Area.[3] The Protocol established a unified administration, the Kommandatura, for "Greater Berlin," or "Gross-Berlin," the capital area as geographically delineated in prewar German law. It divided the city into American, British, and Soviet sectors of military occupation to be administered by the individual sector commanders, not autonomously, but under the instruction of the joint Kommandatura. In the Western view, at least, Berlin was to be a unified city under common rule, not associated with the occupation zones of the three powers or part of them. The three sectors into which the city was originally divided became four in July 1945, when France was associated with the administration of the city and given an occupation sector of its own.

There was no provision in the Protocol of September 12, 1944 for access to Berlin, either for movement of Western military forces in and out of the city from their respective zones of occupation, or for movement of German civilians or civilian goods. On June 14, 1945, before the planned withdrawal of American troops from the territory of the zone allocated to Soviet occupation, President Harry Truman sent a cable to Josef Stalin in which he asked for arrangements to provide unrestricted access to Berlin for American troops by air, rail, and road on agreed routes from Frankfurt and Bremen. Churchill sent a similar message regarding access for U.K. forces. Stalin's reply to Truman on June 16 suggested two weeks delay in the pullback of U.S. and U.K. troops to allow for clearance of mines from Berlin; he pledged that "all necessary measures" would be taken by Soviet authorities, but he did not specifically address Truman's proposal for agreement on free access.

On June 29, 1944, the U.S. and U.K. commanders, General Lucius Clay and Lt. General Sir Robert Weeks, met with Marshal Georgi Zhukov, the Soviet commander-in-chief, at Zhukov's headquarters in Berlin. Oral agreement was reached whereby the two Western forces would have one road, one rail, and one air route to Berlin. (They asked for more, but did not get it.) Zhukov said Soviet military personnel would check documents of British and American personnel, but there would be no inspection of cargo. These points were not committed to writing, and the oral agreement covered only allied military traffic—not interzonal movement of Germans, of which there was little at the time. Yet at the same time, the Western allies were required by circumstances— the nearly complete destruction of Berlin and of the German system for distribution of fuel and foodstuffs—to assume from the outset full responsibility for the supply of the civilian population of their sectors. These circumstances, the dependence of the Western sectors on the Allies, the absence of contractual provision for access, and the location of Berlin in the midst of the Soviet occupation zone, were the source of most of the dramatic developments surrounding the Berlin issue as the wartime allies fell into disagreement.

On November 30, 1945, the Allied Control Council approved in writing the establishment of three air corridors instead of the original single corridor, which had proven insufficient to cope with the traffic. Subsequently, agreement in writing was reached to establish the Berlin Air Safety Center (BASC) to coordinate control of all flights in the congested Berlin Control Zone, the airspace up to 10,000 feet in a circle 20 miles from the Control Council building. The BASC, despite many ups and downs in the smoothness of its operations, continues to function today as part of the Berlin regime.

The single rail line from Helmstedt to Berlin via Magdeburg, which had been agreed to in the Clay-Weeks-Zhukov conversation, also proved inadequate to the demands of Western traffic. Agreement was reached in writing on September 10, 1945 to permit three trains in each direction for Western military use, eight for coal used for both civilian and military purposes, and five for food for the civilian population, or a total of sixteen trains per day in each direction, or sixteen "paths," as they were called.

Road, rail, and waterway traffic of German civilians between the Western and Soviet zones was left to be regulated by occupation authorities competent for those zones. Germans with allied passes were permitted to use allied trains; this practice was questioned by the Soviets as early as 1945, though tolerated by them.

This then was the Berlin regime originally agreed to by the four powers. Its limitations would become evident, but it worked adequately at the outset.

Collapse of the Original Regime

From 1946 on, frictions between the three Western allies and the Soviet Union over governing defeated Germany steadily mounted. The disputes focused mainly on reparations demanded by the Soviet Union from the Western zones, especially the industrial Ruhr, and on the broader question of whether all of Germany was to be governed at subsistence level or helped to recover economically. Western powers wanted recovery in the interest of promoting the general economic recovery of Western Europe, for which the coal of the Ruhr was essential. More fundamentally, the Western governments feared that unless the Western European economy could be pulled out of its postwar low, national communist parties might come to power and the Soviet Union would gain decisive influence over Western Europe.

As the Soviets continued to press for unified administration of all of Germany by consensus among the four wartime allies, the Western allies responded by insisting on prior agreement among the four on a program for administering the German economy. The program was to include currency reform to eliminate the huge wartime accumulation of paper money and to motivate reconstruction, a limit on German reparations, free movement of persons and goods throughout Germany, and approval of an overall export-import plan for Germany as a whole.

In February 1948 the Western Powers and the Benelux countries, meeting in London, agreed to establish a unified German political administration of the three Western zones of occupation and to associate them with the Marshall Plan. As their meeting proceeded, the Czechoslovak communists took over the Prague government. On March 20, Marshal Vasili Sokolovsky, Soviet representative on the Allied Control Council, stated that the London Conference of the Western Powers had decided questions directly within the competence of the Control Council. Consequently, these actions had destroyed the interallied agreement on the control mechanism in Germany. Sokolovsky walked out of the Control Council meeting. On March 30, the Soviets informed the Western powers of new controls on Allied road and rail traffic to Berlin: Allied soldiers and Allied civilian employees and their dependents travelling to Berlin by road and rail would have to identify themselves, and their belongings would be subject to check; freight shipments needed a Soviet permit. The Allies responded that documents of travelers by car would be checked and they would provide passenger lists for trains, but not individual documentation; personal property should not be inspected. In April, the Soviets boarded Allied trains and attempted to inspect documents of individual passengers proceeding to Berlin. The Allies stopped their own passenger train service to Berlin rather than subject themselves to these controls. Also in April, the Soviets closed two of the three lines used by German freight between the Western zones and Berlin, and barge traffic was subject to long delays. Despite these increasing warnings of a tightening noose around Berlin, the United States was not moved to make an explicit commitment to remain in West Berlin. Its failure to do so may have weakened deterrence and facilitated Stalin's decision to clamp down in June.

On June 18, 1948, the Western allies carried out a currency reform for the Western zones of occupation. On June 19, the Soviets completely stopped rail and road traffic from the West to the Western sectors of Berlin. On June 24–25 all incoming and out-going truck traffic and postal services to Berlin were stopped, as well as food deliveries from the Soviet zone. On July 1 the Soviets left the Allied Kommandatura, which governed Berlin, as they had already left the Allied Control Council itself. In doing so, they stated that there was "no longer an Allied Kommandatura." The Western airlift began on June 26, 1948, and continued until May 12, 1949 with a total of nearly 250,000 flights. In September 1948, organized groups of communist demonstrators pushed the elected mayor and city council of Berlin out of the City Hall in the Eastern Sector, and in November a meeting of communist party members appointed a separate admin-istration for East Berlin. A trickle of carefully checked individuals could cross the Berlin sector boundaries and the borders of the Soviet zone of occupation, but both city and country were divided.[4]

In its Note of July 14, 1948, replying to the protests of the Western allies over the imposition of the Berlin blockade, the Soviet Union argued that in violating wartime and postwar agreements providing for unified allied administration of Germany as a whole by moving to set up a separate government for West Germany, the Western powers had "undermined as well the very legal basis which assured their right to par-ticipation in the administration of Berlin. Berlin lies in the center of the Soviet zone and is a part of that zone."[5]

The original Soviet objective in imposing the blockade was probably mainly to dissuade the Allies from their actions in the Western zones and, if that failed, to push the Allies out of Berlin and incorporate the troublesome Western sectors in the Soviet zone of occupation. But although the Soviet Union declared that there was no longer any legal basis for the continuation of Allied forces in the Western sectors of Berlin, it did not in fact urge the withdrawal of these forces or intimate that it would try to expel them. Whatever the original motive, we may assume that the circumstances surrounding the Berlin airlift—its role in mobilizing political and public opinion in the Western sectors of Berlin, in West Germany, and in the Western countries—finally convinced the Soviets that it was not feasible to expel the Allies from Berlin. Consolidation of the Soviet hold over the Eastern Sector of Berlin and the Soviet zone of occupation did take place.

The Soviet Union first made known its willingness to lift the Berlin blockade in Stalin's January 30, 1949, interview with Kingsbury Smith in which Stalin indicated willingness to lift the blockade without requiring, as in earlier statements, that the Allies cancel their currency reform for Berlin.[6]

THE POST-BLOCKADE BERLIN REGIME

The meetings of the foreign ministers and ensuing discussions among representatives of the Four Powers in Berlin restored access to Berlin. But they did not reestablish the Four Power Allied Control Council or the Allied Kommandatura for Berlin. Instead, they established a new Berlin regime for a divided city in a divided country, one in which both the Soviet Union and the Western allies relinquished, for a time at least, their own hopes for a conclusive solution of the Berlin problem, either through incorporation of the Western sectors in the Soviet zone of occupation, or in reestablishing a unified Germany where Berlin would once again become the capital city.

The new Berlin regime, superimposed on radically divergent views about its legal underpinnings that persist to this day, represented the continuation of some pre-blockade procedures and the modification of others. The fact that the Soviet Union was increasingly frustrating the exercise of joint Four Power rights in the Eastern Sector of Berlin did not eliminate these rights. Indeed, the Western powers insisted on retaining remnants of the earlier Four Power system that had survived the blockade: the Berlin Air Safety Center and the circulation of Western military patrols in the Soviet sector.[7]

Yet, on access to Berlin, there were significant differences from the pre-blockade regime. At Soviet order, instead of the earlier West German personnel and locomotives, the East German railroad system operated the Allied military trains to and from Berlin. No Germans were permitted on Allied trains, either as employees or as passengers travelling on Allied passes. The number of permitted trains was reduced. Lists of crews of West German barges had to be submitted for approval to East German officials operating under Soviet control. There was in fact tighter Soviet control over access to Berlin than before the blockade.[8]

Even more significant for the further development of the Berlin regime was the establishment of separate governments in West and East Germany. In May 1949 a constitution for each of these German governments was approved. Significantly, both constitutions laid claim to Berlin, declaring it respectively to be a *Land,* or state, of the Federal Republic of Germany and the "capital city of the GDR."

The establishment of separate governments not only formalized the division of Germany and of Berlin, it began a process of progressive "Germanization" of the Berlin regime on both sides. On the Eastern side, this process took the form of progressive devolution to East German authorities of the Soviet Union's responsibility for its occupation sector in East Berlin and for control of access to Berlin other than access of the military forces of the Western allies. Henceforth, in the Soviet and East German vocabulary, there was only one Berlin: "Berlin, the capital of the GDR," as stated in the GDR constitution. "Berlin-West" was an area on the territory of the GDR temporarily occupied by the three Western powers. In 1953 residents of East Berlin were issued GDR personal identity cards. In 1954 responsibility for foreign trade and foreign affairs involving East Berlin was transferred to GDR authorities.

In September 1955 the Soviet Union and the GDR signed a treaty ending the residual occupation regime for the GDR. The treaty followed similar action by the Western allies in the Paris Agreements of May 1955 to end the occupation regime in the Federal Republic. The Soviet–GDR treaty specified that both the Soviet Union and the GDR retained those obligations under international agreements that concerned Germany as a whole. The treaty was accompanied by an exchange of letters between GDR Foreign Minister Lothar Bolz and Soviet Deputy Foreign Minister Valerian Zorin in which the Soviet Union formally conferred on the GDR responsibility for supervising the border of the GDR with the Federal Republic, the surroundings of Berlin, the sector crossing points in Berlin, and communication routes between West Berlin and the Federal Republic. However, the letter explicitly reserved to the commander of the Group of Soviet Forces in Germany operation of controls over movement of Allied troops between West Berlin and the Federal Republic "for the time being, until a pertinent agreement is reached."[9] The GDR was given responsibility for regulating and controlling German civilian traffic to and from the Western sectors of Berlin. Henceforth, in the event of frequent hindrances by the GDR of civilian traffic to Berlin, the Western allies would protest to the Soviet Union, which disclaimed all responsibility.

The Western allies protested this Soviet action too, stating that the Soviet Union could not unilaterally free itself of earlier Four Power obligations concerning communications between various parts of Germany, including Berlin.[10] But as we have seen, among these earlier Four Power obligations, there was no written commitment by the Soviet Union to assure the access of civilian goods and persons from West Germany to Berlin and the protests remained without effect.

There were major interferences with German civilian access to Berlin in the fall of 1949 and several times in 1951. The Federal German government made clear to the GDR in concluding the 1951 agreement on interzonal trade between the two Germanies that the favorable terms in that agreement could not be repeated if there was interference with movement of persons and goods to Berlin. The outright interferences stopped in the fall of 1951 after a threat by the Federal Republic to stop all interzonal trade, but in September 1951 the GDR nonetheless enacted a stiff road use toll for traffic to Berlin, which was doubled in 1955 and had to be negotiated downward.[11]

In their weaker beleaguered situation in Berlin, the Western allies were deliberately punctilious with regard to their actions associating the Federal Republic with the operation of the Western sectors. In order to avoid undermining their own rights, already directly contested by the Soviet Union, the Western allies suspended application to Berlin of Article 23 of the Basic Law of the Federal Republic, which declared Berlin to be a *Land* of the Federal Republic. They declared that Berlin was not a part of the Federal Republic and not governed by it. Yet the Western allies supported the establishment of close economic ties between the Federal Republic and the Western sectors. In December 1949 the Federal Republic obligated itself at Allied request to give the Western sectors the largest possible economic support. By January 1952, through Bundestag approval of the Third *Ueberleitungsgesetz,* the Western sectors were fully integrated in the economic, legal, finance, and customs system of the Federal Republic. Nearly every law and ordinance adopted by the Federal Republic was applied in Berlin, but only after review by the three Western Allies, who reserved to themselves the final decision in all matters of status and security.

By the end of 1952 Bonn had also committed itself to include the Western sectors in all international agreements it concluded, except for those involving allied reserved rights. Here too, the Allies review all international agreements before application in Berlin, and occasionally suspend their provisions. In order to avoid justified Soviet complaint over deviations from the agreed status of Berlin, the Allies maintain in effect in the Western sectors postwar Four-Power ordinances regarding the demilitarization of defeated Germany that prohibit all organized military activities, including those of the Federal German forces in the Western sectors and conscription for the Federal German Bundeswehr, and the production there of military equipment of any kind. They regularly, if vainly, protest public activities of the GDR armed forces in the Eastern Sector on the grounds that the Eastern Sector too must be kept in fully demilitarized status in compliance with the original Four Power decisions.

To bolster the morale and the economic recovery of Berlin, many agencies of the Federal Republic were located in the Western sectors: technical institutes for physics and for testing of physical substances, the government agency responsible for supervising bank credits, and the Administrative Court. Twenty-two Berlin deputies belong to the German Bundestag. These deputies are prevented by Allied restrictions from voting

to enact legislation. But Berliners can and do preside over the *Bundesrat,* the upper
chamber of the Federal German parliament, belong to the Federal German cabinet, and
vote for the election of the Federal President in the German *Bundesversammlung* or
Federal Assembly, composed of the members of the *Bundestag* and of the *Land* legis-
latures of the Federal Republic.

In order to symbolize the closeness of Bonn and Berlin, the Federal Republic deliberately developed an important "demonstrative presence" of the Federal German
parliament and government officials in the Western sectors: *Bundestag* committees, the
Bundestag in plenary session, the *Bundesrat,* and the *Bundesversammlung.* "Work weeks"
of the committees of the *Bundestag* took place in Berlin, as did meetings of the *Bundestag* caucuses and national conventions of the political parties represented in Berlin.

Interestingly, the GDR welcomed these demonstrative ties in their early stages.
The President of the GDR parliament, the *Volkskammer,* sent the members of the first
Federal Assembly in 1954 an official letter of greeting. *Neues Deutschland,* the official
newspaper of the East German Communist party, welcomed the first plenary session of
the Bundestag in 1955.[12]

But this indulgent Eastern attitude disappeared in 1958 with a new crisis over
Berlin.

THE CRISIS OF 1958–62:
THE BERLIN REGIME UNDER PRESSURE

To deal with European and American concerns following the portentous 1957 success
of the Soviet Union in launching its Sputnik satellite and developing the first ICBM, the
Eisenhower government proposed deployment of American medium-range Thor and Jupiter ballistic missiles in Europe. In December 1957 the NATO Council decided to
accept this proposal. In addition to American bombers already stationed in Europe, the
new missiles could strike Soviet territory more rapidly (and in far greater number) than
Soviet missiles could reach the United States. The American missiles were stationed in
Great Britain, Italy, Turkey, and Greece. Like American Pershings and cruise missiles
twenty years later, they were also intended to be deployed in the Federal Republic.

Then, as later, the Soviet Union reacted with great concern to the prospect of
deployment of intermediate-range American missiles in Germany. As Jack Schick puts
it in his book on the 1958 Berlin crisis, that crisis began with a missile crisis—the
project for American IRBM deployment in Europe—and ended with a second, even
more important one—the Cuban missile crisis. In the settlement of the Cuban missile
crisis, the United States withdrew its IRBMs from Europe.[13] In the event, the American
IRBMs were never stationed in Germany; Chancellor Konrad Adenauer took Soviet
protests seriously and, in the interim, the United States had successfully tested its own
ICBMs.

Prior to the December 1957 decision of the NATO council to deploy the missiles,
the Soviet Union had attempted to forestall their deployment in the Federal Republic by
proposing a confederation of the two German states and adoption of the Rapacki plan
for a zone in Central Europe free of nuclear weapons.

The new Berlin crisis began on November 27, 1958, with Soviet notes to the three
Western powers and the Federal Republic. The Soviet government now declared the
London Protocol of September 12, 1944, null and void and demanded the termination
of the "obsolete" occupation of Berlin, either by transferring the Western sectors to the

sovereignty of the GDR in whose territory the Western sectors were located, or, as a compromise, by converting West Berlin into a demilitarized free city. If this latter compromise solution were not carried out during a six-month grace period, the Soviet Union would withdraw from its remaining occupation functions for Berlin and for access to it and transfer them to the GDR, with which an agreement providing for transit to the free demilitarized city would have to be negotiated by the Western allies.[14]

As in the 1948–49 Berlin crisis, the Soviets again seemed to be testing for two objectives. The first was to use a crisis centered on Berlin to bring the Western allies and the Federal Republic to refrain from actions that the Soviets opposed—in this case, deployment of American IRBMs in Western Europe and especially the Federal Republic. The second objective was to push the Western allies out of the Western sectors. By 1961 a third objective was to limit the flow of East German refugees through Berlin, the most porous point in a tightening system of East German border controls intended to plug the economic drain caused by the loss of many educated professionals and trained workers. Whether the Soviets had serious expectations that the Western allies could actually be pushed out of Berlin is unclear. But, as his later actions in bringing Soviet missiles to Cuba showed, Khrushchev believed that the Soviet system was increasingly powerful and successful, that the Western system was in decline, and that pressure could pay off. In any event, the Soviet intention to challenge and to change the existing Berlin regime was clear.

In his tough meeting with newly elected President John F. Kennedy in Vienna in the summer of 1961, Khrushchev threatened a separate peace treaty with the GDR that would eliminate the occupation regime in West Berlin. If the United States insisted on exercising occupation rights after the new Soviet-East German peace treaty, and if East German borders were violated, Khrushchev said, "force would be met by force—if the United States wanted war, that is your problem."[15]

On his return to Washington, Kennedy responded with a partial mobilization of American forces, reinforcement of U.S. forces in Germany, and the development of plans for a military probe on the autobahn to Berlin. Widely publicized Soviet and GDR threats to cut off access to Berlin resulted in a sharp increase of refugees from East Germany, now totalling up to 2,000 a day. On August 13, 1961, the Soviets and GDR did cut off East Berlin from the Western sectors with barbed wire fences and they began the construction of the Berlin Wall. Elevated railroad and subway connections between the Western sectors and East Berlin were severed, residents of East Berlin were forbidden to visit the Western sectors, and West Berliners to visit East Berlin or East Germany. Postal and telephone connections had already been cut in June and July.

On August 18, the United States sent a combat unit up the autobahn to Berlin. But the Western powers did not carry out recommendations by some officers to challenge the Wall by military measures. They protested against the Wall, but accepted its existence, to the tremendous disillusionment of Berliners and Germans generally. A turning point in German thinking about the division of Germany had been reached, with effects that were not long in coming. But the Soviet and East German actions had changed the Berlin regime immediately, by sealing off the Western sectors from their geographic environment.

The next and final act of the Berlin crisis came after the Cuban missile crisis and its denouement in October 1962. In a speech in December 1962, GDR Party Secretary Walter Ulbricht said "peaceful co-existence is linked up with compromises on both sides" and suggested negotiations between the two German states. Khrushchev in a

January 1963 speech to the East German Communist Party in Berlin said that the Soviet Union had already gained its main point through establishment of the Berlin Wall and by calling the Western powers to order by stepping on their "pet corns." [16] He intimated that, for the time being, he would not press his demands for a change of status in Berlin. The Cuban crisis seems on the one hand to have made the Soviet leadership more sensitive to the risks of continuing the confrontation over Berlin. On the other hand, President Kennedy's indication to the Soviets, as part of the resolution of the crisis, that American IRBMs would be removed from Europe removed what appears to have been a major part of its original motivation. Finally, there had been no effective Western challenge to the construction of the Berlin Wall, which would continue to serve its function of preventing mass exodus from the GDR.

AFTER THE 1958–62 CRISIS

In June 1964 the Soviet Union and the GDR concluded a Friendship Treaty. In a joint communiqué accompanying the treaty, West Berlin is described as an "independent political entity" in the center of the GDR and lying on its territory. The GDR in an accompanying memorandum said that it was proceeding from the present real situation of West Berlin: that West Berlin, which in law belonged to the territory of the GDR, was still occupied by foreign powers. [17]

Khrushchev had complained in a 1959 article in *Foreign Affairs* that the real cause of tensions in Berlin was that the Western powers had progressively permitted Federal Germany to establish so many links to the Western sectors that the resulting situation had undermined the position of the Western powers. Following the wind-down of Khrushchev's Berlin crisis and Khrushchev's removal from office in October 1964, the Soviet Union suspended its pressures on the Allied position in Berlin. Instead, the Soviet Union and GDR shifted their sights to this different target, the Federal German presence in Berlin and Federal German ties with the Western sectors. They attacked the "illegal" practices of the Federal Republic in the Western sectors and the GDR deliberately used its control over access routes to Berlin to register its objections to these demonstrative acts of presence. Through interventions in third countries, the Soviet Union actively contested coverage of the Western sectors in international agreements concluded by the Federal Republic.

The Federal German *Bundestag* planned to hold a plenary session in Berlin on April 7, 1965, as it had in previous years. The GDR prohibited *Bundestag* deputies from using the access routes to Berlin. The Warsaw Pact held large-scale maneuvers in the area between the Western sectors and the Federal Republic, cutting off access completely six times for several hours at a time. The processing of papers for truck transport to Berlin was slowed down, often lasting a day and a half, and huge backups of waiting trucks formed at the crossing points. Canal traffic to Berlin was suspended for a week. On the day of the *Bundestag* session, which took place as planned, Soviet and GDR military aircraft flew through the Berlin air corridors, causing repeated sonic booms over the city.

In January 1968 Soviet Ambassador Semon Tsarapkin presented the Federal German government with a paper summarizing Soviet objections to Federal German activities in Berlin. The memorandum listed as objectionable practices: "Parliamentary Weeks" of Bundestag committee meetings and cabinet sessions in Berlin; the establishment of Federal agencies in Berlin; the execution of official functions by Federal German government leaders while in Berlin; the election of the Berlin mayor as President of the Bundesrat; and meetings in Berlin of Federal German political parties and national associations. This time, the Soviets did not urge that Berlin become an independent entity. Instead, they demanded that the Federal Republic respect the "existing status" of the city. Soon thereafter, a semi-official Soviet publication criticized the inclusion of the Western sectors in the Federal German legal, economic, finance, trade, and customs system and the representation abroad of the interests of the Western sectors by the Federal Republic.[18]

THE RUN UP TO THE BERLIN NEGOTIATIONS

In the middle and late 1960s, the rigid confrontational stance of the Cold War began to erode in both East and West. Khrushchev, who had begun in the summer of 1963 to move toward improved relations with the West, was deposed in October 1964 and replaced by Leonid Brezhnev and Aleksei Kosygin. After a period of initial uncertainty as the new leadership consolidated its internal position, it continued this movement and engaged in active efforts to gain formal Western acceptance of the postwar status quo in Eastern Europe, an effort documented in the 1966 Bucharest Declaration of the Warsaw Pact calling for a conference on European Security. In Federal Germany, the Evangelical Church published in 1965 a significant memorandum calling for reconciliation between East and West, including East and West Germany. In late 1966 a new broad coalition of Christian Democrats and Social Democrats, led by Kurt Kiesinger as chancellor and Willy Brandt as vice-chancellor and foreign minister, succeeded the Christian Democratic-Free Democratic coalition that had governed Germany under Chancellor Adenauer and then Chancellor Ludwig Erhard for the previous fifteen years. In March 1967 President Johnson and Premier Kosygin met at Glassboro, New Jersey. In October, Johnson made a significant speech on East-West reconciliation and pressed for opening SALT talks with the USSR. In December 1967, the NATO foreign ministers adopted the Harmel Report calling for a two-track NATO policy of defense and dialogue with the Warsaw Pact and, in July 1968, the Non-Proliferation Treaty was signed in London and Moscow; one of its most important provisions was to extend to the Soviet Union Federal Germany's earlier commitment to the West not to have nuclear weapons. In August 1968 East German leader Walter Ulbricht offered to hold formal negotiations with the Federal Republic on postal communications and transport issues.

The clear trend toward an East-West thaw stopped abruptly in August 1968, with the invasion of Czechoslovakia by 70,000 Soviet troops. But the momentum toward détente was strong. President Johnson continued to press for the opening of the SALT negotiations. The Soviet Union had received a decisive blow to its international standing and to its authority in the international communist movement as a result of its military repression of Czechoslovak moves toward pluralism. It made energetic efforts to regain its international repute.

Although East and West appeared to be moving toward a somewhat improved relationship, the Western position in Berlin continued to deteriorate as the GDR took firmer hold over the access routes to Berlin and gained in international stature.

In March 1968 the GDR issued an ordinance forbidding Federal Ministers and senior officials to enter the GDR and to use transit routes to Berlin. And in June, the GDR introduced the requirement that all travellers from the Federal Republic to the GDR and to the Western sectors other than members of the Allied garrisons must have

GDR visas. A special tax was levied on freight shipments to the Western sectors. After protesting to the Soviet Union, the Western allies and the Federal Republic accepted the implementation of the new requirements. All pretense of Four-Power responsibility for civilian access to Berlin had been eliminated.

In the same period, the GDR itself was moving rapidly toward international recognition and the vigor of Federal German opposition to this trend was markedly declining. Up to the mid-1960s, the Federal Republic and its allies had expended great effort in maintaining the Federal Republic's claim to be the sole valid representative of the German people in the international arena and in holding back steadily more numerous GDR efforts to gain membership in international organizations. But the continued existence of the GDR and successful Soviet efforts to maintain the Soviet hold over Eastern Europe—through repression of uprisings and strikes in East Berlin, Poland, Hungary and Czechoslovakia—together with the construction of the Berlin Wall and the steady growth of Soviet military power, especially in nuclear arms, had convinced most West Germans that the division of their country was a lasting one that the Western alliance was powerless or unwilling to contest. Every year of continued existence of the GDR made it more difficult to insist on its international nonacceptance.

Between May 1969 and May 1970 the GDR, previously recognized only by communist countries, was recognized by ten noncommunist countries (Algeria, Cambodia, Central African Republic, Congo Brazzaville, Iraq, Somalia, South Yemen, Sudan, Syria and Egypt).[19] Under the policy known as the "Hallstein doctrine," the government of the Federal Republic had declared it would break relations with any country that recognized the GDR and had actually broken relations with Yugloslavia (1957) and Cuba (1963) when these two countries recognized the GDR. But in the face of the many acts of recognition in 1969 and 1970, the Federal Republic contented itself with recalling its ambassadors from Cambodia and a few other countries for consultation.

Indeed, at this point, political and public opinion in the Federal Republic was moving very rapidly towards acceptance of the GDR as a separate independent country on German soil instead of as "the Soviet Zone of Occupation" or the "so-called GDR," as it was still termed at the time. In April 1969 the national convention of the Social Democratic Party, meeting in Bad Godesberg to prepare for the *Bundestag* elections of September 1969, adopted a resolution stating that the existence of the GDR as a state could not be denied. The national convention of the Free Democratic Party adopted in its election platform the demand that the Federal Republic should seek admission to the United Nations even if this meant that the GDR would gain full international acceptance by also becoming a member. Only the Christian Democrats still categorically refused to have any dealings with the GDR, making nonrecognition of the GDR a theme of the CDU campaign for the 1969 *Bundestag* election.

Senior Federal German officials made quite clear their view that further crystallization of German public and political opinion in favor of acceptance of the GDR was inevitable; they urged that the FRG and Western powers should, while it was still possible, try to gain whatever negotiating advantage they could from the GDR by dropping their opposition to its international acceptance.[20]

These forecasts were borne out after the September 1969 elections and the resulting establishment of the Social Democratic-Free Democratic government of Willy Brandt and Walter Scheel. In his October 28, 1969, speech presenting the program of the new government, Chancellor Brandt spoke of "two German states in one nation." Brandt offered a binding contractual agreement with the GDR on non-use of force and said the

FRG would not attempt to block GDR trade and cultural activities in third countries. In the debate on the government program, Brandt and Foreign Minister Scheel abandoned the Hallstein doctrine. Challenged by CDU speakers, they repeatedly refused to state that the FRG would as heretofore consider third country recognition of the GDR as an unfriendly act and break relations with that country.

Under the impact of these developments, the position of the beleaguered Western allies on Allied rights and responsibilities for Berlin was weakening. The Soviet Union had progressively withdrawn from its responsibilities for East Berlin and the GDR had taken on all aspects of controlling Berlin access except for access of allied troops. At the same time, the GDR was moving toward wider international acceptance. The prospect was that the Western allies would, step by step, be obliged to deal on access to Berlin, quite possibly including access of their own forces, with a German Democratic Republic they did not recognize and whose relationship with the West would not necessarily contain any of the restraints that characterized the relationship of the United States and the Soviet Union as nuclear powers. Instead, the GDR, suspected of having instigated on its own many of the recent disturbances involving access to Berlin, could continue to do so or act as the surrogate of the Soviet Union, and the Allies might have no rejoinder but direct force. Behind the Western concern over the GDR was recognition of the growing strength of Soviet nuclear arms, and of the parallel improbability that Soviet control over Eastern Europe could be seriously shaken or—considering the intervention in Czechoslovakia—would evolve to any major extent in the foreseeable future.

Moreover, the morale of the Berlin population was not impervious to the continual difficulties in access of civilian personnel and goods to Berlin. Berliners were apprehensive about growing GDR control over the access routes and Berlin production and trade suffered because of delivery uncertainties. The temporary opportunity to visit relatives and friends in East Berlin and the GDR by means of Christmas passes negotiated by Willy Brandt as mayor of Berlin in the years 1963–66 had not recurred since Brandt's departure from Berlin to become foreign minister and chancellor in Bonn. The Soviet Union had for years refused to even discuss Berlin access with the Western powers. The Berlin regime appeared seriously threatened.

In the customary meetings of British, French, American, and Federal German foreign ministers on the margins of the NATO ministerial sessions at Reykjavik in June 1968 and at Brussels in December 1968, Foreign Minister Brandt urged his Western colleagues to undertake soundings with the Soviets to improve the situation with regard to access to Berlin and easing of visit and travel restrictions for Berliners. The American Embassy in Bonn urged that the Western allies seek to gain some advantage from the efforts of the Soviet Union to reestablish itself internationally after the serious political damage it had received from its invasion of Czechoslovakia; the Soviets should be obliged to give concrete evidence of their intentions through agreement to improvements in Berlin.[21]

Despite these suggestions, the foreign ministries of the three Western powers were reluctant to open discussion with the Soviet Union on the complex Berlin regime. They feared that the Soviets would make far-reaching proposals for change which would have to be rejected, leaving the Berlin situation worse off than before. It took over a year from Western agreement at Reykjavik to look into the issue before the first Allied working paper for possible soundings with the Soviets over Berlin was ready.

President Nixon had visited the Western sectors in February 1969 amid the controversy over the decision to hold the next Federal Assembly there on March 5. In a speech at the Siemens plant, he signalled willingness to make changes in the Berlin situation, which, he said, was not ideal. Henry Kissinger reports that, following President Nixon's return to Washington, Ambassador Anatoly Dobrynin indicated to him Soviet willingness to negotiate on the Berlin question and that President Nixon had expressed his own willingness in a letter to Premier Kosygin.[22]

In their discussion on the margins of the April 1969 NATO ministerial conference, the foreign ministers of France, the United Kingdom, the United States, and the FRG agreed that there should be official soundings of Soviet willingness to discuss the Berlin issue. Foreign Minister Gromyko stated publicly in a July 10 speech in the Supreme Soviet that the Soviet Union was prepared to discuss the future prevention of ''complications over West Berlin.'' The Western allies presented their discussion paper to the Soviets in August 1969. After further preliminaries, the Four Power negotiations began on March 26, 1970, in the building of the Allied Control Authority in the American Sector of Berlin.

THE QUADRIPARTITE NEGOTIATIONS

Given the complexity of their subject matter, the Berlin negotiations were of short duration; they ended on September 3, 1971, after a period of some sixteen months. The specific objectives of both sides were reflected in their negotiating positions. Their broader objectives, which account for the success and rapidity of the Quadripartite negotiations, will be discussed later.

At the outset of the talks, the negotiating objectives of the three Western allies were modest. They were to achieve what were called ''practical improvements'' in the situation in and around Berlin without damage to the structure of Four Power rights and responsibilities—that is, to the existing Berlin regime. This was to be done by assuring access of civilian goods and persons to Berlin; assuring opportunity for further development of economic, financial, and cultural ties between the Federal Republic and the Western sectors of Berlin; making arrangements for less restricted movement of residents of the Western sectors to the Eastern sector of Berlin and to the GDR; and through achieving Soviet acknowledgement in some form that Western rights and responsibilities in Berlin would continue without change.

The immediate Soviet objectives in the Berlin negotiations as assessed in the West reflected interests that the Soviet Union held in common with the government of the GDR: to advance the GDR toward international acceptance; to emphasize GDR sovereignty over its territory, including the access routes to Berlin; to reduce the Federal German presence in Berlin; and to increase the Soviet presence in the Western sectors. One Soviet motive, to preserve some part of its postwar responsibility for Germany as a whole, was somewhat at odds with the rest, but clearly played a role in the outcome of the talks.

The early rounds of the Berlin negotiations were taken up with presentations of the divergent legal viewpoints of the two sides—the Western view that the allies were in Berlin by original right of victory over Nazi Germany and that the structure of Four-Power rights for Berlin and Germany remained intact save for Soviet noncompliance, and the Soviet view that the Soviets had the original rights in all of Berlin whose exercise they had transferred to the Western powers for the Western sectors by agreements that the Western powers had failed to respect. In this initial stage of the negotiation, the Soviets focused on their desire to dismantle Federal German activities and presence in the Western sectors and did not respond to Western suggestions that the negotiations should focus on practical improvements in access to Berlin and access for Berliners to East Berlin and East Germany. By implication, the Soviets suggested relinquishment of the extension of Four-Power status to East Berlin and the political neutralization of the Western sectors, which they described as a center of Western political and propagandistic attempts to subvert the existing order in East Germany. To this end, they argued, the "illegal" political activities of the FRG in the Western sectors should be ended and any arrangements of a practical nature should be based on Western acknowledgement that "West Berlin" was located on GDR territory.

The pace of the Berlin negotiations picked up after the signature on August 12, 1970, in Moscow of the German-Soviet treaty accepting the postwar borders of Poland, the GDR, and the Soviet Union. The first written position papers of the two sides in Berlin were exchanged in September 1970.

By November 1970, the Soviets had indicated readiness to accept several improvements in travel by West Berliners to East Berlin and the GDR proposed by the Western allies. However, there was no resolution of the access issue; the Soviets were asking for further cutbacks in the Federal German presence in Berlin, including elimination of meetings of *Bundestag* committees and the removal of all federal agencies, and there was little progress on the issue of Federal German representation of West Berliners abroad.

The Western powers presented a draft agreement on February 5, 1971, and the Soviets a draft agreement of their own on March 26; the drafts had some similarities on specific points, but diverged widely as regards their statements on legal and status issues. For example, the Soviet draft suggested that arrangements could be made to facilitate visits by residents of the Western sectors to "Berlin, Capital of the GDR," language almost surely pressed by the GDR, but at that advanced stage of the talks probably considered by the Soviets as "bargaining fat." Nonetheless, the unyielding nature of the Soviet draft convinced pessimists in the West that no Berlin agreement was possible. But, by the end of May, the deputy negotiators had developed a partial common text with bracketed language and footnotes indicating continued divergences. On August 23 the four ambassadors orally agreed to a text, which was initialled on September 3. The inner-German agreement was completed in December 1971 and the Final Protocol of the Quadripartite Agreement went into effect on June 3, 1972, the day of entry into effect of the Federal German treaties with the USSR and Poland following a difficult ratification by the *Bundestag*.

The Outcome

The final form of the Quadripartite Agreement is very close to the Western draft agreement of February 5, 1971, at the time considered by some Western experts as a "maximalist" statement of Western objectives. The preamble of the agreement states that the four governments, acting on the basis of their quadripartite rights and responsibilities, were agreed that there should be no unilateral change "in the area." The area is not further identified, reflecting continued divergence of view over the legal status of Berlin. The operative provisions of the agreement are: (1) A declaration by the Soviet Union that transit traffic by road, rail, and waterway of civilian personnel and goods between the Western sectors of Berlin and the Federal Republic "would be unimpeded, and would receive preferential treatment." (2) The three Western powers state that ties between the Western sectors and Federal Republic will be maintained and developed, taking into account that the Western sectors are not a constituent part of the Federal Republic of Germany and not governed by it; the agreement states that the Federal president, the Federal government, the *Bundesversammlung,* the *Bundesrat,* and *Bundestag* would not perform constitutional acts of governing the Western sectors. (3) The Soviet Union pledges improved communications and travel for Berliners to the "surrounding area." (4) The three Western powers declare they would represent the Western sectors abroad in all matters concerning security and status. Subject to this limitation, the Federal Republic could represent the interests of Berlin abroad, Berliners could participate in FRG delegations to international meetings, and international conferences could take place in the Western sectors if jointly invited by the Berlin Senat and the Federal German government. The Soviet Union accepts this statement. (5) The Western powers state that the Soviet Union could establish a Consulate General and trade office in the Western Sectors. (6) The signatories agree that these arrangements would go into effect after satisfactory agreements on access and visits between the Federal Republic and the GDR and between the Senat and the GDR had been concluded. (7 The four governments agree to consult in the event of difficulties in the application of the agreement. The entire agreement with its annexes fills only about eight printed pages.[23]

Evaluation

The Quadripartite Agreement was a success in the sense of achieving specific Western negotiating objectives. Each of the immediate Western objectives was agreed to: reaffirmation of Soviet responsibility for Four-Power rights and responsibilities; improved access to and from the Western sectors guaranteed by the Soviets; arrangements for visits and communications by Berliners to East Berlin and the GDR; Soviet acceptance of ties between the Federal Republic and the Western sectors; a more assured role of the Western sectors in international life. The West paid something for these gains, committing itself vis-à-vis the Soviet Union to maintain the stipulation that the Federal Republic did not govern the Western sectors and permitting a Soviet Consulate General in the Western sectors. The West failed to gain explicit mention of "Berlin" in the agreement and there was no improvement of the Western position regarding the Soviet sector of Berlin. The West also moved far toward agreeing to full international acceptance of the GDR.

In addition to specific objectives already described, the West achieved broader objectives in the Quadripartite Agreement: reducing the risk of confrontation over Berlin, and avoiding a possible Soviet withdrawal from responsibility for Berlin that would leave the Western Powers confronted by the GDR, a nation they did not at the time recognize and over which they had no hold, and which could function, like Cuba, as a surrogate for the Soviets without directly involving the USSR unless it wished to be. The Western allies gained these benefits before it became too late to do so through progressive international acceptance of East Germany. In particular, after the lapse of twenty-five years, the Western allies made good the enormously important omission in the first Berlin regime, the absence of contractual agreement assuring access to Berlin of civilian personnel and goods. They induced the Soviets to drop their efforts to push the Western allies and Federal Germany out of the Western sectors, to reaffirm the "occupied" status of the Western sectors, and to explicitly accept a Federal German role in Berlin at a certain level.

The agreement brought the GDR enhanced international status and the certain prospect of further progress. In the draft agreement on inter-German relations the GDR had given the FRG in 1968, the GDR had proposed simultaneous U.N. entry of the FRG and the GDR following conclusion of inter-German agreements, and this is what occurred. Through the inner-German agreement on transit to Berlin, the GDR also gained a lump sum transit fee for use of the access routes to Berlin. With this agreement, the GDR also received the assurance of a series of annual hard currency payments of about one billion marks, which the FRG makes annually in connection with Berlin access and services to Berlin.

During the negotiations, there were some signs of division of views within the GDR leadership over the Berlin Agreement, especially over the issue of Soviet responsibility for access over GDR territory, which limited GDR sovereignty on this issue; and over the potential effects on GDR control over the East German population of a stream of West German and West Berlin visitors. To explain how it came to assume the responsibility in the Quadripartite Agreement for unimpeded traffic routes to Berlin, the Soviet Union developed the rather artificial theory that, subsequent to its return to the GDR of authority over the access routes, it had been empowered by the GDR to act as its agent in access matters in the Quadripartite talks. In May 1971, GDR leader Ulbricht was suddenly obliged to resign and the Berlin talks moved more rapidly after that.

From the Quadripartite Agreement, the Soviet Union gained the desired advance of the GDR toward international recognition and consolidation, and reduction and limitation of the Federal German presence in Berlin. It overcame much of the onus of its invasion of Czechoslovakia and reestablished its standing in the West. But Soviet motives extended beyond these achievements and were broader than those of the West, which were more closely linked with the Berlin and German issues.

Since the mid-1960s, the post-Khrushchev Soviet leadership had been engaged in an effort to open a new political and economic relationship with the United States and Western Europe. Soviet motivation to do this had been increased by the Soviet clash with the Chinese on the Usuri River in March 1969. The Soviet leadership also probably had a direct interest in defusing the Berlin situation and thus avoiding a direct conflict with the United States over this issue. This was not least because the GDR had more than once apparently taken the initiative to cause difficulties on the access routes without full advance consultation with the Soviets.

But above all, Soviet leaders realized they could not achieve the objectives of their own Western policy without some improvement of the Berlin situation. Beginning in 1969, after the invasion of Czechoslovakia had jeopardized East-West relations, the NATO Council challenged the Soviet Union to give concrete evidence of its professed desire to improve these relations through improvements in the Berlin situation.

Stronger even than its desire to reestablish its post-Prague standing in the West was the Soviet desire to achieve Western acceptance of the postwar borders of Central and Eastern Europe. Federal Germany under Chancellor Brandt believed it was necessary to accept that status quo in order to improve it. It negotiated treaties with the Soviet Union and Poland, accepting the loss of East Prussia and Silesia and the establishment of the GDR and the resulting borders. But after sometimes heated discussion caused by the Federal German government's apparent willingness to proceed with ratification of the Eastern treaties, Federal Germany and the Western allies agreed that the *Bundestag* should not ratify these treaties prior to conclusion of a Berlin agreement.

Not satisfied with Federal German acceptance of the postwar borders, the Soviet

Union also wanted wider endorsement of the borders through a Europe-wide conference, the CSCE, which finally convened in November 1972. But, as shown in successive NATO communiqués in 1970 and 1971, the NATO countries also made their participation in a possible CSCE dependent on prior conclusion of an acceptable Berlin agreement. This linkage was positive linkage, associating a Berlin agreement with something the Soviets wanted to achieve. That the Soviets themselves perceived this linkage became evident. After completion in December 1971 of the inner-German agreement on transit traffic to Berlin and the Berlin Senat–GDR agreements on improvement of travel and visits and on the exchange of enclaves in Berlin, the Soviet Union applied reverse linkage and declined to put the Quadripartite Agreement into effect until after the *Bundestag* had ratified the Federal German treaties with the GDR and Poland; the entire package entered into effect the same day, June 3, 1972. Other linkage factors were the announcement of the SALT I agreement in May 1971, approval of a $500 million American loan to the USSR in connection with the Kama truck factory, and discussion of American sales of grain and oil drilling equipment to the Soviet Union.[24]

Powerful as it was, this linkage or leverage in favor of the Western participants had to move the very considerable weight of near total control over the environs of Berlin by the Soviet Union and GDR, which in the short-range sense had time on their side as the world community—and Federal Germany—moved toward acceptance of the GDR as a separate state.

Significance of the 1971 Agreement
in the East–West Context

Through the 1971 Quadripartite Agreement, the Berlin issue, which had been both product and cause of the East-West confrontation, was deliberately decoupled from the continuing world-wide U.S.–Soviet political and military competition. In the course of decades of confrontation over Berlin, the potential costs of East-West war had grown so great that both sides were willing to insulate the Berlin issue with a new modus vivendi. For the West, the continued effort to block the GDR from international recognition was not worth the ultimate risk of conflict with the Soviet Union. For the Soviet Union, the risks of continued pressure on Berlin as a source of leverage on the West or as a long-term means of squeezing the Allies out of Berlin had become greater than potential benefits. And that pressure had become counterproductive in terms of the Soviet Union's own Western policy: to gain formal Western acceptance of the status quo in Europe, and seek a more advantageous political and economic relationship with the states of the Western coalition.

In concluding the 1971 agreement, both sides suspended their long-term objectives and ambitions for Berlin, accepting that they could not be implemented at the time. By accepting a commitment to the Soviets that the Western sectors were not a constituent part of the Federal Republic, the Federal Republic accepted continued suspension of the provision of the Basic Law declaring Berlin as a *Land* of the Federal Republic. The GDR and Soviet Union relinquished active pursuit of efforts to establish GDR sovereignty over Western sectors or to declare them an international city as a step on the way to eventual incorporation in the GDR. All six powers acknowledged that no final solution was possible at the time, only a modus vivendi or regime to administer an unresolved problem.

The Berlin regime was expanded to cover civilian access to Berlin and, largely for this purpose, further modified through associating the two states which had emerged on German territory with its operation. The Quadripartite Agreement, implemented by the Federal Republic–GDR agreement on transit and the Senat–GDR agreement on visits by West Berliners to the GDR, converted the Berlin regime from a Four Power to a Six Power regime and established a set of rules for the interaction of the six. From the viewpoint of Western legal theory, it is a two-tier regime, with the Four Powers continuing their responsibilities at one level and the Federal Republic and the GDR associated at an implementing level. But in practical terms, the day-to-day significance of the German contribution is considerably greater than that of the original Four Powers—a circumstance that may point the way to further evolution of the Berlin regime in the future.

The complex machinery for administering the Berlin regime has become still more intricate as a result of the 1971 Quadripartite Agreement.[25] In the West, the ambassadors of France, the United Kingdom, and the United States in Bonn retain responsibility for issues affecting Berlin and Germany as a whole, and thus for operation of the Berlin regime. They meet periodically with the Soviet ambassador to the GDR, who also has responsibility for residual occupation responsibilities affecting Berlin and Germany as a whole. On the basis of recommendations and studies from the three Allied missions in Berlin, Allied policy toward Berlin is coordinated with the Federal Republic in the Bonn Group, composed of officials from the three Western embassies and the German Foreign Office. In the Western sectors, still formally governed by the three Allied military commandants, their political advisers coordinate action with one another and maintain contacts with the Berlin Lord Mayor and Senat and also with the working staff of the Soviet Embassy to the GDR. This contact is the main day-to-day East–West coordinating mechanism of the Berlin regime. Since the Western allies formally retain supreme authority in Berlin, the political advisers also maintain a general oversight over the contacts of the West Berlin city administration with GDR authorities.

In turn, the Berlin authorities also oversee a wide range of commercial contacts with the GDR. The Federal Republic and the GDR each maintain a high commissioner in the capitol of the other German state. (The Federal Republic remains unwilling to accord these officials the ambassadorial status desired by the GDR because of the adverse impact on the German unity issue of recognizing the GDR as a foreign state.) The Federal Republic maintains a federal commissioner for Berlin in West Berlin and a senior official of the Berlin Senat represents Berlin interests in the Federal German *Bundesrat* in Bonn and vis-à-vis the Federal German authorities; both liaison activities are much needed in a situation where the Federal German government subsidizes about 50 percent of Berlin's annual budget. The system is intricate, but it works, and usually quite well.

Today's Berlin regime is very much a regime of shared functions. For example, ground military traffic to Berlin is still processed by Soviet military personnel. Air traffic, civilian and military, continues to operate under 1945 rules and is coordinated by the Berlin Air Safety Center mechanism established at that time. In accordance with the 1971 Agreement, civilian ground traffic to Berlin is handled by the GDR under ultimate Soviet responsibility and in cooperation with the Federal Republic, which pays large lump sum transit fees and subsidies for improvement of the land and water routes to Berlin and adjudicates with the GDR the rare cases of travellers stopped or detained by GDR authorities on the land routes. The West Berlin Senat and the GDR operate the mechanism for visits by West Berliners to East Berlin and the GDR. The Federal Ger-

man role in the Western sectors has been formally accepted by the Soviet Union and
the GDR. Under the two-tier system, the interests of Berlin abroad in status and security
matters are represented by the Allies (a function that might be exercised in the Security
Council or in peace treaty negotiations, but which has remained theoretical and unprac-
ticed) and on the second tier, the day-to-day level, by the Federal Republic, again, a
more important function in practical terms.

The FRG–GDR inner-German relationship, with Federal German credits and loans
to the GDR, provides a supportive framework for operation of the Berlin regime and
incentives for continued GDR acceptance of it. The relationship helps assure Soviet
support as well, because the Soviet Union is keenly interested in the political and economic viability of the GDR. The Soviet policy of political, economic, and military
détente toward Western Europe plays a further role in maintaining Soviet support for
the Berlin regime. For the Soviet Union to undercut the Berlin regime and cause serious
difficulties for the Western sectors would be inconsistent with this policy. On the other
hand, if there is a major adverse change in Soviet or East German policy, the Quadripartite Agreement, primarily because of its coverage of civilian access, will provide a
much clearer set of rules for crisis situations than was earlier available, and greater
clarity to Western decision makers and publics as to the specific obligations that the
Soviet Union or GDR would in such a situation have violated.

The Berlin agreement has proved quite satisfactory in implementation. Ground traffic
to and from Berlin has increased enormously, up 300 percent from its 1970 level, and
has moved smoothly; freedom of movement and communication of West Berliners with
East Berlin and the GDR greatly increased to a total of over three million visits a year
in the early 1980s. Federal German ties with Berlin have intensified. Yet there have
been difficulties, and the Agreement has required continuing negotiation and adjustment
to make it work.

Representation by the Federal Republic of West Berlin's interests abroad has been
accepted in principle by Warsaw Pact states, but the experience in this area has not been
entirely satisfactory. West Berlin is still occasionally handled separately from the Federal Republic in exhibits and conferences held in Warsaw Pact countries, and arrangements for Federal German consular representation of Berlin firms in Warsaw Pact states
are not always honored. The Soviet Union still sometimes makes a pro forma protest
when Federal German leaders visit the Western sectors, doing so for example when
Chancellor Helmut Kohl accompanied President François Mitterrand of France on a visit
to Berlin in October 1985. The Soviet Union has blocked representation of the Western
sectors by the Federal Republic in the Federal Republic-Soviet Union agreements on
cultural and scientific exchanges. There is still no agreement on these subjects after
years of negotiation because of the Berlin issue.

Until 1985, the Soviets also held back the GDR from concluding a cultural exchange agreement with the Federal Republic for the same reason. Finally, the GDR
made a side agreement, accepting token participation of West Berlin ensembles in cultural exchanges. The Soviet Union and the Warsaw Pact strongly resisted the Federal
German effort in 1974 to establish in the Western sectors the Federal Office for the
Environment, with responsibility for environmental issues in all of the Federal Republic.
This demonstrative effort to increase Federal ties with the West has led in practice to a
freeze in this area. The Soviet Union has also resisted Federal German efforts to establish offices of the European Community in the Western sectors. Nor have the Soviet

Union and GDR been forthcoming in honoring the right of the Federal Republic and the Senat acting jointly to invite international bodies to meet in Berlin. The Soviet Union and the Warsaw Pact states have blocked some of these conferences and have permitted others; each case has had to be individually negotiated.

Perhaps the main negative development in implementation of the Berlin agreement was the increase in November 1973 of the obligatory exchange of currency for visitors to the GDR and its application to Berliners visiting East Berlin and the GDR. The new requirement worked out to DM 25 per day, per person, a sum that imposes considerable hardship, especially on family visits by Berliners to East Berlin and the GDR (and of course by Federal Germans as well). This requirement countervenes the obligation of the Soviet Union in the Quadripartite Agreement to improve communications between the Western sectors and East Berlin and the GDR. Through assiduous negotiations and loan guarantees to the GDR, the Federal Republic has brought the GDR to reduce the obligation for a few limited groups, such as youngsters under 16.

Other aspects of the Berlin regime require continual attention. In 1984, GDR authorities on short notice closed the Glienicke Bridge crossing point used for access to the Western sectors by personnel of the Allied military liaison missions accredited to the headquarters of the Soviet Group of Forces Germany at Karlshorst, GDR. After Allied authorities protested to the Soviets, the latter intervened and the bridge was reopened. In 1986, after U.S. authorities had accused the GDR of laxness on terrorism by permitting personnel of the Libyan mission in East Berlin to enter West Berlin to carry out bombing of a discotheque there, the GDR responded with tighter security checks and demands for new documentation on personnel of the Western allies entering East Berlin as well as of foreign consulates and military missions in the Western sectors whose documents were provided by the Western allies. After repeated representations from the West, the East Germans shut down flights for inhabitants of Sri Lanka who entered West Berlin as illegal emigrants for economic reasons, but in 1986 they continued to permit a large flow from other developing countries, until this flow too was closed off after further negotiation. This has been a tactic designed to bring Federal German and West Berlin authorities to establish controls on entry to the Western sectors rather than maintaining Berlin as a single entity through minimal controls. The GDR also hoped to gain economic concessions for piecemeal reduction of the flow and these hopes were apparently fulfilled.

Although a practical success, the 1971 Berlin agreement requires continual attention, negotiation, and adjustment. Like East-West arms control agreements and other agreements it has to cover conditions that change continually, and to regulate a continuing competition between participants seeking to accumulate small advantages in the interest of long-term gain for their position.

The Quadripartite Agreement on Berlin did not end East-West competition over Berlin, as these circumstances clearly show. Both sides have accepted that they cannot now press for what they consider a full solution. Yet the competition continues. The Soviet Union and the GDR still hope for a long-term resolution as they define it. Valentin Falin, then Soviet ambassador to the Federal Republic, told Federal German *Bundestag* members and officials at the time of the Quadripartite negotiation that, in the long term, the Soviet Union continued to hope that the Western sectors would become part of the GDR. And the policy of the Federal German government, backed by overwhelming public opinion in the Federal Republic, is insistent that the German unity question must be kept open for ultimate determination by German residents of the GDR. This objective, if ever realized, would provide for a far different final solution of the Berlin question than that envisaged by the Soviet Union and the GDR.

In all probability it will take many decades for either view to develop momentum. In the interim, the expanded Berlin regime agreed to in 1971 insulates the Berlin issue from the ups and downs of other East-West relations, provides a set of rules for managing more safely the continuing competition over Berlin's status, and protects the overall East-West relationship from the negative impact of this continuing struggle. In doing so, it provides a model for application in other areas of the U.S.–Soviet competition that have potential to ignite a general crisis. It is evident that, for the foreseeable future, the relationship between these two countries and the coalitions they head will be a competitive one. No solution of the problems posed by the Soviet Union for the United States is likely to emerge, be it achievement of decisive U.S. military superiority over the Soviet Union, internal collapse of the Soviet system, or its radical change in the direction of Western pluralism. Among the urgent needs created by a situation of continuing East-West competition is for deliberate, step-by-step insulation of the most sensitive areas of U.S.–Soviet confrontation from the general flow of the relationship, neutralizing the interaction of the two, as was done through the Quadripartite Agreement on Berlin.

Notes

1. See "Security Regimes" by Robert Jervis, *International Security* 36, 2 (Spring 1982). I am indebted to Paul Viotti, an originator of the concept, for the description of the present situation in Berlin as a security regime. See his "Berlin and Conflict Management with the USSR," *Orbis* 28, 3 (Fall 1984). For useful bibliographies on postwar Berlin issues, see Jack M. Schick, *The Berlin Crisis 1958–1962* (Philadelphia: University of Pennsylvania Press, 1971); and Honoré M. Catudal, *A Balance Sheet of the Quadripartite Agreement on Berlin* (Berlin: Berlin Verlag, 1978).

2. The meaning of the term "regime" as it is used here is well captured by the term used for the Quadripartite Agreement in the Federal Republic, where it is called the "Berlin-Regelung"; a "regelung" is a set of rules for systematic treatment of some issue; the equivalent French word is "règlement."

3. The documents cited can be found in Wolfgang Heidelmeyer and Guenter Hindrichs, eds., *Documents on Berlin* (Munich: R. Oldenbourg Verlag, 1963), pp. 5, 14, 23, 31, 36, 39.

4. Ibid., pp. 53–78.

5. Ibid., 72, 73.

6. *Foreign Relations of the United States 1949*, vol. III (Washington, D.C.: U.S. Government Printing Office, 1950), pp. 666–67.

7. Ibid., p. 77.

8. See chapter 2 of manuscript of forthcoming book on Berlin by James Sutterlin and David Klein.

9. *Documents on Berlin*, p. 174.

10. Ibid.

11. Gerhard Wettig, *Das Vier-Mächte-Abkommen in der Bewärungsprobe* (Berlin: Berlin Verlag, 1981), pp. 48–49.

12. A good short account of the development of Bonn–Berlin ties is contained in *Die Berlin-Regelung* (Bonn: Press-und-Informationsamt der Bundesregierung, 1971), pp. 218–234.

13. Jack M. Schick, *The Berlin Crisis 1958–1962*, p. 233.

14. Text in *Documents on Berlin*, pp. 180–196.

15. Arthur M. Schlesinger, Jr., *A Thousand Days* (Boston: Houghton Mifflin, 1965), p. 374.

16. *Documents on Berlin,* pp. 342, 351.

17. *Documents on Germany, 1944–70,* Committee on Foreign Relations, United States Senate, May 17, 1971, pp. 654–657.

18. Gerhard Wettig, *Das Vier-Mächte-Abkommen in der Bewärungsprobe,* pp. 78–79.

19. Hans-Adolf Jacobsen, Gert Leptin, Ulrich Scheuner, and Eberhard Schulz, *Drei Jahrzehnte Aussenpolitik der DDR* (Munich: R. Oldenbourg Verlag, 1979), p. 857.

20. Author's own notes, 1969.

21. Author's own notes.

22. Henry Kissinger, *White House Years* (Boston: Little, Brown, 1979), pp. 100, 407.

23. The text of the agreement with useful commentary can be found in Honoré M. Catudal, *A Balance Sheet of the Quadripartite Agreement on Berlin,* (Berlin: Berlin Verlag, 1978).

24. Raymond Garthoff, *Detente and Confrontation* (Washington, D.C.: Brookings, 1985), p. 92.

25. See Viotti, "Berlin and Conflict Management," for an excellent summary of the Four Power coordinating mechanism.

5

Helsinki Accord, 1975

JOHN J. MARESCA

POSTWAR WATERSHED

The Conference on Security and Cooperation in Europe (CSCE) remains the broadest East-West watershed since the Second World War. A wide-ranging, multifaceted negotiation, the CSCE culminated in Helsinki on July 31–August 1, 1975, in a 35-nation summit that has been compared with the Congress of Vienna and the 1919 Peace Conference in Versailles. At Helsinki an unprecedented assembly of national leaders signed the Final Act of the CSCE, a 30,000-word document that serves many functions, some tacit and some explicit. It is a surrogate for a World War II peace treaty. It sets guidelines for interstate behavior, and provides an implicit framework for a continuing system of East–West contacts. It establishes a relationship between all the European countries and the East–West equation, and brings together the many fields available for East–West negotiations. Like an essay, history has its punctuation points as well as its nouns and verbs, and Helsinki provided such a point in the postwar evolution of Europe.

The CSCE was both a product and a reflection of the détente era of the 1970s. The original Soviet idea for a European Security Conference gained ground in a dialogue of communiqués between NATO and the Warsaw Pact in the early 1970s, as interest in détente rose. The concluding summit was held just as détente began to unravel, and would not have been possible later.

The CSCE began with preparatory discussions among representatives of the participating states in Helsinki in 1972–73. All European states were invited to participate; the United States and Canada were included as a result of the insistence of the NATO allies over a period of several years. All the invited countries became CSCE participants except Albania, which has never had anything to do with the CSCE. Monaco joined the Conference after the preparatory talks.

It was agreed that the Conference itself would take place in three stages: an opening meeting of foreign ministers, a period of detailed negotiation, and a final gathering at which the results would be approved. The opening stage was held in Helsinki in June 1973. Negotiations were pursued by hundreds of negotiators in a complex structure of committees and subcommittees during 1973–75 in Geneva, where consensus was reached on the Final Act and the summit-level conclusion.

Since the Helsinki summit there have been three major follow-up conferences to review implementation of the Final Act and consider new proposals. These meetings, in Belgrade, Madrid, and Vienna, have approved a variety of more specialized meetings, all of which have been conducted under the aegis of the Helsinki Final Act.

The CSCE and its spinoff meetings are unique in many respects: they include 35 states that technically participate on an equal footing, and agreements are reached on the basis of consensus among all participants. The list of subjects is vast, and is divided into so-called "baskets," or groupings of related issues. Basket I includes a list of ten principles of interstate behavior, notably a principle of "respect for human rights and fundamental freedoms," and some modest military confidence-building measures. Basket II covers cooperation in fields of economic and commercial relations, science, and the environment. The now-famous Basket III represents pioneering efforts to improve conditions for "human contacts" and freer circulation of information, as well as cultural and educational exchanges. In addition, the Helsinki Final Act includes special sections on cooperation in the Mediterranean area, and on follow-up to the Conference. Because of the number of participants and their widely varying national interests, there were also many wheels within wheels during the CSCE negotiations—sub-issues of importance to only one or two participants, but which had to be dealt with in some fashion.

The central East-West negotiation, however, which led to the signing of the Final Act, concerned the postwar geopolitical situation in Europe—the extent to which it would become fixed and permanent, and the extent to which it could, and should, evolve. This chapter will focus primarily on the treatment of that broad set of issues.[1]

SETTING AND OBJECTIVES

Interest in pursuit of détente grew in the late 1960s and early 1970s, despite a strong Western reaction to the 1968 Soviet intervention in Prague. Each major Western country had its own reasons for seeking improved relations with the Soviet Union, but it was the broadly shared quality of this ambition that made it possible to convene an all-European Conference. The pursuit of détente was consecrated as a major component of Western strategy when the Harmel Report was approved by the NATO alliance in 1967.[2] U.S.–Soviet relations were, of course, the key; if they had not been improving, a CSCE would have been unthinkable. The European political climate was also important, especially the German attitude. The fact that Chancellor Willy Brandt was actively engaged in his *Ostpolitik,* and was determined to settle the FRG's bilateral relations with its neighbors and the USSR, made it possible to think in terms of a broader political improvement. The CSCE thus came about largely as a result of cumulative efforts toward détente with the Soviet Union.

The principal Soviet objective in the CSCE was to obtain the broadest possible international recognition of the European status quo resulting from the Second World War, as the "logical prolongation of Yalta and Potsdam."[3] The absolute top priority was to render the division of Germany irreversible, so that a united, hostile German nation could never again threaten the Soviet Union. This was to be done through agreement on the "immutability" of postwar frontiers. The Soviets made no bones about their main objective during the negotiations, referring privately to the permanent division of Germany as the "key to European security." This objective was also revealed in the importance they attached to obtaining agreement on a "crystal clear" principle of inviolability of frontiers, which they saw as ensuring Germany's division. Everything else in the Conference had a lesser priority.

In their review of the results of the CSCE published on the tenth anniversary of Helsinki, the Soviets revealed just how important this division of Germany continues to be for them: "To hear revanchist circles in the FRG proclaim that the 'German question' remains open, demand the modification of the political map of Europe 'in a historical perspective,' and lay claim to the 1937 borders of the German Reich, one understands better the current relevance and the importance of the efforts of progressive opinion in Europe to guarantee the principle of inviolability of frontiers."[4]

Equally important for the Soviets was to obtain final multilateral recognition of the communist regimes of Eastern Europe, their borders, and the expanded frontiers of the Soviet Union itself resulting from the wartime annexation of the Baltic states and parts of Finland, Poland, Czechoslovakia, and Romania. The Soviets also hoped to establish some kind of system or regime that would permit them to enhance their influence over Western Europe as well. These were major ambitions, touching the very existence of the USSR and its communist buffer states, and their future security. It is not surprising that the Soviets were willing to trade to achieve what they wanted.

The Western side accurately perceived these Soviet ambitions, but in the context of a nascent détente Western governments tended to see them as offering opportunities to reach broad political understanding while advancing the West's own vision of Europe's future. Thus the Soviet desire to convene a CSCE was used to encourage the Kremlin to reach a four-power modus vivendi agreement on Berlin, and to accept an opening date for MBFR negotiations. Later, the Soviet desire to conclude the CSCE at a 35-nation summit was used to shape the Conference agenda and its results.

Within the scope of the CSCE itself, the West was prepared to accept the existing frontiers in Europe, provided the principle of possible peaceful change was preserved. These frontiers had in any case already been explicitly accepted in bilateral treaties between the states concerned. Other CSCE participants had recognized the postwar frontiers implicitly through the maintenance of normal diplomatic contacts; recognition of the two Germanies had occurred with the establishment of diplomatic relations and admission to the United Nations.

The Western countries also had to preserve the principle of self-determination of peoples, and their nonrecognition of the forced Soviet absorption of the Baltic states. At the same time the West wished to improve the human rights situation in the Soviet Union and Eastern Europe, and the availability of information to the peoples of those countries. The general belief was that freer circulation of people and ideas—the concept that eventually produced Basket III—was a worthy objective and could help to bring about a gradual evolution of the communist regimes. These regimes could not in any case be removed by force or fiat.

VIEWS OF NATIONAL LEADERS

Leonid Brezhnev was from the first deeply and personally committed to bringing the CSCE to a successful conclusion. Under his leadership, the European Conference had been made a key element of the so-called "peace program" of the Twenty-fourth Congress of the Communist Party of the Soviet Union. He wanted to report success in this venture to the Twenty-fifth Party Congress, set for 1976, and to portray the Helsinki conclusion as the final culmination of the Soviet victory in the Second World War.

This ambition put the Soviets under some pressure to complete the negotiations in time to link them to the fortieth anniversary of the war's end. The Western side felt no such time pressure, and sought to use Soviet haste for negotiating advantages. The tactic worked fairly well until Western political leaders themselves began to plan on attendance at the final summit. Once such planning was underway it became extremely difficult to slow or stop the momentum.

During the negotiations there were many indications of Brezhnev's direct interest and involvement; for example, he wrote personal letters to Western leaders on several occasions, pressing them to agree to the summit in Helsinki, and raised the subject with every Western visitor. Foreign Minister Andrei Gromyko was similarly absorbed in the CSCE project. He was so well-informed about the progress of the negotiations that Henry Kissinger took to referring to him ironically as "the world's greatest expert on the CSCE." Soviet statements and propaganda consistently focused on the CSCE as the pivotal negotiation for European security.

By contrast, American interest in the CSCE, until 1975, could not have been lower. Since it was a Soviet proposal it was seen primarily as a concession that the United States could give the Soviets in exchange for something more concrete. President Nixon and Secretary Kissinger did not believe the CSCE would add anything to the bilateral treaties that had already recognized postwar frontiers. They did not think the very general declaratory language that would result from the CSCE would differ in any important respect from that of the UN Charter and other such documents. Nor did they believe it would be possible to change the situation in the USSR and Eastern Europe through such a public multilateral conference.

The CSCE was convened at the height of U.S.–Soviet détente, just after President Nixon's landmark 1972 visit to Moscow, which produced a shower of bilateral agreements. The primary objective of the U.S. Administration was to reach agreement with the Soviets on the balance of strategic nuclear weapons, and other aspects of the U.S.–Soviet relationship were secondary. Although the U.S. delegation to NATO played an important role in preparing for the CSCE by suggesting many of the specific Western "freer movement" proposals, this was a relatively low-level effort, did not have real backing from the highest levels of the Administration, and ended with the opening of negotiations.

Although the Nixon Administration saw the CSCE primarily as a concession to the Soviets, this did not mean the American side was prepared to grant important concessions within the negotiations. Positions of principle were to be maintained, and the U.S. delegation, which was not under close instruction until 1975, stuck as closely as possible to the positions agreed to within the NATO caucus. However, the lack of high-level support in the U.S. government led the U.S. delegation to keep a relatively low profile throughout much of the Conference, permitting the West Europeans to form joint positions and to take the lead on many subjects. While some desiderata appeared as the Conference took shape, the United States did not have formal objectives at the beginning of the negotiations.

The U.S. attitude differed from that of the West Europeans and Canadians. Since they were not directly engaged in the American negotiations with the USSR on strategic weapons, the CSCE took a much more central place for them in their relations with Moscow. The United States was skeptical that anything of real significance could be gained in the CSCE, and feared it might raise public expectations about détente that could not be fulfilled. Washington thus wanted to conclude the Conference more quickly than the Europeans, and saw little utility in arguing over "abstruse and esoteric" points of language.[5] From the communiqué of the U.S.–Soviet summit of 1973, which contained a thinly qualified agreement to attend a summit-level conclusion to the CSCE, to the negotiations themselves, when Secretary Kissinger pressed the Allies to be more flexible in order to reach early agreement, there was a continuing tension between the United States and the West Europeans over CSCE.[6] The importance and potential of the Conference were seen differently on the two sides of the Atlantic, and the Allies believed the United States was undercutting Western negotiating leverage in its haste to complete the CSCE.

The U.S. attitude changed abruptly, however, following the fall of Saigon and the beginning of the unravelling of détente. As part of a general stiffening of the U.S. stance toward the USSR, American CSCE negotiators joined the West Europeans in a tough position that evoked a final series of Soviet concessions and made the summit possible.

In the spring of 1975, when the summit conclusion was clearly within reach, the Allied delegations in Geneva made an overall proposal to the Soviets that would settle in one stroke all the remaining issues in Basket III and ensure completion of the Conference. The condition was that Moscow had to accept the offer more or less intact. The Soviets were furious, and tried to sidestep the proposal, but the Allies, including the United States, stuck together. Kissinger himself told Gromyko that the Soviets would have to deal with this Western proposal if they were to have the summit meeting Brezhnev wanted so badly.[7] The Soviets by this time were so deeply engaged, and considered a successful conclusion to the CSCE so important, that they met the essential Western conditions.

When it was announced that President Gerald Ford was going to Helsinki to sign a major East–West agreement, the U.S. public was unprepared. Since the Administration had intentionally downplayed the importance of the CSCE for several years, there was a legitimate question as to why it was suddenly so important as to warrant a presidential signature. There had been only perfunctory consultation with Congress and interested nongovernmental organizations. The fact that the Accord was to be neither a treaty nor an agreement, and thus was not subject to Senate ratification, raised additional suspicions and provoked congressional resentment. Americans with ties to the Baltic states were so hostile to the agreement that Ford felt obliged to issue a special statement on the eve of his departure for Helsinki, denying that signature of the Final Act would change the U.S. position of nonrecognition of the annexation of the Baltic states by the USSR. Even this did not fully satisfy Baltic ethnic groups.

THE DEALS

The CSCE was a bazaar. Every participating state brought its desires to the negotiating table and tried to obtain what it could. Tradeoffs were so intricate that it was hard to keep track of them. Even the major deals entailed numerous subsidiary arrangements to ensure that any country that might object was satisfied. Most important, in exchange for agreeing to convene a CSCE the West ensured completion of the four-power agreement on Berlin, the fixing of a date for the beginning of Mutual and Balanced Force Reduction talks (MBFR), and a CSCE agenda that included the key human rights topics of freer movement of people and ideas. The United States may also have gained a marginally more cooperative attitude on Moscow's part in their bilateral relationship. In return for these Soviet moves the Western countries agreed to participate in a conference that would ultimately put an international stamp of approval on postwar European frontiers.

At the Conference itself, the West obtained measured Soviet commitments on human rights and a number of specific freer movement issues, as well as very modest military confidence-building measures—primarily prior notification of major military maneuvers in Eastern Europe and areas near the USSR's Western borders. The Soviets obtained a qualified recognition by the West of existing frontiers, and the summit-level signing ceremony they wanted. But every clause in the CSCE's Final Act was so thoroughly hedged that the principal achievements on both sides were only meaningful in a political sense.

As a technical matter, the Final Act is not legally binding. While this fact does not detract from the moral and political obligation to carry out commitments publicly undertaken at the highest level, it does provide an ample loophole for avoiding those that are difficult to implement. More specifically, the language on frontiers speaks of their "inviolability" rather than "immutability," which, taken with the text of this principle, suggests that only physical attacks on frontiers (that is, with the use of armed force) are excluded. In addition, the concept of inviolability of frontiers is offset by recognition that frontiers can nevertheless be changed peacefully.

Respect for human rights is clearly established as a principle of interstate relations, one of the main achievements of the CSCE. The seventh of the Final Act's ten "Principles Guiding Relations between Participating States," is the principle of "Respect for human rights and fundamental freedoms, including the freedom of thought, conscience, religion or belief." While from a Western point of view this principle is not ideal (it does not, for example, mention the familiar freedoms of speech and assembly) it reflects a mainly Western conception of human rights, including "the effective exercise of civil, political, economic, social, cultural and other rights and freedoms," the "freedom of the individual to profess and practice, alone or in community with others, religion or belief," and equality of minorities. The principle confirms "the right of the individual to know and act upon his rights," and states that the countries concerned will "act in conformity with . . . the Universal Declaration of Human Rights."[8]

The reference to the Universal Declaration is essential, for it recommits the participating states to the much more detailed iteration contained in that document. The Universal Declaration of Human Rights affirms, inter alia, the right to privacy (art. 12), freedom of opinion and expression (art. 19), the right of assembly (art. 20), the right to marry and found a family (art. 16), and the right to own property alone or together with others (art. 17). The Universal Declaration (art. 13) also states that "Everyone has the right to leave any country, including his own, and to return to his country."[9] Soviet practices do not appear to conform to any of these provisions; for example, the treatment of Andrei Sakharov, Yelena Bonner, and all the thousands of refuseniks is in flagrant violation of Article 13. The USSR abstained when the Universal Declaration of Human Rights was approved by the United Nations General Assembly in 1948, so its commitment to respect the Declaration when Brezhnev signed the Helsinki Accord in 1975 represented a significant new undertaking.

As a result of Helsinki, no one can argue that human rights in one state are the exclusive business of the people of that state, since they have been formally recognized as an element of each state's relations with others. After Helsinki the Soviets argued that the principle of nonintervention in internal affairs prohibited governments from criticizing human rights practices in other states, but more recently they have dropped that line of argument. The fact that human rights are established as a distinct principle makes it difficult to maintain such a line. The Soviets' acceptance at Madrid of a CSCE experts' meeting specifically focused on human rights appears to confirm their recognition that international discussion of human rights practices is not only admissible but is a major component of the CSCE.

EFFECT OF INTERNAL CONSIDERATIONS

Domestic considerations have played a major role in the approaches of both the Soviet and American sides to the Helsinki negotiations and their aftermath. For the Soviets, the effects of specific clauses on such topics as family reunification and the availability of foreign publications, were a major concern. The Soviet delegation included a senior KGB officer whose obvious role was to weigh this angle of any commitment the Soviets were asked to accept. Following the Conference, the Final Act inspired movements in several Warsaw Pact countries, including the Helsinki Watch Group in Moscow, the Charter 77 movement in Czechoslovakia, and the Solidarity labor movement in Poland. The Soviets and their allies cracked down hard to stop the contagion.

In the United States, domestic problems over the CSCE began with the government's failure to inform the public about the Helsinki negotiations, what they entailed, and what they might conclude at the summit. This was partly because the Administration did not believe the negotiations were intrinsically important, and partly because there was a desire not to raise expectations unduly. But there was also a sense of apprehension that public discussion would open a Pandora's Box of problems and opposition similar to that which produced the Jackson–Vanik amendment to the 1974 Trade Act linking the granting of most favored nation status to the Soviet Union with positive performance on Jewish emigration.

The result was a wave of public criticism when President Ford went to Helsinki to sign the Final Act. Those groups with an interest in Soviet and East European policy saw Helsinki as a sellout that recognized the Soviet hold on Eastern Europe but gained nothing in return. Congress was moved to set up a special CSCE Commission largely because they wanted to ensure that the Administration would use the CSCE framework to press actively for human rights improvements in the communist countries.

Another domestic factor was related to the rise and fall of détente. As the Nixon Administration pursued détente with the Soviet Union, apparently successfully, the American public was focused on the improvement of relations with the USSR, and maintained a generally positive attitude toward the overall concept of détente. But as the shortcomings of détente became more evident through public debate about trade and emigration, and particularly following the fall of Saigon, every aspect of the relationship with Moscow came under scrutiny and suspicion, especially those in which the immediate gains for the United States were unclear. This period coincided with the lead-up to the Helsinki summit; public attention zeroed in on the CSCE for the first time, and many conclusions were negative. *The Wall Street Journal*'s editorial headline, "Jerry Don't Go!" summed up the opinion of many Americans about Ford's planned trip to Helsinki.

With this experience in mind, the Carter and Reagan Administrations sought deliberately to build public support for their approaches to the CSCE follow-up meetings in Belgrade (1977–78) and Madrid (1980–83). The U.S. approach to the Belgrade meeting was simplistic and consisted mainly of detailed public criticism of the Soviet human rights record. While it satisfied the American public's desire to call a spade a spade, it made real agreement impossible. The principal achievement in Belgrade was to give meaning to the notion that human rights are an aspect of interstate relations; the taboo on mentioning specific human rights cases was overcome.

The approach to the Madrid meeting was more subtle, complicated by the overall difficulty of East–West relations following Soviet actions in Poland and Afghanistan. The Western strategy was to hold the same kind of frank review of implementation of the Helsinki Final Act as had been conducted in Belgrade, but also to engage the Soviets in real negotiations with a view to building on the Helsinki provisions and improving them. The idea was to try to make Helsinki into a truly dynamic process. A broad range of new proposals was put forward, and negotiations similar to those of 1973–75 were held.

Opinions in the West were strongly divided over whether the West should negotiate at all with the USSR in view of Afghanistan and Poland, and whether it was correct to conclude the Madrid meeting at a high level, an event that was bound to suggest to Western publics that détente was alive and well, and would appear inconsistent with the sanctions many Western countries had invoked against the Soviets because of their behavior on the international scene.

Largely thanks to the skill of U.S. delegation chief Max Kampelman, the divergent views of domestic interest groups and the European allies were reconciled, and the Madrid meeting was brought to a conclusion. Its Final Document, which was similar to the Helsinki Final Act in its scope and content, contained new provisions on combating terrorism, on refraining from support for activities directed toward the violent overthrow of other states' regimes, on ensuring religious freedom, and on the rights of workers to establish trade unions free to conduct legitimate activities. Existing Helsinki provisions were reiterated or expanded in numerous areas. Once again, the principal Western effort was to obtain commitments that would, if implemented, improve the human rights practices of communist countries. But, like the provisions of the original Final Act, these obligations have been largely ignored.

SUPERPOWER INVOLVEMENT

Although in theory the CSCE negotiations were carried out among the 35 participating countries, some key issues were nonetheless negotiated directly between the United States and the Soviet Union. The question of the convening of the Conference was agreed to between Kissinger and Gromyko in Moscow in September 1972, as part of a deal providing for the parallel opening of MBFR talks. The precise language on peaceful changes of frontiers was agreed to between a series of American and Soviet negotiators on the basis of phraseology worked out by the United States and the FRG. The conclusion of negotiations on the Basket III human rights issues was made possible by the frank discussion between Kissinger and Gromyko at their 1975 meeting in Vienna. The timing of the Helsinki summit itself was the subject of last-minute bargaining involving the United States and the Soviets, although it was held hostage to a long string of demands by individual countries that had to be satisfied before the summit could finally be pinned down. Malta produced a unique spectacle when it forced the two superpowers to accept unwanted clauses on the Mediterranean by withholding agreement on the summit date that the United States and the USSR had approved.

There were also a number of issues in the Conference on which U.S. and Soviet interests overlapped, or even coincided. Both of the superpowers had an interest in protecting their rights as wartime victors over Germany. For the United States as well as Great Britain and France, these rights constitute the basis for a continuing presence in Berlin, an essential element of that city's stability and viability. For the Soviets, the four-power rights are an important lever for exercising a special form of pressure on the FRG, and on the GDR as well. There was an extraordinary example of superpower cooperation during the negotiations when the four powers with rights and responsibilities in Germany met and decided to press for language protecting those rights. Other participating states of all political leanings were wary of this language because, if it were not carefully formulated, it could carry other connotations. After a marathon 24-hour negotiating session the four achieved what they wanted, leaving the negotiators from other countries breathless with this demonstration of what could be done through the cooperative efforts of all the major powers.

The United States and the USSR also shared an interest in limiting the arms control content of the CSCE. Since they were deeply involved in bilateral negotiations on strategic weapons systems, and had initiated a NATO-Warsaw Pact negotiation on troop reductions in Central Europe, neither the United States nor the USSR was keen on treating central arms control issues in an all-European forum. Moreover, the presence of neutral and nonaligned participants made the CSCE a more free-wheeling negotiation, and neither military grouping was confident of its ability to control the outcome in such circumstances. As a result, the military content of the CSCE was limited to a few modest confidence-building measures, designed to reduce the uncertainties stemming from large-scale military activities.

A third issue on which U.S. and Soviet views coincided was the need to keep Mediterranean issues out of the CSCE (in the CSCE context "Mediterranean" meant anything relating to the nonparticipating Mediterranean states). For both the superpowers, discussion of the Mediterranean could only raise Middle East issues and add another complex, divisive subject to an already overloaded agenda. Also, the Mediterranean was not central to the East-West focus of the CSCE. Despite the superpowers' opposition, however, the Mediterranean became a major side-issue because of the insistence of Malta, Yugoslavia, Cyprus, Spain, and Italy.

In each of these examples, the parallel interests of Washington and Moscow emerged over time. There was no explicit coordination, except for the one occasion when the four Berlin powers sought language to protect their rights. That case was exceptional in that there was a preexisting forum and logic on which a coordinated effort could be based. In the other instances shared interests only became evident as pressures forced the two sides to take firm positions, and both Soviets and Americans were constantly wary of the other side seeking to profit from their positions.

More important than these isolated examples of shared concerns was the convergence in the early 1970s of U.S. and Soviet interest in a positive bilateral relationship. It was this convergence, of course, that produced the period of détente and led to the easing of rigid positions on both sides. The CSCE could not have taken place without this convergence. In fact, the time window during which the Helsinki summit was politically possible proved to be very brief. By the fall of 1975 the Ford Administration was preoccupied with Soviet and Cuban activities in Angola, and détente was deteriorating rapidly. By 1976 the word "détente" had taken on such negative connotations that Ford actually banned it from his campaign vocabulary.

IMPLEMENTATION

One of the features of the CSCE that has been most disconcerting for Western public opinion is the fact that the effects of the Conference are unbalanced. The principal Soviet gain, recognition of postwar European frontiers, took effect with the signing of the Final Act, whereas the principal Western achievement, a commitment to greater respect for human rights and freer movement of people and ideas in the Soviet Union and Eastern Europe, depended on actions by individual governments after the conclusion of the Conference. Thus the Soviets could pocket what they had achieved, but the Western countries still had to press for implementation in order to show that they had obtained what they sought in the Conference.

Beyond this oversimplified reckoning, the balance between the gains of the two sides is more subtle, and perhaps also somewhat ephemeral. The West, in particular the United States, obtained a recognized, legitimate role with respect to events in the Soviet Union and Eastern Europe. Such legitimacy is sometimes taken for granted by Americans, but as a non-European country, the United States previously had legitimate influence in Europe only within the member states of the North Atlantic Alliance. Through the North Atlantic Treaty those countries had recognized and accepted an active American presence. The Helsinki Final Act had a similar effect with respect to the rest of Europe, and thus legitimized U.S. interest in the area.

It should also be noted that the West has an important continuing interest in providing the East European countries increased breathing space by whatever means can be devised. The Helsinki Final Act, by giving a Soviet blessing to increased contacts and exchanges of virtually all kinds, has done just that. East Europeans have been emphatic since Helsinki in reminding Westerners of how important this aspect of the agreement has been to them.

The overall Conference trade-off was not generally perceived as unbalanced before or during the Conference. The CSCE had been justified as an important element of détente, and each Western country had an investment of its own in détente with the Soviet Union. Thus the perception was that both sides—the USSR and the West—would gain in roughly equal measure through the successful conclusion of the Conference. The total gains for each side included tangible and intangible elements, and was topped by the concept of a dynamic détente leading to a more open and stable Europe, with commercial and human benefits accruing to all concerned. While this perception may appear naive in hindsight, it was not applied solely to the CSCE; on the contrary, it characterized the basic Western approach to détente.

But the Final Act also contains some fairly specific provisions that were meant to be implemented. The Act itself states that it is to be implemented through "unilateral, bilateral and multilateral" efforts. In fact, many of the commitments it contains can only be implemented unilaterally, such as the lowering of fees associated with family reunification (that is, fees charged for exit visas for emigration). The Western view of follow-up meetings was that they would provide a forum for reviewing implementation, and thereby serve as an encouragement to respecting the obligations contained in the Final Act. Thus it was agreed that follow-up meetings would entail "a thorough exchange of views" on "the implementation of the provisions of the Final Act and of the tasks defined by the Conference."[10]

But since the Helsinki meeting, disagreement over implementation of the Final Act has been profound. The Soviets have published long lists of actions they have taken in implementation of the Act,[11] but in fact they have avoided implementing the human rights-related provisions almost entirely, and have openly flouted them by decimating the Soviet Helsinki Watch Group and sending its leaders to prison camp or exile. The Eastern European states have followed the Soviet lead to a greater or lesser degree, adapting Soviet techniques to the needs of their own situations.

These actions have ensured continuing Western interest in the human rights situation in the USSR and Eastern Europe, and continuing criticism of the deal struck at Helsinki. Critics of Helsinki have argued that the overall trade-off of recognition of frontiers for promises on human rights was unbalanced, and should never have been made. According to this thesis, positions of principle should not have been traded for unenforceable and ambiguous promises.

In response, defenders of the Helsinki Accord argue that while there was a multilateral recognition of frontiers at Helsinki, this added nothing to the recognition already accorded through previous Western treaties, agreements, and actions over the years. Moreover, in at least three respects the Helsinki Accord protects, rather than concedes, Western positions of principle on the existing European geopolitical situation: 1) it acknowledges only that existing frontiers will not be violated by force, while reaffirming the sovereign right of peoples to self-determination; 2) it establishes an entirely new international concept recognizing that peaceful changes of frontiers are permissible; and 3) the Final Act specifically asserts that military occupations are illegal and that "No such occupation or acquisition will be recognized as legal."[12] This phrase protects in particular the long-standing American position of not recognizing the Soviet annexation of Latvia, Lithuania, and Estonia.

Western negotiators had to tread a thin line to avoid language that would appear to recognize, or even reinforce, the Brezhnev doctrine that intervention by one state in the affairs of another to defend socialism is permissible. The dilemma for the West was to obtain language that would permit Western governments to press communist regimes for human rights improvements, while excluding the types of state intervention that were exemplified by Soviet repressions in Budapest and Prague. A more acute problem was posed for the wartime allies who retain rights and responsibilities in Germany. They had to find language that would reserve those rights (thus proportionately limiting the rights of the two Germanies) without suggesting that there were other situations in which states might have limited sovereignty.

The balance achieved by the negotiators is reflected in the language of several CSCE principles: those of sovereign equality, inviolability of frontiers, territorial integrity of states, nonintervention in internal affairs, and equal rights and self-determination of peoples. From the Western view a correct balance was found, and the Brezhnev doctrine was contradicted. But the Soviets obviously did not see it this way; only two months after the Final Act was approved they signed a treaty with the German Democratic Republic that specifically reiterated the Brezhnev doctrine.[13]

Many Westerners, including some critics of the Helsinki agreement, see it as a useful yardstick for measuring Soviet and East European human rights behavior, and as an indispensable instrument for pressing those countries to improve. The fact that the Helsinki Accord is neither "a treaty nor an international agreement,"[14] and therefore has no legal effect, is not really relevant since it is unquestionably a central moral and political document whose commitments were undertaken at the highest level. It therefore should carry the same weight for implementation as a treaty of similar scope. In any event, the Final Act would be no more enforceable if it were a treaty than it is in its actual form.

EVOLVING ATTITUDES

During the CSCE, and in the years following the Helsinki summit, attitudes in both the Soviet Union and the West toward the Conference have evolved in important ways. The change has been most easily discernible in connection with the concept of the follow-up to the Conference. Long-standing Soviet interest in a regularized European body suggests that one of the original Soviet objectives in the CSCE was to establish some form of permanent all-European mechanism. Such a device would provide the Kremlin with a framework within which it could exercise more influence over Western Europe as well as the East European satellites.

As early as the meeting of wartime leaders in Teheran in 1943 Stalin spoke of a committee to oversee the postwar affairs of Europe.[15] From the Rapacki Plan of 1958, which suggested "control machinery," to the Budapest Appeal of 1969, which foresaw a European conference leading to "a durable system of European Security," the Soviets clearly had in mind a permanent European security mechanism of some kind. In 1970 a Warsaw Pact communiqué formally suggested that the question of setting up "an appropriate body" be added to the agenda of the Conference. Specifics on the form and functions of such a body were always vague.

But by the time negotiations actually began, the Soviets were back-pedalling. They evidently already foresaw that follow-up meetings could be used to pressure them on human rights. At first they did not explain what they had in mind as a continuing CSCE mechanism. When the communist bloc finally did table its formal follow-up proposal it was carefully hedged to permit meetings to be convened only "whenever its members consider this advisable." This meant the CSCE could be convened only when there was a prior consensus to do so, and thus retained for the Soviets a veto power over any follow-up gatherings. Significantly, the Warsaw Pact proposal avoided commitment even to one follow-up meeting. As the Helsinki negotiations came to a conclusion, the Soviets fought hard to avoid a commitment to regularized follow-up meetings, as was desired by the neutrals. The result was agreement on a single follow-up meeting two years after Helsinki, with a tacit understanding that other meetings would follow.

The Soviets knew they were on the defensive in the CSCE at Belgrade, which surely confirmed their worst fears about how the follow-up mechanism could be used against them. However, since then they appear to have developed considerable tolerance for the follow-up meetings and the criticisms that are now routinely leveled against them for failure to fulfill their human rights obligations. At the Madrid follow-up conference they even agreed to specialized CSCE meetings on human rights and human contacts, where they were sure to be the focus of critical comment on issues such as emigration. The Kremlin had apparently concluded that an avalanche of criticism falls of its own weight, and is therefore tolerable. The Soviets have also taken up an increasingly aggressive policy of defending their own human rights policies (by stressing such "social rights" as the right to work and medical care), while criticizing Western treatment of minorities and other human rights shortcomings.

The Soviets appear once again to see the CSCE as offering them a useful mechanism for influencing Western Europe and separating it from the United States. On the tenth anniversary of the Final Act the Soviets cited the Helsinki Accord as the third step in a process leading toward European security, one which "constitutes a multilateral system of commitments and corresponding measures." [16] The decision of the Twenty-sixth Congress of the Soviet Communist Party in 1981 to accept an enlarged zone of application for military measures to be negotiated at the CSCE spin-off Conference on Disarmament in Europe (CDE) in Stockholm, showed a renewed Soviet commitment to the CSCE process. And in 1985 the new Soviet leader, Mikhail Gorbachev, added his stamp of approval: "The Political Bureau starts from the assumption that the interstate documents of the détente period, including the Helsinki Final Act, have lost none of their value. They are an example of the way in which international relations can be built. . ." [17]

Despite the Western view that the Soviets gained more from the Helsinki Accord, and have failed to live up to their commitments, we can expect the Soviets to seek to use the CSCE forum aggressively in the future to achieve further objectives, including reduction of military readiness in Western Europe, the creation of a pro-Soviet climate among large sectors of Western public opinion, and the encouragement of divisions between the United States and its allies.

The Western attitude toward follow-up has also evolved, almost in mirror image to that of the USSR. Prior to the opening of the CSCE the West was generally leery of the idea of a permanent pan-European mechanism that would give the Soviets a kind of *droit de regard* over Western Europe. This attitude carried over into the beginning of the Conference itself, but was then influenced by two factors: 1) the desire of the neutrals, who were largely Western-oriented, to fix a regular follow-up mechanism to ensure their continuing role in East-West relations; and 2) the growing Western realization that the human rights-related commitments undertaken by the Soviets would need to be pursued if there was to be any chance of their being carried out. The Western proposal on follow-up that was submitted mid-way through the negotiations was a cautious compromise; it suggested a single review meeting two years after Helsinki. This concept was eventually accepted, and the meeting was set for Belgrade.

However, the two years between Helsinki and Belgrade, and the dismal Soviet record of compliance, convinced the Western countries that regular follow-up would indeed be required. Also, the rising interest of Western public opinion in the use of the Helsinki Accord as a human rights prod, and the defensiveness of the Soviets, made it seem clear that follow-up was in the Western, not the Soviet, interest. At the preparatory meeting for the Belgrade Conference both the NATO allies and the neutrals insisted on a commitment to periodic review conferences. The Soviets strongly resisted the concept of regular periodic meetings, but eventually agreed that the Belgrade meeting could not end until the date and place of the next similar meeting had been fixed. This arrangement has served as a precedent since that time.

LESSONS

The experience of implementation has been so disappointing in the human rights field that there has been a recurring debate among Western opinion leaders about possible abrogation of the Helsinki Accord. The reasoning has been that if the Soviets are not prepared to carry out their end of the broad Helsinki bargain by improving freer movement of people and ideas and the status of human rights in the communist countries, the West should withdraw its part of the bargain by renouncing the recognition of postwar frontiers which the Final Act entailed. The counter argument is that such abrogation would have no effect on the myriad acts of recognition of frontiers that were already in the record before Helsinki, such as establishment of diplomatic relations, bilateral treaties and agreements, high-level visits, and membership in the United Nations. At the same time the possibility of using the Helsinki Accord to press for human rights would end. The concept of abrogation could nonetheless gain ground if the Soviets continue to flout their human rights commitments.

But there is no question that the Helsinki experience has brought into focus what is perhaps the most basic dilemma for the West in reaching agreements with the Soviet Union: how to bring such a government to carry out its obligations after agreements have been reached. This question bears on almost every aspect of American-Soviet relations.

In an open, democratic society there are numerous internal forces that encourage a government to respect its international obligations: opposition political parties, an outspoken press, lobbying groups, and pressures from interested allies. All of these forces are at work in pressing the United States government to respect the commitments contained in its bilateral agreements with the USSR.

But in the closed, totalitarian society of the USSR there are no opposition politicians, no free press, and no organized lobbies. Whatever pressure there may be from Warsaw Pact allies is private and muted. At the same time major internal forces are actively engaged in resisting implementation, such as the KGB, the Army, and the bureaucracy of the Soviet state. Pressures from hostile foreign countries generate added resistance from these groups, rather than compliance. Public criticism in the West of the policies of Western governments also tends to stiffen the internal Soviet forces that are resisting reforms, since they are then encouraged to believe that Western policies may be changed.

The failure of the Soviets to carry out their Helsinki human rights commitments has been nothing less than flagrant. While no experienced Soviet-observer expected them to implement every detail of every obligation overnight, it was not an unreasonable hope that the Kremlin would make some effort to demonstrate a respect at least for the spirit of Helsinki. But the Soviets' treatment of dissidents like the Sakharovs, Anatoly Shcharansky and Yuri Orlov, and their extraordinary continuing bestiality toward those who want to leave the USSR, has reflected a determination to move in exactly the opposite direction; to clamp down and strangle any group or individual who aspires to the Helsinki concept of freer movement. The deep-seated Soviet and Russian preoccupation with internal security has far outweighed any inclination there may have been within the Soviet system to permit even symbolic liberalization. Such recent actions as the release of Shcharansky should not mislead us; they are intended to suggest liberalization, but should be seen for what they are—token symbolic exceptions to an overall system that has shown little movement toward civilized standards since the death of Stalin.

The Soviets' post-Helsinki behavior has once again posed the question of whether the West, particularly the United States, should seek further agreements with the USSR in fields where commitments cannot be enforced through some built-in leverage. Indeed, this public demonstration of Soviet bad faith raises questions about entering any agreement with Moscow.

Thus far, no one has found a clear answer to these dilemmas. At the same time, however, there is a basic political need for Western governments, especially the U.S.

government, to show publicly that they are pressing the Soviet Union and the East European regimes on human rights. Thus, whether they are effective or not, Western governments will continue to exert pressures on Moscow to carry out its Helsinki commitments. As Secretary of State George Shultz said in 1985, the Helsinki Accord "provided a standard toward which to strive and against which to measure our behavior. Perhaps we shall not soon see the day when all nations meet that standard, but the effort, in and of itself, could lead to a more secure peace, greater individual freedom, and, thus, a greater fulfillment of Europe's vast potential." On the tenth anniversary of Helsinki, Shultz confirmed America's commitment to it. "My country," he said, "and most other countries represented here remain committed to the goal of putting the program of the Final Act into practice in all of its provisions . . . We believe that the truest test of political intentions are actual steps to improve cooperation among states, to enhance contacts among peoples, and to strengthen respect for individual rights." [18]

The enduring debate as to whether or not Helsinki was in the U.S. interest is likely to continue for years to come. Measured against the clearest Western objective within the Conference—improvement in the human rights situation in the USSR and Eastern Europe—it has thus far been a dismal failure. Nonetheless, there is a large body of opinion, especially in Europe, which believes it is better to have an agreed yardstick for Soviet behavior than none at all. By this logic the post-Helsinki situation is an improvement, for it permits the West to insist on respect for human rights, and puts Soviet behavior under Western scrutiny.

The impact of the launching of what is usually called the Helsinki "process" deserves careful analysis, and can perhaps only be measured at some point in the distant future. Thus far, the Helsinki process appears as an unexpected success, in that it has spawned a broad range of follow-up meetings at the plenary and expert level, including one important new negotiation, the Conference on Disarmament in Europe (CDE), which is treated elsewhere in this book. This process has, in fact, begun to resemble something of a system of European security, with its own rules and taboos, geographic and political limitations, competencies and shortcomings. Thus, while the CSCE has so far been a failure in achieving the West's principal substantive objective, it may have unexpectedly given birth to a European system whose overall implications have never been fully anticipated.

The continuing existence of this process or system is stimulated by the Europeans, especially the smaller European states, but it depends on the acquiescence of the two superpowers, each of which has thus far evidently seen the process as serving its national interests. It would not be possible for the process to continue if one or the other superpower firmly decided that continuation was undesirable. It is this overlapping of U.S. and Soviet interests in Helsinki that keeps the process going.

For the Soviets there is an institutional need to justify the effort they expended to obtain the Helsinki accord, and to laud it as a glorious Soviet achievement. More substantively, the Soviet interest in maintaining the existing geopolitical situation is best served by ensuring that Helsinki is a living document with an institutional existence. In addition, the Soviets have recently shown renewed interest in using the Helsinki forum to divide the West and exercise influence throughout Europe.

The United States, too, must justify its signature of the Helsinki document by being able to show that it has brought human rights improvements. Since these have not been forthcoming, the next best alternative is to continue the Helsinki process, and the pressure it puts on the Soviet Union. Helsinki also has the effect of legitimizing an American role in all-European affairs. American analysts have generally overlooked this because there is a tendency in Washington to assume that the U.S. role in Europe is inherently legitimate. But while a U.S. role in West European affairs was legitimized long ago by the North Atlantic Treaty, there was nothing comparable for the rest of Europe until Helsinki. The point is not an academic one at a time of increasing interaction between East and West in Europe.

European interest in Helsinki, which has an important effect on the American attitude, is far broader. The Europeans think of Helsinki as enhancing the political stability of their continent by establishing agreed behavioral norms for interstate activity—even if these norms may be ambiguous. While the Europeans generally consider this element fundamental, it is difficult for Americans to think in terms of political stability, and the United States thus tends to discount its importance—or not count it at all. Americans emphasize strategic stability, often to the exclusion of other concepts. The desire for political stability is shared throughout Europe, East and West, and there is a widespread belief that the Helsinki process makes a positive contribution. While Washington does not share the analysis, it is influenced by the desires of its European allies, and this has been a continuing factor in the U.S. approach to Helsinki.

The Helsinki Accord has been fully satisfactory to no one. The Western debate about its value is public and well known; the Soviets make positive comments about it, but this is mainly because it was a Soviet initiative, and they are condemned to portray it as a success. Despite the fact that the Accord has put them on the defensive, the Soviets have a great capacity for claiming victory and trying to use even a negative situation to best advantage. Whether we like it or not, the Helsinki system is here to stay, with a proliferating series of spin-off meetings and conferences, and increasing recognition of a set of standards accepted by both the communist and capitalist worlds. The West, particularly the United States, cannot allow the ambiguities of Helsinki to distract us from the central political objectives that it sets, and which remain valid.

Selected Publications on the CSCE

Although there have been many articles on the CSCE, there is a dearth of both source material and scholarly work on the subject. A few books that may be of interest to specialists are listed below.

Ferraris, Luigi Vittorio, ed. *Testimonianze di un negoziato*. Padua: CEDAM, 1977.

Kavass, Igor, I., Jacqueline Paquin Granier, and Mary Frances Dominick, eds. *Human Rights, European Politics, and the Helsinki Accord: The Documentary Evolution of the Conference on Security and Cooperation in Europe, 1973–75*. 6 vols. Buffalo, N.Y.: William S. Hein, 1981.

Maresca, John J. *To Helsinki, The Conference on Security and Cooperation in Europe, 1973–75*. Durham, N.C.: Duke University Press, 1985.

Sizoo, Jan and Rudolf Th. Jurrjens. *CSCE Decision-Making: The Madrid Experience*. The Hague/Boston/Lancaster: Martinus Nijhoff, 1984.

"Symposium: Human Rights and the Helsinki Accord—A Five-Year road to Madrid." *Vanderbilt Journal of Transnational Law*, vol. 13, nos. 2–3, Spring-Summer 1980.

Volle, Hermann, Wolfgang Wagner and Walter Bodigheimer, eds. *Das Belgrader KSZE-Folgetreffen*. Bonn: Verlag für Internationale Politik, 1978.

In addition, the Commission on Security and Cooperation in Europe of the U.S. Congress has published numerous studies and records of hearings on the CSCE, most of which are available through the U.S. Government Printing Office.

Notes

1. For fuller information on the background and content of the CSCE, see the list of Selected Publications above.

2. "The Future Tasks of the Alliance" (known as the Harmel Report after Belgian Foreign Minister Pierre Harmel), was approved by the North Atlantic Council on December 14, 1967.

3. The Soviets come very close to explaining their own objectives in an interesting pamphlet published on the tenth anniversary of Helsinki: "Helsinki: Ten Years Later, Report of the Soviet Committee for Security and Cooperation in Europe" (Moscow: Progress, 1985). The quoted phrase can be found on p. 7.

4. Ibid., p. 40.

5. Secretary of State Henry Kissinger, press conference, February 25, 1975.

6. The communiqué of the Nixon-Brezhnev summit meeting in the United States, June 18–25, 1973, on the eve of the opening stage of the CSCE, contained the following language:

"Reflecting their continued positive attitude toward the Conference, both sides will make efforts to bring the Conference to a successful conclusion at the earliest possible time. Both sides proceed from the assumption that progress in the work of the Conference will produce possibilities for completing it at the highest level."

See also, Kissinger press conferences of March 28 and June 19, 1984, and the report of a Kissinger press conference in the *International Herald Tribune* (July 6–7, 1984).

7. This exchange took place at the meeting between Kissinger and Gromyko in Vienna, May 19–20, 1975.

8. "Final Act of the Conference on Security and Cooperation in Europe," Helsinki, 1975, section 1. a, "Declaration on Principles Guiding Relations between Participating States," Principle VII.

9. Universal Declaration of Human Rights, adopted by the UN General Assembly on December 10, 1948.

10. Final Act, section on "Follow-up to the Conference."

11. Typical of the Soviet approach to CSCE implementation was Brezhnev's proposal shortly after Helsinki that the UN Economic Commission for Europe (ECE) hold a series of grandiose conferences on such issues as the environment. The aim was to pad the international agenda with "cooperative" efforts in relatively uncontroversial areas as a way of demonstrating the "momentum" of détente while distracting public attention from the more difficult issues.

12. Final Act, Principle IV, "Territorial Integrity of States."

13. The "Treaty of Friendship, Cooperation, and Mutual Assistance," signed by the GDR and the USSR on October 7, 1975, contains the following provision:

"[The USSR and the GDR] declare their readiness to take the necessary steps to protect and defend the historic achievements of socialism."

14. Letter from the government of Finland to the Secretary General of the United Nations, dated July 18, 1975, forwarding the Final Act, requesting its circulation, and noting that: "this Final Act is not eligible in whole or in part, for registration with the Secretariat under Article 102 of the Charter of the United Nations, as would be the case were it a matter of a treaty or international agreement." The text of this letter was approved by consensus at the CSCE.

15. Charles E. Bohlen, *Witness to History, 1929–1969* (New York: W. W Norton, 1973), p. 144.

16. "Helsinki: Ten Years Later," p. 10.

17. Ibid., p. 31.

18. Secretary of State George Shultz, address at the commemoration of the tenth anniversary of the signing of the Final Act, Helsinki, July 30, 1985, published by the Bureau of Public Affairs, Department of State, Washington, D.C., 1985 (Current Policy Paper Number 728).

6

The MBFR Experience

COIT D. BLACKER

On October 30, 1973, representatives of seven NATO and four Warsaw Pact countries, including the United States and the Soviet Union, met in Vienna's Kongresshaus in the first substantive round of negotiations on a mutual reduction of armed forces and armaments from the territories of the Federal Republic of Germany, Belgium, the Netherlands, Luxembourg, the German Democratic Republic, Poland, and Czechoslovakia.[1] On July 3, 1986, the delegates gathered to adjourn the negotiations—for the thirty-ninth time—and to agree on a date for their resumption. Although this latest round had been "productive" and "business-like," the negotiators once again departed the Austrian capital without an agreement.

The thirteen-year effort by NATO and the Warsaw Pact to devise a mutually acceptable formula to reduce on a reciprocal basis military personnel and their associated weaponry in Central Europe is the subject of this analysis. Most Western observers long ago dismissed these negotiations, which are among the longest running in the history of U.S.–Soviet arms control, as a dismal failure. Soviet analysts may well share that assessment. The evidence, however, supports a different and less categorical conclusion. Moreover, the past may constitute a less than perfect guide to the future; negotiators for the two alliances may yet produce at least an initial, first-stage accord to reduce the number of U.S. and Soviet forces deployed in the heart of Europe.

The Central European force reduction negotiations, better known in the West as "mutual and balanced force reductions," or MBFR, were in no sense destined to fail. On the contrary, in the period preceding the actual start of the negotiations, both sides had a number of strong reasons (explored at length in the body of this analysis) for wanting the talks to succeed. Some of those reasons still exist.

By October 1973, however, the conditions that had served, in the prenegotiating phase, to underscore for both alliances the perceived utility of an agreement had changed. More than any other single factor, it was the fairly abrupt decline in the intensity of U.S. interest in the negotiations, occasioned by an easing of domestic pressures to withdraw up to 150,000 American troops from Europe, that significantly decreased the likelihood of an accord. The character and degree of Soviet and Warsaw Pact interest have remained more or less constant throughout the talks. As a consequence, the balance, especially for the United States, between the projected benefits and costs of a force reduction agreement shifted dramatically and early-on in the direction of the latter. This is not to suggest, of course, that this negative American assessment must remain fixed for all time. U.S. interests could well change again in the months or years to come, once more making the attainment of an MBFR accord as attractive to American policymakers as it was during the years 1968 to 1972, although very probably for different reasons.

The MBFR experience is best understood as an example of the way in which an initially strong mutuality of interest among negotiating partners can rapidly give way to explicit conflict, producing a situation of deadlock. One purpose of this paper is to investigate the precise nature of these mutual interests. A second and related purpose is to trace how for both sides the balance in the negotiations between the incentives to cooperate and the incentives to "defect," or to resist the conclusion of an agreement, have changed over time.

The analysis is divided into three parts. The first part examines the origin of the MBFR initiative and the essential history leading to the convocation of the negotiations. The second part explores the objectives of the two sides, including an analysis of the major NATO and Warsaw Pact proposals from 1973 to 1986. The third part investigates in detail why—despite the achievement of substantial consensus on most of the major issues that once divided them—the two alliances have been unable to reach even a preliminary agreement to reduce their forces in Europe.

THE ORIGINS OF MBFR

The NATO-Warsaw Pact effort to negotiate reciprocal reductions in their Central European military forces has its origins in domestic U.S. politics.[2] Beginning in 1966 and continuing through 1973, former Senate Majority Leader Mike Mansfield (D.–Montana) introduced a series of non-binding resolutions calling for a partial and unilateral withdrawal of American forces from Europe. Mansfield felt that the maintenance of some 300,000 U.S. troops in Europe twenty-five years after World War II was unnecessary for the physical defense of Europe, a testament to the overcommitment of American military resources worldwide, and an avoidable economic drain. An increasing number of Mansfield's Senate colleagues came to share his conviction. Each year the majority leader's initiatives, as well as similar measures introduced by others in Congress, gained new adherents.

The Johnson and Nixon administrations lobbied hard to defeat each troop reduction resolution. Executive Branch spokesmen cited as a possible consequence of passage an erosion of allied confidence in the American security guarantee to Europe. In the event such a proposal were to become law, they warned, it could well result in a dangerous deterioration in the European military balance. Despite such administration warnings, Congressional pressures for a withdrawal of U.S. forces continued to build.

To undercut support for the resolutions, in 1967 the Johnson Administration initiated discussions with U.S. allies in Europe on a possible mutual reduction of NATO and Warsaw Pact military forces. On balance, the West European governments—eager to promote a relaxation of tensions with the East and to ward off any precipitate withdrawal of U.S. troops—responded favorably to the idea; only France, determined to preserve its independence from NATO and to prevent the imposition of international limitations on its armed forces, resisted the initiative. Notwithstanding French opposition, in June 1968 the North Atlantic Council extended to the Soviet Union and its Warsaw Pact allies an invitation to join with the West in the search for ways to reduce, reciprocally, the level of armed forces and armaments in Central Europe. The offer was repeated every six months at subsequent sessions of the NATO Council.

Although the Kremlin did not respond formally to NATO's offer until 1971, the

Johnson and Nixon administrations were able to stave off Congressional pressures for troop withdrawals by arguing that the matter had become an issue of outstanding international political significance. Any unilateral action to reduce U.S. forces in Europe, they alleged, would only weaken the Western bargaining position once talks began, whatever the domestic economic and political allure of reducing forces through Congressional action. A majority in Congress found the Executive Branch arguments persuasive; however, the number of senators and representatives prepared to vote in favor of troop reductions remained uncomfortably large from the White House perspective.

By the spring of 1971, the Senate, impatient with the apparent lack of progress toward the convocation of negotiations, seemed in a mood to defy the Administration. A Mansfield-sponsored amendment to the Draft Extension Law, mandating a withdrawal of 150,000 U.S. troops stationed in Europe, was scheduled to come to a vote on May 19. Administration allies in the Senate advised the White House that the measure was likely to pass. On May 14, Soviet leader Leonid Brezhnev, in a speech delivered in Tbilisi, the capital of Soviet Georgia, in effect came to the rescue of the Administration by directly communicating the Kremlin's willingness to begin negotiations on the subject. On the strength of Brezhnev's statement, the Mansfield initiative was defeated, 36–61. Three less drastic amendments also failed to secure the necessary votes for passage.[3]

The Soviet leader's strong testimonial on behalf of mutual force reductions came as a surprise to U.S. policymakers. Although Brezhnev had referred positively to the NATO initiative as recently as the Soviet Communist Party Congress in March, his May 15 invitiation to the West to "taste the wine" of negotiations was the strongest Soviet endorsement of the idea to date. In his memoirs, Henry Kissinger suggests that the timing of Brezhnev's remarks had little, if anything, to do with the scheduled vote on the Mansfield amendment. The real Soviet purpose, Kissinger writes, was to accelerate the pace of the Four Power negotiations then underway on Berlin. He also argues that the Soviet proposal, in at least a tactical sense, constituted something of a blunder. "Nothing illustrates better," Kissinger claims, "the inflexibility of the Soviets' cumbersome policymaking machinery than their decision to stick to their game plan even when confronted with the Mansfield windfall."[4]

Other analysts have taken exception to Kissinger's interpretation. Raymond Garthoff, for example, has argued that Brezhnev's clear purpose was to undermine Congressional support for Mansfield's initiative. According to Garthoff, while they had reason to look favorably on a gradual reduction of U.S. forces in Europe spread over a number of years, the Soviets might have feared that a sudden American exit would result in a dramatic expansion in West German military power[5]; a second and related Kremlin concern might have been a revival of interest on the part of some West European countries, including the Federal Republic, in active military collaboration.[6] On the other hand, a negotiated U.S. withdrawal, undertaken in stages, was far less likely to arouse anxiety among NATO countries. While such a redeployment of American power would almost certainly require a companion withdrawal of some Soviet forces from Eastern Europe, it was a price the Kremlin leadership might have been prepared to pay in 1971, depending on the precise character and dimensions of the reductions it would be required to undertake.

The Soviet decision to breathe new life into NATO's MBFR proposal—whatever the proximate cause—significantly heightened West European interest in the negotia-

tions and made much more likely their eventual convocation. Whether NATO and Warsaw Pact representatives would ever meet to consider a reciprocal reduction in armed
forces, however, had less to do in 1971 with the merits of the issue than with the
outcome of an interconnected series of negotiations between East and West, centering
on the normalization of Soviet-West German relations, the Soviet proposal to convene
a European security conference, and the status of Berlin.[7]

In August 1970 the Soviet Union and the West German government of Chancellor
Willy Brandt concluded a treaty, the practical effect of which was to acknowledge the
Oder-Neisse line as the legal and permanent international boundary between the German
Democratic Republic and Poland, thus surrendering all West German claims to former
Reich territories that fell to the east of the Polish-East German border. The signatories
also pledged to renounce the threat or the use of force in their mutual relations. The
Federal Republic and Poland concluded a similar treaty in December 1970.

While clearly pleased with the results of *Ostpolitik,* the Soviets were eager to supplement the essential provisions of the Moscow and Warsaw treaties through the convening of an all-European security conference to which the United States and Canada
would also be invited. Since 1966, Soviet leaders had spoken of the need to undertake
a general relaxation of tensions in Europe so as to confirm postwar "territorial and
political realities" and to "eliminate completely the vestiges of World War II." They
looked in particular to a multilateral security conference to impart legitimacy to that
process and to provide an institutional mechanism to anchor and sustain it.

While cool to the Soviet-West German rapprochement and quietly hostile to the
idea of an all-European security conference, the Nixon administration was prepared to
endorse the former and acquiesce to the latter on the condition that the Kremlin negotiate with the West a new agreement on Berlin.[8] Central to Nixon and Kissinger were a
reaffirmation of the city's special status as occupied territory (thereby subject to continuing Four-Power control) and an explicit Soviet guarantee of the Western right of access. Negotiations began in March 1970. Throughout the proceedings, the Western allies (including the Federal Republic) made clear to Soviet leaders that West German
ratification of the Moscow and Warsaw treaties hinged on the successful outcome of the
Berlin discussions. Eighteen months later, in September 1971, representatives of the
United States, the Soviet Union, Britain, and France initialed the Quadripartite Agreement. Some months later West Germany ratified the treaties with the Soviet Union and
Poland.[9]

With Berlin no longer an obstacle, the Soviets renewed their campaign for a European security conference. The United States, with the support of its NATO allies,
resisted the Kremlin's call, pending a firm Soviet commitment to participate in MBFR.
A bargain was struck. At the May 1972 summit meeting between Nixon and Brezhnev,
the United States agreed in principle to sanction the convening of the Conference on
Security and Cooperation in Europe (CSCE); by the terms of a deal struck by Kissinger
and the Soviet leadership in September, preliminary discussions among the thirty-five
participating countries were set to begin in November. In exchange, the Soviets and
their Warsaw Pact allies agreed to join with NATO in the pursuit of an agreement to
reduce armed forces and armaments in Central Europe. The two sets of negotiations
were to be conducted "in parallel," although progress in one forum was not to be held
hostage in any formal sense to progress in the other.

As scheduled, the preliminary round of the CSCE took place between November
22 and December 15, 1972. Following a three week recess, the conference reconvened.

The preparatory phase of the mutual force reduction negotiations began in January 1973 and ended in late June. Four months later, at the end of October, the MBFR negotiators returned to Vienna to begin their first substantive discussions.

THE NEGOTIATIONS

Western Objectives and Proposals

From 1968 to 1973 the overarching American objective in MBFR (both the initiative and the negotiations) was to prevent Congressionally mandated withdrawals of U.S. military personnel from Europe. Suggestive of the administration's priorities during these years is Kissinger's confession that the proposal to convene the force reduction negotiations was essentially a ploy "to forestall unilateral American cuts."[10] As late as 1971, again in Kissinger's words, American policymakers "had not thought through" what kind of an agreement might be desirable.[11] For the NATO allies, the near-term goal was the same: to head off the redeployment of up to 150,000 American troops from Europe to the United States.

Once committed to MBFR, the United States and its negotiating partners had no choice but to develop a bargaining position. That task was complicated by the realization that virtually every reduction plan seriously examined by the Western allies would, if accepted by the Warsaw Pact, worsen NATO's military position in Central Europe.[12] With the convocation of the MBFR talks no longer in question, however, the Administration felt free to suggest the adoption of less negotiable proposals, secure in the knowledge that Congress was extremely unlikely to sanction unilateral U.S. withdrawals in the midst of an ongoing negotiation.[13] Following a series of intra-alliance consultations, the West Europeans agreed to the American approach.

As a consequence, each of the three major Western MBFR proposals has sought to improve the relative military position of NATO through the negotiation of asymmetrical force reductions. The reductions would be divided into two phases: a first-stage, equal-percentage withdrawal of U.S. and Soviet forces from the "guidelines area" (the Federal Republic, the Netherlands, Belgium, Luxembourg, the German Democratic Republic, Poland, and Czechoslovakia), to be followed by a second and much larger withdrawal or demobilization of forces that would include military personnel from all eleven direct participants. In keeping with this logic, the first NATO offer, tendered in November 1973, called for the redeployment of 29,000 U.S. and 68,000 Soviet troops (constituting reductions of roughly 15 percent for both countries). The West's 1979 proposal urged the withdrawal of 13,000 U.S. and 30,000 Soviet forces. NATO's most recent proposal, made in December 1985, would require a drawdown of 5,000 U.S. and 11,500 Soviet troops.

More ambitiously, the West has also proposed as part of the second stage of an agreement that each alliance reduce its forces (both ground and air force personnel) to a common ceiling of 900,000. Given that Warsaw Pact forces significantly exceed those of NATO (according to Western estimates), the Soviet Union, East Germany, Poland, and Czechoslovakia would be required to undertake much larger cuts than those mandated for the West. NATO's consistent use of the phrase "mutual and *balanced* force reductions" in reference to the negotiations is in keeping with this aspect of the West's bargaining stance.

For the most part, NATO has sought to focus the negotiations on the issue of personnel—where, it is alleged, the most obvious imbalances obtain—and to leave aside the question of large-scale reductions in military equipment, such as aircraft, artillery, and armor. The West's reluctance to consider such constraints reflects the judgment that the conventional weapon systems of the alliance are barely adequate for deterrent purposes and that virtually any drawdown in these weapons stocks could call into question the ability of NATO forces to perform their military missions in the event of war. In addition, to the extent that some Western weapon systems, such as tactical aircraft, are considered superior to their Warsaw Pact counterparts, the West has resisted their inclusion in reduction proposals because of the perceived value of these weapons in compensating for the East's advantage in deployed manpower. Reductions in nuclear weapons and in the number of nuclear delivery systems pose a problem for NATO for essentially the same reason, and because they have come to embody in a highly visible way the American security guarantee to Western Europe.

The West's clear preference for a "troops only" accord highlights the extent to which NATO has pursued two distinct military objectives in MBFR: on the one hand, the alliance has sought to improve its relative standing by proposing that the Warsaw pact accept the imposition of common manpower ceilings; on the other hand, with one exception it has refused to countenance any agreement that would require substantial reductions in either conventional or nuclear weapon systems, thereby seeking to prevent any major *erosion* of the Western military position in Central Europe.

The single exception to NATO's negotiating strategy was the so-called Option III plan of December 1975.[14] To make more attractive to the Warsaw Pact the West's November 1973 proposal to withdraw 29,000 American troops in exchange for a redeployment of 5 Soviet tank armies (containing 68,000 soldiers), NATO also offered to remove from the American military inventory in Europe 54 F-4 nuclear-capable fighter-bombers, 36 Pershing IA surface-to-surface missiles, and 1000 tactical nuclear warheads. Initially considered and then discarded by the allies in 1973, Option III resurfaced during the fall of 1975 at U.S. urging as a device to move the negotiations forward. The Ford Administration was also eager to relieve Congressional pressures to relocate up to 1000 older tactical nuclear weapons from Europe to the United States and to extract a price for their withdrawal. Never very popular with the West Europeans, who have consistently opposed the nuclearization of MBFR, Option III was presented as a one-time, take-it-or-leave-it concession.

In an ambiguous response, Warsaw Pact negotiators characterized the NATO offer as "positive" but "inadequate." In their counterproposal of February 1976, the East sought to advance the dialogue by proposing matching withdrawals of aircraft, missile systems, and tanks. The West rejected the Eastern initiative, emphasizing that Option III had been specifically designed as a kind of "apples for oranges" trade: the withdrawal of U.S. military equipment in exchange for asymmetrical troop reductions. In 1976 Warsaw Pact negotiators were still insisting that all reductions take place on the basis of symmetry. The West did not formally withdraw the proposal until 1979 (although both sides had long considered it a dead letter), when NATO announced the unilateral withdrawal of 1000 nuclear weapons as part of its plan to modernize the alliance's theater nuclear forces with the deployment of 108 Pershing II and 464 ground-launched cruise missiles.[15]

Leaving aside occasional shifts in emphasis, Western MBFR objectives have been remarkably consistent over the years. Since the fall of 1972—and the essential collapse of the threat to remove American forces through legislative fiat—the central Western goal has been to obtain through mutual agreement what NATO spokesmen term a more "stable balance of forces" in Central Europe, by which they mean rough parity in deployed manpower, largely through the mechanism of unequal troop withdrawals.

The West has identified other objectives, of course, such as the negotiation of various measures to increase the "transparency" of the two sides' military establishments in Europe, including prior notification of troop exercises, exchanges of military observers, and provisions for on-site inspection to ensure compliance with whatever agreements might be forthcoming. While potentially valuable in deterring the outbreak of war, however, these measures have been of decidedly secondary importance, especially to the United States, to the more ambitious goal of redrawing the European military balance. Until the late 1970s and the sharp deterioration in superpower relations, many West European governments also looked to an MBFR agreement to lend additional substance to the relaxation of tensions on the continent and to facilitate the development of better relations with the East. But by 1986 few in Europe were prepared to argue that the conclusion of a first-stage force reduction agreement would have much of an impact—one way or the other—on East-West relations.

Soviet/Warsaw Pact Objectives and Proposals

Soviet leaders initially ignored MBFR. From 1968 to 1971 the Kremlin issued no direct response to NATO's semiannual invitation to negotiate a mutual reduction of armed forces and armaments, emphasizing instead the indispensability and timeliness of a multilateral conference on European security. It was only with the explicit linking of the two issues—Western participation in the CSCE in exchange for Warsaw Pact participation in MBFR—that the Soviets began to evidence any real interest in the topic. By the time of the 24th Communist Party Congress in Moscow in March 1971, Soviet attitudes to MBFR had warmed appreciably.[16] Nine months later Warsaw Pact representatives declared that a force reduction agreement, together with a European security conference, "would . . . correspond to the interests of strengthening European security."[17] A military détente between NATO and Warsaw Pact countries, in other words, could help "concretize" the relaxation of tensions in Europe, while also opening up new opportunities for the further improvement of political relations. Soviet leaders had apparently come to the conclusion that an agreement to reduce the armed forces of the two alliances might be a relatively inexpensive way to undergird the developing European détente, depending of course on the degree to which the West was prepared to be flexible in the negotiations and to sign an accord that Moscow might also find acceptable.

Doubtless, the Soviets, no less than their Western counterparts, aspired in MBFR to seize whatever advantages the adversary might be willing to confer. The Kremlin's proximate objective, therefore, was to improve marginally the Warsaw Pact's military position relative to that of NATO. Later Eastern proposals had the more modest goal of preserving the existing balance "at lower levels of armament." While far from perfect from the Soviet perspective, Warsaw Pact military capabilities in the early 1970s were superior to those of NATO in a number of relevant indices, including deployed manpower, armored forces, and artillery tubes. As a consequence, a multilateral agreement that in essence formalized the Central European balance would still be in Moscow's interest.

It came as no surprise to the West that Warsaw Pact spokesmen entered the negotiations by contending that an approximate balance of military forces already obtained along the central front (a position to which they remained faithful throughout the talks). The East's first proposal, tabled one week into the negotiations, urged the withdrawal or demobilization of 20,000 troops for each alliance, to be completed during 1975. Later reductions of 5 and 10 percent were to take place in 1976 and 1977, respectively. In 1974, the Soviets modified their offer to permit an initial reduction of 10,000 Soviet and American forces, to be followed six months later by non-superpower reductions of equal magnitude. In other words, and in sharp contrast to the essential premise of the Western position, the Warsaw Pact negotiators began by arguing for the implementation of reductions on the basis of numerical equality.[18]

Subsequent Warsaw Pact proposals abandoned the notion of strict equality in numbers while retaining the emphasis on symmetry. In 1976, for example, the East proposed a 2 to 3 percent reduction in Soviet and U.S. troop strength. A 1978 initiative urged the withdrawal of 14,000 U.S. and 30,000 Soviet forces, or reductions of approximately 7 percent for each superpower, according to Soviet estimates of deployed manpower in the central region.[19]

Arguably, the most important Soviet concession occurred in June 1978 when the Warsaw Pact agreed, in principle, to the negotiation of the NATO-sponsored provision for common manpower ceilings. Until that time, the Soviets had consistently opposed any such constraint as prejudicial, alleging that the West was seeking to upset the prevailing and, to their mind, stable balance of forces that had taken shape over the preceding two decades.

The Eastern offer was contingent, however, on Western acceptance of the Warsaw Pact's calculations regarding relative force totals. The difference between the figures advanced by the two sides is not trivial. As of 1986, Western estimates of Warsaw Pact troop strength deployed in the guidelines area exceed those of the East by at least 200,000.[20] Efforts to resolve the dispute through exchanges of data have been frustrated, according to the West, by the Warsaw Pact's unwillingness to submit sufficiently detailed information on the number, character, and deployment of its forces. The significance of the disagreement derives from the fact that acceptance of the Eastern figures would require the Warsaw Pact to reduce many fewer troops to reach the agreed common ceiling than would reliance on the NATO estimates. The problem this has posed to negotiators is obvious and until 1985, when the West dropped its demand for a resolution of the data base problem in advance of any first-stage agreement, constituted perhaps the most difficult issue in the talks.

The East has also pressed NATO to accept reductions in weaponry along with personnel as part of any agreement in Vienna. As noted, in 1976 Warsaw Pact negotiators proposed the withdrawal of 54 U.S. and Soviet nuclear-capable tactical aircraft, an equal but unspecified number of Pershing IA and SCUD medium-range missile launchers, and 300 medium tanks to accompany a first-stage superpower reduction in manpower. They also, and for the first time, urged the withdrawal of a proportional (but again unspecified) number of tactical nuclear weapons.[21] Eastern negotiators later abandoned this particular proposal but have never retreated from the position that the forces withdrawn as a result of any agreement be joined by at least some reductions in weaponry.

In keeping with the Kremlin's determination to limit West German military capabilities through MBFR, several Eastern proposals have been specifically designed to prevent the Federal Republic from compensating for any drawdown in U.S. military strength dictated by a force reduction agreement. Foremost among these have been proposals that the military contributions of the European participants be limited by means of national subceilings, that the West commit to a second-stage reduction in non-super-power forces in advance of any U.S.–Soviet withdrawals, and that the two alliances agree to freeze their troop levels following the completion of the first-stage reductions and pending the negotiation of any follow-up accord. The West has acquiesced to the third of these demands; the East has abandoned the second.

On the issue of national subceilings, however, neither side has been prepared to concede—although at the urging of their allies West German officials have repeatedly assured the Kremlin that the Bonn government has no intention of expanding the *Bundeswehr,* even if the other NATO countries should decide to reduce their military contributions in the aftermath of a force reduction agreement.[22] In an effort to attain the same objective through different means, in 1980 Warsaw Pact negotiators proposed that the troops of no country on either side be permitted to exceed 50 percent of the total number of forces allowed each alliance after reductions to a common ceiling.[23] NATO rejects this Eastern proposal.

Narrowing the Differences

Compared to the sharp differences that separated the two sides at the outset of the negotiations in 1973, the remaining obstacles to agreement in Vienna are both few and, with one exception, relatively minor. It is interesting to note in this context that while both sides have amended their proposals in significant ways, the East has made most of the concessions—some substantial and, in keeping with Soviet negotiating behavior, some more cosmetic than real. Warsaw Pact negotiators have conceded, for example, that the superpowers should undertake the first reductions and on an asymmetrical (though roughly equal percentage) basis. They accept that these withdrawals may proceed in the absence of a firm timetable to reduce the forces of the other nine participating countries. They have also agreed that the two alliances should seek, in a second stage, to impose common manpower ceilings. And they have dropped the demand that a first-stage superpower troop withdrawal be accompanied by reductions in nuclear weaponry and in such U.S. nuclear delivery systems as surface-to-surface missile launchers and dual-capable aircraft. The East does not concede, however, that it maintains some 200,000 more troops in the guidelines area than NATO. In 1980, the last year the negotiators exchanged data, Warsaw Pact representatives claimed in fact that NATO forces actually outnumbered those of the East by approximately 12,000.[24]

The West has sanctioned many fewer concessions. It has accepted, in principle, the position that some weaponry (such as small arms) might be withdrawn with the forces that are either demobilized or deployed. Disagreements remain, however, as to the kinds of equipment to be removed, the exact quantity, and what to do with the weapons so designated. As described, NATO has also consented to the interim freeze in manpower levels proposed by the East, but only as a temporary measure to encourage progress toward the conclusion of a second-stage agreement. The West's most significant concession has been its apparent willingness to support a modest first-stage withdrawal of U.S. and Soviet forces without a settlement of the data base controversy.

Since 1981, much of difficulty in the negotiations has centered on the issue of verification. In general, the West has insisted on procedures for monitoring compliance that the Warsaw Pact regards as excessively intrusive. These measures include the maintenance of permanent entry and exit points, manned by personnel of the opposing alliance, through which all arriving and departing forces would be required to pass. NATO also insists on the right to carry out up to thirty on-site "challenge" inspections each year to guarantee that Warsaw Pact force totals do not exceed those permitted under the terms of an agreement.[25] The Soviet Union has been reluctant to agree to either of these Western demands. Early in 1986, however, Soviet leader Mikhail Gorbachev stated that Moscow would be prepared to accept a limited number of permanently manned entry facilities on Warsaw Pact territory to facilitate verification. He also drew attention to what he characterized as an emerging framework for agreement in Vienna, emphasizing that the East was "determined to achieve success" in that forum.[26]

The Soviet leader's relatively upbeat assessment of the force reduction negotiations followed by several weeks both the November 1985 Reagan-Gorbachev summit in Geneva and the submission in December 1985 of revised NATO proposals that one Reagan Administration spokesman claimed had removed "virtually all obstacles to agreement with the possible exception of stringent verification requirements."[27] Whether the Vienna negotiations, long considered the most anemic of the principal superpower arms control ventures, will be sufficiently revived to produce at least a preliminary agreement to reduce U.S. and Soviet forces deployed in the center of Europe is impossible to know as of this writing. What is much more certain is that most of the outstanding issues between East and West that have served to obstruct the achievement of consensus for well over a decade have been removed through patient and sustained effort. Given this substantial convergence of views, why, then, the persistent inability of the two sides to compose their remaining differences?

EXPLAINING THE FAILURE OF MBFR

The Linkage to U.S.–Soviet Détente

One potentially valuable way to understand not simply the longevity of the force reduction talks but also their rather dismal history is by exploring the relationship between these negotiations and the superpower détente of the late 1960s and early 1970s. To do so usefully, however, requires at least a cursory investigation into the nature of this unusual and short-lived period in U.S.–Soviet relations.

In retrospect, it seems that by 1972 Soviet leaders had come to anticipate a period of increasingly cordial and cooperative relations with Washington, building out from efforts to regulate the strategic military competition. During the early years of the relationship, Soviet officials also seemed to regard détente as a kind of great-power compact, enabling them to influence directly political and military developments in such regions of the world as Western Europe and the Middle East that had long been of concern to Soviet policymakers but from which they had felt excluded in the past. From the Soviet perspective, détente implied a kind of implicit hegemonism between the superpowers, through which Moscow and Washington might seek to avoid direct confrontations in those geographic areas where the interests of the two countries were directly engaged. Soviet analysts wrote during this period of a fundamental transformation in superpower relations, dictated by the "all-around" development of Soviet military power, in which the pursuit of mutually advantageous relations had begun to replace the dangerous "unilateralism" characteristic, in their view, of postwar American diplomacy. That the Soviets expected this new relationship to endure, despite occasional setbacks, is suggested by their reference during the early 1970s to détente's pending "irreversi-bility."[28]

American expectations are more difficult to gauge. According to Nixon and Kissin-ger, the primary purposes of détente were to delimit the military competition between the superpowers and to induce a greater degree of restraint in the conduct of Soviet foreign policy than had obtained during previous administrations.[29] To realize the latter, American policymakers sought to entangle the Soviet Union in a complex series of relationships—military, political, and economic—of sufficient importance to the Krem-lin so as to enable the United States to influence its behavior. The notion was to gain enough leverage either to reward or to punish the Kremlin for its conduct, depending on the degree to which Soviet policies accorded with Washington's preferences. This would seem to suggest an expectation on the part of the United States that détente would be an ongoing, evolutionary relationship, likely to persist in one form or another over a period of years. On the other hand, at least during Kissinger's stewardship, the Ameri-can commitment to the relaxation of tensions was always conditional on Moscow's "good behavior"; no senior U.S. official, for example, would have described détente as an irreversible phenomenon.

American conditionality notwithstanding, both sides appear to have believed that they were embarked upon a qualitatively new stage in their relationship that had the potential to endure. The failure of détente to last beyond the mid-1970s should not obscure this fact. Neither country set out to sabotage what Nixon once described as the "emerging structure of peace."[30] Through their words if not always through their deeds, both countries were eager to communicate the message that the Cold War had been displaced by a real, if yet to be tested, relaxation of tensions.

In the end, détente could not withstand the pressures generated against it by U.S. and Soviet unilateralism. A number of prominent Americans, for example, expressed alarm at what they saw as a purposeful Soviet policy to eviscerate at least one major provision of the Interim Offensive Agreement of SALT I.[31] Some communicated dismay at Moscow's unwillingness to warn the United States of the pending Egyptian attack against Israel in October 1973. Still others took strong exception to the Kremlin's direct military involvement, first in the Angolan war for independence and later, following the overthrow of Emperor Haile Selassie, in Ethiopia's struggle against Somalia and the Eritrean rebels. Such behavior, it was alleged, was prejudicial to U.S. interests and, at a minimum, inconsistent with the spirit of détente. For their part, the Soviets com-plained of the Nixon Administration's inability to deliver on its pledge to secure sizeable credits for the USSR through the U.S. Export-Import Bank, of Kissinger's maneuvers to exclude Moscow from the negotiations for a Middle East peace settlement in 1974-75, and of Washington's disinclination to cede the Soviet Union substantial international political as well as military equality following the arrival of strategic parity and the signing of the SALT I agreements.

In the absence of explicit and formalized rules of the road, the two sides became increasingly reluctant to sacrifice short-term advantages in the interest of developing a more robust framework for collaboration and conflict avoidance. Never very hearty to begin with, détente eventually collapsed under the strain of American and Soviet poli-cies designed to optimize near-term opportunities. In this sense, the superpower relax-ation of tensions was never, to use a Soviet phrase, infused with sufficient content; at its most elegant, it remained a mere foundation.

It was in this highly unusual political context that NATO and the Warsaw Pact, led by the United States and the Soviet Union respectively, initiated the Central European force reduction negotiations. It was conventional wisdom in the West that the Soviet Union and its East European allies maintained many more forces along the central front than required for purely defensive purposes. Having expended billions of rubles to field such a potent offensive capability, it was assumed that the Soviets would be loath to surrender that advantage. For the United States, one purpose of MBFR may have been to determine the kinds of concessions the Kremlin might be prepared to make in that forum for the greater good of détente.[32] Would the apparent Soviet interest in "concretizing" the relaxation of tensions extend to the negotiation of a new and, from the Kremlin's perspective, potentially far less favorable balance of forces in Europe?

For Moscow, the link between the force reduction talks and the state of U.S.–Soviet détente was only half the equation. The Soviets were aware of the importance that Nixon and Kissinger attached to the Kremlin's willingness to commit to the MBFR negotiations. At the same time, Soviet leaders were eager to reinforce the relaxation of tensions then underway between the USSR and the countries of Western Europe. The force reduction talks were an important element in that campaign. What did or did not transpire in Vienna, therefore, could have a direct impact on two separate and distinct security regimes to which the Soviet leadership attached considerable importance. An abject failure at MBFR before the conclusion of the European security conference could delay or disrupt those deliberations and retard the effort to secure multilateral confirmation of the essential provisions of both the Moscow and Warsaw treaties, signalling a significant setback for Soviet security policy in Europe.[33] More generally, such an outcome could undermine long-standing Soviet attempts to weaken the bonds of "Atlanticism" by demonstrating to the West Europeans that their reliance on the United States in security matters was both misplaced and unnecessary.

At the outset of MBFR, Soviet spokesmen stressed the potentially positive impact of the negotiations on both sets of relationships. As the détente with the United States began to unravel in the mid-1970s, however, the Kremlin sought to recast the negotiations as largely an intra-European affair, while deemphasizing their significance for U.S.–Soviet relations. It was a strategy designed to preserve and to a degree insulate the security regime in Europe from the visible disintegration of the superpower effort at cooperation. Doubtless, the Soviets were under no illusion that they could obtain a force reduction agreement without U.S. consent; by emphasizing their continuing commitment to an agreement, however, they might have hoped that America's NATO allies would assign at least as much blame to Washington as to Moscow for the deadlock in the negotiations.

While it cannot be demonstrated empirically, the improvement in U.S.–Soviet relations was probably a precondition for MBFR talks. The Soviets first communicated their interest in the negotiations in May 1971, three years after the first NATO proposal but, significantly, at roughly the same time as the breakthrough in the strategic arms talks that Kissinger describes as an essential turning point in those discussions.[34] The reciprocal superpower concessions on MBFR and CSCE between May and September 1972 also occurred within the context of steadily improving U.S.–Soviet relations. At no other juncture during the postwar period did the two superpowers seriously consider negotiations specifically designed to limit or reduce their forces in Europe, strongly suggesting that the coincidence in time between détente and MBFR was not accidental.

The dependence of the force reduction talks on the state of U.S.–Soviet relations is underscored by a second kind of linkage. When the détente of the early 1970s gave way to the acrimony of the early 1980s, the pace of the MBFR talks measurably slowed. Both sides retracted concessions that had been made in previous years, and generally toughened their bargaining stances. During the second year of the Reagan Administration, for example, the West submitted a draft agreement proposing a number of new requirements for monitoring compliance and a more extensive list of "associated measures," including the right to dispatch NATO personnel to the western part of the Soviet Union to observe major pre-notified, out-of-garrison military activities.[35] By contrast, when relations between Washington and Moscow warmed again in 1985, the future of MBFR brightened appreciably.

The relationship between MBFR and détente would appear to constitute what some cooperation theorists describe as "contextual issue linkage," or the placing of a given bargain in the context of a more important long-term relationship in such a way that the long-term relationship affects the outcome of the particular bargaining process.[36] Such linkages may or may not promote consensus in the particular bargaining process, depending on the precise state of the more important relationship.

The virtually perfect correlation between the state of U.S.–Soviet relations and the health of the Vienna negotiations is manifest. It does not, however, explain the inability of the two sides to reach agreement in that forum. There are numerous instances of superpower and East-West cooperation in security-related matters that have been realized in the absence of an "enabling regime." The Austrian State Treaty of 1955, the 1962 agreement on Laos, and the Limited Test Ban Treaty of 1963 were all concluded before the arrival of détente and, with the exception of the last, during periods of considerable tension in East-West relations. Clearly, the state of relations between Washington and Moscow has strongly influenced the course of the MBFR negotiations, but the decline of détente did not prevent consensus in Vienna, nor would its revival necessarily ensure it.

The "Mutuality of Interest" Problem

Three factors may be considered central to the achievement of success in negotiations between adversaries: the number of players, the "shadow of the future," and mutuality of interest.[37] In the MBFR negotiations, the first two have served, on balance, to promote agreement. While the number of countries directly taking part in the force reduction talks is relatively large at eleven, the participants are divided into two groups, each led by a senior partner. Each side maintains a single negotiating position at any given time and changes in posture have been infrequent. Critically, no individual country has ever deviated publicly from the position assumed by its alliance partners, enabling NATO and Warsaw Pact negotiators to project an image of solidarity. Responsibility for representing each side's interests at plenary sessions of the negotiations rotates among the seven Western and four Eastern participants and is therefore shared. In effect and by design, in other words, there are only two "players" in MBFR.

The two sides also recognize that the Vienna talks are but one set of negotiations that take place within the context of a much larger framework of discussions between East and West, many of which are ongoing. The phrase "shadow of the future" refers to the concept that adversaries will be more likely to seek agreement in negotiations when they anticipate that interaction in that and other fora will be both continuous and significant.[38] A long "shadow of the future" is alleged to reduce the incentive to defect in such settings, as noncooperative behavior can lead to retaliation and mutual recrimination, making future collaboration more difficult.

There is every expectation among MBFR participants that they will again have reason to negotiate on a host of political, military, and economic issues. Failure to reach agreement in Vienna need not, of course, prevent the attainment of consensus in these other negotiations; at the same time, the collapse of the negotiations would hardly facilitate the conclusion of any future East-West accords. In theory at least, the "shadow" of the other negotiations to which NATO and the Warsaw Pact are parties should promote rather than retard the search for agreement in MBFR, given the importance both sides attach, or may attach in years to come, to success in one or more of those environments.

The principal problem in the Vienna negotiations has been neither too many players nor the absence of context. The central obstacle has been the lack of a strong mutuality of interest between NATO and the Warsaw Pact.

Historically, *shared* interests have never played much of a role in MBFR. While the two alliances should welcome any steps to reduce the likelihood of war in Europe, one would be hard pressed to characterize this as a particularly salient, let alone a compelling mutual interest; the probability of an intentional armed conflict in Europe is generally assumed to be rather low, with or without a force reduction agreement. For its part, the Soviet Union has been eager to utilize MBFR to advance the relaxation of tensions on the continent, while the United States, always suspicious of the Kremlin's motives, has been decidedly less enthusiastic about the use of arms control as a device to encourage East-West rapprochement. Only at a very high level of abstraction, therefore, can the two sides be said to share certain objectives in the force reduction talks.

Much more important in Vienna, especially in the period preceding the start of the negotiations, was the *complementarity* of NATO and Warsaw Pact interests. The central Western objective in MBFR from 1968 to 1973 was to negotiate a mutual reduction of U.S. and Soviet forces from Europe to relieve the pressures generated by the American Congress for U.S. troop reductions. All other Western goals were secondary to this consideration, whatever the objective appeal to NATO of devising a mechanism to trim Soviet and Warsaw Pact military power in Europe. The major Soviet objective during those years was to underwrite the emerging political détente in Europe by undertaking relatively modest reductions in NATO and Warsaw Pact manpower and military equipment while leaving more or less undisturbed the prevailing balance of forces on the continent. In other words, both sides had a strong interest in seeing the negotiations succeed, although for very different reasons.

Once the negotiations were underway, however, Western, and particularly U.S., purposes began to change. With the formal convocation of the talks, Congressional support for the redeployment of at least some American forces from Germany to the continental United States all but evaporated. Few lawmakers were prepared to endorse a course of action that would undermine, according to the Nixon Administration, American bargaining leverage. As a consequence, U.S. policymakers, in consultation with the NATO allies, were able to formulate a much tougher negotiating position than if the pressures for a unilateral American withdrawal had been maintained.

If Western negotiators had anticipated either a continuation or an intensification of U.S. domestic pressures for a drawdown in American forces in Europe, NATO could have offered proposals designed to produce prompt agreement. For example, the West could have proposed an equal percentage withdrawal of U.S. and Soviet manpower within the guidelines area on the order of 10 percent and a second stage reduction of European forces of perhaps the same magnitude, both of which would have had considerable appeal to the Soviet Union. Concessions on verification requirements or the redeployment of nuclear and conventional weapons could have been offered as well. The subsequent agreement, while far from optimal from NATO's perspective, would have been preferable to an uncompensated withdrawal of U.S. forces.

Instead, the Western reduction plan of November 1973, if implemented, would have redrawn the European military balance. As an initial step, the United States and the Soviet Union were to withdraw an equal percentage of their combat and support troops; in the next phase, however, the two alliances were to reduce their ground forces asymmetrically to realize the goal of common ceilings. In 1973, acceptance of the Western plan would have required the withdrawal or demobilization of 48,000 NATO troops, beyond the 29,000 American forces redeployed in the first round; the Warsaw Pact would have been forced to reduce its forces by 157,000, in addition to the 68,000 Soviet soldiers removed initially. The West also proposed the reduction of 1000 Soviet tanks, without offering to remove any American military equipment. Not surprisingly, the Warsaw Pact condemned the NATO plan as one-sided, complaining that its purpose was to upset to Western advantage the existing balance of forces that had evolved over the preceding two decades and that had "served the cause of peace." NATO spokesmen rejected the Eastern claim, asserting that only a genuine equality of forces could buttress security in Europe.

NATO's determination to negotiate common manpower ceilings offers important insights into Western purposes at MBFR. Had the United States and its allies been eager to conclude an agreement, they would not have sought to use the negotiations to legislate a military outcome that they were either unable or unwilling to achieve through a unilateral buildup of forces. Such a goal would have been perceived as overly ambitious and counterproductive to the process of negotiation. The Soviet Union could hardly be expected to celebrate the notion of common ceilings, given the effort and expense involved in obtaining what Moscow clearly regarded as a desirable margin of safety along the central front.[39] Yet the West submitted a plan that demanded this significant and far-reaching Warsaw Pact concession at the very outset of the negotiations. Moreover, NATO has never retreated from its position on this issue.

Until 1978 the Eastern countries rejected the idea of negotiated common ceilings, proposing as an alternative first equal number and later equal percentage reductions in the forces of all direct participants, as well as the imposition of subceilings on the residual military contributions of the Federal Republic, the Benelux states, the German Democratic Republic, Poland, and Czechoslovakia. The Warsaw Pact's belated endorsement of common ceilings was linked, however, to Western acceptance of Eastern estimates of its own forces, which in 1978 were some 175,000 below the NATO figures. In other words, to obtain an agreement incorporating the goal of at least nominal military equality between NATO and the Warsaw Pact within the guidelines area, the West would have been required to overlook this discrepancy. While the West has now agreed to sanction an essentially cosmetic first-stage withdrawal of U.S. and Soviet forces without the prior resolution of the data base problem, it is not prepared to support any second-stage reductions until the force estimates of the two sides have been reconciled.

The NATO position on common ceilings and the Warsaw Pact's response to that initiative are instructive for what they suggest about the two sides' hierarchies of objectives in MBFR. For the United States, the determination to redraw the military balance in ways more favorable to the West assumed greater importance than arranging for a mutual reduction of U.S. and Soviet manpower within the guidelines area, despite the fact the original American purpose was to achieve the latter. Common ceilings were to be the vehicle to realize that objective. For the Soviet Union, the ordering of the goals has never really changed—to anchor détente in Europe, to preserve the existing balance of power, and to limit West European and especially West German military capabilities. Had Western goals remained unchanged, a compromise agreement—based on a complementarity of interests—might have been attained early on in the negotiations. The Western decision to seek through MBFR a realignment of forces in Central Europe has made such a compromise far less likely, however one assesses the merits or appropriateness of the NATO strategy.

At this level of analysis, MBFR as an opportunity for U.S.–Soviet cooperation on a security-related issue divides into two phases. During the first phase, from the initial NATO proposal in 1968 to the start of negotiations in October 1973, the incentives for both sides to cooperate in the search for a mutually acceptable solution were strong, if significantly different. Immediately upon the convocation of the talks, however, Western enthusiasm for force reductions cooled dramatically. What the West once saw as a distasteful if unavoidable reality had become not just unappealing but also unnecessary. With the sudden disappearance of this complementarity of interests, significant progress toward agreement in the negotiations could not be maintained, in light of the virtual absence of compelling shared interests.

It is critical to note in this regard that for each side, the failure to reach agreement has been, and continues to be, preferable to the conclusion of an accord that would require further concessions on its part. For the West, and especially for the United States, the mere act of negotiating has all but eliminated the pressures to reduce American military forces in Europe. As a consequence, even a situation of deadlock—short of the actual collapse of the negotiations—may be considered to serve an important Western purpose. In addition, without an agreement the NATO states are free to take whatever unilateral steps they may regard as necessary and prudent to maintain a deterrent balance in Europe. Should the Warsaw Pact embark on a major buildup of its military capabilities, the Western calculus could change, of course, making the conclusion of even an unsatisfactory agreement that imposes at least some constraints on Soviet and East European armed forces much more attractive.

For the Kremlin, the calculus has been much the same. While an MBFR agreement might provide a modest boost to détente in Europe, the inability to conclude an accord has not prevented, nor is it likely to preclude in the future, the development of better relations between Moscow, on the one hand, and the United States and Western Europe, on the other. Moreover, the preservation of the status quo in Central Europe between NATO and the Warsaw Pact works on balance to the Soviet advantage; as long as that continues to be the case, there is little military incentive for Moscow to concede on the remaining matters of substance. For the Kremlin as well, in other words, a prolongation of the current deadlock comes at essentially no cost.

CONCLUSION

This analysis began with the proposition that as a case study in security cooperation between the superpowers the mutual force reduction negotiations are best understood as an example of the way in which an initially strong mutuality of interest between negotiating partners can quickly erode, producing a situation of seemingly interminable dead-lock. Logically, even a partial restoration of those mutual interests—either shared or complementary—could also revive the negotiations. The evidence suggests that in the last several months of 1985, the MBFR talks were, for the first time since the early 1970s, again a focus of superpower attention, leading to speculation that some kind of agreement might at last be forthcoming.

Significantly, the catalyst appears to have been the November 1985 Reagan-Gorbachev summit meeting in Geneva. Both leaders left the Swiss capital pledging to improve U.S.–Soviet relations; the long-dormant MBFR negotiations were apparently identified as one forum in which substantial, relatively low-cost, and highly visible progress might be made. The link between the Vienna talks and the state of the U.S.–Soviet relations, always important to the fate of the former, was again evident.

The renewed interest in MBFR proved to be short-lived. Within several months of the Geneva summit, whatever momentary enthusiasm had been generated on behalf of the negotiations had quietly evaporated. Nonetheless, it is important to note that the basis on which the force reduction negotiations returned to favor in late 1985 was dif-ferent from the conditions that led to their convocation. In 1973 it was a perceived complementarity of interest that made the negotiations possible. Thirteen years later, by contrast, it was the potential shared interest of the senior partners in using the negotia-tions to "concretize" the apparent warming of relations that enabled their brief renewal.

If an agreement is eventually forthcoming in Vienna—or in any successor negoti-ation that might be convened to reduce European conventional forces—it will in all probability come about as a consequence of a superpower commitment to ease ten-sions.[40] Moreover, should consensus ever be achieved, it would very likely signal West-ern acceptance of the essential Soviet argument that the purpose of such negotiations is not to alter the military balance in Central Europe but to confirm it at lower levels of armament. Such an accord would probably be of modest scope and therefore unlikely to affect significantly the capacity of the two alliances to wage war; neither would it guarantee subsequent and more sizeable reductions. It might serve, however, to stabilize the situation and to delimit the military competition between NATO and the Warsaw Pact by demonstrating that viable rules and procedures can be devised for the mainte-nance of a balance of forces in Europe, a balance with which neither side is completely satisfied but within which both can coexist.

Notes

1. The negotiations are variously known as MBFR, for mutual and balanced force reduc-tions, MFR, for mutual force reductions, or simply the Vienna negotiations. The Western coun-tries prefer the first designation as it serves to enhance the legitimacy of the NATO argument that Warsaw Pact reductions should be larger in scope, given the latter's numerical advantage in deployed manpower along the Central European front. The East no longer objects to the principle of asymmetrical reductions, but does resist its celebration in the title of the negotiations. The official NATO acronym, MURFAAMCE, for the mutual reduction of forces and armaments and associated measures in Central Europe, is almost never used.

In addition to the eleven direct participants, eight states have observer status in MBFR: Bulgaria, Denmark, Greece, Hungary, Italy, Norway, Romania, and Turkey. Hungary remains something of a special case; while it agreed during the preparatory negotiations that Hungarian forces would not be subject to direct limitation through MBFR, the West reserves the right to reopen that issue at a future date.

2. Much of the material contained in this and the following section of the paper ("The Origins of MBFR" and "The Negotiations") is drawn from the author's "The Soviet Union and Mutual Force Reductions: The Role of Military Detente in the European Security Policy of the USSR," unpublished doctoral dissertation, the Fletcher School of Law and Diplomacy, Tufts University, 1978. For a concise history of MBFR to 1979, see John G. Keliher, *The Negotiations on Mutual and Balanced Force Reductions: The Search for Arms Control in Central Europe* (New York: Pergamon Press, 1980). For an accounting of the negotiations since 1979, see *The Arms Control Reporter* (1986) (Brookline, Mass.: Institute for Defense and Disarmament Studies, 1986), pp. 401.A. 1–12.

3. Raymond Garthoff, *Detente and Confrontation: American-Soviet Relations from Nixon to Reagan* (Washington, D.C.: Brookings, 1985), p. 115; and Henry Kissinger, *White House Years* (Boston: Little, Brown, 1979), p. 947.

4. Kissinger, *White House Years,* p. 947.

5. Garthoff, *Detente and Confrontation,* pp. 115–16.

6. For a discussion of Soviet attitudes toward West European military cooperation and integration, see especially Pierre Hassner, *Europe in the Age of Negotiation,* Washington Papers 8 (Beverly Hills: Sage Publications, 1973), p. 32. See also John Yochelson, "MFR: West European and American Perspectives," in Wolfram F. Hanrieder, ed., *The United States and Western Europe* (Cambridge, Mass.: Winthrop Publishers, 1974), pp. 277–80; and David Holloway, *The Soviet Approach to MBFR,* Waverly Paper 8:1 (Edinburgh: University of Edinburgh, 1972), pp. 7–14.

7. For a more detailed analysis of the interrelationships among the several negotiations concerning European security issues during the period 1969–72, see Jonathan Dean's contribution to this volume. See also Garthoff, *Detente and Confrontation,* pp. 106–26; and Kissinger, *White House Years,* pp. 405–16, 938–49.

For additional documentation, see *The Berlin Settlement: The Quadripartite Agreement on Berlin and the Supplementary Arrangements* (Bonn: Press and Information Office of the Government of the Federal Republic of Germany, 1972): *The Treaty between the Federal Republic of Germany and the People's Republic of Poland* (Bonn: Press and Information Office of the Federal Government, 1971): and *The Treaty of August 12, 1970 between the Federal Republic of Germany and the Union of Soviet Socialist Republics* (Bonn: Press and Information Office of the Federal Government, 1970).

8. Kissinger, *White House Years,* pp. 529–31, 824.

9. Garthoff, *Detente and Confrontation,* p. 121.

10. Kissinger, *White House Years,* p. 400.

11. Ibid., p. 947.

12. Ibid.

13. Again, the source is Kissinger. "The Warsaw Pact had far more troops than we have along the central front; its initial advantage would grow rapidly once mobilization began, particularly because of the proximity of Soviet divisions in European Russia. In such circumstances, agreed mutual reductions, if both sides reduced by an equal percentage, would compound NATO's problem . . . Inevitably, this led to the view that the only safe agreement was 'asymmetrical' reductions, in other words, that the Warsaw Pact would cut its forces by a larger amount than NATO. *This concept first faced tough sledding in a bureaucracy dedicated to the proposition that we needed to put forward 'negotiable' proposals; nobody believed that such an 'unequal' approach would be accepted by the Soviets"* (emphasis added). Kissinger, *White House Years,* pp. 947–48.

14. The best treatment of Option III is contained in Keliher, *The Negotiations,* pp. 99–110. See also Lothar Ruehl, *MBFR: Lessons and Problems,* Adelphi Paper 176 (London: International Institute for Strategic Studies, 1982), pp. 15–18.

15. Keliher, *The Negotiations,* p. 86. At the time of its unveiling by the West, there was considerable speculation that Option III could provide the basis for substantial progress in MBFR, perhaps even an agreement. In retrospect, it is apparent that while the initiative addressed an important Warsaw Pact concern (the inclusion of nuclear delivery systems as part of any agreement), by itself Option III could not have produced a breakthrough. Beyond the fact that the East had yet to accept NATO's proposal for asymmetrical force reductions (leading to the imposition of common ceilings), in 1975–76 the two sides were deadlocked on the issue of force estimates. The East did not even submit formal estimates on deployed manpower in the guidelines area until June 1976, and when it did the figures were at sharp variance with those prepared by NATO. The dispute over numbers still plagues the negotiators. In the absence of Warsaw Pact concessions in both these areas, it is difficult to see how Option III could have led the way to an accord.

16. See "Report of the C.P.S.U. Central Committee to the 24th Congress of the Communist Party of the Soviet Union," *Pravda* (March 31, 1971).

17. "Communique on the Conference of the Political Consultative Committee of the Warsaw Treaty Member-States," *Pravda* (January 27, 1972).

18. Blacker, "The Soviet Union and Mutual Force Reductions," pp. 312–13, 356–358.

19. Keliher, *The Negotiations,* p. 74.

20. *The Arms Control Reporter* (1986), p. 401.A.4.

21. Keliher, *The Negotiations,* pp. 101–103.

22. Ibid., pp. 113–14.

23. Garthoff, *Detente and Confrontation,* p. 767.

24. *The Arms Control Reporter* (1986), p. 401.A.9.

25. Ibid., p. 401.A.7.

26. "Statement By Mikhail Gorbachev," *News and Views from the USSR,* January 16, 1986 (San Francisco: Consulate General, Union of the Soviet Socialist Republics, 1986), p. 7.

27. *Washington Times* (December 6, 1985). As of 1986 the positions of the two sides were extremely close in a number of important areas. For example, in its December 1985 proposal the West called for a withdrawal of 5,000 U.S. and 11,500 Soviet forces as the initial step in reductions; in February 1986 the Warsaw Pact proposed withdrawals of 6,500 U.S. and 11,000 Soviet troops. As noted, by December 1985 the West had also agreed to sanction a first-stage agreement without resolving the long-standing dispute over force estimates within the guidelines area. In addition, both sides were agreed that no substantial reductions in weaponry need accompany any first-round reduction in superpower military manpower.

28. See, for example, address of Nikolai Podgorny in Riga, Latvia S.S.R., December 26, 1973 (Foreign Broadcast Information Service, *Soviet Union,* January 3, 1974, p. R111); Nikolai Kapchenko, "Socialist Foreign Policy and the Restructuring of International Relations," *International Affairs* (Moscow, April 1975): 3–13; and Leonid Brezhnev, "For a Just, Democratic Peace, For the Security of Peoples and International Cooperation," *Pravda* (October 27, 1973), pp. 1–3.

29. See "Prepared Statement of Hon. Henry A. Kissinger, Secretary of State," in *Detente,* Hearings Before the Senate Committee on Foreign Relations, 93rd Congress, 2nd Session (Washington D.C.: U.S. Government Printing Office, 1974), pp. 247–50; "Secretary Kissinger's News Conference of December 23," Department of State *Bulletin,* Vol. 74 (January 19, 1976), pp. 69–70; and Richard M. Nixon, *The Real War* (New York: Warner Books, 1980), pp. 284–90. One of the most detailed accounts of Nixon's and Kissinger's thinking regarding détente is contained in Garthoff, *Detente and Confrontation,* especially pp. 25–36.

30. Richard M. Nixon, *U.S. Foreign Policy for the 1970s,* Report to the Congress, vol. 3 (Washington, D.C.: U.S. Government Printing Office).

31. The provision in question was Agreed Interpretation J of the Interim Offensive Agreement of SALT I in which the parties agreed that "in the process of modernization and replacement the dimensions of land-based ICBM silo launchers will not be increased significantly." They also agreed that "increased significantly" meant any increase greater than 10–15 percent of the di-

mensions of existing ICBM silos. The United States insisted on the provision in order to prevent
the Soviet Union from reconfiguring its silos for "light" ICBMs to accommodate such "heavy"
missiles as the SS-9 (also limited by the Interim Agreement). When in the mid-1970s, the Kremlin
began to deploy the SS-17 and SS-19 missiles in SS-11 silos, many in the United States condemned the Soviet move as a de facto violation on the grounds that both of the new systems were
in fact "heavy" ICBMs—even though Soviet engineers had managed to squeeze the systems into
existing silos for "light" ICBMs. Strictly speaking, of course, the Soviets had done nothing
wrong as only the missiles exceeded the constraints contained in Agreed Interpretation J; modifications to the silos fell within permissable limits.

32. In his memoirs Kissinger is quite clear in saying that his overriding purpose in pressing
for the MBFR negotiations was to save "our whole European defense structure from Congressional savaging." On the other hand, he also notes that the Administration's willingness to promote détente in Europe, and specifically the Soviet initiative for a European security conference,
had "lured" the Kremlin into supporting the force reduction initiative. See Kissinger, *White
House Years,* p. 949.

Clearly, for Kissinger the two initiatives were linked. While he does not say so explicitly,
this would seem to suggest that part of Kissinger's strategy in MBFR was to test just how far
Moscow was prepared to go in promoting a military détente in Europe. If so, the answer came
soon enough in the form of the Warsaw Pact's negotiating proposals: not very far. He also understood that American leverage in MBFR was limited: the Administration's decision not to make
the conclusion of the CSCE in 1975 contingent on a satisfactory outcome in MBFR would seem
to suggest that whatever capacity Kissinger may have felt he had three or four years before to
link the two sets of negotiations had largely dissipated, owing to strong West European pressures
to finish up the work at the Helsinki conference. See Henry Kissinger, *Years of Upheaval* (Boston:
Little, Brown, 1982), pp. 1164–65.

33. That the Soviets were sensitive to the possible implications of an outright failure at
MBFR during the negotiations leading to the signing of the CSCE Final Act in July 1975 and in
its immediate aftermath is strongly suggested by the Kremlin's notably upbeat characterization of
the Vienna negotiations between May and December 1975 and its insistence that the timing for
the conclusion of a force reduction agreement had never been better. See especially Leonid Brezhnev, radio address on the thirtieth anniversary of the end of the Second World War in Europe,
May 8, 1975, (FBIS, *Soviet Union,* May 9, 1975, p. R10); Leonid Brezhnev, radio address to
the Baumanskiy electoral district, June 13, 1975 (FBIS, *Soviet Union,* June 16, 1975, p. R10);
Leonid Brezhnev, "In the Name of Peace, Security and Cooperation," *Pravda* (August 1, 1975);
and Leonid Brezhnev, address in honor of French President Valery Giscard d'Estaing, October
14, 1975 (FBIS, *Soviet Union,* October 15, 1975, p. E3).

34. Kissinger, *White House Years,* pp. 818–23; see also "Background Briefing (SALT negotiations)," 10:55 a.m., May 20, 1971, prepared by the National Security Council Staff.

35. Richard F. Starr, "The MBFR Process and Its Prospects," *Orbis* (Winter 1984) p: 1006.

36. Robert Axelrod and Robert O. Keohane, "Achieving Cooperation Under Anarchy: Strategies and Institutions," *World Politics* (October 1985): 241.

37. Ibid., pp. 228–38; see also Kenneth Oye, "Explaining Cooperation Under Anarchy,"
World Politics, (October 1985): 1–24; and Robert Axelrod, *The Evolution of Cooperation* (New
York: Basic Books, 1984), pp. 124–41, 169–91.

38. Axelrod, *The Evolution of Cooperation,* pp. 169–91; and Oye, *"Explaining Cooperation,"* pp. 12–18.

39. See Leonid Brezhnev, address to the World Peace Congress, Moscow, October 26, 1973
(FBIS, *Soviet Union,* Supplement 40, no. 208, October 29, 1973, p. 10); and Brezhnev, address
to the Baumanskiy electoral district (FBIS, *Soviet Union,* June 16, 1975, p. R10). See also Peter
Vigor, "MBFR: The Soviet View," *Radio Liberty Dispatch* (November 15, 1974), p. 3; and
John Erickson, "European Security: Soviet Preferences and Priorities," *Strategic Review* (Winter
1976): 41.

40. In June 1986 the Political Consultative Committee of the Warsaw Pact urged the creation of a new arms control "forum" to focus on possible conventional and nuclear force reductions "from the Atlantic to the Urals." The Eastern representatives left open the possibility that the MBFR talks might be reorganized to serve this purpose, should the West prefer to reform the Vienna negotiations rather than abandon them. NATO agreed in December 1986 to begin exploratory discussions on the subject. As of this writing, no date has yet been set for the first meeting of the new "forum" and until such action is taken, the MBFR talks are likely to continue in session. For the text of the Warsaw Pact proposal see, "Appeal of the Warsaw Treaty Member-States to the NATO-Member States and All European Countries, Containing a Program for the Reduction of Armed Forces and Conventional Arms In Europe," *Pravda,* June 12, 1986, p. 1.

7

The Stockholm Conference: Negotiating a Cooperative Security System for Europe

JAMES E. GOODBY

The Northern European winter of 1983–84, one of the coldest on record, faithfully recorded the temperature of American-Soviet relations following the downing of a civilian South Korean airliner and the Soviet walkout from nuclear arms controls talks in Geneva. It was apt, if also a little incongruous, that at such a time most of the nations of Europe, as well as the United States and Canada, sent representatives to Stockholm to talk about ways of reducing the risk of war. The delegations that convened in Stockholm's Culture House on January 17, 1984, were led by foreign ministers, as was recommended by a number of West European governments who wanted their publics to see that something was being done about East-West tensions. Inevitably, when the Soviet foreign minister took his turn at the podium, the delegations were treated to some of Andrei Gromyko's harshest rhetoric since the days of the Cold War. Privately, it was put about that senior Soviets were calling the conference "the theatre of the absurd." The Western press saw the occasion only as an opportunity to relaunch other stalled arms control talks. Public interest in this unpromising conference vanished with the departure of the foreign ministers; the chill in the Culture House remained. And yet, the Stockholm Conference became, even by the time of the Reagan-Gorbachev summit meeting of November 1985, the only East-West security negotiation in which the two leaders could note progress and speak of an early and successful completion of its work.[1] When the Stockholm Conference adjourned in September 1986, the participants had agreed to a document that committed each of them to an unprecedented degree of cooperation in explaining the nature of their military operations across the continent of Europe. How did this happen, and how did American and Soviet diplomacy contribute to the negotiation of cooperative security arrangements designed to reduce the risk of war?

THE CHALLENGE OF "CONSTRUCTIVE COOPERATION"

Constructive cooperation between Washington and Moscow has never come easily. The opening of the Conference was preceded by three years of difficult negotiations in Madrid over its mandate. The task amounted to reconciling Eastern interests in a security conference with Western interests in human rights. The negotiators at Madrid succeeded in putting together a delicately balanced compromise, and on September 6, 1983, the 35 participants—all the countries of the Atlantic Alliance and the Warsaw Pact, as well as all the European neutral and nonaligned countries—adopted a document that included agreement "to convene a Conference on Confidence- and Security-Building Measures and Disarmament in Europe," the first stage of which would be held in Stockholm commencing on January 17, 1984.[2] The 35 sponsors were those countries that had adopted the Final Act of the Conference on Security and Cooperation in Europe in Helsinki in 1975. Their agreement to the Stockholm Conference was reached in the context of the latest of the meetings that periodically review the implementation of the Helsinki Final Act.

For the United States, the first step in this "journey of a thousand miles" was a decision made by President Ronald Reagan, at the outset of his Administration, to support a Conference on Disarmament in Europe, under certain conditions, as one possible element of an agreement in the Madrid Review Meeting. The decision was made in February 1981 and thus may have been his first major foreign policy decision as president. In making it, however, he was being responsive, not to the USSR, but above all to French President Giscard d'Estaing. In 1978 the president of the French Republic had proposed a multistage European disarmament conference, the first stage of which would deal only with "confidence-building measures," which were then understood to be measures to provide greater openness about military operations.

As to the U.S.–U.S.S.R. relationship, a much more decisive act by President Reagan came in a speech he delivered on January 16, 1984, the day before the Stockholm Conference convened. It was one of the most important policy statements he has ever made on East-West relations. He spoke of "constructive cooperation" between the United States and the Soviet Union and said that the two countries should "establish a better working relationship with each other, one marked by greater cooperation and understanding." The Stockholm Conference thus became a test of whether "constructive cooperation" was a realistic objective in the post-détente period.

Cooperation was a goal that would not be easy to attain in the face of the alternative and clearly incompatible visions of Europe that underlay much of the discussion leading up to the Conference. The Western countries, in effect, were asking whether Europe must be condemned to a system in which artificial barriers continue to divide the continent, preventing the development of a more natural relationship and resulting in an unnecessary degree of confrontation. Or was it possible that a growing community of interests among all the participants in the Helsinki process—including cooperation in efforts to reduce the risk of war—could begin to knit together the severed connections of the Old Continent "from the Atlantic to the Urals"? Secretary of State George Schultz put the matter squarely in his speech on the opening day of the Stockholm Conference: "The United States does not recognize the legitimacy of the artifically imposed division of Europe. This division is the essence of Europe's security and human rights problem, and we all know it." More than any other point in his speech, the Eastern European governments dwelt on this one for months on end.

In such a situation, confidence-building is obviously in order, but the limited means available for that purpose justify a skeptical attitude. Militarily meaningful agreements in Stockholm perhaps could encourage progress in other negotiations and have an effect on improving the quality of the East-West relationship. But confidence-building is a long-term proposition. One should not look to the immediate but to the cumulative impact of routinely providing information that can dispel unfounded fears and establish a clearer picture of the nature of normal military operations. This practice could serve to underwrite the basic obligation to refrain from the threat or use of force, since it would require tangible, repetitive proofs that military activities in Europe are nonthreatening. Over time, it could also encourage a stable and cautious evolution of the security system in Europe toward one marked by dialogue and cooperation rather than unrelieved confrontation.

A SECOND TRACK FOR ARMS CONTROL

Most delegations in Stockholm probably shared the view that a reliably implemented agreement should ease the way for evolving political and security relationships, but the more direct business of the negotiators was to see what they could do with a relatively untried opportunity for arms control. In the last quarter of a century very few arms control negotiations have tried to deal directly with the proximate causes of war, those triggering mechanisms such as miscalculations and misjudgments about the possibility of a surprise attack. Negotiations typically have tried to grapple with the problem of reducing the levels of conventional, nuclear, or other types of forces. A few successful arms control efforts to deal with the proximate causes of war were bilateral Soviet-American agreements—for example, the hotline agreement of 1963, the Accidents Measures agreement of 1971, and the Incidents at Sea agreement of 1972. One, the Helsinki Final Act of 1975, was multilateral, but its provisions for advance notification and observation of military maneuvers were hardly meaningful in a military sense: the level of activity that would trigger a notification was quite high, the zone of application covered only a narrow strip of the USSR, invitation of observers to watch military activities was voluntary, and there was no real system of verification. Even these simple ideas had not been applied uniformly or to the full extent possible.

Correcting these deficiencies was the primary task of the Stockholm Conference. A widespread desire to move well beyond the rudimentary measures of the Helsinki Final Act was already evident in the Madrid Review Meeting. The mandate negotiated there provided that the zone of applications for confidence-building measures would be the *whole of Europe,* from the Atlantic to the Urals, a very important development in the concept of how to deal with the strengthening of security in Europe. The mandate also pointed to a more demanding security regime by stipulating that agreed confidence-building measures should be militarily meaningful, politically binding, and verifiable, three of the conditions stipulated in President Reagan's 1981 decision to proceed with this type of security negotiation.

The objectives of the Stockholm negotiations, as with other negotiations of this type, were similar to those of the more familiar arms control negotiations. The means chosen to achieve these objectives, however, were quite different. In general, traditional arms control deals with the reduction or limitation of arms, while the purpose of negotiations like the Stockholm Conference is to deal primarily with the reduction or limitation of risks. Traditional arms control negotiations typically have tried, for example, to establish long-term stability by providing greater predictability about the types and levels of forces that would be maintained over a given span of time. In contrast, risk-reduction measures are aimed at establishing a framework for judging the intent behind military operations under normal circumstances, and for enhancing or restoring stability during fast-moving crisis situations. Thus, both types of security regimes should work to enhance stability, provide greater security, and lay a foundation for more civil international relationships.

A negotiation that deals with the elements of chance, ignorance, suspicion, and error, as well as with confidence, is bound to be more difficult to quantify and analyze than those concerned with issues that are mathematical by their very nature, such as strategic arms reductions. The elusive nature of the subject matter is revealed, in fact, in the vocabulary used to describe it: "confidence-building," "security-building," "stabilizing," and "risk-reducing." Each of these terms serves to describe some, but not all, of the objectives of negotiations like the Stockholm Conference, which are aimed at enhancing security through agreement on certain limited forms of cooperation.

Such a cooperative security regime should be risk-reducing: it should prevent or provide the means for dealing with military uncertainties that contain the seeds of potential crisis. Such a cooperative security regime should be stabilizing: it should afford the participants a clear picture of what constitutes a normal pattern of military operations, satisfactorily explain any deviations from this pattern, and enable the participants to restore equilibrium in the event of a disturbance. The terms "security-building" and "confidence-building," in my opinion, should refer to the long-term potential of the routine, customary application of measures of cooperation, since years of successful cooperation will be required in order to replace mistrust and confrontation with both greater security and greater confidence. But even in a nearer-term perspective, it should be possible in such a cooperative security regime for diplomacy to deal more effectively with potential conflict situations.

Because the official title of the Stockholm Conference included the term "confidence-building" and this term is in general usage in the United States, I have elected to use this term hereafter. Confidence-building measures will be defined as those arrangements having the following characteristics:

— they deal with the operations of military forces, not with their capabilities;
— at a minimum they provide a framework for exchanging information about the nature of military operations;
— they should encourage nations to act during normal times in a way that would serve to eliminate causes of tension and reduce the dangers of misunderstanding or miscalculations;
— they should promote habits of cooperation among adversaries;
— preferably, they should serve to reinforce stability or restore equilibrium during period of intense international confrontation;
— agreement on such measures is based on the assumption that the nations involved desire to avoid conflict, but since this assumption could change it is important that such a cooperative security regime should contain measures of verification necessary to deter or detect deception.

JUNK FOOD OR SAFETY FUSES?

Even a brilliant theory fails in the absence of political support. It is a fact that the confidence-building variety of security negotiation does not rank high in the pecking order of arms control negotiations;[3] this was one of the factors affecting the Stockholm Conference. In the United States, no important constituency has strenuously lobbied for confidence-building measures. But neither has there been serious opposition. In fact, there has been a general disposition to favor sharing information if it could lead to better methods of preventing or controlling crises. The Hotline agreement, the Incidents at Sea agreement and other agreements of that type have been seen in the United States as quite useful features of U.S.–Soviet relations. Public awareness of these agreements is limited but, where it exists, the public's attitude is positive. The issue has never been politicized, for better or worse. Preparations for the Stockholm Conference in Washington and in NATO proceeded in an objective and realistic manner.

In the Soviet Union, also, little attention has been paid to confidence-building measures, although from time to time favorable comments have been made about the need to prevent war by miscalculation. General Secretary Yuri Andropov, speaking in the Kremlin on December 21, 1982, just after assuming the leadership role, said:

> Now a few words about what are known as confidence-building measures. We are serious about them. Given the swift action and power of modern weapons, the atmosphere of mutual suspicion is especially dangerous. Even a trivial accident, miscalculation, or technical failure can have tragic consequences. It is therefore important to take the finger off the trigger, and put a reliable safety catch on all weapons. A few things have already been accomplished to this effect, particularly in the framework of the Helsinki accords . . . Surely, the road to confidence, to preventing any and all wars, including an accidental one, is that of stopping the arms race and going back to calm, respectful relations between states, back to détente.

In his speech before the French National Assembly on October 3, 1985, General Secretary Mikhail Gorbachev endorsed the idea when he spoke of "confidence-building measures in the military field, these so-to-say safety fuses to prevent an erroneous interpretation of the actions of the other side in conditions of an aggravation of the military confrontation."

These are important statements, but the historic Soviet attitude towards confidence-building measures has been one of restrained enthusiasm, at best. The Soviets have always seen such measures as secondary to their interests in other political or security objectives.

STOCKHOLM'S SHADOWED PAST

The Stockholm Conference was part of a historical context, from which it could not be divorced. Traveling to Helsinki in 1975 in the face of protests from his countrymen, President Gerald Ford signed there, on behalf of the United States, the Final Act of the Conference on Security and Cooperation in Europe.[4] These accords (which are not in the form of a legally binding treaty) required cooperation across the barriers that divide East from West and established certain agreed standards of behavior in both the human and the security dimensions.[5] In the security field, the 35 participants recognized "the need to contribute to reducing the dangers of armed conflict and of misunderstanding or miscalculation of military activities which could give rise to apprehension, particularly in a situation where the participating States lack clear and timely information about the nature of such activities." On this basis, they organized a rudimentary security regime consisting of notifying one another of their military maneuvers and inviting observers to such maneuvers.

Although the Stockholm Conference was the child of the Helsinki process, it had even more remote ancestors. In 1954 when Soviet Foreign Minister Vyacheslav Molotov called for an all-European security treaty, he was giving expression to a key objective of Soviet policy then and now: a security arrangement for Europe that would ratify postwar borders and, if possible, isolate the United States from European security affairs. With Western Europe thus isolated, the Soviet Union would be left in the position of supreme arbiter on the continent. What the diplomacy of the Soviet Union and its allies eventually settled for was the Conference on Security and Cooperation in Europe (CSCE). But the CSCE was far from what the East had originally envisaged. In fact, it was much closer to Western concepts.

Before the negotiations that led to the Helsinki Final Act could begin, some longstanding issues dividing Europe had to be resolved or accommodated. An example was the signing of the 1971 Quadripartite Agreement on Berlin. Although Soviet accommodations to Western interests were probably regarded by Moscow as tactical concessions necessary for a longer-range strategy, the agreements that preceded or came from the Helsinki meeting created political dynamics that significantly altered the role of the "Helsinki process" as conceived by Moscow.

In fact, the Helsinki process came to support a strategy pursued by the United States and its allies that, broadly, sought to ameliorate the harsher results of the division of Europe, for the Helsinki Final Act also encompassed human rights, human contacts, economic issues, and cultural and educational exchanges. The Helsinki Final Act thus accepted the Western concept that security embodies political, social, and economic concerns as well as strictly military concerns. And of special importance for the Stockholm Conference, by including both the United States and Canada as full partners in the process the Helsinki Final Act reaffirmed the necessity for permanent American involvement in European security matters.

Nonetheless, one of the facts of political life is that the Helsinki accords do not enjoy a good repute in all sectors of American public opinion. They are seen as sanctioning the Soviet domination of Eastern Europe in return for unfulfilled human rights promises.[6] Consequently, the image of the Stockholm Conference was more than a little tainted in the United States. Moreover, the linkage to human rights meant that issues like Andrei Sakharov's hunger strike and the shooting of an American army officer in East Germany were formally raised in Stockholm by the U.S. delegation, a practice not followed in other arms control negotiations. All of this meant that the forum was more explicitly conscious of the political context in which it operated.

The record of promises made and promises kept in the security provisions of the Final Act was also a part of the context of Stockholm.[7] The confidence-building measures accepted in the Helsinki Final Act were modest in scope and imperfectly implemented. Nevertheless, experience with them was instructive. It was possible to see how cooperation in security affairs could work, as well as how this cooperation needed to be improved.

Two measures were central to the Helsinki security provisions. One called for prenotification 21 days in advance of certain military maneuvers involving more than 25,000 troops; the other for invitation, on a voluntary basis, of observers to those maneuvers. There was also a measure calling for voluntary notification of smaller-scale exercises involving fewer than 25,000 troops. The zone of application was intended to apply to relevant military activities throughout Europe but, in fact, it extended only 250 kilometers into the western part of the Soviet Union.

As of the time the Stockholm Conference convened, there had been nearly one hundred notifications of military activities in Europe, involving over two million men.

Although the notification procedures worked well on the whole, there were notable exceptions. Proper notification had not been given for the largest Warsaw Pact military maneuver conducted since 1975, the USSR's Zapad 81, which took place in 1981 in the Soviet Union near the Polish border. This maneuver, which took place during the period when Moscow was pressuring Poland to suppress Solidarity, was clearly an instance of a threat of force to achieve a political end.

In accordance with the Helsinki accords, observers had been invited to about fifty exercises. The NATO countries had extended more than thirty invitations; the United States alone had invited Warsaw Pact observers to ten exercises. The Eastern record was less impressive. The Warsaw Pact had announced more than twenty maneuvers but had invited NATO observers to fewer than half of these. American observers had been invited to Warsaw Pact maneuvers only twice and not at all since 1979.

In the area of smaller-scale exercises, the NATO countries had notified CSCE participants of 29 maneuvers. The Warsaw Pact had notified them of 4.

On the basis of this record, the 35 CSCE participants clearly had not uniformly met the aspirations of the Final Act when the Stockholm Conference convened. They had not succeeded in dealing with the problems of misunderstanding or miscalculation concerning military activities where, in the words of the Final Act, "participating states lack clear and timely information about the nature of such activities." And yet they succeeded in one important way: they created a standard and a model for expected behavior. After Helsinki it was no longer a question of whether less secrecy and less unilateralism about certain types of military operations were desirable but of how to create an even more open and cooperative system.

OPENING MOVES

On January 24, 1984, the NATO countries jointly introduced a six-point proposal, the first of the Stockholm Conference.

In brief, the six measures were:

1. *Exchange of Military Information* provided that participants would inform each other on a yearly basis about the structure of their ground and land-based air forces in all of Europe, giving unit designation, normal headquarters location, and composition of the forces.
2. *Exchange of Forecasts of Activities Notifiable in Advance* called for an exchange of forecasts on a yearly basis of military activities. The forecasts would furnish the name of the exercise, the countries participating, the size and type of forces involved, and the place and time it would occur. The forecasts would also list the purpose of the exercise.
3. *Notification of Military Activities* called for notification, 45 days in advance, of activities involving field training of units at division level or above and notification of certain mobilization and amphibious exercises.
4. *Observation of Certain Military Activities* required states to invite observers from all other states to all pre-notified activities and to certain alert activites.
5. *Compliance and Verification* called on states to agree not to interfere with the "national technical means"[8] of other states and proposed the participating states send observers, on a limited basis, to conduct on-site inspections to assure compliance with negotiated agreements.

6. *Development of Means of Communication* asked that the participating states develop better means and procedures for urgent communications.

Four other sets of proposals were submitted to the Stockholm Conference during the first months of 1984—by Romania, by the neutral and nonaligned participants, by the Soviet Union, and by Malta. The proposals submitted by the neutral and nonaligned countries were of critical importance, since these delegations represented a kind of swing vote in the Conference. Their outlook would help to define the center of gravity of the Stockholm Conference. As it turned out, nine of the twelve proposals included in their package were similar to those introduced by the NATO countries. In fact, three of them went beyond NATO thinking about what was "militarily meaningful": they called for rigorous limitations, or constraints, on the way military forces could be deployed.

Romania's stance in foreign affairs was signalled very early by a proposal introduced in advance of and independently of the formal introduction of the Soviet proposals. The Romanians offered a generous dollop of hortatory measures, but they too suggested some quite concrete notification measures.

The Soviet proposals, when they finally appeared, were drawn, in the main, from political action programs published at past meetings of the Warsaw Pact. These were: a pledge not to be the first to use nuclear weapons; a treaty on the non-use of force; support for nuclear-free zones; a freeze and reduction of military budgets; a ban on chemical weapons in Europe; and improvement in the confidence-building measures of the Helsinki Final Act.

The non-use of force principle is an inherent part of the Helsinki Final Act and had been mentioned in the Madrid mandate. The Soviet call for improved confidence-building measures of the type laid down in the Helsinki Final Act responded to what all delegations, apart from the Warsaw Pact, thought the Conference was designed to do anyway. These two Soviet proposals, therefore, found some support, while all the other proposals eventually were set aside.

Reaffirming the principle of the non-use of force was generally seen in the West as a reward for Soviet concessions on confidence-building measures and, therefore, as a card to be played quite late in the negotiations. A decisive turn in the negotiations came on June 4, 1984, however, when President Reagan delivered a speech that had fundamental consequences in the Stockholm context. Speaking before the Irish Parliament, the President, using rather opaque language, said: "If discussions on reaffirming the principle not to use force, a principle in which we believe so deeply, will bring the Soviet Union to negotiate agreements which will give concrete, new meaning to that principle, we will gladly enter into such discussions." The President had all but played the card; he had forced the pace of the negotiations. Although the public Soviet reaction to the speech was skeptical, there can be little doubt that it both contributed to Moscow's assessment of U.S. intentions in the Conference and created a situation that required the Soviets either to show serious intent or to forfeit their remaining negotiating credibility.

Even after the President's June 4 initiative, the Soviet delegates continued to try to convince the Conference that their other "large-scale political measures" were compatible with the Madrid mandate and that the measures would deal effectively with the "crisis" in Europe. They had little success with either argument. These proposals were seen by nearly everyone as unacceptable on security grounds, inconsistent with the Madrid mandate, likely to be unnegotiable, and essentially designed for propaganda.

But furthermore, the idea of ''confidence-building'' was firmly associated by most participants in the Conference with the idea of the notification and observation of military activities.

Secretary of State George Shultz's opening speech at Stockholm had laid out an agenda that proved to be an accurate reflection of what most delegations thought they were trying to do:

> We should look for ways to make surprise attack more difficult; to make miscalculation less likely; to inhibit the use of military might for intimidation or coercion; to put greater predictability into peaceful military exercises in order to highlight any departures that could threaten the peace; and to enhance our ability to defuse incipient crises.

This definition of an agenda had sunk in. It was clear to most delegates that the Stockholm Conference should deal with confidence-building measures and should not be diverted from that task.

It is also likely—and important to note—that the undeniable tension that existed in East-West relations during much of the first year of the Conference had convinced most delegations that it was necessary to establish the Stockholm forum as a place for serious negotiation rather than for fruitless propaganda encounters. Tense relations produced a positive spin for Stockholm. ''It's the only game in town'' was a common expression in Washington and elsewhere.

MID GAME

In the spring of 1985, the Allies introduced a comprehensive proposal which, for the first time in the Conference, offered the precise language of the obligations that would be undertaken by the signatories to the Stockholm accords. During the summer of 1985 the Warsaw Pact countries introduced working papers that contained clarifications of their thinking on notification and observation of military activities, and on the non-use of force. Romania offered suggestions for synthesizing the approaches under discussion in the Conference. The neutral and nonaligned countries worked intensively and at length on a comprehensive elaboration of their own proposals, which they finally introduced on November 15. The stage was thus nearly set for moving into a more intensive and decisive phase of the negotiation.

Reflecting these moves, the Conference agreed in mid-October 1985 on a definition of the framework for the concluding document of the Stockholm Conference. It essentially established the structure of the final accord.

It should be emphasized here that, unlike most other negotiations, the Stockholm Conference faced a target date that many delegations saw as a deadline. This was the requirement to convene the next review meeting of the CSCE in Vienna in November 1986. This meeting, normally held every five years, would assess developments in the entire process, including the results of the Stockholm Conference up to that point. Most of the participants considered the opening of the Vienna Review Meeting as the date by which the Conference would have to suspend its work, at least temporarily. Time came to be measured in terms of the months remaining before November 1986. This time factor probably contributed to the rather deliberate pace of the negotiations during much of 1984, but as 1985 wore on the need for more intensive negotiations began to be more strongly felt.

During the latter part of 1985 the negotiations increasingly focused on concrete confidence-building measures; as they did, Soviet military requirements and concerns with such measures became more precisely defined, and the tension between the Soviets' perceptions of their political goals and their military needs were revealed. The key issues that emerged as the negotiations moved into the final year prior to the Vienna Review Meeting highlighted the problems that had to be overcome if agreement was to be reached:

— The position of the NATO countries that the unit of account for notification of military exercises should include organizational structures was countered by the Soviets, who held that a manpower threshold expressed in numerical terms would be an equitable and meaningful measure of reckoning military capability.

— In contrast to the position of the NATO countries that the accord should provide for notification of land-force operations down to low levels, and the right of observation by all participants, the Soviets held that the parties should provide notification only for a few large-scale activities (20,000 men and above), which could be seen as a threat to peace; observers from selected countries might be invited to military exercises on some unspecified basis.

— The Allies proposed that all out-of-garrison activities of any type above a certain threshold should be reported, while the Soviets wanted to preserve the Helsinki Final Act's definitions of military operations as "movements" and "maneuvers," arguing that it was excessive to give notification every time troops left their garrisons. They also wanted notification of movements of forces transiting Europe, clearly hoping to include in the agreement any U.S. troop movements through Europe, for example, to the Middle East. The NATO definition would exclude such movements unless these troops moved into the field while in Europe and were thus out-of-garrison.

— The Soviets wanted to include air and naval operations whether or not these were related to land-force activities, on the theory that such operations are capable of sudden, surprise strikes. The Allies maintained that combined arms activities are the real harbingers of the threat or use of force. They argued that independent air activities, for example, would require massive verification measures, and that information on air activities in Europe and naval activities off the coasts of Europe, in accordance with the agreed terms of reference for Stockholm, would be made available under NATO proposals if such activities were functionally a part of land-force operations that warranted notification.

— The Allies believed that on-site inspection should be required by the agreement, while the Soviets maintained that "national technical means" augmented by "consultation" should be adequate.

— The Allies' proposal for an annual exchange of information on the structure and location of land forces and land-based air forces was denounced by the Soviets as "espionage."

— The Soviets wanted to impose a ceiling of 40,000 men on any land-force exercise on the theory that this would inhibit surprise attack. The Allies were prepared to consider constraints on military operations and regarded their proposal for an annual forecast of military activities as exerting a constraining effect.

To discuss these issues is to restate some of the problems that are familiar in any U.S.–Soviet arms control negotiation. The Soviets view secrecy as a positive factor in their security equation, hence their reluctance to volunteer information or to accept direct observation of their military activities. The Soviet delegation, almost from the outset, rejected a NATO proposal for exchange of information as amounting to legalized espionage. The Soviets wanted notifications to cover only large exercises, which were infrequently carried out in the Soviet Union. They thought of observers as coming primarily from neighboring countries. All of these proposals obviously had at their root a traditional Soviet belief that security can be found in secrecy rather than in openness. One of the milder expressions of the Soviet view of the NATO proposals, printed in the July 11, 1984, edition of *Izvestia,* charged that the Allies were making "demands, which they know to be unacceptable, for 'transparency' of the structure and activity of the Armed Forces of the USSR and its allies with a view to securing an advantageous, preferential position for the NATO bloc, and first and foremost the United States."

In fact, Warsaw Pact countries sometimes spoke of NATO proposals as likely to create the opposite of confidence—suspicion. Thus the contrast between the relatively open West and the relatively closed East became a major obstacle to negotiation of a successful agreement.

In addition to this well-known problem, the Soviets also faced another dilemma peculiar to the Stockholm Conference—how to reconcile their interest in a European security conference with their instinct that any agreement emerging from it should apply to U.S. forces and territory with no less rigor than to Soviet forces and territory. At the 26th Soviet Communist Party Congress in 1981 Leonid Brezhnev had offered to extend the area of coverage of the security aspects of the CSCE to all of the European USSR. During the negotiation of the mandate in Madrid, this became the agreed scope of coverage for the subseqent negotiations, a major breakthrough. The fact that U.S. territory was not included evidently rankled, however, for the Soviets were fond of declaiming in Stockholm that "not one inch of U.S. territory" was involved. The usually unspoken implication was that it was unfair for the Soviets to have to accept rigorous confidence-building measures. The Soviets were trying to have their cake and eat it too in this case. From the Soviet standpoint, the Helsinki process was designed to emphasize their "Europeanness" and to distance the United States from European affairs. It was ironic and refreshing to find them making the case, in effect, that in security matters the United States is also European.

The asymmetrical geographical coverage probably caused real concerns in some quarters in Moscow, however, and the Soviet delegates sought to compensate for this by making proposals that affected the West to a greater extent than the East (for example, the proposal for a ceiling on exercises of 40,000 men). They also called for such a high threshold of notification that Soviet territory would seldom be affected. And despite clear injunctions from the Madrid mandate, the Soviets advanced proposals for notification of naval activities on the high seas, even in areas far removed from the continent of Europe. They also emphasized notification of air activities, including those quite independent of any ground-force maneuvers. In both instances they argued that air and naval strikes constituted a major portion of the present danger of sudden surprise attack. Thus they sought to achieve not only a geographic offset to the unequal treatment they tried to portray in the outcome of the Madrid mandate, but also to provide for coverage of those U.S. forces that they perceived to be a special threat to themselves. In addition, the Soviets sought to deal with U.S. reinforcements for Europe and possible U.S. transits through Europe.

A third category of obstacles common to many of the issues cited above stemmed from the asymmetries in the way U.S. and Soviet forces are structured and trained. The differing sizes of divisions and the practice of NATO to conduct larger land-force exercises than the Warsaw Pact contributed to many of the problems encountered in trying to define notifiable activities and to devise a constraint that affected all parties equally.

A major obstacle was also posed by Soviet efforts to secure some form of non-aggression pact between the United States and the Soviet Union or between NATO and the Warsaw Pact. Even in the context of the Stockholm Conference, where neutral and nonaligned countries were strongly represented, the Soviets persisted in giving special emphasis to an alliance-to-alliance treaty on the non-use of force. The United States, strongly supported by the NATO allies, saw the non-use of force as related to confidence-building measures: the principle could be given practical meaning through specific actions designed to demonstrate nonhostile intent. The Soviets, however, wanted to "make more concrete" the non-use of force principle by having the agreement specifically stipulate that the non-use of force applied to certain specific situations, such as, for example, use of force on the high seas, in outer space, or in international air space. The Soviet desire to build into a non-use-of-force agreement a specific reference to the non-first use of nuclear weapons is understandable in terms of neutralizing NATO's nuclear defenses. Their interest in providing for "concrete" applications of the non-use of force is consistent with general Soviet behavior in the United Nations, and could have the effect of limiting the application of the principle to those situations specifically cited.

END GAME

By December 1985 the stage was set for the end game of the Stockholm Conference. The scope of the final accord had been outlined and the specific issues to be negotiated were precisely defined. The pressure of time running out began to be felt as the negotiators agreed on a work calendar for 1986 that set as an effective deadline September 19, 1986.

The first move of the new year was made by General Secretary Gorbachev in a speech on January 15 when he offered to settle the disputed question of notification of naval activities on the high seas. His speech was aimed at assuring public opinion that the Soviet Union was ready to free the world from the threat of nuclear weapons. Gorbachev, significantly for the Stockholm negotiations, also mentioned "on-site inspections," although this was in the context of eliminating nuclear weapons. With specific reference to the Stockhom Conference, Gorbachev said:

> But if it is not possible for the time being to resolve [unresolved problems] comprehensively, why not seek to solve them piece by piece? For instance, to reach agreement now on notifications of major ground and air force exercises and to carry the question of naval activities over to the next stage of the conference.

Gorbachev's personal involvement in this issue was in keeping with the more vigorous diplomatic style with which he had infused the Soviet approach to East-West negotiations. His personal involvement also indicated that in this particular case Soviet political objectives carried more weight in Moscow than narrowly focused military considerations. The negotiating technique of "signalling from the top" continued the practice that both Gorbachev and Reagan already had initiated, a practice that sometimes indicates the presence of bureaucratic gridlocks at lower levels, and which comes close to being an essential element in any successful negotiation between the United States and the Soviet Union.

Despite Gorbachev's initiative, the Soviet position during the first half of 1986 was still characterized by a reluctance to shift ground on issues of special interest to the military. Gorbachev's offer to postpone until a later stage any negotiations on the notification of naval activities, for example, was explained by the Soviet delegation as requiring the Stockholm Conference to agree there and then that this issue would be on the agenda for post-Vienna security negotiations, even though the Stockholm Conference had no competence in such a matter. The Soviet delegation also continued to press the Conference to agree to notification for air activities not tied to ground-force maneuvers. As a result, little progress was made during the first months of 1986 on the fundamental issue of what, exactly, required notification.

The negotiations were still moving slowly when another political impulse was provided by Gorbachev personally in the form of a speech in East Berlin on April 18. The theme of this speech was the Soviet program for peace in Europe. Gorbachev spoke of the powerful conventional armaments deployed in Europe and disputed the "false argument" that "Western Europe cannot give up nuclear weapons, including American ones, because in this case it would allegedly feel less secure in the face of the conventional armed forces and armaments of the Warsaw Treaty Organization."

The General Secretary's key point was that

> agreement [should] be reached on substantial reductions in all the components of the land forces and tactical air forces of the European states and the relevant forces of the USA and Canada deployed in Europe. The formations and units to be reduced should be disbanded and their weaponry either destroyed or stored in national territories. Geographically, reductions, obviously, should cover the entire European territory from the Atlantic to the Urals. Operational-tactical nuclear weapons could be reduced simultaneously with conventional weapons.

In this speech, Gorbachev again spoke of "on-site inspection," this time placing such inspection in the context of "international forms of verification." This reference to verification was connected to the new Soviet proposal for conventional arms reductions. The offer, nonetheless, was to play its part in the end game of the Stockholm Conference.

In fact, the speech made no reference to the Stockholm Conference, which could hardly have been an oversight: conventional arms reduction, even in Giscard d'Estaing's original concept, had been suggested as the subject of a second stage of the Conference on Disarmament in Europe. A possible reason for the omission was that the Soviet proposal might place Moscow in the position of *demandeur* for a second stage of the Conference, which in turn could weaken the Soviet bargaining position in Stockholm. Whatever the reason for the silence about Stockholm, the Soviet initiative inevitably had the effect of placing a premium on reaching agreement in Stockholm. Absent such an agreement, the case for moving on to a second stage of the Conference on Disarmament in Europe would not exist and the case for negotiations on conventional arms reductions would be weakened.

Meanwhile, solutions to negotiating problems were being discussed in Stockholm during the spring months of 1986, but insufficient progress had been made to generate much momentum. The few months left before the Vienna Review Meeting began to look too short to accomplish all the remaining work, and by the end of May the mood in the Conference was pessimistic; participants openly speculated that an agreement might be unattainable.

The next major move affecting the Conference did not alter the situation in Stockholm materially but it was a harbinger of possible future changes in the Soviet position. This move was the Budapest Appeal, a statement issued by a summit meeting of the Warsaw Pact, convened in Budapest on June 11. The appeal clarified the position of the Warsaw Treaty Organization regarding the forum for the negotiations Gorbachev had proposed on conventional force reductions. Although the appeal mentioned the possibilities of convening a special forum and of enlarging the Vienna talks on Mutual and Balanced Force Reductions, the most specific suggestion of the Warsaw Pact countries referred to the forum that would be provided by a second stage of the Conference on Disarmament in Europe: "The present proposals for the reduction of armed forces and conventional armaments in Europe could become the subject of concrete discussion at the second stage of the Conference on Confidence- and Security-Building Measures and Disarmament in Europe." This position underscored the importance of successfully concluding the first stage of the Conference, but broke no new ground in the Stockholm Conference itself. Revisions in the Soviet position, however, were not long in coming. The change again involved Gorbachev personally, for it became known that the Politburo in Moscow had reviewed and ratified a new and more flexible Soviet position for Stockholm. The timing of the Soviet decision was related, partly, to a visit to Moscow by French President François Mitterrand in early July, following Mitterrand's participation in the July 4 Statue of Liberty celebrations in New York. Mitterrand's presence in Moscow had provided a European context for consideration of Stockholm issues, a nuance of some importance for the Soviet government. The French delegation was informed during the visit that the Soviets could agree to set aside notification of air activities, one of the main obstacles to defining the nature of military activities subject to notification and observation. The requirement to define the agenda for a second stage of the Conference also had been dropped and so notifications of independent air and naval activities were now essentially set aside. The Politburo may also have decided by this time that Moscow's repeated references to on-site inspection required a more positive attitude toward this method of verification in the Stockholm negotiations. The Soviet delegation in Stockholm made an important statement to this effect in August.

In the final weeks of the negotiations, therefore, the delegations worked out a series of compromises that produced an accord in September 1986. Nearly all of the Western measures were accepted by the Soviet Union, but with amendments designed to reduce the numbers of notifications, observations, and mandatory on-site inspections. The NATO countries dropped the idea of an initial exchange of information on the structure and location of military forces, agreed that notification would be required for American troops entering Europe for training purposes, and accepted a measure that amounted to a form of constraint on military operations. In brief:

— The threshold for notifications was significantly lowered as compared to the Helsinki Final Act, and the accords now included criteria governing equipment and structure as well as manpower for determining whether notification was required.
— The scope of military operations to be covered was expanded beyond that of the Helsinki accord by including various types of ground-force operations, such as alerts, amphibious landings, parachute assaults, and troop concentrations. Notifications would be provided of movements of ground forces from bases outside the zone to locations within Europe. Certain information would be provided regarding air and naval operations functionally related to ground-force activities, including information about air sorties.

— Observers could include nationals from all participants; they would be invited to all activities for which notification was required above a certain size. The threshold for triggering observations would be higher than the threshold for triggering notifications (a provision known as "split threshold").

— Participants would provide an annual forecast of military activities requiring notification.

— Military activities involving more than 75,000 troops would not be carried out unless two years' notice had been provided; activities involving over 40,000 troops should be announced two years in advance and would not be carried out unless at least one year's notice had been provided.

— The accords required verification, including mandatory on-site inspections, and spelled out the mechanics of carrying out verification operations.

In addition, the non-use-of-force-principle of the U.N. Charter was reaffirmed within the framework of the accord on confidence-building measures.

The agreement on on-site inspection deserves a special comment since it represents a significant new precedent in the history of arms control. It was made possible by Gorbachev's readiness to depart from long-standing Soviet reluctance to accept on-site inspection even for major arms limitation agreements. Gorbachev's speeches in January and in April, referred to above, as well as the Budapest Appeal in June, emphasized on-site inspection. To establish that this was seriously intended, the Soviet delegation in Stockholm was instructed first to accept the principle of on-site inspection for future arms reductions agreements, and then, in the face of a firm Western position, to accept on-site inspection, including the terms of how it would be carried out, for verifying compliance with the Stockholm accords. The question of overflights of the Soviet Union— whether by neutral-nations aircraft or by host-country aircraft—became the last stumbling block. That issue was resolved in favor of host-nation aircraft, provided the inspecting nation could take its own monitoring equipment. This was a decision made personally by President Reagan. The Stockholm Conference thus became the first East-West arms control negotiation to accept the principle and practice of on-site inspection. Although there were restrictions on this right of inspection, which all the countries involved insisted upon to a greater or lesser degree, the precedent should be important for the future.

Another important and innovative feature of the Stockholm accord that deserves special note is the prohibition against carrying out any military activities requiring notification that involve more than 75,000 troops, unless participants in the accord have been informed two years in advance; and against carrying out any such activities involving more than 40,000 troops unless the participants have been notified in the annual calendar forecasting all military activities that require notification. These "constraining provisions," as the Stockholm document terms them, should act to inhibit the threat of force for purposes of political intimidation. Compliance with these procedures would mean that a participant could not suddenly mass troops in excess of permitted levels on the frontier of a neighboring participating nation in response to and in the hope of influencing developments in its neighbor's internal affairs. Noncompliance should call attention to itself in a way that would capture public attention. The issue of what action to take in response to the double violation of the accords—failure to comply with constraining provisions and with the obligation to refrain from the threat of force—would be posed instantly in a way that would be hard to duck.

FACTORS AFFECTING THE NEGOTIATIONS

Progress depends on many factors beyond the substance of proposals or the ingenuity of the negotiators.
George Shultz, Stockholm, January 17, 1984.
The Conference which has begun its work cannot be artificially isolated from today's European world realities, from the impact of developments outside this hall.
Andrei Gromyko, Stockholm, January 18, 1984.

At the outset of the Stockholm Conference, the United States and the Soviet Union were agreed at least that larger political issues presented obstacles to progress towards agreement in Stockholm. Conflicting U.S. and Soviet objectives in Europe, the state of East-West relations, and the leadership transition in Moscow were probably the three key external factors affecting the pace of the negotiations. All these factors were intertwined, but a separate commentary on each can show how each element evolved.

Soviet Objectives in Europe

Little or no headway was visible in the Conference during much of 1984 although there were private exchanges of some value. During that time, and especially during the first half of the year, Moscow constantly attacked American deployments of intermediate-range nuclear forces (INF) in Europe, and Soviet spokesmen did their best to create a crisis atmosphere in East-West relations. The latter effort may have had other motivations, but one was certainly to bring heavy pressure to bear on Western European governments to reconsider the INF decision and to weaken their security connection with the United States. There is little doubt that this was a continuation of the Soviet campaign to prevent deployment of the INF or to roll it back. For Moscow, this campaign took precedence over nearly everything else on the East-West agenda and certainly over the prospect for progress in Stockholm. *Izvestia,* May 8, 1984, contained a typical example of Moscow's propaganda line: "The Pershing-2 and cruise missiles which are being installed in combat positions on American bases in Western Europe cast a sinister shadow on the Stockholm forum. Tension is approaching the danger point."

In the Conference the Soviet campaign took the form of attacking the United States "and its closest allies" for installing first-strike weapons and for seeking superiority over the USSR. The Soviet delegation, of course, was joined in these attacks in varying degrees by its Warsaw Pact allies. They intended to create a mood of crisis, and to blame it solely on the West. What the Soviet referred to as "large-scale political proposals" were presented both as remedies for the "crisis" and as launching pads for denunciations of American and NATO policies. For example, the Soviet proposal to ban chemical weapons in Europe was used to attack NATO's chemical-weapons deployment policies. Their proposal on the non-first use of nuclear weapons became a device for criticizing NATO's strategy of flexible response. The *Izvestia* article of July 11, 1984, cited earlier was quite explicit on this point: "Thus American General B. Rogers, supreme commander of NATO armed forces, states frankly that the bloc's doctrine of flexible response envisages the possibility of the first use of nuclear weapons, and at the earliest stages of the conflict—measured in days, not weeks."

A freeze and reduction of military budgets was advocated by the Warsaw Pact delegations, who pointed to the mounting defense expenditures of NATO and especially the United States. After each such speech, the custom was for TASS or other official Eastern media outlets to publish the gist of the attacks. During the period of this campaign, it is significant that the Soviets' reluctance to engage in serious talks bilaterally with the United States was replicated in their behavior toward all the Western countries in the multilateral forum in Stockholm.

Not until the late summer of 1984, apparently, did the Soviets reach a decision that this policy was proving unproductive and that they should moderate their stance toward the West. Soviet objectives with respect to INF deployment no doubt remained unchanged, but with the moderation of Soviet policy toward the West came more flexibility in Soviet attitudes in Stockholm. Thus, in the fall of 1984 the Soviet delegation began to negotiate seriously on a procedural arrangement to permit more informal discussions. Although not an event of major consequence, this step nonetheless represented a turning point in the Conference, since it was one of the first concrete indications that the Soviets were going to enter into a genuine dialogue with their negotiating partners.

The Impact of East-West Relations

The East-West relationship was the second major external factor affecting the negotiations, but it was, of course, closely related to the first. The negotiation of the Madrid mandate required three years and took place during a period of deteriorating relations between the Western countries and the Soviet Union. The Soviet invasion of Afghanistan, Soviet pressure on Poland, the imposition of martial law in that country, the Soviet government's attempt to eradicate the dissident movement in the USSR, and Moscow's bitter reaction to the INF deployment—all contributed to a mood of tension in Western Europe and naturally affected everything connected with the Helsinki process. And just as the negotiators in Madrid had finished their work, Soviet air defense units downed a South Korean civilian airliner, triggering a burst of outrage throughout the Western world and bringing U.S.–Soviet relations to their lowest point in years.

Despite President Reagan's conciliatory speech of January 16, 1984, despite the fact that the private Stockholm conversations between Foreign Minister Gromyko and Secretary Shultz were businesslike and useful, East-West relations showed few signs of improvement during the first half of 1984. Probably one of the factors affecting Moscow's judgment was the American election campaign.

When Moscow decided to move toward re-engagement with the West, the most dramatic Soviet diplomatic gesture was Andrei Gromyko's call on President Reagan in the White House in August 1984. "The question of questions," as Gromyko put it, was the complex of nuclear weapons issues, and, in addressing these, the United States was central. The Soviet aim was evidently to resume a dialogue with the United States, and with an Administration that Moscow must have assumed would be continued in office. In January 1985 Shultz and Gromyko reached agreement on establishing nuclear and space talks in Geneva. With the accession of Gorbachev to the position of general secretary in March 1985, the President offered a summit meeting, which was ultimately accepted by the new Soviet leader. The summit of November 19–21 in Geneva was characterized by President Reagan as a "fresh start" and constructive. Gorbachev also reported positive results. The effect of this warming trend could only be beneficial to the Stockholm negotiations, and the pace of resolving the outstanding substantive differences gradually began to accelerate during 1986.

Transition in Moscow

No outsider can know what effect the changes in leadership in Moscow had on the Stockholm Conference, but some surmises are possible.[9] It is probable that noticeable progress toward consensus in Stockhom had to await developments in the transition process. This is not because the issues of Stockholm were frequently on the agenda of the Politburo—probably they were not—but rather because Soviet diplomacy in Stockholm must have been influenced in its style, expectations, tactics, and strategy by what was happening at home. Basic decisions affecting Moscow's engagement with the West were probably slow in coming and may have been put on hold pending resolution of the leadership problem. In such a situation the Soviet delegation could do little but mark time.

The first phase of Soviet diplomacy in Stockholm lasted roughly from January through August 1984. It was characterized for the most part by activities that inhibited serious negotiations and promoted the idea that East-West relations were in a troubled state. The basic explanation for this approach must be that it conformed to a general strategy toward the West probably established under the leadership of Yuri Andropov in the latter part of 1983. A caretaker regime like Konstantin Chernenko's, in which security policy was dominated by Gromyko and Defense Minister Dmitri Ustinov, might not have possessed the flexibility to adapt policies to new circumstances. And so the deep freeze continued, well into 1984.

A second phase in Soviet diplomacy became apparent in the period from September to December 1984, when the Soviet delegation negotiated and agreed on a structure for informal negotiations that met Western as well as Eastern needs. This shift, and the broader policy decision with which it coincided, could have been the result of leadership developments in the Kremlin. A Politburo decision to re-engage the West in arms control would be a policy issue of a large magnitude. It is not difficult to imagine that it was taken with a view to who would be occupying Chernenko's chair in the months to come, or that the decision might have played a role in affecting the outcome of the transition.

A third phase of Soviet diplomacy began after the turn of the year. Suddenly, beginning in January 1985, the Soviet delegation began to turn up the heat. They demanded more rapid progress in the negotiations and accused the West of foot-dragging. The constrast between this new sense of urgency and the rather deliberate pace that the Soviets, in fact, had forced on the Conference during most of 1984 was quite striking. This period coincided roughly with the implementation of the Soviet decision to re-engage the West, including the Shultz-Gromyko agreement on re-establishing nuclear arms control talks. Perhaps more significantly, this period coincided with the rise of Mikhail Gorbachev. It is at least possible that the new dynamism being felt in Moscow was also transmitted in some fashion to Stockholm.

The fourth phase, which amounted to a maturing of the general pattern of Soviet diplomacy during January-March 1985, began in May 1985. The Soviets manifested the same vigorous style that had come to the fore in January, but their effort seemed to have a sharper focus and a clearer sense of purpose behind it. For example, it seemed evident by this time that there had been a Soviet decision to begin a period of serious negotiation on a framework consisting of the non-use of force and a series of concrete confidence-building measures. This was the formula suggested by President Reagan on June 4, 1984, and later endorsed at the Fireside Summit. Working papers on confidence-building measures were introduced for the first time by the Warsaw Pact. Although these papers raised a number of new and difficult substantive issues, they at least helped to consolidate the negotiating terrain in a way that bore some resemblance to what the West had been advocating.

In Moscow, it seems likely that a new crispness in style and a reinvigorated decision-making process had made its effect felt by the summer of 1985. The Soviet delegation's activities were probably being more effectively backstopped, and policy direction was being communicated more authoritatively and promptly to Stockholm. The period of uncertainty and stagnation seemed to be over, and one could sense that the long process of leadership transition in Moscow—a process begun in the declining days of Leonid Brezhnev—had come to an end. Despite some fits and starts during the early part of 1986—which may have been tactical—the new leadership in Moscow showed itself capable of brisk and decisive action in guiding its delegation in Stockholm.

Signals from the Top

During 1984–85, public statements by U.S. and Soviet leaders became a principal, but not exclusive, channel for communicating their views and opinions about the Stockholm Conference. In fact, this has been quite a normal practice throughout the history of arms control negotiations. President Reagan's statements were numerous and, frequently, pointed.

The President usually met with the head of the American delegation to the Stockholm Conference during each of the recesses in the Conference, each time issuing a statement of encouragement and support for the negotiations, directed to the general state of the talks. His speech on January 16, 1984, on U.S.–Soviet relations, was of fundamental importance. The speech of June 4, 1984, before the Irish Parliament, as noted, gave a major political impulse to the negotiations by offering to discuss the Soviet proposal on the non-use of force. President Reagan made another important statement regarding confidence-building measures in a speech before the United Nations in September 1984. In 1985, the President continued to speak strongly in favor of progress in confidence-building measures; he did so, for example, in a speech before the European Parliament at Strasbourg on May 8, 1985. All these statements publicly committed the United States in various ways, a fact that was no doubt of some significance to a suspicious Kremlin.

In contrast, Soviet leaders spoke rather more sparingly of the Conference. In April 1984, Chernenko spoke of a combination of political and military measures as the proper solution for the Stockholm negotiations, a concept later endorsed by President Reagan in somewhat different form. Gorbachev, in his speech to the French National Assembly a year and a half later, said:

> As it appears to us, the contours of future accords are gradually beginning to take shape there. They include making more concrete and imparting maximum effectiveness to the principle of the non-use of force. They include a definite set of confidence-building measures in the military field . . .

The Conference did not seem to be high on Gromyko's agenda, since he rarely spoke of it, even in private discussions with Western leaders. It did become, of course, a subject for discussion between Secretary Shultz and Soviet Foreign Minister Eduard Shevardnadze in connection with preparations for the summit of November 1985.

It is likely that in Moscow, as in Washington, the top leadership was required to decide policy issues only infrequently. The personal involvement of President Reagan was very important, however, in the American context. The support he gave the general idea of confidence-building measures enabled the U.S. delegation to speak with confidence about American commitment to a Conference whose history was somewhat suspect in the United States. This was essential in terms of NATO solidarity; it also gave the U.S. delegation a firm, presidentially authorized platform on which to stand and permitted an aggressive negotiating posture. The United States could show that it meant business and could put the Soviets in the position of responding to American and NATO initiatives.

WHO NEEDS IT?

Despite the repeated interventions of President Reagan, it is likely that the Soviet Union correctly deduced that U.S. public interest in the Stockholm Conference was minimal and that neither the Administration nor the Congress had any real political need to reach agreement in Stockholm.[10] The Soviets could and did suggest to Washington that the Stockholm Conference was one method of improving U.S.–Soviet relations at a time when Washington was signalling that an improvement was desired. This had some effect during the early stages of the negotiations, the President's Dublin speech being one important result. The Soviets must have calculated, however, that this carrot would not take matters very far. Exerting pressure—or using a stick—also had only limited usefulness.

If the Soviets hoped that the European allies of the United States would pressure Washington to reach an agreement, they must have been severely disappointed. The Stockholm Conference was not a matter of great political interest in Europe either, and pressure on Washington was practically nonexistent. Only in the event that failure to agree in Stockholm could be seen as clearly the fault of the United States would there be a price to be paid in terms of American relations with European countries. The Soviets had little leverage here either, since the thinking of most West European governments regarding the Stockholm Conference was very close to that prevailing in Washington; the U.S. delegation had sufficient substantive and tactical flexibility to stay with its allies and the ability to provide a measure of leadership.

The accepted view in the West was that the Soviet Union wanted to keep the CSCE process going and, specifically, that the Soviet Union very much wanted to emphasize the security aspect of the CSCE at the expense of the human rights element. The conclusion was that the USSR wanted an agreement.

But it was also recognized that there would be limits on how far the Soviets would go in accepting the philosophy that less secrecy and more cooperation in military affairs would enhance security. The Soviets went out of their way to give the impression that their tolerance for exchange of information was less than zero and that they would impose strict limitations on the extent to which confidence-building measures would be allowed to affect the Soviet Union. The question was whether perceived political benefits, plus any security benefits deriving directly from the operation of confidence-building measures, would bring Moscow within negotiating reach of the militarily meaningful agreement that was NATO's bottom line.

To overcome the negotiating obstacles I have discussed above, both the United States and the Soviet Union had to make an assessment that the benefits of a mutually acceptable agreement would outweigh the costs. A relatively firm cost/benefit analysis could be made only as a deal was about to be cut, of course, but general evaluations had to be made before and during the negotiations. The following description of American and Soviet evaluations would not necessarily be shared by all the policymakers on the American side and is speculative for the Soviet side. To me, however, an analysis along the following lines offered a reasonable guide to judging appropriate U.S. moves and anticipating Soviet moves during the negotiations.

Benefits

The value of confidence-building measures is greater for the United States than for the Soviet Union if such measures are properly conceived and operate effectively, quite simply because greater openness in military activities should better serve the interests of the United States. Confidence-building measures that serve to make more permeable the barriers that divide East and West should also benefit the United States.

But for the Soviet Union, too, the agreement at Stockholm should provide benefits, although mostly of a different character from those just mentioned. The Soviets evidently perceive an advantage in having a voice in the politics of security in Western Europe. An outcome that provided for East-West consultation on some vague basis, particularly if related to an accord on the non-use of force, would provide Moscow with the means for raising questions about Western defense measures. Since the Soviets could never count on gaining such a specific means of influencing Western European governments, however, some more general expectations must inform Moscow's decisions regarding Stockholm. Some likely answers may be found in slogans the Soviets often use: "military détente" and the "European process." Probably they calculate that even without a specific device to give them a *droit de regard* over Western Europe, an agreement at Stockholm could be used to weaken European defense efforts and promote the idea that Europeans should solve their problems without the Americans.

In any case, a failure to reach an agreement in Stockholm would deprive the Soviets of one of their principal motivations for signing the Helsinki Final Act in the first place. Their interest was never in the human dimension of the Final Act but rather in its security dimension. Granted, Moscow sees great advantage in what the Final Act did to ratify post-World War II territorial settlements, but that was certainly only one of the Soviets' objectives. If there were no further movement they could hope to exploit in the security area, the enterprise for which they have labored for so long and in which they have invested so much diplomatic effort would become of diminishing value for them. Probably the Soviets were counting on a second stage in the Conference on Disarmament in Europe, where all the proposals that were rejected in Stockholm—a chemical weapons ban and nuclear-weapon free zones, for example—could be resurrected and others added. They probably assume that such a conference would be much more useful to them than the Stockholm negotiations. They certainly know that they could not hope to get to that promised land without a successful Stockholm Conference.

It is true that even without an agreement the Soviets could use the platform provided by the Stockholm Conference to achieve some of their propaganda goals in Western and Eastern Europe. An endless debate in Stockholm, however, is not an effective way of influencing European public opinion.

In sum, the benefits for the United States flowed directly from the functioning of confidence-building measures. For the Soviet Union, the benefits appeared to derive from anticipated secondary effects—reduced defense spending in Western Europe, for example, and the convening of a second stage of the Conference on Disarmament in Europe where the agenda might be more to their liking. Shifting the balance of the Helsinki process more to security concerns must also have been an important consideration.

Costs

For the United States, there are several potentially negative elements in agreement at Stockholm. That the Soviets might be right in their calculations just cited is one of them, and this cost will be tested in the long term. But the Western countries are counting on the agreement to improve their security without causing debilitating side effects. Another, more immediate, problem is the issue of balanced progress in the human rights and security provisions of the Helsinki Final Act. If the Soviets fail to comply with the human rights provisions of the Helsinki Final Act, any agreement on security would seem to be tilting the balance of interest in the Final Act toward the Soviet Union. Because of these perceived costs, and because the perceived security benefits were not assigned a very high value, it was not difficult to conclude that no agreement at all in Stockholm would have been a quite acceptable and, in some circumstance, a preferred outcome.

As for the Soviets, it can be deduced from their statements and positions that they have little fondness for any agreement that provides for greater openness with respect to Soviet military operations. The leadership in Moscow must know, however, that the information that would be shared in the context of a Stockholm agreement would not be of much intelligence value. Probably the precedents of allowing on-site inspection and accepting a notification regime covering the entire European part of the USSR while excluding all U.S. territory weigh as heavily as any perceived intelligence problem. The problem for Moscow, therefore, was to weigh these disadvantages against the hoped-for political advantages.

COLLECTIVELY NEGOTIATING SECURITY

The security regime under negotiation in Stockholm was multilateral, not bilateral, and this context cannot be given too much stress. The functioning of the confidence-building regime, particularly standards of compliance, will depend heavily on the actions and attitudes of governments other than the United States. Since the nature of the forum also affected the way in which the United States and the Soviet Union interacted in Stockholm, a discussion of conference dynamics is necessary to an understanding of the negotiation.

At the time the Conference convened, Moscow had been boycotting bilateral arms control negotiations with the United States. There was speculation that the Soviets might not appear in Stockholm. This speculation turned out to be incorrect, as the history of Soviet interest in such a conference would have suggested. At the same time, it was obvious that in a period of strained relations, the Soviet Union was more comfortable working with the United States behind the facade of a multilateral conference. Proposals that could be identified as neutral-nation ideas rather than NATO ideas were more apt to be treated sympathetically by the Soviet delegation. During the harsh political climate prevailing during much of the first two years of the Conference, the Soviets clearly preferred to justify shifts in their positions as responses to neutral initiatives, even when bilateral U.S.–Soviet negotiations had paved the way for such shifts. This enabled them to avoid crediting the United States with any positive attitudes while keeping in good standing with the neutral countries. Such motivations were not completely unknown to the U.S. delegation.

There are complications in a multilateral forum that the bilateral negotiator is spared. Solving negotiating problems directly between the two superpowers is a much more delicate process in a multilateral framework than in a bilateral framework. Usually, solutions deriving from U.S.–Soviet consultations were passed on to mediators of the neutral countries in order to multilateralize the process. The U.S. delegation could not speak for the NATO countries on important matters except after lengthy discussions in the NATO caucus, and then only if authorized. Two visits to Moscow by the U.S. chief negotiator and one visit to Washington by the Soviet chief negotiator were quite productive but, in the case of the American representative, could be only a preliminary to consultations within the NATO caucus. A little more flexibility was possible in the more free-wheeling discussions among experts.

A multilateral forum presents another, more intangible problem. The idea of negotiating serious security matters in a 35-nation forum is generally regarded in Washington as little short of ludicrous. Indeed, the experience of the United States in multilateral forums has not been encouraging.

It is true, of course, that in a multilateral conference, and particularly one like Stockholm where security was at stake and consensus the rule, the superpowers cannot have it all their way, even when they happen to agree. From the standpoint of the bilateral negotiator, this introduces distortions in the model of an ideal U.S.–Soviet security regime and also complicates the decision-making procedure. In order to judge whether the multilateral character of the Conference was an obstacle to serious negotiations on security, however, the role of the three groups represented in Stockholm should be reviewed.

As a general observation applying to each of the three groups, one should never underestimate the creativity of an assemblage of highly qualified professional diplomats and military officers from some of the world's most sophisticated governmental establishments. They are not only the heirs of a long diplomatic and military tradition, but also the possessors of a new kind of international lore that has developed with the evolution of the Helsinki process. A skilled diplomat in this setting can make his country count for more than its size would suggest, a phenomenon that usually has worked in favor of the West.

The Neutral and Nonaligned Delegations

The relationship between the United States and the neutral and nonaligned delegations was very close and mutually useful. The role of the neutral and nonaligned countries was of decisive importance throughout the Conference. Their impact on the outcome was constructive, their emphasis always on achieving genuine improvements in security. Without such purposefulness on their part, the Conference might have degenerated into propaganda exchanges. Although their coordinating and brokering roles were important, an even more important contribution was their commitment to achieving a solid outcome from the negotiations. After prolonged and very difficult negotiations among themselves, the neutral and nonaligned countries introduced a detailed description of their proposals in the Conference in November 1985. Like their more generally phrased proposals introduced in 1984, the document pointed towards concrete and rigorous confidence-building measures.

The fact that countries with such disparate security interests as, for example, Sweden, Switzerland, Finland, Austria, and Yugoslavia were able to agree on a single package of proposals showed the intensity of their desire to influence the negotiations in the interest of achieving a genuine improvement in security. The solidarity they achieved, incidentally, could itself contribute to their security in the future.

The substance of their proposals was not, in some respects, acceptable to all of the other countries. At the same time, the neutral and nonaligned delegations viewed some proposals which were acceptable to the United States and the Soviet Union as incompatible with their own security interests. In this category were measures that affected the neutral and nonaligned nations' plans for mobilizing their own armies. The general thrust of these nations' proposals, however, was compatible with the NATO philosophy that the Conference should create militarily meaningful confidence-building measures. Their proposals were not intended to be a compromise between the positions of NATO and the Warsaw Pact but, rather, were their own collective positions agreed upon only after enormous effort, and reflecting their own special concerns. Hence these delegations were somewhat constrained from playing their traditional honest-broker role. The final phase thus involved negotiations between East and West (particularly between the U.S. and Soviet delegations) to a greater extent than had been the case in the previous CSCE conferences.

The Eastern Europeans

It was always clear that the Eastern European countries had a major stake in the success of the Stockholm Conference. In many ways, the Helsinki process has been a test of whether one of the promises of the Final Act—greater permeability in the barriers dividing East and West in Europe—would really benefit the people of Eastern Europe. The verdict has been too slow in coming, but if only as a channel of communications between East and West, the Helsinki process has served at least one of its intended purposes. In Stockholm, the constraints imposed on Warsaw Pact countries by the nature of their political and social system were evident, but the network of relationships among all the delegations brought Eastern European delegations into vigorous dialogue with all the Western delegations. The U.S. delegation sought to maintain an open channel to the Eastern Europeans, including consultations in their capitals. There is no way of estimating the Eastern Europeans' influence on policy decisions, but there was never any doubt that they passionately wanted a successful outcome.

NATO

In Stockholm, maintaining close ties and an identity of views with the Allies was a matter of the highest priority for the United States. The delegations representing members of the Atlantic Alliance pursued a mode of consultation with one another that was similar to the one these countries used in other meetings sponsored by the participants in the Helsinki process. A caucus of all sixteen countries met at the head-of-delegation level, usually twice a week, and meetings of deputies and experts were held separately, often several times a week. The heads of delegations typically reviewed and assessed developments in the Conference, tried to settle on tactics for the near-term, sometimes formulated solutions for negotiating problems, and discussed themes each representative intended to develop in his plenary statements. Every member nation, without exception, participated vigorously and creatively in this work. Deputies and experts worked out more specific analyses and detailed substantive themes and tactics. They also conducted many of the exchanges and negotiations with other participants on the more detailed and technical aspects of the negotiating material.

The truly remarkable achievement of the nations of the Atlantic Alliance during the Stockholm Conference was the consensus they reached and maintained on all of the basic issues. Formal statements, for example, were rarely coordinated among the delegations but there was seldom a significant departure from commonly understood Western tactical and substantive positions. The NATO countries were able to work in close coordination without becoming mired in clearances for everything each country said or did.

The NATO caucus was certainly democracy in action, for the meetings devoted as much time to the views and concerns of each delegation as that delegation wanted. Sometimes it was said that the NATO countries spent more time talking things out among themselves than they did negotiating with counterparts from other groups. But the fact is that solidarity among the NATO countries was not achieved just because each believed in the initial positions their nations jointly had worked out at NATO headquarters in Brussels. It was also, and perhaps even more, a product of trust, openness, and genuine friendship.

The experience and professional skills of the NATO delegates counted for a great deal in Stockholm. So did the individual commitments of the governments of the NATO countries to the proposition that there should be a positive outcome to the negotiations. The support of the capitals was unstinting and understanding.

Soviet Relations with Other Delegations

While the U.S. delegation saw its best interests being served by keeping the focus on the specific business of the Conference, the Soviet relationship to other participants during much of the first year was dictated by the mood of tension and confrontation that Moscow wanted to foster. This did not preclude, of course, bilateral lobbying and public relations work by the Soviet delegation. The objective, however, was not tied directly to achieving results in the Conference.

This approach was replaced by a more accommodating tone when the basic Soviet policy line changed. Ultimately, the Soviet delegation came to speak more or less the same language as other delegations and to lobby for its position in much the same way as Western delegations lobbied for theirs. Although they may not have been greatly influenced by their allies, the Soviets certainly must have recognized that the NATO countries were showing remarkable cohesion, and that the neutral and nonaligned countries were insisting on serious negotiations on improving the Helsinki confidence-building measures. In the end, they realized that to produce an agreement, or even to make a good showing in that setting, they would have to put aside many of their proposals and get on the same wavelength as the other participants.

The Soviets started with several proposals they probably intended to discard ultimately and gradually retreated from their opening position after finding no significant support for their more extreme measures. Their initial proposals on confidence-building measures were vague—in the nature of place-holders designed to keep their options open, rather than indicators of their real thinking. When they finally decided that their large-scale political measures had to be discarded, they began to flesh out their ideas on confidence-building measures, developing in the process negotiating counters they hoped would be useful in countering analogous Western proposals. In contrast, the U.S. delegation started with a realistic, not artificially inflated program that had a solid base of support in NATO, found itself largely in line also with the thinking of the neutral and nonaligned countries, and was able to maintain its basic positions more or less intact through much of the Conference.

DID THE FORUM WORK?

My own conclusion as a participant is that the multilateral character of the negotiations did not adversely affect the effort to establish the type of security regime being discussed in Stockholm. In fact, it is probable that participation of many delegations representing all parts of Europe and North America was beneficial. Pressures for movement toward consensus were directed at the Soviet delegation at least as strongly as at the U.S. delegation. The history of the events that led to this forum on confidence-building measures was well known to 33 other delegations; Soviet efforts to introduce proposals inconsistent with this history were collectively ruled out of order. A high level of professionalism and a sense of responsibility for improving security in Europe were pervasive; game-playing was readily perceived and there was little tolerance for it. The multilateral nature of the negotiations also facilitated shifts in positions when the time came. The mechanics of coordinating positions and negotiating on both procedural and substantive issues were eased by the essentially tripartite character of the Conference. The use of caucuses, supplemented by intense bilateral consultations, enabled the forum to work quite efficiently.

SUMMING UP

The success of the negotiation is attributable to several factors. On the Western side, those engaged in the run-up to Stockholm were moderate in their expectations, and the preparations were characterized by hardheaded realism. This resulted in a negotiating position which, although tough in its demands on the Soviet Union, did not make demands that were totally impossible for Moscow to consider.

At critical points, President Reagan intervened with supporting statements. The most important of these was his Dublin speech of June 4, 1984, which offered the Soviets a negotiating framework they could ultimately accept, since the concepts, if not the specifics, were ideas Moscow had already advanced. The President's offer to discuss the non-use of force was of major importance, since it was an incentive for Moscow to shift its position to a negotiating framework acceptable to all others in the Conference. His repeated support both in speeches and in White House statements was an essential factor in enabling the United States to exercise a leadership role in the Conference.

Although American and Soviet visions of the future of European security were no doubt quite different, each thought that a successful outcome of the Stockholm Conference could contribute to achieving the future it desired. Each was betting, in effect, that the same agreement would work out to its own benefit.

The talks began in a time of troubles, but the adverse political climate acted as a positive factor since it provided a strong motivation to use the Conference to improve the East-West relationship. The United States viewed the Conference that way, and, to an extent, a desire to establish a more constructive working relationship with the Soviet Union prompted the initiatives taken by the U.S. government in the Conference and enabled the U.S. delegation to exercise a positive and constructive leadership role.

The multilateral context promoted progress toward an agreement. All of the participants thought that an agreement was desirable. The NATO allies were united in wanting an agreement that would have a genuine effect in improving their security; they were prepared to be unyielding on that fundamental point. The neutral and nonaligned countries also concluded that if the Conference was to be successful and promote their security interests, it should develop soundly based confidence-building measures. Their tilt in this direction was probably of critical importance in motivating the Soviets to move toward the Western proposals.

The Soviets had a deep interest in a successful outcome, although mainly for reasons external to the subject matter of the Stockholm Conference. The evolving political situation in Moscow, the Soviet delegation's ability to evolve with it, and Moscow's calculations of its relationships with the United States and other Stockholm participants favored movement in the Conference.

The idea of a deadline—the convening of the Vienna Review Meeting—gave a shape and immediacy to the negotiations. At the same time, the idea that not everything had to be resolved in the first stage of this Conference probably provided a way in which unacceptable ideas could be deferred.

The factors operating to slow progress toward an agreement were powerful and quite fundamental. Some of these were: Soviet obsession with secrecy; U.S.–Soviet mutual mistrust; contradictions in fundamental, long-term objectives; differing values placed on the importance of a successful outcome; external considerations, such as, at times, the leadership transition in Moscow; the effect of retrograde developments in human rights matters; and lack of a deep and abiding Soviet interest in the matters under negotiation at Stockholm.

LOOKING AHEAD

In the nuclear age, even an unlikely contingency deserves attention if that contingency poses a threat of nuclear war. War brought on by accidents or miscalculations—that is, a war that no one wanted or planned for—surely is an unlikely contingency. But can anyone say it could never happen? Surprise attack in Europe is another unlikely contingency, but does history suggest that military or political misjudgments are altogether inconceivable?

The document concluded at Stockholm in September 1986 was one of the very few instances of an arms control negotiation that succeeded in putting into place arrangements designed to deal directly with those accidents or miscalculations that could be the proximate causes of the war that no one wants. It remains to be seen how the measures will be carried out, of course, but this accord should encourage further efforts to negotiate confidence-building measures in both multilateral and bilateral U.S.–Soviet negotiations.

The Stockholm document may have been born at a historically opportune moment. The conclusion of the Conference came at a time of considerable flux in East-West relations. The United States and the Soviet Union seemed ready, particularly in the

Reagan-Gorbachev meeting in Reykjavik, to make major cuts in nuclear weapons, which focused renewed attention on the conventional balance in Europe and on deterrence at the conventional level. The conceptual approach underlying the Stockholm accords should be further developed and more fully realized in future agreements, for confidence-building measures can reinforce both arms reductions and defense measures as elements of a comprehensive strategy designed to create a more stable equilibrium in Europe. There should be a rich agenda for future efforts in this promising second track for arms control.

Notes

1. "Attaching great importance to the Stockholm Conference on Confidence- and Security-Building Measures in Europe (CDE) and noting the progress made there, the two sides stated their intention to facilitate, together with the other participating states, an early and successful completion of the work of the Conference. To this end, they reaffirmed the need for a document which would include mutually acceptable confidence- and security-building measures and give concrete expression and effect to the principle of non-use of force." From the Reagan-Gorbachev Joint Statement of November 21, 1985.

2. The agreement specified that: "the aim of the Conference is . . . to undertake, in stages, new, effective and concrete actions designed to make progress in strengthening confidence and security and in achieving disarmament, so as to give effect and expression to the duty of States to refrain from the threat or use of force in their mutual relations. Thus the Conference will begin a process of which the first stage will be devoted to the negotiation and adoption of a set of mutually complementary confidence- and security-building measures designed to reduce the risk of military confrontation in Europe."

3. "Within the government, these were regarded as something of a joke—'arms control junk food' was a common phrase around the State Department." From Strobe Talbott, *Deadly Gambits* (New York: Knopf, 1984).

4. "Yet no journey I made during my Presidency was so widely misunderstood. 'Jerry, don't go,' the *Wall Street Journal* implored, and the *New York Times* called the trip 'misguided and empty.' " From Gerald Ford, *A Time to Heal* (New York: Harper & Row and the Reader's Digest Association, Inc., 1979).

5. *To Helsinki,* by John Maresca (Durham, N.C.: Duke University Press, 1985), is an authoritative description of the negotiations leading to the Helsinki Final Act. Chapter 24 reviews the negotiations on confidence-building measures.

6. President Ford notes in *A Time to Heal* that what he "didn't expect was the outrage that the trip would provoke among Americans of Eastern European descent." He also says that "some members of the White House staff . . . intimated that it was 'another Kissinger deal that was forced down the President's throat.' "

7. "History will judge this conference not by what we say here today, but by what we do tomorrow—not by the promises we make, but by the promises we keep." (President Gerald Ford, at Helsinki, August 1, 1975.)

8. As used in the strategic nuclear negotiations, this term refers to assets that are under national control for monitoring compliance with the provisions of an agreement. National technical means include photographic reconnaissance satellites, aircraft-based systems (such as radar and optical systems), as well as sea- and ground-based systems (such as radars and antennae for collecting telemetry).

9. The chronology of the leadership changes is as follows:

November 1982   Following a protracted decline in health and vigor, Leonid Brezhnev dies and is replaced by Yuri Andropov.

172 *James E. Goodby*

February 1984   After a long absence from view Andropov dies and is replaced by Konstantin Chernenko.

March 1985   Chernenko dies and is replaced as general secretary by Mikhail Gorbachev.

10. The American attitude towards Soviet ideas about a European security conference had remained consistent for more than two decades as President Ford noted succinctly in *A Time to Heal:* ''Ever since 1954, the Soviets had wanted us to attend a thirty-five nation Conference on Security and Cooperation in Europe. Initially, the United States had been cool to the idea because we did not see any advantages to be gained.''

III

CASE STUDIES:
EFFORTS TO COOPERATE ON
ARMS CONTROL ISSUES

8

Nuclear Test Bans: History and Future Prospects

ALAN NEIDLE

The postwar effort to achieve limitations on the testing of nuclear explosive devices has been a saga of remarkable contrasts. There has been historic achievement—and prolonged stalemate. Some negotiations have helped to build safer relations between the two leading powers—and some have contributed to deterioration of relations. There have been unprecedented offers of cooperation—and failures to seize opportunities. There have been swift and skillful negotiations—and indecisiveness and backtracking. There has been courageous and effective leadership—and periods of unmanageable domestic disarray. For some, the test ban has been the best way to push the genie of nuclear explosions back in the bottle; for others, it has epitomized the worst form of arms control. Idealism and cynicism, hope and frustration, serious analysis and nostalgia— all have been engendered by the test ban endeavor.

To sort out the extraordinary tangle of facts, theories, and emotions that surround the issue, and to attempt to assess objectively the extent to which test bans have played and might be able to play in the future a positive role in building a U.S.–Soviet security regime, two complementary approaches must be pursued. One is historical, drawing on a rich and revealing series of negotiations over the last quarter of a century. The other is analytical, dealing with a variety of interrelated topics, including: asymmetries between U.S. and Soviet interests and different perceptions of strategic stability; impact of test bans on weapons capability; the role of cooperative regimes in implementation; the significance of multilateral participation; and, of particular importance, human capacities for leadership and management of highly controversial issues.

The historical material discussed in this essay will focus mainly on three episodes:

1. The negotiation in 1963 by the United States, the Soviet Union, and Great Britain of a treaty banning testing in the atmosphere, in outer space, and under water (the Limited Test Ban Treaty or LTBT). Tests underground were not prohibited unless they caused ''radioactive debris'' to be present outside the testing state's territory. The treaty followed nearly a decade of unsuccessful efforts to achieve a comprehensive prohibition of nuclear testing in all environments.* The LTBT, which has been in force since 1963, now has over a hundred parties.[1]
2. The negotiation by the United States and the Soviet Union in 1974 of a bilateral treaty limiting their underground nuclear tests to a size equivalent to not more than

---

*An appendix provides a brief discussion of terminology and the purposes of nuclear testing.

150 kilotons of conventional explosive force (the Threshold Test Ban Treaty or TTBT); and in 1976 of a complementary bilateral treaty controlling underground nuclear explosions for peaceful purposes (the Peaceful Nuclear Explosions Treaty or PNET). The negotiation of these treaties followed a decade in which work on a comprehensive test ban was kept on the back burner by both governments. The two treaties have never entered into legal force because of the failure of the United States to ratify them although both governments have declared their intention to abide by the 150 kt limit on underground explosions.

3. The effort by the United States, the Soviet Union, and Great Britain from 1977 to 1980 to negotiate a multilateral treaty comprehensively banning tests in all environments, including underground tests (a Comprehensive Test Ban Treaty or CTBT). The early period of this negotiation (from mid-1977 through spring 1978) saw rapid progress in the resolution of basic issues and engendered optimism among many that a comprehensive test ban would be achieved. But in the ensuing years, the negotiations deteriorated into stalemate. After 1980, the United States declined to participate in further CTB negotiations.

What we shall see from the historical material is that the ups and downs of test-ban negotiations have to a great extent been a function of how the test-ban objective has played a role as a political symbol—a symbol of recognition that in the nuclear age there exist some common interests between the two great adversaries, that there are opportunities for expanding U.S.–Soviet cooperation, and that the two countries are not locked helplessly in a zero-sum game relationship. The test ban has been a symbol, in short, for détente and reducing the risk of nuclear war. We will also see that there has been a spectrum of situations. The most favorable circumstances existed when the positive symbolism of a test ban was generally consistent with international political currents and the needs of national leaders and when the scope of the treaty imposed relatively little constraint on weapons development. This was the situation in 1963 when negotiations for the LTBT succeeded. The most adverse circumstances existed in the 1977–80 CTB negotiations when détente was in disrepute within the United States and the ban would have prohibited completely an entire activity related to maintaining and developing nuclear weapons. The result was akin to a diplomatic debacle. Between these two extremes was the 1974–76 experience of the TTBT and PNET negotiations, when support for détente was declining within the United States and the treaties would have narrowed the scope of permitted testing more than the LTBT but less than the CTBT.

In the discussion of analytical factors we will see that the test of whether test bans can positively strengthen the over-all U.S.–Soviet security regime unavoidably depends to a considerable extent on practical, pragmatic factors, such as: the strength and skill of the leadership in both countries; the degree to which the military in each country opposes (or acquiesces in) particular proposals; whether verification procedures can be designed (and, of particular importance, implemented) in ways that promote cooperation; how competing demands in arms control negotiations engage the political prestige of the leaders; and how various test-ban initiatives reinforce, or detract from, these other activities. An examination of such considerations can be quite different from a theoretical analysis of the technical merits of a particular test ban proposal. Because of the importance of these practical and broader policy factors, this paper will of necessity concern itself with domestic arguments, especially within the United States, regarding the desirability of various test bans—arguments that obviously have a fundamental effect on the capacity of leaders to bring about future test bans.

In recent years, the comprehensive test ban has once again been of great prominence in the political relations of the United States and the Soviet Union. The issue was dramatized by a unilateral Soviet moratorium on its own testing which, despite continued American testing, lasted for about nineteen months. There has been no comparable example of self-restraint by either nation, without reciprocity, throughout the nuclear era. In the final section of this essay some thoughts will be offered on the future prospects for additional testing restraints. I will suggest that a comprehensive test ban has relatively little chance of being achieved in the foreseeable future (even beyond 1988)— but that such a prospect is not impossible, provided a rather demanding and perhaps unlikely set of favorable conditions can be brought about. However, the prospects for further partial restraints on testing, such as entry into force of the TTBT and lowering of that treaty's 150 kt level for permitted explosions, are significantly better. In both cases, a crucial factor will be whether the testing restraint is integrated into an over-all U.S.–Soviet relationship in which such measures of cooperation are a logical and supporting element.

THE POLITICAL SETTING FOR THE MAJOR NEGOTIATIONS

Leaders of the United States and the Soviet Union approached the three major negotiations (LTBT, TTBT, and CTBT) giving prominence to political and symbolic factors.

The Limited Test Ban Treaty (1963)

The central political fact regarding the limited test ban is that it was achieved in the wash of the 1962 Cuban missile crisis. Even as the crisis was ending, both leaders expressed the hope in their correspondence that it would open the way to progress on arms control. President John F. Kennedy specifically referred to "the great effort for a nuclear test ban." [2] Lower level diplomatic contacts also reflected this theme. [3] A little time was required, however, for a shift away from the broad objective of a comprehensive ban and toward the negotiation of a limited test ban.

Since the mid-1950s, discussion of a comprehensive test ban between the United States, Great Britain, and the Soviet Union had been dominated by a wide variety of disagreements typical of the contentious Cold War relationship. These included, for example: disagreement over whether the CTBT must be linked to other disarmament and arms control steps, which was advocated at different times by both sides; recriminations regarding the breakdown of a three-year moratorium when the Soviets resumed testing in late 1961; and differences over a host of verification problems, such as the validity and relevance of technical data about conceivable scenarios for cheating, the number of and procedures for on-site inspections, the number and location of seismic monitoring stations, and the organization and composition of an international control commission. When the negotiations resumed in late 1962 following the Cuban missile crisis, they again focused on achieving a comprehensive ban, but once more they foundered on the problem of verification, especially the issues of on-site inspections and seismic monitoring stations.

The ground was prepared for fundamental change with Kennedy's June 1963 commencement speech at the American University. The speech not only stressed a positive common interest of the two countries—their "mutually deep interest in a just and genuine peace and in halting the arms race"; it was also notable for its absence of finger pointing, its recognition that both sides must work for peace and "must avoid those confrontations which bring an adversary to a choice of either a humiliating retreat or nuclear war." This unprecedentedly conciliatory utterance was warmly welcomed by Chairman Nikita Khrushchev.

The focus shifted to a limited test ban in early July 1963, two weeks before the Moscow negotiations began, when Khrushchev made clear that the Soviets would continue to oppose U.S. requirements for on-site inspection, but that they were ready to conclude an agreement banning tests in the atmosphere, in outer space, and under water. This was a reversal of position since the Soviets had previously turned down Western proposals to negotiate a limited ban. When the negotiations began in mid-July, the goal of a comprehensive treaty was rapidly jettisoned in favor of the limited ban, verification of which would not require on-site inspections or the installation of internal seismic stations. Issues on which there were differences now seem, by today's standards, to have been relatively few and susceptible to extremely rapid resolution. Negotiations were completed in ten days.

The shift in objective from a comprehensive to a partial treaty was, of course, important in heightening the symbolic political significance of the first test ban, as opposed to its arms control content or its impact in preventing proliferation of nuclear weapons. At the same time, a treaty preventing nuclear explosions in the atmosphere was responsive to the strong public concern within the United States about contamination of the environment by radioactive fallout. Indeed, public outrage over fallout, especially from the hydrogen bomb tests in the Pacific in the mid-1950s, had been a driving force in establishing a test ban as a goal of American policy.[4]

The LTBT's importance as a symbol of a turning in U.S.–Soviet relations and a step toward reducing the risk of nuclear war became fully apparent after the treaty was concluded. Indeed, the treaty was characterized as a "step" on countless occasions. Immediately after the treaty was initialed, the President set the tone. The treaty was "an important first step—a step towards peace—a step towards reason—a step away from war." He invoked the ancient Chinese proverb: "A journey of a thousand miles must begin with a single step." During the Senate Foreign Relations Committee's hearings, Secretary of State Dean Rusk saw the treaty as "one small step along a new course." General Maxwell Taylor, chairman of the Joint Chiefs of Staff, thought the gains from the treaty might be "a stabilization of international relations and a *move toward* a peaceful environment in which to seek resolution of our differences." The director of the Los Alamos nuclear weapons laboratory thought the treaty was "the *first sign* of hope that international nuclear understanding is possible." The Foreign Relations Committee's report stated that "the treaty offers the prospect of a gradual lessening of tensions, of a *start* toward the progressive elimination of the danger of nuclear war." And finally, Republican Senator Everett Dirksen, in announcing his support for the treaty, declared, "I should not like to have written on my tombstone: 'He knew what happened at Hiroshima but he did not take a first step.' "

These statements should not be downgraded as rhetorical flourishes. Prior to the Cuban missile crisis, U.S.–Soviet relations had been largely dominated by zero-sum thinking about the prospects for conciliation. Despite brief thaws, principally associated with the 1955 and 1959 Eisenhower summits, a great many officials doubted whether it would ever be possible for the two countries to agree on disarmament or arms-control constraints limiting their most important form of strength—nuclear weapons. Everyone knew that Soviet purposes were fundamentally antagonistic to those of the West. The hard-headed men in the Kremlin would not agree to a measure unless it advanced their security, and that surely would be at the expense of the West. How could one expect significant agreement under these circumstances? Indeed, despite all the protestations of earnestness on both sides, and occasional raising of expectations when one side or the other appeared to take a promising initiative, the history of disarmament and arms-control negotiations seemed to be mainly one of stalemates or of consummations avoided. The President's achievement in early 1963 was to establish in a concrete and highly symbolic action that in the nuclear era the two countries shared a genuine mutual interest in working to lessen tensions and reduce the risk of nuclear war. William Hyland has written, "One should date the advent of 'detente' from the American University speech of President Kennedy in 1963 . . . . The basic idea after the Cuban crisis was that there could be gains in stability through the consolidation of overlapping interests, especially in economics and in arms control."[5]

The difficulty of establishing this first détente is attested to by the substantial opposition to the 1963 test ban within the U.S. Senate. In addition to the Foreign Relations Committee, the Armed Services Committee's Preparedness Subcommittee also held hearings and six of its seven members recommended against the treaty. These Senators were of the view that "Soviet secrecy and duplicity require that this Nation possess a substantial margin of superiority in both the quality and quantity of its implements of defense." The final Senate vote in favor of the treaty was 80 to 19. While this may seem a comfortable margin, it is significantly different from the votes for the 1972 SALT I agreements, which were approved with just two negative votes in the Senate.

To achieve adequate support, the President committed the U.S. Government to a program of four safeguards that had been requested by the nation's military leaders. These were: (1) carrying out a vigorous program of underground testing, (2) maintaining readiness to resume atmospheric testing promptly if the Soviets should do so, (3) improving U.S. capability for detecting violations, and (4) maintaining a strong program of weapons development at the weapons laboratories.

From a distance of over twenty years, the LTBT seems to many to be a completely reasonable, perhaps almost inevitable, achievement. But, in fact, it required exceptionally skillful and determined leadership; it involved substantial payments in the form of the testing "safeguards"; and although the treaty had the great attraction of eliminating a threat to health and the environment, about which the public had been deeply concerned, there was still significant opposition. It seems safe to conclude that an atmospheric test ban would not have been achievable but for the occurrence of a grave crisis—the Cuban missile crisis—which was dangerous enough to shake, to some extent, national preconceptions about how relations should be pursued with the Soviet Union, and which was a profoundly sobering reminder of the risk of nuclear war.[6]

The Threshold Test Ban (1974)
and the Peaceful Nuclear Explosions Treaty (1976)

Negotiation of the U.S.–Soviet threshold test ban in 1974 took place under political conditions radically different from those of the LTBT eleven years earlier. While the LTBT was both an opening event, and a stimulus, of U.S.–Soviet détente, the threshold test ban was concluded toward the beginning of a long downward slope after what history now tells us was a relatively brief apogee for détente in 1972.

The LTBT became a live subject in 1974 because of the imminence of the third annual Nixon-Brezhnev summit. Early in 1974, the Soviets had proposed that the two countries agree on a comprehensive ban at the summit. However, the Soviet approach was that all the nuclear powers, including China and France, would have to accept it. Also, the Soviets did not have in mind the type of verification, with on-site inspections, that the United States desired. The Soviet initiative was rejected. Then, in March, during Henry Kissinger's pre-summit consultations in Moscow, Leonid Brezhnev reportedly proposed a threshold ban.[7] Technical discussions proceeded in Geneva, but the treaty was concluded only in the course of the summit, with the participation of the two leaders.

When the summit opened, Brezhnev and Aleksei Kosygin once again argued for a comprehensive ban despite the fact that lower level agreement on a threshold ban had already been worked out. Richard Nixon vigorously rejected a comprehensive treaty mainly on the ground that he would not be able to achieve its acceptance in the United States. There then followed confusion about the level of the threshold. Nixon mistakenly suggested 100 kt, but that proposal was withdrawn rapidly after Kissinger learned that the Defense Department did not want the level to be lower than 150 kt.[8] The Soviets accepted the 150 kt level but some officials close to the negotiation felt they would have agreed to almost any number, including 100 kt.

The higher kiloton level was not a result of weakness in verification capabilities. The main problem in verifying a threshold ban is one of achieving sufficient accuracy of measurement—determining whether particular tests are larger or smaller than the permitted level. This would have been of about the same difficulty whether the limit had been 100 kt, or 150 kt. In contrast, the verification task under a CTBT is one of detecting very small seismic events that might or might not have been deliberately concealed, and then attempting to determine whether they are small earthquakes or explosions. Thus, once again, as they had done in 1963, the two countries in 1974 bypassed the most difficult verification problems.

However, to improve the capability to measure the size of explosions, and also to ensure that the treaty could not be circumvented by conducting explosions having military value under the guise of explosions for peaceful purposes, the Soviets agreed to cooperative verification procedures exceeding any that had been previously incorporated into a U.S.–Soviet arms control agreement. In the TTBT, and the accompanying PNET, which was negotiated in the succeeding two years, these procedures included exchanges of data regarding the geology surrounding test sites, conduct of test explosions for calibration of measuring instruments, and possible on-site observations in the case of certain types of explosions for peaceful purposes. There were also provisions for establishment of a Joint Consultative Commission through which the parties were to consult each other, make and respond to inquiries, and generally promote treaty implementation.

The main political incentives for each side to conclude this agreement are not hard to divine. President Nixon was concerned about the declining health of détente. As he related in his memoirs, Nixon recognized that a breakthrough on the principal arms control project, SALT II, was not possible. He writes: "We both understood that if the process of detente could be maintained through a holding-pattern summit, we might be able to make a breakthrough at the next meeting."[9] Lesser agreements would help to keep the process alive. As to Soviet motivations, Henry Kissinger writes: "The Soviet conciliatoriness with respect to it [the TTBT] must have been to maintain some momentum in the flagging detente.'' [10]

The United States has failed to ratify the TTBT. The treaty has therefore not entered into force. Both countries, however, have said they would abide by the 150 kt testing limit. In the absence of entry into force, none of the cooperative steps to facilitate verification have taken place. The Soviet Union has repeatedly urged U.S. ratification as a step that would contribute to an improvement in relations.

After the second of the two associated treaties (the PNET) was concluded in 1976, the TTBT was disparaged within the United States by traditional supporters of arms control—primarily because the threshold was set so high and because as a consequence the treaty appeared to have very little impact on the U.S.–Soviet arms competition or in promoting a worldwide nonproliferation regime. After President Jimmy Carter took office the treaty was set aside for fear that Senate consideration would complicate prospects for a comprehensive test ban. The Reagan Administration did not seek ratification because of the Administration's position that the Soviet Union may have conducted tests greater than 150 kilotons and that the treaty's procedures for verification are not adequate. (As I indicated earlier, these have never been put into effect; a request by the Reagan Administration in late 1986 that the Senate give advice and consent to ratification, subject to the achievement of improved verification procedures, is discussed later in this essay.)

The Comprehensive Test Ban (1977–80)

When Jimmy Carter became President he inherited a U.S.–Soviet détente policy that seemed well on the way to collapse. A long train of events, including the 1973 October war, Congress's refusal to accord promised economic benefits to the Soviet Union, the domestic American focus on the Soviet government's human rights abuses, Soviet/Cuban actions in Angola, the absence of major arms control agreements, and American dramatization of a ''relentless'' Soviet strategic build-up, all contributed to a deep deterioration in relations.

The new President's basic goals included an improvement in relations with the Soviet Union and a reinvigoration of the arms control process. The most pressing task was to complete the negotiation of SALT II, which had stalled after some five years of effort. But the President had in mind much more ambitious goals for nuclear arms control than those embodied in the Nixon-Ford SALT II negotiations. Achievement of a comprehensive test ban was part of this broader agenda. President Carter reportedly believed that the limited test ban treaty of 1963 had constituted a historic breakthrough and that President Kennedy's stature as a world leader had been greatly enhanced by its achievement.[11] Carter, like Kennedy, was also deeply concerned about the spread of nuclear weapons and believed a comprehensive test ban would be a bulwark against further proliferation.

Accordingly, shortly after his inauguration, President Carter called publicly for an end to all testing; and the objective of a CTB was included in his early correspondence with Brezhnev. The Soviet leader responded positively. Brezhnev, who had been one of the few Presidium members to support prominently Khrushchev's first détente in 1963 and who had built détente with Nixon in 1972, no doubt hoped that a successful CTB negotiation would help to revive that relationship. He continued persistently to advocate détente despite its steady deterioration.

In mid-1977, CTB negotiations got off to an extraordinarily favorable start. In some ways it was a model of how to approach negotiations. The first session was one of exploration, rather than the more frequent and often harmful approach of initially introducing detailed proposals that are then so difficult to retreat from. During the first six months of formal negotiations, U.S., British and Soviet delegations worked out about 90–95 percent of the text of a multileral treaty, including verification provisions; and about 50 percent or more of the provisions of a trilateral U.S.–British–Soviet treaty annex, which was to cover in more detail inspections between those parties and establishment of internal seismic stations.

This unusually rapid progress was possible because the Soviet Union, at U.S. urging, made four major concessions: relinquishing the right to carry out explosions for peaceful purposes (the Soviets had a substantial program); permitting entry into force without Chinese (or French) adherence; accepting the concept of challenge on-site inspections supported by detailed, pre-agreed procedures; and agreeing to the installation in the Soviet Union of a network of automatically recording, tamper-resistant seismic stations. Concessions such as these undoubtedly required decisions at the highest levels of the Soviet leadership, in some cases by Brezhnev, who reportedly overruled parts of the Soviet bureaucracy. During the entire course of the negotiations, which lasted about three years, the United States did not make any moves toward Soviet positions of comparable magnitude.

The negotiations stalled in 1978 primarily because of American adoption of positions (in some cases reversing earlier positions) that added up to advocacy of a short-term, impermanent, and noncomprehensive treaty.[12] At the outset of the negotiation, the United States proposed a treaty of indefinite duration with periodic review. The U.S. position then shifted first to favoring a treaty of five years duration, and soon thereafter to one of three years. What was most important was not the precise number of years for this period, whether five or three, but rather American thinking about continuation of the treaty thereafter. The American position was that the treaty would terminate at the end of three years (not simply be reviewed); and a new decision or negotiation, possibly after an interval of testing, would be required if the treaty were to continue. As to the scope of the treaty, the United States, after introducing the issue of how "laboratory-size" explosions should be dealt with by the treaty, declined throughout the negotiation to provide its considered views on the question. What led the President to approve these various positions, as we shall see in a fuller discussion later, was the strenuous dissent of the U.S. military and weapons establishment from the original goal of a lasting suspension of all weapon tests, primarily on the ground that tests are needed to maintain the reliability of the weapons stockpile.

The significance of these positions for the Soviet Union has not been widely understood. When the Soviet Union early in the negotiations took the major and unprecedented step of accepting provision for a network of automatic seismic stations on its territory, this was not merely an abstract gesture. A large-scale engineering effort would be required, including geological surveys at many locations, testing of equipment, relocation of some sites, and a construction and installation program extending over several years. What, from the Soviet viewpoint, would be the value (and also the risks) of such an effort if the treaty were to end in three years and there were not even a presumption of its renewal?

It was evident in the negotiations that the American posture stimulated primordial Soviet fears regarding arms control as a means of collecting intelligence. It was feared that the American intention was to learn a great deal about monitoring Soviet tests in the three-year term of the treaty and then return to underground testing. Soviet perception that the United States lacked seriousness of purpose could only be deepened by the continuing U.S. refusal to come to grips with the issue of whether, and how, laboratory-scale explosions should be covered by the treaty. These developments must unavoidably have caused Soviet officials to question whether their major concessions had been worth the effort—or even worse, whether they had been taken in. It is not hard, therefore, to see why the negotiation consumed, rather than built, goodwill—why it contributed to the further decline, rather than the rebuilding, of détente.

A number of people have portrayed the negotiation's disintegration as caused by Soviet obstinacy over details of inspection procedure, an explanation that conforms reassuringly to the traditional image of the Soviets giving with one hand and taking with the other—that is, adopting attractive, general postures and refusing later to agree to essential implementing details. It is true that what should have been secondary verification issues came to the fore in the last years of the negotiation. But this was a direct result of the negotiations having lost momentum, and that in turn was caused by U.S. backtracking on fundamental issues.

The U.S. approach to the negotiations was not, of course, an isolated, inexplicable phenomenon. As the SALT II enterprise dragged on through 1978, it came to be appreciated on both the U.S. and the Soviet sides that it would not be a productive strategy to have the CTB come into port ahead of SALT II. This was because of the evident and mounting difficulty within the United States of maintaining sufficient support, particularly within Congress, for nuclear arms control. Moreover, as relations with the Soviet Union continued to deteriorate, stimulated in part by statements from within the Administration that initiated discussion of linkage between Soviet behavior in the horn of Africa and progress in arms control, the atmosphere for progress in arms control generally worsened.

In this situation, it became easier for those within the Administration fundamentally opposed to a comprehensive test ban to press their objections and to gain support for proposals that at first complicated the negotiations and then made success impossible. (The nature of these objections and the manner in which this internal policy disarray was handled will be discussed in later sections of this paper.) In short, the demise of President Carter's comprehensive test ban initiative, which had started with great promise, was caused by a complex, interacting array of factors. Once they began to operate, they caused a downward spiral that, in hindsight, may well have been unstoppable.

U.S.–SOVIET ASYMMETRY

A significant asymmetry appears to have existed between the United States and the Soviet Union regarding the practical impact of constraints contained in the limited test ban, the threshold test ban, and the comprehensive test ban. Notwithstanding the reputation of the Soviet Union as a country extraordinarily tenacious in refusing to give up anything of military value and in preserving every possible advantage, there is good reason to believe that in the area of test bans that country has consistently been prepared to accept agreements that appear to have been to its relative military and technical disadvantage and that probably had the effect of freezing American advantages. This asymmetry has not prevented purposeful negotiations because of a second and perhaps more important asymmetry—the differences in the way the two countries appear to view the purposes of arms control and the risks of nuclear war.

Test ban constraints, in contrast to some other forms of arms control limitations such as reducing levels of specified weapons, involve the cutting off of a type of weapons-related activity. To assess which of several parties comes off better from a military and technical standpoint, one obviously has to try to judge how advanced each side is in the conduct of the relevant activity when the constraint is imposed, and how easily each party can continue to manage the programs it considers essential. With respect to nuclear warhead testing, it is not possible to have a detailed factual picture of Soviet activities in view of the extreme secrecy surrounding such efforts and the greater opaqueness of Soviet programs after testing moved underground. Nevertheless, some deductions would appear warranted.

With respect to the LTBT of 1963, it seems clear that the Soviet Union was at a technological disadvantage. The United States had tested underground for several years. The Soviet Union had not tested underground at all. Moreover, there can be no question that the United States possessed greater technological sophistication, for example, in miniaturization, permitting it to exploit more fully underground testing. Indeed, in the following years, U.S. underground tests outnumbered those of the Soviet Union more than three to one.

The situation with respect to the TTBT of 1974 is perhaps even more unbalanced in the U.S. favor. Not only did the United States almost surely retain relevant technological advantages for conducting underground testing, now there was a limit that cut off testing underground of larger-yield weapons, on which the Soviet Union places greater reliance than does the United States; at the same time, it permitted testing of smaller-yield weapons, on which the United States places greater reliance. This is not a theoretical point. Observance of the TTBT's 150 kt testing limit by the Soviet Union may be preventing it from perfecting warheads with lighter weight, which would permit it to place more high-yield MIRVed warheads on its very large SS-18 missiles.

As to the CTB negotiations in 1977–80, the situation is perhaps not as clear. But I believe that if a CTBT had been concluded, the technological advantage would almost surely have been with the United States. The United States is at least a generation ahead of the Soviet Union in computer technology, which would be very important in simulations and other weapons work in a no-testing environment. Other forms of American prowess and ingenuity in high technology would also come into play. Of most importance, if a CTBT had been concluded in the 1970s, the Soviets would have been seriously impeded in developing weapons with improved yield-to-weight ratios, a capability that has provided advantages for U.S. forces. For example, an improved ratio means that more of a missile's throw weight can be used for increasingly accurate, heavier guidance systems. Yet the Soviet Union not only negotiated seriously toward a CTBT in 1977–78, it made unprecedented offers for verification procedures in order to facilitate progress.

What could explain this seemingly strange state of affairs? The Soviet Union is not noted for its conduct of an eleemosynary foreign policy. The Soviet Union, or more specifically those leaders who make decisions on its behalf, must believe there are benefits from test bans that are significant enough to counterbalance the continuing opposition, which, as we shall see, has existed on the part of the Soviet military.

I believe that Soviet leaders have pursued test ban negotiations seriously for fundamentally important political reasons—because they have believed that the achievement of agreement in such negotiations could help to establish better relations between the two superpowers (in other words, détente) and that this in turn could reduce the risk of nuclear war.

There obviously exists a major asymmetry or divergence here between the Soviet Union and the United States, one that applies not only to test bans but more broadly in the arms control field. With respect to Soviet SALT policy in the early 1970s, Raymond Garthoff has written:

> Numerous Soviet commentaries stressed the role of SALT in contributing to detente and of both SALT and detente in contributing to a reduction of tensions and of the risks of nuclear war. This accords with the Soviet stress on the *prevention* of war by political means—always given higher attention than by the United States, which stresses more the *deterrence* of war by possession of military means. (Emphases are Garthoff's.)[13]

It would be fair to say that there is not merely an asymmetry, but that there has generally existed a gulf between Soviet and American approaches. The American stress on "deterrence of war by possession of military means," to use Garthoff's phrase, has been manifest in an extraordinary preoccupation with precise calculations of the nuclear "balance," as if war or peace depended on whether one side or the other possessed a hundred more or less of varying types of strategic weapons.

The other side of the coin is that there has generally been an American scorn for, even fear of, agreements with an adversary that are largely of a political character. Part of this aversion is historical, deriving from strong distaste for such documents as the 1928 Kellogg-Briand Pact and nonaggression pacts generally. But more fundamentally, there has been a prevailing American belief in the rightness of all of its actions and consequently a belief that if war comes it must be because of the misbehavior of the adversary. Against such an intellectual, or more accurately, emotional backdrop, it is not surprising that American weapons and arms control policy has focused on maintaining perfection of a nuclear deterrent that will always persuade the adversary that his aggression will be defeated.

The underlying asymmetry between the Soviet and American approaches was suggested to me in a comment made by a Soviet official: "The difference between us is that we know that when the piece of bread falls it will always land on the buttered side." A somewhat more erudite formulation has been offered by Michael MccGwire: "In Moscow, the primary danger is seen as unintended global war, whereas in Washington, the danger is Soviet aggression which, if not deterred, would lead to war. The Western viewpoint is shaped by Munich, the Soviet one by Sarajevo."[14]

The distinction is reflected in how the two sides define what constitutes a stable balance of strategic forces. One student of the subject, Douglas Hart, has described the contrast in the following way:

> The Soviet Union appears to view the uncertainty which attends loss of control over both events and forces as the major destabilizing factor in a crisis. This fear of loss of control evidently applies to the Soviet Union, her Eastern European empire, and to a lesser degree, the United States and her NATO allies. Clearly, this notion of instability places far more emphasis on the specifics of the crisis situation than do Western views, which tend to see activity and especially technology as either stable or unstable independent of particular crisis scenarios.[15]

In the judgment of the Soviet government, the détente relationship established in 1972 has made possible U.S.–Soviet consultations and cooperation that have helped to avert at least one serious threat to peace—the U.S.–Soviet confrontation during the 1973 October War in the Middle East, a confrontation that at one stage involved an alert of U.S. strategic nuclear forces.[16] For the Soviets, the risk of another Sarajevo, whether in the Middle East or elsewhere—the bread falling on the buttered side—is the risk of nuclear devastation of the Soviet homeland. It is understandable that pursuit of détente, including test bans, has seemed to them a sensible policy.

This analysis has argued that the Soviets have been motivated by large political goals in pursuing arms control agreements. But the situation, of course, is very complex. A great many factors come into play that can reinforce, or discourage, Soviet readiness to go forward seriously with a major negotiation, particularly if, as I have argued in the case of test bans, there is a military disadvantage or inconvenience for the Soviets. First of all, Soviet decision makers must feel that the Soviet Union has sufficient numbers and quality of nuclear delivery systems and warheads to constitute an adequate deterrent. Obviously, if the Soviets believed at a particular time that there were grave defects in their nuclear forces that affected over-all performance and that could only be corrected by programs that included warhead testing and development, then they would certainly not, at that time, seriously pursue a comprehensive test ban. Another factor in the equation could be some feeling on the Soviet side that a measure calling for a halt to an activity in which the United States has natural advantages (warhead testing using high technology) may have merit even if it means that the Soviets have to forego the opportunity of trying to catch up.

The political benefits which the Soviets sought from agreements like the CTBT and those of SALT, and from détente, are also more complex than simply reducing the risk of nuclear war. Achievement of such major agreements with the United States has no doubt been regarded by the Soviet leadership as a valuable demonstration that the Soviet Union has arrived at superpower status, alongside the United States. These agreements can also be used by the Soviet government to validate throughout the world its credentials as a country working for peace. These various additional factors may all be valid and have their place in the picture. But the most logical over-all explanation of Soviet test ban policy over the years, in my opinion, is that Soviet leaders concluded that major arms control agreements, including test bans, would contribute to the safety of the Soviet Union—by helping to build a relationship of détente that would lessen the risk of nuclear war.

WEAPONS TECHNOLOGY AND RELIABILITY

Bans on the testing of nuclear explosive devices obviously touch directly on the freedom of the parties to develop and exploit technology. They also create controversies about their impact on the reliability of nuclear stockpiles. These issues are important to our general inquiry because they can affect the readiness of both sides to pursue negotiations seriously and thus have direct bearing on whether new test bans are likely to become a part of the over-all U.S.–Soviet security regime. First, we will look briefly at the three historical episodes we have been examining (LTBT–1963, TTBT–1974, and CTBT–1977-1980).

The LTBT

The case of the LTBT is rather straight-forward.[17] Edward Teller, in particular, argued against the treaty on the grounds that freedom to develop new information should not be impeded. Some asserted that the Soviets would gain from the LTBT because they had previously conducted a large series of atmospheric tests and these would give them an advantage in building ABM systems. And some indulged in even less rigorous assertions, such as "The Soviets must know something that we don't."[18] The steam was taken out of these arguments by the continued permissibility of underground testing under the LTBT and by the vigorous program of testing that was promised in the 1963 safeguards. In the event, the Soviet Union was later seen to have no significant advantage in ABMs. The fact that arguments about technology were not a decisive obstacle to approval of the LTBT was doubtless also due to the great political pressure in favor of the Treaty and the determined leadership of the President.

The TTBT

The TTBT of 1974 was also a fairly simple case. The ability to conduct underground tests up to 150 kt would allow considerable scope for testing of value to the weapons program. There was also an additional safety valve; the TTBT, though signed on July 3, 1974, provided that the 150 kt limit would not become operative until March 31, 1976. In fact, the essential companion treaty, the PNET, was not signed until May 28, 1976. (During the two-year interval, it has been reported that both parties conducted about two dozen tests, perhaps more in the case of the Soviet Union, at yields higher than 150 kt.)[19] Some in the military disliked the treaty. For example, Admiral Elmo Zumwalt, Chief of Naval Operations, indicated in his memoir that he believed the TTBT would freeze a Soviet superiority. The Soviets had tested more big warheads than the United States and since the treaty would prevent the United States from catching up in the testing of these warheads, the Soviets would gain.[20] (This is similar to the argument that the SALT agreement prohibited the United States from building heavy missiles— which it did not wish to do anyway.) Nevertheless, the military did not formally oppose the treaty. Nor did the weapons laboratories.

The CTBT

The inherent conflict between the test ban objective and technological concerns became acute during the CTBT negotiation. Objections to President Carter's policy of achieving an end to all testing (which was also, of course, the official U.S. government policy) were at first subdued. But they intensified after major Soviet concessions suddenly made the CTBT seem more than a distant mirage. The objections centered almost entirely on the need to continue testing in order to maintain the reliability of nuclear weapons in the stockpile. This view was supported by virtually everyone holding an official position in the weapons-building community. Those supporting the CTBT effort argued that nondestructive examination of weapons can identify defects, and reliability can be ensured by replacing components or, if necessary, refabricating the entire weapon. Several distinguished weapons scientists who had formerly held key positions came forward in support of this judgement.[21] As we shall see, a single definitive objective answer is impossible. Nevertheless, the argument that testing might be needed in the future to ensure the effectiveness of the American deterrent was one of the most important factors in swaying the President to authorize a change in position from one favoring a treaty of indefinite duration to a treaty of five years, and then to one of three years—changes that would have permitted a resumption of testing just three years after the treaty's entry into force.

Analysis and Implications

A number of observations should be made regarding the issues raised by this history and their implications for present and future policy:

— The over-all context of test ban negotiations must always be kept in mind. Technology, or the impact on weapons, is only one of many factors operating at any particular time. Therefore, its power to influence the outcome depends on the strength of other factors, such as general political currents and qualities of national leadership. In the LTBT episode the latter factors were strong and positive in behalf of arms control and international political considerations, thus preventing preoccupation with fears regarding technology.

— Major issues regarding technology and reliability are seldom susceptible to definitive, quantifiable answers. For example, what is sufficient reliability? Most warheads are said to be well upward of 90 percent reliable. What is the practical significance if, by some theoretical statistical formula, certain weapons without testing become say 88 percent reliable rather than 94 percent? It should be kept in mind that most of the missile delivery systems, and certainly bombers, will have substantially lower reliability percentages in terms of getting through to the target. Another reliability argument is that someday a whole class of warheads might conceivably fail entirely—that is, "catastrophically"—in the absence of testing. However, the probability of this happening also cannot be predicted. What one winds up with is a situation in which CTB opponents cannot demonstrate the certainty of a significant reliability problem in the future; but CTB proponents equally cannot demonstrate a certainty that there will be no reliability problem.

— Inherent difficulties also exist for CTB proponents in trying to make a virtue of loss in reliability, in arguing that it would be a good thing if both sides' weapons were less reliable because then there would be less likelihood of either side ever deciding to launch a first strike. Similar arguments are made by some partisans of the Strategic Defense Initiative (SDI), who recognize that it probably will never bring perfect defense. They argue, however, that SDI will complicate the calculations of the Soviet Union if it ever contemplates strategic aggression. The Soviet Union, they say, would be able to rely less on the performance of its nuclear weapons, and this would surely be a good thing. The argument that loss in reliability enhances stability, when used to support a CTB, has the same underlying weakness as when it is used to support SDI. In both cases there is an unspoken assumption that the main risk of nuclear war is from a Pearl Harbor type aggression—a premeditated attack launched because of the aggressor's calculation of military advantage. A growing number of observers recognize, however, that the greatest danger is probably a Sarajevo type situation in which confusion, fear, and misperception lead to an uncontrollable catastrophe.[22] In such a situation, an incalculable diminution in the reliability of nuclear weapons might, at best, be irrelevant and, at worst, an aggravating factor leading, for example, to pressures for a heavier initial strike to compensate for any conceivable loss in reliability.

— There has also been considerable confusion over the general impact of a CTBT on the arms race. It has been tempting for many to say that a CTBT is needed to end, or at least curb, the arms race. However, a CTBT in the late 1970s would not have prevented development of the MX, the more accurate D-5 missile for the Trident II submarine, or various types of cruise missiles. The situation as of the late 1970s was that a CTBT had lost much of its original relevance. Many experts, in and out of government, have regarded nuclear testing and weapons design as a mature technology. New factors that affect the over-all performance of nuclear weapons systems and do not require testing of the nuclear explosive have risen greatly in importance: for example, development of a variety of guidance systems that give ballistic and cruise missiles a degree of accuracy undreamed of when the comprehensive test ban first became an accepted arms control objective.

— As to how the Soviets regard technological issues, we have very little hard information, but some deductions can be made. There is evidence that the Soviet military, like the American military, has been cool or hostile to every past test ban negotiation. In fact, during the 1977–80 CTBT negotiations, American participants could clearly observe the hostility of the Soviet military, and this was confirmed in a variety of informal contacts. There were also indications that the Soviet military's opposition to the CTBT was based on virtually the same reasons as those of the U.S. military. (The reasons for the opposition of the American weapons community were revealed fully in leaks to the press and therefore were well known to the Soviets.) Opposition within the Soviet military probably had a combination of causes: concerns about weapons reliability; a desire to continue testing to catch up with U.S. technology; and the preference, common to both sides, for protecting one's own programs rather than limiting the adversary's. These comments should not be taken to indicate that today Soviet military officials perceive no benefits at all from a CTBT. For example, they would almost surely welcome a CTBT's inhibition of part of the American SDI program, the nuclear X-ray laser. (Soviet political interests in test ban constraints, which appear to have been very large factors, are discussed in other sections of this paper.)

In recent years, developments have taken place that have intensified the controversy within the United States over the desirability of the CTB objective. First of all, the U.S. testing program has expanded in its purposes to include new or improved designs for warheads for new delivery systems. There has also been intensified work on, and some public discussion of, so-called "third-generation" weapons.[23] With this resurgence in nuclear weapons work has also come a much greater frankness and assertiveness on the part of government representatives in setting forth the need to test for a wide variety of purposes, including specifically design of new warheads.[24] In addition, authoritative government spokesmen have expressed the view that nuclear weapon testing will be needed as long as there are nuclear weapons and nuclear deterrence. For example, Secretary of State George Shultz has stated, "As long as we rely, as we do, on nuclear weapons as our primary deterrent against war, there will be a need for nuclear testing . . . We won't need any more nuclear testing" when "the elimination of nuclear weapons comes about."[25]

Faced with this assault on the validity of the comprehensive test ban objective, it is not surprising that CTB proponents have argued with increasing vehemence that a CTB is needed to limit future arms competition. That a CTBT would restrain the present

U.S. weapons program (and some possible future programs on the Soviet side) can hardly be questioned. What remains debatable is how significant these restraints would actually be and whether a CTBT is the most practical way to limit future nuclear arms competition. For example, a CTBT would probably not have a major impact on the SDI; the nuclear-pumped X-ray laser is only one of several concepts for a nationwide ballistic missile defense—and one that many feel will prove to be particularly impractical. (Indeed, the partial system that was discussed in spring 1987 by Pentagon proponents of early deployment in the 1990s is based on *nonnuclear* rockets that would destroy incoming missiles by colliding with them.) Other third-generation nuclear weapons may also be of doubtful practicality. Of more immediate importance, if testing were to be cut off at present, there would nevertheless exist tested warhead designs for all the main systems to be introduced in the near future.[26]

One is left with the impression, in the end, that the arguments made by both sides in the test ban controversy are somewhat exaggerated. A CTBT would probably be neither as harmful to reliability as opponents allege nor as beneficial in restraining the arms competition as supporters claim. Yet it would be a mistake to regard the situation as a standoff. For our purposes—assessing the potential of test bans as an element in building a U.S.–Soviet security regime—one ought, realistically, to recognize that there will be a strong American sentiment, whether one agrees with it or not, that for our deterrent to be reliable (that is, for it to protect us from "aggression and blackmail") we should know as precisely as possible how it is likely to work. Whether this sentiment is likely to be overwhelming will depend on the strength of other factors, especially the over-all nature of U.S.–Soviet relations and the quality of presidential leadership.

IMPLEMENTATION AND U.S.–SOVIET COOPERATION

Past test ban efforts have not led to the establishment of regimes of active cooperation and problem-solving. The reasons why they have not done so, and what might or might not have occurred in the way of cooperation if a CTBT had been negotiated in the late 1970s, provide insights that will illuminate a central theme of this essay—that the health of test ban projects has depended to a considerable extent on the direction of U.S.– Soviet relations.

First, when the LTBT was negotiated in 1963, there was simply no perceived need for establishing a special consultative mechanism. It was assumed that monitoring and compliance diplomacy would be relatively straightforward tasks accomplished through the use of national intelligence capabilities and occasional ad hoc diplomatic representations. That expectation has proven sound. No questions have been raised suggesting that the Soviet Union has conducted tests in the atmosphere, in outer space, or under water, although there have been some differences between the two sides on what constitutes "radioactive debris" outside territorial limits (an underground test causing such debris is prohibited by the treaty).

The negotiation of the TTBT in 1974 and the PNET in 1974–76 was an entirely different story. The tasks of measuring accurately the size of underground explosions using distant stations, and of monitoring explosions for peaceful purposes, could be considerably assisted by cooperative measures. Those treaties therefore contemplated extensive cooperation for their implementation, including required data exchanges, provision of information about tests, consultations about ambiguous situations, and arrangements for possible visits to sites of explosions for peaceful purposes. Drawing on the provisions of the SALT I agreements, which had established a Standing Consultative Commission (SCC), consisting of representatives of the two sides and their advisors, the PNET contained provisions for a Joint Consultative Commission (JCC), which was to function in a fashion similar to the SALT commission. As indicated earlier, the 1974 and 1976 treaties have not entered into force and so their cooperative procedures, including functioning of the JCC, have not occurred.

The Reagan Administration has asserted that it is likely that the Soviet Union has violated the TTBT's 150 kt testing limit, which both countries have said they would observe. But there is substantial dissent from this conclusion by experts outside and inside the government. The precise difficulty, which arises from the nature of the geological material around Soviet test sites and from differing estimates as to how strongly seismic waves travel through such material, would be significantly alleviated by entry into force of the treaties and implementation of their cooperative measures. The Reagan Administration has said that even with the agreed procedures uncertainties would remain, and it has been unwilling to tolerate such uncertainties. It has therefore proposed renegotiation of those procedures in ways that would make them more intrusive, including emplacement of on-site monitoring devices for many tests planned to be well below the threshold. The Soviet position, at least until fall 1986, has been that the TTBT and PNET should be ratified, the existing procedures should be given a try, and then additional procedures could be considered if needed. At the U.S.–Soviet exchanges on this subject in Geneva in July and September 1986, it is understood that the Soviets listened to U.S. explanations regarding the technology of the proposed additional verification procedures but that their basic stance did not change. Recent developments, from the October 1986 summit in Reykjavik through spring of 1987, will be discussed toward the end of this essay in the section on "CTB Alternatives." Whether or not the TTBT impasse can be resolved in the future, it is worth noting that major factors in its creation were almost certainly the deepening deterioration of U.S.–Soviet relations which took place in 1980–1984 and the evident desire of the Reagan Administration to dramatize a possible case of Soviet noncompliance.

The 1977–80 CTB negotiation is notable for having gone a considerable way toward working out procedures for the most extensive and intimate cooperation that would have taken place under any arms control agreement. The installation of networks of ten automatically recording seismic stations in the United States and the USSR (as well as some stations on British territories) would have required agreement regarding the manufacture of complex equipment, joint testing of the equipment, testing of the suitability of specific sites, agreement on possible relocation of some sites, establishment of installation schedules and agreement on revisions in the schedule, and possible visits in connection with maintenance and repair problems. To complete this huge joint engineering enterprise, which would have been at the forefront of high technology, would have required several years of continuing cooperation.

Just as unprecedented, and perhaps even more remarkable, would have been the cooperation required for on-site inspection. An inspection was to take place if, following a procedure of inquiries and responses about a particular seismic event, the inquiring party was still not satisfied whether the origin of that event was an earthquake or an explosion, and then chose to request the inspection. To conduct an inspection in the USSR around thirty American officials would have to be transported by the Soviets from a port of entry to the area of inspection. Large amounts of equipment—devices for drilling and for chemical and physical analysis, seismic equipment, metal detectors, and computers—would have to be transported. The Soviets would have to be given an opportunity to examine (and probably take apart) duplicate items of equipment they could choose at random. Joint aerial inspection might have to cover hundreds of square kilometers, and subsequent intensive inspection would take place over tens of square kilometers. To narrow down the search, and then to take samples systematically, the inspection team would have to be present many weeks. During this effort, which might well take place in a remote and mountainous region under harsh climatic conditions, the American inspectors would be dependent in many ways on the cooperation of Soviet officials—for example, for transportation, for photography, for living quarters, for food, for communications, and for emergency assistance in case of accidents.

A significant probability would exist that the result of this intensive and lengthy scouring around on Soviet terrain would be inconclusive. If the United States had requested inspection of an area where a clandestine test had actually taken place, then it is hard to believe the Soviets would permit the inspection team ever to arrive. Assuming no such event had taken place, then the task would become that of proving a negative. What would have been demonstrated is that in all the specific places where the inspection team had collected samples no radioactivity was found. This would not be conclusive proof that there was no radioactivity in some other spot within the area subject to inspection, or just beyond the perimeter.[27]

These technical aspects are exposed here because they could have had far-reaching political significance. It is interesting to ask what might have happened if the CTB negotiation had somehow managed to stumble over the goal line and had produced a ratified treaty in the late 1970s. Assuming that broad political trends in U.S. relations with the Soviet Union were the same as they have been in the early 1980s, how would the CTBT's "cooperative regime" have been implemented? Would the United States have been patient and flexible in working out with the Soviets changes in the plans for completing development and deployment of the internal seismic stations, given the inevitable hitches and delays that would occur? Or would there have been irresistible pressures to attribute these difficulties to Soviet plots to frustrate implementation? Would the United States have asked for an on-site inspection only when there was serious reason to fear that one of the many dozens, or hundreds, of small detected (but not identified) seismic events might have been nuclear in origin? How would the United States have portrayed publicly, and to conservative Congressmen, the results of an inspection that was inconclusive? What might have been the quality of cooperation between Soviet host officials and U.S. inspectors if the United States had frequently requested inspections, had stayed for long periods, and if past inspections had not disposed of suspicions? Would the Soviet officials, who might well be suspicious and highly vigilant under the best of circumstances, have been tempted to make things very tough for the inspectors, which surely would not have been difficult to do in a remote and mountainous region of the USSR? Having viewed the general deterioration in cooperation between the two countries in the early 1980s, there would seem little basis for hopeful answers to such questions.

An important extension of a basic theme of this essay emerges. Not only is a favorable political climate in U.S.–Soviet relations required for negotiation of an agreement like the CTBT, but a favorable climate would also be required for its successful implementation.

The question may be asked whether it would not be possible to negotiate verification procedures less complex and demanding than those outlined above—ones placing less strain on limited human capabilities. It certainly would be; and, indeed, if CTB again were to become a live negotiation, efforts should be made in that direction, such as use of existing seismic equipment that has operated successfully over a period of time. For political reasons, however, it would be very difficult for any U.S. Administration to retreat in its verification demands from those that were largely accepted in a prior negotiation. To simplify greatly would require exceptionally strong presidential leadership, a subject I shall discuss shortly.[28]

It would be logical to expect that negotiation of test bans would involve a process of cumulation, a gradual enlargement of a structure of cooperation. But the reality has been quite different. There has been an elusive image of cooperation which, so far, has only shimmered in the distance.

THE MULTILATERAL DIMENSION

Nuclear test bans, especially a CTB, are normally envisioned as having an important multilateral dimension, mainly to reinforce the global nonproliferation regime. This factor appears to have had some, but not predominant, influence in making possible the 1963 LTBT; it had absolutely no significance for the 1974 TTBT; and promised to be a problematic and complicating element in the 1970–80 CTBT negotiations.

Regarding the 1963 negotiation, one phenomenon stands out. Nonnuclear countries were completely excluded from any participation in preparation of the text of the treaty; yet more than 80 of them lined up to sign the treaty almost immediately after it was concluded. The reason for this was certainly not dedication to nonproliferation but rather a desire to be part of and to support a breakthrough in superpower relations. Widespread adherence was also no doubt facilitated by the knowledge on the part of some that the treaty did not foreclose development of a nuclear option. And, indeed, for India, it did not.

The threshold treaty of 1974 was of necessity a bilateral U.S.–Soviet treaty. Its impact on nonnuclear countries that support nonproliferation was, if anything, more negative than positive. For many of them it was primarily a way the two superpowers could create an appearance of progress but evade their commitment to negotiate a CTB. This was not a matter of significant concern to the two powers. For them, the TTBT, like the earlier LTBT, was primarily important in terms of developing a relationship of détente.

With the CTBT negotiations of 1977–80, the situation became more complicated. The treaty would, of course, be multilateral and the maximum number of accessions would be desirable. But the treaty was being negotiated by only three powers, the United States, the USSR, and Britain. Nonnuclear countries participating in the 40-nation Geneva disarmament conference expected that after the three nuclear powers finished a first draft, they would have an opportunity to negotiate meaningfully on the basis of that draft. But this was far from certain.

For the Soviets the preferred course seemed to be for the three negotiating powers to complete their text, and then open it for signatures with no changes, or very minor ones. The 1963 LTBT precedent was clearly in mind. If, as a result of heightened Third-World sensitivities since 1963 and wounded *amour propre*, only twenty or so countries signed the treaty, so be it. The Soviets were clear that the treaty's main importance lay in its significance as an arms control measure between the United States and the Soviet Union.

The issue is not an easy one and it has broad ramifications if CTB should again become a live negotiation. Ideally, it would be desirable to have meaningful multilateral participation in the negotiations and to wind up with a treaty supported by the international community and still acceptable to the nuclear powers. However, this is easier said than done. From the days of the multilateral negotiations of the Non-Proliferation Treaty (NPT) in the mid 1960s, when negotiations were extremely difficult but produced satisfactory results, there has been a major deterioration in the modus operandi of the multilateral negotiating body. It has increasingly been dominated by a style of politics resembling that of large United Nations bodies—much absorption in procedural matters and widespread preoccupation with unrealizable proposals.

Of more basic importance, there is reason to believe that the type of CTBT that was being worked out in 1977–80 by the three powers could not have had smooth sailing in the multilateral arena. It is often said that a CTBT, from the standpoint of the nonnuclear countries, would be an advance over the NPT because all parties would be treated equally: no testing by anyone. There is some general truth to this. But the type of treaty that was emerging would have had some significant elements of inequality. There would, one way or another, have been some form of exception for very small nuclear explosions, an exception that would have provided practical opportunities almost exclusively for the technically sophisticated nuclear powers. There also would have been special and higher quality verification arrangements for the three nuclear powers, as embodied in their trilateral verification annex.

Elements such as these would surely stimulate considerable opposition in a multilateral forum. It may be that, viewed dispassionately, they do not go to the heart of the CTB enterprise and that responsible diplomats from nonnuclear countries would realize this. But it is also probable that such points could become rallying cries from some nonnuclear countries and that given the increasingly U.N. character of the multilateral disarmament forum these objections would be hard to deal with.

A Hobson's choice results: a good possibility of unruly and unproductive discussion if multilateral negotiations take place, or resentment and a relatively small number of acceding states if they do not. This dilemma is likely to persist whenever CTBT negotiations again become serious.

Whatever the procedures for negotiating a CTBT, it would be unrealistic, in my opinion, to expect that significant ''near-nuclear'' countries are likely to adhere to a CTBT, even if it appears to be a less discriminatory measure than the NPT. Such countries desire to preserve a nuclear option because of basic concerns about threats to their security—threats that in some cases raise deep anxieties about their future existence. They are likely to adhere to a CTBT only if there is some significant change in the over-all security situation that caused them to be determined to preserve their nuclear option in the first place. This is not to suggest that a CTBT would not strengthen the worldwide nonproliferation regime. It would do so in a number of ways. The action of the leading nuclear powers in forswearing nuclear weapon tests would form part of the calculations of many nonnuclear powers regarding the future role of nuclear weapons in the world. A worldwide rule against testing would create a greater degree of hesitancy on the part of some governments in deciding whether to proceed with a development and testing program. And the diplomatic leverage of the United States, the Soviet Union, and others working in behalf of nonproliferation would be strengthened.

However, the likelihood that a CTBT might fail to impose direct legal constraints on most, or perhaps any, of the near-nuclear countries of greatest concern underscores a basic reality: nuclear test bans have had, and will probably continue to have, their primary significance in the context of U.S.–Soviet relations.[29]

THE LEADERSHIP FACTOR

It will be apparent from the preceding discussion that successful negotiation and bringing into force of test bans—almost any type and under almost any circumstances—has been an extremely difficult endeavor for American leaders. For Soviet leaders, it may have been somewhat less so, but nevertheless has had its hazards.[30] The test ban history demonstrates just how crucial the leadership factor has been and what elements have been important to success or frustration. It is appreciated that leadership is one of those qualities that can be judged in completely opposite ways depending upon the policy preferences of the writer. Some will think that President Carter showed weak leadership in letting internal dissent about the CTB get out of hand; others that he was more of a leader when having heard about the risks in a permanent CTB he finally moved, however reluctantly, to limit the damage caused by his earlier enthusiasm. A viewpoint is unavoidable and, therefore, this essay discusses leadership in terms of effectiveness in achieving the goal—when it is official policy—of various types of test bans.

The Limited Test Ban Treaty

A successful outcome was made possible in the 1963 LTBT negotiation by a combination of presidential actions now widely viewed as epitomizing wise and strong leadership:

First, Kennedy shaped a broad policy framework of conciliation with the Soviet Union within which the LTBT was a logical, supporting element. He did this through the American University speech, prepared by speechwriter Theodore Sorensen under the direct supervision of the President but without the usual formal inputs from the bureaucracy.[31]

Second, the President closely participated in the preparations for the negotiations and, once they had begun, he followed their progress on a daily basis. The President apparently mastered sufficiently the details of the issues that he was able to approve realistic and flexible instructions to his senior negotiator, Averell Harriman, in whom he invested considerable authority.

Third, the President had appointed a high-level team of senior foreign policy and security officials who basically pulled in the same direction—that is, in support of his policy. This cohesive teamwork, led by the President, was an essential element in containing potentially destructive divisions, especially from the military.

Fourth, the entire effort benefited from a clear and simple sense of priorities. The LTBT was the only significant arms control negotiation taking place in mid-1963. The full weight of the President and his Administration could be put behind the LTBT enterprise.

And finally, the President pursued an extraordinarily skillful and persistent campaign to influence favorably the Senate and public opinion generally. These efforts ranged, on one level, from obtaining the participation of Senators of both parties in the Moscow signing ceremony to the more general and basic level of presenting to the American people a simple, but compelling, theme for supporting the treaty: it was the beginning of a process of cooperation with the Soviet Union and pushing back the risk of nuclear war. The President's strong assurance of implementation of the safeguards proposed by the Joint Chiefs of Staff helped to engender the widest possible support for the treaty. In all these ways, President Kennedy demonstrated consummate skill as a builder of consensus within the nation.

The Threshold Test Ban Treaty

Fewer lessons in leadership emerge from the TTBT negotiation in mid-1974. President Nixon was then deep in the agonies of Watergate. Nevertheless, a few positive aspects of leadership relating to the TTBT can be discerned. The President seemed to have had a clear sense of purpose—to maintain some momentum for the ailing policy of détente. He recognized that SALT II took priority, but this did not prevent achievement of the relatively modest forward step of the TTBT. The favorable outcome of the TTBT negotiation was probably indirectly facilitated as much as anything by the fact that the SALT II negotiations took the brunt of bureaucratic and public dissent, which, in this case, was not successfully managed.

The Comprehensive Test Ban Treaty

The CTB negotiation of 1977–80 got off to a good start in part because of several positive approaches by President Carter. In early 1977 his strong personal commitment to the project stimulated the bureaucracy in its initial interagency studies to seek flexible solutions to problems like verification. At the outset of negotiations in mid-1977, Carter authorized an unusually capable negotiator, Paul Warnke, to conduct an exploration of issues with the Soviets that paved the way for rapid progress in the next six months.

Other aspects of the President's leadership, however, went a long way to ensuring the subsequent collapse of the negotiations:

— There was no consistent framework of policy toward the Soviet Union within which a CTB could have played a recognized role. The Administration's disarray was symbolized in the manner of preparation of the President's major address on policy toward the Soviet Union at Annapolis in 1978. Speechwriter James Fallows has told the story of how the President spliced together détente-oriented material proposed by Secretary Cyrus Vance with hawkish passages submitted by National Security Advisor Zbigniew Brzezinski.[32] Confusion resulted, or rather was perpetuated, and it is hardly surprising that the Soviets reacted negatively to the speech.
— The President established no over-all plan for conducting arms control negotiations. In addition to the SALT II negotiations, and those on NATO-Warsaw Pact forces in Europe and on chemical weapons, all of which were inherited, the Administration added considerably to the breadth of its arms control agenda by initiating negotiations on the comprehensive test ban, conventional arms transfer, antisatellite weapons, and Indian Ocean demilitarization. Interrelationships and priorities were not thought through at the outset.[33] It is possible that if SALT II had been rapidly concluded during 1977 or early 1978 the momentum generated by a large success would have helped to carry the CTBT to a rapid conclusion. But when SALT dragged on for an unexpectedly long period, it became clear that the CTBT would also have to be slowed down. If the CTBT had been completed first, domestic divisions over arms control would have focused on that treaty, and it was clear that the President,

whose public authority on security issues had been steadily shrinking, needed to husband all his influence for the coming SALT battle.

— The President's difficulties were greatly aggravated by his failure to appoint a top level team that was united in working for his objectives. The secretaries of state and defense and the arms control director worked positively for a CTBT. The President's national security advisor, however, according to his own memoir, did not work to promote the President's comprehensive test ban objective. Brzezinski states:

> I saw them [MBFR and CTB] as non-starters, but out of deference to the President's zeal for them I went through the motions of holding meetings, discussing options, and developing negotiating positions . . . I saw CTB as a likely embarrassment to any effort on our part to obtain SALT ratification. I feared that our legislative circuits would become overloaded if we tried to obtain both SALT and CTB, but I respected the President's deep moral concern over nuclear weapons and I did what I could to move the bureaucratic machinery toward meaningful proposals—*yet ones which would not jeopardize our ability to continue the minimum number of tests necessary for our weapons program.* (Emphasis added)[34]

Obviously, working for proposals that permit tests necessary for the weapons program is not the same as working for a comprehensive test ban. Without the genuine assistance of the national security advisor, the President had no realistic prospect of containing the virtually inevitable opposition of the military and weapons establishment.

— Finally, it must be questioned whether the President, despite his reputation as a glutton for details, understood the issues sufficiently to exercise the leadership necessary to prevent his own initiative from sinking. In his memoir, Carter identifies only one controversial issue with the Soviets—a dispute over how many seismic stations should be installed on British territory, a truly secondary issue. There is no indication that the President understood that his successive decisions to shorten the treaty's duration, combined with other American positions, raised for the Soviets fundamental questions about the seriousness of American purposes and deprived the treaty of much of its value.[35]

The contrasts between the Kennedy and Carter approaches revealed by the above summaries are, of course, very striking. However, in fairness to President Carter it must be acknowledged that he faced circumstances much less susceptible to skillful management than did Kennedy. The 1963 missile crisis not only provided Kennedy with the prestige deriving from a great diplomatic triumph, it created an intensified public awareness of the risk of nuclear war, which would inevitably be a favorable backdrop for pursuit of a nuclear arms control measure.

Carter's effort, in contrast, came after a long steep slide in U.S.–Soviet relations that had badly damaged the basic détente concept. It is also true that a limited test ban, for all the reasons I have discussed, is an infinitely easier step to take than a complete halt to testing. And regarding the governmental environment in which the two presidents pursued their policies, there can be little question but that by Carter's day there was an unprecedented lack of discipline in the executive branch. The growing national polarization over security policy had infested the bureaucracy with the practice of dissenting officials taking their complaints to the press and to sympathetic congressmen—a practice which, if it existed in Kennedy's day, was certainly not rampant.

Several questions remain to be asked. Once President Carter had decided to pursue a CTBT seriously could any particular improvements in managing the CTBT project itself have made a decisive difference in the final outcome? Could more thorough and careful planning have anticipated, and found a way to deal with, the strong objections that arose later within the U.S. bureaucracy? For all the reasons described below the answer is probably no to both questions—although no one, of course, can be certain.

A full-scale interagency study was conducted in the early months of the new Administration. That these preparations failed to come to grips adequately with some key issues is beyond question. For example, no clear policy was worked out on the extent of the exception that should be sought for laboratory-scale experiments. Indeed, this issue was never resolved throughout the negotiation. Regarding verification, certain desiderata were set, but there was no rigorous effort to assess how workable these requirements would be if they ever came to be implemented.

Part of the reason for these planning inadequacies was that for many years the goal of a CTBT, while generally given lip service, was not regarded as a serious negotiating objective, and therefore there was no accumulation of practical expertise and technical studies to help in assessing the practicality of various proposals. But there was another, and perhaps more significant, reason for the incompleteness in planning. The question of coverage of very small explosions was recognized early as both difficult and highly controversial within the bureaucracy. There was a desire therefore to put off this sort of decision until later, when the momentum of the negotiations would force a resolution— one which it was hoped would be favorable to the project. In the event, such hopes were not realized. As to the principal specific issue on which internal U.S. consensus was later to crack, the question of weapons reliability, it should be recognized that those opposed to the CTBT initially muted their objections—in part because of a desire not to cross the new President and in part because of an expectation (and hope) that the negotiation would never get anywhere.

The additional question then arises, could the President, once the strength of internal opposition became known, have successfully bargained, as Kennedy had in 1963, for the support of the Joint Chiefs of Staff and the nuclear weapons laboratories? That, of course, was precisely what the President thought he was doing when he approved cutting the treaty's duration down from an indefinite period to five years and then to three years, and particularly when he decided that the treaty should terminate after its short duration, leaving the participants free to resume testing immediately thereafter. But these changes went a long way toward sinking the project. The United States had thus boxed itself in.

Could this trap have been avoided by other well-timed offers of vigorous support for the weapons laboratories and the weapons program generally? Conceivably, if such efforts had taken place against the backdrop of successful presidential leadership in pursuing SALT, in maintaining a strong defense, and in managing U.S.–Soviet relations. But I have used the word "conceivably" because the depth of antagonism for a CTBT was so great that quite possibly no bureaucratic compromises would have stuck, short of destroying the treaty's essential character as a CTBT.

What does seem clear is that such opportunities as might have existed for effective leadership steadily shrank as the SALT II enterprise dragged on and détente deteriorated. For many people, including this writer, a good part of the cause of SALT II's prolongation, and thus the CTBT's demise, must be attributed to misjudgement in the Carter Administration's initial 1977 SALT positions and its mishandling of relations with the Soviet Union; and these developments, of course, also reflected qualities of leadership.[36]

As I noted earlier, there was general agreement within the government (which the Soviets almost certainly understood and never took issue with) that it was politically impractical for the United States to present a completed CTBT to the Senate before SALT. As the SALT II negotiations extended through 1978 and then into 1979, the CTBT negotiations were not deliberately put aside. They were simply allowed to stall. There was thus no compelling need to reconsider the crucial decisions of duration and termination (made in mid-1978) or to settle on a reasonable approach to the definition of laboratory-size explosions. When SALT II finally was concluded in mid-1979, the compelling need within the United States was to concentrate all possible political capital on getting that treaty ratified. In the meantime, the CTBT negotiation was kept barely alive on life-support systems and by then it is hard to see how any effort of leadership could have revived it.

Lessons for the Future

However one assesses the different challenges to leadership in past negotiations, there would seem to be certain constants in leadership qualities that must exist if a President is to have any hope of successfully pursuing a project like the comprehensive test ban. The President must establish an over-all policy framework for relations with the Soviet Union in which the test ban is not an ''embarrassment'' (to use Brzezinski's word) but a logical, supporting element. He must be able to explain this policy convincingly not only to his immediate subordinates but to the public as a whole. He must appoint and maintain a team of top-level civilian officials, all of whom put their shoulders to achieving his policy.

When strategy for the negotiations is prepared and negotiations are actually carried out, the President must take effective charge of the enterprise. Only he can ensure that realistic negotiating goals are established (such as verification procedures that are likely to work in practice), and only he can grant the negotiator sufficient flexibility so that the negotiation is not dragged out to satisfy tenacious bureaucratic longings for tertiary points. And the President must maintain effective leadership throughout the negotiation, for only he can enforce a continuing discipline within the bureaucracy in behalf of his goal.

Of all the challenges for presidential leadership one stands out as paramount. For the American people and the Congress to support arms control—which unavoidably means compromise and imperfect agreements with the Soviet adversary—they must feel a certain amount of confidence about the nation's over-all security and they must feel relatively comfortable about doing business with the Soviets. From the platform of his office, held in great esteem by most Americans, the President has tremendous potential for influencing these American attitudes. President Kennedy, in his 1963 American University speech, used his prestige, which had been enhanced by the successful handling of the Cuban missile crisis, to speak inspiringly to the American people about the need and the opportunities for conciliation with the Soviet Union. No clear message of this sort was delivered by President Carter. Unfortunately, for many Americans the total impression of his national security efforts was one of uncertainty, lack of grip, and ineffectual indignation. Whether or not such an impression was justified, the end result was leadership that did not facilitate arms control but rather undermined it.

Leadership of the sort necessary to achieve major arms control agreements, especially a comprehensive test ban, is obviously a tall order. But even if a future President were able to perform up to such standards, that would not by itself ensure success. If, for example, the Joint Chiefs of Staff maintained formal opposition to a CTBT, even in the face of skillful presidential leadership, it is questionable whether a negotiated treaty would be approved by the Senate. Indeed, there has never been Senate approval of an arms control agreement in such circumstances. It is, therefore, inevitable that a future President even if he is positive about the test ban objective will have to determine whether it seems worthwhile to invest so much effort and prestige in such a difficult project—particularly if he is also pursuing demanding negotiations to limit and reduce further the levels of strategic nuclear weapons. The question we will therefore consider in the next and final section of this paper is: Under what circumstances in the future might skillful and dedicated presidential leadership in behalf of a comprehensive test ban result in conclusion and entry into force of such a treaty?

FUTURE PROSPECTS

In assessing the prospects for achieving U.S.–Soviet agreement on future test bans, five related topics will be discussed: present and future Soviet commitment to a CTBT; the possibility of a CTBT as a separate, early agreement; CTBT as a complement or follow-on to a major strategic arms treaty; CTBT in the context of reassessing the purposes of nuclear weapons; and partial restraints on testing.

Future Soviet Commitment

Soviet desire to have a CTBT and willingness to pay a serious price in cooperative verification measures are essential conditions for achieving a CTBT. Those conditions almost certainly existed throughout the Brezhnev era. They appear, with Mikhail Gorbachev's espousal of a CTBT, to continue to exist today.

The most interesting recent event has been the unilateral moratorium on nuclear testing undertaken by the Soviet Union in August 1985. In August 1986, after two earlier extensions and despite continued American testing, Chairman Gorbachev announced continuation of the moratorium until January 1, 1987.[37] This unilateral and unreciprocated halt in testing stimulated significant dissent within the Soviet Union. On two occasions Gorbachev made the somewhat unusual admission in public statements that his decisions to extend the moratorium were accompanied by internal questioning as to its wisdom.[38] Following the August 1986 extension, the chief of the Soviet General Staff, Marshal Sergei F. Akhromeyev, stated in a news conference that the moratorium caused "damage" to the Soviet Union and gave the United States a military advantage.[39]

What led the leader of the Soviet Union to initiate and sustain this remarkable self-restraint—unmatched throughout the nuclear era? The ostensible purpose, of course, was to bring about an agreed U.S.–Soviet halt to all testing. But there are historical and other factors that make one hesitant to accept such a simple explanation. In the 1977–80 period the Soviets were not in favor of a moratorium to accompany the negotiations. Indeed, they discouraged its consideration. That was probably because early in the negotiations there appeared to be a good chance a CTBT would be achieved and they desired to continue testing to store chestnuts, as it were, for the winter ahead—a winter that at first looked as if it would be permanent. In 1985–86, unless they had lost all touch with political realities, the Soviets could not have expected that the Reagan Administration would be prepared to resume serious negotiations intended to achieve a CTBT. Proposing a moratorium, and accepting one for a period of time on their own testing, was therefore, at least in part, a way for the Soviets to demonstrate their pro-arms control stance and the U.S. government's refusal to negotiate.

Although the Soviet Government ended its moratorium with a test in late February 1987, the episode is likely to have longer range effects, not all of which may be positive for future negotiations. There are likely to be important Soviet officials who will question what was gained by their government's unprecedented self-restraint. It now seems a fair assumption that the moratorium did not produce major concrete gains for the Soviet Union, either in arms control or in the sphere of West European politics. As to the Soviet military, one should not dismiss the degree of pain that was probably caused by a forced interruption of nineteen months in the testing program—one that normally involves about twenty or more tests a year. Whatever some arms control theorists may think about the stability of deterrence with existing weapons, the military establishments of both countries undoubtedly set great store in their activities to improve their nations' security. They do not think they are wasting their time in such major efforts as the nuclear testing programs.[40]

For all of these reasons, the entire episode is not likely to redound to Gorbachev's credit. Whatever his motives in originally launching the moratorium, it does not enhance the prospects for future serious negotiations for the leader of one of the two great nuclear powers to be frustrated and embarrassed as a result of a major initiative. The episode can be used within the Soviet Union by those hostile generally to arms control to prove that efforts to get somewhere with the United States, even when the Soviet Union itself undergoes sacrifice, are futile. And one cannot exclude the danger that the Soviet leadership may try to "recoup" through other maneuvers not primarily intended to promote serious arms control.

These possibilities, while admittedly speculative, seem worth sketching out because it is important to understand that not all arms control gestures, particularly public ones, are necessarily positive. In the long history of test ban diplomacy there have been many initiatives (some might be called maneuvers) which in the end have led to frustration and resentment. I cannot help but fear that the Soviet moratorium has more negative, than positive, potential. Of course, the extent of any such negative impact would be affected by whether the failure of the moratorium comes to typify a pattern of unproductive diplomacy, a question I shall discuss more fully below.

Beyond specific questions associated with the moratorium, there may be more basic reasons for concern about the future possibility of negotiating a CTBT. A great deal of water has flowed over the dam since the promising days of CTBT in 1977–78. There have been, for the Soviets, the sour experiences with SALT II ratification, with the plethora of American charges of Soviet violations, with the continued U.S. refusal to ratify the TTBT and PNET, with American introduction in START negotiations of patently one-sided proposals, and with U.S. launching of an SDI program fundamentally contrary to the purposes of the ABM Treaty. It would hardly be surprising if the Soviets had developed a deep skepticism about American ability to carry through and remain constant with any great arms control enterprise. Such skepticism would naturally create questions for the Soviet Union as to whether they could expect that substantial Soviet investments in forthcoming positions, for example, on verification, would have a reasonable chance of paying off in a satisfactory end result, including a ratified treaty. Their 1977–78 CTB effort did not.

Notwithstanding the large number of Soviet arms control initiatives, I believe we must assume that such basic skepticism exists. To fail to assume this is to presume an improbable degree of insouciance in Soviet policy making. It is also logical to believe that this Soviet skepticism will not readily be dissipated if a new American Administration takes office with what appears to be a positive and conciliatory approach to arms control. The problem on the American side, as the Soviets must see it, has extended over much of the last fifteen years and therefore cannot be dismissed as merely a quirk of the 1980s.[41]

These comments should not be taken as suggesting that the Soviets no longer favor a CTBT or will cease to have an interest in one within a few years. Rather they are intended to underscore that, beyond the difficulty of many of the substantive issues inherent in the CTBT, there may well be larger forces that add to the difficulties and create Soviet hesitations, skepticism, and even greater than normal reluctance to make essential concessions. Nor should these comments be taken to suggest that there are no current arms control activities which, if successful, might cause a turning toward a more favorable arms control environment. Indeed, if U.S.–Soviet negotiations regarding intermediate-range nuclear forces (INF), which as of mid-1987 are considered by both sides to be their most promising arms control negotiations, result in conclusion of a treaty in 1987 or 1988 and relatively prompt U.S. ratification, that would go some distance to improving future long-range prospects. In addition, such a success would also tend to dilute the possible impression within the Soviet Union, described earlier in connection with the failure of the moratorium, that Gorbachev has pursued unproductive and losing arms control policies with the United States. At the same time, it should be stressed that the current optimism about INF negotiations will surely be viewed, at least within the Soviet side, as caused by major Soviet concessions, including particularly acceptance of the U.S. proposal of a zero level of INF weapons. Accordingly, if INF negotiations fail and if this appears to most observers (or at least to the Soviets) to be a consequence of U.S. rigidity—for example, over verification—or of any other type of U.S. or allied reluctance, then there is likely to be a reinforcement of the impression— aroused earlier in the test ban moratorium episode—that there is no point in making concessions to the United States. This, in turn, would almost certainly constitute an additional setback for the prospects for arms control, including achievement of further test ban constraints.

To summarize, a period of building will be needed—the building of mutual confidence in a steady and durable arms control process. This cannot be done by any single set of arms control negotiations, but will require progress on many fronts, on a broad front of arms control and on an even broader political front.

CTBT as a Separate Early Agreement

For many Americans who are eager to promote progress in arms control the CTBT appears to be an attractive short-cut, a way to bypass the protracted struggles inherent in strategic nuclear arms control and to achieve a quick, important agreement. It is popularly believed that virtually all of a CTBT was agreed upon in 1977–80 and since the Soviets seem to remain eager all that is needed is a change of heart by the U.S. government. However, as we have seen, although most of the wording of a CTBT was previously agreed, a number of key issues were not. Moreover, there are additional reasons, particularly affecting the American side of the equation, why giving early priority to a CTBT is not likely to be a successful strategy.

A comprehensive test ban may be described as the type of arms control measure that has a general, or indirect, effect on arms competition. It does not ensure that numbers of weapons are reduced, or even stay at a constant level. It does not result in the reduction of any particular type of weapon that either side finds especially threatening. It does not, in short, improve the stability of the existing balance of strategic forces. In other words, the case cannot be made that a CTBT would lessen the vulnerability or improve the survivability of nuclear forces. What it would do is to impose a blanket restraint on one weapons-related activity—and, as we have seen, not the activity most central to the development of new, more accurate missiles.

It is hard to believe that indirect, general arms control will have the attractions for many Americans in influential positions that it had a quarter century ago. When the limited test ban was negotiated in 1963, it was the first major agreement in which the two leading powers were able to place restraints on their nuclear arsenals. The agreement was thus much more than a technical measure. As we saw earlier, it was a symbolic step that represented a much longed-for turning in the relations of the two countries. In those days there was not a large repertoire of potentially available symbols. Today, the range of possible agreements that could serve this purpose is much larger, including any of the half-dozen or so major areas of arms control.

Since the days of the LTBT, arms control has also progressed greatly in its complexity and its direct relevance to the weapons programs of the two countries. In particular, there have been nearly two decades of SALT and START negotiations in which there have been efforts to deal with specific concerns of each side about the nuclear weapons of the other. Such arms control endeavors are bound to be more absorbing, and to appear more significant, to many Americans than indirect arms control of uncertain impact.[42]

It may be acknowledged that the general indirect advantages that would come from a CTBT—in its political aspects and its effects on nuclear proliferation, and in its long-range constraints on weapons development—are strongly desired by a great many Americans. But this does not ensure American approval of a CTBT if one should be negotiated. The decisive test of success depends on whether two-thirds of the Senate will approve a treaty. And that in turn depends not merely on whether those already converted vote for it but whether enough centrist and somewhat conservative Senators also vote for it. As has been indicated, there would inevitably be objections of all sorts. And some of these would not be easy for many Senators to dismiss, coming, as they would, from officials entrusted by the nation to provide for its security. I believe we must regard the outcome as at best quite chancy. And one thing that certainly would be bad for the building of better U.S.–Soviet relations and the rebuilding of a beneficial arms control process would be U.S. rejection of another major agreement.

CTB as a Complement to a Strategic Nuclear Treaty

Are there any circumstances then in which the CTB objective might be realized? The answer has already been implied. A CTBT might have its best opportunity if it accompanies or follows a major strategic arms limitation treaty. Assuming almost any of the types of strategic treaty that have been widely discussed in this decade, whether a fairly modest improvement of SALT II or something more ambitious along the lines of recent U.S. and Soviet START proposals, it should be possible to show how the CTBT would reinforce those quantitative and qualitative constraints. For example, a CTBT would strengthen any direct, or indirect, limitation on the throw-weight of Soviet ICBMs, which has been a long-standing U.S. objective. This is because a CTBT would prevent the Soviets from testing warheads with improved yield-to-weight ratios and thus make it harder for them to use their existing missile throw-weight more effectively. In ways such as these, the CTBT would be shown as contributing directly, along with the new strategic treaty, to immediate national security objectives.

These arguments would not, of course, counter directly the inevitable objections regarding loss in reliability of the weapons for deterrence. In fact, some CTB opponents could be counted upon to assert these objections with increased vigor on the grounds that with fewer weapons following the reductions required by a new strategic treaty it is all the more important to be sure that the remaining weapons will work as intended. However, the reliability argument might still be less important in the over-all complex of considerations. Moreover, it is probably not testing for reliability that most CTB opponents really want, but rather freedom to make new, improved weapons—a goal that would have decreasing justification against the backdrop of a new strategic treaty that placed comprehensive limits on the future competition. In this situation there would be the best chance of handling reliability concerns by promising strong government efforts, and achieving Congressional support for them, to maintain reliability through nonexplosive testing programs and also by providing incentives for maintaining high-quality personnel at the laboratories.

Reassessing the Purposes of Nuclear Weapons

There is one other circumstance in which it would be possible for the United States to give full support to a CTBT. That circumstance cannot be accorded a high probability of occurring in the near future but it will be briefly summarized here since it involves issues of great importance that deserve public discussion. If a national review were to take place regarding the purposes for which we possess nuclear weapons and if that reassessment resulted in a national consensus that these weapons had essentially no useful purpose beyond deterring their use by others, then a CTBT (and a number of other neglected arms control measures) would become feasible. Indeed, there would also probably cease to be a need for elaborate and somewhat impractical verification schemes designed to thwart farfetched cheating scenarios. It would become clear that the weapons we already have are more than sufficient to meet these much less demanding requirements. Whether the Soviets could manage to cheat with an occasional reliability test or even a test for a new device would become inconsequential in so far as our military security was concerned.

A proposal by Morton Halperin urging a basic shift in how we think about nuclear weapons was published in the spring of 1987.[43] It argues that the risk of nuclear war would be greatly lessened and American security promoted by ceasing to regard nuclear explosives as weapons with which wars can be fought. It describes how the proposal would be implemented with respect to Europe, the U.S.–Soviet strategic confrontation, and Third World conflicts. An attractive aspect of the presentation is that it describes first the desired purposes and strategy for nuclear weapons and then the logical arms control consequences that would flow therefrom, including the appropriateness of a comprehensive test ban. Unfortunately, the opposite approach is all too often taken. A desired arms control end is assumed to be beneficial and then all of its consequences are also assumed to be advantageous. Manifestly, arms control has a nearly crushing burden when it is thrust forward as the leading edge to force changes in basic national security strategy.

As indicated earlier, there may be little likelihood that changes along the lines urged by Halperin will soon be adopted. But for reasons that far transcend the issue of arms control, the subject has been long overdue for serious public attention. According to a recent study of public understanding of nuclear weapons issues, about 80 percent of the public believes that the reason the United States possesses nuclear weapons is solely to prevent their use by the Soviet Union.[44] Few people realize that the United States has a wide variety of plans for initiating nuclear conflict. And most are incredulous or outraged when they occasionally hear about plans for waging nuclear war over an extended period of time. Absolutely profound questions are raised about the functioning of a democratic nation when its government amasses the greatest destructive power in history—power which it now appears can destroy life on the planet—and the people of that democracy do not have a reasonably clear picture of what purposes its government has in mind for that power.

CTB Alternatives

Faced with the difficulties of achieving a CTB, the possibility of seeking lesser constraints on testing should be briefly considered. The most positive alternative of this sort would involve U.S. ratification of the TTBT and PNET, in their present form, which would result in their entry into force, followed by negotiation of a new threshold below the present 150 kt limit. A commitment could be taken to consider further periodic lowering of the limit. The greatest merit of this approach would be the favorable political impact on U.S.–Soviet relations—especially from bringing the two treaties into force. A knowledgeable Soviet official told me that Americans generally had no idea how deeply insulting it was to Soviet officials to negotiate seriously for years on an arms control treaty, making concessions to bring it to a conclusion, and then to be told by a subsequent American government that their work simply wasn't good enough.

But it must be added that there are limitations to this course which are often not recognized. Lowering the threshold by a modest amount, say to 100 kt, while positive symbolically and therefore worth doing, would accomplish relatively little in limiting weapons development and almost nothing in strengthening the nonproliferation regime. On the other hand, a drastic reduction, say to 5–10 kt, would probably elicit opposition from the U.S. military and weapons establishment almost as fierce as against a CTBT. One can expect the idea of a meaningfully low threshold to appear tolerable to many in the weapons community only when the specter of the far greater "evil," a CTBT, looms as a real prospect—as was the case in late 1977 and early 1978.

In addition, effective verification gets more critical, but not necessarily easier to negotiate, as the threshold gets lower. For example, at the 150 kt level, there is little security significance if there is occasional uncertainty over whether a test was, for example 180 or 200 kt. But at a 10 kt threshold, anxiety would be great if the uncertainty extended to 30 kt. The United States would almost surely desire more effective and intrusive verification procedures. But it must be questioned how feasible it would be to achieve such verification, particularly if tighter partial restraints are not primarily what the Soviets seek (as contrasted with a CTBT) and if the United States continues to be unwilling to acknowledge that the ultimate goal of tighter restraints is a CTBT (one not conditioned on the elimination of nuclear weapons).

Another possible partial testing restraint is an annual quota of tests—perhaps a descending quota over time. However, this idea would, if anything, be harder to implement than a descending threshold. First of all, as with the threshold, if the limit were modest, say ten to fifteen tests per year, little would be achieved; but if it were severe, for example, two or three tests a year, opposition within the United States could be expected to be strenuous. But of more importance, verification difficulties would be even greater than with a lowered threshold. There would be two problems. First, it would be hard to distinguish single from multiple explosions unless there was close observation of the test and its preparations. Second, and more serious, fears would exist in the United States that in order to evade the quota the Soviets might conduct small explosions clandestinely without detection. One could argue that to provide reassurance on this score, all the verification needed for a CTBT would also be needed for a quota agreement.

In his address before the U.N. General Assembly on September 22, 1986, President Reagan stated: "In association with a program to reduce and *ultimately eliminate* all nuclear weapons we are prepared to discuss ways to implement a step-by-step parallel program of limiting and ultimately ending nuclear testing." (Emphasis added.)[45] This proposal required, as a first step before negotiation of additional partial testing restraints, agreement on expanded verification procedures for the TTBT and PNET. In addition, the wording of the proposal tied gradual limitations on testing to agreement on a program to reduce and eliminate nuclear weapons. This, as the postwar history of arms control amply demonstrates, must be deemed extremely unlikely. Gradual partial constraints on testing should be viewed as sound and potentially feasible by themselves, or in conjunction with gradual steps of strategic nuclear arms control. But they can only be viewed as rhetoric if tied to goals that are virtually impossible.

Just as the Reykjavik summit was about to open in October 1986, the White House announced that the President would ask the Senate in early 1987 to give its approval to the TTBT and the PNET, with the understanding that the President would not actually ratify the treaties until the Soviet Union agreed to additional verification measures that would be attached to the treaty as a protocol. The Soviet leader was also to be informed of the President's proposal that following ratification of the two treaties there should be parallel negotiations on reducing and ultimately eliminating nuclear weapons and on limiting and ultimately ending nuclear testing.[46] There have been widely varying reports as to how much of a meeting of the minds occurred on these ideas at Reykjavik. It is understood that the two sides worked on, but did not fully agree on, a joint paper that had the character of an agenda.

During the spring of 1987 a number of significant developments took place. As requested by the President, the Senate Committee on Foreign Relations held hearings in January on the TTBT and PNET. The committee recommended that the Senate give its advice and consent to ratification and was prepared to support the President in seeking additional verification. However, a dispute with the Administration remained unresolved as to whether, as desired by the committee, the Senate's approval would now be final or whether, as desired by the Administration, a second Senate vote would be needed after negotiation of the additional verification procedures. The dispute led to questioning of the Administration's good faith in seeking ratification of the treaties. As of May 1987, it is uncertain whether or when the treaties will be brought to the full Senate for action.[47]

As to the U.S.–Soviet negotiations in Geneva, there have been some signs in the first four months of 1987 of new flexibility on the Soviet side. The Soviets reportedly shifted their position in April by offering to discuss at the same time both strengthening the verification of the TTBT and working out lower limits on permitted underground testing. They no longer insisted that work also take place concurrently on a CTBT— provided that the work on new partial limits be recognized as taking place in the context of moving towards a CTBT.[48] However, it is understood that the United States has continued to insist on its preferred sequence for discussions, that is, improvements in TTBT verification must come first. In addition, it is understood that the United States has not been willing to endorse the goal of a CTBT except in conjunction with the elimination of all nuclear weapons.

The Soviet Union has also been reported to have suggested a procedure for calibration explosions to assist in monitoring the TTBT under which the United States and the Soviet Union would each bring one of its own nuclear devices onto the test site of the other country where the device would be detonated.[49] The technical and administrative aspects of this innovative idea will have to be explored by the delegations in Geneva. It is therefore not possible to say at this time whether this potential improvement in the reliability of calibration shots, and thus in verifiability of the TTBT, will satisfy the U.S. requirement for strengthening the treaty or, alternatively, whether this new Soviet initiative might also herald Soviet willingness to consider, or at least participate in, some joint experiments to test U.S. ideas for techniques to monitor individual explosions.

The possibility cannot be excluded that if larger political pressures come into play in late 1987 or in 1988—for example, in connection with a Reagan-Gorbachev summit to conclude an INF treaty—there could also be agreement on some aspect of the testing issue, such as initiation of a joint scientific program to test verification techniques or even conceivably some concrete agreement on strengthening TTBT verification procedures. But regardless of the likelihood of such developments, given the present policies of the two governments, the possibility of their agreement on stricter limitations on underground testing must be considered remote.[50]

In the last 23 years, a comprehensive test ban has been pursued seriously by the United States and the Soviet Union only once—during the Carter Administration—and only for less than a year at the outset of the negotiations in 1977–78. That negotiation was notable for its prolonged demise. Since the LTBT in 1963, there has been only one effort to achieve additional partial constraints on testing, the 1974–1976 negotiation of the TTBT and PNET. Those treaties, although signed, have never entered into force. While their main prohibitions are now being observed, they have also contributed to great power contention.

Can there be a realistic hope of achieving a comprehensive test ban three or four years from now or thereafter? Or is a CTBT destined to remain a chimerical vision supported more by nostalgia than by realism? Will there be a reasonable prospect of achieving new significant limitations, such as a gradual lowering of the 150 kt level for underground explosions? Or will even this more modest objective remain frustrated by conflicting goals for strategic arms control and by larger antagonisms in the U.S.–Soviet relationship? In sum, can the objective of constraining nuclear testing again become a positive element in a mutual U.S. and Soviet effort to lessen the risk of nuclear war?

The answers to these questions will depend on a large number of unpredictable factors. But history and logic would appear to tell us a few things pretty clearly. For the United States, if the objective of limiting nuclear tests can be integrated into American foreign and security policy as a supporting element, it may then have a chance of surviving all the difficulties with which it is inherently burdened. And if that American foreign and security policy includes commitment to building a relationship with the Soviet Union of expanding agreements in the common interest, including an arms control process of enduring achievements, then there is reason to hope that the Soviet commitment to testing restraints on reasonable terms will remain.

But if the CTBT, or even lesser restraints, are pursued by the United States without a backdrop of such policies, there is reason to fear that frustration, or worse, will result. Indeed, the effort would be as hazardous as trying to climb a ladder when it is leaning against nothing.

APPENDIX

A *nuclear test ban* or *nuclear weapon test ban* traditionally refers to limits only on testing of nuclear warheads or explosive devices, not to other parts of weapons such as missiles or guidance systems.

A *comprehensive* test ban has generally meant a prohibition of testing in all physical environments, that is, underground, in the atmosphere, in outer space, and under water. Negotiations on a comprehensive ban over the years have usually not had the objective, at least for the United States, of prohibiting very small detonations. Some of these have been described as "laboratory experiments." But some could simply be very small weapons-related tests. The reason for seeking to exclude them has been the extreme difficulty of verifying whether such explosions occur and the fact that some of them can have scientific purposes not directly related to weapons. The problem of whether and how to specify this type of exemption has haunted, and occasionally plagued, negotiations on a comprehensive ban from the mid-1950s through the CTB negotiations in the late 1970s.

Nuclear testing may be conducted to develop nuclear explosives for a variety of peaceful purposes, such as earth moving to build canals or harbors, or extracting oil from oil shales. The Soviet Union has generally wished not to impede such possibilities, asserting that the objective of negotiations should be a "nuclear *weapon* test ban." But the United States, which has deemed such programs impractical and has therefore abandoned them, has successfully insisted on prohibitions that have the effect of ruling out any tests or explosions for peaceful purposes that could have value for weapons-related work. The technical and diplomatic ways in which this has been done in the different negotiations are complex. These issues do not relate directly to the themes of this essay and therefore a description of them is not included. Moreover, it does not now seem likely that they would be a significant obstacle to further progress if other problems relating to possible future testing constraints can be successfully managed.

Finally, as to the weapons-related purposes of nuclear testing, these can be thought of in three major categories. The first is testing to develop new weapons, which includes both tests to gain knowledge leading to new designs and tests of new designs as they are being developed. The second category is "weapons effects" tests, which has involved nuclear explosions to test the effects on people and equipment of blast, heat, radiation, and fallout. The third category of testing, which has been carried out relatively infrequently, is to maintain the reliability of nuclear weapons in the existing stockpile. This may involve a test of a warhead at random to reveal a defect, or a test to assist in correcting a problem ascertained through nondestructive examination of warheads.

Some persons refer to a slightly larger number of purposes for testing. For example, testing to gain new knowledge can, if one wishes, be called a separate category, rather than a part of testing to develop new weapons. Or testing to improve the safety of weapons, for example, by incorporating "insensitive high explosives" in the warheads, can be listed separately, although such improvements normally require new designs and can therefore be thought of as development testing.

Two works that provide for the nontechnical reader a full discussion of the purposes of testing and the arguments of CTB opponents and proponents regarding their relative importance are the following: National Academy of Sciences, *Nuclear Arms Control: Background and Issues* (Washington, D.C.: National Academy Press, 1985), pp. 204–215; and Herbert York and G. Allen Greb, *The Comprehensive Nuclear Test Ban,* Discussion Paper No. 84 (Santa Monica, Calif.: California Seminar on Arms Control and Foreign Policy, June 1979).

Notes

1. The texts of the LTBT and of the Threshold Test Ban and Peaceful Nuclear Explosions Treaties are contained in *Arms Control and Disarmament Agreements,* 1982 Edition (U.S. Arms Control and Disarmament Agency, Washington, D.C.). The LTBT and the Threshold Test Ban Treaty may also be found in The Stanford Arms Control Group, *International Arms Control: Issues and Agreements,* Coit Blacker and Gloria Duffy, eds. (Stanford, Calif.: Stanford University Press, 1984), second edition. The latter contains a full narrative account of the post-World War II effort to control nuclear arms, including the long effort to limit nuclear testing.

2. The fullest account of the events leading up to the LTBT, its negotiation, and ratification is by Glenn T. Seaborg in *Kennedy, Khrushchev, and the Test Ban* (Berkeley, Calif.: University of California Press, 1981). At the time of the negotiation Seaborg was chairman of the U.S. Atomic Energy Commission. I have drawn heavily on Seaborg's account, including his quotations of U.S. officials regarding the LTBT's negotiation and ratification.

3. See W. W. Rostow, *The Diffusion of Power* (New York: Macmillan, 1972), pp. 177–81, which includes Rostow's account of his dinner conversation with Soviet Ambassador Anatoli Dobrynin. Rostow was then chairman of the Department of State's Policy Planning Council.

4. A full historical study of the debate within the United States over test-ban policy in the 1950s, including the fallout issue, is contained in Robert A. Divine, *Blowing on the Wind: The Nuclear Test Ban Debate, 1954–1960* (New York: Oxford University Press, 1978).

5. William G. Hyland, *Soviet-American Relations: A New Cold War?* (Santa Monica, Calif.: The Rand Corporation, 1981), p. 19.

6. For a development of the thesis that post-World War II arms-control efforts have generally prospered or declined depending on whether or not the United States and the Soviet Union

were seeking to improve their over-all relationship, see Alan F. Neidle, "The Rise and Fall of Multilateral Arms Control: Choices for the United States," in *Arms Control: The Multilateral Alternative,* Edward C. Luck, ed. (New York: New York University Press, 1983), p. 7.

7. Henry Kissinger, *Years of Upheaval* (Boston: Little, Brown, 1982), p. 1167.

8. Raymond L. Garthoff, *Detente and Confrontation: American-Soviet Relations from Nixon to Reagan* (Washington, D.C.: Brookings, 1985), p. 427. This work is notable for its comprehensive historical and analytical treatment of détente over two decades.

9. Richard Nixon, *RN: The Memoirs of Richard Nixon* (New York: Grosset & Dunlap, 1978), pp. 1036–37.

10. Kissinger, *Years of Upheaval,* p. 1168.

11. From an unpublished manuscript by Joel S. Wit of Washington, D.C. Wit conducted interviews with senior Administration officials.

12. Garthoff, *Detente and Confrontation,* pp. 756–59, contains one of the fullest accounts of the 1977–80 negotiations.

13. Raymond L. Garthoff, "BMD and East-West Relations," in *Ballistic Missile Defense,* Ashton B. Carter and David N. Schwartz, eds. (Washington, D.C.: Brookings, 1984), p. 308.

14. Michael MccGwire, "Can We End the Cold War?" in *Before the Point of No Return,* Leon Wofsy, ed. (New York: Monthly Review Press, 1986), p. 106. MccGwire expands on this idea in *Military Objectives in Soviet Foreign Policy* (Washington, D.C.: Brookings, 1986), pp. 362–64. In this major new work, in which he focuses on the Soviet way of thinking, MccGwire describes the three paramount Soviet objectives as avoiding world war, the retention of power by the Communist party, and preserving the capacity for independent national action. MccGwire's thesis is that these three are sufficient and necessary to support the overarching objective of promoting the long-term well being of the Soviet state. The effect of this approach on Soviet arms control policy is set forth in Chapter XI on "Military Objectives and Arms Control."

15. Douglas M. Hart, "Soviet Approaches to Crisis Management: The Military Dimension," *Survival* (September/October 1984): 221.

16. See Garthoff, *Detente and Confrontation,* p. 397.

17. See Seaborg, *Kennedy, Khrushchev,* pp. 271–73.

18. Herbert F. York, "The Great Test-Ban Debate," in *Progress in Arms Control?,* Bruce M. Russett and Bruce G. Blair, eds. (San Francisco: W. H. Freeman, 1979), p. 18. York's article, first published in 1972, contains a full assessment of the technological argument over the LTBT, viewed with the benefit of nearly a decade's experience following the treaty.

19. Robert W. Helm and Donald R. Westervelt, "The New Test Ban Treaties: What Do They Mean? Where Do They Lead?" *International Security* (Winter 1977): 165. The authors were staff members of the Los Alamos nuclear weapons laboratory.

20. Elmo R. Zumwalt, Jr., *On Watch* (New York: Quadrangle/New York Times Book Co., 1976), p. 495.

21. The scientists were Norris Bradbury, a former director of the weapons laboratory at Los Alamos, J. Carson Mark, former head of the Theoretical Division at Los Alamos, and Richard Garwin, a leading consultant on military technology. In a letter to President Carter of August 15, 1978, they stated: "We believe that the Department of Energy, through its contractors and laboratories, can through the measures described provide continuing assurance for as long as may be desired of the operability of the nuclear weapons stockpile." The measures described do not include test explosions of weapons. The letter is quoted and discussed in Herbert York and G. Allen Greb, *The Comprehensive Nuclear Test Ban,* Discussion Paper No. 84 (Santa Monica, CA: California Seminar on Arms Control and Foreign Policy, June 1979), p. 33. York, a former director of the U.S. weapons laboratory at Livermore, agrees with the view of Bradbury, Mark and Garwin. A later, similar letter was written to Congressman Dante Fascell on May 14, 1985. It was signed by Hans Bethe, Norris Bradbury, Richard Garwin, Spurgeon M. Keeny, Wolfgang Panovsky, George Rathjens, Herbert Scoville, and Paul Warnke. The text is reprinted in *Bulletin*

of the Atomic Scientists (November 1985): 11. The case that testing has been, and remains, essential to maintain reliability is argued in a letter to Congressman Henry Hyde of June 7, 1985 by Roger Batzel and Donald Kerr, directors of the Livermore and Los Alamos laboratories respectively. Their letter is also reprinted in *Bulletin of the Atomic Scientists* (November 1985): 12–13.

22. Graham T. Allison, Albert Carnesale, and Joseph S. Nye, Jr., eds., *Hawks, Doves and Owls: An Agenda for Avoiding Nuclear War* (New York: W. W. Norton, 1985), p. 210. In their conclusions, the editors ascribe to Owls, with whom they are in sympathy, concern "focused primarily on loss of control and nonrational factors in history. In this view, a major war would not arise from careful calculations but from organizational routines, malfunctions of machines or of minds, misperceptions, misunderstandings, and mistakes . . . While our Hawks and Doves focus on deterrence of deliberate choices and often cite World War II, Owls are more impressed by World War I, the assassination at Sarajevo, the leaders' misconception of the military situation, and the inadvertent escalation caused by interlocking mobilization plans."

23. Third-generation concepts have been described as including: a nuclear explosion that would induce X-rays as the kill mechanism of an anti-missile defense (this is now one element of the Strategic Defense Initiative); enhanced radiation weapons; and weapons specially designed to create a large electromagnetic pulse to burn out enemy communications. Thomas B. Cochran, William M. Arkin, and Milton M. Hoenig, *Nuclear Weapons Datebook, vol. 1, U.S. Nuclear Forces and Capabilities* (Cambridge, Mass.: Ballinger, 1984), p. 29. See also Fred Hiatt and Rick Atkinson, "Lab Creating a New Generation of Nuclear Arms," *Washington Post* (July 9, 1986), p. A1: "What would distinguish these 'third-generation' weapons from existing arms is that some type of energy produced in every nuclear explosion—X-rays, for example, or microwaves, or gamma rays—would be stepped up and focused on a distant target." Hiatt and Atkinson also report the views of critics: "They worry that third-generation weapons could make nuclear war more likely, as leaders become persuaded that a 'surgical' or 'selective' attack is possible. 'These things are not of any use, but clearly they will be presented to Congress as magical devices,' Kosta Tsipis, a physicist at the Massachusetts Institute of Technology, said."

24. A detailed statement is contained in Deputy Assistant Secretary of Defense Frank Gaffney's letter of January 21, 1986, to Congressman Edward Markey. The text is set forth in *Bulletin of the Atomic Scientists* (April 1986): 11–12.

25. Secretary Shultz's statement was made on October 5, 1986 on the ABC program "This Week with David Brinkley," and was reported by Walter Pincus: "Shultz Backs Continued Nuclear Tests," *Washington Post,* (October 6, 1986), p. A21. For a detailed review of current U.S. policy, see "U.S. Policy Regarding Limitations on Nuclear Testing," U.S. Department of State, Special Report No. 150, August 1986.

26. For the view that a CTBT should have "the highest priority on the global agenda" because of the threat of many new generations of nuclear weapons, see Theodore B. Taylor, "Endless Generations of Nuclear Weapons," *Bulletin of Atomic Scientists* (November 1986): 12. Taylor was formerly a deputy director of the U.S. Defense Nuclear Agency.

27. For a further discussion of these problems, see Warren Heckrotte, "Verification of Test Ban Treaties," in *Verification and Arms Control,* William C. Potter, ed. (Lexington, MA: Lexington Books/D. C. Heath and Co., 1985), pp. 73–76, and especially fn. 20, pp. 78–79. This essay is particularly valuable as a historical and analytical survey of the evolution of test ban verification issues from Eisenhower through Carter. Heckrotte, a member of the staff of the Livermore Laboratory, participated in the negotiations.

28. An encouraging development has been the agreement reached by the Natural Resources Defense Council (NRDC), a private American group, and the Academy of Sciences of the USSR, which provides for the installation of three seismic stations in the Soviet Union and three in the United States, all to be near test sites. See Philip Taubman, "New Yorkers Sign Soviet Test Pact," *New York Times* (May 29, 1986), p. A3. As of late spring 1987, three stations had been fully installed near the Soviet Semipalatinsk site. In the United States, three sites had been se-

lected and surface seismometers (to be replaced later by instruments emplaced underground) have been operating. The Soviets, apparently at the urging of their military, have required that the instruments in the Soviet Union be turned off during Soviet tests in 1987 following the termination of the moratorium. Nevertheless, NRDC stations in the Soviet Union have been able to record explosions in the United States, and those in the United States have recorded explosions in the Soviet Union. It is understood that the seismometers are producing high-quality data which, whatever ultimately comes of the project, should be helpful in understanding the geology around the Soviet test site and therefore should contribute to American ability to monitor the 150 kt limit of the TTBT or any lowered limit.

The most encouraging aspect of the project is that it may be evidence of a continuing easing by the Soviets of their rigid preoccupation with secrecy regarding militarily related activities. However, a few cautions against overextending the significance of this activity as a precedent should be expressed. The project was part of Gorbachev's promotion of his moratorium proposal (an unusually high-powered effort) and such favorable stimulation for cooperation cannot necessarily be counted upon in the future. Moreover, it may be easier for the Soviets to permit a relatively small number of private American scientists unsupported by their government to engage in these activities, than a government team (which would be essential under a CTBT) determined to exercise fully all of its rights under a formal treaty.

Another encouraging sign for the prospects for future verification systems was the position reported to be taken in spring 1987 by the Soviet Union in the Geneva intermediate-range nuclear force negotiations in favor of highly intrusive verification, including on-site inspections. Whether this is primarily a rhetorical position or one that can and will be translated into mutually satisfactory detailed procedures was not clear as of late spring 1987.

29. Nonnuclear countries have vigorously urged the nuclear powers to agree to a comprehensive nuclear test ban, notably at the September 1985 Non-Proliferation Treaty Review Conference, and in a six-nation declaration (Argentina, India, Mexico, Tanzania, Sweden and Greece) issued in May 1984 and renewed in January 1985 and August 1986. The six-power initiative urges many arms control and disarmament steps, including a CTBT, and offers to assist in a worldwide network of seismic monitoring stations. William Stockton, "6 Nations Urge Halt in Nuclear Testing," *New York Times* (August 8, 1986), p. A3. These various declarations and initiatives may be taken as sincere expressions that the nuclear powers should undertake a test ban. They provide no assurance, however, that any particular country, for example, India, would adhere to a CTBT or that it would not insist on conditions for adherence that are likely to be unrealizable, such as, in the case of India, adherence by both China and Pakistan. Nor do they preclude abstention from a treaty, which inevitably will be largely negotiated by the nuclear powers, on the grounds that its provisions are "discriminatory."

30. A senior Soviet official knowledgeable about test ban issues stated in my presence that Khrushchev's handling of the CTBT, specifically his willingness to allow two or three on-site inspections a year in the Soviet Union, had been one of the complaints within the leadership contributing to his removal in 1964. The story of internal dissent in Moscow regarding Khrushchev's test ban policies, particularly the disaffection of the Soviet military, is well told in Christer Jonsson, *Soviet Bargaining Behavior: The Nuclear Test Ban Case* (New York: Columbia University Press, 1979), pp. 195–200.

31. Theodore C. Sorensen, *Kennedy* (New York: Harper & Row, 1965), pp. 730–31.

32. James Fallows, "The Passionless Presidency," *The Atlantic* (May 1979), p. 33.

33. This problem is often referred to as "overloading" the arms control agenda. In my judgment, however, the essence of the difficulty is not the number of subjects on the agenda. In today's political setting there is no way of avoiding half a dozen or more significant arms control topics being worked on concurrently. The U.S. government does have the personnel resources to handle this demand. What is essential is to have a realistic understanding of which negotiations can be pushed forward at what speed in relationship to other topics, and what expectations, within and without the government, should be generated. In other words, a sense of priorities is needed.

The question of how many subjects can be handled at once is, of course, a different question from whether it is wise to attempt seriously any particular one, such as CTBT.

34. Zbigniew Brzezinski, *Power and Principle: Memoirs of the National Security Adviser, 1977–1981* (New York: Farrar, Straus and Giroux, 1983), fn. p. 172.

35. Jimmy Carter, *Keeping Faith: Memoirs of a President* (New York: Bantam Books, 1982), p. 229. The Soviet demand that Britain should install ten stations (which the British rejected) accompanied the Soviet acceptance, without any haggling, of the U.S. requirement that ten stations be installed in the USSR. There was probably an element of confusion since the Soviets had reason to believe that the British were willing to accept at least some stations. The Soviet internal decision to agree to ten stations on its territory was probably facilitated by the idea that none of the three nuclear powers would appear more or less trustworthy than the others; that is, each should be submitted to ten "lie detectors." It is hard to believe that this dispute could not have been fairly swiftly settled on a practical basis if the participants had felt that the negotiation still had momentum and that, therefore, a solution was needed.

36. See Strobe Talbott, *Endgame: The Inside Story of SALT II* (New York: Harper & Row, 1979), especially chapter 3, "The Making of a Debacle."

37. Philip Taubman, "Gorbachev Says Soviet Test Halt Is Again Extended," *New York Times* (August 19, 1986), p. A1.

38. "Excerpts from Gorbachev Speech on Arms," *New York Times* (March 30, 1986), p. 17; and Celestine Bohlen, "Gorbachev Extends Test Moratorium," *Washington Post* (August 19, 1986), p. A1, which reports Gorbachev as stating: "A troubled note justifiably sounds in the letters and pronouncements of Soviet people: is it expedient to preserve the moratorium? . . . Is not the risk too great? Is not the security of our country lessening with time?"

39. Gary Lee, "Gorbachev's Nuclear Test Ban Campaign Controversial in Soviet Military," *Washington Post* (August 31, 1986), p. A25.

40. R. Jeffrey Smith, "Soviet Disputes U.S. on Nuclear Tests," *Washington Post* (August 30, 1986), p. A28: "Stephen Meyer, an expert in Soviet military systems at Massachusetts Institute of Technology, said he believes that development or modification of three Soviet land-based missiles and one submarine-based missile also have been delayed. 'It is absurd to think that they are not being pinched,' he said. 'Our studies of Soviet research practices indicate that they routinely modernize or change the warheads on their deployed systems every four or five years, and to do this they probably need to conduct tests each year.' "

41. Gorbachev certainly has on his mind the inconstancy of U.S. policy. "We also have quite an experience in dealing with the United States. We know how changeable the internal political weather is . . ." Speech to the Soviet people, October 14, 1986, *New York Times* (October 15, 1986).

42. I do not believe that this judgement is inconsistent with the fact that the House of Representatives in August 1986 voted as an amendment to a military spending bill a measure that would limit U.S. tests to those less than one kiloton, providing the Soviet Union reciprocates and agrees to allow on-site monitoring instruments. See Michael Gordon, "House Approves a Year's Test Ban on Most A-Arms," *New York Times* (August 9, 1986), p. 1. The House's amendment was dropped from the legislation finally passed by the Congress just as the President was beginning his summit meeting with Gorbachev in Iceland. William Arkin, a weapons specialist who is a vigorous supporter of a CTBT, has written that the House amendment on testing was "first and foremost . . . a sign of exasperation with the complete lack of progress in arms control negotiations." Arkin, "Test Ban Fever," *Bulletin of the Atomic Scientists* (October 1986): 4. When and if strategic nuclear arms control should again show genuine promise, many who supported a testing halt may be expected to shift their attention to the live negotiating subject and to the questions regarding what constitutes prudent modernization that will inevitably be raised. I would not endorse all of the comments made in a *New York Times* editorial of September 28, 1986, p. 24, entitled, "The Arms Race Has No Quick Fix." Nevertheless, coming from a newspaper that has traditionally supported most arms control efforts, the editorial reinforces my view that once

strategic arms control again has promise it is likely to supplant preoccupation with a CTBT. The editorial states that there is "a deeper flaw in the House's vision: the simplistic belief that the arms race is driven only by technology and can be halted by stifling innovation. The arms race is driven primarily by mistrust, and not all changes in nuclear weaponry are bad. Warhead size reduction, stable basing and improved security contribute greatly to a safer world . . . Further limits on testing are highly desirable, but only after the arms race itself has been contained."

43. Morton H. Halperin, *Nuclear Fallacy: Dispelling the Myth of Nuclear Strategy* (Cambridge, Mass.: Ballinger, 1987).

44. The Public Agenda Foundation in collaboration with the Center for Foreign Policy Development at Brown University, *Voter Options on Nuclear Arms Policy* (New York: The Public Agenda Foundation, 1984), p. 3: " Virtually all Americans (81%) mistakenly believe it is our policy to use nuclear weapons 'if, and only if, the Soviets attack the United States first with nuclear weapons.' This basic misconception about the purposes of the American nuclear arsenal represents a major disconnection between government policy and public understanding." This section of the report was drafted by Daniel Yankelovich.

45. The full text is reprinted in *New York Times* (September 23, 1986), p. A10.

46. Bernard Gwertzman, "Reagan in a Shift on Nuclear Tests on Eve of Talks," *New York Times* (October 11, 1986), p. 1.

47. On the question of allegations of Soviet noncompliance and the need for further verification measures, the committee's report states:

> On balance, most committee members conclude that, without ratification, the United States has been able to ascertain that the Soviet record has been consistent with compliance and that, with ratification, our abilities to monitor compliance would be improved significantly . . .
>
> On the basis of the evidence . . . most of the committee does not feel justified in concluding that additional verification measures beyond those which would be in place upon ratification are required for adequate verification . . .
>
> At the same time, the committee recognizes that some enhancements in verification could be of value in providing additional evidence regarding Soviet compliance and could further dissuade the Soviets from misconduct.

U.S. Congress, Senate Committee on Foreign Relations, *Threshold Test Ban and Peaceful Nuclear Explosions Treaties,* Report together with Additional Views, 100th Congress, First Session, February 27, 1987, pp. 16–17. A description of the conflicts of view within the committee and with the Administration is contained in Michael R. Gordon, "Democratic Fits and Starts on Nuclear Testing," *New York Times* (January 21, 1987), p. A24.

48. Michael R. Gordon, "Moscow Offering to Put Off a Ban on Atom Testing," *New York Times* (April 7, 1987), p. A1.

49. Michael R. Gordon, "Soviet Offering U.S. an Exchange: Nuclear Tests on Each Other's Soil," *New York Times* (April 18, 1987), p. 1.

50. On September 17, 1987, the United States and the Soviet Union agreed on a compromise formula for an agenda which was consistent with each side's main substantive positions but which will allow more formal talks to begin on test ban issues. "Superpowers Agree to INF Treaty, Summit," *Arms Control Today* (October 1987), p. 23.

9

Strategic Arms Control, 1967–87

PHILIP J. FARLEY

Strategic arms control is a central and testing case when examining the possibilities for cooperation between the United States and the Soviet Union to enhance their security, and defining the conditions that facilitate or impede success in reaching agreements to this end and in carrying them out. The topic is a mammoth one; books have been written just on segments of the negotiating history. For purposes of this volume, the topic constitutes a unit and has to be dealt with as such. It is feasible to do so, though a good deal of relevant detail has to be left out and assumed to be generally familiar to readers, and many issues of intrinsic importance are omitted or treated cursorily. This is not a history of SALT/START or a systematic analysis of the issues and positions.

The SALT/START process has now been underway continuously (despite pauses or breaks in formal negotiations) from 1967 to the present—nearly two decades. It is not clear what results can be anticipated over the next two years, even with the impulse given by the November 1985 Geneva Summit and the 1986 Reykjavik Summit. Negotiations are likely to continue, if only for political reasons—both sides have had chastening experience with the political cost of avoiding or breaking off negotiations.

The SALT experience offers neither clearcut failure nor success for our appraisal. SALT agreements—what actually has been agreed on to date whether or not formally ratified—are strongly criticized. Peace activists and disarmament proponents find them halting and inadequate. Arms control skeptics or those who would rely on military strength to keep the peace charge them with inequities and serious flaws (terms used by President Reagan as recently as May 1986[1]). SALT supporters defend the agreements with varying degrees of enthusiasm or apology, but usually with heavy emphasis on their usefulness as the first step in a process they hope will lead to more and greater benefits, and as at any rate better than unregulated U.S.–Soviet strategic competition. Yet most of the agreements remained in effect until late 1986—if only with the grudging promise by both sides not to ''undercut'' SALT I and II, and with the increasingly imminent prospect of U.S. disengagement. The tenacity of their grip on life has been remarkable, and ironic. They have had a real impact on the strategic weapons deployments of both sides.

The SALT experience thus remains highly contentious, especially within the United States. Few would claim objectivity in attempting an appraisal. It is to be hoped, however, that partisans of either a positive or a negative leaning share an interest in examining and reflecting on what has happened, and in drawing some lessons out of the ambiguity and controversy that may be helpful to future efforts to regulate the arms race and reduce the risk of nuclear war.

Other chapters in Part III—those on the Standing Consultative Commission, on compliance, and on avoidance of accidental war—overlap with and supplement this one in major ways. Two others—on reconnaissance satellites and on militarization of outer space—do so to a lesser extent. More broadly, cooperation in regulating the strategic arms race and avoiding nuclear war is central—indeed, integral—to the emergence of any U.S.–Soviet security regime; it is thus treated further in Part IV.

THE SALT LEGACY

The SALT negotiations from 1969 to 1979 are not yet part of past history. The agreements reached are more numerous than is often appreciated. Most of them, in whole or in part, remain elements in the structure of U.S.–Soviet relations. Let us recall what these agreements are, and their present status:

— *The ABM Treaty (1972).* In full legal effect. Of indefinite duration with standard clauses on change and abrogation.
— *Interim Offensive Agreement (1972)* (referred to hereafter as SALT I). Executive agreement,[2] approved by both houses of Congress, of five-year duration. Expired in 1977. After consultation, both governments in 1977 announced their intention to observe its limitations. In May 1986[3] President Reagan announced that the United States will no longer be bound by the ceilings in the SALT agreements.
— *Hotline Modernization Agreement (1971).* Executive agreement remaining in effect, and further amended in 1984, to provide for facsimile transmission capabilities over the direct communication link (U.S.–Soviet "hotline").
— *Agreement on Measures to Reduce the Risk of Outbreak of Nuclear War (1971).* Executive agreement remaining in effect.
— *Memorandum of Understanding regarding Establishment of a Standing Consultative Commission (1972).* Executive agreement of indefinite duration implementing the ABM Treaty; SCC used for SALT II and related agreements as well.
— *Agreement on Prevention of Nuclear War (1973).* Executive agreement of indefinite duration.
— *Protocol to the ABM Treaty (1974).* Ratified by the Senate; of indefinite duration.
— *Vladivostok Accords (1974).* Executive agreement. Important stage in SALT II negotiations, but no continuing status.
— *SALT II Treaty (1979).* The treaty, which was never ratified and thus did not come formally into effect, had an expiration date of December 31, 1985. A *Protocol,* dealing with unresolved issues (such as cruise missiles and mobile missiles) requiring further negotiation had a two-year duration, until December 31, 1981. A *Joint Statement of Principles and Basic Guidelines for Subsequent Negotiations on the Limitation of Strategic Arms* was comparable to the Vladivostok Accords; it was an executive agreement regarding premises for negotiation of SALT III. The Reagan Administration made it clear that it would not seek ratification of SALT II; but on agreement to enter into START negotiations the President announced that the United States "would not undercut" the obligations of the SALT II treaty so long as the Soviet Union did likewise. This policy of de facto reciprocal observance of SALT II treaty obligations (both sides have made it clear they consider Protocol obligations to have lapsed) was not tied to the treaty expiration date. (As noted above, the United States has now ended this policy; in late 1986 it broke through SALT II

ceilings by deploying the 131st bomber armed with ALCMs, without retiring older systems to compensate.)

Thus of these nine negotiated agreements, six—the ABM Treaty and its Protocol, and four executive agreements—are of indefinite duration and remain in full legal effect. Two—the 1972 Interim Offensive Agreement and the 1979 SALT II treaty—have served an important constraining and regulatory function for the strategic arsenals and other activities of the two nations, even though both have expired and SALT II never entered formally into force.

While of a different order, and much broader in scope, the *Basic Principles of Relations* between the United States and the Soviet Union, another executive agreement signed at the Moscow Summit in May, 1972, is relevant. It sets forth some of the political premises which made the SALT negotiations possible, and describes some of the international conditions and modes of state conduct required for international peace and stability and the avoidance of nuclear war. It will thus play a prominent part in the discussion in Part III of SALT as a component of a partial U.S.–Soviet security regime; indeed, it might be conceived as a first effort to describe and codify some major characteristics of such a regime.

MAIN PROVISIONS OF SALT I AND SALT II AGREEMENTS

This paper will not review in detail the history and product of the SALT negotiations. The appended note on basic reference material—official, journalistic, and academic—identifies the main sources drawn on, and the main items in a voluminous and still expanding literature. A brief summary of the structure and major provisions of the main agreements limiting strategic arms may, however, be helpful as a preface to subsequent sections.

The ABM Treaty

The preamble to the treaty states important premises for the agreement (and for the whole SALT process): the devastating consequences of nuclear war, the need for measures to decrease the risk of outbreak of nuclear war, the contribution of limitation of antiballistic missile systems to meeting this need, and the importance of ABM limitations as a prior condition for limiting strategic offensive arms.

The basic structure of the treaty is to prohibit all ABM activities and deployments except as specifically permitted by the treaty. The parties undertake (Article I) not to deploy ABM systems for the defense of the territory of their countries or to provide the base therefore, and not to deploy ABM systems for regional defense except as specifically provided. Article III specifies in detail the missiles, launchers, and ABM radars permitted for defense (1) of the national capital, and (2) of one ICBM field—100 missiles and launchers at each. The 1974 Protocol reduced the permitted deployment to one or the other of these sites.

The prohibitions and limitations are further reinforced (Articles V and VI, and some agreed statements and common understandings). Sea-based, air-based, space-based, or mobile land-based components are prohibited; this is essentially because mobility is inconsistent with the basic prohibition of other than limited regional defense. Upgrading of non-ABM systems or components (primarily air defense systems) to give them ABM capability is banned. Deployment of large phased array radars is limited (for example, geographically, in the case of early warning radars) to prevent building a base for a territorial defense.

Verification is to be by national technical means, and interference with these means, and concealment, are banned. The treaty provides for a standing Consultative Commission to facilitate working of the treaty, including dealing with verification and compliance questions.

The Interim Offensive Agreement of 1972

This agreement was essentially a freeze, applicable to ICBMs and SLBMs but not to bombers, for five-year duration while a broader and more detailed agreement could be negotiated. ICBM launchers were frozen at the number already operational or under construction. New fixed launchers (silos) could not be started; the dimensions of silos could not be significantly increased; launchers for light or older ICBMs could not be converted into launchers for modern heavy ICBMs. Launchers for SLBMs could be increased beyond those operational or under construction, up to an agreed level for each party, but only if a corresponding number of older ICBM or SLBM launchers were dismantled or destroyed. A protocol spelled out the numbers implied by those provisions.

Verification provisions correspond with those of the ABM treaty.

The SALT II Treaty and Other Agreements

SALT II comprised three main elements: the treaty, to expire December 31, 1985; the Protocol, to expire December 31, 1981; and the Joint Statement of Principles for further negotiations.

The treaty continues to focus on "central strategic systems," but deals with heavy bombers and MIRVs as well as launchers for SLBMs and ICBMs. It adds a number of qualitative limitations and is detailed and precise in its definitions and provisions.

Quantitative Limits

— Equal aggregate numerical limits for ICBM and SLBM launchers and heavy bombers, and long-range/air-to-surface ballistic missiles: 2,400 on entry into force, with a reduction to 2,250 by the end of 1981 (since the treaty did not come into force these reduced ceilings have not been considered an obligation that the United States and USSR are committed to observe);
— An aggregate ceiling of 1,320 on MIRVed ballistic missile launchers plus heavy bombers equipped for launching cruise missiles with ranges over 600 km;
— Subceilings of 1,200 on MIRVed ballistic missile launchers, and 820 on MIRVed land-based ICBM launchers;
— Freeze on the number of heavy ICBM launchers and on new heavy ICBMs;
— Ceilings on the throw-weight and launch-weight of light ICBMs;
— A freeze on the number of reentry vehicles (RVs) on current types of ICBMs, a limit of 10 RVs on the one new type of ICBM, and a limit of 14 RVs on new SLBMs.
— A limit of 28 on the average number of air-launched cruise missiles (ALCMs) with

ranges over 600 km deployed on heavy bombers, and a limit of 20 ALCMs on current bombers;
— Ban on heavy mobile ICBMs, heavy SLBMs, heavy air-to-surface ballistic missiles (ASBMs), and certain types of strategic offensive systems not yet deployed by either side, such as ballistic missiles with ranges over 600 km on surface ships.

Qualitative and Verification Provisions

— A ban on testing and deployment of new types of ICBMs during the life of the treaty, except for one new type on each side.
— A ban on testing or deployment of long-range ALCMs on aircraft other than heavy bombers;
— Advance notification of certain ICBM test launches;
— In addition to verification provisions similar to those in SALT I, a specific ban on encryption of telemetry when verification would be impeded;
— Specific counting rules for associating MIRVs and ceilings with corresponding launchers;
— Cooperative measures to distinguish aircraft with different missions by requiring observable differences (FRODS);
— A periodically updated data base to assist verification.

The *Protocol,* in effect, provided a short-term freeze or moratorium on systems on which the parties had been as yet unable to agree. Banned were:

— Flight testing of ICBMs from mobile launchers, or deployment of mobile launchers;
— Testing and deployment of long-range air-to-surface ballistic missiles;
— Deployment of ground-launched and sea-launched cruise missiles (GLCMs and SLCMs) having ranges greater than 600 km.

The *Joint Statement* on guidelines for subsequent negotiations envisaged continued negotiations for further limitation and reduction of strategic arms, not necessarily only the types so far dealt with. The statement specifically called for resolution of the issues addressed on an interim basis in the *Protocol.* It cited cooperative measures reinforcing national technical means as one appropriate means of strengthening verification. Significant and substantial reductions in numbers, and further qualitative limitations, were specific objectives. To help reduce the risk of outbreak of nuclear war, measures were called for which would strengthen strategic stability (such as limiting systems destabilizing to the strategic balance), or measures to avert the risk of surprise attack.

SALT I and II are all limited in scope; individually and even collectively they bring the strategic arms race under only partial control. The ABM Treaty is of unlimited duration, but deals only with one-half of the offense/defense tandem. The Interim Offensive Agreement is explicitly short-term and interim, dealing only with "central strategic systems" and in particular ballistic missile launchers. The SALT II treaty broadens coverage, but is still of limited duration, and has recourse to a Protocol of even briefer duration dealing with disputed systems.

Indeed, geopolitical asymmetries and differing perspectives (to be discussed in a later section) have made a comprehensive or radical approach to strategic arms control unattainable for both parties—in START as well as in SALT. The complexity and intractability of the matters under negotiation led to the progressive step-by-step approach that came to be known as "the SALT process." It is difficult to see an alternative, at least so long as it is politically unacceptable to put off any agreement and stabilizing action until a comprehensive solution can be achieved. There are drawbacks, however. For example, partial measures—even those of the scope of the SALT II treaty—can be seen and characterized as "failures" both by arms control supporters whose grander expectations have been disappointed, and by skeptics or opponents of arms control. Momentum in the process itself can then be slowed or lost.

The agreements reached, even though partial, embrace much more than the numerical limits that are their most prominent feature. The ABM Treaty and SALT II contain several qualitative bans or limits on technological change or innovation viewed as destabilizing. Several executive agreements deal with crisis avoidance or management, or confidence building. Matters of strategic or political principle and policy are treated, not only in the explicitly named *Basic Principles of Relations* in 1972 and *Joint Principles* for future negotiations of 1979, but also in the preamble to the ABM Treaty, which sets forth principles then applied to strategic force posture in the provisions of that treaty and of the accompanying Interim Offensive Agreement. Some of the executive agreements (in particular, the Accidents Agreement of 1971 and the Prevention of Nuclear War Agreement of 1973) set forth principles as well as implementing measures.

The formal SALT negotiations and agreements reached during the decade 1969–79, just briefly reviewed, represent only the conspicuous negotiating phase of the SALT process. Integral to this process and even more protracted was the two-decade period from 1949 (when the Soviet Union conducted its first nuclear text explosion) until the opening of formal negotiations in 1969. During this period, the two superpowers, in a parallel and then interactive process, came to recognize that the primary goal of national security policy in the nuclear age had to be avoidance of nuclear war, that a strategic arms race—even with both sides seeking to deter rather than to win a nuclear conflict— was an inadequate and risky way to pursue security, and that negotiation and agreement on strategic arms might contribute to security in ways that strategic arms alone could not.

Entering into negotiations on such premises would imply acceptance of the other side as a worthy negotiating partner, a nation with compatible even if not identical security goals and standards, thus making it conceivable that a fair, balanced, and verifiable agreement might be arrived at, complied with, and effective. This premise, implicit rather than explicit at least initially during the SALT process, came to be highly contentious—especially in the United States—with the decline of détente beginning in the latter years of the 1970s.

HOW THE UNITED STATES CAME TO ENGAGE IN SALT NEGOTIATIONS

The SALT negotiations, of course, did not occur in isolation. Their context and background are the whole postwar history of the U.S.–Soviet relationship and the nuclear arms race. The political process by which the United States reached the decision to negotiate with the Soviet Union, complex though it is, is thus crucial to an appreciation of the conditions that determined the mixed success and failure of the negotiations and of the agreements they produced. The decision was formally one arrived at by political leaders with the advice of military and political advisers. More fundamentally, both for the negotiations and for the viability of the limited strategic arms control regime that resulted, it was a decision in which the whole American body politic participated. That decision was not only implicit rather than explicit; it was imperfectly understood and formulated, and subject to doubts and fluctuations that proved crucial after the agreements had been negotiated and were subject to Congressional action and came into force formally or de facto.

For present purposes, the evolution of the American attitudes toward nuclear weapons and the Soviet Union in a direction that enabled SALT to commence will be presented schematically rather than in terms of strategic doctrine.

The United States emerged from World War II in a position of unique power and influence. Its undamaged economic and industrial base was a principal factor. But the power and responsibility of the United States in the world were uniquely symbolized by the atomic bomb, which had brought the war in Japan to a dramatic close. As the wartime alliance with the Soviet Union dissolved with the disappearance of the common enemy, and Soviet military power remained entrenched in Eastern Europe, the Cold War emerged to dominate American perspectives on the world. Rather than withdraw within our borders as after World War I, we remained involved worldwide with an active policy of containment of the "Soviet threat." The atomic bomb became our "equalizer" in the face of a perceived massive Soviet conventional superiority. An absolute weapon, it undergirded our security. There was from the outset, however, an awareness of the ambiguity and danger of its longer-term implications, which provided the rationale for the Baruch Plan. That American proposal served our sense of our own altruism and generosity, and Soviet rejection confirmed the image of Soviet intransigence.

The dramatic and unexpectedly early first Soviet nuclear test in 1949 was an unsettling shock. The comforting American nuclear monopoly was short-lived, and the challenge came from our principal rival. The response was to accelerate American nuclear weapons programs—for both producing atomic weapons and developing the H-bomb. Suggestions that the latter be deferred until the possibility of forgoing it could be explored with the Soviet Union were brushed aside. The initial skepticism of J. Robert Oppenheimer as to the H-bomb crash program, and his receptivity to the idea of discussion with the Soviet Union, had significant adverse weight in the hearings that led to withdrawal of his security clearance. Nuclear weapons were increasingly integrated into U.S. force structures, not only of the Strategic Air Command but of the Navy and the U.S. forces in Europe and Korea.

While the emphasis was on nuclear buildup and nuclearization of American military power, there was appreciation of the broader implications of the Soviet test. The Eisenhower Administration, which is associated with the doctrine of massive retaliation, "a bigger bang for the buck," and the accelerating deployment of tactical nuclear weapons in Europe, saw also that premises for American security faced revolutionary change. The Administration recognized its responsibility to inform the American public, and to seek ways to escape the nuclear dilemma. The President's "Atoms for Peace" proposal to the General Assembly of December 8, 1953, was deliberately designed to achieve both ends. Its first part is often overlooked. The opening sections, fittingly entitled "A Danger Shared by All," "The Fearful Potentials," and "No Monopoly of Atomic Power," describe realistically the growth in the size and destructiveness of atomic arsenals, in their deployment, and in the current and prospective number of nations possessing them. As a consequence:

> . . . even a vast superiority in numbers of weapons, and a consequent capability of devastating retaliation, is no preventive, of itself, against the fearful material damage and toll of human lives that would be inflicted by surprise aggression. . . . But let no

one think that the expenditure of vast sums for weapons and systems of defense can guarantee absolute safety for the cities and citizens of any nation. The awful arithmetic of the atomic bomb does not permit of any such easy solution. Even against the most powerful defense, an aggressor in possession of the effective minimum number of atomic bombs for a surprise attack could probably place a sufficient number of his bombs on the chosen targets to cause hideous damage . . . Surely no sane member of the human race could discover victory in such desolation . . . My country wants to be constructive, not destructive. It wants agreements, not wars, among nations.

The particular proposal that followed—for an International Atomic Energy Agency to which nuclear materials would be diverted from nuclear stocks to peaceful uses including nuclear power—was not a particularly promising one. Among other things, it came at a time when Soviet inventories of nuclear material were much smaller than those of the United States, so that proposal could only seem invidious to the former. But a Republican President with the most distinguished military record of any American leader had clearly articulated the nature of the nuclear dilemma, the consequences of nuclear war, and the futility of defense. His statement provided a point of reference for subsequent national debate and policy adjustment.

The Soviet Union, then entering the post-Stalin era, participated constructively in the negotiations leading to the establishment of the International Atomic Energy Agency in 1957, as well as in developing the Agency's functions, which include inspection of civilian nuclear facilities. New nuclear arms control negotiations were not undertaken however until 1958, when the protracted and still deadlocked negotiations for a comprehensive nuclear test ban began. In the mid-1950s, nuclear weapons issues were subsumed in comprehensive phased general disarmament plans under discussion in the UN Disarmament Subcommittee, which ended its work in frustration in 1957.

Thus in the 1950s development and deployment of nuclear weapons and delivery systems dominated the nuclear relationship between the United States and the Soviet Union, with the United States attempting to maintain its nuclear superiority in both strategic and tactical weapons so as to preserve the overall military balance; and the Soviet Union trying to catch up in the nuclear field. The nuclear arms race took on a new significance, particularly for the United States, with the Soviet launch of the first earth satellite *Sputnik* in 1957, which brought home the Soviet technical capability to build boosters for nuclear-armed missiles of intercontinental range. The United States, despite its overall superiority, was now vulnerable to surprise or retaliatory strikes, as Eisenhower had forecast in 1953. Further, once the Soviet Union acquired a substantial arsenal of ICBMs, the retaliatory forces of the United States were exposed to attack so long as they remained fixed and vulnerable. Concern about an imminent "missile gap" led to U.S. acceleration of deployment of ICBMs in hardened silos; to programs increasing the number of SAC airbases and placing bombers on alert; to deploying intermediate range missiles (Thors and Jupiters) in Western Europe to maintain the balance and reassure European allies pending progress in ICBM and Polaris programs; and to developing, producing, and deploying nuclear-powered missile-carrying Polaris submarines, whose mobility and concealment gave them unnparalleled survivability.

Despite the dominance of nuclear competition through the 1950s and indeed until the Cuban missile crisis, sober thinking about the implications and risks of the nuclear arms race continued. The test ban negotiations, while stimulated by the political need to respond to domestic and worldwide concerns about the perils of fallout from large-scale nuclear testing, represented also an explicit desire on the part of many senior

Eisenhower Administration officials to find a way to take specific steps with the Soviet Union to put constraints on the nuclear arms race. Senior Defense Department officials began to ask what the United States could do in its national defense planning to avoid an unending nuclear buildup. The post-*Sputnik* emphasis on survivable and diversified delivery systems provided a concept of force structures under mutual vulnerability that paradoxically would point toward strategic stability.

The prime concern of each nation, even under such a recognition of interdependence, is to look to its own deterrent. By the early 1960s, the U.S. fear of a destabilizing "missile gap" had been alleviated. On the one hand, measures were in hand to diversify and make survivable major elements of the U.S. triad of deterrent offensive forces. On the other hand, the success first of the U-2 surveillance aircraft and then of the much more efficient and politically tolerable reconnaissance satellites made it evident that there had been no missile gap and that the United States had a substantial lead in strategic offensive systems. It took a political shock, however, to lead the two governments to look seriously to negotiations and agreements to reduce the risk of nuclear conflict and turn mutual deterrence into a basis for agreed restraints on the growth and character of strategic forces.

The Cuban missile crisis provided this event. For leaders on both sides, it was a shared experience of being poised on opposite edges of an abyss, with imperfect means of communication or of understanding the acts and purposes of the other, and with the weapons by which each demonstrated resolve but which promised not victory but mutual suicide if they came to be used. While both sides continued to build their deterrent forces (the United States to complete the Polaris and Minuteman programs already underway, the Soviets to accelerate their offsetting sea and land-based missile programs), cooperative measures were promptly undertaken. The "Hotline" was agreed in 1963 as one initial approach to facilitating crisis communications. In the same year, the Soviets dropped their insistence on nothing less than a comprehensive test ban, and the Limited Test Ban Treaty (which both sides agreed could be adequately monitored by national means of verification) was quickly concluded. Similarly, the banning of weapons of mass destruction on satellites was accepted by the Soviet Union as a measure separate from others, such as elimination of U.S. forward bases, and was incorporated in a UN resolution in October 1963. The Outer Space Treaty followed and formalized this measure in 1967. The United States and the Soviet Union also began several years of quiet collaborative diplomacy in the development and negotiation of the Non-Proliferation Treaty, opened for signature in 1968.

Coming directly to grips with the strategic arms race was less easy, however. The simplest measure, freezing deployment of strategic delivery systems, was not feasible while the Soviet Union lagged unacceptably and insisted on catching up for both military and political reasons. In the United States, however, three trends were coming together to suggest that the time for negotiation might be near:

1. The Polaris and Minutemen programs were approaching fulfillment. Secretary of Defense Robert McNamara did not want to get drawn into indefinite follow-on expansion programs, and raised publicly and with the Congress the question of "How much is enough?" His "assured destruction" criterion for the deterrent adequacy of survivable retaliatory forces was an effort to quantify the criterion for force-planning purposes, not a strategy or military goal.
2. The development of a deployable ABM system in the United States and initiation of

limited Soviet ABM deployment around Moscow, were seen by McNamara as stumbling blocks in efforts to put a cap on strategic force levels, unilaterally or indeed even by agreement. Even though the effectiveness of ABM technology in the face of sophisticated offensive forces was no more promising than in the Eisenhower days, ABM deployments—highly expensive in themselves—would have to be taken into account in sizing offensive force requirements. Unless ABMs could be capped or banned, stopping the growth of offensive systems might be unmanageable.

3. While the Soviet Union was clearly highly motivated to close the gap, there could be no basis for U.S. confidence that this force-building momentum would not carry on beyond equality to more numerous strategic systems, leading by reaction to an additional impulse for U.S. strategic force expansion.

The visible outcome of this confluence of trends was the Johnson-McNamara-Kosygin meeting in June 1967 at Glassboro, New Jersey, at which the case for limiting ABM was forcefully put by McNamara. Skeptically received at the time by Kosygin, a process of reflection was started (or reinforced) inside the Soviet Union which led to agreement to begin negotiations on limitation of offensive and defensive strategic arms in 1968. These negotiations were deferred, first by the invasion of Czechoslovakia in 1968 and then by the change in U.S. administration, until 1969.

The change in U.S. administration in 1969 did not result in significant change in the way of thinking about strategic arms limitation (SALT). The Nixon Administration promptly conducted its own review of defense policies and programs, and of the limited ABM program launched by its predecessor. The conclusions, carefully articulated in speeches and official reports, retained the basic premises on which strategic arms negotiations and agreements could serve U.S. interests:

— Nuclear superiority was not attainable against a state with the capabilities of the Soviet Union. "Sufficiency" was therefore the proper criterion for strategic forces— a concept, however fluid, much more easily reconcilable with arms control.
— ABM protection of the nation was not technically feasible, and pursuit of more than strictly limited defense would not only be expensive but destabilizing and an obstacle to limitation of offensive forces.
— SALT was a timely venture in view of approaching strategic parity: it would not be possible to reach an agreement freezing the strategic balance as long as the United States was strategically predominant.

More generally, the President stated succinctly his rationale for arms control, and for strategic arms limitation in particular, in his first Annual Foreign Policy report to the Congress:

— The traditional course of seeking security primarily through military strength raises several problems in a world of multiplying strategic weapons.
— Modern technology makes any balance precarious and prompts new efforts at even higher levels of complexity.
— Such an arms race absorbs resources, talents and energies.
— The more intense the competition, the greater the uncertainty about the other side's intentions.
— The higher the level of armaments, the greater the violence and devastation should deterrence fail.

  For these reasons I decided early in the Administration that we should seek to maintain our security whenever possible through cooperative efforts with other nations at the lowest possible level of uncertainty, cost, and potential violence.[4]

That same report restated at its outset the underlying character of the nuclear dilemma as first presented by Eisenhower in 1953:

> Today, a revolution in the technology of war has altered the nature of the military balance of power . . . Both the Soviet Union and the United States have acquired the ability to inflict unacceptable damage on the other, no matter which strikes first. There can be no gain and certainly no victory for the power that provokes a thermonuclear exchange. Thus, both sides have recognized a vital mutual interest in halting the dangerous momentum of the nuclear arms race.[5]

More broadly, the Nixon Administration also reexamined and redefined U.S. foreign policy, globally and in relation to the Soviet Union. The same Foreign Policy Report describes this review, made timely by the changing international environment and the relative decline in U.S. power. SALT became a major element of the new "era of negotiation" and the pursuit of détente with the Soviet Union.

THE SOVIET UNION ARRIVES AT A SIMILAR POINT

The course by which the Soviet Union came to see strategic arms negotiations with the United States as desirable is now reasonably clear.

The implications of nuclear weapons for modern warfare, for the military balance, and for Soviet security were generally apparent from the outset. The Soviet state would remain insecure if it failed to master this revolutionary new weapons technology. As the shape of the postwar power structure became apparent, it behooved the Soviet Union in particular to match American capabilities. The United States thought of nuclear weapons primarily as adding a new dimension of power to bombardment capabilities of the Strategic Air Command and naval carrier forces, and only secondarily to their tactical applications. The Soviet Union initially saw nuclear weapons as a more powerful artillery; but it could not be blind to U.S. strategic concepts. Less capable with long-range air and naval bombardment forces, the Soviets gave priority to development of long-range rockets, making full use (as indeed did the United States) of captured German scientists. The Soviet Union also developed long-range bombers, however; indeed, its first nuclear weapons were for delivery by bombers.

Soviet military thinking first sought to assimilate nuclear weapons to basic concepts of overwhelming fire power, preemptive attack on opposing fire power, and the requirements for victory over any aggressor against the Soviet homeland. But even under Stalin, ways of thinking began to change; he was especially affected by the development of the vastly more powerful H-bomb. After his death, Georgi Malenkov echoed the Eisenhower theme that nuclear war would mean the destruction of world civilization. By the end of the 1960s the basic principles of Soviet policy came to be that the Soviet Union could not accept nuclear superiority by any other power, but was not itself seeking such superiority; it had achieved and would maintain the capability to inflict a crushing blow on anyone who attacked it; nuclear war would have catastrophic consequences and could not constitute a rational course of policy or action; and thus as an objective condition it had to be recognized that mutual deterrence obtained between the two superpowers.

The classic expression of this Soviet way of thinking is not any public statement, but the first official presentation of the Soviet rationale for SALT, in the opening private statement by the Soviet chief negotiator, Vladimir Semenov, in November 1969. According to Gerard C. Smith:

> Semenov began by stating that both sides recognized the importance of curbing the strategic arms race. It could only contribute to a general increase in the threat of war. Mountains of weapons were growing, yet security was not improving but diminishing as a result. A situation of mutual deterrence existed. Even in the event that one of the sides was the first to be subjected to attack, it would undoubtedly retain the ability to inflict a retaliatory blow of destructive force. It would be tantamount to suicide for the ones who decided to start war. However, in the Soviet view, mutual deterrence did not entirely preclude nuclear war. Each side has its own understanding and interpretation of the numerous factors and complex interactions of the evolving military political situation. This could lead to major miscalculations. The strategic situation by no means excluded the risk of a nuclear conflict arising from unauthorized use of nuclear missiles or from a provocation on the part of some third power possessing nuclear weapons.
>
> Semenov went on to make a point he would often repeat. It was obvious that mutually acceptable solutions should be sought along lines that would insure the security of each side equally rather than through efforts to obtain unilateral military advantages. He rejected any idea that arms limitation be linked to other issues. While concrete results would contribute to the improvement of relations between our countries, the subject matter of our deliberations was so complex in itself that to link it to other international problems would mean directing the matter into a blind alley.[6]

Such a way of thinking about nuclear weapons tracks closely with the American thinking as it developed over the years from 1949 to 1969. Some elements have become debatable in the United States during the past few years; it is thus thought-provoking to juxtapose with Semenov's remarks the first substantive paragraph of the *Joint Statement* issued at the end of the November 1985 Geneva Summit:

> The sides, having discussed key security issues, and conscious of the special responsibility of the U.S.S.R. and the U.S. for maintaining peace, have agreed that a nuclear war cannot be won and must never be fought. Recognizing that any conflict between the U.S.S.R. and the U.S. could have catastrophic consequences, they emphasized the importance of preventing any war between them, whether nuclear or conventional. They will not seek to achieve military superiority.[7]

Such general principles are of course important, but the real test comes in reaching concrete agreement to apply them to strategic forces.

Noteworthy in the Semenov statement is the concern about the risk of war even in a regime of mutual deterrence and joint effort to avoid nuclear war. As noted, the Cuban missile crisis brought this danger to the fore and the Hotline represented one agreed means of dealing with it. One of the main American concerns about strategic defense was the strain opposing ABM systems would place on crisis stability; this theme has been taken up in Soviet statements from the time of SALT I, and recently by Yuri Andropov and Mikhail Gorbachev. The theme seems not to be just an echo of American statements. A good example is a precursor speech by Andrei Gromyko to the Supreme Soviet in July 1969, setting forth the Soviet interest in the approaching SALT talks. He said:

> The point of the matter is primarily whether the big powers come to an agreement to arrest the race of creating increasingly destructive means of attack and counterattack,

or whether each of them is to try to break out ahead in one sphere or another to obtain military advantage against his rivals, which will force the latter to mobilize even greater national resources for the arms race. And thus ad infinitem.

There is also another side of the matter that cannot be ignored by a state's long-term policy. It is linked to a considerable extent with the fact that the systems of weapons control and direction *[upravleniye]* are becoming increasingly autonomous, if one can put it this way, from the people who create them. Human capacity to hear and see are incapable of reacting at modern speeds. The human brain is no longer capable of assessing at sufficient speed the results of the multitude of instruments. The decisions adopted by man depend in the last analysis upon the conclusions provided by computers. Governments must do everything possible to determine the development of events and not to find themselves in the role of captives of events.[8]

Such concerns lie behind Soviet interest in the Accidents Measures Agreement of 1971 and the Prevention of Nuclear War Agreement of 1973, as well as the ABM Treaty. The convergence with American concern is evident. The persistence of Soviet concern is seen in Gorbachev's press conference following the November 1985 Summit:

The U.S. side does not wish to acknowledge that SDI means putting weapons into space. These are indeed weapons. They—U.S. and Soviet weapons—would be flying in waves above people's heads. We would all gaze at the sky and anticipate what would rain down from it. Let us imagine—and we said this to the U.S. side—the consequences of even an accidental collision in space, let us say that something breaks off a missile—the tip *[golovnaya chast]*, shall we say, carries on while the delivery vehicle *[nesushchaya chast]* falls away and collides with a cluster of these space weapons. Signals would go out, which would be interpreted almost as an attempt by the other side—in this instance I am not talking about our side or any particular side—as a signal that an attempt is being made to destroy these weapons. All the computers are switched on, and in this situation politicians can do nothing sensible at all. What, are we going to be the prisoner of these events? Many pictures of this kind could be painted.[9]

One additional instance of convergence appeared early in the presentation of Soviet thinking about strategic weapons at the opening sessions of SALT I. In 1967 Aleksei Kosygin had treated strategic defense as beneficent and non-threatening, in contrast with offensive systems; a small ABM defense deployment was underway around Moscow. But Semenov, in a prepared statement early in the exchange, noted the ambiguous character of the terms "offensive" and "defensive" weapons. It was not the weapons themselves that were offensive or defensive, but how they were used. "Offensive" weapons could in fact be defensive if they were used to make clear that nuclear war would be profitless, and thus to deter its outbreak. "Defensive" weapons would be offensive if they were used to make a nuclear attack feasible by frustrating a retaliatory response. Neither side would of course permit such frustration but would build up its offensive forces to prevent it. The rationale of the preambular clauses of the ABM Treaty is "that the limitation of anti-ballistic missile systems . . . would contribute to . . . . further negotiations on limiting strategic arms." And similarly, the Interim Offensive Agreement takes into account "the relationship between strategic offensive and defensive arms."

SEEKING AGREEMENT: UNDERLYING ASYMMETRIES
AND DIFFERING APPROACHES

After the first exploratory session of SALT I at Helsinki in late 1969, both sides found sufficient convergence in views and interests to move from exploratory discussion to negotiation. A process began that yielded two major, though partial, sets of agreements in 1972 and 1979; a halt and reappraisal, especially on the U.S. side, from 1979 to 1982; and a resumption of negotiations in 1982 with broader scope but less convergence in goals and approaches. Many of the roots of the present impasse can be seen in the long drawn out and tortuous process by which agreements were reached from 1969 to 1979, and in the forces that led to widespread disillusionment and opposition in the United States and a consequent pause in negotiations. The reasons why specific areas of agreement have been difficult to reach and subject to tension are instructive both as to the negotiating process and the future prospects for strategic arms limitation.

The problems encountered arise from the basic systemic rivalry between the United States and the Soviet Union, from more specific geopolitical asymmetries, and from the inherent difficulties and dilemmas involved in seeking to apply ''arms control'' to an ongoing strategic arms race between two major powers in such a situation of rivalry.

The first of these dimensions, the over-all U.S.–Soviet rivalry, has some concrete impact on SALT issues and on the viability of SALT or START accords. One element of U.S.–Soviet systemic rivalry is the disposition in the United States to see the Soviet Union as driving for world dominance, seizing every opportunity to move toward that goal even by armed force, and expecting historical forces to assure it victory in the end.

On the Soviet side, the U.S. role as leader of the imperialist camp conversely makes it plausible that the United States might seek to arrest inevitable historical processes for a time by recourse to military superiority. As a result, each is all too ready to see in the military doctrines, strategic weapons developments and deployments, and SALT/START proposals of the other side features and motivations that reflect pursuit not of equality and equal security but of overall advantage and superiority. Arms control agreements, however carefully balanced, will be suspected as traps that a priori favor the rival—or he would not have agreed. Similar suspicions can arise as the implementation of an apparently balanced agreement gives rise to tensions and uncertainties. At root is the always latent doubt whether there really is a common base of interests and values, without which no agreement or looser understanding can be viable.

A second source of tension and instability arises from attempted strategic cooperation between a closed and an open society. In negotiating an agreement, the U.S. side does not know (except from its own intelligence estimates) what are the program goals of, say, the Soviet ICBM construction and development activities or continued Soviet ABM research; nor does it know when such programs are modified and Soviet budget allocations are reduced or shifted, except retrospectively and after contentious interpretation of observable activities in progress. A debate over the Krasnoyarsk radar and its ABM treaty implications can thus rage over years while it is still incomplete and its operational characteristics differently imputed by the two sides. Similarly, U.S. critics of SALT and détente insist there has been a ''relentless'' Soviet military and strategic buildup at a 5 percent to 7 percent annual rate of increase over the late 1970s and early 1980s; only in 1982 did retrospective firmer CIA estimates correct the Soviet budgetary increase levels to roughly the rate of Soviet GNP increases (about 2–3 percent annually) and show Soviet strategic investment to have held about level as Soviet launcher/missile levels under SALT ceilings remain constant despite an active modernization program.

Many highly concrete geopolitical asymmetries complicate the process of finding and defining areas of agreement and limitation, against these background factors of mutual suspicion and uncertain information. For example, the United States has Canada and Mexico on its borders; the Soviet Union has China to the east, NATO to the west, and the Moslem world to the south. The other three nuclear powers, the United Kingdom, France, and China, are rivals of the Soviet Union. And the Soviet Union has limited access to the open oceans, which hampers its navy and increases the vulnerability of its SLBM submarines; while the United States with its long coast lines, enjoys naval advantages but suffers far greater vulnerability to even relatively short-range Soviet cruise missiles.

A third troublesome systemic difficulty relates to continuity and consistency. These are important over the course of a long sequential series of negotiations and are vital to building mutual understanding and confidence. In this case, the difficulty is created for the Soviet Union, and the source is both in the way Americans approach issues, and in the American political system. Examples are many. Throughout the negotiations, the United States has shifted emphasis on the subject of mobile land-based missiles—whether they should be permitted or banned, whether a limitation or ban could be verified, whether they are stabilizing (because relatively survivable as a result of mobility) or inequitable (both because of verification uncertainties we consider more awkward for us than for the Soviets, and because the sheer size and the political system of the Soviet Union make it easier for them to deploy them). Recently, U.S. thinking has appeared to move toward viewing them positively, as increasing survivability and thus stability; we have shown interest ourselves in a mobile Midgetman. Yet we have at the same time continued to find fault with the Soviet development of mobile ICBMs; and the U.S. START proposals at the end of 1985 called for mobile ICBMs to be banned. Another example was the handling of ABM limitations in SALT I. There we developed four "options" (a mysterious concept for the Soviets) and presented first one calling for limiting ABMs to a small deployment around national capitals. The Soviets promptly accepted it. We refused to accept their acceptance, and put forward a series of alternatives, with a good deal of ambiguity as to whether we would ourselves accept each or any of them. Broader instances of discontinuity, of course, are the initial radical SALT II proposal of the Carter Administration, which the Soviets promptly rejected as inconsistent with the Vladivostok principles recently agreed; the shift in 1981 from SALT to START; and President Reagan's "Star Wars" speech and SDI program, which diverged radically from the premises of the ABM Treaty and the basic U.S.–Soviet understandings on the offense-defense relationship, mutual deterrence, and crisis stability.

A related matter of some bewilderment to the Soviets, whatever their abstract understanding of it, is the role of the Congress and American public opinion with regard to arms control agreements and their ratification and viability. After years of experience, the Soviets accept these phenomena as a fact of life, but as a minimum they regard each American claim that concessions by the Soviet Union are needed to satisfy these separate centers of domestic political power as a U.S. negotiating ploy to pressure them to reopen an agreed deal, and yield something which logic and equity alone would not justify.

Asymmetries are particularly troublesome, since (as will be discussed shortly) strategic arms limitation is inconceivable between two leading powers on any other basis than that of equality. Yet in very fundamental senses the two nations are not equal. The United States since World War I—the time of origin of the Soviet Union—has been incontestably the principal advanced industrial state. Its relative position was at its peak when at the end of World War II it emerged with an undamaged economy yielding almost half the world's output. It remains the leader even though its GNP share is now under a quarter of the total. The Soviet Union has been turning itself into a modern industrial society from its inception, and explicitly seeking to overtake the West and the United States. It has recovered remarkably from the devastation of World War II. It is the third national economy in overall output, but less than half the gross size of the American economy. In efficiency, dynamism, and high technology it lags further—and its leaders are well aware of this. Because of the Soviet obsession with security, and the priority given to military power, Soviet military expenditure is at least equal to that of the United States and its weapons development and production complex is the most advanced segment of the Soviet economy. In most areas of strategic weaponry, the United States has been the innovator and maintained a technical edge, and the Soviet Union has played "catch up."

Given the size, diversity, and sophistication of the strategic arsenals on both sides, it is generally conceded that "essential equivalence" (another key concept for strategic arms control) obtains, and is unlikely to be lost by either side. But such an objective appraisal is hard for national political and military leaders to maintain in the face of technical change and the background of mutual suspicion and uncertain information. Where the Soviet Union sees itself as catching up, the United States sees relentless momentum that is about to achieve a lead unless we launch compensating buildups. When the Soviet Union builds a first-generation ABM system of a limited size around Moscow, we see the prospect of a nationwide Soviet ABM defense frustrating our retaliatory deterrent forces; when we launch a limited Sentinel/Safeguard ABM, they see the prospect of a technically much more sophisticated and effective American ABM negating their deterrent forces. For once—in the ABM Treaty—these reciprocal concerns were balanced off and eased, not by an ABM race but by a restraining agreement. It is now proving to be an uneasy bargain.

Other asymmetries complicate perceptions and agreed limitation. The geographical positions and military histories of the two nations have produced differing emphases in their military concepts and force structures. The United States has a long naval tradition and concept of its role as a naval power; since World War II, the Air Force and the Strategic Air Command have been prominent and influential. The Soviet Union is a landlocked nation which has only recently become a global seapower; its emphasis has been on ground forces and artillery. The composition of the respective strategic forces reflects these factors. Roughly three-fourths of American strategic warheads are on sea- and air-based delivery systems, and one-fourth on ICBMs and European-based Pershing-IIs and GLCMs. About two-thirds to three-fourths of Soviet warheads are on ICBMs, and somewhat over one-fourth on bombers and SLBMs. Soviet naval and bomber technology is also inferior, which would make altering the mix—if they came to see that as desirable in the interests of greater survivability—not easily achievable quite aside from cost and time considerations. Even the ICBMs of the two sides offer a further major asymmetry—in size and throw-weight. While there may be developmental reasons for the size and power of Soviet launchers—difficulty in developing solid fuel boosters, a lag in miniaturization of warheads, even a cultural respect for sheer size and power in the modern successor to artillery—the result is a significant advantage in missile payload capability as the technical lags are gradually overcome and accompanied by accuracy improvements. Fitting these asymmetries into formulas for limitation that will be equal in appearance and equivalent in effect has been a taxing challenge for negotiators. And while (as the Scowcroft Commission suggests in its second report) [10] the asymmetries may have non-sinister origins, the consequence may be destabilizing—and difficult to deal with.

One other fundamental asymmetry has far-reaching implications for SALT. The Soviet Union is not only landlocked. It has to the east and west of it states that are historic rivals, and which it continues to view with suspicion and a good deal of hostility—particularly Germany in the west, and China and Japan in the east. Even its southern borders, if not presenting the same perceived threat, are areas of instability, past and present. These factors help account not only for the well-known Soviet land and air-defense establishment, but also for the powerful forward deployments of forces which, whatever their defensive purpose, have by doctrine and structure powerful strike or attack capabilities. Further, after their final expulsion of the Nazi invasion in World War II (after two earlier major invasions from the west over the previous century and a half), the Soviets established a postwar *cordon sanitaire* of dependent states in East Europe, with communist governments set up under Red Army occupation. Interpreted in the light of Marxist-Leninist revolutionary pronouncements, as well as postwar social ferment, the forward deployments were found extremely threatening by West European governments, as well as by the United States. Formation of the NATO Alliance was a response to the perceived threat in Europe; the United States responded to the active Soviet foreign policy worldwide, with its policy of "containment." The United States, insulated by oceans on two sides, and with friendly smaller states to the north and south, never having suffered more than local invasion since its independence, tended to see only the threatening, rather than the defensive component of the size and disposition of Soviet forces. And given the perceived disparity in conventional forces between NATO and Warsaw Pact alliances, nuclear weapons—strategic as well as tactical—came to be valued as an offset, and were deployed and integrated into NATO and U.S. deterrent and defensive strategy in ways that complicated the SALT process.

This complex situation, with different and often divergent trends and capabilities and perspectives on the two sides, with a sense of high stakes, and with a mutual sense of suspicion, was the context within which areas of SALT agreement had to be found, spelled out, and judged acceptable. In searching for agreement, the touchstone came to be what is called "the principle of equality and equal security" in the preamble to the SALT II Treaty and in the *Joint Statement of Principles* for future negotiation. This principle is a criterion of a sound agreement that does not require perfect symmetry within the agreement itself. Perhaps more important, the principle refers not just to a single agreement or even a set of strategic limitation agreements, but to the over-all strategic balance and relationship between the two sides within which the negotiation takes place, and within which its acceptability must be judged. Even if the balance cannot be precisely described or analyzed, it must be judged satisfactory by each; neither would be willing to accept inferiority with or without limitation agreements. One might prefer more precise and demonstrable criteria and measures of balance; but the necessity for qualitative judgment of an odd mix of technical, political, and other factors is inescapable. The Joint Chiefs of Staff tend to recognize this in their annual appraisals of the balance, with a final formula to the effect that, all tangible and intangible factors allowed for, a rough strategic balance obtains (though at risk if we do not continue appropriate modernization and readiness programs). Politicians and public opinion find this more difficult to accept.

Even if only a rough, overall assessment of agreements is possible, agreements to be acceptable and viable must not be or appear unequal and disadvantageous. This issue was dominant in the 1972 debate in the United States over the SALT I Interim Offensive Agreement. As a freeze of ballistic missile launchers, leaving out bombers and MIRVs, which were areas of U.S. advantage in numbers and dynamism, the agreement in its own terms was unequal, specifying higher numbers of missile launchers and submarines for the Soviet Union. As a freeze in construction or enlargement of silos (insisted on by the United States to stop the Soviet build-up of this category of launchers) it meant also that the United States would for at least five years be barred from matching the Soviet Union in the sensitive category of "modern heavy missiles" with its tie to potential destructive capability. The supporting arguments for approval of the agreement were that taking into account the over-all strategic forces, excluded as well as included, the balance was fully satisfactory; and that as the Soviet Union was building missile forces toward an unknown program level while the United States had completed its program of ICBM and SLBM launchers, the freezing did not stop us from doing anything we planned, but halted the ongoing Soviet program, including the addition of heavy missiles. Additionally, further negotiations were to follow in which more comprehensive limitations would be applied.

These arguments carried the day, and the agreement was approved by large majorities in both houses of Congress (it was not a treaty). There was enough discontent expressed, however, about the lack of "equality" so that Congress passed an accompanying so-called Jackson "sense of Congress" non-binding resolution. The resolution is of such broad scope and addresses issues of such future prominence that it deserves summary here.

1. Section 3 declares that the principle of equality would be followed in future offensive-limitation agreements as in the ABM Treaty and that the United States should not accept inferior levels. Support was stated for a vigorous U.S. program of research, development, and modernization in the interests of a prudent strategic posture.
2. Section 4 notes that the Interim Agreement is only a preliminary step, and "urges the President to seek at the earliest practicable moment Strategic Arms Reduction Talks (SART) with the Soviet Union, the People's Republic of China, and other countries . . . in order to bring about agreements for mutual decreases in the production and development of weapons of mass destruction."
3. Section 5 states that Congress considers that "the success of the interim agreement and the attainment of more permanent and comprehensive agreements are dependent upon the preservation of longstanding United States policy that neither the Soviet Union nor the United States should seek unilateral advantage by developing a first strike potential."

Leaders in both houses stressed for the record that although the United States could never accept inferiority, an "acceptable balance" should not overemphasize any one factor such as throw-weight or a rigid numerical formula while overlooking qualitative factors. In effect, they endorsed what came to be known as "essential equivalence." [11]

The domestic U.S. debate about the SALT I Interim Offensive Agreement was public. The Soviets also had difficulty during negotiation with such an interim and partial agreement; their concern related to the absence of limitations on American "forward based systems" (mainly land- and carrier-based aircraft with varying degrees of capability of delivering nuclear weapons against the Soviet Union), and on the strategic forces of U.S. allies—France and the United Kingdom. They put the United States formally on notice that these were matters of security importance to them, germane to the strategic balance, and had to be dealt with in continuing negotiations. (Leonid Brezhnev made the same stipulation to Jimmy Carter at the signing of SALT II in 1979.)

As is evident, "equality" is an ambiguous term, even if an indispensable criterion. Even in SALT and SALT-related documents, the word sometimes has only the most general political sense in which all nations are "equal" in the UN General Assembly. For instance, the eleventh principle of the 1972 Basic Principles of U.S.–Soviet Relations states that the two nations "recognize the sovereign equality of all states," and neither claim nor recognize any special rights or advantages. What "equality" means as applied to SALT agreements is not defined. In practice, particularly in SALT II, its meaning was embodied in "equal aggregates" for strategic delivery systems covered by the agreement, and for MIRVed systems. Negotiators also used a general drafting technique of stating provisions in such a way as to apply equally to both sides—even if the impact of a particular provision (such as constraints on heavy missiles or on numbers of ALCMs on bombers) might weigh more heavily on one side temporarily or even over the long term. Thus within a general structure of equality some scope is left for offsetting asymmetries, some explicit, some implicit. As a practical matter, the term "essential equivalence" probably best captures the desired result, even if the form and appearance must come closer to strict "equality."

The coupling of "equal security" with "equality" was a matter of special importance to the Soviet Union. It reflects the geopolitical asymmetry already referred to—in the current international situation, the Soviet Union is opposed by all of the other four nuclear powers, two of which are formally allied with the United States under the North Atlantic Treaty and coordinate nuclear strategy more or less closely (in Soviet eyes at least). Even the prospective Nth nuclear weapons powers are more threatening, by geography or political orientation, to the Soviet Union. Thus strict U.S.–Soviet strategic equality means Soviet inferiority in a broader geopolitical context. This issue, while specifically identified by the Soviet Union in SALT I, was never dealt with head-on in SALT agreements. It took on new prominence with the 1979 NATO decision to deploy American Euromissiles in Europe to offset Soviet deployments of SS-20s to replace and modernize older SS-4s and -5s. It is a central issue in the Geneva START talks of the mid-1980s.

"Equality" is not only a criterion of fair and acceptable agreements, but a precondition of successful negotiation. As is noted in Richard Nixon's fourth Annual Foreign Policy Report, "some years ago, when the United States was strategically predominant, an agreement freezing the strategic balance was unrealistic."[12] This factor was recognized within the U.S. government at the outset of SALT, but was initially muted. "Parity" with the Soviet Union was difficult for the United States to come to terms with after years of strategic superiority. U.S. officials feared that confidence in the American deterrent might be shaken, at home and also abroad among allies and clients. There were of course solid grounds for this concern; strategic parity and American vulnerability did indeed lead to questioning in NATO Europe as to the likelihood that the United States would fulfill its guarantee to use nuclear weapons to forestall a successful Soviet attack on NATO. The NATO INF deployments were in good part a consequence of this concern. On the other side, the Soviet Union showed evidence of attaching political importance to "equality" with the hitherto dominant superpower. Beyond the acceptance of a strategic balance, the Soviet Union saw political prestige and status, a fulfillment of its claim to a special mission both as a great power and as the leader of the socialist camp. It was this apparent Soviet sense of achievement that contributed to the initial—and recently resurgent—U.S. sense of uneasiness with explicit admission of equality between the two nations and by implication their social systems. And on the other side, the Soviets have shown discontent on occasion with the fact that the United States, and other nations, evidently do not see the two nations as in practice equal outside the military area.

FINDING AGREEMENT, COUNTERING OBJECTIONS

The forces of convergence described in Sections 4 and 5 above were strong enough in SALT I and II to overcome the obstacles and inherent complexities and dilemmas outlined in Section 6. For offensive weapons, the solutions were interim and partial, even though of increasing scope in SALT II. For defensive missiles, the ABM Treaty was considered at the time, and for over a decade, to be a sound and comprehensive treatment, of indefinite duration.

Between the United States and the Soviet Union, the basic and interlinked issues were how "strategic nuclear weapons" were to be defined, and the coverage of the agreements. From the opening of SALT I, the Soviet Union adhered tenaciously and explicitly to its concept that strategic weapons are those which can strike the territory of the other side. It has been similarly explicit and tenacious in its "principled" position that the forces of the United Kingdom and France that meet this test are relevant to the U.S.–Soviet strategic balance and the criterion of "equal security," and must in due course be "taken into account." These remained "principled" positions in 1986. This does not, of course, mean that compromise or postponement are not again possible: the Soviet Union, like other great powers, is capable of again "rising above principle" when its interests so dictate.

The debate on these matters went on throughout SALT I and II. The United States advanced many arguments as to why dealing with FBS and British and French forces was unwarranted and unduly complicating (Gerard Smith's *Doubletalk* reviews the debate in detail), and why "central strategic systems" (ICBMs, SLBMs, intercontinental bombers, and their MIRVs and eventually ALCMs) should be the focus. The arguments that appeared to persuade the Soviets were that these central systems were the dynamic ones that were driving the strategic arms race; and that American FBS and British and French forces were static and, whatever the logic of their inclusion, not major factors in the strategic balance at current and prospective permitted levels of launchers and MIRVs. By the time of SALT II, the imminence of ground- and sea-based cruise missiles and the prospect of British modernization of SLBMs with Trident, as well as growing French forces, undermined this case, but not enough that the Soviets wished to defer putting some effective limits on American strategic modernization in an agreement of limited duration.

The first years after the 1972 Moscow Summit and the signing of SALT I saw an internal U.S. debate over the structure of a SALT II agreement. The general view was that equity and public opinion as reflected in Congress called for some form of explicit equality as embodied in the equal aggregates and sublimits of the Vladivostok Accords and eventually the SALT II Treaty. Kissinger argued initially for an asymmetrical structure, explicitly permitting more U.S. MIRV delivery systems as against larger numbers of Soviet launchers and heavy missiles. The argument for "equality" triumphed and continues to prevail, despite the ambiguities and the continuing tension with the avowed principle of "equal security" already discussed.

I have already described the objections raised in Congress during SALT I hearings concerning numerical inequalities, and the outcome. The principal disappointment of SALT advocates, within the executive branch as well as in the Congress, was the failure to ban MIRVs. The destabilizing consequences of MIRV deployment were all clearly perceived and argued within the executive branch and in public in the late 1960s and early 1970s. These were: the multiplication of strategic warheads, the vulnerability of fixed landbased ICBMs in the face of more attacking warheads of steadily improving accuracy, an exchange ratio favoring the offense, the advantage in potential MIRV payload given to the Soviets by their larger throw-weight, and the resultant U.S. fear of a "window of vulnerability" and the attendant premium on striking first with enhanced crisis instability. The debate was not pressed when the Interim Offensive Agreement came before the Congress, however. Pro-defense congressmen, both critics and supporters of the agreement, were relieved that U.S. MIRVs were not limited. Pro-arms control proponents of a ban or limitation on MIRVs were aware that they did not have the votes to carry their position, and did not want to imperil an agreement they saw as a valuable, even if only limited, breakthrough and beginning in strategic arms control.

SALT II dealt with MIRVs indirectly, to some extent moderating the destabilizing effects. Multiplication of nuclear warheads was not blocked. The criticism that the SALT agreements did little to halt the strategic weapons buildup was thus available to pro-disarmament critics of SALT—to the satisfaction of pro-defense critics. Failure to limit MIRVs adequately is frequently cited as a major missed opportunity. This is plausible in the abstract, but less so in historical perspective. Just as SALT itself was not ripe until the Soviet Union saw prospect of negotiating on a basis of equality, it was not realistic to expect the Soviet Union to agree to ban MIRVs when the United States had a tested capability nearing readiness for deployment while the Soviet Union had not yet reached readiness to test. In the United States, the MIRV program had acquired high status. It was urged by the McNamara Defense Department as a rational strategic response to the Soviet ABM program, which MIRVs would overwhelm and penetrate, thus assuring the deterrent effectiveness of the U.S. retaliatory forces. The MIRV program also provided a justification for capping the expensive deployment of U.S. offensive ICBMs at 1000, and SLBMs at 41 missile-carrying submarines. By the time it became apparent both that the deployment scale and capability of Soviet ABMs had been grossly overestimated, and that the ABM Treaty could forestall its expansion, MIRVs were well entrenched, and were being justified as an area of U.S. superiority not constrained by SALT. When Soviet preparations for MIRV testing were discerned, it was belatedly recognized that the U.S. lead would be brief, that the Soviets would have MIRVs of their own with the usual five to seven-year lag, and that their MIRVS would threaten a part of the U.S. deterrent force. Strategic instability would be enhanced. Yet U. S. policy makers resisted the conclusion that we would be better off if neither side had MIRVs than if both sides had them, even with some timing and perhaps qualitative edge to the United States. There was a reluctance to admit that a symbol of U.S. superiority was a wasting asset and perhaps even a trap. There was also concern over the feasibility of verifying limitation of MIRVs, and a slowness to recognize that monitoring of testing of missiles and MIRVs offered a valid way to define and verify useful limitations. Here is a classic instance of the ambiguities and dilemmas of the strategic arms race and its action-reaction mechanism, which plague the effort to find viable arms limitation alternatives.

As for SALT II, Secretary of State Cyrus Vance observes that it was recognized in sending the treaty forward to the Senate that "... unlike SALT-I, this time the Congress, the executive branch, and critical sectors of public opinion would be drawn into a prolonged debate over U.S.–Soviet relations, the military balance, and Soviet intentions. SALT would be the anvil on which the differences would be hammered out." [13] As he also notes, SALT had been oversold in the early 1970s. Critics on both the left and right found common ground in complaining that SALT II did not go far enough, and had no "deep cuts." Vance's summary of the main objections to the treaty advanced during the hearings gives a fair presentation of American concerns;

— Negotiating compromises were weighted in favor of the Soviets, especially their retention of 308 heavy ICBM launchers, versus none for the United States;
— Soviet compliance could not be verified, and there were ambiguities in the treaty;
— the treaty and its protocol would impede U.S.-NATO defense cooperation, and prejudice cruise missile development and deployment;
— the treaty did not provide for sufficient deep cuts, especially in MIRVed ICBMs;
— more generally, the U.S. was not keeping pace with the Soviets because it was lulled into complacency by SALT; thus the treaty should be "held in abeyance" until defense deficiencies had been corrected. (Kissinger took a position close to this.) [14]

Senior officials, including the chairman of the JCS, strongly defended the treaty and disputed those objections. For example, NATO had been given explicit assurances, and the United Kingdom had been given a commitment for a supply of Trident missiles to modernize British SLBM forces. NATO countries took positions supporting SALT. Defense officials argued that "a ceiling on the overall Soviet MIRVed ICBM force would be strategically as advantageous to us as a sub-ceiling on heavy missiles alone ..." [15] Whether the treaty would have been ratified were it not for the Soviet military intervention in Afghanistan will never be known. Vance's judgment is plausible: "Ratification was blocked because the opponents were successful in creating political linkage between the treaty and the problem of restraining Moscow's attempt to expand its influence." [16]

SUMMARY OF DEVELOPMENTS, 1979–86

After the Soviet intervention in Afghanistan, ratification of SALT II was clearly infeasible. At the President's request, the Senate suspended consideration of the Treaty, though it was not withdrawn. The U.S. position then was that even though the Treaty was not formally in force, actions would not be taken which would undercut it.

As a candidate, Ronald Reagan had repeatedly characterized the SALT II treaty as "fatally flawed." During the first year of his presidency, the status of SALT II—and indeed of SALT I—was obscure, as was the U.S. position on resuming strategic arms control negotiations. In 1982, the Administration agreed to engage in parallel negotiations on intermediate range nuclear missile forces (INF) in Europe and on strategic arms reduction (START). It then was necessary to define the U.S. view of the status of SALT agreements. President Reagan summarized it in his report to Congress of June 10, 1985, concerning U.S. interim restraint policy:

> In 1982, on the eve of the Strategic Arms Reduction Talks (START), I decided that the United States would not undercut the expired SALT I agreement or the unratified SALT II agreement as long as the Soviet Union exercised equal restraint. Despite my serious reservations about the inequities of the SALT I agreement and the serious flaws of the SALT II agreement, I took this action in order to foster an atmosphere of mutual restraint conducive to serious negotiations as we entered START.[17]

The Soviet position was similar. As stated by then Foreign Minister Gromyko in a Moscow television interview January 13, 1985:

> Concerning the SALT I treaty, which was concluded when Mr. Nixon was the U.S. President, despite the fact that the period of validity for the treaty expired, in due time the sides agreed to exchange official statements to the effect that the obligations assumed by the sides under this treaty remained in force. We therefore may reply that they remain in force today. We are prepared to regard this treaty as such in future.

> Concerning the second treaty, SALT II, which was duly signed in Vienna by Leonid Ilich Brezhnev and on the U.S. side by former President Carter: This Treaty, as is known, was not ratified by the United States. The obligations assumed by the sides under this treaty therefore are not legally in order and do not remain valid.

> But the sides reached an agreement that whatever is of positive significance would, in fact, operate under this agreement, too. Why such a formula? Because the contents of this agreement are complicated in many respects, in particular in the respect that some of the points of the agreement . . . for instance, those on cruise missiles, no longer apply. This was a temporary factor—some points no longer apply and are no longer operating. There was a protocol as an addendum to the accord. It does not exist any more. That is why it is correct to say that what is positive now in connection with this accord should be in operation. There is an understanding between the two sides here and this is good.[18]

These respective positions are an illuminating example of how a de facto "security regime" can prevail when a formal one remains elusive.

In the first year of the Reagan Administration, priority was given to an expanded strategic modernization program. It was characterized as necessary (1) to redress an adverse strategic balance due to neglect on the part of previous administrations, (2) to match a relentless Soviet strategic buildup, and (3) to put the United States in a strong negotiating position. Similar justfications were advanced for pressing ahead with INF deployments in Europe. As for strategic arms control, the Administration asserted that U.S. positions were under study, though it is not clear that much was actually done. There was a harsh and challenging tone to public statements about the Soviet Union, of which the famous presidential allusion to the "evil empire" at the root of conflict and disorder in the world was perhaps the most extreme. The clear implication was left that the Soviet Union was an unreliable and unworthy negotiating partner.

Political pressures that built up in both the United States and Western Europe played a major part in the decision to resume negotiations in Geneva in 1982. INF deployment faced strong opposition within a number of prospective NATO host countries, and their governments feared that in the absence of a plausible effort to negotiate limits on NATO and Soviet deployments the program might not be possible to implement. The original

NATO "two-track" decision of December 1979 had called for parallel negotiations on INF with the Soviets, along with preparations to deploy if these negotiations were unsuccessful. These negotiations were explicitly presumed to take place in the SALT context. More broadly, there was much unease in Europe about the erosion of détente and the deterioration of U.S.–Soviet relations, and the cessation of all arms control talks. In the United States an active peace movement gathered strength, fed by major military budget increases and the absence of any arms control efforts. Broad voter support for a "nuclear freeze" appeared in many states and was reflected in Congress. The Administration viewed this approach as simplistic and dangerous. Proposals on INF and START were developed and negotiations undertaken in 1982.

The new U.S. positions were in sharp and deliberate contrast with previous ones in SALT. The principal emphasis for START was on "deep cuts," in conformity with campaign accusations that SALT agreements, in addition to their other flaws, were not even "real disarmament." Instead of using launchers and numbers of MIRVs per launcher as the units for numerical limitation, the focus became numbers of missiles and warheads in inventories—presumably all those that had been produced, rather than only those actually deployed. There was stern insistence on strict verification including on-site inspection, but little detail on just how, or how well, this might be done for missile and warhead production and stockpiles. Initial priority among strategic delivery systems was to be given to missiles and their warheads, and especially large fixed land-based missiles (the backbone of the Soviet strategic force structure) as the most threatening and most destabilizing. Bombers were not included in initial ceilings, though recognized as proper for negotiation in due course. Cruise missiles, FBS, and allied strategic missiles were excluded. For INF, the U.S. proposal called for a "Zero option"—a ban on all intermediate range missile forces worldwide, not only those in or targetable on Europe. Medium-range bombers were not covered; British and French SLBMs were excluded as independent strategic forces.

The initial Soviet position in START can be reasonably characterized as their SALT III position. It called for a 20 percent reduction in strategic delivery vehicles below the never-activated SALT II common ceiling—from 2250 to 1800 intercontinental bombers and missile launchers. Long-range cruise missile deployment—whether land-, sea-, or air-based—would be banned. No additions to FBS would be made—thus blocking the NATO INF deployments.

In the INF talks, the basic Soviet position was that there was already a nuclear balance in the European theater, and that they were willing to negotiate to a lower balance at any level, even zero. The SS-20s, which had stimulated the NATO INF reaction, were simply a modernization of the older SS-4s and 5s, which were being retired; the replacement SS-20s would have fewer missiles and less total megatonnage (probably true, though they would also have more warheads as well as being mobile and more modern and accurate). British and French forces would have to be taken into account either in INF or in START. As for the planned NATO INF deployments, if they were not abandoned as envisaged in Soviet START proposals, the Soviet Union would be entitled to match them by additional SS-20 or other deployments—and would do so with or without an agreement.

I will not trace here the course of successive modifications in positions; Strobe Talbott's *Deadly Gambits* gives a useful account through 1983. No common ground or serious negotiations emerged in START; the two sides simply made changes to remove conspicuous weaknesses or inequities in their proposals, or to try to capture the high ground in public opinion. In INF negotiations there was some interaction. The Soviets showed special concern at the prospect of facing 108 Pershing IIs with their high accuracy and short time of flight. There are even signs that this prospect made them appreciate for the first time the uneasiness with which the West Europeans viewed the formidable SS-20s facing them. For whatever reason, the Soviets were quite active in seeking a formula for a solution or even an interim deal. They put forward a succession of modified proposals, the final one before the breakoff in talks being to reduce their number of SS-20s and warheads to the total of French and British SLBM and land-based missiles and warheads, if the NATO deployments were abandoned. Their negotiator engaged in intensive exploratory talks which, after the famous "walk in the woods" with his U.S. counterpart, resulted in a compromise plan calling for offsetting reductions on both sides but with a partial NATO deployment. This was rejected by both governments amid public recriminations. Interestingly, heads rolled on the U.S. side but both the U.S. and the Soviet negotiator remained.

In March 1983 a wild card was introduced with President Reagan's "Stars Wars" speech. Deploring the threatening mutual assured destruction posture of the two superpowers, he asked rhetorically if it would not be better and more moral to *defend* against nuclear weapons rather than menace each other with retaliation. On this premise, he launched his Strategic Defense Initiative (SDI) to find ways to remove the threat of nuclear attack by defensive measures, and thus point the way to elimination of nuclear weapons themselves. The implementing program that took shape was asserted to be confined to "research" as permitted by the ABM Treaty. The scope of the program ($26 billion over five years) and some of the anticipated experimental activities were, however, hard to reconcile with a restricted laboratory research program and strict avoidance of development and testing as banned by that treaty. Most fundamentally, the speech and the program challenged the basic premises of SALT in general and the ABM Treaty in particular: that avoidance of nuclear war through mutual deterrence was the only sensible position for both governments, that "offensive" systems to deter war could not be limited or reduced significantly in the face of actual or prospective area defenses, and that deployment of defenses would foster acceleration of the arms race rather than facilitate reductions and in addition would be a grave element of instability in crises, putting an additional premium on striking first. The program was thus highly controversial both in the United States and among allies; it went ahead nevertheless.

Critics of the SDI in the United States argued from the outset that the goals of the program were inconsistent with the strategic premises of the ABM Treaty and with the preconditions for limitation of offensive weapons—let alone deep cuts in strategic arsenals. Citing Articles I and V and Agreed Statement D, they pointed out that the defensive systems envisaged by the SDI, particularly space-based components, could not even be developed and tested under terms of the treaty.[19] Thus challenged, the Administration undertook a reexamination of the treaty and its confidential negotiating history, and produced a new interpretation which would permit full SDI development and testing. This was formally contested by a group of senior SALT I negotiators.[20] It was also challenged in Congress, both as to validity and on constitutional grounds, since the Senate had ratified the treaty on the basis of testimony different from the new interpretation.[21] A truce was arrived at through Administration assurances that, while the new intepretation was still considered to be well grounded, the SDI program would be carried on within the bounds of the original interpretation. However, the President held firmly to his position that the SDI concept and program might be discussed at Geneva, but they would not be negotiated away.

The Soviets challenged the SDI and its premises promptly. A statement by Andropov three days after Reagan's March 1983 speech made points about unilateral change in agreed U.S.–Soviet principles of strategic arms control such as those just summarized. Beyond that, he spoke strongly of this latest U.S. initiative as further evidence of a U.S. push for strategic superiority and a first-strike capability. Soviet statements to this effect had begun with the Senate's failure to ratify SALT II and the Carter strategic modernization program. They intensified with the expanded Reagan strategic modernization program and associated rhetoric about the need to recover the U.S. edge. The Soviets also cited the deployments under the NATO INF program (especially the Pershing IIs), the U.S. commitment to aid Britain in modernizing its SLBM force with Trident systems, and the deployment of sea-launched Tomahawk cruise missiles and NATO GLCMs after the December 1981 expiration of the SALT II Protocol deferring cruise missile deployment. Some of these Soviet assertions were designed to appeal to arms control, peace movement, and anti-nuclear elements of public opinion in Western Europe and the United States; they are also to be taken seriously as reflecting Soviet perceptions of the changing strategic balance and the implications for arms control and U.S.–Soviet relations.

With the first deployments of NATO INF imminent, the Soviet delegation broke off INF negotiations in November 1983. A little later, when START talks recessed, they refused to set a date for resumption on grounds their whole position had to be reassessed in the light of developments. In public statements they stressed the need to ban space weapons in general (those aimed at targets in space as well as those deployed in space) as well as space-based ABM system components, and demanded the withdrawal of NATO INF missiles as a precondition to resumption of talks.

Boycotting negotiations is an uncomfortable public posture, however. A new formula for resuming negotiations in Geneva was reached by Secretary of State George Shultz and Foreign Minister Gromyko on January 8, 1985, with the tasks stated to be ". . . to prevent an arms race in space and to terminate it on earth, to limit and reduce nuclear arms, and enhance strategic stability."[22] Within overall umbrella negotiations, three parallel negotiations proceeded on START, INF, and space. Basic differences persisted, however, including U.S. insistence that the SDI was fully consistent with the ABM Treaty and not negotiable.

The Geneva Summit in November 1985 did not produce specific guidelines for the negotiators. The President and General Secretary did agree to accelerate the negotiations and called for early progress, citing common ground on the principle of a 50 percent cut in nuclear arms and the idea of an interim INF agreement. Given the basic differences, perhaps more important was the first substantive paragraph of the Geneva Joint Statement, which restated some of the common premises of strategic arms control that had led to the SALT agreements:

> The sides having discussed key security issues, and conscious of the special responsibility of the U.S.S.R. and the U.S. for maintaining peace, have agreed that a nuclear war cannot be won and must never be fought. Recognizing that any conflict between the U.S.S.R. and the U.S. could have catastrophic consequences, they emphasized the importance of preventing any war between them, whether nuclear or conventional. They will not seek to achieve military superiority.[23]

As negotiations resumed in January 1986, Gorbachev unveiled a dramatic new formula for elimination of nuclear weapons by the end of the century in three phases— a 50 percent cut in U.S. and Soviet nuclear weapons by the year 1990, inclusion of other nuclear weapons states in negotiations thereafter, and a comprehensive phase-down and elimination of all nuclear weapons in the year 2000. Various counter-proposals and refinements and modifications of the positions of the two sides then followed in inconclusive negotiating sessions, with increasing sense of frustration and mutual re-crimination, and with attendant jockeying for public support. The speeches by Paul Nitze identified in the Appendix to this chapter summarize these developments.

The apparent convergence in START positions seen by some during the brief period of post-Summit optimism quickly showed itself to be illusory. The Shultz-Gromyko formula of January 1985, which was the premise of the negotiations, had simply papered over differences. Limiting the ''arms race in space'' was an integral part of the Soviet approach; the United States saw nothing to negotiate, either over ASATs or over the SDI and its prospective space-based components. For the United States, the SDI was fully consistent with the ABM Treaty; for the Soviet Union, it was not a simple research program but a challenge to the basic SALT premises on the offense-defense relationship that are a prerequisite for reductions in deterrent offensive warheads and delivery systems. The proposals of the two sides tended to converge toward a 50 percent reduction, but the reductions would apply to very different things.

The Summit reference to a possible interim INF agreement failed to lead to agreement, despite ingenious U.S. proposals for reductions to produce a U.S.–Soviet INF balance in Europe and worldwide. There were also new INF complications. The United States, in large part at the insistence of NATO allies, stipulated that even a lower or zero U.S.–Soviet INF balance had to be supplemented by Soviet redeployments or reductions of shorter-range theater delivery systems such as those the Soviets had deployed forward in East Europe in response to the NATO INF deployments beginning in 1983. There is clearly some logic to this U.S. proposal—as there is to the analogous Soviet position that all weapons threatening their territory must be counted in strategic limitations—but it added a new factor in an already complicated calculation.

At the beginning of March 1986, the United States finally presented in Geneva the INF verification proposal on which Administration officials had been working for five years. The U.S. requirements were high:

1. An on-site inspection by field inspectors of the other country to establish the starting count of each side's INF missiles as a basis for agreed reductions. The background for this proposal was the U.S.–Soviet data dispute over whether the Soviets had 270 or 243 SS-20 missiles deployed within range of Europe, and other uncertainties about SS-20 reloads.
2. In connection with the inspection, initial data exchange on deployed missiles was to be followed by subsequent exchanges of updated data.
3. No encryption of telemetry for tests.
4. Restriction of missile deployment to designated areas around their operational bases. Missiles would be limited to these areas to aid verification. Because an agreement would be formulated in terms of limiting the number of warheads deployed on missiles of both sides, but verification of the agreement would be largely in terms of launchers deployed, any missile seen outside the designated area, unless in a designated production or maintenance facility, would be classed as a violation.
5. Supervised destruction of withdrawn missiles.
6. Follow-on on-site inspection on a random basis of certain facilities or suspected

deployment sites. U.S. authorities were still considering various alternatives for this, including inspection of production plants, and did not advance a specific proposal on this topic.[24]

These requirements merit close examination, since they foreshadow U.S. requirements for START verification. The current Administration has consistently stressed the inadequacy of previous verification arrangements, both in negotiation and in application. While one focus of verification would be numbers of launchers—relatively easy to observe from satellites—limits are also stated in terms of numbers of missiles and warheads. Here satellite observation is unsatisfactory. Even on-site monitoring of destruction of missiles and associated warheads leaves the difficult problem of ascertaining whether all units have actually been identified and destroyed, whether new production is offsetting the destroyed weapons, and—in the case of warheads—whether weapons material from previous stocks or operating nuclear power reactors is feeding clandestine weapons manufacture. Such questions become particularly compelling as arsenals are reduced to low levels, where modest levels of clandestine stocks or production can change the equation, thus placing heavy demands on monitoring capabilities. These considerations are highly relevant to START proposals for sharply reducing or eliminating strategic delivery systems and setting a ceiling on associated nuclear weapons. Agreeing on, and then installing, the machinery of verification will be a formidable task; the verificaton experience in test ban negotiations described in another chpater might be recalled here. Given the current U.S. emphasis on Soviet unreliability and noncompliance, it will difficult to soften requirements. Indeed, the disposition to date has been to insist that verification machinery must be in place before actual reductions begin.

Gorbachev's sweeping January 1986 proposal for a phased elimination of strategic nuclear systems by 2000 A.D. was in good part a propaganda move to capture the high ground and upstage the U.S. claim to be the champion of deep cuts and the progressive elimination of nuclear weapons. Similarly, the Soviet Union extended its unilateral moratorium on nuclear tests, and publicized its detection of unannounced U.S. underground tests, both to emphasize U.S. refusal to follow its example and also to support its claim that unilateral national monitoring of a comprehensive test ban is an adequate means of verification. Their propaganda also exploited U.S. preparations for ASAT tests. The targets of all this activity were European and U.S. public opinion. The United States responded, stressing particularly its charges of Soviet noncompliance with existing arms control agreements in order to bring into question Soviet sincerity and trustworthiness.

The impasse in Geneva START talks, against the background of reiterated charges of systematic Soviet violation of existing agreements, has served increasingly to bring into doubt the U.S. policy of not undercutting SALT I and SALT II. In June 1985 the issue took concrete form as U.S. Trident deployments were about to exceed SALT II limits unless corresponding existing systems were retired. At that time the President decided to dismantle a Poseidon submarine to remain within SALT ceilings, while expressing deepening concern about inherent SALT agreement flaws, the lack of progress in START, and "the pattern of Soviet noncompliance with their existing arms control commitments increasingly affecting our national security."[25] He called on the Soviet Union "to join us in establishing an interim framework of truly mutual restraint," which would involve "reversing their unwarranted military buildup."

On December 31, 1985, the unratified SALT II Treaty reached its formal expiration date. In the following spring, the United States again faced concrete decision regarding compliance with SALT limits. On May 27, 1986, the President announced the impending U.S. disengagement from these limits, justifying it as a response to Soviet noncompliance, intransigence in START, and continued strategic force buildups "which challenge seriously the essential strategic balance" and thus do not constitute Soviet restraint comparable to that shown by the United States.[26] While two additional Poseidon submarines were retired in the summer of 1986, thus maintaining a little longer the de facto U.S. conformity with SALT limits, the retirement was carefully attributed to military and budgetary reasons, not to arms control obligations. In the absence of "constructive steps" by the Soviet Union, the President said, he intended to authorize the disengagement action. The Soviet Union denounced his statement promptly and vigorously, and declared that as soon as the United States in fact went beyond SALT limits it would consider itself free from the relevant commitments and would take the necessary practical steps "to prevent the military-strategic parity from being upset . . . and rule out the possibility of the United States acquiring advantages . . ."[27] At the end of 1986, an additional heavy bomber was equipped with cruise missiles, thereby putting the United States over SALT limits. The Soviet Union did not immediately carry out its threat to respond in kind however.

A second Reagan-Gorbachev Summit in late 1986 thus came to be looked to as an occasion for finding the way to avoid reciprocal breakout from the SALT limits as well as from the impasse in Geneva talks. But the Summit proved to be equally problematic and the object of diplomatic and propaganda maneuvering. The November 1985 Summit, and its amicable conclusion, had been greeted with widespread relief and expectations about arms control and improved U.S.–Soviet relations. As the insubstantial nature of Summit results become apparent, Geneva talks remained at impasse, and U.S.–Soviet relations frequently became acrimonious, the value of a second Summit became dubious. While neither side looked forward to another empty event, neither wanted to assume the onus of backing out. The Soviet position was to stress the primacy of arms control and the need for concrete arms control results if a Summit was to occur; the United States pointed to a broader agenda of world political problems on which changed approaches (mainly by the Soviet Union) were needed and which should be taken up.

In late September came the dramatic announcement that Gorbachev had proposed, and President Reagan had accepted, a meeting in Reykjavik on October 11–12, in lieu of a formal 1986 Summit. There appears to have been no formal agenda and there was no agreed final public statement. While other topics were discussed, the focus was on the arms control impasse and on the respective views as to how to move ahead on the two areas of prospective convergence identified at the November 1985 Geneva Summit: a 50 percent reduction in U.S. and Soviet nuclear arms and an interim INF agreement.

Such a sudden meeting could not be compared to the 1972 Moscow Summit or even to the November 1985 Geneva Summit. It was more analogous to the 1974 Brezhnev-Ford Summit at Vladivostok, which produced guidelines for the SALT II negotiations. Nothing so concrete emerged from Reykjavik, and the immediate mood at the end was one of disappointment. Both sides shortly assumed a more positive posture, and not without reason. Despite the lack of careful and concerted preparations, the discussions were intensive and the positions of the two sides forthrightly presented and confronted. While many important details of the discussion are obscure, the main outlines are clear and contain seeds of promise, despite substantial differences.

The picture on INF is clearest. There would be zero INF in Europe, and each side could have 100 INF warheads elsewhere—the Soviet Union in Asia, the United States within the United States. Verification details were of course not addressed. British and French forces were implicitly referred to the START process. The Soviet Union was prepared to have a freeze on shorter range INF while negotiations on them proceeded.

The START picture is more complicated, with two phases. In the first five years, both sides were prepared to reduce to 1600 central strategic delivery vehicles (ICBMs, SLBMs, long range bombers)—roughly a one-third reduction from current Soviet levels. Associated warheads would be limited to 6000—down from some 10–12,000 now, or approximately back to Soviet levels when the SALT process was suspended in 1979. The Soviets wanted a single over-all ceiling for delivery vehicles and for warheads, with each side to establish its own mix. The United States wanted a series of subceilings designed to restructure the Soviet strategic forces away from land-based ICBMs, with subceilings on ballistic missiles, on land-based missiles, on heavy missiles and total throw-weight, and on mobile ICBMs (which would be banned unless the Soviet Union could show the United States how they could be verified).

In the next five years, there would be movement toward elimination—but of *what* is unclear now, and perhaps at Reykjavik too. Gorbachev proposed elimination of *all nuclear arms* at the end of the ten-year period (presumably not just those of the United States and the Soviet Union). Reagan apparently accepted that as an ultimate goal, but not on such a schedule. His counterproposal was that *all offensive ballistic missiles of all ranges* would be eliminated at the end of the ten-year period. U.S. spokesmen have been explicit that the United States would retain sea-launched cruise missiles (SLCMs) as well as remaining strategic bombers with their ALCMs. They justify this as necessary to offset Soviet conventional force advantages and thus maintain an overall military balance—particularly in Europe.

Such differences within the over-all ceiling numbers are major, and directly related to the strategic situations of the two sides and their long-established force structures and phases. Equally integral to the strategic balance is the other main disagreement—on SDI. Reagan took the position (first clearly stated in his September 22 address to the UN General Assembly) that the ABM Treaty, now of indefinite duration, should be renegotiated to expire in ten years, after which either side would be free to deploy any type of ABM system. In the meanwhile, SDI research would proceed under his Administration's liberal interpretation of permitted development and testing. Gorbachev insisted that offensive reductions would have to be preceded by a reaffirmation of the ABM Treaty and the original restrictive interpretation of permitted development and testing activities (modernization of fixed land-based ABM deployments, but laboratory work only on mobile or exotic systems). Both sides would undertake not to exercise their treaty right of withdrawal for ten years, after which the future of the treaty could be discussed in accordance with its provisions.

The first post-Reykjavik meeting of Shultz and Eduard Shevardnadze in early November confirmed the disagreements. Geneva negotiations resumed, with the United States presenting its views on subceilings under the 1,600/6,000 ceilings for strategic delivery vehicles and warheads, and with verification discussions still ahead. No signs of a 1987 Summit emerged.

STATUS AND PROSPECTS, END OF 1986

Geneva negotiations cannot be expected to reach concrete agreements until the negotiators have been given some common goals and principles by their leaders. Establishing these is the proper task of a 1987 Summit. The elements are discernible in the Reykjavik discussions, despite current disputes and acrimony. For example, a 1987 Summit might charge the Geneva negotiators (and perhaps others) with the task of working out the following next-stage agreements:

a. An INF accord providing for zero INF in Europe and 100 for each side elsewhere, with a freeze on shorter-range nuclear missiles.
b. An initial START agreement providing for 1,600 central strategic delivery systems and 6,000 associated warheads, with cooperative as well as national verification measures including carefully defined on-site inspection.
c. A new impulse to MBFR negotiations, in recognition of the importance of a conventional military balance in Europe in relation to further cuts in strategic nuclear forces; shorter-range nuclear force reductions might be taken up in this forum.
d. Resumption of negotiations on a phased approach to a comprehensive nuclear test ban (CTB).
e. Each of these is a demanding task, given the definitional and verification problems. Some symbolic concrete actions might be possible shortly after or even at the Summit: ratification and bringing into force of the Threshold Test Ban, for example; or a freeze and perhaps even some token withdrawals of INF pending working out of dismantling and verification procedures for full withdrawal.
f. The key to such agreed guidance to negotiators would be relaxation of the U.S. principled position on SDI; the President would have to drop his insistence on revision of the ABM Treaty now to provide for expiration at the end of ten years. The SCC might then be charged with working out agreed understandings as to permitted development and testing of ABM components under the ABM Treaty.
g. On at least a de facto basis, the two sides would have to pledge themselves to stay within SALT I/II ceilings, while negotiations proceed.

While the concession by the President in *f* above would be difficult, it would be offset by the dramatic movement of the Soviet Union toward U.S. positions: the elmination of SS-20s targeted in Europe, without reduction in British and French forces; lowered ceilings on central strategic delivery systems and their warheads; and omission of sea-launched cruise missiles as well as British and French forces from initial START reductions. He would not have to abandon his vision of the future, his conviction that the security of the world and of the United States could over the longer term best be founded on the combined elimination of nuclear arms and the installation of nonnuclear SDI; nor would he have to relinquish a moderate research and development program consistent with the classic interpretation of the ABM Treaty.

There are obvious interrelationships among these elements: links exist among INF and the strategic balance, and the defense of NATO and the U.S. nuclear guarantee; SDI and the readiness of the USSR to move to actual reductions in strategic offensive systems; and the feasibility of defining and moving toward radical nuclear cuts—whether of all ballistic missiles, all strategic nuclear systems (however defined), or all nuclear arms. To attempt to agree in any but the most general terms on a subsequent START stage, as reportedly discussed at Reykjavik, would be sterile. An agreement in principle along lines I have just suggested, and its early incorporation in ratified agreements, would be a major breakthrough. Such steps would create the basis for the necessary cooperative approach to realizing such of them as prove feasible.

Such an accord on principles and negotiating goals is not inconceivable in 1987. It would be a major achievement but a difficult one. Each of the major participants—the Soviet Union; Western Europe (at least in the wings); and the United States—would have to solve certain dilemmas.

The Soviet Union

We in the United States tend to see the Soviet Union as unpredictable and unreliable as a partner in negotiation and cooperation. The Soviet Union feels similar suspicion and bewilderment. Gorbachev remarked, at the end of his television report on the Reykjavik meeting to the Soviet people in October 14, 1986, that "We also have quite an experience in dealing with the United States. We know how changeable the internal political weather is. . . ." [28] The reference goes beyond such things as the differences between Nixon and Carter and Reagan, the U.S. failures to ratify SALT II, or the Threshold Test Ban Treaty. There have been more fundamental shifts in the very premises of strategic arms control. As we saw in Sections 4 and 5 earlier, three of the key premises of SALT were:

a. Mutual vulnerability in the event of nuclear war, and the resultant recognition of mutual deterrence as the fundamental means of living with it;
b. The recognition of the link between so-called offensive and defensive strategic forces, and the need to limit the latter if offensive forces are to be limited and reduced.
c. Strategic parity, and the renunciation of pursuit of strategic superiority.

The SDI, and the proposal to renegotiate and terminate the ABM Treaty represent explicit rejections and abandonments of premises (a) and (b). The U.S. proposal at Reykjavik for the second-stage of START—elimination of all offensive ballistic missiles—represents abandonment of (c), parity. The United States justified the proposal on the basis of a U.S. need to retain strategic bombers and sea-launched cruise missiles (in which we have a substantial numerical and technological lead) to offset Soviet conventional advantage. If this position is sustained (and it is a highly debatable one), it poses a virtually insoluble dilemma for Soviet leaders: eliminating ballistic missiles would deprive them of their effective deterrent, while returning the United States for at least a time, to strategic dominance comparable to that of the 1950s when the SAC bomber force was unmatched.

Such U.S. SALT revisionism does not mean that the Soviets will abandon START. They have already experienced in the 1980s (as did we) the political costs of boycotting negotiations. And as Gorbachev noted, they know how changeable the political weather is in the United States. But their primary concern is with Soviet security, and they will move cautiously, and look to the necessary enduring prerequisites before dismantling any of their deterrent systems.

The same Gorbachev speech refers several times to Soviet opposition to SDI as "a matter of our national security." Americans have trouble understanding this and suspect its sincerity. Perhaps another quotation will help—this one from Secretary of Defense Caspar Weinberger. In his report to the President on the security significance of suspected Soviet SALT violations, he had this to say about ABM:

> The Krasnoyarsk radar together with other indications suggesting a possible future territorial defense could have a profound effect on our strategic deterrent forces. Even a *probable* (emphasis in original) territorial defense would require us to increase the

number of our offensive forces and their ability to penetrate Soviet defenses to assure that our operational plans could be executed.[29]

This is the mirror image of the Soviet reluctance to reduce sharply its deterrent offensive missiles in the face of the U.S. commitment to develop and deploy SDI. They are reportedly as skeptical as many U.S. scientists as to the feasibility of such a strategic defense concept; but so long as the United States takes it seriously and pursues it in a bipartisan-supported multi-billion dollar program, coupled with efforts to end the ABM Treaty, they have to ask whether "deep cuts" in START are prudent.

The Soviet position on this point is clear, but there is another issue, relating to the conceivable initial agreement, that could cause difficulties. If throw-weight and the number of MIRVed missiles and associated warheads for the United States and the Soviet Union are to be significantly reduced, will it be tolerable to the Soviets for the United States at the same time to go ahead and transfer to the United Kingdom some 64 Trident missiles with up to ten or a dozen reentry vehicles each? We would certainly think it an odd kind of end-run if the Soviets proposed it for one of their allies.

None of these issues (and several others could be cited) is insoluble, but each of them poses difficult dilemmas for the Soviets and for the negotiations.

Western Europe

The confused accounts of what happened at Reykjavik caused a number of expressions of concern from political and military leaders in European member countries of NATO. The principal reason was the reported agreement to move toward elimination of "all nuclear arms" over a ten-year period. Since NATO's "flexible response" doctrine assumes the backing of U.S. tactical and strategic weapons as an integral part of the NATO deterrent against Soviet conventional attack, questions were raised. No such agreement was reached, even for a second-stage START agreement. But further nervousness and alarms are to be expected. Europe depends on the U.S. alliance and the American nuclear guarantee, but is often ambivalent about nuclear weapons as well as plagued with domestic controversy. The NATO INF program originated from concerns expressed by European leaders about Soviet SS-20s; the INF negotiations as part of the NATO two-track program were insisted on by Europeans. But the prospect of the long-sought withdrawal of U.S. GLCMs and Pershings in return for similar withdrawal of SS-20s has had a mixed reception. It is partly that political leaders who have just succeeded in overcoming vigorous internal opposition and protest in order to go ahead with the INF deployments, see the whole issue being reopened, with the outcome of negotiations by no means certain. That is an objection that cannot be sustained. But there are other reasons for concern. One is the shorter-range missiles that the Soviets moved up close to West Germany, in East Germany and Czechoslovakia, when the NATO INF deployments began. European leaders see for the first time what was true all along—and what the Soviets may have come to realize first—that SS-20s were really unnecessary, given the thousands of Soviet strategic warheads, the hundreds of shorter-range delivery systems, and the relatively small number of sensitive NATO targets. Even if the new forward deployments were reversed, the vulnerable NATO situation would be little affected.

There is an elusive but weighty psychological consideration which should be recognized. At the root of the initial European reaction to the SS-20s was the way in which it dramatized an imbalance: the Soviets had weapons directed from their soil specifically at Europe, and NATO had none in Europe that were directed at Russian soil. There is much that is illogical in this attitude (many Europeans saw clearly enough that surviv-able sea-based weapons were more effective and less destabilizing and attractive targets) but it is understandable. If the SS-20s and the NATO INF are both withdrawn, Europe is still targeted by Soviet missiles, near and far, but there is no direct European match.

Against the background of the NATO two-track approach to INF, such agonizing dilemmas cannot stand out against a practicable U.S.–Soviet "zero option" for INF in Europe. The closest consultation between the United States and the rest of NATO will be required, however, and will complicate working out the terms of an agreement. More constructively, a renewed examination should be undertaken of the role of tactical nu-clear weapons in NATO defense plans and deterrence doctrine.

As for arms control, such an examination is likely to introduce a new element, already foreshadowed at Reykjavik. Just as the INF issue led to introduction of INF into strategic arms talks, shorter-range nuclear delivery systems are likely to be found to be part of the arms control equation. The West Germans have already discovered that there is some merit to the consistent Soviet position: strategic weapons are weapons that can attack your territory, and they all have to be taken into account, if not in devising limitations, then in appraising the acceptability of the resulting military balance. Limi-tations on numbers, types, and/or deployment areas and numbers may be called for. If so, in view of their relationship to the European theater military balance, the obvious place for negotiations is Vienna, where the European nations are full participants. An agreement on the other systems is unlikely as part of an initial INF package, but follow-on negotiations might be charged with pursuing the issue.

The United States

In the United States, no solid consensus exists for a foreign policy and defense posture that would accommodate cooperation with the Soviet Union on normal inter-state terms, particularly in such sensitive areas as limitation and reduction of strategic arms. As one looks ahead to the longer term, however, it is noteworthy that the confrontational con-sensus that prevailed since the last year and a half of the Carter Administration—that the Soviet Union is a dubious and untrustworthy partner in international agreements and activities, and is actively seeking and perhaps achieving a dangerous military superiority which (in President Reagan's repeated words) requires us to "play catch up"—is com-ing under challenge. The hesitant but continuing presidential pursuit of summitry is one reflection in the political sphere. There are concrete signs in the defense sphere as well.

The sharply increasing Reagan defense budget initially went through Congress al-most without opposition or change. Both in Europe and in the United States, concern, protest, and pressure appeared first among the public. The protests diminished markedly in Europe in the mid-1980s, after the commencement of INF deployments in Western Europe and the resumption of START talks. The nuclear freeze movement dwindled away in the United States. The center for informed criticism of the defense program and associated budget increases, and for pressure for more effective arms control efforts, shifted to the Congress. Resolutions were passed, particularly in the Democratic-con-trolled House, in support of SALT offensive and defensive limitations, of negotiations to ban chemical weapons and nuclear tests, and of a moratorium and eventual agreement on ASAT testing. They were for the most part "sense of Congress" resolutions, and had only limited and temporary impact.

More fundamental and significant was the increasingly bipartisan opposition to full approval of defense budget requests. As over-all budgetary deficits and the national debt rose steadily in the mid-1980s, and cuts in non-defense budgets reached the practical limit, scrutiny of defense requests became respectable, and cuts were made both in over-all levels and in particular programs. Polls showed that the majority of voters no longer considered that greater defense expenditures were needed, but instead that defense appropriations were "about right." In 1986, in the face of a Defense Department budget submission calling for sharp increases to retrieve the previous year's cut, the issue in Congress was not whether to endorse the proposed budget, but rather whether to hold appropriations at the prior year's level, thus requiring absorption of inflationary cost, or to increase the budget just enough to allow for inflation. In the face of this Congressional resistance, the President in his May 27 statement on imminent disengagement from SALT limits used the occasion for a strong call for full funding of his strategic modernization program, including the 50 MX missiles Congress was refusing to fund. In a subsequent press conference he asserted that the Soviets under SALT were increasing their superiority over us ("they were building while we were dismantling") and repeated his claim that the United States is still "playing catch-up" militarily.[30] The House and Senate Armed Services and Appropriations committees were not moved to reconsider their respective budget cuts. The implication in an election year was that members of Congress were not afraid to face their electorate while not fully supporting the President on defense needs—an estimate borne out by 1986 election results.

The situation is paradoxical, since the steadily rising defense costs over the last few years do not for the most part represent new programs. The bill is simply being presented for the Reagan strategic modernization program and other force buildups that were added to the already beefed-up final Carter defense budget. These were overwhelmingly adopted by Congress in 1981–82; the SDI program is the only substantial later addition. But in any defense buildup the initial budget installment is a fairly modest down payment. It is later budgets that rise sharply as equipment is purchased and added to the force structure. Thus the President and Secretary of Defense have some grounds for protesting budget cuts as inconsistent. On the other hand, not until the full bills begin to come in can responsible defense critics get a hearing for their objections: e.g., that the program is overly ambitious and expensive; that some bomber and fighter aircraft programs are duplicative; that missiles such as MX are vulnerable and threatening and thus destabilizing; that the strategic rationale for an enlarged Navy is obscure; and that the SDI research program tries to do too much too fast.[31] Many of these controversial programs have direct bearing on particular START and INF proposals and issues, as we have seen above. Over all, they are related to broader issues: Is there a current strategic balance? Is either the United States or the Soviet Union seeking or gaining superiority? How might strategic arms control reinforce parity and stability? How might reductions be equitably defined and carried out?

With some U.S. strategic programs under domestic challenge, the case for disengagement from SALT limits also becomes debatable; it received skeptical appraisal from a number of Congressional defense specialists. If we free ourselves from SALT constraints, we also free the Soviet Union. SALT limits have not hobbled the United States: retirement of aging Poseidon submarines, as the President has acknowledged, has been favored by the Navy for budgetary and operational reasons as Trident submarines have entered the inventory. The Soviet Union has ready options for expansion, however. It could, for example, stop dismantling older ICBMs as it is now doing as it deploys the new mobile SS-25 and imminent SS-24. Over all, SALT limits have so far constrained the Soviets more than us. Since the conclusion of SALT I, they have stayed within the SALT limits on numbers of strategic delivery systems, systems with MIRVs, and MIRV fractionation. To do so, they have destroyed or retired over 1,250 strategic missiles as newer models have been deployed, as well as some 20 ballistic missile submarines.[32] They have, indeed, also in conformity with SALT provisions, deployed thousands of MIRVs, as we too did with roughly a five-year lead time during the 1970s, so that they have begun to reach our MIRV level. But without SALT limits, they could deploy thousands more MIRVs on their heavy missiles.

The future of strategic arms control is uncertain. The trend is clearly toward disengagement from the constraints of previously negotiated agreements, and toward protracted but sterile negotiations for new agreements. But this is only half the picture that emerges from the foregoing facts. Just as noteworthy is the phenomenon that there is discomfort with this situation, and not only on the part of single-minded arms controllers. Neither in the United States nor in Europe was it politically tolerable in the early 1980s to drop out of strategic arms negotiations. Once talks are begun, it is not enough to be seen to be negotiating; some results are expected. Dramatic and radical proposals—"deep cuts" and "zero options"—come to be seen as desirable but impractical; it becomes necessary to consider "interim" measures for INF in Europe, and a pragmatic approach to reductions by stages. The scenario begins to take on a resemblance to the old SALT process. The absence of broader political negotiations also is not tolerable. Despite false starts and obstacles, the pursuit of summitry goes on, and provides an incentive and an occasion for striking deals—arms control preeminent among the topics—which, whatever their intrinsic merit, keep the process alive.

More fundamentally, the risks and costs of protracted military confrontation cannot be overlooked. The prospective abandonment of SALT limits forces the questions: Will we be better off from the gesture? Can we achieve reciprocal restraint with no agreed premises and benchmarks? Is it only arms control that has risks, or does the arms race have risks too, and might the latter be lessened by dialogue and concerted action? If we wish to level off defense programs and budgets, can agreements help us to do so with added assurance of balance and reciprocity? Has the experience, even if mixed, been all bad—and have the flaws been fatal, or should they be seen as matters for correction?

Such questions are now on the agenda, implicitly and at times explicitly, in debates and decisions, on summits and defense budgets as well as on arms control proposals. Arms control thus loses its *sui generis* or *deus ex machina* image, and becomes one of many possible avenues by which states can pursue security or economic interests that oppose or overlap with those of other states. The practical issue for leaders then becomes, not "Has arms control failed?, Can arms control solve our security problems?," but "Can we use agreements or concerted action on arms and military activities to help reduce risks and costs, and strengthen confidence and stability?"

In Part IV we turn to examining such broader questions, in the light of the experience discussed in this and other chapters, as they bear on conditions for constructive U.S.–Soviet cooperation on arms control and related political and military measures.

APPENDIX: SOURCES AND DOCUMENTATION

I have made no attempt to document every statement of fact and opinion. A list of major basic documents may be of use to some readers.

The texts of almost all of the agreements appear in *Arms Control and Disarmament Agreements* 1982 edition (Washington, D.C.; U.S. Government Printing Office), prepared by the U.S. Arms Control and Disarmament Agency; each is preceded by a brief negotiating history. A few additional texts can be found in the appendices to *International Arms Control: Issues and Agreements,* second edition (Stanford, CA: Stanford University Press, 1984). Fuller accounts of negotiating history, together with useful analysis and discussion of pros and cons for major issues, are presented in *Nuclear Arms Control: Background and Issues* (National Academy of Sciences Press, 1985).

The fullest accounts of SALT/START negotiations that have so far appeared are:

1. For SALT I, *Doubletalk,* by Gerard C. Smith, (Garden City, N.Y.: Doubleday, 1980); reissued in paperback by University Press of America, Inc., 1985
2. SALT II, *Endgame,* by Strobe Talbott (New York: Harper & Row, 1979)
3. For START, *Deadly Gambits,* Talbott (New York: Knopf, 1984)
4. For the whole sequence, the relevant chapters in Raymond L. Garthoff's *Detente and Confrontation* (Washington, D.C.: Brookings, 1985) contain many additional details and explanations. The book is particularly valuable as an account of U.S.–Soviet interaction, a process integral to success or failure in reaching agreement.

Henry Kissinger had a leading role in SALT negotiations, both for SALT I and to a lesser degree the early years of SALT II; his memoirs—*White House Years* (Boston: Little, Brown, 1979), and *Years of Upheaval* (Boston: Little, Brown, 1982), provide additional information and comment. Cyrus Vance played a similar role for SALT II in the Carter Administration, described in his memoirs, *Hard Choices* (New York: Simon and Schuster, 1983). Secretary of Defense Harold Brown was also a major actor in U.S. policy-shaping for SALT II; his discussions of SALT in relation to U.S. defense programs and policies in his annual ''posture statements'' at the time of presentation of the defense budget to the Congress are both analytic and informative. The testimony of the Secretaries of State and Defense, the Chairman of the Joint Chiefs of Staff, and the Director of the Arms Control Agency when the SALT I and SALT II agreements were being considered by the Congress present the case for the agreements; the most trenchant criticism of SALT II is that by Paul Nitze in his 1979 testimony before the Senate Foreign Relations Committee.

A lucid and recent account of Soviet thinking about these matters, and its development, is contained in David Holloway's *The Soviet Union and the Arms Race* (New Haven: Yale University Press, 1983). Garthoff's book mentioned above is useful in the same connection. Both provide many references to statements by Soviet leaders and spokesmen, as well as to other official and scholarly volumes.

There is no comprehensive account of the negotiations over the past two to three years. Only the general outlines and a few details of the various proposals and counterproposals have been made public. Three speeches by Paul Nitze, while naturally not devoid of polemics and advocacy, give clear and coherent accounts: ''The Soviet Arms Control Counterproposal,'' October 24, 1985, Department of State *Bulletin* (December 1985), p. 35; ''The Nuclear and Space Arms Talks: Where We Are After the Summit,''

December 5, 1985, *Bulletin* (February 1986), p. 58; and "Negotiations on Nuclear and Space Arms," March 13, 1986, *Bulletin* (May 1986), p. 50.

The Department of State *Bulletin* is generally the most convenient single source for statements of the views and actions of the Reagan Administration on strategic arms control. It contains the texts of speeches by the President and Secretary of State; White House statements and reports on such subjects as Soviet noncompliance and U.S. interim restraint policy (the rubric for announcements as to U.S. positions on adhering to the ABM Treaty or to SALT II limits); and a steady flow of speeches by U.S. arms control negotiators, especially by Paul Nitze, the senior and most experienced of them.

Notes

1. Ronald Reagan, "U.S. Interim Restraint Policy: Responding to Soviet Arms Control Violations," Presidential Statement of May 27, 1986, in Department of State *Bulletin* (August 1986), p. 36f.

2. Basic U.S. legislation provides that the United States shall not be obligated "to disarm or to reduce or to limit the Armed Forces or armaments of the United States, except pursuant to the treaty-making power of the President . . . or unless authorized by further affirmative legislation by the Congress . . ." (Sec. 33, Public Law 87-297, 75 Stat. 631: Arms Control and Disarmament Act.) The interim, partial, and short-term nature of the Interim Offensive Agreement made the Congressionally approved executive agreement appropriate. This is a precedent with important implications for future arms control procedures, to be discussed in Part III.

3. Reagan, "U.S. Interim Restraint Policy."

4. Richard M. Nixon, *U.S. Foreign Policy for the 1970s,* a Report to the Congress, February 18, 1970 (Washington, D.C.: U.S. Government Printing Office, 1970), pp. 142–43.

5. Ibid, p. 3.

6. Gerard C. Smith, *Doubletalk: The Story of SALT I* (Garden City, N.Y.: Doubleday, 1980), p. 83.

7. Department of State *Bulletin* (January 1986), p. 7.

8. *Documents on Disarmament, 1969* (Washington, D.C.: U.S. Government Printing Office, 1970) p. 315.

9. *Foreign Broadcast Information Service (FBIS),* November 21, 1985.

10. *(Second) Report of the President's Commission on Strategic Forces,* March 21, 1984, p. 4. Released by the White House.

11. House Joint Resolution 1227, 92nd Congress, passed, September 30, 1972 as Public Law 92-448.

12. Richard M. Nixon, *U.S. Foreign Policy for the 1970's: Shaping A Durable Peace,* May 3, 1973 (Washington, D.C.: U.S. Government Printing Office, 1970), p. 36.

13. Cyrus Vance, *Hard Choices* (New York: Simon & Shuster, 1983), p. 135.

14. Ibid, p. 354.

15. Ibid, p. 61.

16. Ibid, p. 350.

17. Ronald Reagan, "Report to Congress," June 10, 1985, Department of State *Bulletin* (August 1985), p. 33.

18. *FBIS,* January 14, 1985, p. AA5.

19. For example, see Sidney Drell et al., *The Reagan Strategic Defense Initiative* (Cambridge, Mass.: Ballinger Publishing Co., 1985).

20. Press statement, National Campaign to Save the ABM Treaty, Washington, D.C., May 26, 1986.

21. See speech by Senator Sam Nunn, August 8, 1986, in *Congressional Record,* vol. 132,

no. 108, p. s-10810; and letter of December 1, 1986, from Senator Carl Levin to Secretary of State George Shultz.

22. Department of State *Bulletin* (March 1985), p. 30.

23. Department of State *Bulletin* (January 1986), p. 8.

24. Drawn from Jonathan Dean, *Watershed in Europe* (Lexington, Mass.: Lexington Books, 1987), pp. 145–56.

25. Ronald Reagan. "Building an Interim Framework for Mutual Restraint," Presidential Statement of June 10, 1985, Department of State *Bulletin* (August 1985), p. 33.

26. Ronald Reagan, "U.S. Interim Restraint Policy: Responding to Soviet Arms Control Violations," Presidential Statement, May 27, 1986, Department of State *Bulletin* (August 1986), p. 36.

27. See excerpts in *New York Times* (June 1, 1986), p. 8; from TASS text of Soviet Government statement of May 31.

28. See excerpts in *New York Times* (October 15, 1986).

29. "Responding to Soviet Violations Policy," memorandum for the President from the Office of the Secretary of Defense, November 13, 1985.

30. Department of State *Bulletin* (August 1986), p. 17 f.

31. For one discussion of the complex budgetary issues, see William W. Kaufmann, *The 1986 Defense Budget* (Washington, D.C.: Brookings, 1985).

32. Report No. 85-768S, "Soviet Compliance with the SALT I and SALT II Agreements on Offensive Arms," June 13, 1985, Congressional Research Service, pp. 4, 10, 11.

10

The U.S.–Soviet Standing Consultative Commission

ROBERT W. BUCHHEIM AND PHILIP J. FARLEY

Cooperation in security affairs goes well beyond reaching and signing agreements: that is only the first step. Agreements must be carried out—by parallel and to some extent coordinated action. If such action is to satisfy the parties involved, it cannot be automatic or without problems. Few agreements—especially pathfinding and complex ones such as the SALT I and SALT II treaties—would ever be concluded if all eventualities had first to be foreseen and all necessary implementing procedures and actions spelled out in detail. Provided sound general provisions can be reached, many implementing procedures and actions, as well as detailed interpretations of language, can better and more realistically be dealt with in an ongoing process of interaction among the parties after the agreements come into force.

Such a process cannot, however, be left to chance. The ABM Treaty, of indefinite duration, specifies to this end the establishment of a Standing Consultative Commission of the parties (Article XIII), and also joint reviews of the treaty at five-year intervals and an amendment procedure (Article XIV). The SALT I and SALT II agreements on offensive strategic arms, which are short-term and limited in their coverage of relevant systems, provide integrally for further negotiations, in addition to the work of the SCC.

For a study of U.S.–Soviet security cooperation, the SCC has special interest. Designed to institutionalize key aspects of cooperation in carrying out formal obligations, the SCC with its nearly fifteen-year history constitutes an experiment deserving separate examination here. In the interests of brevity, we have omitted many of the details that are contained in the chapters on compliance and on strategic arms negotiations. Sources and additional material are identified in the references at the end of this chapter.

SCC ORIGINS AND FUNCTIONS

From the outset of the SALT negotiations in 1969, the United States and the Soviet Union were conscious of the novelty, complexity, and difficulty of their task of achieving effective limitation of strategic arms. After three and a half years, they were able in 1972 to reach only partial and interim agreement on limiting some offensive arms. While the ABM Treaty dealt more comprehensively with defensive systems and could thus be of indefinite duration, many problems of implementation and verification were foreseeable. Thus it was recognized early in the negotiations that a special standing unit would be needed to deal with problems of implementation of both agreements, including questions relating to compliance with treaty provisions and adaptation to changing circumstances.

Only routine difficulties were encountered in drafting Article XIII of the ABM Treaty creating the SCC and listing its functions. The SALT I Interim Agreement on offensive arms provides for use of the SCC in carrying out that agreement also. The mandate of the SCC is quite broad:

To promote the objectives and implementation of this Treaty, the Parties shall establish promptly a Standing Consultative Commission, within the framework of which they will:

(a) consider questions concerning compliance with the obligations assumed and related situations which may be considered ambiguous;

(b) provide on a voluntary basis such information as either Party considers necessary to assure confidence in compliance with the obligations assumed;

(c) consider questions involving unintended interference with national technical means of verification;

(d) consider possible changes in the strategic situation which have a bearing on the provisions of this Treaty;

(e) agree upon procedures and dates for destruction and dismantling of ABM systems or their components in cases provided for by the provisions of this Treaty;

(f) consider, as appropriate, possible proposals for further increasing the viability of this Treaty, including proposals for amendments in accordance with the provisions of this Treaty;

(g) consider, as appropriate, proposals for further measures aimed at limiting strategic arms.

The SALT II Treaty concluded in 1979 provides in Article XVII for use of the SCC. In view of the broader scope of that treaty, the SCC functions are expanded somewhat to deal with additional types of offensive arms and to provide for regular data exchanges on strategic inventories, as well as for ICBM test notifications stipulated in the treaty.

On December 21, 1972, the United States and the USSR concluded a Memorandum of Understanding which established the SCC. This founding memorandum provides that, in addition to its responsibilities under the SALT I agreements, the SCC shall also promote the objectives and implementation of the Agreement on Measures to Reduce the Risk of Outbreak of Nuclear War between the United States and the USSR signed on September 30, 1971. It is supplemented by agreed regulations to guide SCC operations.

The Memorandum of Understanding provides, among other things, that the SCC shall meet no less often than two times per year, that the SCC shall meet in Geneva (but other sites may be used as agreed), and that each government shall be represented on the SCC by a commissioner and a deputy commissioner assisted by such staff as is deemed necessary. In addition to general procedural matters, the regulations provide for written or oral communications between commissioners during intervals between SCC sessions so that the SCC is, in effect, in permanent session, and further provide that the SCC may not make its proceedings public except with the express consent of both Commissioners.

On both sides, the delegations* include advisers assigned by interested agencies, and both civilian and military personnel. The interactions among people from the two sides within the SCC have been correct and directed to the business at hand. There have been only three Soviet and three U.S. commissioners over the more than fourteen years of the SCC's existence, all with a high level of relevant experience, competence, and professionalism.

Within the U.S. government, the SCC commissioner and deputy commissioner are appointed by the President upon the recommendation of the secretary of state, secretary of defense, chairman of the Joint Chiefs of Staff, director of the Arms Control and Disarmament Agency, director of central intelligence, and the President's special assistant for national security affairs. Although SCC proceedings are not made public, the executive branch provides full accounts of any substantive understandings reached in the SCC to six Congressional committees: the Senate Committee on Foreign Relations, the House Committee on Foreign Affairs, and the committees in both houses on Armed Services and Intelligence. In addition, the executive responds to requests from these committees for further information.

The SCC does not determine compliance or settle compliance issues; it is not an independent tribunal or decision-making body. It is indeed "consultative," discussing questions or issues in an effort to clarify facts and intentions and to find possible ways to reconcile differences regarding implementation of agreements. The delegations are agents of their respective governments, acting according to instructions and reporting fully their formal and informal discussions. Within the U.S. government, the interested agencies work within the National Security Council framework to review treaty application and compliance and to determine matters to be taken up in the SCC and their disposition. Backstopping of SCC meetings is handled by a similar committee apparatus.

The SCC is not primarily a negotiating body. Ongoing negotiations on strategic arms control have consistently been the responsibility of other delegations in Geneva. However, if SCC discussions clarify issues and lead to consensus between governments on matters of procedure or interpretation concerning implementation of agreements, the SCC commissioners may be charged with negotiating and signing appropriate protocols or understandings. In dealing with questions relating to the implementation of established agreements, both components of the SCC routinely have recourse to the records of the negotiations leading to formal agreement.

While compliance questions have been the main and the most prominent SCC topics, the basic purpose of the SCC is the broader one of promoting the implementation and viability of agreements within its responsibility. In the next section we will cite several examples of such activity, which includes exchanging data and establishing procedures for dismantling and replacement of excess or obsolete systems, and for implementing the Accident Measures agreement.

On compliance-related issues, the role of the SCC is to help clarify and deal with uncertainties or suspected violations; it does not determine whether the agreements are being complied with. Nor does the SCC *verify* compliance. It may be useful to distinguish here among *compliance, monitoring,* and *verification,* and the relationship of the SCC to each. *Compliance* refers to conduct of the parties to an agreement in carrying out their obligations and acting in conformity with the provisions. *Monitoring* refers to

---

*In standard SCC parlance, these are referred to as "the U.S. component" and "the USSR component" of the joint body.

the measures taken by each party to observe what the others do with regard to the subject matter of the agreement; monitoring is in general carried on by national technical means of observation and other data collection methods familiar in intelligence gathering. *Verification* is the process by which each party compares the data obtained from monitoring with the obligations of other parties, in order to judge whether there is satisfactory compliance, or, instead, a degree of uncertainty that would justify asking for clarification. All of these functions are internal governmental matters for the respective parties. The SCC is a joint instrument to assist in resolving doubts over compliance; such doubts can arise from ambiguities in actions or in treaty interpretation, or from actions that appear to contradict obligations. The SCC discussions may also provide some help to monitoring and verification, from the data exchanges called for by the SALT II Treaty, or from other information or explanations provided in the SCC consultations. But the main SCC contribution in this area is assistance to governments in assessing and assuring compliance, which is of course central to treaty implementation and viability.

To this subordinate but important role, the SCC brings valuable assets in the privacy and regularity of its consultations. The privacy provided for in SCC regulations helps make it possible to raise and deal with compliance issues in a non-challenging and cooperative way. On technical weapons issues of considerable security sensitivity to one or both sides, the privacy requirement has on occasion enabled a degree of plain talk that is difficult for both the United States and the Soviet Union, but particularly for the latter. SCC secrecy has, however, occasioned the one controversy of real substance that has arisen regarding SCC procedures. The problem is rooted in the sharply different societies and governmental systems of the two countries, and will be examined later along with other issues relating to the value and future usefulness of the SCC.

The continuity and regular meeting schedule of the SCC also facilitate its consultative mission. As noted already, there have been three Soviet and three American commissioners, all non-political and with professional backgrounds and competence. In addition to dealing with the highly contentious compliance questions they have worked together regularly on concrete tasks of applying specific agreements, exchanging data, and working out necessary procedures. Not only have such activities constituted achievements of substance; dealing with them has maintained the SCC as a channel of U.S.–Soviet contact and communication even when other channels were temporarily unused. Along with the provision for regular meetings, this has made it possible for some questions and issues to be broached in a routine and noncontentious way, in time to clarify and defuse them before the two sides could become entrenched in opposing positions.

While the SCC is the most specific and continuing device for assessing and reinforcing the viability of strategic arms agreements, it is not the only one. Others are the provisions in the ABM Treaty for treaty review every five years and the amendment procedure (Article XIV); and the ongoing SALT/START negotiations themselves, which are explicitly recognized in the SALT I and SALT II accords as essential to the viability of the offensive arms agreements. The first two five-year reviews of the ABM Treaty, in 1977 and 1982, were considered by some to be little more than pro forma, and were conducted in the SCC. The 1987 review might involve more fundamental policy issues, arising from the U.S. Strategic Defense Initiative and its implementation program and from the Soviet position on the link between the SDI and the Geneva strategic arms negotiations. The SCC may thus not be the appropriate venue.

The SALT I Interim Offensive Agreement was partial in scope as well as limited to five years in duration. It thus did not deal broadly or definitively with the problem of limiting offensive strategic arms and Article VII commits the parties to continue active negotiations. During the visit of Leonid Brezhnev to the United States in June 1973, he and President Richard Nixon signed a statement of Joint Principles to guide these negotiations. At Vladivostok in November 1974, Brezhnev and President Gerald Ford reached a more detailed understanding on the main outlines of what became SALT II. While the SALT II Treaty was not signed until 1979, two years after the formal expiration of the SALT I Interim Agreement, these sequential understandings kept the negotiating process alive and prevented the long-drawn-out negotiations—slowed because of both technical and political complexities—from putting strategic arms control in peril. The SALT II Treaty, while broader in scope, was also not comprehensive and of limited duration, in this case seven years. In addition to a continuing treaty commitment to further negotiations, it includes a protocol of two-year duration placing certain restrictions on some systems (particularly cruise missiles and mobile missiles) while negotiations on them continued; and a Joint Statement of Principles as general guidance for future negotiations. The premise of these provisions, as well as of the SCC, is that partial agreements cannot be indefinitely viable unless outstanding issues of scope and treatment of strategic arms limitation are systematically addressed and resolved in a way that produces a mutually satisfactory strategic balance. The fragile status of SALT II at the end of 1986 shows the validity of this premise.

SCC EXPERIENCE AND ACHIEVEMENT, 1973–86

Consultation on compliance-related questions has been the main, and the most prominent, preoccupation of the SCC. Compliance issues themselves, their merits and status, are the subject of another chapter. Here we will focus on the SCC's role and its contribution to dealing with these issues.

The SALT I accords specifically provided for destruction, dismantling, or replacement of strategic systems in accordance with agreed procedures, and for the SCC to work these out. Accordingly, the SCC took up these matters after convening in May 1973. Two protocols on Procedures Governing Replacement, Dismantling or Destruction, and Notification—one for strategic offensive arms and one for ABM systems and their components—were agreed in the SCC in June 1974 and signed by Secretary of State Henry Kissinger and Foreign Minister Andrei Gromyko in Moscow on July 3, 1974. These documents govern the replacement of certain older ICBM launchers and launchers on older submarines by ballistic missile launchers on modern submarines in accordance with the Interim Agreement. The protocols also set procedures for the dismantling or destruction of weapons systems and components in excess of those permitted by the ABM Treaty and the Interim Agreement.

In October 1976 the two SCC commissioners signed a supplementary protocol regulating the replacement of ABM systems and their components, and the exchange of ABM system deployment areas, to take account of the protocol to the ABM Treaty that had been signed in Moscow on July 3, 1974.

Also in 1976, a protocol was agreed that codified means for facilitating and speeding the transmission of immediate notifications, as called for by the Agreement on Measures to Reduce the Risk of Outbreak of Nuclear War of September 30, 1971. Discussions of this matter had begun in the SCC in early 1975. Implementation of the Accident Measure agreement remained on the SCC agenda. In June 1985 an additional common understanding was reached, extending the provision for "immediate notification" to cover any suspected threat or actual use of nuclear arms by a third country or by a terrorist group.

In 1976, the United States became concerned that the Soviet Union would not meet requirements for timely dismantling of land-based missiles to offset the introduction of new sea-based launchers. It was decided to raise the question in the SCC, but before this could be done the Soviets acknowledged that the dismantling of 41 older ICBM launchers had not been completed on time. They predicted that all dismantling would be completed by June 1, 1976, and agreed that no more submarines with replacement SLBM launchers would begin sea trials before such completion. Both conditions were met.

A recurring topic of SCC discussion has been ABM and air defense radars or surface-to-air missiles (SAM). The ABM Treaty stipulates that radars other then ABM radars may not be given the capability to counter strategic ballistic missiles or their elements in flight trajectory, or to be tested in an ABM mode. An SCC Agreed Statement in 1978 clarified treaty obligations regarding the use of radars in an ABM mode or for range safety and instrumentation purposes. Discussion of the general topic, which had begun in the SCC as early as February 1975, continued and led to a further common understanding in June 1985. Parties are therein obligated to turn off surface-to-air missile radars at test ranges during ABM tests, unless potentially hostile aircraft have clearly approached the test range; in the latter eventuality, a written explanation must be provided within 30 days and at the following SCC meeting.

The first five-year review of the ABM Treaty came due in 1977 and was conducted in a special session of the SCC. A Joint Communiqué was issued on November 21, 1977. The parties agreed that the treaty was operating effectively, that the SCC consultations during the five-year period had been productive and useful in promoting understanding, working out procedures, and resolving issues, and that they would seek to maintain and further increase the viability and effectiveness of the treaty.

In 1982, the SCC conducted the second five-year review of the ABM Treaty. There was no communiqué, but the Annual ACDA Report to Congress for 1982 states tersely that "Each party reaffirmed its commitment to the aims and objectives of the Treaty and to the process of consultation within the framework of the SCC." This conclusion, of course, pre-dated President Reagan's "Star Wars" speech of March 1983, which set the United States on a course looking to possible abandonment or change of the ABM Treaty and its strategic premises.

COMPLIANCE AND THE SCC

Compliance has been the main preoccupation of the SCC, and in recent years it has become increasingly contentious. A separate chapter by Gloria Duffy deals with changing U.S. views of Soviet compliance and the various reciprocal questions or charges of noncompliance. Here these matters will be viewed primarily for the light they cast on the role of the SCC. It is convenient to divide review of the SCC experience with compliance into two periods—one from 1972 to 1980; the other from 1981 to the present, after Soviet intervention in Afghanistan and the suspension of Senate consideration of the SALT II Treaty.

In the period of the 1970s, the SCC worked in a regular and private way to deal with a number of compliance questions, in addition to the sometimes overlapping tasks of implementation of provisions of SALT I. Charges of Soviet noncompliance appeared increasingly in the U.S. political arena, however, as the spirit of détente weakened and the SALT II negotiations moved into their final stages in 1978–79. Even before the signing of the treaty in 1979, the Carter Administration found it necessary to address publicly the question of the Soviet record of compliance in a letter from Secretary of State Cyrus Vance to the chairman of the Senate Committee on Foreign Relations. That letter describes the issues taken up in the SCC at the initiative of either the United States or the Soviet Union, and the disposition of each. The list embraces the following questions:

Raised by the United States

— Nature of new silos in Soviet ICBM fields, claimed to be launch control facilities by the Soviets;
— Concealment measures;
— Soviet conformity with restrictions on modern large ballistic missiles;
— Possible testing of an air defense system (SA-5) radar in an ABM mode;
— Reporting on dismantling of excess ABM test launchers;
— ABM radar on Kamchatka Peninsula;
— Dismantling or destruction of replaced ICBM launchers; and
— Concealment at a test range.

Raised by the Soviet Union

— Shelters over Minutemen silos undergoing modification;
— Status of Atlas and Titan launchers;
— Radar on Shemya Island;
— Privacy of SCC proceedings;
— Dismantling or destruction of ABM radar under construction at Malmstrom AFB; and
— Various radar deployments.

The lists are quite symmetrical. This is not by chance; in addition to the fact that the topics reflect some of the most difficult issues in the drafting of SALT I agreements, it is fair to say that the Soviets engaged to a considerable degree in what might be termed "counterpunching" to U.S. questions. The only kind of issue raised initially by them is that of SCC privacy, which is not only important to SCC effectiveness, but a preoccupation reflecting Soviet secretiveness.

The conclusion of the Carter Administration was that in each instance raised by the United States, the Soviet activity in question had either ceased or additional information had allayed U.S. concern. In retrospect, that positive assessment, while warranted, is somewhat sweeping. For example, the issue of permissible dimensions of ICBM launchers deployed under SALT I provisions limiting "modern large ballistic missiles" was one that had not been resolved in the SALT I negotiations. It was not resolved in the SCC either, whether by reaching a common understanding or by a change in Soviet action. However, the simultaneous SALT II negotiations did reach agreement on the boundary between "large," or "heavy," and "light" missiles. On the concealment issue, an acceptable outcome was reached, but much too slowly, so that later it was possible to charge that concealment only ended after dubious concealed activities had been completed. In any case, the Carter Administration's positive assessment was not shared by SALT skeptics in the United States in the late 1970s. In the 1980s, several of these items appeared in reports to Congress on "Soviet noncompliance," as examples of past violations or highly questionable behavior.

As Gloria Duffy explains in the chapter on compliance, the Reagan Administration assumed a much more aggressive posture from the outset. In addition to initial statements that the SALT II Treaty was not only "fatally flawed" but "dead," and a delay of a year and a half in resuming strategic arms control negotiations, it provided the Congress a series of detailed reports of Soviet acts of noncompliance, variously characterized as suspected, probable, or proven. These included a number previously considered as disposed of. The prior work of the SCC, and even its inherent value, were vigorously disparaged. The most extensive negative treatment of the SCC came in a letter and enclosed memorandum for the President from Secretary of Defense Weinberger on Soviet noncompliance and possible U.S. responses, on November 13, 1985. Some excerpts follow:

Verification is not a substitute for compliance. It is vital to know what the Soviets are doing and to be able to judge when violations take place. But verification does not guarantee compliance. Some of the most troubling violations are also the most easily verified. The Krasnoyarsk radar and the SS-25 are examples of violations that the Soviets must have known we would detect . . .

The Standing Consultative Commission, the body assigned to deal with violations, has failed to gain Soviet compliance and will continue to do so. Indeed, it has, I think, generally discouraged more effective measures to gain Soviet compliance by pushing compliance issues into the recesses of a languid, confidential and ineffective forum . . .

The United States might not be faced with the Krasnoyarsk radar today if, more than a decade ago, we had effectively protested the construction, also illegal under the ABM Treaty, of a Soviet radar at Kamchatka . . .

SALT I and II and the ABM Treaty all provided for a Standing Consultative Commission (SCC) for the drafting of technical implementing agreements and the resolution of compliance issues. It consists of representatives of the U.S. and Soviet Union who negotiate on the occasion of their meetings. Its deliberations are secret.

Contrary to the claims often made for it, the SCC has failed to resolve any significant compliance issue in the approximately 1,500 days that it has been in session over the last 13 years. A less productive forum for the resolution of disputes would be difficult to find.

Far from resolving disputes over compliance, the SCC has become a diplomatic carpet under which Soviet violations have been continuously swept, an Orwellian memory-hole into which our concerns have been dumped like yesterday's trash. Unwilling to face up to a mounting record of Soviet violations, successive administrations have consigned our concerns to the SCC where they have been "discussed," often for years on end, with wholly unsatisfactory results.

Violations raised by the U.S. in the SCC were dealt with in slow motion while they continued and until they had run their course, at which time they were declared to have been resolved. A good case in point is the Soviet program for testing air defense components in an "ABM mode" in violation of the ABM Treaty. Well over 100 suspicious tests were conducted over twelve years while the SCC painted an attenuated arabesque that served to obscure their continuation. When their tests were completed the Soviets announced, and the United States gratefully received, the news that they would cease. Even this dismal result proved ephemeral; after a brief interval, the Soviets resumed the prohibited tests—and back we went to the SCC.

Our Administration has been the first to acknowledge the ineffectiveness of the SCC, and the first one willing to report publicly Soviet violations.

There are those who believe that the inadequacies of the SCC can be overcome by redoubled effort. I believe this misses the essential point about the SCC. If the Soviets comply with agreements, the issue of violations will not arise in the SCC or anywhere else. If they wish to violate them, they will not be deterred by semi-annual meetings of the SCC. The SCC is merely a forum for discussion, a date and place and list of attendees. While, in theory, it could be used to dispel misunderstandings, misunderstanding is not the source of Soviet behavior; rather Soviet behavior is motivated by a desire to gain advantage and the SCC is powerless to affect it.

A constituency has developed around the SCC composed, as is the SCC itself, of Soviets and Americans who believe that violations of agreements must not be permitted to become prominent features of the arms control dialogue. Only a clear declaration from the President that the SCC has failed offers any prospect that we will find the will and opportunity to make the appropriate responses that will create incentives for Soviet compliance and disincentives to Soviet violations.[1]

To this should be added a more succinct response by Assistant Secretary of Defense Richard Perle to a question by Senator John Tower, chairman of the Senate Armed Services Committee:

Senator Tower. Both you, today, and Ambassador Rowny, in a recent appearance before the Committee, have expressed serious concern about the effectiveness of the Standing Consultative Commission (SCC) in resolving our concerns about Soviet noncompliance. What can be done to enhance the SCC effectiveness?

Secretary Perle. The issue is not really the SCC. The SCC is not a judicial commission. It does not make decisions, and it cannot order the Soviet Union to comply with arms control agreements. It is merely a negotiating forum. The problem is Soviet unwillingness to live up to the obligations that they have undertaken, not SCC effectiveness.

I have put emphasis on the failure of the SCC to resolve compliance concerns because previous Administrations, in efforts to sell unverifiable arms control agreements to Congress, have created a virtual mythology about it. The fact of the matter is that serious compliance problems have generally not been resolved by the SCC or in any other manner.[2]

Such sweeping condemnation of the SCC goes beyond the actual experience and attitude of the Reagan Administration. As we have noted, in June 1985 the SCC commissioner, under Washington instructions, worked out and agreed to two new common understandings in the SCC; one of these established a procedure to resolve concerns about operation of Soviet air defense radars during ICBM tests. While extreme, the general thrust of the statements by Weinberger and Perle is similar to that of the series of Administration reports on "Soviet noncompliance," in which the objects of criticism are not the SCC but alleged deliberate Soviet patterns of violation of agreements, and conscious complicity of previous U.S. Administrations.

The Perle quotation thus goes to the heart of the matter for present purposes, in saying that "the issue is not really the SCC." If the SALT agreements are unverifiable, if there have been serious compliance problems reflecting a basic Soviet unwillingness to live up to their obligations, and if previous administrations have been interested in selling unsound agreements rather than in insisting that the Soviets live up to them, then the SCC, which is an agent, not a principal or independent actor, cannot correct these outrages. The current compliance situation is, however, much more nuanced, as Duffy's chapter and related studies argue. Over-all Soviet fulfillment of major obligations under agreements, whether ratified or in effect on a de facto basis, has been generally good; the security significance, or "seriousness," of Soviet violations is limited in the few instances in which they have not given at least a plausible explanation or response. Despite the assertive tone of the Perle and Weinberger quotations, questions remain open as to: the potential value for U.S. security of present or prospective strategic arms agreements, which are still being actively pursued; the possibility of adequate (even if never 100 percent) verification; and the Soviet Union's security and political interest in carrying out agreements and being seen to do so. So long as such questions remain open, there remains a role for the SCC—which thus still continues to function.

Some of the recurring—one might even say perennial—questions that arise in the SCC illuminate the interrelationship between the texts of strategic arms control treaties and the institutional bodies or procedures related to their implementation and viability, such as the SCC itself, the five-year ABM Treaty reviews, and the ongoing incremental process of further limitation and reduction of strategic arms. Discussion of SCC activities is often cast in terms of efforts to make up for inadequacies or ambiguities or mistakes in treaty drafting which should have been avoided. Such defects occur, and ought to be avoided if at all possible. But in complex and contentious negotiations between adversary states with a high degree of reciprocal incomprehension and distrust, it is surprising that so few cases in this category have arisen. Going further in the direction of trying to anticipate all contingencies in treaty drafting would add to the already formidable structure of treaty provisions, common understandings, agreed statements, and so on, which make the ABM Treaty and SALT II Treaty so bewildering and even impenetrable for the layman. And if everything is to be foreseen before anything is agreed and put into practice, the arms control process would be even slower than it is; it might even become more abstract and theoretical in the absence of experience with first-stage limited agreements that enable the parties to see without excessive risk what problems will actually arise and what solutions are most practical.

Thus treaty language stating commitments in general terms may not always be a second-best solution to more concrete and comprehensive spelling-out. The latter alternative may result in lists that prove not to be inclusive and thus can be used to justify anything not listed, even though it is arguably inconsistent with overall treaty premises. Also, specific provisions appearing satisfactory when drafted may, with the passage of time and changes in technology or in the strategic situation, become inappropriate or otherwise defective. Even ambiguity may be the best that can be agreed, in taking initial account of a problem whose importance is clear to both sides but for which there is no agreement as to the right solution, or perhaps not yet political readiness by one party or both to commit themselves to it.

The SCC then becomes a crucial part of the strategy of dealing with such treaty-drafting dilemmas. The legacy for the SCC will be the duty of dealing with intricate, changing, and often contentious problems of treaty interpretation and application. But this dual approach to cooperation under agreements—establishing norms and principles in the optimum attainable form at time of conclusion of an agreement without seeking premature precision and detail, and leaving much to be worked out in the SCC—may be the pragmatic and wiser course.

One of the perennial SCC topics illustrates these considerations. The ABM Treaty could not, and did not, ban all relevant radars or all surface-to-air missiles and their launchers. Air defense systems are extensive, particularly those in the Soviet Union facing U.S. (and some other) long-range bombers and strike aircraft and various cruise missiles. Radars for this purpose, and for others such as early warning or air traffic control or space tracking, have been deployed and are constantly being improved. The system capabilities required for an effective ABM defense far exceed those for current air defense; but that does not mean that a concrete technical dividing line for all time could be written into a 1972 treaty (anymore than a specific dividing line between national air space and outer space has been practical or prudent). High-powered radars, whatever their stated or primary purposes, can be used for other purposes, as in the case of Soviet or American early warning radars which, if an ABM system were to be deployed, could contribute importantly to initial detection and tracking of attacking ballistic missiles. Air defense technology must cope with constantly changing threats, such as the U.S. development of the B-1B penetrating bomber and a prospective Stealth bomber; deployment of ALCMs and SLCMs and Europe-based GLCMs; Soviet deployment of SS-20s and forward deployment of shorter range ballistic missiles facing NATO Europe, as well as U.S. Pershing IIs within range of the USSR. The cruise missiles and other theatre nuclear forces suggest a possible case for development and deployment of anti-tactical ballistic missile systems (ATBM), posing new problems of distinguishing ABM systems and components from otherwise acceptable non-ABM systems. The consequence is constant evolution in air defense and other systems, which must be assessed and taken into account in implementing the ABM Treaty and maintaining its viability.

The treaty, rather than trying to anticipate and regulate all these developments and responsive actions, is structured as follows, in a way made possible by the planned provision for the SCC:

— A general formula in Article VI(a) obligates the parties not to give missiles, launchers, or radars, other than ABM interceptor missiles, ABM launchers, or ABM radars, capabilities to counter strategic ballistic missiles or their elements in flight trajectory.
— Two important elaborations of this formula, in categorical terms that themselves require evolving interpretation, ban testing such non-ABM components in an ABM mode, and limit deployment of early warning radars to the periphery of the country and facing outwards.
— Several "Agreed Statements" were drawn up, on which consensus was possible but formal treaty incorporation judged undesirable.
— One unilateral U.S. statement was included (on testing in an ABM mode), which in effect was illustrative rather than an obligation.

With this body of guidance, the SCC has dealt with a succession of issues as they have arisen in concrete form, including such matters as SAM testing, location and mission of large phased-array radars, mobility of air defense radars, and SAM activity during ICBM/SLBM tests. As the chapter on compliance reflects, some of these have been resolved at least temporarily (one as recently as June 1985), by changes in national SAM activities or procedures; some are still hotly contested (Krasnoyarsk early warning or space tracking radar); some still may lie ahead (limiting or adapting to ATBM development if it occurs; issues arising from SDI development).

New understandings may become necessary and emerge from the SCC. For example, the Krasnoyarsk radar issue might lead to agreement that additional "other large phased-array radars" (OLPARs) are not needed and will not be deployed, or, more modestly, that in future any OLPARs for permitted purposes (space tracking, verification, early warning) will be submitted for discussion in the SCC before construction starts. The outcome might be a treaty amendment, or a common understanding, perhaps negotiated in the SCC in either case.

The SCC experience offers another example to suggest that preciseness of treaty terms, especially before experience in treaty implementation, is not always the solution to a complex and dynamic problem, though treaty language can serve as a benchmark or rough criterion provided there is a body such as SCC to apply it. The SALT II Treaty provides that only one new type of ICBM will be developed and deployed by each side during its lifetime, and defines "new" to mean differing from existing types in certain parameters by more than 5 percent. For the SS-25, compliance has been hotly debated. The 5 percent criterion has been of doubtful value, both because of the questionable ability of national technical means of verification to make such fine distinctions and quantitative measurements; and because of the dubious significance of such small deviations. This uncertainty applies to both existing and new ICBM types, so that the task becomes one of trying to define a small percent of relative change in two uncertain factors. (The same difficulty of precise measurement and evaluation of compliance has notoriously plagued the Threshold Test Ban Treaty with its ceiling of 150kt equivalent yield.) The point is not that such criteria are to be rejected, but that they must not be expected to eliminate the need for consultative or even cooperative measures for treaty interpretation and application. A consultative instrumentality such as the SCC remains essential, and such benchmarks have their value as aids in consultation rather than as simple and infallible discriminants.

The SCC role in cooperative approaches to implementing strategic arms agreements, even if never-ending and rarely producing tidy definitive solutions, ought to be familiar and comprehensible to Americans. National or state legislation is regularly tested or contested as to its relevance or detailed application or even its soundness. It is interpreted and adjudicated by courts, supplemented by administrative organs and their regulations, amended when appropriate. The institutional structure and context are of course very different for the national and international cases, but the realities of human nature and society, which impose the need for an ongoing adaptive and evolutionary process, are similarly compelling.

Other recurring issues in the SCC history could be reviewed to illustrate the concept we have described of its role and achievements. So long as strategic arms control is partial in scope and national strategic programs of development, testing, and deployment continue, problems of treaty interpretation and application, and new challenges to viability, will arise and will have to be dealt with cooperatively in a body such as the SCC. Adaptations in procedures for implementation and verification, and corresponding adaptations in national strategic programs, will succeed each other. The role of the SCC will continue to be constructive and integral to the process, not only as a forum of consultation on issues and questions, but also as a domain of cooperation between rival nuclear powers over an indefinite future period of technical and political change and interaction. As long as engaging in this tentative path of cooperation remains contentious in the United States, the SCC will not be exempt from criticism and contention in its turn—even while it is grudgingly made use of, as in establishing the June 1985 understandings.

SOME SUGGESTIONS FOR FUTURE CONSIDERATION

In the light of the SCC history, some observations can be made about the future role of the SCC in support of U.S.–Soviet arms control cooperation.

1. There is a direct relationship between the attitude and approach of the two countries and the success of the SCC's work. The Soviet Union has been relatively circumspect in the SCC, or has engaged in "counter punching" in response to U.S. challenges. When well-formulated U.S. questions or issues have been presented in private, the Soviet delegation has reportedly often been quite detailed and forthcoming in discussions of dismantling procedures for retired systems, or of relevant physical characteristics of the SS-25. Only rarely has the Soviet delegation taken the initiative, as it did in 1976, when the Soviets acknowledged delay in completing dismantling of some land-based missile launchers before the United States could raise the question. A more anticipatory and forthcoming Soviet approach would be helpful; in its absence, a suspicion by some Americans that the Soviets only acknowledge a problem when they are caught out will be natural.

The United States has been more active in using the forum, but has increasingly tended to be accusatory rather than inquiring. Questions and issues need to be raised, but with the reasons for concern presented, at least initially, in a factual way without implied presumption of guilt pending response.

The United States cannot always afford to delay in raising questions until its case has been perfected; possible Soviet infringements can too easily become a matter of U.S. public knowledge, debate, and prejudgment, and put the Soviets on the defensive in a way that will be counterproductive when the matter is addressed in the SCC. Also, the longer questionable activities go on, the harder they are to rectify.

2. It is sometimes suggested that the SCC should be more active on functions identified in Article XIII of the ABM Treaty but rarely if at all exercised.

Article XIII.*d* provides for consideration of changes in the strategic situation that have a bearing on the provisions of the treaty. Where such changes arise, it is clearly appropriate for them to be addressed in the SCC as they relate to implementation or compliance. (More broadly, it would in the view of many officials and observers of U.S.–Soviet relations be advantageous if the two governments also made a practice of exchanging views on changes in the strategic situation and their implications among senior policy officials, at the cabinet or NSC level or by deputies or senior advisers.) Out of such exchanges, rather than initial SCC discussion, might be drawn instances for SCC dialogue or action regarding treaty implementation.

Article XIII.*f* envisages possible proposals from the SCC for actions to increase the viability of the ABM Treaty, including proposed treaty amendments. Such proposals are more likely to emerge in policy circles of governments. However, SCC consultations on compliance issues, on interpretation and application of treaty provisions, or on new technical developments might well on occasion point to the need to go beyond common understandings to amendment of treaty text. So far, the SCC has found it possible to have recourse to clarifications of interpretation or action, to additional common understandings or agreed statements, or to changed procedures or national patterns of activity, rather than to treaty amendment. Should such procedurally simpler solutions prove infeasible or inadequate, the way is open for the SCC or one delegation to raise the possibility of amendments, and perhaps obtain authority to negotiate it. Where fundamental treaty principles are at stake, such as arise from the SDI or the recent unilateral U.S. reinterpretation of some treaty provisions, a different forum from the SCC would probably need to take up any proposals for changing the treaty. For offensive arms, any required amendment in previous agreements would be better handled in Geneva, where active negotiations on that subject are currently taking place.

Article XIII.*g* envisages considering proposals for further measures aimed at limiting strategic arms. So long as a forum such as the Geneva talks is active, a division of responsibility leaving such proposals to it is clearly desirable.

3. The regulations for the SCC provide that the proceedings shall be private, and shall not be made public except by mutual consent. Privacy for the exchanges, and for sensitive data exchanged, is necessary for frank and effective consultation, and for maintenance of an atmosphere in which potentially contentious issues can be freely discussed. This consideration has been for the most part recognized and observed. On the U.S. side, however, there has also been a need for regular and responsible reporting of SCC proceedings to competent committees of the Congress. Since compliance issues are hotly debated both in the executive branch and in Congress, leaks and references to SCC actions or exchanges in the press or public documents are frequent occurrences. This in turn has been met with Soviet objection and protest. The problem here is intrinsic to the differences in the two political systems, and will not go away or lend itself to neat solution. The privacy of the actual SCC proceedings and of sensitive technical and other data can be fairly well maintained. Some information on the results of SCC consultations must be made public in the United States to enable confidence in arms control agreements and compliance; this will probably be more than the Soviets would like and less than would be desirable in the United States. Leaks are inevitable, for both interested and disinterested purposes, and will have to be contained or the damage to the SCC working relationship repaired to the best extent possible. While a matter of U.S.–Soviet contention and irritation, the problem is neither unique nor unmanageable so long as there is mutual interest in arms control.

4. There has been speculation the SCC might be given responsibilities as a risk reduction center, or as a focus for crisis communications or support of crisis management. Such activities or institutions, discussed in the chapter by Barry Blechman, have attracted a good deal of interest but have not as yet taken on clear definition. They would deal with significantly different aspects of U.S.–Soviet strategic relations from those arising in the SCC at present. The experience and some of the organizational arrangements and procedures of the SCC would no doubt offer valuable insights as to how to proceed if such ideas come to fruition. The SCC function in regard to treaty implementation is quite different, however, and the fact that the SCC exists and has done its job well is little reason to regard it as the proper agent for these sensitive and different new functions.

5. There have also been suggestions that the SCC be charged with facilitating implementation and compliance for other arms control agreements than those dealing with strategic arms. For all arms control agreements, implementation is crucial if they are to have meaning and value, and requires mechanisms for positive action or for dealing with problems. This need is addressed in virtually all agreements, through five-year reviews, consultative mechanisms, technical advisory groups (standing or ad hoc),

and various verification arrangements. Some are extensive or regularly used, as, for example, in implementing the Nonproliferation Treaty or the Antarctic Treaty. Some of these procedures are imperfect but are receiving renewed attention, as in the case of the Biological Weapons Convention. These agreements, and others, are of course multilateral. The subject matter, the nature of the limitations or other provisions, the compliance problems and approaches are so diverse that none is obviously readily assimilable by the SCC. Most fundamentally, the SCC appears appropriate only for bilateral U.S.–Soviet agreements, but even there only where strategic arms, or closely related ones such as INF, are concerned.

FINAL COMMENTS

At the outset of SALT I negotiations, President Richard Nixon wrote to his principal negotiator, Ambassador Gerard Smith:

> I will accept limitations on our forces only after I have assured myself of our ability to detect Soviet failure to implement limitations on their own forces in sufficient time to protect our security interests . . . I am determined to avoid, within the Government and in the country at large, divisive disputes regarding Soviet compliance or noncompliance with an understanding or agreement. Nor will I bequeath to a future President the seeds of such disputes.[3]

These are admirable principles. The first, concerning verifiability, has proven generally feasible by the Nixon criterion. The second, regarding avoidance of compliance disputes, has proven illusory. It may gradually become possible to escape from the bitter and polarized U.S. internal debates on Soviet compliance that have raged over the past ten years. However, suspicions, questions, charges, and debates are not likely to disappear; to some extent they are healthy as well as inevitable. A more pragmatic spirit might come to prevail both in the dialogue with the Soviet Union and in internal U.S. debates. The proper SCC role then is well summed up by the experienced and bipartisan Presidential Commission on Strategic Forces, headed by former Lt. General and National Security Assistant Brent Scowcroft:

> Compliance consists of verification and a procedure for consultation and explanation of questionable events or procedures, plus a resulting determination as to whether the observed act or condition is in fact a violation. In the event of noncompliance, the first step is to take action on any violation which significantly affects the strategic balance. The second step is to decide what to do about other activities or conditions which constitute violations of agreements but which have only marginal or inconsequential military significance.
>
> Decisions regarding minor violations can be very difficult. Even though they may not have significant military impact, such violations erode the confidence of the American people and government in the agreements themselves. In addition, failure to take action may encourage the Soviets to believe they can act with impunity. There may not always be available, however, effective responses proportionate to the violations themselves. The proper course of action is to maintain a system of communication for review and correction of such incidents.[4]

The SCC has shown itself well adapted to discharge this and associated functions of maintaining the viability of arms control agreements. Some role for the SCC remains open even when—as at present—it is unclear whether U.S.–Soviet differences can be bridged and arms control momentum restored. Agreements on secondary but substantive points such as those covered in the two 1985 SCC common understandings have value in themselves, serve to keep a cooperative channel open, and keep a useful institution alive. Similarly, if in 1987 at the time of the third five-year review of the ABM Treaty the two governments wish to avoid coming to grips—and probably to stalemate—over their fundamental differences concerning the SDI, the SCC could be used for a low key review followed by continuing adherence to the ABM Treaty, with or without a statement of intention to do so, into the next five-year period.

References

The texts of the SALT I and SALT II agreements, and of the 1971 "Accident Measures" agreement, can be found in ACDA publication, *Arms Control and Disarmament Agreements: Texts and Histories of Negotiations* (Washington, D.C.: U.S. Government Printing Office, 1982).

The texts of the "Memorandum of Understanding Regarding Establishment of the Standing Consultative Commission" of December 21, 1972, and the "Protocol and Regulations" of the SCC of May 30, 1973, are in Coit Blacker and Gloria Duffy, eds., *International Arms Control: Issues and Agreements* (Stanford, Calif.: Stanford University Press, 1974), pp. 431–433.

Robert W. Buchheim and Dan Caldwell, "The U.S.–USSR Standing Consultative Commission: Description and Appraisal," Working Paper No. 2 (Center for Foreign Policy Development, Brown University, Providence, R.I., May, 1983).

Sidney N. Graybeal and Michael Krepon, "Making Better Use of the Standing Consultative Commission," *International Security* (Fall 1985): 183ff. This article and the one cited above are primary sources since Graybeal and Buchheim were the first two U.S. commissioners on the SCC.

Compliance and the Future of Arms Control, 1987, a report of a Working Group of the Stanford Center for International Security and Arms Control directed by Gloria Duffy, is a thorough and up-to-date review of compliance history and problems and contains a full up-to-date account of the SCC.

Letter on compliance and the SCC, from Secretary of State Cyrus Vance to the Chairman of the Senate Committee on Foreign Relations, February 21, 1978, contained in Department of State Publication 8939, March 1978. (Similar information is contained in testimony during hearings on the SALT II Treaty, in Department of State publications at the time, and in ACDA Annual Reports from 1973 to the present.)

Notes

1. Memorandum from the Secretary of Defense to the President, "Responding to Soviet Violations Policy (RSVP) Study," 13 November 1985.
2. Hearing before the Committee on the Armed Services, U.S. Senate, March 14, 1984.
3. Gerard C. Smith, *Doubletalk* (Garden City, N.Y.: Doubleday, 1980), p. 99.
4. Presidential Commission on Strategic Forces, *Second Report to President Ronald Reagan,* released by the White House Press Office March 21, 1984.

11

Conditions That Affect
Arms Control Compliance

GLORIA DUFFY

In the evaluation of U.S.–Soviet security regimes, a great deal of attention is devoted to the factors that affect the ability of the two sides to reach an initial agreement or a major change in direction in one aspect of their relationship. However, the test of a regime's success is not simply whether it is initiated, but whether it endures over time through the adherence of both parties. A sometimes neglected but important set of questions has to do with the factors that may encourage or discourage the survival of a regime over time.

One of the main phenomena affecting the state of security regimes is the tension that arises from conflicting perceptions of national self-interest when countries must choose between cooperation with an adversary and the unilateral pursuit of security. When an agreement is reached setting forth the terms and purposes of a regime or a single element of a regime, it represents a point of coincidence along the continuum of the parties' alternation between the poles of unilateralism and cooperation. A regime is initiated at the point where the interests of the two sides are perceived to overlap at that time.

But the perceptions of either side about whether elements of the regime continue to be in its interest can shift over time in response to the evolution of the regime, to extraneous factors, and to the interaction between the two adversaries. The continuing tension between conceptions of self-interest may put stress on compliance with a regime, throw into uncertainty the further development of a regime, and in fact threaten to roll back past progress in constructing a regime.

The purpose of this chapter is to examine how the tension between interests in cooperation and interests in unilateral measures has affected compliance with arms control agreements. The focus will be on the period of the end of the 1970s and early-to-mid 1980s, when the arms control regime seemed to reach its most shaky point to date in terms of continued confidence and compliance. I will attempt to identify not only the factors that decreased confidence in the arms control regime during this period, but, on the other side of the coin, those that may contribute in a positive way to continued compliance with agreements.

THE COMPLIANCE "CRISIS"

Until 1979–1980, leaders of the United States and the Soviet Union projected a sense that, in broad terms, they were satisfied with the operation of the arms control regime and with the quality of compliance with the terms of agreements. A number of questions about compliance were raised during the 1970s by the two sides through the Standing Consultative Commission (SCC), the bilateral body in Geneva charged with hearing complaints and working out mutually satisfactory means of addressing disagreements. In general, the SCC was praised for its effectiveness in working out disputes. U.S. officials, ranging from Defense Secretary James Schlesinger in 1975 to Secretary of State Cyrus Vance in 1978, expressed the view that the Soviet Union had largely complied with the terms of arms control agreements.[1] No public Soviet complaints were heard about U.S. compliance.

But in the late 1970s this situation changed. The first major sign of dissatisfaction about the functioning of the arms control regime came from the United States, in the form of questions raised about Soviet adherence to the terms of two agreements restricting the production, stockpiling, and use of chemical, biological, and bacteriological weapons.[2] The first official sign of U.S. displeasure occurred in 1979, when the Carter Administration questioned whether an outbreak of anthrax virus near the Soviet city of Sverdlovsk indicated Soviet engagement in the production of anthrax for biological warfare purposes. Dissatisfied with Soviet responses to direct inquiries about the Sverdlovsk incident, the Carter Administration sought an investigation of Soviet behavior through the United Nations, as provided by the 1972 multilateral Biological Weapons Convention (BWC). A second group of questions involving the BWC, and the 1925 Geneva Convention as well, was raised by the Reagan Administration in 1981, with regard to suspected Soviet chemical or biological warfare activities in Afghanistan and Southeast Asia.

Between 1982 and 1986, a number of official U.S. pronouncements were made, charging the Soviet Union with widespread noncompliance with the terms of existing arms control agreements.[3] The Soviet Union responded in kind, accusing the United States of similar violations.[4] The charges of noncompliance were made in the public arena; the SCC had functionally ceased to operate as a mechanism for resolving disputes by 1981. The two countries expressed dissatisfaction about compliance with nearly every major element of the arms control regime, including provisions of SALT I, SALT II, the ABM Treaty, limitations on nuclear testing, the Helsinki Final Act, and chemical and biological weapons agreements.

By 1986, the United States stood ready to extricate itself from the constraints of the Interim Agreement, the SALT II Treaty, and possibly the ABM Treaty, citing Soviet noncompliance as justification.[5] As a result of an interaction involving decreased U.S. confidence in arms control, Soviet stretching of the limits of agreements, and U.S. seizing on Soviet behavior as justification for its withdrawal from agreements, in 1986 the crisis of confidence about arms control threatened to become a real compliance crisis after all.

In the early 1980s, the governments of the United States and the Soviet Union, led primarily by the United States, created the impression that compliance with arms control agreements was undergoing a severe crisis, the first in the history of the arms control regime. This conception that compliance with the terms of agreements had broken down bears scrutiny, though. A close look at the charges made by both sides indicates that there was a crisis in confidence about the arms control regime, rather than a severe downturn in compliance. This crisis of confidence was due to shifting perceptions on the part of each side about whether its own self-interest continued to be served by the terms of the agreements both had signed during the 1960s and 1970s. The compliance behavior of the Soviet Union, in particular, served as something of a whipping-boy for a more negative U.S. evaluation of the United States's relative security position under the arms control regime.

Yet, the record shows far less, in terms of concrete violations of agreements, than both sides attempted to convey through their official pronouncements alleging noncompliance in the 1982-86 period. Nearly all the charges of noncompliance were either patently invalid or somewhat questionable.[6] They fell into several categories: charges where the behavior in question was ambiguous; charges where the provisions of agreements in question were ambiguous; and tit-for-tat charges, especially from the Soviet side. Most of the problems that were raised between 1982 and 1986 had to do with differing interpretations of provisions of agreements which were, in fact, somewhat ambiguous in their meaning. Such ambiguities had been reduced through the work of the SCC in the past, but the process of resolving disputes through the SCC was stalemated in the early 1980s.

Despite the impression created in the early-to-mid-1980s, the over-all pattern up to that point had been one of U.S. and Soviet compliance with agreements. By whatever measure is used—compliance with the sheer number of arms control provisions contained in treaties, or compliance with the most significant treaty provisions—the over-all pattern on both sides was clearly one of compliance rather than noncompliance. The number and the significance of the provisions, that were adhered to by both parties vastly outweighed the problem areas.

More specifically, until the United States withdrew from the SALT I Interim Agreement and the SALT II Treaty in November 1986, both sides had upheld the over-all ceilings on strategic offensive launchers established by SALT I and SALT II. These ceilings contributed crucially to maintaining the deterrent balance between the United States and the USSR, and were an essential ingredient of both past restraints on defensive weapons and potential future offensive limits.[7] Had the process of handling disagreements been working, the disputes that arose most likely would not have continued long enough to give the impression that compliance was breaking down.

CAUSES UNDERLYING THE CRISIS

The compliance crisis of the 1980s really had its roots in U.S. and Soviet ambivalence about whether their security needs were being met by the relinquishing of some autonomy in order to obtain the greater degree of cooperation to which the numerous arms control agreements of the 1960s and 1970s had committed them. In the mid-to-late 1970s, both countries tended towards the perception that their security needs would be better served by unilateral steps than through mutual security arrangements. Each side's perception of the interests that had led them to institute the various elements of the arms control regime had shifted significantly since the time the agreements were negotiated and signed. This shift created mutual dissatisfactions, resulting in the charges of noncompliance. And these charges provoked a sequence of actions leading towards actual withdrawal from parts of the arms control regime.

The factors that led the United States and the USSR to the brink of dismantling parts of the arms control regime in the early 1980s were of two types: those internal to the arms control regime itself, and those external to the agreements. The internal causes included ambiguities in the terms of agreements, which are natural for agreements between adversaries. Some of these internal causes also represented flaws in the agreements' approaches to dealing with specific issues, which, in light of experience, should be avoided in the future. A third cause of compliance difficulties internal to the arms control regime was lack of adequate verifiability of some agreements or their provisions.

Many of the external causes were related to the trend away from cooperative security measures, and they exerted a much more forceful influence on the compliance situation, leading both sides to exploit rather than attempt to ameliorate the natural imperfections of the regime. These factors included internal politics and policies in both countries; shifts in the strategic relationship underlying the regime, some of which were caused by the development of new weapons technologies; verification problems that resulted from the new weapons developments; a trend towards greater secrecy and less sharing of information by the USSR; the misuse of consultative mechanisms; and an absence of further development of the arms control regime. This last factor had profound consequences, including diminished interest in adherence to the arms control regime and failure to provide follow-up measures to deal with ongoing problems that had only been provisionally addressed by previous agreements.

PROBLEMS INTERNAL TO THE REGIME

Treaty Provisions

Several of the compliance disputes in the first half of the 1980s concerned provisions of agreements that were an imperfect compromise at the time they were negotiated, establishing qualitative constraints on weapons or behavior, but doing so in a way that contained substantial ambiguities. Such deficiencies provided ample room for differing U.S. and Soviet interpretations of their obligations under the agreements. Such ambiguities were involved in each of the central compliance disputes between the United States and the USSR in the 1980s. Three examples of treaty ambiguities follow, each of which was involved in a major U.S.–Soviet compliance dispute.

SALT II/Encryption

The SALT II provision restricting encryption of telemetry was one such ambiguous, qualitative measure. The treaty prohibits either party from impeding the ability of the other to verify compliance with treaty provisions by using deliberate concealment measures, including the encoding of ballistic missile flight test telemetry. Verification of compliance with certain limits of SALT II, such as restrictions on warhead fractionation, requires intelligence about Soviet systems obtainable most efficiently through monitoring Soviet flight test telemetry.

The use of the term ''impede'' was a result of the two countries' inability to reach agreement on a complete ban on encryption of telemetry in the SALT II negotiations, due to the habitual Soviet desire to protect the secrecy of its military programs to the greatest extent possible, and to the United States's unwillingness to relinquish its own option to encrypt telemetry at some future time.[8] But the use of this term allowed widely differing interpretations of the amount of encryption permissible.

ABM Treaty/LPARs

Certain provisions of the 1972 ABM Treaty also contain ambiguities that contributed to the compliance disputes in the early 1980s. The agreement prohibited deployment of large, phased-array radars (LPARs) for tracking incoming ballistic missiles and relaying their flight path to ABM radars and interceptors, except at the one permitted ABM site chosen by each country. The intent of the negotiators in including this provision was to prevent deployment of the most costly, longest lead-time component of an ABM system, the existence of which could allow one of the parties to most easily and quickly break out of the treaty limits to mount a regional or nationwide ABM defense.

The precise wording of Article VI of the ABM Treaty was designed to distinguish LPARs that could be used for purposes of attacking incoming missiles from those used for early warning, since from external observation LPARs for both uses would appear to be the same. In 1972, both the United States and the USSR were beginning modernization programs for their early-warning networks involving the deployment of new LPARs. Article VI committed the parties not to deploy new early-warning radars except at the periphery of their national territories, and oriented outward. Due to their location and vulnerability, radars deployed in this fashion would be ill-suited for ABM battle-management.

But at Soviet instigation, a further qualification to the limits on LPARs was appended to the treaty by Agreed Statement F. This clause stated that an exception to the rule would be provided for LPARs used for space-tracking or verification; such LPARs could be located other than on the periphery of the country and other than oriented outward. The Soviet LPAR at Abalakovo is located inland and is oriented toward the northeast, giving it coverage over at least 3,000 kilometers of Soviet territory, which certainly does not qualify as "oriented outward."

But due to the loophold provided by Agreed Statement F, the USSR has been able to claim that the radar is for space-tracking purposes. The overwhelming likelihood is that the radar is for early-warning. Abalakovo closes the last complete gap in the Soviet early-warning network, which would lack radar coverage without this installation. It is specifically oriented to detect launch of U.S. long-range C-4 and D-5 SLBMs deployed on the *Trident* submarine force in the northern Pacific Ocean. It is thus most likely a technical violation of the ABM Treaty, even though it may not violate the spirit of the agreement, which seeks to prevent the deployment of ABM defenses.

But until the radar operates, the Soviet case cannot be proved or disproved. The differences between LPARs for spacetracking and for ballistic missile early warning are not physically observable by national technical means of verification, and relate mostly to the software, or control systems, which govern the radar's operation. Once the radar begins to operate, it emits signals that may be monitored to determine the function it is serving at that time. But its function can be changed at any time, by manipulating these same internal controls. The ABM Treaty contains no specific criteria or guidelines for distinguishing prohibited LPARs from those that are permitted for space tracking and verification, which has allowed varying U.S. and Soviet claims about how the treaty provisions relate to their radar programs.

The ABM Treaty provisions governing LPARs have permitted the United States, as well as the USSR, to move towards actions that may not be consistent with the spirit of the agreement. Article VI of the treaty clearly prohibits the deployment of new LPARs except as permitted for spacetracking, verification, use at test ranges, and for early warning if on the periphery and oriented outward. But it does not explicitly prohibit the modernization of existing LPARs, wherever they may be.

The USSR charged in 1985 that U.S. upgrading of two LPARs at Thule, Greenland and Flyingdales Moors in the United Kingdom violated the Article VI strictures that new radar for early-warning could not be deployed except on the periphery of U.S. national territory and oriented outward.[9] According to the Soviets, modernization of these two sites actually involved building new radar, and clearly neither of them were located on the U.S. periphery and oriented outward. The Soviets also hinted, just as the United States charged with regard to Abalakovo, that they believed the purpose of upgrading these radar was to provide ABM battle-management capabilities. The United States responded that these radar were not for ballistic missile defense, and that their modernization was not prohibited under treaty terms.[10]

The extent of the planned U.S. improvement of these two facilities raised the question of the dividing line between modernization of existing systems and the creation of radars that represent a new level of technology and thus are essentially new systems. In the case of Fylingdales, a separate radar will be built at some distance from the original installation, apparently for the operational reason that locating it at a distance would allow the old radar to continue operating during the construction of the new facility. The new radars also represent a change in the operating principle of the installations: the updated facility will be electronically scanned, while the old radars were mechanically steered.

ABM Treaty/Strategic Defense

Most strikingly, the Reagan Administration announced in March 1983 that it intended to mount a national research effort directed towards deploying a nationwide, space-based ballistic missile defense for the United States. The Soviet Union promptly took the position that such a program would violate the ABM Treaty, Article I of which states that

> each party undertakes not to deploy ABM systems for a defense of the territory of its country and not to provide for such a defense, and not to deploy ABM systems for defense of an individual weapon except as provided for in Article III of this Treaty.

Article III of the ABM Treaty permitted two ABM systems to be deployed by each country, around their national capitals and around a single ICBM field. A 1974 protocol to the treaty restricted each side to a single site.

Several key treaty ambiguities surrounded the issue of whether the U.S. Strategic Defense Initiative (SDI) program would violate the ABM agreement. Perhaps the most important of these was contained in Agreed Statement D of the treaty. This provision stated that in the event of the emergence of ABM systems based on "other physical principles," in which components not foreseen by the treaty but serving functions restricted by the treaty would emerge, specific limitation on these systems and their components would be subject to discussion through the SCC and possibly serve as the basis for amendments to the treaty.

This provision means that systems based on "other physical principles" could be pursued only if legitimized by future amendments to the treaty; otherwise, they would be prohibited under Article I of the Treaty. Proponents of SDI have rejected the latter alternative and advanced a more permissive interpretation, while opponents prefer the more restrictive reading of the treaty.

Other ambiguities in treaty provisions have led to similarly diverging interpretations. The treaty prohibited "development or testing of ABM systems or their components which are sea-based, air-based, space-based, or mobile land-based" (Article V).

Was the U.S. SDI program purely a research program even if its ultimate aim was to produce an ABM system? At what point does research end and development begin? The treaty provided no guidance on these points. What constituted a "component" of an ABM system? Were some technologies under development in the early 1980s, such as lasers, permitted because they were not *prima facie* connected with an ABM system; or prohibited because they could be components of such a system? Again, the treaty provided little guidance.

These ambiguities allowed an intense debate to develop within the United States in 1985 and 1986, and between the United States and the USSR, as the Reagan Administration sought to justify its SDI program by re-interpreting ABM Treaty provisions to permit research and development on "exotic" SDI systems.[11] Critics alleged that such interpretations did not reflect the intent or negotiating history of the treaty.[12] But the ambiguities in the actual text of the treaty permitted the Administration to build something of a case for its reinterpretations.

Nonverifiability

A few agreements that became embroiled in compliance controversies beginning in 1981 contained provisions that were quite simply unverifiable by national technical means of intelligence-gathering. The 1974 Biological and Toxin Weapons Convention fell into this category. The convention banned the production, stockpiling, or use of biological or toxin weapons.

Since such weapons may be manufactured and stockpiled virtually anywhere and potentially used secretly, the lack of any provisions for on-site inspection or other effective means of verification made compliance with this ban nearly impossible to ascertain with any certainty. U.S. suspicions that the Soviets were producing and stockpiling biological weapons, and using toxic gasses and/or mycotoxins in Afghanistan and South East Asia (the so-called "yellow rain"), were therefore impossible to prove or disprove.

CAUSES EXTERNAL TO THE ARMS CONTROL REGIME

Having just reviewed some of the deficiencies of the existing arms control agreements, it is important to recognize that it is probably not possible to write a perfect arms control treaty. Every agreement is imperfect, and contains substantial ambiguity which can be exploited by parties if they choose. In the practice of diplomacy, there is even a certain incentive to avoid being overly precise in constructing agreements, so as not to convey the impression that anything that is not expressly prohibited will be permitted.

It stands to reason that even with the best of agreements, disputes are bound to arise. This is true of domestic contracts such as labor-management agreements, marriage contracts, and business agreements. The likelihood that disputes will arise is even greater when the parties to an agreement are military adversaries, when the agreement concerns their key security interests, when there is no functioning judiciary as in domestic affairs to which both parties are bound to submit in case of dispute, and when there is only a minimal history of cooperative measures in pursuing security.

The real issue involved in the compliance problems of the 1980s is not simply that disputes arose, but why each country tended towards a restrictive interpretation of its adversary's obligations under agreements coupled with a permissive view of its own obligations, leading to numerous disputes; and why the two sides were unable to resolve disputes when they arose. Underlying the tendency to push at the limits of agreements and the inability to resolve compliance disputes was the resurgence of unilateral approaches to seeking security by the United States and the USSR, which undermined the structure of the arms control regime as it had developed in the 1970s.

Internal Politics and Policymaking

Much of the blame for the threatened compliance crisis of the mid-1980s lay with trends taking place outside the arms control regime, but strongly affecting the regime. Among these causes, few had an effect comparable to that of the tendencies in internal politics and policymaking in the United States and the USSR that ran contrary to the perception of mutual interests in security measures, the foundation upon which the arms control regime rested.

Trends in the United States

The U.S. domestic political environment went through a metamorphosis in the late 1970s, as a result of which the political leadership and elements of the public became more skeptical of the ability of the mutual security arrangements with the USSR to serve U.S. security needs. For a variety of reasons, which may have included a reaction to the decade of questioning about U.S. foreign policy that followed the Vietnam War (the so-called post-Vietnam syndrome), the United States was more inclined to rely on unilateral means of pursuing security objectives beginning in the late 1970s. Under attack from the political right in the 1980 election season, and initially condemned publicly by the new Reagan Administration in 1981, arms control fell into disfavor in the United States as a means of pursuing security.

The arms control regime seemed to those jockeying for political power in the late 1970s and to the new U.S. political leadership in 1981 to come up short in several respects. The agreements that had been reached did not seem to solve major American security problems. Despite the SALT I and SALT II offensive arms limitations, for instance, the United States was still faced in the late 1970s and early 1980s with the problem of at least theoretical vulnerability of the fixed land-based element of its strategic triad. The arms control agreements achieved in the 1970s had not led to Soviet restraint in deploying new systems; the USSR had put in place a variety of new land-based and sea-based strategic systems, and intermediate-range forces directed against Western Europe and Asia during the tenure of these agreements. The arms control regime had not lessened U.S.–Soviet competition in regional conflicts; in fact, during this period geopolitical competition with the USSR seemed, if anything, to intensify.

It was during the abortive U.S. domestic debate over ratification of the SALT II Treaty in 1979 that arms control skeptics first began to express their doubts about the process in terms of concerns about the Soviet compliance record. Senator Gordon Humphrey (R-NH), in particular, compiled a long list of alleged Soviet violations of the ABM Treaty, the SALT I Interim Agreement, the Threshold Test Ban Treaty, the Limited Test Ban Treaty and two agreements circumscribing Soviet military activities in Cuba.[13]

Shortly after the election of Ronald Reagan, a member of the Arms Control and Disarmament Agency (ACDA) transition team, former CIA analyst David Sullivan, compiled an extensive list of alleged Soviet violations. Sullivan pressed the new Administration to make the list public and to confront the Soviets with his charges. He succeeded in initiating a study of Soviet compliance by the General Advisory Committee on Arms Control and Disarmament (GAC), an official advisory body to the executive branch. As a staff member serving a group of conservative Senators including James McClure (R-Idaho), Steve Symms (R-Idaho), and Jesse Helms (R-NC), Sullivan stoked Congressional sentiment to pressure the Administration for an official compliance review.

In 1983, Congress attached an amendment to the FY1984 Defense Authorization Act that required an Administration report on Soviet noncompliance. In January 1984, following an interagency review process coordinated by the National Security Council Staff, the Reagan White House produced its first report on Soviet noncompliance. The Gac report had been delivered confidentially to the President in October 1983. At Congressional insistence, it was released in the fall of 1984, expanding the number of U.S. charges.[14] Two subsequent White House reports followed in January and December 1985. By the summer of 1985, the Congress had passed Public Law 99–145, requiring an Administration report on Soviet compliance by December 1 each year, as part of the defense budget authorization process.

The negative domestic U.S. attitude towards arms control beginning in 1979 led to a variety of concrete effects. SALT II remained unratified by the United States, as did the 1974 Threshold Test Ban and Peaceful Nuclear Explosions treaties. By 1981, all arms control negotiations that had been underway between the United States and the USSR were abandoned at the instigation of the new Administration, and no new efforts were undertaken for nearly two years.

In dealing with the compliance issue over time, the Reagan Administration proved unable to escape the confines of the anti-arms control political strategy adopted at the very outset of its tenure. During its first months in office, it will be recalled, the Reagan Administration asserted that only the USSR had gained through past arms negotiations, that the SALT II agreement concluded by the Carter Administration was "fatally flawed," and that it would be unwise to negotiate any further with the USSR until the United States "rebuilt" the military strength it had lost during the 1970s. Sullivan's early investigations and the GAC's undertaking were to some extent attempts to rationalize a U.S. policy of no arms negotiations with the Soviets, using the argument that the Soviets had not respected their past arms control commitments.

After public pressure for a nuclear freeze or other arms control measures intensified in 1981–82, causing the Administration concern about the fate of Republicans in the 1982 mid-term Congressional elections, the Reagan Administration felt obliged to restart arms negotiations with the Soviets. President Reagan initiated the Intermediate Nuclear Forces (INF) negotiations in 1982, and the Strategic Arms Reduction Talks (START) in 1983.

But the process of alleging Soviet noncompliance with arms control agreements had already become, in a sense, institutionalized. Pressure from Congress forced the Administration to continue generating annual reports on Soviet noncompliance, after 1983. The Department of Defense, in particular, became prone to using charges of Soviet noncompliance as a means of justifying new U.S. weapons programs that would risk abrogating U.S. arms control commitments.[15]

This continued emphasis on massive Soviet noncompliance put the Reagan Administration in the curious and contradictory position of asserting an incorrigible Soviet tendency to cheat on arms control agreements while at the same time it was involved in a number of different negotiations, from 1983 on, to reach new arms accords with the Soviets.

Soviet Policies

For the Soviets, despite their commitment to various mutual security agreements, the tendency towards unilateral steps to meet their security needs remained strong. Due to the internal organization of defense policymaking in the USSR, which offers less-than-adequate compliance oversight, Soviet military programs pushed as close as possible to the limits of the agreements.[16] In one instance, the Soviets may have gone over these limits, while in other instances their compliance was debatable.

Into the U.S. climate of skepticism about mutual security fell several Soviet military programs in the early 1980s, the characteristics of which were perilously close to exceeding the terms of arms control treaties. Three of these activities—encryption of most Soviet ballistic missile flight test telemetry, testing and deployment of the SS-25 mobile ICBM, and construction of a large phased-array radar at Abalakovo in Siberia—eventually became central issues among the U.S. charges of Soviet noncompliance. In the past, particularly in the 1970–1971 period, the Soviet political leadership had taken steps to bring Soviet military programs in line with arms control requirements.[17] In the early 1980s, however, the uncertain status of SALT II and other agreements may have decreased the incentives for the political leadership in the USSR to intervene in favor of a conservative interpretation of Soviet obligations under arms control treaties.

ABALAKOVO RADAR

As a result, if deployment is completed as scheduled in about 1988, the Abalakovo radar will probably violate Article VI and Agreed Statement F of the ABM Treaty. These provisions restrict each country's deployment of LPARs, except those used in the one ABM system permitted to each side, and those for tracking space objects and verification to the "periphery of its national territory and oriented outward." Despite Soviet claims that the Abalakovo radar is for tracking space objects, its orientation is not that of a space-tracking radar. Additionally, such radar are in reality capable of various functions, including early warning, which is prohibited for radars in its locale. The location of Abalakovo, several hundred kilometers from the nearest periphery of the USSR, will place it in violation of the ABM Treaty. Abalakovo was the sole clear case of a Soviet arms control violation in the 1982–86 time period, and the second clear case in the history of the arms control regime.[18]

TELEMETRY ENCRYPTION

The other two compliance issues are instances where Soviet behavior is questionable in light of treaty provisions, but not uncategorically in violation. Both instances represent permissive Soviet interpretations of treaty provisions that are, all the same, somewhat ambiguous.

From 1981 on, the USSR reportedly encoded over 95 percent of the telemetry on its flight tests of new missiles.[19] The United States has complained that Soviet encryption impedes U.S. verification of Soviet compliance with SALT II provisions. The USSR has responded that the United States can obtain the necessary data through the small portion of telemetry transmitted in the clear, and from other sources, and that U.S. requests for further telemetry are simply intelligence-gathering gambits.[20] The ambiguity in this case revolves around the subjectivity of the term "impede." SALT II contains no definition of how much encryption constitutes "impeding," although the U.S. SALT II delegation reportedly pointed to a heavily encrypted Soviet SS-18 flight test in December 1978 as a level of encoding the United States would find unacceptable under the terms of the treaty.[21] But there is no evidence that the Soviet delegation agreed with this interpretation.

SS-25 ICBM

The third case, also involving ambiguity, stems from Soviet deployment of a new mobile, single-warhead ICBM, in possible contravention of the SALT II limit that restricts both sides to only one "new type" of ICBM. The USSR claimed as its one permitted "new type" the SS-24 ICBM. When challenged about the testing of another new ICBM in 1983, the USSR responded that it was only a modernization of an existing missile, the SS-13. But while modernization of existing systems is restricted by the treaty to 5 percent changes across several specified categories, the Soviet SS-25 ICBM appeared to exceed this 5 percent modernization limit in throwweight, and also to field a reentry vehicle representing less than 50 percent of the throwweight of the launcher. This last limit was set by SALT II in an effort to prevent proliferation of warheads as a result of ICBM modernization.

The ambiguity in this case stems partly from the lack of a dependable baseline from which to gauge whether or not the SS-25 exceeds the throwweight of the SS-13 by more than 5 percent. In the mid-1960s, when the SS-13 was flight-tested, verification capabilities were not sufficiently good to gauge the throwweight of the system with great accuracy. The USSR contends that U.S. figures for calculating the throwweight of the SS-13 do not include guidance and other devices deployed on the third stage of the missile, which would raise the throwweight of the SS-13 to within 5 percent of that of the SS-25.[22]

Interaction of U.S. and Soviet Policies

The rise of U.S. complaints about Soviet arms control compliance was closely related to the trend towards defining self-interests in terms of unilateral solutions to security problems. As questions about the advantageousness of arms control agreements became more prevalent, the United States became less inclined to accept the constraints on its forces and behavior embodied in the existing arms control agreements. Charges that the Soviets were in violation of the agreements cast doubt not only on the value of the agreements, but on the future of the arms control enterprise. If the Soviets habitually cheat on arms control agreements, then further mutual security agreements with them would seem unwise.

In the atmosphere of skepticism in the United States about the benefits of arms control, critics of the process seized upon certain Soviet activities as evidence that the USSR does not abide by the terms of agreements. The Director of the Arms Control and Disarmament Agency, the Secretary of Defense, and his vocal deputy Richard Perle pointed to these Soviet activities as evidence of a wide pattern of Soviet violations. By

1986, the White House was charging the USSR with eighteen specific violations of arms control agreements.

The public nature of the U.S. charges against the USSR, and the demand that the Soviets adhere to a restrictive U.S. interpretation of Soviet obligations under provisions of arms control agreements, provoked a Soviet response of denial and countercharges. As a result, the SCC was stymied, unable to reach a common understanding or agreed statement on any of charges made by either country in the early 1980s. As compared with seven agreed statements or common understandings and numerous tacit agreements reached during the 1970s, in the 1979–1986 period the SCC reached just two agreements, only one of which related to the recent noncompliance charges. The terms of this one agreement, related to concurrent testing of SAMs and ABM radar at Soviet ABM test ranges, had actually been worked out during the Carter Administration, but final action was delayed in the SCC until 1985.

In the absence of an effort to make the dispute resolution process work, the charges of Soviet noncompliance may have been serving as something of a rationale for U.S. movement away from its own adherence to arms control agreements. President Reagan and other officials cited Soviet behavior as justification for a number of unilateral U.S. moves designed to enhance security. But the announced U.S. programs were not really analogous to the Soviet behavior. For instance, the Reagan Administration cited the Soviet Abalakovo radar in justifying U.S. movement towards a space-based strategic defense that could violate the ABM Treaty. The President also referred to the pattern of Soviet violations in May 1986, when he announced that the United States would abrogate the SALT II sublimit on MIRVed launcher/cruise-missile carrying aircraft by the end of 1986.[23] He also stated that the United States would cease at that time to be bound by the SALT I Interim Agreement on Offensive Weapons. The President also announced an acceleration in the *Midgetman* ICBM program. When tested, *Midgetman* would violate the SALT II provision restricting both countries to one ''new type'' of ICBM; the United States has already declared its MX missile to be the one permitted ''new type.''

But the prospective U.S. withdrawal from arms control limits was not strictly a response to Soviet activities. The Soviets had not breached the MIRVed launcher ceilings of SALT II, and the Abalakovo radar was likely an early warning radar as little suited for ABM battle management (as alleged by the United States) as it was for space-tracking as claimed by the USSR. THe U.S. *Midgetman* missile could not possibly be counted a modernization of any existing U.S. ICBM, as the Soviet SS-25 could arguably be called an update of the SS-13.

Shifts in the U.S.–Soviet Political/Strategic Relationship

As I suggested earlier, at least some elements within the U.S. political leadership had come to believe by 1981 that the basis of the U.S.–Soviet strategic relationship on which the arms control regime rested had undergone fundamental changes that made the terms of agreements no longer advantageous to the United States. Soviet behavior, if not Soviet public statements (which continued to favor arms limitations) indicated that the USSR also was skeptical that strict adherence to the terms of agreements served its interests, an interpretation one would have to make based on the permissive reading by the USSR of several provisions of agreements.

Some of the elements in the strategic situation that had given rise to the arms control regime had indeed altered by the early 1980s. The arms control regime had been based on a number of factors that made such mutual approaches to security seem both palatable and advantageous to both countries. Primarily, of course, rough parity in strategic forces existed at a level sufficiently high that increments to forces were likely to be met by countermeasures that tended to neutralize any strategic advantage. And reconnaissance and intelligence capabilities had developed sufficiently on both sides to provide confidence in the verifiability of arms control agreements. But developments in weapons technology in the 1970s served to upset the perception that unshakable parity existed, and to decrease confidence in the verifiability of agreements.

Unconstrained by any ban on warhead fractionation in SALT I, the USSR had proceeded to MIRV its force of heavy missiles in the 1970s, calling into question the survivability of the U.S. land-based ICBM force. The United States had continued to deploy a new class of *Trident* submarine-launched ballistic missiles, putting an ever larger number of strategic targets in the USSR under time-urgent threat of accurate attack. The arms competition proved to be quite dynamic during the 1970s, despite the SALT agreements.

While neither side necessarily saw the potential for obtaining strategic superiority through continued modernization, worst-case perceptions of one another's forces driven by increased political tensions compelled each side to pursue programs to offset the other side's perceived advantage. The possibility for modernization of forces within the limits of the existing agreements was still great enough to permit this sort of competition. The incentives were thus high for both sides to push the limits of the agreements as far as possible, and to circumvent them where useful.

Developments in military technology also rendered verification more difficult. The Abalakova radar was a case in which the evolving technology of weapons systems made verification more problematic. As mentioned above, it is not possible, using national technical means of verification, to determine the specific application for which such a multi-use system is intended. Once again, this verification limitation left the issue of compliance with the ABM Treaty mired in uncertainty and public controversy.

To some extent, Soviet deceptive practices also complicated the already difficult U.S. task of verifying Soviet compliance with arms accords. Soviet interference with U.S. national technical means of intelligence through encrypting telemetry contributed to verification problems. Soviet encryption created some uncertainty about the parameters of the SS-25 and other systems, raising questions about their compliance with agreements. SALT II provisions such as the rules governing new types of missiles relied upon non-interference with national technical means of intelligence gathering and would have benefited even more from cooperative means of verification.

The net effect of these developments in the political/military realm was to decrease confidence in the effectiveness of the arms control regime, and to raise questions about the desirability of further efforts to develop the regime.

Soviet Secrecy

A mutual security regime relies for its success on the willingness of the participants to give up some of their autonomy in trade for the benefits of the regime. One such compromise for the Soviet Union had been to curtail its traditional emphasis on secrecy in its military programs. Gradually during the 1970s the USSR became a bit more open about providing data or clarifying its activities when challenged through the SCC. The

USSR also agreed, in the SALT II Treaty, to an exchange of data bases on strategic weapons and to semi-annual updates of these data bases through the SCC.

A key signal that Soviet perceptions of their interests were shifting away from mutual security measures and back towards unilateral approaches was that from about 1980 onward the USSR reversed its trend toward openness and returned to its habitual secrecy about military activities. The Soviets became noticeably less forthcoming in the SCC when asked by the United States about their activities related to compliance with agreements. No SALT data-base exchanges went forward. The Soviets also increased their level of encryption in both 1979 and 1981, to provide the bare minimum, if even that, of the information required for verification of SALT II.

Misuse of Consultative Mechanisms

Another important cause of compliance problems with a source external to the regime was misuse of the Standing Consultative Commission, the U.S.–Soviet body created by SALT I to review disputes related to that and subsequent agreements. The status of the SCC provides an excellent opportunity to take the pulse of the arms control regime. A consultative body like the SCC is at the heart of the ability of a mutual security regime to function, since it is the mechanism by which the initial structure of the regime on the one hand, and subsequent behavior and developments on the other hand, are accommodated to one another. It is the most immediate forum for the maintenance, expansion, or contraction of the regime.

Through the fate of the SCC during the first half of the 1980s, it is possible to see the contraction of the arms control regime. The SCC has no power to actually alter the behavior of parties to agreements. Prior to 1980, however, it had been able to register objections, allow an accused party to provide explanations, and achieve mutual U.S.–Soviet understandings about the practical meaning of agreements. On occasion, discussion in the SCC was followed by changes in the behavior that had provoked the complaint.

During the 1970s, the United States and the USSR had what has been described as a "problem-solving" approach to compliance issues in the SCC. The approach assumed that agreements contained ambiguities which permitted differing interpretations of treaty obligations. Without assuming malice on the part of either country in taking differing interpretations, the SCC's approach was to achieve compromises in which either new agreements were reached that rendered treaty terms more precise and restrictive, to the equal benefit of both parties, or else explanations for ambiguous behavior were accepted in the interest of maintaining the treaty regime. The goal of the process was to maintain and strengthen the arms control regime through accommodation.

From the outset of the Reagan Administration, the United States abandoned the problem-solving approach. The SCC was initially in disfavor with the new U.S. leadership because if the SALT regime were not to be continued, then what purpose would be served by continuing to use the forum attached to those agreements? The regular session of the SCC scheduled for spring 1981 was delayed until late in the season, as the Reagan Administration debated whether or not to use the forum, and avoided appointing a U.S. delegation.

When the United States did send a delegation to the SCC, it was with instructions to charge the Soviets with numerous violations of U.S. unilateral and restrictive interpretations of Soviet obligations under provisions of the SALT agreements, as well as to register some valid concerns about Soviet behavior. The Soviets responded with their own, sometimes permissive, interpretations of their obligations, and with counter-charges against the United States. The sessions of the SCC during 1981–1985, as described by U.S. participants, took on the quality of meetings at which American and Soviet representatives each simply presented the contrary positions of their respective governments, without any impetus to move towards common understandings.

By late 1985, the SCC had reached a stalemate on encryption, Abalakova and the other compliance disputes. Each country had taken an opposing position on these issues, and it was not at all clear to SCC representatives what was the next step, or what higher authority on each side could step in to further pursue a resolution of the dispute where the SCC had failed. Once an impasse has been reached at the SCC, no mechanism has been developed to pursue SCC issues at the level of foreign ministers or heads of state.

The rules of the SCC call for the Commission meetings and the resulting common understandings to be secret, partly in order that complaints of noncompliance might not take on a public, sensationalistic quality that would prevent the country being questioned from taking quiet steps to meet the objections of the complaining party. Seemingly frustrated by what they regarded as an intransigent Soviet response in the SCC, the Reagan Administration went public in early 1984 with charges of Soviet noncompliance. This infuriated the Soviets even further. Making these charges public, they said, was in clear violation of the agreed-upon SCC procedures which demand that Commission deliberations be conducted in strict confidentiality.[24] Indeed, even the common understandings reached by the SCC in the 1970s were not made public. In 1981–85, compliance problems became so politicized that the entire debate was taking place in the public arena, outside the SCC.

In the fall of 1985, the SCC produced its first U.S.–Soviet common understanding since the mid-1970s. The culmination of a discussion begun during the Carter Administration, the SCC achieved a common understanding on concurrent testing of SAMs and ABM radar.[25] The restrictions on "concurrent testing" were broadened to preclude "concurrent operation" of these systems at ABM test sites, which might actually have permitted the country engaging in such operation to derive some testing benefits.

But on more major compliance issues, such as encryption, new U.S. and Soviet systems that were questionable in light of the SALT II "one-new type only" provision, early warning radars, and movements towards nationwide ballistic missile defenses, the SCC proved incapacitated. The SCC's impotence reflected the high level of accusation and frustration characteristic in general of relations between the two countries at the time.

The Soviet Union did propose new approaches to the LPAR and encryption problems in 1985. On encryption, the USSR proposed that the United States specify the data, telemetry for which it needed to receive unencrypted.[26] And the Soviets suggested that construction be stopped on the Abalakova radar and the Thule and Flyingdales installations, after which their status would be discussed together.[27] The United States rejected both propositions. In the case of encryption, the United States argued that by specifying channels of telemetry it needed, the United States would be revealing the capabilities and limitations of its intelligence-gathering effort to an unacceptable degree. And the United States held that the Thule and Flyingdales installations were not comparable to Abalakova, because the Soviet radar was an arms control violation, while the U.S. modernization program was not.[28]

The SCC was so much in disfavor within the Reagan Administration that in 1985

Secretary of Defense Caspar Weinberger called in his RSVP ("Responding to Soviet Violations Policy") Report for the United States to publicly denounce the SCC and to abandon it as a forum for dealing with compliance issues. The SCC, Weinberger said, was an "Orwellian memory hole" into which U.S. concerns had been "dumped like yesterday's trash."[29] In a climate such as this, the SCC could hardly perform effectively.

The fact that the SCC operated in a less than optimal fashion in the early-to-mid-1980s interacted negatively with the ambiguities in treaty provisions, since one of the main functions of the SCC is to clarify the precise meaning or application of treaty language.

Decline of the Arms Control Process

The breakdown of progress towards constructing a more extensive arms control regime was probably the most significant external cause of the threatened compliance crisis. Lacking progress towards new agreements, the incentives for both sides to comply with the agreements of the past declined. The general lack of success of arms control talks after 1972 also harmed compliance by permitting the exploitation of new technologies, unconstrained by arms control agreements, which further changed the strategic situation and the basis for the arms control regime.

Nonratification of Agreements

One early sign of the downturn in arms control was the failure of the United States to ratify several agreements negotiated during the 1970s. No U.S.–Soviet arms control agreement was actually ratified after 1972, although several were concluded. In international law, the Vienna Convention on the Law of Treaties holds that no action prohibited by an agreement which is signed but not ratified shall be taken, as long as it is pending ratification.[30] Once it ceases to be pending ratification, it need not be considered in force. SALT II was pending ratification until 1982, when the Reagan Administration withdrew it from Senate consideration.[31] The United States and the USSR subsequently announced that they would continue to adhere to the agreement, and do nothing to "undercut" its provisions.[32] In June 1985, however, the United States added a qualification to its position, stating that it would observe the treaty, but reserve the right to make "proportional responses" to Soviet violations.[33]

Both the United States and the USSR interpreted their commitments to adhere to the terms of SALT II to mean only that they would hold to the treaty limits but would not make the reductions to 2400 delivery systems that the treaty required by 1979, or to 2250 launchers that the treaty required by January 1981. And both sides hedged their commitments to SALT II in other ways.

The ambiguous, signed-but-not-ratified status of agreements contributed to the rise of compliance controversies related to these treaties. The uncertain legal status of SALT II contributed to the fact that its provisions became the focus of compliance controversies, particularly with regard to Soviet behavior. As James Schear aptly puts it, Soviet encryption may simply be an act of defiance against the United States, a refusal by the Soviets to curtail their habitual secrecy in order to uphold an agreement that the United States had refused to ratify.[34]

The Threshold Test Ban Treaty (TTBT) of 1974 was also left unratified. This treaty included provision for consultation about compliance, and exchange of data on nuclear tests. Since these measures would only come to fruition through ratification of the treaty, they were never pursued. The compliance dispute involving testing by both countries that was allegedly beyond the 150 KT limits of the TTBT may have had its roots in inaccurate measurement of tests on both sides. Consultation as the treaty directed might have helped to resolve this dispute by instituting an exchange of the appropriate data in order to correct the models being used on both sides to calculate yield. Had the agreement been ratified and the consultative procedures and data exchange come into effect, disputes involving the TTBT might more easily have been resolved.

Lack of Incentive to Uphold Agreements

Viewing the future of their military competition as one unconstrained by additional arms control provisions, the superpowers naturally saw disadvantages to continuing to respect arms control agreements. Soviet leaders likely concluded that if the United States was not going to be constrained by future agreements, then they had best prepare for the worst-case instance of increased U.S. military power, eschewing conservatism in compliance with agreements where that conflicted with their priority goal of military readiness.

Such worst-case planning on the Soviet side could explain their behavior in the cases where their compliance practices came close to exceeding treaty limits. If the Soviets believed, for example, that the United States would not consider itself bound by ABM Treaty strictures or participate in any agreement limiting space weapons, then the most obvious Soviet response would be to build offensive warheads and delivery systems to overcome any U.S. strategic defense. This might explain why the Soviets moved ahead with programs to build not only the SS-24 and questionable SS-25 ICBMs, but towards testing other ICBMs in the pipeline as well. Worst-case planning, against a threat that would be unconstrained by arms control, may have contributed to the compliance problem involving the "one-new-type" limit of SALT II.

No Agreements to Deal with New Threats to the Regime

Far from imposing additional constraints, those new negotiations that were begun after 1981 proved unsuccessful, causing the provisions of existing treaties to become further and further out of date. With no updated specific constraints on developments such as space-based anti-ballistic missile defense systems, the ABM Treaty became a less effective deterrent to strategic defense activities when new, unconstrained technologies began to push against existing treaty limits.

Lack of progress in developing the arms control regime was the underlying cause of two of the factors discussed above that have fostered compliance difficulties. The SCC has been unable to produce common understandings on compliance problems due to the perceived lack of prospects for the arms control regime. If the regime is not developing, then what point is there to resolving disputes and solidifying the gains of the past through a consultative mechanism?

Likewise, the halt in development of the arms control regime exacerbated the difficulties that arose from the lack of adequate verification methods and by the movement towards military technologies nonverifiable by national technical means. The SALT I and SALT II agreements and the ABM Treaty, in particular, were based on the premise that they would be followed by future agreements placing additional constraints on coming generations of defensive and offensive weapons. Some of the provisions of SALT II, for instance, were specifically designed to be the basis for future agreements. Restraints on the deployment of long-range cruise missiles, which present considerable verification challenges, were pushed into a two-year protocol to SALT II, on the assumption that this issue would be dealt with in subsequent negotiations.

CONCLUSIONS

As we have seen, the arms control compliance crisis of the 1980s actually had little to do with arms control compliance per se, and a great deal to do with decreased Soviet and American confidence in the mutual security regime they had constructed during the two previous decades. Beginning in the late 1970s, both countries moved back towards reliance on unilateral measures to deal with their security problems.

DEFICIENCIES IN THE REGIME

To a minor degree, the cause of the lowered U.S. and Soviet desire to rely on mutual security measures is to be found in deficiencies in the regime itself, which created dissatisfactions. Measures to decrease the ambiguities in provisions of specific agreements would certainly clarify the obligations of parties to arms control treaties, and thus reduce the opportunity both for stretching the terms of agreements and for accusations sparked by less-than-conservative compliance behavior.

Verifiability of compliance with agreements is also a crucial ingredient of a successful arms control regime. Several existing agreements are either virtually unverifiable (the Biological Weapons Convention, the Geneva Convention of 1925) or contain provisions supported by verification arrangements that require continuing consultation regarding interpretations and application (SALT II, the ABM Treaty). A variety of approaches could be pursued to improve the verification situation. Efforts could be made to negotiate cooperative measures to improve the verifiability of existing agreements. Provisions could be written into new agreements to supersede and improve verifiability of provisions found in present treaties. Meanwhile, the United States could unilaterally work to develop more effective technologies and methods of intelligence analysis for verification.

But most of the causes of the compliance frustrations of the 1980s have been external to the arms control regime. Even if the internal problems of the arms control regime were under control, trends in the external context within which the regime operates are likely to periodically become volatile, and could at any time in the future again disrupt its functioning. Thus, for the arms control regime to become stronger and to function more smoothly, it will be necessary to see an evolution in some of the factors affecting the regime.

RECOGNITION OF REGIME'S IMPERFECTIONS

Several developments in the general context of the U.S.–Soviet relationship would foster maintenance of the arms control regime. The first would be a recognition that disputes are bound to arise in an arms control regime between two nations as adversarial as the U.S. and the USSR. Put another way, it will be a long time—if ever—until the two countries consistently see their own self interests and their mutual interests in the security realm as being the same. Indeed, it will be a long time until those interests really do consistently match up, if ever they do. Unilateral interests and mutual security interests will continue to pull and tug one against the other, in a shifting balance that will affect the success of any elements of a mutual security regime between the two countries.

The fact that disputes are inevitable should not be considered to represent the failure of the regime, a conclusion the U.S. political leadership was prone to jump to in the early 1980s. Since it is highly likely that disagreements about obligations under the terms of treaties will surface, special attention should be given to the process of resolving disputes. Under what circumstances does it function best? How can it be improved?

A better utilization of the Standing Consultative Commission, and the other consultative and dispute resolution mechanisms of existing arms control agreements is a key ingredient in helping the regime to work. The problem-solving approach to the SCC, which assumes that agreements are ambiguous and may be variously interpreted, is crucial to the success of that body. The SCC and other consultative mechanisms such as those mandated by the Threshold Test Ban Treaty are not simply aspects of the arms control regime that can be penalized along with other elements of the regime when it does not seem to be working optimally. These are the very mechanisms for allowing the regime to work, and for helping it to survive inevitable fluctuations in U.S.–Soviet relations. When unilateral security drives push U.S. and Soviet behavior in directions that threaten the arms control regime, this is precisely the time that smooth functioning of the dispute resolution mechanisms is most needed.

A variety of suggestions could be made about improving and developing consultative mechanisms. No new agreements should be outside the jurisdiction of some consultative body or process, either the SCC itself or mechanisms attached to other agreements. U.S. and Soviet ratification of the Threshold Test Ban Treaty is crucial in order to bring into being the data exchange and consultation required by the treaty. Both that agreement and the Limited Test Ban should be brought under the jurisdiction of a consultative forum, as should all other security agreements of the past that do not involve such procedures.

How to prevent the SCC and other consultative mechanisms from becoming arenas for greater deterioration of the regime, rather than forums for preserving it, is a more difficult question. For these mechanisms to operate as a binding force in times when the United States and USSR seek to pull away from the regime would require not only the assumption that disputes are an inevitable part of the process, but a longer-term concept of self-interest on both sides that was demonstrated in the period of the late 1970s and early 1980s.

DEVELOPMENT OF LONGER-TERM CONCEPT OF SELF-INTEREST

It is interesting to observe what happened to U.S. national security policy between 1981 and 1986, and to a lesser extent to Soviet security policy also during this period. The United States made a sharp detour in the early 1980s, and then came full circle back to an avenue very similar to that of the 1970s, at least in its stated approach to national security policy. The Reagan Administration moved from an extremely negative attitude towards mutual security approaches to national security in 1981, to at least verbal embrace of arms control objectives by 1986. Indeed, some of the arms control concepts under discussion by the mid-1980s, including eradicating ballistic missiles by the mid-1990s, exhibited a far more radical reliance on mutual security concepts in the nuclear weapons area than did those of any of President Reagan's predecessors in the White House.

This assessment should be qualified by noting that no actual arms control agreements along these lines are produced through the mid-1980s. But even if advocacy of such mutual security arrangements with the Soviets was partly rhetoric or an attempt by the U.S. government to appease American public opinion, it still serves to show how, over time, the power of the mutual security idea exerted itself on an American leadership deeply drawn towards unilateral security measures at the outset of its tenure in office.

Does this suggest that there was a certain inevitability about the implications of the nuclear arms competition during this period for the governments involved? Perhaps. After several years of poor-mouthing arms control, the Reagan Administration did find itself essentially embracing the type of mutual security approach to arms control characteristic of the 1970s. The realities of mutual vulnerability, essential parity, more-than-sufficiency of existing nuclear forces, the moral and political unacceptability of nuclear war, and the ever-present danger of a nuclear exchange resulting from any of a number of circumstances were eventually found by the Reagan Administration to be persuasive incentives to seek mutual U.S.–Soviet constraints on forces and behavior. U.S. self-interest was pushed back towards being defined at least partially in terms of mutual security interests.

The cycle of behavior engaged in by the United States and the USSR in the early 1980s clearly had destructive effects on the arms control regime. The compliance crisis ensued, calling into question adherence to existing treaties; treaties that had been negotiated were not ratified; there was a several-year hiatus in seriously pursuing new agreements. The cyclical nature of the sequence of actions during this period of time suggests that a longer-term perspective by each country about its security interests might have led to the conclusion that mutual security measures continued to be a promising means of dealing with security problems facing each country.

Influence of Domestic Politics on Definition of Self-Interest

Much of the definition of self-interests in the security realm, of course, proceeds within the context of the domestic politics of each country. In both the United States and the USSR, the domestic structures are far from ideal in terms of encouraging a longer-term view of self-interests in mutual security measures. The extreme volatility of domestic politics in the United States means that sharp detours such as that of the Reagan period are possible, followed by developments which to a certain extent represent reinvention of the wheel with regard to mutual security measures. In the USSR, the system contains too few internal watchdogs on compliance and too great an emphasis on secrecy at the cost of sharing information with the United States that is needed to sustain mutual security measures.

Although these problems arise from different sources on each side, the net effect of the domestic structure on both sides is to create a tension between built-in tendencies towards unilateralism on the one hand, and mutual security approaches on the other hand, hampering the functioning of the security regime. There is no easy answer to this problem of the short-term nature of domestic perceptions about national self-interest in security policy. The most that can be said is that some promising trends are underway under the Gorbachev leadership in the USSR that could lead both to greater openness in sharing data with the United States on military programs in the service of arms control agreements, and perhaps to a stronger internal constituency for mutual security measures and compliance with existing agreements. If these trends represent a major shift in the Soviet approach, this could bode well for Soviet interest in developing mutual security approaches with the United States in the future.

In the United States, the Congress, the press, and the public interest sector have tended to constrain the executive branch when it has been inclined to pursue solely unilateral security measures. The U.S. return to the acceptance of mutual security measures in the mid-1980s represents a recognition of the limitations of a strictly unilateral approach to dealing with security issues, even if that realization has not yet been fully assimilated by the public and the government.

ADDRESSING DEFECTS IN THE REGIME
THROUGH DEVELOPMENT OF THE REGIME

As confidence in the security regime flagged in the late 1970s, the United States and the USSR fell back on traditional unilateral means of pursuing security. The United States engaged in a major strategic modernization and expansion program, while the USSR continued and expanded its already robust weapons programs. Neither side pursued the possibility that the means to address the problems in the regime lay within the regime, rather than with a return to the unilateral measures traditionally employed. Through consultative mechanisms, some avenues did exist within the regime to address its deficiencies and the dissatisfactions of both parties.

But to a great extent, the drop in confidence in the regime had to do with dissatisfaction because it could not solve problems that it was not designed to solve. The lack of confidence had to do primarily with disputes over regional conflicts and with the continued qualitative nuclear arms competition. The security agreements of the 1960s and 1970s either did not address these problems, or did so only minimally and poorly, as in the case of attempted constraints on the qualitative race in the SALT II agreement.

The mutual security regime of the 1960s and 1970s was in a tenuous position partly because it involved bilateral measures set into a context where modes of behavior in general were not based on mutual security principles. Further development of the regime, and its extension into new areas would probably improve the functioning of arms control agreements. If agreements seeking to moderate or resolve regional conflicts were in operation, and effective mechanisms for moderating or restraining the qualitative nuclear arms competition existed, then dissatisfactions in these realms might cause fewer reverberations in the arms control regime. The broader the mutual security regime, both within the arms control realm and otherwise in the security relationship, the better the functioning of arms control agreements will be.

Notes

1. Testimony of James Schlesinger, Subcommittee on Arms Control, Senate Armed Services Committee, 94th Congress, 1st Session, March 6, 1975, p. 3; U.S. Department of State, "SALT ONE: Compliance, SALT TWO: Verification," Special Report No. 7 (Washington D.C.: U.S. Government Printing Office, 1978).

2. The 1925 Geneva Protocol for the Prohibition in Use in War of Asphyxiating, Poisonous or Other Gases, and of Bacteriological Methods of Warfare; the 1972 Convention on the Prohibition of the Development, Production, and Stockpiling of Bacteriological (Biological) and Toxin Weapons and on Their Destruction.

3. *The President's Report to the Congress on Soviet Noncompliance with Arms Control Agreements,* White House, Office of the Press Secretary, January 23, 1984; "Soviet Noncompliance with Arms Control Agreements," *Special Report* No. 122 (Bureau of Public Affairs, U.S. Department of State, February 1, 1985); *The President's Unclassified Report on Soviet Noncompliance with Arms Control Agreements* (White House, Office of the Press Secretary, December 23, 1985); "Soviet Noncompliance" (U.S. Arms Control and Disarmament Agency, February 1, 1986).

4. "US Violates Its International Commitments," Aide Memoire, Embassy of the USSR, Washington, D.C. Released by TASS, January 29, 1984.

5. "Presidential Statement on Interim Restraint" (White House, May 27, 1986), pp. 2–3.

6. For a case-by-case evaluation of the charges, see the report, *Compliance and the Future of Arms Control* (New York: Ballinger, 1987).

7. For a fuller discussion of the positive record of U.S. and Soviet compliance with arms control agreements, see the section "The Compliance Record," in *Compliance and the Future of Arms Control.*

8. On the encryption debate during the SALT II negotiations, see Strobe Talbott, *Endgame: The Inside Story of SALT II* (New York: Harper & Row, 1979), pp. 237–244.

9. Leslie H. Gelb, "Moscow Proposes to End a Dispute on Siberia Radar," (*New York Times,* October 29, 1985), p. 1.

10. Ibid.

11. For Reagan Administration reinterpretations, see "The ABM Treaty and the SDI Program," Testimony by Ambassador Paul H. Nitze, special advisor on arms control matters, and Abraham D. Sofaer, legal advisor to the state department, before the Subcommittee on Arms Control, International Security, and Science of the House Foreign Affairs Committee, October 22, 1985. U.S. Department of State, Bureau of Public Affairs, *Current Policy* No. 755.

12. Among many critiques, see Testimony of John B. Rhinelander before the Subcommittee on Arms Control, International Security, and Science of the House Foreign Affairs Committee, Testimony April 24, 1985; Christopher Paine, "The ABM Treaty: looking for loopholes," *Bulletin of the Atomic Scientists* (August/September 1983): 13–16; Gerard Smith, "How the Administration Amended the ABM Treaty," Letter to the *New York Times* (October 23, 1985); Tom Wicker, "Subverting a Treaty," *New York Times* (October 25, 1985); R. Jeffrey Smith, " 'Star Wars' Tests and the ABM Treaty," *Science* (July 5, 1985): 29–31.

13. Gordon J. Humphrey, "Analysis and Compliance Enforcement in SALT Verification," in William Potter, ed., *Verification and SALT: The Challenge of Strategic Deception* (Boulder, Colo: Westview Press, 1980), pp. 113–117.

14. Summary, "A Quarter Century of Soviet Compliance Practices Under Arms Control Commitments: 1958–1983," General Advisory Committee on Arms Control and Disarmament, October 1984.

15. See Gloria Duffy, "Administration redefines Soviet 'violations,' " *Bulletin of the Atomic Scientists,* vol. 42, no. 2 (February 1986): 13–17

16. See the section on the "Sources of Soviet Compliance Behavior" of *Compliance and the Future of Arms Control,* for a discussion of the Soviet internal process for compliance decisionmaking.

17. See Raymond L. Garthoff, *Detente and Confrontation* (Washington, D.C.: Brookings Institution, 1985), p. 183.

18. The one previous instance of clear Soviet violation involved Soviet lagging behind in dismantling submarine-based ballistic missile launchers as new systems were deployed in 1976, putting the USSR temporarily over the Interim Agreement launcher limit. The USSR requested

an extension due to practical delays, then dismantled the requisite number of systems within a time limit as agreed by the United States and the USSR.

19. "Verification: Peacekeeping by technical means," *IEEE Spectrum* (July 1986): 61.

20. Marshal Sergei F. Akhromeyev, Press Conference, Soviet Foreign Ministry, June 4, 1986. Reported in *Pravda* (June 5, 1986), p. 4; *FBIS/USSR Daily Report,* June 5, 1986, p. AA1.

21. "US Warns Russians to Stop Encoding Missile Data," *New York Times* (February 1, 1979), p. 7.

22. See Marshal Akhromeyev Press Conference.

23. "President's Statement on Interim Restraint."

24. "US Violates Its International Commitments," Aide Memoire, Embassy of the USSR, Washington, D.C. Released by TASS, January 29, 1984.

25. R. Jeffrey Smith, "Arms Agreement Breathes New Life into SCC," *Science* (August 9, 1985).

26. Leslie H. Gelb, "Moscow Proposes to End a Dispute on Siberia Radar," *New York Times* (October 29, 1985), p. 1

27. Letter from V. Isakov, Minister-Counselor, Soviet Embassy, Washington, D.C. to Congressman Stephen Solarz, April 23, 1985.

28. Gelb, "Moscow Proposes to End a Dispute."

29. "Responding to Soviet Violations Policy," Memorandum for the President, Office of the Secretary of Defense, November 13, 1985, p. 9.

30. Article 14, Vienna Convention on the Law of Treaties, U.N. Document A/CONF 39127 (1969), reprinted in *American Journal of International Law* 63 (1969): 875. For a discussion of this point, see Phillip R. Trimble, *Soviet Violations of Arms Control Agreements: A Legal Perspective,* Working Paper No. 53, Center for Strategic and International Affairs, University of California at Los Angeles, November 1985.

31. Secretary of State Alexander Haig told the Senate Foreign Relations Committee on May 11, 1982 that "We consider SALT II to be dead and have so informed the Soviet Union." *Washington Post,* (May 12, 1982), p. A9. For clarification on this point, see Leo Sartori, "Will SALT II Survive?" *International Security,* vol. 10, no. 3 (Winter 1985–86): 149.

32. This U.S. policy came to be referred to as "interim restraint." Statement by President Reagan in his speech announcing the beginning of the START talks in Geneva, *New York Times* (June 1, 1982).

33. *New York Times* (June 11, 1985).

34. James Schear, "Arms Control Treaty Compliance: Building Up to a Breakdown," *International Security,* vol. 10, no. 2 (Fall 1985): 164.

12

SALT and the Search for a Security Regime

CONDOLEEZZA RICE

Strategic arms control is a central case in the examination of American and Soviet efforts at cooperation. The SALT experience (which includes the Interim Offensive Arm Agreement and Anti-Ballistic Missile Treaty [ABM] of Salt I and the unratified SALT II treaty) has been neither a clear cut failure nor success. It is, perhaps, the most remarkable illustration of a cooperative impulse in U.S.–Soviet relations. In the SALT process and its successor START, the United States and the Soviet Union have attempted to augment unilateral security measures (independent defense policies) with negotiated security arrangements. The process has been concerned with the most central systems at the disposal of the two countries: those that are capable of deterring and, should war break out, destroying the adversary. SALT does not deal with tangential security issues. Strategic arms control explicitly recognizes that, in spite of the superpowers' adversarial relationship, American and Soviet security are inextricably linked.

Cooperation and regime theorists have paid insufficient attention to the regime aspects of the SALT/START experience. Regime theory, when transferred to the security realm, has tended to examine détente in its entirety in trying to understand the nature of U.S.–Soviet cooperation. Arms control has rightly been identified as one of the institutions of the cooperation, not as an end in itself. Nevertheless, the SALT process, while clearly embedded within the larger effort at cooperation, was an attempt to establish a regulatory mechanism for the development of the strategic arms postures of the United States and the Soviet Union. Confined to a rather narrow, if essential, sphere of the competition, SALT can be thought of as an attempt to lay the groundwork for a strategic arms control regime based on principles and rules that would have regulated the development of U.S. and Soviet strategic forces.

The successes, failures, and finally the pressures for defection from the SALT treaties are instructive for refining our concepts of security regimes. A regime is based upon principles, norms, rules, and decision-making procedures.[1] If it is truly a regime, it will have a discernible impact on national patterns of conduct and action. SALT, though highly contentious, was an effort by the United States and the Soviet Union to constrain in some (though not in all) respects independent decision-making in a larger bilateral decision-making framework. But intent and effect are not synonymous. The SALT experience has been characterized by adherence to the letter of the treaties, but expectations that it would mature and be extended have been frustrated. Principles, rules, and machinery for consultation were all a part of the SALT experience. But a regime must also provide a set of norms around which actors' expectations converge. The SALT process failed to mature to that point. Ultimately, the most important lesson of the SALT experience may be the problem of expectations in a security regime between adversaries.

There were many difficult issues in the strategic interaction that the early SALT treaties could not accommodate. In order to keep the negotiations on track, difficult issues were sometimes postponed to the next round. There was, in the headier days of the experience, an expectation that each successive round, building on the successes of the last, would lead to ever more beneficial agreements. The hope was that the momentum of the process and the trust it would engender would then become instruments for helping to solve even more difficult problems of force asymmetry and different views of the nature of deterrence in the future. If the strategic arms control effort disintegrates altogether, as it is currently in danger of doing, frustrated and unfulfilled expectations will be a major reason for its demise.

THE DEMAND FOR A REGIME

Why bother? The critics of SALT on the left and right ask precisely this question. Peace movement or disarmament proponents point to the fact that the arms race has not been halted by strategic arms control. In fact, the superpowers have seemingly exploited loopholes and built their forces to the limits allowed. Skeptics on the other side argue that the impact of the agreements has been one-sided. The United States believes in bilateral security, but the Soviets do not. SALT is said to detract from the real means of securing the peace—the maintenance of American power. The stronger the United States the better. Yet the state actors, the United States and the Soviet Union, have pursued arms control continuously. Why do they bother? What preference ordering would lead any analyst to expect that adversaries would engage in arms control?

The conditions that were necessary for the initiation of efforts at strategic arms control were: (1) the realization by both sides that strategic parity between the United States and the Soviet Union was approaching and that an effort should be made to stabilize it; (2) the recognition of the ''objective condition'' of deterrence and the belief that it precluded ''meaningful superiority''; (3) the realization that unilateral security measures could not alter those conditions and might, in fact, lead to decreased security at greater cost. In the parlance of cooperation theory, the Soviet Union and the United States realized that to pursue a unilateral course would not lead to an optimal outcome. There was a need to regulate their decision-making jointly. The rationale for arms control was put most succinctly by Richard Nixon in his first Annual Foreign Policy report to Congress:

> The traditional course of seeking security primarily through military strength raises several problems in the world of multiplying strategic weapons. Modern technology makes any balance precarious and promotes new efforts at ever higher levels of complexity. Such an arms race absorbs resources, talents and energies. The more intense the competition, the greater the uncertainty about the other side's intentions. The higher the level of armaments the greater violence and devastation should deterrence fail.

The timing of the decision to initiate strategic arms control is no accident. There were throughout the latter half of the 1950s proposals and counter proposals on disarmament, long before the SALT process. What was missing, though, was strategic parity, or rather the expectation of parity in the immediate future, and the acceptance of it as a desirable end point if it could be stabilized. Until the Soviet Union's own military power was sufficient to deter an American attack on the Soviet Union, the Soviets were interested only in broad sweeping proposals for disarmament. The fear of inferiority made bilateral security impossible. Conversely, as long as the United States enjoyed superiority and could expect to maintain it for some time, bilateral security arrangements were not very attractive. Once parity was achieved, however, the United States and the Soviet Union faced the prospect of a costly, if not also risky, arms race in which neither would be able to gain superiority.

The problem is that the concept of ''parity'' is difficult to operationalize in precise terms. The SALT process, in the absence of an agreed upon definition, attempted to give meaning to parity through constructing rules for equating the arsenals of both sides. The Interim Offensive Agreement (SALT I) and subsequently SALT II were, in effect, attempts to cap the arsenals of the two sides. Since asymmetries in force structure, threat environment, and strategic preferences existed between the two sides, this turned out to be a difficult process. Moreover, since force modernization was allowed, the maintenance of parity demanded the search for an elusive dynamic equilibrium rather than a static force relationship. Nevertheless, one of the contributions of the SALT process was the development of a set of rules (primarily through numerical limits and explicit tradeoffs) that implicitly defined parity. Not surprisingly, the form of cooperation was arms limitation.

The rules themselves caused a political problem, however, For a variety of reasons several types of forces were not covered in the agreements and slippage in those areas led to fears that the other side was attempting to break out of or circumvent the treaty. The clearest example of this problem was the SS-20 controversy. Because European-based systems were not limited, many have argued that the Soviets used this gap in the treaty to gain a military advantage in that theater. Moreover, important domestic constituencies in the United States have never been satisfied with the ambiguity contained in the Soviet-inspired phrase ''equality and equal security.'' The Soviets have argued continually that it was necessary to accommodate differences in the threat environment facing the two sides. The independent nuclear forces of Great Britain and France, the former a member of NATO and the latter a participant in the political, though not the military, NATO machinery, were cited as examples of the aysmmetrical threat. The United States has never recognized this claim, though adjustments in the over-all SALT I totals may have taken tacit account of the asymmetry.

Asymmetries in force structure were also accommodated. Perhaps the most controversial of these provisions allowed the Soviets to retain a significant throwweight advantage (a function of larger but, at the time, less accurate Soviet land-based systems), in exchange for a few more American missiles. For Senator Henry Jackson of Washington and others, this gross parity or essential equivalence, was unacceptable. The probably necessary definition of parity as ''gross parity'' has thus led in the political arena to a constant fear that the other side is not really satisfied with parity but seeking superiority. This has made the situation in which both sides prefer cooperation to mutual defection potentially unstable and subject to continual pressure from technology and domestic politics.[2]

A second condition for the creation of a strategic arms limitation regime was the acceptance of the ''objective condition'' of mutual deterrence. The underlying principle is first and foremost the unacceptability of nuclear war as a policy instrument. If nuclear war cannot be won, regardless of the size and sophistication of one's arsenal, there is a strong impulse toward cooperation. The first principle advanced in the ABM treaty states this precisely by saying that both sides were "proceeding from the premise that nuclear war would have devastating consequences for all mankind." The paradox is, though, that cooperation is possible *because* unilateral measures have been taken and could be taken again in order to preserve parity. Arms control is thus premised on an implicit agreement that neither side will allow the other to exploit it. Unilateral strength and cooperation measures go hand in hand. Though critics of the arms control process often obscure the link between bilateral and unilateral measures, the reality of the process is that it is de facto recognition and codification of the balance of terror. Neither the United States nor the Soviet Union has throughout the process been ready to allow arms control to become a substitute for mutual deterrence. Again it is not surprising that the form of cooperation is arms limitation, not disarmament.

Acceptance of the condition of mutual deterrence also turned out to be a politically sensitive issue. Asymmetries in American and Soviet forces, stemming from different strategic preferences and technological strengths, continued to worry many. The Soviets' doctrinal insistence on "damage limitation and war winning," married to a heavy land-based arsenal, made it difficult for Americans to accept the premise that the Soviets believed in their own vulnerability to a retaliatory strike. In recent years, the emphasis on damage limitation has been less pronounced in Soviet military doctrine. At the political level, they have incorporated the thesis that "a nuclear war would have no winners,"[3] and a number a notable Soviet military authorities have admitted that the initiation of nuclear was is probably tantamount to suicide.[4] Nonetheless, even if it were possible to argue that the Soviets accepted mutual vulnerability (not necessarily mutually assured destruction), they exhibited little enthusiasm for it as a military strategy and even less willingness to allow the United States to define the types of forces that could keep the situation of mutual deterrence stable. This was particularly true in the mid- to late 1970s when the Soviets argued vociferously that their force posture was no more threatening than that of the United States.

In fact, American operational doctrine has not resembled a strategy of mutually assured destruction since the mid-1960s either. Flexible response, limited nuclear options, and a wide range of targeting options have always given an American President options short of mutual suicide. The United States, too, simply realized that protection from an all-out nuclear attack was infeasible. The political fallout caused by the ambiguities in Soviet doctrine was heavy, however, and SALT, with its emphasis on essential equivalence and mutual deterrence, was hostage to the resulting opposition.

Having accepted the conditions of parity and mutual deterrence, the United States and the Soviet Union were able to cooperate. The demand for the regime was thus somewhat more complicated than an interest in "preventing nuclear war." As Robert Jervis and others have done, it could be argued that nuclear war is prevented by power capabilities alone.[5] But interestingly, the fact of mutual deterrence was not deemed to be enough. The Soviets in particular were insistent that efforts to relax political tensions between the two sides and measures to "reduce the risks of nuclear war," were also necessary.[6] But the real demand for the regime stemmed from the realization that mutual deterrence needed to be codified. Rules were needed to constrain independent decision making so that certainty could be introduced into the relationship. In order to do this, principles, rules, and norms, as well as policing machinery were established.

REGIME PRINCIPLES

Two of the conditions that led to the demand for the regime also became sustaining principles of the strategic arms control effort: political acceptance of parity as a virtually irreversible condition, and the recognition of mutual vulnerability as an objective technological fact of the nuclear age.

A third principle, stemming from mutual vulnerability, was the offense-defense link: the recognition that the acquisition of defensive weapons would drive the other side to acquire more offensive firepower in order to overwhelm the defense. As the document that establishes this link, the ABM Treaty is somewhat more than an effort to limit ballistic missile defense. The treaty states in two places that the limitation of antiballistic missile systems would be a substantial factor in curbing the strategic arms race. A few lines later it makes the link again: "With respect to the limitation of strategic offensive arms, it would contribute to the creation of more favorable conditions for further negotiations on limiting strategic arms." The ABM Treaty was, then, an enabling agreement for the entire SALT process. Without limitations on ballistic missile defenses, the desire to overwhelm them would drive military planners to proliferate offensive weapons.

The Americans in fact feared that simply responding to the Soviet buildup of ABM by developing its own would do nothing to enhance security. Defensive technologies were, at the time, judged to be ineffective and certainly costly. Further, defensive systems were destabilizing when linked with offensive systems and it would be impossible to obtain limitations on offense without prior limitations on defense. The United States did think it necessary to demonstrate American's willingness to build an ABM in the absence of a treaty. President Nixon explicitly asked for a Congressional vote to develop and deploy an ABM system on the grounds that the Soviet Union could then, faced with the prospect of a superior American system, be persuaded to sign the ABM Treaty. This "bargaining chip" strategy was designed to show the Soviets that they could not contemplate the attainment of superiority. Though bargaining chips are probably used too loosely and too often, their use is understandable. Since arms control is premised on the implicit understanding that neither side will accept inferiority, periodic demonstrations of resolve in defending parity should be expected. This introduces a self-reinforcing dynamic into the agreement.

SALT, then, was based on three key principles: the maintenance of parity and the renunciation of superiority; the acceptance of mutual vulnerability; and acceptance of the link between offense and defense. On this basis a number of agreements were then concluded. The agreement actually had an impact on the security forces of the two sides. The criticism levelled at SALT that offensive forces grew during the period misses the mark. The purpose of the first two agreements was to stabilize the growth of the arsenals at an agreed upon limit.

A broader set of rules for preventing nuclear war was encompassed in auxiliary executive agreements. These include provisions for the notification of parties in the event of accidental, unauthorized, or other unexplained incidents; detection of unidentified objects by missile warning systems; and an agreement to maintain and improve organizational and technical arrangements to guard against accidental or unauthorized use of nuclear weapons.

In addition to the principles and carefully delineated rules of SALT, regime characteristics include a mechanism for policing and regulating the parties (the Standing Consultative Commission), to which the United States and Soviet Union send permanent representatives of ambassadorial rank; a counting mechanism (the SALT counting rules); and rules to ensure transparency in SALT-related matters. The latter, an agreement not to encrypt (encode) SALT-related data, has been difficult to enforce because the line between SALT-related and other data is difficult to establish. The provision itself is interesting, however, suggesting that both sides were willing, at the time, to give up a modicum of secrecy for the sake of bilateral treaties.

THE IMPACT OF SALT ON DEFENSE POLICY

Even if one argues that SALT was to be the basis for a strategic arms control regime, it is necessary to demonstrate that it was more than a diplomatic exercise but had the potential to alter unilateral decision-making.

Under the terms of the SALT I and unratified but largely respected SALT II limits, the United States and the Soviet Union had dismantled old systems as they have modernized. The Soviet Union has removed 1,027 ICBMS, 229 SLBMs, 7 Hotel class submarines, and 13 Yankee class submarines as newer ones have come into service. In the same period, the United States has fully dismantled eight Polaris missile-carrying submarines as new Trident subs have come into being.[7] It is well to note that the Soviet Union's military is known for its propensity to hold on to even obsolete weapons and that dismantling is a break with this tradition. After all, this is an army that only recently stopped deploying World War II vintage T-34s. Another indication of the impact of the regime comes in examining Soviet force posture. Stephen Meyer and Peter Almquist, using a force posture model developed by I. I. Anureyev, the influential Soviet operations research specialist and military planner, have shown that the current Soviet nuclear force posture is not the best that they could acquire to meet military and economic efficiency requirements as designated by the model. Another force posture would have been preferable, but it would have violated SALT I limits. Obviously, this is only indirect evidence but it is suggestive of the potential impact of the regime on defense policy.[8]

Until recently, the United States also followed the limits of the treaty. This was in spite of the Reagan Administration's rejection of the SALT treaties. The decision to continue to abide by the limits of the treaty as long as the Soviet Union did (the "no undercut" provision) is instructive in thinking about the potential impact of regimes on security policy.

The Reagan Administration has made it clear that it is an opponent of arms control as it was previously practiced and that it considers the SALT treaties fatally flawed. But in the absence of agreements more to the President's liking, the SALT limits provided a point of coalescence for supporters of arms control as a process both inside and outside of the Administration for almost six years. Legislators, U.S. allies, and until 1986 the Joint Chiefs of Staff, were particularly vocal in imploring the President to continue compliance with the unratified SALT II treaty.[9]

The view that some rules are better than no rules triumphed for the better part of six years. A decision in December 1985 to dismantle two Poseidon submarines while deploying the new Trident II submarine was made over the objections of Secretary of Defense Caspar Weinberger and ACDA Director Kenneth Adelman. Then, at the end of 1986, the President announced that the United States was no longer bound by the numerical limits of the SALT II Treaty. The decision to launch additional B-52s retro-fitted with air-launched cruise missiles placed the United States in technical violation of the treaty. Interestingly, the decision passed with only a mild response from Moscow that they also were no longer obligated by the limits of the treaty but would remain in technical compliance for the time being. The important point is that it did not derail the START talks.

In spite of the eventual revocation of the ''no undercut'' policy, the way in which the policy was structured also throws light on the concept of regimes. The existence of this unratified treaty made the President's job of breaking out of the SALT limitations very difficult.

This difficulty illustrates that when a bilateral arrangement is in place, a unilateral decision to violate it is a challenge to an existing body of rules, and there are therefore costs associated with such decisions that might otherwise go by largely unnoticed. In fact, the Administration has justified its decision to break out of the treaty limits through a skillfully orchestrated campaign of charges that the Soviets have already violated the treaty. The desire to show domestic and international opponents of the breakout that it is, in fact, the Soviets who have defected from the regime is important. It is not clear whether the Administration will reverse its course, but the unratified treaty is now a rallying point in Congress. There has even been discussion of tying a favorable response to the President's defense budget request to an agreement to respect the treaty limits.

Even as the SALT limitations are receding into the history books the United States and the Soviet Union continue to draw upon the residual machinery of the process. The transition from rules based on the SALT formula to those of START was facilitated by what had already been negotiated. Launchers had originally been the primary unit of counting at START, but the decision to use warheads instead was accepted by both sides with relative ease. Moreover, the SALT counting rules that established the war-head limit on the basis of test data have not been challenged by either side. Without the SALT counting rules and the agreement that test data were acceptable as a defining characteristic of warhead totals, it would not have been possible to make the shift from launchers to warheads.

A second point about regimes and unilateral defense policy is illustrated by the experience of the last five years. When states enter regimes, the necessity of managing and complying with the regime fosters bureaucratic mechanisms and institutions within the domestic policy-making arena that must be accommodated or (with some effort) deliberately circumvented in order to break out of the regime. The process of issuing arms control impact statements, of verifying regime compliance, and of justifying po-tential violations to the Legislative branch has built a kind of inertia into the system.

Little is known of the Soviet policy-making process in this regard, but they too have new bureaucratic players as a result of the arms limitation regime. The General Staff's Legal and Treaty Department apparently monitors Soviet defense programs to ensure compliance. Moreover, in a system infamous for compartmentalization and bur-eaucratization of the defense policy process, arms control arguably pushes certain de-fense decisions to the highest political levels when they might otherwise be left to the General Staff. The considerable continuity of personnel on Soviet arms control delega-tions suggests that the arms control process has created a cadre of experienced civilian defense experts in a Soviet system notorious for the absence of a civilian staff to aid in the defense decision-making process.[10]

A final argument about the impact of regimes on defense policy is that they help to place boundaries on reality by reducing relevant uncertainties affecting force planning. The Soviet Union is a closed society. It is impossible to estimate Soviet defense spending in advance or to know what will emerge from the defense planning process in five or ten years. The "transparency" provided by an agreed upon data exchange and numerical limits helps to diminish the "worst" that needs to be taken into account in worst-case planning. This has been the primary argument in favor of SALT by the Joint Chiefs of Staff, who after all must oversee military planning. For them, planning, especially against a secretive adversary, is made easier by the existence of some limits.

IS THE SALT REGIME AT AN END?

Whatever the past value of the SALT agreements, as of 1987, two challenges appear to be close to undoing it. The first, the Strategic Defense Initiative, is a challenge to the basic principles underlying the process. The second, the problem of compliance, threatens the confidence of the contracting parties in the stability of the regime and their expectations of its benefits.

Volumes have been written about the President's strategic defense initiative, which seeks to lay out the vision of an alternative future to continued mutual vulnerability. In the President's words, "it will be more humane to defend lives than to avenge them." For the purposes of this discussion, the merits of this program are not of immediate relevance. Rather, it is the impact of the search for a defense-dominated world on strategic arms control that is of interest. It will be remembered that the principles of mutual vulnerability and offense-dominance underlie SALT. The offense-defense link means that efforts by one side to increase the defensive component of its arsenal will stimulate the other side to increase its offensive capability. When regime theorists argue that security regimes are more stable in a defense-dominated world they leave out an essential fact. Even if defense dominance were possible, a highly unlikely proposition in the nuclear age, the transition period would be highly unstable. Paul Nitze, special advisor to the secretary of state, has pointed this out very effectively. He and others argue that the transition period will have to be managed carefully, and probably bilaterally. This is a tall order. The problem is that defenses are extremely threatening to the other side in the nuclear age because of the fear that they will be used to blunt a retaliatory strike. The range, speed, and distance that nuclear weapons cover practically obliterate the offense-defense distinction. Fortifying one's territory against another's attack is threatening unless one has no offensive forces.

At this point, the reality of the offense-defense link is bedeviling attempts at arms control. The United States has tried simultaneously to convince the Soviets that SDI is a research program and to make the case that defense dominance is, in any case, preferable. In the first instance, the Soviets argue that they cannot agree to constrain their own forces as long as deployment of an SDI is a high priority American goal. They point to the principles of the ABM treaty, supported by former American administrations, in support of their position. The Soviets have also sought public relations victories by demanding a ban on "space-strike weapons." In fact, the Soviets maintain a healthy research program on defensive technologies and have the world's only operational ABM system. If arms control is to move forward, both sides will have to back away from current positions and agree upon acceptable and verifiable limits on research activities. At Reykjavik, the two sides seemed to be moving toward an agreement to adhere to the terms of the ABM Treaty for some agreed period of time. But the Reagan Administration proposed a "reinterpretation" or a "broad interpretation" of the treaty to allow testing of SDI. The Soviets made it clear that they would not agree to a liberal interpretation in order to accommodate SDI.

The second set of problems, charges of noncompliance with existing treaties, is a danger to strategic arms control for other reasons. Soviet violations, especially of the provisions of the ABM Treaty through the construction of the Krasnoyarsk phased-array radar, have led to lowered expectations, in some quarters, of the value of arms control treaties. Regime theorists point to the importance of regimes for establishing the credibility of the parties. While Soviet acts of compliance far outstrip those of noncompliance, the charges, particularly in reference to the Krasnoyarsk radar (a violation of little military significance), have sullied the Soviet record. In a less politically charged environment, these charges might have been dealt with by the machinery established to do so: the Standing Consultative Commission. But the Reagan Administration has chosen to make a very public case and Krasnoyarsk has become the lead item in support of the view that the Soviets are engaged in systematic noncompliance.

The question has been what to do about the violation. The Administration clearly recognizes the difficulties of enforcement but has failed to articulate a coherent compliance strategy. Some in the Administration have argued for an explicit tit-for-tat or proportional response. In this scheme, the United States would selectively violate the treaty to demonstrate its unwillingness to tolerate Soviet noncompliance. The danger, of course, is that the Soviets would then feel compelled to respond in kind. The spiral of escalatory retaliation would then endanger what is left of an already weak set of agreements. Compliance problems do raise significant challenges for security arrangements among adversaries. It is absolutely imperative that treaties of the SALT type be self-enforcing, because there is no authority to enforce compliance when one of the partners sees it to be in its interest to violate the treaty terms. In relations between adversaries, already short on good will, there is little willingness to give the other side the benefit of the doubt.

HOW VALUABLE ARE LIMITED SECURITY REGIMES?

Even if it can be shown that SALT has had an impact on unilateral decision-making, the question "So what?" still lingers. Given the myriad military programs not limited to SALT, it is difficult to know how to judge the impact of the attempt at forming a strategic arms regime. European-based systems, both Soviet INF and U.S. forward-based systems and INF, are not currently limited by SALT (although the INF forces are currently under negotiation). Cruise missiles, except ALCM, provide another non-treaty-controlled area for breakout. The same could be said for conventional forces. So the question remains: even if SALT limits the central strategic arsenals of the two sides, does it reduce the chances of war between the two sides by significantly restraining their military capacity?

The answer in the short term, under existing treaty limits, is probably no. But it is fair to ask whether security regimes can be expected to have such an impact overnight. Consideration must be given to the need for maturation of regimes before they can be extended. This is especially true in the security area where the costs of being exploited are very high. The problem with transferring concepts from political economy to security regimes is that peculiar characteristics of security regimes may be ignored. Adversaries attempting to develop cooperative arrangements have an entire menu of conflicting interests. This is likely to mean that any effort at cooperation is going to be relatively isolated. In an economic regime like GATT, the Western capitalist countries are attempting to regulate harmful trading practices among themselves. The conflicts of interest that need to be mediated are economic and concern regime issues. Since the period immediately following World War II, there has been a community of interests among these nations on a range of issues, and a supporting network of cooperative security, political, and economic arrangements. Strongly held shared values also contribute to the spirit of shared interests.[11] It is well to remember that even economic regimes are weak in restraining the unilateral pursuit of self-interest. When one turns to security regimes, which generally exist without supporting cooperative arrangements and are attempting to moderate policies of adversaries, their weakness is predictable. The order is reversed in the security realm. The only areas of agreement are within the regime, the entire range of other issues is usually subject to strong conflicts of interest. Cooperation among adversaries is not the norm. When it occurs, it will be subject to all of the pressures that make the parties adversarial in the first place.

It has been correctly noted that there are few examples of comprehensive security regimes among adversaries. The Concert of Europe is sometimes cited as one such example.[12] It is, however, an example with limited applicability to the broader phenomenon of cooperation among adversaries. The Concert, essentially a new version of the European balance-of-power system, did manage to keep the peace among adversaries with territorial conflicts. It was a regulating mechanism based on the principles of conservation and agreement that the balance of power served all members better than territorial expansion at one another's expense. They were able to agree, however, because there was a bond between these conservative governments based on mutual fear of the revolutionary tides emanating from the French Revolution.

The important point is that the community of interest was stronger than the impulse toward war. The satisfaction with the status quo and the drive toward cooperation were based on shared interests among adversaries that are not likely to be matched again. One could argue that economic pressures in the United States and the Soviet Union leading to fears of internal stress might be the modern day version of the revolutionary tides the Concert feared. Such fears would, in turn, make the shared interests very strong, and deeper than just the desire to avoid nuclear war. But this expectation seems to be rather farfetched. The desire to save money, even in difficult times, is probably not a strong enough motive, or likely to be strong enough, to drive the United States and the Soviet Union to broad cooperation, although it might strengthen the demand for limited regimes. Moreover, the economic pressures are likely to be highly asymmetric and would not necessarily be recognized as a common bond. There is at least as great a chance that one or the other side would try to exploit the other's economic weakness.

The fear of exploitation on the part of both nations is understandably very strong and it is not surprising that SALT takes the form that it does: an explicit bargain to limit central forces undergirded by a promise by each side that it will aggressively pursue parity as may be required. The maintenance of bilateral parity as it has been defined is still a unilateral responsibility. As such, parity must be preserved via certain permissible (or not excluded) changes in overall strategic forces. It is a dynamic equilibrium over time, not a static situation. Hence, the steps that one side takes to maintain parity over time can be viewed by the other side as threatening parity at best and at worst as a bad faith search for superiority. This leads to exacerbation of the security dilemma.

What arrangements of the SALT type might do is provide a basis for the next step.

The expectation that SALT I would lead to restraint in increasing offensive forces did not materialize. Nevertheless, regimes, especially security regimes, cannot be expected to emerge full-blown. At the earliest stage, one would expect a SALT-like regime, with the balance between unilateral and bilateral security measures favoring the former heavily. At later stages, arms reductions might actually begin to take place and the balance between unilateral and bilateral measures might be roughly equal. It could be argued that the limitations imposed by SALT are the starting point for the more ambitious efforts at arms reduction that are now underway. Without those numerical limits, which gave meaning to parity, it is likely that the establishment of a ceiling would have been necessary before negotiations on reductions could have proceeded. The final stage, however, where cooperation means a substantially disarmed world, is difficult to foresee. Cooperation theorists have been known to say that adversaries prefer a disarmed world, but that fear of exploitation makes this difficult to achieve.[13] It is more likely that state actors cannot even conceive of a disarmed world. In any case, a rational great power would not necessarily prefer one. Considerable power and prestige flow from possession of overwhelming military force, even if it is not used. The avoidance of war may be a primary concern but it is not the only one. Prestige and the ability to extend one's influence and shape the outcome of the international system are often as much a part of the security equation as the avoidance of war. Given the complexities of the "security dilemma," the possibilities are slim for supplanting reliance on unilateral military preparedness with exclusively cooperative security arrangements.

This is the real dilemma facing adversaries who wish to regulate their behavior. Anything more than a very limited regime is likely to be a mixed motive game. Yet the maintenance and furthering of a limited regime is difficult in the absence of broader political cooperation. It is remarkable that SALT, including ratified and unratified agreements, has had an impact in spite of the soured political relationship and even though there has been no progress in arms control since 1979. The situation suggests the interesting possibility that although arms control progress is linked to the larger political relationship, existing agreements can continue to govern the security relationship in the absence of a larger regime. Perhaps cooperation between adversaries will always move in fits and starts. If limited instances of formal cooperation provide a brake during a period of heated rivalry, the mechanisms of regulation will grow incrementally over time. If this is the case it would be happy news because an examination of the effort to build a larger security regime (détente) based on wide acceptance of principles of cooperation is not very encouraging.

SALT AND DETENTE: AN EMBEDDED REGIME

The SALT process began at a time when expectations for broad improvement in U.S.–Soviet relations were running high. The Nixon-Kissinger notion of a security regime recognized the principle that such security regimes are very difficult to achieve unless they are supported by a network of common interests and cooperative arrangements. Even in retrospect, the principle seems sound. The United States and the Soviet Union had managed to avoid war for twenty-five years in 1969 and a kind of modus vivendi had emerged for managing the intense political rivalry without resorting to war. The tenets of the "nuclear peace," are well stated by Lewis Dunn, presently serving in the State Department.

The stakes of the Soviet-American confrontation remained limited even at the height of the Cold War. Neither country sought to challenge the territorial integrity or political independence, let alone the physical survival, of the other. Despite periodic East-West crises from the late 1940s to the early 1960s over Western Europe's political orientation, neither superpower believed that recourse to military force and the risk of escalation to a nuclear exchange were justified.[14]

One could add the Soviet dominance in Eastern Europe, though reprehensible from the American point of view, went unchallenged. The risks were just too great.

With this twenty-five year history in mind, Kissinger and others developed policies aimed at codification of the status quo and the search for explicit rules and norms of behavior to replace the tacit practice of restraint. Some theorists have argued that patterned behavior inevitably generates convergent expectations leading to conventionalized behavior. This description most certainly fits postwar Soviet and American behavior. Arguably, the next step was the one that the United States and the Soviet Union took, the development of "Basic Principles of Relations." The question is whether it was wise to replace a tacit regime with one that was explicit. In trying to define a broad security relationship, the United States and the Soviet Union probably learned that their relationship is governed simultaneously by a mutual desire to avoid war and by a drive to extend their prestige, support "friendly" governments, and, when necessary, reverse political change not to their liking. Therefore, while the preferences were pretty straightforward in SALT, they are more complex when it comes to détente. In areas of the world where interest asymmetries do not favor one side, so called grey areas like the Third World, competition is bound to continue. The avoidance of war is only one of several agenda items. This makes the search for a broader security regime difficult.

More important for our consideration of SALT, the impact of these different interest calculations is immense. It has been said that the broad political atmosphere matters for the successful conclusion of arms control. But why should this be the case? Why can't the United States and the Soviet Union de-link the broader regime from the limited areas where their impulses toward cooperation are very strong? Certainly there is a strong tendency to link issue areas implicitly even if not explicitly. President Reagan is said to have decided to abide by SALT in 1985 to avoid endangering the summit. He is also said to have almost changed his mind when the Soviets, linking the Libyan crisis to U.S.–Soviet relations, cancelled the Shultz-Shevardnadze planning session. Policy makers do not deal in discrete policy packages. It is perhaps only natural to expect that the adversary, seeing the benefits of, say, arms control, will show more restraint in other areas in order to achieve it. Interestingly, policy makers do not seem to see their own behavior in the same fashion. They expect that the adversary should be able to see that a given action had nothing to do with the desire for better relations or for an arms control agreement.

There is another reason that de-linkage is difficult. The real link between an embedded regime like strategic arms control, and the broader security relationship, is that in the pursuit of interests that conflict, the perception that the adversary is engaging in exploitation in the broader political relationship links automatically to perception of one's own military inferiority as a result of the limitations imposed by cooperation. Put simply, the regulation of Soviet military power through SALT did not lead the Soviets to abandon their attempts to extend their influence throughout the world. The United States, in turn, linked this perceived exploitation directly to the limits placed upon American power by détente and SALT. It is illogical to believe that different launcher limits under SALT would have prevented the Soviets from actively supporting rebels in Angola and Ethiopia. But the arms race itself, in the absence of the resort to war, has become a kind of measure for the relative strength of the two sides. American power, prestige, and the ability to defend the allies were all called into question precisely because of the codification of parity. The most telling example of this linkage was the questioning of American credibility as a member of NATO. West European leaders explicitly questioned the willingness of the United States to defend Europe under conditions of parity. The Gaullist formula ''Would the United States risk New York for Paris?'' took on new meaning with the American admission of vulnerability to Soviet strategic nuclear forces. The entire INF episode, with the American deployment of Pershing II and ground-launched cruise missiles to counter the Soviet SS-20s and show resolve toward the alliance, was one of the legacies of SALT. The Soviets, of course, bombastically proclaimed that their more active role in the world was linked to parity, thus contributing to the perception that SALT was actually an American admission of weakness.

THE PROSPECTS FOR COOPERATION UNDER THE "COMPLEX SECURITY DILEMMA"

Clearly, the decision to cooperate in a SALT-like regime is not simply the result of a calculation of how to avoid war or an arms race. It is deeply embedded in great power rivalry and the desire to extend influence. Given the probable continuation of U.S.–Soviet rivalry, attempts to form limited regimes no matter how difficult and fragile, may be the best that one can expect. One could posit that better relations are necessary for the conclusion of new strategic arms agreements and the extension of existing ones. But during periods of relatively unconstrained rivalry, existing agreements might provide regulation and play a moderating role until the larger political environment improves.

It may be characteristic of security regimes that they are made up of a series of limited, fragile, but useful sets of rules and principles that guide and govern superpower behavior. Whether these rules and principles can engender mutually accepted norms of behavior around which actors' expectations can converge is difficult to say. The history of the effort to build a strategic arms control regime is not encouraging in this respect. But the SALT treaties, which at least attempted to codify mutual vulnerability, the link between offense and defense, and parity rather than military superiority as the pillars on which strategic arms cooperation would rest were probably on the right track. The SALT process was arguably quite mature in this regard and only a few steps short of becoming a limited regime in and of itself.

Its successor START, as it is currently conceived, is far less mature in that it lacks a framework of principles on which to base agreements. The point can be most clearly seen in the disagreement over the role of defensive systems in the arsenals of the two powers. Until the two sides agree on the relationship of offense to defense, a principle that is not self-evident, it will be difficult to agree on reductions in the arsenals. Those who argue both within the Administration and outside of it, that some semblance of the ABM Treaty must survive for START to have a chance, understand the significance of underlying principles on which to build.

Because of the complexity of the security dilemma, the step-by-step approach characteristic of SALT, though delicate and difficult to manage, is probably ultimately more promising than efforts to achieve a comprehensive security regime. Were the avoidance of war the only concern, broad arms agreements, even disarmament, might be feasible.

But between two great powers there is considerably more at stake. A comprehensive security regime will probably be a very long time in coming. It is possible to imagine a series of limited regimes, however, which taken together could form a basis for a stable and less dangerous relationship between the superpowers. In light of the complexity of their relationship, lower expectations of what security cooperation can do will probably contribute more to U.S.–Soviet efforts to manage their rivalry than any other single political factor.

Notes

1. Stephen D. Krasner, "Structural Causes and Regime Consequences: Regimes as Intervening Variables," in Stephen D. Krasner, ed., *International Regimes* (Ithaca, N.Y.: Cornell University Press, 1982).

2. The Soviets in fact went through quite a protracted debate before the military finally dropped the notion of "superiority." Political intervention may have been the reason for the conversion. In 1977 at Tula, Leonid Brezhnev finally stated forthrightly that the Soviet Union did not seek military "superiority."

3. Leonid Brezhnev, *Pravda,* October 21, 1981.

4. M. A. Gareyev, *M. V. Frunze: Voennyi teoretik* (Moscow: Voenizdat, 1985).

5. Robert Jervis, "Cooperation Under the Security Dilemma," *World Politics* (Winter 1978).

6. Many of these ideas are incorporated in the 1971 agreement on measures to reduce the risk of nuclear war and the 1973 agreement on the prevention of nuclear war.

7. "Soviet Compliance with the SALT I and II Agreements on Offensive Arms," *Congressional Research Service Report* 85–768.

8. Stephen Meyer and Peter Almquist, *Insights from Mathematical Modelling in Soviet Mission Analysis:* Part II. DARPA Study (April 1985). Anureyev is the most influential operations research specialist in the Soviet military. He has worked for the General Staff, is a member of the Council (ruling body) of the Academy of the General Staff, and has had the distinction of writing the entries in the Soviet Military Encyclopedia on operations research and mathematical modelling in military planning. This particular force model has also gained wide attention and use throughout the Soviet military-technical literature.

9. The Joint Chiefs of Staff have traditionally supported SALT as "useful." Recently, Admiral William Crowe, chairman of the Joint Chiefs, was more equivocal, saying that the decision about the "no undercut" provision was a "political" not a military issue.

10. On the problem of civilian expertise at the staff level in Soviet military planning see Stephen Meyer, "Civilian and Military Influence in Managing the Arms Race in the USSR," in Robert J. Art, et al., *Reorganizing America's Defense: Leadership in War and Peace* (Washington, D.C.: Pergamon-Brassey, 1985).

11. For a clear picture of the importance of shared values, read the preamble to the NATO treaty, which talks about a community of interests and shared beliefs about political life and political institutions. *NATO: Facts About the North Atlantic Treaty Organization* (Paris: NATO Information Service, 1962).

12. On one occasion Robert Jervis suggested that the Concert was the primary example of a security regime. See his "Security Regimes," in Stephen Krasner, *International Regimes.*

13. Arthur Stein, "Coordination and Collaboration: Regimes in an Anarchic World," in Krasner, *International Regimes.*

14. Lewis A. Dunn, *Controlling the Bomb* (New York: Twentieth Century fund, 1982). See also the more detailed explanation of John Lewis Gaddis in "The Long Peace," *International Security* 10, 4 (Spring 1986).

13

Antarctica: Why Success?

DEBORAH SHAPLEY

The tangled history of East-West relations since the Second World War includes few chapters in which the United States and the Soviet Union have had stable, mutually reinforcing relations. Still fewer chapters describe successful multilateral arrangements that have helped third parties as well. If the purpose of this study is to identify when and why such stability has occurred, the Antarctica case is strikingly relevant.

Four features of this case give it special interest:

1. For twenty-six years, the only obvious code for the Antarctic—a term which refers to the ocean and land areas south of 60 degrees south latitude, or one-fifteenth of the earth's surface—has been a brief 2,300-word document, the 1961 Antarctic Treaty. The treaty dedicates the region to peaceful uses and international scientific research. It bans military activities or maneuvers and nuclear storage and testing. It permits unilateral inspection of all ships, stations, and cargoes. The United States and the Soviet Union are among the original twelve voting parties to the treaty, which now number eighteen. The treaty, besides working as intended to govern scientific work in the region, also has dampened U.S.–Soviet rivalries and brought about cooperation between the two. The arms control provision of the document are more valuable today than when they entered into force. These are rare achievements in international relations and so deserve examination.

2. Supplementary rules for national conduct in Antarctica consist of agreed measures adopted jointly by the treaty parties and regulations adopted by the separate governments to implement them. The means of administration entail no secretariat and no permanent employees. Administration is aided by a private committee of scientists, the Scientific Committee on Antarctic Research (SCAR), whose subcommittees coordinate national research agendas and tackle special problems such as resource development and environmental protection. Finally, there are unwritten customs for national behavior in Antartica derived from the experience of the explorers, the demands of large-scale scientific research, and the exigencies of Antarctica's frontier character. So the Antarctic is governed by a regime of which the treaty is a critical part.

3. Although inspired in part by Western fears of Soviet military expansion in the region, the Antarctic Treaty and regime are strongly multilateral. The original group consisted of the twelve historically interested nations, including the United States and the Soviet Union.* Today there are eighteen voting parties and seventeen

*The original twelve "consultative," or voting, parties were: Argentina, Australia, Belgium, Chile, France,

307

"acceding" parties. The latter are nations which have agreed to the treaty's terms but do not have a national scientific program in Antarctica and so are not qualified to vote. The United States and the Soviet Union, potential rivals in the region, have used this multilateral forum to accomodate each other's needs and evolve now-entrenched patterns of cooperation.

The Antarctic regime is also multipurpose. In twenty-six years, it has expanded its reach into preservation of historic sites, tourism, sealing, the environment, and marine living resource conservation. The group is now trying to finalize rules for oil and mineral development in the region. There has also been an evolution in the membership: the original members were the superpowers and major European countries and Japan, as well as southern hemisphere nations with an interest because they faced Antarctica across the southern oceans. Recently, major developing nations with no polar tradition—India, Brazil and China—have achieved voting status.

4. The political future of Antarctica is not solely led by this "club" of treaty parties. Nonparties to the treaty have challenged its exclusivity and legitimacy at the United Nations. So Antarctic diplomacy has changed in recent years as these challenges spur adaptation and change. One result is that the mutual interest of the United States and Soviet Union in the present system has come fully to light. Even when over-all U.S.-Soviet relations were strained during the first Reagan term, the U.S. and Soviet representatives ardently defended the treaty at the United Nations. What this regime is, and whether it can adapt to these latest concerns, are relevant questions for this study and for Antarctica's future.

Antarctica is the fifth largest continent on the planet, the only one with no native human inhabitants, and the last which man discovered and tried to colonize. Its land area is approximately the size of the United States and Mexico combined, and almost completely covered with ice. The giant, domed icecap has formed over thousands of years from snow falling through the dry cold air of the interior. At its thickest, the Antarctic ice sheet is 4,770-meters thick—cores of this ice reveal samples of air and volcanic ash dating back thousands of years. The ice inches outward over the landmass towards the coasts, where the water warms it from below and it calves off into great icebergs. There are few exposed beaches and fewer natural harbors. The only temperate region is the Antarctic Peninsula, which extends up towards the southern tip of South America. Its Andean-type mountains and steep coasts create few suitable landing strips or good harbors. Antarctica's climate is mainly the result of its isolation from other continents; the Southern Ocean, which encircles it, comprises one-fifth of the world's ocean water by volume. It beats around the continent, carrying wind and weather, and enclosing it, in effect, behind a wall of cold.[1]

This chapter has three parts. Part I briefly describes the political development of the region from earliest times to 1961 when the Antarctic Treaty capped the larger,

Great Britain, Japan, New Zealand, Norway, Republic of South Africa, the Soviet Union, and the United States. Those achieving voting status after 1961, and the year they did so, are: Brazil (1983), Federal Republic of Germany (1981), India (1983), People's Republic of China (1985), Poland (1977), Uruguay (1985).

Acceding parties as of early 1987 and year of accession are: Bulgaria (1978), Cuba (1984), Czechoslovakia (1962), Democratic Republic of Korea (1987), Denmark (1965), Finland (1984), German Democratic Republic (1974), Greece (1987), Hungary (1984), Italy (1981), Netherlands (1967), Papua New Guinea (1981) (succession), Peru (1981), Republic of Korea (1986), Romania (1971), Spain (1982), Sweden (1984).

unwritten regime with which national governments experimented during the 1957–58 International Geophysical Year.

Part II discusses how the treaty and regime have maintained themselves in the years since 1961. It shows they have succeeded not because of the treaty's idealistic phrases but because they balance underlying political conflicts—including U.S.–Soviet rivalry—and hold them in check. The regime has been strained three times: (1) by the advent of krill fishing, an extensive new economic activity; (2) by the need to settle the issue of mineral exploration and development; and (3) by the challenge of nonparties to the treaty at the United Nations.

Part III discusses why the treaty and regime have succeeded thus far, what factors caused an innovative regime to emerge in the first place by 1961, what factors have enabled it to adapt and maintain itself, and how the Antarctic regime compares to some others discussed in this volume. A key theme is the evolution of U.S.–Soviet cooperation over Antarctica, and the buttressing of these mutual interests by the larger regime. U.S.–Soviet cooperation in turn, helps the larger multilateral system adapt to challenges. In closing, the paper notes what the now-emerging Antarctic regime bodes for international relations generally.

FROM TRADITIONAL SECURITY TO INNOVATIVE REGIME

Early Conceptions of Antarctica

The ancient Greeks, who knew only the geography of the northern part of the world, postulated the existence of a large landmass that balanced it in the south. This became known as Terra Australis Incognita, and on early maps was often given fabulous characteristics. On the other side of the world, the ancient Polynesians, venturing south in their canoes, saw icebergs and believed them to be the souls of the dead.

On his voyage of Pacific exploration of 1772–1775, Captain James Cook repeatedly turned his ships southward. He thus circumnavigated the far southern region and determined that Terra Australis Incognita was not as large as rumored. He concluded there was land over the South Pole, but so locked behind stormy seas, threatening ice, and "the inexpressibly horrid aspect of the country" that "the world will derive no benefit from it."[2]

Cook's dour conclusion discouraged far southern exploration for another generation, but his report of bountiful seals on the coasts of southern South America spurred a sealing boom, which brought British and American sealers to that region in the 1820s to engage in lucrative trade. In November 1820, Nathaniel Brown Palmer, the twenty-one year old captain of a fourteen-meter sloop from Stonington, Connecticut, apparently sighted the mainland of the Antarctic peninsula, while looking for untapped sealing beaches.[3]

National rivalry followed. A British captain, Edward Bransfield, probably saw the mainland before Palmer, in January of 1820, but his log was lost, so the British claim to prior discovery was weak. In addition, the tsar of Russia had sent Admiral Thaddeus von Bellingshausen to explore the Pacific. Von Bellingshausen's two men-of-war circumnavigated the region in 1819–21, and even met up with Palmer in his little boat in the fog off Antarctica. But von Bellingshausen never claimed to have seen the unknown southern land and the next published Russian map labeled it "Palmer Land."

After the sealing era—which rendered the fur seal almost extinct—ships mapped southern oceans mainly to determine their magnetic characteristics, for compasses became unsteady in far southern latitudes. The busy maritime traffic of the age required precise navigation. The Briton James Weddell penetrated a great bay south of the Atlantic in 1823, and in 1840 James Clark Ross found another huge indentation on the opposite side of Antarctica, south of New Zealand. Dumont D'Urville, a Frenchman hunting for the south magnetic pole, touched the coast south of Australia in 1840. And an American expedition under Charles Wilkes followed a long stretch of the east Antarctic coast south of Australia and New Zealand in the same period.[4]

The growth of international science in the late nineteenth century sparked a coordinated "polar year" in 1882–83 that studied the Arctic, using strings of observing stations across Russia and northern Europe. This led geographers and scientists to turn to the Antarctic. Around the turn of the century several expeditions went: the British *Discovery* expeditions, and later those of Robert Falcon Scott and Roald Amundsen, who raced to the South Pole in the austral summer of 1911–12. Scott undertook this heroic journey, on which he died, for politically insignificant reasons: though British explorers were still trekking to remote regions and planting the flag, the Golden Age was ending and the British Empire fading.[5]

Traditional Security Concepts Make Conflicts

Seven nations made formal claims to Antarctic territory between 1908 and 1947. Great Britain in 1908 extended by Letters Patent the area included in the Falkland Islands Dependencies south to the South Pole. Britain was concerned with its naval power and sought better control of the Drake Passage around the tip of South America. It was also concerned with commerce: British station-masters in the region were assigned to collect fees from whaling captains who had to port locally to process their catch. In 1923 London claimed a wedge of Antarctica south of New Zealand and assigned it to that country. The New Zealanders were to collect taxes from the whalers, most of them Norwegian, who operated in those waters. In 1924 France, without revisiting Antarctica, announced ownership of the area D'Urville visited, which was next to the New Zealand claim. Paris moved to preempt another British claim and London announced one in 1933, when it asserted claim to two huge wedges of Antarctica on either side of the French claim and extending inland to the pole, and assigned them to Australia.

In 1938, the Third Reich dispatched an expedition to Antarctica. Ship-based planes overflew a part of the coast, dropping swastikas. The Norwegian government learned of the impending expedition, and declared ownership to the area for which the Germans were headed, for it had been mainly seen by Norwegian whalers. The third Reich's priorities were patently not in Antarctica, however, and nothing further was done about a German claim.[6]

In 1940 Chile announced ownership of a slab of the continent south of its landmass and including part of the peninsula claimed by Britain. In 1947 Argentina claimed a seventh wedge. This overlapped the conflicting Chilean-British claims. The Argentinians were militant in asserting sovereign rights: tearing down unoccupied British bases, and on one occasion, in 1952, firing on a British landing party and driving them back to their ship. In the late 1940s and early 1950s, a local shooting war over Antarctic territory seemed possible—a war that might have resembled the Falkland Islands war of 1982.

American supporters of the Antarctic Treaty later maintained that the U.S. role in

Antarctica was always scientific and international. In fact, in the 1930s and 1940s, the U.S. government supported extensive efforts by private expeditions to map and claim Antarctica for the United States. Since Alaska had been a valuable acquisition for the United States, Antarctica should be too, they reasoned. The American claim effort was not publicized at the time for fear of offending European allies; the records of the claims efforts were classified. But this use of America's raw power and technology, which dwarfed anything the Europeans could mount at the time, made the United States the main determiner of Antarctica's future.

The American position was ambivalent. As I have written elsewhere:

> The ambivalence that runs through US Antarctic history about whether Antarctica is ours or not or whether it is domestic or foreign territory stems from the obvious opportunities for expansion afforded by US power and its image of itself as an antidote to imperialism.[7]

These contradictory impulses were one reason that an innovative regime, which dodged the question of colonization, took root so quickly in the period of innovation in 1957–1961.

With Richard E. Byrd's first flight over the South Pole in 1929, aircraft revolutionized Antarctic exploration by enlarging the scale on which Antarctica could be discovered, mapped, and claimed. Moreover, the families of Byrd and of Lincoln Ellsworth, another prominent Antarctic explorer of the period, were influential in Washington. They got the small world of American politics in the interwar period interested in an Antarctic claim. As the expeditions became too expensive for Tidewater Oil and John D. Rockefeller to sponsor, the government took over. In 1939, Franklin Roosevelt authorized establishment of a U.S. Antarctic Service in the Department of the Interior. A U.S.A.S. expedition went to Antarctica in 1939 under Byrd with the goal of colonizing the region by continuous occupation and discovery. The expedition was cut short almost at the outset by World War II.[8]

After the war, the government sponsored two postwar expeditions. First Operation Highjump of 1946–47 in which 4,700 servicemen aboard thirteen ships assaulted most of the periphery of Antarctica, extended the area previously claimed by the United States. Highjump was followed by a similar but smaller expedition, Operation Windmill, in 1947–48. By this time, U.S. explorers had seen some 80 percent of the continental area, whereas foreign expeditions—Scott, Amundsen, and the others—had seen only approximately 5 per cent.

By the early 1950s the dispute over Antarctica had become a minor international crisis. France, Great Britain, Norway, Australia, and New Zealand recognized one another's claims. Chile and Argentina disputed the British claim and refused to recognize the other European claims. Great Britain tried unsuccessfully to take Chile and Argentina to the World Court. Meanwhile, the significance of the big American expeditions and their extensive aerial exploration was not lost on the seven announced claimants: the United States was laying the basis for a huge claim that would contradict all of theirs.

With the U.S. government, the issue of formalizing its claim raised all the ambiguities clouding U.S. Antarctic policy. An Antarctic claim would put the United States at odds with its allies, particularly Great Britain. A U.S. claim would contest those of Chile and Argentina and make U.S. leaders look like the Yankee imperialists they were forever telling Latin leaders they were not. All the claimants assumed Antarctica would be valuable for its minerals one day; also, the development of long-range aircraft for civilian and military uses made Antarctica seem to be important real estate.

But who owned it? The international legal literature of the period is rife with theories; it was assumed that if the rivals were not to fight over Antarctica, they would have to take their problems to the World Court or to the conference table.[9]

In the late 1940s the State Department applied traditional concepts to try to settle the issue. It considered tabling the U.S. claim and then calling for an international conference. It queried the British as to whether to propose making Antarctica an international trust territory. The British objected, reflecting traditional maritime power concerns: the Soviet Union would have to be included and this could jeopardize control of the strategic Drake Passage. At that point, the U.S. government assured the British that it would not allow the Soviets to be part of any settlement. The British suggested an eight-way condominium but when the United States made this proposal to the others, they all objected. They were not about to relinquish the power they presumed would accompany territorial sovereignty. Traditional concepts held fast.[10]

The dispute might have rattled on for years, except that word of an impending settlement reached Moscow. In 1949, a Soviet geographical congress resurrected von Bellingshausen's voyage and proclaimed him the discoverer of Antarctica. Since discovery of new lands has been the legal basis for title to them, the import of the Soviet message was clear. Still clearer was a diplomatic note circulated in 1950 to the United States and the seven governments with announced claims. "The government of the USSR cannot agree that such a question as that of the regime of the Antarctic be decided without its participation . . . [It] cannot recognize as legal any decision regarding the regime of the Antarctic taken without its participation."[11]

The Soviet note dashed hopes for an all-Western settlement and gave the Antarctic dispute new gravity. In the United States, the private explorers and military officers stepped up their plans. Another expedition was planned but canceled at the last minute. In 1956 the group presented President Eisenhower with a ten-year "National Program" for mapping Antarctica at a cost of $56 million.

Political Innovations Lead to a Regime

Meanwhile, a new constituency was emerging which needed Antarctica for different purposes. This was a group of scientists in the United States, Great Britain, Belgium, and France who planned a third polar "year," named the International Geophysical Year (IGY), to run for eighteen months from July 1, 1957, through December 31, 1958. The dates would coincide with a solar maximum when the sun's effect on the earth's magnetosphere and ionosphere could be observed best. Plans were laid for coordinated observations from many points on the earth and from balloons and rockets. Because the lines of the earth's magnetic field bend inwards at the north and south magnetic poles, Antarctica offered an ideal laboratory for observing these effects. While making coordinated observations up into the sky, scientists would have an unprecedented chance to examine Antarctica itself in a coordinated fashion. The explorers' small-scale investigations of the vast continent would give way, then, to the methods of modern big science.[12]

The scientists were strong-willed, organized, and had strong institutional bases in each of their respective national academies of science. In the United States, they managed to edge out the explorers and military group, whose influence was waning. Meanwhile, the framers of the IGY Antarctic program painted themselves as the voice of science, the future, and a better way. There was much conflict between the two factions. One of the explorers, Paul Siple, complained that though he had been to Antarctica four times, he was regarded by the scientists as a know-nothing and was brushed aside.[13]

In order to carry out a program in Antarctica the scientists needed to seek innovative departures from the rules that had governed past national activities in Antarctica.[14] In the United States, such suggestions were eased by the long-standing discomfort with asserting U.S. ownership and exclusivity.

The scientists lobbied with their respective governments for new Antarctic policies for the duration of the IGY. They secured a gentleman's agreement on free access by scientific stations and trail parties, and aircraft; anyone could go anywhere without affecting a sovereignty claim. Since the first principle of sovereignty is the sovereign's right to prohibit outsiders from entering his turf, for claimant states this was quite a concession, especially when the result was that the Australian Antarctic territory would be the site of Soviet stations. To promote this "sterilization" of expeditions and stations, the IGY group changed the lingo: instead of "base" the term "station" was adopted because the former implied military and political intent. So the claims dispute, the source of long-standing unresolved tensions, was temporarily put on ice.

Nonetheless, claimant states did not ignore their long-standing stakes in certain regions of Antarctica. The seven claimants put stations in "their" respective sectors, and only reluctantly acceded to have "foreign" stations in them. The United States planned several stations around the coast and two inland. At a 1955 planning meeting in Paris the Russian delegation suddenly announced plans to put a station at the geographic South Pole. The French chairman of the meeting replied that the Americans already planned a station there (they had not, until that moment). The Soviets could have a station at the "other" pole, called the "pole of inaccessibility," where man had never been and where there was a gap in the planned coverage.

The Soviets agreed. They trekked to the deep interior to "their" pole, in the Australian sector. The Americans airdropped Navy Seabees and equipment, and built a station at the South Pole, the symbolic heart of the continent, where the sector claims met. The pole station was useful for science—though any deep hinterland spot would have done as well—and it also symbolized the continent-wide reach of the unspoken U.S. claim.

Another innovation was the demilitarization of Antarctica for the IGY. Past expeditions had involved military activity of some sort. But military activities or maneuvers were banned for the IGY. For many nations, however, the military was the only institution with the ships, personnel, and equipment capable of operating in the hostile Antarctic, so military logistics were allowed in support of a nation's scientific program. (Inside the United States, when the military wanted to use the IGY to begin its National Program of Mapping and Claims, the scientists objected that it was contrary to the spirit of the IGY, and Eisenhower dropped the program. Nonetheless, some mapping was done during the IGY and one of the private explorers, Finn Ronne, went on making claims.)[15]

Another innovation was the pooling of weather and rescue services, formerly provided on a national basis. Even weather was politically sensitive, however, for weather data can make the difference to survival in the Antarctic. Larger weather-gathering stations were called "mothers"; each "mother" gave data to smaller stations and trail parties, nicknamed "daughters." The network was devised so that no "daughter" would be dependent on a politically rivalrous "mother."

Through personnel exchange, potentially rival national efforts were made interdependent. Visits to others' stations and camps is an important feature of Antarctic life; these create comradery and mutual understanding. Further, it was decided that an American would winter over at a Soviet station while a Soviet scientist wintered over at an American station. Walter Sullivan wrote: "Nothing could have done more to allay fears and suspicions than the series of personnel exchanges." Since then, this exchange has continued during every austral winter, apparently without incident. While there have been benefits, there are risks: the meetings of the U.S. Antarctic Policy Group regularly discussed the question of "asylum" in the 1970s. The State Department will not comment on whether a Soviet guest has ever sought asylum, but clearly, such a request could precipitate a serious incident, given the unresolved legal status of Antarctica.[16]

One further innovation was the creation of the Special Committee on Antarctic Research, or SCAR (later the Scientific Committee on Antarctic Research). Based in Cambridge, England, it provided a forum in which the senior scientists exchanged research plans and results. SCAR evolved an important role in coordinating national research programs in the 1960s. When the regime was challenged in the 1970s and 1980s, SCAR served as an informal sounding board for representatives of the treaty parties. Thus, although nowhere mentioned in the treaty text, SCAR is a crucial piece of the over-all Antarctic regime.

Despite mishaps and tensions, the IGY was a political as well as a scientific success. As the year got under way, and the politically complex Antarctic program proceeded smoothly, the governments considered making their temporary gentleman's agreement a permanent one. The Antarctic Treaty is the result of that wish.

The immediate spark was a request by Australian Minister R. G. Casey to U.S. Secretary of State John Foster Dulles in 1957: What if the Soviets stayed on in Australia's Antarctic territory after the IGY? Could Dulles look into the matter? Dulles assigned the Antarctic question to Paul C. Daniels, a career diplomat. Daniels' background in Latin America showed that Dulles thought the Latin claimants could be the most reluctant to acquiesce in an agreement. Daniels persuaded the twelve governments with IGY Antarctic programs to meet in Washington in 1958 to draw up a treaty. President Eisenhower had sent a letter to each government outlining some proposed terms, including a moratorium on claims. The goal was to reach agreement before the IGY ended on December 31. The launch of Sputnik in October of 1957 created an air of urgency. Eisenhower backed Daniels' effort completely. The negotiation created little backlash within the United States. The content of the twelve-nation talks remained secret but for one minor news leak.

Some minutes of the meetings have been released.[17] The Soviets agreed quickly to the ban on military activities and maneuvers in the region. Since neutralization of the Soviet presence had been a main objective, the West thereby quickly got what it sought. The speed of the Soviet acceptance suggests that the West misgauged Soviet motives: these may have been to seek not military advantage but prestige. From the Soviet viewpoint, a treaty offered a chance to stay on in the region and appear equal to the West.

Demilitarization was to be verified by a right of unilateral inspection by any party of all ships, stations, and cargoes in Antarctica. Soviet agreement to this proposal is striking, in view of their later resistance to subsequent proposals for on-site inspection of their own territory. In all likelihood, the Soviet Union did not think of Antarctica as its home territory and this eased acceptance of the inspection provision.

The crux of the proposed treaty, Article IV which froze the dispute over claims, was likewise quite quickly agreed. It was proposed by Daniels in virtually its final form, which stated that nothing in the treaty should be construed as a renunciation or diminution of a claim or basis of claim while the treaty was in force. Also, no new claim could be asserted.

Article IV satisfied crucial national interests and balanced historic national competition in the region. In it, the European and Latin claimant states gave up nothing; they could go on asserting their national positions. They also obtained the guarantee that no new power, or the United States or the Soviet Union, would trump their claims while the treaty remained in force. The treaty thus correctly anticipated the difficulty the European nations in particular would have in enforcing their claims militarily, a sign of their diminished power in this period.

Finally, such nations as Belgium, Japan, and South Africa were helped by not being shut out of Antarctica by virtue of their nonclaimant status, and indeed by winning equal voting power in Antarctic decision making with the claimants and the superpowers.

The freezing of the claims dispute served the United States by not forcing the resolution of its own sovereignty position. Was Antarctica ours or not? Domestic or foreign territory? Article IV permitted the parties to preserve any "basis of claim to territorial sovereignty in Antarctica . . . as a result of its activities or those of its nationals in Antarctica, or otherwise." Thus, the United States could maintain its ambivalent position at little cost while other U.S. priorities in Antarctica—namely scientific research—went forward.

Argentina suggested the ban on nuclear weapons tests in the Antarctic area south of 60 degrees south latitude. It did not want fallout from Antarctic blasts drifting over its country. Since Argentina would have difficulty getting the treaty accepted at home— for Article IV would appear to dilute Argentina's claim, no matter what it said—the others quickly agreed to the proposal. At the time, the United States, the Soviet Union, and Great Britain tested their nuclear bombs in the atmosphere. (Indeed, some nuclear explosions were set off to help scientists study the ionosphere during the IGY!) Nuclear-free zones were a popular idea in the growing arms control movement, and this feature particularly pleased President Eisenhower. He was also pleased with the right of overflight in the verification provision in Article VII, which echoed his "Open Skies" proposal.

The treaty negotiators sidestepped the question of the rights of nonparties and the corresponding rights of the twelve to negotiate a permanent agreement for Antarctica. They also sidestepped resource issues on the grounds that they were too sensitive, and long term in any event. The brevity of the document suggests their eagerness to get an agreement fast. They covered for their omissions by providing in Article IX for regular meetings of the voting members to "consult together on matters of common interest pertaining to Antarctica." This arrangement seemed to permit room for it to evolve.

On the other hand, the apparatus was made quite rigid; it can be modified only by unanimous consent of all voting parties. Moreover, at their first such consultative meeting, the parties decided to vote by consensus. This made agreement appear particularly difficult and gave them an incentive to sidestep difficult issues that might produce a veto. Consensus voting was adopted at the insistence of the claimants who then—and today—wanted to be able to veto measures which threaten their sovereignty positions.

Another weakness was the treaty's silence about the rest of the world's relationship to it, and to Antarctica. The treaty's preamble asserted that the parties were acting in the interest of "all mankind," but if other representatives of mankind wished a voting role, they first had to establish a scientific presence, and so on. The legal basis on which the twelve were acting in the first place remained unclear.

In any event, the document was finalized at a conference in Washington in October 1959 and signed by the twelve governments. Ratification came quickly and it entered into force June 23, 1961. When the U.S. Senate considered ratification, some witnesses objected that the treaty foreclosed the chance for Antarctica to become a U.S. possession and permitted the "reds" to encroach there. Government spokesmen countered that the United States would retain the "basis" of its sovereignty claim and was not giving anything away. The Senate ratified by a vote of 66 to 21 on August 18, 1960.

REGIME MAINTENANCE, ADAPTATION, AND CHALLENGES

The treaty legitimized and perpetuated the de facto regime that had evolved rapidly in 1957–61, making rules hand-tailored to immediate, practical needs, and sidestepping awkward problems like sovereignty and U.S.–Soviet rivalry in the interest of getting on with immediate work.

Circumstances helped the new arrangement take root in the 1960s. No new uses of Antarctica arose in the 1960s and no rival constituencies appeared on the scene. Indeed, after a brief flurry of publicity in 1957–1961, Antarctica dropped from prominence on the public and diplomatic scene. Being offstage from the main events and conflicts of the period obviously helped the new Antarctic regime develop in its own way and gain authority in its own right.

After the Berlin crisis of 1961 and the Cuban missile crisis of 1962, there was halting progress towards arms control, which created a hospitable international environment for the treaty. The creation of the U.S. Arms Control and Disarmament Agency also helped: one of ACDA's first projects was to make the United States a model adherent to the treaty's arms control provisions, and to get other governments to follow suit. So the first on-site inspections were carried out by a new, young agency eager to be, and be seen as, successful.[18]

During this period, more or less the same people went back to Antarctica each season and turned the experimental arrangements of the IGY into traditions. The same diplomats returned to the biennial consultative meetings. They got to know one another and the different national interests, and the unique problems of human activity in hostile Antarctica. SCAR became permanent; it proliferated committees. These in turn developed a large international network of experts on the region who communicated with one another frequently. A pragmatic tradition of Antarctic administration was established: rules were adopted only for immediate problems; sweeping principles were eschewed in favor of limited measures. With time, the scope of the rule making broadened: at first the group regulated how to treat historic sites like Scott's hut and whether dogs should be leashed. Then it moved on to protect sensitive sites and to rules on tourism. A sealing scare caused the negotiation of a convention to regulate Antarctic sealing, though the commercial effort never materialized. There was much other yearly business relating to activities "down on the ice."[19] Thus developed a low-key, but extensive informal structure—in short, a regime—which would be challenged in the 1970s and 1980s.

Strains Over Fishing

Compared with the other six continents, Antarctica is more uniform in its climate and ecology. The continental landmass and icecap are surrounded by the powerful ocean current that beats around the periphery of the continent, aided by the spin of the earth. The ocean current distributes weather, water temperature, nutrients, and species more or less evenly throughout the region. The biological result is that while there are relatively few individual species in the Antarctic, their members tend to exist in huge numbers, all around the coastal area. For example, the crabeater seals that live in the pack ice have a collective biomass of 2,868,000 tons—possibly the largest biomass of any single species on earth.

This ecology has economic implications. Whales visit the region in great numbers. Since the turn of the century whalers have hunted them in the austral summer. Once man finds an efficient technique for catching a species in this Antarctic environment, he can apply it with devastating effect. By the 1960s, the blue, humpback, and sei whales were nearly extinct, and there were fewer than 100,000 fin whales left, compared to 400,000 at the turn of the century.[20]

In the late 1960s, Soviet whaling vessels could find few whales left so instead began hauling in krill, another Antarctic organism which exists in great abundance. Krill are tiny crustaceans which swarm near the sea surface. Swarming makes them easy to catch with ordinary trawling gear. Since they can be 16 percent protein, they can be a useful human or animal food. In 1968 P. A. Moiseev, a Soviet scientist, told a SCAR working group that Antarctic krill stocks could support harvests of 150 million metric tons (MMT) a year—more than twice the entire world fish catch, which was then 60 MMT![21]

The Soviets and Japanese distant water fleets began to fish there, followed by vessels from Poland, Taiwan, East and West Germany, and Spain. The extension of 200-mile exclusive fishing zones in northern waters was driving the fleets southward and large-scale fishing seemed a real possibility. Catch rose from 22,000 MMT in the 1973–74 austral season to 334,000 MMT in the 1978–79 austral season.[22]

Krill happen to be central in the simple Antarctic marine food chain: many higher species, including many whales, depend on them. Overfishing of krill could take away food from the the whales and possibly hurt the stocks' recovery.[23] The United States and Great Britain, as well as other governments alerted by the concerns of scientists and environmental groups, wanted to set up a mechanism for limiting krill fishing. But this was not easy, as both the Soviet Union and Japan had for years resisted efforts by the International Whaling Commission to limit their activities. In dealing with Antarctic krill, the United States and the Soviet Union were again on opposite sides of the issue.

The Antarctic Treaty seemed the appropriate forum to address the problem, yet the treaty group had never regulated an ongoing economic activity. Moreover, Soviet and Japanese fishing captains operating on the high seas and only sporadically reporting to their governments, were not obviously within the treaty group's jurisdiction.

The treaty itself had to be stretched to have jurisdiction over the issue. Resources were sidestepped in the original negotiation as too controversial, and the treaty's text mentions them only once, in a list of topics the parties might discuss at their biennial meetings ("preservation and conservation of living resources in Antarctica"). On the other hand, this language and many of the administrative measures the group had agreed earlier suggested the parties did have a mandate to protect the environment of the Antarctic region. On this basis the group proceeded, discussing the matter itself and, as usual, referring sensitive questions to SCAR. After 1977 the group held "special" meetings to try to work out a regime, so regular Antarctic business would not be derailed by the novel undertaking.

An agreement within the treaty's framework could encompass the activities of the Soviet Union and Japan, the two largest fishing nations that were also prominent Antarctic Treaty parties. But it could not regulate the fishing of South Korea, Taiwan, Spain, and others not parties to the Antarctic Treaty. Moreover, though the fishing takes place south of 60 degrees south latitude and therefore in the Antarctic Treaty area, it is also a high seas activity and difficult to regulate in any event. Should the group make an agreement among themselves, like the "agreed measures" already passed to protect Antarctic flora or fauna? In the end, they decided to make a separate convention which any nation could join even if it was not a party to the Antarctic Treaty. (They inserted in the convention text an "umbilical cord" provision in which all parties to the convention agreed to abide by the Antarctic Treaty.)[24] Thus, by a seemingly small decision on a fine point, the group asserted its right to create free-standing conventions dealing with economic questions.

A crucial part of the negotiation was to convince the Soviet Union and Japan that large scale krill harvests could hurt the Antarctic ecosystem. The multiplicity of forums and contacts which make up the Antarctic regime helped; data from the British *Discovery* expeditions dating back to the turn of the century were studied to see what the whales' biomass was originally, hence how much krill the whales had eaten, and thus if there was a "surplus" of krill caused by the demise of the whales now available to man. Within SCAR and informal scientific meetings, British scientists and their colleagues discussed the ecosystems issue with Moiseev and other Russians, and eventually—though after great resistance—the Soviet representatives agreed that an "ecosystem standard" could be required in the convention's text.

What incentive did fishing states have to participate in the negotiation? Their reluctance did modify the conservationists' proposal for an interim standard limiting krill fishing before the agreement entered into force. Conservationists sought the interim standard in case the parties dragged their heels on ratification of the agreement; in the meantime fishing could reach large proportions and hurt the ecosystem. By defeating this initiative, the fishing states fought off regulations they considered unwarranted.

The Convention for the Conservation of Antarctic Marine Living Resources (CCAMLR, pronounced camlar) was signed in 1980 and entered into force in 1982 after the required eight states ratified it. All the Antarctic Treaty voting parties, including Japan, Poland, and the Soviet Union, joined. East Germany, West Germany, and the Netherlands also signed, even though they were only acceding parties to the Antarctic Treaty at the time. So the treaty group won some international acceptance for its right to legislate Antarctic fishing. The regime, in short, had been strengthened.

But whether meaningful regulation will be achieved remains an open question; fishing agreements are notoriously hard to implement. After a brief decline, krill-fishing levels began rising in the mid-1980s, reaching 446,000 in 1985–86. And several species of Antarctic finfish found near the peninsula where the fleets (and whales) congregate are already overfished. The scientific determination of how to measure the stocks of

Antarctic species and how to determine overfishing remains an unsolved problem. The solution rests on adequate research by individual national Antarctic programs. So the verdict is not yet in.

However, one episode from the convention's early workings shows how it has strengthened the Antarctic regime and insulated it from conflicts in the outside world. The first meeting of the CCAMLR commission was held in Hobart, Australia in May and June 1982. There, representatives of Argentina and Great Britain sat at the same table, discussing data collection, ecosystem management, and so on. Meanwhile in the South Atlantic, soldiers and sailors of both nations fought each other over their arcane territorial claims to the Falkland Islands. In the room in Hobart, one diplomat said, "You never would have known there was a war on."[25]

The krill-fishing issue shows how potential U.S.–Soviet conflicts regarding Antarctica are diluted by the multilateral, multipurpose character of the Antarctic regime. The Soviet Union is allied with Japan on the fishing issue; the United States with Great Britain and other powers. The story contains no particular bilateral conflict; both the superpowers' interests were accommodated as part of the general settlement.

The Minerals Dispute

The Antarctic regime was not immune from the global shocks created by the Arab oil embargo of 1973 and the worldwide fear of future shortages of oil and strategic minerals that dominated the international scene afterwards.

Antarctica doubtless has as many mineral deposits as the other continents, since it formed from the same processes. The few exposed rock areas show evidence of minerals: a giant coal seam runs through the Transantarctic Mountains; there is a "layered intrusion" in West Antarctica which has never been drilled but which looks from the surface like the extraordinarily rich Bushveld intrusion in South Africa; and there are copper-lead-zinc deposits in the Andean-type mountains of the peninsula. But the absence of economic deposits found so far and the obvious difficulty and expense of exploitation make mining the continent remote.

In the nearer term—if it can be called that—is the prospect of finding and extracting oil from Antarctica's continental shelves, particularly the Ross and Weddell seas. In summer, parts of the surface of both seas are ice-free. Drilling is technically possible even though the icecap depresses the continental shelf an average of 1500 meters below the sea surface. In 1973, the Arab oil embargo and price rise was followed by a journal report that a U.S. scientific ship drilling core rock from the Ross Sea shelf, had found traces of hydrocarbons, plugged the hole, and pulled away.[26]

Strains appeared immediately among the twelve Treaty consultative parties. Efforts to air the issue privately at a meeting sponsored by the Fridtjof Nansen Foundation in Polhogda Norway, in 1974, revealed the problems within the group. One claimant—the country was unnamed—said it would not consider a minerals agreement until its claim was recognized by the others. Another participant told the group they should fuse ownership in a condominium. Outside the group, environmentalists tried to have Antarctica declared a world park to forestall development.[27]

The group was not immune to pressures to keep all "frontiers" that might have big deposits available for exploration in the future. Some nations favored a permanent moratorium on all Antarctic exploration and exploitation. But the Ford Administration instructed U.S. delegates to the Eighth Consultative meeting in Oslo in 1975 to prevent a permanent moratorium and none was adopted. Instead, at the next meeting, in 1977 in London, treaty members adopted SCAR's suggestion that they have a policy of "voluntary restraint" regarding exploration. In it they "urge their nationals and other states to refrain from all exploration and exploitation of Antarctic mineral resources while making progress toward timely adoption of an agreed regime concerning Antarctic mineral resource activities."[28] Nothing, they realized, would upset a minerals negotiation more than sudden discovery of an economic deposit, with its attendant worldwide publicity and political pressures.

Already in the mid-1970s, political pressures were strong enough to generate expeditions to make "scientific" surveys of the Antarctic continental shelves. "Voluntary restraint" tested the degree to which the regime could regulate important national actions. The result was uneven.

The Antarctic continental shelf is key to the puzzle of how the continent once fit with the other pieces, South America, Africa, India, and Australia, into the large supercontinent of Gondwanaland. The shelf has been so little explored that there are no good maps. Any survey is manifestly basic research. So expeditions went: the Norwegian Antarctic Research Expedition to the Weddell Sea in 1976–77; West Germany to it also in 1978 and to the Ross Sea in 1980; and the Institut Francais du Petrol examined parts of the East Antarctic coast in 1981–82. In 1979 the Japan National Oil Corporation began a three-year seismic survey of different parts of the shelf. In the 1970s, the United States turned down an offer of an advanced industry seismic exploration ship; officials said that such a survey could violate the voluntary restraint policy. (In the 1980s, the U.S. government reversed itself and sent down a government seismic ship which was much less capable.) None of these surveys was detailed enough to count as exploration so none violated the letter of the policy. But the policy could not hold back the race for an edge in knowledge of Antarctica's oil potential, which is what the expeditions really were seeking.

The sudden interest in collecting seismic data eroded the open exchange of scientific information that had become a long-standing tradition of the regime. Norway did not make its seismic data available to others for years after its expedition. West Germany showed similar secrecy. Such secrecy was unusual, even granting the difficulty and expense these nations' small scientific institutions have in processing such data (data processing is a major expense in commercial oil exploration). The secrecy suggested that the participants wanted an edge on knowledge: if the data showed any sign of a Saudi-sized field off Antarctica, the nation holding it wanted to know first.

As with the krill issue, U.S. and Soviet interests initially appeared in conflict. In the mid-1970s, U.S. oil companies were at the forefront of evolving technology for exploration deep offshore and in the Arctic. So, while the United States was not as dependent on OPEC oil as some other Antarctic Treaty parties, the nature of its industry meant it would favor easing the way for eventual Antarctic exploration. The Soviet Union, by contrast, did not seem eager to facilitate oil exploration in Antarctica. A common explanation was its lag in offshore drilling capability; at that time, Soviet rigs were only exploring the shallow, temperate Caspian Sea. Observers concluded that the Soviets would be interested in facilitating Antarctic offshore exploration only when they could mount a respectable effort of their own.

But these differences were minor compared to the pressing needs of other parties to the Antarctic Treaty. Japan and New Zealand, for example, are highly dependent on Arab oil, and eager to see rules developed for exploring the Antarctic, which is closer to them than the Persian Gulf and requires tankers to pass through fewer strategic straits. Great Britain and Norway had advanced polar technology, thanks to their development of the North Sea, but felt no urgency about sending their rigs to Antarctica. To varying degrees, countries with oil reserves and strong environmental movements could argue for delaying or forswearing Antarctic development. Claimants with a strong sense of nationalism, such as Australia, held views contrary to the interests of nonclaimants such as Japan or South Africa. Thus, the U.S.–Soviet differences were subsumed by the more complex needs of the group.

As of this writing, it is unclear whether the treaty group can conclude a convention for minerals development parallel to the CCAMLR. Every part of the regime's extensive network is being brought into play. Groups appointed by SCAR have studied and reported on the environmental impacts of exploration and development. SCAR holds technical meetings that compare national positions, seek consensus, and send ideas to the negotiators. The negotiations for a regime are held in separate special meetings so that normal Antarctic business can continue. There is much informal discussion.

The negotiations have become more complex since 1983 when India and Brazil joined, and since China became a full voting party in 1985. As the next section will discuss, these entrants were spurred in part by a wish to have a voice in the minerals discussions. According to R. Tucker Scully, the chief U.S. Antarctic negotiator, some of the developing nations want a minerals agreement to make it possible for developing nations to participate directly in Antarctic minerals development.

Another complication is added by the observer status at the negotiations now accorded to the eighteen acceding powers to the treaty; their delegates can advise and consult with the negotiators. Environmentalists and other nongovernmental organizations are also weighing in. The likelihood that the superpowers—or the superpowers along with a small group of like minded nations—could divide Antarctica's mineral wealth among themselves has passed.

Scully discussed the emerging minerals agreement publicly in July, 1986, after draft texts had been leaked and published by environmental groups.[29] The signs are that in this regime, the historic problems of sovereignty that the minerals question raises will be sidestepped in favor of pragmatic compromise. The dispute over who owns the land or continental shelf where an economic deposit is found can be sidestepped if rights and royalties are agreed in a way that is satisfactory to investors, industry, and the international system. According to the drafts and Scully's talk, "prospecting"—ordinary geologic investigations that are general and scientific—could be undertaken unilaterally with provisions for advance notice, as it is now under the treaty.

The agreement would establish a commission of its voting parties with ultimate decision-making power over every subsequent stage of exploration and development. If a private consortium or national group wanted to explore in a given area—exploration being more specific, more intrusive than "prospecting"—a plan for exploration and statement of environmental impact would be submitted to the commission. At that point, the region of Antarctica in question would be known, be it the Ross Sea or the inland site of the layered intrusion mentioned above, or the peninsula. The commission would appoint a regulatory committee, representing the treaty powers, to be the working group charged with provisional decision making for that region. Separate committees are visualized for separate regions, since the legal aspects, resources, and environmental circumstances will differ in most instances. The regulatory committee would make the initial judgments about whether the resource would be developed or even explored at all, or whether environmental damage would be too great. Since the commission could only approve or reject committee recommendations but not modify them, the committee would be the real locus of decision making and power.

The composition of the committee would reflect the power balance for that particular region. The fact that both superpowers have an interest in the entire region is reflected in their inclusion on any committee formed. Each committee would also include two states, including the state sponsoring the exploration application and another chosen by it, and up to four additional states, including ones chosen by the one or more states that claim the area. This committee would work up a management scheme for the proposed activity, in effect a contract between the would-be developers of the resource and the nations that feel they have rights over the specific area.[30]

Other features of the proposed convention include a general environmental standard for any development activity, a scientific advisory committee, and "umbilical cord" provisions like those in CCAMLR binding all parties to the chief provisions of the Antarctic Treaty.[31] There are two important points about the drafts: first, they show the extensive accommodation being made regarding resource development, an historic thorn in the side of the regime; second, they show the mutuality of U.S., Soviet, and mid-sized power interest in reaching an accommodation on Antarctic minerals.

The Charge of Political Inequity

The rush to complete a minerals agreement stemmed from something besides an idealistic wish to perfect the Antarctic legal system. The underlying motive was to keep control over Antarctic decisions in the hands of the treaty group. The minerals negotiations began in earnest after 1982 and coincided with the strongest attacks on the treaty from outside the group in its history. The extreme form of the assault was the argument that Antarctica was the "common heritage of mankind" so that decisions should be made by a one nation-one-vote forum of all nations, such as the Law of the Sea meeting or the United Nations. Fear of loss of control drove the treaty parties to find a solution themselves, but one the outside world might also find equitable.

The debate over Antarctica that has followed at the United Nations shows the extent to which the United States and the Soviet Union now complement one another's interests in Antarctic decision making—a powerful contrast to the rivalry and mistrust of the 1950–57 period. At the United Nations, the Soviet representatives were among the staunchest defenders of the treaty system. The debate coincided with a general U.S. position, articulated by U.N. Ambassador Jeane J. Kirkpatrick, that showed little support for Third-World political equity. Ironically, while U.S.–Soviet relations were at their lowest point in decades during the first Reagan term, the Soviet and U.S. representatives echoed each other in defense of the Antarctic Treaty at the United Nations.

Critics often call the Antarctic regime "weak" and "fragile," but its response to attacks suggests robustness. The first challenge came after the start of the Third U.N. Conference on the Law of the Sea (LoS) in 1974. There, representatives of more than 150 nations began updating the 1958 legal code for virtually all man's activities in the world's oceans and territorial seas, including fishing rights, rights of passage through straits, and others. In 1970, the U.N. General Assembly unanimously passed a resolution declaring "the deep seabeds beyond the limits of national jurisdiction" to be the "common heritage of mankind." Mining companies, primarily American, had plans to scrape minerals from the ocean floors, which are strewn with potato-sized nodules rich in manganese, copper, cobalt, and nickel. The seabeds committee of the LoS meeting interpreted the "common heritage" label to mean that no private or state operator could mine the seabeds without prior approval of all co-owners, that is, 150-odd nations. They devised a new U.N.-like structure to regulate ocean mining, with a giant legislative body to make decisions. This structure was especially pushed by the Group of 77, led by minerals-exporting nations, over the opposition of mining interests represented by the U.S. delegation and those of other advanced industrial nations.[32]

During the seabed mining debate, representatives of the Group of 77 argued that Antarctica was also a common heritage and covered by the 1970 General Assembly resolution.[33] It fit the resolution's definition, they argued, because Antarctica was "beyond the limits of national jurisdiction." But the treaty parties saw the move for what it was: an attempt to wrest control of decision making away from them. There was some corridor conversation, and it is noteworthy that Chile and Argentina, two Antarctic claimants threatened by the "common heritage" approach, were also key members of the Group of 77. As the seabeds mining controversy swelled to unexpected proportions spokesmen began to say they would take up Antarctica *after* the LoS convention was over.

Promptly in 1982, Datuk Seri Matahir bin Mohamad, prime minister of Malaysia, rose at the 37th U.N. General Assembly to say that now that the LoS was finished, "a new international agreement" for Antarctica should be negotiated. Sri Lanka had shown an interest earlier, and Antarctica had been discussed at a Non-Aligned Movement meeting chaired by India. The prospect of another seabeds-type controversy loomed, possibly pitting "mankind," in the form of a bloc of developing nations, against the "club" of treaty powers, largely rich industrial nations. Some Western law experts put forward sweeping new schemes for Antarctica at the time.[34]

But the diplomats who launched into the Antarctic issue expecting another LoS-style confrontation underestimated the extent to which Antarctica was not a tabula rasa waiting for them to erect political institutions at will. They would discover that Antarctica was already the object of longstanding political interests met by the treaty and its regime. Moreover the treaty parties were not about to become the easy ideological targets which the mining interests had become in the LoS.

The first discussion of Antarctica at the United Nations was scheduled for the 38th U.N. General Assembly opening in September 1983. Earlier the treaty parties began a backstage effort to educate nonparties about the merits of the Antarctic system, trying to persuade them to join rather than fight. Perhaps certain outside governments saw a chance to exert leverage between the two camps. In any event, India, which sent an expedition in 1981, became an acceding party in August 1983 and a full voting member that October. Brazil, which had acceded in 1975 and sent a shipboard scientific expedition, became a voting party in October 1983. Italy and Peru had become acceding parties in 1981; Spain did likewise in 1982. In 1981 the treaty had aquired its first "developing" country, Papua New Guinea. China expressed an interest and in 1985 became an acceding party. Besides a longer list of voting parties, the list of acceding parties was long enough to carry weight. So when the U.N. debate got under way, the treaty parties could argue that a large part of "mankind" had sided with the treaty.

So Malaysia had difficulty finding cosponsors for its U.N. initiative and recruited only one, Antigua and Barbuda. The result of the debate was referral of the question to the secretariat for study, but the treaty parties had guidance inserted which assured that the study would not prejudice their interests. In subsequent debates at and around the

United Nations, Malaysia softened its original call for " a new international agreement" for Antarctica while continuing to assail the Treaty as "exclusive, comprehensive, and unaccountable." At an unusual privately sponsored meeting in the Antarctic wilderness in January 1985, attended by old polar hands and some Third World challengers, the Malaysian ambassador to the United Nations did not urge that the treaty be thrown out.[35]

These glimmerings of compromise receded in 1985 and 1986, when South Africa's role as one of the original twelve treaty parties fanned criticism of the treaty at the United Nations, particularly from black African states. These debates took place during the South African regime's crackdown on blacks and the news media, and amid a storm of criticism by other governments and world opinion. The treaty party governments—many of which were condemning South Africa with one hand—found themselves defending South Africa's right to be included in the treaty system. Their argument was that the United Nations did not have authority to meddle in the treaty group's internal affairs. The treaty, they argued, was a functioning regional peacekeeping arrangement under Chapter VIII, Article 52 of the U.N. charter. So long as the arrangement was working, the United Nations had no right to tell it what to do. When the United Nations asked for reports on the minerals negotiations, the treaty powers declined that request also; they were willing to give information of their own accord, but not take instruction from the United Nations.[36]

Even the Antarctic regime's critics acknowledge it has adapted tremendously from only a few years ago. Most of "mankind" is represented in the voting membership, now that India and China have been added as members. The list of voting and acceding powers numbers thirty-five and includes most major regions and power blocs, with the exception of Middle Eastern and black African nations. Some developing nations participate in the minerals negotiations, which are closed to nonparties but now open for acceding states to attend as observers. Information is published, if not on instruction from the United Nations. But the foregoing story shows that much of this adaptation and innovation has come as a reaction to threats from the outside—much as in the 1957–61 period the historic, traditional Antarctic conflicts were solved quickly when the Soviet threat appeared.

ANALYSIS OF SUCCESS AND LESSONS

What Is Success?

The story told here suggests the Antarctic regime has been successful. The two superpowers faced competition over Antarctica in the 1950s; through the treaty and regime U.S.–Soviet relations have become cooperative and now mutually reinforcing with respect not only to arms control but to the over-all viability of the regime. Medium-sized claimant nations—Great Britain, France, New Zealand, Australia, Norway, Chile, and Argentina—formerly in conflict with one another and with the United States over claims, have found a modus vivendi through the treaty and regime. If the measure of a successful regime is whether it modifies the way the parties would have behaved in the absence of the regime, then the Antarctic regime has been a success.

The Antarctic regime has also been dynamic. An assessment of its achievements in 1970 would have celebrated improvement in U.S.–Soviet cooperation and multilateral relations. But an assessment in 1987 must also acknowledge that the regime has broadened from the original goals: CCAMLR has given it a foothold in regulating the major economic activity of fishing, and it has made progress towards resolving the most difficult resource issue of mineral rights. The regime now includes new voting members such as India and China, and a greater role has been given to acceding parties and nongovernmental organizations.

But in at least four respects the treaty and regime have failed to meet the hopes of some supporters.

First, the arrangement has not fulfilled early hopes that the setting aside of the claims dispute would lead to a formal internationalization of the continent. Instead, Article IV of the treaty holds in place the web of competing national interests that have retained their domestic appeal: the potential U.S. claim, Soviet aspirations, Chile's strong nationalism, and claims by Argentina and Australia in particular regarding "their" respective Antarctic territories. The Falkland Islands War is a reminder that such national feelings—however quaint they seem to those who do not share them—can be powerful forces, even when applied to remote regions of the world. The rise and persistence of nationalism has been a prominent trend of modern times, which those who held such hopes for the Antarctic Treaty failed to take into account.

Second, the Antarctic regime is not the orderly legal system some of its defenders claim. Some spokesmen for the original twelve parties, such as the Chilean diplomat, Fernando Zegers Santa Cruz, have argued that there is an "Antarctic system" of the law due to the terrestrial, naval, and aerial transportation networks and other services the parties provide to users of the region.[37] Further, because the parties to this system provide responsible administration of the region, they have *earned* the right to make decisions for the region regardless of their original rights. This view is expressed in the CCAMLR text, which requires all parties to it—including those that are not parties to the Antarctic Treaty—to recognize the "special obligations and responsibilities" (which are undefined) of the Antarctic Treaty parties.

Critics counter that the vaunted "system" is merely a patchwork of half-measures conveniently lax in their enforcement. F. M. Auburn, for example, contends the group does not even obey its own rules: environmental regulations go unenforced, requirements for data exchange have not been met. The foregoing story shows that some parties ignored, in effect, the group's stated policy of voluntary restraint on minerals exploration. As another example, in 1979, when a commercial airliner crashed into a mountainside near the Ross Sea killing all 257 on board, there was no clearly assigned authority for air navigation and safety south of 50 degrees south latitude—the boundary at which world navigation charts issued by the International Civil Aeronautics Organization leave off.[38]

Western conservatives could raise a third criticism, namely that the treaty covers a failure by the West in 1950–57 to keep the Soviets out of Antarctica. Arguably, the United States and the seven announced claimants could have reached a settlement despite the 1950 Soviet note; instead they took it as a given that the Soviets should be allowed to participate in Antarctic diplomacy. The Soviets were even invited to go there during the IGY, and the treaty that came after only made their presence permanent.

This argument could be developed to emphasize the importance the Western treaty powers have placed on preventing Antarctica from becoming the "scene or object of international discord." While subscribing to the rhetoric of international harmony, the Soviets have expanded their Antarctic presence without a murmur from the West. In the years just after the IGY, the Soviet Antarctic program shrank, only to build up again later. To its two bases in the Australian section the Soviet Union added additional ones around the coast, each placed near different sector claims. The seventh Soviet station is in the ''unclaimed'' piece of the Antarctic pie, nicknamed the American sector because it was explored by Byrd. This ring of stations could be seen as Soviet encirclement of the continent, and evil motives could be imputed despite the lack of evidence of Soviet intentions to violate the spirit or letter of the treaty. A benign interpretation of the expanding Soviet program is that Antarctica offers Soviet polar specialists and icebreakers something to do in the Arctic winter—which is the relatively hospitable austral summer in Antarctica.[39]

Fourth, from a different political perspective, the treaty and regime can be criticized for not going far enough in the direction of cooperation and innovation. As we saw, the recent adaptation has been reactive, a response to threats from outsiders. And although the regime has changed, it could be argued that all that has happened is that the historically interested nations have retained their political power over the region—and even extended that power into areas not granted specifically in the original text.

Members of the group have not gone as far as they could in setting old security concepts aside and exploiting opportunities for further international cooperation. The United States, for example, spends more than $50 million per year to maintain its own scientific station at the South Pole and to man it year-round. The reason is partly scientific: there is an important role for a year-round station in the deep hinterland. The primary reason for this investment is to prevent the Soviets from occupying the pole.[40] The United States also maintains a ''presence'' symbolizing the continent-wide U.S. claim in case the treaty should ever break down. Yet a decade ago the United States could have begun serious planning for an international consortium of invited nations (exclusively Western nations if it so chose) to share the expense and use of the facility, much as oceanographic vessels are now jointly funded. In an era of brutally rising costs for advanced scientific installations of all kinds, the U.S. failure to consider this obvious step is hard to understand.

Another opportunity thus far missed would be to soften the continued requirement that to qualify for voting status within the treaty an applying nation must have in Antarctica its own national station or ship-based expedition, thereby demonstrating ''substantial scientific interest'' in the region. This requirement forces any nation wanting a voice in Antarctic decisionmaking to make a large investment in polar equipment and research—not neccessarily the first call on funds for developing nation governments with urgent needs at home. Moreover the proliferation of stations on the few ice-free coasts of Antarctica, which happen to be where fish and bird life feed, has become an environmental concern. The obvious solution is joint station management and joint scientific programs, but the treaty group has given little serious study to this potential innovation.

Why Success?

Despite these criticisms, the Antarctic Treaty and regime have endured with surprising robustness. Seven factors have caused this success. Three factors explain how a traditional conflict situation was transformed into an innovative, cooperative regime. Three more factors explain how the resulting regime maintained itself and adapted with time. The seventh and last factor is the complementary character of U.S. and Soviet interests, which has both helped advance multilateral cooperation and been helped by it.

1. As I mentioned earlier, the transition from conflict to cooperation was prepared by the political innovations adopted for eighteen months during the IGY. Though not intended as such by its organizers, the IGY in Antarctica amounted to a period of experimentation with alternative political arrangements.

The Antarctic story suggests that temporary arrangements can be useful in demonstrating cooperation among states, and thereby making some more permanent accommodation possible. The IGY organizers got concessions from governments of claimant states in part because they were intended as temporary concessions. Indeed, if the IGY organizers had asked for a permanent change in the political landscape of Antarctica, they probably would have been unable to win support.

The Antarctic Treaty would have been difficult or impossible to negotiate in the absence of the IGY, which demonstrated how its political innovations would work "on the ice." In fact, something like the Antarctic Treaty was proposed earlier. In 1948, when Secretary of State Dean Acheson was casting about for solutions, a Chilean jurist, Julio Escudero Guzman, drafted a plan for a five-year moratorium on claims, while Antarctica would be dedicated to scientific research, free access, and political neutrality for scientific expeditions.[41] When Acheson's trusteeship and condominium proposals were rebuffed, he put forward the Escudero plan. It got nowhere. There was no organized international constituency for an Antarctica dedicated to science in 1948. Moreover, the plan appeared to threaten the claims. Thus it seems clear that only after the IGY showed that such arrangements could work in practice, could the temporary innovation be made permanent.

2. After 1961 when the treaty entered into force, it had more than ten years without major external shocks in which to develop norms and practices and accumulate authority. Indeed, after a few years of public visibility in 1957–59, Antarctica sank, figuratively speaking, from international view. This early phase of protection strengthened the agreement so it could withstand external shocks better when they came.

3. The third factor that brought about cooperation from the conflict-ridden Antarctic diplomacy of the 1940s and 1950s was the existence of a powerful constituency for the new arrangement, who remained active after it came into force. The scientists were well organized, influential in many governments around the world, and in the United States had a coherent institutional base in the U.S. National Academy of Sciences, (after the IGY, in the National Science Foundation). The arms controllers had an institutional base in ACDA.

During the early years of the treaty no rival users of the Antarctic appeared. Clearly, the ongoing interest of scientists and the arms controllers in the agreement, and the absence of competitors, strengthened the original accord.

The Antarctic regime continued and broadened because scientist-users in other nations lobbied their governments as well. It seems clear that the Soviet scientists were effective in maintaining political leaders' support for the agreement. This factor helps explain the consistency of the regime over such a long period. In some countries, scientific interest did decline; Norway and Belgium for example, have shut down their Antarctic stations, though they remain active in treaty diplomacy. Finally, the scientists had no rivals; if a serious rival group had appeared, the evolution of the regime might have been different.

4. Why is the Antarctic Treaty stronger as an arms control measure now than it was when it was signed? A major reason is the complementarity of U.S. and Soviet interests, mentioned in the story above and analysed below. But luck has also played a

part, the lucky chance that military technology in the intervening thirty years has evolved to make Antarctica less, rather than more, militarily useful.[42]

In the late 1950s, the United States depended heavily on its bomber force to project U.S. power around the world. These required air bases in many foreign countries. There were relatively few sites for such bases in the southern hemisphere, despite U.S. military requirements for a presence there. Thus in the late 1950s Antarctica was considered a possible site for air bases.

Sputnik suggested to some that Antarctica could be militarily threatening: the Australians were afraid the Soviets would put their new ballistic missiles in Antarctica and threaten nations in the southern Pacific region. In the 1960s, another threat materialized in the form of a possible Soviet Fractional Orbital Bombardment System (FOBS). The FOBS could fire missiles on a trajectory around the south side of the earth instead of the north to hit North America from her unguarded southern flank. Also, early polar-orbiting satellites required continuous ground tracking, and Antarctica was considered seriously for this purpose. (However, early on, Antarctica was ruled out as a port for naval vessels. The coast offered no useful harbors, and, after the disastrous effort of the submarine *U.S.S. Sennett* to operate in the pack ice during Operation Highjump, when it had to be towed to the safety of the open sea, submarines could not operate near its coasts.)

Antarctica was also expected to be useful in the age of plentiful nuclear power, which was supposed to be dawning in the late 1950s. It was predicted that nuclear power plants would spread rapidly all over the world, providing cheap energy and, in the phrase of the day, to make the deserts bloom. These would generate much radioactive waste, and among the storage schemes seriously considered was burial in the Antarctic icecap. These possibilities for Antarctica were serious when the treaty was drawn up; they explain the urgency with which demilitarization was sought at the time.

Little more than a decade later, most of these uses were not seriously considered, however. The rise of nationalism spelled the end of the network of farflung U.S. air bases; carrier-based aircraft replaced land-based bombers for U.S. power projection. The installation of long range ballistic missiles in the U.S. and Soviet homelands and on submarines made most foreign-based missiles obsolete, especially the idea of putting them in Antarctica. Satellites became less dependent on ground tracking, requiring fewer ground stations. FOBS faded, as did the specter of quantities of nuclear waste requiring storage in the Antarctic icecap. The 1963 treaty banning nuclear tests in the earth's atmosphere relieved pressures to test in the Antarctic.

Thus, while the United States and the Soviet Union still need to deny hegemony over the region to each other, they have found ways of doing so through their national presences—not by direct military means. Fortunate circumstances have not bred pressure for abrogating or changing the treaty's arms control provisions.

5. The outstanding feature of the Antarctic story is Antarctica itself: beautiful, evocative, dangerous, a frontier having a vast, empty desert of ice for its mainland and churning, ice-and-bird-flecked seas for its coasts.

Clearly the ongoing success of the regime for Antarctica has derived in part from the need for each step agreed by the nations to meet a test of real world practicality: it must be useful to the hundreds of people who work in the region every year, some in considerable danger. The Antarctic imposes its own limitations, creates a bias for pragmatism, incremental approaches, and practicality at every step.

In rebutting those at the United Nations who would impose a one-nation-one-vote administration for Antarctica, the treaty parties have raised practical objections. Suppose a new regime supersedes the treaty and gives each nation of the world an equal vote in Antarctic administration. What incentive would they have to spend money there, or send ships and personnel? When some black African nations objected to South Africa's presence in the treaty group, other treaty parties countered that because South Africa subscribes to the treaty, it is banned from testing nuclear weapons south of 60 degrees south latitude. Did the others really want that nation, widely rumored to be developing nuclear weapons, to be freed from the treaty's restraints on such tests?

Some retrospectives, such as that by Stephen D. Krasner, conclude that the UNCLOS deepsea mining negotiation was driven by considerations of political equity more than real world practicality.[43] As evidence, he cited the UNCLOS' prescription of having more than 150 nations voting in a General Assembly-like forum as to whether a bit of the seabed may be scraped or not, with dozens of committees, a secretariat, a big regulatory arm and an "enterprise" through which the Third World would mine the deep seabed itself. The draft Antarctic minerals regime is more pragmatic, deferring even the creation of administrative arrangements such as the all-important regulatory committees until some would-be explorer submits an application for a specific activity in Antarctica. Even after being signed and ratified, very little of the agreement's machinery will come into existence if no one cares to explore Antarctica's minerals seriously in years to come. So the draft regime reflects the pragmatic tradition of previous Antarctic diplomacy. Krasner favorably compares the more flexible Antarctic arrangements with the cumbersome ones drawn up for seabed mining in UNCLOS.

Agreements having high technical content, which are also needed for the conduct of ongoing business, can insulate themselves from outside pressures. Krasner discusses the allocation of frequencies on the radio spectrum for worldwide communications through the World Administrative Radio Conferences.[44] Attempts by the Group of 77 to allocate space on the basis of political equity were attenuated by fear of the massive disruption in worldwide communications which would occur if the regime broke down.

6. A final reason the Antarctic regime has been both strong and adaptive is the layered networking within the system. Problems are taken up in many ways at different levels. Most of these forums communicate with each other so the status of the problems is known throughout the system.

The regime's communication system can be thought of as a lattice, with each vertical bar being a party to the treaty. At the highest level for each nation is the diplomat charged with Antarctic affairs, and the official who manages the national Antarctic program. Below this level on the bar come the senior scientists, many of them IGY alumni, who sit on polar committees of their respective national academies of science, participate in SCAR, and have broad policy responsibilities. Below them are staff experts in polar research programs and diplomatic offices. At a lower level on the bar—lowest because it is the closest to what happens in the field, in Antarctica itself—are the working scientists and technical support people.

The regime's communication system also includes the Non-Government Organizations (NGOs), which have won increasing status as observers and advisers to the regime. These are mostly environmental groups whose individual members and press are important sources of lateral and vertical communication within the regime. One of their main complaints is the treaty parties' secretiveness; it was no surprise that the written draft of the minerals regime was leaked to an NGO newsletter. The leak served a purpose. The many treaty party governments would have had difficulty clearing the release of such a document; this way outsiders learned the general shape of the settlement under discussion.

Finally, part of this lattice are the acceding parties. These were originally given no role in the workings of the treaty group. Now they are accorded observer status at consultative meetings. These form a large group: there are now seventeen (see note, pp. 307–8). Particularly in the U.N. debate, they have been a source of communication about the treaty system to nonparties. Presumably, they are a source of criticism and change within the treaty group.

The system is a "lattice" because there are similar structures in each participating country, and because people engaged in similar activities in the different countries communicate laterally with one another, not just vertically within their own national team. This structure offers many chances for problems to be discovered and discussed.

7. As a final factor in success, the United States and the Soviet Union engage in cooperation and competition regarding Antarctica through the mechanism of the Antarctica Treaty and the larger regime that has evolved around it. This is not to say that U.S. and Soviet interests have not collided. They have, and in many of the negotiations mentioned above the Soviets have been among the last holdouts, leaving it unclear to others whether they would sign on at all. In the end, however, Moscow has opted for courses of action which were consonant with the group's interest and parallel to those of the United States.

The United States has preserved the large basis of claim laid down by private and government expeditions in the twentieth century for two reasons: (1) to be able to play a controlling role in deciding secondary Antarctic questions such as arms control, resource development, and general administration and (2) to be prepared to exercise its rights in the unlikely event the treaty ever breaks down. The United States has had a geopolitical interest in denying a free hand in the region to the Soviets ever since the USSR expressed interest in it, and in having a major presence centered on the South Pole. These U.S. geopolitical interests are less military than preclusive; its national interest is only underlying and indirect.

In the policy deliberations that led to the IGY and the treaty, the government discovered a corollary, namely, that it had a stake in avoiding the expense and distraction of an arms race in the far south. The general U.S. interest in global stability made it useful to try to "zone off" a large portion of the southern hemisphere from likely military activity or conflict.

The Soviet Union behaves as though its fundamental interests in the Antarctic mirror those of the United States. Events over the past twenty-six years have shown that so long as the Antarctic remains militarily useless to both sides, this complementarity of interests will remain. Recent history suggests that even powerful shocks in the central U.S.–Soviet relationship have had very little effect on the underlying complementarity of superpower interests in Antarctica. The Soviet Union's interests are to protect whatever territorial claim it believes it has in Antarctica—though the nature of these have never been defined publicly—and to be "present" in the region in as wide-ranging a manner as the United States. (Hence its early interest in a pole station and subsequent ring of stations around the coast. Hence its attempts to "infly" from a neighboring land—Madagascar—to land at a Soviet-built runway in Antarctica just as the Americans "infly" from New Zealand to McMurdo. It is still extraordinarily difficult to fly into Antarctica from neighboring continents and most national programs provide station resupply only by sea.) Finally, the Soviets appear to recognize the cost advantages of a demilitarized Antarctica; the strong Soviet defense of the treaty as an arms control measure may stem from a need to avoid spending rubles on an arms race.

One of the most instructive aspects of the Antarctic case is that the United States and Soviet Union maintain this balance of interests not through a bilateral exclusive agreement, but through a multilateral one serving many other political, economic, and regional purposes for many nations whose Antarctic interests differ from those of the superpowers. Several episodes described earlier indicate how the multilateral and bilateral aspects reinforce one another. The krill story showed how the United States, which had no direct interest in harvesting krill itself, had two interests in the issue: 1) to assure the protection of the ecosystem because of previous policies to protect marine mammals worldwide and 2) to strengthen the Antarctic Treaty and regime through helping the whole group adapt successfully, no matter what their positions and problems. The Soviets had an interest that was contrary to that of the United States, namely, to clear the way for its fishermen to catch what they needed from the rich Southern Ocean.

But a second Soviet interest, in maintaining the Antarctic Treaty system by allowing it to address this new problem through an agreed convention, motivated the USSR to compromise. The krill issue also did not become a bilateral problem because neither superpower was alone in its respective position; Great Britain was pro-conservation along with the United States, while Japan was aligned with the Soviets as a pro-fishing state. The multilateral character of the issue prevented U.S.–Soviet confrontation.

Something similar appears to be happening in the minerals negotiations, though little is known about them publicly. The United States has an interest in assuring access in the medium term to its oil and mining interests—technologically among the most advanced in the world. There are also U.S. interests in conservation and maintenance of the treaty system. The Soviets are unlikely to make a showing in near- or mid-term Antarctic oil development but also have a stake in not allowing the minerals question to break the treaty apart.

Finally, the story of the challenge from the United Nations shows how mutual U.S.–Soviet interests bolstered the Antarctic regime and helped fend off outside attack. While the joint U.S.–Soviet response may be reactionary—more a wish to preserve past gains in Antarctica than to reach creatively for new horizons of cooperation—the story shows that mutuality of interests is a powerful factor, possibly the key one, in the robustness of the regime. While it is possible that U.S.–Soviet differences will arise in future—over the expanding Soviet presence, over access to oil, or some other issue—it seems unlikely that the fundamental complementarity of interests will change anytime soon.

Implications

Does the story of the Antarctic regime hold any larger lessons beyond those that apply to the unique part of the world south of 60 degrees south latitude? As I have mentioned, the techniques of the 1961 Antarctic Treaty did not transfer into other arenas (such as unilateral on-site inspection, aerial inspection, nuclear weapons free zones) as some hoped, and this shows that the achievements in Antarctica may not necessarily be transferable elsewhere.

However, in an oblique way developments in Antarctic governance did anticipate trends in the international system, many unforeseen at the time they appeared in the Antarctic regime. In 1958–59 the Cold War still prevailed. For Soviet scientists to cooperate with their Western colleagues in Antarctica seemed remarkable—an oddity in the tenor of the time. Similarly, the Soviets agreed to Antarctic demilitarization, and battened down to cooperate there over the long term.

Was it a fluke? Looking back, we can see now that this acceptance of cooperation anticipated the search for coexistence which followed the 1962 Cuban crisis—the 1963 test ban treaty, the Glassboro summit, and the fuller détente of the 1970s.

Similarly, the multilateral aspect of the treaty was much criticized at the time—for weakening national sovereignty, for downplaying all-important national conflicts among European, Latin, and American claimants. A rich literature between 1957 and 1961 doubts whether the treaty means anything since individual national claims would inevitably dominate. (Other articles of the period predicted the opposite extreme of complete *internationalization* as a result of the treaty.) Yet through the Antarctic regime, these medium-sized powers came to cooperate on essential services such as providing weather and scientific data, and rescue. But each retained individualistic national programs and styles. Over-all, their participation was shaped by the United States and the Soviet Union, which held ultimate power over the region.

The adapted Antarctic regime that emerges from the present challenges may signal future trends as well. One of the most striking features is the cooperation between the United States and the Soviet Union. In the first Reagan term, the superpowers' close cooperation at the United Nations seemed a fluke. Moscow's decision to avoid costly adventures in Antarctica—and to harmonize with the West rather than score points against it—may presage Soviet behavior on other fronts. Certainly this would be a fitting stance for a nation already burdened by the arms race and troubled by internal social, political, and economic problems.

Two other trends can be seen in current Antarctic geopolitics. One is the obvious: the United States is no longer dominant. Gone are the days when only American planes, cameras, and mapmakers explored the Antarctic wilderness while an Acheson or a Daniels led negotiations with the other Antarctic nations. The recent challenges to the treaty have come from outside the United States; they have concerned questions the United States probably would not have raised. The Antarctic agenda is being set elsewhere: this may explain why U.S. policy has become reactive rather than spontaneous.

The last trend is the differentiation among mid-sized industrial states and developing countries that have become key actors in the Antarctic drama. The newcomers, such as Brazil, India, and China, are influential. Because they have respectable polar scientific programs, none can be said to be "underdeveloped" on Antarctic matters. Yet they show that the developing world is not left out of the circle, even while Malaysia, Antigua and Barbuda, and some black African states stay outside. The situation belies any simplistic division into "North" and "South." This trend is becoming general, as the gaps between the poorer, still-developing nations and the more proficient ones become as large as those between North and South, or between the First and Third Worlds, with the more advanced developing nations playing larger more independent roles in world affairs.

Antarctica is remote but not irrelevant. Disputes and defects remain within the regime, but it remains strong and is still evolving. Its history and techniques for reconciling varied national interests suggest lessons both for U.S.–Soviet relations and for multilateral cooperation in other areas.

Notes

1. Central Intelligence Agency, *Polar Regions Atlas* (Washington, D.C.: U.S. Government Printing Office, 1978) p. 41.

2. *The Voyages of Captain James Cook Round the World* (London: Richard Phillips, 1809), vol. IV, pp. 208–210, 216, 217.

3. A good, detailed, comprehensive history of early exploration in the southern hemisphere is C. Hartley Grattan, *The Southwest Pacific to 1900, A Modern History* (Ann Arbor, Mich.: University of Michigan Press, 1963). Most references to early expeditions below are based on Grattan.

4. The United States Exploring Expedition, as Wilkes' operation was called, is described in Kenneth J. Bertrand, *Americans in Antarctica 1775–1948,* Special Publication Number 39 (New York: American Geographical Society, 1971). Hereafter referred to as Bertrand.

5. A devastating portrait of Scott's mistakes, which were known but little discussed after his martyrdom, is Roland Huntford, *Scott and Amundsen* (London: Hodder and Stoughton, 1979). The futility of Scott's Antarctic conquest in the context of the empire is mentioned by James Morris, *Farewell the Trumpets: An Imperial Retreat* (New York: Harcourt Brace Jovanovich, 1980).

6. C. Hartley Grattan, *The Southwest Pacific Since 1900: A Modern History* (Ann Arbor, Mich.: University of Michigan Press, 1963), pp. 652–653. Earlier references to twentieth century claims are also based on this source. The Germans named the area—which the Norwegians call Queen Maud Land—New Schwabenland, but neither the Reich nor postwar Germany has ever broached the issue of a claim.

7. Deborah Shapley, *The Seventh Continent: Antarctica in a Resource Age* (Washington, D.C.: Resources for the Future, Inc., 1985), p. 21.

8. Bertrand, *Americans.* This book is based on the official records of the major American expeditions and is especially authoritative for the twentieth century. However, Bertrand omits mention of claims activities which were apparently classified at the time he was given access to the records. U.S. Archives, Record Groups 59 and 330 contain the State Department materials relating to Antarctic claims. A list based on written records of where claims markers were put down in Antarctica from 1928 to 1957, probably compiled by Henry Dater, is in Records of the Secretary of Defense, Records of the U.S. Antarctic Projects Officer, Record Group 330, National Archives. See also Shapley, *Seventh Continent,* pp. 32–63 passim.

9. The changing preoccupations about Antarctica of governments, the media, and the legal community are shown in a bibliography of Antarctic literature, with English abstracts of a remarkable number of foreign articles, books, and official documents. See Robert D. Hayton, *National Interests in Antarctica* (Washington, D.C.: U.S. Antarctic Projects Office, 1959).

10. National Intelligence Survey—Antarctica (NIS-69), (Central Intelligence Agency, 1956) pp. V-67 to V-69. U.S. Department of State, *Foreign Relations of the United States, 1948,* vol. 1, pp. 997–1001. See New York Times Index for 1948, for the responses of Chile, Great Britain, Australia and Norway.

11. Memorandum, The Embassy of the Soviet Union to the Department of State, *Foreign Relations of the United States, 1950,* vol. 1, pp. 911–913.

12. An excellent readable account of the origins and politics of the IGY, and why the Antarctic was regarded as a unique scientific frontier, is Walter Sullivan, *Assault on the Unknown* (New York: McGraw-Hill, 1961).

13. Paul A. Siple, *90° South* (New York: G.P. Putnam's, 1959) p. 23.

14. See Sullivan, *Assault,* for the understandings during the IGY. The insertion of these in the treaty is described in Richard S. Lewis and Philip M. Smith, eds., *Frozen Future* (New York: Quadrangle Books, 1973).

15. Siple, *90° South.* Evidence of Ronne's claims made after U.S. policy was changed, for

example the one he made October 23, 1957, after the IGY began, is in the Dater list (see footnote 8).

16. Sullivan, *Assault,* pp. 325–331. References to asylum are in "Summary of Antarctic Policy Group (APG) Meetings," Office of Oceans and Polar Affairs, U.S. Department of State.

17. Though they are still classified by the State Department, daily summaries prepared for the American negotiators are found in Papers of Rear Admiral George Dufek, George Arents Research Library for Special Collections, Syracuse University, Syracuse, N.Y.

18. These efforts, including the participation of other governments in the early implementation of the regime, are described in "United States Policy and International Cooperation in Antarctica, Message from the President" (Washington, D.C.: U.S. Government Printing Office, 1964).

19. See "Message from the President," and U.S. Department of State, *Antarctic Treaty, Handbook of Measures in Furtherance of the Principles and Objectives of the Antarctic Treaty,* (1979). See also Lewis and Smith, *Frozen Future.*

20. A brief description of the ecosystem and its unique aspects is in John R. Beddington and Robert M. May, "The Harvesting of Interacting Species in a Natural Ecosystem," *Scientific American,* vol. 247, no. 5 (November 1982), p. 5 ff.

21. P.A. Moiseev, "Some Aspects of the Commercial Use of the Krill Resources of the Antarctic Seas," in Martin W. Holdgate, ed., *Antarctic Ecology* vol. 1 (London: The Academic Press for the Scientific Committee on Antarctic Research, 1970), pp. 213–216. The other papers in this volume stress the abundance of marine life, large volume of planktonic food, estimates of krill biomass, and related issues.

22. United Nations Food and Agriculture Organization, *Yearbook of Fishery Statistics, Catches and Landings* (Rome: Food and Agriculture Organization of the United Nations, 1979). FAO data also indicate large catches of Antarctic finfish, found mainly in the more temperate waters east of the Antarctic Peninsula and south of the Falkland Islands, in this period.

23. Barbara Mitchell and Richard J. Sandbrook, *The Management of the Southern Ocean* (London: International Institute for Environment and Development, 1980).

24. James N. Barnes, "The Emerging Convention on the Conservation of Antarctic Marine Living Resources: An Attempt to Meet the New Realities of Resource Exploitation in the Southern Ocean," in Jonathan I. Charney, ed., *The New Nationalism and the Use of Common Spaces* (Totowa, N.J.; Allanheld, Osmun, 1982).

25. Deborah Shapley, "Antarctica Up for Grabs," *Science 82,* vol. 3, no. 9 (November 1982), p. 75.

26. Two U.S. Geological Survey reports summarize the state of knowledge in the early 1970s and the present. These are: N.A. Wright and P.G. Williams, "Mineral Resources of Antarctica," Geological Survey Circular 705 (Reston, Virginia; USGS, 1974), and John C. Behrendt, ed., "Petroleum and Mineral Resources of Antarctica," Geological Survey Circular 909 (Alexandria, Va.: USGS, 1983).

27. Report of the meeting held at the Fridtjof Nansen Foundation, May 30–June 10, 1973, Polhogda, Norway. The unnamed claimant state was referred to by the British diplomat Brian B. Roberts, "International Cooperation for Antarctic Development: the Test for the Antarctic Treaty," *Polar Record,* vol. 19, no. 119 (May, 1978), p. 112 ff.

28. The moratorium story has been told only in part, in different places. The U.S. Antarctic negotiator, R. Tucker Scully, admitted in testimony that in effect it was U.S. reluctance which scotched the permanent moratorium within the treaty group. See *U.S. Antarctic Program,* Hearings before the Subcommittee on Science, Research, and Technology of the Committee on Science and Technology, U.S. House of Representatives, 96th Congress, 1st Session, May 1, 3, 1979.

29. Successive draft regimes have been leaked to the environmental press. This account is based on "Antarctic Minerals Regime: Beeby's Slick Solution," in *Eco,* vol. 23, no. 1, 1983.

30. R. Tucker Scully, "The Antarctic Mineral Resource Negotiations, A Report," U.S. Department of State, unpublished. July 1986. p. 27.

31. Ibid.

32. This history is described in testimony of Leigh Ratiner, *Law of the Sea Conference,* Hearings before the Subcommittee on Domestic and International Scientific Planning, Analysis and Cooperation, Committee on Science and Technology, U.S. House of Representatives, 95 Congress, 1st session, April 26–28, 1977, pp. 42–51.

33. See statement of Alvaro de Soto, Peruvian representative at the Law of the Sea negotiations, quoted in Barbara Mitchell and Richard Sandbrook, *The Management of the Southern Ocean* (London: International Institute for Environment and Development, 1980), p. 26.

34. See for example, Edward E. Honnold, "Thaw in International Law? Rights in Antarctica Under the Law of Common Spaces," *The Yale Law Journal,* vol. 87, no. 4 (March 1978): 804–859.

35. The state of the debate, as well as the ingenious ways in which it was conducted, is reflected in Robert Jones, "History in the Making at South Pole," *Los Angeles Times* (January 24, 1985). See also Deborah Shapley, "Delegates Debate Antarctic's Future," *New York Times* (January 29, 1985).

36. Deborah Shapley, "At the pole, fighting for a piece of the ice," *WorldPaper,* vol XII, no. 3 (March, 1986), p.8 ff.

37. Fernando Zegers Santa Cruz, "El Sistema Antartico y la Utilizatione de los Recursos," *University of Miami Law Review,* vol. 33, no 2 (December, 1978). See also R. Tucker Scully, "Alternatives for Cooperation and Institutionalization in Antarctica: Outlook for the 1990's." (Presented at Teniente Marsh Station, Antarctica, October 1982).

38. F.M. Auburn, *Antarctic Law and Politics* (London: C. Hurst, 1982). Also "257 Believed Killed as DC-10 Crashes on Antarctic Peak," *New York Times* (November 29, 1979).

39. The details of the Soviet logistics effort in Antarctica and its attempt to rival the more air-intensive logistics presence of the United States, are in Shapley, *The Seventh Continent,* pp. 200–202.

40. They are interested. For example in February 1981, as the summer personnel prepared to leave and the wintering-over parties were readied, there were rumors in Antarctica that the United States, due to budget cuts in Washington, would shut down its South Pole station. One afternoon at the pole, the roar of an engine announced the arrival of an IL-14 aircraft which had flown partway across the continent to the pole from the Soviet station Druzhnaya. The Soviet visitors were, of course, welcomed by the Americans, shown around, fed, and then got back in their plane and departed, offering no explanation for their unannounced visit.

41. The Guzman proposal and U.S. use of it is in *Foreign Relations of the United States, 1950,* vol. 1, pp. 905–906, and *Foreign Relations of the United States, 1948,* vol.1, Pt. 2, pp. 962–1016.

42. This technology evolution is discussed in Deborah Shapley, "Pax Antarctica," *Bulletin of the Atomic Scientists,* (June/July 1984), p. 30–33.

43. Stephen D. Krasner, *Structural Conflict* (Berkeley, Calif.: University of California Press, 1985), pp. 244, 245.

44. Ibid., pp. 229–231.

14

U.S.–Soviet Cooperation in a Nonproliferation Regime

JOSEPH S. NYE, JR.

The large majority of states in the world today adhere to a set of norms that establish a presumption against the spread of nuclear weaponry. That most states adhere to a regime in which they foreswear the right to use the ultimate form of self-help in technological terms is quite an extraordinary situation.[1]

The beginnings of the current nonproliferation regime date back to 1953. In the aftermath of the failure of the Baruch Plan, and with it the international effort to totally restrict the control of nuclear technology, President Dwight D. Eisenhower launched his Atoms for Peace Program. This program was meant to assist countries in the development of nuclear energy in return for their guarantees that such assistance would be used only for peaceful purposes. The policy was oversold and poorly thought through in its execution at a time when too little was known about the likely pace and cost of peaceful nuclear development. Nonetheless, the central accomplishment of the Atoms for Peace Program was the creation of an institutional framework in the form of the International Atomic Energy Agency, established in 1957 with headquarters in Vienna. Under the IAEA safeguard system that was developed in the 1960s, non-weapon countries agreed to file with the Agency regular detailed reports on civilian nuclear activities and to allow international inspectors to visit their facilities to verify the reports and to ensure there had been no diversion of materials from peaceful to military purposes.

This regime was further developed and strengthened by the signing in 1968 of the Non-Proliferation Treaty. This treaty originated in a 1958 Irish proposal in the United Nations that was repeated through the early 1960s. Eight significant countries—Argentina, Brazil, China, France, India, Israel, Pakistan, South Africa—have refused to sign the NPT, usually on grounds that it is a discriminatory treaty. Of the eight, France, it is worth noting, has indicated that it will not undercut the purposes of the treaty. In Latin America a regional treaty limiting nuclear weapons, the 1967 Treaty of Tlatelolco, helped to fill the normative gap. Skeptics have dismissed the NPT as a modern equivalent of the infamous Kellogg-Briand antiwar pact, since any state can simply quit on three months' notice. Other detractors have argued that the treaty is imperfectly drafted and involves promises that cannot fully be kept. Third World states have complained that the weapons states have not fulfilled their obligations to transfer technology or to curb their own arsenals. Nonetheless, by establishing a normative presumption against proliferation and by creating procedures to verify intentions, the NPT has helped to build confidence and a degree of predictability in states' behavior. While the nonproliferation regime is a multilateral framework, it also provides an interesting example of U.S. and Soviet cooperation in the security area.

At first glance, slowing the spread of nuclear weapons looks like an easy case for U.S. and Soviet cooperation. In a multilateral context, both superpowers have an interest in maintaining their nuclear preponderance. Thus skeptics might argue that there is not much to learn from analyzing U.S.–Soviet efforts to cooperate in slowing the spread of nuclear weapons. Such a quick dismissal, however, would be too facile on several counts.

Cooperation on nonproliferation, like many other areas, is a mixed motive game involving elements of both cooperation and competition. The positive sum and zero sum aspects of the game are tightly intertwined. Even when cooperation can produce a Pareto optimal solution, there can still be zero sum competition about the place of final equilibrium on the contract curve. Although the United States and the Soviet Union share a common interest in maintaining a nuclear duopoly, that interest need not be symmetrical. For example, some American analysts have suggested that we should make the Soviets pay a higher price for cooperation in nonproliferation because most of the new entrants into the nuclear category will target their weapons primarily on the Soviet Union.[2] Moreover, measures to slow the spread of nuclear weapons can be costly in terms of relations with other countries. Thus it is not surprising that even in the current well-developed phase of U.S.–Soviet cooperation in this area, discussion is easier about general issues than about specific hard cases. It is more difficult for the Soviets to discuss Libya and Cuba, or for the United States to discuss Pakistan and Israel, than it is to get agreement on new guidelines for restricting nuclear exports.

Another puzzle for the skeptics is why, if cooperation in this area is so obvious and so easy, did it take so long to develop? It was nearly two decades after both countries had the bomb before they signed a nonproliferation treaty. The skeptics fail to ask how national interests were defined and changed over time. For example, in the 1950s both countries gave a relatively low priority to nonproliferation. That priority began to increase in the late 1950s and early 1960s. But each country's first efforts to deal with proliferation were unilateral rather than cooperative. Only after those unilateral efforts failed did they begin to define an interest in cooperating to slow the spread of nuclear weapons. Moreover, the changing political context of loosening bipolarity and concern over allies as well as the developing political interest in partial détente played important roles in the redefinition of interests. In short, the proliferation case can help us to understand how nations learn.

Finally, it is important to look at how cooperation may change after agreement has been reached. One of the interesting aspects of the proliferation case is the evolution of cooperation and its institutionalization. After the nonproliferation treaty was signed in 1968, both nations relaxed the priority that they gave to the issue. Nonetheless, during the 1970s they developed an impressive degree of cooperation and developed institutions for maintaining that cooperation.[3] These features of the regime survived the return of renewed hostility in U.S.–Soviet relations in the early 1980s. Scholars who have looked at the literature on regimes in economic interdependence have tended to dismiss its relevance to security issues.[4] In part this is because they have focused too simply on the overall nature of the U.S.–Soviet security relationship. Had they separated security issues into various subissues, they might have noted more significant developments in international regimes. The nonproliferation case is a good example of the development of an international security regime as a subissue of the overall U.S.–Soviet relationship.

EFFORTS TO REACH AGREEMENT

One of the reasons for the slow development of cooperation between the United States and the Soviet Union in nonproliferation was the difference in technological capability and the resultant differences in the perception of how proliferation relates to the overall U.S.–Soviet relationship. After all, the first American nonproliferation plan, the Baruch Plan of 1946, was universal in form, but would have had the practical effect of preventing the Soviet Union from developing their bomb. Not too surprisingly, the Soviets launched a counter proposal in the United Nations.[5] The Americans developed the bomb first and severely underestimated the time it would take the Soviets to catch up. Stalin was determined to match the American capability. While the Soviets tested a thermonuclear device in 1953, it was not until 1955 that they developed a full-scale hydrogen bomb.[6] For much of the first decade of the nuclear era, Soviets were busy becoming the first "proliferator."

William Potter has suggested that the United States and the Soviet Union have gone through similar periods in their nuclear export policy.[7] Both went through a period of secrecy and denial until 1953, then an "Atoms for Peace" phase (1954 to 1974 for the United States, but only to 1958 for the Soviet Union), and then both entered a technology control period lasting to 1980. The major difference is that the Soviets switched from nuclear sharing to technology control in 1958 because of China's efforts to build a bomb, while the United States did not switch to technology control until after India's explosion of 1974. In both cases the definition of policy interest was redefined after a Third World country made significant progress toward nuclear weaponry. This calls to mind the aphorism of a French nuclear official who once told me that "each nation makes one big mistake before it learns its interest in nonproliferation; the Soviet lesson was China, the French lesson was Israel, and the American lesson was India."

While this periodization is a useful approach to nuclear export policy, it is not fine-grained enough to explain the politics of nonproliferation before the NPT. An alternative description of phases is presented in Table 1.

TABLE 1. Policy Phases Before the NPT

	U.S.	*USSR*
1. Unilateral restriction	1946–53	1949–54
2. Share with allies	1954–60	1954–58
3. Control ally by confronting opponent	—	1958–63
4. Balance alliance sharing and global norms	1961–66	—
5. Global regime as solution	1966–68	1963–68

After the failure of the Baruch Plan, the United States followed a policy of restriction and secrecy to prevent the spread of nuclear technology. For example, the Atomic Energy Act of 1946 went so far as to curtail cooperation with America's wartime ally, Britain. American policy entered a new phase at the end of 1953. Eisenhower's Atoms for Peace program was to make fissionable materials available under international control and thus check the spread of nuclear weaponry. But the Atoms for Peace proposal was also designed to advance America's interest in its political competition with the Soviet Union. By stressing the peaceful role of the atom, the United States hoped to counter Soviet propaganda that sought to delegitimize American nuclear weapons. Indeed, a key feature of American policy from 1954 to 1960 was the sharing of nuclear defense capability with our NATO allies. Except in the case of Britain (after it had already become a weapons state), this sharing related to the deployment and control of American weapons rather than to the design of independent weapons. Nonetheless, in William Bader's description, the Eisenhower Administration "placed a higher premium on nuclear weapons cooperation with our allies—even at the price of encouraging and stimulating independent atomic weapons programs—than it did on seeking international agreements retarding the spread of nuclear weapons." Until at least 1958, the United States believed that the Atoms for Peace approach to the control of fissionable materials and technological barriers to independent programs would prevent what John Foster Dulles called "promiscuous spread."[8] Thus America could design NATO nuclear defenses as it saw fit. In 1953, the first American nuclear artillery were deployed in Europe. In 1955, the Atomic Energy Act was loosened to permit NATO allies to have information on the external characteristics of nuclear weapons and training in their use. In 1957, Dulles reassured NATO that "if war comes, they will not be in a position of supplicants, as far as we are concerned, for the use of atomic weapons."[9]

In 1958 the Act was loosened again to permit the transfer of fissionable materials and sensitive information to allies. After Sputnik, there were fears of a Soviet missile gap advantage and Eisenhower worried about the pressures on the defense budget. Allied nuclear sharing was seen as an inexpensive way to offset the rising Soviet threat. In Eisenhower's words, it was wasteful for "Allies to expend talent and money in solving problems that their friends have already solved—all because of artificial barriers to sharing." Nonetheless, the American Congress was "considerably more conservative and skeptical over extending the areas of atomic cooperation than the White House." Thus, Congress restricted the sharing of sensitive information to allies who had already "made substantial progress," in other words, to Britain. A meeting between John Foster Dulles and General Charles de Gaulle in June 1958 left the French leader with the impression that the United States would not fully share nuclear technology with the French.[10]

At the same time the United States hoped to restore European confidence by deploying intermediate range ballistic missiles (Thor and Jupiter) in Europe with release authority given to NATO commanders. In addition, changes in the technology of delivery systems were creating what George Quester called "de facto proliferation in Europe."[11] Long-range NATO aircraft equipped with American nuclear weapons were stationed in European countries under so-called "dual control," but in many cases the only thing standing between a German pilot's capability to take off and drop an American nuclear weapon on the Soviet Union without authorization was a single American sentry who could easily be overcome. As Bader describes it, in the 1950s the United States "put flexibility in the use of our nuclear weapons above the first fretful international efforts to erect barriers to the acquisition of nuclear weapons."[12]

Soviet policy in the 1950s went through similar phases but in foreshortened form. After a period of restriction, the Soviets followed the American lead by sharing with its allies. They went further than the Americans by transferring design information to China, but they learned their lesson and drew back more quickly. In July 1954 the Soviet Union declared that it was willing to share for peaceful purposes both within the Soviet bloc and beyond. But this would be "true sharing," not conditional on military and political restrictions involving inspection.[13] In 1954, a Sino-Soviet science and technology commission was established and in October 1957 the Soviet Union signed a defense agreement that involved helping China to develop a nuclear weapon.[14] At the same time the Soviet Union was using devices such as the Rapacki Plan to discourage the proliferation of nuclear weapons to Germany. The Soviet need for Chinese support in the aftermath of events that shook the Soviet system in 1956 may help to explain the contradiction between Soviet proliferation policy in the East and in the West in 1957.[15] Subsequently the Soviets approached China with proposals for bases and joint military command structures. In April 1958 they even proposed a joint fleet. They hoped to control Chinese weapons through military cooperation. They may also have hoped that a test ban might help to ease their dilemma. But the Soviets met Chinese resistance to all such proposals, and in May the Chinese announced their intention to acquire their own nuclear weapons. According to Lambeth, the turning point in Soviet policy was the Taiwan Strait crisis of 1958. Ironically, Nikita Khrushchev's bravado bluff about gaining superiority over the West encouraged Mao to ask for Soviet support in recapturing the offshore islands in the Taiwan Strait.[16] In his memoirs, Khrushchev complains that Mao backed down but Khrushchev's caution in reserving his threats until the crisis had peaked shows that he had no intention of risking nuclear war for Chinese goals. Whether this incident affected Soviet views by raising the prospect of catalytic war launched by a nuclear ally is uncertain.[17] Sino-Soviet nuclear cooperation was not abrogated until June 1959. Khrushchev later justified his action as a response to a Chinese "smear campaign" and territorial claims. When he finally reneged on his promise to provide a sample bomb to the Chinese, Khrushchev said the atomic weapon was all packed up and ready to go.[18]

The end of the nuclear agreement accentuated the Soviets' proliferation dilemma. How could they restore control over their Chinese ally and also prevent the spread of nuclear weapons to Germany? Cooperation with the United States might help in Europe but would have weakened their efforts to renew control over the Chinese. It might have also required costly political concessions to the West. Faced with this dilemma, Khrushchev adopted a confrontational rather than a cooperative strategy for his new nonproliferation policy. Tension with the United States would help solidify the Eastern bloc alliance, and, as he put it in his memoirs, Berlin was a "blister" that he could step on to pain the Americans. He could trade stability in the status of Berlin for Western assurances that the Federal Republic of Germany would not get nuclear weapons. According to this analysis, it is no accident that the Berlin Crisis of autumn 1958 followed so closely after Khrushchev's failure to support his Chinese ally earlier in the summer.[19] This also helps to explain Khrushchev's 1959 proposal of the Far East nonnuclear zone as a means to constrain China, while at the same time the Soviets were very shy about discussing proliferation publicly in the United Nations as a universal problem. Despite the failure to alter Chinese policy, Khrushchev pretended that there were no problems between the Soviet Union and China during his 1959 meetings with Eisenhower.

In March 1960, after General Lauris Norstad announced a plan for integrating nuclear forces with the ultimate objective of making NATO a nuclear power in its own right, the Soviet ambassador delivered a protest to Eisenhower threatening similar Soviet behavior. However, the Soviets withdrew their nuclear experts from China in the middle of the year. After the election of President John F. Kennedy in 1960, Khrushchev continued his confrontational policy. He may have hoped that a diplomatic victory over the United States would help him with China and Germany at the same time. When John McCloy visited Moscow in July 1961, Khrushchev continually raised the issue of German nuclear weapons. At the same time the Soviets resisted U.S. multilateral approaches such as the Test Ban Treaty and developing safeguards at the International Atomic Energy Agency (IAEA). In fact they derided the test ban as a nonproliferation instrument, arguing that Germany would get weapons by transfer from the United States, not by testing its own.[20]

Khrushchev heightened the tension in 1961 with the Berlin Wall and resumption of particularly large nuclear tests. Nonetheless, at the United Nations the United States and the Soviet Union both voted for the first time in favor of the Irish resolution supporting nonproliferation. In July 1962 Soviet Ambassador Valerian Zorin told the Eighteen Nation Disarmament Conference of the United Nations (ENDC) that nonproliferation "cannot be discussed in an abstract fashion. It is primarily the question of the spread of nuclear weapons to West Germany."[21] In the East, the Soviet Union was trying to create a rapprochement with China by offering trade agreements, jet planes, and subdued rhetoric. In August, Khrushchev raised the prospect of a nonproliferation agreement with the Chinese, but was rebuffed. At the same time the first Soviet medium range ballistic missiles were being sent to Cuba. Khrushchev's motives are still unclear. At least one Sovietologist, Adam Ulam, argues that Khrushchev sent the missiles to Cuba not to redress the balance of nuclear power, but to create something to be traded for a Berlin agreement. Such a diplomatic victory would, in turn, help deprive the Germans of nuclear weapons, and impress the Chinese with Soviet leadership.[22]

Whatever Khrushchev's motives may have been, the Cuban missile crisis proved to be a turning point in U.S.–Soviet cooperation on nonproliferation policy. The confrontational approach had failed. China was proceeding toward a nuclear explosion and the Americans were proceeding with plans to share nuclear capabilities with their NATO allies. Under these circumstances the Soviets turned to détente as a new tactic. In March 1963 the Soviets officially protested the American plans to go forward with a multilateral force for NATO (MLF), but to no avail. By June they reversed their policy of opposing American efforts to reach agreement on international inspections by the IAEA, and in the summer they agreed to the establishment of the Hotline and quickly negotiated a Limited Test Ban Treaty with the United States.[23]

China's explosion of a nuclear device in 1964 relieved the Soviets of at least part of their dilemma over reconciling their Eastern and Western nonproliferation policy.[24] Henceforth they would try to seek by détente and diplomatic cooperation at least part of what had eluded them in their confrontational nonproliferation policy. From 1964 to 1968, the Soviets sought a nonproliferation treaty as a means of curtailing NATO nuclear cooperation and particularly German access to nuclear capabilities. Much of the diplomacy from 1964 on, when the ENDC began to work on proliferation on a steady rather than an occasional basis, consisted of German efforts to gain some concessions for foreswearing nuclear weapons and Soviet efforts to grant nothing to the Germans and to weaken Germany's political position with NATO. But lest the German question be seen as the sole Soviet interest in nonproliferation, it is worth noting Heikal's testimony that the Soviets did not respond to Nasser's efforts to gain Chinese support for developing nuclear capabilities.[25]

American policy in the early 1960s is a story of gradual transition in priority from NATO sharing to global nonproliferation norms. The United States had always been concerned about proliferation, but "during the fifties, the restrictive spirit of the

McMahon Act was gradually eroded.'' Some in the military believed nuclear weapons ''were inevitably the means of modern warfare and that political restriction on their use constituted an inconvenient and even dangerous impediment to military operations.''[26] American policy during the early 1960s was an effort to control nonproliferation by balancing NATO sharing with global nonproliferation norms. After the French explosion in 1960, there was fear that Germany would be tempted to follow suit. This could be forestalled by giving Germany a sense of greater participation in sharing in NATO nuclear planning.

The first signs of a switch in priority from NATO sharing to a more balanced approach antedate the 1960 election. In the late 1950s, the Joint Committee on Atomic Energy became concerned about the lax control over American weapons in allied countries. The Kennedy Administration moved to develop and install Permissive Action Links (electronic combination locks) to increase control over such weapons.[27] Also in the late 1950s, some of the State Department officials who developed the idea of a multilateral force (MLF) thought of NATO sharing less as a means of enhancing military capabilities than as a means of reassuring the Germans and thus heading off their incentives for proliferation. This approach became more important after the election. In May 1961 Kennedy referred to a European seaborne force as a possible nonproliferation measure. After the Cuban missile crisis and the meeting with Harold Macmillan at Nassau in late 1962, Kennedy advanced the MLF as a device for solving the European nuclear problem. When he encountered European (particularly French) resistance, he downgraded the priority but did not entirely drop the MLF approach, and many State Department officials continued to give the MLF a top priority. While Americans saw the MLF as a means of reconciling their nonproliferation and alliance objectives, the Soviets bitterly opposed it.

Kennedy, like Eisenhower before him, also saw the test ban as in part a nonproliferation measure. Averell Harriman was instructed to raise the prospects of Chinese adherence to the test ban during his talks in Moscow. Khrushchev, however, was not willing to discuss China at that point. Kennedy agreed to a quick resolution of the test ban issue despite the absence of time for prolonged consultation with allies. President Lyndon Johnson continued Kennedy's policy, gradually switching U.S. priority from NATO sharing to a nonproliferation treaty. But as late as the American draft treaty of August 1965, the United States was not willing to foreclose for all time the possibility of a European or NATO nuclear force.[28] As Arthur Dean put it in 1966, ''Washington has apparently not as yet decided that the time is right for a supreme and unconditional effort to win an antiproliferation agreement.''[29]

In 1966 during a political debate, Franz Joseph Strauss asked Robert Kennedy, ''NATO or Geneva? What is your priority?''[30] By the end of the year, President Johnson had settled on Geneva. There was still jockeying over diplomatic details. A section of the U.S.–Soviet joint draft referring to safeguards was left open because of the difficulties of reconciling the Euratom safeguards arrangements with the new NPT plans. The United States strongly supported West European integration and did not want to undercut the role of Euratom in inspecting West European facilities. But a compromise was reached in the joint draft of early 1968, and the treaty was signed in July.[31] With the signing of the NPT, the Soviets also agreed to the talks on strategic weapons that Johnson had suggested in 1967.

The final diplomatic compromises were facilitated by the increased interest in détente both in the United States and in the Federal Republic of Germany. The entry of the Social Democratic Party into a grand coalition brought to German foreign policy the hope of easing the reunification problem by building bridges and increasing engagement rather than by trying to bargain for reunification as a reward for foreswearing nuclear weapons. In short, détente and the loosening of diplomatic bipolarity eased the American dilemma of balancing alliance interests and pursuing global nonproliferation norms, just as the defection of China from the Soviet alliance had resolved the earlier Soviet dilemma. In that sense the NPT was facilitated by two major trends of the 1960s: the Sino-Soviet split and the development of European détente.[32] These developments allowed the superpowers to redefine their interests by relaxing the constraints imposed upon them as alliance leaders.

In the late 1950s and early 1960s, both countries became more concerned about the dangers posed by the spread of nuclear weaponry and redefined their interests to give nonproliferation a higher policy priority. But in the early 1960s both countries were constrained by an equally high priority of alliance maintenance demands. In the changed setting of the late 1960s, the relaxation of these constraints allowed them to agree on formal norms for achieving their nonproliferation interests. The role of détente in advancing cooperation was not to create goodwill or trust so much as to permit the relaxation of these alliance constraints. Détente was an instrument in the continuing larger political competition. In metaphoric terms, détente was not a new volcanic force of trust thrusting an island of cooperation above the sea of hostility in the Cold War era. Rather it was a tactical lowering of the level of hostility to allow a submerged island of common interest to appear.

Another way of making the point is to survey the efforts at bilateral cooperation. In 1957 Harold Stassen believed that the Soviets might be willing to discuss the nonproliferation issue. He tabled a talking paper at the London Disarmament Conference that suggested that all except three nations be prohibited from manufacturing or using nuclear weapons. This proposal did not address transfer of weapons through NATO. It also irritated the British who complained to Eisenhower that it would inhibit the development of their capability. Eisenhower reassured the British and interpreted the Soviet rejection as a lack of interest in what he called the "fourth country problem."[33] Also in 1957, the IAEA, which had been proposed in the Atoms for Peace speech, was established within the U.N. system. The Soviets joined, but they tended to support Indian and Third World positions that prevented development of significant agency safeguards capabilities until after the Cuban missile crisis. Test ban talks were held in 1958, but they were unsuccessful. In 1958 Ireland first proposed a nonproliferation resolution in the United Nations that the United States refused to support because it would have blocked any transfer of nuclear information. Thirty-seven countries supported the resolution, including the Soviet Union, and 44 abstained, including the United States. In 1959 the United States voted in favor of a slightly different Irish resolution but the Soviet Union (and France) abstained. In 1960, the positions were reversed again. The Soviets supported a slightly different Irish resolution and the United States (and France) abstained. Not until 1961 did both countries vote for the same Irish resolution, but as we have seen, this did not really signify an underlying change of policy in the direction of cooperation. Neither did bilateral talks in 1961 and 1962 lead to significant changes in policy. It was only after the change from confrontation to limited détente, in 1963, that the basis was set for cooperation on nonproliferation. Even then, the multilateral talks in the ENDC from 1964 to 1966 made little progress until détente eroded the bipolar diplomatic constraints that had previously inhibited cooperation.

IMPLEMENTING THE AGREEMENT

Ironically, one of the first effects of agreement on the nonproliferation treaty was to lower the priority given to the issue of nonproliferation in both countries. To the extent that the NPT tied down the West Germans, a major source of Soviet concern about proliferation had been relaxed. In the United States, the Nixon Administration was critical of the extent to which its predecessor had damaged alliance relationships on "the altar of the NPT." There was a feeling that the United States had been too dogmatic in its approach to nonproliferation. Faced with nonnuclear weapon states' complaint of discrimination, both superpowers wished to avoid damaging their bilateral relations with such countries. For example, they did not cooperate on pressing difficult cases such as India for adherence to the NPT.

On the other hand, cooperation in more technical areas was enhanced by the agreement. The role of the IAEA in promoting safeguards was further strengthened and a committee (the Zangger Committee) met from 1971 to 1974 to develop a trigger list of items that would require safeguards. Both the United States and the Soviet Union participated in the Zangger committee, but it did not deal with restriction of sensitive exports such as enrichment and reprocessing plants.

Several events in the period 1973–74 dealt shocks to the fledgling nonproliferation regime, and had an especially strong impact on American policy. The first was India's explosion of a nuclear device in 1974, using a Canadian research reactor and heavy water supplied by the United States under the Atoms for Peace program. The Indians proceeded with their explosion despite a unilateral American interpretation that it was not permitted under the existing agreement for cooperation between the United States and India. Though the Nixon Administration did not respond very strongly to the Indian explosion, the American Congress was quite incensed by what it regarded as India's violation of the spirit and perhaps the letter of the agreement for cooperation.[34]

A second event was the energy crisis of 1973–74. The quadrupling of oil prices in the aftermath of the 1973 Middle East War led to exaggerated projections of demand for nuclear energy. There were widespread views that uranium would be in short supply and that it would be necessary to extract plutonium from spent fuel to run power reactors. The projections of widespread reprocessing and commercial trade in plutonium (a weapons-useable fuel) caused alarm because of the inadequacy of the current IAEA capabilities for safeguarding such facilities. The prospect loomed of the entire elaborate structure of international safeguards breaking down.[35]

The third shock was related to the second. France and Germany both announced plans for significant exports of sensitive nuclear facilities that could be used to produce nuclear weapons materials. France announced the sale of reprocessing plants to South Korea and to Pakistan (which, it was later discovered, did intend to use them for developing nuclear weapons), and Germany announced a massive plan to supply reactors, enrichment plants, and reprocessing facilities to Brazil. This German-Brazilian deal threatened the Argentines, who advanced their plans to develop sensitive nuclear facilities.

In this context and in the face of growing Congressional and public concern, the State Department proposed in late 1974 that the major nuclear supplier nations meet in London to discuss the situation. Seven supplier nations (later expanded to fifteen) met to discuss conditions for transferring nuclear supplies. The suppliers eventually agreed on such measures as safeguards on all transferred materials, restrictions on the export of sensitive facilities such as enrichment and reprocessing plants, a promise not to undercut one another's efforts at sanctions, and promise of consultation in future cases. One of the interesting points about the suppliers' group meetings was that the United States and the Soviet Union often found themselves in closer rapport on policy positions than the United States did with its allies France and Germany. This gave the Soviets a splendid opportunity for provoking difficulties, but in September 1977 when the United States decided to compromise with the French and Germans by not requiring full-scope safeguards in order to get agreement on a set of guidelines that could be forwarded to the IAEA, the Soviet Union resisted the temptation to cause trouble and instead acquiesced in the compromise. The United States held regular bilateral meetings with the Soviet Union (as it did with other member countries) in the context of these supplier group meetings.

The Soviets were not merely responding to American initiatives. On the contrary, it appears that the same three events were forcing them to reevaluate their own policy. Previously, the Soviets had taken care of their own by requiring the return of spent fuel from the reactors they exported to Eastern Europe. Their initial reaction to the Indian explosion was as mild as that of the Nixon Administration. However, the prospects of a Pakistani bomb and concern about the German-Brazilian deal seemed to stimulate a more active approach. They cooperated with the United States in preparing for the 1975 NPT Review Conference and resisted temptations to play for Third World popularity. Subsequently, in 1976–77, they insisted on stringent safeguards on a sale of heavy water to India.[36]

Early in 1977 the new Carter Administration found itself involved in diplomatic imbroglios with Germany and France as it sought to reverse the Brazilian and Pakistan deals. The Administration also encountered trouble with Japan when its agreement for cooperation required approval for reprocessing in a new plant the Japanese were building, while at home it had taken steps to refuse permission to develop a commercial reprocessing plant in South Carolina. U.S. approval for the Japanese project was withheld at first, but later granted. A number of nonnuclear weapons states were also resentful of the restrictions imposed by the nuclear suppliers' guidelines, and by the tightened American restrictions being discussed by the Congress for the Nuclear Nonproliferation Act that subsequently passed in 1978.

The State Department devised a plan for an international nuclear fuel cycle evaluation (INFCE) to address the various dimensions of how research and commercial nuclear facilities might be involved in the proliferation of nuclear weapons. INFCE was a considerable success. Sixty-six countries and organizations came together in Vienna between 1977 and 1979, including consumers and suppliers, both rich and poor, East and West, and, most important, a dozen countries that had not signed the NPT. In all, some 519 experts from 46 countries participated in 61 meetings of 8 working groups producing 20,000 pages of documents. As a diplomatic device, INFCE helped to reestablish a basis for consensus on a more cautious approach to the nuclear fuel cycle. INFCE helped the U.S. government set the agenda for other governments, and helped to defuse the dispute between the United States and its allies.

The Soviet Union could have been disruptive in the INFCE context as a means of exacerbating American problems with its allies but chose not to be. The Soviets were not much worried about fuel cycle problems. They believed in the development of plutonium for breeder reactors and did not share the United States' concern, in part because they required the return of spent fuel from their Eastern bloc allies. Despite the fact that fuel cycle issues were not a high priority for the Soviets, they resisted the temptation to play a disruptive role and in fact were quite cooperative both in chairing an important working group and in the plenary sessions. Moreover, INFCE provided an opportunity for regular bilateral U.S.–Soviet consultations in the context of its meetings.

In addition to the bilateral meetings that took place in the context of supplier group, INFCE, and IAEA board meetings, special bilaterals were held in June 1977 and July 1978. These had been agreed upon by Secretary of State Cyrus Vance and Foreign Secretary Andrei Gromyko in March 1977. Particular problem countries were discussed in such bilaterals, though the depth of discussion of hard cases was often limited by the competitive nature of the political relationship. One striking exception, however, was the case of South Africa.

In August 1977 a Soviet reconnaissance satellite discovered a suspicious drilling site in the Kalahari desert that looked like a nuclear test site. The Soviets notified the United States of what it had found and where to look. The Americans confirmed the Soviet siting and entered a period of intense bilateral diplomacy with South Africa in which President Carter extracted a South African pledge not to go ahead with a nuclear test. The situation on the ground, as seen from reconnaissance satellites, remained ambiguous from the Soviet point of view. They had to take the American word on any progress. A certain amount of information was shared with the Soviets, but intelligence sources and methods placed limits on what could be shared. Faced with criticism by African states in the United Nations, the Soviets were tempted to take a disruptive stand in support of U.N. resolutions that would interfere with American efforts to persuade the South Africans to hold back on their nuclear program. In the ad hoc bilaterals, the Americans pleaded for Soviet restraint on supporting some of the most extreme U.N. sanctions resolutions, and the Soviet Union complied.

As Table 2 by William Potter shows, a rich web of contacts in various settings arose in the nonproliferation area in the latter half of the 1970s.[37]

The rise of renewed hostility in the late 1970s and early 1980s caused concern that the nonproliferation regime might be disrupted. In 1978 in reprisal for human rights jailings in the Soviet Union, President Carter halted a science and technology mission to the Soviet Union. This did not, however, interfere with nonproliferation discussions. After the Soviet invasion of Afghanistan in December 1979, however, consultations became more difficult to arrange. Moreover, the incoming Reagan Administration had an even more suspicious view of the Soviet Union, and of some of the global political programs of its predecessor. As a candidate, Reagan announced that nonproliferation was not any of our business, and during the first six months of the Reagan Administration the issue was given low priority. According to National Security Council officials, the Israeli raid on an Iraqi reactor in June 1981 raised the proliferation issue to a higher priority for the new Administration.[38] Now it was a question that could affect other security interests. Nonetheless, there was no rush to reinstitute regular bilateral consultations with the Soviet Union. Some rather technical issues were discussed in the context of IAEA board meetings, but many of the difficult cases were not addressed. Moreover in 1982, when Arab countries at the IAEA general conference proposed a resolution that would have expelled Israel from the organization, the United States withdrew from the general conference and withheld part of its annual contribution on the grounds that the organization had become too politicized. During this time, the Soviet Union supported the Arab position.

In the fall of 1982, however, during the Shultz-Gromyko talks at the United Nations, both countries agreed that their interest in maintaining the nonproliferation regime would be best served by establishing semiannual bilateral meetings.[39] Such meetings between Ambassador-at-Large for Nonproliferation Richard Kennedy and his Soviet counterparts have been held at roughly six-month intervals since December 1982. These consultations last several days and cover a wide range of issues. In the words of a high level participant, "Our early discussions were somewhat rigid regarding the hard cases, but after seven or eight meetings, they have become more frank. They now give us detailed information, and when they bring up our hard cases, it is not in the old rhetorical way. The talks definitely improved with time."[40]

Since that time there have been a number of cases of Soviet cooperation and/or restraint. For example, at the 1983 IAEA general conference, the Soviets moderated their support for the Arab condemnation of Israel's attack on the Iraqi reactor. In 1982 the Soviets followed the American example of making a voluntary offer to put some of their commercial nuclear facilities under IAEA safeguards as a means of proving to nonnuclear weapons states that IAEA safeguards do not impose an unhealthy burden on commercial nuclear activity. At the end of 1983, when the Soviet Union walked out of other arms control talks in protest of NATO's decision to go forward with the deployment of intermediate range nuclear missiles in Europe, they did not interrupt the bilateral talks on nonproliferation.

The 1985 nonproliferation treaty review conference provided another opportunity for the Soviet Union to reap short-run diplomatic gains at the cost of the nonproliferation regime. The Soviet Union had announced its support of a comprehensive test ban, a measure that many of the nonnuclear weapons states regarded as a litmus test for seriousness about compliance with Article 6 (reducing superpower arsenals) of the NPT. The United States had announced that it had put CTB negotiations on a back burner and was distinctly uninterested in the more recent Soviet offer. But before the conference, in an intensive series of diplomatic contacts, both official and unofficial, the Soviet Union agreed that it would not be in the interest of the nonproliferation regime for the two superpowers to use the review conference to embarrass each other and thereby provide ammunition to nonnuclear weapons states that might be interested in wrecking the regime.[41]

CONCLUSIONS: THE ROLE OF THE REGIME

The rediscovery of cooperation on nonproliferation by the United States and the Soviet Union in the early 1980s, when other areas of security cooperation were disrupted and when the rhetoric surrounding the overall relationship between the two countries had become particularly harsh, suggests that the institutionalization of a regime in which there are explicit norms and multiple opportunities for contact may help to preserve an area of cooperation when the overall climate has turned sour. The multilateral nature of the regime probably helps. It provides opportunities for meeting without an explicit bilateral initiative. The universal nature of the norms helps to stress areas in which cooperation is possible, rather than only the hard cases. The multilateral nature of the contact also allows intra-issue coalitions to develop, with the United States and the Soviets on the same side rather than in strict opposition to each other on all issues.

The legal and political obligations that each country has undertaken in the context of the regime seem to have given greater predictability to its behavior and therefore

TABLE 2. Fora for U.S.–Soviet Consultation on Nonproliferation Issues During the Ford, Carter, and Reagan Administrations

Forum	Administration	Frequency	Focus	Remarks
Zangger Committee	Ford Carter Reagan	1/yr.*	Export guidelines	Set up in 1970. Last met in June 1983. Continues to be chaired by Zangger. Relatively dormant between 1977 and 1981. More active in 1982 and 1983.
London Suppliers Group	Ford (1975–76) Carter (1977–78)		Export guidelines	First met in 1975. Has not met since 1978.
INFCE	Carter (1977–80)	3 plenary conference meetings and 61 working group meetings	Nuclear fuel cycle	
Threshold Test Ban and PNE Negotiations	Ford (1974–76)		Nuclear test limitations	
CTB	Carter (1977–80)		Nuclear test limitations	
IAEA Board of Governors	Ford (1974–76) Carter (1977–80) Reagan (1981–84)	4/yr.		Usually involves lower-level representation than General Conference
IAEA General Conference	Ford (1974–76) Carter (1977–80) Reagan (1981–84)	1/yr.		Very important forum for U.S.–Soviet consultation. Usually involves lengthy review of wide range of proliferation issues.
IAEA Experts Consultant Groups** 1. International Spent Fuel Management	June 1979 to July 1982			
2. International Plutonium Storage	1st convened September 1978; concluded at end of 1982			
3. Committee for Assurances of Supply	1st convened June 1980			
Scientific Advisory Committee of the Director General of IAEA	Ford (1974–76) Carter (1977–80) Reagan (1981–83)		Discussions of technical issues	

Forum/Committee	Administration (dates)	Subject	Notes
Joint Committee established by the U.S.–Soviet Agreement for Cooperation in Atomic Energy	Carter (1977–79) Reagan (1983–84)		Meetings ceased after 1979 Soviet invasion of Afghanistan. Agreement was renewed in summer 1983.
UN General Assembly and First Committee of the UN (Political and Security)			
NPT Review Conference	Ford (May 1975) Carter (August 1980)		
Ad hoc	Carter (March 1977)		Vance discussed holding meeting on proliferation with Soviets when he presented Carter's comprehensive arms control proposals.
	Carter (June 1977)		1st meeting held to follow-up March 1977 proposal. Chaired by Warnke and Nye (U.S.), Morokhov (USSR).
	Carter (August and September 1977)	South Africa	Exchange of intelligence information regarding South African nuclear test site. Discussions at Ambassadorial level.
	Carter (May 1978)	South Africa	Nye and Timerbaev met in Geneva
	Reagan (December 1982, June, 1983, February 1984)	IAEA, Export Controls NPT Review Conference	Kennedy and Morozov met in Washington, D.C. (1982). Kennedy and Petrosyants met in Moscow (1983) and Vienna (1984)
Embassy to Embassy (in some Nth countries)			

*Chairman may call additional meetings and has done so in past.

**The United States ceased to participate in these meetings following the IAEA vote to withdraw Israel's credentials at the September 1982 General Conference. In February 1983, after a five-month reassessment of its participation, the United States announced its intention to resume participation at an "early, appropriate date." It resumed participation that same month.

helped both countries to orient their expectations accordingly. For example, a 1985 American study of Soviet writings and actions on proliferation concluded that the strengthening of the nonproliferation treaty would prevail over ''the longstanding desire to enhance its authority and image in the Third World.'' It found that Soviet official writings about U.S. nonproliferation policy took into account the restraints imposed by the regime in a manner that was different from their other writing. The nuanced qualifications to be found in analyses of the Reagan Administration's nonproliferation policy are absent when Soviet commentators examine other aspects of U.S. defense and arms control policy.[42] The authors of such analyses included not only academicians, but also high level foreign ministry officials. Top Soviet leaders have explicitly supported the nonproliferation regime.[43]

Of course the very nature of the subject matter, in which the object of the policy is to coopt and limit others in a normative framework that leads them to forgo their sovereign right to the most destructive weapon, creates incentives for the superpowers to maintain the regime. Could cooperation have survived or been relearned in the absence of a regime? Possibly. But it certainly would have been much more difficult than in a situation in which the structure and expectations of the regime already existed.

It is also worth noting the change in the structure of power within the nuclear supply area as an incentive for maintaining the regime. Whereas the United States was the predominant international supplier in the 1960s, by the early 1970s the development of French capability to supply reactors and fuel, a German-British-Dutch consortium to provide fuel, and the prospect of a second tier of subsidiary suppliers in the 1980s, made it clear to both superpowers that their leverage within the nuclear supply area was eroding. With this diffusion of power, the prospects of return to unilateral policies look less promising than they might have earlier. In short, the incentives to maintain the regime were probably strengthened by the diffusion of power that occurred in the 1970s. All signs point in the same direction and seem certain to eventuate in a third tier of nuclear supplier countries.

It is also worth noting that the linkage of the nonproliferation issue to the overall U.S.–Soviet relationship has become progressively looser over time. As we saw with the efforts to reach agreement on the regime in the 1950s and 1960s, it was difficult to make progress in the period of tight bipolarity when there was hostility in the overall U.S.–Soviet security relationship. The need to maintain alliance structures created a tight linkage between the proliferation issue and the overall security relationship. Détente seemed to be a necessary condition for initial progress on nonproliferation. But by the 1980s, détente was no longer a necessary condition for maintenance of the nonproliferation regime. In the context of looser diplomatic structures and diffused power in the particular issue area, the United States and the Soviet Union were able to maintain their cooperation in the nonproliferation area despite the renewal of hostility. To go back to the metaphor used at the end of the first section, when the sea of hostility rose again, it did not submerge this island of cooperation. In part this was because hostility did not rise to its previous Cold War levels (despite rhetorical excesses), and in part because a superstructure of regimes constructed in the 1970s raised the level of cooperation and made it less submersible by a rising tide of hostility. If one believes that periods of good and poor relations in the U.S.–Soviet relationship tend to be cyclical,[44] then the fact that not all subissues in the relationship mirror the pattern of the overall cycles is of particular importance in understanding the evolution of U.S.–Soviet cooperation in the security area.

Notes

I am grateful to John Wertheimer and William Jarosz for research assistance, and for comments from Alex George, John Lewis Gaddis, Philip Farley, John Lewis, Robert Keohane, Ernest May, Henry Trofimenko, Vitaly Zhurkin, and participants at the Stanford Conference, May 1986.

1. For definitions and discussion of regimes, see Stephen Krasner, ed., *International Regimes* (Ithaca, N.Y.: Cornell University Press, 1983). For a discussion of nonproliferation as a regime, see J. S. Nye, "Maintaining a Non-Proliferation Regime," *International Organization*, vol. 35 (Winter 1981).

2. See Paul Zinner, "The Soviet Union in a Proliferated World," in John Kerry King, ed., *International Political Effects of the Spread of Nuclear Weapons* (Washington, D.C., U.S. Government Printing Office, 1979), p. 122.

3. For example, when the Soviets warned Pakistan not to develop a nuclear bomb in 1986, U.S. officials complained that "even though Washington was also strongly opposed to Pakistan's development of nuclear explosives, they felt the Soviet warning was an attempt to intimidate Pakistan over the Pakistani support for the Afghan guerrilla forces." *New York Times* (July 16, 1986).

4. See, for example, Robert Jervis in Krasner, ed., *International Regimes*. See also J. S. Nye, "Nuclear Learning and U.S.–Soviet Security Regimes," paper presented at the American Political Science Association, Washington, D.C., 1986.

5. See Joseph L. Nogee, *Soviet Policy Toward International Control of Atomic Energy* (Notre Dame, Ind.: Notre Dame Press, 1961).

6. David Holloway, *The Soviet Union and the Arms Race* (New Haven: Yale University Press, 1983), Ch. 2.

7. William Potter, "Nuclear Proliferation: U.S.–Soviet Cooperation," *Washington Quarterly* (Winter 1985).

8. William B. Bader, *The United States and the Spread of Nuclear Weapons* (New York: Pegasus, 1968).

9. John Steinbruner, *The Cybernetic Theory of Decision* (Princeton, N.J.: Princeton University Press, 1974), p. 177.

10. Bader, *The United States*, pp. 28–34.

11. George Quester, *Nuclear Diplomacy* (New York: Dunellen, 1970), p. 172. In Steinbruner's words, "American control was very tenuous for some of the weapons." *The Cybernetic Theory*, p. 179.

12. Bader, *The United States*, p. 40.

13. Stephen R. Sestanovich, "Nuclear Proliferation and Soviet Foreign Policy 1957–68: The Limits of Soviet-American Cooperation," Ph.D. thesis, Harvard University, 1979, p. 48.

14. John Gittings, *Survey of the Sino-Soviet Dispute* (London: Oxford University Press, 1968), pp. 102–9.

15. Walter Clemens, *The Arms Race and Sino-Soviet Relations* (Stanford, Calif.: Hoover Press, 1968), pp. 36 ff.

16. Benjamin S. Lambeth, "Nuclear Proliferation and Soviet Arms Control Policy," *Orbis* (Summer 1970). "That event thus marked a significant watershed not only in the erosion of the Sino-Soviet relationship but also in the evolution of Moscow's opposition to nuclear spread." p. 311.

17. Clemens also dates the split from 1958, but he puts the point in more general terms of Soviet concern about the Chinese drawing more radical conclusions than Moscow from Soviet space and strategic successes. "It was hardly accidental that Soviet spokesmen began in the fall of 1957 to warn of the dangers of broad escalation from local military conflicts." p. 41.

18. Nikita Khrushchev, *Khrushchev Remembers: The Last Testament.* Translated and edited by Strobe Talbott (Boston: Little, Brown, 1974), p. 269.

19. See Sestanovich, "Nuclear Proliferation," p. 181. See also Adam Ulam, *The Rivals* (New York: Viking Press, 1971), Ch. 10.

20. Sestanovich, "Nuclear Proliferation," p. 189.

21. Ibid., p. 221.

22. Ulam, in *The Rivals,* speculates that "The Soviets wanted to force not only the United States to agree on a German peace treaty with absolute prohibition of nuclear weapons for Bonn, but also for Taiwan. It is possible that Khrushchev intended to demand as a condition for removing the nuclear missiles in Cuba that the United States remove its protection of Formosa," p. 329.

23. Lawrence Scheinman reports the most significant turning point in the IAEA was "the cessation of systematic Soviet opposition to the agency's safeguards system." The Soviet tone began to moderate in 1962, but became patent in 1963. "IEAE: Atomic Condominium?" in Robert Cox and Harold Jacobson, eds., *The Anatomy of Influence* (New Haven: Yale University Press, 1974), p. 223.

24. Shortly before the Chinese explosion, the United States considered joint actions with the Soviet Union (up to and including military) to stop China, but the idea was never implemented. John Lewis Gaddis, *Strategies of Containment* (New York: Oxford University Press, 1982), p. 210.

25. Mohamed Heikal, *The Cairo Documents* (Garden City, N.Y.: Doubleday, 1973), p. 305.

26. Steinbruner, *The Cybernetic Theory,* pp. 169, 216.

27. Report of a conference on Permissive Action Links, Harvard Center for Science and International Affairs, February, 1986.

28. Bader, *The United States,* p. 59. Even at the time of ratification, Secretary of State Dean Rusk said that the NPT "would not bar succession by a new federated European state to the nuclear status of one of its former components." Hearings on Non-Proliferation Treaty, Senate Foreign Relations Committee, July, 1968 (Washington, D.C.: U.S. Government Printing Office, 1968), pp. 5–6.

29. Arthur H. Dean, *Test Ban and Disarmament* (New York: Harper & Row, 1966), p. 122.

30. Bader, *The United States,* p. 60.

31. Lawrence Scheinman, "Nuclear Safeguards: The Peaceful Atom and the IAEA," *International Conciliation* 572 (March 1969).

32. Sestanovich, "Nuclear Proliferation."

33. Dwight D. Eisenhower, *Waging Peace: 1956–1961* (Garden City, N.Y.: Doubleday, 1965), pp. 472–434.

34. Scheinman, "Nuclear Safeguards."

35. See Nye, "Nuclear Learning." Sections below are also based on personal experience.

36. See Gloria Duffy, "Soviet Nuclear Exports," *International Security,* vol. 3 (Summer 1978); and W. Scott Spence, "Soviet Strategies for the Non-Proliferation of Nuclear Weapons: 1965–1985," Columbia University seminar paper. Also confirmed in conversations with academicians in Moscow, June 1986.

37. Potter, "Nuclear Proliferation," pp. 144–5.

38. Conversation with NSC official, Autumn 1981.

39. Secretary of State George Shultz, "Preventing the Proliferation of Nuclear Weapons," Department of State *Bulletin* (December 1984).

40. Interview with State Department official, Washington, D.C., October 1986.

41. Interview with U.S. Arms Control and Disarmament Agency official, August 1985.

42. Charles Glickham, "The Non-Proliferation Treaty: A Rarity in Soviet American Efforts at Nuclear Arms Control," Radio Liberty Research, RL269/85, August 19, 1985.

43. In the words of Gorbachev's message to the 1985 NPT Review Conference, "an international non-proliferation regime has emerged on its basis and become an effective instrument of peace." *Soviet News* No. 6239, August 28, 1985; Moscow citing, August 27 TASS.

44. See J. S. Nye, ed., *The Making of America's Soviet Policy* (New Haven: Yale University Press, 1984), ch. 1.

15

The Evolution of
a Reconnaissance Satellite Regime

JOHN LEWIS GADDIS

Espionage, the philosopher Michael Walzer has suggested, might—under certain circumstances—promote rather than hinder communication among nations.[1] The idea seems improbable at first glance, given the efforts great powers have always made to guard against the loss of state secrets. Certainly the history of the Cold War does not appear to contain very many instances in which Washington and Moscow welcomed each other's attempts to ferret out such information. But if one effect of espionage were to be to reduce the danger of surprise attack, then, in theory at least, states should derive mutual benefits from tolerating a certain amount of it. And, in practice, something like this has happened in relations between the United States and the Soviet Union during the past quarter century, albeit discreetly and without explicit agreements governing the procedures involved. The fact that in one major arena of their competition Americans and Russians have actually cooperated in spying on one another was in itself, for many years, one of the better kept secrets of the Cold War; the fact that they have come to regard such activities as consistent with the principles of international law is certainly one of that conflict's least expected developments.

Reconnaissance satellites are no longer a secret, although both governments remain cautious about formally acknowledging their existence.[2] The critical role these instruments have played in verifying arms control agreements is now generally understood;[3] the threat that anti-satellite weaponry might pose to them is now openly discussed.[4] But what has not received attention, until recently, is the question of how the Soviet Union and the United States came to tolerate, and even to rely on, the collection of sensitive intelligence about each other from these devices in the first place.[5] Their decision to do so represents the clearest example in postwar Soviet-American relations of tacit cooperation on matters of mutual interest. It was also an implicit acknowledgement that certain forms of espionage can not only facilitate communication: they can also serve the cause of peace.

I

There was, to be sure, little in the history of great power rivalries to suggest that nations might willingly allow potential adversaries to reconnoiter their territories.[6] Observation balloons had been used, but also fired upon, as early as the Wars of the French Revolution.[7] Military reconnaissance conducted from aircraft came into its own during World

353

War I, but so too did countermeasures: the first true fighter aircraft were developed for the purpose of shooting down observation planes.[8] World War II provided few instances in which belligerents perceived it to be to their advantage for their adversaries to conduct successful overhead reconnaissance,[9] nor were such flights left unopposed during the Korean War.[10] And, of course, the most famous reconnaissance aircraft of all time, the U-2, entered the public's consciousness only as a result of being shot down over the Soviet Union in May, 1960; still another U-2 would be destroyed at the height of the Cuban missile crisis two years later.[11]

The U-2 program had grown out of a series of efforts Washington had made since the onset of the Cold War to compensate for one of that conflict's most obvious asymmetries: the disparity between an almost totally closed Soviet Union, given to making available virtually no accurate information about its military capabilities, and the almost totally open United States, where details about new technologies appeared regularly in newspapers and periodicals,[12] and in which the location of sensitive military installations could be pinpointed from the detailed road maps available—in those days, free—at corner service stations.

During the first postwar decade, that disparity had stimulated several ingenious but not always effective attempts by the United States to penetrate Soviet secrecy: they included the use of defectors, emigres, and—more rarely—actual spies; the careful analysis of World War II and even tsarist-era maps; eavesdropping in the form of intercepted cable and radio communications; the use of radar to track early Soviet missile experiments; regular monitoring of the upper atmosphere to detect Soviet nuclear tests; the launching of balloons equipped with cameras designed to float across Soviet territory for subsequent recovery; and regular reconnaissance flights along Soviet and East European borders and on several occasions deep into Soviet territory itself.[13] None of these efforts, with the exception of those directed toward the monitoring of nuclear tests, had produced much useful information. There were "shortcomings of a serious nature" in the accuracy of intelligence estimates regarding the Soviet Union, CIA Director Allen Dulles admitted to the National Security Council early in the Eisenhower Administration: "We must remain highly critical of our intelligence effort . . . but we must not be defeatist in the face of the difficulties of securing adequate information."[14]

As if in response to Dulles's injunction, Eisenhower in the months that followed authorized two separate but related initiatives—one covert, the other conspicuously overt—aimed at improving the collection of intelligence about the Soviet Union. Early in 1954, he established a Technological Capabilities Panel, headed by James R. Killian, president of the Massachusetts Institute of Technology, to investigate ways of reducing the danger of surprise attack. Placing its faith in rapidly developing remote-sending technology, the Killian Committee advised immediate construction of a high-altitude photoreconnaissance aircraft (which turned out to be the U-2), and, as a longer term measure, investigation of the potential of reconnaissance satellites. Eisenhower accepted these recommendations, thus committing his and subsequent administrations to reliance on overhead reconnaissance as the primary method of breaching Soviet secrecy.[15]

But the President authorized an overt approach to this problem as well: one that sought to legitimize these new reconnaissance techniques through diplomatic means. The world first learned of Eisenhower's "open skies" inspection plan when he suggested it to the Russians—in what appeared to be a spontaneous gesture—at the Geneva four-power summit conference in July, 1955.[16] We now know that a working group headed by presidential assistant Nelson Rockefeller had originated this plan, which would have involved an exchange of information on military facilities and the unrestricted right of aerial photoreconnaissance over both Soviet and American territory. Eisenhower had approved it, and indeed had insisted on presenting it over the objections of a skeptical John Foster Dulles.[17] What is interesting about this sequence of events is that Rockefeller's working group apparently knew nothing of what the Killian Committee had recommended regarding the U-2.[18] Only the President and a few trusted top advisers were aware that the United States would soon have the capacity to institute its own wholly unilateral "open skies" plan.

The question arises, then, as to why Eisenhower undertook the Geneva initiative at all. Surely he must have expected the Soviets to reject it, given the disproportionate benefits it would have provided to the United States.[19] Surely Eisenhower was aware that the U-2 and satellite reconnaissance programs could proceed, at least for a while, without the Russians' permission, since it would take them time to develop effective countermeasures. That situation would not last indefinitely, though, and it is this prospect of countermeasures that makes one wonder whether Eisenhower's "open skies" plan might not have been a farsighted attempt to build a climate of legitimacy for overhead reconnaissance, in anticipation of the day when the Russians would develop the capability to act against it.

As is often the case with the elusive Eisenhower, his intentions in this matter are not easy to pin down. But there is no question that his World War II experience had thoroughly sensitized him—as few other political leaders at the time could have been— to the potential military significance of overhead reconnaissance.[20] We know as well that he worried about how the Soviets might respond to unilateral American reconnaissance efforts: in May, 1956, for example, he warned of the need "to be wise and careful in what we do" because he wanted "to give the Soviets every chance to move in peaceful directions and to put our relations on a better basis."[21] But the underlying motive of the "open skies" plan appears most clearly, if obliquely, in a comment Eisenhower made to a group of advisers shortly after the launching of Sputnik in October, 1957: the Russians, he argued, "have in fact done us a good turn, unintentionally, in establishing the concept of freedom of international space."[22]

II

Unfortunately, the U-2 incident of May, 1960, confirmed a somewhat different proposition: that the Soviet Union, once it had the capacity to do so, would shoot down whatever flew over its territory. Russian secretiveness had long been a matter of state policy, one that not even collaboration in the wartime anti-Hitler coalition had in any significant way breached.[23] This attitude continued after the war, with the Soviet government refusing—almost alone among independent states at that time—to participate in international civil aviation agreements providing for the right of "innocent passage" through sovereign airspace.[24] And although it acknowledged in principle the need for verification in monitoring arms control agreements, the USSR insisted on defining the concept in the narrowest possible way, with a view to minimizing opportunities for espionage;[25] as a result, the immediate postwar years saw no progress made toward the international control of atomic energy, or toward mutually agreed-upon reductions in conventional forces. Moscow also protested, loudly and frequently, the various unilateral efforts the United States had made prior to Eisenhower's "open skies" proposal to carry out overhead reconnaissance, and had, on occasion, taken more active counter-measures as well.[26]

Even so, the Russians' initial response to "open skies" was not entirely negative. In a shift from their earlier position that disarmament should *precede* the establishment of verification procedures, they themselves had put forward in May 1955 a proposal that would have had the United Nations set up "control posts at large ports, at railway junctions, on main motor highways and in aerodromes" for the purpose of ensuring "that no dangerous concentration of military land forces or of air or naval forces takes place."[27] And even though party chief Nikita Khrushchev dismissed "open skies" at Geneva as "nothing more than a bald espionage plot,"[28] there is reason to think that the Russians saw both advantages and disadvantages in Eisenhower's proposal, and did not immediately rule out the possibility of accepting it.[29]

In the end, though, the Soviet Union did reject the plan, ostensibly on grounds that aerial inspection alone would not prevent the concealment of military forces, that the "open skies" plan made no provision for reconnaissance over the territories of countries other than the United States and the USSR, and that the proposal did not provide for arms reduction.[30] The real reason was probably closer to the concerns Khrushchev had expressed, as the official history of Soviet foreign policy retrospectively acknowledges: "All [the plan] had in mind was espionage . . . and in this respect it was of immense interest to those who were contemplating war and working on military plans."[31]

As Eisenhower had anticipated, the launching of *Sputnik* in October 1957, presented difficulties for Soviet legal experts who had earlier asserted the inviolability of sovereign airspace: one of them ingeniously—but unconvincingly—took the position that *Sputnik* did not actually fly over other countries' territories, but rather that those territories rotated beneath it.[32] As the prospect of American reconnaissance satellites became more immediate, however, the Russians found it necessary to reassert the principle of vertical sovereignty, without at the same time calling into question the right of their own satellites to overfly the United States. They did this by attempting to distinguish between "innocent" passage and espionage: it was permissible for satellites to pass overhead, but not if they were to be used for purposes of reconnaissance.[33]

However difficult this principle might have been to enforce, it did carry disturbing implications for the U. S. reconnaissance satellite program. The Americans were already some years ahead of the Russians in developing such systems; clearly they stood to benefit from them far more than did the Russians, who had the advantage of monitoring a society in which little was kept secret in the first place. With these considerations in mind, Eisenhower early in 1958 authorized the beginning of research on an American anti-satellite system, designed to deter the Russians from interfering with the reconnaissance satellites Washington expected soon to launch. He did so, though, with considerable misgivings, lest such a program compromise the possiblity—implicit in the "open skies" plan—of eventually persuading the Russians that reconnaissance could provide mutual benefits. It was for this reason that Eisenhower and his advisers strongly resisted pressures actually to deploy anti-satellite weaponry.[34]

Convinced of the value of satellite reconnaissance—the Central Intelligence Agency's "Discoverer" system had returned the first satellite photographs of the Soviet Union in August, 1960, only three months after the U-2 had been shot down[35]—the Kennedy Administration quickly embraced Eisenhower's goal of seeking to legitimize this new and impressive form of reconnaissance. It did so, though, by means that were at once more energetic and more imaginative than anything its predecessor had contemplated:

First, the White House imposed a strict news blackout on information concerning the development and launching of reconnaissance satellites. There had been no effort to conceal American programs in this area prior to 1961. The Eisenhower Administration had prided itself on the openness of the American space program, successes and failures alike, and since the latter had outnumbered the former during the late 1950s, the Air Force had not been at all reluctant to publicize the success of its SAMOS reconnaissance satellite in late 1960 and early 1961.[36] This all changed shortly after Kennedy took office: henceforth "Discoverer" and SAMOS launches received only minimal publicity, if any. The purpose of this news blackout was not to deny information about launches to the Russians, whose own tracking systems were fully capable of monitoring them. Instead it appears to have been an attempt to avoid provoking Moscow into categorical public condemnations of overhead reconnaissance;[37] there may also have been the assumption that the Russians would have less of an incentive to develop their own anti-satellite system if the success of American reconnaissance satellites were kept quiet.[38]

Second, and somewhat contradictorily, the Kennedy Administration undertook to let the Russians know—although very discreetly—something of the intelligence collection capabilities of reconnaissance satellites. It did this in the form of a carefully worded speech by Deputy Secretary of Defense Roswell Gilpatric in October, 1961, in which Gilpatric acknowledged that "the Iron Curtain is not so impenetrable as to force us to accept at face value . . . Kremlin boasts" about Soviet missile capabilities.[39] Made at the height of the Berlin crisis, this decision to reveal what the United States knew about the absence of a "missile gap" had the obvious purposes of precluding any further attempts by Khrushchev to extract political advantages from weapons he did not possess, while at the same time reassuring the American public and allies overseas. An indirect effect, however, could only have been to confirm for the Russians the value of the intelligence Washington was now receiving from reconnaissance satellites.[40]

Third, the Defense Department late in 1962 unilaterally "reoriented"—in effect, cancelled—the major American anti-satellite system then under development. This was the Air Force's satellite interception (SAINT) program, an effort that had been underway since 1958 to develop methods of locating and inspecting Soviet satellites in orbit; once that capability was perfected, it had been assumed, actual destruction of the satellite would be a simple matter.[41] Anti-satellite development did not entirely end with the phasing out of SAINT: both the Army and the Air Force were allowed to continue work on "direct ascent" systems, which would work by firing rockets from the ground directly at satellites. The capabilities of these systems were severely limited, however; there were never any more than two launch sites, and only a handful of missiles were actually produced. The pattern of the early 1960s was one, then, of refraining from developing the full-scale anti-satellite systems that could have been put in place by that time.[42]

Finally, the United States began a diplomatic offensive in the United Nations aimed at establishing international legal precedents for satellite reconnaissance. The U.N. General Assembly had created a Committee on the Peaceful Uses of Outer Space in 1958, but because of procedural objections raised by the Soviet Union the new organization remained inactive until 1961. By the end of the year, though, it became clear that the Russians had decided to use the committee as a forum in which to press their case against satellite reconnaissance, and in June 1962 they introduced a resolution that would have declared "the use of artificial satellites for the collection of intelligence information in the territory of foreign states . . . incompatible with the objectives of mankind in its conquest of outer space."[43] Washington had anticipated this initiative, and responded to it by stressing the difficulty of separating peaceful from military uses of space, the potential scientific value of observations made from satellites, and, very quietly, the possibility that satellites could be useful in monitoring arms control agreements.[44]

These U.N. discussions got nowhere, with the Soviet delegate still insisting that satellite reconnaissance was inconsistent with international law, that "the object to which such illegal surveillance is directed constitutes a secret guarded by a Sovereign State," and that "regardless of the means by which such an operation is carried out, it is in all cases an intrusion into something guarded by a Sovereign State in conformity with its sovereign prerogative."[45] By the summer of 1963, it appeared that the campaign to get the Russians to accept the legitimacy of overhead reconnaissance—begun with Eisenhower's "open skies" proposal and continued on several different fronts by Kennedy—had flatly failed.

III

But then a surprising series of events took place. They began in July 1963, with a newspaper report that Khrushchev—in the characteristically improbable setting of a picnic along the banks of the Dnieper—had half-seriously offered to show the Belgian Foreign Minister Paul Henri Spaak a selection of Soviet reconnaissance satellite photographs.[46] The following month, Moscow abruptly dropped its previous objections to the use of photography from weather satellites. Then in September, in the U.N. Committee on the Peaceful Uses of Outer Space, the Russians expressed a willingness to modify their previous insistence on the illegality of reconnaissance from satellites. And in October 1963, the Soviet Union proposed—without requiring as a precondition the banning of reconnaissance satellites—a U.N. resolution prohibiting the placement of nuclear weapons or other weapons of mass destruction in outer space. The Americans quickly agreed, and the General Assembly approved the resolution unanimously that same month. Two months later, the General Assembly endorsed as well, also by a unanimous vote, a "Declaration of Legal Principles Governing the Activities of States in the Exploration and Use of Outer Space" that made no mention at all of reconnaissance satellites.[47]

The reasons for this sudden shift in the Soviet position can only be surmised, but there are several possibilities. One is simply that the Americans had made it clear, by this time, that they did not propose to negotiate away the right to send satellites over the Soviet Union for reconnaissance purposes; they had also shown that they would develop the means to deter attacks on such satellites if necessary. In this sense, the Soviet Union confronted a *fait accompli,* and had little choice but to accept it.

But the Russians had also now developed their own reconnaissance satellites, and had presumably come to recognize the value of the intelligence derived from them. The first Soviet reconnaissance satellite went into orbit in April 1962, and others soon followed.[48] There is no way to know how good the photographs from these Soviet satellites were, except to point out that they were apparently good enough for Khrushchev to be boasting about them by the following summer.[49] It had previously been assumed that reconnaissance satellites would benefit the United States more than the Soviet Union, and that the Russians would find it preferable to call for banning them rather than tolerate them. But it may well be that their first actual satellite photographs were of greater use to the Russians than they themselves had expected. Certainly the Cuban missile crisis, which occurred between the first Soviet reconnaissance satellite launch and Moscow's change of heart on the legality of such reconnaissance, could well have illustrated the value of intelligence collected in this way; it is worth noting also that Sino-Soviet relations had seriously deteriorated by this time, and that a capacity to monitor Chinese military developments might not have been unwelcome in Moscow.[50]

It is also possible that the Russians had now come to recognize the value reconnaissance satellites could have in stabilizing the arms race. Soviet spokesmen as early as 1960 had informally acknowledged the possibility of such an effect;[51] clearly U-2 overflights had played a demonstrably vital role, first in alerting the United States to the Soviet missile buildup in Cuba, and then in monitoring Soviet compliance with the Kennedy-Khrushchev agreement that ended the crisis.[52] And, of course, the Limited Nuclear Test Ban Treaty of August 1963 had just established the precedent of maintaining arms control agreements by nonintrusive means of inspection.[53]

It has also been suggested—although there is no way to prove it—that the realization had now begun to dawn in the Kremlin that its policy of secrecy regarding military capabilities had backfired: the result had been an American proclivity for worst case analysis that had produced military buildups larger than otherwise would have been the case. The very fact that the one successful breach of Soviet secrecy prior to the advent of satellites—the U-2 program—had led Eisenhower to reject demands to close the nonexistent "missile gap" only confirmed the point. As Deputy Defense Secretary Gilpatric suggested in 1962: "The Soviets are forced to work very hard to keep up with what *they know* we are doing in order to keep up with what *we think* they are doing."[54]

The overall improvement in Soviet-American relations that followed the Cuban missile crisis should also be taken into account in explaining the Soviet decision to tolerate satellite reconnaissance. For had the Russians not developed some sense of mutual interest in stabilizing the arms race—a sense that had been noticeably absent during the years of Khrushchev's "strategic deception" between 1957 and 1962—then it is hard to see how very much progress could have been made toward the mutual toleration of satellite reconnaissance.

Was there any direct connection between the Kennedy Administration's efforts to legitimize satellite reconnaissance and the tacit Soviet agreement to do so? One possibility is that the Americans' unilateral decision to phase out the SAINT satellite interception system, and to exhibit restraint in developing other anti-satellite programs, may have induced the Russians to respond by not pushing their anti-reconnaissance campaign.[55] Whether or not the cancellation of SAINT was intended as a gesture to the Russians[56], it is undeniable that the United States did refrain from pressing ahead with the development of full scale anti-satellite systems during the late 1950s and early 1960s, and that one reason for this was Washington's determination to do nothing to interfere with the possibility of legitimizing satellite reconnaissance.[57] But whether the Russians were sophisticated enough to recognize this restraint—particularly in view of the fact that a limited anti-satellite program did continue through the mid-1960s—is highly questionable. Certainly their commitment to maintaining a tacitly agreed-upon satellite reconnaissance regime did not prevent them from initiating their own considerably more ambitious and, in its effects, highly destabilizing anti-satellite program in the mid-1970s.[58]

There may be another sense, though, in which unilateral American restraint did contribute to the Soviet decision to tolerate such reconnaissance. The most obvious change that the Kennedy administration made from its predecessor's policy on reconnaissance satellites was to minimize publicity about their existence. This may well have been an important consideration in making these satellites more tolerable to the Russians; they had reason to expect, not least from the quiet way in which the October 1961 Gilpatric speech had been handled, that although the United States would take maximum possible intelligence advantage of its reconnaissance satellite capabilities, it would not trumpet the fact, thereby embarrassing the Soviet Union. Certainly Kennedy's sensitivity to the importance of not humiliating Khrushchev is acknowledged to have played an important role in the successful resolution of the Cuban missile crisis;[59] there is no reason to think that such an approach might not have had an equally beneficial effect with regard to satellite reconnaissance as well.

IV

The reconnaissance satellite regime tacitly agreed upon in 1963 has been in existence now for almost a quarter of a century. This record of durability suggests the extent to which both Moscow and Washington have found it advantageous to tolerate this new nonintrusive form of espionage, but both governments have been reticent about revealing just what these advantages are, or how they are brought to fruition. Nevertheless, enough information has filtered into the public domain to make possible certain basic generalizations about both the capabilities of reconnaissance satellites and—to a lesser extent—their political purposes.[60]

The capabilities of reconnaissance satellites fall into four general categories:

1. *Photoreconnaissance.* Taking photographs from outer space was the original purpose of reconnaissance satellites, and it remains their most important function. Quite early in its history space photography attained a remarkable capacity to distinguish even minute features on the face of the earth; today's satellites are said to be able to detect objects as small as ten centimeters. Infrared and ultraviolet spectra are employed, in addition to visible light, with the resulting photographs returned either through capsules ejected from the satellite or, more frequently now, direct transmissions. Orbits are usually low, and most reconnaissance satellites are now maneuverable.[61]

2. *Early warning.* Satellites have also been used since the early 1970s to detect missile launchings and surreptitious nuclear tests. Their capacity to do this takes advantage of the same infrared detecting capacity used in low-orbiting photoreconnaissance satellites, but early warning satellites are generally placed in geosynchronous orbit some 22,000 miles above the earth so that their coverage of targeted areas is broad and constant.[62]

3. *Radar reconnaissance.* These satellites rely upon the development of side-looking synthetic-aperture radar, which makes it possible not only to penetrate cloud cover over land targets but to measure wave-heights and other ocean conditions. They are of obvious value in monitoring the movement of surface vessels, and they may have some potential in the future to track submerged submarines.[63]

4. *"Ferret" or electronic surveillance satellites.* The function of these satellites is the one about which least is known, but presumably it includes eavesdropping on military and civilian telecommunications, as well as analyzing radar signals and monitoring the telemetry from missile tests.[64]

Determining the political functions of reconnaissance satellites is not as easy as describing their physical functions; here one is forced to rely on a small number of official disclosures—both intentional and inadvertent—and on a very large amount of well-informed speculation. Such an analysis suggests the following:

1. *Guarding against surprises.* The most important political function reconnaissance satellites have served has been to increase the confidence of each superpower that it will be able to detect preparations by its rival to launch a surprise attack. Early warning satellites double the time that would otherwise be available to respond to an ICBM launch; photoreconnaissance and radar satellites can easily track movements of conventional forces; and "ferret" satellites have the capability to intercept communications that might reveal adversary intentions. This array of warning systems also provides useful safeguards in the case of false alarms, as recent experience has indicated.[65] There remains, of course, no guarantee against one superpower achieving surprise in using force against the other or against its allies. But reconnaissance satellites do greatly reduce the chances of that happening.

2. *Assessing adversary forces.* Reconnaissance satellites have also been valuable in providing a means by which each superpower can evaluate the configuration of the other's military arsenal, and hence make more informed decisions about its own military priorities than had been possible prior to their development. Obviously, as a relatively open society seeking to learn the secrets of one largely closed, the United States has benefited more from this use of satellite intelligence than has the Soviet Union. Its very first reconnaissance satellites torpedoed Khrushchev's strategy of seeking political benefits from nonexistent rockets,[66] and ever since the Russians have found it much more difficult than it had been during the first decade and a half of the Cold War to obscure the size and nature of their military establishment. But the Americans have managed to maintain some secrets of their own,[67] and presumably Moscow has found it convenient to be able to check what appears in the open literature against what its own reconnaissance systems reveal about military research, development, and deployment in this country and among its allies.

3. *Monitoring compliance with arms control agreements.* This is the only function of reconnaissance satellites that Washington and Moscow have explicitly—if euphemistically—agreed to endorse. Both the Strategic Arms Limitation Interim Agreement and the Treaty on the Limitation of Anti-Ballistic Missile Systems, signed in Moscow in May 1972, provide for "assurance of compliance . . . [by] national technical means of verification . . . in a manner consistent with generally recognized principles of international law." The SALT I package further provided that no interference with "national technical means" would take place, and that neither side would seek to impede such means of verification through "deliberate concealment measures."[68] The SALT II agreement of 1979, which the United States never ratified, carried these arrangements even further by providing for the deliberate incorporation into aircraft and cruise missile design of "functionally related observable differences" and "externally observable design features"—external characteristics intended to be visible from satellites as a means of ensuring compliance with the agreement.[69]

4. *Keeping track of third party crises.* One byproduct of the long postwar Soviet-American rivalry has been that all of the actual fighting that has gone on since 1945 has taken the form of limited regional conflicts involving third parties. At times—as in Korea, Vietnam and Afghanistan—these conflicts have drawn in one of the superpowers as a belligerent; more often, however, Moscow and Washington have been content to

watch these confrontations nervously from the sidelines. Reconnaissance satellites, of course, greatly enhance their ability to do so. Careful reconstruction of satellite orbital paths has demonstrated a tendency on the part of both the Russians and Americans to increase coverage of those parts of the world where regional conflicts are taking place; the pattern can be clearly seen in crises as diverse as the 1969 Sino-Soviet border clash, the 1971 India-Pakistan War, the 1973 Arab-Israeli War, the 1974 Cyprus crisis, and the 1982 Falklands War.[70] There have even been instances of superpowers sharing satellite reconnaissance information about third parties; the clearest example is the warning conveyed from Moscow to Washington in 1977 that the South Africans appeared to be about to test a nuclear weapon in the Kalahari desert.[71]

5. *Evaluating an adversary's resource base.* The launching of the American Earth Resources Technology Satellite (since renamed Landsat) in July 1972 immediately demonstrated the ability of even low-resolution satellite photography to detect, and distinguish between, specific varieties of minerals and vegetation on the earth's surface.[72] Although the Landsat program was public from its inception, its techniques of using false-color and infrared photography to bring out contrasts in geological features and even patterns of agricultural cultivation have no doubt been available to intelligence analysts as well, probably at higher levels of resolution.[73] Such information makes possible calculations of harvest yields; it may also provide at least a basis for estimating certain mineral resource reserves as well. Information of this type obviously could be useful in estimating the future performance of the Soviet economy.

It is very doubtful that this short list exhausts the benefits, actual and potential, that reconnaissance satellites provide to the Soviet Union and the United States. But it should at least provide a partial explanation of why a mutually tolerated reconnaissance satellite regime has survived as long as it has, and with so few attempts at interference from either side.

V

Consideration of how one might in fact interfere with the operation of reconnaissance satellites has been going on, in both the United States and the Soviet Union, for as long as the satellites themselves have been in place,[74] but it is only within the past decade that the two superpowers have made serious efforts actually to develop means of doing this. The relatively low priority given research on anti-satellite weapons until the mid-1970s provides striking evidence of the benefits both sides saw in preserving the satellite reconnaissance regime; but what has happened since then does create the possibility that that regime may not remain as sacrosanct in the future.

The United States developed the first operational system for destroying orbiting satellites—a system that relied upon the use of Thor missiles armed with nuclear warheads—and maintained it from 1964 through 1975. But Project 437, as it was known, was intended primarily as protection against an anticipated threat from Soviet orbital bombardment weapons that never materialized. It never had anything more than a limited capability against reconnaissance and other kinds of satellites; its nuclear warhead would have endangered American satellites as much as whatever Soviet target at which it might have been aimed; and after 1967 the Outer Space Treaty, which banned altogether the placement of nuclear weapons beyond the earth's atmosphere, appeared to remove the threat of orbital bombardment that Project 437 had been intended to counter. By 1970, the program's operational readiness had been cut back to such an extent that it would have taken 30 days to launch a single missile.[75]

Soviet anti-satellite weapon development began—a good deal more purposefully— in 1968, and involved the actual launching of "killer" satellites, capable of intercepting and destroying target satellites in low earth orbit. These tests were suspended from 1971 until early 1976, but they have since continued periodically.[76] Moscow's motives for beginning to develop true "killer" satellites just as a much more primitive American anti-satellite system was being phased out remain unclear. It has been suggested that the Soviets had acquiesced all along only in the use of satellites to verify arms control agreements, not to gather military intelligence; but their tacit acceptance of the recon- naissance satellite regime dates from 1963, long before arms control agreements specif- ically dependent upon satellite verification had been concluded. The more plausible explanation is that the Russians saw the need to have a capability in wartime to destroy American satellites whose functioning they were willing to tolerate as long as war did not occur.[77]

American officials did not regard the first series of Soviet anti-satellite tests as a significant threat: they went ahead with the phase-out of Project 437 even after the Soviet experiments had taken place, and despite some puzzlement over Moscow's inten- tions they did not respond by initiating an updated American program. The general atmosphere of détente during the early 1970s no doubt contributed to Washington's relaxed attitude, as did the fact that Moscow refrained from further anti-satellite testing after 1971 and that provisions for "national technical means of verification" in the 1972 SALT I agreements appeared to constitute a binding, if inexplicit, obligation on the Russians' part not to impede satellite reconnaissance when used as an instrument of arms control.[78]

But when the second series of Soviet anti-satellite tests began in 1976, the political climate was much less auspicious. Détente had begun to crumble, both as the result of domestic pressures within the United States and growing signs of Soviet interventionism in Africa.[79] Rumors of Soviet experiments with directed-energy weapons had begun to surface, and in an ambiguous series of incidents late in 1975, the infrared sensors on three American satellites had been blinded by what may—or may not—have been laser beams directed from Soviet territory.[80] Concern about levels of Soviet military expen- diture had begun to grow as well, as had disputes about the adequacy of American intelligence in assessing Moscow's intentions.[81] It was within this context that the Ford Administration, just before leaving office in January 1977, directed the Defense De- partment to begin development of a new American anti-satellite weapon system.[82]

Just as the Soviet anti-satellite program had constituted a significant advance in sophistication over the primitive Project 437, so now the new American development effort produced a system that exceeded the capabilities of its Soviet counterpart. Relying on the use of a small but highly accurate rocket launched from an F-15 fighter, the system works by directly ramming the target satellite. It does not require, as does the Soviet "killer" satellite, time-consuming orbital rendezvous maneuvers; moreover its reliability, at least in the limited tests conducted so far, appears to exceed that of the Soviet anti-satellite system.[83] And, of course, since the surprise announcement of Pres- ident Reagan's Strategic Defense Initiative in March 1983, research has been proceeding on a much wider variety of systems—including laser and particle beam weapons—that if developed could destroy enemy satellites as well as the enemy missiles that are the officially announced targets of a space-based defensive capability.[84]

Meanwhile, efforts to negotiate agreements that would safeguard the right of satellite reconnaissance have come to nought. The Carter Administration coupled its pursuit of a new anti-satellite system with an offer to the, Russians to begin discussions on how such weapons might be prohibited altogether, and in June 1978 talks on this subject began in Helsinki, followed by two further sets of talks that took place in Bern and in Vienna in 1979. But because of the difficulty of specifying in advance just what kinds of activities might threaten reconnaissance satellites, neither government found it a simple matter to formulate a negotiating position, or to address the problem of how an anti-satellite treaty might be verified. Asymmetries in capabilities on both sides also created difficulties. The Americans, noting that the Russians already had an operational anti-satellite system but that they did not, resisted any ban on research and testing; the Russians pointing to the well-advertised satellite interception and retrieval potential of the soon-to-be-launched American space shuttle, countered with demands for guarantees against its use as an anti-satellite weapon.

Further discussions might have narrowed these differences, but the increasingly acrimonious debate over SALT II inside the United States froze all progress on arms control for the remainder of 1979; the Soviet invasion of Afghanistan at the end of that year ensured that none would take place during what was left of Carter's term. The Russians now took the initiative, proposing a draft space weapons treaty in the United Nations in 1981, but the Reagan Administration quickly decided not to follow Carter's example of simultaneous negotiations and anti-satellite weapons development, but rather to concentrate upon the latter altogether.[85]

Does the development of anti-satellite weaponry, together with the failure of negotiations on their control, mean that the reconnaissance satellite regime is now at risk? It clearly does, in the sense that the capability to destroy satellites on short notice with reasonable accuracy now exists on both sides, and can be expected to improve. But whether capability produces intention is another matter entirely. One characteristic of the nuclear age has been precisely the distinction between these two things: the capability for mutual destruction has been present for at least three of the four decades during which nuclear weapons have existed; but the intention to commit such destruction has been mercifully absent.

There is little reason to think that this distinction between capabilities and intentions will not apply to the satellite reconnaissance regime in the future, much as it has to the nuclear arms competition in the past. For it is precisely the connection between the two—the value of satellites in providing some measure of protection against surprise nuclear attack—that would cause any actual employment of anti-satellite weapons against reconnaissance satellites to be regarded as an act almost as provocative as a full-scale missile launch would be. The existence of anti-satellite weapons, therefore, may have no greater effect upon the security of satellites in peacetime than the proliferation of highly accurate missiles armed with nuclear warheads has had on the likelihood of nuclear weapons actually being used.

VI

The quiet evolution of a reconnaissance satellite regime that both Washington and Moscow could find reasons to want to perpetuate was at least as important an example of Soviet-American cooperation to lower the risk of war as the highly publicized Limited Test Ban Treaty of 1963 or the Strategic Arms Limitation Agreements of 1972. Cooperation on reconnaissance was all the more remarkable for the way in which it came about: in this case, the superpowers identified mutual interests and evolved procedures for enhancing them without resort to the formal negotiations that are generally thought necessary to accomplish such results. This fact raises interesting questions about the respective advantages of tacit as opposed to explicit agreements as a means of managing superpower rivalries.[86]

Tacit cooperation has the definitive advantage of minimizing the extent to which prestige on either side is engaged. It would have been considerably more difficult for the Russians to have accepted American reconnaissance satellite overflights had the existence of such satellites been given the publicity accorded other elements of the U.S. space program. Certainly one senses that at least some of the Soviet Union's current vociferous objections to the American Strategic Defense Initiative grow out of the highly public manner in which that program has been pursued, and the implications of Soviet technological inferiority that are so explicitly drawn from it.[87] The American reconnaissance satellite program was handled in a very different way in the early 1960s, and that may account in part for the ease with which the Russians accepted its legitimacy.

The absence of publicity also makes it possible for governments to act quickly, without the requirement for intensive consultation within the bureaucracy and among affected constituencies that is normally required for initiatives taken openly. It is illustrative to contrast the speed with which Eisenhower and his immediate advisers put together the "open skies" proposal in 1955, or with which the Kennedy Administration was able to develop a combination of initiatives in 1961–62 intended to persuade the Russians to accept the legitimacy of satellite reconnaissance, with the length of time it has taken both the U.S. and Soviet governments to resolve internal disagreements prior to publicly presenting their positions on the control of strategic arms since negotiations on that subject began in 1969.[88]

Finally, tacit cooperation tends to lift delicate issues in Soviet-American relations out of the arena of political debate inside the United States. It is interesting to contemplate what the Kennedy Administration's domestic opposition might have made of the fact that Soviet reconnaissance satellites were overflying the United States after 1962, had that information become widely known. Recent intrusions of domestic political considerations into foreign policy—the Jackson-Vanik Amendment of 1972, the manner in which the term "détente" became unacceptable during the 1976 presidential campaign, and the 1979 controversy over a suddenly discovered Soviet "combat brigade" in Cuba are only the most prominent examples—provide little assurance that mutual interests in Soviet-American relations will always override the narrow partisan interests of American political leaders.[89] The fact that cooperation in reconnaissance has proceeded on a tacit basis has made it possible to avoid these difficulties as well.

But the tacit pursuit of mutual interests is not without its disadvantages. First, one is never quite sure what is included within a tacit agreement and what is not. The fact that research on anti-satellite weapons has proceeded alongside reliance on satellite reconnaissance illustrates the point; nor is there any clear understanding between the superpowers as to the kinds of actions that would constitute abrogation of the informal reconnaissance regime.[90] If one believes—and there is some reason to do so—that deterrence is best achieved through ambiguity,[91] then the very vagueness of the superpower understanding on reconnaissance satellites could be an asset. But this does nothing to lessen the danger of misperception or accident; it is all too easy for casual, thoughtless, or even unintended behavior on one side to appear purposeful, calculated, and sinister to the other.[92]

Second, tacit cooperation requires that each side continue to value it, regardless of circumstances or changes of leadership. Formal treaties provide protection—admittedly imperfect—against future uncertainties; informal arrangements like the satellite reconnaissance regime do not. There is nothing to prevent leaders in either Washington or Moscow from simply abandoning, at any point, their practice of tolerating each other's remotely conducted espionage, should they choose to do so.

Third, the very secrecy on which these programs depend narrows the range of those who are knowledgeable about them, whether within government or outside of it. This makes it difficult to conduct informed public discussion about such important issues as the verification of arms control agreements, a fact that became painfully apparent during the debate over the ratification of SALT II.[93] Secrecy can also raise questions about the appropriate uses of such publicly financed programs as the space shuttle, as the recent controversy over that vehicle's classified military missions has shown.[94]

But whatever its advantages and disadvantages, the emergence of a tacitly agreed-upon satellite reconnaissance regime does illustrate that nations need not always confine themselves to traditional forms of negotiation to achieve meaningful cooperation in areas of mutual interest. It also suggests the extent to which long-term systemic interests—the interests both sides share in avoiding nuclear war and in preserving the international system as it has evolved since 1945—can, at times, override the immediate national interests of the two nations whose rivalry has defined that system during the four decades it has been in existence.[95]

Notes

1. "Another form of great power communication, this one undervalued, is espionage, which makes for a sharing of information about new weapons systems and recent troop deployments and so, perhaps, reduces the risks involved." Michael Walzer, "The Reform of the International System," a paper delivered at the 1985 Nobel Institute Symposium on "The Study of War and Peace," p. 23. For one possible confirmation of Walzer's theory, see Christopher Andrew's recent account of Anglo-Italian relations during the Italian-Ethiopian War (1935–36) and the Spanish Civil War (1936–39), in which both countries were intercepting each other's military and diplomatic cable traffic. *Her Majesty's Secret Service: The Making of the British Intelligence Community* (New York: Viking Press, 1986), pp. 401–403.

2. The first official, if inadvertent, acknowledgement of the benefits of satellite photography came in what was supposed to have been an off-the-record comment by Lyndon Johnson in March, 1967. *New York Times* (March 17, 1967). There was also an oblique reference to the use of satellites for the verification of arms control agreements in Secretary of State William P. Rogers' letter of June 10, 1972, formally transmitting the Anti-Ballistic Missile Treaty to President Nixon prior to submission to the Senate. *Weekly Compilation of Presidential Documents,* VIII (June 19, 1972), p. 103. There was no further public reference to the role of reconnaissance satellites until Jimmy Carter described them, in October, 1978, as "an important stabilizing factor

in world affairs in the monitoring of arms control agreements.'' *Public Papers of the Presidents: Jimmy Carter, 1978* (Washington: U.S. Government Printing Office, 1979), p. 1686. The first published photograph from a reconnaissance satellite appeared in *Jane's Defence Weekly* in 1984 as the result of a security breach for which former navy employee Samuel Loring Morison was sentenced to two years in prison. *New York Times* (December 5, 1985).

3. For two early journalistic accounts, see Philip J. Klass, *Secret Sentries in Space* (New York: Random House, 1971); and John W. R. Taylor and David Mondley, *Spies in the Sky* (New York: Scribners, 1972). John Newhouse provided the first good discussion of the importance of satellite reconnaissance in verifying the SALT I agreement in *Cold Dawn: The Story of SALT* (New York: Holt, Rinehart & Winston, 1973), especially pp. 14–17.

4. See, for example, D. L. Hafner, ''Anti-Satellite Weapons: the Prospects for Arms Control,'' in Bhupendra Jasani, *Outer Space—A New Dimension of the Arms Race* (London: Taylor & Francis, 1982), pp. 311–323; also the special supplement on ''Space Weapons'' in the *Bulletin of the Atomic Scientists* XL (May, 1984): 1S–15S.

5. There are now two important books on this subject, based on access to U. S. official sources. They are Gerald M. Steinberg, *Satellite Reconnaissance: The Role of Informal Bargaining* (New York: Praeger, 1983), and Paul B. Stares, *The Militarization of Space: U. S. Policy, 1945–84* (Ithaca, N.Y: Cornell University Press, 1985). The following essay relies heavily upon them. Two other recent accounts that deal extensively with this topic are John Prados, *The Soviet Estimate: U. S. Intelligence Analysis and Russian Military Strength* (New York: Dial Press, 1982); and Walter McDougall, *The Heavens and the Earth: A Political History of the Space Age* (New York: Basic Books, 1985).

6. One possible exception to this generalization would be the custom, prior to World War I, of allowing foreign officers to attend military maneuvers, but even that access tended to be cut off in periods of crisis. See, on this point, Ernest R. May, ed., *Knowing One's Enemies: Intelligence Assessment Before the Two World Wars* (Princeton: Princeton University Press, 1984), especially pp. 42–44, 179–180.

7. L. T. C. Rolt, *The Aeronauts: A History of Ballooning, 1783–1903* (New York: Walker, 1966), p. 162.

8. Taylor and Mondley, *Spies in the Sky*, p. 22; Andrew, *Her Majesty's Secret Service*, pp. 133, 136–137.

9. The exception here would be instances in which specific measures were undertaken to deceive enemy observers. For examples, see R. V. Jones, *The Wizard War: British Scientific Intelligence, 1939–1945* (New York: Coward, McCann & Geoghegan, 1978), pp. 405–412; and Stephen E. Ambrose, *Ike's Spies: Eisenhower and the Espionage Establishment* (Garden City, N.Y.: Doubleday, 1981), pp. 83–86.

10. Taylor and Mondley, *Spies in the Sky*, pp. 56–59.

11. The best account of the U-2 incident is Michael Beschloss, *Mayday: Eisenhower, Khrushchev and the U-2 Affair* (New York: Harper & Row, 1986).

12. The magazine *Aviation Week and Space Technology* has long been an important source of information on new U. S. military technologies. For some examples of its role in this regard in the 1950s, see Prados, *The Soviet Estimate*, pp. 36–37, 105. See also, on the question of U. S. anxieties about the difficulty of penetrating Soviet secrecy, Harry Rositzke, *The CIA's Secret Operations: Espionage, Counterespionage, and Covert Action* (New York: Readers' Digest Press, 1977), pp. 13–17; and W. S. Rostow, *Open Skies: Eisenhower's Proposal of July 21, 1955* (Austin: University of Texas Press, 1982), p. 12.

13. Almost no documentary evidence has been declassified concerning these efforts, but their general outlines have been reconstructed in Rositzke, *The CIA's Secret Operations*, pp. 18–100; Prados, *The Soviet Estimate*, pp. 24–30; Thomas Powers, *The Man Who Kept the Secrets: Richard Helms and the CIA* (New York: Knopf, 1979), pp. 42–58; James Bamford, *The Puzzle Palace: A Report on America's Most Secret Agency* (Boston: Houghton Mifflin, 1982), pp. 181–183, 232–239; John Ranelagh, *The Agency: The Rise and Decline of the CIA* (New York: Simon

& Schuster, 1986), pp. 135–142, 226–228; and David Alan Rosenberg, "The Origins of Overkill: Nuclear Weapons and American Strategy, 1945–1960," *International Security* VII (Spring 1983): 15.

14. Minutes, NSC meeting, March 31, 1953, U. S. Department of State, *Foreign Relations of the United States: 1952–54,* II, 268.

15. James R. Killian, Jr., *Sputnik, Scientists, and Eisenhower: A Memoir of the First Special Assistant to the President for Science and Technology* (Cambridge, Mass.: MIT Press, 1977), pp. 79–85. The theoretical possibility of reconnaissance satellites had been the subject of speculation within the U. S. government since at least 1945. See, on this point, Stares, *The Militarization of Space,* pp. 23–33.

16. Eisenhower statement, July 21, 1955, *Public Papers of the Presidents: Dwight D. Eisenhower, 1955* (Washington, D.C.: U.S. Government Printing Office, 1959), pp. 715–716.

17. Rostow, *Open Skies,* pp. 26–56.

18. For the relationship between the Killian Committee report and the "Open Skies" proposal, see ibid., p. 10; also Stephen Ambrose, *Eisenhower: The President* (New York: Simon & Schuster, 1984), p. 258; and Ray S. Cline, *Secrets, Spies, and Scholars: The Essential CIA* (Washington, D.C.: Acropolis Books, 1976), pp. 158–159. Rockefeller was presumably aware of the potential benefits of satellite reconnaissance. See his memorandum of May 17, 1955, included in NSC 5520, "U. S. Scientific Satellite Program," May 20, 1955, Dwight D. Eisenhower Papers, White House NSC Assistant, NSC Series, Policy Paper Subseries, Box 16, Dwight D. Eisenhower Library.

19. Admiral Arthur Radford, Chairman of the Joint Chiefs of Staff, candidly acknowledged that "it would be to the advantage of the U.S. to make such an agreement, since the Soviets already have most of the information they could obtain through such a privilege, whereas we have little or none." Quoted in Rostow, *Open Skies,* p. 53.

20. See, on this point, Ambrose, *Ike's Spies,* p. 267.

21. Goodpaster notes, Eisenhower conversation with Radford, Twining, Herbert Hoover, Jr., and Allen Dulles, May 28, 1956, Eisenhower Papers, Ann Whitman File, DDE Diary, Box 8, "May 56 Goodpaster." Eisenhower's comment was made in the context of a discussion concerning a Soviet protest over what had probably been an RB-47 reconnaissance flight in the Arctic. (The document in question is partially sanitized.) The first U-2 overflight of the Soviet Union took place on June 14, 1956. Prados, *The Soviet Estimate,* p. 33. For other Eisenhower expressions of concern about overflights, see the transcript of an Eisenhower telephone conversation with John Foster Dulles, December 18, 1956, Eisenhower Papers, Whitman File, DDE Diary, Box 11, "Dec. 56 Phone Calls"; and Dulles notes, conversations with Eisenhower, January 22 and March 7, 1958, John Foster Dulles Papers, White House Memoranda, Box 6, "Meetings with the President, January–June, 1958 (6, 7)," Dwight D. Eisenhower Library.

22. Goodpaster notes, Eisenhower conversation with Donald Quarles and other advisors, October 8, 1957, Eisenhower Papers, Whitman File, DDE Diary, Box 16, "Oct. 57 Staff Notes (2)." See also Quarles's comment at the cabinet meeting of October 18, 1957, L. L. Minnich notes, ibid., "Oct. 57 Staff Notes (1)." A RAND Corporation report had speculated about the legality of satellite reconnaissance as early as 1950, and in May 1955, NSC 5520, which dealt with future satellite programs, had stressed the importance of establishing a legal precedent for satellite overflights. See NSC 5520, May 20, 1955, p. 3; also McDougall, *The Heavens and the Earth,* pp. 108–110, 120–121.

23. See John Lewis Gaddis, *The United States and the Origins of the Cold War, 1941–1947* (New York: Columbia University Press, 1972), pp. 81–86.

24. See, on this point, McDougall, *The Heavens and the Earth,* p. 109; also Irvin L. White, *Decision-Making for Space: Law and Politics in Air, Sea, and Outer Space* (West Lafayette, Ind.: Purdue University Press, 1970), pp. 102–111.

25. Allen S. Krass, "The Soviet View of Verification," in William C. Potter, ed., *Verification and Arms Control* (Lexington, Mass.: Lexington Books, 1985), pp. 37–39.

26. The U-2 was by no means the first U. S. reconnaissance plane to be shot down by the Russians. See, on this point, Bamford, *The Puzzle Palace,* pp. 181–182. For Russian protests over balloon and U-2 reconnaissance, see Ambrose, *Eisenhower: The President,* pp. 309–310, 341, 563.

27. Department of State *Bulletin,* XXXII(May 30, 1955), pp. 900–905.

28. Eisenhower, *Waging Peace,* p. 521.

29. See Rostow, *Open Skies,* pp. 79–83.

30. Ibid., pp. 63–64.

31. A. A. Gromyko and B. N. Ponomarev, eds., *Soviet Foreign Policy, 1945–1980,* Fourth edition (Moscow: Progress Publishers, 1981), II, 234.

32. McDougall, *The Heavens and the Earth,* p. 258.

33. Ibid., pp. 258–261; Steinberg, *Satellite Reconnaissance,* pp. 27–28; Stuart A. Cohen, "The Evolution of Soviet Views on SALT Verification: Implications for the Future," in William C. Potter, ed., *Verification and SALT: The Challenge of Strategic Deception* (Boulder, Colo.: Westview Press, 1980), pp. 56–58. Khrushchev did suggest, in an offhand remark at the abortive Paris summit that followed the U-2 incident in May, 1960, that the Russians objected only to reconnaissance from airplanes, not satellites. Dwight D. Eisenhower, *The White House Years: Waging Peace, 1956–1960* (Garden City: Doubleday, 1965), p. 556; George B. Kistiakowsky, *A Scientist at the White House: The Private Diary of President Eisenhower's Special Assistant for Science and Technology* (Cambridge, Mass.: Harvard University Press, 1976), p. 334. But this was not the consistent Soviet position at the time.

For an overall summary of attempts by Soviet and East European scholars to wrestle with the legal implications of earth satellites, see C. Wilfred Jenks, *Space Law* (New York: Praeger, 1965), pp. 133–147.

34. Kistiakowsky, *A Scientist at the White House,* pp. 229–230; also Steinberg, *Satellite Reconnaissance,* pp. 31–35; and Stares, *The Militarization of Space,* pp. 49–54. NSC 5814/1, approved by Eisenhower on August 18, 1958, pointed out that "reconnaissance satellites are of critical importance to U. S. national security." They would have "a high potential use as a means of implementing the 'open skies' proposal or policing a system of international armaments control." There was, as a consequence, an urgent need to seek "a political framework which will place the uses of U. S. reconnaissance satellites in a political and psychological context most favorable to the United States." NSC 5814/1, "Preliminary U. S. Policy on Outer Space," August 18, 1958, Eisenhower Papers, White House NSC Assistant, NSC Series, Policy Papers Subseries, Box 25.

35. Steinberg, *Satellite Reconnaissance,* p. 24.

36. Ibid., pp. 40–42. The CIA had been more discreet about its "Discoverer" series, but the first successful recovery of a "Discoverer" film capsule in August 1960 had been fully covered in the press.

37. Philip J. Farley to the author, May 27, 1986. Former Secretary of Defense Robert S. McNamara, who played the major role in cutting off information about reconnaissance satellite launches, has confirmed to me in a private conversation that his intention was to avoid the kind of public challenge the U-2 incident had presented to the Russians.

38. See Stares, *The Militarization of Space,* pp. 62–65; Steinberg, *Satellite Reconnaissance,* pp. 30–31, 44–45.

39. For the Gilpatric speech, see the *New York Times,* October 22, 1961. Its background is best discussed in Roger Hilsman, *To Move a Nation: The Politics of Foreign Policy in the Administration of John F. Kennedy* (Garden City, N.Y.: Doubleday, 1967), pp. 163–164, although Hilsman mistakenly dates the speech as November 1961.

40. Steinberg, *Satellite Reconnaissance,* pp. 50–51. Prados suggests, unfortunately without providing a source, that Kennedy actually showed Gromyko satellite reconnaissance photographs in September 1961. *The Soviet Estimate,* p. 122. The best discussion of Khrushchev's "strategic deception" strategy, which he followed from 1957 to 1961, is Arnold Horelick and

Myron Rush, *Strategic Power and Soviet Foreign Policy* (Chicago: University of Chicago Press, 1966).

41. Steinberg, *Satellite Reconnaissance*, pp. 83–84. For details on the SAINT system, see Stares, *The Militarization of Space*, pp. 112–117.

42. Steinberg, *Satellite Reconnaissance*, p. 85; Stares, *The Militarization of Space*, pp. 80–82, 117–128. Stares points out that SAINT was cancelled primarily for technical and financial reasons, and that the decision to do so was not intended as a signal to the Russians. He does acknowledge, though, that the Kennedy Administration did deliberately refrain from full-scale anti-satellite weapons development, in an effort to avoid jeopardizing satellite reconnaissance legitimacy.

43. Quoted in ibid., p. 69. For discussion of the Soviet diplomatic offensive of 1962 on this subject, see Steinberg, *Satellite Reconnaissance*, pp. 54–55.

44. Ibid., pp. 56–62. One part of this campaign was a full set of briefings for American allies on the capabilities of reconnaissance satellites. See, on this point, Stares, *The Militarization of Space*, p. 69.

45. Quoted in ibid., p. 71.

46. *New York Times* (July 15, 1963). The report was by C. L. Sulzberger, but curiously Sulzberger does not mention the comment about satellites in his July 11, 1963, diary entry about the Spaak-Khrushchev picnic. C. L. Sulzberger, *The Last of the Giants* (New York: Macmillan, 1970), pp. 994–995. For a similar Khrushchev offer to William Benton in May 1964, see Klass, *Secret Sentries in Space*, p. 127n.

47. Steinberg, *Satellite Reconnaissance*, pp. 64–65; Klass, *Secret Sentries in Space*, pp. 127–129. For the General Assembly resolutions, see Jenks, *Space Law*, pp. 317–319, 326–327.

48. Klass, *Secret Sentries in Space*, pp. 119–122.

49. See footnote 46, above.

50. Klass, *Secret Sentries in Space*, pp. 120–122; Stares, *The Militarization of Space*, p. 238.

51. See Rostow, *Open Skies*, pp. 82–83.

52. Taylor and Mondley, *Spies in the Sky*, pp. 72–79.

53. See, on this point, Glenn T. Seaborg, *Kennedy, Khrushchev, and the Test Ban* (Berkeley: University of California Press, 1981), pp. 226–228.

54. Quoted in Klass, *Secret Sentries in Space*, p. 217. For a discussion of the "Gilpatric principle," see ibid., pp. 216–218.

55. Steinberg, *Satellite Reconnaissance*, pp. 71–87.

56. Stares, *The Militarization of Space*, pp. 116–117.

57. Ibid., pp. 50–53, 127.

58. For the Soviet anti-satellite program that began in 1976, and its effect in stimulating comparable U. S. programs, see Stares, *The Militarization of Space*, pp. 176, 187–192, 243.

59. See Hilsman, *To Move a Nation*, p. 224.

60. Reconnaissance satellite launchings are generally announced—although without specifying their function—and their orbital parameters are provided. With the voluntary cooperation of both the United States and the Soviet Union, the U.N. Secretary General began maintaining a public registry of all objects launched into space in March 1962. With the coming into force of the U.N. Convention on Registration of Objects Launched into Outer Space in September 1976, this procedure became mandatory. Jenks, *Space Law*, pp. 221–224; J. E. S. Fawcett, *Outer Space: New Challenges to Law and Policy* (Oxford: Clarendon Press, 1984), pp. 27–28, 154–159. For an indication of what can be learned about satellite missions from a careful analysis of orbital parameters, see G. E. Perry, "Identification of Military Components Within the Soviet Space Programme," in Jasani, ed., *Outer Space*, pp. 135–154. An excellent introduction to the military uses of satellites in general is Ashton B. Carter, "Satellites and Anti-Satellites: The Limits of the Possible," *International Security* 10 (Spring 1986), especially pp. 46–72.

61. David Hafemeister, Joseph J. Romm and Kosta Tsipis, "The Verification of Compliance

with Arms-Control Agreements," *Scientific American* (March, 1985): 40–41. For technical details, see Bhupendra Jasani, "Military Space Technology and Its Implications," in Jasani, ed., *Outer Space*, pp. 43–50; T. Sakata and H. Shimoda, "Image Analysis and Sensor Technology for Satellite Monitoring," ibid., pp. 197–214; also T. Orhaug and G. Forssell, "Information Extraction from Images," ibid., pp. 215–227.

62. B. G. Blair, "Reconnaissance Satellites," ibid., pp. 125–130.

63. Jasani, "Military Space Technology," ibid., pp. 54–56; Blair, "Reconnaissance Satellites," ibid., pp. 132–133. See also Charles Elachi, "Radar Images of the Earth from Space," *Scientific American* (December 1982): 54–61.

64. Jasani, "Military Space Technology," in Jasani, ed., *Outer Space*, pp. 50–54. See also Bamford, *The Puzzle Palace*, pp. 252–255.

65. See Prados, *The Soviet Estimate*, pp. 3–4, 290.

66. See footnote 40, above.

67. The U-2 is perhaps the best example of a secretly developed American military system that the Russians probably would have detected if they had had reconnaissance satellites functioning at that time. "Stealth" bomber development might have been another, had the Carter Administration had not chosen, for reasons that must certainly have puzzled the Russians, to reveal the fact that it was underway. See, on this latter point, Elizabeth Drew, *Portrait of an Election: The 1980 Presidential Campaign* (New York: Simon & Schuster, 1981), pp. 267–268.

68. U. S. Arms Control and Disarmament Agency, *Arms Control and Disarmament Agreements* (Washington: U.S. Arms Control and Disarmament Agency, 1982), pp. 141, 151.

69. Ibid., pp. 249, 261.

70. K. Santhanam, "Use of Satellites in Crisis Monitoring," in Jasani, ed., *Outer Space*, pp. 269–271. For the Falklands conflict, see "America's Falklands War," *Economist* (March 3, 1984): 30–31.

71. Santhanam, "Use of Satellites in Crisis Monitoring," p. 271; Stares, *The Militarization of Space*, pp. 140–141; Raymond Garthoff, *Detente and Confrontation: American-Soviet Relations from Nixon to Reagan* (Washington, D.C.: Brookings, 1985), p. 763.

72. For some dramatic examples, see Nicholas M. Short, et al., *Mission to Earth: Landsat Views the World* (Washington, D.C.: National Aeronautics and Space Administration, 1976).

73. Landsat operates at 30 meters resolution. A new French satellite, launched in 1986, provides similar photographs, but at 10 meters resolution. D. D. Edwards, "Making Remote Sense Out of Space Commercialization," *Science News* (December 21 and 28, 1985): 393.

74. See Stares, *The Militarization of Space*, p. 49.

75. Ibid., pp. 120–129, 201–202. On the danger to other satellites of nuclear explosions in outer space, see ibid., p. 108.

76. Ibid., pp. 136–146. Raymond Garthoff has suggested that a significant opportunity was lost during the SALT I negotiations to trade off the American operational anti-satellite capability for a complete ban on anti-ballistic missile systems, in which the Soviets were leading at that time. *Detente and Confrontation*, pp. 189–190. This argument may exaggerate the extent to which Project 437 can be considered a workable anti-satellite system, however.

77. Stares, *The Militarization of Space*, pp. 146–156. See also Richard L. Garwin and John Pike, "Space Weapons: History and Current Debate," *Bulletin of the Atomic Scientists*, XL (May 1984): 2S–3S.

78. Stares, *The Militarization of Space*, pp. 162–166.

79. These events are most fully discussed in Garthoff, *Detente and Confrontation*, pp. 360–537.

80. Stares, *The Militarization of Space*, pp. 145–146.

81. Prados, *The Soviet Estimate*, pp. 245–257.

82. Stares, *The Militarization of Space*, pp. 168–171.

83. For recent American anti-satellite weapons development, see ibid., pp. 206–209; also Garwin and Pike, "Space Weapons," pp. 3S–4S.

84. On the anti-satellite implications of SDI, see ibid., pp. 2S–9S.

85. For discussions on an anti-satellite weapons ban during the Carter and Reagan adminis-trations, see Stares, *The Militarization of Space,* pp. 181–187, 192–199, 216–220, 229–235; and National Academy of Sciences, Committee on International Security and Arms Control, *Nuclear Arms Control: Background and Issues* (Washington, D.C.: National Academy Press, 1985), pp. 159–186.

86. The discussion that follows owes much to Steinberg, *Satellite Reconnaissance,* espe-cially pp. 99–101, 111–112, 116–119, 122–124, 129–135, 166–167.

87. See, on this question, David B. Rivkin, Jr., "Star Wars: The Nagging Questions: What Does Moscow Think?" *Foreign Policy* 59 (Summer 1985): 85–105.

88. The SALT I negotiations took three years, from 1969 to 1972; SALT II negotiations required seven years, from 1972 to 1979. For the Reagan Administration's difficulties in formu-lating a position on strategic arms control, see Strobe Talbott, *Deadly Gambits: The Reagan Administration and the Stalemate in Nuclear Arms Control* (New York: Knopf, 1984).

89. Two recent discussions of the impact of domestic politics on recent American foreign policy are Joseph S. Nye, Jr., *The Making of America's Soviet Policy* (New Haven, Conn.: Yale University Press, 1984); and I. M. Destler, Leslie H. Gelb, and Anthony Lake, *Our Own Worst Enemy: The Unmaking of American Foreign Policy* (New York: Simon & Schuster, 1984). There is also a fine brief case study of the Soviet "combat brigade" controversy in Richard E. Neustadt and Ernest R. May, *Thinking in Time: The Uses of History for Decision-Makers* (New York: Free Press, 1986), pp. 92–96.

90. For some possibilities, see Carter, "Satellites and Anti-Satellites," pp. 73–88.

91. See Alexander L. George and Richard Smoke, *Deterrence in American Foreign Policy: Theory and Practice* (New York: Columbia University Press, 1974), pp. 527–530, 565.

92. See, on this point, Robert Jervis, Richard Ned Lebow, and Janice Gross Stein, *Psy-chology and Deterrence* (Baltimore: Johns Hopkins University Press, 1985), pp. 15–18; also Deborah Welch Larson, *Origins of Containment: A Psychological Explanation* (Princeton: Prince-ton University Press, 1985), pp. 34–42.

93. Prados, *The Soviet Estimate,* pp. 278–282.

94. See William M. Arkin, "Waging Secrecy," *Bulletin of the Atomic Scientists* (March 1985): 5–6.

95. For the durability of systemic interests in Soviet-American relations since 1945, see John Lewis Gaddis, "The Long Peace: Elements of Stability in the Postwar International System," *International Security* 10 (Spring 1986): 99–142.

16

Attempts to Regulate Military Activities in Space

STEVEN WEBER AND SIDNEY DRELL

The expanded use of space for military purposes is a central case study in the examination of American and Soviet cooperative behavior in security issues. The two superpowers have—to a varying extent over the course of the last 25 years—achieved and
sustained limited cooperative arrangements regulating the conduct of security-related
activities in space. This chapter examines the history of the development, management,
and deterioration of a complex web of both tacit and formal arrangements regulating
U.S.–Soviet interaction in the militarization of space. Our purpose is to contribute to a
more general understanding of the conditions and processes that favor the development
of cooperation in security issues between essentially adversarial states.

Since the early days of space exploration, there has existed on the part of much of
the public and the technical community a vague moral presumption that space ought
somehow to be a sanctuary of peace and international cooperation. Civilian activities in
space have in fact been the subject of significant international cooperation. The International Geophysical Year, during which scientists from the United States, the USSR,
and other countries joined to prepare and analyze fly-bys of Halley's Comet, was a
particularly visible example of scientific collaboration in the extension of knowledge
about space.

Concurrently, however, both superpowers have vigorously pursued military and
security objectives in space much as they have on the earth, on the seas, and in the air.
As a result, space is already highly militarized, and has been an arena of active military
competition since the first ICBMs flew through space in 1957. Since the early 1960s,
more than 2,000 military payloads have been placed in orbit by the United States and
the USSR. While comparable figures are not available for the Soviet Union, the U.S.
Department of Defense (DoD) has invested over $70 billion in military space activities
over the past 25 years.[1] Accordingly, we proceed from the assumption that there is
nothing sacrosanct or even unusual about military and national security activities in
space.

There is a clear contrast between space and the Antarctic as areas of military competition. The Antarctic was not believed to be an area of potential military importance
by the nations claiming sovereignty over parts of the continent, who agreed in 1959
that:

> Antarctica shall be used for peaceful purposes only. There shall be prohibited, inter
> alia, any measures of a military nature, such as the establishment of military bases and

fortifications and the carrying out of military maneuvers, as well as the testing of any type of weapons.[2]

Space, however, is widely recognized to have important military uses, only some of which may be amenable to present technology.

Military missions in space pose unique opportunities for, as well as threats to, the national security interests of both the United States and the Soviet Union. The two states face a complex structure of shared and conflicting interests, within which lie opportunities for, and impediments to, the achievement of limited cooperative arrangements beneficial to both sides. While a good deal of the competitive behavior that is seen in this relationship is simply the result of conflicting interests, of greater theoretical interest is conflictual behavior arising in areas of potential cooperation. These cases can be thought of as "missed opportunities"—describing points of parallel or shared interests that for any number of reasons are not realized in agreements or tacit coordination of behavior.

In this chapter we will examine the manner in which certain subsets of shared interests have been realized in the development and management of a space regime that has evolved to constrain, in limited ways, the military aspects of superpower competition in space. We will focus primarily upon restraint (cooperative and unilateral) and competition in the development of anti-satellite weapons. Analysis of success and failure in placing mutually desirable limits on the competition will contribute to an understanding of the factors that led to the realization and, more recently, the eventual breakdown of limited cooperative arrangements in the militarization of space, a phrase used henceforth to describe the extension of military uses of space.

THE SPACE THREAT AND THE SATELLITE SECURITY DILEMMA

In considering the nature of the potential threat posed by military activities in space, it is useful to categorize current and potential military satellite (MILSAT) missions within a tripartite classification on the basis of their impact on the security interests of the adversary. The first category of MILSAT functions can be described as those that are relatively benign and stabilizing in peacetime. A number of missions currently carried out by satellites fall within this category. For example, the use of photoreconnaissance and other satellites has enabled the superpowers to achieve some degree of confidence in verification of mutually beneficial arms control agreements, whose conclusion and successful management might have otherwise not been possible. Other functions that can be called benign and stabilizing in peacetime include early warning of nuclear attack, and reliable communications. Both early warning systems and communication capabilities are particularly useful in reassuring both sides that an attack has *not* occurred; importantly, they also provide means for each side to communicate to its own forces and to the adversary that it believes the situation is stable.

A secondary category of MILSAT functions, considerably less benign, are those that enhance or multiply the value of terrestrial forces. These functions are by themselves nondestructive, but they act in support of destructive forces, multiplying by varying degrees the latter's military utility. Examples of this category include Soviet electronic and radar ocean reconnaissance satellites (EORSAT and RORSAT), which can be used to locate and direct Soviet forces toward U.S. Navy battle groups. Some communication and reconnaissance capabilities fall within this category: for example, satellites can provide real-time information and communications to tactical battlefield units that significantly enhance the destructive power of conventional forces.

The final category of satellite functions can be described as direct application of force from space. At the present time, neither side has chosen to deploy satellites capable of such functions. However, the technological constraints that have contributed to restraint in this area are undergoing change: there are now a large (and increasing) number of potential missions in which the direct application of force from space might be both controllable and useful. For example, space-based components of an advanced ballistic-missile defense (BMD) system would clearly maintain capabilities for the direct application of force. Similarly, anti-satellite (ASAT) weapons based in space, or defensive systems for satellites that relied on destructive capabilities would also represent the direct application of force from space.

The problem confronting a state in its attempt to manage the threat from space is thus extremely complex. Some satellites that provide capabilities for force support and force enhancement have no benign or stabilizing role in peacetime; they contribute to the security of one side by threatening the security of the adversary. Offensive satellites, capable of the direct application of force from space, would similarly have no potential benign function, and would contribute to the exacerbation of the classic security dilemma between hostile states. As capabilities within these two categories provide no potential benefits to the adversary state, and may in fact threaten its vital interests, each state maintains a strong incentive to deny to the other side the ability to perform these missions. This is of course balanced by each side's interest in providing sanctuary for its own offensive or force-supporting satellites.

The unique characteristic of the ''satellite security dilemma'' is that the incentive to place satellites at risk is also balanced (on both sides) by the desire to provide sanctuary for benign, stabilizing satellite functions that serve the shared interests of the states. Since these satellite functions may increase the security of both states under a wide variety of conditions, both sides may have a net interest in assuring the invulnerability of particular satellite-based capabilities. The situation is further complicated by the fact that most forms of denial are insufficiently discriminating to place at risk only those satellites which pose a threat to a state's security, while not threatening satellites that perform benign, stabilizing functions.[3]

A second important characteristic of the satellite security dilemma is that the mere existence of the capability to destroy benign and stabilizing satellite systems may decrease their utility and stabilizing effects in time of crisis. If State A is highly dependent on certain satellite-based capabilities, the benign functions of these satellites will be stabilizing only if the satellites are believed to be invulnerable to preemptive attack. Thus, if State A fears that its space-based communication and early warning systems are vulnerable to preemptive attack by State B, and if it is highly dependent on these systems, it will experience pressure to attack State B in a preemptive fashion (while A's essential systems remain intact), should war be perceived as imminent or likely. In a classic example of Schelling's ''multiplier effect'' the side that threatens the adversary's satellites may become aware of its potential enemy's tenuous position, and experience pressure to preempt before the adversary does so.[4] As a result, the capability to destroy essential satellites may eventuate in a dangerous and unstable ''solution'' to the problem of managing the militarization of space.

MANAGING THE THREAT: COOPERATIVE
AND COMPETITIVE RESPONSES

Recent developments in cooperation theory suggest an analytically useful means of characterizing policies chosen to manage threats arising from the militarization of space. State policy choices can be considered as a series of decisions regarding the most efficient strategies to adopt in response to a developing requirement of an interdependent security relationship.

The development and deployment of ASAT weapons, to deter and/or deny offensive MILSAT capabilities, is a means of managing the threat which creates new threats against the adversary's security interests, as well as against benign and stabilizing satellite capabilities. This form of response is usefully categorized as *competitive;* it represents unilateral action that results in exacerbation of security dilemmas, and promotes escalation of the competition. Although the competitive response has the advantage of deterring the development and deployment of space-based offensive capabilities, the adversary may choose to engage in a measure-countermeasure race to ascertain whether he can achieve some functional advantage. At the minimum, the adversary will experience incentives to redress the diminution in his security brought about by the impact (part of which may be inadvertent) of the existence of ASAT capabilities. A series of competitive responses may deteriorate into a costly, destabilizing, mixed offensive-defensive arms race in space. From the point of view of economic costs, arms race stability, and strategic stability, this is likely to be a non-optimal means of managing the threat.

Other means of responding to the threat may be usefully categorized as representing *cooperation.* These are actions which contribute to the security of the state without threatening the security of the adversary, and thus ameliorate the severity of security dilemmas. Cooperative actions promote relatively stable solutions that do not require escalation of the competition by the adversary in order to protect his interests.

In the case of the militarization of space (as in many security issues), cooperative policies can be subdivided into *unilateral cooperative* measures and *bilateral cooperative* measures. Unilateral cooperative measures are those actions a state can take on its own initiative to enhance its security position without exacerbating security dilemmas (i.e., without posing new or more severe threats to the adversary). Unilateral cooperative measures do not require policy coordination with the adversary in order to contribute to the security of the state. Examples include passive satellite survivability measures (such as "hardening" of satellites, or moving them to higher altitudes), as well as selective countermeasures to MILSATs that do not pose additional threats to the adversary (emission control, deceptive sailing techniques, and reduction of radar cross-sections by Navy battle groups, as countermeasures to Soviet ocean reconnaissance capabilities).

Bilateral cooperative measures are those means of dealing with the threat which require coordination of policy between the adversaries in order to be efficacious. In the context of the militarization of space, bilateral cooperative measures for managing the threat can be described as various forms of arms control. Arms control measures need not, of course, be formal negotiated agreements; in space, arms control has in fact more often taken the form of tacit agreements or coordination of policy.

Bilateral cooperative solutions to interdependent security issues are most difficult to achieve and to sustain between adversarial states. The impediments to stable cooperation in the international system have been discussed, in a general sense, in the introduction to this volume. Nevertheless, the interdependent status of security relations between the United States and the Soviet Union in the militarization of space opens up a wide variety of opportunities for the development of mutually beneficial cooperative arrangements that would contribute to the security of both states (or at a minimum, close off areas of mutually undesirable competition).

Over the course of the past 25 years, the two sides have cooperated to a varying extent in the management of particular aspects of the competition in space. The complex web of tacit and formal agreements regulating superpower behavior in space that has evolved over time can be said to constitute an international regime for space, defined as "principles, norms, rules, and decision-making procedures around which actor expectations converge in a given issue area."[5] Conceptualizing the history of U.S.–Soviet efforts to regulate the militarization of space as posing the task of creating and managing a regime is valuable in a number of respects. It permits the analyst to draw selectively on the practical experience and theory related to the evolution of regimes in non-security areas. Thus, the regime orientation provides a number of candidate hypotheses and suggests variables potentially relevant to the success or failure of cooperative arrangements in international relations.

The regime framework also focuses attention on the strategies states may adopt to promote cooperative outcomes. It suggests analysis of state policies as appropriate or inappropriate means of influence in an interdependent decision situation. Attempts to overcome the impediments to cooperation may take the form of strategies seeking the establishment of behavioral norms, procedural or substantive rules for the regulation of competition, or appropriate institutional arrangements to aid in the implementation and stabilization of cooperative solutions.

THE ARGUMENT

In an attempt to explore questions relevant to cooperation in security issues, this chapter examines the history of U.S.–Soviet interaction in the militarization of space. Due to limitations on available data regarding Soviet decision-making, the emphasis is on American strategy and policy for managing the developing threat from space. The period 1960–1986 is divided (somewhat roughly) into four segments, each of which is characterized by a particular American strategy for managing the threat from space.

The first period, 1960 to 1968, is characterized by an American strategy of contingent restraint in military space activities. This period witnessed the evolution of a partial regime governing the militarization of space, as a result of limited policy coordination between the two states (not simply as an epiphenomenon of technological constraints). The second period, covering the late 1960s and early 1970s, is characterized by the maintenance of the strategy of contingent restraint, and the relatively successful management of the limited regime, despite a number of significant challenges to cooperation in space. The third period, beginning in the mid-1970s and continuing to 1980, witnesses a significant shift in American strategy towards a two-track approach—contingent threats of escalation, linked to a drive for the negotiation of formal agreements limiting military activities in space. The third period also witnesses significant deterioration of the partial space regime that had evolved over the course of the previous decades. Finally, the fourth period, beginning in 1980 and continuing to the present (1986), is characterized by an American strategy of unrestrained competition in military space activities. Cooperation in space underwent further deterioration during this period. Although the future of the partial space regime remains uncertain at the time of writing, the maintenance of even limited cooperative arrangements between the United States and the Soviet Union in managing the militarization of space seems increasingly unlikely. (Since this paper was written, the U.S. Congress has reinjected an element of contingency into the U.S. ASAT program by restricting funds for the continued testing of the Miniature Homing Vehicle (MHV) system unless and until the Soviet Union resumes tests of its ASAT. As of August 1986, the Administration has been unsuccessful in its attempt to argue against this restriction, and the MHV testing program remains, at present, on hold.)

This chapter seeks to account for shifts in American strategy as a partial result of the interaction of technological possibilities with factors affecting reciprocity in the international system and in the U.S.–Soviet relationship. The basic argument explores the conditions under which strategies based on the norm of reciprocity are viable and efficacious in the context of interdependent, mixed-motive "games" in security between the superpowers.

Five clusters of variables are traced through the history of the interaction. They are: the interests and incentives of the states (incorporating the impact of progress in space-related technologies), the general political environment between the superpowers, the development of military and strategic theory, the impact of bureaucratic politics, and the importance of "saliencies." (The term "saliency" refers to a focal point around which the players' expectations converge in a particular game or scenario. Saliencies in international politics are shared perceptions of a potential boundary or point around which coordination of the independent states' policies can occur. We will give greater empirical content to the term in the course of the historical discussion.) Shifts in the state of these variables are used to explain changes in the viability of reciprocity as a norm governing superpower strategy and behavior in the competition over the militarization of space.

The 1960s

Following the launch of Sputnik in 1957, and the subsequent rapid development and deployment of reconnaissance satellites, expectations of an arms race in space were widespread among American policy makers and analysts. Only a few months prior to the deployment of the first successful reconnaissance satellite (Discoverer 13) in August 1960, the Soviet Union had shot down a U-2 high altitude reconnaissance aircraft. This act was accompanied by considerable bellicose rhetoric, and by Soviet proclamations that overhead reconnaissance constituted a violation of the sovereignty of Soviet airspace, and thus of international law. It was assumed by many American policy makers that the USSR would do its utmost to shoot down or otherwise interfere with American reconnaissance satellites as soon as the technological capability to do so was available.[6]

Contrary to expectations, reconnaissance and other satellites continue to operate unhindered, some 26 years after the first successful launch. Neither the Soviet Union nor the United States has deployed ASAT systems capable of destroying or disabling the vast majority of satellite systems. This stands in sharp contrast to the Soviet response to the use of U-2 aircraft, which the Soviet Union succeeded in shooting down only three years after its initial use.

The following section traces the development through the 1960s of a regime concerning satellite reconnaissance activities. We begin by examining the initial response to the deployment of reconnaissance satellites. We then trace the evolution of a pattern of mutual restraint in ASAT activities through the 1960s, constituting a necessary prerequisite to the development and tacit acceptance of a satellite reconnaissance regime. The conditions and processes that contributed to this unexpected outcome are considered within the analytic framework discussed at the outset of this chapter.

The successful launch of Sputnik in October of 1957 created the possibility that the military aspect of the security competition between the USSR and the United States would be extended to the previously unexploited realm of outer space. As technology achieved the ability to penetrate outer space, scientists, political scientists, policy makers, and military strategists generally came to accept the belief that these capabilities were likely to be applied to the development of space weapons.

In fact, the technology that had permitted the Soviet Union to launch the world's first earth satellite was soon brought to bear upon the problem of intercontinental delivery of nuclear warheads. Within several years of Sputnik, the Soviets had successfully tested an ICBM, employing technology similar to that required to place weapons in orbit. As the ICBM race began in earnest, there seemed little reason to believe that the competition would end with weapons that merely travelled *through* space.

The perception that an arms race in weapons *based* in space was a likely occurrence was shared by those who desired such an outcome, and by those who profoundly wished to avoid it. Despite the small advantage the Soviets had achieved by orbiting Sputnik prior to the first American satellite, some Americans were confident that the development of the arms race in a direction increasingly dependent on high technology was profoundly advantageous to the United States. Whereas the Soviets maintained a numerical advantage in conventional weaponry and in the size of their land-based armies, the "coming age of space combat" played directly to the technological superiority of the United States.[7]

Mixed with the belief that the United States maintained a technological edge over the Soviet Union was the perception that this advantage was fleeting, and must be continuously exploited lest the Soviets catch up and perhaps even overtake the United States. As a result, the hope of potential American "command" of space was mixed with a fear that delay might mean the squandering of American advantages. Furthermore, the significance of Soviet technological proficiency demonstrated by Sputnik was not to be underestimated. According to the dominant perception at the time, "the country that controls the moon will control the earth."[8] If the United States were not to fall dangerously behind in the overall competition, it had little choice but to meet the perceived Soviet challenge and extend the arms race to outer space.

The growing perception that the militarization of space had become inevitable can be partially explained on the basis of structural features of international politics. The Soviet Sputnik, passing as it did over the heads of the American population, engendered a security dilemma of extreme proportions between the two states. Regardless of whether the Soviets intended Sputnik to be a gesture or capability threatening to American national security interests, it was in fact perceived as such by the American public and policy makers. The military potential of weapons based in space could not be ignored.

Given the uncertainty of Soviet intentions, and the structural anarchy that characterizes the international environment, the United States was in a sense constrained to act as if Sputnik and its potential offspring posed a direct threat to American security interests.

The impact of the security dilemma upon American perceptions is nicely illustrated by the fear, prominent at the time, that the United States might be denied access to space (and to whatever future advantages access to space might entail) by an advancing Soviet capability in satellite and ASAT systems.[9] If the United States were to prevent this scenario—spoken of at the time as the "Panama Hypothesis"—from becoming reality, it would have to not only deny the advantage in space to the Soviet Union, but in fact seize the advantage itself. According to the journal *Astronautics,* there were "strategic areas in space vital to future scientific, military, and commercial programs— which must be occupied by the United States lest their use be forever denied us through prior occupation by unfriendly powers."[10] When both sides feel the need to pursue unilateral advantage solely to maintain and protect their security position and options, the security dilemma between states is severe and may be the source of inadvertent—or mutually undesirable—escalation of arms competition.

A closer examination of the threat posed (or potentially posed) by the development of Soviet space capabilities reveals that U.S. fears were not totally unjustified, although they might have been somewhat premature. Soviet space activities as early as 1961 began to suggest the simultaneous development of both aspects of the dual space threat (both the denial of the use of space to the United States and the potential for the direct application of force from space).

As early as 1961, the Soviets succeeded in placing a very large spacecraft in orbit, which was then used to launch a Venus probe. Demonstration of this technology suggested a developing capability to launch weapons from space both at other space targets and at targets on earth, thus posing a dual threat.[11] Soviet detonations of large (30 and 58 megaton) nuclear weapons later that year, which terminated the moratorium on nuclear testing that had lasted up until October, were seen not only as a bargaining tactic in the Berlin crisis, but also as a part of a Soviet ABM and ASAT development program.[12] Finally, the successful rendezvous of the two manned spacecraft Vostok 3 and 4 suggested the possibility that the Soviets might soon possess the capability to intercept and destroy American reconnaissance satellites.[13]

Soviet statements regarding the capabilities and direction of their active space development programs served to exacerbate American perceptions of threat. On the subject of capabilities, Marshal Sergei S. Biriuzov, chief of the Soviet Strategic Missile Forces, proclaimed that "it had now become possible, at a command from the earth, to launch rockets from a satellite at any desired time, at any point in the satellite's trajectory."[14] While this capability could presumably be directed either at objects in space or on the earth, Defense Minister Rodion Malinovsky stressed the ASAT mission in his announcement that defense forces had been tasked to study means of combating "an aggressor's . . . attempt to reconnoitre our country . . . from space."[15] The combination of potentially threatening capabilities with uncertainty regarding Soviet intentions, exacerbated by hostile Soviet rhetoric, nearly guaranteed that a worst-case analysis of the potential threat would become the basis of an American policy response to Soviet space activities.

Early U.S. perceptions of the threat arising from Soviet space activities did indeed suggest that the two sides were about to embark on an escalation of the arms race into outer space. Perceptions of a serious threat to American security interests were aired both in the public press and in testimony before the Congress. General James Ferguson, Air Force deputy chief of staff for research and technology, testified before Congress in early 1962 that

> the Soviets have demonstrated increasing competence in space technology which may have application to a broad spectrum of military systems. Since we cannot know the Soviet's intentions, we must be prepared to respond to a variety of threats.

The perception of threat, and pressure for an American response, was further exacerbated by the aerospace industry and its press organs, as well as by Republican candidates in the 1962 Congressional elections.[16] By mid-1962, it appeared as if an escalatory American response, in the form of a new and intensive emphasis on military space activities, was indeed forthcoming. Priorities within the American military space program were reshuffled so as to place great emphasis on the development of ASAT technology.[17] An American ASAT capability, it was argued, would deter the Soviets from carrying out attacks against American satellites, for fear of retaliation. In addition, the American ASAT could be adapted for active defense of American satellites, and might at some point be used to attack hostile Soviet space assets.

A number of specific ASAT development programs received boosts in 1962 in accordance with this policy. While Project SAINT, designed primarily as a satellite *inspection* (rather than destruction) system, received less attention, new emphasis was placed on the development of ground-based ASAT systems capable of intercepting and destroying hostile satellites. Program 505, an Army proposal to employ a variant of the Nike Zeus missile in an ASAT role, finally received a go-ahead in 1962 (after several years of controversy).[18] Project 437, an Air Force system employing a modified Thor booster in a "non-orbital collision-course satellite interceptor system capable of destroying satellites in an early time period," also began serious development in 1962.[19]

By late 1962, the United States and the USSR appeared to be poised on the brink of an arms race in space. New emphasis on military space missions and ASAT development programs was reflected in public perceptions, Congressional sentiments, and thinking among strategic analysts.[20] A sense of inevitablity had crept into the behavior of the two states: their policies and their rhetoric did little to suggest the possibility for a cooperative solution to the threats posed to the security of both sides by the militarization of space.

The massive new emphasis on U.S. military space programs prompted the Kennedy Administration in 1962 to undertake a detailed re-examination of the efficacy and direction of the U.S. space program. During the course of this evaluation, the threat posed to American security interests by Soviet space activities was judged to be far less severe than previously thought. This new evaluation, based for the most part on a re-interpretation of previously available information (rather than on newly received information), stressed the limitations, rather than the potential strengths of the Soviet military space program. For example, the rendezvous achieved by Vostok 3 and 4 was reinterpreted as a demonstration of a relatively rudimentary capability, achieving at best a three-mile separation after launching the spacecraft from the same point into identical orbits. Although this approach would have been close enough to permit disruption of a target satellite by a nuclear warhead, it was known at the time (on the basis of high altitude nuclear tests) that such an explosion would interfere with satellites at a much greater distance, disabling a number of satellites (belonging to both sides) in addition to the specific target of the attack. The military utility of nuclear explosions in space was thus known to be severely constrained by the inability to control the application of force. The importance of the use of a satellite as a launch platform was downplayed, and it was emphasized that the Soviets had yet to solve the central problems of accuracy or command and control that would be essential to the operation of a viable ASAT system. According to Steinberg, information regarding Soviet activities in space was reinterpreted to yield the conclusion that "the Soviet space threat was not immediate and that the development of U.S. ASAT systems was not urgently required."[21]

The reinterpretation of the Soviet threat preceded a shift in American strategy that was to set the tone of U.S. space policy for the next decade. In early 1962, the United States prepared to manage the threat from Soviet space programs by a strategy of competition, or "defection"; that is, by posing new threats to the Soviet Union in response to Soviet actions. During 1962, American strategy shifted gradually toward contingent restraint, designed to promote bilateral cooperative solutions to the problem of managing the threat from space. This shift can be demonstrated both in changes in public statements by U.S. officials and in changes in emphasis of military space development programs in the 1960s.

In late 1962, public statements by members of the Kennedy Administration shifted away from the comparatively bellicose rhetoric toward a new policy of contingent restraint regarding the militarization of space. Three major themes of policy were evident: the militarization of space was a mutually undesirable outcome, the United States would be willing to forgo efforts in this area to the extent that such restraint was reciprocated by the Soviet Union, and limits on activities in space could be coordinated without necessarily relying on formal negotiations or treaties. Deputy Secretary of Defense Roswell Gilpatric echoed these themes in the following comments of September 5, 1962:

> The U.S. believes that it is highly desirable for its own security and for the security of the world that the arms race should not be expanded into outer space and we are seeking in every feasible way to achieve that purpose . . . I can think of no greater stimulus for a Soviet thermonuclear arms effort in space than a US commitment to such a program. This we will not do . . . We will, of course, take such steps as are necessary to defend ourselves and our allies *if the Soviet Union forces us to do so.*[22]

Gilpatric's comments clearly indicate the shift from a competitive strategy to one of contingent restraint in both offensive and defensive military space activities. To the extent that the Soviet Union demonstrated reciprocal restraint, the United States would not move to develop ASAT weapons or otherwise extend the arms race into outer space. Furthermore, continued restraint was predicated on the demonstration of reciprocity, rather than (necessarily) upon the conclusion of a formal treaty limiting the activities of the sides.

Proclamations of a policy of contingent restraint were in fact matched by concrete demonstrations of a willingness to limit American military activities in space. During the course of the mid 1960s, American ASAT development programs were curtailed and/or reoriented to conform to the strategy of contingent restraint. The most obvious indication of this redirection of policy was the cancellation of the SAINT program in December of 1962. (Although the defense department officially referred to this action as a "reorientation," the extent to which the program was functionally curtailed justifies calling this action cancellation). In conceptual terms, SAINT had proven itself to have little military value as a satellite inspection system. An alternative course of action to cancelling the program would have been to reorient it as a satellite kill mechanism— but this the Administration, in accordance with the new policy of contingent restraint, was not prepared to do.[23] Although the DoD did not offer an official explanation of the decision to cancel SAINT, Steinberg argues on the basis of interviews with a number of participants in the decision that "a fear of escalation of military conflict and arms competition in space was a primary reason for the demise of SAINT."[24]

The cancellation of SAINT was accompanied by decisions to proceed with several other ASAT programs such as Projects 505 and 437, as previously described. These development programs were pursued, however, within limited bounds and can arguably be said to have been hedges against Soviet ASAT "breakout," rather than unrestrained attempts to develop a dedicated ASAT capability. Both programs were of limited military utility, and little effort was expended to significantly enhance their capabilities against Soviet satellites. After achieving operational readiness in 1963, Program 505 was maintained with the limited capability to launch one nuclear-tipped ASAT weapon against a hostile Soviet satellite. This severely limited program was phased out by 1967, as it was largely replaced by Program 437. This project, an attempt to construct a quick-fix ASAT system with conventional technology and available boosters, achieved operational capability in June of 1964. Full operational capability, however, was limited to two nuclear-tipped missiles with a reaction time of at least 24 hours, capable of destroying satellites up to an altitude and range of 200 and 1500 nautical miles, respectively.[25]

It is clear that American ASAT development programs in the 1960s operated under a policy of fiscal and political, as well as military restraint. Cuts in program funding began in 1964, and testing of the 437 system (for both operational and developmental purposes) decreased in frequency throughout the 1960s.[26] In public statements, President Lyndon Johnson stressed the limitations, rather than the strengths, of American ASAT capabilities.[27] The 437 system, for example, was constrained by its inability to attack satellites other than those passing directly overhead, and by its limitation to only two launch pads and several missiles; further, the operational readiness of the system was at most times uncertain. At no time did Program 437 pose a militarily significant threat to Soviet space assets. It did, however, serve as a reminder of the fact that the United States maintained a technological base from which to pursue more dedicated ASAT development, should Soviet activities demand this course of action.

The argument that ASAT development activities during the 1960s were part of a strategy of contingent restraint is strengthened by the observation that nonhostile capabilities relevant to activities in space underwent extensive development during this decade. Significant work on the improvement of space-track facilities began in the late 1950s and continued unabated throughout the 1960s. Similarly, the United States placed increasing emphasis on sophisticated sensor technologies directly relevant to the mission of identifying objects in space.[28] The 1960s also witnessed the development by both the United States and the Soviet Union of increasingly sophisticated satellites and spacecraft for use in civilian scientific and exploratory programs. Significant advances in the use of space by both sides lends credence to the argument that demonstrated restraint in ASAT activities cannot be explained simply as an epiphenomenon of technological constraints. Rather, ASAT restraint appears to have been a deliberate attempt to coordinate a policy of contingent restraint designed to prevent the militarization of space, and manage the threat to the security of the states by cooperative means.

Up to this point we have described the development, in the early 1960s, of a potential arms race in space. The outright, unrestrained militarization of space that seemed inevitable in 1962 did not, however, take place. The explanation for this cooperative outcome lies partly in the technological constraints on ASAT possibilities—given limited guidance capabilities and the resulting necessity for the use of nuclear kill mechanisms. The adoption and implementation of a strategy of contingent restraint on the part of the United States was an important additional factor contributing to the outcome of this case during the 1960s: it helped to restrain what might otherwise have been a vigorous (but mutually undesirable) competition in ASAT development.

An examination of the conditions and processes that contributed to the cooperative outcome described should begin with an analysis of the interests and incentives of the two states. In the case of the potential militarization of space in the 1960s, neither side possessed clear and compelling incentives to compete—that is, to unilaterally pursue hostile military objectives in space. As a result of technological constraints, the potential for well-controlled (and thus militarily useful) application of force from space was at best uncertain. The United States, for example, had considered—and rejected as militarily nonadvantageous—the placing of nuclear weapons in orbit around the earth. U.N. Resolution 1884, accepted by both the Soviet Union and the United States in 1963, enjoined all states from stationing in space "nuclear weapons or any other kinds of weapons of mass destruction." It is significant, in terms of demonstrating the extent of common interest involved, that this de facto arms control agreement, which lay the foundations for the Outer Space Treaty of 1967, contained no specific provisions for verification of compliance.

Both the United States and the Soviet Union did, however, maintain unilateral interests in the stationing of reconnaissance satellites in orbit to monitor the adversary's military activities (the incentives in this regard were probably much greater on the American side). In the early 1960s, the Soviets apparently judged American satellite reconnaissance activities to be detrimental to Soviet national security interests. Strategic analysis in the United States, however, had evolved towards the view that information exchange of the type made possible by satellite reconnaissance could in fact be stabilizing to the nuclear balance. Although the Soviets refused at the time to explicitly accept this logic, their shift in attitude (as documented by Steinberg) regarding satellite reconnaissance in the 1960s seems to indicate at least tacit acceptance of the mutual benefits of information exchange. (See Chapter 15 by John Lewis Gaddis.) On balance, neither side had a pressing interest in the pursuit of military activities in space that would explicitly be perceived as threatening the essential security interests of the adversary.

On the contrary, both sides shared a strong interest in preventing the unrestrained militarization of space. Space was an entirely new arena of national security competition. Both sides were forced to consider the long-term uncertainty of what an arms race in space might look like, against the potential short-term incentives for a side to defect (in hope of achieving some limited advantage). While uncertainty is likely to lead to worst-case analysis and escalation of arms races in security dilemma interactions between states, *extreme uncertainty* may in some cases contribute to cooperative outcomes. Indeed, when the risks of mutual defection are potentially extreme for both sides, incentives for cooperative restraint may appear more compelling, particularly when the rewards for exploitation (the temptation to defect) are moderate (and themselves uncertain). In this sense, the cooperative solution to the threat of the militarization of space in the 1960s may to some extent be explained as a regime of "shared aversion."[29]

A predominance of shared interests does not, however, guarantee the evolution of a cooperative solution to the management of security problems between hostile states (as a number of other chapters in this book demonstrate). Although shared interests are undoubtably a necessary condition of cooperation, they are clearly not, historically, a sufficient condition.

Both deductive theories and empirical studies of cooperation point to the importance of clear saliencies for the actors involved, or what Schelling referred to as "focal points for the convergence of expectations."[30] Cooperation is more likely when the two sides have a shared, unambiguous perception of a focal point around which their policies can be coordinated. In the case of the militarization of space, the fact that space had not yet become an arena of hostile military action provided a clear saliency around which actors' expectations converged. The perception of this saliency by the actors at the time is illustrated by a variety of statements incorporating the notion that it would be significantly easier to prevent the militarization of space altogether than it would be to limit military activities in space once they had begun. In the words of Senator Albert Gore:

> It is especially important that we do everything now that can be done to avoid an arms race in outer space—for certainly it should be easier to agree now not to arm a part of the environment that has never been armed than later to agree to disarm parts that have been armed.[31]

Gore's statement demonstrates another important aspect of existing saliencies that may be important in the evolution of cooperation. If the number of potential saliencies in the situation is seen to be small, a sense of urgency may enter the bargaining process, as the actors may come to believe that there is a small window of opportunity (before either side violates the saliency) during which agreement can be reached. In the case at hand, the sense of urgency that something be done to limit the activities of the two sides prior to erosion of the saliency and the development of a full-fledged arms race in space appears to have contributed to a cooperative outcome.

Theories of cooperation emphasize the role played by environmental factors—often referred to as the "context" or the the "rules" of the game. In the empirical case under study, relevant factors can be considered as features of the general political environment of the U.S.–Soviet relationship. Particularly important in this regard are the perceptions of the two sides regarding the nature of the competition between them, and of their adversary in that competition.

As always, problems in the collection of data plague the investigator's attempt to study the state of these variables from the perspective of the Soviet Union. The following remarks are thus limited to perceptions of the decision-making elite of the United States regarding the superpower competition and the Soviet Union.

By the mid-1960s, the image of the competition with the Soviet Union had evolved so as to include elements more conducive to the conclusion of cooperative agreements than had been the case previously. The American decision-making elite had largely accepted that the competition with the Soviet Union was to take place over the long term: the bipolarity of the postwar world had been established and was relatively stable. The image of the competition with the Soviet Union took on many of the characteristics of an "iterated game"—the problems of the U.S.–Soviet relationship could not be solved but would instead have to be managed over the long term. Although U.S. and Soviet interests were seen to be in opposition at many points throughout the world and on a variety of issues, the two states also shared a number of common interests. The most obvious of these, but only the most obvious, was of course the prevention of nuclear war.

This image of the superpower competition was accompanied by images of the Soviet Union, which, although varied, shared certain elements essential to the development of cooperation. Both hard-line and soft-line thinkers shared the belief that the Soviet Union had become a viable long-term opponent: the communist leadership of the USSR was not likely to collapse under its own weight or succumb to internal revolution in the near future. The Soviet Union was a viable state with legitimate security and other interests in the world, as well as a military power to be reckoned with. Further, the demonstration of Soviet technological proficiency in space dispelled illusions that the United States would be able to easily outpace the Soviets in the development of military and other technologies. The Soviet Union was a serious and capable adversary, a state that would have to be dealt with carefully over the long term. While this perception of the Soviet Union may have intensified American competitive impulses to some extent, it also made possible a variety of cooperative arrangements designed to regulate the competition within the bounds of common interests shared by two superpowers.

Developments in strategic thought at the time also served to enhance the possibilities for cooperative management of the threat from space. (By strategic thought we mean the body of military and strategic theory that defines the *role* of the state's military power in contributing to the realization of state goals. Strategic theory also studies the *means* by which military power serves state goals.) The 1960s witnessed an evolution in strategic thought that centered around changes in the relationship between force and politics that had been the result of the technological development and improvement of nuclear weapons and delivery systems. While nuclear weapons did not make war obsolete (as some advocates of disarmament had hoped), they did widen the scope for cooperative management of some threats via arms control and other agreements between adversaries. It should be stressed that the weapons themselves did not enhance the prospects for cooperation. Rather, it was the way of thinking about the weapons, and their role in the superpower competition, that suggested ways in which the two sides might cooperate in the management of threats to their security.

The application of game theory and other theories of interdependent decision-making (as in Schelling's *Strategy of Conflict*) to security competition between states contributed to an increased understanding of the role of interdependent decision-making and action-reaction phenomena in bringing about seemingly non-optimal political and military outcomes. The theory-based assessment that an action-reaction cycle, exacerbated in severity by the operation of a severe security dilemma (made more severe by the fact that nuclear weapons enhanced the advantage of the offense as compared to the defense), contributed in insidious ways to the development and escalation of an arms race, received increased attention among American policy-making elites.[32]

Additional developments in strategic theory contributed to the identification of a number of areas in which the United States and the Soviet Union could best manage the threat to their security via cooperative means. Theories of strategic stability and the importance of a survivable second-strike retaliatory capability rested on two notions: that the Soviets would achieve a nuclear capability comparable to that of the United

States, and that in the ensuing situation of functional parity, nuclear weapons would be useful only as a deterrent, to prevent the use of nuclear weapons by the other side. Acceptance of the notion that functional parity would be an inevitable development— that is, that the United States could not maintain a militarily significant advantage in nuclear weapons—opened up the possibility for cooperative arrangements to codify and stabilize the situation of parity at lower rather than higher levels of weaponry.

Theories of *arms control,* rather than general and complete disarmament, began to stress the importance of limited cooperative agreements designed to manage (rather than eliminate) threats to the two sides' security. Particularly important was the perceived need to limit and otherwise tailor the growth of the two sides' strategic arsenals, so as to both decrease the costs of the arms race and manage the potential for inadvertent escalation of conflict to nuclear war. Space seemed an ideal realm in which to apply these developing ideas, not least because of its importance in the two sides' ability to conduct information exchange deemed essential to the conclusion and management of arms control agreements on what was to become known as the "SALT model." The potential for new cooperative arrangements engendered by developments in strategic theory is nicely illustrated by the comments of Secretary of Defense Robert McNamara in his 1963 Defense Posture Statement:

> As the arms race continues and the weapons multiply and become more swift and deadly, the possibility of a global catastrophe, either by miscalculation or design, becomes ever more real. More armaments, whether offensive or defensive, cannot solve this dilemma. Mutual deterrence underscores the need for a renewed effort to find some way, if not to eliminate these deadly weapons completely, then at least to slow down or halt their further accumulation.[33]

An important additional factor permitting the cooperative management of the threat from space in the 1960s can be identified in the alignment of decision-making power within the U.S. bureaucracy. While bureaucratic politics does not appear as a structural variable affecting opportunities for cooperation, it is extremely important as a process variable by which potential cooperative agreements are or are not reached. Bureaucracies do not create necessary or sufficient conditions for cooperation. Bureaucratic politics can, however, act as a spoiler, negating the possibility of realizing potential cooperative solutions. In the case under consideration, bureaucratic politics were properly aligned so as to permit the development of cooperative arrangements limiting the militarization of space.

The history of the bureaucratic infighting that took place over space weaponry in the early 1960s is far too complex and convoluted to repeat here. (Paul Stares' book is excellent on this subject.) Rather, we will concentrate on what we believe to be two of the most important factors in the interplay of bureaucratic forces.

The most important bureaucratic factor in the 1960s was the role played by presidential leadership in accepting the risks of cooperation. President Kennedy's willingness to push the bureaucracy to accept an arms control agreement lacking provisions for completely effective verification is notable in this regard.[34] Given the complex nature of the decision-making process for defense policy in the United States, it is essential in most cases that the President exert personal leadership in the conclusion and maintenance of cooperative arrangements with the Soviet Union. This President Kennedy, in the issue of militarization of space, was both willing—and able—to do. Although presidential leadership cannot in and of itself create possibilities for cooperative arrangements, it is almost always essential that the President exert control over the bureaucratic impediments to the construction and consistent implementation of a strategy designed to promote cooperative outcomes.

Also valuable was the establishment, in 1961, of a specific bureaucratic actor devoted to the analysis of arms control—the Arms Control and Disarmament Agency (ACDA). The ACDA, despite its relative weakness as a bureaucratic player, provided an institutional base for proponents of arms control to voice their theories for serious consideration by the decision-making elite. ACDA also provided an institution for the study, design, and control of policies enacting the general strategy of contingent restraint. Although the existence of ACDA did not in and of itself increase the potential for cooperation, it did help to insure that some potential cooperative arrangements could be enacted and maintained between the states.

In summary, the 1960s witnessed the evolution of a partial, cooperative arrangement to manage the threat posed by the militarization of space. The American strategy of restraint contingent on Soviet reciprocity contributed in important ways to the development and successful management of the limited regime. A number of important variables were seen to contribute to the explanation for this unexpected, cooperative outcome.

The Early 1970s

Reciprocal restraint in the militarization of space appears to have been successfully maintained by the two sides in the period 1963–1968. Neither the United States nor the Soviet Union placed great emphasis on ASAT development programs during this period. The United States, in fact, acted to scale down its fiscal commitment to a number of follow-on projects to Program 437. In particular, the cancellation in 1968 of Project 922, a relatively advanced ASAT system employing a nonnuclear kill mechanism, demonstrated a willingness on the part of the United States to forgo the development of promising ASAT technologies at this time.[35]

The major perceived threat from Soviet space activities at the time concerned the development of a fractional orbital bombardment system (FOBS). When Soviet tests of a FOBS were announced by McNamara in 1967, however, the secretary of defense stressed that the FOBS neither violated the 1963 U.N. resolution nor represented a grave threat to American national security. In response, the United States did not choose to reverse its decision (taken in 1965) to halt development of its own FOBS system. Rather, American policy was designed to counter the threat in non-escalatory fashion, by improving OTH radar and other capabilities for early warning over the Southern part of the United States.[36] The controlled nature of the American response to Soviet FOBS activities represented a sober evaluation of American interests and Soviet threats. A restrained response seems to have been successful in limiting unnecessary damage to the embryonic space regime, and may have contributed to the successful conclusion of formal restrictions on stationing nuclear weapons in space.

The Outer Space Treaty of 1967 thus represented a partial codification of limited arrangements for reciprocal restraint in space that had evolved between the United States and the Soviet Union. Signatories to the treaty agreed ''not to place in orbit around the earth any objects carrying nuclear weapons or any other kinds of weapons of mass destruction, install such weapons on celestial bodies, or station such weapons in outer space in any other manner.'' The Outer Space Treaty can be seen as a reaffirmation of a previously existing arrangement, many of whose provisions were (and remained) tacit. While it did not foreclose any militarily significant options, the treaty probably contributed to each side's expectations that the partial regime governing the militarization of space would continue to be managed in cooperative fashion.

While the mid-1960s saw the demise of the FOBS threat, the late 1960s witnessed a rebirth of the Soviet ASAT threat and the development of a significant second aspect of the militarization of space—the threat from MILSATs. While the nature of the threat evolved considerably during this period, American perceptions of the severity of the problem remained restrained. American policy for managing the threat relied upon a continuation of the strategy of contingent restraint, leading to a reaffirmation of the space regime in the early 1970s.

The potentially hostile military applications of Soviet space programs began to receive increased attention in the United States during this period. This was a result of two factors: the increased sophistication of satellite photoreconnaissance, and the development of EORSAT and RORSAT systems capable of tracking U.S. and NATO naval forces. The Soviets demonstrated significantly enhanced photoreconnaissance capabilities by launching several extra satellites in a short time frame, during border conflicts with the Chinese in 1969 and during the India-Pakistan War of 1971.[37] During the Yom Kippur War of 1973, there were suggestions that the Soviets had shared militarily significant satellite photoreconnaissance data with their Egyptian allies.[38] Thus by the early 1970s the Soviets had demonstrated a capability to selectively employ satellite photoreconnaissance in crisis monitoring and perhaps, significantly, in direct support of terrestrial military activities (in this case by proxy states). This was considered to be a potential threat of significant proportions to American security interests.

The second element of the evolving threat in the late 1960s concerned the development of a dedicated Soviet ASAT system capable of attacking certain American space assets. In the period 1968–1970, the Soviets carried out a series of tests involving high speed fly-by and detonation of what appeared to be a co-orbital satellite interceptor system. American information regarding these tests remained ambiguous; apparently, the Pentagon did not conclude that the system was in fact an ASAT weapon until early in 1970.[39] Tests of the system continued through 1971, and ended rather abruptly in November of that year with an interception of a target satellite whose explosion in the nighttime sky was witnessed by observers in Sweden as a large flare that lasted for about 20 seconds.[40] In a period of about three years, the Soviets had demonstrated a limited but nevertheless significant capability to place at risk a number of U.S. satellites in low earth orbit.

The technical capabilities and limitations of the Soviet co-orbital satellite interceptor system have been widely discussed in the open literature. (Since the current Russian ASAT system is basically similar to that introduced in 1968, the following discussion is of both historical and immediate interest.) The Soviet ASAT weapon sits atop a modified SS-9 liquid-fueled ICBM booster. The Soviets apparently maintain a single facility (at Tyuratam) with only two launch pads capable of handling the system, although several interceptors per day could presumably be launched from this complex. Once the interceptor is launched, it maneuvers into an orbit where after one or two trips around the earth its orbit will cross that of the target satellite. The interceptor then maneuvers close to the target under the guidance of an on-board radar or infra-red sensor.[41]

As a result of its technological limitations, the Soviet ASAT system suffers from a number of basic conceptual flaws that severely limit its utility as a military system. Co-orbital interception can take as long as three hours (from launch to intercept); this provides significant warning time, as well as an opportunity for the target satellite to employ deceptive countermeasures or evasive maneuvering. The co-orbital method of interception limits potential targets to satellites whose ground tracks run close to the launch point of the system. As this occurs only twice a day for satellites that would be vulnerable to the system, the attacker must wait an average of six hours to attack any given satellite.[42] The difficulty of reloading launch facilities and firing several massive liquid-fueled boosters from a single launch facility further constrain the number of attacks that could be carried out within a given time period.

The most significant limitation of the Soviet system is that the vast majority of U.S. satellites are not within its reach, as the system is operationally limited to attacking satellites in low earth orbit. (At the present time, the system has been tested at a maximum altitude of only 2400 kilometers; the Pentagon estimates that the system may be capable of attacking satellites at an altitude of 5000 km.)[43] As a result, the system poses its most significant threat to the constellation of American photoreconnaissance satellites, all of which are in LEO. It is highly unlikely that the system's capabilities could be extended to attack satellites in geosynchronous orbit. Such an adaptation would require the use of a much more massive booster, would severely tax the homing and maneuvering capabilities of the interceptor's guidance system, and would in any case increase the time lag between launch and interception to a period of many hours. On balance, most technical assessments conclude that the Russian ASAT weapon is a cumbersome, inflexible system whose techological constraints make it a threat of only limited significance to a small subset of U.S. satellites.

Despite the inherent limitations of the Soviet ASAT weapon, it did pose a threat to the stability of the space regime that had evolved in the mid-1960s. American decision makers at the time were uncertain of Soviet intentions regarding the ASAT mission, and as a result were divided over the issue of how to respond to this apparent violation of tacit arrangements limiting the militarization of space. After a period of study and debate, the Nixon Administration chose to adopt policies that continued the strategy of contingent restraint. The following section chronicles the emergence of this policy, and seeks to account for this outcome on the basis of the variables that conditioned the development of a strategy of contingent restraint in the 1960s.

The early American response to Soviet ASAT system tests in the late 1960s was surprisingly restrained, given the seriousness with which this system would later come to be viewed. American decision-makers apparently chose to adopt a wait and see attitude with regard to two questions: the military significance of the Soviet ASAT system, and the strength of the Soviet commitment to the ASAT mission.[44]

As the Soviet ASAT test series continued, concern within the Nixon Administration mounted, but in a slow and restrained fashion. In October 1970 National Security Advisor Henry Kissinger called for an interagency working group—which would come to be known as the Eimer group after its chairperson Deputy Director for Research and Engineering (DDR&E) Manfred Eimer—to be established to study the nature of the Soviet ASAT threat and possible American responses. The lack of immediate concern with which the Nixon Administration viewed this subject is evidenced by the fact that the Eimer group's report, originally designed as a "quick study," was not submitted to the National Security Council until 1973.

On the subject of capabilities, the Eimer group reportedly concluded that the Soviet ASAT system represented a limited threat to certain American space assets, as outlined above. The question of Soviet intentions regarding the ASAT mission remained confused. Unable to isolate "a specific target" for the system or even an "identifiable reason" why the Soviets had chosen to test the system, the Eimer group apparently failed to reach consensus on why the Soviets had chosen to jeopardize the existing arrangements for restraint in the militarization of space. Some members of the group apparently argued that the Soviet program represented an unintended output of bureaucratic politics, and was thus not part of an overall strategy to defect from the space regime.[45] It was decided, in any case, that the Soviet program did not represent an intensive effort to develop militarily significant ASAT capabilities, and thus did not pose an immediate and serious threat to U.S. security interests.

In accordance with this relatively sanguine view of the Soviet threat, the Eimer group's recommendations for an American policy response emphasized continued restraint as a means of reaffirming tacit cooperation and mutual restraint in space. Unilateral cooperative measures (which would increase the security of the United States without posing any threat to the Soviet Union), such as reducing the vulnerability of satellites, were recommended as immediate steps to further reduce the military significance of the Soviet ASAT system.

On the question of whether the United States should develop its own ASAT system in response, the Eimer group reportedly came to the conclusion that Soviet ASAT activities did not provide sufficient justification for the United States to reciprocally defect from the regime. It was the judgment of the group that current and potential Soviet space threats could be managed through a mixture of non-hostile countermeasures that posed no additional threat to the Soviet Union. On the basis of assessments of the relative vulnerability of each side to ASAT attacks, the group argued that U.S. possession of comparable ASAT capability would not, in and of itself, be a robust deterrent to Soviet use of ASAT. On the contrary, a vigorous U.S. ASAT development program might have the insidious effect of further stimulating Soviet ASAT development, and thus contribute to the deterioration of the space regime, leading to an overall decrease in American security.[46]

The Eimer group concluded that in the area of ASAT development, the United States should "maintain a minimum ASAT development lead time, which would be proportional to the warning that the United States could expect to have before a particular threat materialized."[47] This policy appears consistent with a strategy of contingent restraint. A limited ASAT development program of the sort called for in the Eimer group report would not produce a weapon system capable of fulfilling military missions. Rather, the objective of a limited ASAT program appears to have been to provide incentives for Soviet restraint by demonstrating a willingness to maintain the regime, contingent on Soviet reciprocal behavior. While avoiding activity that would contribute to the breakdown of reciprocal restraint in space, American policy had the dual advantages of protecting the United States against an unforeseen Soviet ASAT breakout, as well as demonstrating American willingness to maintain restraint *or* to defect, contingent on Soviet behavior. The goal of this policy, presumably, was to create a structure of incentives so that Soviet decision-makers would perceive it to be in their interests to demonstrate reciprocal restraint in ASAT activities.

Three themes can thus be said to characterize the Nixon Administration's response to Soviet military activities in space. The first theme, concerning the military response, emphasized restraint in American military space activities and a policy of conservative development. A relatively mild assessment of the ASAT threat, combined with the military's primary investment of both attention and resources in the Vietnam War, produced increasingly stringent budget restrictions for the military space program. This in turn spawned technological conservatism and an increased concern with cost-efficiency in terms of fulfilling well-defined military missions. U.S. military space programs would thus

> be carefully structured in the context of the threat, economic constraints, and the national priorities placed on defense. In particular the DoD will embark on new military space programs only when they can clearly show that particular mission functions can be achieved in a more cost-effective way than by using more conventional methods.[48]

In accordance with this strategy, research directed at the development of a nonnuclear kill mechanism for ASAT systems continued, but at a relatively slow pace. The Air Defense Command proposed in 1971 to develop and test a nonnuclear system code-named Project Spike, but this proposal was rejected on the grounds that it represented "a rather sophisticated development whose potential risk could not be easily assessed." Although Miniature Homing Vehicle (MHV) technology research began in 1970, funding for this and other projects within the Space Defense Program suffered severe cuts each year from FY 1972 to FY 1975.[49]

The fate of Project 437 during this period is of particular interest. In recognition of its severely limited utility, the operational readiness of this nuclear-tipped system was downgraded from 24 hours to 30 days in October of 1970. Exercises designed to test the ability of the launch crews to redeploy and reactivate the missiles had been planned to take place semiannually; however, the first of these exercises did not take place until November 1971, and future exercises were cancelled altogether.[50] Although Project 437 was not officially cancelled until March 1975, its credibility as even a potentially useful military asset had disappeared five years earlier.

Stares notes, however, that in the period 1970–1975, Program 437 "proved remarkably resistant to closure even from natural causes."[51] Following a 1972 hurricane that caused considerable damage to the Johnston Island launch facilities, the Air Defense Command chose to reconstitute the system at considerable cost. This is particularly surprising in light of the fact that a decision to phase out Program 437 by late 1974 had already been taken.[52] Despite the fact that the Johnston Island facilities were being used for other (non-ASAT) programs in addition to 437, the decision, during a period of fiscal restraint, to invest significant funds in a moribund program requires further explanation. It may be argued that the decision to maintain a rudimentary ASAT capability in Project 437 was primarily a political action, designed to communicate to the Soviet Union the *contingent* nature of American restraint in ASATs. The reconstitution of 437 demonstrated to the Soviets that while the United States on its own initiative was not about to escalate the ASAT competition, we did maintain both the capability and the resolve to reciprocate Soviet activities in this area.

The second theme of Nixon Administration policy towards the militarization of space could be described as a cautious and prudent evaluation of the threat posed by Soviet activities. The Administration, hoping to avoid unnecessary deterioration of the space regime, was careful not to overestimate the severity of the challenge posed by limited Soviet ASAT development activities. Even as concern with Soviet ASAT tests began to mount in 1970, DDR&E John Foster stressed that there had been no attempted interceptions of U.S. satellites, and that the DoD did not consider Soviet tests as threatening.[53] A moderate interpretation of the Soviet threat served to support the Administration's strategy of managing the threat via nonescalatory means, so as to prevent the development of an action-reaction conflict spiral in the militarization of space.

The third theme of the Nixon Administration's strategy was to emphasize the political (as opposed to military) response to Soviet activities, in an attempt to revitalize tacit cooperation in space. Although the ASAT issue was not explicitly addressed in the SALT I treaties, a number of provisions within the ABM Treaty placed implicit constraints on some potential ASAT missions. In particular, the provisions regarding non-interference with national technical means of verification seemed to codify the legitimate right of the states to operate photoreconnaissance satellites. While the two sides did not agree on a precise definition of "interference," the approval of these provisions by the Soviet Union was interpreted by some observers as demonstrating Soviet willingness to forgo continued ASAT activity.[54]

Several additional treaties agreed to by the United States and the Soviet Union during this time placed additional (if implicit) limitations on ASAT activities. In the Agreement on Measures to Reduce the Risk of Outbreak of Nuclear War (signed September 1971) the two sides agreed to consult in the event of interference with early warning or communication systems, both of which were dependent upon satellites (Article III). The Hot Line Modernization Agreement (signed September 1971) committed the two states to the use of Soviet Molniya and American Intelsat satellites for Hot Line communication. In addition, the states agreed to take measures "to insure the continuous and reliable operation of the communications circuits and the systems of terminals" (Article II). While neither of these agreements specifically mentioned ASAT, they did seem to signal a joint commitment to protect the invulnerability of specific space assets from interference. Coupled with the conclusion of the Soviet ASAT test series in 1971 (the apparent "last" test took place in November of 1971), the accession of the two states to these treaties seemed to indicate a revitalization of political will underlying the space regime.

An examination of the Nixon Administration's record regarding the militarization of space reveals a great degree of continuity with the strategy of its predecessors. The United States in the late 1960s and early 1970s maintained a strategy of contingent restraint in military space activities, in an attempt to structure incentives for the Soviet Union to demonstrate reciprocal restraint. The strategy combined unilateral cooperative measures (increasing the commitment to satellite survivability programs) with contingent restraint designed to demonstrate to the Soviets that the United States would prefer to maintain the space regime, but would defect if Soviet activities made such action necessary. The strategy of contingent restraint appears to have succeeded in bringing about a revitalization of both political and military commitment to the space regime in 1971.

The conditions and processes that contributed to the strategy of contingent restraint (and cooperative outcomes) in the early 1960s remained operative through the early 1970s. The developing nature of the U.S.–Soviet relationship during this period in fact strengthened the conditions that underlay the evolution of limited cooperation in space. Although new challenges to the regime (of a political, military, and technological nature) emerged, limited cooperation in the form of a partial regime governing military space activities proved surprisingly robust.

The basic, objective interests of the two sides continued to provide large incentives for the cooperative management of threats while providing comparatively little incentive for the unilateral pursuit of hostile military objectives in space. Technological constraints continued to place limits on the potential for the controlled application of force from space. Having come to the conclusion that nuclear weapons based in space were of limited military utility, and in fact might be a source of inadvertent or accidental war, the states agreed to codify what had been a more or less tacit arrangement within the Outer Space Treaty of 1967. However, developments in MILSAT technology, to be discussed further in the following section, were laying the groundwork for a change in the structure of incentives that would become important in the mid- and late 1970s.

Regarding ASAT technology, this period witnessed the development and testing of the first dedicated nonnuclear ASAT weapons system. The military utility of the Soviet system remained, however, extremely limited, a fact that American evaluations acknowledged. The threat posed by the Soviet ASAT system could be successfully managed through unilateral cooperative (nonescalatory) means, such as reducing the vulnerability of American space assets. There was no compelling reason for the United States to develop an ASAT of its own, either to attack Soviet satellites, or to deter attacks against American satellites (such a deterrent posture was not considered to be robust in any case). As a result, there was little incentive for the United States to immediately defect from the regime in reciprocation for Soviet activities.

The incentives to practice restraint in the militarization of space remained relatively compelling. Considerable uncertainty remained regarding the potential outcomes of an arms race in space, and the impact such a competition might have on the stability of the superpower relationship (in both political and military terms). In this sense, a degree of shared aversion underlay the incentive to cooperate. But powerful positive incentives were at work as well. In particular, the states had begun to perceive shared benefits from the limited success of arms control on the SALT model. Essential to the SALT process was the verification of treaty provisions by national technical means (NTM), primarily reconnaissance satellites. Shared confidence in each side's ability to conduct satellite reconnaissance without interference was in fact made explicit in the NTM provisions of the SALT treaties. This signalled a realization on the part of both sides that information exchange of this type operated to the mutual benefit of the states.

The maintenance of a clearly defined saliency around which expectations of cooperation converge retained its importance, as coordinated restraint in the development of weapons systems capable of the direct application of force from space was sustained. But as we said earlier, erosion of this saliency at the margins began in the late 1960s. Developments in MILSAT technology began to erode the distinction between the cooperative use of space for activities of mutual benefit, and the hostile, or threatening uses of space. Advances in technology were increasing the potential for the use of space assets in the support and enhancement of terrestrial military force, both conventional and nuclear. In particular, the use of satellite reconnaissance capabilities to monitor the movement of conventional military forces during international crises (and the possibility that such information could be shared by a superpower with its proxy states) began to erode the significance of the saliency that had been an established part of the space regime. Also important in this regard was the Soviet development of EORSAT and RORSAT systems capable of monitoring U.S. and NATO naval deployments on the high seas. These developments were to play a significant role in the deterioration of the space regime in the mid- and late 1970s.

Specific features of the general political environment—namely perceptions of the adversary and of the competition—continued to favor the development of limited co-operative arrangements between the superpowers in the 1970s. The image of a détente with the Soviet Union that prevailed during this period, and the image of the Soviet Union that supported that vision, were both conducive to the development of limited cooperative agreements. The superpower relationship under détente has been described as "non-confrontational competition" or as a "mixed competitive-collaborative relationship" by Alexander L. George and George Breslauer, respectively.[55] The concept of détente, although poorly defined in many of its specific manifestations, included a recognition by the United States that the competition with the Soviet Union would take the form of a long-term struggle between great powers, neither one of which would come to predominate in the foreseeable future. Détente described an existential bipolarity in world politics, in which the two superpowers could cooperate in limited ways to manage the inevitable processes of adjustment that would be required to maintain the stability of the system. The two sides would thus act as partial collaborators in an attempt to avoid potentially disastrous consequences of unrestrained competition in a world with nuclear weapons. In addition to supporting the development of cooperation to avoid shared aversions, the concept of détente opened up new possibilities for limited cooperation in areas where the two sides shared common interests that could be more efficiently pursued under conditions of policy coordination between the states.

The grand design of détente identified a number of areas in which limited cooperative agreements could contribute to the welfare of both states. Cooperation, in the post-hegemonic world of détente, would be enforced via norms of reciprocal restraint. Neither side was to seek unilateral advantage, by defecting from cooperative arrangements judged to be in the long-term interests of both sides, in order to achieve short-term advantages. While the terms of reciprocity were never precisely defined by the states, the concept of détente and its associated images (of the desired relationship, and of the nature of the adversary) strongly supported both the concept of limited cooperative agreements between adversaries, and the strategy of contingent restraint based on reciprocity as a tactical means for achieving cooperation.

A number of continuing developments in strategic theory also contributed to the evolution of the space regime. Action-reaction theories continued to hold an important place in the debate about the dynamics of seemingly irrational and undesirable arms races. As a result, American decision makers were sensitive to the possibility that certain weapons systems might undesirably exacerbate the security dilemma between the United States and the Soviet Union, and lead to an eventual decrease in security for both sides.

An essential development in strategic thought concerned the acceptance by most American decision makers of the concept of strategic parity as a fait accompli from which neither side could hope to emerge. The acceptance of functional strategic parity as an inescapable (if undesirable) consequence of nuclear evolution had a number of consequences of its own, most of which were conducive to the development of limited cooperation in the management of strategic stability.

Parity made possible the development of cooperative arms control measures on the SALT model. These agreements added a measure of predictability and control to the cooperative management of strategic stability. The acceptance of parity also enabled strategic analysts to give increasing attention to the problems of inadvertent escalation and of accidental war. Strategic theory stressed the shared nature of these problems, indicating that they could be managed in part through limited cooperative arrangements (an example of a regime based, in part, on shared aversion). Particularly important in the management of these threats was the stabilizing role played by space-based Command, Control, Communications, and Intelligence (C3I) systems, which strengthen confidence in managing one's own forces during crises, and provide a mechanism for information exchange with the adversary. The maintenance of these capabilities, and their invulnerability during both peacetime and crisis, contributed to the development of a strategic stability that would potentially be instrumental in the successful management of a superpower crisis.

Two additional developments of a primarily political nature served to reinforce the possibilities for cooperative arrangements suggested by the evolution of strategic thought. The first of these concerned the relatively stable situation in Europe, given de facto recognition and legitimation of the postwar division of the continent. Although the conventional forces of the Warsaw Pact nations were thought to be superior, the apparent stability of the superpower stand-off in Europe ameliorated the strategic demands of extended deterrence. This decreased the perceived need for American strategic forces to actively threaten the Soviet Union, and reinforced the tendency to accept as a sufficient deterrent the maintenance of an invulnerable and somewhat flexible retaliatory capability. This development in turn reinforced Nixon's concept of "strategic sufficiency," as well as its logical correlate, the codification of parity within SALT.

The second development involved increasing concern with the economic consequences of unrestrained security competition. As the costs of the Vietnam War mounted, and the consequences of declining American economic hegemony became apparent, U.S. decision makers became increasingly concerned with the costs (both direct and potential) of U.S.–Soviet competition. Increasing recognition of the potential for mutually beneficial trade between the superpowers was one result of this concern. Another was an increased awareness that only limited resources could be devoted to the pursuit of security. Limited cooperative agreements between the superpowers, if correctly designed and implemented, might permit each state to purchase greater security at lesser cost, in the context of a limited security regime based on certain shared interests.

Finally, bureaucratic politics once again assumed a shape that was receptive to the development of limited cooperation between the superpowers. The late 1960s and the early 1970s were a time when the executive branch succeeded in exerting rather tight control over America's Soviet policy. The Nixon Administration was exquisitely sensitive to the need to achieve "policy legitimacy" for its strategy vis-à-vis the Soviet Union. Kissinger, in particular, was aware of the challenge facing American policy makers wishing to obtain domestic support for a consistent and carefully managed policy of limited cooperation with the Soviet Union. In the early years of détente, the Administration's multifaceted response to this challenge largely succeeded in limiting the negative intrusions of bureaucratic politics into the process of formulating grand strategy.[56]

It was also fairly successful in limiting intrusions into the formulation of tactical policy consistent with the grand strategy. The perceived legitimacy of détente as a long-term strategy for managing the superpower relationship permitted Nixon and Kissinger (in the early and successful years of détente) to pursue a fairly consistent policy vis-à-vis the Soviet Union in the militarization of space, and in other areas.

In sum, limited cooperation in the militarization of space continued throughout the early years of détente. Although both aspects of the dual threat in space underwent considerable evolution during this period (primarily as a result of technological developments relevant to MILSAT and ASAT capabilities), the challenge to the limited space regime was successfully managed by the two sides. The American strategy of contingent restraint appears to have contributed to a reaffirmation of limited cooperative arrangements to manage the threat from space. The conditions and processes that had contributed to American strategy were, however, beginning to change in ways that would have significance for the future of the space regime in the mid- and late 1970s.

American policy regarding the limited space regime underwent a significant shift in the period 1975–1977. The weakening of tacit arrangements regarding the militarization of space, as a result of both increased Soviet activities and changes in the American perception of the threat, led to an American commitment (in early 1977) to develop, test, and possibly deploy a dedicated ASAT system based on the MHV concept (which had previously been a research program). Developments in Soviet space activities prompted a re-evaluation of American policy regarding the space regime. The change in the *objective nature* of the threat from space, however, does not suffice to explain the nature of the change in American policy, nor does it explain the particular response to the threat that was chosen from among a number of possible alternative responses. A changing American *perception* of the nature of the threat from space can be discerned, followed by a fundamental shift in American strategy for managing the threat. This new strategy can be characterized as one of contingent threat of escalation, replacing the previous strategy of contingent restraint and reciprocity.

In the period 1975–1977, Soviet military activities in space progressed along two lines: ASAT and MILSAT. U.S. concern with Soviet ASAT-relevant activities had been mounting, even prior to the resumption of testing in February of 1976. Of particular interest at the Pentagon and elsewhere were Soviet research developments in laser and other directed energy weapons relevant to the ASAT mission.[57] Suspicions were thus raised when three U.S. satellites experienced "blinding" incidents in October and November of 1975. The apparent illumination of these satellites by an intense beam of radiation emanating from the western part of the Soviet Union was eventually attributed, however, to a fire along the trans-Siberian pipeline.

American perceptions regarding the Soviet commitment to the ASAT mission became of paramount concern when, in February 1976, the Soviets resumed testing of their ASAT system. A number of candidate explanations have been proposed for this seemingly provocative decision;[58] all suffer from a lack of evidence. We will leave aside the question of Soviet intentions and concentrate primarily on American evaluation of the Soviet threat, and proposed responses.

The Soviets carried out at least four tests of the ASAT system in 1976, representing the largest number of tests in any one year up to that time. In addition, American observers judged that technological improvements in the system might contribute to more than a marginal improvement in capabilities. The Soviets had begun to test a technologically more advanced, passive infra-red (IR) sensing system for target acquisition, to replace the more easily countered, active radar sensor. The operational readiness of the system's various components at Tyuratam were judged to have been significantly improved.[59] Although technological constraints still limited the military significance of the Soviet ASAT (in particular, all tests employing the new IR sensor were judged to have been failures), U.S. policy-makers were concerned with Soviet intentions regarding ASAT, as well as the technological potential for further development of the IR sensor system.

Technical progress in MILSAT capabilities continued to expand the role of military satellites in the U.S.–Soviet security competition. Ocean reconnaissance by Soviet satellites continued to progress, as did the use of satellites for other forms of electronic intelligence, tactical communications, and the gathering of geodetic targeting data for ICBMs.[60] The total number of Soviet satellite launches per year bypassed comparable American totals during this period, and Soviet launch rates continued to increase at a considerable pace.[61] The high launch rate was in fact a reflection of a less sophisticated Soviet technology; their satellites are individually less capable and do not last as long as their American counterparts. Nevertheless, the increasingly active and visible Soviet space program engendered a considerable degree of concern among American policy-makers during this period (despite the fact that the precise nature and severity of the threat remained highly uncertain).

The impact of these activities on the perceptions of Soviet military intentions in space was considerable, but uneven, within the American decision-making elite. It is interesting to note that the perception of the threat tended to be more severe in the White House than in the Department of Defense. Thus the major impetus behind the shift in strategy for managing the threat derived from the political rather than the military bureaucracy.

The relatively restrained attitude of the Defense Department regarding the threat from Soviet space activities underwent only mild change during this period. DoD posture statements, which had not mentioned the existence of a Soviet ASAT since 1972, began in FY 1976 to include only brief statements about the growing threat from space. In response to what was described as a limited threat, Defense requested only small increases in its budget for "space defense research." Emphasis was placed on reducing the vulnerability of American space assets through a variety of nonhostile satellite survivability measures. Although concern about the potential use of Soviet MILSATs in various scenarios was expressed, the DoD remained hesitant regarding the efficacy of a U.S. ASAT to counteract this threat. In sum, the DoD chose to reaffirm the American strategy of restraint contingent on reciprocity. Policy statements throughout the period stressed the contingent nature of American restraint in ASAT development. One official told members of the Air Force Association:

> The Soviets have developed and tested a potential war-fighting antisatellite capability. They have thereby seized the initiative in an area which we hoped would be left untapped . . . I would warn them that they have started down a dangerous road. Restraint on their part will be matched by our own restraint, but we should not permit them to develop an asymmetry in space.[62]

The restrained nature of the DoD's response to the Soviet threat from space was echoed by the Air Force. With few exceptions, enthusiasm among top Air Force officials for military space missions had declined dramatically since the 1960s. While partially a result of bureaucratic factors and financial constraints, the Air Force's lack of interest in ASAT development can be attributed at least in part to the lack of a clearly defined military mission or deterrent function for an American ASAT. The ASAT mission was not considered a high priority Air Force responsibility, nor was it the subject of significant enthusiasm or funding, until the Air Force was directed by the White House to develop the MHV system.[63]

Just as the major concern with Soviet military activities in space arose within the executive branch rather than the military, the impetus to ASAT development likewise came from the National Security Council (NSC) and the White House; to some extent, it encountered a rather reluctant military bureaucracy. The perception of threat during this period thus seems to have derived to a significant extent from the political rather than the military consequences of Soviet space activities.

Following the resignation of President Nixon in 1974, U.S. policy regarding military activities in space was reevaluated by an NSC-appointed panel, chaired by Dr. Charles Slichter. Largely as a result of a perceived increase in Soviet "adventurism" in the Third World, the Slichter panel was tasked to study the dual issues of MILSAT and ASAT technology from the perspective that space assets might be used (or attacked) in support (or denial) of conventional terrestrial force capabilities. The panel concluded (in 1975) that particularly with regard to force projection in the Third World, the United States had become dangerously dependent on a relatively small constellation of potentially vulnerable satellites.[64]

Another study panel, under the chairmanship of Dr. Solomon Buchsbaum, was established in 1975 to explicitly consider the problem of satellite vulnerability. The Buchsbaum panel's concern on this issue was heightened significantly by the resumption of Soviet ASAT tests. An interim report issued to President Gerald Ford in response to Soviet test activities resulted in the issuing of policy memorandum NSDM-333, which called for enhanced measures to reduce the vulnerability of American satellites (by nonhostile means).

The final report of the Buchsbaum panel (delivered in December 1976) called for primarily compensatory, nonescalatory countermeasures to the Soviet space threat. The report explicitly considered the question of whether the United States should develop its own ASAT system, concluding that this would not in fact enhance the survivability of U.S. space assets. A U.S. ASAT would be useful neither for specific military missions against Soviet satellites, nor as a deterrent to Soviet use. Rather, an ASAT system would be useful only as a bargaining chip with which to negotiate a comprehensive agreement banning ASAT development, testing, and possession. The panel argued that because the possession of only a few ASAT weapons on one side could be of military significance, an effective ASAT arms control measure would have to include the dismantling of existing systems. It was judged unlikely that the Soviets would agree to dismantle their system unless the United States had something to dismantle in return.[65]

Troubled by the report's conclusions regarding satellite vulnerability, President Ford became "very upset and concerned about the relaxed approach of the Defense Department" to the issue of ASAT research and space defense.[66] In the face of another Soviet ASAT system test on December 27, Ford apparently came to the conclusion that the American policy of contingent restraint had failed to induce reciprocal Soviet restraint.

As a result of this assessment, the Ford Administration (during its final days in office) issued NSDM-345, which directed the DoD to immediately develop an operational ASAT system. The decision to proceed with development and testing of the MHV represented a major shift in American strategy for managing the threat from space. The new strategy was based on the threat of escalation rather than contingent restraint.

Although NSDM-345 represented the end of the American policy of contingent restraint in ASAT, it did not guarantee an outcome of unconditional defection from the regime. Apparently, the original document did not mention the possibility of an arms control agreement to forestall system development on both sides. Kissinger, in particular, had come to the conclusion that meaningful negotiations could not take place until the United States demonstrated both a willingness and a capability to build an ASAT system of its own.[67] The Ford Administration, however, was in its last days, and with the coming to power of the Carter Administration, the arms control option would receive new consideration.

Under Jimmy Carter, the decision to proceed with the American MHV ASAT system became part of a two-track policy, whose other track involved the pursuit of direct, formal arms control negotiations. The preferred objective of the two-track policy remained a cooperative solution (coordinated restraint) to the problem of military activities in space, but the proposed strategy for achieving this objective had shifted in important ways.

The development track of the two-track policy involved a steady program capable of producing a technologically sophisticated, operational ASAT system within a reasonable time. The ASAT development and testing program was primarily intended to demonstrate the willingness and the capability of the United States to develop its own ASAT system in response to Soviet activities in this area. Such a demonstration, it was argued, would be useful in providing incentives for the Soviet Union to negotiate a formal agreement on ASAT limitations.

The nature of the contingent threat embodied in the U.S. program was not, however, one of tit-for-tat reciprocity. Rather, the decision to proceed with the MHV system can be usefully thought of as returning two tits for a tat, or as a contingent threat of escalation. The MHV system, unlike previous U.S. ASAT projects, was designed to exploit to full advantage the American technological edge. The result was to be a far more capable ASAT system than its Soviet counterpart.

The U.S. MHV system (entering its final stages of testing at the time of this writing) employs a direct-ascent kinetic kill interceptor mechanism. The MHV, a small cylinder with a diameter of about 30 centimeters and a weight of approximately 15 kilograms, is carried (along with its booster) to high altitude by an F-15 fighter specially adapted to carry the weapon. On the basis of target acquisition and tracking data supplied by the U.S. space surveillance network, the MHV is launched (on top of a small, two-stage short-range attack missile [SRAM]) directly into the path of its target. The MHV uses passive infrared sensors to home in on its target, and it is equipped with a series of small boosters that permit final course correction. The MHV destroys its target by direct impact, as the cylinder smashes into the satellite at high velocity. No explosive mechanism is required.[68]

The MHV system, like the Soviet ASAT, suffers from a number of operational limitations. The maximum altitude at which the MHV system could be effective has not been determined. Its kill mechanism (which demands direct impact, and thus can tolerate only extremely small homing errors) and the limitations of its booster rocket suggest that it will be useful only against satellites in LEO (or perhaps against satellites in Molniya orbits, if they can be attacked at their orbital perigee). The second major limitation of the system arises from the requirement that it be launched from an F-15 fighter directly into the path of the target satellite.

Despite these limitations, the MHV system is far more capable than the Soviet ASAT. The MHV system is compact and operationally simple to manage; the United States could maintain a large stockpile of these weapons and carry out multiple attacks in a very short period of time. The direct-ascent interception method chosen for the American system has two distinct advantages. First, the MHV need only cross the orbit of its target (rather than having to actually maneuver into the orbit of the target); as a result, the time from launch to intercept is dramatically reduced. Second, because MHV-equipped F15s could be based in the Southern Hemisphere, the system may place at risk Soviet early warning and other satellites in Molniya orbit. Military experts generally agree that the MHV, although currently at a lesser stage of development, will when fully operational exceed the operational capability of the Soviet system in militarily significant ways.

The decision to proceed with the development of an extremely capable ASAT system can be seen as a contingent threat to escalate the competition in ASAT, rather than manage the threat by nonescalatory means. This argument is supported by the fact that there were available, to both the Ford and the Carter administrations, a number of alternative options for managing the Soviet ASAT threat. Some of these would have approached the problem in reciprocal, tit-for-tat fashion, while others would have minimized the impact of Soviet activities upon American security interests without posing any threat to the Soviet Union.

A full spectrum of unilateral cooperative measures to minimize the threat from Soviet ASAT activities was available to American decision makers in the mid-1970s, had they chosen to continue the strategy of contingent restraint. The military significance of the Soviet ASAT system (already limited) could be further reduced by a number of passive and active satellite survivability measures. Most satellite survivability measures would pose no direct threat to Soviet security. Although it was judged that decreasing the vulnerability of satellites would significantly increase the costs of the U.S. MILSAT program, these costs had to be balanced against both the immediate and potential long-term costs of an unrestrained competition in ASAT weaponry. The American commitment to reducing the vulnerability of satellites did in fact increase during this period of time; the most obvious manifestation of this policy was the attempt to place satellites in high orbit (semi- or geosynchronous) whenever this was consistent with technological possibilities and the satellite's mission. (In addition, steps were taken to increase maneuverability and to harden satellites so as to reduce their vulnerability to simple or unsophisticated threats). However, the priority of the space defense program lay clearly with the threat of escalation (the MHV system) and not with unilateral cooperative measures.

Had the United States desired to continue its strategy of contingent restraint and demonstrate its resolve to match Soviet activities in reciprocal fashion, without escalating the competition to a higher level of technology, a number of alternative ASAT system options other than the MHV were available. For example, the United States might have demonstrated contingent restraint by limiting ASAT research and development to *ground-launched* systems with limited capabilities roughly comparable to the Soviet ASAT. An ASAT Working Group had, in the early days of the Carter Administration, suggested that the United States pursue the development of an interim ASAT capability using existing technology in order to reinforce a potential American negotiating position. Apparently this system would have employed the co-orbital method of interception, and disabled its target with a shower of metal pellets.[69] The proposed system was in fact rejected by Defense on the grounds that it might impair commitment to the ongoing MHV program and by State and ACDA on the somewhat paradoxical grounds that an operational U.S. ASAT might complicate the attempt to negotiate an agreement banning ASATs. Another potential means of demonstrating reciprocity might have been the reactivation of the nonnuclear follow-on to Project 437, Program 922, which, as originally designed, would have also closely matched the operational capabilities of the Soviet ASAT system.

Apparently, at least some decision makers believed that the threat to escalate the competition and exploit American technology to its fullest would act as a powerful incentive for the Soviets to negotiate comprehensive limitations on ASAT. A cooperative solution was still the desired goal but the means of achieving it had changed to a strategy of contingent threat of escalation. In accordance with changing U.S. evaluations of Soviet intentions, a tacit or informal agreement was no longer judged to be sufficient. Instead, the second track of the two-track policy demanded formal negotiations leading to an explicit ASAT treaty.

Further empirical evidence of the shift in American strategy can be found both in funding decisions and in DoD statements regarding the nature and intentions of the U.S. ASAT program. Actual funding for space defense, which had amounted to less than $4 million per year through 1976, underwent a major expansion starting with FY 1977. In FY 1978, the budget for space defense had increased to $41.6 million (more than double the amount that had been projected for FY 1978 just two years earlier).[70] By FY 1981, the budget had again more than doubled, to $110.4 million. Of this money, the preponderant share was in fact to be devoted to research on the MHV. Lesser amounts ($19 million in FY 1978, $33.3 million in FY 1981)[71] were budgeted for programs aimed at reducing the vulnerability of American satellites by nonhostile means. The evidence suggests a commitment to rapid expansion of ASAT research with less emphasis placed upon options designed to manage the threat from space by cooperative means.

While the scope of the American commitment to ASAT development increased, public statements (by the DoD and others) continued to stress the fact that the American program represented a contingent response to Soviet activities, and that the United States continued to prefer a bilateral, comprehensive ban on ASAT systems. The Military Posture Statement for FY 1977 briefly mentioned the problem of space defense, but limited its discussion of American activities in this area to unilateral cooperative measures (such as satellite survivability and space surveillance programs). The FY 1979 Posture Statement placed increased emphasis on the subject of space defense. The dual nature of the threat was, for the first time, explicitly acknowledged: an increased American commitment to space defense was demanded by both Soviet ASAT and Soviet MILSAT activities. The American strategy is clearly outlined as one of contingent threat of escalation, coupled with a strong, primary desire to avert an arms race by arriving at a formal negotiated agreement.

> It would be preferable to join in on an effective, and adequately verifiable ban on anti-satellite (ASAT) systems; we certainly have no desire to engage in a space weapons race . . . We hope that negotiations on ASAT limitations lead to strong symmetric

controls. But in the meantime we must proceed with ASAT programs (for the present, short of operational or space testing), especially since we do not know if the Soviets will accept the controls on these weapons that we would think necessary.[72]

The shift in American strategy in the mid-1970s away from the use of contingent restraint can be partially explained by new technological and political challenges that had weakened the limited cooperative regime. By the late 1970s, the behavior of the two sides showed evidence of a sharp deterioration in the cooperative management of the threat from space.

The limited space regime had been based partially on a consensual understanding that certain MILSAT capabilities contributed to the shared interests of the two sides by enhancing strategic stability. Advancing technology, however, was increasing the hostile capabilities of satellites (particularly photoreconnaissance, ocean reconnaissance, and navigation systems), overshadowing their stability-enhancing functions. As technology enabled relatively benign satellite capabilities to expand into hostile applications, the interests of the two sides in regulating military activities in space began to diverge radically.

Partially as a result of technological opportunities, the United States (and to a lesser extent, the Soviet Union) had come to rely more heavily upon MILSATS to provide military and other capabilities essential to national security interests. In the mid-1970s, the United States was probably somewhat more dependent on space-based assets than was the Soviet Union, largely because its military forces were spread more widely throughout the world. (It should be stressed that general comparisons of this sort are notoriously unreliable and usually underexamined. Nevertheless, one can argue that an asymmetry of interest did exist in the mid-1970s. It has probably decreased progressively since that time, as we shall see.) Asymmetries of interest on this score may have produced opposite impacts on the two sides' perceived incentives. While the United States had greater reason to maintain sanctuary status for certain space assets, the Soviets may have had a greater incentive to place these assets at risk, or perhaps decrease American propensity to take advantage of its technological edge in space by posing at least a potential threat to U.S. satellites.

Concomitant with the growth of MILSAT technology were significant advances in technology relevant to ASAT. While systems capable of attacking satellites in GEO remained out of immediate reach, advancing technology (embodied in the MHV) had solved many of the problems relevant to an effective LEO ASAT. The incentive to proceed with LEO ASAT was strengthened by the impact of this new technology, despite the fact that the LEO-GEO distinction does not parallel the presumed interests of the two sides in placing at risk threatening satellites, while providing sanctuary to those judged benign.

Developments in technology also contributed to the erosion of important saliencies that had been focal points for U.S.–Soviet cooperation in space. With regard to ASAT weaponry, what was in any case an ambiguously defined saliency between dedicated and residual ASAT capabilities suffered erosion as a result of both technological developments and political decisions. Technology had enhanced the potential utility against satellites of a number of weapons designed primarily for other military missions, including ICBMs, SLBMs, and even sophisticated surface-to-air missiles (SAM). Increased research by both sides in ballistic missile defense systems promised to produce additional technologies (in particular, high power lasers) which would be applicable to the ASAT mission. The decision of the Soviets to resume testing their dedicated ASAT system signalled a possible shift in their intentions regarding the ASAT mission, and thus prompted American military analysts to take a worst-case view of potential residual ASAT capabilities. The perception by the United States that a number of Soviet systems posed a significant threat against satellites (particularly those in LEO) helped erode a saliency delineating dedicated ASAT activities from those Soviet systems with only residual ASAT capability.

With regard to MILSAT technology, a relatively unambiguous saliency between nonhostile, stabilizing activities, and the multiplication and enhancement of terrestrial forces was also undergoing technological erosion. Satellite functions considered to be in the mutual interest were progressively less clearly delineated from related functions that would be a source of military advantage to one side should war occur. For example, the existence and invulnerability of early warning satellite systems was judged to be in the mutual interest of the two sides. When it was suggested, however, that technology would soon permit early warning satellites to identify (in near real-time) the precise silos from which ICBMs had been fired, these satellites took on potentially threatening capabilities in the context of war-fighting scenarios. A number of additional developments in MILSAT technology served to further erode the distinction between benign and threatening satellite functions.

Two effects of the erosion of this saliency were evident. First, the focal point for coordination of policy—the use of space for nonhostile purposes—was increasingly blurred, as a single satellite could serve both hostile and nonhostile functions. Second, the structure of interests and incentives in the militarization of space was becoming increasingly complex. In particular scenarios (in peacetime, for example), it would be in both sides' self-interest to maintain certain satellites in an invulnerable position. In other scenarios (particularly in war-fighting of different kinds), a side might have a strong incentive to deny to the adversary certain military capabilities provided by satellites. At the same time, he might wish to maintain the invulnerability of his own satellites, *as well as* the invulnerability of certain of the adversary's satellites. For example, in a conventional war between proxy states, one superpower might wish to deny photoreconnaissance capabilities to the adversary. However, it would also be in that side's interest to insure that the adversary remained confident of the invulnerability of early warning satellites, to protect against the possibility of inadvertent escalation to central war. It was clear that no ASAT system could in fact discriminate between hostile and nonhostile satellites; at best, a saliency could be temporarily enacted between LEO-capable ASAT systems, and systems posing a threat to satellites at higher altitudes. Unfortunately, a saliency based on satellite altitude would only be partially successful in safeguarding satellites that perform mutually beneficial and stabilizing satellite functions.

By the mid-1970s, the general political environment of détente, which had been favorable to the development of limited forms of cooperation, had come under increasing stress. Détente, conceived of as a "mixed competitive-collaborative" relationship[73] based on norms of reciprocity and restraint, declined at least in part because of the failure of the states to define a mutually acceptable, shared definition of reciprocity by which the relationship would be governed. Unable to define agreed upon terms of exchange, the superpowers failed to capitalize on many shared or complementary interests. Conflicting interests, which were supposed to be managed through shared restraint and reciprocity in forgoing unilateral advantages, often became areas in which the two sides defined the terms of exchange so as to benefit themselves asymmetrically, to the detriment of the other's interest.

Particularly with regard to activities in the Third World, the two sides' operational definitions of reciprocity soon revealed themselves to be incompatible. As a result, disillusionment with détente was becoming increasingly widespread within the United States. In the judgment of much of the American decision-making elite, Soviet activities both in the Third World and in the continuation of a vigorous build-up of strategic nuclear weapons, seemed to indicate that the Soviets had defined "the terms of competition, and the terms of collaboration, in ways geared more toward maximizing unilateral advantage than toward expanding the mutual interest."[74] The introduction of SS-20 missiles into the European theater, which first attracted significant attention in 1977, was taken by many in the West as a definitive indication that the Soviets had not adopted a policy of reciprocal restraint with regard to its partner in détente.

Soviet behavior contradicted American expectations of reciprocal restraint, calling into question the robustness of the norm of reciprocity, as well as the efficacy of strategies of influence based on that norm. The belief that the Soviets would respond positively to both positive and negative incentives underwent a significant change as a result of the détente experience.

A reevaluation of the image of the Soviet Union as a partial collaborator was one result of this experience. The grand design of détente began to look less plausible, as the Soviet Union appeared increasingly opportunistic and aggressive. Apparently, the Soviet Union was a state that did not respond to Western conceptions of reciprocity. What was actually contingent restraint on the part of the West was likely to be perceived by the Soviets as unconditional conciliation, based on weakness.

The efficacy of strategies of reciprocity for dealing with Soviet threats was inevitably called into question. In its place, a new strategy—that of contingent threat of escalation—was suggested as being more appropriate. The optimal way to deal with the Soviets was not from a position of equality, but rather from a position of strength. According to this image of the adversary, the United States had to threaten to escalate the competition to the comparative detriment of the Soviet Union, in order to create sufficient incentive for the Soviets to work towards limited cooperative solutions to shared problems.

Developments in strategic theory, some of which were linked to changes in the image of the Soviet Union as an adversary, also served to weaken the basis for contingent restraint in the militarization of space. The Soviet strategic build-up, interpreted as a bid for unilateral advantage rather than as an attempt to satisfy legitimate security requirements, reduced the perceived viability of strategic nuclear policies based on a standard of parity. An increasingly influential school of thought argued that parity might be insufficient to insure extended deterrence in Europe, or even the deterrence of war between the superpowers.

U.S. policy-makers increasingly interpreted the requirements of deterrence and the continuing political stability of the Western alliance as requiring the United States to match or exceed Soviet capabilities for war-fighting. These developments in strategic thought became manifest in the evolution of the countervailing doctrine, adopted as American declaratory policy in Presidential Directive (PD)-59. The argument, essentially, was that the nature of the Soviet threat (with regard to both intentions and capabilities) precluded reliance on cooperative arrangements to insure U.S. security. Rather, the United States would have to actively threaten the Soviets in order to achieve viable deterrence, as well as strategic and political stability. As the United States's primary advantage remained its technological edge, areas of high technology were seen as a potential means of offsetting Soviet advantages in other areas.

An additional source of deterioration in cooperative behavior in space was the rapidity with which changes were taking place (and additional complexities and uncertainties introduced) in the underlying issues, and thus in the interests of the two sides with regard to military activities in space. Shared definitions of what types of behavior constitute reciprocal restraint are extremely sensitive to changes in underlying interests. When the potential of technology is expanding as rapidly as it was during this period, the two sides may encounter additional difficulties in developing and accepting shared norms of behavior that include "a mutually recognized definition of what constitutes an innovation, a challenging or assertive move, or a cooperative gesture."[75] Particularly with regard to advances in MILSAT capabilities, technology may very well have outrun the tortuous process by which norms of behavior are established in interdependent fashion between adversaries.

Rapidly increasing complexity and uncertainty of issues may help to account for American efforts to revitalize the space regime through formal negotiations rather than continued attempts at tacit cooperation or coordination of policy. Tacit arrangements may be particularly vulnerable to radical and/or rapid redefinitions of the structure of the underlying issue area. When issue structure changes rapidly, tacit processes of communication and policy coordination may not respond quickly enough to forestall deterioration of the regime.[76] Formal institutions may, in such instances, provide a valuable framework for modifying the shared referent points which define cooperation.

Bureaucratic politics supported the shift in American strategy and the deterioration of the space regime. As we have seen, the shift in perception of the threat from space was at first a political and not a military assessment. Predictably, when political pressure began to produce larger funds for space defense programs without removing funds from other programs, the Air Force's perception of the importance of ASAT weaponry underwent noticeable change. By the late 1970s, the DoD had become a major bureaucratic force behind the ASAT program.

In attempting to arrive at a viable U.S. negotiating position for formal talks with the Soviets, Pentagon officials questioned not only the *verifiability* of ASAT limitations, but also the *desirability* of such limitations even if they were verifiable. Other bureaucratic actors, most importantly ACDA and State, argued that the potential benefits of a negotiated agreement limiting the ASAT threat would outweigh the risks of minor Soviet violations, and would on balance contribute to American security interests. The two-track strategy satisfied both sides of the bureaucratic struggle. A vigorous ASAT research and development program satisfied the demands of the DoD, while the promise of negotiations held out the ultimate goal of arms control to ACDA and State. It would be incorrect to argue (as Paul B. Stares does) that the two tracks were inherently contradictory.[77] Rather, the threat of escalation of the arms race in space, and the promise of arms control, were linked as part of a strategy of contingent threat. The goal of the Carter strategy remained the revitalization of the limited space regime, and the identification of new cooperative measures to partially manage the shared threat from space.

In sum, American strategy for continued management of the limited space regime underwent a significant shift in the mid-1970s. Broad trends in international politics and technological developments affected the conditions and processes that had supported limited cooperation in the previous decade. The underlying basis of the partial space regime had weakened considerably by 1977. As perceptions of the Soviet Union and of the threat from space began to shift, American strategy for managing the regime shifted away from contingent restraint and conciliation towards threat of escalation. The American ASAT program became part of a two-track policy, whose preferred goal remained a partial cooperative solution via formal negotiated limits on military activities in space. The difference from previous policy lay primarily in the strategy for achieving this goal.

The Late 1970s

In accordance with the goals and strategy of the two-track policy, full-scale development of the MHV ASAT system continued while the Carter Administration prepared for— and eventually entered into—formal negotiations seeking limits on ASAT weaponry. The following section describes the impediments the Administration encountered in its attempt to formulate a coherent negotiating stance that would serve American security interests and be consistent with the strategy of influencing the adversary to seek cooperative solutions by contingent threat of escalation. A short history of the formal negotiations that took place during the Carter Administration illustrates the additional difficulties encountered in the attempt to implement the two-track policy. The history of the negotiations indicates that the failure of formal negotiations to contribute to a cooperative solution can be partially explained by the failure of the United States to construct early on and maintain a negotiating stance that was precisely attuned to the larger strategy by which the United States sought to influence Soviet behavior.

Formal talks between the United States and the Soviet Union on the issue of ASAT weapons began in Helsinki on June 8, 1978. This first negotiating session was considered preliminary in nature, but sufficient progress was apparently made to justify continuing the talks. Two subsequent rounds of ASAT negotiations were held, in Bern in the early winter of 1979, and in Vienna in the spring. The details of draft texts developed in these negotiations have not been made public. Significant progress appears to have been made, although opinions vary widely as to how close to agreement the two sides actually came in these talks.[78] According to Raymond Garthoff, the two sides had succeeded in drafting a "largely agreed joint draft text." Agreement was apparently extremely close on a "no-use" accord, and a more elaborate agreement, including a complete ban on testing and deployment, was considered within reach by at least some of the principal negotiators.

Despite both sides' apparent interest in exploring the several unresolved issues blocking agreement, the talks were put on hold in June of 1979, as a result of Carter's decision to give absolute priority in the arms control field to the ratification of the SALT

II Treaty. Following the invasion of Afghanistan in December 1979, the ASAT negotiations, like the SALT Treaty, fell victim to the new chill in U.S.–Soviet relations.

The failure of the formal negotiating process can be partially explained as a result of the inability of the two sides to translate their recognized mutual interest in cooperative limitations on the militarization of space into a concrete basis for a mutually advantageous agreement. On the American side, a lack of presidential leadership early in the process was evident in the failure to define a desirable direction and/or outcome for the negotiations. The American negotiating team did not present a consistent position (and one that made sense as part of the two-track strategy) to the Soviets until the final round of negotiations, by which time the domestic and international political climates were far less conducive to the conclusion of a meaningful agreement.

When the American delegation entered the first set of negotiations, apparently their only specific instructions were "to explore the extent of Soviet interest and thinking on this issue."[79] As a result, the American team promoted a number of options, ranging from a complete prohibition of ASAT systems to interim agreements encompassing a moratorium on testing and various kinds of operating rules. It could not have been clear to the Soviets what were the precise goals of the United States in the negotiations, or how these might have been linked to pursuit of superior capability through the MHV system.

The second set of negotiations, taking place in Bern between January and February of 1979, produced little in the way of progress towards an agreement. While the Soviets had unilaterally refrained from testing during the course of the talks (the last test of the Soviet ASAT system had been in May of 1978, just prior to the first set of negotiations), the U.S. delegation refused to accept the idea of a joint testing moratorium, arguing that this would have left the Soviets with an asymmetrical ASAT capability since the Soviets were unwilling to dismantle their system. The only common ground identified was the possibility of some type of agreement on procedures incorporating a "non-use" pledge, although the problems of arriving at shared definitions of "ASAT use" remained.

Prior to the final set of negotiations, the Carter Administration agreed on precisely what types of ASAT limitations to pursue in the context of the formal negotiations. A negotiating position calling for a short-term testing moratorium in conjunction with a non-use agreement, followed by an effort to ban the possession of ASAT weapons, was forged and supported by the various elements of the arms control bureaucracy. The U.S. negotiating team returned to the table (this time in Vienna) with clear instructions as part of a coherent strategy for achieving a limited cooperative agreement with the Soviets.

At what was to be the final negotiating session, the United States and the Soviet Union did in fact make some progress towards reaching common definitions of ASAT-relevant activities as part of a no-use agreement. A number of problems remained, however, and the negotiations were adjourned just prior to the SALT II signing ceremony. Important unresolved issues centered around the definition of ASAT-relevant activities, and the extent of coverage of a potential agreement. The Soviet Union apparently wished to place limits on the operations of the U.S. space shuttle because of its limited, residual ASAT capability; the United States argued that the shuttle could not be considered as either an ASAT or an ASAT launch platform. American concerns included the difficulty of placing limits on development of directed-energy ASATs, as well as the question of whether ASATs could be used for purposes of self-defense against "hostile" acts. Another important issue concerned the applicability of the treaty to space assets belonging to third nations—the United States was concerned lest a bilateral treaty appear to legitimize attacks on satellites belonging to nonsignatories.[80]

At the signing ceremonies for the SALT II Treaty in Vienna, the United States and the Soviet Union agreed in a joint communiqué "to continue actively searching for mutually acceptable agreement in the continuing negotiations on ASAT systems." It was expected that a fourth round of talks would take place the following autumn; however, the attention of the Carter Administration quickly became consumed by the domestic political issues surrounding ratification of the SALT Treaty. As a result, the issue of ASAT weaponry was relegated to a low priority. Some Administration officials believed that the SALT II Treaty approached the limits of what the domestic system could bear; asking support for cooperative limitations on ASAT as well might jeopardize support for ratification of SALT II.

In any case, the unwillingness or inability of the Carter Administration to exert sufficient control over the bureaucracy and over the input of public opinion contributed to what may have been a missed opportunity for achieving a formal agreement limiting ASAT activities. With the Soviet invasion of Afghanistan in December of 1979, prospects for continued progress in ASAT arms control dimmed considerably. As if to underscore the demise of the opportunity to re-establish some degree of cooperation in space, the Soviets resumed testing of their ASAT system in April of 1980.

The difficulty of constructing a coherent and logical negotiating stance for ASAT arms control arose in part as a result of the complexity of the issues involved in the militarization of space, and the uncertain impact on U.S. security interests. Uncertainty over the eventual impact of an unrestrained arms race in both ASAT and MILSAT led to significant controversy within the Carter Administration over what type of cooperative restraints, if any, were in fact desirable. It was generally thought that some degree of shared restraint in space would contribute to American security interests; however, the precise nature of a desirable limited regime in space remained a matter of uncertainty.

The controversy over what type of agreement the United States ought to pursue fell out along bureaucratic lines of division. Representatives of State and ACDA generally argued that a more comprehensive agreement, up to and including a complete ban on possession of ASAT systems, would be the most desirable outcome. Pentagon officials, in contrast, felt that a comprehensive agreement would not be in the best interests of the United States, arguing instead for a limited agreement on "non-use" or "rules of the road."[81] The concrete basis of the controversy lay in varying evaluations of the problems of *defining* ASAT capabilities, *evaluating* Soviet intentions and capabilities in the ASAT mission, and *monitoring* Soviet ASAT-relevant research, testing, and development activities.

The most difficult issue to be overcome in the negotiations was the problem of definition. While the two sides might have agreed relatively easily on the definition of a dedicated ASAT system, a number of other weapon systems maintain a degree of residual ASAT capability that might or might not be militarily significant. Certain of these systems or activities might have been constrained by limitations on testing in an ASAT mode, but others probably could not have been defined in a way that was acceptable to both sides. While insufficient constraints might leave a side with a potential advantage in ASAT capabilities, neither side would accept limits so constraining as to impede other non-ASAT activities that were judged to be in the security interests of the state. For example, Soviet insistence that the United States guarantee that manned, maneuverable space vehicles would not be used as an ASAT weapon would have required the United States to accept severe limitations on the activities of the space shuttle. The American position was that the space shuttle could not be considered as either an ASAT or an ASAT platform, and thus would not be a subject of discussion in the negotiations.[82]

The second category of difficulty in constructing a coherent negotiating stance concerned the problem of evaluating Soviet intentions with regard to ASAT. American analysts were perplexed by the Soviets' on-again off-again ASAT testing program; it was not immediately clear that the Soviets were highly committed to developing and maintaining a significant capability to destroy American satellites. The evaluation of intentions is of course a recurrent problem in exploring potential avenues of cooperation in security issues. In lieu of a reliable assessment of intentions, additional emphasis is placed on the task of monitoring capabilities.

The third category of difficulty concerns the problem of monitoring Soviet research, development, and testing activities relevant to ASAT. Strategies that incorporate contingency can operate only when each side is able, with high confidence, to recognize the actions of the adversary as instances of cooperation or of possible violations of an agreement. In arms control, the problem of recognition is managed via procedures for verification of compliance, by NTM and other means.

Once agreement had been reached (if in fact it ever was) about what particular ASAT systems and activities ought to be limited, the feasibility of such limits would have had to be considered in terms of verification capabilities. It is important that the requirements for verification of ASAT limitations were considered to be particularly stringent. Given the relatively small number of U.S. satellites, it was judged by some American decision-makers (particularly those in the Pentagon and in the intelligence community) that a small degree of cheating, allowing the Soviets to maintain even a limited covert ASAT capability, would be of significance.

As the perceived payoff from minor noncompliance was judged to be of potential military significance, U.S. policy-makers were adamant in their pursuit of stringent verification arrangements. The problem was further exacerbated by the assessment of the intelligence community that unilateral means of verification by NTM would by themselves be inadequate. Even currently existing, dedicated ASAT systems were seen to pose significant verification problems. The Soviet ASAT interceptor unit was relatively small, complicating the problems of verifying dismantlement and preventing potential stockpiling. The SS-9 booster, on top of which the interceptor was launched, was employed by the Soviets for a variety of other purposes; hence, its elimination was out of the question. The fact that the Soviet ASAT system operated from only two specific launch pads in Tyuratam provided a potential means of verifying operational limitations on the system, but any such arrangement would have required somewhat elaborate cooperative measures, such as previous announcement of launches, designed to improve American recognition capabilities. The American MHV system is so small that it too is essentially unverifiable by NTM without cooperative measures designed to improve Soviet recognition capabilities.

The problem of residual ASAT capabilities further complicated issues of verification. The large number of systems that have residual ASAT capability (in particular, ICBMs and the Galosh ABM interceptor) could not in themselves be meaningfully limited by an agreement, although restrictions on testing of these systems in an ASAT mode could be a means of limiting their significance. Although assessments vary, it is the general consensus that such limitations could be verified to significant (although not to 100 percent) levels of confidence by unilateral means.[83] In contrast, potential future systems, based on principles such as directed energy weaponry, might be more difficult to monitor, and might pose a threat to satellites at higher altitudes (including, potentially, those in geosynchronous orbit).

As is generally the case with arms control negotiations, problems of definition and verification exacerbate the difficulty of designing and implementing cooperative agreements that would be acceptable to both sides. Given imperfect verification capabilities, and uncertainty concerning the impact of certain kinds of limitations on American security interests, presidential leadership assumes a critically important role in the conclusion and management of cooperative agreements.

It is incumbent upon the President to assume leadership of the situation and exert control over the arms control and military bureaucracies. In the 1960s, President Kennedy's leadership in accepting the risks of imperfect verification was crucial to the conclusion of treaties and the acceptance of tacit arrangements which on balance were judged to contribute to American security interests. Where Kennedy had succeeded, President Carter noticeably failed. It should be appreciated, in fairness to Carter, that advancing technology had considerably complicated the task of the President. Whereas the risks incurred by the acceptance of imperfect verification in the 1960s were calculably small, the technological momentum of the intervening decades had made the risks of imperfect verification significantly greater, and certainly more difficult to estimate. As a result, the U.S. government's position on verification of ASAT limitations was never well defined. (The CIA, ACDA, and the DoD each carried out its own ASAT verification studies, reaching what were in many cases contradictory conclusions.)[84] An interagency working group, whose task it was to define the American position on these issues prior to the start of the negotiations with the Soviets, apparently did not succeed in its attempt to reconcile the differing positions within the bureaucracy.[85] The American negotiators never had a clear sense of precisely what type of agreement would be both desirable in terms of serving American security interests, and feasible given the impediments to verification.

The efficacy of the formal negotiation track of the two-track policy was further inhibited by a conceptual failure on the part of American decision-makers and strategic analysts. In attempting to structure incentives for the Soviet Union, so as to revitalize partial cooperation in the management of the threat from space, the Carter Administration's negotiating position took heed of only one aspect of the dual threat from space. While developing a relatively advanced ASAT weapon as the contingent threat of escalation, and pursuing formal negotiations as the means for arriving at a partial cooperative arrangement, the American strategy failed to take account of the increasingly important second aspect of the threat from space—the use of MILSATS for force enhancement, multiplication, and (perhaps) the direct application of force from space.

As long as unrestrained development of MILSAT technology and capabilities was allowed to proceed, the incentives for each state to maintain and improve ASAT capabilities would probably increase. Certainly no ASAT agreement could be completely sheltered from other types of military activity in space, particularly as saliencies that had existed in the use of MILSATs were progressively eroded by advancing technology. The failure of the Carter Administration to perceive, or to act upon, the inevitable linkage between ASAT and MILSAT in the context of the negotiations is difficult to explain. Perhaps it was simply a failure of strategic analysis, or a result of the complexities encountered in trying to deal with only the ASAT aspect of the militarization of space. In any case, the inadequacy of the U.S. negotiating position detracted from the efficacy of the two-track policy, and made it unlikely to succeed as part of the larger American strategy regarding the militarization of space.

The 1980s

When the Reagan Administration assumed office in January 1981, the space regime was near dissolution. The Soviets had resumed a vigorous ASAT testing program, and the U.S. MHV system was in advanced stages of development. Both states were proceeding without obvious restraint in the development and deployment of increasingly threatening MILSAT systems. Limited cooperation in space, even to avoid the most detrimental effects of an unconstrained arms race, seemed increasingly unlikely.

Further deterioration of cooperation in space came about in conjunction with another shift in American strategy at this time. Soon after President Reagan assumed office, American strategy shifted from one of *contingent* threat of escalation to one of unconditional defection from the regime, or *noncontingent* escalation. The adoption of this competitive strategy by the Reagan Administration entailed a significant shift in the perceived goals of the U.S. military space program in general, and the MHV ASAT system in particular. It also spelled the end of efforts to reach an arms control agreement for space.

In August 1981 President Reagan directed an interagency working group under the National Security Council to evaluate the impact of American space policy on national security interests. Apparently in accordance with the findings of the review, American military strategy in space underwent a shift to a policy of unconditional, noncontingent competition. Despite some obligatory rhetoric about cooperation in the peaceful use of space, the Reagan Administration—both in its statements and in its actions—demonstrated a clear commitment to the unilateral pursuit of military capabilities in space that it deemed beneficial to American security interests. Limited cooperation with the Soviets would play little or no part in managing the threat from space.[86]

Regarding ASAT capabilities, the Reagan Administration rejected the previous strategies of contingent restraint, and contingent escalation, as means for arriving at cooperative arrangements with the Soviets. No longer was the American ASAT development program conceived of (even in part) as a hedge against Soviet ASAT development, or as a threat of escalation designed to increase Soviet incentives to negotiate

ASAT limitations. According to DDR&E Richard DeLauer, "the US ASAT program is not a bargaining chip and never was."[87]

The Reagan Administration viewed the MHV system as a weapon with specific military utility, and offered a dual rationale for its development and deployment. First, U.S. officials maintained, an operational MHV system would act to deter the Soviets from using their ASAT system against American satellites. Second, the MHV system would be applicable to a number of plausible military missions. It was argued that within particular crisis or conflict scenarios, the United States might need to disable Soviet space assets that provide support to, or otherwise enhance, terrestrial military forces. The changed rationale for the U.S. ASAT program is illustrated by the following White House policy statement of late 1982:

> The United States will proceed with development of an antisatellite (ASAT capability), with *operational deployment as a goal*. The primary purposes . . . are to deter threats to space systems of the United States . . . and to deny any adversary the use of space-based systems that provide support to hostile military forces.[88]

In accordance with this shift in strategy, the United States at the same time moved to initiate research on follow-on systems to the MHV. DeLauer, in a 1984 statement before the House Armed Services Committee, stated that it was now the Administration's policy to intensively investigate the possibilities for a "follow-on system with additional capabilities to place a wider range of Soviet satellite vehicles at risk."[89] The implied objective was to develop the capability to attack satellites in GEO.

A similar shift in strategy occurred with regard to the development of MILSAT systems. The Reagan strategy dictated that the United States attempt to capitalize on its presumed technological superiority in order to develop space assets for the support and enhancement of terrestrial forces, and perhaps even for the direct application of force from space. Much of the discussion of MILSAT technology is classified; nevertheless, the Fiscal 1984–8 Defense Guidance Document was reported to have stated that "the Department of Defense will vigorously pursue technology and systems both to provide responsive support and to project force in and from space as needed."[90]

The change in American strategy was closely associated with a change in the evaluation of Soviet space activities, both actual and potential. Soviet ASAT tests were continuing, with at least three tests taking place between January 1981 and August 1983. The Pentagon found the last of these tests particularly troublesome, as it was carried out in conjunction with a major exercise involving other elements of the Soviet strategic forces, simulating the actual integrated operations that would take place during conflict.[91]

The Reagan Administration characterized Soviet space activities as potentially hostile, escalatory to the competition, and thus a threat to American security interests. In fact, the Soviet ASAT system that was tested successfully during this period was indistinguishable from and no more capable than the system that had been tested in the 1970s. It was the political evaluation of the threat rather than the nature of the threat itself that had changed. A worst-case analysis stressed the technological potential of the new IR sensor system—despite the fact that all tests employing the new sensor system failed.[92] A worst-case assessment was similarly made of the potential of the Soviet ASAT to attack satellites in GEO, if it could be carried to high altitudes by a larger booster (such as the Proton). The considerable technical difficulties to be overcome, as well as strategic problems arising from the fact that such an attack would necessarily include a tactical warning to the adversary of many hours, were apparently discounted in the Administration's evaluation of the threat.[93]

What had been a steadily growing concern regarding Soviet potential in the area of directed energy weapons (DEW) took on additional importance, given the Reagan Administration's worst-case assessment of Soviet intentions and capabilities in ASAT. While previous administrations had not considered the development of a Soviet DEW capability likely in the near term, the Reagan Administration stated openly (in 1982) that it believed the Soviet Union might demonstrate a militarily significant space-based laser capability by 1983. *Soviet Military Power,* the annual Pentagon document describing developments in Soviet military capabilities, described in 1983 a "directed energy research program including the development of laser-beam weapon systems which could be based either in the USSR, aboard the next generation of Soviet ASATs, or aboard the next generation of Soviet manned space stations."[94] The DoD argued that the Soviets had the potential to construct and deploy, sometime in the 1990s, a DEW ASAT system threatening American satellites in LEO, and possibly in GEO as well.

Although there was reason to be concerned about Soviet DEW research, a majority of scientists within the intelligence community considered the DoD's assessment to be highly unrealistic.[95] A White House Science Council Study, completed in 1984, concluded that considerable conceptual and engineering problems had to be resolved before informed estimates of the potential military utility of DEW ASAT weapons could be made; no such technological breakthroughs were foreseen for the next decade.[96] The perceived threat from Soviet research in laser and other DEW technology was apparently based more on a political assessment of Soviet strategy and intentions than on a sober evaluation of the technological potential of the program.

The more alarming assessment of the potential Soviet ASAT threat was associated with the shift in American strategy to unconditional defection from the space regime. The character of the new American strategy is illustrated by the shift in tone and content of the government's Military Posture statements over the period FY 1980 to FY 1986. Former Secretary of Defense Harold Brown's statements for FY 80 through FY 82 had included a clear statement of the U.S. desire for a cooperative solution, linked to a contingent threat of escalation, as part of the Carter Administration's strategy:

> The President has stated our preference for an adequately verifiable ban on ASAT systems and our opposition to a space weapons race . . . In the absence of an agreement and in the face of the potential threat, we will have to continue working to defend our satellites, and to develop an equivalent capability to destroy Soviet satellites, if necessary.[97]

Up through FY 1982, the American ASAT program was described as a research and development program whose near-term goal was the development of a prototype ASAT capability. The ultimate goal of the strategy remained (and this was quite clearly stated) a cooperative solution banning or otherwise limiting ASAT capabilities on both sides.

The Military Posture statement on space policy underwent significant change in FY 1983. American interest in ASAT was no longer contingent on Soviet activities. Deployment of a technologically sophisticated ASAT system capable of threatening Soviet satellites was the clear goal of the policy; arms control measures and/or coordinated restraint were no longer considered desirable. According to Secretary Weinberger:

> We are pursuing an operational ASAT system . . . The Air Force plans to deploy the
> Air Launched Miniature Vehicle, which will be launched by F-15's against enemy
> satellites. To support an ASAT capability beyond this decade, we are currently assess-
> ing the feasibility of space-based laser weapons[98]

In moving towards a policy of noncontingent escalation in which the competition would
be unrestrained, the Reagan Administration assumed, apparently, that in such unrestrained competition, the United States was likely to come out the winner.

While American policy evolved in an increasingly competitive fashion, the Soviet
Union in 1983 began to exhibit renewed interest in cooperative agreements in space.
(The change in Soviet policy may have been partially or even largely due to American
policy, but it would be incorrect to draw this causal link without further evidence, little
or none of which is available.) The Soviet policy initiative took two directions, the first
of which was a contingent moratorium on ASAT tests, announced by Chairman Yuri
Andropov in August of 1983:

> The USSR assumes the commitment not to be the first to put into outer space any type
> of antisatellite weapon, that is, imposes a unilateral moratorium on such launchings for
> the entire period during which other countries, including the USA, will refrain from
> stationing in outer space antisatellite weapons of any type.[99]

Andropov's statement committed the Soviet Union to a moratorium on ASAT activities, if and only if the United States were to exhibit reciprocal restraint. The contingent moratorium can be characterized as a strategy aimed at a cooperative solution to
the ASAT problem, based on the strategic consensus that the military significance of
the two sides' current capabilities was roughly equal, and in any case, quite low.

The second aspect of the Soviet policy initiative was a draft treaty on the militarization of space submitted to the United Nations the day after the moratorium had been
announced. This treaty corrected many of the inadequacies of a previous draft that had
been submitted in 1981, and included a number of significant Soviet concessions. The
Soviet draft treaty addressed both the ASAT issue and the related question of MILSAT
capabilities. Outlawing the use of force in space, it called for a prohibition on testing
and deployment of space-based weapons capable of striking against targets in space or
on the earth. It banned the testing and deployment of new anti-satellite systems. In a
significant concession to American criticisms of the earlier draft, this proposed treaty
called for the elimination of current ASAT systems.[100] This was the first indication that
the Soviets would be willing to dismantle their current ASAT system in the context of
a cooperative agreement.

In accordance with the Reagan Administration's strategy of unrestrained competition, the United States rejected the thrust of the Soviet initiative. The Pentagon argued
that a moratorium on ASAT activities would remain undesirable until the United States
had achieved an operational capability matching or exceeding that of the Soviet Union.
The State Department argued that the United States could not verify with acceptable
confidence the dismantling of the Soviet interceptor system. (The question of whether
several covertly maintained and untested ASAT interceptors, dependent upon a large
and vulnerable launch facility for their use, would be of military significance, was not
addressed.) The problem of residual ASAT capabilities was also cited as a reason for
rejecting the Soviet offer.[101]

The Administration's objections to the Soviet draft treaty were for the most part substantive; the treaty presented several operational problems. Nevertheless, the Soviet draft might have formed the basis for negotiations between the two sides. Given observed Soviet interest in an agreement, American intransigence at this juncture may have contributed to what could be labelled a missed opportunity for revitalizing limited cooperation in space. That the Reagan Administration chose to reject Soviet overtures outright, rather than move to negotiate on parts of the treaty it found potentially interesting, is a clear indication of the way in which American strategy had shifted in the preceding years.

Through the period 1983–1985, the Soviets periodically raised the issue of space arms control with the United States, but received little encouragement in response. Meanwhile, the MHV testing program proceeded on schedule. Two partial tests of the system had been conducted in January and November 1984; the function of the booster's guidance system and the ability of the MHV to track an infrared source (in this case, a star) had been demonstrated.[102]

The third test, originally scheduled for early summer 1985, was to be the first actual intercept trial, in which the MHV was to be launched at a specially instrumented target balloon whose function it would be to assess the performance of the system. The decision to proceed with the test in the face of technical constraints and Soviet offers of coordinated restraint illustrates the interaction between the political and military aspects of the Reagan strategy.

In May 1985, an Air Force technical review group recommended that the test be postponed, as a result of a number of technical concerns considered to pose a medium or high risk to achieving the objectives of the test. Only seven days after the review group filed its report, the Air Force Systems Command's Space Division approved the technical readiness of the hardware for the third test. The review group noted, in response, that the probability of accomplishing mission objectives remained somewhat less than 50 percent, as the technical concerns it had identified had not been adequately addressed. Reflecting the primarily political assessment that the test had to proceed as scheduled (regardless of its military utility), the Air Force countered with the argument that there were "no further reasonable actions that can be taken prior to the third test that would increase the 50 percent probability."[103]

Additional technical difficulties similarly failed to postpone the target date for the third test. The MHV unit itself was in midsummer returned to the manufacturer for changes and repair.[104] Even more serious difficulties plagued the instrumented target balloon. In August, the objective of the test was changed from a launch against the target balloon, to the destruction of a defunct American satellite currently in orbit.[105]

The change in target objective placed severe constraints on the military value of the test for the purposes of development. If the test were a success, the United States would have demonstrated (in rather spectacular fashion) an operational ASAT capability, but would not in fact learn a great deal about the performance parameters of the MHV. If the test failed, almost no information about the performance of the MHV, and the cause of the failure, would be available. From the point of view of a military scientist wishing to evaluate the capability and performance of the MHV system, it would seem far from optimal to carry out the test under these conditions.

Additional incentives to refrain from carrying out the scheduled test were provided by the Soviet Union. In June 1985, the Soviets proposed a joint moratorium on ASAT development, to accompany the Soviet moratorium on testing. The United States refused to consider this proposal outside of the larger framework of the Geneva umbrella negotiations. As the date of the U.S. test approached, the Soviets reemphasized that the testing moratorium they had adopted in 1983 was contingent on American activities: "The peoples (of the Soviet Union) will put the responsibility for the beginning of a race in space weapons on those who are prepared to start dangerous experiments in near-earth orbits."[106] The Soviets thus underscored their perception that coordinated restraint in space had reached a critical juncture. Given the tenuous state of the space regime in 1985, the American decision to proceed with the test series signalled a clear intention on the part of the United States to withdraw from cooperative arrangements limiting military activities in space.

On August 21, 1985, the Administration informed the Congress that it would within several weeks proceed with the third test of the MHV. The Department of Defense justified its decision to proceed on the basis of three familiar arguments.[107] An American ASAT system was needed to deter attacks against U.S. satellites, as well as to address the growing offensive capability of Soviet MILSATs. If bilateral ASAT limitations were seen as desirable, extremely stringent standards of confidence in verification would have to be met. Finally, parity in operational ASAT capabilities was considered to be important in and of itself. The Reagan Administration's view of the concept of parity will receive detailed consideration subsequently; suffice it to say here that the Administration considered "optical equivalence," rather than an objective consideration of threats and capablities, to be the necessary prerequisite of parity.

The third test of the MHV system was carried out on September 13, 1985, and was judged an "absolute success" by the Air Force.[108] The MHV directly struck and destroyed a small target at a height of 290 miles above the earth's surface. The target was, however, an old defunct satellite, rather than the specially instrumented target balloon whose technical difficulties had threatened to postpone the test. As previously explained, the decision to proceed with the test under these circumstances severely limited the potential scientific and military information about the system's performance that could be gleaned from the test, "Pentagon officials acknowledged that using a dead satellite would reduce the scientific value of the trial, but they said the Air Force decided it would be worse to delay the test for months while the target vehicle was prepared."[109]

American policy in this case appears to have been designed in part to demonstrate that the United States had committed its resources to unrestrained competition in space. It is noteworthy that the test was carried out a number of weeks prior to the Geneva summit; it seems reasonable to assume that this aspect of timing was at least partially the result of political intention. The presumed imperative to carry out the test prior to Geneva constitutes further evidence of a strategy designed to make the Soviets more "tractable" by escalating the competition in space, suggesting new and direct threats to Soviet security interests.

Political, military, and technological developments of the early 1980s further weakened the basis of limited cooperation in space, contributing to the deterioration of the space regime. Accompanying these changes was a shift in American strategy for managing the competition in space, which can be partially explained with reference to the framework of variables previously described.

The incentives and interests of the United States continued to shift so as to make competitive options appear increasingly attractive and mutual restraint less so. Technological developments applicable to MILSAT, ASAT, and the promise of space-based ballistic missile defense (BMD) enhanced the perceived incentives for development of military assets in space.

American technological proficiency was rapidly expanding the potential use of space-based systems for force support and force enhancement, as well as the direct application of force from space. In the 1980s, the United States orbited the first photoreconnaissance satellite capable of digital imaging and real-time transmission of data to ground stations. (The KH-11 and succeeding systems thus were able to overcome a serious limitation of previous systems, which periodically eject film canisters for retrieval and processing.)[110] Concurrently, the United States moved towards deployment of the NAVSTAR GPS, an advanced navigational system that also offers significant tactical support to ground-based artillery and tactical air operations.[111] Improvements in ELINT technology, such as the use of side-looking synthetic aperture radar, promised a significant expansion of all weather, high altitude imaging and tracking capabilities.[112] The lure of technological possibilities, seemingly offering asymmetrical advantages to the United States, made restraint in the militarization of space appear increasingly unattractive.

At the same time, improvement in Soviet MILSAT capabilities, although somewhat less impressive than U.S. developments, increased the perceived incentive of some U.S. decision-makers to proceed with ASAT. As Soviet satellite ocean reconnaissance capabilities continued to improve, some American strategists questioned the sufficiency of passive countermeasures to deal with the potential vulnerability of U.S. and NATO naval forces during a prolonged conflict in Europe. (In the 1980s, the Soviet Union sought to maintain both an EORSAT and a RORSAT on station at all times. Since countermeasures against the two different types of ocean reconnaissance are different, and to some extent mutually exclusive, this complicated to a considerable degree the U.S. Navy's attempts to defeat ocean reconnaissace by passive countermeasures.)[113] It was argued that protection of sea lines of communication and resupply might require the destruction of Soviet EORSAT and RORSAT satellites. The possible application of ocean reconnaissance and other satellite capabilities to anti-submarine warfare (ASW) operations also became of increasing concern.[114] Although multiple, "point-by-point" countermeasures could defeat each of these threats individually, a viable ASAT seemed an efficient way to manage all these threats at once, as well as to deter the Soviets from investing additional resources in space-based military systems capable of threatening U.S. security interests.

Perhaps the strongest incentive for the United States to eschew limited cooperation in space derived from potential developments in BMD employing space-based systems. President Reagan's commitment to the SDI, and the resulting emphasis on space-based defensive systems, impacts directly on the perceived interests of the United States with regard to cooperation in space.

BMD and ASAT are intimately connected in both a technological and military-strategic sense. Technologies applicable to BMD (search, acquisition, tracking, and destruction capabilities) are in many cases similar to ASAT technology; and the task of attacking satellites is far less complex than the attempt to defend against ballistic missiles. A moderately effective BMD system with exo-atmospheric capabilities would pose a substantial threat to satellites. In addition, some BMD technologies would provide or enhance capability to project force directly from space against other targets, such as airplanes, cruise missiles, or perhaps ground targets. While it is true that certain types of DEW systems would not be capable of penetrating the atmosphere (X-ray lasers, for example), other components of BMD systems (such as lasers in the visible region of the spectrum) might pose a direct and multifaceted threat to the military forces and other security interests of the adversary.

American strategic analysis generally accepts the contention that the Soviets will not permit the United States to achieve a unilateral, invulnerable strategic defense capability in space, *if* it is within the Soviet capability to prevent it. In short, the development of increasingly threatening space-based systems enhances the incentive of the Soviet Union to develop its ASAT capability. As long as the United States is committed to placing increasingly hostile capabilities in space, the Soviets will have little reason to agree to cooperative limits on ASAT. From the American perspective, such limitations could only be arrived at by placing constraints on strategic defense and other MILSAT systems based in space, which the United States is not now willing to do.

The requirements for relative invulnerability of strategic defense systems based in space demand that the goal of American space policy be to establish an operational superiority in space, and to deny meaningful access to space for the Soviet Union. This is obviously inconsistent with cooperative management of a bilateral space regime. Rather, American strategy demands that the United States compete vigorously in a bid to overwhelm the Soviet Union and "seize the high ground" in space.

Saliencies in space, which had been relatively unambiguous in the 1960s, and had progressively eroded since that time, underwent further deterioration in the 1980s as a result of both technological developments and the political commitment of the United States to strategic defense. As a result, it became increasingly difficult to envision focal points around which cooperation would be judged feasible by both sides.

Regarding MILSAT, the previous distinction between benign and threatening satellite capabilities was further blurred by technology and doctrine. The revised American strategic posture, with renewed emphasis on war-fighting scenarios, placed increasing reliance on satellites. Space-based systems would be essential in targeting mobile military assets; they would also provide damage assessment data essential to efficient retargeting in the conduct of protracted nuclear war. Technological possibilities seemed to support these changes in doctrine. Early warning sensors, for example, were being upgraded to provide a measure of sensitivity (i.e. impact prediction) that would presumably be useful in nuclear war-fighting scenarios. The ability to transmit and process photoreconnaissance data in near real-time enhanced the threatening aspect of photosatellites as well. Space-based systems promised to play an essential role in strategic defense, and in each sides' repertoire of countermeasures. As a result, few if any satellite capabilities could be said to serve the shared interests of the sides independent of political-military context. Almost all, in some scenario, would pose direct threats to the adversary.

Regarding ASAT, the continuing development of DEW technology further blurred the distinction between dedicated and residual ASAT capabilities. DEW technology, regardless of its primary purpose, poses a militarily significant threat to the survivability of space systems. Specifically, lasers might make possible a prompt, large-scale attack against some or all MILSATs without significant tactical warning. In this case, redundancy of satellites would be of no defensive value; a successful "sky-sweeping" attack could pose a threat of great magnitude to a side dependent on satellites for essential military missions. Given the two sides' commitment to DEW research, the military significance of a distinction between dedicated and residual ASAT capabilities was becoming increasingly problematic.

New developments in both ASAT and MILSAT technology received further impetus as a result of President Reagan's commitment to the SDI. As previously noted, strategic defense systems based in space will pose significant threats to other space-based systems, and perhaps to targets in the atmosphere and on earth as well. The objective of developing a space-based strategic defense system will finally erase any significant saliencies in controlling the militarization of space.

Specific features of the general political environment contributed to the demise of cooperation in space during the 1980s. The American image of the Soviet Union as an adversary and of the superpower competition detracted from both the perceived desirability and feasibility of superpower cooperation in security issues.

The predominant image of the Soviet Union among the American decision-making elite, which had undergone a shift starting in the mid- to late 1970s, continued to deteriorate in the 1980s. Soviet actions in Afghanistan and in Poland, allegations about the use of chemical warfare by Soviet troops and proxies, and other suspected Soviet activities (such as involvement in the plot to assassinate the Pope) reinforced the tendency of many Americans both within and outside the Administration to view the Soviet Union not as a status quo great power in the Western sense, but rather as a revisionist state seeking to undermine the basic structure of the international system. According to this view, cooperative behavior and restraint on the part of the Soviet Union represented only tactical maneuvering, designed to support a long-term struggle for unilateral advantage and a quest for political and military ascendance over the West.

This perception of the Soviet Union derived largely from an assessment of Soviet political and military activism during this period. The Soviets were seen by many American observers as seeking superiority in both conventional and nuclear weaponry.[115] The conventional build-up extended not only to the long-standing Soviet emphasis on land forces, but also to the rapidly expanding Soviet Navy, and other capabilities useful for conventional force projection. In the area of nuclear capabilities, the Soviets continued a build-up of strategic systems that was judged to violate at least the shared understandings underlying SALT, and in some cases, the letter of the treaties as well. New Soviet ICBM deployments, the construction of a large phased array radar at Abalakovo, and other compliance concerns, as well as continued deployment of SS-20 IRBMs in Europe contributed to the American perception that the Soviet Union was actively in pursuit of military superiority. Such superiority, if not usable in the classical military sense, served as an enabling condition for unprecedented political activism, risk-taking, and the pursuit of unilateral advantage in third areas.

In accordance with this set of beliefs, the Reagan Administration chose to reject the concept of cooperative security arrangements with the Soviets, preferring to rely on unilateral means of meeting security goals. They were convinced that Soviet behavior would not be influenced by positive inducements, as the Soviets would construe conciliatory gestures or contingent restraint not as an invitation to shared restraint, but rather as an indication of American weakness. The Soviet Union was best dealt with by isolation, threat, and intimidation. Constant pressure would at least make the Soviets more tractable; at best, it might even lead to a breakdown of the internal stability of the Soviet system.

The image of the superpower competition, which changed drastically with the demise of détente, further detracted from the prospects of cooperation in security issues. The Reagan Administration brought to power the long-standing conservative view that the concept of a détente-type relationship with the Soviet Union had been inherently flawed. According to this view, the superpower relationship could not be based on managed coexistence with mutual limits on competitive behavior. Rather, the United States and the USSR were seen as contradictory social and political systems with few shared interests in the international environment. It was argued that American détente policy had not only failed to elicit reciprocal Soviet restraint, but had aided and abetted the Soviet Union in its drive to extend power and influence over Europe and the Third World. While the United States pursued conciliatory policies, the Soviets continued to compete in unrestrained fashion.

To rectify the errors of détente, the Reagan Administration sought to pursue competition with the Soviet Union in a variety of areas. The first step in correcting the abuses of détente was to disengage from cooperative arrangements that were judged to be one-sided in the distribution of benefits. For example, the new Administration worked to reduce technology transfer to the Eastern bloc, as well as to place limits on economic ties that were seen as yielding asymmetrical benefits to the Soviet Union. The second step in revitalizing American competitiveness was to capitalize on those areas in which the United States held a comparative advantage. A primary example was in the area of military technology: American technological strength could compensate for, if not overwhelm, the Soviet advantages of secrecy, manpower, and the ability to extract resources from the population.

Military activities in space were a particular area in which the unrestrained exploitation of technology would be a source of comparative advantage for the United States. The logical correlate was that cooperative agreements or mutual restraint yielded asymmetrical benefits to the Soviet Union, and thus were not in the interest of the United States. This line of argument, which in fact takes a rather long-term perspective on the superpower competition, appears to have contributed to President Reagan's vision of space-based BMD, with its accompanying arms competition in space (in which it was judged the United States would achieve, over the long run, clear superiority).

These changes in the general political environment of the superpower relationship had an important impact on American judgments about the most efficient means of influencing Soviet behavior. Given the character of the Soviet state, and the unremittingly competitive nature of the superpower relationship, strategies based on the norm of reciprocity would be perceived by the Soviet Union as a manifestation of American weakness. The Soviets did not view American restraint as contingent on Soviet behavior, but instead took advantage of these opportunities to compete with added vigor. Accordingly, it was judged that influence over Soviet policy required a position of American superiority, from which the United States could make credible coercive threats against central Soviet interests. This line of reasoning was obviously inconsistent with significant cooperation in security issues.

The deteriorating U.S–Soviet political environment had important implications for strategic theory, which was evolving at the time to assess the significance of the Soviet military build-up. An important development concerned the redefinition of the concept of parity in the strategic competition. Strategic analysts within the Administration rejected the previously dominant definition of parity as "functional equivalence," or shared "strategic sufficiency." This was replaced by a concept of "optical equivalence," which demanded strict equivalence in essential weaponry. American security required at least the maintenance of parity at a level defined by this new, more demanding concept; more desirable (and feasible, according to some) would be a return to an era of American strategic superiority.

Changing definitions of parity meant that it would be both politically and militarily insufficient to negate the Soviet ASAT threat solely by nonthreatening countermeasures. Rather, the new concept of parity required the United States to maintain its own operational ASAT system to match or exceed the Soviet capability. This policy was judged to provide incentives for the Soviets to negotiate; failing that, it would allow the United States to escalate the competition to its own advantage.

Changing interpretations of parity interacted with perceptions of a continuing Soviet military build-up to further expand the perceived requirements of strategic and political stability. Cooperative management under the SALT regime was judged to have detracted from these important goals, as a result both of asymmetries written into the treaties, and an alleged pattern of Soviet violations. A "decade of neglect" of American military programs was said to have permitted a shift in the strategic balance to the favor of the Soviet Union. Regardless of the military significance of the nuclear imbalance, some analysts believed that perceived American quiescence in the face of Soviet military expansion impacted negatively upon the credibility of extended deterrence in Europe. (The "window of vulnerability," for example, did not imply that the Soviets were about to launch a counterforce against American ICBMs. However, it was argued to have an important, if ambiguous political value in Soviet competition with the United States, and perhaps an impact on perceptions of American power and resolve in Europe and the Third World.)

This evolution in strategic thought underlay the American strategic modernization programs that began during the Carter Administration. Under President Reagan, the strategic modernization program was accelerated, and doctrinal commitments to the concept of nuclear war-fighting were made more explicit. Renewed emphasis on damage limitation as a strategic goal underlay the Administration's commitment to the development of counter-force capable systems, and the Strategic Defense Initiative.

Linked to these changes in American strategic thought, and particularly to the concept of strategic defense, was an enhanced effort in military space programs. The unrestrained exploitation of the American technological edge in space was a logical consequence of the renewed emphasis on strictly unilateral and competitive pursuit of security goals.

The Reagan Administration's space strategy was supported by an extraordinary degree of bureaucratic control up through late 1985. Despite wavering public sentiment and a number of Congressional attempts to impose restraint or contingency on the U.S. ASAT program, the Administration was largely successful in implementing the policy of unrestrained ASAT development.

As early as the fall of 1982, the Congress began to express serious concern over the Administration's apparent unwillingness to engage in serious negotiations with the Soviets on the ASAT question.[116] In its defense, the Administration claimed that it was committed to a continuous and serious "study of space arms control," but that "no arrangements or agreements beyond those already governing military activities in outer space have been found to date that are judged to be in the overall interest of the United States and its Allies."[117] The Congress agreed to accept as proof of the Administration's interest in exploring possible cooperative restraint an annual report certifying that the United States "was negotiating in good faith" with the Soviet Union.[118]

Further Congressional challenges arose in June 1984, when the House voted to cut off funds for any additional tests of the American ASAT system unless the Soviets were to violate their unilateral testing moratorium.[119] In response, the Administration mounted a large lobbying effort and succeeded in preventing the Senate, and the conference committee, from enacting constraints on the MHV program.

The presidential election of 1984 further complicated the Administration's attempt to consistently implement its preferred strategy in space. Given the level of public concern with issues related to nuclear weapons, and the apparently widespread belief that President Reagan would be more likely to involve the United States in war than would his opponent Walter Mondale, Republican leaders grew concerned that the Administration's position on space arms control could jeopardize Reagan's reelection.

In June 1984, President Reagan hinted in a news conference that the United States was actively considering potential options for cooperative management of the arms race in space.[120] Perhaps to the Administration's surprise, the Soviets responded by calling on the United States to begin formal negotiations on the militarization of space. In turn, the United States agreed to meet with the Soviets to discuss "feasible negotiating approaches."[121] However, the U.S. position was that negotiations on ASAT would have to be a part of comprehensive discussions that also dealt with intermediate range (INF) and strategic weapons.[122]

As the Soviets had walked out of the INF talks and refused to set a resumption date for strategic arms negotiations in response to American deployment of GLCMs and Pershing IIs in Europe, the American condition for negotiations on ASAT was essentially a nonstarter. Predictably, the Soviets rejected the conditional American offer of negotiations. For the Reagan Administration, the incident provided a further justification for unyielding American policy on ASAT. It was, in effect, an exemplary illustration of bureaucratic control. Leslie Gelb, describing the Administration's position, noted

> there was something in it for everyone: for the State Department, willingness to meet with the Russians; for the Pentagon, nothing to jeopardize the new antisatellite testing program; and for White House aides, the prospects of a good domestic political reaction.[123]

In 1985, continued legislative pressure for restraint in ASAT activities achieved some success, as the Congress voted to make the availability of funds for further tests of the MHV contingent on Soviet activity:

> None of the Funds appropriated by this Act or any other Act may be obligated or expended to carry out a test of the Space Defense System (anti-satellite weapon) against an object in space until the President certifies to Congress that the Soviet Union has conducted, after October 3, 1985 a test against an object in space of a dedicated anti-satellite weapon.[124]

The Administration responded negatively to this intrusion into its strategy, arguing:

> The antisatellite (ASAT) program is central to our efforts to improve defensive capabilities in space . . . We must caution that congressionally imposed restrictions or

prohibitions against further tests would adversely affect the prompt development of this needed capability.[125]

However, the Congressionally imposed contingent moratorium on ASAT tests survived 1986. A similar bill has been proposed by the House for 1987. (Its fate, as of May 1987, remains uncertain.)

In sum, the United States in the 1980s pursued a highly competitive strategy with regard to ASAT and MILSAT development. Under the Reagan Administration, cooperation with the Soviet Union to place constraints on military activities in space was rejected as detrimental to American security interests. The future of this strategy, as well as its impact on the continuing superpower competition (in outer space and elsewhere) is as yet uncertain. It seems clear that limited cooperation in managing the detrimental effects and shared threats resulting from the unrestrained militarization of space is becoming increasingly unlikely.

This analysis began with the proposition that military activities in space involve a complex set of shared and conflicting interests for the United States and the Soviet Union. The extent to which shared interests have been realized in the context of limited cooperative arrangements has varied over the course of the past 25 years. The interesting question is not whether a space regime can be said to have existed, but why at certain times the superpowers were more or less successful in managing threats to shared security interests by cooperative means.

Strategies of restraint, contingent on reciprocity, were relatively successful in the management of limited cooperative arrangements in space up until the mid-1970s. In the context of a limited but robust regime, tacit coordination of policy was deemed sufficient to insure the stability of restraint in space. Despite increasing technological challenge to policies of restraint, the regime was successfully managed and continued to contribute to the shared security interests of the two states.

When the conditions that had supported reciprocal restraint deteriorated in the mid-1970s, perceptions of strategies based on reciprocity underwent comparable change. U.S. strategy shifted to a two-track approach, whose underlying rationale was the perception that influence over Soviet policy was best achieved by making contingent threats. Changes in beliefs about how reciprocity operated in the context of a competitive relationship influenced the United States to pursue cooperative outcomes via formal negotiated agreements, rather than continuing to rely upon tacit coordination of policy.

The political challenge to the space regime was accompanied by new technological challenges, which were raising the stakes of both cooperation and conflict in space. The failure of the Carter Administration to forge a coherent tactical linkage between the development track and the negotiation track of the two-track strategy, as well as its failure to adequately address the growing threats posed by MILSAT technology, contributed to the deterioration of the regime in the face of these challenges.

The 1980s witnessed a further deterioration in the conditions that had favored reciprocity as a norm of strategy in the superpower relationship. Concurrently, the Reagan Administration rejected the limited regime in space, choosing instead to pursue a strategy of unconditional military competition in space. This strategy derived from the perception that unrestrained competition in space would benefit the United States asymmetrically, and would on balance serve U.S. security interests more efficiently than any cooperative arrangements with the Soviet Union.

The Reagan Administration's strategy presupposed a different understanding of the nature of the superpower relationship than had been expressed by the American decision-making elite in the previous 25 years. While détente had been the most extreme enunciation of a mixed competitive-collaborative relationship, the vision of U.S.–Soviet competition both before and after the détente era had taken as given the interdependence of the superpowers in many strategic areas. Nuclear weapons, and the bipolarity of the postwar world, had created certain shared interests in managing threats to the security of both superpowers. Some of these shared security interests could best be managed (and others could *only* be managed) in the context of limited cooperative agreements between adversaries.

The Reagan Administration's perception of the superpower competition rejected the notion that the United States had no alternative but to accept the interdependent nature of its security relationship with the Soviet Union. In security issues, unilateral solutions were both preferable and feasible. According to the Reagan view, American security interests are best served by pursuing unilateral advantage whenever and wherever American comparative strength makes such a strategy possible. The militarization of space, depending as it does on high technology, seemed an ideal arena in which to pursue American advantage.

The deterioration of the partial space regime has currently progressed beyond the point where a comprehensive ban on ASAT systems, even if judged desirable, would be feasible. An important question for the future is whether new, limited forms of cooperation in space might contribute to the shared security interests of the two states, given the constraints imposed by the current strategic, political, and technological environments.

One possibility that has been widely discussed is a "deep space sanctuary" regime, which would permit the superpowers to maintain and test their current dedicated ASAT systems, but would prohibit the testing in an ASAT mode of any additional or new systems (essentially a "no-new-types" agreement). Each side would take unilateral measures to enhance the survivability of satellites at altitudes above LEO. The Soviets, in particular, would experience incentives to move as many of their satellites as possible to higher orbits. In addition, measures of a bilateral cooperative nature (such as keep-out zones and additional rules of the road) could be enacted to further constrain the threat posed to high-altitude satellites. The primary purpose of the limited regime would be to provide sanctuary to satellites based in orbits outside LEO.

The military significance of deep space sanctuary based on a no-new-types agreement would be twofold. First, such restrictions would provide relative sanctuary to satellites in high orbit, increasing perceived confidence in the invulnerability of essential early warning and communication capabilities (assuming the Soviet Union were to increase its commitment to placing such assets in GEO orbit). Given the limitations on ASAT development, the regime would, over time, permit the design of countermeasures that would presumably decrease the vulnerability of even LEO satellites. Second, restrictions on testing new systems in an ASAT mode would forestall the development, on either side, of the ability to carry out a prompt, sky-sweeping attack against the adversary's satellites.

A limited regime of this type would contribute to the shared security interests of the states by preventing the development of the most highly destabilizing ASAT capabilities. Both states would be assured of the relative invulnerability of essential systems based in GEO orbit. In addition, both states might be deterred from employing LEO assets in directly threatening ways in the course of a limited conflict. (For example, the limited ASAT threat might help to deter the transfer of photoreconnaissance data to a superpower client state during a proxy war.)

The impediments to the successful realization and management of a partial regime (based on no new types and deep space sanctuary) arise primarily from political and strategic barriers to the management of cooperative agreements. At the conceptual level, an American policy that sought to establish such a regime would have as a primary goal the structuring of incentives for the Soviet Union so as to make the desired agreement appear to be in the best interests of that state as well. A strategy incorporating U.S. restraint contingent on Soviet reciprocity would presumably be an efficacious means of influence, perhaps eliciting the desired Soviet behavior. However, in light of the current political and strategic relationship between the superpowers, strategies based on reciprocity are not likely to be perceived as viable means of influence.

At the strategic level, the primary impediments to cooperative agreements in space continue to arise from the Reagan Administration's commitment to the SDI, and the failure to demonstrate interest in constructing a coordinate regime for the limitation of threatening MILSAT activities. In this environment, each side will continue to experience incentives for ASAT development, rendering unlikely any potential cooperation in an ASAT regime.

The general political environment of the superpower relationship remains unsuitable to the development of limited cooperation in space. Of greatest importance is the perceived imperative on the part of the United States to capitalize on its technological superiority in order to threaten and place at risk a variety of Soviet security interests. As a means of influence in an interdependent situation, noncontingent threats are less likely to yield cooperative outcomes than are strategies based on reciprocity. In unrestrained competition, the push of technological innovation will further exacerbate trends toward discord and collectively nonoptimal solutions. In such an environment, the most likely outcome appears to be mutual defection from any limited cooperative arrangement. In the case of the militarization of space, this has, and will continue to result in missed opportunities (the political correlate of economic market failure). Agreements that would potentially contribute to the interests of both sides will not be made.

Notes

1. Bhupendra Jasani, ed., *Outer Space: A New Dimension of the Arms Race,* SIPRI (London: Taylor and Francis, 1982), pp. 41 and 112.

2. Antarctic Treaty, Article 1, Paragraph 1.

3. It may be possible for ASAT systems to discriminate between low and high altitude satellites, that is, one could imagine a regime under which low altitude satellites were vulnerable to attack by current low earth orbit (LEO) capable ASATs, while both sides refrained from development and testing of new ASAT systems capable of threatening satellites in geosynchronous orbit (GEO). This would provide relative sanctuary to satellites in GEO orbit. However, discrimination on the basis of altitude does not parallel the functional discrimination that has been drawn between benign and threatening satellite capabilities. Both levels of orbit hold satellites of both categories. Indeed, in some cases, a single satellite may perform a variety of functions, some of

which are benign and others of which are threatening. Unilateral measures such as ASAT are thus not selectively capable of placing at risk only those functions seen as threatening.

4. Thomas C. Schelling and Morton Halperin, *Strategy and Arms Control* (Washington, D.C.: Pergamon-Brassey's, 1985).

5. Stephen D. Krasner, "Structural Causes and Regime Consequences: Regimes as Intervening Variables," *International Organization,* Vol. 36, No. 2 (Spring 1982).

6. Gerald M. Steinberg, *Satellite Reconnaissance: The Role of Informal Bargaining* (New York: Praeger, 1983), pp. 4–6.

7. James R. Killian, *Sputniks, Scientists and Eisenhower* (Cambridge, Mass.: MIT Press, 1977).

8. Herbert F. York, *Race to Oblivion* (New York: Simon & Shuster, 1970) p. 1.

9. Gerald M. Steinberg, *Satellite Reconnaissance: The Role of Informal Bargaining* (New York: Praeger, 1983), p. 5.

10. *Astronautics,* Vol. 6, No. 6 (June 1961): 36.

11. Walter R. Dornberger, "Arms in Space, Something Else to Worry About," *U.S. News and World Report* (October 9, 1961), p. 76.

12. Theodore C. Sorensen, *Kennedy* (New York: Harper & Row, 1965), p. 699.

13. *Science* (August 24, 1962).

14. Quoted in Walter C. Clemens, Jr., *Outer Space and Arms Control* (Cambridge, Mass.: Center for Space Research, MIT, 1966).

15. V. D. Sokolovskii, ed., *Soviet Military Strategy,* translated by Herbert S. Dinerstein, Leon Goure, and Thomas Wolfe (Englewood, N.J.: Prentice-Hall, 1963), p. 430.

16. Steinberg, *Satellite Reconnaissance,* pp. 75–76.

17. See Raymond L. Garthoff, "Banning the Bomb in Outer Space," *International Security,* Vol. 5, No. 3 (Winter 1980/81): 25.

18. Paul B. Stares, *The Militarization of Space; U.S. Policy, 1945–84* (Ithaca, N.Y.: Cornell University Press, 1985), pp. 117–118.

19. Ibid, p. 120.

20. Steinberg, *Satellite Reconnaissance,* p. 78.

21. Ibid., p. 80.

22. *Congressional Record* (September 21, 1962), pp. 7007–9. Emphasis added.

23. Max Berger, *The Air Force in Space,* FY 1961 (USAF Historical Division, April 1966), pp. 70, 71.

24. Steinberg, *Satellite Reconnaissance,* p. 84.

25. Stares, *Militarization of Space,* pp. 118–119, 124–127.

26. Ibid. p. 124, Table 6.1.

27. *Aviation Week and Space Technology* (September 21, 1964), p. 21.

28. Stares, *Militarization of Space,* pp. 131–134.

29. See Arthur A. Stein, "Coordination and Collaboration: Regimes in an Anarchic World," in Stephen Krasner, ed., *International Regimes* (Ithaca, N.Y.: Cornell University Press, 1983), pp. 115–141. See, in particular, p. 125.

30. Thomas C. Schelling, *The Strategy of Conflict* (London: Oxford University Press, 1960), ch. 3.

31. From a speech by Senator Albert Gore, U.S. Representative to the First Committee of the U.S. General Assembly, on the peaceful uses of outer space, December 3, 1962. ACDA, *Documents on Disarmament,* Vol. 2 (Washington, D.C.: U.S. Government Printing Office, 1963), pp. 1119–1124.

32. Arthur M. Schlesinger, Jr., *A Thousand Days; John F. Kennedy in the White House* (Boston: Houghton Mifflin, 1965), pp. 502–504.

33. *1963 Hearings on the Military Posture,* Committee on the Armed Services, U.S. House of Representatives, 88th Congress, 1st session (Washington, D.C.: U.S. Government Printing Office, 1963), p. 307.

34. Raymond Garthoff, "Banning the Bomb in Outer Space," *International Security,* vol. 5, no. 3 (Winter 1980/1981).

35. *Aviation Week and Space Technology,* vol. 81, no. 19 (November 1964), p. 19; vol. 82, no. 12 (March 22, 1965), p. 13.

36. *Department of Defense Appropriations for 1969.* Hearings before the House Committee on Appropriations, 90th Congress, 2nd Session, 1968, part 1, p. 252.

37. Jasani, *Outer Space,* p. 105.

38. *Soviet Space Programs, 1971–75,* Staff Report of the Senate Committee on Aeronautical and Space Sciences, Vol. 1 (1976).

39. "Launching the Killer Cosmos," *Newsweek* (February 16, 1970).

40. G. E. Perry, "Russian Hunter-Killer Satellite Experiments," *Royal Air Force Quarterly* vol. 17 (Winter 1977): 332.

41. U.S. Congress, Office of Technology Assessment, *Anti-satellite Weapons, Countermeasures, and Arms Control* OTA-ISC-281 (Washington, D.C.: U.S. Government Printing Cffice, September 1985), p. 52. Also see U.S. Department of Defense, *Soviet Military Power* (Washington, D.C.: U.S. Government Printing Office, 1985), pp. 55–56. (It should be noted that tests of the system employing the active radar sensor have had mixed results. All tests employing the IR sensor have been judged to be failures.)

42. Richard L. Garwin, Kurt Gottfried, and Donald L. Hafner, "Antisatellite Weapons," *Scientific American* (June 1984), pp. 45–55; 49.

43. See *Soviet Military Power,* 1985, p. 56.

44. Stares, *Militarization of Space,* p. 162.

45. Ibid., pp. 163–165.

46. Ibid., p. 164.

47. Ibid.

48. *Aeronautics and Space Report of the President,* Washington, D.C., January 1970, p. 32.

49. Stares, *Militarization of Space,* p. 204. (See p. 203 for quotation from Memorandum on Project Spike, September 21, 1971.)

50. *History of Air Defense Command,* FY 1972, pp. 143–44.

51. Stares, *Militarization of Space,* p. 201.

52. *History of Air Defense Command,* pp. 192–194.

53. *Department of Defense Appropriations for 1971.* Hearings before the House Committee on Appropriations, 91st Congress, 2nd Session, 1970, Part 6, p. 88.

54. See John Newhouse, *Cold Dawn: The Story of SALT* (New York: Holt, Reinhart and Winston, 1973), and Gerard Smith, *Doubletalk: The Story of SALT I* (New York: Doubleday, 1980). For a discussion of why the United States did not pursue formal limits on ASAT in SALT I, see Raymond L. Garthoff, *Detente and Confrontation* (Washington, D.C.: Brookings, 1985), ch. 5, especially pp. 189–192.

55. Alexander L. George, ed., *Managing U.S.–Soviet Rivalry: Problems of Crisis Prevention* (Boulder, Colo.: Westview Press, 1983), pp. 17, 320.

56. For a more detailed discussion of this point see Alexander L. George, "Domestic Constraints on Regime Change in U.S. Foreign Policy: The Need for Policy Legitimacy," in *Change in the International System,* Ole R. Holsti, Randolph M. Siverson, and Alexander L. George, eds. (Boulder, Colo.: Westview Press, 1980), pp. 233–262.

57. John Douglas, "High Energy Laser Weapons," *Science News,* vol. 110, no. 1 (July 3, 1976), p. 12.

58. See Stares, *Militarization of Space,* pp. 146–154.

59. Stephen M. Meyer, "Soviet Military Programmes and the New 'High Ground,' " *Survival,* vol. 25 (September/October 1983), p. 212; and "Satellite Killers," *Aviation Week and Space Technology* (June 21, 1976), p. 13.

60. Craig Covault, "Geodetic Launches and Soviet Targeting," *Aviation Week and Space Technology,* vol. 104, no. 23 (June 7, 1976), pp. 23–24.

61. Jasani, *Outer Space,* pp. 94–95.

62. Malcolm Currie, quoted in "Warning to Soviets," *Aviation Week and Space Technology,* vol. 105, no. 19 (November 8, 1976), p. 13.

63. Stares, *Militarization of Space,* p. 176.

64. Ibid., p. 169.

65. Ibid., p. 170.

66. Quote from a former NSC staff member in Ibid., p. 171.

67. Donald Hafner, "Averting a Brobdingnagian Skeet Shoot: Arms Control Measures for ASAT Weapons," *International Security,* vol. 5, no. 3 (Winter 1980/1981) pp. 50–51.

68. Garwin, Gottfried, and Hafner, "Antisatellite Weapons."

69. Stares, *Militarization of Space,* p. 183.

70. *Military Posture and Department of Defense Authorization for Appropriations* for FY 1976, 1977, 1978. House Committee on the Armed Services, U.S. Congress.

71. Stares, p. 210.

72. *Military Posture Statement,* FY 1979, by Secretary of Defense Harold Brown, p. 125.

73. George Breslauer, "Why Detente Failed," in George, ed., *Managing U.S.–Soviet Rivalry,* p. 321.

74. Ibid, p. 320.

75. Schelling, *The Strategy of Conflict,* p. 168.

76. For a theoretical discussion of these issues, see Duncan Snidal, "Coordination versus Prisoner's Dilemma: Implications for International Cooperation and Regimes," *American Political Science Review* (December 1985): 940.

77. See Stares, *Militarization of Space,* p. 200.

78. Committee on International Security and Arms Control, the National Academy of Sciences, *Nuclear Arms Control: Background and Issues* (Washington, D.C.: National Academy Press, 1985), p. 162. See also Raymond Garthoff, *Detente and Confrontation* (Washington, D.C.: Brookings, 1985), p. 760.

79. Stares, *Militarization of Space,* p. 196.·

80. NAS, *Nuclear Arms Control,* p. 162.

81. "Killer Talks," *Aviation Week and Space Technology* (November 28, 1977), p. 13.

82. "Anti-Satellite Move," *Aviation Week and Space Technology* (August 21, 1978), p. 11.

83. See Donald Hafner, "Potential Negotiating Measures for ASAT Arms Control," and Theodore Ralston, "Verification of Negotiated Limits on Anti-Satellite Weapons." Background papers for the Aspen Strategy Group Summer Workshop on Anti-Satellite Weapons and the Evolving Space Regime, Aspen Institute for Humanistic Studies, August 1985.

84. Robert Toth, "U.S.–Soviet Talks Seen Soon on Anti-Satellite Arms Ban," *Los Angeles Times* (November 5, 1977), p. 1.

85. Stares, *Militarization of Space,* pp. 193–197.

86. *Hearings on National Space Policy,* Subcommittee on Space Science and Applications of the House Committee on Science and Technology, 97th Congress, 2nd Session (August 4, 1982), p. 13. See also "White House Fact Sheet Outlining United States Space Policy" (July 4, 1982).

87. *Arms Control and the Militarization of Space,* Hearings before the Subcommittee on Arms Control, Oceans, International Operations and Environment of the Senate Committee on Foreign Relations, 97th Congress, 2nd Session (September 20, 1982), p. 27.

88. "White House Fact Sheet" (Emphasis added).

89. "Anti-Satellite Weapon Research is Pressed," *Washington Post* (February 28, 1984), p. 3.

90. "Pentagon Asks Arms Capability in Space," *Washington Times* (January 19, 1983), p. 4.

91. Stares, *Militarization of Space,* p. 223.

92. Garwin, Gottfried, and Hafner, "Antisatellite Weapons," p. 47.

93. Stares, *Militarization of Space,* p. 223.

94. Department of Defense, *Soviet Military Power* (Washington, D.C.: U.S. Government Printing Office, March 1983), p. 67.

95. See, in particular, testimony by Robert M. Gates and Lawrence K. Gershwin on Soviet Strategic Force Developments, before a Joint Session of the Subcommittee on Strategic and Theater Nuclear Forces of the Senate Armed Services Committee and the Defense Subcommittee of the Senate Committee on Appropriations, June 26, 1985.

96. Stares, *Militarization of Space,* p. 224.

97. *Report of the Secretary of Defense to the Congress on FY 1979 Budget and Its Implications for the FY 1980 Authorization Request* (U.S. Department of Defense, 1979), pp. 129–130.

98. *Military Posture Statement* FY 1984, pp. 226–227.

99. "Andropov Urges Ban on Weapons to Attack Satellites," *Washington Post* (August 19, 1983), p. 1.

100. *Text of Soviet Draft Treaty on Banning the Use of Force in Space and From Space with Respect to the Earth,* Proposal to the U.N. General Assembly in August of 1983, quoted in U.S. Congress, Office of Technology Assessment, *Anti-satellite Weapons, Countermeasures, and Arms Control,* OTA-ISC-281, September 1985, pp. 145–146.

101. Stares, *Militarization of Space,* p. 232.

102. *Status of the U.S. Antisatellite Program,* Report to the Honorable George E. Brown, Jr., United States General Accounting office, GAO/NSIAD-85-104, June 14, 1985, p. 3.

103. Ibid., p. 4.

104. *New York Times* (August 25, 1985), p. E2.

105. Ibid.

106. *New York Times* (August 25, 1985), p. E2. (Translated and reported from TASS.)

107. "U.S. Will Proceed with an Arms Test on Space Target," *New York Times* (August 21, 1985).

108. "Air Force Missile Strikes Satellite in First U.S. Test," *New York Times* (September 14, 1985), p. 1.

109. Ibid.

110. Jasani, *Outer Space,* Appendix 1A, pp. 331–343.

111. Ibid., p. 178.

112. Ibid., p. 132.

113. See Stephen M. Meyer, "Soviet Military Programmes and the 'New High Ground,' " pp. 209–211.

114. Meyer, "Soviet Military Programmes," p. 210; and Jasani, *Outer Space,* p. 133.

115. For example, see Richard Pipes, "Why the Soviet Union Thinks It Can Fight and Win a Nuclear War," *Commentary* (July 1977), pp. 31–34.

116. For an example of Congressional expressions of concern, and the Administration's responses, see: *Arms Control and the Militarization of Space,* Hearings.

117. Report to the Congress on U.S. Policy on ASAT Arms Control, March 31, 1984; covering letter by President Reagan.

118. Stares, *Militarization of Space,* p. 232.

119. "Antisatellite Tests Backed, With Condition," *Washington Post* (June 13, 1984).

120. U.S. Considering Controls on Use of Arms in Space," *Washington Post* (June 16, 1984), p. 1.

121. U.S. Says It Weighs Kremlin's Motives in New Arms Offer," *New York Times* (July 1, 1984), p. 1.

122. OTA, *Anti-satellite Weapons, Countermeasures, and Arms Control,* p. 101.

123. ''U.S. Agreed to Talk About Space Arms Without Clear Plan,'' *New York Times* (July 3, 1984), p. 1.

124. *Congressional Record,* House of Representatives, H12035, December 16, 1985, Section 8097.

125. *Posture Statement,* FY 1986, p. 215.

IV

CASE STUDIES: REGIONAL SECURITY, CRISIS AVOIDANCE, AND CRISIS MANAGEMENT

17

The Laos
Neutralization Agreement, 1962

DAVID K. HALL

Geography and political history destined the Kingdom of Laos to become a focal point for Soviet-American competition in the late 1950s. At the conclusion of the Geneva Agreement of 1954, which ended the first Indochina War, Laos emerged as a sparsely populated land of mountains and jungles separating the communist and noncommunist nations of Southeast Asia. To the north, Laos shared a 263-mile border with communist China and a 146-mile border with neutralist Burma. To the east Laos shared a frontier of 818 miles with the new communist state of North Vietnam and a boundary of 301 miles with the new pro-Western state of South Vietnam. To the south Laos bordered neutralist Cambodia for 277 miles, while in the west Laos shared a 1,090-mile boundary (of which 500 miles traced the Mekong River) with the pro-Western state of Thailand.[1]

The modern political history of Laos began in the late nineteenth century when France wrested control of the three Laotian kingdoms of Luang Prabang, Vientiane, and Champassak from Thailand. France ruled Laos until 1944, was driven out by Japanese troops in 1945, and then reoccupied Laos in 1946. Pressured by the growing Indochina War, France took a series of political steps that eventually culminated in Laotian independence in 1953.

A moderate level of guerrilla activity occurred in Laos during the Indochina War, mostly as a part of communist Vietminh operations in bordering Vietnam. The communist Pathet Lao (PL) movement was organized in North Vietnam in 1951 under the leadership of Lao Prince Souphanouvong. During 1953 and 1954, communist Vietminh forces attacked French forces in northern and central Laos and helped firmly establish the Pathet Lao in the two northern Lao provinces of Sam Neua and Phong Saly.

The 1954 Geneva Agreement required the Vietminh to withdraw north of the 17th parallel in Vietnam, and the Pathet Lao were regrouped in Sam Neua and Phong Saly provinces pending their negotiated integration into a national unity government and the Royal Lao Army. All nations except France were proscribed from establishing military bases and training missions in Laos. External economic and military aid, such as the U.S. programs begun in 1950, were permitted to continue. An International Commission for Supervision and Control in Laos (ICC), composed of members from India (chairman), Canada and Poland, was created to police these agreements and report any violations to the permanent co-chairmen of the Geneva Conference, the United Kingdom and the Soviet Union.

When French colonial rule in Southeast Asia collapsed in 1954, defense against further communist expansion in that region was taken up by the U.S. government. Despite formal agreement at Geneva to national unity elections in both Laos and Vietnam, the Eisenhower Administration remained hostile to any governmental arrangements that permitted communist representation. Instead, the Administration embarked on a policy of strengthening the Western-oriented governments of Laos and South Vietnam.

To counter the threat of a Korean-style invasion of Southeast Asia, the Eisenhower Administration helped create the Southeast Asia Treaty Organization (SEATO) in September 1954. Initial signatories included the United States, United Kingdom, France, Thailand, Australia, New Zealand, the Philippines, and Pakistan. The Administration considered internal communist subversion of Southeast Asian governments to be an equally serious threat, and economic and military assistance programs were begun to shore up the pro-Western elements in the region. In 1955 the United States began direct military assistance to Laos to augment the declining French program. To avoid open violation of the 1954 Geneva Agreement prohibiting such a U.S. mission, American military personnel in Laos were given civilian status and clothing.

American violations of the Geneva Agreement were easily justified by comparable violations of the accords by communist forces in Laos. The Pathet Lao showed little interest in completing the negotiations leading to their integration into the political and military institutions of the country. Throughout 1955–1956 the Pathet Lao devoted their efforts to recruiting peasants in Sam Neua and Phong Saly provinces and harassing elements of the Royal Lao Army garrisoned there. The Pathet Lao's efforts were assisted and encouraged by cadres of the Vietminh left behind in Laos in violation of the Geneva Agreement.

Despite the recalcitrance of the Pathet Lao, Prince Souvanna Phouma, the first Laotian prime minister, patiently pursued his goal of peacefully reuniting his nation. American officials considered Souvanna's negotiations toward the legal integration of Pathet Lao personnel into the national parliament, army, and bureaucracy to be politically naive and dangerous. Pathet Lao leaders were considered to be far more organized than their Royal Government counterparts and fully capable of taking control of the political and military institutions of the nation if they were granted an official role within them. American officials believed that if a national unity government permitted the establishment of Soviet and Chinese diplomatic missions in Laos, this would further enhance the subversive capabilities of the Pathet Lao.

In late 1957 the worst fears of the Eisenhower Administration began to materialize, as Pathet Lao leaders finally agreed to terms for their reintegration into the Royal Government and Army. The new political arm of the Pathet Lao, the Neo Lao Hak Xat (NLHX), was recognized as a legal political party, two communist leaders were accepted into the Cabinet, two battalions of Pathet Lao soldiers were integrated into the Royal Lao Army, and special national elections were called. In the 1958 elections for the National Assembly, the NLHX and an allied party captured 13 of the 21 contested seats. Souvanna Phouma viewed the elections as the final reintegration of Lao political elements into a national community and as Laos's fulfillment of its obligations under the 1954 Geneva Agreement. As a result, he asked that the ICC discontinue its monitoring activities in Laos. This request was acted on favorably by the three-member commission.

The Eisenhower Administration and pro-American leaders in Laos were unwilling to accept the growing political influence of the Pathet Lao and the neutralist foreign policy that Souvanna intended to pursue. Two new conservative parties emerged in Laos during the summer of 1958, the Rally of Lao People (RLP) and a young military officer reform party called the Committee for Defense of National Interests (CDNI). The most vigorous and ambitious leader of these noncommunist elements was then-Colonel Phoumi Nosavan of the CDNI, who was privately assisted by the U.S. Central Intelligence Agency and Defense Department. Spurred on by congressional criticism of its loosely administered aid program in Laos, the Eisenhower Administration held up payments to the Laotian government in August 1958. The anti-communist elements in Laos took advantage of this development to precipitate a parliamentary crisis and oust Souvanna Phouma on a no-confidence vote. A new pro-American government was formed under the leadership of Prime Minister Phoui Sananikone.

The new Laotian government removed the two Pathet Lao ministers from the Cabinet, pushed ahead with integration of the two PL battalions into the Lao national army, and ultimately threw several Pathet Lao leaders in jail. In May 1959, one of the two PL battalions mutinied, and aided by North Vietnamese advisers, it began driving Lao government soldiers and officials out of Sam Neua and Phong Saly. The Lao government claimed that regular elements of the North Vietnamese army had invaded its northern territory, and it appealed for military help from the United States and the United Nations. The Eisenhower Administration responded by boosting its military aid by 30 percent and augmenting its covert military assistance advisory group, the Program Evaluation Office (PEO), with one hundred Special Forces advisers. A U.N. fact-finding team was unable to document the movement of North Vietnamese troops into Laos, but the U.N. investigation helped dampen the conflict.

Growing fear of civil war and disappointment in the United States' failure to take direct military action moderated the Laotian government's behavior towards the Pathet Lao, but rigid anticommunism recommenced in December 1959 following a military coup led by General Phoumi Nosavan. Government policy was reversed one more time in August 1960 when Phoumi was overthrown by Captain Kong Le, commander of the Second Lao Paratroop Battalion. Kong Le viewed the Laotian government's departure from international neutrality as the cause of growing bloodshed and corruption in his country, and he called upon the King to reappoint Souvanna Phouma as prime minister.

In August 1960, Souvanna Phouma was once again asked to form a government. After briefly joining Souvanna in a national unity Cabinet, General Phoumi broke away to establish his own government in southern Laos, where he established Prince Boun Oum as "president" of those Lao politicians and generals unwilling to support Souvanna. Phoumi quickly rallied support for a countercoup from his cousin, Thai Premier Sarit Thanarat, and from Defense Department and CIA advisers long associated with him. Soon Thailand had imposed an unofficial blockade on all food and fuel bound for the Lao capital of Vientiane. Meanwhile, Pathet Lao troops began occupying towns in northern Laos and were ordered by their leaders to avoid clashes with Souvanna's neutralist soldiers.

When Thailand's economic warfare began to strangle Vientiane, Souvanna asked for U.S. rice and oil deliveries to relieve the growing shortages. The Eisenhower Administration failed to respond. Souvanna pressured Washington further by establishing diplomatic relations with the USSR and reopening national unification talks with the Pathet Lao. When Vientiane's fuel supplies ran out on October 25, the prime minister indicated that he would accept the new Soviet Ambassador's offers of economic assistance. On November 16, with evidence that General Phoumi's troops were moving toward Vientiane, Souvanna denounced the United States for failing to honor its promise to prevent Phoumi from using American equipment to overthrow the new Lao government. That same day Souvanna's Cabinet voted to establish "good neighbor relations" with China and to send goodwill missions to Peiping and Hanoi. The Soviet Union commenced an emergency airlift of rice and oil from Hanoi to Vientiane on December 3, 1960.

When General Phoumi's troops attacked Vientiane on December 8, Souvanna Phouma abandoned the capital to Kong Le and flew to Cambodia. Meanwhile, Souvanna's information minister struck a deal with Hanoi: in exchange for military supplies to be delivered to Kong Le's troops, Souvanna Phouma's government agreed to a formal alliance between Kong Le and the Pathet Lao. On December 15, the first Soviet arms and ammunition arrived for the neutralist soldiers. Kong Le's forces were driven out of the capital by Phoumi's advancing army the following day. A new Laotian government, headed by Prince Boun Oum as prime minister and Phoumi as deputy prime minister and defense minister, was ratified by the Lao National Assembly. While the United States, Britain, France and Thailand quickly extended official recognition to the new government, the Soviet Union, China, India and other nations continued to recognize Souvanna Phouma as the legal ruler of Laos.

Despite his control of Vientiane, General Phoumi was slow to pursue Kong Le's soldiers retreating northward. Each passing day the 10,000 neutralist soldiers and 15,000 Pathet Lao troops grew stronger because of new arms, ammunition, and food airdropped by Soviet and North Vietnamese aircraft and with the help of North Vietnamese troops and advisers arriving by land and air. American intelligence estimated that 184 Soviet and North Vietnamese cargo sorties were flown into Laos between December 15, 1960, and January 2, 1961.[2]

Kong Le's troops advanced northward to the all-weather landing field at the strategic Plain of Jars. On December 31, in combined attack with the Pathet Lao, his forces seized the airfield and surrounding villages from the Royal Lao Army and French advisers guarding the Plain. The area was quickly transformed into a fortified staging point, with 45 tons of Soviet supplies landing daily from Hanoi. A provisional government under Souvanna Phouma was established at Kong Le's headquarters in Khang Khay. The outgoing Eisenhower Administration passed on the crisis to the incoming Kennedy Administration, warning that the United States was now close to war in Laos.

The broad policy that the Kennedy Administration would pursue in Laos for three years was sketched out during its first two weeks. At his first press conference on January 25, President John F. Kennedy stated that he favored an "independent, peaceful, uncommitted" Laos. On February 5 the Laos Task Force provided Kennedy a "concept telegram," jointly drafted by the State Department, Defense Department, NSC staff, CIA, JCS, and the U.S. Ambassador to Laos, which was subsequently sent to key embassies and allies. The telegram stated that:

> US wishes leave no stone unturned find peaceful solution and has therefore joined in attempt find conditions under which ICC might function. . . .
>
> We are acting in conformance with the guidance in the President's inaugural address that, while we do not fear to negotiate for genuine peace and understanding, we will not abandon our friends. . . .
>
> Having taken positive step toward peaceful solution onus passes to the USSR for recalcitrance. . . .
>
> Because Soviets may feel time favors Pathet Lao and Communist cause in Laos,

they will probably be reluctant acquiesce unless pressure brought to bear. We feel such pressure must be not only political in terms . . . but also military and must involve clear collaboration between US and our closest allies. . . .

We conceive of Laos as a neutral state, unaligned in her international relations but determined to preserve her national integrity. In order to exist in this special status, enjoy independence and territorial integrity, some temporary international machinery to guard this neutrality will have to be devised. Neutralized state would permit, except as provided by previous agreements, no foreign military bases, no foreign troops and no military alliances. State of Austria may serve as precedent. An underlying assumption is that it is in best interest of US and USSR avoid widespread hostilities in Laos.[3]

The remaining 34 months of the Kennedy Administration were spent trying to achieve these desired outcomes.

Developments within Laos soon threatened Kennedy's objectives. By the end of April 1961, the combined forces of Kong Le and the Pathet Lao, with the growing assistance of North Vietnam and the Soviet Union, had mounted a counteroffensive that threatened Vientiane and the royal capital Luang Prabang. While the Kennedy Administration agreed to join a new, enlarged Geneva Conference designed to negotiate an end to the war, President Kennedy also readied U.S. military forces for possible intervention in Laos.

A shaky ceasefire was arranged in Laos under the supervision of the reactivated ICC, and the Geneva Conference on Laos convened May 12, 1961. At Vienna on June 4, Soviet Premier Nikita Khrushchev and President Kennedy agreed on the need for Soviet and American withdrawal of military forces from Laos and for international agreements to protect Laos's neutrality. In October, Souvanna Phouma, Boun Oum, and Souphanouvong agreed to create a new coalition government with Souvanna Phouma serving as prime minister. In December, envoys from the fourteen nations represented at the Geneva Conference completed a draft agreement guaranteeing the international neutrality of Laos.

Final approval of the new Geneva agreement awaited, however, actual formation of a provisional coalition government for Laos that could initial the new accords. Such a unity government could not be arranged during the first months of 1962 because of General Phoumi's insistence that the rightists be assigned the cabinet portfolios of Defense (which controlled the Army) and Interior (which controlled the police and courts). Despite U.S. pressure on Phoumi to concede the Defense and Interior ministries to the neutralists, the political stalemate persisted until early May, when 5,000 of Phoumi's troops were defeated at Nam Tha. The Kennedy Administration responded to this major breakdown in the ceasefire by landing 5,000 U.S. combat troops in neighboring Thailand.

The defeat of Phoumi's troops and the arrival of American combat forces in Thailand helped bring the Geneva Conference to conclusion. On June 11, 1962, the neutralists, communists, and rightists agreed to an internationally neutral coalition government in which the prime minister, defense minister, and interior minister would be neutralist officials and the communists and rightists would hold an equal number of the remaining ministries. On July 23, 1962, the foreign ministers of the fourteen nations assembled at the Geneva Conference initialed the "Declaration on the Neutrality of Laos."

INCENTIVES FOR THE KENNEDY ADMINISTRATION'S
ACCEPTANCE OF THE 1962 GENEVA AGREEMENT ON LAOS

International Incentives for Cooperation

As the contents of the new Geneva agreement suggest, the Kennedy Administration altered the nature of U.S. policy toward Laos in 1961. In doing so, it reduced the risk of a direct military confrontation between the United States and the USSR in Southeast Asia, and it removed Laos from the agenda of major disputes between the two superpowers. It is important to understand the international and domestic forces that led Kennedy to accept this neutralization agreement, for it was not an outcome easy to accept. It was widely understood within the Administration that the specific terms of the agreement would be extremely difficult to enforce and would probably leave much of Laos in de facto control of North Vietnam, communist China and the Pathet Lao.

First and foremost, President Kennedy and his key advisers were in no mood to begin their White House tenure with a military confrontation with the USSR. They hoped, instead, to improve the quality of Soviet-American relations through a resumption of the high-level negotiations that had broken down after the May 1960 U-2 incident. As early as December 1960, Kennedy's Deputy National Security Adviser Walt Rostow and White House Science Adviser Jerome Wiesner had discussed strategic arms control and the German problem with Soviet officials in Moscow. Khrushchev's subsequent release of two U.S. reconnaissance pilots shot down over the North Sea encouraged further action. At a lengthy White House meeting on February 11, Kennedy and his top Russian experts agreed that it would be helpful for the new President to meet Khrushchev as soon as possible, so that each leader could increase his understanding of the other's interests, concerns, and reactions. Word of Kennedy's desire for such a meeting was personally carried back to Moscow by U.S. Ambassador Llewellyn Thompson.[4]

As the Laos crisis grew in intensity during spring 1961, the increasing possibility of a disruption in Soviet-American relations or even a Soviet-American armed confrontation weighed heavily on Kennedy's mind. Throughout his entire term in office, Kennedy's greatest fear was that some unnecessary or unintended superpower clash arising from "miscalculation" might spiral out of control and into a nuclear exchange.[5] In Laos, where American military advisers were actively supporting the frontline troops of the Royal Lao Army and Soviet military technicians were delivering and maintaining arms for Pathet Lao and neutralist soldiers, the potential for a Soviet-American armed exchange grew daily. On March 27, Kennedy emphasized this danger of war through miscalculation directly to Soviet Foreign Minister Andrei Gromyko. In a background briefing that same week, National Security Adviser McGeorge Bundy said that U.S. military intervention in Laos would probably force the Administration to abandon most of the diplomatic initiatives it had planned, perhaps for the duration of its term.[6]

Adding to the Administration's desire to find a cooperative solution to the Laotian civil war was its early recognition that the Boun Oum-Phoumi regime lacked international credibility and support, even among the United States' closest allies. Neither Great Britain nor France, the other two key members of SEATO, were willing to commit military forces in defense of the Boun Oum-Phoumi government, viewing it as an unrepresentative and unviable leadership imposed on Laos by U.S. hardliners. The French

Military Mission in Laos officially responsible for training the Lao Army was so antagonistic toward General Phoumi by early 1961 that it had stopped performing its function. British officials were strongly influenced by their government's role as co-chairman of the Geneva Conference and their responsibility for upholding its agreements. The Kennedy Administration quickly perceived that Great Britain and France would provide military support in Laos only for the purpose of bringing about a new national unity government.

A third factor encouraging the Kennedy Administration's acceptance of a negotiated neutralization for Laos was the existence of an acceptable political and administrative alternative to the Boun Oum-Phoumi regime in the form of Lao Prince Souvanna Phouma. While the competence and neutrality of Souvanna had been strongly doubted by senior officials in State, Defense, and the CIA during Eisenhower's presidency, there were also American officials—most importantly Winthrop Brown, the U.S. Ambassador to Laos since July 1960—who felt that Souvanna Phouma was sincerely committed to extricating his country from Cold War politics and capable of doing so. Ambassador Brown made this point directly to Kennedy on February 3, 1961, when he was recalled to Washington for consultations. Brown told the President that a national coalition of centrist, rightist, and leftist elements under the leadership of Souvanna Phouma was the only political alternative capable of putting an end to the raging civil war. Brown's views were soon reinforced by then-Roving Ambassador Averell Harriman, who met with Souvanna in New Delhi in late March 1961. As Washington increasingly recognized that Souvanna was the key to any stable Laotian government, the objective of protecting him from pressures and coups from the left (the Pathet Lao) and the right (Phoumi) became central to the Kennedy Administration's strategy.[7]

Of related importance to a negotiated settlement in Laos was the assumed political neutrality of Captain Kong Le, the commander of the Second Lao Paratroop Battalion and the military strength behind Souvanna Phouma. Kong Le's strong criticism of U.S. influence in Laos and his military collaboration with the Pathet Lao beginning in December 1960 convinced most Eisenhower Administration officials that Kong Le was a communist agent. The Kennedy Administration accepted the opposing view of Ambassador Brown and certain CIA analysts, who considered the young Lao officer to be a sincere patriot who was angry at the civil chaos and corruption created by longstanding American manipulation of Lao internal affairs.

One other precedent that facilitated a negotiated settlement of the Laotian war was the existence of the International Control Commission (ICC) as a peacekeeping mechanism in Laos during 1954–1958. While the United States was not pleased with the ICC's composition (India, Poland, and Canada) or its prior effectiveness, this organization still became the ceasefire enforcement solution to which all parties gradually turned during spring 1961. When the Kennedy Administration proposed in February 1961 the creation of a new Neutral Nations Commission of Cambodia, Burma, and Malaya to police Laos's independence, this suggestion was quickly rejected by the international community. Virtually all other governments favored reactivating the original ICC, and the Kennedy Administration was strongly pressed in this direction by Great Britain, the co-chairman of the Geneva Convention and the United States' closest ally throughout the crisis.

The final incentive compelling the Kennedy Administration to seek a negotiated settlement to the Laotian war was the overall military situation confronting the United States. First, there was early and growing disillusionment in the Administration with the fighting spirit of the 50,000-man Royal Lao Army (RLA) under the command of General Phoumi. Despite the increasing infusion of White Star advisory teams from the U.S. Green Berets down to the company level, the RLA was repeatedly routed by the 25,000 Pathet Lao and Kong Le soldiers opposing it. One explanation for this lack of aggressiveness was the peaceful character of the Lao people. Another was the growing presence of North Vietnamese troops in support of the Pathet Lao-Kong Le troops. Centuries of contact with the more martial Vietnamese and the latter's victory over the French had left Lao soldiers terrified of confronting North Vietnamese soldiers on the battlefield.

By early 1962, North Vietnamese troops in Laos were a critical factor in the calculations of U.S. policymakers. While the North Vietnamese went to great lengths to conceal the strength and location of their units in Laos, U.S. intelligence reports officially estimated that by 1962 the number had reached 9,000 soldiers—3,000 as cadres integrated into Pathet Lao/Kong Le units and 6,000 more in independent combat units. Washington recognized that should these North Vietnamese troops be fully committed to the civil war, Laos would be completely overrun by the communists in a matter of days unless the United States quickly intervened.[8]

Equally sobering to the Administration was the realization that no matter how much money and energy the United States poured into expanding and training the pro-American army in Laos, it could never match the power that North Vietnam could quickly commit on behalf of the Pathet Lao. In an attempt to compensate for the limited effectiveness of the Royal Lao Army, the United States increased its material support for the more aggressive Meo tribesmen fighting in the mountains of northern Laos and it helped introduce Thai volunteer units into Laos. But despite ongoing assistance to 11,000 Meo soldiers by late 1961, U.S. officials were aware that such measures could never fully offset North Vietnam's escalatory advantage.

Although the United States possessed the military capability to offset North Vietnamese troops in Laos, American decisionmakers were confronted by a daunting list of costs and risks when they contemplated such a ground war. The mountainous jungle terrain, the tropical climate, and the almost total absence of communication and supply lines made Laos a military nightmare for modern conventional forces. In fact, so large was the logistical problem that some military leaders argued that fighting in Laos was out of the question. Army Chief of Staff George Decker told Kennedy's top advisers on April 29, 1961, that "we cannot win a conventional war in Southeast Asia; if we go in we should go in to win, and that means bombing Hanoi . . ."[9]

Because of the weakness of the Royal Lao Army and the difficult conditions under which U.S. soldiers would have to fight, Defense Department representatives insisted that any use of American forces include enough troops to respond effectively to all possible contingencies. This insistence on large numbers of troops irritated those Kennedy advisers simply interested in "signalling" U.S. intent, but it was a position advocated by Secretary of Defense Robert McNamara as well as by the Joint Chiefs of Staff. In May 1962, when Pathet Lao advances led to serious discussions about putting U.S. combat forces into Laos, McNamara wrote Kennedy that if 5,000 U.S. troops were to land in Laos's Mekong River Valley, as the State Department proposed, they would have to be backed up by 35,000 additional troops landed in Thailand.[10] With the Defense Department advocating the movement of 40,000 U.S. soldiers to Southeast Asia if the United States were to intervene in Laos, the White House was under considerable pressure to find some negotiated solution short of such a drastic step.

A related factor in the Administration's reluctance to commit troops to Laos was the belief that there were better places in Southeast Asia to make a decisive stand against North Vietnam. Both South Vietnam and Thailand had armed forces of greater size and fighting spirit, better logistical support, and more stable anticommunist governments than existed in Laos. On April 29, 1961, during one of the Administration's many discussions of Laos, "The Attorney General [Robert Kennedy] asked where would be the best place to stand and fight in Southeast Asia, where to draw the line. Mr. McNamara said he thought we would take a stand in Thailand and South Viet-Nam."[11] While all of the President's senior advisers recognized that it would be harder to hold South Vietnam and Thailand if Laos fell to the communists, discussions invariably drifted toward the question of what minimal Laotian territory needed to be held to make a military stand possible in the bordering pro-Western countries.

Laos's location on China's southern border further complicated the military situation. Kennedy's advisers assumed that Peking would be acutely sensitive to any application of American ground and air power in that region, and they officially estimated that China would respond with some type of military counterattack should the United States introduce a large force into Laos.[12] The fact of China's interest in Laos was supported by U.S. intelligence reports in spring 1962 that a sizable contingent of Chinese military advisers had entered northern Laos, primarily for the purpose of completing construction of a road linking China and northern Laos. In addition, construction to improve Chinese airfields near northwest Laos was detected. The Administration realized that China was undergoing severe economic stresses that would make Peking extremely reluctant to confront the United States, but the specter of fighting Chinese troops in the Laotian jungles often limited serious debate to consideration of smaller, symbolic uses of force in Laos that could not threaten communist China's security.[13]

Domestic Incentives for Cooperation

Domestic considerations were certainly relevant to the Kennedy Administration's quick decision to commit the United States to a negotiated resolution of the Laotian civil war, although these considerations were rarely spoken of at length. Primary among them was the lack of congressional support for any major U.S. combat role in Laos and the obvious political risks to the Administration from a messy and prolonged guerrilla war in the jungles of Southeast Asia.

Particularly important were the views of Senate Majority Leader Mike Mansfield, who on the first day of the new Administration began intensively lobbying Kennedy to accept a neutralized, nonaligned Laos. Mansfield was the Senate's preeminent expert on Asia and was in direct contact with Prince Souvanna Phouma. His own assessment of the domestic situation facing the Administration was spelled out in a March 22, 1961 memorandum to Kennedy and Secretary of State Dean Rusk:

> At home—to take the grimmest prospect in the present situation—the loss of all of Laos to the Pathet Lao will hurt the Administration. To a considerable extent, however, the hurt will be mitigated by some public awareness that the problem was inherited from the previous Administration. If the home-front reaction to the complete loss of Laos will be painful, the effect of a major financial drain on the nation from a prolonged involvement will be even worse. And if the involvement includes American casualties, the effect will be politically disastrous for the Administration.[14]

When Kennedy and his aides consulted the top Democratic and Republican leaders of the House of Representatives and the Senate at critical points during 1961 and 1962, they always found these congressional views on Laos similar to Mansfield's. Leaders in both parties invariably opposed the direct use of American combat troops in Laos because of the terrain and the Laotians' reluctance to fight, and they suggested instead that South Vietnam and Thailand were better locations for "drawing the line" against communism in Southeast Asia. Such House and Senate views were expressed not only in the privacy of the Oval Office but later on various television and radio news programs.[15]

To be sure, there were brief periods during 1961 and 1962 when some Republican politicians sharply criticized Kennedy's handling of the Laos problem. When Kennedy suspended foreign assistance to the Boun Oum-Phoumi regime in spring 1962, to force Phoumi into accepting Souvanna's terms for a national unity government, the official organ of the Republican National Committee criticized the Administration for "forcing the legitimate government of Laos into a perilous coalition with the Reds."[16] When some of Phoumi's best battalions were defeated by the Pathet Lao in May 1962, a few Republicans took the floor of the Senate and the House to attack the Administration for failing to support the rightists. At that time former President Eisenhower publicly expressed his doubts about the planned coalition government in Laos, observing that this was "the way we lost China."[17]

But none of this criticism drew political blood. It was brief in character, associated with those periods when Laos was front-page news, and it was offset by equally credible congressional voices describing the costs and risks of deeper military involvement in Laos. It was clear that those at the top of the Administration were ready to listen to these voices of caution. At a press background briefing in late March 1961, National Security Adviser Bundy stated that no matter how effectively Kennedy argued that military intervention in Laos was the only alternative to appeasement, the Republicans would eventually resort to the charge that "Democrats cause wars" and would score points against the Administration.[18] Clearly the potential domestic costs of getting bogged down in Laos were perceived as greater than any temporary price Kennedy might pay for not lending greater military assistance to the Laotian government.

INCENTIVES FOR KHRUSHCHEV'S ACCEPTANCE OF THE 1962 GENEVA AGREEMENT ON LAOS

International Incentives for Cooperation

At the time John Kennedy assumed office, Soviet Premier Nikita Khrushchev had little incentive for reducing the diplomatic, economic, and military assistance which the USSR was providing to Souvanna Phouma and the Kong Le-Pathet Lao soldiers backing him. From the Soviet perspective, the United States had caused the civil war in Laos by undermining the national unity government of Souvanna Phouma in 1958 and by repeatedly violating the 1954 Geneva agreement through covert military assistance to the anticommunist elements in Laos. The latest chapter in this growing civil war had begun with the September 1960 economic boycott against Laos established by the pro-American regime in Thailand, followed by General Phoumi's armed attack on Souvanna's supporters in December.

In the eyes of most non-SEATO governments, the Soviet Union was assisting the still-legitimate leader of Laos. Souvanna had officially requested Soviet economic and military assistance in October 1960, and this aid was being continued despite his exile. With Hanoi and Peking actively assisting the Soviet Union's air and land delivery of supplies to the Kong Le-Pathet Lao soldiers, logistical problems were manageable. With the military assistance of North Vietnam, the neutralist-communist forces had every prospect of capturing most of Laos. In short, Laos was a trouble spot where the United States would have to create a new set of political and military incentives for the Soviet Union in order to persuade Khrushchev to wind down his opportunistic involvement.

The new diplomatic environment which the Kennedy Administration constructed for the Soviet Union in early 1961 depended on the new American President's acceptance of a truly neutralized Laos and his willingness to convene another Geneva conference and reactivate the ICC in support of this outcome. Kennedy's basic inclination was to favor a truly neutralized Laos, as he made clear in his first news conference on January 25. The new President said, in response to a question, that the United States was seeking to establish an "independent, peaceful, uncommitted country" in Laos.[19] His use of the adjective "uncommitted" suggested a shift away from the Eisenhower policy of promoting a pro-Western government in Laos. The United States had to take several subsequent actions, however, in order to give credibility to Kennedy's statement. First, therefore, this meant accepting the seating of the Pathet Lao and neutralist delegates at the Geneva conference on equal footing with the Boun Oum government's representative officially recognized by Washington. Then, during the negotiations at Geneva it became clear that no stable Laotian government could be constructed without the inclusion of Pathet Lao members in the Lao Cabinet. (This was an action that Eisenhower had strongly warned Kennedy away from, privately describing it as "fatal" one day prior to Kennedy's inauguration.)[20] And ultimately a negotiated settlement of the war required Kennedy to pressure the United States' own clients in Laos, Thailand, and South Vietnam into accepting Laos's neutralization under Souvanna Phouma's leadership.

The proposal to reconvene a new international conference on Laos had first been made by Prince Sihanouk at the United Nations in September 1960. On December 23, with Souvanna's supporters in retreat, the Soviet Union called for a renewal of the Geneva conference to discuss the war. This proposal was endorsed by the Peoples Republic of China (PRC) in a note to the conference co-chairmen on December 28. On January 1, Prince Sihanouk proposed a larger, fourteen-nation conference, to include those nations which had been at Geneva in 1954, the members of the ICC, and the Asian nations bordering Laos.[21]

While the Eisenhower Administration had been unreceptive to each of these proposals, viewing any such international conference as a communist propaganda forum that would never generate useful measures, Kennedy finally accepted such a conference in April 1961 when it became clear that this was essential to the formation of a Laotian government on which the Western and communist blocs could agree. The only precondition Kennedy attached to his acceptance of a new, expanded Geneva conference was the arrangement of a stable, verified ceasefire prior to the opening of the conference.

Verifying a truce in Laos, however, required ground observers acceptable to all parties. The Eisenhower Administration had opposed reactivation of the International Control Commission for this purpose in December 1960 when this was requested by Prime Minister Jawaharlal Nehru of India and then endorsed by the Soviet and British governments. The ICC was viewed by Eisenhower as hopelessly ineffective during 1954–

1958 because of the veto power exercised by its Polish member and because of the obstructionist tactics of the Pathet Lao, which had hampered investigations. Moreover, the United States had little incentive to support the ICC in December 1960 when General Phoumi's troops appeared to have the upper hand.

Despite his own misgivings about the ICC's effectiveness, Kennedy called in March 1961 for the ICC's reactivation and its verification of a truce in Laos prior to a new Geneva conference. The United States' request was directed to India as chairman of the ICC and to Great Britain and the USSR as co-chairmen of the Geneva convention. Moscow quickly acknowledged in principle its support of the ICC, but the Soviet government delayed the ICC's actual reactivation in Laos through a series of debates over ICC procedures. As Moscow's delaying tactics soon made clear, Kennedy's diplomatic concessions to the USSR in February and March of 1961 were insufficient to induce Khrushchev to terminate the Soviet airlift and other forms of assistance to the Pathet Lao and neutralist forces. There was no compelling reason for the Soviet Union to restrain its communist clients until there was a greater risk of military confrontation with the United States than was evident during the first weeks of 1961. Only when President Kennedy publicly threatened to intervene in Laos and then, in March–April 1961, backed this threat with a series of overt military steps including the mobilization of several thousand troops in Asia, the movement of additional soldiers toward Laos, and the massing of three aircraft carriers off Thailand, did Khrushchev begin pressuring the Pathet Lao and the North Vietnamese to halt their military advances in Laos and commence negotiations in Geneva.[22]

As the United States prepared for military action in spring 1961, it became clear that Khrushchev, like Kennedy, had no desire for a superpower confrontation in Laos. "If we all keep our heads and do nothing provocative," he told the U.S. ambassador, "we can find a way out of our problems in Laos."[23] Like the new American President, Khrushchev wanted an early summit meeting and tangible progress on the more important issues of Germany and strategic arms control. The Kennedy Administration directly informed both Khrushchev and Gromyko that any negotiated progress on these vital issues hinged on first settling the Laotian crisis.[24]

It was as important for Khrushchev as it was for Kennedy that an acceptable alternative existed to the Boun Oum-Phoumi regime in the person of Souvanna Phouma. With Souvanna recognized by all communist nations as the legitimate prime minister of Laos, Khrushchev could comfortably support a new coalition government under Souvanna's lead as a substitute for the Pathet Lao's full military victory. Souvanna arrived in the USSR on April 16, 1961, to consult with Khrushchev about a negotiated solution to the war. This meeting soon led to the Soviet premier's decision to ask Prince Souphanouvong, the head of the Pathet Lao, to fly to Moscow as well. The three leaders eventually issued a Soviet-Lao communiqué calling for a ceasefire, an enlarged Geneva conference, and reactivation of the ICC as measures to end the crisis. Then the two Laotian leaders flew to China, where they conferred with Mao Tse-tung and Chou Enlai, and then on to Hanoi, where they spoke with North Vietnamese leaders. On May 2 Hanoi radio broadcast a ceasefire order for the Pathet Lao, to take effect the following morning.[25]

When Khrushchev and Kennedy met in Vienna on June 3 and 4, Laos was the only topic on which they reached a useful consensus. Their joint communiqué, issued on June 4, "reaffirmed their support of a neutral and independent Laos under a government chosen by the Laotians themselves, and of international agreements for insuring that neutrality and independence, and in this connection they have recognized the importance of an effective ceasefire."[26] Privately, Khrushchev and Kennedy agreed to withdraw their armed presences from Laos upon successful completion of these international negotiations so as to reduce the chances of an unwanted superpower confrontation.[27]

Even after the Geneva negotiations began, the United States had to rely on diplomatic and military pressures to keep the ceasefire from completely collapsing. The Pathet Lao and North Vietnamese were in no mood to give away at the conference table what could be won without significant risk on the battlefield. As early as June 6, chief U.S. delegate Averell Harriman temporarily suspended U.S. participation in the Geneva conference because of continuing attacks on U.S.-supported Meo tribesmen living in remote villages behind Pathet Lao lines. As the Geneva conference recessed in August 1961, Harriman and chief British delegate Malcolm MacDonald wrung from their Soviet counterpart, Georgi Pushkin, the agreement that each conference co-chairman would insure adherence to the ceasefire by those parties in its political camp until the conference resumed. Meanwhile, Kennedy himself turned away Khrushchev's request for a summit meeting on Berlin until the Soviet Union showed better faith in controlling its clients in Laos.[28]

The Laotian ceasefire was seriously strained in December 1961 and again in February 1962 because of military probes and counterprobes by the Pathet Lao and General Phoumi's troops. Then the truce appeared to disintegrate completely in early May 1962 when 5,000 of Phoumi's best troops were routed by the Pathet Lao and North Vietnamese at Nam Tha, fifteen miles from the PRC's border. Fearing full collapse of the Royal Lao Army and a loss of all communist incentive for peacefully settling the civil war, Kennedy ordered the U.S. Seventh Fleet back into the Gulf of Siam and landed 5,000 U.S. combat troops in neighboring Thailand. At the same time, word went out to the Soviet Union through multiple channels, including meetings between Ambassador Thompson and Khrushchev and between Secretary Rusk and Ambassador Anatoly Dobrynin, that the U.S. political objective remained a neutralized Laos but that Moscow must dissuade the communist forces from further military action.[29] If Moscow's ability to achieve the latter was in doubt, the Kennedy Administration hoped that U.S. troop landings in Thailand would strengthen the Soviets' hand vis-à-vis the more aggressive Chinese and North Vietnamese.

OBSTACLES TO AMERICAN–SOVIET COOPERATION IN LAOS

Obstacles to American Cooperation

The principal impediments to U.S. cooperation with the Soviet Union over Laos were the differences between the interests of the United States and those of its clients. The most important American client during the Laotian civil war was the Thai government under the leadership of Marshal Sarit Thanarat.[30] U.S. officials recognized that Laos had little intrinsic value, but harmonious relations with the important nation of Thailand depended on U.S. willingness to prevent a communist victory in Laos. Thailand's preeminent security threat was communist control of the Mekong River valley in Laos, and the increased infiltration and subversion among the Lao and Vietnamese living in northeastern Thailand that such a development could bring. During the late 1950s, while the Eisenhower Administration was openly striving for a pro-American government in

Laos, Thailand had funneled soldiers, arms, and money into Laos to support General Phoumi Nosavan, Marshal Sarit's Laotian cousin.

The Thai government was profoundly shaken in spring 1961 when SEATO dead-locked on collective action against the successful Pathet Lao-neutralist offensive and the United States refused to intervene unilaterally. Thai fears grew in late 1961 when Kennedy accepted Souvanna Phouma as the next Lao head of government and tried to coerce General Phoumi into dropping his demand for control of the Defense and Interior ministries in Souvanna's future Cabinet. Bangkok opened talks with the USSR on trade and cultural exchanges, and speculation began that Thailand might move toward neutralism and withdraw from SEATO.

During the first half of 1962 the Kennedy Administration took several steps to shore up its relationship with Thailand and to obtain Marshal Sarit's acceptance of the 1962 Geneva agreements. In March the Thai foreign minister and Secretary of State Dean Rusk negotiated an agreement which formally pledged the United States, without prior consent from other SEATO members, to meet militarily any communist attack on Thailand. Two weeks later Averell Harriman flew to Bangkok to promise that, in exchange for Thai support of Souvanna Phouma's coalition government, the United States would prevent the communists from seizing full control of Laos. Immediately following Phoumi's defeat at Nam Tha, Thailand announced support for Souvanna's coalition government. Kennedy's decision to send 5,000 American soldiers to Thailand in May was motivated in part by the Administration's determination to demonstrate the reliability of its commitment. Finally, even before the Geneva Accords were signed, the Defense Department had concluded plans for improving the roads and landing fields in northeast Thailand to deter both conventional and guerrilla attacks in that area abutting Laos. Although U.S. combat troops were withdrawn from Thailand between July and November 1962, the United States left all the necessary combat and logistic equipment ready in Thailand for another deployment.

While events in Laos appeared less threatening to South Vietnam than to Thailand, the Kennedy Administration recognized that conceding eastern Laos to the communists would increase guerrilla infiltration into South Vietnam and put Saigon under greater pressure. By April 1961, Walt Rostow recalls, Kennedy had decided that

> If he had to engage American forces in Southeast Asia, he would do so in Vietnam rather than Laos. . . . Vietnam appeared to have relative advantages, which Kennedy once tersely ticked off to me in these terms: relatively speaking, it was a more unified nation; its armed forces were larger and better trained; it had direct access to the sea; its geography permitted air and naval power to be more easily brought to bear; there was the cushion of North Vietnam between South Vietnam and the Chinese border.[31]

In May 1961, after forgoing military intervention in Laos on behalf of Boun Oum and Phoumi Nosavan, Kennedy approved a series of measures designed to reassure Saigon and prevent South Vietnam from building "to a situation like that in Laos."[32] Kennedy secretly ordered 400 Special Forces advisers to South Vietnam, approved sabotage and harassment inside North Vietnam by CIA-trained South Vietnamese, doubled U.S. military assistance to South Vietnam, and approved South Vietnamese intelligence and harassment missions into southeastern Laos.[33] In November 1961, while negotiations were underway at Geneva on neutralizing Laos, Kennedy further escalated U.S. involvement in South Vietnam in an attempt to contain the Viet Cong. National Security Action Memorandum number 111 authorized significant increases in U.S. military advisers and support units in South Vietnam; enhanced ground, sea, and air mobility; expanded training; improved arms; and upgraded logistics. Between November 1961 and June 30, 1962, the number of U.S. servicemen in Vietnam grew from 948 to 5,579.[34] Kennedy had decided to make his stand in South Vietnam.

The most recalcitrant U.S. client during the Laotian civil war was General Phoumi Nosavan, the long-time favorite of Defense Department and CIA advisers in Laos; Phoumi was the commander-in-chief of the Royal Lao Army and the true leader of the Boun Oum government. The President and his advisers were well aware that Phoumi presented them with an excruciating dilemma. On the one hand continuing U.S. assistance to Phoumi's army was essential to the pro-American government's capability to prevent the Pathet Lao-neutralist forces from occupying all of Laos and to keep alive the perception that the U.S. would intervene if necessary. On the other hand this assistance reinforced Phoumi's belief that the United States was dependent on his political and military survival. Phoumi stubbornly refused to accept Souvanna Phouma's terms for a national unity coalition and instead clung to the opinion that Souvanna would eventually resign in frustration or that the United States would be compelled to intervene militarily when the communists finally broke the ceasefire. Phoumi's obstinacy made it impossible to reach a final political settlement of the war.

By February 1962, the Kennedy Administration had become so frustrated by Phoumi's unwillingness to compromise with Souvanna Phouma that it had suspended its monthly $3 million payroll assistance to the Lao government, hinted that it might terminate the delivery of military equipment as well, and fired the CIA agent in Laos long associated with Phoumi. In late March, at a meeting in Vientiane with Phoumi and his Cabinet, Averell Harriman was extraordinarily blunt. The only alternative to a neutral Laos was a communist one, Harriman said, and if the current Cabinet members would not accept Souvanna's terms, then they would soon have to swim the Mekong River to Thailand because the United States would not protect them.[35] In April, as another element of the squeeze on Phoumi, Kennedy gave Harriman approval to withdraw the Military Assistance Advisory Group training teams operating with the Royal Lao Army in forward field positions.[36] Before this could be implemented, however, 5,000 of Phoumi's best troops were overrun at Nam Tha in early May.

Some U.S. officials suspected that Phoumi had intentionally provoked the battle at Nam Tha to coerce Kennedy into resuming full support for the rightists. Instead, Harriman told the Lao ambassador in Washington that Phoumi's political career was now finished. The U.S. government refused to replace the $1 million in equipment lost at Nam Tha and actively discouraged Thailand, South Vietnam, South Korea, Japan, Taiwan, Malaya, and the Philippines from extending any of the political or economic support immediately sought by Phoumi and Boun Oum.

Yet the original dilemma persisted: how to force Phoumi and his associates to join the coalition government without openly suggesting to the Pathet Lao-North Vietnamese that the United States would under *no* circumstances react militarily in Laos. The deployment of U.S. combat troops to Thailand following the collapse of Nam Tha was an effort to signal that the United States might intervene if the ceasefire collapsed but engage in such signaling without actually lending assistance to Phoumi or reinforcing his obstinacy.[37]

By May 15 Phoumi and Boun Oum had finally cracked under the weight of military humiliation and U.S. pressure. They indicated their willingness to accept a coalition government in which the Interior and Defense ministries were led by neutralists provided that Souvanna Phouma could "prove he is not working for the communists." On June 8, in the first full exchange of views among the three Lao factions in several months, Phoumi agreed to cede the Foreign Affairs, Defense and Interior portfolios to Souvanna. The last major obstacle had been cleared for the official signing of the coalition agreement, which came on June 12.[38]

Obstacles to Soviet Cooperation

While the Soviet Union's limited strategic and political interests in Laos did not warrant a direct military confrontation with the United States, its cooperation with Washington over Laos was nonetheless constrained by its growing competition with the PRC for influence in the communist and socialist world. In Southeast Asia, this Soviet-Chinese competition centered on the political allegiance of the Democratic Republic of Vietnam (DRV). The Soviet campaign for influence over the DRV had begun in 1960, with the extension of $200 million in credits for DRV industrial expansion. The USSR could not remain aloof from the escalating Laotian civil war in late 1960, while the United States installed a pro-Western Boun Oum-Phoumi regime, without significantly strengthening the hand of the pro-Chinese faction in Hanoi.

Hanoi had a major stake in the outcome in Laos. North Vietnam had founded the Pathet Lao organization, trained it, armed it, and developed it. Souphanouvong, leader of the Pathet Lao, was married to a Vietnamese communist party official, and had spent much of his life in Vietnam. By 1962, at least 10,000 of the 35,000 communist and neutralist troops in Laos were North Vietnamese regulars, and Hanoi was well aware that this military force could completely defeat the Royal Lao Army in a matter of days unless the United States and its allies intervened to prevent this.

Particularly critical to Hanoi was its continued ability to use the Ho Chi Minh infiltration trails, which ran through the jungles of eastern Laos into South Vietnam and constituted the principal supply route to the communist insurgents in the South. During the December 1960–May 1961 fighting before the ceasefire, the North Vietnamese and Pathet Lao had been able to establish complete military control over eastern Laos. Any settlement at Geneva that North Vietnam could support would have to permit some use of this corridor into the South.

Several aspects of Soviet behavior were driven by the constraints and obstacles created by the DRV and the PRC. First, Moscow was obliged to provide vital advisory, material, and logistical assistance to the communist and neutralist forces in Laos until an outcome had been reached that was acceptable to the communist bloc. Initially, in spring 1961, Kennedy had indicated that a discontinuation of the Soviet airlift into Laos would be a precondition for the commencement of another Geneva conference. The Soviet Union was unwilling to accept this demand, and this position was soon dropped by the U.S. government.

A second feature of Soviet behavior was to paint the risks and consequences of U.S. intervention in Laos in highly dramatic terms, for the apparent purposes of deterring the communist forces there from provocative military action and justifying Moscow's own efforts to reach a negotiated solution to the war. Soviet reaction to the introduction of U.S. troops into Thailand in May 1962 followed this pattern. While the Soviets were carefully informed of the defensive and limited goals of this American troop movement, Khrushchev seemed determined to exaggerate its dangers for his Vietnamese, Chinese, and Laotian comrades. He publicly predicted that U.S. forces would become involved in a shooting war: "They arrived with their weapons. They did not come to play golf. They will shoot, and those they shoot will shoot back." [39] Two days later, *Pravda* condemned the United States for "preparing for intervention in Laos," which "would certainly widen the military conflict and enhance the danger of war not only on the borders of Laos but also in the whole of Southeast Asia. . . . In that case the military intervention of the United States in Laos also would turn into a collective intervention and would inevitably provoke a counteraction by the other side." *Pravda* concluded that the failure to peacefully resolve the Laos problem was the worst possible outcome for all parties, including the communist bloc. [40]

A third element of Khrushchev's approach to Laos was to convince the other concerned communist parties that whatever immediate concessions might be made to American military power, the long-term outcome in Southeast Asia was an inevitable communist victory. In spring 1961, in the face of Kennedy's first threats to intervene in Laos, Khrushchev had commented to the U.S. ambassador in Moscow, "Why take risks over Laos? It will fall into our laps like a ripe apple." [41] When U.S. troops actually moved into Thailand in May 1962, Khrushchev returned to the theme of inevitable communist victory in his public observations. "The Americans may fight fifteen years if they want to, but it will not help." The masses in Southeast Asia, he assured *Pravda*'s readers, were certain to win over the capitalists in the end. [42]

Ultimately, the neutralization of Laos under Souvanna Phouma's leadership was sufficient improvement over prior events in Laos to gain Chinese and North Vietnamese support. International guarantees of Laotian neutrality would require the withdrawal of U.S. military personnel from Laos and remove that country from the protective orbit of SEATO. At the same time, the mechanisms envisioned for policing this neutrality would be inadequate to prevent discreet use of eastern Laos by North Vietnamese soldiers. The negotiated withdrawal of U.S. forces from Laos was an important precedent which Hanoi hoped to apply in future talks on the status of South Vietnam.

Souvanna Phouma's elevation to power was perceived as a positive development both by Hanoi and Peking. During the 1961–1962 ceasefire, the DRV had actively pursued a series of bilateral agreements with Souvanna's exile government in northern Laos that legitimated the DRV's presence in Laos: agreements on broadcasting, foreign training grants, commercial relations, exchange of payments, economic assistance, road construction, and Lao students in North Vietnam. China had also cultivated Souvanna Phouma during 1961–1962. In a joint statement signed with Chinese Premier Chou En-lai in April 1961, Souvanna had agreed to establish diplomatic, economic, and cultural relations with Peking. In January 1962 Souvanna agreed to Chinese construction of a major road running from Mengala, China to Phong Saly in northern Laos. [43] And the withdrawal of the Soviet Union's 500 military advisers, as required by the 1962 Geneva agreements, would give Peking an inherent advantage over Moscow in Laos because of its natural economic and cultural ties with this bordering nation.

Finally, neutralization of Laos and the withdrawal of American advisers would eliminate the frightening possibility of a direct military confrontation with the United States and its allies. As Moscow frequently reminded Saigon and Hanoi, no one's interests would be well served by provoking the United States into a fullscale intervention. Such a war would probably escalate to Chinese and North Vietnamese territory, and the United States' SEATO allies would find it difficult to stay clear of such a war. Chinese radio broadcasts charged that "in Thailand a large number of U.S., Thai, Philippine, and South Vietnamese troops . . . have been grouped in readiness to invade Laos at any time."[44] A negotiated resolution of the civil war, which contained every prospect of eventual communist domination, was superior to confronting these troops.

THE INITIAL CONSEQUENCES OF AMERICAN-SOVIET COOPERATION

Several formal and informal domestic, bilateral, and international agreements flowed from the one and a half years of Soviet-American efforts to remove Laos as a threat to superpower relations. The first of these formal agreements was the "Three Princes' Agreement on Formation of the Provisional Government of National Union" officially signed by Lao Princes Souvanna Phouma, Boun Oum, and Souphanouvong on June 12, 1962. In this document the neutralist, communist, and rightist factions in Laos formally agreed to the future structure of the next Cabinet, the allocation of portfolios among the three competing political factions, and the basic decision-making procedures for the Lao Cabinet. With this agreement, Prince Souvanna Phouma was selected prime minister of the new government, and his neutralist colleagues were allocated control of the key positions within the Cabinet.[45] Both Khrushchev and Kennedy had been maneuvering their respective Lao clients toward this accord for a full year, and its final completion offered the potential for putting an end to the civil strife which had drawn the United States and the Soviet Union into its vortex.

Equally significant was the statement of neutrality issued by the new Royal Government of Laos on July 9, 1962. In it, the Lao leadership declared that:

1. It will not enter into any military alliance or into any agreement, whether military or otherwise, which is inconsistent with the neutrality of the Kingdom of Laos; it will not allow the establishment of any foreign military base on Laotian territory, nor allow any country to use Laotian territory for military purposes of interference in the internal affairs of other countries, nor recognize the protection of any alliance or military coalition, including SEATO; and
2. It will require the withdrawal from Laos of all foreign troops and military personnel, and will not allow any foreign troops or military personnel to be introduced into Laos.[46]

The formation of the new Lao government and its July 9th statement of neutrality cleared the way for final approval of the "Declaration on the Neutrality of Laos" signed on July 23, 1962, by the fourteen foreign ministers assembled at the Geneva conference. Explicitly incorporating the Lao government's solemn pledge of neutrality into its text, the "Declaration on the Neutrality of Laos" specifically required its fourteen signatories to:

1. Do nothing to impair the sovereignty, independence, neutrality, unity, or territorial integrity of the Kingdom of Laos;
2. Refrain from direct or indirect interference in Laotian internal affairs;
3. Refrain from attaching political conditions to any assistance which they might offer or which Laos might seek;
4. Refrain from bringing Laos into a military alliance;
5. Respect Laotian wishes not to recognize the protection of any military alliance, including SEATO;
6. Refrain from introducing any military personnel into Laos;
7. Refrain from establishing in Laos any foreign military bases or strongpoints; and
8. Refrain from using the territory of Laos for interference in the internal affairs of other countries.[47]

This last clause was inserted at the urging of the South Vietnamese delegation to prevent North Vietnam from using Laos as a corridor for infiltrating men and equipment into the south. The communist delegations accepted this provision only in exchange for a reciprocal commitment by the Western bloc not to interfere again in Laotian political affairs.

An equally vital element of the Geneva agreements of 1962 was the "Protocol to the Declaration on the Neutrality of Laos," which dealt with the difficult problem of interpreting, supervising, and enforcing the general terms found in the Declaration. In general, the Protocol:

1. Mandated the withdrawal of all foreign troops and advisers within 30 days after the Royal Lao Government declared that ICC inspection teams were in place along government-designated withdrawal routes for foreign troops. (As an exception to this rule, the Protocol provided for the Laotian right to request that a limited number of French military instructors be left in Laos.) It provided for the release and return of all military and civilian personnel captured or interned during the 1960–1962 civil war.
2. The Protocol defined the terms by which the International Control Commission would supervise and control the ceasefire in Laos and the withdrawal of foreign military personnel from that country. It partially addressed the past complaints about ICC ineffectiveness by authorizing the ICC to make procedural changes and initiate investigations by majority vote, although unanimity among the Indian, Canadian, and Polish representatives was still required on "major questions." It defined the financial obligations of all Conference members to support the ICC in Laos. China, France, the USSR, UK and USA would each contribute 17.6%, with the other signatories paying much smaller amounts; and
3. Provided that the co-chairmen of the Geneva conference exercise supervision over the observance of the Protocol and the Declaration of the Neutrality of Laos. Required that the co-chairmen receive routine reports from the ICC, receive reports of any violations of the agreements on Laos, assist the ICC in its functions, circulate routine and emergency reports to the members of the conference, and when appropriate consult with the members of the conference.[48]

Given the long history of both Western and communist violation of the 1954 Geneva accords, it is not surprising that both political camps would seek some additional guarantees that the 1962 Geneva agreements would be more faithfully implemented. To this end, the terms of the Protocol were reinforced by a continuation of the private 1961 agreement among Harriman, British delegate MacDonald and Soviet delegate Pushkin that each Geneva co-chairman would ensure compliance with the accords by the members of its political bloc. In other words, Great Britain promised to keep the United States, Thailand and others from meddling in Laos's internal affairs while the Soviet Union promised to hold China, North Vietnam, and the Pathet Lao in check. These private promises came to be referred to as "the Pushkin agreement."[49]

Certainly the Kennedy Administration was well aware that even with the formal and informal agreements made at Geneva, the future prospects for a stable, neutral, coalition government in Laos were highly uncertain. Internally, it was problematic that a functioning tripartite government could ever be established. As the State Department's Bureau of Intelligence described the situation on the eve of the 1962 Geneva agreements:

Initially a coalition government would be presiding over a country unified in name only since the dominating political factor would be the existence of three separate military forces and three separate civil administrations, with the communist and anti-communist wings each seeking to dominate the center. How long it would take to extend the government's control over all Laos would depend principally on how long it took to integrate the three armed forces into one national army. Based on past experience in Laos, this could well be a matter of years. Meanwhile the coalition government would be a government in name only, presiding over a divided country. While the United States may wish to hasten as much as possible the transition to a truly unified Laos, there are too many factors out of US control, too much incipient obstructionism and too much built-in inertia for any optimism on this score.[50]

Those U.S. officials knowledgable about Laos's external situation were equally pessimistic that any dramatic change would occur because of the Geneva accords. All were aware of the military's warnings, such as those cabled by Admiral Harry Felt, commander-in-chief of the Pacific Command, that:

> If coalition Govt is formed as currently contemplated, routes for NVN infiltrate agents, troops and supplies to SVN and Thailand through Laos will not be closed.
>
> A neutral Laos springing out of present negotiations will look neutral on a map. However, back in mountainous jungle areas adjacent to the borders of SVN, Communist control will prevail.
>
> Interests of a neutralized Laos cannot be served adequately by an ICC which will probably function in the areas of main centers of population along the Mekong and be frustrated in other parts of Laos.[51]

Yet Kennedy and his chief advisers were prepared to accept their failure to fully neutralize Laos provided the Mekong River valley separating Laos and Thailand did not fall to the Pathet Lao-North Vietnamese. American intelligence estimated that 2,000 North Vietnamese personnel would infiltrate South Vietnam via the Ho Chi Minh trails during 1962. The White House considered this to be a threat that could be neutralized within South Vietnam itself.[52] So long as neither Kennedy nor Khrushchev were visibly humiliated by events in Laos, both could withdraw their military personnel and eliminate the potential for a dangerous superpower clash. Thailand was now reluctantly willing to concede northern and eastern Laos to the communists. And even if the Laotian coalition never functioned, this was not a major problem. As State's Bureau of Intelligence advised Harriman:

> If coalition proved unfeasible, the most probable and feasible adjustment of the Laotian problem would be some sort of partition. Such a partition would be strictly *de facto;* all concerned including the US would probably continue to profess a desire to reunite Laos peacefully but with little hope or real desire that it should or could be done. It would be particularly useful for the West, which is militarily weak in Laos, to profess continued allegiance to the principle of a political solution as this would lessen the pretext for the bloc to denounce and disregard the cease-fire.
>
> If the rightists and the Western powers handled things skillfully it is possible that Souvanna's dependence on the Communists for support could be lessened with a consequent lessening of Communist influence over him. In this case the present "neutralist" Laos and RLG Laos might eventually be merged into a viable and stable neutral Laos.[53]

A new test of will and capability was under way within the constraints of the 1962 Geneva agreements.

IMPLEMENTING THE 1962 GENEVA AGREEMENTS

Obstacles to Implementation

The United States began the implementation of the new Geneva agreements with three specific objectives: (1) to secure maximum—if possible, complete—North Vietnamese military withdrawal from Laos; (2) to remain on friendly terms with Prime Minister Souvanna Phouma; and (3) to prevent General Phoumi Nosavan from taking actions that could jeopardize the coalition and provoke communist military action.[54]

The Geneva agreements signed on July 23, 1962, required that all foreign military personnel depart Laos within 75 days. Kennedy concluded that only through full compliance with this provision—even if it were violated by the DRV—would the United States defuse the threat to Soviet-American relations, maintain a cooperative relationship with Souvanna Phouma, and be able to bring effective political pressure on Khrushchev to restrain the North Vietnamese. Therefore, 666 American military advisory personnel were withdrawn from Laos through designated checkpoints and under the supervision of the International Control Commission prior to the October 7, 1962, deadline. In addition, 403 Filipino technicians maintaining Lao equipment under contract to the U.S. Military Advisory Assistance Group (MAAG) departed under ICC supervision. Given the communists' superior forces in Laos, in the form of several battalions of North Vietnamese regulars, there was considerable military risk in these actions. CINCPAC believed that it was essential to keep the U.S. MAAG in Laos if Phoumi's army were to remain a viable force. "Removal of the MAAG," Admiral Felt said, "would sacrifice Laos."[55]

Because of such concerns, arrangements were made with the tacit approval of Souvanna Phouma to ensure that U.S. military clients in Laos remained supplied. A special Requirements Office run by retired military personnel was established within the U.S. Embassy in Vientiane to maintain contact with the Royal Lao Army and validate its military aid requirements. Seventy members of the former Laos MAAG were reassigned to the U.S. Military Advisory Group in Thailand, from where they assisted with the delivery of military supplies.[56] Meanwhile, CIA agents continued their recruitment and training of Meo tribesmen operating in the Laotian jungles, and CIA-contracted Air America aircraft continued to assist the Meos through supply drops originating in Thailand and South Vietnam. Souvanna Phouma's attitude appeared to be that so long as the United States did not attach political preconditions to this military assistance, he would tolerate—and in some cases encourage—it so as to counterbalance North Vietnam's pressure on Laos. (Hanoi, however, viewed such U.S. actions as justification for its own refusal to fully respect the 1962 Geneva agreements.)[57]

During the second half of 1962, the Kennedy Administration took several other steps to strengthen the centrist elements under Souvanna Phouma—steps which were fully legal within the Geneva framework. The United States actively encouraged its allies to establish diplomatic, consular, and commercial relations with the new Lao government. It pressured France to send the best possible military trainers to Laos, as permitted under the agreements. Kennedy personally hosted Souvanna in Washington at the end of July 1962 and met with him again at the United Nations that September. Under economic assistance programs openly negotiated with the Royal Lao government, Washington provided subsistence for the 150,000 refugees created by the civil war, and rural development programs in villages in noncommunist areas.[58]

However, given the unstable nature of the new Lao coalition, the Kennedy Admin- istration also continued to plan for possible military intervention in Laos. The Defense Department reviewed several possible actions: (1) air strikes in response to a communist rupture of the ceasefire; (2) an occupation of the Mekong River valley with the back-up capacity in Thailand to proceed beyond this point; (3) an occupation of the Mekong River valley and an advance to take over southern Laos; and (4) an occupation of the Mekong River valley and an advance on part of southern Laos. These contingency plans called for various applications of U.S., Thai, and South Vietnamese forces.[59]

In addition, actions for preventing or reversing a Pathet Lao coup against Souvanna Phouma were discussed, with heavy emphasis on compelling the Soviets to control their clients. As Assistant Secretary Roger Hilsman wrote to Harriman:

> We [in the Bureau of Intelligence and Research] believe that our most useful diplo- matic target would be Moscow—on the premise that agreement over Laos is essential to the edifice of tacit American-Soviet understanding on other issues and areas. Our approach to Moscow—which in present circumstances could be effective—would start from the contention that any attempt to disturb the balance in Laos would undermine the concept of the negotiated and peaceful settlement of international crises as a basis for American-Soviet relations.[60]

American officials passed the word to Pathet Lao leader Souphanouvong that any coup against Souvanna Phouma would destroy the accords and resurrect the possibility of U.S. intervention.

Effective U.S. intervention in Laos required the further development of the logis- tical infrastructure of northeast Thailand abutting the Mekong River border. Through use of the Secretary of Defense's contingency funds, improvements were begun in Thai- land's roads, pipelines, fuel storage, and railway equipment to pave the way for the introduction of U.S. forces. These projects had the additional benefits of supporting the defense of Thailand itself and the economic development of northeastern Thailand where domestic insurrection had long been a security concern.[61] Meanwhile, the American combat troops sent to Thailand in May 1962 were gradually withdrawn during autumn, with all of the ground troops gone by November 1962.

The Soviet Union very carefully adhered to the terms of the 1962 Geneva agree- ment. By October 7, Moscow had withdrawn all of the 500 military technicians and pilots it had sent to Laos during 1960–1961. It turned over to the Pathet Lao the Soviet road building machinery and six hundred trucks which had constituted the overland supply train originating in North Vietnam. And, despite strong protests from both Hanoi and Peking, it terminated its airlift of supplies between Hanoi and northern Laos for the Pathet Lao and neutralist forces. Ten Soviet cargo planes involved in this airlift were turned over to the DRV, with the understanding that the USSR would assist in the training of additional North Vietnamese air crews. Soviet supplies continued to flow into North Vietnam, but it was Hanoi that violated Laos's neutrality by transporting these goods across the border. Meanwhile, Pathet Lao leaders complained bitterly that the Soviets failed to provide the level of financial assistance that the Laotian rightists were receiving overtly and covertly from the United States. These complaints were ignored in Moscow.[62]

The private explanation which the Soviets provided to their communist allies for their careful adherence to the Geneva agreements revealed the secondary importance that Khrushchev had come to assign to the Laos problem. The departing Soviet ambas- sador to Laos explained to Poland's ICC representative in August 1962 that:

Moscow hoped that the Laotian success would pave the way for the reopening of the Berlin negotiations, which Soviet Deputy Foreign Minister Kuznetsov was instructed to take up in Geneva with U.S. representatives. Moscow attached importance to the correct implementation of the Laotian experiment: the general aim was to turn the Laotian settlement into profit in European affairs.[63]

When Peking complained about Moscow's decision to discontinue its military airlift into Laos, V. V. Kuznetsov wrote the PRC that

surely you will agree that the transport of military material to Laos on Soviet planes with Soviet crews would not go unperceived . . . We would put in the hands of our enemies a great political trump; enabling them to say in their propaganda that socialist countries do not meet their obligations. For example, how would socialist proposals to guarantee a free city status for West Berlin look if socialist countries began to violate the only recently signed Geneva agreement?[64]

Hanoi's interests were quite different from Moscow's, and it quickly became apparent that the DRV had no intention of adhering to the Geneva agreement's required departure of foreign military personnel. In particular the DRV would insist on retaining military control and use of the infiltration routes entering South Vietnam through eastern Laos. Only forty North Vietnamese technicians withdrew from Laos through ICC checkpoints. U.S. intelligence acquired through Meo trail watchers and overhead reconnaissance flights indicated that Hanoi withdrew about 1,500 of its approximately 9,000 ground troops by the October 7 deadline and regrouped some of its battalions within Laos closer to North Vietnam's border. Sanitized versions of these assessments were shared with Souvanna Phouma, the British, the Soviets, and the ICC. However, precise knowledge of DRV troop movements was hampered by the rugged terrain and sparse population of Laos and by the complex nature of the North Vietnamese presence in Laos, which included regular military battalions, mixed Vietnamese-Pathet Lao military units, military advisers attached to the Pathet Lao, civilian technicians and laborers working on construction projects, and individual agents at the local level. When ICC representatives attempted to investigate North Vietnamese violations, the Pathet Lao denied them access to certain zones within the country. Even noncommunist members of the Laotian Cabinet were refused entry to sensitive areas.[65]

During autumn 1962 the North Vietnamese and Pathet Lao began sharply reducing the Soviet supplies that Kong Le's neutralist soldiers had been receiving since December 1960. Some neutralist officers defected to the Pathet Lao; others, including several of Kong Le's commanders, were assassinated by the communists. Exchanges of fire began between neutralist and Pathet Lao personnel. In November 1962, after Kong Le asked Souvanna Phouma for U.S. supplies to sustain his neutralist army, Air America transport planes began landing food, fuel, and ammunition for them at the Plain of Jars, adding to the tension between the neutralists and the communists.

By late March 1963, Kong Le had openly broken with the Pathet Lao. The spiraling tension culminated in the April 1, 1963, assassination of Foreign Minister Quinim Pholsena, a Pathet Lao sympathizer, by one of Kong Le's supporters. That same week, Pathet Lao and North Vietnamese troops launched major attacks against Kong Le's units at the Plain of Jars, with the apparent goals of destroying his forces and seizing his territory. The intensity of the attacks and the accompanying propaganda by the Pathet Lao, Hanoi, and Peking led the American Embassy in Laos to conclude that the communists had "reached the end of the road with Souvanna and have no further intention of cooperating in a government of national union."[66] Only troops sent to the area by General Phoumi and by Meo tribal commanders slowed the communists' advance against Kong Le.

After considerable vacillation, Souvanna Phouma asked the British and Soviet co-chairmen of the Geneva conference, through their ambassadors in Vientiane, to stop the communists' attacks, send ICC inspection teams to the Plain of Jars, and pressure Hanoi to remove its troops from his country. Frustrated by the continuing communist offensive, Souvanna called a press conference to accuse the Pathet Lao and North Vietnamese of trying to destroy his neutralist units and of bringing back the civil war.[67] With U.S. encouragement, the British ambassador in Moscow repeatedly pressed the Soviet Foreign Ministry to rein in the communists in Laos and dispatch ICC teams to investigate the fighting.

Despite Soviet claims that they were working on behalf of a new ceasefire in Laos, Washington and London saw little evidence of it. By refusing to delete charges of U.S. responsibility for the fighting from the draft version of the Geneva co-chairmen's reply to the Laotian government, Moscow effectively blocked any public statement by the conference, since London and Washington could not accept such official accusations. Furthermore, the obstructionist tactics of the Polish ICC representative in Laos blocked the dispatch of an ICC inspection team to the Plain of Jars, and there was no evidence that Moscow was attempting to end this delay. American officials could only conclude that "Moscow intends to avoid commitment to a course which might be detrimental to communist interests in Laos and harmful to Moscow's position in its struggle with Peiping."[68]

Kennedy saw Khrushchev's inaction as a violation of the "Pushkin agreement" that the Soviet premier would continue to restrain his fellow communists in Laos. In a last attempt to save the Geneva settlement through diplomacy, Kennedy dispatched Averell Harriman, Harriman's aide William Sullivan, and NSC staff member Michael Forrestal on an urgent mission to Khrushchev. The U.S. emissaries hurriedly left for Moscow and held two meetings with Khrushchev. The first session with the Soviet premier was given over to reminiscences about Harriman's service as U.S. ambassador to the Soviet Union during World War II and to banter about the capitalist and socialist systems. The meeting of substance occurred the following day, in a three-hour discussion of Cuba, Berlin, and finally Southeast Asia.[69]

Khrushchev made it clear that he wanted to wash his hands of the Laos problem and had grown exceeding weary of being caught between the demands of Asia's communist leaders and the pressures from Kennedy. It was a mistake for the two superpowers to have gotten so involved in Laos, he said. He contrasted the problem to Berlin, where real interests were engaged.[70] Then throwing up his hands, Khrushchev said: "Laos, Vietnam, all Southeast Asia. You and the Chinese can fight over it. I give up. We give up. We don't want any of it."[71] Khrushchev suggested that he had lost virtually all control over the Pathet Lao's behavior because of his decision to withdraw Soviet advisers from Laos and to halt the Soviet airlift of military supplies. He made harsh jokes about the Laotians in general and about the nature of the country. "What can you do with such crazy people?" he asked.[72]

Harriman, Sullivan, and Forrestal returned to Washington in late April with the opinion that because of the Soviets' lack of military presence in Laos and their ideological struggle with Peking, Khrushchev could no longer be relied on to restrain the communist forces there. The "Pushkin agreement" was largely irrelevant to defending

American interests. If Khrushchev were to play any role at all, it would only be because the United States threatened to take some action that raised the risks for all, including Moscow. As Ambassador David Bruce observed from London, "The Soviets' principal bargaining position with Peking is American belligerency" and a "military situation which could threaten to get of hand."[73]

The Harriman-Sullivan-Forrestal assessment was compatible with the views of State's Bureau of Intelligence. Its director, Thomas Hughes, wrote Roger Hilsman on April 20:

> The USSR cannot be expected to exert a restraining influence in Hanoi and Peiping simply for the sake of saving the Geneva Accords. If Moscow saw a real likelihood of U.S. military reinvolvement, however, it would probably attempt to use what leverage it has to restrain Hanoi and the Pathet Lao. It probably wishes to avoid a major problem in an area of peripheral national interest but one where Soviet prestige is engaged as a Geneva agreement overseer. United States military deployments in the vicinity of Laos credibly signaling intent to intervene seem the only possible means of stimulating Soviet pressures on Hanoi to desist from further military support for the Pathet Lao and to seek a new *modus vivendi*.[74]

Whether Soviet pressure on Hanoi would have much effect on the latter's decisions was by no means clear, however. In March the North Vietnamese had openly tilted in the direction of the PRC in the Sino-Soviet dispute, stressing that armed struggle was superior to peaceful revolution in the confrontation with capitalism.[75]

The State Department also worried that an absence of U.S. military action in response to the communists' violation of the Laos ceasefire would be misinterpreted:

> The Pathet Lao and Hanoi will interpret a U.S. failure to respond vigorously to their attacks on the neutralists as a U.S. decision to abandon Laos and an invitation to apply similar tactics to Phoumi that they have successfully used on Kong Le.

> First the neutralists and later the Phoumi forces will make the same interpretation as the Pathet Lao and Hanoi—that the United States has decided to abandon Laos—and disintegrate, leaving us with nothing to support.[76]

In late April 1963, therefore, the Kennedy Administration once again found itself reaching for military threats to stabilize Laos. First, a carrier task group and an amphibious ready group were ordered into the waters off South Vietnam, with instructions to be prepared to steam into the Gulf of Tonkin if necessary, for the purpose of threatening North Vietnam. The two groups were ordered to conduct normal radio communications and air operations en route to their destination to ensure that Hanoi, Peking, and Moscow were aware of the deployment. State Department intelligence suggested that this movement of Seventh Fleet ships

> may be more effective in argument with Moscow than movement of ground forces into Thailand. This is precisely because it suggests the possibility of action against North Vietnam to protect the neutralists rather than a precautionary movement into Thailand to protect Phoumi. It raises the question of Soviet as well as Chinese commitments more directly than would the dispatch of forces to Thailand, potentially for Laos.[77]

A second action was to send Admiral Felt to Bangkok to lobby for advancement of the SEATO ground defense exercise already scheduled in Thailand for mid-June. This exercise was to include the deployment of one U.S. infantry battle group from Hawaii, one airborne brigade from Okinawa, one tactical fighter squadron, and supporting air units. If SEATO did not agree to advance the exercise, Felt was to arrange for accelerated deployment of the U.S. forces. These ground actions were given no special publicity in order to avoid complicating Souvanna Phouma's ceasefire negotiations with the Pathet Lao and giving General Phoumi any encouragement to take the military offensive.[78]

What little political cohesion still existed within Laos's coalition government fully dissolved during the next weeks. While a shaky ceasefire was established during May with the beginning of the monsoon season, the communist members of Souvanna's Cabinet permanently departed Vientiane for the Pathet Lao's headquarters at Khang Khay. On June 6, Souvanna for the first time publicly accused the Pathet Lao of relying on weapons and soldiers from North Vietnam. On June 24 he terminated military budget funds for the Pathet Lao and then turned to the United States for additional military assistance.

By the time Laos's monsoon season ended in November 1963, the lives of South Vietnam's President Ngo Dinh Diem and the United States' John Kennedy had been taken by assassins' bullets. Kennedy's successor, Lyndon B. Johnson, quickly stated his attitude toward the situation he inherited in Asia: "I am not going to lose South Vietnam. I am not going to be the President who saw Southeast Asia go the way China went."[79]

During spring 1964 Souvanna Phouma made one last effort to reestablish the domestic and international conditions envisioned for Laos by the Geneva agreements. He travelled to Hanoi and Peking, then threatened to resign unless the Geneva signatories fulfilled their pledges to observe Laotian neutrality. In April he went to the Plain of Jars for what turned out to be the last tripartite negotiations with Souphanouvong and General Phoumi. When the conference failed to reach consensus on plans to demilitarize the royal capital of Luang Prabang, Souvanna flew back to Vientiane and announced his intention to resign. On April 19 Souvanna was overthrown and arrested by two Laotian generals but was quickly restored to power when the U.S. government threw all of its diplomatic and financial pressure against the coup. The Johnson Administration realized that Souvanna Phouma had become the indispensable politician holding together the loose rightist-neutralist coalition opposing the Pathet Lao and North Vietnamese.[80]

Meanwhile, in late April 1964, the communists again launched their annual dry-season offensive. Following a brief effort to reconstitute the national unity government, Souvanna announced on May 2 that he had merged the neutralist and rightist political factions under his leadership. As the Pathet Lao broke through the neutralists' defense lines and drove Kong Le's forces from the Plain of Jars, plans for merging the neutralist troops with the Royal Lao Army were announced. Laos was now formally polarized between pro-American and pro-Vietnamese political factions. The domestic influence of the 1962 Geneva agreements had come to an end.[81]

The spring 1964 communist offensive also precipitated a decisive break in U.S. adherence to the Geneva accords. Faced with a crumbling neutralist army and the meager capabilities of the Laotian Air Force, the Johnson Administration authorized bombing strikes against the advancing Pathet Lao-North Vietnamese troops by Air America pilots and U.S. jet aircraft based in Thailand. Then, when the communist offensive stalled in the face of American and Laotian bombing, U.S. Army advisers helped plan a counteroffensive by the Royal Lao-neutralist army and accompanied the Laotian regiments into battle. Meanwhile, pressure also built on the Johnson Administration to counter the rising level of North Vietnamese trucks, weapons, and personnel infiltrating South Vietnam via the improved and enlarged Ho Chi Minh "trails" (actually, roads) through Laos. In December 1964 the U.S. Air Force began its effort to interdict this threat through systematic aerial bombing.[82]

As U.S. military efforts in Laos escalated, the Johnson Administration and then the Nixon Administration were mindful of the need to pay lip service to the 1962 Geneva agreements and prevent widespread awareness of the American combat role in Laos. The "U.S. secret war in Laos" during the period 1965–1972 rested on the combined efforts of U.S. Army advisers, CIA agents, CIA contractors, and Air Force pilots operating airplanes based in neighboring countries. During these years U.S. ambassadors to Laos strongly resisted any plans for large-scale American and South Vietnamese ground operations in that country. In the end, sustained operations by U.S. Army units were avoided.

The U.S. government adhered to operational secrecy and restraint in Laos to avoid embarrassing Souvanna Phouma and to avoid provoking the Soviet Union into some undesired response. Washington feared the possible consequences of an overt repudiation of the 1962 Geneva agreements and the pressure this might place on Moscow to once again become directly involved in the Laotian civil war.[83] In this limited sense, then, the influence of the Geneva agreements was felt until 1973, when American military activities in Laos officially ended as a part of the negotiated conclusion of the Southeast Asian war between the United States and North Vietnam. In September 1973 Souvanna Phouma and Pathet Lao leaders agreed on yet another coalition government and administration for their nation. This new Lao government collapsed in 1975 when, in conjunction with Hanoi's final military offensive in South Vietnam, Pathet Lao and North Vietnamese troops defeated Souvanna's rightist, neutralist, and Meo armies operating without U.S. assistance. The Kingdom of Laos was rapidly transformed into the Lao People's Democratic Republic and was reduced to permanent political dependency on the new Vietnam.[84]

SUMMARY

In summary, both President John Kennedy and Premier Nikita Khrushchev quickly came to recognize the escalatory danger inherent in their governments' military commitment to opposing political factions in Laos's civil war. Neither Kennedy nor Khrushchev perceived Laos to be worth this growing risk to superpower relations, even though both were willing to use military and political threats to defend their limited interests in that country. Nor did Kennedy perceive Laos to be the optimal location in which to confront the growing military challenge by North Vietnam to the United States' position in Southeast Asia. The alternative to armed confrontation between the superpowers or a U.S.–North Vietnamese war in Laos was a negotiated definition of Laos's domestic and international status among those governments with a stake in that fragile nation.

Despite considerable pressure from their Asian allies for increased military involvement in Laos, both Kennedy and Khrushchev managed to arrange a ceasefire among the warring Lao factions and an international conference on Laos attended by fourteen concerned governments. The eventual success of this conference was facilitated by the existence of Prince Souvanna Phouma, a longtime leader of Laos whom both Kennedy and Khrushchev could trust to steer Laos toward neutrality, and the existence of an international Control Commission which had supervised Laos's neutrality during 1954–1958. The new agreement on Laos's domestic and international status and the means for guaranteeing this agreement were spelled out in the 1962 Geneva "Declaration on the Neutrality of Laos,'' signed by all fourteen negotiating governments, and in the unofficial "Pushkin agreement" reached among the United States, the USSR and the United Kingdom.

Preventing a superpower confrontation in Laos required both Kennedy and Khrushchev to accept some significant political and military losses in Southeast Asia. For Khrushchev, the accords resulted in a loss of political and military leverage over the Pathet Lao and greater influence by the People's Republic of China over North Vietnam. For Kennedy, the 1962 Geneva accords required permanent acceptance of communist control over much of Laos and acceptance of North Vietnam's use of Lao territory in pursuit of its war aims against South Vietnam.

Within a year, the coalition government envisioned for Laos under the 1962 Geneva accords had once again dissolved into pro-American and pro-Vietnamese factions occupying a partitioned country. While the domestic elements of the Geneva accords failed to function after 1963, the international terms of the accords on Laos proved to be an influence until 1973. For Moscow, the 1962 Laos neutralization agreement was a convenient rationale for its permanent extrication from a messy civil war in which it had minimal strategic interests and which, to its surprise, had brought it near armed conflict with the United States. For succeeding American administrations, the 1962 Geneva accords provided an international mechanism for preventing Soviet-American friction over the status of Laos, for constraining North Vietnam's military operations in Laos, and for acknowledging Souvanna Phouma's dream of returning his country to a unified neutral status. As the war in Southeast Asia escalated, both North Vietnam and the United States increasingly violated Laos's territorial integrity. Nonetheless, until final U.S. withdrawal from Southeast Asia, the political bargains struck at Geneva in 1962 remained a restraining force on the visible military actions which the signatories were willing to undertake in Laos.

Notes

1. Unless otherwise indicated the following historical summary is compiled from: Charles A. Stevenson, *The End of Nowhere* (Boston: Beacon Press, 1973); Arthur J. Dommen, *Laos: Keystone of Indochina* (Boulder: Westview Press, 1985); Alexander L. George, David K. Hall, William E. Simons, *The Limits of Coercive Diplomacy* (Boston: Little, Brown, 1971), pp. 36–85; and David K. Hall, "The Laotian War of 1962," in Barry M. Blechman et al., *Force Without War* (Washington, D.C.: The Brookings Institution, 1978), pp. 135–175.

2. Department of State Press Release, January 3, 1961. National Security Files. Boxes 131–139. Laos. John F. Kennedy Library.

3. Dean Rusk to John F. Kennedy, Draft circular telegram on Laos, February 5, 1961. National Security Files. Boxes 131–139. Laos. John F. Kennedy Library.

4. Walt W. Rostow, recorded interview by Richard Neustadt, April 11, 1964, pp. 28–30, John F. Kennedy Library Oral History Program; Theodore C. Sorensen, *Kennedy* (New York: Bantam Books, 1966), pp. 609–611.

5. This was Kennedy's principal theme in his meetings with Khrushchev in Vienna, June 3 and 4, 1961. Arthur M. Schlesinger, Jr., *A Thousand Days* (Greenwich, Conn.: Fawcett World Library, 1967), pp. 334–339.

6. Michael V. Forrestal, recorded interview by David K. Hall, January 2, 1987; Stevenson, *End of Nowhere*, pp. 147–148.

7. Winthrop G. Brown, recorded interview by Larry J. Hackman, February 1, 1968, pp. 14–16, John F. Kennedy Library Oral History Program; Michael V. Forrestal, recorded interview by David K. Hall, January 2, 1987.

8. CINCPAC to the Secretary of State, January 11, 1962. National Security Files. Boxes 131–139. Laos. John F. Kennedy Library.

9. Memorandum of Conversation, April 29, 1961. National Security Files. Boxes 131–139. Laos. John F. Kennedy Library.

10. The Secretary of Defense. Memorandum for the President. June 1962. National Security Files. Boxes 131–139. Laos. John F. Kennedy Library.

11. Ibid.

12. For instance, see: Roger Hilsman to Dean Rusk. Bloc Reactions to Contingent U.S. Actions in Laos and North Viet-Nam. June 7, 1962. National Security Files, Boxes 131–139. Laos. John F. Kennedy Library.

13. Memorandum of Conversation, April 29, 1961. National Security Files. Boxes 131–139. Laos. John F. Kennedy Library; Department of State. Discussion Paper for White House Meeting, May 10, 1962. National Security Files. Boxes 131–139. Laos. John F. Kennedy Library.

14. Senator Mike Mansfield to President John F. Kennedy. March 22, 1961. Presidential Office Files. Box 87. Departments and Agencies. John F. Kennedy Library.

15. "Senators Call Laos Poor Place to Fight," *New York Herald Tribune* (May 8, 1961), p. 2.

16. *New York Times* (February 15, 1962).

17. Ibid. (May 11, 1962).

18. Stevenson, *End of Nowhere*, p. 148.

19. *Public Papers of the Presidents of the United States, John F. Kennedy, 1961* (Washington, D.C.: Office of the Federal Register, 1962), p. 16.

20. Quoted in Clark Clifford's Memorandum for the Record. Larry Berman, *Planning a Tragedy* (New York: W.W. Norton, 1982), p. 17.

21. George, Hall, Simons, *Coercive Diplomacy*, pp. 51–52.

22. The fine details of U.S. actions during these months are spelled out in: George, Hall, Simons, *Coercive Diplomacy,* pp. 53–59.

23. Quoted in Hugh Sidey, *John F. Kennedy, President* (New York: Fawcett World Library, 1964), p. 86.

24. George, Hall, Simons, *Coercive Diplomacy,* p. 57.

25. Stevenson, *End of Nowhere*, p. 150.

26. Department of State *Bulletin* (June 26, 1961), p. 999.

27. Michael V. Forrestal, recorded interview by David K. Hall, January 2, 1987.

28. Stevenson, *End of Nowhere*, pp. 165–66; Michael V. Forrestal, recorded interview by David K. Hall, January 2, 1987.

29. Hall, "The Laotian War," pp. 144–45.

30. The following analysis of Thai-American relations is drawn from: Hall, *"The Laotian War,"* pp. 139–142.

31. Quoted in Berman, *Planning a Tragedy,* p. 19.

32. Walt Rostow to Kennedy, May 26, 1961. President's Office Files, Staff Memoranda. Rostow 3/61. John F. Kennedy Library.

33. Neil Sheehan et al., *The Pentagon Papers* (New York: Bantam Books, 1971), pp. 87–93.

34. Berman, *Planning a Tragedy,* p. 29.

35. Michael V. Forrestal, recorded interview by David K. Hall, January 2, 1987.

36. National Security Action Memorandum No. 149. National Security Files. Boxes 131–139. Laos. John F. Kennedy Library.

37. For a detailed account of the Nam Tha incident, see: Hall, "The Laotian War," pp. 135–175.

38. Hall, "The Laotian War," pp. 162–63.

39. Quoted in *New York Times* (May 19, 1962).

40. Ibid. (May 21, 1962).

41. Quoted in Roger Hilsman, *To Move a Nation* (New York: Dell Publishing, 1967), pp. 130–131.

42. *New York Times* (May 19, 1962).

43. Hall, "The Laotian War," p. 156.

44. New China News Agency in English to Asia. September 9, 1961. National Security Files. Boxes 131–139. Laos. John F. Kennedy Library.

45. The text of this agreement can be found in: Marek Thee, *Notes of a Witness* (New York: Vintage Books, 1973) pp. 412–14.

46. For the entire statement of neutrality, see: Thee, *op. cit.,* pp. 417–418.

47. Ibid., 417–18. Signing this declaration were the governments of Burma, Cambodia, Canada, China, France, India, Laos, North Vietnam, Poland, South Vietnam, Thailand, the United Kingdom, the United States, and the USSR.

48. Ibid., 420–26.

49. Stevenson, *End of Nowhere,* pp. 164–66.

50. Roger Hilsman to Averell Harriman. May 7, 1962. National Security Files. Boxes 131–139. Laos. John F. Kennedy Library.

51. Admiral Felt to Secretary McNamara. June 1962. National Security Files. Boxes 131–139. Laos. John F. Kennedy Library.

52. Michael V. Forrestal, recorded interview by Joseph Kraft, August 14, 1964, p. 131, John F. Kennedy Library Oral History Program.

53. Hilsman to Harriman. May 7, 1962. National Security Files. Boxes 131–139. Laos. John F. Kennedy Library.

54. Hilsman to Harriman. September 24, 1962. National Security Files. Boxes 131–139. Laos. John F. Kennedy Library.

55. Admiral Felt to Secretary McNamara. June 1962. National Security Files. Boxes 131–139. Laos. John F. Kennedy Library.

56. General Robert J. Wood to Major General Chester Clifton. September 12, 1962. National Security Files. Boxes 131–139. Laos. John F. Kennedy Library.

57. Thee, *Notes of a Witness,* pp. 303–13.

58. United States Operations in Laos and the Geneva Agreements, April 22, 1963. National Security Files. Boxes 131–139. Laos. John F. Kennedy Library.

59. National Security Action Memorandum No. 157. May 29, 1962; and Contingency Planning for Laos. June 12, 1962. National Security Files. Boxes 131–139. Laos. John F. Kennedy Library.

60. Hilsman to Harriman. April 4, 1962. National Security Files. Boxes 131–139. Laos. John F. Kennedy Library.

61. Contingency Planning for Laos. June 12, 1962. National Security Files. Boxes 131–139. Laos. John F. Kennedy Library.

62. Thee, *Notes of a Witness,* pp. 324–32.

63. Ibid., p. 326.

64. Ibid. p. 329.

65. Hilsman to Harriman. September 24, 1962. National Security Files. Boxes 131–139. Laos. John F. Kennedy Library.

66. Ambassador Leonard Unger to Secretary of State Rusk. April 20, 1963. National Security Files. Boxes 131–139. Laos. John F. Kennedy Library.

67. Stevenson, *End of Nowhere,* pp. 189–193.

68. Thomas L. Hughes to Secretary Rusk. Soviet Intransigence on Laotian Crisis. April 23, 1963. National Security Files. Boxes 131–139. Laos. John F. Kennedy Library.

69. Michael V. Forrestal, recorded interview by David K. Hall, January 2, 1987.

70. Ibid.

71. Quoted in William H. Sullivan, recorded interview by Dennis O'Brien, June 16, 1970, p. 27, John F. Kennedy Library Oral History Program.

72. Michael V. Forrestal, recorded interview by David K. Hall, January 2, 1987. See also: Stevenson, *End of Nowhere,* pp. 191–192.

73. Ambassador Bruce to Secretary Rusk. April 28, 1963. National Security Files. Boxes 131–139. Laos. John F. Kennedy Library; Stevenson, *End of Nowhere,* p. 307, fn. 35.

74. Thomas L. Hughes to Roger Hilsman. April 20, 1963. National Security Files. Boxes 131–139. Laos. John F. Kennedy Library.

75. Stevenson, *End of Nowhere,* p. 191.

76. Diplomatic Moves on Laos. April 20, 1963. National Security Files. Boxes 131–139. Laos. John F. Kennedy Library.

77. Thomas L. Hughes to Secretary Rusk. April 22, 1963. National Security Files. Boxes 131–139. Laos. John F. Kennedy Library.

78. Daily Report to the Secretary of Defense. April 22, 1963. National Security Files. Boxes 131–139. Laos. John F. Kennedy Library.

79. Quoted in Tom Wicker, *JFK and LBJ: The Influence of Personality on Politics* (New York: William Morrow and Co., 1968), p. 205.

80. Stevenson, *End of Nowhere,* pp. 195–197.

81. Ibid., pp. 197–99.

82. Ibid., pp. 201–208.

83. Ibid., pp. 208–10.

84. Arthur J. Dommen, *Keystone of Indochina* (Boulder, Colo.: Westview Press, 1985), pp. 92–136.

18

Efforts to Reduce the Risk of Accidental or Inadvertent War

BARRY M. BLECHMAN

If there is one interest that the United States and the Soviet Union hold in common, it is not to become embroiled in a military conflict that neither of them wants. Such a conflict could result accidentally, the result of a technical failure or the unauthorized use of military equipment, or it could happen inadvertently, the result of international events escalating beyond the point either of the great powers intended. The worst situation, of course, would be one in which nuclear weapons were used in an accidental or inadvertent conflict. Insofar as any military conflict between the two powers would incorporate a substantial risk of nuclear use, however, in the first instance this mutual interest of the United States and the USSR can be considered to extend to avoiding any accidental or inadvertent war.

Over the past three decades, the two nations have discussed a number of steps that might be undertaken in pursuit of this mutual interest; a subset of these measures actually has been implemented. Some of the measures are technical in character, pertaining both to the means available to the two governments to communicate with one another and to the risks associated intrinsically with the existence and operations of their military forces. Others are more political, pertaining primarily to the avoidance of situations in which the risk of inadvertent conflict might increase substantially. Both technical and political measures to reduce the risk of accidental or inadvertent conflict have sometimes resulted from unilateral actions, and in other cases have been implemented following negotiations and formal agreements. Examples of each type of measure are listed in Table 1.

We may consider those cases in which either power exercised restraint in its military response to an action by the opponent that it was likely to have considered provocative as constituting unilateral political actions to avoid inadvertent conflict. Two clear examples are the very limited Soviet response to the U.S. mining of Vietnamese harbors in 1972, an action that directly harmed Soviet merchant vessels, and the restrained U.S.–NATO response to the Soviet invasion of Czechoslovakia in 1968, an action that the United States perceived as not only offensive in itself, but as suggesting a broader threat to the status of Romania and Yugoslavia. In both cases, the restrained power seems to have recognized the overriding stake that its rival perceived in the situation and chose to curtail its own response lest a situation develop with a risk of inadvertent (or deliberate) conflict.

TABLE 1. Illustrations of Measures to Limit the Risk of Accidental or Inadvertent Conflict

Unilateral	Negotiated
Political Measures	
1. Soviet restraint when the U.S. mined Haiphong (1972)	1. Agreement on the "Prevention of Nuclear War" (1973)
2. U.S. restraint when the Soviets occupied Czechoslovakia (1968)	2. Talks on limiting arms sales (1977–79)
	3. Discussions of regional issues (1984–)
Technical Measures	
1. Measures to improve command and control systems*	1. "Hotline" (1963, 1971, and 1984)
2. Improvements in the safety of nuclear weapons	2. "Accidents" agreement (1971)
3. Improvements in the survivability of offensive forces	3. "Incidents at Sea" treaty (1972)
	4. "Nuclear Risk Reduction Centers" (1987–)

*Undated illustrations have occurred continuously.

Indeed, there is evidence that the great powers have tacitly developed certain norms that have governed their military actions in virtually all potential confrontations. Inferring these norms from a study of the behavior of the great powers' navies, James McConnell has suggested that essentially the United States and the Soviet Union act to minimize their potential losses, and the losses of their allies. All else being equal, there is a bias in their confrontations that favors the great power defending the political status quo, he argues, as seeking to revise the status quo would be to risk a significant conflict. The power whose ally is challenging the status quo may deploy military forces, he notes, in order to be seen to be playing a role in the situation, and also to prevent the dominant power from pursuing outcomes that would go beyond a restoration of the political status quo, but the challenger typically avoids any action that could lead to confrontation.[1]

Thus, the Soviet Union moved warships into the South China Sea in 1972, but kept them well away from the U.S. taskforce that was carrying out mining operations in response to the North Vietnamese Easter offensive. Similarly, the direct Western response to the Soviet reassertion of its authority in Prague was limited to a low level alert and a warning by President Lyndon Johnson to Soviet leaders not to press beyond Czechoslovakia.[2]

In addition to these unilateral measures, there have been negotiations and consultations involving the great powers that aimed to avoid the development of situations in the Third World that could lead to inadvertent war. In 1973 the two nations concluded the "Agreement on the Prevention of Nuclear War," in which they committed themselves to practice restraint in their relations with each other and with other countries "in circumstances which may endanger international peace and stability," and to consult with one another urgently should there ever appear to be a risk of nuclear conflict. The impact of this agreement is hard to discern, however, and many Americans believe that the Soviet Union violated the treaty almost before the ink was dry by not discouraging, and perhaps encouraging, the Egyptian-Syrian offensive in October 1973.[3]

As Janne Nolan describes separately in this volume, some American policy makers saw the U.S.–Soviet talks on arms transfers in 1977–78 as the beginnings of an effort to develop a common understanding of military activities in the Third World that might jeopardize the great powers' relationship and incur the risk of inadvertent conflict. Little came of these talks, however. More recently, the Reagan Administration initiated a series of consultations with the Soviet Union on specific regional situations, including South Asia, southern Africa, the Middle East, and Latin America. The results of these talks have not been made public, but it has been reported reliably that they have consisted largely of recitations of the two sides' public positions on each region, with little, if any, give and take, and no progress toward agreement.[4]

On the technical side, as well, far more has been accomplished through unilateral actions than through negotiations and agreements. Based on technical factors alone, it seems clear that the risk of accidental nuclear war is far lower today than it was thirty, or even twenty, years ago. The United States (and presumably the Soviet Union) has developed elaborate systems and procedures to control the possible use of its nuclear weapons, including the placement on most weapons of electronic devices that would preclude their detonation even if they were seized by unauthorized individuals. Both nations have also invested heavily to improve the ability of their strategic forces to survive preemptive attacks, thus reducing pressures they might otherwise feel in a crisis to initiate a nuclear exchange. Land-based missiles no longer require hours at unprotected sites to prepare for launch, bombers no longer have to be kept in the air to avoid being destroyed in a surprise attack, missiles launched from submarines have greater ranges, a factor that can be used to increase their survivability. These and many other steps that both great powers have taken would enable them to exercise restraint in a crisis, confident of the continued viability of the weapons each views as the ultimate guarantor of its security.

Technically oriented agreements to reduce the risk of accidental or inadvertent war, on the other hand, have proven relatively difficult to achieve. This is not due to a paucity of such ideas; there have been proposals for technical measures to reduce nuclear dangers virtually since the beginnings of the nuclear age. Indeed, the basis for "arms control" as an approach to international security—as contrasted to the then more familiar notion of "disarmament"—was a series of proposals in the 1950s for negotiated, technical means of reducing the risks associated with the existence of nuclear weapons and the operations of military forces. Preparations for the 1958 Surprise Attack Conference were particularly important in this regard. The idea behind the new approach was that although it did not seem possible to resolve the underlying political causes of U.S.–Soviet competition and thus to bring about disarmament, the independent risks implied by the continued existence of the two nations' nuclear forces might at least be contained through technical agreements.

Yet the Surprise Attack Conference failed miserably, and relatively little else has been set in place or even pursued seriously. The question of why the great powers have been slow to establish a more elaborate set of technical measures to reduce the risk of accidental or inadvertent nuclear war is compelling for anyone who believes, as does the writer, that much more could and should be done. To answer this question, I first describe those agreements that it has been possible to conclude and sketch the broader range of measures that could be considered, and then analyze the history of these efforts, seeking an understanding of these negotiations in the shifting context of U.S.–Soviet political relations.

THE RECORD AND POTENTIAL AGENDA

William J. Lynn has described more than twenty international agreements, conventions, and treaties in which both the United States and the Soviet Union participate, including measures to help manage crises or to build signatories' confidence that others do not intend to initiate conflict. A chart summarizing his list is reproduced as Table 2. Additional measures are now being discussed by the two countries. The contributions of most of these agreements to a reduced risk of accidental or inadvertent conflict, however, are relatively marginal and incidental; only four clusters of agreements deserve serious attention in this context.[5]

1. *Agreements intended to reduce the risk of inadvertent conflicts resulting from military deployments in Europe.* Adjacent deployments of very large concentrations of U.S. and Soviet military forces in Central Europe suggest considerable potential for incidents and inadvertent conflicts; several efforts have been made to reduce these dangers, but with only limited success.

The 1946 Berlin Air Corridor Agreement established flight rules and safety measures covering access to the divided city. It also established a quadripartite Berlin Air Space Center, in which air controllers from the four occupying powers exchange information (and complaints) about aircraft entering the corridors to the city. By all accounts, the center has served in this very limited capacity fairly well.

In the 1975 Helsinki Final Act, the United States, the Soviet Union, and the nations of Europe agreed to notify one another in advance of all military maneuvers exceeding a certain size, and established certain other voluntary measures intended to build confidence against surprise attacks. In the 1985 Stockholm agreement, these confidence-building measures were extended to require mandatory notification of virtually all maneuvers and to require observers at most large exercises. The agreement also permits challenge inspections of suspected violations.

These agreements barely scratch the surface of what might be undertaken to reduce the risk of accidental or inadvertent conflict in Europe. Additional measures have been discussed in both the Vienna talks on Mutual and Balanced Force Reductions, now in their twelfth year, and in negotiations in Stockholm that were part of a follow-up process to the Helsinki Agreement. In September 1986, the Stockholm talks were concluded successfully with a new agreement tightening the requirements for prior notification of maneuvers and extending requirements for observers to be invited from other nations. The new agreement, in an important precedent, also includes provisions specifying that charges of noncompliance are to be verified by on-site inspections on a challenge basis. Additional negotiations on confidence-building measures are expected to be held in Stockholm, beginning in late 1987 or 1988.

2. *Agreements to improve official communications links between the United States and the USSR.* In the first instance, the ability of the two powers to manage crises requires that appropriate officials be able physically to communicate and exchange information in a timely manner. Although normal diplomatic exchanges are the appropriate channel for most consultations between the great powers, the very short period of time required by modern armed forces to carry out operations of the gravest consequence suggests the desirability, under certain circumstances, of supplementary means of communication being available.

TABLE 2. Existing U.S.–Soviet Confidence-Building Measures

	Restrictions on Military Activities						Informational Confidence-Building Measures			
	Ban on Class of Weapon	Numerical Limits	Regional Demilitarization	Non-Proliferation	Limits on Testing	General Conduct Limits	Special Comm. Links	Mutual Inspections	Notification Rqmts	Implementing Body
UN Military Staff										X
Berlin Agreement										X
Antarctica Treaty			X	X	X			X		
Hotline Agreement							X			
Limited Test Ban					X					
Outer Space Treaty			X	X	X			X		X
Treaty of Tlatelolco			X	X	X			X		X
Non-Proliferation Treaty				X	X			X		X
Seabed Arms Control			X	X	X			X		
Nuclear Accident Agmt.							X		X	X
Biological Weapons Conv.	X				X					X
Space Cooperation Agmt.										
Incidents at Sea Agmt.						X			X	
U.S.–Soviet Basic Principles Agmt.						X				
ABM Treaty	X									X
SALT I		X								X
Prevention of Nuclear War						X				
Threshold Test Ban					X				X	
CSCE									X	
PNE Treaty					X			X	X	X
Envrnmtl Modification									X	X
SALT II		X			X				X	X

Source: Barry M. Blechman, *Preventing Nuclear War* (Bloomington, Ind.: Indiana University Press, 1985), p. 25.

The 1964 film, "Fail Safe," which concerns a prolonged attempt by an American president to persuade his Soviet counterpart that an atomic bomb about to be dropped on Moscow was the result of a technical failure—and thus avoid a Soviet retaliatory attack and the initiation of a major war—assumed that dedicated telephone lines existed between the two heads of state and also between the two sides' military headquarters. Even so, at one point, the film made clear the desirability of an additional capability to transmit electronic displays between the two capitals.

In reality, the two nations have chosen to establish only rudimentary channels of communications between their governments. In 1963, the United States and the USSR set up their first direct, official communications link—the Hotline. In a memorandum of understanding, the two great powers agreed to provide for direct communications between the two heads of state through the use of single telegraph-teleprinter terminals in each capital linked by both wire telegraph and radio telegraph circuits. In 1971 the two nations agreed to modernize this equipment, replacing the existing system with multiple teleprinters in each capital linked by a satellite circuit. In July 1984 the two agreed to modernize the system again, supplementing the existing system with a capability to transmit facsimiles, meaning that full pages of text could be exchanged instantaneously, as well as such printed graphic material as maps and charts.

An official listing of the instances in which the great powers have made use of the Hotline has never been released to the public. Reportedly, U.S. and Soviet leaders have exchanged urgent messages via this direct communications link on several occasions, including the 1967 Arab-Israeli War and the 1973 war in the Middle East, and the 1980 Polish crisis; its use has been hinted at, less reliably, on other occasions as well. There remains no official channel for real-time communications between the two governments, however. Even communications between each government and its embassy in the other's capital are constrained well short of the levels and means possible with modern technologies. Commercial telephone circuits or other means of communications might be available in an emergency, but the disadvantages of such ad hoc arrangements—not least of which being their susceptibility to eavesdropping—should be apparent.

In addition to improving the Hotline, the United States proposed in 1983 to establish a dedicated communications channel between the Defense Department and the Soviet Defense Ministry, and also to improve embassy communications capabilities. The USSR had refused to discuss either proposal.

At their summit in November 1985, President Ronald Reagan and Soviet General Secretary Mikhail Gorbachev agreed to "study the question at the expert level of centers to reduce nuclear risk . . . ." The proposal was to create centers in Moscow and Washington, parts of their respective governments, linked by modern means of communications, to carry out a variety of measures intended to reduce nuclear risks in normal times, and to be available as a supplemental channel for intergovernmental communications in the event of a crisis or other extraordinary situation (see below). The two sides' experts met initially in Geneva in May 1986 to study nuclear risk reduction centers. Assistant Secretary of Defense Richard Perle headed the American team and General Obukhov, the Soviet delegation. After four rounds of negotiations in Geneva, and supplementary discussions in Moscow and Washington, in May 1987 it was announced that the negotiators had initialed a draft agreement to establish nuclear risk centers. The formal agreement was signed in September 1987 by Secretary of State George Shultz and Soviet Foreign Minister Eduard Schevardnadze. The agreement established only a limited version of the Center concept, including limiting its communications channel to a non-real time system.[6]

3. *Agreements to reduce the risk of inadvertent incidents on the high seas.* As described separately in this volume by Sean Lynn-Jones, the United States and the Soviet Union concluded the Agreement on the Prevention of Incidents On and Over the High Seas in 1972, ending a series of incidents involving the two sides' naval forces that had been an increasing source of tensions and potential calamity. The agreement bans the harrassment of each other's ships and aircraft on the high seas and specifies rules of conduct to govern the surveillance of each other's naval forces in international waters. The two nations also agreed to notify one another of actions on the high seas that might represent a danger to navigation, and to arrange for their naval officers to meet annually to review compliance with the treaty. It was under the terms of this agreement that the United States informed the Soviet Union of its exercises in the Gulf of Sidra in March 1986 that led to combat with Libyan forces.

By all accounts, the agreement has worked very well, resulting in a greatly reduced number of incidents involving the two sides' navies. Additional measures intended to reduce the risk associated with military operations might also be desirable. In 1982 both the United States and the Soviet Union proposed in the bilateral arms control talks in Geneva to require the prior notification of certain types of long-range missile tests and bomber exercises; no agreement has been reached, however. These types of measures have the potential to reduce the risk that routine operations of strategic forces might be misunderstood and thus trigger a military response by the other side which, in turn, might lead to a confrontation. The two sides might also consider prohibiting certain types of military operations that raise particular concerns. No serious official attention has been given to operational restrictions, however, and serious arguments have been raised against such confidence-building measures.[7]

4. *Agreements intended specifically to reduce the risk of accidental nuclear war.* In the 1971 Agreement on Measures to Reduce the Risk of Outbreak of Nuclear War (known as the "Accidents Agreement"), the United States and the Soviet Union recognized officially that despite the most elaborate unilateral control procedures, the existence of nuclear weapons implied a continuing risk of war as a result of a technical malfunction, an unauthorized action, or a misinterpreted incident. The agreement seeks to contain these dangers by establishing certain procedures to be followed in the event of such an error. In the agreement, each side pledged to maintain and improve its own organizational and technical arrangements to guard against the unauthorized or accidental use of nuclear weapons. The sides also agreed to notify one another immediately in the event of such an accident or any other incident involving a possible nuclear detonation that could create a risk of nuclear war. And they agreed to notify one another prior to launching missiles beyond their national territory in the other's direction. The Accidents Agreement also includes a commitment to further consultations on the implementation of these provisions and on the possibility of additional measures serving the purposes of the Agreement.

Fortunately, there have been only one or two occasions in which the parties may have considered it useful to notify one another of a possible detonation leading to a risk of nuclear war.[8] They have discussed the specific procedures that would be followed, and have worked out coded messages that would be transmitted over the Hotline in the event of accidental or unauthorized missile launches; these negotiations took place in the Standing Consultative Commission, a body established by the Agreement. They also agreed in the summer of 1985—again in the Commission—that the possibility of nuclear terrorism would be considered one of the types of incidents requiring immediate notification under the terms of the agreement. The specific terms of this understanding have been kept secret.

A great deal more could be done to elaborate upon or expand the Accidents Agreement, or to implement the commitments the two nations already have undertaken in that document. For example, Victor Utgoff has proposed that the two sides agree to install certain devices at each other's missile sites that would warn of a missile launch, thus providing a double check on unilateral warning satellites and helping to avoid needless, and possibly provocative, responses to false alarms.[9] As a second example, a number of writers have suggested that the two sides could usefully discuss possible nuclear contingencies, seeking to develop guidelines for cooperative actions in the event such events occurred. The discussions would not seek agreements mandating specific courses of action, but only more general and necessarily tentative understandings of voluntary actions that could be attempted. The point would be to provide a script that might facilitate an effective joint response in a fast-breaking situation. Neither government has expressed interest in such proposals.[10]

CHRONOLOGY

The previous discussion has attempted to suggest something of the potential agenda of negotiated, technical measures to reduce the risk of accidental or inadvertent war. It would be a diversion from the present purpose to delve more fully into the substance of this agenda. But I would assert that more potentially could be accomplished, more than has been indicated in the prior discussion, and far more than has actually been achieved. Given their mutual interest in avoiding a war that neither wants, why have the great powers not seriously explored this more ambitious agenda? An understanding of the answer to this question can be obtained by looking closely at those instances in which measures to reduce the risk of accidental or inadvertent war have been concluded. Of particular importance, as we shall see, is the context of great-power relations in which the measure was negotiated, and the political agendas then being pursued by each nation's leaders.

To simplify the analysis, I will put aside the measures pertaining to the risk of conflict in Europe. These agreements are a subsidiary aspect of a special set of great-power concerns and are mediated by their respective allies in Europe; both factors complicate the question. Separate articles in this volume by Coit Blacker, Jonathan Dean, James Goodby, and others discuss this broader context of great-power relations in Europe.

The remaining agreements pertain specifically to the risk of accidental or inadvertent conflict deriving directly from the bilateral great-power relationship. They were achieved essentially in three periods: (a) during the two years following the Cuban missile crisis; (b) during the period of détente in the early 1970s; and (c) during the limited improvement in U.S.–Soviet relations since 1984. In this section I briefly describe each period. In the following section, the primary characteristics of the three periods are analyzed.

Post–Missile Crisis

The initial Hotline agreement was concluded on June 20, 1963, eight months after the Cuban missile crisis. The crisis had underscored the inadequacy of existing diplomatic channels for crisis communications. The two sides had found themselves compelled at times to indicate their own, and to try to understand their opponent's, intentions through the unspoken signals emitted by military movements—the idiom of military action, as Tom Schelling has termed it. They also resorted to a variety of irregular meetings outside normal diplomatic channels in their effort to bring the crisis to a peaceful resolution.

The idea of a direct communications link between the two heads of state had first been raised in the United States in connection with discussions of means to prevent surprise attacks in the mid-1950s, and at the abortive conference on that subject in 1958. The Soviet Union generally had denied the desirability of such measures except in the context of a treaty for general and complete disarmament. In December 1962, six weeks after the crisis, the United States presented a paper to the Eighteen Nation Disarmament Committee in which it proposed the creation of a direct communications link as one of several so-called "collateral measures" to prevent war. The break came in April, when the USSR announced its willingness to negotiate a separate agreement on the Hotline; the rest was easy.

It was also possible to make rapid progress toward a limited nuclear test ban during this period. The treaty banning tests in the atmosphere, under the seas, and in space was concluded in August. There also were reciprocal cuts in military budgets later in the period and a flurry of proposals to reduce certain types of nuclear forces. Additional measures to control arms and reduce the risk of inadvertent war proved elusive, however, and by the end of 1964, with a struggle for power within the Soviet Union and a deepening American involvement in Vietnam, the "window" seems to have closed.

Détente Period

Three of the technical agreements described in the previous section were negotiated and concluded in the brief period of U.S.–Soviet détente during the first Nixon Administration, coinciding with the successful negotiation of the Treaty Limiting Anti-Ballistic Missile Systems and the Interim Agreement on Offensive Weapons. The period can be said to have begun with the diplomatic initiatives leading to the opening of the Strategic Arms Limitation Talks in 1969; the end of the period is less clear. A case can be made that this brief flowering of apparently cooperative U.S.–Soviet relations had ended as early as the 1973 war in the Middle East. A number of additional agreements were concluded subsequent to the war, however, including two limited agreements on nuclear testing, and it was possible to conclude the SALT II Treaty as late as 1979. Some would thus argue that the period extended to the Soviet invasion of Afghanistan at the end of that year. Regardless, it is evident that beginning with the 1973 war, the combination of a shifting balance of military power, a more assertive Soviet stance in the Third World, and a series of U.S. setbacks—particularly the fall of allies in Saigon and Tehran—eroded the political foundations that had made possible unprecedented progress in arms control negotiations, including technical measures to reduce the risk of accidental and inadvertent war.

The Accidents Agreement and the first improvement to the Hotline were concluded in September 1971. They had been negotiated by a working group within the strategic arms limitation talks. At the opening of the talks in 1969, in a reversal of their usual roles, the Soviet Union had proposed that the two sides consider technical means of precluding accidental or unauthorized uses of nuclear-armed missiles, and the United States had agreed to discuss the subject. The Soviet Union continued to press the subject during the first two rounds of talks. Soviet negotiators argued for agreements on these subjects separate from the overall treaty on anti-ballistic missiles and offensive weapons, and they suggested a wider range of measures than were finally agreed to, including a requirement of prior notification of certain missile launches and bomber operations. The United States opposed the conclusion of a separate agreement until 1971, a reluctance that stemmed from its overall strategy for the talks, not from substantive reservations. During this early period, the United States was seeking to ensure that constraints on ABMs would be accompanied by constraints on offensive forces. Policymakers feared that the precedent of separate agreements on accidents and the Hotline would harm the effectiveness of this strategy.[11]

The Incidents at Sea Treaty was signed by President Richard Nixon and General Secretary Leonid Brezhnev at their summit in May 1972. A series of episodes involving Soviet and Western warships in the late 1960s, particularly—but not only—in the Mediterranean, had made clear that the two powers' efforts to maintain a close watch on each other's navies implied a serious risk of conflict. Quite apart from the simple danger of collisions, given the potential vulnerability of surface warships there was a risk that these interactions could lead one or the other to fire on a surveying vessel or aircraft in the mistaken belief that the monitoring force was actually preparing to attack.

The United States had first proposed negotiations on means to reduce naval incidents in 1967. The Soviets responded positively in 1970. Two rounds of talks, one in Moscow in the fall of 1971, the second in Washington in the spring of 1972, were sufficient to reach agreement.

There were of course many other agreements concluded during this period. The establishment of the Standing Consultative Commission by the 1971 Accidents Agreement did provide a forum that potentially could be helpful in negotiations about technical measures. The 1979 SALT II Treaty included a requirement of prior notification for certain types of missile tests and also established a mutually agreed data base on certain types of forces, but these measures have not been implemented as the treaty was never ratified. The other agreements concluded during this period had no direct relevance to reducing the risk of accidental or inadvertent nuclear war.

1984–85 Thaw

The deterioration of U.S.–Soviet relations, which began in the mid-1970s and accelerated markedly both with the invasion of Afghanistan in 1979 and the inauguration of the Reagan Administration in 1981, seems to have bottomed out at the end of 1983 when the Soviet Union walked out of both the START and INF arms negotiations, ostensibly in response to NATO's first deployments of intermediate-range missiles. The counterproductivity of this posture soon became apparent, however, and by September 1984, then Foreign Minister Andrei Gromyko had visited Washington unexpectedly to reinitiate the arms control dialogue; talks resumed in the Spring of 1984. In November 1985, President Reagan and Soviet General Secretary Gorbachev met in Geneva in what was perceived in the West, at least, as a useful meeting heralding both an improvement of relations and more rapid progress in arms negotiations.

By 1988, an agreement banning all intermediate-range missiles appeared imminent and progress had been made toward a treaty on central strategic systems as well.

It was possible during this brief period of improved relations, moreover, for the two nations to conclude several potentially useful, if very minor, measures to reduce the risk of accidental or inadvertent conflict.

In July 1984, the two great powers agreed to supplement the Hotline with a facsimile transmission capability. This ability to transmit instantaneously full pages of text from one capital to the other would reduce somewhat the time required for the two leaders to communicate with one another, and also make possible the receipt of charts or other visual materials. The requirement that each statement be written out prior to its transmission would preclude the sort of real-time exchange that would be possible on a telephone link, however. Most experts believe that such a delay is desirable, given that any ill-considered or misunderstood statement by the leader of a great power in a crisis situation could have catastrophic consequences.

The proposal to upgrade the Hotline was one of three means of improving communications that the United States had proposed to the USSR early in 1983. Expert groups met alternately in Washington and Moscow four times over the next year until the agreement was concluded. Throughout the process, the Soviets had expressed concern that the U.S. proposals were intended primarily to divert pressures for conclusion of an agreement to reduce nuclear arms in the Geneva talks. They clearly delayed conclusion of the Hotline agreement so as not to cloud the political signal intended by their walkout from the talks at the end of 1983, and then insisted successfully that the signing ceremony be handled in a very low-key fashion. Interestingly, though, they did agree to hold the meetings of experts, and then conducted them in a businesslike fashion at the very depth of the U.S.–Soviet relationship in the winter of 1983–84.[12]

The "understanding" that instances of nuclear terrorism would be considered subject to the provisions of the Accidents Agreement was reached in the Standing Consultative Commission in the summer of 1985, thus demonstrating the potential utility of this forum for negotiating technical arrangements. Both the talks that led to the understanding and the terms of the agreement itself have been kept secret by the two governments.

The joint statement issued by President Reagan and General Secretary Gorbachev at their November 1985 summit included a commitment to "study" the question of nuclear risk-reduction centers. This resulted from an unofficial initiative. In November 1982, a working group cochaired by Senators Sam Nunn and John Warner issued a report calling for the establishment of such centers. After receiving overwhelming Congressional endorsement of the idea, the two Senators elicited a letter from Robert McFarlane, then the President's national security advisor, in which the Administration expressed support for a limited version of it. The two senators took the letter to Moscow in September 1985 and brought back a favorable evaluation of the concept from Gorbachev. The mutual commitment to study the idea was then expressed in Geneva and meetings of experts on the subject were initiated in May 1986. As noted previously, conclusion of an agreement to establish a limited version of the nuclear risk-reduction center was announced in May 1987.

Conceived as a natural extension of the 1971 Accidents Agreement, the creation of nuclear risk-reduction centers could facilitate the negotiation and implementation of technical measures and institutional arrangements to reduce nuclear risks in normal times, and also provide a means of instantaneous communications between experts in the event of extraordinary situations. In normal times, the centers' agenda might be set by an annual meeting of the two nations' foreign and defense ministers. Among the measures they might agree to discuss would be exchanges of data on nuclear forces, dialogues on nuclear doctrines, prior notifications of certain types of nuclear operations, and possible cooperative actions in the event of contingencies involving nuclear threats by subnational organizations. Carrying out such discussions in normal times could help allay suspicions on the two sides, develop bureaucratic routines that might facilitate cooperation in unknown contingencies, and also build confidence in the efficacy of this technical channel, enabling it to be used to help manage crises.

It is difficult to predict the character of crises that may arise in the future. In case of extraordinary events, such as incidents involving nuclear terrorism or the destruction of civilian nuclear power reactors, the centers could provide the means for experts, working under the direction of national leaders, to communicate important technical and operational information rapidly and comprehensively. Although the centers would not be used to resolve the substantive aspects of great power confrontations, they could provide a means of supplementing diplomatic exchanges with technical expertise.

This *ambitious* concept of nuclear risk reduction center *is* far from a reality, however, and both governments continue to express serious reservations. The primary Soviet complaint—as in the case of the Hotline upgrade—is that the topic is a diversion from "more serious" arms control issues; accordingly, the Soviets are unlikely to permit the idea to move very far ahead in the absence of progress in the talks on offensive and defensive nuclear weapons in Geneva. The United States appears to be prepared to move forward with the concept independent of progress in the Geneva talks, but the official position envisions only a limited version of the centers being established in at least the first phase of implementation.[13]

ANALYSIS

Four factors are most important in understanding the great powers' poor record in negotiating technical measures to avoid accidental or inadvertent war: (a) the broader context of their relationship; (b) the interests that each side perceives in such agreements; (c) their respective perceptions of the other's interests and objectives; and (d) internal political and bureaucratic considerations.

The three periods during which these technical measures were negotiated have similar characteristics in terms of the great powers' broader relationship. Each was a time of improving relations; each followed a particularly difficult point in the relationship. In each period, the technical agreements were the consequences of the improvement in relations stimulated by other considerations. In no sense can the conclusion of these technical agreements be considered to have constituted a first order contribution to the broad improvement of relations. In effect, it appears that in each case the improvement in political relations made possible the implementation of ideas that had been around for some time. Primarily, the improving political context made it possible for advocates of these ideas within the bureaucracy to push them to a successful conclusion. To a degree, the political leaders' desire to impart some momentum to the improving relationship, and also to provide tangible evidence of its benefits to domestic and foreign audiences, may have added to the likelihood of success.

This was true for both nations in the post-missile crisis period. Sobered by the seriousness of that confrontation, both President Kennedy and General Secretary Khrushchev appear to have been determined to improve relations and to take steps that would make the management of future crises somewhat easier. They each perceived domestic political reasons to pursue such a course, as well as its substantive benefits. Given the rudimentary character of preparations in both countries for arms negotiations at the time, the Hotline (along with the Limited Test Ban Treaty) was one of the few measures readily available for quick agreement, and had practical benefits as well. Nothing else of lasting significance was accomplished during this period.

During the détente period of the early 1970s, the Soviets appear to have had the stronger motive to reach these kinds of agreements and, indeed, pushed harder for them. General Secretary Brezhnev appears to have been anxious to elicit evidence of the Soviet Union's equality with the United States as a "superpower"; what better evidence than special arrangements involving the two powers, and them alone, to deal with the dangers of nuclear weapons. As the U.S. opening to China was revealed to them, the Soviets' motives no doubt intensified, as they sought to impart the idea that U.S. moves with China were only games, while serious business could only be accomplished in Moscow. Only later in his first term, as President Nixon sought progress in arms control as means of offsetting the electoral consequences of the continuing war in Vietnam, did the conclusion of such technical arrangements as upgrading the Hotline become of interest to U.S. political leaders.

In the third period, political motivations were reversed and restored to their more common context. The Soviet Union was unenthusiastic about progress toward technical arrangements for fear of diverting pressures on the Reagan Administration to make concessions in the talks on the size and characteristics of strategic arsenals. During this time, they also believed that they benefited politically, particularly in Western Europe, from the image of President Reagan as an opponent of arms control—an image they did not want to dissipate by signing minor agreements, no matter how technical. The Reagan Administration's political motives were the opposite—to play up the importance of the arrangements under discussion in order to undercut the adverse political effects of the lack of progress in the arms talks. Only when Soviet leaders concluded that their stiff-necked approach was counterproductive, particularly among European audiences, did even the limited progress contained in the minor agreements negotiated during this period become possible.

Broadly speaking, there is an important, and probably permanent, asymmetry in the ways in which the United States and the USSR view technical agreements to reduce the risk of accidental or inadvertent war. The whole concept of arms control, after all, is an American one. The idea that the stability of political relations, and the risk of war, might depend to some extent on the technical characteristics of military forces and weapons and, therefore, that technical means to contain those risks are possible and worth pursuing, is not one that fits comfortably in the Soviet worldview. On the strategic level, the Soviets are inclined to look at the underlying policy context associated with the deployment of a weapon system—the political objectives it is intended to serve—in determining its effect on stability. Their term for stability used in this context is *ustoichivost*. Very recently, Soviet arms control specialists have begun to refer to the word *stabilnost* when referring to stability, a word that appears closer to the Western technical connotation. This latter word is not found in Soviet military dictionaries, however, and appears to have gained favor solely because Soviet spokesmen found it a useful argument against the Pershing II missiles being deployed in West Germany.[14]

It is not that the Soviets do not understand the technical risks that these measures are intended to reduce. They simply attribute far less importance to them among the complex of factors that might lead to a war than would many Americans. Moreover, the great discipline and tight control that characterizes the Soviet military (and society generally) probably causes them to discount the risk of unauthorized uses of nuclear weapons more than might be the case in the West. In addition, the Soviets probably perceive some benefit in the continuance of public concerns about the danger of nuclear war; this unease in Europe and the United States clearly increases political pressures on American leaders to make concessions in arms talks.

It is thus only in extraordinary circumstances, such as the period in the very early 1970s, that the Soviets will perceive greater incentive than U.S. policymakers to pursue technical arrangements to reduce the risk of accidental or inadvertent conflict. More often, the Soviets may wish to avoid concluding agreements that might serve to ease public concerns about nuclear war and, thus, pressure on Western leaders to make concessions in other arms talks, particularly as the Soviets may not believe that such technical arrangements would be particularly important in reducing nuclear dangers. Moreover, the Soviets know that most often the United States will take the lead in proposing technical arrangements, as it did in the 1950s and 1960s, and in the later 1970s and 1980s. This is to the Soviets' tactical advantage, of course, as a technical proposal then becomes a U.S. position, to which Soviet representatives may "reluctantly" agree, regardless of their true evaluation of the proposal, in exchange—formally or tacitly—for an American concession on a Soviet initiative.

The greater U.S. emphasis on technical aspects of arms control problems has been remarked on with regard to virtually every negotiation. In general terms, what this means is that if technical arrangements are to be negotiated, they must be proposed by the American side. The two nations may have a symmetrical interest in avoiding accidental or inadvertent war, but their interest in concluding measures to reduce that risk is asymmetrical and perceived as such by both parties.

As a result, if technical arrangements are to be concluded, in most cases the United States must be prepared to pay a price for them. Perceiving the conclusion of such measures to be more in the American interest than in their own, the Soviets typically seek to trade movement in this area for American concessions on subjects of greater interest to them (or related political issues). The successful negotiation of technical arrangements, therefore, requires that American decision makers must perceive the proposals to be of sufficient importance to give ground elsewhere. Given this Soviet perspective, and insofar as American political leaders and foreign policymakers typically have attributed relatively little importance to the types of technical arrangements discussed in this article, little progress has been made in their implementation.

It is instructive that in his 1200-page memoir of the first Nixon Administration, Henry Kissinger never mentions the Accidents Agreement or the Hotline improvement.[15] The subject typically is seen as something that probably should be dealt with, but not of great interest or consequence—a matter that can be left to specialists. It is certainly not something that merits any significant concession on the American side.

Given the potential cost of an accidental or inadvertent war, one might think that both nations would be more enthusiastic about negotiating measures that seem likely to help reduce these risks. The lack of enthusiasm is understandable, however. To begin with, the risk of such a war is generally believed to be extremely low already. The controls that have been placed on nuclear forces are quite substantial and redundant; decision makers have confidence in them. No one likes to contemplate catastrophic events, in any case, and the historic behavior of the two powers has been very cautious—so far, at least.

Second, the contribution of any single technical measure is likely to be very small, and a conditional one in any case, which means that it cannot be quantified in tangible terms; thus the value of any measure is likely to be perceived as minute. In arguing for the negotiation of a technical arrangement, one can only describe the extremely far-fetched circumstances the measure is designed to avoid. While the case may be clear intellectually, it is only rarely compelling politically—particularly when the Soviets may be demanding a tangible price for their acquiescence. Decision makers are concerned lest they be seen to have traded away an important concession for a technical step of little value; or, at least, they do not perceive any political gain in taking the risk that such would be the eventual judgment of the media and the public.

Within both governments there are also bureaucratic obstacles to the conclusion of technical arrangements. Most such potential arrangements pertain to military forces; neither country's armed forces are enthusiastic about providing information to the other and are distinctly hostile when it comes to arrangements that might limit the flexibility of their operations. Whereas the State Department might often see diplomatic reasons to seek to offset this hostility when it comes to the structural arms talks, the technical character of the arrangements being discussed here is so far removed from the experience of most foreign service officers that such proposals rarely draw backers at State. At the same time, the idea of the two sides' armed forces establishing communications channels or other exchanges has problems of its own. Both the Soviet Foreign Office and the U.S. State Department see communications between the two countries as their own bailiwick; neither encourages competition. On the Soviet side, there is also a special problem concerning political control of the armed forces. The U.S. proposal to establish a direct communications link between the two defense ministries appears to have been dismissed out of hand for this reason.

As has been noted, U.S. leaders have at times perceived political motivations for moving on technical arrangements, even if a price has to be paid for it. At times, public concerns about the risk of nuclear war have seemed to be getting out of hand. Both in the post-missile crisis period and in the early 1980s, the Administration probably perceived technical measures—in addition to their substantive benefit—as helping to ease these public concerns and thus to reduce the political cost of tense U.S.–Soviet relations. They may also have viewed concessions in this area as diverting pressures for concessions in what were seen as more important negotiations—precisely why the Soviet leadership was unenthusiastic.

Even so, just as technical measures are not valued highly within the government, their value as political currency is not great either. Indeed, the two are no doubt related. In short, neither the United States nor the Soviet Union has perceived any urgency in negotiating technical measures to reduce the risk of accidental or inadvertent nuclear war. Although each side in special circumstances has perceived political incentives to conclude such arrangements, for the most part such ancillary benefits have constituted only weak arguments for the concessions necessary to obtain agreement.

Thus, the conclusion of technical arrangements to reduce the risk of accidental or inadvertent war has proceeded at only a slow pace, awaiting the juxtaposition of the maturation of such ideas within the two governments and a favorable constellation of political relationships that would enable the proposals' supporters to advance the measures in the wake of the main focus of arms negotiations. These propitious circumstances still seem a long way off.

Notes

1. James M. McConnell, "The 'Rules of the Game': A Theory on the Practice of Superpower Naval Diplomacy," *Soviet Naval Diplomacy,* Bradford Dismukes and James McConnell, eds. (New York: Pergamon, 1979), pp 240–80.

2. These and related incidents are described in Barry M. Blechman and Stephen S. Kaplan, *Force Without War* (Washington, D.C.: Brookings, 1977) and Stephen S. Kaplan, *The Diplomacy of Power* (Washington, D.C.: Brookings, 1981).

3. Descriptions and text of the agreements cited in this article can be found in U.S. Arms Control and Disarmament Agency, *Arms Control and Disarmament Agreements* (Washington, D.C.: 1980).

4. The recent U.S.–Soviet regional discussions are described in the articles by Alexander L. George and Harold H. Saunders in this volume.

5. William J. Lynn, "Existing U.S.–Soviet Confidence-Building Measures," *Preventing Nuclear War,* Barry M. Blechman, ed. (Bloomington; Ind.: Indiana University Press, 1985), pp. 24–51.

6. The summit statement was reprinted in the *New York Times* (November 22, 1985). Articles reporting conclusion of the agreement appeared in the *New York Times* (May 6, 1987) and the *Washington Post* (May 6, 1987). The final agreement is available from the White House press office. A discussion of the concept can be seen in Barry M. Blechman and Michael Krepon, *Nuclear Risk Reduction Centers* (Washington, D.C.: Center for Strategic and International Studies, 1986). Proposals for improving U.S.–Soviet direct communications are discussed in Michael Landi, et al., "Improving the Means for Intergovernmental Communications in Crisis," *Survival* (September/October 1984): 200–14.

7. An evaluation of operational confidence-building measures can be found in Alan J. Vick and James A. Thomson, "The Military Significance of Restrictions on the Operations of Strategic Nuclear Forces," in *Preventing Nuclear War,* pp. 99–125.

8. U.S.–Soviet cooperation to avert what appeared to be an imminent South African test of a nuclear weapon is an exception. The unexplained flash in the South Atlantic in 1979 that appeared to have been a nuclear explosion might also have been an exception. See Richard K. Betts, "A Diplomatic Bomb for South Africa?" *International Security* (Fall 1979): 91–115; and E. Marshall, "Flash Not Missed by Vela Still Veiled In Mist," *Science* (November 30, 1979): 1051–52.

9. The proposal is explained in Victor Utgoff, "On-Site, Automated Monitoring: An Application for Reducing the Probability of Accidental Nuclear War," in *Preventing Nuclear War,* pp. 126–43.

10. Recent books pertinent to this discussion include: Albert Carnesale, et al., *Hawks, Doves, and Owls* (Cambridge, Mass.: Harvard University Press, 1985); *Preventing Nuclear War,* and William Ury, *Beyond the Hotline* (Boston: Houghton Mifflin, 1985).

11. Gerard Smith, *Doubletalk: The Story of SALT I* (New York: Doubleday, 1980), pp. 280–300).

12. This information is based on confidential interviews with U.S. government officials.

13. Blechman and Krepon, *Nuclear Risk Reduction Centers.*

14. The writer is indebted to Douglas Hart for pointing out this usage in Soviet writings.

15. Henry Kissinger, *White House Years* (Boston: Little, Brown, 1981).

19

The Incidents at Sea Agreement

SEAN M. LYNN-JONES

The 1972 Agreement on the Prevention of Incidents at Sea[1] is an example of successful U.S.–Soviet cooperation in security matters. Although it was almost ignored in both the American and Soviet announcements of the various agreements that emerged from the May 1972 Moscow summit, the agreement has helped to avert potentially dangerous incidents between the U.S. and Soviet navies. Before the agreement, encounters between U.S. and Soviet warships on the high seas frequently led to tense situations as opposing vessels maneuvered to disrupt one another's formations. Since the agreement was signed, fewer serious naval confrontations have occurred, and those that take place have not generated dangers of escalation or political crises. The U.S. and Soviet navies have cooperated at the working level to implement the agreement, despite the fluctuations in U.S.–Soviet relations since 1972.

This chapter will review the history of the Incidents at Sea Agreement and the nature and possible causes of the naval incidents that led to its negotiation and signing. After a discussion of the process of negotiation and the provisions of the agreement, the factors contributing to its successful negotiation and implementation will be considered.

BACKGROUND AND HISTORY OF THE INCIDENTS AT SEA AGREEMENT

Defining Incidents at Sea

The term "incident at sea" can be applied to a variety of situations resulting from different maritime activities. At the most general level, it means an action on the high seas by a ship or plane that endangers, or is alleged to endanger, another vessel or aircraft. Some actions of U.S. and Soviet naval units that fit into this category include violations of the International Regulations for Preventing Collisions at Sea ("Rules of the Road"),[2] close, high-speed surveillance ("buzzing"), simulated attacks on ships or planes, accidental firing upon vessels during naval exercises, and other actions that interfere with the safe navigation of ships, such as shining searchlights on the bridge of vessels.

1. *Dangerous Maneuvers.* Naval units in close proximity can engage in a variety of maneuvers that force other vessels to take evasive action to avoid imminent collisions. Former U.S. Chief of Naval Operations Admiral Elmo Zumwalt has described such activities "as an extremely dangerous, but exhilarating, running game of

'chicken'."[3] Many incidents of this sort have occurred between U.S. and Soviet ships, including some that have led to collisions. Although the Rules of the Road are intended to prevent such maneuvers, Soviet vessels often have exploited ambiguities in the rules to play "chicken" or to "shoulder" U.S. vessels off course, particularly during carrier operations or refueling at sea. The Rules of the Road are intended for use by civilian vessels, and thus do not cover all the situations that might arise between military vessels. Under the Rules of the Road, for example, a Soviet destroyer might technically have the right of way as it maneuvered in front of a U.S. aircraft carrier, even though the American vessel would not be able to give way without endangering its planes as they landed or took off. Although the U.S. Navy generally has blamed the Soviets for such incidents, senior naval officials admit that the United States has been at fault in some cases. As Admiral Zumwalt has written, "as any teen-aged boy knows, it takes two to make a drag race."[4] Prior to the 1972 agreement, the United States and the Soviet Union often issued diplomatic protests that accused the other side of violations of the Rules of the Road.

2. *Close Air Surveillance ("Buzzing").* U.S. and Soviet aircraft have frequently flown close passes near opposing vessels for reconnaissance purposes. The Soviets have protested that such actions violate the Rules of the Road and threaten the safe navigation of their vessels; but their own actions are not significantly different.[5] They have been particularly concerned over the U.S. practice of dropping sonar buoys from aircraft to track Soviet submarines, as such actions, they claim, endanger the safety of their submarines.[6]

3. *Simulated Attacks.* Soviet and U.S. naval vessels often have simulated attacks by aiming guns, missile-launchers, torpedo tubes, other weapons, and sensor systems at each other's ships and planes. For example, in an encounter between a U.S. ship and accompanying naval aircraft and several Soviet warships during the 1970 Jordanian crisis, the Soviet ships "went to battle stations . . . ran surface-to-air missiles out on their launchers, and appeared to track the departing U.S. aircraft with their fire control radars."[7] Such actions are at least unnerving to the naval officers and men who experience them. In times of acute international tension, they could increase the incentives for preemptive strikes.

4. *Accidental Firing During Exercises.* Naval exercises involving the use of live ammunition obviously can endanger stray warships or merchant vessels. Such an incident apparently occurred on March 8, 1963, when a Soviet trawler allegedly came under fire from U.S. naval vessels seventy miles east of Norfolk, Virginia. The United States dismissed the possibility that there was any danger to the Soviet vessel, noting that the incident took place in a U.S. Navy operations area.[8] The absence of prior notification of exercises and the interest of both countries in observing the other's maneuvers as closely as possible increase the probability of such incidents. In this case, the Soviet trawler was almost certainly engaged in surveillance of U.S. naval activities.

5. *Other Harassment.* There are a variety of other ways in which U.S. and Soviet vessels can harass one another at sea. The warships of both countries have illuminated the bridges of opposing vessels with powerful searchlights. The Soviets, for example, alleged that a U.S. patrol vessel off Florida passed within 100 meters of the Soviet passenger steamer *Turkeniya* on May 28, 1964, "and repeatedly lit up the hull and the captain's bridge of the vessel with a powerful searchlight, blinding the navigating personnel and creating a danger of collision."[9] Soviet vessels have en-

gaged in similar behavior on a number of occasions. U.S. and Soviet ships can also engage in harassment by firing flares at one another.

There have been hundreds of incidents involving U.S. and Soviet surface ships and aircraft, although the details of these encounters have not always been made public. Many of these incidents occurred in the late 1960s and early 1970s, when the Soviet Navy began to assert itself on the world's oceans. Former U.S. Secretary of the Navy John Warner has said that the two superpowers "were just waiting for an accident to happen" during this period.[10] Additional incidents have involved collisions between Soviet and U.S. submarines, some of which were carrying nuclear weapons. Such collisions have taken place in Soviet territorial waters, as well as under the high seas.[11] The 1972 Agreement on Incidents at Sea, however, covers primarily surface and aerial maneuvering. This paper will therefore concentrate on incidents involving surface ships and aircraft.

The Motivations and Causes of Incidents at Sea

The most difficult question to be addressed in considering the causes of incidents at sea is whether the United States or the Soviet Union has deliberately authorized its naval commanders to harass the vessels of the other. Some incidents doubtless are the result of the excessive zeal or incompetence of local naval commanders. Admiral Zumwalt has argued that ship captains bear the primary responsibility for naval incidents: "It was always my opinion that the leadership on both sides was less anxious to play the kind of game I have described than peppery young ship captains were."[12] Given the intense rivalry between the United States and the Soviet Union, it would be surprising if naval personnel did not occasionally play chicken with their opponents at sea. The increase in incidents that seems to have occurred in the late 1960s and early 1970s, by this account, was the inevitable result of the larger Soviet presence at sea and more frequent interaction with U.S. forces. The inexperience of Soviet captains also may have played a role during this period.

But incidents also may serve some political purposes, possibly justifying their deliberate use as instruments of policy. Seen in this light, naval harassment and dangerous maneuvering are variations on the venerable practice of gunboat diplomacy.[13] These actions constitute limited applications of naval force to achieve some political objective. The Soviet Union and the United States may have purposefully engaged in some instances of harassment or dangerous maneuvering at sea, or at least given such actions de facto approval by not disciplining the commanders involved.

Although any discussion of Soviet motivations is necessarily speculative, Soviet harassment of U.S. naval vessels appears to have served several purposes. First, and most generally, Soviet harassment of U.S. ships, particularly simulated attacks on aircraft carriers, demonstrated to the U.S. Navy that Soviet warships can deny the United States the freedom of action that it has traditionally enjoyed on the high seas. Soviet anticarrier forces have been deployed in crises to deter possible actions directed against Soviet interests.[14] The awareness of the Soviet presence and capabilities may constrain U.S. actions in a crisis, as Admiral Zumwalt has suggested.[15] The Soviets appear to have at times had this objective in mind. Admiral Sergei Gorshkov, commander-in-chief of the Soviet Navy for 29 years, has written:

> In a series of instances, our ships and naval aviation have demonstrated operational and active actions as a result of which some foreign governments became convinced

that they could not consider their aircraft carriers and submarines "invisible," "untouchable," and in the event of war "invulnerable" in whatever areas they may be located.[16]

Second, the Soviets clearly have used harassment as a means of conveying their resentment over U.S. naval operations in areas the Soviet Union apparently regards as home waters. These areas include the Black Sea, the Baltic Sea, and the Sea of Japan. The United States has sent two Sixth Fleet destroyers into the Black Sea every six months to assert its rights under the Montreux Convention. Regarding these actions as provocative, the Soviets have dispatched naval vessels to shadow and harass U.S. ships throughout their voyage through the Black Sea.[17] Similarly, in the Sea of Japan, Soviet land-based attack aircraft routinely have simulated missile attacks on U.S. carriers.[18] Many incidents of harassment of U.S. naval vessels have occurred in this region, including the well-known collisions of the U.S. destroyer *Walker* with Soviet vessels in 1967 and the March 1984 collision of the U.S. carrier *Kitty Hawk* and a Soviet submarine. Although these actions could be attributed to the aggressiveness or incompetence of local Soviet commanders, it seems more likely that at least some of them were the result of deliberate policy. Soviet diplomatic protests following incidents in the Sea of Japan claim that "U.S. ships show no regard for existing international norms, grossly violate international norms for the prevention of collisions of ships at sea, and take a number of illegal actions against the Soviet ships in this area, coming dangerously close to them." But the real motivation for Soviet actions seems to be their belief that "the very fact of U.S.–Japanese exercises close to Soviet shores cannot be regarded as anything but a premeditated, organized provocative military demonstration."[19]

Third, the Soviet Union may use harassment for tactical military purposes. Interfering with the flight operations of U.S. carriers and otherwise obstructing U.S. naval activities can prevent the launch of an aircraft that might deliver an attack or, more probably, track a Soviet submarine. Soviet vessels may attempt to disrupt U.S. naval operations even when there is no immediate U.S. threat, as such maneuvers must be practiced in order to be performed successfully in actual naval combat. Moreover, harassment may enable the Soviets to obtain information on the likely U.S. responses to attempts to interfere with combat operations.

Finally, Soviet harassment, especially simulated attacks, may demonstrate naval capabilities to internal Soviet audiences. Overflights of U.S. aircraft carriers, for example, demonstrate the value of naval aviation and the need for increased spending in this area. Many Soviet naval activities and writings may be intended for domestic consumption by political decision makers, as naval expenditures have not always been given priority in the Soviet Union.[20]

Many of the U.S. reasons for harassment of Soviet warships probably do not differ significantly from Soviet motivations. Like the Soviets, U.S. units have harassed opposing vessels to impede their operational effectiveness. U.S. warships also may have harassed Soviet merchant ships or trawlers on the grounds that such vessels were probably engaged in surveillance of U.S. naval forces and operations. Some naval officers even have suggested that harassment be employed deliberately to reduce the ability of Soviet vessels to launch a surprise attack.[21]

There are, however, some differences between possible U.S. and Soviet motivations for provoking incidents at sea. The U.S. Navy long has been established as a preeminent force on the world's oceans; it need not engage in deliberate harassment to make its presence felt. In addition, U.S. forces have different missions and capabilities than their Soviet counterparts. Air surveillance of Soviet warships may be considered vital due to the paucity of naval information released by the Soviet Union. The United States also has a much greater capability to engage in aerial reconnaissance, given its monopoly on larger aircraft carriers. U.S. naval units are able to track Soviet submarines and to force them to the surface. The Soviets lack comparable antisubmarine warfare (ASW) capabilities. These differences in capabilities and objectives tend to produce asymmetries in motivations.

Incidents also are produced by an action-reaction process. In the Sea of Japan, for example, the commander-in-chief of the U.S. Seventh Fleet, exasperated by continued Soviet harassment, issued instructions that his ships were to maintain course and speed even if a collision resulted, and he recommended claiming damages from the Soviet Union in the event of a collision.[22] This sort of reaction to incidents at sea can create a vicious circle in which incidents begin to take on a life of their own and provoke continued reprisals. Regardless of the potential utility of some forms of harassment, there are clearly inherent dangers in incidents at sea. Both the United States and the Soviet Union eventually recognized that the risks of naval harassment undermine any justification for its unconstrained continuance. The 1972 agreement was the result of this mutual recognition of the dangers of naval incidents.

Negotiating the Agreement

The increasing frequency and severity of U.S.–Soviet naval incidents led the United States to propose negotiations on the subject in 1967.[23] This overture was ignored for over two years until the Soviets surprised U.S. officials in 1970 by proposing that negotiations be opened in the spring of 1971. The United States did not respond immediately, but initiated an interagency review of the problem to formulate a position. The interagency process was chaired by Ambassador Herbert Okun, a State Department Soviet expert, and involved representatives of the Navy, Department of Defense, and the National Security Council (NSC). National Security Adviser Henry Kissinger and senior NSC staff member Helmut Sonnenfeldt were directly involved. The interagency review team compiled and analyzed information on all previous U.S.–Soviet incidents at sea and the subsequent protests by either party. It sought to develop a negotiating position that would not constrain U.S. or allied naval missions or activities while preventing dangerous Soviet maneuvers. The United States could not accept the inclusion of limitations on submarine activities, since senior naval officers feared such a provision might lead the Soviet Union to propose the establishment of submarine operating zones in which ASW would be prohibited.[24] Given the U.S. lead in ASW technology, this step would benefit the Soviet Union. Moreover, the United States was reluctant to discuss submarine incidents, as any negotiated provisions might force the disclosure of submarine locations and compromise strategic and reconnaissance missions.

Navy representatives also were concerned over the possible negotiation of a distance formula that would govern how closely U.S. vessels and aircraft could approach their Soviet counterparts. Any form of distance limitation could interfere with naval operations and complicate surveillance of Soviet warships. Soviet protests following previous incidents indicated that they were particularly irritated by U.S. close air surveillance. The question of a distance formula thus became a critical issue in the subsequent negotiations.

The U.S. delegation formulated detailed proposals prior to the start of any talks and considered the likely Soviet responses. The U.S. negotiating position essentially called for clarifying and expanding the Rules of the Road. The United States was particularly interested in preventing Soviet vessels from shouldering U.S. aircraft carriers and thus disrupting their flight operations. Having formulated its position, the United States accepted the Soviet offer to negotiate in June 1971, and discussions were scheduled to begin in Moscow in October of that year.

The U.S. delegation to Moscow consisted primarily of participants in the interagency review process. It was headed by John Warner, then undersecretary of the Navy. Okun was the vice-chairman. Vice-Admiral Harry Harty, senior military advisor to the delegation, represented the Joint Chiefs of Staff. Other members of the U.S. delegation included Charles Pittman of the State Department's legal office; Commander William Lynch, special assistant to Warner for law of the sea; Captain Edward Day, an expert in naval aviation assigned to the State Department's Bureau of Politico-Military Affairs; Captain Robert Rawlins of the Navy's policy planning branch; and Captain Robert Congdon of the Defense Department's Office of International Security Affairs.

The U.S. negotiating team was the highest-ranking U.S. military delegation to visit the Soviet Union since 1945. But the Soviet delegation consisted of even higher-ranking officials, conveying a clear interest in the talks. Headed by Admiral Vladimir Kasatonov, deputy commander of the Soviet Navy, the team also included Admiral V. A. Alexeyev of the naval staff, Rear-Admiral Motrokhov, chief navigator of the Soviet Navy, and Colonel-General Vishinsky of Naval Air. The delegation thus included the second, third, fourth, and fifth highest-ranking officers of the Soviet Navy. In addition to demonstrating their interest, the high rank of the Soviet delegation may have reduced the constraints that central authorities generally impose on Soviet negotiators.

Although many naval officers and some U.S. experts on Soviet foreign policy had been skeptical about the prospects for the talks,[25] the Soviet delegation warmly welcomed their American counterparts. In the negotiations, the Soviets accepted the U.S. agenda and agreed that geographical constraints on submarine operations would not be discussed. The announcement of President Richard Nixon's planned visit to Moscow on October 12 created an even more propitious political atmosphere.

The actual negotiations were conducted in surface and air working groups. The surface working groups discussed the Rules of the Road, signaling, disruption of flight operations, the definition of naval platforms, and the training of weapons and sensor systems on enemy vessels. Among these issues, the most contentious was the matter of a distance formula that would modify the Rules of the Road by, for example, prohibiting maneuvers within a certain distance of opposing warships. In contrast to the general U.S. pattern of seeking highly specific agreements, the American negotiators refused to accept Soviet proposals for a distance formula, preferring to stress good judgment and general principles. Similar disagreements arose in the talks between U.S. and Soviet negotiators in the air working group.

Despite the lack of agreement on any distance limitations, the negotiations made considerable progress. In talks that often lasted up to 16 hours per day, the two delegations reached agreement on most issues. The U.S. negotiators were not surprised by the Soviet proposals, having anticipated them in their preparations. This advance preparation, as well as Soviet concessions on critical issues such as the dropping of sonar buoys from aircraft, enabled the two delegations to initial a memorandum of understanding covering points on which they had reached agreement and listing outstanding issues, including the distance formula, which were to be discussed in Washington in May 1972.

On the American side, the negotiations and the memorandum were subjected to a second, more intensive, interagency review before the talks resumed. As the initially skeptical military departments now confronted the possibility that an agreement actually would be reached, they increased their level of representation and vigorously objected to any suggestion that a distance formula be accepted. The Navy argued that such a provision would interfere with surveillance activities. As the Navy was concerned that the State Department might be overly conciliatory, Lawrence Eagleburger of the Pentagon's Office of International Security Affairs chaired the second interagency review.

The seemingly intransigent attitude of the Navy at this stage of the review might be traced to naval opposition to the very idea of agreement with the Soviets. Naval officers accustomed to thinking of their Soviet counterparts as rivals might understandably be reluctant to enter into any form of cooperation with the "enemy." Indeed, some naval officers might even favor the continuation of incidents at sea that demonstrate the intensity of U.S.–Soviet hostility and thus provide a basis for increased naval appropriations. They might fear that an agreement would exert a lulling effect on Congressmen who would interpret any evidence of reduced tension and rivalry at sea as grounds for reductions in U.S. naval expenditures.[26]

The distance formula was the principal issue in the second round of talks. Although the Soviets intially seemed adamant on the distance issue, they eventually dropped their objections in return for an agreement to discuss it in the future. They apparently continued to feel strongly about the issue, as indicated by Soviet Captain First Rank V. Serkov, a member of the Soviet negotiating team, in the September 1972 issue of *Morsky Sbornik*:

> It is quite evident that the Agreement would more fully serve its purpose if it contained fixed maximal permissible distances for the approach of ships and aircraft . . . Therefore the Commission appointed in accordance with Article X will have to develop practical recommendations relative to concrete fixed distances which must be observed when approaching warships and aircraft.[27]

Despite their misgivings, the Soviets were apparently satisfied with the rest of the agreement. Their interest in negotiating some form of constraints on dangerous maneuvers and harassment at sea overrode their desire for a distance limitation. Soviet negotiators wanted an agreement and were reconciled to making serious concessions to obtain it. Soviet interest was demonstrated not only by the warm welcome accorded to the U.S. delegation in Moscow, but also by the complacent Soviet naval reaction to the U.S. mining of Haiphong harbor, which occurred in the middle of the Washington negotiations. Admiral Kasatonov actually watched Nixon's speech announcing the mining at John Warner's Georgetown house. After a pause, he remarked: "This is a very serious matter. Let us leave it to the politicians to settle this one." This comment implicitly ackowledged that the naval talks were too important to be disrupted even by U.S. actions that endangered Soviet merchant ships. As Okun later remarked of the incident: "We were highball to highball, and they were the first to clink."[28]

The agreement was initialed by Warner and Kasatonov in Washington and formally signed by Warner, then secretary of the navy, and Admiral Gorshkov on May 25, 1972, during the Moscow summit meeting. It represented the first important military agreement between the two superpowers since World War II. In announcing the results of the summit to Congress, Nixon contended that the agreement would have a "direct bearing on the search for peace and security in the world" and was "aimed at significantly reducing the chances of dangerous incidents between our ships and aircraft at sea."[29]

The Provisions of the Agreement

The 1972 Agreement on the Prevention of Incidents at Sea serves four basic purposes: (1) regulation of dangerous maneuvers; (2) restriction of other forms of harassment; (3) increased communication at sea; and (4) convening regular naval consultations and exchanges of information. Its provisions address many of the possible causes of U.S.– Soviet naval incidents, particularly those arising from misunderstanding or misinterpretation of the other party's action.

1. *Regulation of Dangerous Maneuvers.* The agreement reaffirms the Rules of the Road, and Article II specifically requires ships to remain well clear of one another to avoid hindering the evolution of formations, and to show particular care in approaching ships engaged in launching or landing aircraft, as well as ships engaged in underway replenishment.
2. *Restriction of Other Harassment.* Articles II and IV of the agreement also prohibit simulated attacks or the launching of objects in the direction of passing ships of the other party, the use of searchlights to illuminate navigation bridges, the performance of "various aerobatics" over ships,[30] and the dropping of various objects that would be hazardous to ships or constitute a hazard to navigation. This last provision apparently reflects Soviet concern over the U.S. practice of dropping sonar buoys from aircraft, but the ambiguous wording probably allows the United States to continue to act as it did before the agreement. It is always possible to claim that the sonar buoys did not actually endanger safe navigation.
3. *Increased Communication at Sea.* Article III of the agreement requires the use of internationally recognized signals to convey information about operations and intentions and to warn ships of the presence of submarines in an area. Article V requires signals to announce the commencement of flight operations and also mandates that aircraft flying over the high seas display navigation lights "whenever feasible." Finally, Article VI requires three to five days' advance notification of actions (naval exercises or missile test launches) on the high seas that represent a danger to navigation or to aircraft, as well as requiring increased use of informative signals to signify intentions of vessels maneuvering in close proximity to one another.[31] These provisions reduce the danger of accidental attacks during exercises and limit the possibility of collisions arising from misunderstanding or misinterpretation.
4. *Regular consultations and Information Exchanges.* Article VII stipulates that the Soviet and U.S. naval attachés in each other's capitals shall serve as the channel for the exchange of information concerning incidents and collisions. This provision may help to minimize the diplomatic consequences of incidents at sea by ensuring that such matters are handled primarily by the two navies.[32] The Soviets during the negotiations were apparently pleased that incidents could be discussed between "brothers at sea"; this type of attitude may provide a basis for fruitful exchanges on the details of any incidents. Article IX provides that the United States and the Soviet Union shall conduct annual reviews of the agreement. Every three years, these meetings are used to renew the agreement for an additional three-year period, as specified in Article VIII. Article X specifically establishes a committee to meet within six

months to "consider the practical workability of concrete fixed distances to be observed in encounters between ships, aircraft, and ships and aircraft."

U.S. and Soviet negotiators did not reach any agreement on a distance formula,
although the Soviets continue to raise the issue and both countries agree to study it
further at the annual reviews of the agreement.[33] Subsequent negotiations did, however, produce a protocol to the original agreement on May 22, 1973.[34] The protocol
extends some provisions of the 1972 agreement to nonmilitary ships. Article I states
that measures shall be taken to notify each party's nonmilitary ships of the provisions
of the agreement directed at securing mutual safety. Article II prohibits simulated
attacks on nonmilitary ships and the dropping of objects near them in a hazardous
manner. The protocol seems to be a logical extension of the original agreement, as
several incidents at sea have involved merchant or fishing vessels. Although the
protocol obviously is meant to safeguard the nonmilitary ships of both parties, it may
confer somewhat greater benefits on the Soviet Union. Its provisions could serve to
protect Soviet trawlers or other nonmilitary vessels that actually serve some military
purpose, particularly surveillance. Moreover, the large and growing Soviet merchant
fleet is more exposed to Western harassment. The bulk of Soviet merchant and fishing vessels operate in waters that can be controlled by the West, whereas only an
insignificant portion of U.S. shipping is usually found in Soviet-controlled waters.[35]

FACTORS CONTRIBUTING TO THE NEGOTIATION OF THE AGREEMENT

The manner in which the Incidents at Sea Agreement was negotiated suggests that the
talks can be classified as a relatively easy success for U.S.–Soviet cooperation. Although it is difficult to weigh the relative importance of the factors discussed below,
both parties had incentives for reaching an understanding and worked hard to complete
the agreement in intensive negotiations. Nevertheless, there were still a number of obstacles that might have prevented a successful outcome. This chapter therefore also
examines some potential obstacles, particularly domestic factors in the United States,
and the way in which they were overcome.

U.S.–Soviet Common Interests in Avoiding Incidents at Sea

Perhaps the most important factor in the successful negotiation of the 1972 agreement
is that the United States and the Soviet Union recognized that they shared a common
interest in preventing incidents at sea. The United States and the Soviet Union apparently concluded that the benefits of deliberate harassment were outweighed by the dangers of unregulated incidents. These dangers can be divided into three categories: (1)
the physical danger to lives and vessels posed by a collision; (2) the possibility that an
incident, even if relatively minor in itself, will provoke a crisis or even war; (3) the risk
of direct and immediate combat and escalation as a result of misperception or misinterpretation of an incident by local commanders.

Removing the Physical Dangers of Collisions

The most obvious danger of incidents at sea is the threat to sailors and vessels posed by
practices that interfere with safe navigation. Although collisions in times of relative
international calm may not have grave political repercussions, they still threaten injury

to men and damage to ships involved. With the exception of several incidents in the 1950s and early 1960s in which the Soviets shot down U.S. military aircraft over international waters, few naval incidents appear to have caused significant damage or loss of life. A Soviet TU-16 bomber attempting to buzz U.S. vessels apparently crashed into the Norwegian Sea in May 1968,[36] but most actual collisions between ships appear to have involved the scraping of hulls, not broadside or head-on collisions. Nevertheless, both governments have stressed the threat to human life posed by acts that impede safe navigation.[37] U.S. naval officers generally first mention the threat to lives and ships when they assess the risks of naval incidents. Admiral Zumwalt, for example, stresses "the immediate damage to property and the loss of life that any one of them might cause."[38] The importance of avoiding collisions to minimize risk to ships and men should not be underestimated as a factor leading to the 1972 agreement, as both navies presumably regard their vessels as significant military assets that should not be jeopardized. Admiral Robert Hilton, a participant in several of the annual reviews of the agreement, argues that "neither country wants to have its valuable ships damaged by inadvertent or imprudent actions of its naval officers."[39]

Avoiding Incidents That Could Increase Tensions and the Risk of War

The United States and the Soviet Union also have a common interest in reducing the possibility that collisions or other confrontational naval encounters might increase tensions or even lead to war. Although an incident itself might not directly escalate to major armed conflict, it could create grounds for political demands or reprisals.

Historically, naval incidents have often increased tensions and provided the catalyst for the outbreak of war. The bizarre incident that triggered the War of Jenkins' Ear between Great Britain and Spain (1739–1741) is perhaps the most unusual example of such an encounter on the high seas.[40] The Dogger Bank affair between Great Britain and Russia during the Russo-Japanese War is a classic case of a naval incident that brought the countries involved to the brink of war.[41] Incidents at sea precipitated the War of 1812 and brought the United States and Germany into conflict in both world wars. More recently, the Gulf of Tonkin "incident" and the seizure of the *Mayaguez* provoked significant U.S. military responses. Although these two incidents did not involve Soviet forces, and strictly speaking, entailed different types of actions than those defined as incidents above, they do indicate that even low-level naval clashes could lead to escalatory U.S. military actions.

Under conditions of international tension and great-power rivalry, public opinion in a liberal democracy is likely to demand retaliation after a provocation by a major rival. Naval incidents seem to elicit particularly emotional responses in the United States. Reflecting on the Gulf of Tonkin incident, former White House aide Chester Cooper observed:

> There is something very magical about an attack on an American ship on the high seas. An attack on a military base or an American convoy doesn't stir up that kind of emotion. An attack on an American ship on the high seas is bound to set off skyrockets and the "Star-Spangled Banner" and "Hail to the Chief" and everything else.[42]

The reaction to an incident, even if it is clearly accidental, will depend on the subjective interpretation of events, which may be independent of the level of damage or loss of life. American reactions to the sinking of the *Maine* indicate that a probable accident can be given the most negative possible interpretation by a nation predisposed to war.

It is, of course, unlikely that a naval incident could provoke a major conflict leading to a nuclear exchange between the United States and the Soviet Union. Political leaders would have the opportunity for reflection—provided that the incident did not immediately escalate. An incident could, however, increase tensions and needlessly disrupt negotiations or other political discourse, much as the U-2 incident of 1960 forced the cancellation of the Khrushchev-Eisenhower summit. The cumulative impact of a succession of incidents could undermine the stability of superpower relations even further. As Thomas Schelling has written, "nothing is more threatening to the nuclear fate of the world than the loss of confidence on each side in the other's restraint, patience, and security."[43] Public reaction to incidents at sea could create such a loss of confidence.

Preventing Incidents and Escalation During Crises

The most alarming, although not necessarily the most likely, danger posed by U.S.– Soviet incidents at sea is the possibility that harassment of warships or aircraft will accidently escalate to actual combat. U.S. and Soviet vessels generally have acted with restraint, but in September 1971 a Soviet ship in the Sea of Japan apparently opened fire on a U.S. naval patrol aircraft.[44] Initial hostilities involving only local naval units could escalate to a more general conventional or even nuclear conflict, particularly if the incident occurred during a period of acute international tension.[45] Naval officers in the United States and the Soviet Union apparently share this view. Admiral Zumwalt has suggested that a naval incident "could lead people to shoot at each other with results that might be by that time impossible to control."[46] Soviet Captain V. Serkov wrote in 1981 of the "dangerous consequences" that might be the result of incidents in the absence of the 1972 agreement.[47]

This type of escalation is distinct from the possibility that an incident might increase international tensions and raise the risk of war. In the latter case, the incident serves only as a catalyst that triggers or increases hostility between the parties involved; it does not immediately lead to sustained fighting. Political leaders would have the opportunity to assess the incident and then act. In a crisis, however, the incident itself might lead to significant hostilities and direct escalation. The political leadership of both countries might eventually have the opportunity to reflect and decide upon further military measures, but major combat already would have taken place at the local or theater level.[48]

An incident between U.S. and Soviet vessels could lead to accidental and unintended hostilities if some form of harassment were interpreted as a sign of imminent attack. An American commander might, for example, view Soviet actions such as the training of weapons and fire-control radars on U.S. vessels as the prelude to a large-scale attack. Under such circumstances, he might react by launching a preemptive attack against the threatening Soviet warships or aircraft, or, more likely, he might engage in countermeasures to reduce the likelihood of a successful Soviet strike.[49] Options include maneuvering away from the threatening Soviet vessels, jamming Soviet equipment or deceiving it with feints and decoys, and harassing the Soviet forces. This last category of acts includes shouldering the Soviet ships onto a nonthreatening course, forcing submarines to surface, and escorting Soviet aircraft away from the U.S. vessel. Although these actions might reduce the probability of a successful Soviet attack, they could also increase Soviet apprehensions over the possibility of imminent hostile actions by U.S. forces. Indeed, some of these acts might even end with the destruction of Soviet units.[50] Thus U.S. countermeasures intended to reduce the chances of a successful attack could increase Soviet fears of a U.S. attack and prompt the very preemptive attack that they were meant to avoid. The nature of the interaction between hostile naval units creates an inherent instability at the tactical level. This instability is likely to be most pronounced during crises, when tension is heightened and actual fighting appears more likely. Under such circumstances, the temptation to strike first could increase.

Several factors contribute to the inescapable instability of contemporary naval interaction. First, current naval technology gives an overwhelming advantage to the side that strikes first.[51] This condition increases the military temptation to launch a preemptive attack when threatened. Moreover, most observers believe that Soviet naval doctrine emphasizes the importance of striking first in any naval engagement. Soviet forces, lacking aircraft carriers and their attendant tactical air support, are configured for a first strike against U.S. aircraft carriers. The writings of Soviet naval commanders, including Admiral Gorshkov, stress "decisive, offensive actions" and "the struggle for the first salvo."[52] Soviet naval exercises usually involve attacks on passive targets, indicating a desire to achieve surprise in war at sea. During Okean 75, a major Soviet exercise, the Soviet navy simulated a surprise attack by over 200 warships and 300 submarines within 90 seconds of each other.

Some analysts question whether the Soviets actually plan to launch preemptive strikes to initiate naval warfare with the United States. George Quester suggests that the Soviet naval literature emphasizes preemption to impress domestic audiences and to increase the Soviet Navy's share of military expenditures. Michael Klare argues that the Soviet Navy lacks the capability to engage the United States in conflict at sea. And apparent changes in Soviet tactics may indicate a reduction in Soviet confidence in their ability to preempt U.S. naval forces.[53]

Despite the uncertainty over the possibility of a Soviet preemptive strike on U.S. vessels, U.S. commanders probably will not become complacent. The proximity of U.S. and Soviet forces during a crisis would enable the Soviets to launch an attack from point-blank range without advance warning.[54] Under such conditions, dangerous maneuvering or simulated attacks by Soviet vessels could provoke a U.S. response.

A second factor contributing to the instability of naval interaction at sea is that information can easily be misinterpreted in the confusion caused by a proximity of large numbers of vessels from various countries, including third parties. The Israeli attack on the American ship *Liberty* in the June 1967 war could, for example, have been misinterpreted as a Soviet attack.[55] Similarly, in several of the wars in the Middle East, Soviet vessels might have reacted mistakenly to Israeli naval actions, assuming that Israeli units were hostile U.S. forces. Attempts by national command authorities to control local units might be disrupted or otherwise prove unsuccessful, as occurred in the case of *Liberty* and the Cuban missile crisis.[56] The "fog of crisis" could also lead to a misinterpretation of a nonhostile act. Harassment meant as a political signal might be misread by a local commander. An attempt by U.S. or Soviet vessels to shake enemy "tattletales" (surveillance ships) might be viewed as a prelude to offensive action, not as a legitimate defensive maneuver. The use of decoys to deceive trailing vessels could be misinterpreted, as such decoys can sound like antisubmarine torpedoes.[57]

Finally, the danger of naval conflict and escalation is heightened by the tendency of naval confrontations to assume a life of their own, prolonging competitive deployments after the crisis has abated. Although the October 1973 Middle East war ended in late October, the U.S. Sixth Fleet continued to operate at DEFCON III readiness until mid-November.[58] The 1971 Indo-Pakistani war ended on December 17, but intense U.S.–Soviet naval interaction did not begin until December 22 and ended on January 8, 1972.[59] These extended confrontations multiply the risks inherent in shorter crises. Moreover, naval units may enjoy greater scope for autonomous action after political authorities are no longer preoccupied with the crisis.

Neither the United States nor the Soviet Union has attempted deliberately and consistently to raise the risks of naval confrontations. Indeed, many American observers argue that Soviet naval activity, like Soviet crisis behavior in general, has been remarkably circumspect.[60] Nevertheless, dangerous incidents have taken place during international crises. Although the Soviets maneuvered carefully in the Mediterranean in June 1967 to avoid any incident with the U.S. Sixth Fleet that might be misinterpreted or escalate out of control, on June 8 a Soviet escort and destroyer interfered with the operations of the carrier *America*'s task group.[61] (This incident may have been the result of indiscretion or an attempt to stop U.S. ships from tracking a Soviet submarine.) In the aftermath of the seizure of the *Pueblo* by North Korea in January 1968, Soviet vessels engaged in harassment of U.S. warships in the Sea of Japan. U.S. Navy records show a dozen violations of the nautical Rules of the Road by Soviet vessels during this period, as well as a collision between the Soviet merchant ship *Kapitan Vislobokov* and the U.S. destroyer *Rowan*.[62] U.S. forces also have engaged in provocative naval acts during crises, including following, harassing, and forcing Soviet submarines to surface during the Cuban missile crisis. According to Robert Kennedy, President John F. Kennedy was extremely concerned over the possible dangers of this harassment and sought to control the actions of local naval commanders as much as possible.[63]

The risks of superpower naval confrontation should not be overestimated or exaggerated. The overall stability of the strategic nuclear balance adds to the incentives for caution and reduces the possibility that either side will see any advantage in initiating war at sea. Moreover, naval officers and political leaders are aware that the stakes in any crisis probably do not justify the launching of a surprise attack at sea. In most cases, even the most extreme forms of harassment are likely to be regarded as a bluff. Nevertheless, naval commanders on the scene will not become complacent.[64] Even if the probability of war at sea is low, it may be higher than the chance of U.S.–Soviet hostilities in Europe or other regions.[65] It certainly appears greater than the odds of a bolt-from-the-blue nuclear strike by either side. Although most scenarios envisage the start of U.S.–Soviet hostilities on land, the risks of naval incidents were apparently perceived as great enough to give the United States and the Soviet Union a mutual interest in negotiating the 1972 agreement. In the nuclear age, even a relatively low risk of superpower conflict can justify significant precautions.

Complementary U.S. and Soviet Interests in the Agreement

The United States and the Soviet Union may have had complementary interests that increased the likelihood that they could cooperate in reaching the Incidents at Sea Agreement. The Soviets may have seen the agreement as a recognition of their status as the equal of the U.S. Navy on the high seas.[66] After a period of marked inferiority in which they harassed U.S. vessels to make their presence felt, the Soviet Navy may have decided to seek the agreement as a symbolic recognition of parity on the world's oceans. The United States, on the other hand, would have no need for a recognition of its status but would have an interest in reducing Soviet harassment of U.S. vessels. As the location of U.S. allies and naval bases makes it more likely that U.S. warships will find themselves operating in or near Soviet home waters, the United States may have had a greater interest in restricting dangerous maneuvers.[67]

It is also possible that asymmetries in the force structure, capabilities, and missions of the U.S. and Soviet navies created a set of complementary interests and provided a basis for tradeoffs between different areas discussed in the negotiations. The Soviets, for example, lack significant naval aviation or ASW capabilities and seemed to be concerned over U.S. aerial harassment of Soviet submarines. The U.S. Navy, on the other hand, appears to be most interested in protecting its ability to perform strategic deterrence and surveillance missions, while also minimizing disruptions of carrier operations.

Overcoming Domestic Impediments in the United States

The mutual and complementary interests of the United States and the Soviet Union in regulating naval incentives created powerful incentives for an agreement. But more than mutual interest is required for the successful negotiation of an agreement between the superpowers, as the history of U.S.–Soviet arms control negotiations demonstrates. Inept diplomacy can frustrate even the most promising arms control initiatives.[68] The United States successfully overcame these obstacles in negotiating the Incidents at Sea Agreement.

The relative ease with which the text of the agreement was negotiated can be attributed in part to the careful and thorough U.S. preparations and the intensive involvement of the U.S. Navy in the preparations and negotiations. The participation of the Navy may have facilitated an agreement by ensuring that the U.S. proposal and the memorandum of understanding were acceptable to the operational commanders of the service directly affected. There were substantial internal disagreements between the State Department and the Navy over the question of a distance formula, but these were ultimately resolved in a way that satisifed the Navy. The extensive and high-level participation of naval representatives in the actual negotiations may have helped reduce any fears that the agreement might prevent the U.S. Navy from performing what it saw as its vital missions. Although the U.S. Navy initially feared that the Soviet offer to open negotiations was a ruse to set up zones in which ASW would be banned, naval representatives were able to ensure that the U.S. stance in the talks would rule out any such accord. The U.S. negotiating position and the eventual agreement did not jeopardize any of the missions that the Navy deemed vital. The agreement did not interfere with the highly risky reconnaissance activities by U.S. submarines in Soviet territorial waters.[69] The U.S. delegation refused to entertain the possibility of any agreement that might restrict the traditional principle of freedom of the seas by limiting the geographical scope of submarine or surface deployments. The agreement also did not restrict how closely U.S. ships and planes could approach their Soviet counterparts. This issue of a distance formula was the subject of many internal disagreements during the U.S. preparations for the negotiations, but the Navy's resistance to any distance limitation was incorporated into the negotiating position and the Soviet Union's desire for a distance formula did not prevent an agreement.

The nature of the Incidents at Sea Agreement may have reduced any U.S. domestic obstacles to its negotiation. As the agreement does not establish numerical limits on U.S. and Soviet weapons, it is less vulnerable to attacks from congressional and other critics who might allege that it codifies a U.S.–Soviet imbalance. It does not require the U.S. Navy to forgo any ship-building programs. The absence of constraints on force levels also eliminates many of the thorny issues of verification that have plagued other U.S.–Soviet agreements. Either because the issue of naval incidents is inherently non-controversial or because the absence of quantitative limits reduces the potential for controversy, there has been virtually no public debate in the United States over the agreement. This absence of debate may be attributable to the fact that the agreement is not a treaty and was not subjected to public debate in the U.S. Senate. The announcement of the agreement was overshadowed by the flurry of agreements that emerged from the 1972 Moscow summit, particularly the SALT I interim agreement and the ABM Treaty. The U.S. Navy appears to believe that the absence of publicity contributes to the success of the agreement and did little to call attention to it in 1972 or since.[70]

The General Political Climate: Détente and the Agreement

The Incidents at Sea Agreement was negotiated and signed during a period in which U.S.–Soviet détente appears to have been at its peak. This general climate of good relations probably increased U.S. and Soviet incentives for an agreement, although it is difficult to find specific connections between the negotiations and the political atmosphere. The improvement in U.S.–Soviet relations may have influenced the Soviet decision to accept the U.S. offer to negotiate in 1970—over two years after the United States had made its initial proposal. Senior officers of both navies may have believed that negotiating the agreement not only served their interests, but enabled them to demonstrate their support for the general strategy of détente pursued by the political leadership in both countries. Finally, the emergence of détente may have encouraged U.S. high-level political involvement in the preparations for the talks and support for an agreement.

The Level and Nature of Representation in the Negotiations

The high status of both the Soviet and the U.S. delegations to the negotiations may not have been an independent factor contributing to the success of the talks. It may have been little more than a reflection of the various incentives that the United States and the Soviet Union had for reaching an accord. But the high level of the negotiations also may have helped to convince both sets of negotiators that the other was serious about reaching an agreement. The U.S. Navy appears to have been skeptical about the prospects for a significant agreement, but at least some of this skepticism was dispelled once the negotiations began. The extremely high level of the Soviet delegation could have dispelled American concerns that the Soviets had ulterior motives; the status of the representatives may have altered a previously held image of the opponent in this case.

Naval representatives from both countries may also have been encouraged by the navy-to-navy nature of the negotiations. As the issues under discussion were often technical and required some familiarity with naval practices, the involvement of a large number of naval representatives may have facilitated mutual understanding. In addition, it is possible that both navies felt that it would be better to reach an agreement between themselves than to rely on the political leadership to negotiate an accord. The similarities in outlook and experience of U.S. and Soviet naval officers may have contributed to a "brothers at sea" spirit that enabled the two parties to negotiate the agreement.[71]

FACTORS CONTRIBUTING TO THE SUCCESSFUL IMPLEMENTATION OF THE AGREEMENT

Assessing the Success of Implementation

The 1972 Agreement on the Prevention of Incidents at Sea generally is regarded as a success.[72] Incidents have continued since it was signed, but they have become less frequent and less severe. Although information on the number and type of incidents generally is not released by the U.S. Navy, available data suggest that the agreement is working. The number of serious incidents apparently exceeded one hundred per year in the late 1960s, but Secretary of the Navy John Lehman, Jr., reported that there were only about forty potentially dangerous incidents between June 1982 and June 1983.[73] Lehman has attributed this substantial reduction in collisions and near-collisions to the 1972 agreement.[74] The most dangerous maneuvers and attempts to disrupt formations are no longer commonplace. Numbers alone, however, may not be the best indicator of the success of the agreement, which is intended to resolve questions about incidents as well as prevent them. When incidents do occur, they are resolved by the U.S. and Soviet navies through the the channels established by the agreement. Naval commanders are less likely to retaliate on their own, thereby provoking further incidents. The existence of established channels also reduces the likelihood that incidents will become the source of diplomatic controversies. Lehman feels that the annual meetings to review the accord have produced a "stable pattern" of dealing with incidents and that they provide "pretty good resolution" of any disputes in a "rather businesslike" manner.[75]

U.S.–Soviet naval interaction in the October 1973 Arab-Israeli war apparently exemplifies the positive impact of the agreement. The Soviets deployed a peak of 96 vessels during the war, confronting a slightly smaller number of U.S. ships. Despite the heightened political tensions and the increased probability of incidents due to the proximity of so many hostile vessels, incidents were relatively rare. Some Soviet warships trained guns or searchlights on U.S. vessels, fired flares near U.S. aircraft, or engaged in close maneuvering. But, as Stephen Roberts notes, these actions were probably "clumsy efforts at reconnaissance" or were performed for "operational reasons." The "gun movements (which tended to occur around 8:00 a.m.)" may have been "routine checks of equipment." On the whole, Soviet ships observed the agreement and avoided harassment of their U.S. counterparts.[76] Admiral Worth Bagley, commander-in-chief of U.S. Naval Forces in Europe at the time, remarked that the "Soviets weren't overly aggressive. It looked as though they were taking some care not to cause an incident."[77]

Soviet assessments of the agreement also indicate that it has been a success. In 1981, Captain Serkov wrote in *Morsky Sbornik:*

> Nine years have elapsed since the aforesaid agreement was signed and put into effect. In that comparatively short time the safety of sea navigation and overflight has noticeably improved, and the role of the norms and principles of international law has grown greater in dealings between the two Navies on the high seas. The number of serious incidents between ships and aircraft of the two countries have been curtailed.[78]

Although Serkov went on the note that "regular, professional contact has been established between representatives of the two Navies" he also pointed out that "there have

been certain negative phenomena'' and reiterated the Soviet belief that a distance formula would be effective. He concluded that naval commanders needed to display ''un-
deviating observance of the provisions of the said Agreement.''[79]

The agreement was never entirely insulated from the overall state of U.S.–Soviet
relations. Naval commanders report that the Soviets tend to engage in more harassment
when superpower relations deteriorate. Nevertheless, the agreement has continued to
function despite the decline of the détente that provided the atmosphere for the negotiation of the agreement. The 1980 annual review took place in Moscow, despite the
suspension of most other U.S.–Soviet contacts in the wake of the invasion of Afghanistan.

Events of recent years, however, seem to suggest that the agreement is not faring
so well. Soviet vessels interfered with salvage operations by U.S. and allied vessels in
the Sea of Japan following the downing of the Korean airliner in 1983, making low
passes over ships, dashing at U.S. salvage vessels to force them to change course, and
running parallel to them to drown out signals from U.S. underwater listening equipment.[80] A Soviet guided-missile frigate apparently attempted to disrupt flight operations
of the U.S. carrier *Ranger* in the Arabian Sea before colliding with the U.S. frigate *Fife*
in November 1983. The U.S. Navy protested the incident through its attaché in Moscow, claiming that the Soviets had clearly violated the agreement. Although the Soviet
ship signaled that it had steering difficulties, it appeared to be under full control at all
times.[81]

Additional incidents were reported in early 1984. In March, a Soviet Victor-I class
submarine running without lights collided with the U.S. carrier *Kitty Hawk* in the Sea
of Japan. Although the carrier was not seriously damaged, the submarine was apparently
disabled. The U.S. Navy began an inquiry to determine whether the Soviet submarine
was at fault, although Lehman indicated that the collision appeared to be ''inadvertent.''[82] Several days later, the Soviet carrier *Minsk* fired eight flares at the U.S. frigate
Harold E. Holt. Three hit the U.S. vessel, including one that passed within three feet
of the captain. The *Holt* was within thirty yards of the *Minsk*, which had stopped for
unexplained reasons. The *Holt* apparently had signaled that it planned to pass the *Minsk*
on the starboard side and did so despite several warnings from the Soviet vessel. The
U.S. Navy decided to raise the incident at the annual meeting in May 1984.[83]

These incidents do not necessarily signal the demise of the agreement. Soviet vessels in the Sea of Japan may have been reacting to the extraordinary tension that followed the downing of the Korean airliner, or they may have been attempting to prevent
the United States from recovering the flight recorder. U.S. naval officials believe that
the harassment was politically motivated, at least in part because of the proximity to
Soviet borders and bases. Even under these circumstances, the agreement apparently
helped to limit Soviet harassment. Admiral Sylvester R. Foley, Jr., then commander of
the U.S. Pacific Fleet, recalls that during the search the Soviets ''gave us trouble and
hassled us, and we said, 'If the Incidents at Sea Agreement means anything, cut it out,'
and they did.''[84] The collisions with the *Fife* and *Kitty Hawk* and the firing of flares at
the *Holt* were all potentially dangerous incidents, but Lehman stated that he believed
that relations between the U.S. and Soviet fleets are still ''very professional and work-
manlike.'' Commenting on the *Minsk* incident, he said: ''I don't see anything sinister
in the incident with the *Minsk*. Let's say there are two plausible sides to that story. The
Minsk skipper may not have been all on the wrong side.''[85] Other senior U.S. officials
have reaffirmed that the incidents of 1983 and 1984 have not changed their interpretation

of Soviet behavior, arguing that the "Soviets have made it very clear that they believe in the Incidents at Sea agreement. They want it to continue. They want it to work. They want to live up to it." U.S. officials also pointed out that "each year we've seen basically a decrease" in the number of incidents.[86]

The May 1984 meetings in Moscow of U.S. and Soviet representatives to review the agreement provided further evidence of its success. The talks were reportedly conducted in an open, frank, and professional manner. U.S. Chief of Naval Operations Admiral James Watkins said the session was "well run" and drew a "higher caliber" of Soviet officer.[87] Both sides acknowledged the concerns of the other and avoided political rhetoric and unreasonable demands. A State Department participant is said to have been amazed by the contrast between the frankness and professionalism of the naval talks and previous U.S.–Soviet diplomatic intercourse.[88] U.S. admirals, who said the sessions were the best such meetings in memory, and their Soviet counterparts agreed to renew the agreement for three years. Announcing this renewal to a conference on U.S.–Soviet exchanges, President Reagan described the agreement as "useful." In addition, the Soviet delegation reportedly proposed extending the principles of the agreement to cover additional activities of military aircraft.[89]

Ironically, the successful 1984 meeting was followed by the postponement of the 1985 meeting for political reasons. The annual meeting was scheduled for Washington, D.C., but Secretary of Defense Caspar Weinberger decided to shorten the meeting and cancel all its social events in retaliation for the killing of Major Arthur Nicholson by a Soviet sentry in East Germany. The Soviets then informed the State Department that they would not be coming. Several Reagan Administration officials apparently resented this linkage between the Nicholson shooting and the Incidents at Sea Agreement. John Warner, now a U.S. Senator (R.–Virginia), argued: "We should not link the operation of the agreement to problems elsewhere in the world." Some Administration officials reported that Weinberger's decision was taken without consulting Secretary of State George Shultz or then National Security Adviser Robert McFarlane. The Navy also opposed the changes in the schedule of the meetings, suggesting that Weinberger's decision reflected political considerations, not any problems with the agreement itself. Admiral Watkins later said: "We like the sessions. They like the sessions . . . It is important that we get back to the table."[90] The two countries reached agreement on resuming the annual meetings in November 1985. The 1986 annual review was held quietly in Moscow in June of that year.[91]

Reasons for the Successful Implementation of the Agreement: The Criteria for "Success"

One of the most basic, but easily overlooked, reasons for the apparent success of the Incidents at Sea Agreement is the fact that it does not have to prevent all incidents in order to be judged a success. The agreement may fail in some cases, but a reduction in the number of incidents still counts as an overall success. There are important benefits from reducing the number of incidents and from providing regular procedures to deal with incidents that do arise. The criteria for evaluating the success or failure of other agreements may be quite different. The Hotline, the Accident Measures Agreement, or the Agreement on the Prevention of Nuclear War would all be judged harshly if they failed on even one occasion. The amount of alleged Soviet cheating on the SALT I and SALT II agreements is relatively small when compared to the instances of Soviet compliance, but these examples of apparent violations are often used as evidence in arguments that the agreements have failed. The Incidents at Sea Agreement is not only more obscure than the SALT agreements, which tend to be the focus of public debate, but is also more robust in the sense that it continues to work even if some violations take place. The agreement itself operates on the implicit assumption that some possible violations will occur and provides a set of procedures for their communication and resolution.

The Basic Conceptual Approach: Regulation of Inevitable Competition

The success of the agreement also can be attributed to the basic conceptual approach that underlay its negotiation and execution. The Incidents at Sea Agreement accepts the reality of U.S.–Soviet competition and competitive interaction. Unlike naval arms control measures that would impose geographic limitations on deployments,[92] it implicitly assumes that U.S. and Soviet warships will continue their rivalry at sea and engage in gunboat diplomacy to influence political outcomes in crises. Article III, in particular, assumes that naval surveillance will continue, but establishes ground rules to keep it within limits.[93] Observance of the agreement makes U.S.–Soviet competition safer; it does not alter the basic terms of that competition.

In contrast to the U.S.–Soviet Basic Principles Agreement of 1972, the Incidents at Sea Agreement does not call for general political restraint by either superpower. Instead, it provides for specific measures to deal with a particular problem. It does not raise expectations, as a more nebulous statement of principles might. The agreement serves to prevent crises that could lead to escalation as well as those with political ramifications, but it explicitly defines the behavior it attempts to prevent, rather than prohibiting undefined actions that one superpower perceives as leading to unilateral advantages for the other. Implementation of the agreement increases predictability in U.S.–Soviet relations, prevents possible crises that neither party intended, and controls the possibility of escalation in incidents.[94]

Absence of Problems of Enforcement and Verification

The Incidents at Sea Agreement lacks any provisions for formal enforcement, but mutual interests and continuing U.S.–Soviet naval encounters create the basis for a system of self-enforcement through reciprocity.

If both countries share an interest in minimizing incidents at sea, tit-for-tat enforcement may work to limit the number of incidents. Each navy is in a position to respond to harassment by the other by initiating similar harassment on its own. Although neither navy would want to see such retaliation escalate into a spiral of harassment and counterharassment, the threat of tit-for-tat behavior may increase mutual incentives for restraint.[95]

Although verification issues have plagued many U.S.–Soviet arms control agreements, they have not arisen in regard to the Incidents at Sea Agreement. Obviously, an incident can only take place when the other party is present to observe it. Both navies are able to present evidence in the form of photographs or videotapes at the annual meetings as they attempt to demonstrate that the other party was at fault in a particular incident. Because the agreement does not impose any quantitative restrictions on armaments it avoids many of the compliance issues that have plagued other agreements. It therefore may be more difficult to apply any lessons for the Incidents at Sea Agreement to more traditional types of arms control.

Institutionalization and Internalization of Norms

The same incentives that led the U.S. and Soviet navies to negotiate the agreement continue to motivate both navies to implement its provisions. As both countries will continue to deploy their fleets on the world's oceans, some interaction between U.S. and Soviet vessels will be inevitable and both parties will retain an interest in regulating such encounters. The agreement did create new rules for naval encounters and procedures for handling incidents, but, as Admiral Zumwalt has argued, the agreement "was less significant for what it said, which was little more than a reaffirmation of the Rules of the Road, than for what it represented, which was a desire on the part of the Soviet leadership to normalize maritime behavior."[96]

Both navies appear to have internalized and institutionalized the norms reaffirmed by the agreement. Despite the deterioration of U.S.–Soviet political relations after 1972, the regime for naval incidents appears to have acquired its own momentum. Representatives of the U.S. and Soviet navies reaffirm the importance of the agreement from time to time and, at least in the United States, the Navy now seems to be the most vigorous defender of the agreement.[97] According to Admiral Hilton, both navies have published the agreement and circulated it among their fleets. The Special Signals devised by the agreement are posted on the bridge of every U.S. and Soviet vessel. The procedures for reporting incidents to the naval attaché of each country are often used. The U.S. Navy also requires captains to make detailed reports of every incident so that it can be determined whether the matter is serious enough to raise with the Soviets.[98]

Interest of Agencies Charged with Implementation

The interest of the U.S. and Soviet navies in upholding the agreement can be at least partly explained by the fact that the agreement is designed to serve naval interests and is implemented by both navies. Unlike some arms limitation agreements that may win only grudging support from the services they affect,[99] the incidents at sea agreement amounts to arms control that serves military purposes. The agreement actually increases the organizational autonomy of the U.S. Navy instead of constraining it, and it may have a similar effect on the Soviet Navy. Admiral Hilton suggests the professional officers of each navy may be able to communicate more effectively with one another than with other agencies of their own government.[100] As it is implemented largely by the two navies, it can generally be insulated from political considerations. Neither the U.S. nor the Soviet Navy has an interest in exploiting the agreement for propaganda purposes. Thus the agreement has continued to operate despite the vicissitudes of U.S.–Soviet relations since 1972.

CONCLUSIONS

The successful negotiation and implementation of the 1972 Incidents at Sea Agreement suggests that U.S.–Soviet security cooperation can occur when both countries have mutual interests and are willing to separate a particular issue from broader political considerations. In this case, the two navies have been able to establish a professional, working relationship to attempt to regulate the problem of naval incidents. The U.S. and Soviet navies have institutionalized the norms on which this cooperation is based and, at least in the United States, seem determined to continue to uphold the agreement and to resist political pressures to link it to other issues.

There may be areas in which similar approaches could be equally successful. The success of the agreement suggests that arms control agreements that attempt to address the operational causes of instability, may prove less controversial than those that reduce levels of armaments. The agreement should be classified as a confidence-building measure, an arrangement "designed to enhance such assurance of mind and belief in the trustworthiness of states and the facts they create." [101] No agreement can prevent the deliberate initiation of war, but agreements can reduce the possibility of unintentional conflict arising from mutual suspicion. The Incidents at Sea Agreement reduces the possibility of misinterpretation of potentially dangerous behavior at sea, thus increasing U.S. and Soviet confidence in the nonthreatening nature of each other's naval actions.

It is tempting to attempt to identify a number of areas in which the approach used in the Incidents at Sea Agreement might prove equally fruitful. There remain, however, some limits on the applicability of the methods used to negotiate and implement the agreement. In other areas, it might not be possible to find such a strong set of mutual interests that would give the affected U.S. and Soviet military services compelling reasons for negotiating an agreement. Whether the agreement could have been negotiated in the absence of U.S.–Soviet détente remains an open question. In other areas, the involvement of a variety of U.S. and Soviet government agencies might complicate implementation. The agreement's scope is narrow but important and it can be regarded as a success even if it breaks down on occasion; similar conditions do not always exist for security issues.

Nevertheless, the Incidents at Sea Agreement provides a modest, yet encouraging example of successful U.S.–Soviet security cooperation. Modesty in expectations may be a prerequisite for success in any U.S.–Soviet negotiations. The Incidents at Sea Agreement demonstrates that important results can emerge from modest expectations.

Notes

1. The full title is: Agreement Between the Government of the United States of America and the Government of the Union of Soviet Socialist Republics on the Prevention of Incidents on and over the High Seas, May 25, 1972. The complete text of the English and Russian versions appears in U.S. Department of State, *United States Treaties and Other International Agreements,* vol. 23, pt. 1, 1972 (Washington, D.C.: U.S. Government Printing Office, 1973), pp. 1168–1180.

2. The Rules of the Road govern nautical lighting, maneuvering, and signaling procedures to ensure safe navigation. For a discussion of recent revisions see T. J. Cutler, "More Changes to the Rules of the Road," *U.S. Naval Institute Proceedings,* vol. 109. no. 6 (June 1983), pp. 89–93.

3. Elmo R. Zumwalt, Jr., *On Watch* (New York: Quadrangle, 1976), p. 391.

4. Ibid.

5. D. P. O'Connell, *The Influence of Law on Sea Power* (Annapolis: Naval Institute Press, 1975), p. 165.

6. This issue arose in the negotiations leading to the 1972 agreement. The 1983 incident in the Atlantic in which a Soviet submarine was apparently disabled and forced to surface after U.S. sonar equipment became entangled in its propellor demonstrates the validity of Soviet concerns,

although that sonar array was towed by a surface ship, not dropped from the air. Even if buoys and cables do not become entangled in Soviet submarines, they may be extremely irritating. According to a U.S. official, when such buoys are dropped near submarines, "the pinging really drives them crazy." See *Washington Post* (June 8, 1984), p. A15.

7. Abram N. Shulsky, "The Jordanian Crisis of September 1970," in Bradford Dismukes and James M. McConnell, eds., *Soviet Naval Diplomacy* (New York: Pergamon, 1979), p. 176.

8. See the exchange of U.S. and Soviet notes on this incident in Historical Office, U.S. Department of State, *American Foreign Policy: Current Documents 1964* (Washington, D.C.: U.S. Government Printing Office, 1967), pp. 562–563.

9. Note from the Soviet Embassy in Washington to the U.S. Department of State, in ibid., p. 672.

10. Quoted in Michael R. Gordon, "At Sea," *National Journal* (July 6, 1985): p. 159.

11. The collisions in Soviet territorial waters involved U.S. submarines on intelligence missions. Such missions entailed monitoring Soviet submarines and plugging into underwater communications cables. On one occasion a U.S. submarine surfaced under a Soviet ship during naval exercises. In another incident an American submarine was temporarily grounded beneath Vladivostok harbor. Other incidents have doubtless occurred as U.S. and Soviet submarines have played a running game of cat and mouse under the high seas. See "Operation Holystone," *Nation* (July 19, 1975), pp. 35–36; Dan Caldwell, *American-Soviet Relations: From 1947 to the Nixon-Kissinger Grand Design* (Westport, Conn.: Greenwood Press, 1981), p. 128; Desmond Ball, "Nuclear War at Sea," *International Security,* vol. 10, no. 3 (Winter 1985/86): 4–6; "Critics of U.S. Spy Subs offer Mission Details," *International Herald Tribune* (May 26, 1975), p. 1; and James Coates and Jack Fuller, "U.S., Soviet Subs treading dangerous waters," *Chicago Tribune* (December 4, 1977), p. 1. For additional information on submarine intelligence operations code-named "Ivy Bells," as well as Reagan Administration efforts to prevent their disclosure, see Bob Woodward's *Veil: The Secret Wars of the CIA, 1981–1987* (New York: Simon and Schuster, 1987), pp. 30, 448–463.

12. Zumwalt, *On Watch,* p. 394.

13. For a seminal discussion of this subject, see James Cable, *Gunboat Diplomacy, 1919–1979: Political Applications of Limited Naval Force* (New York: St. Martin's Press, 1981).

14. Stephen S. Roberts, "Superpower Naval Confrontation," in Dismukes and McConnell, eds., *Soviet Naval Diplomacy,* pp. 211–212.

15. Elmo R. Zumwalt, Jr., "Gorshkov and his Navy," *Orbis,* vol. 24, no. 3 (Fall 1980): 491–510.

16. Quoted in David R. Cox, "Sea Power and Soviet Foreign Policy," *U.S. Naval Institute Proceedings,* vol. 95, no. 6 (June 1969), p. 41.

17. Richard T. Ackley, "The Soviet Navy's Role in Foreign Policy," *Naval War College Review,* vol. 24, no. 9 (May 1972): 55; and Frederic N. Smith, "USSR: Black Sea Fleet As Counter-Force," *Defense and Foreign Affairs Daily,* vol. 12, no. 23 (February 9, 1983), pp. 1–2. This practice apparently continued after the agreement was signed in 1972. In 1979, Soviet planes, including Backfire bombers, conducted more than 30 mock attacks against the U.S. destroyers *Caron* and *Farragut.* See *New York Times* (August 11, 1979), p. 4. More recently, on February 18, 1984, the destroyer *David R. Ray* was harassed in the Black Sea near Novorossiysk when a Soviet plane fired cannon rounds into its wake and a Soviet helicopter came within 30 feet of its deck. See *The Washington Post* (June 8, 1984), p. A15. In March 1986 the *Caron* and the cruiser *Yorktown* actually sailed into Soviet territorial waters in the Black Sea. See "2 U.S. Ships Enter Soviet Waters Off Crimea to Gather Intelligence," *New York Times* (March 19, 1986), pp. A1, A11. Also note that the incident described by Admiral Zumwalt in *On Watch,* pp. 391–393 took place in the Baltic.

18. Abram N. Shulsky, "Coercive Diplomacy," in Dismukes and McConnell, eds., *Soviet Naval Diplomacy,* p. 123. These simulated attacks apparently have intensified as the United States has conducted exercises with aircraft carriers near Vladivostok. Over 100 Soviet planes reacted

504   *Sean M. Lynn-Jones*

to a December 1984 exercise that brought U.S. vessels to within 50 miles of the Soviet coast. A Defense Department spokesman said: "When we operate in certain waters or in close proximity to foreign territorial waters, we anticipate a reaction." See Hedrick Smith, "Soviet Reacts to Operation By U.S. Navy," *International Herald Tribune* (December 20, 1984), pp. 1, 2.

19. See statement issued by the official Soviet News Agency TASS, May 13, 1967, in Historical Office, U.S. Department of State, *American Foreign Policy: Current Documents 1967* (Washington, D.C.: U.S. Government Printing Office, 1969), pp. 457–458.

20. Steven E. Miller, "Assessing the Soviet Navy," *Naval War College Review,* vol. 32, no. 5 (September–October 1979): 65.

21. Frank Andrews, "The Prevention of Preemptive Attack," *U.S. Naval Institute Proceedings,* vol. 106, no. 5 (May 1980), p. 139.

22. O'Connell, *The Influence of Law on Sea Power,* p. 178.

23. The following chronology is based on a personal interview with Ambassador Herbert Okun, a principal negotiator of the 1972 agreement, Washington, D.C., November 29, 1983; and Anthony F. Wolf, "Agreement at Sea: The United States–USSR Agreement on Incidents at Sea," *Korean Journal of International Studies,* vol. 9, no. 3 (1978): 57–80. See also Robert P. Hilton, Sr., "The U.S.–Soviet Incidents at Sea Treaty," *Naval Forces,* vol. 6, no. 1 (1985): 30–37.

24. For an example of such a proposal, see Ken Booth, "Law and Strategy in Northern Waters," *Naval War College Review,* vol. 34, no. 4 (July–August 1981): 3–21.

25. Some experts were optimistic, however, including former U.S. Ambassador Llewelyn Thompson.

26. For prominent examples of the general "lulling effect" argument see Norman Podhoretz, "The Future Danger," *Commentary* (April 1981): 29–47; and Eugene V. Rostow, "The Case Against SALT II," *Commentary* (February 1979): 22–32. For a detailed explication and assessment of the argument, see Sean M. Lynn-Jones, "Lulling and Stimulating Effects of Arms Control," in Albert Carnesale and Richard Haass, eds., *Superpower Arms Control: Setting the Record Straight* (Cambridge, Mass.: Ballinger, 1987), pp. 223–273. At least one observer has suggested that Admiral Gorshkov also feared that the agreement might "attenuate the climate of Soviet-American conflict necessary for substantial Soviet naval spending." See Franklyn Griffiths, "The Tactical Uses of Naval Arms Control," in Michael MccGwire, Ken Booth, and John McDonnell, eds., *Soviet Naval Policy: Objectives and Constraints* (New York: Praeger, 1975), p. 65.

27. Quoted in Anne Kelly Calhoun and Charles Petersen, "Changes in Soviet Naval Policy: Prospects for Arms Limitations in the Mediterranean and Indian Ocean," in Paul J. Murphy, ed., *Naval Power in Soviet Policy* (Washington, D.C.: U.S. Government Printing Office, 1978), pp. 244–245. *Morsky Sbornik* is a professional naval journal intended primarily for Soviet naval officers.

28. Marvin Kalb and Bernard Kalb, *Kissinger* (Boston: Little, Brown, 1974), p. 306. In his account of the same event, Admiral Zumwalt points out that the only Soviet official who became angry was a civilian. See *On Watch,* p. 393.

29. Richard M. Nixon, "The Moscow Summit: New Opportunities in U.S.-Soviet Relations," Department of State *Bulletin,* June 26, 1972, p. 856.

30. In practice, this provision has meant that U.S. and Soviet planes fly no lower than 1,000 feet and do not pass directly overhead. See Dick van der Aart, *Aerial Espionage* (Shrewsbury, Great Britain: Airlife, 1985), p. 144. The Soviets apparently object to lower overflights. In July 1981 a Soviet destroyer fired a warning shot at a CBS chartered aircraft carrying cameramen and flying at 800 feet near Cyprus. See "Soviet ship fires at cameramen off Cyprus," *The Times* (London) (July 7, 1981).

31. Special signals have been developed for U.S.-Soviet communication at sea. These convey messages such as "I am testing my gun systems" and "Dangerous operations in progress." Naval officers report that they have had a significant impact. See Hilton, "The U.S.-Soviet Incidents at Sea Treaty," p. 33.

32. The channel is used relatively often. Between June 1982 and June 1983, for example, the U.S. government called in the Soviet naval attaché for consultations seven times, while the U.S. attaché was summoned to the Soviet Ministry of Foreign Affairs eight times. See van der Aart, *Aerial Espionage,* p. 144.

33. Hilton, "The U.S.–Soviet Incidents at Sea Treaty," p. 33.

34. Protocol to the Agreement Between the Government of the United States of America and the Government of the Union of Soviet Socialist Republics on the Prevention of Incidents on and over the High Seas, Signed May 25, 1972. English and Russian texts can be found in U.S. Department of State, *United States Treaties and Other International Agreements,* vol. 24, pt. 1, 1973 (Washington, D.C.: U.S. Government Printing Office, 1974), pp. 1063–1066.

35. Michael MccGwire, "Soviet Naval Policy for the Seventies," in MccGwire, ed., *Soviet Naval Developments: Capability and Contest* (New York: Praeger, 1973), p. 509. Although there are no recorded cases of deaths from U.S.–Soviet collisions, at least two Soviet sailors were killed when their destroyer collided with the British aircraft carrier *Ark Royal* in 1970. See David Fairhall, *Russia Looks to the Sea* (London: Andre Deutsch, 1971), p. 217.

36. Thomas W. Wolfe, "Soviet Naval Interaction with the United States and its Influence on Soviet Naval Developments," in MccGwire, ed., *Soviet Naval Developments,* p. 266.

37. See diplomatic notes in Historical Office, U.S. Department of State, *American Foreign Policy: Current Documents 1964,* pp. 669–673.

38. Zumwalt, *On Watch,* p. 393. The amount of property damage obviously will vary from incident to incident, but one 1976 U.S.–Soviet collision caused $500,000 in damage to a U.S. frigate in the Ionian Sea. See "U.S. Ship Crash Blamed on Russia," *International Herald Tribune* (March 16, 1977).

39. Hilton, "The U.S.–Soviet Incidents at Sea Treaty," p. 37.

40. The unfortunate Captain Robert Jenkins, a British smuggler, allegedly lost his ear in 1731 when it was cut off during a fracas after his ship had been boarded by a Spanish vessel. The incident became an issue in Britain in 1738, when Jenkins exhibited his severed ear to Parliament and the uproar was exploited by proponents of war with Spain.

41. After Japanese torpedo boats had attacked the Russian fleet in the Far East in 1904, the Russian Baltic fleet began the long voyage that eventually ended on the bottom of the Tsushima Straits. Fleet commanders feared further attacks by Japanese torpedo boats—possibly disguised as trawlers—in the North Sea. A jittery Russian captain, confused in a fog at night, bombarded British trawlers, sinking one, damaging five, and leaving two fisherman dead and six wounded. The British public was incensed. King Edward VII, Admiral John Fisher, and others urged a military response. Even Foreign Secretary Lord Lansdowne, an advocate of entente with Russia, was outraged, and felt that Britain's reputation as a great power was at stake. Arthur Balfour estimated the probability of war to be about 50 percent. The British fleet was poised to intercept the Russians as they steamed southward. Eventually, however, the Russians complied with the British demand that those responsible for the incident be put ashore to face a tribunal. They also pledged to avoid any repetition of such errors in judgment. See Richard Ned Lebow, "Accidents and Crises: The Dogger Bank Affair," *Naval War College Review,* vol. 31, no. 1 (Summer 1978): 66–75.

42. Quoted in "The 'Phantom Battle' that Led to War," *U.S. News and World Report* (July 23, 1984): 65–66.

43. Thomas C. Schelling, "Confidence in Crisis," *International Security,* vol. 8, no. 4 (Spring 1984): 57.

44. See van der Aart, *Aerial Espionage,* p. 144.

45. For an excellent discussion of the risks of war and escalation at sea, see Ball, "Nuclear War at Sea."

46. Zumwalt, *On Watch,* p. 393.

47. Quoted in Hilton, "The U.S.–Soviet Incidents at Sea Treaty," p. 33.

48. For a discussion of various scenarios involving escalation induced by naval warfare, see

Francis Fukuyama, "Escalation in the Middle East and Persian Gulf," in Graham T. Allison, Albert Carnesale, and Joseph S. Nye, Jr., eds., *Hawks, Doves, and Owls: An Agenda for Avoiding Nuclear War* (New York: W. W. Norton, 1985), pp. 115–147.

49. Present NATO rules of engagement prohibit preemptive strikes and preparations for attacks during crises, but the United States apparently has attempted to change this doctrine. See "NATO Issue: When to Let Its Ships Fire," *New York Times* (April 2, 1984). For a discussion of the problem, see George Bunn, "International Law and the Use of Force in Peacetime: Do U.S. Ships have to Take the First Hit?" *Naval War College Review*, vol. 39, no. 3 (May–June 1986): 69–80.

50. Andrews, "The Prevention of Preemptive Attack," p. 133.

51. See George H. Quester, "Naval Armaments: The Past as Prologue," in Quester, ed., *Navies and Arms Control* (New York: Praeger, 1980), pp. 1–11.

52. Sergei Gorshkov, quoted in Raymond G. O'Connor and Vladimir P. Prokofieff, "The Soviet Navy in the Mediterranean and Indian Ocean," *Virginia Quarterly Review*, vol. 49, no. 4 (Autumn 1973): 491–492.

53. See Quester, "Naval Armaments"; Michael T. Klare, "Superpower Rivalry at Sea," *Foreign Policy* no. 21 (Winter 1975–76): 86–89; and Charles C. Petersen, "About-Face in Soviet Tactics," *U.S. Naval Institute Proceedings*, vol. 109, no. 8 (August 1983), pp. 57–63.

54. Stansfield Turner, "The Naval Balance: Not Just a Numbers Game," *Foreign Affairs*, vol. 55, no. 2 (January 1977): 350.

55. The first reaction of then Secretary of Defense Robert McNamara was to consider the possibility that the Soviet Union was responsible for that attack and to plan retaliation against Soviet forces in the area. Fortunately, however, the United States soon concluded that a Soviet attack was unlikely and the Hotline was used to assure the Soviets that U.S. aircraft dispatched to assist the *Liberty* were not going to threaten Soviet forces. McNamara later said that Soviet Premier Alexei Kosygin misunderstood U.S. military maneuvers in the Mediterranean and sent a "very tough" message over the Hotline, warning "if you want war you will have war." See Phil G. Goulding, *Confirm or Deny* (New York: Harper & Row, 1970), pp. 97–98; and Anatole Kaletsky, "Russia and U.S. 'Were Near to War in 1967,' " *Financial Times* (September 15, 1983).

56. Repeated orders instructing the *Liberty* to move away from the battle zone were misrouted or delayed. During the Cuban missile crisis, a U.S. plane strayed over Soviet territory and naval commanders preferred to use standard operating procedures for conducting a blockade instead of the risk-minimizing practices desired by President Kennedy and Secretary of Defense McNamara. On the latter point see Graham T. Allison, *Essence of Decision* (Boston: Little, Brown, 1971), pp. 127–132; Dan Caldwell, "A Research Note on the Quarantine of Cuba, October 1962," *International Studies Quarterly*, vol. 22, no. 4 (December 1978): 625–633; and Scott D. Sagan, "Nuclear Alerts and Crisis Management," *International Security*, vol. 9, no. 4 (Spring 1985): 100–118.

57. O'Connell, *the Influence of Law on Sea Power*, p. 180.

58. F. C. Miller, "Those Storm-beaten Ships, Upon which Arab Armies Never Looked," *U.S. Naval Institute Proceedings*, vol. 101, no. 3 (March 1975), p. 24. For a discussion of the 1973 alert and the problem of nuclear alerts in general, see Sagan, "Nuclear Alerts and Crisis Management."

59. James M. McConnell and Anne Kelly Calhoun, "The December 1971 Indo-Pakistani Crisis," in Dismukes and McConnell, eds., *Soviet Naval Diplomacy*, p. 191.

60. See, for example, Adam Yarmolinsky, "Department of Defense Operations During the Cuban Missile Crisis," *Naval War College Review*, vol. 32, no. 4 (July–August 1979): 88; and Dismukes and McConnell, "Conclusions," in *Soviet Naval Diplomacy*, p. 289.

61. Anthony R. Wells, "The June 1967 Arab-Israeli War," in Dismukes and McConnell, eds., *Soviet Naval Diplomacy*, p. 165.

62. Donald S. Zagoria and Janet D. Zagoria, "Crises on the Korean Peninsula," in Stephen

S. Kaplan, ed., *Mailed Fist, Velvet Glove: Soviet Armed Forces as a Political Instrument* (Washington, D.C.: U.S. Department of Commerce, National Technical Information Service, 1979), pp. 9–6.

63. See Robert F. Kennedy, *Thirteen Days: A Memoir of the Cuban Missile Crisis* (New York: W. W. Norton, 1971), pp. 48–50, 97.

64. Hilton discusses his "frayed nerves" as he describes a March–April 1972 naval confrontation in which he was involved. See "The U.S.–Soviet Incidents at Sea Treaty," pp. 30–31.

65. See Ball, "Nuclear War at Sea," and Fukuyama, "Escalation in the Middle East and Persian Gulf."

66. See Wolf, "Agreement at Sea," pp. 76–77; Donald W. Mitchell, *A History of Russian and Soviet Sea Power* (New York: Macmillan, 1974), p. 554; and Gorshkov's claim that the United States had obtained a recognition of parity from Great Britain at the interwar naval conferences and that the Soviets may have achieved the same in 1972, in Abram N. Shulsky, "Gorshkov on Naval Arms Limitations: KTO KOGO?," in Murphy, ed., *Naval Power in Soviet Policy,* p. 250.

67. In the Protocol to the agreement, however, the situation is reversed and the Soviets have a greater interest in preventing harassment of nonmilitary vessels.

68. For a discussion of the U.S. domestic impediments to arms control, see Steven E. Miller, "Politics over Promise: Domestic Impediments to Arms Control," *International Security,* vol. 8, no. 4 (Spring 1984): 67–90. Any discussion of domestic impediments to arms control in the Soviet Union is speculative, particularly in the case of the Incidents at Sea Agreement. Nevertheless, the military and political leadership may have had different motives for seeking an agreement and these differences could have provoked internal disputes.

69. Ball argues for changes in U.S. submarine deployments as a way to reduce the probability of naval incidents. See "Nuclear War at Sea," pp. 29–30.

70. See Hilton, "The U.S.–Soviet Incidents at Sea Treaty," p. 37.

71. Ibid. Former Chief of Naval Operations Watkins has also suggested that "Mariners have a common bond." Quoted in Gordon, "At Sea," p. 159.

72. For arguments that the agreement has been successful, see Hilton, "The U.S.–Soviet Incidents at Sea Treaty," p. 33; Senators Sam Nunn and John Warner, "A Nuclear Risk Reduction System," excerpts from the Report of the Nunn/Warner Working Group on Nuclear Risk Reduction, *Survival,* vol. 26, no. 3 (May–June 1984): 135; William Langer Ury and Richard Smoke, *Beyond the Hotline: Controlling a Nuclear Crisis* (Cambridge: Nuclear Negotiation Project, Harvard Law School, 1984); and Paul D. Wolfowitz, "Preserving Nuclear Peace," *Naval War College Review,* vol. 36, no. 2 (March–April 1983): 78.

73. "Superpowers Maneuvering for Supremacy on the High Seas," *Washington Post,* April 4, 1984, p. A18. The annual number of incidents may not be the best indicator of the success of the agreement. Incidents vary in severity and may be more likely now than in the late 1960s, when the Soviet Navy was smaller and the U.S. Navy conducted fewer exercises near Soviet waters.

74. "Soviet Sub Bumps into U.S. Carrier," *Washington Post* (March 22, 1984), p. A28.

75. "Stable pattern," "pretty good resolution," from ABC-TV *Nightline,* April 3, 1984; "rather businesslike," from CBS radio news, 8:12 A.M., April 4, 1984.

76. Stephen S. Roberts, "The October 1973 Arab-Israeli War," in Dismukes and McConnell, eds., *Soviet Naval Diplomacy,* p. 196. The Soviets did, however, simulate attacks after the U.S. alert. See ibid., p. 210.

77. Quoted in Caldwell, *American-Soviet Relations,* p. 228.

78. Quoted in Hilton, "The U.S.–Soviet Incidents at Sea Treaty," p. 33.

79. Quoted in ibid., pp. 33–34.

80. See "Soviets Harass Searches for 747 Debris," *Aviation Week and Space Technology,* September 12, 1983, p. 28; and "Race for the Black Box," *Time* (October 3, 1983), p. 26.

81. "Soviet Warship, US Naval Vessel Collide in Mideast," *Boston Globe* (November 18, 1983), p. 6.

82. See "Soviet Sub Bumps into U.S. Carrier," p. 1; and "Soviet Sub and U.S. Carrier Collide in Sea of Japan," *New York Times* (March 22, 1984), p. A7. If the submarine was under water at the time of the collision, the Incidents at Sea Agreement probably would not even apply.

83. William E. Smith, "Moscow's Muscle Flexing," *Time* (April 16, 1984), pp. 28–30.

84. Gordon, "At Sea," p. 159.

85. Ibid., p. 30.

86. "High Seas Diplomacy Continuing," *Washington Post* (June 8, 1984), p. A15.

87. Gordon, "At Sea," p. 159.

88. Hilton, "The U.S.–Soviet Incidents at Sea Treaty," p. 37.

89. William Beecher, "Election Clouds Weapons Talks," *The Boston Globe* (July 17, 1984), p. 4. The full text of Reagan's speech appears in *Weekly Compilation of Presidential Documents,* vol. 20, no. 26 (July 2, 1984), pp. 944–946.

90. See Leslie H. Gelb, "U.S.–Soviet Session on '72 Naval Accord Canceled," *New York Times* (June 19, 1985), p. A1; and Gordon, "At Sea," p. 159.

91. *International Herald Tribune* (November 8, 1985), p. 2; and "Superpower Contacts: A Variety of Forums," *New York Times* (August 31, 1986), p. 18.

92. See the chapter in this volume by Richard Haass on the 1978 U.S.–Soviet talks on demilitarization of the Indian Ocean.

93. Hilton, "The U.S.–Soviet Incidents at Sea Treaty," p. 31.

94. For an extended discussion of the Basic Principles Agreement of 1972, see Alexander George, ed., *Managing U.S.–Soviet Rivalry: Problems of Crisis Prevention* (Boulder, Colo.: Westview Press, 1983), pp. 107–118.

95. On the theory of tit-for-tat, see Robert Axelrod, *The Evolution of Cooperation* (New York: Basic Books, 1984) pp. 27–54.

96. Zumwalt, *On Watch,* p. 394.

97. Note that the U.S. Navy objected strongly to Weinberger's decision to cancel the 1985 annual review. On the Soviet side, Captain Serkov's support for the agreement presumably reflects the views of the Soviet Navy.

98. Hilton, "The U.S.–Soviet Incidents at Sea Treaty," p. 37.

99. In many cases military acceptance of arms control agreements has required "assurances" or "safeguards" that guarantee that the agreement will be accompanied by additional military programs. This was the case with the Limited Test Ban Treaty of 1963 and SALT I. See U.S. Congress, Senate, Committee on Armed Services, *Nuclear Test Ban Treaty. Hearings Before the Committee on Armed Services,* 88th Cong., 1st Sess. (Washington, D.C.: U.S. Government Printing Office, 1963), pp. 274–275; and U.S. Congress, Senate, Committee on Armed Services, *Military Implications of the Treaty on the Limitations of Anti-Ballistic Missile Systems and the Interim Agreement on the Limitation of Strategic Offensive Arms. Hearings Before the Committee on Armed Services,* 92nd Cong., 2nd Sess. (Washington, D.C.: U.S. Government Printing Office, 1972), pp. 17, 146. Although the Senate never voted on the question of consent to ratify SALT II, approval of the treaty almost certainly would have been tied to increased military spending. See, for example, Stephen J. Flanagan, "The Domestic Politics of SALT II: Implications for the Foreign Policy Process," in John Spanier and Joseph Nogee, eds., *Congress, the Presidency, and American Foreign Policy* (New York: Pergamon, 1981), pp. 44–76.

100. Hilton, "The U.S.–Soviet Incidents at Sea Treaty," p. 37. Joseph S. Nye, Jr., has suggested that a similar procedure might be effective for discussing broader military issues. In his "ReStarting Arms Control," *Foreign Policy,* No. 47 (Summer 1982): 109–11, he suggests that the chairman of the U.S. Joint Chiefs of Staff meet regularly with his Soviet counterpart to discuss military forces and doctrines.

101. Johan Jorgen Holst, "Confidence-Building Measures: A Conceptual Framework," *Survival,* vol. 25, no. 1 (January/February 1983): 2. Numerous authors have offered various defini-

tions of confidence-building measures. See Jonathan Alfred, ed., *Confidence-Building Measures,* Adelphi Paper No. 149 (London: International Institute for Strategic Studies, 1979); John Borawski, ed., *Avoiding War in the Nuclear Age* (Boulder, Colo.: Westview Press, 1986); E. M. Chossudovsky, "Confidence Building and Confidence-Building Measures in East-West Interactions," *Coexistence,* vol. 21, no. 1 (1984): 23–36; and Kevin N. Lewis and Mark A. Lorell, "Confidence-Building Measures and Crisis Resolution: Historical Perspectives," *Orbis,* vol. 28, no. 2 (Summer 1984): 281–306.

20

The U.S.–Soviet Conventional Arms
Transfer Negotiations

JANNE E. NOLAN

In what was intended to be a sweeping departure in U.S. policy, President Jimmy Carter assumed office in 1977 pledging to reduce sharply the global trade in advanced conventional armaments. Partly in response to the legacy of the Nixon Doctrine—the effort to substitute sales of sophisticated military equipment to key allies for direct U.S. military involvement in the Third World—concern in the Congress and the public about the potential dangers of escalating U.S. arms sales had been growing since the mid-1970s. Symbolized most dramatically by the sales of extremely sophisticated technologies to Arab states and to Iran during the "oil shocks" of the decade, the perceived risks arising from the proliferation of such weapons in volatile regions of the world became a major issue for the Carter presidency.

Reducing the global arms trade was a matter of personal commitment for President Carter, a commitment shared by a number of his most senior advisers—including Vice-President Walter Mondale and Secretary of State Cyrus Vance, as well as several key officials in the State Department of the U.S. Arms Control and Disarmament Agency. Originating in the campaign for the presidency, this commitment reflected domestic as well as international considerations.

Domestically, the Carter Administration, like all new administrations, was engaged in a concerted effort to disassociate itself from the military policies of its predecessors, of which the perceived profligacy of the Nixon and Ford Administrations' arms sales policies were a part. Key Democratic members of Congress had helped arouse public sentiment about the onerous image of the United States as a "merchant of death," and candidate Carter had made strong appeals to this constituency during his campaign. Once in office, his Administration was anxious to fulfill campaign promises and defuse this source of domestic pressure.

Internationally, a number of President Carter's advisers came to office with a heightened awareness of the implications for U.S.–Soviet relations of the spread of advanced weapons to strategic areas of the world. The Soviet Union had made substantial strides in its own arms exports, with a steady pattern of escalation in the quantity and sophistication of armaments sold to its Third World clients. Competitive arms supplies to Middle East states in the 1970s already had resulted in several superpower confrontations.[1]

Consequently, a key element in the development of arms restraint policies was the perception of an urgent need to address increasing Soviet activism in the Third World—

a major force behind the continued deterioration in U.S.–Soviet relations. The policies developed to guide arms sales represented only one of the many efforts of the Administration to recapture the momentum of détente, and where possible to substitute negotiations for confrontation. For some in the Administration, engaging the Soviets in a direct dialogue on arms sales policies was seen as a way to develop a common understanding and codes of conduct for U.S. and Soviet military operations and policies in the Third World—a way to reduce tensions and avoid inadvertent superpower conflict.

As a result, President Carter and his advisers, although by no means unanimous in their views, agreed early in the Administration to initiate talks with the Soviet Union concerning arms sales. This was one element of a three-part strategy to bring about a reduction in the world's arms trade that included unilateral restraints on U.S. arms sales, a pledge to seek multilateral negotiations among all major suppliers, and an effort to encourage recipients to curb their demand for weapons.[2] The resulting Conventional Arms Transfer Talks (CAT)—four rounds of bilateral negotiations on ways to limit arms sales held between 1977 and 1979—are the subject of this article. Although the talks failed, rather quickly becoming both the victim of, and a catalyst for, the deterioration in superpower relations that took place during the Carter Administration, the negotiating effort provides interesting lessons for any future attempt to moderate U.S.–Soviet military rivalry in the Third World.

The talks also provide a prism through which to analyze Soviet perceptions of regional security. The Soviet Union had developed a marked dependence on arms sales as its primary means of gaining access to the Third World and as a source of badly needed foreign exchange. Still portraying its weapons exports as a means of championing national liberation movements, the Soviet Union had in fact become increasingly active by the late 1970s in supplying arms to countries that owed it little allegiance and, in some cases, actively suppressed domestic communist movements—including, for instance, Algeria and Guinea.[3] Such transfers, divorced from ideological motivations, were and remain the leading instrument available to the Soviet Union for expanding its influence in the developing world.

At the same time, the CAT initiative coincided with intensifying Soviet concern about growing Western military involvement in areas close to Soviet borders—notably, Iran and the People's Republic of China. An element of Soviet interest in discussing arms restraint reflected the traditional Soviet objective of reducing Western "encirclement" in areas proximate to the Soviet Union, an objective that could be served by restricting U.S. and West European military sales to a number of these countries.

The CAT talks represented an avenue for the Soviet Union to attempt to legitimize its own activities in the Third World and push for restraint on Western actions, while maintaining an image of cordial relations with the United States. Cautiously receptive throughout, the Soviet Union clearly understood these talks to be an American initiative, driven as much by U.S. domestic forces as geopolitical concerns. Unencumbered by any such political pressures, the Soviet side was free to participate in the CAT talks as a means of nurturing an image of détente without jeopardizing its interests in the Third World—possibly even gaining enhanced status among Third World countries. To the extent that there were mutual interests in CAT, they tended for the most part to be corollary to fundamental Soviet security objectives, as is discussed below.

The talks also illustrate the interplay between domestic politics in the United States and the fate of U.S.–Soviet negotiations. Although one major reason the talks failed was that they were conducted against a backdrop of worsening U.S.–Soviet relations and volatility in the Persian Gulf region, bureaucratic confusion and personal rivalries ensured a failure to develop domestic consensus in favor of the effort. From their inception, the CAT talks were associated with broader political perceptions of an Administration bent on unilateralism, excessive efforts to conciliate the Soviet Union, and global military disengagement. The sheer number of competing arms control efforts undertaken by the new Administration—of which SALT II was clearly the highest priority—also ensured that concerted high-level attention to the CAT effort would be difficult. And partly as a result of exaggerated rhetoric coming from the Administration itself about the objectives of arms restraint, the Carter Administration's arms sales policies were doomed to incite opponents and disappoint proponents. In reality, the measures proposed by the Administration were quite modest. As was the case in a number of other arms control efforts adopted by the Administration, however, even modest efforts became casualties of domestic sabotage in the face of insufficiently coherent objectives.

THE CONTEXT

The transfer of military technology to allies and friends is a policy instrument of central significance for virtually all of the industrial countries, an instrument that cuts to the heart of several fundamental, often competing, national interests, including, inter alia, diplomatic relations, economic/trade interests, and defense. Until the mid-1950s, arms transfers by the superpowers consisted for the most part of grants of obsolescent equipment to their respective allies in Europe. For the past twenty-five years, however, and especially since the mid-1970s, the focus of U.S. and Soviet arms sales has been on commercially advantageous exports of advanced weapons to countries in the Third World— many of which owe little or no allegiance to either superpower.[4]

Arms sales in the contemporary environment have become an increasingly salient aspect of the superpower competition for influence in the Third World, serving in many instances as the cutting edge of great power involvement in local conflicts and complicating efforts by the United States and the Soviet Union to reach accommodation at the strategic level and in Europe. As documented elsewhere, great power involvement in local conflicts—involvement that often originated in arms supply relationships—has contributed to superpower confrontation and in several instances posed the risk of direct military conflict.

By the time of the 1976 presidential campaign, arms sales were the target of widespread public opposition in the United States. Although Soviet and West European supplies of arms to Third World countries had grown significantly, the U.S. role as leading arms merchant—especially to countries of questionable stability, such as Iran—prompted public outcries. The Nixon Doctrine had culminated in the late 1970s in a perception of arms sales as an instrument out of control; or, as Senator William Proxmire put it, "the old sell-anything-to-anyone-at-anytime policy."

As analyzed by Paul Hammond and others,[5] two contradictory trends were evident in the late 1970s: increased domestic pressure to restrain arms sales and the growing importance of arms sales in the pursuit of foreign policy objectives traditionally fulfilled by other means. The inherent conflict between efforts to appease domestic opposition and the various pressures intrinsic to the structural dependency of the United States on arms sales was translated into the policies that the Carter Administration attempted to implement, resulting in a chronic tension that ultimately undercut the policies' effectiveness.

From the Soviet standpoint, there is no evidence that arms transfer restraint had ever been considered seriously at senior levels of the government prior to the Carter initiative.[6] As discussed above, arms sales had come to occupy an increasingly prominent place in Soviet geopolitical strategy. As part of their overall development of global military power, the Soviet Union had by the mid-1970s achieved the "global reach" incumbent on a superpower—of which the ability to arm clients in distant areas formed a part. Soviet doctrine continued to portray arms supplies to the Third World as consistent with the image of the Soviet Union as champion of liberation movements and incipient Marxist regimes—although this image was clearly of dubious credibility in the face of growing Soviet exports to anticommunist countries. Absent serious domestic pressures arising from public opinion or international opprobrium, however, any Soviet concerns over its role as an arms supplier were clearly not commensurate with those of the United States.

At the same time, however, the Soviets were not entirely immune from some of the costs of expanded arms supplies to Third World countries. Unceremoniously expelled from Egypt in 1972, the Soviet Union had also experienced far less than decisive gains from major arms exports to Indonesia, the Sudan, Guinea, and Nigeria—as well as a serious setback in Somalia in 1977 as a result of its refusal to sanction Somali aggression against Ethiopia. In addition, Soviet recognition of the dangers of providing advanced technologies to strategic regions of the Third World was implicit in certain tacit demonstrations of restraint—including the refusal to supply North Korea with ground-mobile air defense systems (which would have greatly enhanced Pyongyang's ability to mount an invasion against the South, an objective the Soviets did not support) and denials of Syrian requests for advanced systems, such as the SS-12 short-range ballistic missile.[7] In view of the direct superpower confrontation witnessed in the Middle East, there were at least in principle security considerations that could prompt sincere Soviet attention to the prospect of conventional arms restraint.

Moreover, President Carter's unilateral policy contained elements that could advance Soviet objectives. Restrictions on exports of advanced technology would by implication have a more direct effect on Western countries, given the Soviet Union's restraints on state-of-the-art arms exports. Prohibitions on coproduction agreements and the retransfer of arms from one client to a third country were also already part of Soviet restrictions. And, as discussed earlier, the negotiations provided an opportunity to the Soviet Union to try to restrict Western transfers to critical regions while helping to legitimize Soviet activities in the Third World. All told, however, there is simply no basis for suggesting that any systematic attention to conventional arms restraint informed Soviet policy prior to the Carter initiatives.

THE NEGOTIATIONS

The Carter Administration discussed the subject of arms transfer negotiations at the first meeting of the National Security Council and the issue was raised with the leaders of several European countries by Vice-President Mondale during his trip to Western Europe in late January of 1977. The subject was raised again in a series of less publicized bilateral meetings between U.S. and British, French, and German officials. The European reaction, perhaps predictably, was pure skepticism. Until the United States reduced its own share of the arms market—a market that it dominated so overwhelmingly—and demonstrated concretely that the Soviet Union would do the same, the Europeans saw no compelling reason to join in.

Accordingly, the United States issued its first démarches to the Soviets. In March 1977, arms transfer restraint was one of eight subjects discussed by Secretary Vance during his trip to Moscow. The result was an agreement to establish working groups, one of which was to be devoted to conventional arms sales. Initial formal consultations were held in Washington in December 1977, led on the American side by the State Department's Director of Political-Military Affairs, Leslie Gelb, and on the Soviet side by Ambassador Oleg Khlestov, Chief of the Treaty and Legal Department in the Ministry of Foreign Affairs.[8]

The first meeting, described variously as "exploratory" and "procedural," consisted largely of U.S. explanations to the Soviet side of the Carter arms restraint policy, underscoring the point that the U.S. unilateral policy, were it to be sustained, would require multilateral cooperation. Key to the U.S. presentation—and to the fundamental U.S. perspective—was the idea of conventional arms restraint as a means of blunting U.S.–Soviet competition so as to avoid inadvertent conflict and reduce the risk of war. Such efforts, it was argued, would flow directly from obligations that the two sides assumed in the 1972 Declaration of Principles and reinforced with the 1973 Agreement on the Prevention of Nuclear War—a paradigm which seemed to make an impression on the Soviet delegation. Although Gelb described the meeting as "perfunctory" and stated "it was unclear whether the Soviets would agree to meet again,"[9] the Soviets requested subsequent talks.

By the time of the second round held in Helsinki in May 1978, U.S. officials had decided that for both domestic and international reasons it was important to produce tangible signs of progress that could be disseminated publicly—at a minimum, a joint communiqué demonstrating that the two sides were serious. Keyed in part to encouraging European and Third World support for CAT, the growing pressure for rapid and concrete signs of progress was also the result of incipient doubts among certain Carter advisers about Soviet motives in the negotiations.

In the effort to emphasize the mutual obligations of the two sides in reducing global tensions—of which arms transfer restraint was to form a part—the U.S. strategy at Round II was to link CAT more explicitly to the 1972 Basic Principles Agreement. The ensuing discussion in this round proved extremely encouraging. Aside from agreeing on certain ground rules for the negotiations, the two sides issued a joint communiqué that unmistakably reflected U.S. strategy. The United States and the Soviet Union acknowledged that "the problem of limiting international transfers of conventional arms is urgent" and that "these meetings, being a component of the Soviet-American negotiations on the cessation of the arms race, are held in accordance with the Basic Principles Agreement."[10] The delegations also pledged their governments' support for CAT at the forthcoming U.N. Special Session on Disarmament (SSOD). The subsequent Soviet public statement at the SSOD mentioned CAT in the text of its proposal "On Practical Paths Toward Ending the Arms Race," referring to the issue as an "urgent" problem that "must be resolved" and was "attainable in the general context of the relaxation of international tension."[11]

These developments lent significant impetus to that CAT talks, permitting them to move from exploratory sessions to the recognized status of formal negotiations. The Soviet delegation at Round II had a new and more senior chief negotiator, Lev Mendelevich, also the head of the Soviet delegation to the Indian Ocean negotiations, indicating to some American officials a higher level of commitment to the talks on the part of the Soviet government. The Final Document of the SSOD, supported by both superpowers, had called for consultations "among major arms suppliers and recipients on the limitation of all types of international transfer of conventional weapons"—the first time, as Leslie Gelb stressed, that the "concept of restraint . . . [received] an international blessing." [12] Together with the receptivity of the Soviet delegation during Round II and the wording of the final communiqué, there was sufficient collective optimism to permit the scheduling of a third round for July—barely ten weeks after Round II.

Although still inchoate, evidence of serious differences among U.S. officials' approaches to the talks and between the United States and the Soviet Union was already emerging, however. On the U.S. side, preparation for Round III revealed a crucial difference of perspective within the Executive Branch over how to proceed—a difference that led ultimately to the demise of the effort and has a significant bearing on the question of whether regulation of arms sales may ever be an effective mechanism for reducing U.S.–Soviet tensions.

The principal division over U.S. strategy was between those who believed that the most advantageous way to proceed was to emphasize technical rather than political issues, and those who viewed CAT as primarily a political exercise aimed at reaching a common understanding of the U.S.–Soviet rivalry in the Third World. In the context of planning for negotiations and their aftermath, the use of the term "technical" referred to an emphasis on weapons characteristics and capabilities as the guiding criteria for the negotiations, emphasizing the need to define a priori the types of technologies that both sides believed to be in their security interests to restrain. Conversely, the term "political" was used to denote the way in which arms transfers were actually used as instruments of state behavior—the political/military consequences of arms transfers in specific regional and subregional contexts.

Advocates of the first approach, led by the Arms Control and Disarmament Agency but joined on occasion by representatives from the Joint Chiefs of Staff and the Office of the Secretary of Defense, shared two major assumptions. The first was that arms transfers could at least initially be seen as stabilizing or destabilizing according to the character of the weapons involved. For example, advanced systems easily diverted to terrorist use, such as man-portable air defense systems, could be categorized as inherently destabilizing throughout most of the Third World and thus possibly subject to a complete ban. Similarly, systems that accorded a country clear advantage in a preemptive strike, such as long range surface-to-surface missiles, could be discussed as candidates for comprehensive restraint.

Since the key long-term objective was to develop guidelines to limit the transfer of equipment whose sophistication significantly exceeded that already contained in regional arsenals, however, it was understood that it would be necessary over time to develop more specific and regionally distinct criteria—recognizing that what constituted an advanced system in East Asia would not necessarily be so in the Middle East. Proponents of the technical approach argued that as the talks progressed from systems subject to blanket prohibitions to more complex criteria affecting systems such as fighter aircraft or ground combat vehicles, regional differentiations would be implicit.

But the second and more important assumption guiding the "technical" approach was tactical. Given the absence of any prior agreements on arms transfer restraint—and the extreme sensitivity of the subject—advocates of the technical approach saw advantage in steering the initial discussions towards areas of least controversy. To this end,

516   *Janne E. Nolan*

even developing a common data base with the Soviets as to what they understood to be an "advanced" system—such as ranges and capabilities of surface-to-surface missiles, for instance—would be useful. As in the initial stages of strategic nuclear negotiations, developing a common understanding of which systems both sides believed to be the highest priority for control was a critical, and time consuming, first step.

More important, advocates of this approach believed that modest agreements were necessary to provide momentum for more ambitious discussion. At issue was how best to develop the fundamental infrastructure—both bureaucratic and international—that would permit the institutionalization of arms restraint mechanisms. Making progress in areas that incited a minimum of political controversy, they stressed, could in turn lead to the development of agreed criteria for more far-reaching application—to weapon systems of clear significance to both countries' political/military policies, applied on a regional or subregional basis.

In contrast, Secretary of State Vance and Chief Negotiator Gelb favored an approach that emphasized political objectives in both the immediate and long-term. The utility of the talks, they maintained—and the criteria by which to measure their success—derived from the ability of the two sides to reach agreements about appropriate norms of behavior in the Third World. The talks should at the outset emphasize discussion of regions and subregions, rendering explicit the full scope of political and military forces in the U.S.–Soviet competition. As such, weapon systems were only the conduits by which the two sides would arrive at a broader understanding of their respective overall regional interests. Advocates of this approach were concerned that ACDA's technical emphasis would produce only marginal agreements, could drag on for years, and, most significantly, would divert attention from the real issue: the political rivalry of the superpowers for influence in the Third World.

The U.S. internal debate was finally resolved in favor of the State Department, and the U.S. brought regionally oriented proposals to the bargaining table at Helsinki in July, proposing that the two sides focus on Latin America and Subsaharan Africa as initial regions for discussion. The rationale for choosing these regions was largely that they were then areas of relatively lesser superpower interest and local military capability. The regional orientation did not supplant continued work on the development of lists of potential weapons for restraint, but relegated this to one of several activities in support of regional proposals.

In the interim, the Soviet Union had itself developed certain proposals. As they had alluded to in their statements at the SSOD, the Soviet Union stressed two critical themes: first, that détente was the overwhelming objective of CAT, and second, that political imperatives were the ultimate determinant of any negotiations in this area.

As such, the Soviet Union came to Helsinki stressing the primacy of agreements on legal principles to govern arms transfers on a global basis. As they had stated in their UN proposal:

> Reasonable and precise political/legal criteria must be elaborated that would determine in what situations and for which recipients arms deliveries are justified and permissible and in which cases they should be banned or severely restricted. Such criteria must be based on the UN Charter and on the decision of the United Nations regarding the provision of material and moral support for peoples struggling for liberation from colonial and racist oppression.[13]

Formal Soviet proposals at Round III drew heavily on U.N. documents, and pressed for the establishment of eligibility criteria for recipients of the type referred to above, such as the permissibility of arms transfers to countries for defense against external aggression but not for violation of the territorial integrity of another country. A key rhetorical rallying point for the Soviets was the legitimization of military support to "national liberation groups." The Soviet approach was opposed sharply by the United States, evoking reactions ranging from concern that it would lead to a meaningless exercise that delineated broad guidelines absent any enforceable criteria, to a more pronounced fear that this preoccupation with general legal principles proved the essentially propagandistic Soviet motives in CAT.

The Soviet Union, however, agreed over the course of Round III to adopt major elements of the U.S. approach. The United States had proposed to discuss arms transfers to specific regions—beginning with Latin America and Subsaharan Africa—and to develop precise military-technical criteria to regulate arms sales on a global basis. These criteria were directly derived from the Carter policy for unilateral restraints of U.S. arms sales, and included proposed restraints on either side being the first to introduce an advanced weapon system into a region; on the development of weapons solely for export; on retransferring weapons from one recipient to a third country; and on coproduction agreements between a superpower and a regional ally.

Quite to the surprise of the American side, the Soviets not only agreed to discuss criteria of this kind and arms restraints tailored to specific regional contexts, but also accepted the U.S. proposal that interim regional restraint agreements could be negotiated in advance of any final decisions on overall criteria. They also indicated they would consider interim agreements consisting of lists of specific candidate weapons for restraint, an important U.S. position thought to be key to the achievement of early progress. Finally, the Soviets agreed to recognize the essential equality of political and technical criteria for the purpose of the negotiations.

By the end of the July round, the two sides had agreed on the need to develop a three-part framework consisting of (1) commonly-agreed political/legal criteria to determine recipient eligibility; (2) commonly-agreed military/technical criteria to govern the types and quantities of technology transferred; and (3) mechanisms to implement principles and guidelines in specific regions.

From the standpoint of key U.S. negotiators, major strides had been achieved. As the deputy U.S. negotiator, Barry Blechman, argued, agreement on the framework could establish "a common set of criteria and a common approach to their implementation, which can serve as models for both suppliers and recipients in framing arms transfer policies and designing regional restraint agreements."[14] Similarly, Leslie Gelb, in testimony to the Congress, suggested there was a "realistic possibility" that there could be a "development of harmonized national guidelines for transfer restraints."[15] A number of officials and commentators pointed to the London Suppliers' Group for nuclear exports as a possible model.

Unexpected successes aside, the two sides' approaches throughout Round III revealed fundamentally different security preoccupations and serious asymmetries in objectives. A Soviet proposal that each side should ban military transfers to the other's "neighbors" surfaced in Round III, for instance, demonstrating a Soviet preoccupation with limiting U.S. security assistance to countries close to Soviet territory that were central to U.S. interests: Turkey, Iran, and the People's Republic of China. In spite of the Soviet agreement to accept the equality of legal and technical criteria, moreover, public pronouncements by Soviet commentators continued to emphasize the preeminence of legal principles.[16] And the Soviet side continued to emphasize the need to include Western European arms transfers in the discussions. As one Soviet commentator put it, conventional arms control "cannot, in the final analysis, be resolved by the efforts of the USSR and USA alone without the participation of other major arms suppliers."[17]

The most significant schism emerging at this point, however, concerned negotiations on regions, exposing the underlying conflict of interest in discussing regions at all and the asymmetry of interests in specific regions. As was predicted by those officials who had opposed early discussions of regional restraints, Soviet agreement in principle to discuss U.S. candidate regions would lead to an inevitable confrontation between the two sides when the Soviets put forward their own regional proposals at Round IV. During a visit to Moscow in the fall of 1978, Leslie Gelb was informed by Ambassador Mendelevich that the Soviets would clearly want to discuss regions other than Latin America and Subsaharan Africa, citing China as an example. Gelb responded that China did not constitute a region and would not be an acceptable subject for discussion; but that any other legitimate "region," geographically and politically distinct, could be proposed.

The overall foreign policy context in the United States at the time of the preparations for Round IV was hardly propitious for regional discussions. Although not known to the majority of officials involved in CAT, normalization of relations with the People's Republic was reaching its delicate final stages, under the personal direction of National Security Adviser Zbigniew Brzezinski. In West Asia, the stability of the Pahlavi regime in Iran was eroding daily.

U.S. preparations for the fourth round of talks, to be held in Mexico City in December 1978, nevertheless focused almost entirely on the regional issue. Preliminary diplomatic contacts had indicated the Soviets wanted to discuss "East Asia," by which they still principally meant China, and "West Asia," by which they meant the Persian Gulf. U.S. officials notified the governments of South Korea and Saudi Arabia of the likelihood that the Soviets would propose arms limitations in these regions, but assured them that discussions would be of regions, not specific countries.

Opposition to discussions of these countries escalated throughout the Executive Branch during this period and a number of senior American officials, including Brzezinski and Secretary of Defense Harold Brown, stated categorically that even pro forma discussions of Iran and China could jeopardize U.S. interests. The issue of whether the United States should uphold its pledge to discuss regions proposed by the Soviets was taken up subsequently by the Special Coordinating Committee of the National Security Council in several contentious meetings.

Not previously extensively involved, Brzezinski began at this point to play a key role in the planning of the CAT talks. He argued forcefully at an SCC meeting on November 27 that the American delegation should be instructed to break off negotiations if the Soviets raised either East or West Asia—and that the Soviets should be informed of this position in advance. Chief negotiator Leslie Gelb argued that while the United States was clearly not interested in negotiating restraints on arms transfers to these regions in the near-term, the Americans should at least to listen to Soviet proposals, if only to reject them. A staunch refusal to even entertain the other side's proposals was an unprecedented act in U.S.–Soviet arms control negotiations. Moreover, it was a breach of the U.S. commitment made to the Soviets at the previous round.

A protracted bureaucratic dispute ensued involving all of the President's most senior foreign policy advisers. Preoccupied with the SALT II negotiations, however, neither Secretary of State Vance nor U.S. Arms Control and Disarmament Agency Director Paul Warnke proved willing to become directly involved, leaving the matter for adjudication by their deputies. It was not an even match. When the issue was brought to the attention of President Carter, Brzezinski, supported by Secretary of Defense Brown, persuaded the President to instruct the American delegation to discuss only Latin America and Subsaharan Africa and, if other regions were raised, to walk out.

Prior to the opening of the fourth round, held in Mexico City in mid-December, Gelb presented the U.S. position to Ambassador Mendelevich. The Soviet negotiator, at first astonished, became increasingly angry at the U.S. refusal to even listen to the Soviet position. The Soviet delegation had obviously come prepared to discuss regions, with several new delegates known to be specialists in Middle Eastern and Far Eastern affairs.

After nearly a week of strained procedural meetings involving only the heads of the delegations—and a now infamous exchange of cables between Gelb and Brzezinski in a last ditch effort by the U.S. delegation to gain more flexibility in the negotiating instructions[18]—a modest compromise was reached. The regional working group was not convened, regions were not discussed, but the two sides tabled candidate lists of political/legal and military/technical criteria, worked on common text, and agreed on the need to develop overall consultative mechanisms to oversee the implementation of guidelines.

The two sets of criteria contained some elements of commonality, particularly on the political/legal side, with both sides drawing on the U.N. Charter for development of principles. There was in fact so little serious disagreement in the political/legal drafting group that the U.S. working group chairman had to be instructed to slow its progress so as to ensure keeping its pace consonant with that of the military/technical group. Differences between the two sides were much more significant in the latter, but the Soviets seemed to agree on some candidate systems for global prohibition, including cluster bombs and napalm.

But in spite of some perfunctory references to CAT and minor diplomatic exchanges in 1979, for all practical purposes the CAT talks ended in Mexico City in December 1978. As a final, pointed epitaph, delegates arrived at breakfast on the last day in Mexico to find newspaper headlines heralding the formal U.S. recognition of the People's Republic of China. If there were any lingering doubts on the part of the negotiators that the CAT talks had been operating as, at best, a modest sideshow to the overarching concerns of American foreign policy—in this case, a major policy initiative to which no officials involved in the talks had been privy—this certainly laid any such doubts to rest.

LESSONS FROM THE FAILURE OF CAT

The CAT talks fit all too clearly the category of efforts in which the obstacles were so formidable that one might have predicted failure or assigned very low probability to achievement of an agreement. They also illustrate a missed opportunity—an opportunity to at least begin to develop guidelines for arms transfer diplomacy, an area of endeavor which remains moribund.

But the root causes of the failure of CAT were more fundamental. Most significantly, the talks failed as a result of two fundamental contradictions in the choice of both objectives and strategy. First was the decision that the talks should bear the burden of mediating the entirety of U.S.–Soviet differences in the Third World—in spite of the almost unexplored nature of this type of diplomacy. Second was the fact that the U.S.–Soviet rivalry in the Third World and the international political relations on which discussions of this rivalry could impinge were simply too sensitive to be discussed by the great powers—either in global terms or more particularly in regional terms—at the current stage of their relationship. The schismatic strategy reflected critical divisions within the Carter Administration; in some cases, in the thinking of single individuals.

Seen as a missed opportunity, the failure of the talks obviated potentially promising discussions and agreements to restrain transfers of highly destabilizing weapon systems, such as hand-held air defense systems. The danger of the proliferation of such systems to volatile regions has been pointedly underscored by two recent developments: the shooting down of a Sudanese civilian aircraft by insurgents using Soviet SA-7 missiles in August of 1986 and the Congressional effort in mid-1986 to prohibit the sale of Stinger air defense missiles to countries experiencing severe instability. The demise of the talks also prevented the achievement of a better understanding of how the Soviets view arms transfers as an instrument of their global objectives. One particular approach of great promise for such discussions might have been to reaffirm and build on existing arrangements that were honored tacitly—such as on the Korean Peninsula in the late 1970s. The Reagan Administration's violation of this tacit restraint with the sale of F-16 fighter aircraft to South Korea in 1981 certainly will complicate any future efforts in this region. This decision might well have been forestalled had there been a more formal U.S.–Soviet agreement to mutually forego certain advanced technology sales to North and South Korea.

Clearly, the objectives pursued by the United States in the CAT talks were never in consonance with the realities of either the domestic or international environment. Domestically, the collapse of the talks both contributed to, and was abetted by, the repeated revisions of the Carter arms transfer restraint policy: a policy that began as a sweeping revolution, evolved into a selective application of criteria when denials of sales posed no serious political complications, and culminated in its abandonment. It was widely perceived that while arms restraint may have been an initial commitment of the Administration, it was transitory, given the perfunctory efforts to develop a durable political consensus on its behalf. The serious structural impediments to U.S. restraint—from industry pressures to competition from European arms suppliers—were not accorded sufficient attention. As one commentator put it, "Reality forced the administration to abandon for all practical purposes another of its third world policies—one calculated to curtail the sales of arms to developing countries . . ."[19] Like the CAT talks, the restraint policies self-destructed in the maelstrom of exaggerated expectations.

The CAT talks were also casualties of a worsening geopolitical environment, deteroriating U.S.–Soviet relations, and eroding domestic support for the Carter Administration. From the time of the first discussion in 1977 to the final round in 1978, the Carter Administration—and the world—had changed. The moral optimism that had guided much of the President's thinking in earlier stages was by 1978 increasingly giving way to more pragmatic assessments of the prospects for U.S.–Soviet conciliation—what many have characterized more colorfully as an ascendance of Brzezinski over Vance.

The coalition developed within the American bureaucracy in favor of the CAT effort was fragile from the outset but was made even more so by the pressure to achieve early progress in regional discussions—in this case, within a year. The pressure for early success was never realistic; but, in addition, the regional emphasis helped to destroy prospects for the talks by inciting those who had authority for the conduct of diplomatic relations with key Third World countries. Bureaucratic disputes arose not only between agencies but on an intra-agency basis as well, marked by profound suspicions on the part of regional bureaus in the State Department who were kept insufficiently informed of objectives and developments by the key CAT negotiators.

In the Latin American bureaus of the State and Defense Departments, for instance, any support for restricting Soviet arms sales to these regions competed with broader concerns that U.S.–Soviet negotiations would interfere with regional developments by undercutting ongoing efforts among a number of Latin American countries to develop regional arms restraint arrangements, and encouraging a perception of a superpower condominium insensitive to local concerns. In regions of greater political importance, moreover, including Asia and the Persian Gulf, such discussions were simply anathema to regional specialists in light of the complex and sensitive challenges they were facing in relations with Iran and China. In short, once regional relations became the subject of the talks, the effort moved out of the jurisdiction of arms control and into the realm of geopolitics. This in turn underscored the fact that the CAT initiative should never have been been pursued in a manner that permitted the separation of arms control interests from overall foreign policy objectives, applied in specific areas.

Internationally, the initiation of talks with the Soviet Union preceded, rather than followed, any effort to develop an understanding of Soviet interest in and potential commitment to arms restraints. With all evidence to the contrary, the United States seemed to assume that the Soviet Union would share U.S. concerns and a sense of urgency about the dangers of arms transfers. In fact, without any of the pressures of public opinion, international opprobrium, an outspoken Congress, or even seriously imperiled allies, like Iran, whatever Soviet interest existed was clearly derived from other sources, as previously discussed.

Without any clear understanding of Soviet motives, the U.S. bureaucracy left itself open to damaging speculations about Soviet objectives that were difficult to dispel. Opponents of the CAT effort advanced a number of theories about why the Soviets agreed to participate and in turn to go along with significant elements of the American strategy: the Soviets hoped to generate domestic pressures in the United States and West Europe against NATO arms sales in order to drive wedges in the NATO alliance; they planned to use the talks as a propaganda tool to enhance their prestige in the Third World and legitimize their arms sales to Africa and elsewhere; or they hoped ultimately to demilitarize their frontiers. In the end, perceptions of purely nefarious motives on the Soviets' part prevailed.

Although U.S. and Soviet motives clearly diverged, some common or parallel interest in CAT might have been identified and served as a basis for cooperation. Thus, there is evidence that the Soviet Union did not exploit CAT purely for reasons of propaganda. Soviet willingness to abide by common definitions contained in the U.N. Charter, for instance, as well as Soviet agreement to consider the London Suppliers' Group as a model for a CAT agreement would not have been possible if Soviet efforts were directed entirely at image building in the Third World. Most important, however, Soviet willingness to discuss technical limitations on advanced arms sales reflected a recognition of the risks to the superpowers of escalating shipments of arms to volatile and strategic regions of the world. Given the truncated nature of the talks, however, no firm conclusions about long-term Soviet objectives and whether they could provide a basis for some kind of CAT agreement can credibly be drawn.

Any future efforts in this area should draw on three key lessons from the failure of CAT:

1. The talks proved that it is not possible to discuss U.S.–Soviet rivalry in the Third World under the guise of arms control or any other subterfuge. The putative objective of the CAT effort—to seek limits on sales of advanced armaments—was quickly overwhelmed when the talks took on the burden of mediating U.S.–Soviet geopolitical rivalry. The failure demonstrates the need for an incremental approach to arms transfer restraint that emphasizes the technical over the political in the early stages. Clearly, arms transfers were and remain far too significant for the security and political objectives of the superpowers to be subject to immediate restraints along regional lines.
2. The failure of CAT shows the importance of clear objectives, backed up by domestic political support—support that is only possible when there is strong and consistent presidential leadership to ensure bureaucratic discipline and careful planning of objectives and strategy. The CAT talks were clearly a casualty of competing international objectives and contradictory perspectives among senior officials, which precluded the development of any reasonable foundation for their implementation.
3. The CAT experience demonstrates that a tolerable level of cooperation between the superpowers is a prerequisite for success in any such effort. At the time of the first démarche to the Soviet Union, however, the spirit of U.S.–Soviet détente, which had made possible the 1972 Basic Principles agreement, and other important signs of conciliation, had all but disappeared.

Discussions of technical issues—from global bans on destabilizing weapons to tighter restrictions on clients' disposition of weapons received from the superpowers—need not be seen as either a substitute for, or a sacrifice of, the larger objective of developing more general codes of conduct for superpower behavior. There is much to be learned about what the Soviets believe to be "destabilizing" weapons; how they would define advanced and long-range systems; and their views about acceptable client behavior. Developing norms to guide even these limited types of transfers could lend some measure of predictability to what is at present an area of great uncertainty. Moreover, once an infrastructure of cooperation were developed, ranging from agreed candidate systems for restraint to a consultative framework for implementing agreements, more comprehensive efforts could be undertaken.

Ultimately, if any such efforts are to be undertaken in the future, they must be preceded by serious efforts to articulate the importance of the objectives, the security risks of escalating arms supplies, and the benefits to be derived from arms restraint. Otherwise, the controversies associated with even modest efforts in this area will always overwhelm any potential gains—in a permanent ascendance of short-term over long-term interests.

Notes

1. For a more complete discussion of superpower confrontations in the Middle East, see Barry Blechman, Janne E. Nolan and Alan Platt, "Negotiated Limitations on Arms Transfers: First Steps Toward Crisis Prevention," in Alexander L. George, ed., *Managing U.S.–Soviet Rivalry: Problems of Crisis Prevention,* (Boulder, Colo.: Westview Press, 1983).
2. The Carter Administration policy, enunciated in Presidential Directive 13 of 1977, set

forth controls for arms transfers to be applied to all countries outside of NATO, ANZUS, and Japan. In addition to an annual ceiling on the dollar volume of government-to-government arms transfers, these categories included: a) prohibition of transfers of advanced equipment that would introduce a qualitatively higher combat capability into a region; b) a ban on the development of weapons solely for export; and c) restrictions on coproduction agreements, retransfers of U.S. equipment, and on the promotion of weapon sales by agents of the U.S. government or private manufacturers. All of these provisions were to apply except "in instances where it can clearly be demonstrated that the transfer contributes to national security interests." For a complete discussion of the Carter Administration's arms restraint policies, see, inter alia, Paul Hammond, et al., *The Reluctant Supplier* (Cambridge, Mass.: Oelgeschlager, Gunn & Hain, Inc., 1983) and U.S. Congress, Senate, Committee on Foreign Relations, *Implications of President Carter's Arms Transfer Policy* (Washington, D.C.: U.S. Government Printing Office, 1977).

3. For a more complete discussion of Soviet arms transfer policy, see Jo Husbands, "Soviet Weapons Exports: Russian Roulette in the Third World," *The Defense Monitor* vol. 8, no. 1 (January 1979).

4. The arms transfer phenomenon is cogently discussed in Andrew Pierre's book *The Global Politics of Arms Sales* (Princeton, N.J.: Princeton University Press, 1982).

5. Hammond, *The Reluctant Supplier,* Chapter 6.

6. There are unfortunately no comprehensive studies of Soviet motives and objectives in CAT. One exception is Cynthia Roberts' unpublished paper "Soviet Arms Transfers and Perspectives on Conventional Arms Restraint," January 1982.

7. For further discussion of this, see Barry Blechman, et al., "Pushing Arms," *Foreign Policy* (Spring 1982): 139–140.

8. In addition to Gelb, the U.S. delegation was composed of representatives of the Arms Control and Disarmament Agency, the National Security Council Staff, the Department of Defense and the staff of the Joint Chiefs of Staff. Regional specialists and weapons experts supplemented the delegation as necessary. The Soviet delegation was led by two career diplomats successively, Ambassadors Khlestov and Mendelevich. Various specialists, some with practical experience in negotiating experience and several with experience at the United Nations, comprised the rest of the Soviet negotiating team.

9. Hammond, *The Reluctant Supplier,* p. 173.

10. "Joint U.S.–U.S.S.R. Communique, May 11, 1978," reprinted in the Department of State *Bulletin,* (July 1978), p. 36.

11. *Pravda,* (May 31, 1978), quoted in Roberts, "Soviet Arms Transfers," p. 22.

12. Statement by Leslie H. Gelb to the House Armed Services Committee, Special Panel on Conventional Arms Transfers and the Indian Ocean, October 3, 1978.

13. *Pravda,* quoted in Roberts, "Soviet Arms Transfers," p. 22.

14. Barry Blechman, "Controlling the International Trade in Arms," speech to the Woodrow Wilson International Center for Scholars, May 29, 1979, p. 10.

15. Leslie H. Gelb, statement before the House Armed Services Committee, October 3, 1978.

16. A Soviet commentator writing in *Novoe Vremia* singled out desirable restraints on armaments to "militarist states . . . which torpedo disarmament efforts" (China): "racist regimes" (South Africa and Rhodesia); and to countries "recognized as having unjust territorial claims on other states" (Israel). Quoted in Roberts, "Soviet Arms Transfers," p. 24.

17. V. Petrovsky, "The Soviet Union's Struggle for Real Disarmament," *International Affairs* (Moscow, 7 July 1978), p. 19; quoted in Roberts, "Soviet Arms Transfers," p. 24.

18. See for instance Don Oberdorfer, *Washington Post* (December 19, 1978), p. 1.

19. Edward Laurence, Professor, Naval Post-Graduate School, in a statement before the Subcommittee on International Security and Scientific Affairs, Committee on Foreign Affairs, U.S. House of Representatives, March 4, 1980.

21

Arms Control at Sea:
The United States and the Soviet Union
in the Indian Ocean, 1977–78

RICHARD N. HAASS

What turned out to be the final session of the U.S.–Soviet negotiations on arms control in the Indian Ocean took place in Berne in February 1978, just eight months after American and Soviet negotiators first met in Moscow to discuss Indian Ocean matters. Between the June 1977 and February 1978 sessions there were two others, in Washington and Berne respectively. Soviet involvement in the Horn of Africa constituted the proximate cause for U.S. termination of the endeavor. Until then, considerable progress had been realized, although substantial issues remained unresolved. Notwithstanding the failure of this diplomatic enterprise—to the contrary, in large part because of it—these negotiations offer valuable insights into the U.S.–Soviet relationship and in particular its dimensions of arms control and regional competition. It is to these insights and the lessons that may be drawn from them that this essay is addressed.

THE BACKGROUND TO THE NEGOTIATIONS

For much of the postwar era, the Indian Ocean was with few exceptions a veritable backwater of international relations, less significant than either the Atlantic or Pacific oceans. By the late 1960s and early 1970s, however, both the reality and the perception of the Indian Ocean began to shift. The decision by the United Kingdom in the mid-1960s to withdraw from its responsibilities east of Suez gave rise to fears in the West that a geopolitical vacuum was being created. What was at stake was not simply influence but the vital commodity of oil; only the producers of southwest Asia, and in particular those of the Middle East, Persian Gulf, and North Africa, could meet the increasing demands of Western Europe, Japan, and (to a much lesser degree) the United States. The late 1960s also witnessed the extension of the forward deployment of the Soviet Navy to the Indian Ocean, while both the 1971–1972 subcontinent war and the 1973 Middle East conflict reminded observers of the region's potential not only for local conflict but for escalation involving the two superpowers.

Both the United States and the Soviet Union had good reasons to follow Indian Ocean developments carefully. Energy was a vital concern for the West; the United States grew increasingly concerned over both adequate access to supplies for its allies and itself and the unimpeded transit of tankers moving to and from producing areas.

The United States retained a continuing stake in Israel's security, and under the Guam (or Nixon) Doctrine, looked to the Shah's Iran and Saudi Arabia to help protect Western interests at a time when an overburdened and reluctant America was subject to political and military constraints stemming from the war in Vietnam. But the day when either of the so-called twin pillars could be counted on to assume major security responsibilities was some way off, and for the time being the United States had no alternative but to provide them the means for their own defense as well as the promise of more direct assistance if needed.

The Soviet Union also had reason to pay close attention to the Indian Ocean; that said, such Soviet interest was hardly new. From the time of Peter the Great, Russian leaders had eyed covetously the warm waters of the Indian Ocean and its promise of year-round access and egress for the fleet. In 1946 Soviet reluctance to withdraw from Iran constituted an early chapter of the emerging Cold War. By the 1960s, the USSR had developed modest fishing and mercantile interests in the ocean. More important, though, were emerging geopolitical concerns. The deepening Sino-Soviet split, heightened struggles for influence in South Asia, the 1969 Brezhnev proposal for a collective security system for Asia—all pointed to mounting Soviet preoccupation with its south and east. At the same time, European withdrawals—including those of Portugal, Italy, and France as well as Great Britain—from areas of traditional influence around the Indian Ocean, together with the emergence of energy as a possible Achilles heel of the industrialized West, suggested that the Indian Ocean area could well provide valuable new opportunities for Soviet involvement.

A reflection as well as a source of this mutual increase in superpower engagement in the Indian Ocean and its periphery was the role played by their two navies. The U.S. Navy had long been present in the area; a three-ship Middle East Force was established in 1949 and homeported out of Bahrein. In the early 1970s, this force was upgraded modestly with a more capable flagship; more important, in the late 1960s, the United States initiated a pattern of deploying carrier or major surface combatant task forces into the Indian Ocean three or four times a year. The United States and Great Britain agreed in late 1966 that selected Indian Ocean islands could be developed for military purposes; several years later, Congress approved funds to establish a communications facility on Diego Garcia. This augmented presence was intended to signal resolve and continued interest in the wake of the British withdrawal; at the same time, naval presence was an essential element of the Nixon Doctrine's mix of complementing local ground forces with U.S. air and naval capabilities. The trend was reinforced further by Secretary of Defense James Schlesinger who, in the aftermath of the 1973 Middle East conflict and the increased concern over energy supplies, announced a policy of more frequent and more regular naval deployments to the area, a step soon to be complemented by an Administration request for funding to expand Diego Garcia's capacities.[1]

Soviet naval combatants first appeared in the Indian Ocean in 1968, when a three-ship force entered the ocean and called at ports of several littoral states. A permanent Soviet presence was established less than a year later, and by the early 1970s averaged some twenty vessels, divided evenly between combatants and support ships. (The relatively large number of support vessels resulted from limited Soviet access to local facilities.)

If the pattern of Soviet deployments is clear, the rationale is less so. Some have argued this extension of deployments reflected a Soviet concern over actual or possible U.S. use of the Indian Ocean as a patrolling area for strategic submarines armed with

long-range nuclear missiles that could reach Soviet territory. This is a possible explanation, although it fails to take into account reports that the Indian Ocean was not a
regular area for such patrols and would have been a poor one (offering little target
coverage) for the generation of submarines armed with the relatively shorter range Po-
laris/Poseidon missile and an unnecessary patrol area for the Trident submarine and its
much longer range missiles. The fact that the Soviet presence in the Indian Ocean
included only limited anti-submarine warfare (ASW) assets suggests that any Soviet
concern with a strategic threat to the homeland emanating from the Indian Ocean was
oriented more towards the future than the present. Even less likely as an explanation of
Soviet naval activity is the thesis that the Soviet Navy entered the Indian Ocean to
threaten the passage of oil; if indeed that had been a Soviet objective, there were available alternative means of doing so far more efficiently. Instead, the most plausible
analysis of Soviet motives emphasizes naval diplomacy and the Soviet desire to use
naval forces to bolster what Admiral Gorshkov termed "the interests of a country beyond its borders."[2] More specifically, the Soviet Navy could by its presence symbolize
Soviet global strength and, in times of crisis, actually act in ways to further specific
Soviet interests. By so doing the USSR would also be denying such unimpeded use of
the ocean to the West.[3]

Parallel to this rise in U.S. and Soviet interest and military presence in the Indian
Ocean came a rise in interest in arms control. The first impulse in this direction, however, came neither from Washington nor Moscow but from the Indian Ocean's littoral—
the states of east Africa, the Persian Gulf and above all south Asia. The desire for some
form of Indian Ocean arms control had its roots in the nonaligned movement. Resentment was widespread over the prediction that the British withdrawal would somehow
create a political or military vacuum. At the Third Non-Aligned Conference, held at
Lusaka in 1970, the representatives endorsed a resolution calling on the United Nations
to declare the Indian Ocean a "Zone of Peace," free of great power military presence
and bases and free of nuclear weapons. The high-water mark of this multilateral approach to arms control came just months later, when, in December 1971, the UN General Assembly passed a similar declaration—ironically just weeks before the United
States (quickly followed by the Soviet Union) dispatched naval task forces into the
Indian Ocean to symbolize their support for Pakistan and India respectively.[4]

But other than being reaffirmed with some regularity, and despite the controversial
surges in superpower naval presence coincident with both the 1971–72 South Asian and
the 1973–74 Middle East crises, the Zone of Peace movement never gained serious
momentum.[5] Part of the problem lay in the resolution itself; its text was vague in terms
of which states were to be affected and in what sequence. More important, the resolution suffered from the simple fact that no consensus existed among the littoral states of
the Indian Ocean as to the wisdom of establishing an area free of great power presence;
voting for a resolution was one thing, acting on it quite another. For local powers such
as India the idea was attractive, but for the small and weak there was little to be gained
in trading the protection afforded by outsiders for the possible hegemony of neighbors.
India's championing of the resolution also set back the prospects of the movement, due
to hostility to India itself. The 1971–1972 conflict with Pakistan in which India played
midwife to Bangladesh, India's ties to Moscow, the breakdown of Indian democracy—
all created doubts in the area as to how much New Delhi could be trusted.

What was decisive, however, in the failure of the Zone of Peace effort to move
beyond rhetoric was the opposition of the great powers the resolution sought to restrain.

Of the five permanent members of the UN Security Council, only the People's Republic of China supported the effort, and only China of the five had no military presence in the ocean to limit. The Western powers—Great Britain, France, and the United States— voiced their specific opposition to a proposal that would jeopardize the access and transit protected by international law and required by foreign policy; the USSR was only some- what more circumspect in its opposition to the resolution, mixing expressions of sym- pathy with reminders that it had no alternative but to deploy military forces in a body of water that constituted a vital link between its east and west.[6]

The failure of the multilateral approach to arms control did not discourage those who were drawn to a more pragmatic bilateral process. In the United States, interest in some form of U.S.–Soviet arms control regime for the Indian Ocean can be traced back to the early 1970s when concern mounted in some quarters—notably among Democratic members of the Congress and in several think tanks—that the Indian Ocean could well become the venue of a costly and avoidable arms race if action was not taken to nip such a race in the bud. One concern was money—one study estimated that keeping a carrier task force in the Indian Ocean would entail $5–8 billion in acquisition costs and some $800 million annually in operating expenses.[7] Another concern was precedent. How the United States, already overburdened in Asia, reacted to the British withdrawal east of Suez, and what role, if any, military force would play in U.S. policy, became for many congressmen a test of whether the United States had "learned the lessons of Vietnam."

Much of the effort to affect the course of U.S. policy concentrated on stopping or slowing the planned construction program for the U.S. facility on the British-owned island of Diego Garcia. At issue was less the cost of the construction itself, which was relatively modest, than the policy of incorporating a significant military dimension into the U.S. approach to this part of the world.[8] Congressional critics argued that going ahead with the Diego Garcia project would make any naval arms limitation pact impos- sible to negotiate, while agreement on a naval arms control arrangement would make Diego Garcia's expansion unnecessary. Pushing the Administration (then that of Presi- dent Ford) into naval arms limitation talks (NALT) became their key objective; although they failed in this goal—the Ford Administration argued in 1975 that delaying Diego Garcia construction would only weaken Soviet incentive to negotiate, and in 1976 that negotiations were in any event inappropriate given Soviet behavior in Angola—members of Congress did make the issue a regular staple of Democratic Party foreign policy thinking in 1976 and hence a likely initiative for any Democratic administration that might take over after the November 1976 election.[9]

Soviet interest in arms control, both as regards naval forces in general and in the specific context of the Indian Ocean, also predated the advent of the Carter Administra- tion. In 1971, General Secretary Leonid Brezhnev criticized the United States for alleg- edly maintaining a double standard that the global deployments of the U.S. Navy were legitimate whereas those of the Soviet Navy were not. But he went on to say that "we have never considered it an ideal situation to have the fleets of the great powers plying the seas for long periods at great distances from their own shores. We are prepared to resolve this problem, but on an equal footing."[10] Only months before, Soviet Ambas- sador to the United States Anatoly Dobrynin had raised the possibility of an arms control dialogue on the Indian Ocean with Secretary of State William Rogers; when the United States followed up, however, there was no further indication of Soviet interest. A congressional delegation encountered a similar Soviet disinterest in the notion of Indian

Ocean arms control during a 1975 visit to Moscow. It was thus something of a surprise when in the autumn of 1976 Soviet Foreign Minister Gromyko tabled for the consideration of the UN General Assembly a memorandum on arms control which, among other things, stated that "the Soviet Union will be prepared to seek, together with other powers, for ways to reduce, on a reciprocal basis, the military activities of non-littoral states on the Indian Ocean and directly adjacent regions." The Soviet statement was replete with conditions: there could be no foreign military bases in the area (existing ones would have to be dismantled) and allowance would have to be made for the right of the Soviets (and presumably others) to navigate freely in the ocean and visit the littoral states. Taken as a whole, the Soviet statement could be interpreted as a conditional acceptance of naval arms limitation talks and a repudiation of the movement to declare the Indian Ocean a Zone of Peace.[11]

Soviet motives were no doubt several. Their approach allowed them to appear to favor arms control while protecting their own right to use the Indian Ocean. (Moscow sought to mollify the Zone of Peace adherents by expressing a willingness to consider attending a conference to discuss implementing such a zone so long as the conference would agree to recognize Soviet exceptions to the zone.) Perhaps more important, their embrace of naval arms limitation offered the Soviets a means to place a ceiling on U.S. use of the Indian Ocean, while the emphasis on the exclusion of bases might influence the Diego Garcia debate then underway in the U.S. Congress. There was even the possibility that Soviet interest in arms control reflected a desire by some in the Politburo to clip the wings of the increasingly visible and costly Soviet Navy. But whatever the reason or reasons, by the beginning of 1977 the Soviet Union found itself well positioned to respond favorably to the new American Administration's call for a dialogue on Indian Ocean arms control.

THE CARTER INITIATIVE AND THE 1977–78 NEGOTIATIONS

The specific impetus for bilateral talks on the Indian Ocean came from the newly elected American President. "As a clear signal to other nations that we could make progress towards peace, I wanted to work with the Soviet leaders to establish strict limits on the permanent deployment of naval forces in the Indian Ocean," Jimmy Carter wrote in his memoirs.[12] Consistent with this aim, he voiced support for the complete demilitarization of the Indian Ocean early in his presidency.[13] Only afterwards did his top foreign policy advisors—Secretary of State Cyrus Vance, Secretary of Defense Harold Brown, and National Security Advisor Zbigniew Brzezinski—meet to determine just how this presidential initiative would be interpreted and implemented.[14] At a March 1977 Special Coordination Committee (SCC), one of the Carter Administration's principal interagency bodies managing national security affairs, the three agreed that an offer to begin bilateral negotiations on an Indian Ocean arms control agreement would constitute one element of the package Secretary Vance would present during his trip to the Soviet Union that same month. President Carter concurred, and Vance so proposed to the Soviets. When the Soviets in turn agreed, the Indian Ocean negotiations became one of the eight U.S.–Soviet arms control working groups established during the March visit—the same visit in which the Soviets unceremoniously rejected the new Administration's proposals on strategic arms limitations.

The events of March led to intense activity within the U.S. government. The interagency community examined the Indian Ocean question in depth. A spring 1977 review, benefitting from a late 1976 study undertaken by the outgoing Ford Administration, included a full range of possible negotiating objectives, from a minimal "declaration of intent" by the two parties not to contribute to an arms race to full and formal demilitarization. Quite quickly a consensus was reached: the immediate goal for the bilateral negotiations would be some form of modest limitations while, at the President's insistence, demilitarization would remain the ultimate U.S. objective. This consensus represented agreement on some key policy elements: the United States would not need a large permanent presence or a new "numbered" fleet; the probability that the United States would not be offered a base by any littoral state; an assumption the United States would retain peacetime access to Diego Garcia and additional crisis access to other area facilities; and the belief that the United States stood to benefit from limits on Soviet naval presence and access to local facilities.

That those on the National Security Council staff, in the Arms Control and Disarmament Agency, in the Office of the Secretary of Defense, and the State Department supported this enterprise is not surprising; institutional missions aside, key individuals involved in Indian Ocean decision making were on record as supporting the idea. (Secretary of State Vance, for example, had chaired a study group before the Administration took office that among other things proposed a more ambitious arms control policy for the Indian Ocean.[15]) More difficult to explain is why the Navy and the Joint Chiefs of Staff went along with an initiative that could threaten the ability of the United States to project and sustain military forces in the Indian Ocean. Potentially dangerous precedents were involved as well. The behavior of the military was in part tactically inspired: the early Carter Administration embraced an optimistic view not only of U.S.–Soviet relations but of what arms control as an instrument of policy could be expected to produce; to have opposed this dominant thrust of the President and his top advisors would have risked not only an early bureaucratic defeat but alienating the top level of a new administration just as it was assuming office and with it the power to make life miserable for the military if it so chose. It is also possible that military leaders concluded that they would be wiser to shape specifics of the U.S. negotiating position rather than oppose the negotiation per se. Closely associated with this view was the estimate that the talks were unlikely to result in agreement. Last, the Navy had recently concluded its own study of Indian Ocean arms control considerations, and was far more able to accept the enterprise when it became clear that limitations, not demilitarization as initially indicated by the President, would be the principal determinant of U.S. policy.

The negotiations themselves convened in Moscow in late June. Symbolizing the importance the two governments attached to the talks, both delegations were led by experienced negotiators—Ambassador Lev Mendelevich for the USSR, Arms Control and Disarmament Agency (ACDA) Director Paul Warnke for the United States, and each was backed by a team of relatively senior officials. With little fanfare the talks got underway. Both sides were quick to characterize them as serious; both agreed that they would operate under the confidentiality rule so that negotiations would not be disturbed by public posturing or scrutiny.[16]

Certain issues were settled with relative ease. The two countries agreed that any Indian Ocean pact would be a bilateral one of limited duration. (Not settled was the related matter of what would constitute the escape or withdrawal clause.) Any agreement would affect only the forces of the two parties; unaffected would be the forces of littoral states and those of other outside powers such as the United Kingdom and France, each of which maintained a modest level of naval and other forces in the area. The two delegations were also able to agree to a considerable extent on what was to be limited—naval vessels (both combatant and auxiliary) and logistic facilities and bases—and what would not—ground forces and commercial vessels, such as fishing and merchant fleets. Also excluded were certain activities such as transferring arms to littoral states; at least in principle, that dimension of superpower competition would fall under the purview of the arms control working group (also established in March 1977) that was considering constraints on the conventional arms transfer policies of the United States and the Soviet Union.

The limits themselves were intentionally imprecise, so as to avoid difficult definitional problems inherent in trying to construct a balance between two fleets of contrasting unit and overall composition. The understanding would have stabilized force levels where they existed in March 1977 when the negotiations were set up. For the United States, stabilization would have meant the continued presence of the three-ship Middle East Force in the Persian Gulf and periodic (three or four times a year) visits of naval task forces. The Soviets would have been allowed to continue maintaining a presence of approximately 18 to 20 vessels split evenly between combatants and auxiliaries. Each side would have been permitted to retain existing levels of facilities: for the United States, Diego Garcia as it then stood, for the USSR, presumably some blend of access to local facilities (such as the Somali port of Berbera, which until mid-1977 was the principal Soviet logistic site in the Indian Ocean) and anchorages. Only in later phases of the negotiations were actual reductions to be considered, although this issue was by no means settled, given the adamant U.S. Navy opposition to any reductions. Leslie Gelb, Director of the State Department's Politico-Military Bureau and Deputy Head of the U.S. delegation, summed up the approach as follows: "Under a stabilization agreement neither the U.S. nor the Soviet Union could increase the size of its military presence in the Indian Ocean or significantly alter its pattern of deployments . . . an agreement would maintain the U.S.–Soviet force balance."[17]

There were two principal sticking points. The Soviets wanted assurances regarding U.S. use of the Indian Ocean for strategic purposes; more specifically, they sought a ban on any use of the Indian Ocean for basing either long-range nuclear-capable bombers or submarines carrying long-range ballistic missiles armed with nuclear warheads. The former was at least in principle easy for the United States to agree to as there were no plans for stationing B-52 long-range bombers in the region;[18] the only question was what the United States could expect in return for such a commitment. The issue of nuclear-armed submarines was far more complex. Even though the arithmetic of missile ranges and submarine operating tempos made the Indian Ocean an unattractive strategic submarine basing or deployment area for the United States, the United States would not declare the Indian Ocean off limits. Any such declaration would allow the Soviets to concentrate their limited anti-submarine warfare (ASW) assets elsewhere; moreover, such a declaration would compromise the principles of free access to nonterritorial waters for all U.S. ships and the U.S. Navy's policy of neither confirming nor denying the presence of nuclear weapons on board its ships. Thus, while the United States was willing to agree not to establish dedicated bases in the Indian Ocean for the purpose of supporting nuclear-missile-firing-submarines, the Soviets would have had to make do with informal assurances and understandings that the United States would not use the Indian Ocean for strategic submarine patrols.[19] Whether this would satisfy the Soviets was never determined.

The principal U.S. concern that could not be settled satisfactorily in the course of the four negotiating sessions was the status of land-based Soviet strike aircraft. The United States sought to constrain Soviet ability to introduce or base fighter and bomber aircraft on the Indian Ocean periphery. This was the sine qua non of the U.S. position; without such a provision the Soviet Navy would have been able to operate under the protection of land-based Soviet naval aviation while the Soviet air force could introduce large and potentially decisive amounts of power into the area. Stabilization of force levels would limit U.S. air and power projection assets to the periodic appearance of carrier task forces; without some corresponding ceiling on Soviet land-based tactical air power, the United States and its allies in the littoral could have found themselves at a marked disadvantage. Such a constraint was resisted by the Soviets, however—they saw their ability to deploy air forces as compensation for U.S. advantages at sea (and in particular for U.S. sea-based air power) and as a necessary means of promoting security objectives to their south.

There were other major problems as well. A basic difficulty stemmed from an inability to agree on the geographic scope of the Indian Ocean pact. The Soviets wanted limits on facilities and strategic forces to include U.S. assets in Western Australia; given commitments to the ANZUS alliance as well as the worldwide functions of some of its Australian sites, the United States wanted them exempt from any regional Indian Ocean arrangement. At the same time, the United States had a clear interest in extending any Indian Ocean agreement northwards into the Asian littoral; constraints on Soviet land-based aviation made little sense if the Soviets could still deploy forces within easy operating range of the Indian Ocean and key portions of its periphery.[20]

Finally, there were problems of verification. The Soviets were worried about the prospect that some of the aircraft aboard U.S. carriers would be nuclear-capable; demonstrating they were not would have been extremely difficult. More important, there was the fundamental problem of verifying that the stabilization agreement was being honored. Soviet and U.S. forces were far from identical; in the words of one participant, "How does one compare a permanent pack of wolves with an occasional foray of elephants?"[21] Ship substitutions, unit modernizations, schedule alterations, facility access and upgrades—all would have raised serious compliance issues. The problem was exacerbated by U.S. concern with Soviet land-based aircraft and Soviet concern with alleged or possible U.S. strategic submarine deployments. The approach of the negotiators—to finesse the problems through a web of explicit and implicit understandings—may not have withstood the scrutiny of either government. Even if it had, the smooth functioning of any such regime could well have required a degree of trust and communications between the parties that was simply beyond their capacity or willingness to sustain.

THE END GAME

Before these issues could be resolved either within the U.S. delegation or between the United States and the Soviet Union, the course of the Indian Ocean talks was truncated by developments on the periphery of the ocean. For much of 1977 the Soviet Union had supported with economic and military assistance the new radical leadership of Ethiopia in its struggles against its domestic opponents, Eritrean separatists and its neighbor Somalia. By November 1977, Soviet support for its new client proved too much for Somalia; Soviet hopes for maintaining good relations with the two protagonists of Africa's Horn proved impossible, and the Soviet Navy suddenly found itself without access to the Somali port of Berbera. Three months later, in February 1978, the United States concluded the fourth and what turned out to be the final round of the Indian Ocean negotiations by announcing that Soviet support for Ethiopia also proved too much for Washington. Leslie Gelb provided the official explanation in open testimony before the Congress: ". . . Soviet naval operations in support of their political activities in the Horn called into question whether we had a common understanding of how a stabilization agreement would actually affect the behavior of our two states . . . the intention here was to limit the degree to which the [political] competition would be supported by military activities. For our part, the way the Soviets supported their political activities in the Horn by increasing the level of their naval forces in the Indian Ocean was not consistent with a stabilization agreement. Unless we understand such an agreement in the same way it would be meaningless.''[22]

As a logical proposition, the explanation is not fully satisfactory. It is not clear that the Soviets ought to have felt bound (or been so considered) by the terms of an agreement still being negotiated. More important, and there is not a little irony here, the increase in Soviet naval presence was incidental to Soviet policy in the Horn of Africa. To the extent the Soviets destabilized the area, they did it not with their naval vessels but with their arms-laden merchant fleet—assets that would not have been affected by the Indian Ocean agreement even had it been in effect. What is clear, though, is that the announced U.S. concept of ''stabilization''—one that implied a shared code of behavior affecting both the means and ends of U.S.–Soviet regional competition—went beyond anything being formally negotiated and beyond any Soviet understandings. The U.S. side appeared to have in mind a political regime regulating superpower competition in the Indian Ocean and its littoral; the Soviets sought only a narrow military pact placing a ceiling on naval forces and possibly facilities.

The U.S. decision to terminate the negotiations can only be understood in the context of the broader U.S.–Soviet relationship. Soviet diplomacy in the Horn of Africa was symptomatic of a more assertive Soviet diplomacy throughout the Third World such as was seen in the Middle East in 1973 and in Angola a few years later. That the Horn was cited by the Carter Administration as grounds for breaking off the Indian Ocean talks reflected nothing so much as the evolution of the Carter Administration in its perception of and attitude towards Moscow.[23] In particular it reflected the ascendancy of the increasingly hardline views of Carter's national security advisor, a change the Navy and the Joint Chiefs were only too happy to support given their own mounting misgivings with those aspects of the Indian Ocean negotiations that might have constrained U.S. facilities and compromised U.S. conventional and strategic options in the area.

The negotiations came close to being resumed only once when, in September 1978, Soviet Foreign Minister Gromyko broached the subject with Secretary of State Vance. Vance indicated his willingness, a decision that touched off a considerable bureaucratic tempest in Washington, as neither the military nor National Security Advisor Brzezinski was anxious to agree to the Soviet request. Months later, on the margins of the U.S.–Soviet Conventional Arms Transfer Talks (CATT) being held in December in Mexico City, Soviet Ambassador Mendelevich (who headed both their Indian Ocean and CATT delegations) pressed Leslie Gelb (the head of the U.S. CATT team and deputy head of the Indian Ocean delegation) for a starting date, offering to stop in Washington on his way back to Moscow to resume the Indian Ocean talks if the U.S. side wished. Gelb reportedly cabled back this offer, suggesting that he hold informal conversations on the

Indian Ocean with Mendelevich in Mexico City. Brzezinski conditionally approved the Gelb proposal, instructing him to walk out of the room if Mendelevich raised the subject of Iran, then in the throes of revolution. Gelb's appeal of these instructions was rebuffed; when he in turn described the ground rules under which any discussion of the Indian Ocean would have to occur, Mendelevich refused to accept, and the talks never resumed.[24]

Any renewed possibility of restarting the talks was closed off by the December 1979 Soviet invasion and resulting occupation of Afghanistan; not only did it create a climate in which no proposed arms control agreement could survive the American political process, but, together with the events in Iran, created pressures for a fundamentally different U.S. approach to southwest Asia and the entire Indian Ocean area. In a span of only a few years the Carter Administration had moved from choosing between naval arms limitation and complete demilitarization to establishing the Rapid Deployment Force and promulgating a new doctrine in which "An attempt by any outside force to gain control of the Persian Gulf region will be regarded as an assault on the vital interests of the United States of America, and such an assault will be repelled by any means necessary, including military force."[25]

THE INDIAN OCEAN NEGOTIATIONS IN RETROSPECT

How does one characterize the Indian Ocean talks with the advantage of hindsight? A missed opportunity to close off yet another avenue of superpower military competition with all its attendant costs and risks? An impossible quest to bring arms control into an area simply too complex and dynamic to be constrained by such formal political arrangements? Or, and in particular from the American perspective, a misguided initiative which, if it had succeeded, would only have done so to the detriment of U.S. interests?

It is tempting to embrace the first two epitaphs; indeed, several of the American participants still look back on the experience as a negotiating effort that came close to fruition and that would have served U.S. interests had it been successful. Each side had reasons to want to conclude an agreement, whether to cap or eliminate certain capabilities of the other or to avoid unwanted investments of its own. And the record indicates that the two delegations agreed on several important elements of what would comprise any Indian Ocean agreement.

Despite these areas of accord, however, it is not at all certain that the United States and Soviet Union could have bridged their differences. Coming up with a mutually acceptable formula to constrain Soviet land-based aircraft could well have proven impossible to negotiate. The United States would have found it impossible to compromise on its refusal to provide formal assurances regarding strategic (nuclear) use of the ocean; accepting limits on access to and use of facilities in Western Australia may too have proved an insurmountable obstacle. With such fundamental issues as definition, inclusion, and verification unresolved, subsequent rounds of the Indian Ocean talks could only have been complicated and time consuming. Nevertheless, what might have been more important than any agreement was the negotiation itself; it is quite possible that the talks provided the Soviet side with some useful insight into American strategic thinking and the low priority attached to the Indian Ocean as a venue for basing submarines armed with long-range nuclear missiles. Thus, a potential rationale for an expanded Soviet naval presence was weakened.

But what if the two sides had been able to bridge their differences and conclude an agreement? Would it have mattered? Obviously, the precise terms agreed to would in large part dictate the answer to this question. If the arrangement had been limited to stabilizing naval force levels, the agreement would have had a measurable but modest impact. Before the negotiations, there was not much of an Indian Ocean naval arms race to speak of, and even without the agreement not much of one materialized, although U.S. force levels increased significantly in the early 1980s. If the stabilization regime had covered not simply naval forces but also facilities and land-based aircraft, it would have had a far greater impact on superpower competition, although again important elements of that competition—notably the transfer of all forms of military assistance to local states—could have continued unconstrained.

A more important question to ask, however, is whether the entire enterprise constituted a desirable diplomatic initiative for the United States. The Indian Ocean, and in particular its northwest arc, emerged in the late 1970s as an area of major and possibly vital strategic importance to the United States. An arms control arrangement of the sort envisioned by the Carter Administration would have limited U.S. ability to maintain peacetime presence and severely reduced U.S. capacity to introduce and support augmented forces in changed circumstances or crises—all in a part of the world where the USSR enjoyed decided geographic advantages and where a number of local states possessed the strength to jeopardize U.S. interests. An agreement in 1978 could have created as well a false sense of security for the United States on the eve of the crisis in Iran and just a year before the Soviet invasion of Afghanistan. Indeed, it is instructive to note that by the end of the Carter Administration the Middle East Force had been expanded from three to five combat vessels; deployment of at least one aircraft carrier had become a permanent feature of the U.S. presence; ships filled with materiel for ground forces were prepositioned off Diego Garcia; military access agreements had been negotiated with Somalia, Oman, and Kenya; and Diego Garcia itself was undergoing new expansion. None of these steps was consistent with the stabilization regime being negotiated only two years before.[26]

There are also lessons to be drawn about the negotiation effort itself. The Indian Ocean ought to have constituted a relatively simple venue for arms control. If it was more complex than Antarctica and thus did not lend itself to a purely preclusive approach to limiting military presence, it was still a long way from the complexity and density of the European theater or the strategic nuclear relationship. Yet the Indian Ocean presented formidable negotiating difficulties, difficulties which, as noted earlier, were likely to have proven an obstacle to agreement. There were three alternatives in the circumstances: to conclude a simple pact limited to naval deployments and possibly facilities; a regime of confidence-building measures, in which the two superpowers would agree to provide advance notification of and information about such activities as military exercises, major alterations to their presence, or facility upgrades;[27] or a more general dialogue in which the two would discuss the full range of their own and each other's interests and policies in the area in an attempt to reduce misunderstanding and miscalculation and possibly mute competition. The first of these three alternatives would have been clearly disadvantageous to the United States, given its far greater dependence on the sea as a means for projecting power into the area's key northern reaches. The second of the two alternatives was only partially explored, while the third was introduced in part both within the negotiations—for example, the reassurance provided to the Soviets about the absence of plans for U.S. strategic use for the ocean—and outside the negotiations, in the statements issued by the United States indicating the inconsistency and ultimate unacceptability of Soviet efforts to affect the balance in the Horn of Africa.

The 1977–78 experience highlights too the political obstacles to regional arms control. Such efforts are highly vulnerable to any event in the region, even if much of what transpires falls outside the formal purview of the negotiations. What took place in the Horn of Africa underlines this point, as did the Afghan crisis some two years later. Linking the fate of the negotiations to such events is far less artificial or contrived than it is in the case of strategic arms control; the justification for responding includes not only any political rationale but a more immediate strategic one as well.

Attempts to build a U.S.–Soviet regime in any region are vulnerable as well to the activities of other states. What matters in many situations is not overall strength or inventories but the level of force that can be brought to bear quickly; in certain circumstances, littoral or local states can outgun a superpower, particularly if the external power has established only a low level of peacetime presence. Many of the U.S. force increases in southwest Asia or the Indian Ocean more generally, in the late 1970s and 1980s, were tied not to Soviet threats or actions but to those of local states. Bilateralism for the most part continues to make sense on the strategic nuclear level, but it has less and less appeal on other levels, given the actual and potential proliferation of conventional, chemical, and nonstrategic nuclear capabilities.

A related problem was one of "break-out." Traditional deployment accords such as that contemplated for the Indian Ocean placed no direct constraints on inventory. In a crisis each side would have the ability to alter significantly its level of military force in the area; the only real constraint would be the ability to support such additional men and equipment and the resulting increase in activity or operations. Given geography, however, the Soviet Union was far better positioned to take advantage of a crisis to increase the level of its forces. Using air and ground assets the Soviet Union could bring considerably more force to bear in much of southwest Asia (or the northwest quadrant of the Indian Ocean) in a short period of time than could the United States, given the greater distances facing the United States, its reliance on sea power, and its limited access to area facilities.

Many of these considerations hold true for crises involving the United States but not the Soviet Union. There have been a number of incidents in which littoral states acted in a manner hostile to U.S. interests in the area: India in 1971–72 comes to mind, as does postrevolutionary Iran or both Iran and Iraq at various times during their conflict in the 1980s. In such situations as these, conditions could easily arise in which the United States would want to increase its presence beyond the level permitted by a stabilization agreement. Were a stabilization accord in effect, the United States could find itself lacking the means to introduce forces quickly (because of deployment ceilings), unable to support significantly augmented forces (because of limits on facilities), or forced to choose between increasing its military presence and continuing to honor the agreement. The potential for crisis raises questions about the wisdom of agreeing to a formal bilateral stabilization agreement in a part of the world containing multiple threats to important U.S. interests and where the United States is heavily dependent on deploying military forces necessarily maintained outside the area in normal circumstances. Either a stabilization agreement would preclude specified peacetime measures and crisis responses, in which case it would diminish the ability of the United States to act on behalf of its interests, or it would not, in which case the concept of stabilization is denuded of much of its significance.[28]

Lastly, there is the basic question of whether arms control can play a useful role in limiting U.S.–Soviet regional competition. History suggests caution, as one can only point to the preclusive Antarctic agreement (and similar agreements for the seabed and outer space) and the limited set of confidence-building measures introduced into Central Europe by the Helsinki accords. These accomplishments must be kept in perspective; preclusive accords came about because of the absence of major interests at stake, while the rules of the road for Europe are distinguished mostly by their modesty in scope and impact.

Indeed, what this record demonstrates above all is the negligible contribution formal arrangements (especially arms control pacts) have made or can make to moderating superpower competition. Selecting certain forces for limitation from a desire to reduce the chances for direct confrontation in regions lacking a consensus over the proper ends and means of change is a questionable enterprise. Limiting forces will not necessarily make a crisis less likely to occur. Nor will such constraints necessarily make a direct superpower confrontation less likely if a crisis does come about. On the contrary, such limits can invite circumvention, that is, actions not expressly prohibited or constrained by some formal arrangement but that all the same can prove decisive in shaping some conflict. Limits on forces can also undermine deterrence or the ability to manage crises or both.

The Indian Ocean negotiations were thus flawed; what might have been in the U.S. interest—a regime of substantial restraint—could not be negotiated, while what might have been negotiated—a naval arms control accord—was unlikely to be in the U.S. interest. A more valuable diplomatic approach might have emphasized limited confidence-building measures for military forces and discussions aimed at defining one another's legitimate interests in the area and acceptable means of furthering them. There was also the possibility of reaching some accord on constraining the transfer of conventional arms and technologies relevant to the proliferation of chemical and nuclear capabilities. Anything more was out of reach; the U.S.–Soviet relationship was not yet ripe for an initiative to apply the 1972 Basic Principles or some other form of significant restraint regime to either the Indian Ocean or its periphery. Nor was the Indian Ocean area yet ripe for controls that would have significantly constrained the ability of the United States to introduce and maintain military forces in the region to safeguard its national security interests. In such circumstances, it should surprise no one that the 1977–1978 arms control initiative met with little success.

Notes

1. For useful background on U.S. policy see Gary Sick, "The Evolution of U.S. Strategy Toward the Indian Ocean and Persian Gulf Regions," in Alvin Z. Rubenstein, ed., *The Great Game: Rivalry in the Persian Gulf and South Asia* (New York: Praeger, 1983).

2. For background into Gorshkov's thinking, see Sergei G. Gorshkov, *Red Star Rising at Sea* (Annapolis: U.S. Naval Institute Press, 1974) and *The Sea Power of the State* (New York: Pergamon Press, 1979).

3. There exists a vast literature on the evolution of the Soviet Navy's capabilities and missions, both as pertains to the Indian Ocean and more generally. See, for example, Geoffrey Jukes, *The Indian Ocean in Soviet Naval Policy* (London: International Institute for Strategic Studies, 1972); Oles M. Smolansky, "Soviet Entry into the Indian Ocean: An Analysis," in Alvin Cottrell and R. M. Burrell, eds., *The Indian Ocean: Its Political, Economic and Military Importance* (New York: Praeger, 1972); M. MccGwire, "The Soviet Navy's Shift to Forward Deploy-

ment,'' in M. MccGwire and J. McDonnell, eds., *Soviet Naval Influence: Domestic and Foreign Constraints* (New York: Praeger, 1977); and the testimony of then CIA Director William Colby, reprinted in the *Congressional Record* of August 1, 1974, p. S. 14094.

4. The United States may also have sought to deter India from any further dismemberment of Pakistan and to demonstrate to the leadership of the People's Republic of China that there was value in developing diplomatic connections. The official U.S. rationale, that Task Force 74 (headed up by the aircraft carrier *Enterprise*) was dispatched to evacuate American nationals from East Pakistan, made little sense, as the force entered the Indian Ocean several days after all foreign nationals wanting to leave Dacca had done so. Moreover, a British force was already in the area. For further background to this episode see J. McConnell and A. Kelly, *Superpower Naval Diplomacy in the Indo-Pakistani Crisis* (Arlington, Va.: Center for Naval Analysis, 1973) and Jack Anderson, *The Anderson Papers* (New York: Random House, 1973).

5. The Zone of Peace Resolution is available as U.N. General Assembly Resolution 2832 (XXVI) of December 16, 1971. The fate of the resolution and the zone of peace initiative can be traced through the annual publication of the Ad Hoc Committee on the Indian Ocean, published by the United Nations as Supplement No. 29 to the U.N. General Assembly Official Records.

6. See "USSR Memorandum on Questions Concerning the Ending of the Arms Race and Concerning Disarmament," tabled by Soviet Foreign Minister Andrei Gromyko in the U.N. General Assembly on September 28, 1976; reprinted in *Soviet News* (October 19, 1976).

7. See Barry Blechman, et al., *Setting National Priorities: The 1975 Budget* (Washington, D.C.: Brookings, 1974), pp. 122–123.

8. A speech on the Senate floor by Senator John Culver (D-Iowa) captured well the flavor of the debate. "It is true that the island of Diego Garcia is a flyspeck of coral atoll [and] that most Americans do not know what Diego Garcia is or where it is or how it relates to such urgent close-at-hand problems as unemployment or the cost of living. But only a few years ago, the Tonkin Gulf was similarly unknown to most of us . . . If we proceed with this expansion in the Indian Ocean at this time—without even trying the peaceful, less costly, no-risk alternatives— then we will indeed be simply replaying the first act of a scenario identical with that which took us into the quagmire of Vietnam . . . We have, in effect, come to the first major test of our ability and determination to chart a new, more constructive direction in foreign and defense policy that does not rely exclusively on automatic military escalation and gunboat diplomacy . . . We are at the crossroads." (*Congressional Record,* July 28, 1975, pp. S. 13934, 13936).

9. More specifically, in 1975 the State Department stated that "From extensive experience in negotiations on arms control, we believe that chances for any useful talks with the Soviets would be improved were the Diego Garcia matter resolved in such a way as to demonstrate that the United States is determined, and has the means, to protect its security interests in the Indian Ocean." A year later, following the Angolan crisis, the Department noted that "We have concluded that although we might want to give further consideration to some [Indian Ocean] arms limitation initiative at a later date and perhaps take up the matter with the Soviet government then, any such initiative would be inappropriate now . . . an arms limitation initiative at this time in a region immediately contiguous to the African continent might convey the mistaken impression to the Soviets and our friends and allies that we are willing to acquiesce in this type of Soviet behavior." (*Congressional Record,* July 28, 1975, p. S. 13934 and May 6, 1976, p. S. 6626).

10. The Brezhnev speech is reprinted in translation in *Current Digest of the Soviet Press,* vol. 23, no. 24 (July 13, 1971), p. 20.

11. The full text of the Soviet memorandum is printed in *Soviet News,* no. 5854 (October 19, 1976). See especially p. 365.

12. Jimmy Carter, *Keeping Faith: Memoirs of a President* (New York: Bantam books, 1982), p. 217.

13. Carter spoke of his goal of "demilitarizing" the Indian Ocean in a news conference held March 24, 1977 on the eve of the initial Vance mission to Moscow. The text of his remarks can

be found in *Public Papers of the Presidents of the United States* (Jimmy Carter, 1977, Book I), page 497.

14. The idea of Indian Ocean arms control had been examined by the Carter transition team, but the new Administration did not produce any initiatives or proposals until after President Carter declared his intent in this area. For much of the detail on the background to the 1977–1978 negotiations I am beholden to various members of the U.S. government at the time who discussed their experiences with me as I prepared this essay.

15. See *Controlling the Conventional Arms Race* (New York: United Nations Association of the United States of America, 1976), especially pp. 29–31.

16. Considerable information about the negotiations emerged nonetheless. The best public sources are two congressional documents: *Indian Ocean Arms Limitations and Multilateral Cooperation on Restraining Conventional Arms Transfers,* Hearings before the Panel on Indian Ocean Forces Limitations and Conventional Arms Limitation of the Intelligence and Military Application of Nuclear Energy Subcommittee of the Committee on Armed Services, House of Representatives (Washington: USGPO, 1978) and the report under the same title by the same panel (House Armed Services Committee No. 95-100) published in 1979. The best public source for the Soviet view of the negotiations is S. Vladimirov, "Indian Ocean: Urgent Problem" in *Pravda* (January 18, 1978).

17. Testimony of Leslie Gelb in *Indian Ocean Arms Limitations,* Hearings, p. 6.

18. In the late 1970s and early 1980s the United States did introduce B-52 flights in the Indian Ocean for surveillance purposes. These were conducted out of Guam, as Diego Garcia's runway lacked the strength and width to handle B-52s. In 1985, however, the United States completed rebuilding the runway so that the island could accept B-52s on a regular basis.

19. See the comments by one of the U.S. participants in *India, the United States and the Indian Ocean,* Report of the Indo-American Task Force on the Indian Ocean (Washington, D.C.: Carnegie Endowment for International Peace, 1980), especially p. 101.

20. For additional discussion of the considerations relating to the creation of an arms control agreement for the Indian Ocean see Richard Haass, "Naval Arms Limitation in the Indian Ocean," *Survival* (March–April, 1978), pp. 50–57; Barry M. Blechman, *The Control of Naval Armaments: Prospects and Possibilities* (Washington, D.C.: Brookings, 1975); and Dale Tahtinen, *Arms in the Indian Ocean: Interests and Challenges* (Washington, D.C.: American Enterprise Institute, 1977). See also *Means of Measuring Naval Power with Special Reference to U.S. and Soviet Activities in the Indian Ocean,* a study prepared for the Subcommittee on the Near East and South Asia of the House of Representatives Committee on Foreign Affairs by the Congressional Research Service (Washington, D.C.: U.S. Government Printing Office, 1974).

21. Private communication to author.

22. Gelb's testimony can be found in *Indian Ocean Arms Limitations,* p. 7.

23. The Soviets never accepted the American explanation. Soviet commentators cited alleged U.S. plans to expand Diego Garcia and U.S. intentions to increase military cooperation with Iran and Saudi Arabia as prompting U.S. disinterest in continuing the negotiations. See Alexei Nikolayev, "Why Soviet–U.S. Talks on Indian Ocean Have Been Suspended," *Soviet News,* no. 5941 (August 8, 1978), pp. 276–277.

24. The bulk of the account of this episode comes from interviews with participants in the negotiations. Brzezinski, for his part, mentions this exchange of cables with Gelb in his memoirs, but does so only in the context of the conventional arms transfer talks, not the Indian Ocean. See Zbigniew Brzezinski, *Power and Principle: Memoirs of the National Security Advisor, 1977–1981* (New York: Farrar, Straus & Giroux, 1983), p. 175.

25. This statement, commonly known as the Carter Doctrine, was announced in President Carter's January 23, 1980 State of the Union address.

26. It is worth noting that Brzezinski makes no mention of Indian Ocean arms control when it comes to listing the accomplishments of the Carter Administration. Instead, he cites "the reinjection of American military presence into the Indian Ocean and the initiation of a regional se-

curity framework for the area, including the Carter Doctrine.'' Brzezinski, *Power and Principle,* p. 528.

27. For additional discussion of such ideas, see three chapters by Richard Haass: ''Confidence-Building Measures and Naval Arms Control'' in Jonathan Alford, ed., *The Future of Arms Control: Part III Confidence-Building Measures* (London: International Institute for Strategic Studies, 1979); ''Arms Control and the Indian Ocean'' in Richard Burt, ed., *Arms Control and Defense Postures in the 1980s* (Boulder, Colo.: Westview, 1982); and ''Naval Arms Control: Approaches and Considerations'' in George Quester, ed., *Navies and Arms Control* (New York: Praeger, 1980).

28. Jimmy Carter stated in his memoirs that any U.S.–Soviet Indian Ocean agreement should ''. . . require prior notification if such permanently deployed naval forces had to be strengthened to protect the special interests of either nation.'' *Keeping Faith,* p. 217. Such an allowance for surges was raised with the Soviets in the negotiations but no agreement was reached. This attempt—clearly different from the less flexible notion of stabilization outlined by Gelb in his testimony cited earlier—represented an evolution of the U.S. approach away from a stabilization pact and towards a confidence-building regime.

22

Regulating Soviet–U.S. Competition and Cooperation in the Arab–Israeli Arena, 1967–86

HAROLD H. SAUNDERS

THE PURPOSE

The overall purpose of this book is to enhance understanding of ways in which the Soviet Union and the United States have regulated their competition or have cooperated to avoid nuclear confrontation. "Regulating" competition implies common interest in avoiding confrontation, and recognition on each side—tacit or explicit—that certain complementary practices or understood rules of the game can make confrontation less likely.[1] The few official efforts to write down such practices and rules have only been very general, as in the Basic Principles Agreement of 1972. Normally, tacit rules of practice in particular situations have grown out of experience to provide the essence of an informal regulation. In those circumstances, we are still trying to identify the precise interests of each side and what actions will be seen as tolerable and intolerable in each side's eyes. In nonofficial dialogue, we are still trying to understand and articulate the practices and rules that might contribute greater assurance that competition will be regulated within bounds short of nuclear confrontation. Although regulation involves some cooperation, we usually think in this context of cooperation as involving action toward an agreed goal.

Much attention is given in other chapters to agreements that address obvious areas of potential confrontation—either across clearly defined lines in Europe or in cases where the military forces of the superpowers interact, either directly as at sea or indirectly through aspects of the arms race. These are areas where each side has made clear that interests defined as literally vital to its security are at stake. They are areas where interests can normally be precisely defined.

A few chapters, such as this one, address Soviet–U.S. competition in areas where neither interests nor the lines between them are as clearly defined or as precisely drawn. In these areas, competition for influence continues with sometimes only general indication of areas of special interest or sensitivity and with a changing picture of the exact nature of the influence sought. The task in examining the arena of Arab-Israeli conflict is to identify conditions, policies, and interactions that have increased or decreased incentives and opportunities for the USSR and the United States to regulate their competition or to cooperate.

This chapter deals with Soviet and U.S. experience in interacting with each other in the arena of the Arab-Israeli-Palestinian conflict from the years leading up to the 1967 war through 1986. The chapter does not attempt to deal with Soviet–U.S. interaction in other parts of the larger Middle East area such as the Persian Gulf or Afghanistan.

In order to make this complex of events more manageable, I have chosen—I hope not too arbitrarily—to divide these two decades into six "experiences." Each experience seems in retrospect to be marked by a new departure, a particular dynamic, and a conclusion or shifting of gears to a new approach. As an aid to the reader, I have included a one-page table summarizing how the experiences are defined and the principal developments in each period.[2] To treat these experiences discreetly is not to deny the elements of continuity threading through them. I will attempt to reflect on those in the final section of the paper.

A FRAMEWORK FOR ANALYSIS

Each experience is discussed against the background of a conceptual framework that I find useful in trying to understand policymaking and behavior in any international relationship, especially one characterized by conflict. This framework identifies questions that will help us probe each experience for what it may teach about the conduct of the Soviet–U.S. relationship in a regional conflict.

Let me introduce the framework by explaining the distinction between "conflict" and "crisis." I view conflict as a condition characterized by a long-term competition or clash of interests serious enough to prevent or disrupt a normal relationship and to threaten on occasion the outbreak of violence. Within the context of basic conflict, a crisis is a particularly intense period of confrontation when violence seems imminent or actually breaks out. I view the conduct of a relationship in which basic interests conflict as a continuous exercise in conflict management because the aim is to conduct the relationship in such a way as to prevent dangerous crises. By conflict management I do not mean, as Soviet colleagues often fear, the exploitation of conflict for unilateral advantage; I mean the regulation of conflict and competition.

If we are to identify those elements in our experience that have particularly contributed to regulating competition, we need some framework that alerts us to the important questions we should ask in reviewing our experience. I will have in mind the following framework as I discuss and analyze the six experiences. It describes three sets of questions that leaders deal with as they go through the policymaking process. As is common in political life, leaders constantly revisit their earlier judgments and preserve their flexibility to make midcourse corrections. Still, it is useful to identify the questions that need to be held in mind.

A. *Defining the problem, analyzing threats to interests, and deciding to try to change a situation.* In analyzing any policymaking process, it is important at the start to understand how each side pictures the problem, defines its interests and the threats to them, and decides whether it can live with continuation of the present situation or whether efforts must be made to change it. There is an analytical stage in any policy process when a leader asks himself and his colleagues: What is happening and where does this situation lead? Why should I care? Must I try to change the situation? More specifically:

1. Each leader's definition of the problem posed by a situation and the course that situation seems to be taking reflects not only an objective description of what is happening but also how that leader interprets developments in light of his own world view and personal, national, and global objectives. Defining a problem can often be the cause of heated political controversy because how policymakers define a problem will begin to determine the policy they will eventually set. In the Soviet–U.S. relationship, it makes a policy difference whether Americans see the Soviet Union as an "evil empire" or as another world power with its own unique objectives. It makes a difference whether Soviets make policy as communist ideologues or mainly as protectors of Soviet security, which might be assured in various ways. Beyond that, it makes a difference whether policymakers in Moscow and Washington think of the Middle East as another field for superpower competition or whether they judge that relationships with key states in the region, creatively pursued on their own merits, will best serve the aim of blocking domination of the region by the other power.

2. Each side's leaders will determine how their interests are being affected by developing conditions. At this point, leaders ask whether a present situation could go on without harming their interests. In my view, interests are defined by governments on two levels.

    a. To begin with, an analytical statement of interests usually reflects as precisely and as objectively as possible the government's stakes in a given situation.

    b. Then leaders must take into account questions raised in the political arena: What relative priority does the leader assign to those interests? How do interests analytically defined stand up in competition with one another for resources, political support of key constituencies, or high-level attention? It is also in this arena, for instance, that leaders consider the impact, if any, of any significant policy change on the overall Soviet–U.S. relationship. Each side's definition of its interests in the Middle East, for instance, derives at least partly from its interest in keeping the other side from gaining exclusive influence there.

3. If continuation of the present situation seems to harm one side's interests or not to advance them at a desirable pace, its leaders begin thinking about whether they must try to change the situation. This is a critical moment in the policy process and in the conduct of a relationship. Change can destabilize and even lead to military conflict; change can also lead, after some tension, to a more desirable and more stable situation. In understanding how to avoid military confrontation or how to end it, for instance, it becomes essential to understand what produced the compulsion to risk confrontation in order to change the situation. Or, if a leader wants to change a situation peacefully, he needs to understand what might cause others to share his compelling desire for change.

    a. In the Arab-Israeli arena, for instance, Moscow wants to become a partner in changing the present situation so as to bring about Israeli withdrawal from territories occupied in 1967 and the establishment of a Palestinian state. The United States wants to produce a settlement that will crystallize an Arab change of position to acceptance of a normal relationship with Israel. A question is whether and how each side's interest in change can be dealt with peacefully in relation to the other's interest in change.

B. *Developing alternatives.* If policymakers conclude that change is necessary, they begin to think about what they should and can do. They ask themselves whether they can visualize alternative situations they could live with politically. Alternatives may involve short-term limited objectives or fundamental changes in a relationship over a long period of time. They analyze the obstacles to moving in a particular direction. Although a leader at this stage begins to think about ways of moving, he is still essentially in a stage of analysis and exploration. Specifically, he begins to ask these questions:

1. Can our side envision an alternative situation that might be preferable to the present one and politically supportable?

2. If one side can view a preferable alternative situation, what is its perception of the other side's interest, readiness, and ability to move toward that new situation? Do leaders recognize shared or complementary interests in achieving that alternative situation? Do the two sides have a common interest or at least separate interests in achieving that situation? A key point is whether each party is able to understand and incorporate the other side's concerns into its own picture of a desirable alternative situation. It is this step for instance, that underlies the concept of common security—recognition that the other side's insecurity produces an unstable situation, or, in the Middle East, that one side's efforts to exclude the other can increase the likelihood that competition will lead to confrontation.

3. How will the balance of forces constrain or impel moving to the alternative? What are the obstacles to change? Can they be removed peacefully? At this point, policymakers will begin analyzing what needs to be changed in moving to an alternative situation. Again, a leader reaches a critical moment. Once he knows where he wants to go and might realistically do so, how he identifies the obstacles to getting there will begin to shape his strategy for removing them so he can achieve his objectives. How he understands what influences the other side's position will begin to shape his thinking about what needs to be done. At this moment, a leader's analysis of the obstacles to change and of ways to reduce the other side's opposition can provide a base for decisions on strategy that will involve choices between peaceful and destructive ways of bringing about change.

C. *Devising a strategy.* As policymakers move closer to this point in their decision making, they will already have begun thinking about the strategy for changing the balance of forces in the situation so as to move toward the preferable alternative situation. They also begin looking at the practical politics of changing the situation. What goes on in a leader's mind is one thing; how leaders act in the political arena in trying to bring constituencies into line with their own reasoning is another. There are two dimensions to the politics of pursuing a policy. One is building political support among domestic constituencies. Without this essential political support a leader cannot sustain any course of action. The second dimension is conducting the interaction—or relationship—with other parties in such a way as to change the relationship and move to an alternative situation. As a leader translates analysis into political strategy, he must consider both dimensions and the interaction between them. To understand how a leader begins to operate in the political world, it may be useful to think in terms of functions to be performed at three stages: exploration, political engagement, and making change happen.

1. Exploration. An extended period of exploratory exchanges, mostly private, will mark much of the period before the leader finally decides on a course of action.

During this period, he will begin to test his thoughts against political reality among his advisers, in his own body politic, and even in the adversaries' political arenas by reaching quietly across international boundaries into the other camp. Often a leader's public will be debating the same issues he is considering, and his concern will be to shape the debate to lead to the conclusion that he would most like to see, or perhaps simply to learn from it. The main characteristic of a leader's actions during this period is flexibility; he is still not committed to a course of action and can back off or change course at minimum political cost.

2. Political engagement. At some point, even during the period of exploration, a leader will begin to take his first deliberate, though still tentative, steps to change the political environment. The first moves will normally be made within his own body politic, but as he begins to operate publicly, he will be aware that he is communicating at least indirectly with the constituents of the other party. In today's world, some leaders have begun to recognize that the conduct of an international relationship is a process of continuous interaction between policy-making and policy-influencing communities on both sides of the relationship. Actions to create a political environment in one body politic will influence opinion in the other. Any effort to examine this aspect of decision making on the Soviet's part is necessarily speculative. On the U.S. side, it is apparent that the President must not only sift out the normal analyses of interests that affect any foreign policy decision but must also cope with the American public's interpretation of Soviet statements and actions.

3. Making change happen. As a leader feels he has built some political support and begins developing a strategy, he will review the instruments of statecraft available for use in changing the situation. In my view, leaders today have a need and an opportunity to move beyond the traditional instruments in conducting international relationships. For instance, competition between the United States and the USSR for influence in the Middle East, and the regulation of that competition, can involve a number of instruments.

   a. Military force. The armed forces of the superpowers could confront each other on Middle Eastern battlefields, but their possession of nuclear weapons imposes limits on even their use of conventional weapons against each other. Their competition has more often taken the form of supplying regional states and movements with military equipment. Their prestige vis-à-vis each other then becomes in some degree a hostage of the abilities and hostilities among those regional powers. At that point, regulating the superpower competition becomes a function of determining exactly how the interests of each superpower are affected by the regional contest. Defense of interests and security remains a basic duty of government, but security and protection of interests may come from political arrangements as well as from military capability. Those political arrangements may actually substitute for a test of force. They may be explicitly agreed to between the superpowers or they may be tacitly arrived at through a sequence of experiences. Some of those experiences are the subject of this chapter.

   b. Economic pressures or inducements. Economic assistance has been an important tool in the superpower contest for influence in the Middle East, and the perceived Soviet threat to control the Gulf and cut off the source of NATO's oil supplies—whether a realistic perception or not—has played a significant role in the Soviet–U.S. competition. But with the boom in oil revenues in the 1970s, instruments of government were not the only factors to be taken into account. As Middle Eastern nations laid out elaborate economic development plans, they turned mainly to the private sectors in Western nations for technology, management, and equipment. As they invested their rapidly accumulating oil revenues in Western economies, they experienced limits on their abilities to use such instruments as the oil embargo—which the Soviet Union had applauded in 1973 and 1974. Economic interdependence has reshaped the balance of economic advantage in the superpower competition from the days when the Soviet Union could simply offer to finance the Aswan Dam project, which the United States had dropped.

c. Diplomatic discussions or negotiations. Traditional diplomacy may be used in any situation where efforts to change a situation could escalate tension. The United States and the USSR certainly have an incentive for direct communication to avoid nuclear confrontation between them and for negotiated deescalation of a regional crisis that could involve them. But they also have an interest in developing a Soviet–U.S. political relationship in which they can build experience and confidence in tacit rules of interaction between them and among their allies to serve as guides to crisis prevention. They may further act jointly or in parallel—with explicit or only indirect communication—to change the regional political environment and reduce the deeper causes of Arab-Israeli conflict. In that context, the Soviet–U.S. competition has sometimes taken the form of demonstrating which power has the greater ability to influence the course of events in the Arab-Israeli arena. For instance, the United States between 1974 and 1979 acted unilaterally to mediate five Arab-Israeli agreements while the Soviets mounted a major effort to return those mediating efforts to an international conference where they would have at least the appearance of equal participation.

d. Propaganda. Opinion-molding acts are no longer limited to traditional propaganda. What each party does will be assessed by the other body politic and that assessment will have more influence on the other's actions than formal statements of policy. Substantive proposals and acts that embody genuine alternatives can be designed for their impact on opinion in the other side's body politic. For instance, the Soviet Union's relationship with Israel and its treatment of Jews in the Soviet Union and their emigration will have more influence on Soviet–U.S. interaction in the Middle East than any public statement the Soviets could make on the superpowers' common interest in moving the Arab-Israeli conflict toward resolution. In the Helsinki process, we have designed formal confidence-building measures to reduce the likelihood of a crisis. In a region like the Middle East, measures that repeatedly demonstrate common interests could play an important role in regulating competition.

My purpose here is not to develop this framework further but only to explain the source from which questions and vocabulary will be drawn in discussing and assessing experiences in regulating Soviet–U.S. competition in the Arab-Israeli arena. Posing questions in a conceptual context can often cause us to look at familiar material in a fresh light. In short, we will be analyzing the six experiences that follow with three sets of questions in mind reflecting this analytical framework:

- Why is a party trying to change the situation? What is the basis of its perception of the problem; what political needs must be met; how are its interests seen to be threatened?
- What is the party trying to change? What are its views of available alternatives and its understanding of the obstacles—both at home and on the other side—that would have to be removed in moving toward those alternatives?
- How does the party try to achieve the desired change? What strategy does it devise for conducting a relationship to change a situation and what instruments does it use?

In applying this framework to Soviet–U.S. competition in the Middle East, one point needs to be underscored. In dealing with the Middle East, policymakers in Moscow and Washington must think simultaneously of two sets of relationships and the interaction between those two sets: Each must think of its own interests and roles in the region, but each must also consider how its policies toward the Middle East will affect its relationship with the other. The latter set of interactions will also include the alliance systems surrounding the superpowers, as was evident in 1973 when Moscow tried to use Western Europe's concern about the Arab oil embargo to mobilize European pressure against Washington. In fact, it often becomes difficult to determine whether it is Soviet–U.S. competition or Middle Eastern considerations that primarily determine policies in Washington and Moscow. Whichever is the case at a given moment, attempting to understand the mix of concerns can shed light on the instruments available to regulate superpower competition. A superpower's actions in the Middle East can often only be fully explained in terms of the signal they send to the other superpower in their bilateral relationship.

Each of the following sections will include two parts: (1) a discussion of the experience from the perspective described above and (2) reflections on ways in which Soviet–U.S. competition was or was not regulated. At the end of the paper a concluding section will draw together some overall thoughts from those reflections on the six experiences (see Table 1).

THE 1967 WAR: BEFORE AND AFTER THROUGH 1968

Discussion of the Experience

In this period, the superpowers experienced increasingly complex political, military, and economic competition in an arena of regional conflict where few clear lines were drawn between their interests. They experienced the first moment when, realistically, they could see a Middle East conflict drawing them into direct confrontation. We can usefully think of the experience in this period as evolving through three successive circumstances: (1) the perspectives that leaders in Moscow and Washington developed on each other's purposes in the Middle East before the June 1967 war, (2) the hotline exchanges between the superpowers during the war to avoid confrontation between them, and (3) the parallel efforts through the end of the Johnson Administration to put the long-term Arab-Israeli conflict into a diplomatic and therefore hopefully more manageable—or at least less dangerous—context. The lessons drawn from this experience began to shape our thinking about interaction in situations of this kind.

In the years before the war, the Arab-Israeli conflict increasingly became a vehicle for superpower competition, with the Soviets responding to Arab concerns and the United

TABLE 1. The Six Experiences

The 1967 War: Before and After through 1968

Pre-1967	Intensifying USSR–U.S. competition and mounting Arab–Israeli tension
June 5–10, 1967	Arab–Israeli war and hotline exchanges
June–Nov., 1967	UNGA, Glassboro summit, and UNSC Res. 242
1968	Resumption of military assistance with some restraint
Nov.–Dec. 1968	U.S. and USSR take positions on Egyptian–Israeli settlement

The State Department Effort, 1969–71

March–Dec. 1969	Detailed Soviet–U.S. talks on Egyptian–Israeli settlement
April 1969–Aug. 1970	War of Attrition on Suez Canal
—April 1969	Egypt begins artillery barrages across Canal
—Sept. and Jan.	U.S. F-4s to Israel; Israeli raids deep in Egypt
—Feb.–Aug. 1970	Soviet buildup of Egyptian air defenses
—April–Aug.	U.S.-mediated ceasefire-standstill
Sept. 1970	Jordan's conflict with PLO; Syrian invasion of Jordan
1971	U.S. initiative on interim Egypt-Israel agreement to open Canal

The White House Becomes Involved, 1971–1973

July 8, 1971	Kissinger trip to Peking announced
Aug.–Sept. 1971	Soviet–White House talks on Mid-East opened
Dec. 1971, April 1972	Israel–Kissinger, Egypt–Kissinger channels opened
May 1972	Brezhnev-Nixon issue bland summit communiqué on Mid-East
Jan. 20, 27, 1973	Nixon's second inauguration; Vietnam agreement signed
Feb., May 1973	Secret Kissinger meetings with Sadat's adviser, Hafiz Ismail
April–Oct. 1973	Sadat steps up preparations for war
June 1973	No Mid-East progress at Brezhnev–Nixon summit
Oct. 1973	Yom Kippur War; U.S. airlift to Israel; Arab oil embargo; Kissinger to Moscow; UNSC Res. 338
Dec. 1973	USSR, U.S. co-chair Geneva Mid-East Peace Conference

Step-by-Step Diplomacy, 1974–76

Jan. 1974	First Egypt-Israel disengagement, first Kissinger "shuttle"
Feb. 1974	Saudis agree to lift oil embargo
May 1974	Israel-Syria disengagement, 35-day Kissinger shuttle
Feb.–May 1974	U.S. relations restored with Egypt, Algeria, Syria
June 1974	Nixon visit to Mid-East; third Brezhnev-Nixon summit
Aug. 1974	Nixon resigns; Ford assesses next steps
Oct. 1974	Rabat Arab summit—PLO "only legitimate" Palestinian representative
Nov. 1974	Brezhnev–Ford summit at Vladivostok, main topic is arms control
March 1974	Kissinger shuttle ends without agreement
Aug. 1974	Kissinger shuttle produces second Egypt-Israel agreement

Carter and Camp David, 1977–80

Feb.–Oct. 1977	Efforts to resume Geneva conference
Oct. 1, 1977	Joint USSR–U.S. statement
Nov. 1977	Sadat visits Jerusalem
Sept. 1978	Camp David accords; Iranian revolution into high gear
March 1979	Egypt-Israel peace treaty
May 1979	Palestinian autonomy talks begin
Fall 1979	SALT treaty in trouble in Senate
Nov. 1979	Iran hostage crisis begins. U.S. naval buildup in Indian Ocean
Dec. 1979	USSR invades Afghanistan

TABLE 1. The Six Experiences *(Continued)*

Reagan, 1981–86	
1981	Haig's "strategic consensus." Habib's ceasefire in Lebanon. Camp David talks on Palestinian autonomy sidelined. Multinational force for the Sinai
April, June 1982	Israeli withdrawal from Sinai. Israeli invasion of Lebanon
Aug. 1982	Habib ceasefire in Lebanon. U.S. Marines ashore
Sept. 1982	Sabra and Shatilla massacres. Marines return
Sept. 1, 1982	Reagan's speech—a "fresh start" on Arab-Israeli negotiations
Sept. 1982–May 1983	Discussions on Israeli-Jordan-Palestinian negotiation parallel negotiations on Israeli withdrawal from Lebanon, ending May 13
Aug. 1983–Feb. 1984	Marines take casualties. Sixth Fleet guns and aircraft deployed. Marines withdrawn
Nov. 1984–Feb. 1986	Hussein concludes agreement with Arafat Feb. 11, 1985, on Jordanian-Palestinian confederation. Extensive efforts to arrange an international conference falter Feb. 1986.

States increasingly drawn to Israel's support. In the regional context, competition for influence steadily escalated, with each side using the by then usual instruments of economic and military aid and cultural exchange plus active efforts to develop relationships with like-minded political leaders and movements as Arabs and Israelis confronted each other. In the global context, each was conscious of the larger Soviet effort to change the strategic balance so that it would not again be at a power disadvantage in a showdown as it had been in the 1963 Cuban missile crisis.

In such a situation both sides recognized the need to continue efforts begun by the two superpowers after the Cuban crisis—such as installing the "hotline"—to manage their interaction so as to reduce the risk of nuclear war. Avoiding a direct confrontation was an explicitly stated interest on each side. Each walked a tightrope between taking advantage of regional conditions to build its own influence and exercising restraint to avoid confrontation, but for all of that, neither had experienced exactly how, or how dramatically, Arab-Israeli violence could escalate into major war. The 1956 Suez crisis had come only at the beginning of deeper Soviet involvement, and both powers had opposed the Anglo-Franco-Israeli action against Egypt. In the period immediately after 1956, the violence—apart from the Lebanon crisis—had remained episodic.

Soviet leaders, for their part, defined the problem in terms of steadily enhancing the Soviet bilateral relationship with key governments in the Middle East as a way of pursuing the longstanding Soviet interest in pushing "encircling" Western positions away from Soviet borders. By the mid-1960s, they were aware of increasing Arab restiveness over the contest with Israel and of the deep disagreements within Arab ranks over how to deal with the problem. Moscow sought to maintain its strong position in Cairo, where President Gamal Abdel Nasser opposed the use of force against Israel, while trying to establish its influence in the more militant Arab group clustering around the regime in Syria and the Palestine Liberation Organization, which was recognized at the first Arab summit conference in 1964. As Arab coordination improved after a new government came to power in Damascus in February 1966, the Soviets saw increased opportunity for influence in both Arab quarters. Developing that influence required, in Moscow's view, some measure of Soviet support for Arab positions.

Moscow's interest in building influence in both camps led to an ambivalence in its stance. As violence increased with a pattern of guerrilla attacks and Israeli retaliation along its Jordanian and Syrian borders in late 1966 and early 1967, the Soviet position in Western eyes became unclear. While Moscow appeared not to want to see the situation run out of control because of the danger of confrontation with the United States, it also appeared to block U.S. efforts to deal with the conflict diplomatically in the U.N. Security Council by supporting Arab positions. At the same time, Moscow denied Syria's requests for the most advanced military equipment. In short, the Soviets seemed to recognize that Arab restiveness was a potential threat to Soviet credibility in Arab capitals if Moscow did not support Arab positions, and they did not sense an approach that might provide both Arabs and Israel with a constructive alternative. Since the Middle Eastern parties were not prepared for a diplomatic settlement, Moscow seemed unready to develop one as a realistic alternative.

The United States, on its side, had focused on three main aspects of the problem. First, the Kennedy Administration had recognized that neither Arabs nor Israelis were ready for a comprehensive effort to resolve their conflict and so had tried to build a base for a Palestinian refugee settlement. Second, it had come under increasing pressure from Israel for military assistance in response to mounting Soviet military shipments to the Arabs. In that context, Kennedy moved slowly in providing conventional arms and made a persistent, though ultimately unsuccessful, effort to prevent Israel from developing nuclear weapons. Third, the United States had attempted to build a political relationship with Nasser to avoid leaving the nonaligned camp entirely to the Soviets. It remained important to prevent Soviet predominance in an area that provided vital oil for European and Japanese allies.

After 1964, Johnson had been increasingly watchful of Soviet efforts to enhance their position in the Middle East by deepening their political relationships. Johnson later recalled that he "had watched this process with growing concern" and late in 1966 had "asked for a special study of Soviet penetration in the Middle East."[3] A substantial study and debate within the foreign affairs bureaucracy followed. One side took the position that the Soviets were steadily and effectively infiltrating the political mechanisms of the Middle East and improving their position in irreversible ways that could eventually exclude significant U.S. influence. Another school of thought held that the built-in resistance to communism in Middle Eastern bodies politic would establish limits on how substantial that Soviet position could become. Nevertheless, in the context of the global relationship with the Soviet Union, the President was aware of the combined danger of growing Soviet influence and the possibility that the Middle East could become the next arena for a nuclear showdown.

Johnson did not see an immediate threat to U.S. interests but rather the threat of steady erosion. With growing frustration he had tried—albeit with less personal enthusiasm for the nonaligned perspective—to continue the Kennedy policy of developing at least a mutually respectful working relationship with Nasser's Egypt while maintaining the U.S. commitment to Israel. By 1966 and 1967, Johnson above all feared the possibility of a Soviet–U.S. confrontation on top of the already heavy U.S. involvement in Vietnam. He also recognized that escalating tension between Arabs and Israelis would provide an opportunity for the Soviets to improve their position with the Arabs while the United States maintained its commitments to Israel. For both reasons, Johnson sought to avoid a crisis in the Middle East and, after it had erupted, to bring it to a quick close and put it into a diplomatic context that would involve some measure of Soviet–U.S.

cooperation. Like Soviet leaders, he could not see a clear-cut alternative that he could manage politically, given Middle Eastern attitudes and his own preoccupations.

Before the 1967 war, the superpowers had a theoretical choice between (1) pursuing their individual interests and bilateral competition by building relationships with their respective clients, and (2) seeking to address the underlying causes of the Arab-Israeli conflict without waiting for a crisis to erupt. In the prewar period, the Soviet government seemed intent on consolidating its position with the emerging Egyptian-Syrian-Palestinian coalition to the extent that it felt constrained from taking a position at the United Nations that would have enabled that body to deal impartially with the escalating tension. The United States, while momentarily trying to move the conflict into a U.N. context, did not engage in any significant direct diplomatic effort to reduce the potential for conflict. As has often been the case, preoccupation with domestic programs in 1964 and 1965, as well as with Vietnam, put the Middle East lower on the U.S. priority list. Each side was wary lest the other side's influence in significant sectors become exclusive, but within that context seemed prepared to live with an ongoing competition for influence. In addition to regional considerations, the two superpowers were still in the exploratory stages of trying to develop new elements in their bilateral relationship, particularly in arms control.

The 1967 war threatened that relationship basically because it raised the possibility of direct superpower military involvement and, particularly at the end of the war, because it threatened the credibility of the Soviets' political relationship with Syria. Geography permitted Egypt to preserve its heartland—the Nile Valley—while the Israeli advance on Damascus threatened Syria's capital.

The crisis began on May 14, 1967, when President Nasser ordered Egyptian troops into the Sinai in violation of an understanding between the United States and Israel which had led to Israeli withdrawal from the Sinai in March 1957 after the Suez War. The crisis intensified on May 16 when Nasser requested removal from the border areas of the U.N. Emergency Force established as part of that 1957 agreement. It took on an even more dangerous coloration on May 22 when Nasser closed the Strait of Tiran, an act that Israel had made clear at the time of its 1957 withdrawal it would regard as a cause of war.

On May 27, the Soviets told President Johnson they had reports that Israel was planning an attack, and Johnson used the Soviet message as an occasion to repeat his warnings to Israel not to attack. At the same time, Johnson and Secretary of State Dean Rusk sent messages to Premier Aleksei Kosygin and Foreign Minister Andrei Gromyko urging a Soviet–U.S. effort to calm the situation and particularly suggesting that Nasser suspend his closing of the Strait for two weeks. In theory, there was an option of joint action, but this exchange seemed a communication in the spirit of normal diplomatic base-touching to suggest complementary actions rather than the start of a concerted cooperative effort. In situations of this kind, there was a common feeling—at least in Washington—that separate approaches would be more effective because a joint approach could be read in the Middle East as evidence of an attempt to impose another great power condominium.

When the war broke out in the early hours of June 5, 1967, each superpower turned earnestly to avoiding confrontation with the other. Early on June 5, Kosygin activated the Moscow-Washington hotline for its first substantive use. The Soviet Union and the United States each took steps to reassure the other that it did not intend to involve itself militarily in the crisis and would make efforts bilaterally and at the United Nations to bring about a ceasefire. Through the six days of the war the two sides used the hotline almost two dozen times for a variety of purposes. In addition to exchanging messages on achieving a ceasefire through the U.N. Security Council, when the Israeli air force attacked the U.S. intelligence ship *Liberty* on June 8, Johnson assured Kosygin that U.S. naval movement would be limited to investigation and rescue. In the final hours of the war on June 10, as Israel seemed determined to press toward Damascus, the Soviets let the United States know that allowing Israel to inflict further damage on Syria would touch Soviet raw nerves. Moscow threatened to take steps, including military involvement, if Israel did not observe the ceasefire. Johnson responded by turning key Sixth Fleet elements toward the eastern Mediterranean to show U.S. opposition to Soviet military action, but by that time efforts to make the ceasefire effective were already well advanced. The fighting stopped within hours. The hotline had served its purpose in enabling Soviet and U.S. leaders to deal with the crisis as a shared effort to avoid a direct face-off.

When the war ended, the two powers faced two questions: First was the basic question of how to help position the long-standing Arab-Israeli conflict in an international diplomatic context, where it might be contained and moved gradually toward resolution. The diplomacy of that effort included the first meeting between Johnson and Kosygin and diplomatic efforts at the United Nations in which both parties cooperated to some extent. The second question concerned the continuing Soviet and U.S. relationships with the parties to the conflict, as expressed in terms of political support, resupply of military equipment, and continuing military assistance programs.

The Middle East was not the only issue on the agenda when Johnson and Kosygin met in Glassboro, New Jersey, on June 23 and 25. Ever since becoming President, Johnson had exchanged views with General Secretary Nikita Khrushchev and Kosygin on the possibility of a meeting, and the two sides had taken a number of steps together to reduce tension between them in the nuclear field. By that time, the U.S. involvement in Vietnam was also a factor in the relationship. As Johnson recalled, he began the conversation focusing on possible efforts to lessen Cold War tension, but each time he raised strategic arms talks, Kosygin—who did not have authority to negotiate—shifted the conversation to the Middle East.

In the Special Emergency Session of the U.N. General Assembly, which began on June 19 and continued through much of July, American and Soviet representatives sought some common ground between the positions of Arabs and Israelis. By the time of the Glassboro summit, the two sides could state in the communiqué the equation that called both for the right of every state to live in a durable peace and for Israeli troop withdrawals. Johnson had laid out five points for peace in a speech on June 19, including that equation and the importance of negotiation and of limiting the Middle East arms race. In mid-July, the two sides were close enough to produce a tentative joint draft resolution in the General Assembly calling for total Israeli withdrawal in return for an end to the Arab war with Israel. The Arabs rejected that position and in late August in a summit meeting at Khartoum took a position of no recognition, no negotiation, and no peace with Israel.

Finally, on November 22, 1967, U.N. Security Council Resolution 242 was passed with the support of both powers, calling for "withdrawal of Israel armed forces from territories [not *all* territories] occupied in the recent conflict" and "termination of all claims or states of belligerency and respect for and acknowledgement of the sovereignty, territorial integrity and political independence of every State in the area and their right to live in peace within secure and recognized boundaries free from threats or acts of force.'' That resolution also called on the U.N. Secretary General to appoint a representative to work with the parties to develop the basis for a negotiated resolution of the conflict.

In short, both the United States and the Soviet Union seemed in the summer of 1967 willing to take political positions at a distance from those of their friends and to reflect in their policies a common interest in putting the Arab-Israeli conflict into an international diplomatic context. The Soviets were willing to support a negotiated peace between Israel and the Arabs, while the United States for a moment that summer supported total Israeli withdrawal from all territories occupied in the conflict. As time passed, each superpower retreated in some degree from those positions to be closer to the positions of their friends, but they did not give up continued concern to advance the diplomatic position, albeit without in 1968 involving themselves firmly and directly in that diplomacy.

In 1968, each side turned to the question of rearming the parties to the conflict, and Johnson became increasingly enmeshed in the domestic politics of the escalating war in Vietnam. At the same time, the foreign ministries on each side maintained a dialogue with U.N. emissary Ambassador Gunnar Jarring. In November and December, each of the superpowers made known its position on the terms of a final Egyptian-Israeli settlement. On November 2, Secretary of State Rusk told the Egyptians that the United States would support full Israeli withdrawal from the Sinai in the context of a genuine peace. During the year, Egypt had begun artillery fire across the Suez Canal, while Moscow and Washington continued the flow of arms to their respective clients. They did so with some restraint, in an effort to avoid the appearance of endorsing an unqualified return to a military solution. After a visit by Soviet Foreign Minister Gromyko to Cairo in early December 1968, the Soviet government presented to the United States its own position on a settlement. By that time, the transition to the new Nixon Administration in Washington had already begun.

Reflections on the Experience

First, the period before the 1967 war was still a time of active and self-conscious competition between the United States and the USSR for greater influence with individual countries. Each side saw the situation as not serving its interests because of what it regarded as the actual or potentially excessive influence of the other side.

The Soviets since the early 1950s had felt threatened by what they saw as a U.S. network of relationships in the Middle East intended to encircle the Soviet Union, contain its influence, and deny it an active presence. A high Soviet priority had been to change a situation in which the United States seemed to be trying to establish an exclusive position in an area the Soviets regarded as their backyard.

The United States throughout this period remained acutely sensitive to possible Soviet exploitation of post-colonial change to achieve exclusive positions, especially by establishing communist governments as it had in Eastern Europe. In addition to being concerned about the strategic aspects of the Cuban missile crisis, Americans saw Cuba as a nation taken over by Moscow to be used as a jumping-off place for spreading revolution to gain advantage in the global contest. The United States was concerned about Soviet efforts to develop relationships of that kind in the Middle East.

Second, in the 1960s each side saw its alternatives in terms of building political, economic, and security relationships with key Middle Eastern countries almost as quasi alliances. Neither superpower gave much thought to whether cooperation might enhance its position. The only alternatives with any character of cooperation stemmed from their recognition of the need to limit competition to the extent necessary to reduce the danger of confrontation, and that cooperation was not explicit before the 1967 war. Each party seemed to accept the competition as a given, and each recognized that the other would react sharply when special relationships were threatened. Each was also especially sensitive to any effort by the other to achieve an exclusive relationship, although that did not stop either from trying. Joint action in the absence of a crisis was not seriously considered.

Third, the Arab-Israeli conflict became an instrument in that Soviet–U.S. competition until the 1967 war forced consideration of limiting exploitation of the conflict for unilateral advantage. Before the war, the United States saw Moscow as responding to Arab concerns in order to strengthen its own position, and Moscow saw the United States as using Israel as a proxy for attacking its growing relationships as part of a continuing U.S. effort to deny the Soviets a legitimate presence in the area. Once the Arab-Israeli crisis exploded, leaders on both sides immediately gave priority to developing a relationship with each other for at least the limited purpose of managing the regional crisis so as to avoid a Soviet–U.S. nuclear confrontation. I believe it is fair to say—acknowledging possible American bias—that the United States was much more active than the USSR in efforts between May 22 and June 5 to defuse the mounting crisis. Once the war began, there was little hesitation about agreeing through direct communication to stand aside and to consult on steps to end the war. More significant, neither then seemed to use the war as an instrument in their competition, and each was straighforward in communicating specific interests in particular situations.

The crisis left them more willing to consider alternatives to using the Arab-Israeli conflict as an instrument in their competition. They were more willing to agree on a general framework for negotiating resolution of the Arab-Israeli conflict, but both shied away either from joint mediation or from a unilateral mediator's role. They were not ready to lean on their regional friends to adjust the basic Arab-Israeli relationship so as to reduce the long-term causes of a conflict that could embroil them. In addition to revealing perhaps their sense of the intractability of the Arab-Israeli conflict, their keeping a distance also seemed to reveal a concern that cooperation in trying to produce a settlement would somehow allow the other side some advantage. To use the U.S. concept, cooperation would legitimize the Soviet Union as an arbiter of events in a way that could reshape the future of the area.

After the war it was also openly recognized that restraint or lack of restraint in supplying arms to Middle Eastern parties could influence the superpower relationship. In the years before 1967 each superpower was still experimenting to see what influence could be achieved through active economic and military assistance programs and political efforts. The United States since 1950 had been only a reluctant supplier of arms until Soviet shipments to Arab states increased the pressure from Israel and brought the United States slowly into the arms race. The Soviets found in 1967 that the humiliating defeat of Soviet arms in the hands of Arab armies could affect the balance of superpower influence.

In short, the competition for influence would continue, but the war had dramatized the dangers of using the Arab-Israeli conflict as an instrument in that competition. The two powers began to identify how individual instruments in the competition could affect the Soviet–U.S. relationship. They cooperated—though they did not for the most part act jointly—to put the conflict into an internationally approved and more current diplomatic framework for working toward its resolution. Making the U.N. Secretary General responsible for mediation avoided at least for that moment the question of either power ceding primacy to the other as mediator. In addition, it is probably fair to say that the two powers had not at this point developed an ability to cooperate in dealing with critical bilateral issues, so it was not surprising that their ability to go beyond a certain point in cooperation on a regional issue was limited. The perception of the Middle East as a powder keg continued and was an important factor in shaping the Nixon Administration's picture of the problem, both in its Soviet–U.S. and its Middle East dimensions.

THE STATE DEPARTMENT EFFORT, 1969–71

Discussion of the Experience

This period combined some of the most sustained Soviet–U.S. talks on the conditions of an Arab-Israeli peace settlement with remarkably intense superpower competition through clients—Egypt and Israel—that were engaged in heavy and sustained fighting just short of all-out war. Turning to proxy military competition after failure of a serious diplomatic effort seriously affected judgments on both sides about the possibility of cooperation in a regional context.

More important, this period also coincided with the efforts of President Richard Nixon and National Security Advisor Henry Kissinger to end U.S. involvement in Vietnam, establish a new basis for the Soviet–U.S. relationship, and add a U.S. relationship with the People's Republic of China to the big-power global balance. The period is characterized on the American side by the conduct of the relationship in the Middle East mainly through conventional diplomatic channels, with White House approval but with only episodic White House interventions. Those interventions normally brought to bear on Middle East developments concerns arising from the global superpower competition and efforts to change that relationship.

The experience evolved through a sequence of four circumstances: (1) a period of active Soviet–U.S. dialogue in 1969 reaching toward a common approach to resolving the Arab-Israeli conflict; (2) a time of intensified military action in the War of Attrition across the Suez Canal until the U.S.-mediated ceasefire of August 1970; (3) the Jordan crisis of "Black September" 1970; and (4) the eventual renewal of diplomatic activity, in 1971, by the United States alone.

The change of administrations in Washington in January 1969 created a new situation for both sides. It was a time for each to review definitions of the problem, threats to interests, aims, and alternatives.

The Soviet Union, for its part, saw the need to get back for its Arab friends Arab territories lost in the 1967 war, as a means of recouping its position in the Middle East after the humiliating defeat of Soviet arms and clients. Moscow saw an opportunity to enlist a new U.S. Administration, free of the Johnson Administration's preoccupation with Vietnam, in a new effort to achieve Israeli withdrawal. The Soviets saw cooperation for that purpose as serving their interests. The Soviets recognized the importance of U.S. involvement in pressing Israel to withdraw, and the disadvantage Moscow suffered from not being able by itself to gain Arab territory back from Israel. Although this assessment is open to debate, it appears that the Soviet leaders did not then want another Arab-Israeli conflict because they knew that their Arab clients were in no position to win and that they consequently might be called upon to send troops, which would have brought them into confrontation with the United States. They saw continuation of the existing situation as harmful to their interests by demonstrating their inability to serve the interests of their Arab clients. In my view, that analytical judgment would have coincided with an interest at the political level in developing a relationship including some degree of collaboration with the incoming U.S. Administration on bilateral issues. Moscow's preferred alternative to letting the Israeli occupation of Arab territory drag on was an Arab-Israeli settlement negotiated in accordance with the Arab interpretation of U.N. Security Council Resolution 242.

The new U.S. leadership, on its side, viewed the situation in the Middle East in the context of two much more compelling interests: (1) ending the involvement in Vietnam, and (2) establishing a relationship with the Soviet Union based on recognizing Soviet nuclear parity and the consequent need to substitute negotiation for military force in resolving potential disputes between the superpowers. Given the overriding interests of Nixon and Kissinger in reordering the global balance by negotiating with the Soviet Union and bringing the People's Republic of China into that balance, they considered regional situations—even one as important as the Middle East—in the context of that reordering. The issue for them in the Middle East was how to relate to the Soviet Union in such a way as to demonstrate that the United States did not consider itself at a disadvantage and that even in a situation to be resolved by negotiation, the United States could marshal sufficient political and military resources within the region to underscore that it was not acknowledging inferiority in agreeing to negotiate. In the regional context, the Americans saw it as in their interest to demonstrate that the United States remained the principal arbiter of events.

The new Administration was divided in defining the problem. The Nixon team in the White House recognized the dangers of the Middle East situation and could probably see some advantage in opening a dialogue with the Soviet Union, but given their other preoccupations, they were not themselves prepared to pay detailed attention to the problem and viewed talks by the State Department as putting the Middle East in a holding pattern and preparing for later attention. They approved but did not become personally involved in those talks. In view of Israel's general military superiority, they saw themselves as holding the stronger regional cards and were prepared to wait for the Soviets to take a position independent of their Arab friends. Secretary of State William P. Rogers and Assistant Secretary Joseph Sisco, on the other hand, were more inclined to deal with the Middle East in terms of trying to make progress within the regional context, taking advantage of Soviet interest in moving the situation.

Soviet efforts to change the situation began with persistent Soviet approaches to start a diplomatic dialogue with the United States to try to advance mediation of an Arab-Israeli settlement. The Soviets from their closer relationship with Egypt understood Nasser's growing impatience in 1968 with continued Israeli occupation of Arab territory following the June 1967 war. They tried to lay the groundwork for diplomatic collaboration with the new Nixon Administration by presenting to the U.S. government in December 1968 a diplomatic note containing a proposal for a comprehensive settlement. At the same time, the Soviets reportedly refused to respond positively to Nasser's full request for advanced military equipment, while Johnson had temporized on a decision to provide Phantom aircraft to Israel. Nixon and Kissinger did not give high priority to responding to the Soviet initiative but permitted Rogers and Sisco to engage in detailed talks with Soviet Ambassador Anatoli Dobrynin and eventually Foreign Minister Gromyko. These talks began in March 1969.

Just after those talks began, Nasser in early April 1969 stepped up what came to be called the War of Attrition across the Suez Canal, beginning with heavy artillery barrages. According to reports, the Soviets pressed Nasser to bring the war to a quick end. During May and June, the talks between Sisco and Dobrynin made substantive progress, with both sides taking significant distance from the positions of Egypt and Israel. After a visit by Gromyko to Cairo at the end of June, while the War of Attrition was still going Egypt's way, the Soviets suddenly took a step back in the negotiation. On July 20, the Israeli air force began systematic heavy attacks on Egyptian positions and by October had virtually destroyed Egyptian anti-aircraft defenses. In July also, the diplomatic exchanges picked up again, justifying a Sisco visit to Moscow. They continued during Gromyko's October visit to the U.N. General Assembly, producing a U.S. paper of October 28, which came to be called the "first Rogers Plan." That paper called for complete Israeli withdrawal to the pre-1967 borders—the former international border—in the context of a peace agreement negotiated between Egypt and Israel. This U.S. proposal, however, came against a background of the collapse of Egyptian defenses and the U.S. delivery to Israel in September 1969 of Phantom jet aircraft that represented introduction of a new generation of air capability into the Arab-Israeli military balance. In that context, the Egyptians, Israelis, and Soviets rejected the U.S. proposal.

At the end of 1969 each superpower seemed constrained in its ability to change the situation diplomatically by the reluctance of its client to make the concessions that an agreement would require—or by its own unwillingness to press for such concessions in the circumstances. Each of the superpowers nevertheless went beyond its client at individual points in the diplomatic exchanges, but in the end neither was willing to press that client beyond verbal urging to concur.

It seemed that once the diplomatic and military tracks were operating simultaneously, the military track eventually took over. Between September 1969 and August 1970, military exchanges escalated, with the Soviet Union and the United States each supporting its client in the face of what it regarded, rightly or wrongly, as a direct challenge from the other superpower.

The Soviets apparently decided in principle in early 1970 that they would have to do what was necessary to restore Egypt's defensive capability. When the Israelis in January 1970 began using the Phantom jets to attack deep into Egypt—now in an effort to topple Nasser—the Soviets during a late-January Nasser visit to Moscow promised quick installation of a new missile defense system in Egypt. Later in the spring, Soviet pilots actually flew patrols over those Soviet-manned missiles and were shot down in combat by Israeli aircraft. The Soviets saw Israel's deep penetration raids as an escalation of the conflict that threatened to bring on Nasser's collapse and a major setback to the Soviet position in the Middle East. It was a challenge they did not feel they could ignore. Kissinger saw the raids as a normal response to Nasser's War of Attrition. It is not clear whether he condoned Israel's raids. Whereas the Soviets saw their military response in early 1970 as their only choice in the light of the Israelis' escalation of both political objectives and military strategy, Kissinger saw the Soviet response as a challenge to the United States in the global context. Neither superpower saw the other as attempting to restrain its side. The Nixon White House also saw Soviet moves in the Middle East in the context of Soviet support for the North Vietnamese, which was making more difficult the U.S. exit from Vietnam.

From April 1970 through August, diplomacy was dominated by a unilateral U.S. effort to bring the War of Attrition to an end and to launch new efforts to negotiate an Egyptian-Israeli settlement. On June 19, the United States proposed without prior consultations with Moscow—despite Soviet involvement—that Egypt and Israel "stop shooting and start talking." In August the ceasefire came into effect. In its first days, the Egyptians, with Soviet assistance and in violation of the agreement continued to move into place defensive missiles that would cover the Suez Canal, but eventually the ceasefire took hold. Soviet–U.S. diplomatic efforts had resumed briefly in June at U.S. initiative. The Soviets responded with new concessions from Nasser. Both sides moved further beyond their clients in July, but at that point violations of the ceasefire and standstill put an end to this collaboration. In U.S. eyes, the Soviets appeared guilty of trying to undermine the U.S. initiative.

That impression was reinforced by what Kissinger assumed was Soviet acquiescence in the movement of Syrian armed forces into Jordan during the "Black September" internal showdown between the Jordanian government and the Palestine Liberation Organization. Interpreting the Syrian invasion against the background of Soviet involvement in the Egyptian violation of the standstill agreement, Nixon and Kissinger could not believe—given the number of Soviet advisers with the Syrian armed forces—that the Soviets had not at least known of the Syrian plan and permitted the Syrians to challenge the moderate government of Jordan. Rather than raise the Syrian invasion immediately in the U.N. Security Council, Kissinger chose to make it an issue between the White House and the Soviet government. U.S. carrier aircraft were moved to the eastern Mediterranean with the capability of striking the invading Syrian armored column, and the Administration worked out with the government of Israel an Israeli mobilization that threatened Syria proper. Jordanian combat aircraft hit the invading Syrians hard. The Syrians did not commit their air force, and after the Jordanian counterattack they withdrew. Kissinger felt that the stern approach to Moscow had played a significant role in bringing the crisis to an end.

After those events plus Nasser's sudden death in September, both sides stood back for a moment to allow the new leadership in Egypt to settle down. In renewed diplomatic efforts, the United States unilaterally sought resumption of talks under the U.N. mediator, but when those lost momentum got behind an effort to negotiate an interim agreement that would have resulted in an Israeli pullback from the Suez Canal and an Egyptian reopening of the Canal. When that effort foundered in the summer of 1971, the White House began to reappraise the U.S. position. During 1971, the Soviets deepened their military supply relationships with other Arab countries but made clear to Egyptian President Anwar Sadat that they would not support resumption of the War of Attrition. They continued to deny the advanced weaponry that might have encouraged Sadat to go to war with Israel. Meanwhile, after the August 1970 standstill violations, the United States accelerated delivery of A-4 and F-4 aircraft to Israel.

At that point, for global and domestic reasons, Nixon and Kissinger moved discussion of this issue into the White House's back-channel dialogue with the Soviet government. It was in July 1971, as efforts to achieve an interim agreement along the Suez Canal ended, that the Nixon Administration announced Kissinger's secret trip to Peking.

Reflections on the Experience

The United States and the Soviet Union saw the Middle East problem from two different perspectives. For the Soviets, the problem stemmed from Arab humiliation and military defeat in 1967 and the Soviet inability to return to Arab sovereignty the Arab lands that Israel had occupied. The Soviets recognized their disadvantage in this arena and sought to change the situation by enlisting U.S. cooperation. The U.S. view of the problem had two dimensions. First, in a regional context, the United States sought a final Arab recognition of Israel and a commitment to live in peace and security in return for Israeli withdrawal from occupied territories. Although Moscow recognized Israel, its interests since 1948 had shifted to building relationships with key Arab states and it was unwilling to press them beyond their own willingness to recognize Israel. Second, the United States sought a relationship here as elsewhere of genuine negotiation with the Soviet Union, which would form the basis for—if not cooperation—parallel approaches to the problem. The two pictures of the problem and the different priorities that resulted produced quite different motives for trying to change the situation.

The two powers did not differ much in their view of the substantive alternative to the existing Arab-Israeli relationship. They largely agreed on the outlines of a settlement based on Resolution 242. Where they differed was in their views about the alternative power relationships between them that the process of achieving a settlement would produce. Moscow saw that process as including U.S.–Soviet collaboration as equals in producing a settlement that was necessary to restore Soviet credibility with the Arabs. The White House saw no reason to enhance the Soviet position in the Arab-Israeli arena while a friendly nation, Israel, held superior regional power—unless the USSR showed willingness to cooperate in other areas, such as Vietnam, in ways that would lessen damage to the U.S. position. For Nixon and Kissinger, the Middle East, where a friend of the United States held the strong cards, was a place to make the point that cooperation helpful to Soviet aims would be possible only if reciprocated elsewhere.

In short, the effort to cooperate diplomatically foundered when the United States saw the Soviets as unwilling to move beyond Arab positions and when the Soviets saw the United States as working through Israeli military forces again to humiliate the Arab parties and weaken the Soviet position. For the Americans, a continuing assessment of Soviet readiness to establish a new Soviet–U.S. relationship of negotiation dominated every judgment of Soviet actions in the Middle East, as it did elsewhere.

One has to ask what the result would have been had both sides decided to test fully in a political context alone the other's readiness to press its friends toward a settlement within the framework of Resolution 242. It could at least be argued that both sides missed an opportunity to work together toward a settlement that would not have demonstrated American weakness. Why was this opportunity missed? There may be several answers.

First, by conceptualizing elaborate linkage across areas—real as such linkage may be in the political arena—the Nixon Administration may have missed an opportunity in the Middle East. One can argue, as Kissinger did, that the overriding purpose was to demonstrate to Moscow at every turn what a relationship of negotiation required. On the other hand, one could respond that persistence in developing diplomatic cooperation could have contributed to an accumulation of experience in working toward an outcome that reflected each side's interests.

Second and more compelling, it can be argued that neither side saw an incentive to pay an excessive price with its friends for the sake of producing agreement. The diplomatic dialogue of 1969 showed that Moscow and Washington were not far apart in their own substantive views of how an Arab-Israeli settlement should be shaped. Their inability to come to final agreement stemmed not so much from their own differences as from constraints imposed by inability or unwillingness to gain agreement from their clients, particularly Egypt and Israel.

Third—but perhaps most important—each side allowed military considerations to displace negotiation. Both Moscow and Washington went remarkably far in efforts to shift or to maintain the Arab-Israeli military power imbalance as an instrument for influencing efforts to achieve a negotiated settlement. The War of Attrition was started by the Middle Eastern parties, but the superpowers seemed more inclined to let it play itself out militarily than to join in efforts to stop it. With direct Soviet military participation and with the United States carefully supplying Israel with advanced electronic equipment to deal with Soviet-supplied defensive missiles, the War of Attrition represented the most direct superpower engagement in Middle Eastern military action to date. With Soviet military personnel actively engaged in combat and suffering casualties because of newly supplied U.S. electronic equipment, still there was no suggestion that either Moscow or Washington was inclined to make their competition direct. Why? For all of the difficulities in the main Soviet–U.S. relationship, it may be that the back-channel efforts to improve the relationship gave the two sides a framework within which they were confident they could avoid escalation into direct confrontation.

Finally, the experience of Soviet–U.S. diplomatic and military interaction in the Middle East led the two powers away from efforts to work together there. Each successive diplomatic initiative by Washington from the spring of 1970 on reflected a judgment that the Soviets would not contribute effectively to a peace effort but would only use such an initiative for their own advantage. The Administration felt that collaboration was not an alternative and began to see advantages in unilateral action if it could demonstrate that the United States alone had the ability to influence events. The Soviets saw the United States as continuing to take advantage of Israeli military superiority to promote itself as the primary arbiter of events in the region.

THE WHITE HOUSE BECOMES INVOLVED, 1971–73

Discussion of the Experience

By the summer of 1971, Nixon and Kissinger had begun to draw the Middle East more tightly into their global strategy. By that point in Nixon's first Administration, secret talks on Vietnam had begun in May 1971; Kissinger's back-channel relationships with the Soviets had been active since early in the Administration but the question of a summit was now on the agenda; and Kissinger's secret trip to Peking was announced on July 8, 1971. In the Middle East, talks on an interim settlement along the Suez Canal were losing momentum, and Nixon became increasingly eager to keep the Middle East from exploding into a domestic political issue during the coming 1972 presidential election campaign.

This period evolved through three stages: (1) a long period through the 1972 election to the January 1973 Vietnam settlement when the primary aim was to assert White House control of Mid-East policy and to keep it in a holding pattern; (2) the period from January 1973 to the October war, when Kissinger began to explore more actively how he might tackle the problem but without really coming to grips with it; and (3) the collaboration between the superpowers to end the 1973 war and to try to move the conflict into a negotiating context through the Geneva Middle East Peace Conference in December 1973.

Those years were marked by maturation in the Soviet–U.S. effort to develop what came to be called détente. Top leadership on neither side put the Middle East high on the agenda, and each saw the Middle East as a field on which to test the overall relationship and gather advantage to offset disadvantage elsewhere. In that context, it was clearly the Soviet Union—unable to move Israel off its Arab friends' lands without U.S. cooperation—that felt its disadvantage. The period ended in the crucible of the 1973 war when the issue was whether genuine cooperation would be forged or whether postwar peace efforts would become the vehicle for resumed competition.

The Soviet Union, on the one hand, in mid-1971 saw the United States still desperately trying to disengage from Vietnam but, on the other hand, recognized that its Arab clients were still no match for superior Israeli power. The Soviets were unsettled by the U.S. opening to China, and began to see the potential economic advantage of their own broadening relationship with the United States. The Soviets recognized their inability alone to produce a settlement that would meet the full demands of the Arab parties. They were troubled by the fact that the United States since the spring of 1970, following the breakdown of the Soviet–U.S. talks, had increasingly turned to unilateral efforts to deal with the problem, leaving the Soviet Union on the sidelines. In his June 1973 summit talks with Nixon at San Clemente, Brezhnev argued vigorously late into the night for Soviet–U.S. cooperation on a settlement to prevent another Arab-Israeli war.

While wanting to play a more active role, the Soviets did not seem to have a relationship with their Arab partners, or perhaps the flexibility in their policymaking, that would have permitted them to advance creative proposals for breaking the stalemate and moving the negotiations forward. They continued to press for a comprehensive settlement based on maximum Arab demands. As Kissinger frequently told them, they gave the United States little incentive to work with Moscow since the United States itself could cope directly with those Arab demands.

As Kissinger described his objectives, the Nixon-Kissinger team sought to create a situation in which either the Soviet Union would adopt a position more flexible than the Arab position or one of the Arab states would recognize that the Soviet Union could not produce a settlement and would take its own distance from Moscow. As Kissinger described the strategy, it became a process of stalling any efforts at a settlement that would require the United States to lean on its friend, Israel, in order to produce concessions demanded by the allies of the Soviet Union. Kissinger sought to change the negotiating style of the USSR, which he considered intransigently pro-Arab, while the Soviets saw the United States as standing uncritically behind Israel and seeking to change what they regarded as the intent of Resolution 242.

In short, neither side saw the situation as satisfactory but neither saw reason for taking a major initiative to change it. Rather each waited for change to come from some other quarter.

To try to cushion the shock of the opening to China and to assert closer White House management of Middle East diplomacy, Nixon in a letter to Brezhnev on August 5, 1971, held out the possibility of superpower cooperation in the Middle East. During the months that followed, the Soviets during Sadat's visit to Moscow in October pledged continued Soviet efforts to stregthen Egypt militarily, while in September Gromyko proposed to Nixon putting the Middle East into the special Kissinger-Dobrynin channel. In that channel, the Soviets persistently held out for maximum Arab demands in a comprehensive settlement, while Kissinger experimented further with ways of breaking down the overall problem into attainable objectives. Through the Nixon-Brezhnev summit of May 1972, Americans and Soviets exchanged views on principles that might govern a settlement, while each side continued the flow of military assistance to its Middle Eastern clients. The discussion of principles was more of a process of mutual probing than an effort to advance agreement. Neither side went much beyond the positions it had taken in the 1969 talks.

To the Soviet–U.S. back-channel was added a separate dialogue between Kissinger and Israeli Ambassador Yitzhak Rabin at the end of 1971. Then in early April 1972, Kissinger received a proposal for opening a parallel channel with President Sadat's national security adviser, Hafiz Ismail. Kissinger made plain in each of these channels that serious progress was unlikely until after the November 1972 presidential election and the conclusion of negotiations to end the war in Vietnam. The Egyptian expulsion of Soviet military advisers in July 1972 provided encouragement for greater U.S. involvement, but on the eve of the presidential election the Administration was not inclined to take new initiatives.

With Nixon's second inauguration and the signing of the Vietnam agreement on January 27, 1973, Nixon's and Kissinger's more active personal involvement in Middle East diplomacy became possible. In February and in May 1973, Kissinger met secretly outside New York and Paris with Ismail and continued the separate dialogues with the Soviet Union and Israel, especially during the preparation for the second Brezhnev-Nixon summit in June 1973. Between the 1972 and 1973 summits, the Soviets finally agreed that the terms of an Arab-Israeli settlement would have to be negotiated between the Middle Eastern parties. This had been a critical issue in the breakdown of the 1969 talks. Still, the United States, in Kissinger's strategy, sought to arouse enough Arab frustration with Soviet inability to produce diplomatic progress to cause key Arabs to turn to the United States for help in getting their territory back. Despite Brezhnev's strong argument in June 1973 that the Arabs were considering war, and despite similar warnings from friendly Arabs, the United States was not sensitive enough to Arab frustration to recognize that Sadat was preparing to change the political environment by going to a limited war.

Soviet leaders recognized that they could not, in the foreseeable future, dislodge the Israelis from Arab territory by any but diplomatic means without direct Soviet military involvement, which they did not want. The Soviet Union was continuing its military assistance to its Arab clients, but was doing so with restraint in an effort to avoid actually encouraging its clients to attack Israel. The Soviets recognized that the American body politic could not allow its President to stand idly by and see Israel threatened. In exercising some restraint in responding to Egyptian requests for equipment, the Soviets recognized that they were jeopardizing their political relationship, especially since they seemed to offer no diplomatic way of achieving Arab political objectives. Their only viable strategy in the near future seemed to be enlisting the United States in a diplomatic initiative. In Kissinger's eyes, they seemed unable to make that an attractive alternative to the United States.

This step-up in White House diplomatic exploration coincided with the step-up in Sadat's preparations for military confrontation. While Sadat was planning with Syria to go to war to change the political environment, Israeli and U.S. analysts were discounting that possibility on grounds that Sadat seemed to have no effective military capability.

During this period, Nixon and Kissinger may have had different senses of the urgency of engaging in a serious diplomatic effort. Nixon writes that he urged movement while Kissinger felt the situation was not politically ripe. In any case, the Egyptians did not find in exchanges with Washington a sense of seriousness or urgency. In concentrating their efforts on changing the Soviet relationship with the Arab parties, in one direction or the other, U.S. policy makers made assumptions about Arab motivations and capability that caused them to minimize the possibility of war. At the June 1973 summit—despite the progress in the overall relationship—neither side seemed able to find a way to put the problem in the context of bilateral cooperation.

The outbreak of war on October 6, 1973 brought the Soviet Union and the United States into closer cooperation, both in framing U.N. Security Council Resolution 338 to bring the war to an end and in incorporating in that resolution a call to begin negotiation of an overall settlement within the framework of Resolution 242. To that end, Gromyko and Kissinger, during Kissinger's visit to Moscow just before the end of the war, also agreed that the Soviet Union and the United States would co-chair a Middle East peace conference in Geneva.

Once again—as in 1967—the last moments of the war produced a moment of sudden escalation in Soviet–U.S. tension. Despite the U.N. ceasefire, Israeli forces continued fighting, with the clear intention of destroying the Egyptian Third Army. The Soviets could not tolerate another humiliation of an Arab friend and felt the United States had agreed to help stop the war. Brezhnev sent Nixon a message proposing that U.S. and Soviet forces intervene jointly to stop the fighting but stating that Soviet forces would intervene unilaterally if the United States chose not to join. The direct U.S. response was to put its nuclear forces on alert to signal that the United States would strongly object to such a unilateral Soviet military intervention, but it also let Israel know that the time had come to stop fighting. In retrospect, the alert seems to have been more a signal, and understood as such on both sides, than serious threat of nuclear war. In any event, Israel stopped, and the issue became moot. The experience demonstrated the limits of tolerance on both sides—Soviet fear of excessive harm to its position if an Arab friend suffered serious damage, and U.S. concern about the possible establishment of a further Soviet military foothold in the area.

The meeting of the Geneva conference in December represented the visible peak of Soviet–U.S. cooperation in the Middle East, which had already been passed as Kissinger laid the groundwork himself for a unilateral U.S. diplomatic effort to move the negotiations forward. Although one may ask in looking back whether active cooperation was ever intended, analytically, at least, the possibility existed.

Reflections on the Experience

Until early 1973, Moscow and Washington were working with two very different perceptions of the problem. The Soviets' picture of their problem in the Middle East remained the same, with the added awareness in 1972 and early 1973 of steadily mounting Arab frustration with the continuing stalemate. They continued to see their primary problem as moving the United States to play its role in moving Israel to withdraw. For Nixon and Kissinger in 1971 and 1972, the problem was to keep the Middle East in a holding pattern while they completed an agreement on U.S. withdrawal from Vietnam and conducted the political campaign for Nixon's reelection. In the domestic context, Nixon could not be sure that his strong military support for Israel during and after the War of Attrition had overcome deep suspicion in the Jewish community, aroused by the "first Rogers plan," that Nixon would pressure Israel to withdraw. The White House opened a channel with the Soviets and Middle Eastern parties to show concern about the problem, but frankly stated that the United States could take no action until after the election and completion of the Vietnam negotiations. Both Soviets and Arabs seem to have decided it was worth waiting until the United States could focus its full attention on the Middle East.

An important point to consider at this moment in terms of conflict management is that channels were established to communicate political as well as diplomatic positions. This made it possible for each side to make clear the reasons for its actions and to communicate what it expected from the other side. While the 1971–73 experience was characterized by negotiation over diplomatic solutions to the problem and by a test of power in the War of Attrition, the eighteen months from mid-1971 through January 1973 were characterized by explanation of the political constraints on U.S. action. In the back-channel with the Soviets, Kissinger also stated explicitly that the United States would not play the role of pressing Israel alone unless the Soviets were prepared to play an independent role in moving the Arab position. The point is not the character of the communications channel, although a White House channel carried special authority; the point is that the subject of the communication was political constraints and what each side expected of the other if their relationship was to include cooperation in the Middle East.

As a result of its position in 1971 and 1972, the United States faced a serious challenge on the Middle East issue in early 1973, when the two heavy political constraints were removed by Nixon's re-election and the Vietnam agreement. The problem in Soviet eyes remained how to move the United States to produce Israeli withdrawal, thereby removing a burden from Soviet shoulders in their relations with their Arab friends. As long as the Soviets could not regain lost Arab territories, the Arabs saw the United States as having superior ability to influence events. To the United States, the problem was how to move either Arabs or Soviets closer to its view of how to resolve the conflict. The United States and the Soviet Union differed over the purpose of cooperation. Would cooperation produce Israeli withdrawal to its 1967 borders? Or would cooperation serve only to bring about a negotiation of those borders?

After five months of probing the Nixon-Kissinger position, Sadat decided to launch a limited war for three purposes: (1) erasing the humiliation of 1967 so the Arabs could negotiate from a position of restored honor; (2) forcing more active superpower diplomatic involvement; (3) demonstrating to Israel that it could not impose a solution based on existing borders. In the context of Soviet–U.S. relations, the question arises: To what extent did the Soviets concur in Sadat's recourse to limited war to change the political balance?

The critical factor here is that the Soviets pressed hard in the June 1973 summit for superpower cooperation, on grounds that the likelihood of another Arab-Israeli war was increasing rapidly. Kissinger seemed to discount the probability of war but felt that if an unlikely war did take place it could create a political situation in which the burden for making concessions to produce a solution would be shared rather than falling on the United States. The Soviets apparently warned Sadat against going to war, but they did not prevent him. Since they could not change the situation themselves—even by holding up to Nixon the specter of another war—they felt unable to prevent Sadat from trying. Both superpowers seemed to have basic confidence that they could avoid a nuclear confrontation over this issue.

At this point, the two superpowers were each trying to engage the other on the basis of positions set down by their Middle Eastern friends. Neither was giving significant attention to changing those positions. As long as the issue was on the superpower agenda, genuine cooperation would not be possible if one side felt it was being pressured to grant concessions in order to give advantage to the other. Cooperation would only be possible if both superpowers in more or less equal measure gave resolving the Arab-Israeli conflict a higher priority than using the conflict to gain advantage in their own contest for global influence. As long as they felt they could avoid a nuclear crisis in the Middle East, they seemed willing to risk another regional war. That required a precise recognition of each other's most sensitive interests and the ability to communicate about them. Despite the threat of Soviet military intervention and the responding U.S. nuclear alert, the two powers seemed again able to avoid direct confrontation without unusual difficulty.

The Kissinger-Gromyko meeting at the end of the war did produce reciprocal concessions in the superpower context. In agreeing on Resolution 338's call for negotiations and on Soviet–U.S. co-chairmanship of a peace conference to follow the war, the Soviets ostensibly conceded the point that negotiations would precede Israeli withdrawal and the United States ostensibly conceded the Soviets' right to equal involvement in the effort to end the conflict. That subsequent U.S. unilateral mediation denied the Soviets even the appearance of equal involvement remains a source of deep Soviet bitterness over the possibility of cooperation.

STEP-BY-STEP DIPLOMACY, 1974–76

Discussion of the Experience

This period encompasses the unique Kissinger shuttles and then the familiar "down time" of a presidential election year. This was also the period when the limits of détente came into sharper focus. The predominance of unilateral U.S. efforts in the Middle East caused some disillusionment with the relationship in Moscow, and in late 1975 Washington's disillusionment with détente deepened following Soviet action in Angola.

Above all, this period marked a shift to increased attention, especially by the White House, to how the political dynamics within the Middle East affected efforts to resolve the Arab-Israeli conflict. Instead of simply dealing in the currency of their clients' diplomatic positions, the United States began to think about how to hasten the peace process by changing the regional political environment. As the United States realized it could influence the course of negotiations this way, it also found practical ways to enhance its position vis-à-vis the USSR by demonstrating its ability to influence events and produce results.

No sooner had the Geneva Middle East peace conference met under Soviet–U.S. co-chairmanship than Kissinger was reflecting on ways to consolidate distance between the Arab and Soviet positions. The pattern of unilateral U.S. mediation was confirmed in January 1974 when Kissinger visited the Middle East to follow up on his December discussions with Sadat. The purpose of this trip was to produce an agreement on Egyptian-Israeli disengagement along the Suez Canal, which could become the first step in what we later called the "peace process" leading to an overall settlement. When Kissinger arrived in the Middle East, Sadat asked him to stay until agreement had been reached. Thus was born the first "shuttle."

For the U.S. team, the peace process became more than the mediation of Arab-Israeli agreements. It became the centerpiece of U.S. diplomacy for broadening U.S. influence across the Middle East. Following the Egyptian-Israeli disengagement in January 1974, Kissinger promised to try for a similar agreement between Israel and Syria and, with that promise, won Saudi Arabia's agreement to lift the oil embargo. The Israeli-Syrian disengagement was completed after a 35-day shuttle in late April and May. In the period from January through May, the United States restored normal relations, which had been broken during the 1967 war, with Egypt, Algeria, and Syria. This was also the period of rapidly accumulating oil revenues in the hands of the Arab oil producers, and cooperation between finance ministers in the interest of global economic stability became a part of the Arab–U.S. relationship. In addition, a number of joint economic councils were established to strengthen the relationship between the U.S. private sector and the development programs of key Arab countries as a means of building a safety net against a downturn in political relations.

Each in this series of interim agreements was designed to produce enough movement toward an overall settlement to be politically manageable and to be significant enough to change the political environment and make possible further movement in later steps. Nixon and Kissinger had come to the judgment back in 1971 that attempting a comprehensive negotiation was more than any body politic—Arab or Israeli—could digest at one time and that it was necessary to move by carving out manageable pieces of the problem to deal with on a step-by-step basis.

The Soviet leadership was increasingly irritated by the unilateral U.S. effort, especially in the wake of the apparent beginnings of cooperation in Geneva. Kissinger tried to mollify them by periodic consultation. For instance, during the May 1974 Israeli-Syrian shuttle, he met in Geneva with Gromyko on the way to the Middle East, broke off the shuttle in the middle to meet with him on Cyprus, and met briefly with him at the conclusion of the negotiations; but without question, this was strictly "lip service" consultation. Kissinger repeatedly told his Middle Eastern negotiating partners that the Soviet negotiating style was too ponderous for such an operation and that it seemed to him more important to make progress in the negotiations, while keeping channels of communication open to the Soviet Union so that it might return to the process at some later appropriate point.

The last half of 1974 was a momentous period in setting the political environment for the Arab-Israeli peace process. In August, President Nixon resigned, and Gerald Ford became President of the United States. By happenstance, a steady stream of Middle Eastern visitors had been scheduled to come to Washington during Ford's first six weeks in office to discuss the peace process. The main issue was what the next step in the U.S.-mediated peace process should be. Involving Moscow again was not an active consideration.

A principal substantive issue was whether to move toward some kind of Israeli-Jordanian agreement in order to establish movement on all three fronts, including the Israeli-Palestinian front. That effort became the victim of political changes in the Middle East. When Yitzhak Rabin succeeded Golda Meir as prime minister of Israel in early June, he had asked Kissinger for time to get his feet on the ground before he had to tackle the difficult West Bank problem. Almost simultaneously, significant political scuffling took place in the Arab world over who should represent the Palestinians; in October a summit meeting of Arab leaders in Rabat declared that the Palestine Liberation Organization would be the "only legitimate representative of the Palestinian people," thereby apparently blocking efforts by King Hussein to negotiate for areas important to the Palestinians. The result was an almost year-long effort by Washington to achieve a second Egyptian-Israeli agreement, over the strong objections of Syria and the Soviet Union. As that agreement was concluded through another shuttle in August 1975, the Soviet–U.S. showdown in Angola through proxy factions was coming to a head.

Following the conclusion of the second Sinai agreement, the American shuttle team, even including Kissinger, began to wonder how much longer step-by-step diplomacy could go on. For one thing, the second Sinai agreement had secured as substantial an Israeli withdrawal as was possible without a full peace, so there were no more significant segments of the Sinai to carve out in another interim agreement. The Israeli-Syrian disengagement had taught us that it would be difficult to find one more stone on the Golan Heights for another Israeli withdrawal there, and we were precluded from working on the West Bank for the time being. Therefore, thinking in the quiet presidential election year of 1976 began to shift hesitatingly back toward some kind of international conference, which would inevitably involve the Soviet Union. That choice was ultimately left to the next Administration.

The years 1974–76 saw an increasingly complex combination of interactions between the superpowers. This period included the third Brezhnev-Nixon summit in June 1974 and the Brezhnev-Ford summit in Vladivostok in November, which began to crystallize the main elements of a strategic arms limitation agreement. During this period as well, the contest for influence in the Third World continued, particularly in the Middle East and Angola.

If one were to attempt to describe the perspective of the Soviet Union on its relationship with the United States, one would find increasing Soviet bitterness at Washington's disregard for what the Soviets saw as their legitimate role in the Middle East. One would also find, particularly with regard to the Middle East, a sense that the United States by its unilateral diplomatic efforts was making a major effort to exclude significant Soviet presence from an area the Soviets regarded as their backyard and where they felt they had legitimate interests. As Kissinger proceeded, Moscow seemed to adopt a posture of waiting for the U.S. effort to run out of steam so the Soviet Union could move in and pick up the pieces, thereby restoring its legitimate position in the area. At this point, the Soviets would have been closer to the Syrian than to the Egyptian position in urging a return of negotiations to an international conference in Geneva. Other than stating their position, they did little either to promote their own position or to block U.S. progress.

Reflections on the Experience

The 1973 war seemed to open the door to fundamental change in the Middle East—both in the relations among parties to the Arab-Israeli conflict and in relations between the superpowers.

Sadat seemed ready to end the conflict with Israel so he could devote Egypt's energies and resources to solving his country's internal economic problems. Sadat also saw the United States and the rest of the Western world as far more likely than the

Soviet Union to help Egypt deal with its chronic economic problems, and he was prepared to make a basic shift in Egypt's international orientation. That was one reason Kissinger focused as heavily as he did on trying to involve the American private sector in Egyptian economic development.

The United States on its side, could not resist the opportunity offered by Sadat and even by Syrian President Hafez al Assad to appear as the great power which alone could produce diplomatic results. The Middle East states looked to the United States as the one great power that might have a capacity to move Israel. The United States defined its goal as moving Arab-Israeli negotiations forward as a means of consolidating a significant shift in great-power relationships with key countries in the region.

In any case, this period was marked less by a contest for power via military shipments and support for allies than by intensive diplomatic and political efforts by the top U.S. leadership in a Middle Eastern diplomatic process. The diplomatic instruments used were at that time virtually unprecedented on the scale employed, required greater political dexterity than the Soviet establishment seemed in Kissinger's eyes able to muster, and combined that diplomatic ability with broader efforts to establish a stronger U.S. political position throughout the Middle East.

At least from the American perspective, Soviet efforts to change the situation during this period were minimal. Even an effort to block an American success was hardly noticeable on the American side. The Soviets seemed to concentrate on ways of re-entering the picture at an appropriate time. In any case, the intense activity of the Kissinger shuttles seemed to give them little alternative but to wait.

This period represented a time of the greatest U.S. prestige and Soviet eclipse in the area. It also represented a period of minimal Soviet–U.S. cooperation in the region but one where the potential for direct confrontation between the two sides was also at a low ebb because the instruments used for changing the situation were diplomatic and political rather than military, and the regional parties were actively engaged in a negotiating process. The two superpowers relied on other aspects of their relationship to sustain their bilateral enterprises. The Soviets smarted under their exclusion from the peace process, but they maintained their relationships with individual states. They kept alive their pressure on the United States for re-involvement in the process.

A central analytical question rooted in this period relates to how the détente relationship was intended to play itself out in Third World areas. The Basic Principles Agreement signed in 1972 at the first Brezhnev-Nixon summit recognized that "efforts to obtain unilateral advantages at the expense of the other, directly or indirectly, are inconsistent" with efforts to build a new superpower relationship.[4] Kissinger later wrote:

> Détente did not prevent us from seeking to reduce the Soviet role in the Middle East nor the Soviets from scoring points with the Arabs now and then. But fairness compels the recognition that Moscow never launched an all-out campaign against us. And we took pains not to humiliate the Soviet Union overtly even while weakening its influence. Détente is the mitigation of conflict among adversaries, not the cultivation of friendship.[5]

Soviet actions through this period and later raised questions in American minds whether Soviet leadership saw the relaxation of détente simply as a way of throwing the United States off guard while the Soviets continued their military buildup in Europe and thrust into the Third World. Neither side seems to have seen the other as ready to suspend the basic competition for influence or to give up any advantage that a situation provided.

As long as diplomacy continued to engage the Middle Eastern parties in the search for a settlement, the danger of a war that might embroil them was diminished.

CARTER AND CAMP DAVID, 1977–80

Discussion of the Experience

Once again administrations changed in Washington. The Carter Administration committed itself to continuity both at the core of the Soviet–U.S. relationship and in the Middle East peace process, and to a different perspective on both problems. President Jimmy Carter and Secretary of State Cyrus Vance came to office seeing the world in terms of the necessity of preserving progress toward regulating the Soviet–U.S. military relationship and broadening the U.S. commitment to principles of human rights in its international relationships and practices.

Building from the experience of the Kissinger team at the end of the Ford Administration, Carter and Vance felt that the next step in the Arab-Israeli peace process would be a return to the Geneva Middle East peace conference. They recognized the need to focus on final settlements but at the same time to work through procedures that would preserve some of the advantages of step-by-step diplomacy in not ensnarling each negotiation in lowest common denominator positions across the Arab world. The Carter Administration spent its first nine months in an active diplomatic effort to develop agreement by the Middle Eastern parties on terms of reference that would permit resumption of the Geneva conference before the end of 1977. Secretary Vance went to the Middle East in February and August for consultations especially in Egypt, Israel, Jordan, Syria, and Saudi Arabia. Between those trips, he made an intensive effort through diplomatic channels to develop agreement around working papers—some of them highly sensitive—which were designed to produce terms of reference and organization for the conference.

It was natural in the context of those efforts to resume the Geneva conference that, at some point, the United States should also consult with the Soviet Union. By August and September, with the prospect of the annual meeting between the U.S. secretary of state and the Soviet foreign minister at the U.N. General Assembly, it was logical that the two should begin their consultations as co-chairmen of the Geneva conference. Before Gromyko came to New York, he and Vance exchanged drafts of a statement that could be issued reflecting their views of the terms of reference. The final draft was actively negotiated by staff over most of a week during their talks in New York. Vance also showed an early draft to the Egyptian and Israeli foreign ministers, who did not offer any significant comments. The joint statement was issued on October 1, 1977. From the U.S. perspective and in retrospect, the statement did not reflect significant U.S. concessions on the major issues, which principally dealt with the Palestinian part of the problem. The purpose was to resume a conference where the main negotiation would take place in working groups.

It was the reaction of the Israeli government in Jerusalem, reflected in vehement opposition of American Jewish groups, and eventually President Sadat's visit to Jerusalem in November that determined the ultimate outcome of this exercise. The Israeli reaction came despite Vance's advance consultation with Foreign Minister Moshe Dayan, presumably because of right-wing political opposition in Israel to negotiation about the Palestinian issue. Almost immediately, the sharp reaction of the Israeli government caused

President Carter and his team to produce an Israeli–U.S. working paper that diluted the impact of the joint Soviet–U.S. statement. The reaction of Egypt is less certain. Some argue that President Sadat was so concerned about the United States drawing the Soviet Union into the negotiations that he decided to make his historic visit to Jerusalem. This seems an extreme interpretation, since Sadat had accepted throughout 1977 the efforts to try to reestablish at least the framework of the Geneva conference. Even after he went to Jerusalem, his first efforts were devoted to translating the trip into preparations for Geneva. It was only later that Sadat's initiative, almost by default, brought the parties back to an intensive Egyptian-Israeli negotiation.

The October 1 statement proved to be the high point of Soviet–U.S. cooperation in the Arab-Israeli context during the Carter Administration; within a year, Carter invited Israeli Prime Minister Menachem Begin and Sadat to Camp David and then unilaterally mediated the Egyptian-Israeli peace treaty. In the Carter Administration, this way of proceeding seemed to result more from pragmatic judgment of what was possible than from actions designed—as Kissinger's had been—to affect the Soviet–U.S. relationship. Arms control negotiations with the Soviet Union proceeded on a separate track, and the Soviet–U.S. relationship had to absorb the Soviet-Cuban intervention in Ethiopia.

At the end of the Carter Administration, it was events in the Middle East apart from the Arab-Israeli conflict that caused a fundamental shift in the Soviet–U.S. relationship. First, the Iranian revolution brought down the security system that had existed in the Persian Gulf since the early 1970s and seemed to open the way for Soviet intervention both in Iran and in the Gulf area. Second, the Soviet invasion of Afghanistan in December 1979, after the taking of U.S. hostages in Tehran, administered a telling blow to the Soviet–U.S. relationship. These events led to inclusion in President Carter's early 1980 State of the Union address of words that would come to be called the "Carter Doctrine," stating that the United States would oppose by all means, including military, efforts by any outside power to gain control over the Gulf area. At the same time, in response to the Soviet missile buildup in Eastern Europe, NATO decided to increase defense spending and ultimately to deploy intermediate-range nuclear missiles in Europe—the so-called "two track decision."

Reflections on the Experience

The Carter Administration came to office with a firm commitment to continue both the Strategic Arms Limitation Talks and the Middle East peace process in some kind of common effort with the Soviet Union. Perhaps because of the background of negotiations in the previous two administrations, those efforts by Carter and Vance took the form of renewed diplomatic efforts, with less attention given early in the Administration to balance-of-power considerations. They seemed committed to changing the situation only in ways that would follow from successful negotiations, and their alternatives were defined in the aims of these negotiations. It was only later in the Administration that Carter and Vance reflected the opinion of most Americans that the Soviets had not shown restraint in either the military or in Third World areas. They became painfully aware that those perceptions made it politically impossible for the United States to sustain the détente relationship.

In each negotiating arena, the Americans seemed to rely primarily on diplomatic rather than traditional coercive instruments until later in the Administration when they perceived that Soviet actions had gone beyond limits of American tolerance. In the Middle East, the United States seemed more concerned with moving the negotiations forward than with gaining advantage in the U.S.–Soviet competition, although the outcome was continuation of solo U.S. mediation efforts. Soviet leaders, according to their later statements, professed to feel that, at least by 1979, détente was dead. The NATO two-track decision; the U.S. retreat from the October 1, 1977, joint statement on the Middle East; the difficulty of achieving Senate ratification of the SALT agreement in the fall of 1979; the issue of the Soviet brigade in Cuba; and eventually the November–December U.S. naval buildup in the Indian Ocean all were reasons—in the Soviet view—to see little left in détente to preserve.

For different reasons, each side pursued the Soviet–U.S. relationship in its own way, dealing with each issue on its own terms rather than explicitly as part of the larger relationship. While no less committed to the aims of détente, Carter and Vance seemed less inclined than Kissinger and Nixon to link all the elements of the relationship so as to use one as a lever on others. In the Middle East, that approach made it possible to take advantage of Sadat's positions and to produce significant progress in the peace process. One can only speculate on whether progress would have been broader if we had been able to bring all the parties to the Geneva conference instead of abandoning that effort for the sake of another—albeit important—Egyptian-Israeli step. The Soviets and Arabs would argue that case, but they cannot demonstrate, for instance, that Syria and the PLO were ready to negotiate peace if the Geneva conference had been convened.

THE REAGAN ADMINISTRATION, 1981–86

Discussion of the Experience

Soviet–U.S. interaction in the Middle East was heavily affected during the first Reagan Administration by the most prolonged low point in the bilateral Soviet–U.S. relationship in more than two decades. Consistent with that relationship was a U.S. perspective on regional problems that was heavily military and strategic. In the Middle East, the Administration's energies became deeply absorbed in Lebanon, where Syria was seen as a Soviet proxy and the potential for a Soviet–U.S. incident increased in late 1983 as Sixth Fleet aircraft overflew Lebanon and Soviet personnel manned Syrian air defense missiles. When the Arab-Israeli peace process became active, tension arose between a U.S. policy of attempting unilaterally to arrange direct Israeli-Jordanian-Palestinian negotiations and Arab insistence on an international conference involving the United States and the USSR as well as the other permanent members of the U.N. Security Council. Although the period through 1984 saw almost no official Soviet–U.S. dialogue on the Middle East, interaction between the superpowers remained a live issue. As official talks resumed in 1985 and 1986, each side held to standard positions and at the end of 1986 were no closer to common positions than before.

This was also a period when the leadership in Moscow experienced three state funerals in three years and was deeply concerned by President Reagan's early defense buildup and subsequent emphasis on the Strategic Defense Initiative. The uncertain and confrontational character of the bilateral relationship precluded any serious efforts at cooperation in the Middle East, though in the context of Lebanese hostilities each side again acted to avoid confronting the other. Apart from relatively sterile exchanges on the Arab-Israeli conflict at the assistant secretary level in 1985 and 1986, the steps to avoid confrontation in Lebanon were the main achievement of this period.

On the Middle East issue, Reagan Administration policy during the first six months was dominated by Secretary of State Alexander Haig's conviction that there was a "stragegic consensus" among friends of the United States in the region, and that it needed to be consolidated. This approach started from the premise that all who were part of that consensus agreed that the Soviet Union was the primary threat to security in the area and that the Arab-Israeli conflict was subordinate to that larger threat. In that context, Haig put the post-Camp David talks on autonomy for the Palestinians in the West Bank and Gaza on the back burner. He concentrated instead on forming a multi-national force to monitor compliance with the Egypt-Israel peace treaty after final Israeli withdrawal from the Sinai, scheduled for April 1982. Given Haig's emphasis on U.S. strategic interests, the Soviet Union saw formation of that force as the Administration's effort to establish an advance U.S. military foothold for future U.S. military deployments to the area.

The summer of 1981 was marked by a number of violent episodes by the Middle Eastern parties, particularly in Lebanon. Without considering joint Soviet–U.S. action, President Reagan sent Ambassador Philip Habib to the Middle East eventually to work out a ceasefire on the Lebanese-Israeli border. Washington dealt with this situation mainly in a Middle Eastern context, although Secretary Haig tended to see any actions by the Syrians or Palestinians as the actions of Soviet proxies.

As the moment for final Israeli withdrawal from the Sinai approached in the spring of 1982, Defense Minister Ariel Sharon's plans for the Israeli invasion of Lebanon were also maturing. Secretary Haig's motives in relation to that invasion were complex, but some part of them, again, seemed to include notions that an Israeli defeat of Syrian military units would serve as a put-down for the Soviet Union, as would a defeat of the Palestine Liberation Organization, which Haig regarded as a Soviet pawn. It was thoughts such as these that led Haig at least to refrain from opposing the invasion actively. His handling of this episode as well as cumulatively bad working relationships with the White House staff led to President Reagan's acceptance of his resignation in June 1982.

The first weeks in office of the new secretary of state, George Shultz, were characterized by a shift of attention to the Arab-Israeli conflict, with Washington again staking out a unilateral position generally consistent with the U.S. position in the Camp David Accords rather than considering joint superpower actions. The United States relied on its own diplomacy to try to avoid an Israeli-Syrian clash in Lebanon and eventually to bring the Israeli invasion to an end. The President's speech of September 1, 1982, called for a "fresh start" in efforts to achieve an over-all Arab-Israeli settlement, but the President and Secretary Shultz only involved themselves intermittently in the immediate follow-up to the speech. Unlike their three predecessors they seemed to give low priority to changing the Arab-Israeli political environment, even as a way of promoting the United States as the principal great-power arbiter of events in its competition with the Soviet Union for influence in the region.

The months that followed President Reagan's September 1 speech were characterized largely by heavy and increasing U.S. military involvement in Lebanon. The U.S. Marines were first landed in Lebanon in the summer of 1982 to cover the withdrawal of the PLO from Beirut. They were withdrawn early in September and were sent back after the massacres in the Palestinian refugee camps, Sabra and Shatilla, later in the month. Diplomatic efforts to arrange withdrawal of all foreign troops continued through the winter, but the Israeli-Lebanese agreement of May 1983, which Secretary Shultz had personally helped to arrange, was never implemented because it did not include Syria. At that moment, analysts in Washington reflected frequently on whether the United States could produce major political developments in the region without Syria and whether Syria could be moved without involving the Soviet Union. Had Syria become the instrument for blocking U.S. efforts to influence the course of events in the Arab-Israeli arena alone?

The Soviet Union saw the U.S. military forces in Lebanon, along with the deployment of U.S. troops as part of the multinational force in the Sinai, as the vanguard of a significant new U.S. military posture in the Middle East. In the wake of a brief Israeli-Syrian confrontation at the beginning of the invasion of Lebanon, the Soviet Union provided new surface-to-air missiles to build up the Syrian air defense system, and the personnel to man them. In fact, the growing contest between leftists and U.S. forces in Lebanon, which intensified in the fall of 1983, remained essentially a Syrian-U.S. confrontation. Nevertheless, in late November 1983, in the course of a visit to Moscow by American private citizens, a Soviet participant passed privately to some U.S. participants a clear statement of the Soviet view that the situation was dangerous, given the proximity of the U.S. and Soviet forces, and the United States should understand that the principal Soviet interest lay in the defense of Syria, not in the defense of Syrian forces in Lebanon. The purpose of this communication was to make clear that Soviet radar could not distinguish between Israeli and U.S. aircraft and that if Soviet-manned missiles were fired at aircraft violating Syrian airspace this should not be read as an act explicitly directed at the United States.

After the withdrawal of the Marines in February 1984—partly because the Reagan White House was looking forward to the 1984 presidential elections—the Soviet–U.S. dimensions of Middle East hostilities quieted. But that spring the bilateral relationship reached its nadir with the withdrawal of the Soviet Union from the Olympic Games. It was also during this period that popular pressure for a nuclear freeze began to build in the United States. The nuclear freeze movement was not only a movement in support of a particular approach to arms control; it was also an expression of deep popular concern in the United States at the absence of a serious working relationship between the nuclear superpowers. By fall, President Reagan used his speech before the U.N. General Assembly to propose an improvement in that relationship. One of the means he proposed was official dialogue between the two superpowers on regional conflicts such as that in the Middle East. A sterile exchange of views on the Middle East took place in Vienna in February 1985 and there was a similar meeting in Washington, on Afghanistan, in the late spring of 1985. Two somewhat more substantive exchanges took place in 1986, but these still fell short of serious proposals for joint action, except for the possible expression of common interests in seeing the Iran-Iraq war end.

Despite the fact that Arab parties to the Arab-Israeli conflict were pressing for an international conference with the five permanent members of the U.N. Security Council attending, positions exchanged in the official talks did not approach the level of creativity needed to lay the foundations for Soviet–U.S. cooperation in making such a conference happen. The Reagan Administration remained opposed to such a conference on grounds that this would "bring the Soviet Union into the Middle East." Although that position began to give way in the wake of the Hussein-Arafat agreement in February 1985 and a shift in the Israeli position in mid-1985 after Israeli-Jordanian exchanges, the Administration did little directly to foster such cooperation with the Soviet Union.

The Soviets, on their side, seemed to concentrate on strengthening their relations with key parties to the conflict, even putting out feelers to restore an Israeli-Soviet working relationship.

Reflections on the Experience

Soviet–U.S. interaction in the Middle East during the first Reagan Administration was dominated by an emphasis on global strategic competition between the two powers and the existence of only a minimal working relationship between them. The weakness of this relationship raised questions about cooperation even on bilateral issues and certainly precluded serious cooperation to reduce the underlying tensions of the Arab-Israeli conflict. The Soviet Union was preoccupied with the rhetoric of the Reagan Administration, particularly the rhetoric surrounding the substantial increases in the first Reagan defense budgets. That rhetoric plus Reagan's eventual proposal of a Strategic Defense Initiative caused Soviet leaders to suspect that the Administration believed it could win a nuclear war and was preparing for one. On the U.S. side, the President represented a part of the political spectrum that regarded the Soviet Union as, at most, "evil" or, at best, unreliable in keeping agreements. Its approach to the world was based more on maintaining a superior military position than on trying to build a political relationship within which common interests might be explored. This new American leadership's approach to the over-all Soviet–U.S. relationship coincided with the death in Moscow of Brezhnev and his two successors.

Second, the leaderships of both powers—each for its own reasons—gave low priority to pressing toward an Arab-Israeli settlement. Insofar as the U.S. Administration gave attention to the issue it focused on the dynamics of the region and generally opposed Soviet involvement in efforts to deal with the conflict. U.S. policy was aimed primarily at using regional developments to reduce Soviet influence. President Reagan gave his name to an initiative for getting the Arab-Israeli peace process moving again, but in the end his Administration was unwilling to risk a serious political investment in the attempt. In July 1984 the Soviet government through TASS issued a statement calling for an international conference to achieve peace in the Middle East, thereby reasserting its long-standing support for a multilateral international approach to a peace settlement with equal Soviet and U.S. participation. One clear purpose was to end U.S. domination of the peace process, but the Soviet government made no sustained effort to develop the working relationship with Israel that effective Soviet participation would require. In that context, the two powers held no serious official discussion about what they might do jointly or through complementary action to advance the peace process.

Private dialogue highlighted the difference in approach to breaking the Arab-Israeli impasse that had characterized the superpowers since the 1973 war. With varying degrees of effectiveness, the United States had engaged itself actively in detailed dialogue with the Middle Eastern parties to find ways to overcome obstacles to negotiation by changing the political environment. The Soviet Union for the most part had either watched the United States or engaged with it in developing principles that might guide a comprehensive negotiation, but the Soviets had not engaged persistently with the parties— either competitively or in collaboration—to try to change the political base for negotiation. It was possible in nonofficial dialogue to discuss these differences analytically, but the absence of a larger official relationship limited the incentive to go beyond that analysis. The absence of high-level political commitment meant that neither government would pursue its efforts vigorously.

Third, despite their cooled relationship and the low priority both sides gave to moving the peace process forward, the two powers continued to give careful attention to avoiding confrontation between one another. This was demonstrated when the fighting in Lebanon was at its height. Even though the Soviet Union saw the Reagan Administration as supporting the Israeli effort to destroy the PLO and to damage Syrian forces, it made clear that its important interests would become involved only if Syria proper were threatened. The two powers retained the capacity—even if only through nonofficial channels—to communicate basic interests and to try to avoid misperceptions about them.

CONCLUSIONS

My fundamental observation about Soviet–U.S. interaction in the Arab-Israeli arena is that the two powers have continued to compete for influence on the Middle East stage as on others throughout this period. They have refined their understanding of each other's interests, have sensed some tacit rules for regulating their competition, and have experimented with forms of cooperation and learned their limits. They have not yet reduced their level of competition to the point of moving to cooperation as the norm in their interaction.

Recalling that several sets of problems and relationships are involved, I want to underscore that our focus here is the problem posed to policymakers in Moscow and Washington by the interaction of the two powers themselves in the Arab-Israeli arena. The following points reflect what Washington and Moscow seem to have learned about governing that interaction.

Defining the Problem and Interests in Change

Since the early 1950s, the Soviet Union and the United States have competed for influence in the Middle East both because of an interest in strengthening their global positions vis-à-vis each other and because of specific security interests in the region. An analysis of their interests in shaping change to their own advantage suggests why continuing competition has not given way to cooperation except in one area of common interests—avoiding nuclear war.

The Soviets moved from concern after the Cuban missile crisis never again to be caught at a power disadvantage, to nuclear parity in the late 1960s, and then in the 1970s to demands for political parity commensurate with their nuclear capability. Overall, they sought to shift the balance of influence in the Middle East. Specifically, they sought to push back what they regarded as Western encirclement. They deeply resented attempts to keep them in an inferior position or to exclude them altogether from their own "backyard."

The United States sought to prevent Soviet political domination of the inevitable process of post-colonial change in the region. It perceived a need to protect NATO and Japanese access to oil through that period of change in Arab countries. It also sought ways of encouraging Arab acceptance of Israel as a state in the Middle East.

Throughout this period, one overriding common interest limited the superpowers' pursuit of their respective interests—their interest in avoiding a Soviet–U.S. collision in the Arab-Israeli arena that could lead to nuclear war. In this region, each side has demonstrated a high degree of commitment to avoiding a direct confrontation. Avoiding such a confrontation required as precise a picture as possible of where each side's raw nerves are.

Each of these moments of mutual restraint seemed to reflect a rule of the game that the superpowers will state their specific interests clearly when they are threatened and will avoid allowing an Arab-Israeli crisis to draw them into direct confrontation. To clarify their interests, they have used a variety of communication channels—from the hotline in 1967 to the backchannel relationship of 1973 and the messages passed through private channels precisely defining Soviet interests in Syria in 1983. At some points, direct communications have included threats and signals of military actions, as in the case of the Soviet threats at the end of the 1967 and 1973 wars and the U.S. nuclear alert in October 1973.

Each power also seems to have agreed that it is important to move each Arab-Israeli crisis as quickly as possible back into a diplomatic framework—normally under U.N. auspices—for dealing with the fundamental issues in the long-term conflict. Diplomatic consultations and even coordination have ranged from the joint drafting of Resolution 338 and the co-chairmanship of the Geneva Conference in 1973, through extensive private talks in 1969 and 1971-1973, and the joint statement of October 1, 1977. Most of these exchanges produced some clarification of the exact nature of each side's interests in an Arab-Israeli settlement.

With the safety net of such a diplomatic framework to fall back on, each side has been willing to use the Arab-Israeli conflict as a vehicle in their competition, but each side has recognized some limits of tolerance in the other's willingness to accept setbacks. That recognition seems to include acknowledgment of asymmetries in the two sides' interests in the area. Moscow could tolerate the decisive defeat of Egyptian and Syrian armed forces in peripheral areas in 1967, but not threats to their heartlands (the Nile Valley and Damascus). The Mid-Eastern parties themselves have mostly avoided attacks on population centers, with the exception of Israeli-Palestinian exchanges in Lebanon and in northern Israel. The U.S. threshold in supporting Israel is less flexible; in 1973 the U.S. airlift to Israel was set in motion before any of Israel's basic frontiers had been crossed. The two superpowers have cooperated in ending wars short of those thresholds. Outside the Arab-Israeli area, the Soviet Union seems to understand the intensity of American interest in Persian Gulf oil. Governments have difficulty in drawing such lines because doing so would seem to indicate tolerance for action up to those lines, but such limits distilled from experience can provide a guide to future policymakers.

In addition to recognizing these thresholds of danger, or "raw nerves," the two powers' perceptions of the influence they sought in their competition also evolved. In the 1950s and early 1960s, both parties aimed at developing exclusive positions. The United States in the 1950s tried to form an anti-Soviet alliance that would block Soviet military expansion into the Middle East. After the USSR leap-frogged that effort by using military and economic aid to gain influence, U.S. policymakers saw the ultimate Soviet aim as infiltrating politically to turn key states into quasi-Soviet satellites. From the mid-1960s into the early 1970s, each side increasingly sought influence by trying to increase the military strength of its friends in the Arab-Israeli conflict. After the 1973 war, when three military showdowns (1967, 1969–1970, 1973) had demonstrated that neither the Middle Eastern parties nor the superpowers could impose a settlement by force, the superpowers renewed diplomatic efforts to achieve a settlement. At that point, Moscow and Washington began to recognize that diplomatic and political instruments skillfully used to lay the foundations for a settlement provided yet another source of influence—not the influence of establishing control over a state but the capacity to influence the course of events.

From 1967 through 1979, the superpowers working behind their friends in the Middle East used a constantly shifting mix of military and diplomatic instruments to show their ability to influence the situation. From the viewpoint of Middle Eastern states, the function of these instruments was to achieve a settlement. For Moscow and Washington, the added aim was to demonstrate that one power surpassed the other in its ability to influence the course of events. At times, one power moved to demonstrate the other's ineffectiveness by acting alone without the other power. Whatever the instrument used, as instruments changed in usefulness, the aim of the competition shifted over time from seeking exclusive positions to exercising the greater influence in the constantly changing Arab-Israeli scene.

In this area where continuing competition for influence is the norm and assures that interests remained intertwined, it has not been possible to draw dividing lines between the superpowers' respective interests. Perhaps the most refined statement regarding these interests is to say that neither side seems prepared to accept over time the other's exclusive position in an important country. Another way of saying this might be that each superpower is prepared to accept as a norm competition for influence over states that preserve their sovereign capacity to make independent decisions about their relationships.

Since the 1967 war, when Israel occupied territories of Egypt, Jordan, and Syria, an increasingly pressing Soviet interest has been to demonstrate that Moscow has the influence to produce Israeli withdrawal. Moscow saw its influence in the Arab states diminished as long as it could not produce that result. Because of Israel's superior military power, the United States has sometimes used that power to demonstrate to the Arabs that Israeli withdrawal, if any, would only follow a peace in which Israel was accepted as a state within negotiated boundaries, and to the Soviets that they could only produce withdrawal by producing that Arab acceptance.

It is a Soviet and Arab dilemma that acceptance of Israel within negotiated boundaries is the prerequisite of ending the drain of continuing conflict. Debate over whether to end the conflict goes on in the Arab states, but the center of gravity in the Arab position has shifted to accepting Israel within its 1967 borders and stipulating the creation of a Palestinian state. The Soviet Union would probably prefer to end the conflict by negotiation because—given Israel's military superiority—they have no other way of demonstrating their influence, but Moscow has not come to grips with Israeli positions that would have to be dealt with in negotiation. A key element in the Soviet–U.S. relationship in this area has been Washington's unwillingness to share its influence over the peace process unless that process hit a dead-end and Moscow seemed able to move the Arabs and Israelis in a way that Washington could not.

As long as the Soviet Union and the United States define the problems they face in the Arab-Israeli arena in different ways, it seems unlikely that they will willingly share influence in the area. For the Soviet Union, the problem since 1945 has been to push back Western encirclement in this area. When supporting the Zionists seemed a way to undermine the British position in Palestine and when Zionism was seen as a philosophy heavily influenced by socialism, Moscow supported Zionism and Israel. As time passed, Moscow—without changing its relationship with Israel until 1967—began to recognize that its ability to reduce Western influence mainly required a relationship with the Arab states. As that interest became more important, the nature and degree of Moscow's interest in Israel changed. The United States, on the other hand, has defined the problem as winning ultimate Arab acceptance of Israel while also building its own relationship with key Arab states to limit Soviet influence. This difference in approaching the problem puts limits on the two sides' ability to cooperate.

In short, neither side has been comfortable for long with the status quo in the Arab-Israeli arena. Because their perceptions of the problem and their interests in trying to change the situation have differed, their ability to cooperate in changing it has been limited. Their common interest in avoiding nuclear confrontation has led only to momentary cooperation to end crises resulting from regional powers' efforts to change the situation. Each side's picture of the problem includes a fear that the other seeks an exclusive position as the outcome of their competition. In the U.S. body politic, that general apprehension is interwoven with deep-rooted fear that Moscow would be willing to accept a subordination of the Jewish state comparable to the subordination of the Jewish people imposed in the USSR by the Soviet government. Soviets would say that they deeply resent the fact that the United States will not accept them as equals with legitimate interests in their own backyard. Until each side can resolve the difference between these perspectives, their ability to cooperate will be limited to practical measures for avoiding confrontation.

Alternatives. Repeated Arab-Israeli crises have caused both powers to think of peaceful alternatives that would contain the conflict by attacking its root causes. However, other priorities have repeatedly overshadowed efforts to achieve a settlement, and it is here that the limits on cooperation become evident. As each side has thought about moving the Arab-Israeli conflict toward a settlement, it has considered how such an alternative would affect its own interests. Moscow and Washington differ on only two major elements of a settlement—creation of a Palestinian state and the scope of Israel's withdrawal. The greater issue is how the process of achieving a settlement would change each side's influence vis-à-vis the other. Alternative processes and outcomes of negotiation are judged in significant measure by how the superpowers envision their relative positions after a settlement.

In retrospect, the United States seems to have invested more unilaterally than the Soviet Union in trying to achieve a settlement. That may simply reflect three points: (1) the special U.S. commitment to Israel's acceptance as a state and the judgment that Israel cannot survive in the long run unless the roots of the crisis are resolved; (2) the fact that the United States' special relationship with Israel enables it to gain diplomatically by using this relationship to facilitate mediation; and (3) U.S. experience that preserving a relationship with the Arabs requires a U.S. effort to achieve an Arab-Israeli-Palestinian settlement. The Soviets could bargain with Israel over Jewish emigration and Arab acceptance—valuable cards—but have chosen not to. Both sides recognize the limits on their ability to move the fundamental positions of Middle Eastern parties, but neither seems ready to cooperate with the other if cooperation would result in enhancing the other's position.

The United States has acted from different motives at different times in pursuing a settlement, but it invariably has sought enhanced U.S. influence coupled with a closer relationship with key Arab states. Nixon and Kissinger, for instance, invested heavily after the 1973 war in the diplomacy of moving the Arab-Israeli conflict in the direction of settlement as a means of completing Egypt's—and potentially Syria's—reorientation away from Moscow. The State Department, even in the Nixon period, concentrated on ending the regional conflict as a means of enhancing U.S. influence rather than using the conflict as a vehicle in pursuing the superpower competition. Carter and Vance, on the other hand, acted more out of concern for the human suffering that has resulted from the perpetuated conflict. Carter himself has said that he approached the conflict in a human rights context, feeling that a morally right position would also strengthen the United States. At the same time he acknowledged familiar strategic concerns. The Reagan Administration did not make a consistent high-level political investment in its sporadic efforts.

It is an open question whether there are comparable differences of approach within the Soviet government. As Moscow considers alternatives, one school may well hold the view that Soviet influence will not achieve parity with that of the United States until Soviet client states such as Syria become Israel's military equal. They may well see the United States as unwilling to cooperate until Israel's military superiority has been diminished and a real military balance has been established. Others may believe this would take too long to accomplish, and argue that if the Soviets could play an equal role in political efforts to achieve a peace settlement, the USSR would gain the appearance it wants of being an equally influential arbiter of events in the Middle East. Professionals in each capital have argued that it would be better to deal with the problem now by sharing the burden of mediation than to wait until the Middle Eastern parties are ready to try dealing with it as military equals or with nuclear weapons. Neither of those threats has seemed to political leaders to be imminent enough to warrant priority attention or parallel action.

Moscow and Washington are not far apart in their views of the substance of an Arab-Israeli settlement. However, neither has persuaded the other that it is not simply using the process of achieving a settlement as a way of building its own influence. In that context, both sides have yet to consider at high policy levels whether, in view of the dangers of recurring Arab-Israeli crises, a realistic alternative might be to create a positive sum situation where each might gain stature through collaboration. That thought process might begin if leaders decided that they could not alone make the political investment necessary for a settlement and that the other side could make a contribution that would make the investment affordable.

Conducting the Relationship

If both sides could visualize a roughly similar Arab-Israeli settlement they could live with but that neither could achieve alone, then Moscow and Washington would face two options in conducting their relationship in the Arab-Israeli arena. First, they could go on defining their own and each other's interests in the Middle East more sharply in order to avoid threatening those interests in a way that might lead to nuclear confrontation. In other words, they could go on trying to regulate their competition. Or, they could go further and try to find a way of addressing the Arab-Israeli conflict in a way that would not seem to concede an undue advantage to one side in its outcome.

At the competitive end of the spectrum, the two powers have gone remarkably far in using the Arab-Israeli conflict as a vehicle in their competition. Interestingly, they were most cautious in 1967 and 1983 when their bilateral relationship was least well developed. They were most daring in terms of their own competitive military involvement in 1970, when they had begun to develop enough of a relationship to be more confident of their ability to avoid confrontation but were still testing each other in the process of building that relationship. They came closest to actual cooperation in late 1973 and 1977, when cooperation on bilateral issues was at its most mature, although in neither case could that cooperation be sustained. In 1974, the temptations and asymmetries in continuing the competition peacefully short-circuited cooperation. In 1977, the failure was caused in part by domestic political opposition in the United States and objections from Israel. Since 1967, the two powers have repeatedly talked about the possibility of curbing the arms race in the Arab-Israeli area—and in the Carter Administration talks actually began—but they were unable to sustain such efforts in the absence of an agreed political context in the Middle East.

With the notable exception of the first Reagan Administration, the two powers have seemed able to talk seriously up to a point about the terms of an Arab-Israeli settlement, but they were limited in the distance they could take from the positions of their Middle Eastern friends. Two reasons for this provide important insight into the limits on collaboration.

First, each power has become quite open since the early 1970s in acknowledging to the other that it cannot force its friends to take positions those friends judge not to be in their interest. Even if Moscow and Washington could absorb the negative reactions at home and in the Middle East that would follow a joint effort to impose a settlement, they have not answered the fundamental question of *how* they would go about persuading the parties to comply with a settlement they felt did not fulfill their objectives.

Second and more basic, each of the powers seems in the end unwilling to surrender the appearance of individual ability to influence the course of events in the Middle East. The Soviet–U.S. contest for influence in the Middle East goes on, and neither power appears ready to share with the other the appearance of being able to shape events. Again, the absence of understanding about the character of their interaction in the Middle East limits their ability to cooperate.

Reasons for this stem largely from the fundamental suspicion and fear that underlie the relationship between the Soviet Union and the United States, and from the deep-rooted concerns on each side about the other's basic intentions in the contest for world power. One important element is the fact that the United States' friend, Israel, retains predominant strength in the area, and the United States has been reluctant to undermine that advantage in the absence of a clear-cut Soviet or Arab commitment to final acceptance of Israel within negotiated borders. Another is the conviction in the United States—right or wrong—that the Soviet interest lies more in enhancing its influence with Arab states than in assuring Israel's security. If this is an accurate description of the two powers' interests, it explains why cooperation is guarded.

Even if Moscow and Washington perceived a common interest in achieving a settlement, they have learned that their ability to cooperate in the Arab-Israeli arena is limited by what is going on in other areas of their relationship. At a maximum, the Arab-Israeli arena has been used, as it was between 1970 and 1973, to convey messages both ways about the desired nature of the Soviet–U.S. relationship. At a minimum, American public opinion about the Soviet Union's actions, such as those in Angola, Ethiopia, and Afghanistan, or its military build-up in Europe, can limit collaboration in the Middle East. Opinion among Soviet policymakers was clearly affected by Kissinger's statement, as the Soviets paraphrase it, that he used détente as a cover under which to reduce Soviet influence in the Middle East.

Although the two powers have learned to talk extensively about the substance of these issues in their diplomatic relationship, there seems to have been remarkably little sustained conversation—with the possible exception of Kissinger's conversations with Dobrynin and Gromyko—about the conduct of the relationship itself. This kind of communication has been most productive when it has taken place at the political (often in a back-channel setting) rather than at the diplomatic level because political leaders seem freer in discussing real interests and constraints. When such communication is not taking place, the two powers still tend to rely in communicating with each other on sending indirect signals—military alerts, visible increases in defense spending, unfriendly political rhetoric—rather than in talking directly about the conduct of the relationship. Official conversations are still not marked by much self-revelation on either side. As far as the Middle East is concerned, there have been few such exchanges in the 1980s, and the talks that have taken place have largely been limited by highly restrictive instructions on both sides. These talks have not only failed to grapple with real Middle Eastern issues, they have not been used by either government as a vehicle for understanding more fully the larger purposes of the other side. Developing that dialogue on the basis of studies such as those in this series offers the opportunity of a quantum jump in the quality of official exchanges.

A short concluding word: The quality of the Soviet–U.S. relationship in dealing with the Arab-Israeli conflict reflects the quality of their political relationship itself. The obstacles to cooperation are the deep-rooted obstacles of fear, suspicion, and mistrust that continue to fuel the two powers' global competition. In the Middle East significant progress has been made in developing an experience of apparent tacit acceptance by both parties of those rules of behavior minimally necessary to avoid a superpower nuclear confrontation. The task now is to bring those rules into the routine explicit official dialogue and to broaden that dialogue to deal politically with differing perceptions of each other's motives, with alternatives that do not give one side an advantage it is not willing to work for equally, and with building a relationship that would lead to collaboration designed to benefit each side in ways tolerable to the other.

Notes

1. It is worth noting that the definition of "regulate" includes the ideas of controlling or governing according to rule, and "regulation" reflects the notion of a rule prescribed for the management of some situation or for regulating conduct. How the rule comes into being and whether it is explicit or informally understood are important further questions in refining the concept of regulating competition in the conduct of international relationships.

2. For more detail, see George W. Breslauer, "Soviet Policy in the Middle East, 1967–1972: Unalterable Antagonism or Collaborative Competition?" and Alexander L. George, "The Arab-Israeli War of 1973: Origin and Impact," in Alexander L. George, ed., *Managing U.S.–Soviet Rivalry: Problems of Crisis Prevention* (Boulder, Colo.: Westview Press, 1983); and William B. Quandt, *Decade of Decisions* (Berkeley, Calif.: University of California Press, 1977) and *Camp David: Peacemaking and Politics* (Washington, D.C.: Brookings, 1986). In addition to published materials, I have referred to my own files and experience.

3. Lyndon Baines Johnson, *The Vantage Point: Perspectives of the Presidency 1963–1969* (New York: Holt, Rinehart and Winston, 1971), p. 288.

4. Quoted in George, *Managing U.S.–Soviet Rivalry*, pp. 107–108.

5. Henry Kissinger, *Years of Upheaval* (Boston: Little, Brown, 1982), p. 753.

23

U.S.–Soviet Efforts to Cooperate in Crisis Management and Crisis Avoidance

ALEXANDER L. GEORGE

It is remarkable that all U.S.–Soviet diplomatic confrontations—over Berlin, Korea, the Middle East, Cuba, and in South Asia—have been successfully terminated without any kind of shooting war between American and Soviet military forces. The mutual fear of igniting a fuse that could trigger thermonuclear holocaust is undoubtedly the major factor that accounts for this success. Moreover, during forty years of global competition the two superpowers have learned some fundamental "rules of prudence" for managing their rivalry and for dealing with occasional confrontations without becoming embroiled in warfare.

At the same time, however, it needs to be recognized that the two superpowers have been more adept in managing war-threatening crises than in avoiding them. This chapter discusses the factors that have contributed to success in crisis management and it also identifies the major "threats" that U.S. and Soviet crisis managers have had to overcome in order to avoid war. Finally, this chapter will also discuss some of the efforts that the two superpowers have made to improve cooperation in crisis avoidance and assess some suggestions that have been advanced to improve crisis avoidance.

We begin by noting the critical importance of incentives for crisis management and for crisis avoidance. Incentives for managing war-threatening confrontations are much stronger and more clear cut than the incentives for avoiding them. In contrast to crisis management, crisis avoidance is a more amorphous objective and, judging from past experience, is *not* one that both superpowers are equally committed to in every situation. Soviet-American competition for global influence results in different kinds of crises, some clearly more war-threatening than others. Some of these conflicts are tolerable to one side, if not both, because they are thought to carry with them either no risk of a superpower military clash or an easily controllable one. Further, as some students of international relations have noted, in the thermonuclear era crises are sometimes a *substitute for war*. Thus, a confrontation may be deliberately initiated by a superpower (as by Stalin over West Berlin in 1948) or by a regional actor with the blessings or acquiescence of its superpower ally, in the hope of bringing about desired changes in a situation it regards as intolerable. In other words, the initiation of a controlled crisis may seem to offer an opportunity for achieving foreign policy goals.

Not only do incentives for crisis management and crisis avoidance differ; the requirements for these two aspects of U.S.–Soviet relations also differ. Fortunately the general principles for managing crises are stark and simple. Leaders of the two superpowers quickly grasped these requirements in their very first war-threatening confrontation over Berlin in 1948–49. To be sure, the general requirements for crisis management must be operationalized and tailored to the idiosyncratic configuration of each confrontation, and this is a challenging, demanding task. But at least these general principles for crisis management remain pretty much the same from one situation to another. As a result not only is crisis management easier to learn than crisis avoidance, but the learning experiences from successfully managed crises are, in principle at least, more easily accumulated and adapted for the management of subsequent crises.

In contrast, crisis avoidance is a more complex task because there is no single, prototypical set of general requirements for preventing U.S.–Soviet conflict of interests in a particular area from erupting into a confrontation of some kind.

CRISIS MANAGEMENT

Although the frequency of war-threatening crises involving the superpowers appears to have declined, there having been no dangerous U.S.–Soviet confrontation since the October 1973 war between Israel and Egypt and Syria, it would be ill-advised to conclude that the United States and the Soviet Union can be counted upon to manage their relations in the future without plunging into another dangerous confrontation.

Concern over the danger of nuclear war has in fact increased in recent years in response to developments in military technology and changes in force postures. Increased missile accuracies, the deployment and forward basing of highly accurate strategic systems that reduce available warning time, and developments in warning and alert systems have raised the possibility of so-called decapitation strikes against vulnerable political and military command posts. As a result of these developments in the strategic environment in which deterrence must operate, both American and Soviet analysts have expressed concern over the heightened danger of crisis instability and the associated possibility of inadvertent and accidental war.

Both Moscow and Washington, as already noted, are familiar with what we refer to here as the general principles and operational requirements of crisis management. Briefly summarized here, what may be called the *political requirements* for effective management of war-threatening U.S.–Soviet confrontations are that one or both sides limit the objectives they pursue in the crisis and/or limit the means employed for achieving those objectives. In addition, analysis of past U.S.–Soviet crises enables one to identify a number of more specific *operational requirements* that are relevant for avoiding an undesired escalation. While the importance of these requirements or principles varies, they provide useful guidance for crisis policymaking. Some six such principles or desiderata have been identified and their role in past crises can be documented:

1. Top-level political authorities must maintain knowledge and informed control over the selection and timing of military alerts, movements, and actions.
2. Top-level political authorities must carefully coordinate movements of military forces and force options with diplomatic actions as part of an integrated strategy for pursuing crisis objectives at acceptable cost-risk levels.
3. Each side shall slow down the tempo of military movements and, if necessary, deliberately create pauses in the momentum of the crisis in order to provide time for

assessing the situation, making decisions, exchanging diplomatic signals and communications, and preparing proposals.
4. Each side shall avoid military movements and threats that give the mistaken impression that it is about to resort to large-scale warfare, thereby forcing the other side to
consider preemption.
5. Each side shall ensure that military alerts and force movements undertaken to reduce
vulnerability, increase readiness, and signal resolve are consistent with its limited
diplomatic objectives in the crisis; and, correspondingly, it shall avoid military moves
that may send conflicting or incorrect indications of its intentions.
6. Each side shall select diplomatic proposals and military moves that leave the other
side a way out of the crisis that is compatible with its fundamental interests.[1]

However, mere awareness of crisis management principles does not guarantee that they
will be effectively implemented in a new confrontation. It is a challenging and difficult
task for policymakers to adapt their general knowledge of crisis management principles
to the specific, idiosyncratic configuration of each new crisis situation. This is particularly difficult when the two superpowers are drawn into wars between their regional
allies, as in the Middle East. Moreover, given the above-mentioned developments that
contribute to crisis instability, it has become more urgent than ever to address the question whether crisis management concepts and procedures will prove robust and flexible
enough to withstand the possibly destabilizing and escalatory potential of military alerts
and actions that each side may feel obliged to take to protect interests believed to be at
stake in a confrontation, and to hedge against the possibility that crisis management
may break down in a new confrontation.[2]

THE BASIC RULE OF PRUDENCE IN U.S.–SOVIET RELATIONS[3]

Soviet-American rivalry has been regulated by a basic rule of prudence to which both
sides have adhered, namely that *neither superpower shall initiate military action against
the forces of the other superpower*. The mutual fear of thermonuclear war lies at the
root of this "rule" and helps to explain why there has been no shooting war of any
kind between the military forces of the two superpowers.

Adherence to the basic rule, it should be emphasized, is dependent upon observance of several corollary rules. The first corollary requires that *neither superpower
shall exploit its advantage in a crisis to impose on the other a policy dilemma between
backing down in defeat or desperately initiating the use of force*. Both superpowers
have pushed this corollary to the limit on past occasions, succumbing to the temptation
to utilize an advantage in a crisis to exploit the other's reluctance to initiate direct
combat. Thus, in the Berlin crisis of 1948 the Soviet Union chose to exploit the advantage inherent in the geographically isolated position of Berlin deep in the Soviet occupation zone of East Germany to impose a blockade on ground access to West Berlin.
Confronted with a grim choice between backing down or using force to break the blockade, thereby risking war, President Harry Truman turned instead to a hastily organized
airlift to West Berlin which eventually proved to be successful. The United States, too,
came close to violating this important corollary when, during the Cuban missile crisis
in 1962, President John F. Kennedy found it expedient to exploit the U.S. Navy's
superiority in the Caribbean to force Soviet submarines to the surface. Soviet authorities

584   Alexander L. George

decided not to counter the U.S. Navy's actions, presumably fearing that to do so might trigger a shooting war on the high seas that would escalate.

The second corollary to the basic rule of prudence requires that *each superpower shall operate with great restraint in its policies and actions towards areas of vital interest to the other superpower.* This corollary is subject to interpretation because the superpowers do not accord each other comprehensive, uncontested spheres of influence.

Two additional corollaries are of considerable significance in regional conflicts, such as in the Middle East, between local actors each of which has the backing of one of the superpowers. The third corollary requires that *neither superpower shall permit a regional ally to drag it into a confrontation or shooting war with the other superpower.* Moscow and Washington do not always find it easy to honor this imperative. An acute policy dilemma sometimes arises from a superpower's need to lend support to its regional ally while restraining it from actions that could draw Moscow and Washington into a dangerous confrontation. The superpowers' lack of perfect control over their regional allies compounds this dilemma.

Out of the superpowers' experience in dealing with this policy dilemma in several Middle East crises there has emerged a pattern of restraint that can be formulated as a fourth corollary to the basic rule of prudence: *each superpower shall accept military intervention by the other superpower in a regional conflict if such intervention becomes necessary to prevent the overwhelming defeat of a regional ally; moreover, in order to remove the other superpower's incentive to intervene in such situation each superpower shall accept responsibility for pressuring its regional ally to stop short of inflicting such a defeat on its local opponent.* Thus, in the Arab-Israeli wars of 1967, 1970 and 1973 the Soviet Union felt obliged to threaten military intervention in order to obtain a cessation of hostilities before its Arab client suffered a catastrophic setback. In 1967 and again in 1973 the Soviet threat of intervention was quickly countered by U.S. deterrence measures—President Lyndon Johnson moved the U.S. Sixth Fleet toward the Syrian coast as a signal that Washington opposed Soviet intervention; President Richard Nixon put strategic forces on alert in answer to Leonid Brezhnev's threat of, and preparations for, Soviet intervention. At a critical time for Egypt during the War of Attrition in late January 1970, the Soviet Union issued a somewhat ambiguous warning to Washington that it would not remain idle in the face of the Israeli deep-penetration air raids that were threatening to topple Egyptian president Gamal Abdel Nasser. The Soviet warning was not correctly interpreted or taken seriously by Washington, which neither undertook strong deterrence measures to dissuade Moscow from intervening nor pressed the Israelis to curtail their deep-penetration air attacks so as to remove the reason for possible Soviet intervention.

In this connection it should be noted that in 1967 and 1973, in contrast to 1970, U.S. leaders not only promptly countered Soviet intervention threats but also pressed Israel to accept a cease-fire, thereby removing the necessity or excuse for Soviet intervention. In a sense, therefore, Soviet intervention threats in these two crises achieved their purpose: the United States was induced to curb its ally, something which it had been unable or unwilling to do prior to the Soviet threats of intervention. Soviet-American interaction in these two crises can be characterized, therefore, as a pattern of last-ditch "coerced cooperation" in crisis management and crisis resolution. Developments in the 1970 War of Attrition took a different course, as already noted, but not one that is inconsistent with this interpretation. When the United States failed either to curb the Israeli deep-penetration raids against Egypt or to deter Soviet intervention, the Soviets gradually introduced major air defense forces of their own to defend Egypt—a development American policymakers accepted and, however reluctantly, tacitly acknowledged as legitimate under the circumstances.

These rules of prudence, it should be understood, are at most tacit understandings and shared expectations that can be inferred from patterns of behavior exhibited by Moscow and Washington. So far as is known Soviet and American leaders have never discussed and agreed upon such rules. Still, one is perhaps justified in referring to these rules and the shared U.S.–Soviet understanding of the principles of crisis management as constituting a tacit regime.

THREATS TO CRISIS MANAGEMENT

Let us turn now to a discussion of various "threats" to effective crisis management that were noted in past confrontations and may well emerge in future crises as well. The fact that these threats were experienced but effectively surmounted in past crises does not guarantee similar success in new confrontations that may occur under quite different circumstances. Analysis of past U.S.–Soviet confrontations has enabled us to identify a number of dangerous threats to effective crisis management, some already alluded to, which are briefly listed here:[4] (1) The tension that policymakers on both sides in a crisis may experience between a desire to utilize strong coercive threats on behalf of their objectives and, on the other hand, the requirements to slow down the momentum of events and avoid actions that would give the impression of preparing for a major escalation; (2) the temptation to exploit an advantage in the crisis situation which, if pursued, might force the other side to choose between backing down or initiating the use of force; (3) the difficulties experienced in backing one's allies in regional conflicts without being dragged into a war with the superpower that is backing a rival regional actor; (4) the difficulty of controlling the possible destabilizing and escalatory consequences of military alert measures and other actions that seem prudent to take in a crisis in order to reduce force vulnerability, improve readiness, signal resolution, etc.; (5) the difficulty of controlling one's own military forces in a crisis through reliance on standing orders and rules of engagement; (6) the possibly harmful effects of crisis-induced stress and fatigue on policymakers.

At various times in the past twenty-five years Moscow and Washington have taken steps to solidify and improve cooperation in crisis management and, for that matter, to avoid certain types of crises. These developments were discussed by Barry Blechman in Chapter 18. It suffices here to note that after the Cuban missile crisis, Kennedy and Nikita Khrushchev moved quickly to set up a direct communications link, the "hotline," between Washington and Moscow. It was used by President Johnson, apparently for the first time, during the Middle East war of 1967, to avoid Soviet misapprehensions as to U.S. intentions after he ordered U.S. aircraft to search the water near Egypt for survivors of an American vessel sunk, it turned out, by Israeli planes. However, conversations between heads of state over the hotline are not a substitute for carefully prepared, more formal diplomatic communication. During the Nixon-Brezhnev era, direct communication between Soviet and American leaders increased in many ways. The Dobrynin-Kissinger "back channel" played an important role in preparing various agreements; it also served as a vehicle for important diplomatic communications during crises such as the Syrian invasion of Jordan in 1970, and in heading off incipient crises such as the building of a base in Cuba for Soviet submarines in 1970. One of the most

Alexander L. George

dramatic instances of direct communication in the interest of cooperation in crisis management occurred during the October 1973 war in the Middle East when Brezhnev invited Henry Kissinger to Moscow to work out details of a cease-fire.

CRISIS AVOIDANCE

We noted earlier that crisis avoidance is a much more amorphous objective than crisis management, and that the superpowers' incentives for moderating and regulating their global competition in the interests of crisis avoidance are much weaker and less clear-cut than for crisis management. As a matter of fact, incentives for crisis avoidance conflict with incentives for enhancing one's global and regional influence. The incentives that feed U.S.–Soviet global and regional competition, moreover, do not stem solely from the urge for more power or, more specifically, to achieve and maintain a position of relative power advantage over the adversary. That is to say, the nature of Soviet-American global rivalry cannot be adequately understood in terms of classical realistic theory as simply a competition for power and influence. Rather, the rivalry of the two superpowers is much accentuated and complicated by fundamental ideological differences. Thus, any attempt to comprehend the challenging task of crisis avoidance must recognize that the United States and the Soviet Union are engaged in continuing competition to shape the direction and forms of global and regional political and economic change and development in accord with their ideological preferences as well as their perceived security needs. A further complicating factor is that the distinction between security needs and ideological preferences becomes blurred in the conduct of foreign policy.

During the era of the Cold War, the United States relied largely upon the various instruments of its containment strategy—deterrence, alliance commitments, military and economic aid—to prevent challenges to the Free World that could result in tense diplomatic crises, if not also war. The problem of how the United States and the Soviet Union might moderate their rivalry and competition to avoid dangerous confrontations received much less attention than problems of deterrence, crisis management, coercive diplomacy, preventing limited conflicts from escalating, and arms control. The great gulf that divided the United States and the Soviet Union appeared to make it futile to utilize classical diplomacy and negotiation to resolve or moderate conflicts of interest between the two superpowers.

Even during the Cold War, however, the two superpowers occasionally found ways of limiting the potential conflict in their relationship. In Europe, as David Schoenbaum has depicted in his chapter, the wartime agreement for dividing Germany into occupation zones was gradually transformed into a tacit, if also somewhat ambiguous and uneasy, sphere-of-influence arrangement. Despite the Eisenhower Administration's moral support of the "captive peoples" of Eastern Europe and its talk of "liberation," it acted with great prudence when crises erupted in that area that challenged Soviet control. Washington stood aloof when the East German rebellion was crushed in 1953. A non-interventionist policy was articulated by Secretary of State John Foster Dulles during the Polish crisis of October 1956, and it was adhered to again by the Eisenhower Administration during the Soviet invasion of Hungary in 1956 and by President Johnson in the face of the Soviet invasion of Czechoslovakia in 1968. In the recent Polish crisis as well, both the Carter and Reagan administrations clearly indicated that the United States did not have any military option.[5]

Washington's acceptance of Soviet primacy in Eastern Europe during the Cold War was consistent, of course, with Roosevelt's and Truman's earlier decision to recognize the special security interests of the Soviet Union in Eastern Europe while at the same time engaging in abortive efforts to couple that recognition with insistence on self-determination and free elections in the countries liberated from the Nazi yoke. Other instances of unilateral actions or coordination of policies in the interest of crisis prevention can be found during the Cold War. The Soviet Union withdrew from northern Iran under U.S. pressure in 1946 and, soon thereafter, in response to U.S. opposition, gave up its demands on Turkey for guaranteed passage of Soviet vessels through the Straits of Bosphorus.

There were also instances of U.S.–Soviet cooperation that harked back to some of the practices that the great powers had utilized from time to time during the nineteenth century to reduce sources of potential conflict. Thus, as Kurt Steiner's chapter traces in detail, prolonged negotiations between the Western powers and the Soviet Union finally led in 1955 to the Austrian State Treaty, which created a neutral buffer state and removed it from the ongoing competition between the two sides in Europe. Another instance of U.S.–Soviet cooperation of this kind occurred during 1961–62 when President Kennedy, as David Hall shows in his chapter, induced Khrushchev to help bring about a cease-fire in Laos as a prerequisite to American participation in a reconvened Geneva conference on that country. At their Vienna summit talks in June 1961, Kennedy and Khrushchev agreed that what was at stake in Laos was not worth the risk of a superpower confrontation and, in the year that followed, they cooperated to bring about a cease-fire and the Declaration on Neutrality of Laos.

As these examples from the Cold War period demonstrate, the goal of crisis avoidance in the U.S.–Soviet relationship can be pursued—through either unilateral policies or cooperative action—even in a period otherwise marked by acute mutual hostility and distrust. One might assume that the goal of crisis avoidance would have been facilitated when the relationship between the United States and the Soviet Union was marked by détente. Our brief review of this period, however, reveals a mixed picture of major disappointments as well as important achievements. New opportunities emerged for reducing the conflict potential in U.S.–Soviet relations. There was now a shared disposition to utilize negotiation and accommodation to settle some of the long-standing conflicts of interest that had been bones of contention during the Cold War, particularly in Europe where the vital interests of both sides were engaged. The chapters by Jonathan Dean and John Maresca provide a detailed analysis of the complex but successful negotiations leading to agreements that stabilized the situation in Berlin, recognized the existence of the two German states, and tacitly formalized the division of Europe that had emerged following World War II.

Europe was an area in which both superpowers had vital interests, a fact that facilitated cooperation in crisis prevention. The two sides were less successful in making arrangements for moderating their competition and regulating their involvement in the Middle East, Africa, Asia, and other Third Areas—areas characterized either by low-interest symmetry or by disputed or uncertain symmetry of U.S.–Soviet interests.

The new relationship that Nixon and Brezhnev set out to create between their countries was burdened from the start by crucial ambiguities and latent disagreements on important issues that created mutually inconsistent expectations regarding the benefits each side hoped to derive from the détente process. We cannot examine all aspects of these developments and shall focus on those most directly relevant to the task of managing their rivalry in Third Areas.

The Basic Principles Agreement (BPA) that Nixon and Brezhnev signed at their first summit meeting in Moscow in May 1972 included general principles that committed the United States and the Soviet Union to avoid dangerous crises and the outbreak of nuclear war. Not only were these general principles extremely abstract and ambiguous, but the agreement to cooperate in crisis prevention itself was, in important respects, a pseudo-agreement. Article 1 of the BPA contained the Soviets' favored formulation that "in the nuclear age there is no alternative to conducting . . . mutual relations on the basis of peaceful coexistence." Earlier, when preparations for the Moscow summit were under way, Nixon had instructed Kissinger to state clearly and explicitly ₔo the Soviet leaders that the United States could not accept either the Soviet concept of "peaceful coexistence" or the "Brezhnev Doctrine," whereby the Soviet Union claimed the right to support "national liberation" movements all over the world and to intervene militarily in East European countries that deviated from the path laid down by Moscow. For reasons we need not go into here (which have to do mainly with the desire to obtain Soviet help in seeking a Vietnam settlement), Kissinger did not follow Nixon's directive; nor did Nixon himself pursue the matter at the Moscow summit. Instead of opposing the inclusion of "peaceful coexistence" in the BPA or insisting that the document include a statement of their disagreement with the Soviet concept, Nixon and Kissinger contented themselves with introducing elsewhere in the BPA (Article 2) language that reflected their long-standing exhortation to the Russians to forego "efforts to obtain unilateral advantage" at the expense of the West and to "exercise restraint" in their foreign policy.

Thus, the BPA gave the erroneous impression that the Soviet Union and the United States were in substantial agreement on the general rules of the game and the restraints to be observed in their competition in Third Areas. Thereby Nixon and Kissinger contributed to what their domestic critics were later to refer to as the "overselling" of détente.

As subsequent events were to make clear, each side read its own hopes and desires into the language of the general crisis-avoidance principles of the BPA. In the first place, Washington and Moscow had rather different conceptions of the crises that these two agreements were supposed to help avoid. Soviet leaders were interested primarily in using the general principles to avoid crises carrying the danger of nuclear war with the United States. Nixon and Kissinger were interested, in addition, in using the agreements (together, of course, with positive inducements offered to Moscow for good behavior) to moderate Soviet efforts to make gains in Third Areas at the expense of the West, whether or not such assertive Soviet behavior should lead to dangerous crises of the kind feared by the Soviets. But for Moscow the virtue of U.S. adherence to the concept of peaceful coexistence was precisely that it should make it more acceptable and safer for the Soviet Union to engage in low-level, controlled efforts to advance its influence in these areas.

For the Soviets, the notable achievement of having U.S. leaders accept "peaceful coexistence" as the basis for their relationship in the future was reinforced by what they regarded as a formal acceptance by Nixon of the political equality of the Soviet Union with the United States. For Moscow the value of Article 1 of the BPA was that it committed the United States to developing "normal relations" with the Soviet Union on the basis of the principle of "equality." Although the language of these articles was phrased as applying to both sides, it had special significance for Soviet leaders as constituting an acknowledgement by the United States that Soviet achievement of strategic military parity entitled the Soviet Union to be treated by the United States as political-diplomatic equal as well.

From Moscow's perspective, this entitled the Soviet Union to participate as an equal with the United States in settling all international problems that, in Moscow's view, affected its security in areas that were in geographical proximity to the Soviet Union, such as Europe, the Middle East, and, to a lesser extent, Northeast Asia.[6]

Consistent with this, in the Soviet view, was the apparent fact that the Nixon Administration was already working together with the Soviet Union, however unsuccessfully up to that point, to develop general principles for a Middle East settlement. To the Soviets this constituted practical recognition by the United States of Soviet security interests in the Middle East and an acceptance by Washington of the necessity to act jointly with the Soviet Union in settling the Arab-Israeli conflict. As a matter of fact, however, this was a gross misperception by Moscow of the American attitude and an incorrect appraisal of the Middle East policy Nixon and Kissinger were actually pursuing. Thus, even while going through the motions of trying to work out a basis for a joint U.S.–Soviet approach, Nixon and Kissinger had in fact embarked on a concealed policy aimed at removing the Soviets from the area. As Kissinger put it in his memoirs: "To some extent my interest in détente was tactical, as a device to maximize Soviet dilemmas and reduce Soviet influence . . . in the Middle East.[7]

Far from providing solid norms of restraint on which to base the further development of the détente relationship, the general principles of the BPA were viewed by each side as a vehicle for imposing constraints on the foreign policy of the other side, not on its own. Given the generality and ambiguity of the principles and the fact that no provision was made for interpreting or enforcing them, they were bound eventually to provoke charges and countercharges of nonfulfillment and thus to generate disillusionment and additional friction in U.S.–Soviet relations.[8]

Developments leading to the Arab-Israeli war of October 1973, just a few months after the signing of the Agreement on the Prevention of Nuclear War (APNW), provided the first test of these two agreements. The Soviets did not go as far as they might have (or as far as they ought to have gone, according to one interpretation of their responsibilities under the BPA and APNW) to prevent the Arab attack or to consult adequately with the United States to enlist its cooperation to this end. As a matter of fact, however, at their second summit meeting in the United States in June 1973, Brezhnev had strongly warned Nixon about the danger of war in the Middle East. Brezhnev's warning, however, was of a general character. He did not state that Anwar Sadat had definite, firm plans for an attack. Washington dismissed Brezhnev's warning as scare tactics designed to pressure the United States to change its Middle East policy. It is also possible that the Soviets attempted to give the United States indirect warning of the Arab attack a few days before it occurred when they suddenly ordered the evacuation of Soviet civilian personnal from Egypt and Syria. For various reasons, however, U.S. leaders did not regard this as an indication that Soviet leaders knew that an Arab attack was imminent.

The origins of the October War reveal the difficulties of implementing the APNW provision for urgent U.S.–Soviet consultations to head off the development of dangerous situations carrying with them the threat of war. The Soviets were caught in a situation in which honoring the requirement for consultation conflicted with their responsibilities to their Arab allies. Viewed more broadly, the origins of the October War, if analyzed in more detail than is possible here, would reveal the complexities of the Middle East situation that made it a particularly severe test of détente and the crisis-prevention agreements. After an initial effort by the State Department during the first year or two of the Nixon Administration to find a basis for diplomatic cooperation with the Soviet Union in settling the Arab-Israeli conflict, Washington and Moscow pursued divergent objectives and strategies in the Middle East that in effect ruled out cooperation between them in the interest of crisis prevention. Even while ostensibly favoring a cooperative solution, each superpower covertly pursued a self-seeking policy of its own toward the Middle East conflict—the United States attempting to bring about a reversal of alliances that would exclude Soviet influence in Egypt, and the Soviet Union arming Egypt and Syria and condoning their resort to war.

The competition and diplomatic disunity of the superpowers gave Egypt, the local actor most dissatisfied with the status quo, an opportunity to maneuver and to use force to pursue its own policy objectives. This case is a reminder, therefore, that prevention of crises is not under the exclusive or reliable control of the two superpowers. Competition between them in Third Areas may allow highly motivated local actors to play one superpower off against the other and to pursue their own interests in ways that generate crises into which the superpowers are then drawn.

In the aftermath of the October War the interests of the two superpowers collided even more sharply in the Middle East, and soon in Africa as well, in ways that exposed the ambiguities and shallowness of the general principles to which Nixon and Brezhnev had ostensibly subscribed. By January 1975, when the United States and the Soviet Union entered into covert competition to influence the internal struggle for power in Angola, many of the expectations and hopes generated in the Kremlin by the Basic Principles Agreement of 1972 had turned sour. Kissinger's success in excluding the Soviets from meaningful participation in Middle East negotiations was itself a source of deep frustration, being viewed as contradicting the principles of "equality" and "reciprocity" that were to have governed superpower relations in the era of détente. Moreover, the promise that détente would yield the Soviet Union substantial trade and credits had foundered on Washington's inability either to moderate Senator Henry Jackson's determined effort to link trade with Moscow's policy on emigration of Jews or to forestall Senator Adlai Stevenson's amendment that sharply limited credits to Moscow. By early 1975, moreover, prospects for a SALT II agreement had dimmed as a result of increasing domestic controversy over its merits that extended to some of the highest levels of the Ford Administration itself.

As a result of these developments, Soviet leaders were hardly disposed to withdraw from the competition in Angola when, in January-February 1975, Washington decided to give covert assistance to an anti-Marxist movement rather than support efforts of the Portuguese authorities, backed by the Organization of African Unity, to set up a transitional government in Angola composed of representatives of the three indigenous independence movements. Developments in Angola during the remainder of 1975, it is generally agreed, constitute a particularly important instance of the failure of the United States and the Soviet Union to manage their rivalry in Third Areas so as to avoid a diplomatic confrontation. One emerges from a study of the origins and development of the Angola crisis with the conclusion that a superpower confrontation there was not preordained and might have been avoided. Neither Washington nor Moscow foresaw or planned the scenario that unfolded in 1975.[9]

The Ogaden war of 1977–78 led to another Soviet-Cuban intervention in an African conflict and resulted in further damage to what remained of the détente relationship. As in Angola, the general principles for crisis avoidance agreed to in 1972 and 1973 seemed entirely irrelevant and ineffectual. And again, as in Angola, U.S. policymakers were unable to improvise ways of deterring or otherwise inducing the Soviets to act with restraint. In the early stages of the war, when it appeared that Somalia would win, Washington lacked incentives to limit the conflict. A Somali success was not unwelcome, since it might help to undermine the Soviet position in the strategic Horn of Africa. At the same time, diplomatic efforts to induce Moscow to use its influence with Ethiopia to bring about a cease-fire were not a wholly attractive option, since this would tend to legitimize a Soviet role in the area. It was only after Soviet-supported deployment of Cuban troops to Ogaden reversed the local balance that Washington overcame its reluctance to engage Moscow in direct talks with a view to limiting and terminating the conflict. Soviet readiness to use force was encouraged by several aspects of the situation over which Washington had little leverage. Moscow could justify its support for Ethiopia as legitimate assistance to the victim of unprovoked aggression by Somalia, a position that many African states found persuasive. Moreover, whatever the risks of Moscow's intervention, they were reduced by the domestic constraints on U.S. policy occasioned by Vietnam, Watergate, and revelations of CIA activities. On the other hand, while the United States was unable to prevent the Cuban-Ethiopian counterattack from retaking Ogaden, Washington was more successful in discouraging any temptation Moscow might have felt to support an invasion of Somalia itself. Diplomatic exchanges between the two superpowers eventually resulted in a formula whereby the United States agreed not to carry out its threat to arm Somalia in return for a Soviet-Ethiopian pledge to stop the Cuban-Ethiopian advance in Ogaden at the Somalian border.[10]

What Angola, Ogaden, the Middle East, and other cases demonstrate is that both superpowers are often unwilling to forego perceived opportunities to advance their own interests at the other's expense *unless and until the threat of a dangerous confrontation appears to be imminent.* This makes one side or the other reluctant to initiate timely diplomatic consultations to work out an ad hoc understanding for avoiding or limiting their competition in any particular Third Area.

Despite the unsatisfactory experience with these two agreements and the gradual demise of détente, interest in the possibility of developing a set of general ground rules for limiting involvement of the superpowers in Third Areas persists among some students of U.S.–Soviet relations. An ambitious proposal for a formal explicit agreement was put forward in 1982 by the American Committee on East-West Accord, based on the ideas of one of its members.[11] The proposal urges that the United States and the Soviet Union negotiate "a precise set of ground rules having to do with specific geography and a specific ban on direct or indirect use of combat forces in those areas." The prohibition would apply to the Middle East, Southwest Asia, Africa, the Indian subcontinent, and Southeast Asia—presumably also to Latin America and the Caribbean, although these two areas were not explicitly mentioned in the American Committee's statement. It may be noted that the proposal also suggested that the prohibition against introduction of U.S. and Soviet forces into these areas should be extended to include a ban on "covert, paramilitary, or so-called 'volunteer' combat forces." Also, the Committee proposed, the agreement should stipulate "that neither power would intervene with combat forces *even if* 'invited' to do so by one of the Third World countries" (emphasis supplied).

While many types of superpower intervention would be excluded by these proposed ground rules, the prohibition does not extend to the transfer of weapons or the sending of military advisers; nor were proxy forces and those of superpower allies to be explicitly prohibited. Therefore, as is often the case with efforts to define what is not permitted, the result is to make it implicitly legitimate to do everything that is not explicitly forbidden by the agreement.[12]

It should be noted that a superpower's acceptance of general ground rules of this kind would mean that it was willing to accept *any* outcome of a regional conflict, however harmful to its interests the outcome might turn out to be. Similarly, unless otherwise specified, adherence to such sweeping ground rules would cancel commitments the United States and the Soviet Union have made to allies in the geographical areas in question to assist in their defense against external attack or armed insurrection. General ground rules of this kind make no allowance for the difference in the relative interests of the superpowers in different areas. The proposed prohibitions would apply across the board to areas in which a superpower had substantial and vital interests as well as to areas in which it has quite limited interests.[13]

For these reasons, perhaps others as well, it is doubtful whether either superpower would regard ground rules of the kind proposed by the American Committee as acceptable. Both the desirability and the feasibility of such a comprehensive, across-the-board set of prohibitions would be questioned.

The type of cooperation between the superpowers called for in the American Committee's proposal is in the nature of a formal explicit agreement to forego certain kinds of intervention in many different geographical areas. It is important to recognize that superpower cooperation to limit competition and involvement in Third Areas can take other forms. Instead of agreeing to a general contractual arrangement that applies equally to many regions, the superpowers can make an agreement that is limited to a specific country or region, as in the case of the Austrian State Treaty and the neutralization of Laos. An agreement to limit competition in a particular area can be quite explicit without taking the form of a treaty. Thus, as noted earlier, in the winter of 1977–78 the two superpowers made use of traditional diplomatic modalities to reach an understanding regarding the war between Ethiopia and Somalia over the Ogaden. The United States sought and received explicit assurances from the Soviet Union that Ethiopian-Cuban troops would not invade Somalia after expelling Somalian troops from the disputed Ogaden area.

Thus far we have discussed formal, explicit superpower agreements that are either comprehensive in geographical scope or limited to a particular area or country. Superpower rivalry can be limited and regulated also through mutual adjustment and the development of "norms of competition"—i.e., less formal and often less explicit understandings. Norms of a tacit character, such as the "basic rule of prudence" and its corollaries discussed earlier in this chapter, can emerge during the course of superpower competition or reflect patterns of restraint that have emerged through past experience which the two sides find it useful to observe in new situations that arise. In contrast to the legal or quasi-legal type of formal agreement referred to earlier, norms of competition are analogous to a "common law" that develops through experience and offers useful precedents or benchmarks.

It is important to recognize that the utility of norms and patterns of restraint are often weakened because they contain ambiguities and loopholes that may tempt one side or the other to probe or to take advantage of the inadequacies of the understanding. While such challenges can weaken or destroy existing norms, nonetheless probes and tests of ambiguous norms sometimes have a beneficial effect by forcing a clarification of ambiguities and closing of loopholes, thereby enhancing the usefulness of the norms for regulating superpower competition.

Tacit and verbalized norms of competition can play an important role, if only because more explicit and formal agreements on rules of competition are lacking. But such norms tend to be unstable. Compliance with existing norms or patterns of restraint cannot be taken for granted when new situations arise. It may be necessary for one superpower to take steps to activate the norm, to insist upon its relevance and applicability in the situation at hand. The other superpower may or may not agree.

Thus, an inherent weakness of norms of competition is that they lack precisely the kinds of institutionalized arrangements and procedures for their clarification and application to new situations that the superpowers have found it necessary to create in order to facilitate implementation of formal negotiated agreements such as the ABM treaty, SALT I, the Accidents at Sea Agreement of 1972, and the Berlin Quadripartite Agreement of 1971.

Another limitation of many norms of competition is that they are area-specific; that is, they grow out of experience in a particular region in which the superpowers have been competing and may not be easily transferable to other areas of their competition. This is certainly the case with the norms of competition that have developed with respect to the Middle East, which we discussed earlier in this chapter, and also with respect to Cuba.

The uses and limitations of norms of competition are well illustrated by the subsequent history of the quid pro quo agreement between Kennedy and Khrushchev that helped to bring the Cuban missile crisis to a close.[14] As will be recalled, Kennedy expressed willingness to declare that the United States would not invade Cuba in the future in return for removal of the missiles and an assurance that offensive weapons would not be reintroduced into Cuba. Nonetheless, in the following years ambiguity remained as to whether the understanding was still in force and as to its scope. In early August 1970, for reasons that remain unclear, the Soviet Union utilized diplomatic channels to inquire whether the Kennedy-Khrushchev understanding remained in force; the Nixon Administration responded affirmatively. Shortly thereafter, the Nixon Administration successfully invoked this understanding as the basis for its objection to the beginnings of the construction of a base in Cuba to service Soviet submarines. Other ambiguities remained, however, and Soviet probing that took the form of visits by various types of Soviet submarines to Cuban ports continued, though certain restraints were observed.

A second potential diplomatic crisis over Soviet compliance with the 1962 agreement was more expeditiously and clearly deflected in 1978. This time the question was whether the Kennedy-Khrushchev agreement that banned reintroduction of offensive weapons systems into Cuba extended to fighter aircraft capable of striking targets in the United States. Intelligence indicated that the Soviet Union may have been replacing Cuban MIG-23 fighter-interceptor aircraft designed for air defense with MIG ground-attack planes capable of delivering nuclear weapons against U.S. targets. Diplomatic talks between high-ranking U.S. and Soviet officials resulted in a policy decision by the

Carter Administration not to make an issue of the matter, given the difficulty of ascertaining whether the new MIG aircraft were capable of carrying nuclear weapons, and to accept Soviet assurances in the matter so long as the number of MIG aircraft remained quite limited.

Within a year's time, a major U.S.–Soviet diplomatic confrontation erupted in 1979 over the "discovery" of what appeared to be a Soviet combat brigade in Cuba. A State Department review of the 1962 agreement and prior U.S.–Soviet discussions of it failed to turn up evidence that Soviet ground forces had been included in the original Kennedy-Khrushchev agreement or in its 1970 elaboration. But from various past U.S. statements and President Jimmy Carter's 1978 commitment to oppose Soviet bases in the Western Hemisphere, the State Department concluded that a Soviet combat force in Cuba could be regarded as in conflict at least with unilateral, publicly expressed U.S. policy. However, the Soviet Union refused to accept the U.S. demand for the brigade's withdrawal or to change its equipment to make it more consistent with its stated training mission. On the other hand, the Soviet Union did reaffirm that the brigade's mission was confined to training Cuban forces and promised not to change its function or status. Washington's inept handling of this affair inflicted additional damage on the overall U.S.–Soviet relationship and contributed to the non-ratification of SALT II.

AN ENHANCED ROLE FOR DIPLOMACY

We have noted the reasons for regarding as impractical the possibility of a general nonintervention agreement and the possibility of formulating general principles or norms that apply equally to all parts of the globe. At the other extreme is the idea of a superpower "condominium," a concept loosely applied to refer to the possibility that the superpowers would end their competition in a particular region by cooperating to impose and enforce arrangements that would protect their own interests and bring stability to the region. This type of crisis avoidance regime must be regarded as neither feasible nor desirable. Instructive in this regard, as Harold Saunders' chapter documents, are the difficulties Moscow and Washington have encountered in attempting to cooperate to help bring about an over-all settlement of the Arab-Israeli conflict, efforts that stopped well short of an attempt to impose a settlement. Indeed, so strong is the antipathy of other states and leaders to the possibility of a superpower condominium at their expense that much more benign forms of actual or possible U.S.–Soviet cooperation are often viewed suspiciously as portending such a development. Regional situations are not empty stages on which the United States and the Soviet Union pursue their interests competitively. The primary interests are those of the local states, and these may intersect or clash with the interests of one or the other of the superpowers.

A more promising alternative to the adoption of general principles or a nonintervention agreement—indeed, it has been successfully employed on occasion—is an ad hoc, case-by-case approach whereby Moscow and Washington jointly consider how they might clarify their interests in a particular situation, and whether and how they might put brakes on their involvement in that area. Thus, the two superpowers should seek to develop—through timely, intensive discussions—a series of individual understandings as to how to limit competition and involvement in a particular country or region. Such diplomatic discussions should illuminate and take into account the specific configuration of each particular case—i.e., what was at stake for each side; what was the danger of unwanted escalation; whether other external actors were or might become involved, and what might be done to discourage or limit their involvement; what development and outcomes of the local situation would and would not be acceptable; whether diplomatic solutions could be worked out.[15]

An important advantage of the proposed case-by-case approach is that it would bring the two superpowers together in the most serious kind of diplomatic conversations at an early stage in the development of a local situation that threatened to get out of hand. Even if their effort to devise an ad hoc agreement covering a specific situation proved abortive or only partially successful, the timely diplomatic exchanges between the two superpowers could have the useful result of mutual clarification of interests engaged by that situation, correction of possible misperceptions of each other's intentions and activities, and encouragement of efforts by third parties or the United Nations to arrive at solutions before the superpowers were drawn in more actively.

To urge that the superpowers undertake timely, serious diplomatic discussions to clarify their interests in a particular area and to identify actions by the other side that they would regard as threatening those interests is to do no more than to enjoin U.S. and Soviet leaders to make greater use of traditional diplomatic practices. Indeed, Washington and Moscow have made sporadic efforts of this kind, some successful and others not, for many years. Given the need for confidentiality, diplomatic efforts of this kind often take place without publicity. Thus it is reported that in 1982–83 "several rounds of unpublicized U.S.–Soviet diplomatic exchanges took place that dealt with regional issues and potential crises in southern Africa, the Middle East (in particular the Iran-Iraq war), and Afghanistan." According to Raymond Garthoff:

> These quiet diplomatic discussions were one of the most successful aspects of American diplomacy with the Soviet Union in the early 1980's. One main reason was their confidentiality. Another was the interest on both sides in pragmatically probing "rules of engagement" in the regional geopolitical competition. To cite an example, both the United States and the Soviet Union not only warned the other not to exploit the Iran-Iraq war, but also used the opportunity to explain some of their own activities in the region (including U.S. military preparations for contingent action to ensure world access to the Persian Gulf), as those actions might have been subject to misinterpretation by the other side.[16]

The question is how to institutionalize such traditional diplomatic practices and make them more effective. A useful step in this direction—but as it turned out a quite limited one—was taken by President Ronald Reagan in his address to the United Nations on September 24, 1984, in which he proposed a series of Soviet-American regional discussions to alleviate tensions. This led to a series of meetings to discuss Middle East issues, southern Africa, Afghanistan, and Far East issues.[17] These talks were restricted to a rather sterile exchange of already familiar positions and views, and were primarily of symbolic importance. Somewhat more substantive exchanges are said to have taken place in 1986.

Although these meetings constitute an important first step towards creation of a procedural mechanism for serious bilateral discussion of regional issues, they appear to have been utilized thus far largely for exhortation.

At the same time, it must be noted, Moscow and Washington have made no progress in developing better written norms, a "code of conduct," or general principles for regulating their involvement in Third Areas. Here we must reckon with the fact that ideological differences between the two superpowers make it difficult for either side to accept written norms that seem to legitimize the ideological thrust of the other's foreign policy. It must be assumed that Soviet leaders will not in the foreseeable future accept any proposed code of conduct that implies modification or abandonment of the ideological position that the Soviet Union is bound to lend assistance to "progressive forces" in the rest of the world. Similarly, it is unrealistic to expect that American leaders, after the disillusioning experience with the Basic Principles Agreement and the souring of the Nixon-Brezhnev version of détente, will once again accept inclusion of the Soviet concept of "peaceful coexistence" in a statement of general norms.

The Reagan Administration has not only rejected "peaceful coexistence," it has in fact articulated a strong counter to it in the so-called Reagan Doctrine.[18] Thus the Administration has openly committed itself to provide meaningful support to "freedom fighters" in Afghanistan, Southeast Asia, southern Africa, and Central America who are resisting Soviet-supported communist regimes. The Reagan Administration challenges the legitimacy of these regimes as it also challenges Moscow's long-standing insistence that Soviet gains are irreversible. Thus, insofar as communist regimes in Angola, Afghanistan, Cambodia, and Nicaragua are concerend, the Reagan Doctrine goes beyond the policy of containment. The message the Administration seeks to convey to Moscow is that it must reconcile itself to giving up its recently acquired positions of influence and control in these countries. In his message to Congress, Reagan rejected the view that regional wars in which the Soviet Union is embroiled provide an opportunity to "bleed" the Soviets: "This is not our policy . . . military solutions are not the goal of American policy." Rather the goal of American policy is to "require both sides in these struggles to lay down their arms and negotiate political solutions." But, at the same time, as Robert W. Tucker notes, the Administration has made clear that it is prepared to negotiate only the manner by which communist regimes accept democratic processes.

Therefore, despite the introduction of a procedural mechanism for U.S.–Soviet discussion of regional issues, a moderate form of superpower competition exists in Afghanistan, Angola, Cambodia, and Nicaragua. At the same time, it must be recognized that the Administration's policy of going beyond containment is restricted to areas that are not of vital interest to the Soviet Union. Moreover, while the Administration does pursue ambitious objectives vis-à-vis these countries, it seeks to limit the risks of escalation by limiting the means employed for these purposes. Underlying the Reagan Doctrine and lending a certain optimism to its objectives is the belief that U.S. military and economic strength have been reestablished and that Moscow, having overreached itself globally and encountering severe domestic economic problems, will eventually have to come around to the President's way of setting the terms of overall U.S.–Soviet relations. "For the United States," Reagan stated in his message to Congress, "these regional conflicts cannot be regarded as peripheral to other issues on the global agenda. They raise fundamental issues and are a fundamental part of the overall U.S.–Soviet relationship." Not surprisingly, therefore, the Reagan Administration attempts to use the periodic discussions of regional issues with the Soviets to press for diplomatic solutions of the type it favors.

While the difficulties standing in the way of U.S. and Soviet efforts, taken unilaterally or cooperatively, to moderate their global rivalry will remain formidable, it is possible to be too pessimistic on this score. Among developments in the international system that can be envisaged is the possibility that the superpowers may eventually redefine and delimit their global aspirations. In fact both the United States and the Soviet Union are drawing, and may be expected to continue to draw, sober lessons from their experiences in the Third World. For a variety of reasons, both superpowers have ample cause to come to a better understanding of the limits of military power and of their economic resources for maintaining and extending their global positions.

This process of learning is not confined to the United States, where the earlier impact of the Vietnam experience on public attitudes toward foreign policy has by no means dissipated.[19] For a variety of reasons the Soviet elite, too, has ample cause to reassess its policies and aspirations. Careful study of Soviet statements indicates the existence of a policy debate that reflects important differences regarding priorities and cost-benefit evaluations of extending Soviet influence in the Third World. Moreover, visitors to the Soviet Union have reported a new tendency on the part of some of their contacts to entertain second thoughts about the wisdom of the assertive Soviet policies of the mid- and late-1970s in parts of the Third World that, they now acknowledge, helped to undermine support for détente in the United States and led to a marked deterioration in the overall U.S.–Soviet relationship.[20] There is recognition, too, that trends in the Third World toward even greater turbulence and instability will confront both superpowers, the Soviet Union as well as the United States, with the prospect of declining influence and control in those areas.

In view of these developments and prospects, the analyst of U.S.–Soviet relations might well predict that both the United States and the Soviet Union will be pressed to redefine and shrink their conception of what kind of global role remains a viable goal for the superpowers. Not only will this task be difficult and painful; it could also accentuate the competitiveness and instability of superpower global rivalry, especially if one side attempts to exacerbate, and gain advantages for itself from the difficulties the other is experiencing in maintaining positions of influence in the Third World. One can hope, however, that pressures to reduce both superpowers' involvements abroad might lead instead to their mutual restraint and tacit cooperation in achieving this end.

Notes

This chapter draws directly from the author's earlier publications: "Political Crises," in Joseph S. Nye, ed., *The Making of America's Soviet Policy* (New Haven, Conn.: Yale University Press, 1984), pp. 129–157; *Managing U.S.–Soviet Rivalry: Problems of Crisis Prevention* (Boulder, Co.: Westview Press, 1983); "Crisis Management: The Interaction of Political and Military Considerations," *Survival*, vol. 26, no. 5 (1984): 223–34; *Inadvertent War in Europe: Crisis Simulation* (together with David M. Bernstein, Gregory S. Parnell, and J. Philip Rogers), Center for International Security and Arms Control, Stanford University (June 1985); "Problems of Crisis Management and Crisis Avoidance in U.S.–Soviet Relations," in O. Osterud, ed., *Studies of War and Peace* (Oslo: Norwegian University Press, 1986), pp. 202–226; "The Impact of Crisis-Induced Stress on Decision Making," in *The Medical Implications of Nuclear War*, Institute of Medicine (Washington, D. C.: National Academy Press, 1986); pp. 529–552; "U.S.–Soviet Global Rivalry: Norms of Competition," *Journal of Peace Research*, vol. 23, no. 3 (1986): 247–262.

1. For a more detailed discussion see the author's earlier writings in *Inadvertent War in Europe*, and his article "Crisis Management" in *Survival*.

2. This question was the subject of the 8th Conference on New Approaches to Arms Control held by the International Institute of Strategic Studies in England on April 9–11, 1984. For a partial report of the conference see *Survival*, vol. 26, no. 5 (1984): 200–234.

3. The ideas presented in this section have benefited from my opportunity to participate in the series of dialogues of the Harvard-Soviet group on Prevention of International Crises sponsored by the International Research and Exchange Board (IREX).

4. For a more detailed discussion see citations of the author's earlier publications: "Crisis Management," in *Survival*; "Political Crises," in Nye, ed., *America's Foreign Policy*; "Prob-

lems of Crisis Management and Crisis Avoidance in U.S.–Soviet Relations,'' in Osterud, ed., *Studies of War and Peace;* and ''The Impact of Crisis-Induced Stress on Decision Making,'' in *The Medical Implications of Nuclear War.*

5. For an analysis of U.S. responses to crises in Eastern Europe, see Jiri Valenta, ''Toward Soviet–U.S. Prevention of Crises at the Soviet Periphery,'' paper presented at the International Political Science Association, 12th World Congress, Rio de Janeiro, August 9–14, 1982.

6. Coit D. Blacker, ''The Kremlin and Détente: Soviet Conceptions, Hopes and Expectations,'' in George, *Managing U.S.–Soviet Rivalry.*

7. Henry Kissinger, *White House Years* (Boston: Little Brown, 1979), p. 1255.

8. It may be noted that neither Moscow nor Washington attempted to engage the other in follow-up conversations after signing the Basic Principles Agreement and the Agreement on Prevention of Nuclear War in order to consider the operational implications of the agreements for cooperation in crisis prevention. Nor did the two sides attempt to set up institutionalized procedures for periodic meetings to discuss how the general principles would apply to countries and regions of potential crisis. Neither did the U.S. government initiate any policy-planning studies to consider the implications of the agreements or to devise procedures for making effective use of them.

9. For detailed analyses see the chapters by Larry C. Napper and Alexander L. George, in George, *Managing U.S.–Soviet Rivalry.*

10. Larry C. Napper, ''The Ogaden War: Some Implications for Crisis Prevention,'' in George, *Managing U.S.–Soviet Rivalry.*

11. The proposal was briefly discussed in a newsletter, *Basic Positions,* issued by the American Committee on East-West Accord (1982). It was described in more detail by a member of the Committee: Arthur Macy Cox, *Russian Roulette: The Superpower Game* (New York: Times Books, 1982), pp. 156–164.

12. This point, rarely acknowledged in Soviet writings, was sharply stated in a recent article by Yevgeny M. Primakov, director of the Moscow Institute of World Economy and International Relations and a member of the U.S.S.R. Academy of Science. Commenting on the limited utility of '' 'rules of conduct,' however thoroughly thought over, agreed upon in detail, and linked to specific situations,'' he noted that ''the formulation of such rules is fraught with some danger, because they may be taken for the 'limits of the permissible.' Thus interpreted, which is inevitable, they may even stimulate activity, which in itself would lead to a dangerous aggravation of the situation.'' (Y. Primakov, ''The Soviet Union's Interests: Myths and Reality,'' in ''The Superpowers in the Middle East,'' Harold H. Saunders, ed., a special issue of the *AEI Foreign Policy and Defense Review,* vol. 6, no. 1 (1986), p. 30.

13. For a more detailed discussion of the fact that the relative interests of the superpowers vary in different parts of the globe and the implications of this fact for crisis avoidance, see George, *Managing U.S.–Soviet Rivalry,* pp. 381–389.

14. The following discussion is based on Gloria Duffy, ''Crisis Prevention in Cuba,'' in George, *Managing U.S.–Soviet Rivalry,* pp. 285–318.

15. See, in this connection, the experience of the Dartmouth Conference Task Force on Regional Conflicts, reported by Harold H. Saunders, the chairperson of the American delegation, in his introduction to the special issue, ''The Superpowers in the Middle East,'' of the *AEI Foreign Policy and Defense Review.*

16. Raymond L. Garthoff, *Detente and Confrontation* (Washington, D. C.: Brookings, 1985); p. 1061. Garthoff states that this information was obtained from ''informed U.S. officials on a background basis.''

17. *New York Times* (February 13, 20, and 21; June 19; September 7, 1985).

18. The most comprehensive statement of these policies was provided in President Reagan's message to Congress on March 14, 1986, which was entitled ''Freedom, Regional Security, and Global Peace.'' See also the commentary by Leslie Gelb in *The New York Times* (April 5, 1986),

and the op. ed. column by Robert W. Tucker, ''The New Reagan Doctrine Rests on Misplaced Optimism,'' *New York Times* (April 9, 1986).

19. See Ole R. Holsti and James N. Rosenau, *American Leadership in World Affairs: Vietnam and the Breakdown of Consensus* (Boston: Allen & Unwin, 1984); William Schneider, ''Public Opinion,'' in Joseph S. Nye, Jr., ed., *The Making of America's Soviet Policy* (New Haven, Conn.: Yale University Press, 1984); pp. 11–35.

20. See, for example, Elizabeth K. Valkenier, *The Soviet Union and the Third World: An Economic Bind* (New York: Praeger, 1983); Stephen Sestanovich, ''Do the Soviets Feel Pinched by Third World Adventures?'' *Washington Post* (May 20, 1984); S. Neil MacFarlane, ''The Soviet Conception of Regional Security,'' *World Politics,* vol. 37, no. 3 (April 1985): 295–317.

V

ANALYSIS AND LESSONS

24

Soviet Approaches to Superpower Security Relations

ALEXANDER DALLIN

WHY ANALYSIS IS DIFFICULT

How do the Soviet policymakers define security, and what is the place of negotiated agreements in their search for it? Do they want agreements at all or merely the appearance of agreements? Do they believe that international instability creates unique opportunities for them, while stability favors their enemies, or have they come to believe that the calculability of a stable world is much to be preferred to the dangers of instability? If the former, how to explain their signature on some significant accords with the United States? If the latter, how to explain some of their behavior, from Angola to Afghanistan?

Soviet assumptions and calculations regarding international affairs and international security are often difficult to establish with any measure of certainty. To a far greater degree than is true in regard to the United States, the outside observer (or, for that matter, probably a Soviet scholar too) faces a number of serious obstacles in seeking to identify a Soviet mindset (or, more likely, the several relevant mindsets of Soviet political analysts and decision makers). The same difficulties arise in identifying Soviet objectives, as well as the underlying beliefs concerning the international system and the United States in general and Soviet security policies in particular.

In significant measure this is due to the gap—whose width there is no precise way to gauge—between "ideological" formulations, on the one hand, and operational behavior and decisions, on the other; and also to the gap between public pronouncements and private calculus. It is due as well to the unadvertised and unacknowledged changes in Soviet operating assumptions over time. It is compounded by the inadequacy of the available sources, Soviet and non-Soviet alike; by our lack of access to Soviet decision makers with whom one might knowledgeably and seriously discuss some of these questions; by the not infrequent limitations—be it bias, linguistic inadequacy, hostility, or misunderstanding—of foreigners who have dealt with Soviet diplomats on security matters; and by the uncertainty as to whether or not there is a close fit between Soviet academic views and arguments (about which we know a good deal) and those of Soviet policymakers (about which we know very little). Important though it has been in other areas of public affairs, the recently touted *glasnost'* has scarcely extended to security affairs. All this points up the need for a separate discussion here of the Soviet side of our equation.

TRENDS AND TENDENCIES

To put the problem in its simplest and most extreme form: There is little doubt that the initial outlook of the Bolshevik leaders, in 1917, would have dismissed as ludicrous, naive, and "objectively subversive" the very notion of sustained Soviet cooperation with a leading capitalist state in matters involving the security and survival of the Soviet state. Any joint arrangement (such as the Treaty of Brest-Litovsk, in 1918) could be tactical, limited in scope, short-term, and instrumental at best; cooperation with your adversary that required relying for your very existence to some significant degree on your potential enemy's good will and playing by some set of "bourgeois" rules of the game, was unthinkable and suicidal.[1]

It is equally self-evident that in fact the Soviet authorities have negotiated and, as a matter of their own self-interest, have concluded a long list of agreements with other powers—some, of considerable importance, on matters involving international security. This is a trend that began even prior to World War II but has been particularly obvious in the years after Stalin's death, ranging across the fields of arms control, such as SALT I and II and the Non-Proliferation Treaty; territorial questions, such as Austria, Berlin, Laos, Antarctica, the Helsinki accord; and a variety of other issues as well.

How are we to explain this seeming contradiction? Some would try to accommodate these seemingly incompatible approaches and attitudes in the capacious—if amorphous—vessels labeled Russian (or Communist, or Soviet) political culture.[2] But such an effort registers, rather than explains, the apparent tension; it tends to write off the cultural baggage as immutable; and methodologically, "political culture" raises at least as many questions as it purports to answer. Ultimately, we cannot tell which elements are the product of Marxist-Leninist indoctrination, which should be attributed to centuries of authoritarian rule, which are to be ascribed to Russian backwardness, which to the "Tatar yoke," and which to Stalin; and, perhaps more important, we cannot tell under what conditions such a political culture may be changed. A more satisfactory explanation must be sought elsewhere, in an historical and situational approach.

In the seventy years since the October Revolution, Soviet Russia has been gradually transformed from a pariah state in the international system into one of the two superpowers. Its capabilities and its ambitions, as a state, have grown apace. Although initially they were among those who pressed for a reversal of the post-World War I settlement, during the mid-1930s Soviet leaders favored defending some part of the international status quo—at least insofar as it was being challenged by Hitler's Germany and its allies. World War II dramatized this orientation.

Since then the Soviet Union has become the second nuclear superpower, the hegemon in Eastern Europe, gradually acquiring a global reach and seeking to extend its influence and press its claims elsewhere in the world. Its military power, conventional and strategic, is probably second to none. The reasons for its military build-up are complex and have been amply discussed and debated elsewhere; so have its changing views of war as an instrument of policy, and nuclear war in particular.

For at least a generation now Moscow has asserted that no major problems in the world may be settled without its participation. Rather than being excluded from the councils of the mighty—as it was from the Paris Peace Conference and again at Munich, half a century ago—it strives to be engaged and involved everywhere: some have referred to the Soviet self-image as manifesting a global vocation.

Despite occasional blunders and missteps, this effort has been accompanied by a general Soviet tendency toward risk-aversion and an awareness of the limits of Soviet power (and indeed, most recently, a keen resentment of the stagnation now identified with the Brezhnev years). Especially with the successive change of generations among Soviet decision makers and foreign-affairs experts, we have witnessed the emergence of a new Soviet orientation stressing interdependence, mutuality, and a ''non-zero sum'' perspective in world affairs. Undoubtedly a consciousness of the potential destructiveness of nuclear weapons and of looming world problems—in such areas as energy, the environment, and epidemiology, for example—has contributed to a Soviet attitude that rejects self-isolation of the Stalin type. Also contributing to this attitude is the realization that there is much that the Soviet Union can achieve, procure, or learn jointly with the outside world that it cannot so easily, rapidly, or cheaply do alone; and a consciousness of the immensely stronger base from which the Soviet Union has been able to wield political and other forms of power abroad, including its ability to negotiate with its fellow superpower.

At the same time, the trend over time has been an unadvertised shrinking of communist ideological pretensions. From the early expectations and imagery of inevitable ''world revolution,'' Moscow has moved to greater realism and moderation: international communism has proved to be both a withering promise and a brittle and unreliable tool.

In turn, without any explicit surrender of earlier beliefs, the orthodox doctrinal perspective on world affairs has become much attenuated and increasingly ritualized—a trend that was both revealed and reinforced by the exchanges between the Soviet and Chinese leaderships in the early 1960s. Responding to Mao Ze-dong, who insisted that weapons technology could not arrest the inevitable course of the laws of history, Nikita Khrushchev remarked that in selecting their victims nuclear weapons did not follow the class principle.[3] After first proving unhelpful or worse in explaining or predicting trends in the developed West, ''class analysis'' turned out to be disappointing and misleading in the Third World as well. At the same time, the Marxist-Leninist orthodoxy has proved to be of little help to Soviet policy makers in dealing with ICBMs and SDI. Soviet acceptance of the notion of a ''mutual hostage posture'' (in SALT I) did not square with the assumptions of orthodox Leninism. Instead, Moscow has begun to assimilate and adapt to the complexities of the modern world.

In fact, in the process of interacting with the United States and other advanced societies, the Soviet Union appears to have unwittingly engaged in a significant process of learning. At the same time, the structuring of the foreign-policy and international-security agenda in the Kremlin has moved from the party bureaucrats and ideologists into the hands of more pragmatic and more expert professionals. This need not mean that the Soviet Union has been, or will be, easier to deal with or that its special objectives will disappear, yet this process too marks a noteworthy change.

In practice, it has not been the case that one orientation suddenly replaces an earlier one. If we think of one as the go-it-alone perspective based on the assumption of inevitable class and hence world conflict, and the other as the—perhaps reluctant—recognition of inevitable, if limited, international cooperation (as well as competition and perhaps conflict), it might be suggested that many leading Soviet actors have exhibited elements of both these orientations. Even more pronounced has been the functioning side by side of decision makers who fit primarily in one or the other camp. Stalin could use a Litvinov, after a fashion, despite—or precisely because of—their profoundly divergent mindsets, but beyond 1946 he would not tolerate him. Khrushchev and Molotov represented fundamentally contrasting approaches to world affairs: the showdown between them in 1955 (as illustrated in Kurt Steiner's Austrian case study) symbolizes the gradual prevalence of the more complex, interactive orientation over the primitive, isolationist. The later mindset, despite zigzags, would find expression both in the Soviet calculus that led to détente and again in the foreign-policy initiatives of Mikhail Gorbachev.

Often, then, one might expect to find side by side (or even in the same Soviet negotiator or decision maker) elements of both these approaches. (Not that such incompatibilities have been unknown within American administrations or even in individual key actors.) This finding—while it conflicts with the conventional stereotype of a single set of Soviet assumptions and signals, hierarchically passed down from the top—is reinforced by the evidence of the simultaneous existence—indeed, advocacy—of different Soviet images of the outside world, and in particular of the United States and of Soviet-American relations. Different sets of images, it has been shown, often serve to inform and reinforce different policy priorities in Moscow.[4]

The preceding discussion might help to establish why, despite stereotypes to the contrary, in the Soviet case we lack a credible, single, coherent, authoritative view of the international system and international security. Indeed, at different times different Soviet actors have adopted significantly divergent positions, for example, on such questions as whether a stable international system is desirable, or whether one can "do serious business"—say, in the arms control field—with the United States.

THE SOVIET VIEW OF INTERNATIONAL SECURITY

While the subject deserves more thorough and detailed analysis than it can be given here, it appears clear that the Soviet view of security has evolved considerably over time. On the one hand, it has become more explicit, more systematic, and more professional.[5] In 1950 international security would be discussed and defined in Moscow, at least publicly, by a small clique consisting largely of party officials, mostly rigid in outlook and scarcely knowledgeable about world affairs; in 1980 it would be analyzed and commented on by several constituencies, including academics, military officers, diplomats, and journalists, typically more competent and in some cases more open-minded than their predecessors.

No less important, the fundamental orientation has begun to change. It has been remarked that for Stalin, Soviet security was essentially a function of everyone else's insecurity. For Gorbachev, Soviet security presupposes a sense of security not only for allies of the Soviet Union but also for its adversaries: as he remarked, there can be "no security for the USSR without security for the United States."[6] True, that rhetoric remains to be translated into consistent conduct; yet the gulf between past and present concepts informing Soviet policy choices could scarcely be more profound.

Tactically, the Soviets could seek security in a number of different ways—by going it alone or by alliances, by building up military might or by appeasement of adversaries, by deterrence or by bluffing, by stimulating revolutions in the enemy camp or by arming clients, by self-isolation or by international agreements, or by a combination of the above. But the Soviet strategic perspective was traditionally to equate security with control—and, in its most concrete application, territorial control: political dominance based on military power.

Here, over time, the accents have shifted. The instinct for territorial control dies only slowly and with difficulty, but it surely has weakened, if only because the Soviet leadership has understood that the risks and costs of expansion have risen (as the fighting in Afghanistan has dramatically brought home to the Kremlin) and because in an age of jets, ICBMs, and Chernobyls, real estate hardly represents a fair measure either of power or of security. By the same token, the Stalinist instinct for isolating Soviet society, the Soviet economy, Soviet science, and Soviet thought from the outside world is gradually being shed as not only a costly but a disastrous prescription. Though the sense of interdependence with the outside world is still fragile and, in some sense, largely rhetorical, the confrontational assumptions have begun to slip. "From insulation to interdependence" is the span that Soviet conceptions have traversed—not for everyone in Moscow, to be sure, nor irreversibly, but at least for the dominant policymakers and their attentive constituencies.

Not unrelated has been the recognition, growing in the course of the post-Stalin decades, that international security is not a "zero-sum" game (a world inevitably divided between "us" and "them," as the whole Leninist tradition led Soviet theorists and practitioners alike to expect), but on the contrary involves a perceived mutuality of interests in at least some issue areas (several of which are illustrated in the case studies in this volume). Such a deepening sense of the positive "non-zero sum" approach still encounters impatient hostility and incomprehension in some Soviet quarters, provoking charges of "surrender" and "appeasement" (as it does at times in the United States as well). Moreover, if such an insight has spurred Soviet flexibility in some areas of arms control negotiations, it has not informed, and need not inform, all Soviet conduct or objectives in all other security-related negotiations.

Finally, the Soviet perspective has gradually shifted from seeking instability in the largely hostile international system to preferring predictability and order in an environment of which its leaders increasingly wish to see themselves as major actors. Indeed, there are good indications that the Gorbachev leadership is concerned precisely about the unpredictable international security environment which American advances in weapons technology—including spinoffs of SDI—are apt to produce in the years ahead.

Much of this change in authoritative Soviet thinking has been an unacknowledged process. Except for some of the more obvious (and propagandistically useful) reformulations about the necessity of avoiding nuclear war, the changes have not been explicitly advertised in Moscow as doctrinal revisions and they have often been underestimated abroad. At the same time, they cannot all be taken to be entirely irreversible, and of course they have not in fact removed all the difficulties in Soviet-American dealings, even those for which the Soviet side has primary responsibility.

TOWARD A SOVIET "OPERATIONAL CODE"?

Typically, the search for negotiated understandings with its principal adversary or adversaries on the world scene has been subordinate to unilateral action in the Soviet pursuit of international security, although in the Soviet perception the relative importance of security regimes has varied considerably over time. In fact, Soviet specialists on world affairs might agree with the proposition that unilateral behavior of each of the two superpowers (or their alliance systems) has been the single most important ingredient in making deterrence work throughout the second half of this century.

But insofar as security negotiations are concerned, at times the Soviet Union has chosen to act first and then to confront its adversary with a *fait accompli,* either as a substitute for or as a prelude to negotiations. At times it has introduced proposals that were palpably intended as propaganda (the General and Complete Disarmament proposals of the Khruschev era are some of the most obvious examples). At other times, the boundary between propaganda and "serious" negotiating purpose has been hard to define. Indeed, the two objectives need not be mutually exclusive, as is demonstrated by the Soviet proposal for total elimination of nuclear weapons by the year 2000. At times (as several of the preceding studies show) Soviet negotiating behavior appears to have reflected a decision that stalling was preferable to any possible change in the status quo. From Stalin's days to the present, bluffing under conditions of maximum secrecy—primarily by pretending to deal from greater strength than the facts warranted, or concealing critical weaknesses—has been standard operating procedure, and never more so than in the days of Nikita Khrushchev. Albeit in different proportions, other states have naturally exhibited similar characteristics.

If, eschewing such generalities, we seek to distill from our repertoire of cases some traits that might be called distinctive elements of a Soviet "operational code,"[7] several salient characteristics deserve attention.*

1. Soviet policy has typically exhibited, over the years, a strong sense of "first things first," being grounded in a broad authoritative definition—no matter whether right or wrong, doctrinally pretentious or pragmatically informed—of the "nature of the epoch" or, more usefully, of the strategic priorities for the present and the years immediately ahead. Typically, this has been based on an elaborate assessment of the "correlation of forces" on a world scale. Such an exposition of overriding priorities entails making policies at all subordinate levels congruent with them. Examples abound from the Soviet past, be it in the "popular front" and "collective security" era, or the "ultraleft" swing, or the relentless isolation of the Soviet population from the outside world, down to more recent zigzags in policy toward China and the United States. Typically, the overriding priority becomes a broad political objective, such as the forging of a new alliance system, or a new attempt to mobilize friends and neutrals against a perceived common foe, or the improvement of relations with the rival superpower.

The fate of particular security arrangements abroad has been influenced in important ways by the broader context and the dominant orientation of Soviet foreign policy. Examples abound in the cases examined in the preceding chapters. The prospects of an Austrian settlement were greatly enhanced by the victory of the Khrushchev orientation, which favored a settlement of pending issues, in the aftermath of Stalin's death. The Antarctica Treaty came about when Soviet scientists were again allowed to travel abroad. The Berlin accord in 1971 came at a time when the Brezhnev leadership was eager to improve relations, first with the European West, and then with the United States—a course that culminated in the Nixon-Kissinger visit to Moscow in 1972. As our contributors have established, both the Helsinki and the Stockholm accords benefitted from the priority Moscow assigned, just prior to their conclusion, to an improvement of relations with the United States and its allies; a similar consideration is identified as one of the facets in the MFBR talks and unilateral overhead reconnaissance technology. The limited test ban treaty and the "hotline" agreement were negotiated when, in the aftermath of the Cuban missile crisis, Khrushchev hoped to compensate for his rift with China by an improvement of relations with the United States, just as (according to Joseph Nye)

---

*This section makes no effort to provide an exhaustive listing of such features.

the Chinese factor played a part in the Soviet agreement to the Non-Proliferation Treaty.

Though significant, this relationship between a specific accord and a broader Soviet policy of seeking cooperation need not always be a precondition for agreement (the nonproliferation treaty came at a time of deteriorating superpower relations); nor does it guarantee a successful outcome of negotiations (apparently the time has never yet been ripe for an MBRF agreement; and regional security issues—for instance, in the Middle East—have typically defied all efforts at bilateral resolution). Nor of course does this nexus imply Soviet indifference to the specific terms of agreement. But, everything else being equal, a propitious context of Soviet foreign-policy priorities has repeatedly made—and may again make—a crucial difference between success and failure in security negotiations.

Just what constitutes such a "propitious" context remains to be explored more precisely. The available cases point overwhelmingly to a congruence between a particular agreement and the dominant thrust of Soviet foreign policy orientations and initiatives. With the possible exception of the settlement of the Cuban missile crisis—an exceptional case indeed—not a single agreement to date appears to be the result of pressure successfully exerted or threats made by the United States to secure Soviet acceptance of terms otherwise rejected or deemed unacceptable by the USSR.

On the other hand, negotiations may be influenced by both sides' perceptions of parity (either in particular weapons systems or, more broadly, in strategic power) or by the effort of either side to match the other's assumed advantage in research and development (for instance, in ICBMs or anti-ballistic missile systems). Nor should we ignore the importance of efforts by the United States to change the international environment—for instance, by normalizing relations with China in the 1970s—as one way to make Moscow more inclined to negotiate with greater speed and flexibility.

2. Soviet behavior also exhibits a rather consistent bias in favor of a broad political, rather than technical, approach to problem solving. In contrast to a widespread American tendency to look for apolitical "solutions," the typical Soviet approach (as Barry Blechman convincingly points out) has been skeptical of such devices as "risk reduction centers" to be established in both Moscow and Washington, if these were to be staffed by citizens of the "other" superpower. Even when agreeing to explore and negotiate such proposals, Moscow has usually regarded them as frivolous gimmickry, suggesting a flight from "serious" (i.e., political) issues.

Moscow has been equally reluctant to deal with neutral abstractions such as crisis prevention: in the Soviet view (as Alexander George argues elsewhere) its pursuit would deprive Soviet policy of opportunities and would place a higher value on the avoidance of crises than on the pursuit of Soviet objectives.

Similarly, Soviet negotiators have been characteristically leery of pursuing such techniques as dealing with a complex problem piecemeal and trying to find solutions to individual parts; such an approach, in the Soviet view, tends to lose sight of the dominant political essence of a given problem. Rather than negotiating such piecemeal arrangements, what needs modifying—the Soviet approach suggests—is the underlying outlook on the other side.

This likewise applies to Western attempts to formulate "rules of conduct." As Yevgeny Primakov, an influential Soviet academic and policy adviser, wrote in regard to the Middle East:

"Rules of conduct," however thoroughly thought over, agreed upon in detail, and linked to specific situations, cannot serve as an alternative to an overall settlement. This should also be emphasized because there is a strong trend in American political sciences to concentrate on the formulation of rules of conduct, which are regarded as a panacea even against a situation threatening war. . . .[8]

Substance, in other words, must not be sacrificed to process.

While this has been the dominant Soviet orientation, it stands not without exceptions; indeed, it may have begun to crumble. It has not prevented agreement on a White House-Kremlin "hotline" (and its technological upgrading later), as Blechman's chapter shows. As far back as 1969 it was the Soviet side that raised the technical questions regarding the prevention of accidental or unintended nuclear exchanges. The "Incidents at Sea" agreement belongs in this category. Moreover, the Stockholm agreement in 1986 did—in a different international setting—show Soviet interest in enacting certain types of "confidence-building measures" without resolving underlying political questions, presumably because Stockholm marked an extension of the Helsinki process favored by the USSR. Perhaps the modest agreement concerning "risk-reduction centers" reported in May 1987 is another case in point. Once again the broader context of Soviet-American relations and, in the case of Stockholm, the multilateral setting no doubt contributed to this switch.

3. There is also a rather persistent pattern that reveals a far stronger Soviet interest in, and desire for, declaratory policy than have been true for U.S. foreign-policy making. The "Basic Principles" adopted at the Nixon-Brezhnev summit in 1972 are perhaps the outstanding example, but other instances abound.[9]

It has been impossible to find an entirely satisfactory explanation for this proclivity. On the face of it, one might expect the lingering effects of Bolshevik suspicion of "scraps of paper" signed by imperialist statesmen to militate against taking seriously any pronouncements of principles or any declaratory promises. But, unlike the American reluctance to make any sweeping commitments to ethical universals in dealing with foreign powers, Soviet negotiators seem eager, time and again, to enshrine rhetorical achievements in formal pronouncements, be it recognition of superpower parity or abjuring the use of force in the resolution of disputes. Soviet analysts and negotiators must realize that such pronouncements do not in fact alter the balance of forces one iota; nor would they inhibit either side in a major crisis. But presumably the symbolic political effect is deemed worth the effort, which Western negotiators have often had some difficulty in taking seriously. Moscow must value the inhibitions that such verbal commitments may impose on the other side. At times, to be sure, the anticipated Soviet gain is somewhat more specific, as was true of the implicit (or expected) recognition of East European boundaries in the Helsinki Accord of 1975.

4. Soviet negotiating techniques have been the subject of a number of American studies and memoirs.[10] It would go too far to summarize them here, but—allowing for oversimplifications and exaggerations—no doubt there was a basis in fact for the immobility, chicanery, stalling, and studied insensitivity of Soviet negotiators often reported by foreign interlocutors and observers. Soviet negotiating behavior has all too often been marked by a self-righteous refusal to take seriously the other side's arguments, and by a stubborn self-serving commitment to extreme and at times unrealistic positions. The instinct of Soviet political and military planners has frequently tended toward totalist "solutions" and toward worst-case assumptions in attributing motives and capabilities to potential adversaries. Even when "equal security" became the

watchword, the phrase remained strikingly devoid of operational content. It remains to be seen whether this will be equally true of the "new political thinking" of the Gorbachev years.

What also deserves mention, however, is that all this is not, and need not, always be the case. There is also the fact that when they are so instructed, Soviet negotiators have had the skill and the will to reach agreements with remarkable speed. This was true in the Soviet-German talks in August 1939 that produced both a nonaggression pact and a secret partition of Eastern Europe, and in the Stalin-Churchill "percentages agreement" on the Balkans reached in October 1944; it was true in the limited test ban negotiations in 1963. It may yet apply to the proposals made by Mikhail Gorbachev in 1986–87, which suddenly reversed a number of Soviet negotiating positions (for instance, on on-site inspection, and on medium- and short-range missiles in Europe); although more than once in recent years Soviet negotiators in Geneva have markedly lagged behind the changing terms and proposals enunciated in Moscow.

Moreover, the change of generations among Soviet diplomats has recently brought to the fore a cohort that is more subtle, more informed, more familiar with the language and style of their opposite numbers than were their predecessors. The new negotiators are sometimes provided with instructions allowing them more flexibility, and are therefore able to respond to different negotiating situations with a wider range of signals than had been true before. Of course, this tendency is neither universal nor irreversible, and there are reasons to think that it is easier for the decision makers in Moscow to proclaim dramatic shifts in negotiating positions than for their subordinates to implement these proclamations in dealing with their negotiating partners.*

5. Another area that deserves attention but—virtually by definition—lacks hard data is that of tacit understandings between the superpowers. What is meant here are not secret deals struck that were perhaps not formally codified (the Churchill-Stalin "percentages agreement" had some such characteristics) but rather similar or parallel assumptions shared by the two sides.

For some years it seemed plausible to assume that both Moscow and Washington were in fact operating on the basis of some spheres-of-interest axioms even while verbally denouncing them. The United States refrained from intervening militarily in Eastern Europe when the Soviet Union used force, or threatened to use force, in Hungary, Czechoslovakia, and Poland; and much of the American rhetoric with regard to Cuba, Grenada, and Nicaragua was couched in terms of their proximity to the United States and their importance to U.S. concerns. The Soviet Union's caution in regard to Central America suggests some similar appreciation on the Soviet side. But the "terms" and the boundaries of such tacit understandings are inevitably vague, and their perceived "violations" by either side can scarcely be protested. Thus Soviet intervention in Afghanistan manifestly went beyond its tacitly accepted sphere even if Moscow correctly surmised that there would be no direct American counterintervention. On the other hand,

---

*On the other hand, what had long been an accepted Soviet practice—the use of informal and "back channels" to explore the possibility of negotiated settlements—appears to have come to an end. Such explorations—for instance, in the Nazi-Soviet talks in the summer of 1939, in the Jessup-Malik talks that led to the end of the Berlin blockade in 1948, in the efforts in Washington to end the Cuban missile crisis in 1962, and on other occasions—took place with the obvious approval of the highest Soviet authorities. One reason for their termination was the withdrawal of Ambassador Anatoli Dobrynin from Washington in 1985. Another may have been the effort of the Soviet Foreign Ministry to reassert tighter control over the conduct of foreign policy. There is no reason to think that Moscow would in principle be unwilling to renew such informal feelers or launch new trial balloons in the future.

in most other instances the Soviet Union's restraint in the use of armed forces and weapons beyond its boundaries (and those of its allies) does suggest a measure of risk-aversion that implies the expectation of reciprocity.

The inevitable lack of precision and lack of enforcement mechanisms are among the reasons why tacit understandings—more easily arrived at than formally negotiated documents—ultimately cannot commend themselves to Soviet policymakers as substitutes for more binding accords (or, for that matter, for full freedom of action), least of all in the security realm.

CONSTRAINTS AND LINKAGES

In addition to its chronic (through lessening) misperception of events in the outside world, perhaps the single most serious variable constraining and shaping the conduct of Soviet foreign policy generally, and security policy in particular, has been domestic politics, Soviet style. Usually kept out of public view, and therefore often denied at home and ignored abroad, Soviet elite and bureaucratic politics are concerned not only with power and jurisdictional rivalries but also with characteristic differences over policies and priorities. Granted that, typically, foreign and security issues have been less frequent sources of dispute than domestic issues, the former have nonetheless figured prominently for at least two reasons: 1.) there has frequently been a close connection between domestic and foreign policy preferences of particular actors, and 2.) over the past generation the salience of foreign and security issues has increased.[11]

It is true that in many instances our knowledge of specific alignments in the Soviet leadership is highly imperfect. This was particularly true in the Stalin days. In his chapter on the Postdam agreement, David Schoenbaum reminds us of the divisions and changes of policy in Moscow over postwar policy toward Germany. It is still not certain whether they pitted higher against lower officials (a hypothesis supported by some American participants) or civilian (party) against military elements, and/or whether some leading Soviet personalities simply changed their minds as the war approached its end and as inter-Allied relations began to deteriorate.

In other instances the picture is clearer. Reference was made earlier to the Khrushchev-Molotov dispute over foreign policy in 1955, in which the Austrian question was but one of a number of issues separating two distinct views, each reasonably consistent across a number of cases. Indeed, in this instance what was involved was not only the specific case of Austria but also a shifting view of both security and neutrality. Was greater control of territory to be equated with greater security, or was its denial to the adversary a warrant of sufficient security? Was neutrality no longer to be seen as immoral and inimical? Interestingly, both these questions had also been confronted by American analysts.

As Jonathan Dean appropriately shows, the Berlin settlement in 1969–71 similarly coincided with the resolution of a policy debate in Moscow that was triggered by the expectation of superpower parity in strategic weapons. The outcome of the debate was to have implications across the board, from resource allocation decisions and the abandonment of autarchy in Soviet economic and technological development, to the search for know-how, credits, goods, and services abroad in preference to a destabilizing restructuring of Soviet institutions at home.[12]

In 1986–87, it seems clear, the announcement of Soviet consent to on-site inspection in arms control agreements (albeit thus far untested by the American side for reasons of their own) was the outcome of a dispute between the traditionalists who equated security with secrecy, and those modernizers who saw greater benefit in openness, here as in other areas of Soviet life.

Undoubtedly there have been many cases of Soviet elite conflicts relevant to the issues discussed in this volume, which have remained unknown to the uninitiated. Though perhaps to a lesser degree than in Washington since the mid-1970s, such disputes have probably accounted for some stalling and irresolution in negotiations. In other cases, such differences on the Soviet side have apparently not had much bearing on official policy. The Paul Nitze-Yuli Kvitsinsky "walk in the woods" during the 1982 INF negotiations in Geneva was condemned in Moscow as it was in Washington (though on both sides the "perpetrators" remained in their administrations' relatively good graces) and did not alter the established policy. Time and again (especially in recent years, when Soviet diplomats and academics have been more relaxed in talking with foreigners) it has become clear that negotiators do not necessarily agree with the official positions or negotiating instructions that have come down from Moscow, but (as is probably almost as true in other establishments) are typically well advised to keep their reservations to themselves.

Only in the Gorbachev era have differences of opinion on foreign policy begun, slowly and cautiously, to be ventilated in the public media. The questions raised have included whether to go to Reykjavik in October 1986, whether Soviet intervention in Afghanistan had been a mistake, and whether Moscow had miscalculated in counting on West European opinion to oppose the deployment of Pershing IIs and cruise missiles in NATO countries. Still, security issues continue to be handled most gingerly by Soviet commentators who on other issues permit themselves a fair degree of independent judgment. Only a minor reason for this is the near-absence of Soviet civilian specialists on matters of international security who are conversant with the entire technical arsenal of Soviet and Western weapons systems and numbers.

In the Soviet case, one need hardly dwell on the importance of the individual leader. Stalin's self-satisfied inflexibility prevented not only the conclusion of particular agreements but more broadly, the adaptation of his state to the nuclear age. Khrushchev's impulsive improvisations opened the door both to fresh strategic thinking and to near-catastrophes such as the Cuban missile crisis. Gorbachev's accession to power has again changed the deck as well as the dealer.

At the same time, any leader is dependent on the advice of experts, especially in areas of relatively esoteric information, concerning science and weapons technology as well as obscure corners of the globe; over time the role of consultants has been institutionalized—first and foremost, through the Central Committee staff that structures and services the Politburo's agenda. The experts' access to the decision makers has been made easier—both through personal consultation and through the mechanism of *zapiski* (notes) passed up through bureaucratic channels—and the importance of their input has increased. It is not to belittle their role that we must also record the impression that the Politburo—and the Defense Council, customarily headed by the "number one" in the Soviet system—on occasion may ignore the advice of its expert consultants.

Typically, Soviet negotiators and staffs have had little latitude in doing their work. Key decisions are normally made back in Moscow and, in matters of national importance, at the very top. This is not to deny that the bureaucracy can—and does—drag its feet and officials can—and do—try to stack the deck. Most important in matters of international security is of course the state of civil-military relations.

There is a good deal of circumstantial and anecdotal evidence to support the view that—especially on matters relating to arms control—senior military commanders have more than once voiced reservations or objections to the agreements being negotiated. This may have been true when the partial test ban was concluded in 1963; it was apparently true at the Brezhnev-Ford meeting in Vladivostok; as James Goodby reports in this volume, this was the case even at the Stockholm talks; and there is good reason to think that there was objection on the part of some military commanders to the extension of the Soviet moratorium on nuclear testing in 1986. (See the chapter by Gloria Duffy on questions relating to compliance with arms control agreements.) Other such instances may yet come to light. Naturally, the whole conception of a future war, as presented by the marshals and admirals, has a direct bearing on Soviet research and development, procurement, and deployment and thus impacts the negotiation of mutual constraints.

Any competent leader, in Moscow or Washington, will want to consult "his" military chiefs and make sure to have them on board in concluding sensitive security agreements. In fact, given (at least, until recently) the paucity of Soviet civilian expertise on arms control and weapons issues, it appears that the party leadership has typically required—in fact, depended on—a substantial military input into relevant decision making, both informational and judgmental. Yet this does not seem to have provoked major political crises.

The Soviet experience to date suggests that in the end the uniformed commanders accept the principle and practice of civilian supremacy even when they do not like particular policy choices. The public visibility of the Soviet marshals has varied greatly, even in recent years. No doubt they have contributed powerfully to the internal debates. Individuals such as Marshal Georgi Zhukov in the 1950s and Marshal Nikolai Ogarkov in the 1980s have found themselves on the outs but to date there is no indication of any attempt by the armed forces to impose their will or defy the country's civilian leadership. The prompt and unceremonious ouster of Marshal Sergei Sokolov as Minister of Defense and Politburo candidate member in May 1987, in reaction to a West German teenager's unimpeded flight of a Cessna to Red Square, only underscored the civilians' continued preponderance.

Changes in Soviet negotiating positions, including those that ultimately make agreements possible, have often been associated with—or, more precisely, preceded by—changes in Soviet decision-making or diplomatic personnel, especially of course when these have represented different policy orientations. We have seen the difference that the replacement of a Chernenko by a Gorbachev can make; inversely, the ouster of a Khrushchev led to a period of marking time and stalling while his successors sorted out their priorities. At the foreign minister level, the replacement of a Molotov and, more recently, of a Gromyko opened the door to a new flexibility and dynamism even while the losers were still part of the official Soviet family. Changes in the policy-making process and in the institutions involved in it may also make a difference in the conduct of security negotiations.

In the perception of Soviet policymakers there are various domestic factors that affect the negotiating stance in security arrangements. Resource constraints are perhaps the most obvious. An awareness of the total "defense burden," some observers have argued, may similarly help shape Soviet reactions to arms control proposals. However, insofar as they are significant, such variables figure only as they are mediated through the perception of the responsible actors and their advisers. Over the whole range of negotiated security arrangements, over the course of nearly half a century, it is difficult to generalize about continuities on this score.

Indeed, it is this time dimension that makes it difficult to discern lasting patterns or permanent predilections on the Soviet side: American observers may well have taken far too much for granted a continuity of Soviet impulse, outlook, and style.

What remains is the pertinent but perhaps unanswerable question whether, in view of the many strains on the Soviet system, Soviet leaders can be counted on to carry out obligations they have assumed by the terms of international security agreements. The answer may hinge on contingent and unknowable developments, but it may be reasonable to assume that the authorities in Moscow are bound to maintain sufficient control over politics and resources to be able to live up to their commitments—if they so desire.

LEARNING AND THE GORBACHEV ERA

Notwithstanding the insistence—by both Soviet and anti-Soviet commentators—on the unchanging characteristics of the Soviet state, a look at Soviet conduct and outlook over time reveals, in addition to the obvious continuities and changes, one other major feature: a continual process of learning. As I suggested earlier, the Gorbachev era in particular provides an interesting example, not only of behavioral but also of cognitive learning; and one of the most important areas in which Soviet leaders and scholars have claimed to be embarked on "new thinking" is precisely international affairs, including problems of international security.

Perhaps not surprisingly, given both Soviet behavior and the public image created by government propaganda and the media over the years, the Western public has been much bedeviled by the doubt, fed by repeated earlier disappointments, whether these changes in Soviet rhetoric are "genuine"—that is, whether they reflect a change in outlook and policy objectives as a result of a process of learning or whether they are meant to impress "useful idiots" abroad with the pretense of Soviet reasonableness and moderation.

Whatever our individual convictions on this score, the only proper response to such proposals is to test them in the process of negotiations. To dismiss them a priori as "mere propaganda" or "grandstanding," is not only to prejudge the issue but to risk missing valuable opportunities—to close "windows of opportunity" that may not long stay open. If, moreover, the new climate and the new insights should make for a more benign setting for negotiated agreements, their success would in turn anchor the acceptance of the "new thinking" more solidly on the Soviet side as well.

Perhaps in the Soviet case in particular it is well to be mindful of the possibility of "unlearning"—and of learning the wrong lessons. It is reasonable to assume that a good deal of private learning is going on that is not publicly acknowledged. For instance, the perceived shortcomings of orthodox Marxism-Leninism for a realistic understanding of world affairs will be indirectly recognized but cannot be fully spelled out. Given the nature of public life in the Soviet Union, there more than elsewhere the critical, distinctive learning is done by individuals, not by the "system." When it comes to "government learning" or "organizational learning" in the West,[13] in the Soviet case the insights or lessons learned by individuals are apt to be "unlearned" as far as public institutions are concerned when there is a change in their core personnel. Discontinuities in mindset and hence in ensuing middle-range objectives and policy are most readily identified with individual changes at the top of the Soviet machine, and without a doubt alternative Soviet sub-elites tend to represent and promote a far more closed, conventional, and fundamentalist outlook on international security.

The Soviets can be—and have been—difficult to deal with, on security problems as on others. In significant ways their outlook, their underlying assumptions, and their style have differed from those of American policy makers and negotiators. But to explain Soviet behavior we scarcely need posit the decisive role of various esoteric belief systems—be it medieval Muscovite folkways, Byzantine or Tatar political culture, or Marxist-Leninist dogmatism—that have at times been invoked. An awareness of Russia's historical experience—its past backwardness, protracted isolation, and the impact of Stalinism—and a recognition of the instrumental payoff of certain techniques, such as secretiveness and reiteration, can help us understand some of the "peculiarities" of Soviet behavior. But if our analysis is right, their role and weight have in fact begun to shrink to a significant degree.

That trend, welcome though it is, will not by itself assure international security or concord. Indeed, great expectations risk once again being dashed. But, provided it persists and deepens, the trend might substantially improve the prospects for bringing about a more stable superpower relationship—if the United States knows how to make the most of the opportunities it provides.

Notes

1. For a collection of references to early Soviet sources, see for instance Timothy A. Taracouzio, *The Soviet Union and International Law* (New York: Macmillan, 1935).

2. On Soviet political culture, see e.g., Archie Brown, ed., *Political Culture and Communist Studies* (Armonk, N.Y.: M. E. Sharpe, 1985); and Stephen White, *Political Culture and Soviet Politics* (New York: St. Martin's Press, 1979).

3. Open Letter of the CPSU Central Committee, *Pravda* (July 14, 1963).

4. See Franklyn Griffiths, "The Sources of American Conduct: Soviet Perspectives and Their Policy Implications," in *International Security,* vol. 9, no. 2 (Fall 1984).

5. On the Soviet view of international security, see Helmut Sonnenfeldt and William G. Hyland, "Soviet Perspectives on Security," *Adelphi Papers,* no. 150 (London: IISS, 1979); David Holloway, "Military Power and Political Purpose in Soviet Policy," in *Daedalus* (Fall 1980); See also Jiri Valenta and William Potter, eds., *Soviet Decisionmaking for National Security* (London: Allen & Unwin, 1984); S. Neil MacFarlane, "The Soviet Conception of Regional Security," *World Politics* (April 1985); Michael MccGwire, *Military Objectives in Soviet Foreign Policy* (Washington, D.C.: Brookings, 1987).

6. *Pravda* (February 8, 1986).

7. On the concept of an "operational code," as used here, see Alexander L. George, "The 'Operational Code': A Neglected Approach to the Study of Political Leaders and Decision-Making," *International Studies Quarterly,* vol. 13, no. 2 (June 1969).

8. Yevgeny Primakov, "The Soviet Union's Interests: Myths and Reality," *AEI Foreign Policy and Defense Review,* 1986, no. 1, p. 30.

9. See Alexander L. George, "The Basic Principles Agreement of 1972: Origins and Expectations," in his *Managing U.S.–Soviet Rivalry* (Boulder, Colo.: Westview Press, 1983), pp. 107–117.

10. Works (of uneven value) dealing with Soviet negotiating techniques and styles include Raymond Dennett, ed., *Negotiating with the Russians* (Boston: World Peace Foundation, 1951);

Joseph G. Whelan, ed., *Soviet Diplomacy and Negotiating Behavior* (Washington, D.C.: Library of Congress, Congressional Research Service, 1979; also Boulder, Colo.: Westview Press, 1983); Leon Sloss and M. Scott Davis, *A Game for High Stakes: Lessons Learned in Negotiating with the Soviet Union* (Cambridge, Mass.: Ballinger, 1986); Edward Rowney, "The Soviets are still Russians," in *Survey,* no. 111 (Spring 1980); Christer Jönsson, *Soviet Bargaining Behavior: The Nuclear Test Ban Case* (N.Y.: Columbia University Press, 1979). See also Raymond Garthoff, *Detente and Confrontation* (Washington, D.C.: Brookings, 1985).

11. See Alexander Dallin, "The Domestic Sources of Soviet Foreign Policy," in Seweryn Bialer, ed., *The Domestic Context of Soviet Foreign Policy* (Boulder, Colo.: Westview Press, 1981).

12. See e.g., Bialer, ed., *The Domestic Context of Soviet Foreign Policy;* George W. Breslauer, *Khrushchev and Brezhnev as Leaders* (London: Allen & Unwin, 1984); Peter M. E. Volten, *Brezhnev's Peace Program* (Boulder, Colo.: Westview Press, 1982).

13. See e.g., Lloyd S. Etheridge, *Government Learning* (Cambridge, Mass.: MIT Press, 1979); Hugh Heclo, *Modern Social Politics* (New Haven, Conn.: Yale University Press, 1974); and Robert Axelrod, ed., *Structure of Decision* (Princeton, N.J.: Princeton University Press, 1976).

25

Arms Control and U.S.–Soviet Security Cooperation

PHILIP J. FARLEY

Arms control is a major strand in post-World War II efforts by the United States and the Soviet Union to introduce elements of cooperation into their security relationship. The other major strand, as reflected in the case studies in this volume, is European security. They are interwoven to a considerable degree.

The United States and the USSR have been and are the principal actors in postwar arms control, as befits their status as by far the leading military powers. They are by no means the only actors, even if their bilateral arms control negotiations and their often uneasy accords are the most conspicuous. In the current imperfect international system, comprising over 160 sovereign states subject to no higher authority, arms control is a principal means of gradually enhancing and extending international order in the interests of international peace and security. Here arms control is likely to be part of broader political efforts, even more than in U.S.–Soviet security relations. In such multilateral settings, U.S. and Soviet security interests often clash less directly, and even converge, as we have seen in some of the earlier chapters and will discuss further below.

A brief overview of arms control efforts and results to date—by no means all of which are dealt with even incidentally in our case studies—is the first step in appraising the significance of arms control for U.S.–Soviet security relations and cooperation. Table 1 lists arms control negotiations and agreements, all but one (the Geneva Protocol of 1925) post-World War II. Those examined in our study in detail are identified by an asterisk (*), and those treated only incidentally by double asterisks (**). Of twenty-four negotiated agreements, eleven are bilateral in form; but for several of the thirteen multilateral agreements (including the Limited Test Ban Treaty, the Biological Weapons Convention, even the Non-Proliferation Treaty) U.S.–Soviet bilateral negotiations either preceded or paced the over-all negotiations. Of the four failed negotiations three were bilateral and only one (the comprehensive test ban negotiations) was trilateral (though the third party, the United Kingdom, is a close partner of the United States in nuclear weapons development and testing). Of ongoing negotiations, three are multilateral; the fourth (the Geneva nuclear-space talks), while bilateral in form, involves basic interests of U.S. NATO allies and continuous close consultation with them.

The groupings in the table are designed to highlight arms control purposes and motivations, but are somewhat arbitrary, with important overlap and interrelations. U.S. and Soviet interests and roles in the negotiations and agreements, and the implications for U.S.–Soviet security cooperation, call for systematic comment, as follows.

TABLE 1. Arms Control Agreements and Negotiations

I. *Negotiated Agreements*	*Negotiated*	*In force for U.S.*	*Signatories (end 1985)*
A. *Ban or Limitation on Use of Specified Weapons*			
**1. Geneva Protocol	1925	1975	130
2. Convention & Protocols on Inhumane & Indiscriminate Conventional Weapons	1980	1982 (Signed but not ratified)	?
B. *"Preclusive" agreements* (banning deployments in new environments; banning specified new developments)			
*3. Antarctic Treaty	1959	1961	32
**4. Outer Space Treaty	1967	1967	123
**5. Latin American Nuclear Weapons Free Zone	1967	(1971 & 1981, protocols only)	32
*6. Non-Proliferation Treaty	1968	1970	136
7. Seabeds Arms Control Treaty	1971	1972	108
8. Environmental Modification Convention	1977	1978	72
9. South Pacific Nuclear Free Zone	1985	Rejected association 1987	13
C. *Risk Reduction Agreements*			
*10. U.S.–Soviet "Hotline" Agreement (Updated 1971 and 1984)	1963	1963	***2
*11. "Accidental Nuclear War" Agreement	1971	1971	2
*12. "Avoiding Incidents at Sea" Agreement	1972	1972	2
*13. Prevention of Nuclear War Agreement	1973	1973	2
*14. "Confidence Building" Measures, in Helsinki Accords on Security and Cooperation in Europe	1975	1975	35
*15. Agreement on Confidence Building and Security Measures in Europe	1986	1986	35
**16. Nuclear Risk Reduction Centers	1987	*(Ad referendum)*	2
D. *Arms Limitation/Reduction Agreements*			
*17. Limited Test Ban Treaty	1963	1963	127
*18. ABM Treaty	1972	1972	2
*19. Protocol to ABM Treaty	1974	1976	2
*20. SALT I Interim Agreement Limiting Offensive Arms	1972	1972 (Expired 1977)	2
*21. Threshold Test Ban Treaty	1974	—	2
*22. Underground PNE Treaty	1976	—	2
**23. Biological Weapons Convention	1972	1975	131
*24. SALT II	1979	— (Expired end of 1985)	2

TABLE 1. Arms Control Agreements and Negotiations _(Continued)_

I. _Negotiated Agreements_	_Negotiated_	_In force for U.S._	_Signatories (end 1985)_
II. _Failed Negotiations_			
	Began	_Composition_	_Ended_
*25. Comprehensive Test Ban	1958	UK–U.S.–USSR	1979
*26. Anti-satellite Weapons	1978	U.S.–USSR	1979
*27. Indian Ocean Naval Forces	1978	U.S.–USSR	1979
*28. Conventional Arms Transfers	1978	U.S.–USSR	1979
III. _Ongoing Negotiations_			
*29. Mutual Balanced Force Reductions in Europe (MBFR)	1975	NATO & Warsaw Pact Nations	
*30. Conference on Disarmament in Europe (CDE)	1984	Nations of East & West Europe Plus U.S. & Canada	
*31. START (Including strategic weapons, INF, and space arms)	1982	U.S.–USSR	
**32. Chemical Weapons Ban	1982	U.N. Committee on Disarmament, Geneva	

* Agreement discussed in separate chapter.
** Agreement incidentally discussed.
*** Similar agreements involve other nuclear powers.

Sources: Most texts can be found in _Arms Control and Disarmament Agreements_ (1982 edition, U.S. Government Printing Office), prepared by the U.S. Arms Control and Disarmament Agency; each is preceded by a brief negotiating history. Additional texts and history are contained in appendices to _International Arms Control: Issues and Agreements_, 2nd edition (Stanford, Calif.: Stanford University Press, 1984); and in _Nuclear Arms Control: Background and Issues_ (National Academy of Sciences Press, 1985). Signatories and parties are tabulated in the first named document, and supplemented annually in the ACDA annual reports to the Congress.

LIMITATIONS ON WEAPONS USE

Agreements in this category are best understood as examples of the Laws of War, rather than as arms control. Development, possession, and even deployment of the weapons in question are not limited—only the use. The use (in practice, the first use) may be _banned,_ as for chemical or biological weapons; or _regulated_ (as for mines or booby traps or incendiaries or certain exotic arms), with respect to emplacement, risk to civilian noncombatant population, etc. For comparison, other Laws of War deal with such things as treatment and protection of prisoners of war, or the status of noncombatants and medical personnel and hospitals. Since they concern actions in wartime, enforcement and verification possibilities are limited. The recourses include complaints to and investigation by the United Nations, deterrence by the threat of retaliation against weapons use, or "tit-for-tat" reaction for mistreatment of prisoners or noncombatants if appropriate.

In effect, then, in this category the agreements establish _norms of conduct_ in wartime. They supplement and extend others developed in the Hague convention and other international accords over the past century, often with active preparatory work under the sponsorship of the International Red Cross with governmental participation. After the conclusion of the Geneva Protocol of 1925, chemical weapons (CW) were not used in World War II, for mixed reasons including the influence of the Protocol, the fear of retaliation, and the perception of the limited likely military gains from use. Use of CW has occurred or been suspected in a number of less central conflicts, however—most recently in Vietnam, Southeast Asia, Afghanistan, and the Iran-Iraq conflict.

Actual or suspected violations have not tended to undermine the agreements. General outcries or protests, or official protests in the United Nations, have led to investigations to the extent feasible in wartime conditions, and on occasion to U.N. resolutions of condemnation. Criticism of U.S. use of tear gas and harassing agents in Vietnam, as well as use of defoliants and napalm not covered by the Geneva Protocol, contributed heavily to belated U.S. ratification of the Geneva Protocol in 1975 (the United States had taken the position earlier that it would follow its principles) and to U.S. participation in the negotiations on use of certain so-called inhumane or indiscriminate weapons. According to State Department reports, the Soviet Union appears to have been somewhat sensitive to charges of involvement in use of chemical and possibly even biological agents in Kampuchea and Afghanistan, as was inferred from the subsequent fading away of instances of suspected use. More generally, violation of these international norms of conduct has motivated heightened interest in negotiations to reinforce them by banning chemical weapons, and by interim actions to limit their acquisition, which is technically within the capability of any nation with modern chemical laboratories and plants.

The United States and Soviet Union are parties to the Geneva Protocol on the same footing as other nations. They are the principal nations with substantial admitted stocks of agents and means of delivery. The focus of our present inquiry is on the charges of Soviet violations of the Protocol as part of the U.S. case against the Soviets for deliberate and systematic noncompliance with arms control accords in the 1980s. The Protocol itself has not been brought into question.

PRECLUSIVE AGREEMENTS

The agreements in this category have in common that they attempt to anticipate threatening or destablizing trends in the development or spread of weapons, and to prevent or preclude them. Four have as their central purpose the blocking of the spread of nuclear weapons—the Latin American Nuclear Weapons Free Zone, the Non-Proliferation Treaty, the recent South Pacific Nuclear Free Zone, and the Seabed Arms Control Treaty (which bans stationing of either nuclear weapons or other weapons of mass destruction on the seabed or the ocean floor). The Antarctic Treaty and the Outer Space Treaty have broader nonmilitary scope and purposes, but include similar preclusive arms control stipulations. The former prohibits any measures of a military nature in Antarctica, including establishment of military bases, military maneuvers, and any weapons testing including nuclear explosions. The Outer Space Treaty has a similar provision regarding activities on the moon or other celestial bodies, and also bans placing nuclear weapons or other weapons of mass destruction in orbit or stationing them in outer space in any other manner. The remaining agreement in this group, the Environmental Modification Convention, bans military or other hostile use of major environmental modification techniques (which are carefully but broadly defined).

The United States and the Soviet Union have played a major, and generally cooperative, role in the development of a nonproliferation regime, which is itself a component of a larger regime governing peaceful use of nuclear energy. The Eisenhower "Atoms for Peace" speech in December 1953, which called for international cooperation in the regulated peaceful exploitation of nuclear energy for civilian purposes and proposed establishment of an International Atomic Energy Agency (IAEA) to these ends, directly invited the Soviet Union to participate from the outset. The Soviet Union participated fully in establishment of the IAEA in the mid-1950s. In the 1960s the two nations, in their capacity at the time as Co-chairmen of the U.N.-related Geneva Disarmament Conference, took the leading role in drafting the Non-Proliferation Treaty, though with continuous hard bargaining with nonnuclear weapons states. Nonproliferation is by no means a monopolistic venture of the nuclear "haves," however. The Latin American Nuclear Free Zone was local in origin, and negotiations were completed before those for the NPT. The South Pacific Nuclear Free Zone was also the creature of the regional states. Both have provisions for limited association by the nuclear powers; all five nuclear powers have acceded to the relevant protocols to the former treaty, but the United States has refused to associate itself with the latter on grounds that it unacceptably hampers essential nuclear deterrent operations.

The other preclusive agreements have been at times denigrated or even ridiculed as prohibiting what no one wants or is able to do anyway. Just now this charge has some force for the agreements on seabeds and environmental modification—though agreement on the latter was in part motivated by worldwide concerns among environmentalists about U.S. defoliant and incendiary operations of considerable scale in Vietnam. The argument for preclusive agreements is simply that one cannot be sure what may be possible in the future, and it is easier and wiser to agree not to do something when no one wants to. That bit of common sense takes on more pertinence as the peaceful and military exploitation of outer space continues to expand and diversify. If the burst of national pride attending the first landing of man on the moon and the planting of the national flag is recalled, the possibility suggests itself that after that event it might have been more difficult to renounce claims to sovereignty or consideration of military activities. In contrast with occasional expressions of regret about "missed opportunities" in arms control, these preclusive agreements offer cases of "opportunities seized" in a timely way.

The Outer Space Treaty is less sweeping than the Antarctica Treaty in its proscription of military activities other than logistic support of scientific and other peaceful activities. Weapons other than those for mass destruction are not barred from satellites or space stations.

Military satellites of the two superpowers have proliferated for a variety of non-weapons uses—communication, weather observation, navigation, and early warning, as well as reconaissance. The superpowers' reciprocal tolerance for each other's reconnaissance satellites is chronicled in Chapter 15. They have major importance for both nations: for military operations, for intelligence, for strategic warning, for command and control, and for verification of arms control accords. The question has arisen repeatedly: should the Outer Space Treaty be supplemented with an agreement to ban or limit anti-satellite weapons (ASAT)? Development of ASAT has proceeded apace, as described in Chapter 16, and exploratory U.S.–Soviet negotiations were undertaken in 1977–78 without success. The dilemmas are familiar ones. Once ASAT weapons have been developed and tested, is it possible to frame an agreement banning or limiting them or their use? If an agreement were to prove feasible and mutually acceptable, could it be verified? And most basic of all, given the military value of satellites, is the net benefit for the United States (or for the Soviet Union) to be found in preserving the ability to destroy hostile satellites—or in saving one's own from destruction in time of crisis or conflict? The Soviet Union appears to have come down on the side of a reciprocal ban;

in the 1980s it tabled successive draft treaties banning weapons in space, whether for attacking satellites or for "space strike" against earth targets, as well as weapons launched from earth against satellites. The Strategic Defense Initiative gave impetus to the Soviet concern, with its prospect of kill mechanisms and associated systems which, whatever their capability as ABMs, would have clear ASAT capabilities. To enable convening of the current Geneva strategic arms negotiations with their START and INF components, the United States had to agree to add to the agenda consideration of "preventing an arms race in space." The explicit U.S. position, however, is that an ASAT agreement does not appear desirable or verifiable, and this part of the Geneva talks remains stalemated. Within the United States, the issue of the desirability of an ASAT agreement remains under active debate. The Congress, in a unilateral preclusive measure of its own, has barred using defense-appropriated funds for any ASAT test so long as the Soviets continue to refrain from further tests. The rationale appears to be that the contribution of an ASAT ban or limitation to strategic stability outweighs the value of an unhampered U.S. capability to destroy Soviet satellites, and technical developments should not be permitted to preempt the possibility of a negotiation. Pending a clearcut resolution of where the U.S. interest lies, both arms control negotiations on this issue, and further evolution of the outer space regime pertaining to satellites, remain in suspense.

Regimes

The nuclear nonproliferation agreements as well as the outer space and Antarctica agreements have a scope and implications extending beyond arms control. The Outer Space Treaty and the Antarctic Treaty deal with realms outside of national sovereignty—in the former case, by formal exclusion of claims to national sovereignty; in the latter, by in effect suspending assertion of new or pre-existing claims. The Outer Space Treaty and the nonproliferation agreements attempt to come to grips with new technology that has dual military and civilian applications, and transcends national boundaries in its implications and the problems of regulation. In addition to the challenge for arms control, then, the United States and the Soviet Union along with the rest of the international community have faced the challenge of how to provide some elements of international order for these new realms and technologies, in ways that extend the imperfect international system constructively. The challenge for international security extends beyond the role of arms control, and the conduct of the United States and the Soviet Union in responding to that challenge is as illuminating of their ability to engage in security cooperation as is arms control per se. Aside from the issue of military activity in outer space, U.S.–Soviet cooperation in this extended realm, whether direct or at arms length has generally been good.

Outer space activities by satellites, however, bear in a major way on the strategic balance, strategic stability, and the risk of nuclear war. Whatever position one takes on ASAT, it is clear that the stakes and the dilemmas are major, and it is not surprising that the positions of the two countries have been slow and difficult to develop. (The problem for the Soviet Union as described by John Lewis Gaddis, has been in accepting space observation; for the United States, the problem is determining the desirable degree of militarization or demilitarization of space beyond the 1967 treaty restrictions.) But if one does not focus solely on the ASAT issue, the extent and richness of the outer space regime are noteworthy. In addition to the ban on claims of sovereignty, the Outer Space

Treaty formally subjects outer space to international law including the U.N. Charter. For communications or weather satellites, international organizations either new (Intelsat and Comsat) or old (the World Meteorological Organization and the International Tele-communications Union) have provided services and a framework for operating and regulating these new international ventures. Less formally, and without formal legal definition, the distinction between national air space and outer space, and between what is permitted in each and what are the rights of nations with regard to them, has been handled satisfactorily even if some issues remain (for example, those regarding direct broadcast from satellites, or the dissemination of imagery). Arrangements regarding liability, and return and rescue of astronauts, have been worked out. Commercial ventures, particularly in the field of communications, have operated effectively despite differences among market and planned economies, or industrialized and developing states. Symbolic of these arrangements is the solution for modernization of the U.S.–Soviet "hotline": the United States provided the Soviet Union with ground stations for access to Intelsat space channels (though the Soviet Union was not an Intelsat member), and the Soviets in turn provided *Molniya* ground stations for the United States. The arrangement may not appear efficient, but it is cooperative, and redundancy has merit for crisis communications. Through these and other measures, a viable and still evolving regime has emerged to facilitate exploration and exploitation of space and to make civilian and military activities compatible; it includes international law, intergovernmental and private organizations, tacit understandings, and established procedures and practices. The contribution to international and national security and the avoidance of conflict is substantial. The role of the United States and the Soviet Union was essential, given their dominant current position in space activities, and has been constructive over-all, with the two superpowers acting both in parallel and at times in coordination.

The Antarctic case is similar in many respects. Though simpler, it may face increasing difficulty in avoiding disputes and even conflicts, if resource exploitation becomes an important option and the issues of conflicting territorial claims or of the relationship between the present treaty partners and the United Nations can no longer be held in suspension. The treaty provides a valuable and flexible foundation of law and practice for confronting these problems, as Deborah Shapley shows. Here the United States and the Soviet Union have had little occasion for more than tacit or routine cooperation, but they have shown that they share an interest in the preservation and evolution of the regime, for security and peacekeeping as well as practical reasons.

The regime that governs the seas has not been one of our cases, though it has security dimensions and a longstanding history of U.S.–Soviet consultation. As Leigh S. Ratiner, long a U.S. official and negotiator, notes: "The Law of the Sea Treaty has been under negotiation since 1966, when the United States and the USSR agreed to consult all nations on the question whether they would agree to a new global conference on the law of the sea." Soviet security interests cannot be directly cited, but probably have geostrategic roots similar to those of the United States. On the latter, Ratiner comments:

> The Department of Defense had in previous Administrations (before the 1980s) been a strong unyielding supporter of the successful conclusion of the treaty. It had always felt that the stability of international law which would accrue from this treaty, which contains many provisions favorable to the mobility of its air and sea forces, was a significant national security benefit when compared with the uncertainty of potential arguments with coastal states which might exist in the absence of this treaty[1]

As a codification of a regime with long roots in international law and practice, the treaty's provisions of interest to the Department of Defense have some standing as customary international law, though in the absence of U.S. adherence to the treaty they do not have the additional force of interstate commitments. In addition to these security interests, the United States and Soviet Union as trading and fishing nations have an interest of broader security character in the treaty and the regime, which it codifies and extends.

The Seabed Arms Control Treaty of 1971 bans emplacement of nuclear and other weapons of mass destruction on the seabed. Viewed at the time of signature as somewhat farfetched, that treaty seems more prescient in view of increasing international interest in mining the minerals of the seabed. Ratiner notes that the Law of the Sea Treaty provides for a historic global organization, for the first time one which regulates, manages, and produces globally shared resources, possesses and develops technology, has taxing power, and brings international disputes under the jurisdiction of the International Court of Justice. The United States refused to sign the treaty because of opposition to such an innovation in international authority, but Ratiner speculates that faced with the alternative of an anarchic situation for the seabeds, in time the Soviet bloc and U.S. allies as well as Third World countries will sign and ratify the treaty. If this happens, U.S. and Soviet positions will have diverged in a domain where there has heretofore been a convergence of interests.

It should be added that the regime governing exploitation of nuclear energy has broader security dimensions than avoiding the spread of nuclear weapons. Nuclear power and its associated nuclear fuel cycle have international safety and health implications, whether in such tasks as controlling radioactive emissions and disposing of nuclear wastes from normal operations, or in coping with the transborder consequences of accidents such as the recent Chernobyl disaster. The Statute of the International Atomic Energy Agency negotiated in the mid-1950s with Soviet participation gives the agency various regulatory, educational, and advisory functions, which have taken on added scope and importance with the spread of nuclear power facilities and heightened public and governmental concern. The Antarctic Treaty banned disposal of nuclear wastes and the recent South Pacific Nuclear Free Zone Treaty provides tight disposal restrictions to supplement nonproliferation provisions. As Joseph Nye shows, the Soviets have been cautious but consistently cooperative. In the 1980s, they took two further steps: they reached agreement with the agency to open their nuclear power facilities to agency inspection (following the example of the United States and United Kingdom); and they worked closely with agency experts and officials immediately after the Chernobyl incident, both to ascertain its effects and to strengthen international procedures relating to future incidents.

These observations about regimes in relation to preclusive arms control are not extraneous. While all the regimes have broader scope and purposes, the regimes could not emerge or be codified without some provisions regarding military activities. Arms control is not their central core, but is one necessary element. Because they relate to international or transnational domains, they require participating nations to view their security interests from a broader perspective than often obtains among nations. While none of the regimes arose in international relations with a *tabula rasa,* they have been taken up internationally in a sufficiently timely way to permit preclusive actions (such as banning or suspending territorial claims, arms control, or dispute-resolution procedures) with clear security implications for avoidance of conflict or arms races. These circumstances have in most cases eased U.S.–Soviet cooperation. For those who wonder whether the Soviet Union can be a reliable partner in international action, they furnish an instructive body of some decades of experience. Here the point of interest is only incidentally direct U.S.–Soviet cooperation; rather, it is the readiness of the Soviet Union to work with the rest of the world in establishing institutionalized arrangements for international order, and in carrying them out effectively in the interests of international peace and security.

RISK REDUCTION AGREEMENTS

Concern about the risk of nuclear war, and interest in concerted action to reduce that risk, have been evident at least since the Cuban missile crisis. That concern underlies the Washington-Moscow "hotline" for crisis communications, established in 1963 and updated twice since—most recently under the current Administration in 1984. The concern was formally articulated in the Accidental Nuclear War agreement of 1971 and in the preamble to the ABM Treaty of 1972. Active interest in extending such measures currently focuses in the United States on the possibility of "risk reduction centers," jointly manned by U.S. and Soviet military and diplomatic personnel. Different concepts of the purpose and activities of such centers have been under discussion in the United States, as Barry Blechman shows. In May 1987, agreement was reached in Moscow *ad referendum* for establishment of nuclear risk reduction centers in the two capitals, though not on a jointly manned basis.

Risk reduction measures have the support of politicians and military men as well as arms controllers. This is most clearly seen in the Incidents at Sea agreement, which has been primarily sponsored and negotiated and carried out in the United States by Navy Department personnel. With such a base in the military establishment, an agreement is clearly not primarily political and symbolic, but incorporated in the operational structure of armed forces with the support and interest of their military and civilian chiefs.

This observation suggests one other dimension to future risk-of-war measures. Most of them are essentially instrumental, providing for furnishing of data or notices or for consultation in certain situations. Such instrumentalities are better used if there is some previous dialogue among top political and military leaders regarding political and military trends and issues of direct bearing on the military interaction in question. Isolated summits have their role; but more regular, less dramatic, consultations and discussions not burdened with the stakes of success or failure could make their different and valuable contribution to increased understanding and to stability and lowered risk of loss of control in any crisis.

The other side of risk reduction is confidence building. The latter face is the one which has been put on arms control measures in Europe, as a constituent part of the 1975 Helsinki accords, and as the main content of the 1986 Stockholm Agreement on Confidence Building and Security Measures in Europe. The focus is on removing unnecessary fears of surprise attack or of a threatening posture or composition of opposing alliance military forces and movements. Changes in the forces are not stipulated. The measures consist of such things as advance notice of maneuvers and other major military movements; data exchanges about forces involved; and opportunity for observation by the other side, including some aerial surveillance.

Here the United States and Soviet Union are participants not only with their allies of NATO and the Warsaw Pact, but with neutrals and other nonaligned countries of Europe. To the extent that limited war in Europe is one of the most likely ways in which nuclear war might come about by escalation, the Stockholm agreement has its link with avoidance of superpower nuclear confrontation. Beyond that, the agreement has another broader dimension. For the first time, such an agreement applies to Europe from the Atlantic to the Urals, thus bringing Soviet territory under coverage. The aerial surveillance provisions, while applying to limited situations, also represent a breakthrough of historic character—the United States has sought such observation measures since the Eisenhower "Open Skies" proposal of the mid-1950s. Both the geographic scope and the surveillance provisions open up new possibilities for arms control in Europe, conventional as well as nuclear.*

FAILED NEGOTIATIONS

The negotiations in this category are quite diverse. A comprehensive test ban was the object of formal U.S.–Soviet (and U.K.) negotiations from 1958 on, as well as continuing discussion in the Geneva Disarmament Committee. While ASAT weapons were only once the topic of formal talks, they are still technically on the agenda of U.S.–Soviet Geneva talks under the rubric of "space arms." Conventional arms transfer limitations, and Indian Ocean naval forces, have disappeared from the active agenda.

What all these issues have in common is that, even when they were the topic of intensive formal negotiation, they did not have a solid basis of political and strategic understanding and support within one or the other country, or an adequate and mutually acceptable verification base, or both. The changing and divisive U.S. debate on the desirability and verifiability of ASAT limitation is thoroughly outlined by Steven Weber and Sidney Drell. Alan Neidle shows how shallowly rooted was the formal U.S. commitment to a verifiable comprehensive nuclear test ban (CTB). Quite aside from the still continuing debate about verification of an underground test ban, the Congressional and military support necessary for ratification of a treaty has been shaky—at the time of the Limited Test Ban Treaty after the Cuban missile crisis, when Kennedy's Senate soundings showed it would be imprudent to send up a CTB; in the Carter Administration, when it was decided that after the bruising Panama Canal Treaty fight it would be unwise to seek ratification of both the SALT II and CTB treaties and the former was given priority; and in the Reagan Administration, when the goal of a CTB was formally renounced, on grounds that testing should continue so long as nuclear weapons remain a major component of U.S. defensive and deterrent forces.

Arms control is not a solution appropriate to every facet of the arms race. The levels of conventional arms transfers are forbiddingly high; arms imports feed and sustain regional conflicts and confrontations expensive in money and blood. Whether agreement among suppliers to limit arms transfers is the solution is more debatable. As Janne Nolan points out, methods of designing and formulating limitations on arms supply are technically feasible; the political and security preconditions are more difficult to satisfy. The principal arms recipients are allies or clients of the United States and the Soviet Union (and increasingly of other intermediate-sized military powers). Unless the interests of regional states and their external allies or patrons can be reconciled, and regional situations stabilized, the common ground for defining limitations on the flow of arms

---

*Arms Limitation/Reduction Agreements are discussed on pp. 629–37.

will be elusive. The failure of Conventional Arms Transfer (CAT) talks was thus not the result of poor preparations or negotiations; it was fundamental. The obverse is, however, that if (for example) a Middle East settlement is reached of broader scope than the Camp David accords, or appropriate understandings become possible in parts of Africa or Latin America or Asia, provisions relating to supply or acquisition of arms, as well as perhaps military deployments, are likely to be part of any accords. Here again, arms control provisions must have a minimum political and security context, and cannot by themselves create stability or the resolution of conflict or tension.

The Indian Ocean naval negotiations, like the CAT talks exploratory in character, failed for similar reasons. The technical problem of defining limits on naval deployments were forbidding enough, in view of the very different composition of naval forces. The Soviets have nothing comparable to American carrier task forces, but can bring to bear land-based aircraft not to be left out of account in any naval balance. Thus, defining relevant units of account for any limitations was in itself conceptually difficult. More fundamentally, the Indian Ocean constitutes a dubious zone for limitation. The United States and the Soviet Union do not as a practical matter deploy forces for the Indian Ocean. It is a zone of transit to the areas of primary military and political concern: the Horn of Africa; the Persian Gulf; the arena of Arab-Israeli confrontation. Requirements for naval forces and operations are dictated by these areas, not by the Indian Ocean and its littoral. And as for Soviet influence on the areas of conflict just cited, Richard Haass points out that Soviet merchant ships carrying military supplies affect the regional security situation at least as much as Soviet naval forces. The failure of these negotiations is thus not to be viewed as a "missed opportunity," but as an opportunity that did not exist.

One of the ongoing negotiations can be conveniently mentioned here because of its subject matter—the Geneva negotiations for *chemical weapons elimination*. These are well advanced, and could conceivably result in an agreement in 1987–88 in the Geneva U.N. Committee on Disaramation. These negotiations have long roots. The Geneva Protocol of 1925, briefly discussed above, deals only with *use* of chemical and biological weapons in war. Since World War II there has been U.N. discussion of a possible treaty limiting development, production, and deployment of CW and BW weapons. The Biological Weapons Convention of 1972 was broken out of those negotiations and explicitly declared in its preamble to be a first step toward a CW treaty. That BW Convention is instructive for two other reasons. It was preceded by one of the few acts of unilateral disarmament: the unilateral renunciation by the United States of further research, production, or deployment of BW weapons. Contrary to the common wisdom that such a unilateral step removes all incentive and leverage for negotiation, the convention was quickly negotiated with the Soviet Union and others; there are now 131 signatories. The convention has no verification provisions, only provision for consultation, and for review conferences at five-year intervals. Recent concern over disputed allegations of the use of toxin weapons in Southeast Asia, and more basically over the implication of developments in biotechnology, made the 1986 review conference the occasion for serious and searching examination of what should be done. Agreement was reached on strengthened consultation measures, on identification and open access to biotechnology research facilities, and in particular on convening a meeting of experts in Geneva in April 1987 to develop these concepts. The Soviet Union has engaged fully in these developments and promised cooperation in implementing them. This is an important matter for arms control compliance and verification. Treaties can never anticipate all the challenges of verification and compliance, particularly where novel technology is involved; this kind of updating and strengthening as requirements become clearer will be imperative. And if such adaptation always has to go the cumbersome, time-consuming route of spelling out and ratifying treaty amendments, implementation of arms control agreements will be difficult indeed. New formal agreements, or amendments to old ones, will be needed from time to time; but the continuing need will be for general procedural measures such as the Standing Consultative Commission or five-year review conferences, to adjust to technical or political change within the scope of the over-all agreement, or to resolve questions of interpretation and application of texts.

CENTRAL ARMS CONTROL NEGOTIATIONS ON LIMITATIONS AND REDUCTIONS

We will not review one by one the major agreements and negotiations on limitation and reduction of strategic and other major weapons, but instead look at them as a group and consider their interconnections. Recent developments before, at, and after the Reykjavik summit of 1986 have thrown these interconnections into sharp relief. Even before that summit, the major talks had been consolidated at Geneva in view of the links evident among strategic arms, Euromissiles, and space arms. The imminence of an agreement on longer-range intermediate missiles and the possibility of sharp cuts in strategic missiles or even more radical measures called attention to the link with the conventional arms balance in Europe.

These interconnections are not novel. Some go back to the unfinished business of SALT I; some go back even to the 1950s and the first serious efforts of American and Soviet leaders to understand the implications of their expanding nuclear arsenals and their mutual vulnerability in event of nuclear war. The current arms control situation has to be viewed in the context of the development of U.S.–Soviet relations since World War II, and their gradual efforts, first separate and then to some extent cooperative, to adapt their security policies and measures to the imperatives of nuclear weapons.

The first effort to control nuclear weapons was a radical one, the Baruch plan. Its concept—surrender of U.S. and other national nuclear programs to a supranational authority—reflected the globalism that engendered the U.N. Charter in the last years of the war, just before the Grand Alliance against Hitler began its rapid dissolution into the Cold War. Quite aside from the chill in U.S.–Soviet relations, the concept of a veto-free international authority over the superpowers was quixotic. The Soviet Union bore the onus of rejection; it is not easy, however, to imagine the U.S. Senate ratifying such a renunciation of sovereignty and of the U.S.-developed absolute weapon.

A different kind of global approach to arms control followed in the 1950s. The objective was general and complete disarmament (GCD), with elimination of nuclear weapons in the final stages, after balanced reduction of conventional arms and armies to levels approaching that of police forces, and the firm establishment of an international verification and dispute resolution organ. Much dedicated and imaginative thought went into plans for GCD, but the negotiations were sterile in the harsh political atmosphere of the mid-1950s.

In the changing political scene of the later 1950s, a more pragmatic case-by-case approach emerged. In Europe, a modus vivendi regarding Germany and East-West relations was reached following the death of Stalin and emergence of a less autarchic and uncompromising Soviet approach to international relations. The implications of nuclear weapons for national security, rooted in the reality of mutual vulnerability, began to be perceived, as first enunciated in Eisenhower's "Atoms for Peace" speech to the United Nations of December 1953. A more pragmatic approach to nuclear weapons control was tried in 1957–58—combining a focus on one relatively small measure (a nuclear test ban) and quiet preparatory talks by experts to see if there was mutual interest in the measure and if verification appeared feasible. After an encouraging start in 1958, impasse soon obtained in the CTB talks (as it did more quickly in the innovative multilateral conference on measures to prevent surprise attack in 1958). Despite these checks, an invaluable learning process, both national and international, had been launched regarding nuclear weapons, the arms race in the nuclear age, and the possible role of arms control in enhancing national and international security.

The Cuban missile crisis was the watershed, with its lessons on the dangers of confrontation between possessors of nuclear arsenals, and also on the possibility of communication and negotiation. In the succeeding years of the mid-1960s, a number of bilateral and multilateral agreements were reached (Limited Test Ban, Hotline, Outer Space Treaty, Non-Proliferation Treaty). They did not affect the central strategic balance, but were significant for international stability and for encouragement as to the value of negotiation. They began an arms control process which, in the last year of the Johnson Administration and the first Nixon term, moved on to strategic negotiations and the SALT I package of agreements, as well as a number of others set forth in Table 1.

Not coincidentally, this was the period of détente, beginning in Europe with Willy Brandt and *Ostpolitik* and NATO's 1967 Harmel Report articulating a dual NATO philosophy of defense and détente, later expressed in the United States by Henry Kissinger in his own terms. As a number of chapters in this volume describe, a group of European agreements from 1971 to 1975 constituted a movement from the narrow modus vivendi of the 1950s to a de facto postwar settlement. Then came the beginning of a process (the Helsinki process) of reestablishing in Europe more normal and even cooperative East-West relations to the extent possible between sharply differing economic and social and political systems which nevertheless shared common historical and cultural roots. The process is broad in scope. European security has been a major topic; the negotiations on mutual force reductions (MBFR) and on Euromissiles are supplemented by multilateral talks on confidence-building measures. More broadly still, and explicitly of equal importance, the process embraces explorations of improved economic, cultural, scientific, and personal dealings and relationships between East and West; and a formal acceptance of standards for human rights followed by frank debates and painfully slow adjustment of East European national practices to conform to these standards.

Détente unravelled in the United States (but not in Europe) in the Ford and Carter administrations, under strains in U.S.–Soviet relations most immediately linked with events in Africa, Southeast Asia, and the Middle East, and culminating in Afghanistan. Arms control was nominally exempt from this chill in relations, but few agreements were reached, and these for the most part failed of ratification. The chill deepened in the last year of the Carter Administration, with nearly all arms control activities suspended, and became a virtual revival of the Cold War in the first years of the 1980s.

The atmosphere was not propitious for arms control in the first Reagan term. In addition to using anti-Soviet rhetoric, the Administration gave priority to sharp increases in military budgets and programs, justified as necessary to compensate for a "decade of neglect" in which a relentless Soviet military buildup had given the Soviets nuclear as well as conventional superiority, which could only be overcome by acceleration of U.S. defense efforts.

While the dominant tone of remarks about arms control remained one of scorn, by the end of 1981 negotiations on intermediate-range Nuclear Forces (INF) had been resumed. The basic NATO decision of 1979 called for a two-track program of parallel NATO INF deployments and U.S.–Soviet negotiations. For Germany and Benelux, deployment was not politically practical without a visible effort to negotiate INF limitations. By mid-1982, strategic arms control talks had also resumed in a reincarnation as Strategic Arms Reduction Talks (START), again largely for domestic and international political reasons. The predominant U.S. concern in both talks was to facilitate NATO INF deployment (and on the Soviet side to block it), and to get ahead with U.S. programs of strategic modernization and over-all force buildup.

Gradually the Geneva talks took on a different character. The Soviet Union showed unexpected flexibility on both INF and START, as well as receptiveness to the possibility of strengthened verification procedures including on-site inspection, even before the advent of Mikhail Gorbachev and more pronouncedly thereafter. Over all, a change in tone toward dealing with the Soviets began to appear in the United States, marked by the presidential speech of January 16, 1984, on U.S.–Soviet relations. Summits took place in Geneva in late 1985 and Reykjavik in late 1986. Despite accomplishing little of substance other than exchanges of views, they created expectations of substance which had to be met or countered. And at the Reykjavik summit, while confusion and imprecision in U.S. positions occasioned much alarm and criticism in both Western Europe and the United States, remarkable convergence on essential elements of an INF agreement, and the outlines of an initial START agreement, was apparent in retrospect. The Soviets accepted the U.S.-proposed "zero option" for European INF, agreed in principle to reductions in strategic arms which could be portrayed as "deep cuts" for warheads as well as delivery systems, and spoke positively about the role of on-site inspection where needed.

Ambiguities of the Present Situation

Negotiations on INF and START have intensified in 1987, even dealing with actual treaty drafts. The extent of general agreement on the major elements of an INF accord suggests that, given sustained purposeful negotiation, an agreed text could be attainable within the year (and even a START text is not inconceivable). A closer examination shows obstacles and pitfalls which discourage such optimism. They also illustrate well the inherent difficulties and dilemmas of efforts to achieve strategic arms control agreements between heavily (and differently) armed rivals such as the two negotiating parties and their allies.

The mixed reaction in Europe is revealing. The Soviet acceptance of the NATO INF proposal exposed divergent views. The original European support for the "zero option" was based on disparate viewpoints. One group hoped negotiations would succeed and would limit or reverse INF deployments. Another, however, wanted the deployments to proceed, and viewed negotiations as pro forma and a politically necessary charade. If this difference were all that was at stake, NATO would have little choice after acceptance by the Soviets but to honor NATO's commitment to its own proposals and give the green light to U.S. negotiators. But previously muted underlying concerns about the role of nuclear weapons in Europe emerged. One related to Soviet shorter-range INF (SRINF), which had been deployed forward in East Europe in response to commencement of NATO's INF deployments, and which could cover many of the likely SS-20 targets. As a minimum, there was a strong case that such systems should be pulled back and the previous situation restored (as the Soviets gave indications they might be willing to do). However, more fundamental dilemmas about NATO's nuclear posture were reopened when the Soviets suggested the possibility of a "zero SRINF" in Europe to accompany dismantlement of INF, and restated their long-standing interest in full denuclearization of West and East Europe up to their borders. In the face of Soviet conventional superiority and offensive posture, NATO's flexible response doctrine required the option of first use of nuclear weapons if NATO's forces were faced with defeat and a Soviet takeover of Western Europe. Such a course would in practice be of debatable military advantage and would have certain catastrophic consequences for Western Europe in view of opposing Soviet theater nuclear strength at least equal to NATO's; yet the doctrine had rough common sense as a deterrent strategy to bring home to the Soviets the high risks and unlikely gain from any aggression. But faced with the prospect of radical change—in the form of removal of U.S./NATO INF weapons and possibly SRINF—Europeans revived old debates concerning the "coupling" of U.S. strategic nuclear forces to deterrence and the defense of NATO Europe, and concerning the attractions or dangers of moving toward denuclearization in Central Europe. The uneasy consensus favoring an INF agreement was severely tested.

Familiar arms control issues are visible here. One is the *separability* of partial measures (here, limiting theater nuclear weapons). Eliminating INF on both sides does not solve (though it does not necessarily intensify) the problems of nuclear balance in Europe, a balance which includes SRINF; tactical nuclear weapons in the thousands; the U.K. and French nuclear forces; Soviet ICBMs, some of which can target Western Europe; and U.S. sea-based cruise and ballistic missiles (some of them committed to Supreme Allied Commander Europe [SACEUR]). The first question is whether a specific limited measure will improve (or at least not reduce) security, rather than increase risks. NATO advanced the "zero option" on the explicit premise that eliminating LRINF targeted on Europe would correct an imbalance favoring the Soviet Union at least as well as deploying NATO missiles in smaller numbers. Unless NATO were to abandon this premise, the appropriate arms control course following Soviet acceptance would be to proceed to finalize a satisfactory treaty, with whatever supplementary provisions on related limitations or reductions might be quickly agreed. Follow-on negotiations on SRINF and perhaps tactical nuclear weapons might be called for, with or without agreed guidelines, as necessary to the viability of the initial agreement, and as a possible mutually advantageous next step.

But the issues go deeper. Connections are involved—*structural linkages*—not only among theater nuclear weapons, but between those and strategic weapons, those of other NATO allies (United Kingdom and France) as well as the superpowers; and between nuclear forces and conventional forces and the over-all military balance. Structural linkage should determine the degree to which, or the conditions under which, partial arms control measures can be undertaken separately, or must be linked to concurrent or sequential measures affecting other forces.

From the start, NATO has viewed INF as not linked to a START agreement; the Soviets recently conceded that point. The other related negotiation is the Vienna MBFR conference. If NATO is concerned about the conventional balance in Europe, and that concern is exacerbated by the prospect of INF elimination, it has two courses open. One would be to improve the military balance by the buildup and modernization of NATO conventional forces—not, in theory, outside the reach of a wealthy, populous and highly industrialized alliance. Or, a balance could be established by agreement for mutual reductions to equal levels, as pursued in MBFR. The former course has been urged by the United States and some Europeans for two decades. It remains unlikely, in view of European budgetary and political obstacles, and (paradoxically, in view of current security concerns) disbelief in the imminence of any Soviet attack.

What about MBFR? The sterility of the negotiations over the past ten years has been exaggerated. Coit Blacker describes the amount of agreement reached on principle and detail, including establishment of a common ceiling to which the force levels of both sides should be reduced. What has been lacking is political incentive to press to some initial agreement. Principal specific issues relate to the factual situation—the actual numbers and character of opposing forces—and verification measures such as data exchanges, observation posts and inspection teams, and aerial surveillance. There has also been the question whether even intensive verification procedures can suffice unless they are applicable to Soviet territory. Political motivation to give higher priority to conventional arms negotiations should now emerge from the nervous concerns aroused by the prospect of an INF agreement and also from the broader doubts as to long-term U.S. alliance policy occasioned by vague presidential statements at Reykjavik about elimination of nuclear weapons. For the substantive aspects of verification of an MBFR agreement, the Conference on Disarmament in Europe (CDE) experience opens new vistas; the recent Stockholm CBM agreement covers the area from the Atlantic to the Urals, bringing in the Western USSR. While the CBM monitoring and notification provisions are not directly transferable to MBFR, they point to possible routes to dealing with outstanding verification issues in Vienna. To match this broader geographic scope, a new negotiating forum superseding the Vienna conference is in prospect. Participants would come only from NATO and Warsaw Pact nations and would make reports to the CDE but not be subordinate to it.

There is a further stumbling block for INF agreement, also pertinent for other major arms control measures. The U.S. verification proposals envisage not only verification of *removal and destruction* of current Europe-related INF deployments on both sides, but also inspection of facilities for *production and storage* of missiles (how warheads would be handled is unclear at this point). Treaty-drafting problems are formidable, and will be even more time consuming in application. Inspection would be called for in Western Europe as well as in the United States and Soviet Union. It is not often appreciated that in Western Europe as well as the United States, intricate legal and practical problems for handling Soviet inspectors would be posed. The interminable problems in working out arrangements for IAEA inspectors at civilian nuclear facilities in the United States are instructive, though simpler. Perfectionism on verification and inspection could easily make agreement in principle on the INF zero option a dead letter. There are alternative solutions, of course, but they represent the sort of pragmatic approach to arms control and verification that has been condemned as a matter of principle by the Reagan Administration. INF deployments appear to be verifiable, judging by the precision and speed with which SS-20s have been tallied by U.S. intelligence and DOD public reports over past years. A possible agreement might thus focus on limiting deployments and destroying excess or removed systems and their missiles. On-site observation would be limited to destruction; national means of verification would suffice for deployment and withdrawal. At present levels of strategic warheads (even under the prospective START agreement), the strategic risk should be tolerable. The broader verification problems with regard to production and stocks and disposition of nuclear warheads would not be overlooked, but would be assigned to START rather than the more limited INF agreement. Since verification of production and storage of missiles and warheads is impractical on a sector-by-sector basis, it should cover the Soviet strategic weapons industry as a whole rather than be limited to INF.

Whether an INF agreement should be undertaken promptly, then, is a standard arms control problem of the separability of a limited measure. Even if such an agreement is viewed positively, with its costs and risks outweighted by advantages, certain problems would remain. Questions involving the link to further arms control, verification, and the unprecedented legal and procedural problems of on-site inspection in the United States and Western Europe as well as the Soviet Union offer infinite possibilities for long drawn-out debate and haggling. Disagreement on arms control is vastly easier than agreement.

On START, the situation is even more complex and less promising, again for reasons of exemplary value. It should be noted at the outset that the convergence at Reykjavik had misleading aspects. The concept billed as a 50 percent "deep cut" in strategic forces boils down in fact to somewhat less—cuts from around 10,000 warheads on each side to 6,000; and from 2,000–2,500 delivery vehicles to 1600. The systems covered are only those covered by SALT: ICBMs, SLBMs, and strategic bombers. Sea-launched cruise missiles (SLCMs) and U.K. and French forces are not included. Only some two hundred British and French strategic warheads are deployed at present—but both nations have modernization programs that could lead to as many as a thousand warheads. The United States is in the process of deploying several hundred SLCMs with strategic missions (either for *horizontal escalation*—responding to Soviet attack in one area, such as Europe, by counterattack in another region of Soviet sensitivity or vulnerability—or as *strategic reserve* freeing up other strategic systems for warfighting or limited nuclear attacks). The Soviets also deploy some SLCMs, and are developing an improved missile. Further, at Reykjavik the U.S. participants reportedly got Soviet acceptance of counting ALCMs individually against the warhead ceiling, but counting all bombs and short-range attack missiles on each bomber as only one. If the United States were, for example, to retain 100 penetrating bombers (such as the B-1B or the prospective *Stealth* bomber), each with 10 to 20 such weapons, another 1,000 to 2,000 warheads would be exempt from the 6,000 ceiling.

These factors are to some extent a problem for the future, and primarily a security concern for the Soviets (though the United States might examine more closely the net benefit to the United States of being able to attack the Soviet mainland with SLCMs— at the cost of exposing to Soviet SLCM attack the much longer and more heavily populated U.S. coastal and adjacent areas). But if one looks at the overall strategic picture, the prospective START accord is more a breakthrough in the recent impasse than a radical breakthrough in strategic arms control. It represents a delayed version of SALT III as forecast in the Joint Statement of Principles for future negotiations appended to the 1979 SALT II treaty. Indeed, it deals only with the subset of systems limited in SALT, rather than dealing also with cruise missiles as equivocally forecast in SALT II. The ceiling of 1,600 delivery systems is not much below the first Soviet position—1,800—when START began in the early 1980s. The warhead limitation is an innovation, but a logical next step from the MIRV fractionation limits in

SALT II. Thus, the START accord would be essentially the sort of SALT III agreement that might have been expected in the first half of the 1980s had SALT II been ratified and SALT III proceeded in accordance with agreed guidelines (including expanded cooperative measures of verification).

If it happens, better late than never. But present convergence is on numbers only. For strategic arms limitation, concepts and premises are as important as quantities. As I explained in the chapter on strategic arms control the three main previously agreed premises of nuclear arms control have been challenged by the SDI and its rationale, and by other U.S. doctrinal statements. SDI explicitly seeks to move away from *mutual deterrence* based on recognition of the objective condition of mutual vulnerability; it would also go counter to the second principle, of *interdependence of offensive and defensive weapons*. The third principle, of *equality and equal security in the strategic arms equation*, is also under challenge; strategic equality is not enough for the United States, which may claim to need superior nuclear strength to counterbalance Soviet superiority in conventional arms.

The Soviets continue to profess the previous joint premises and insist that they are essential for a definitive agreement. An initial START agreement acceptable on its own terms would not, however, appear to be ruled out, if accompanied, say, by an equivocal formula that did not abandon the indefinite duration of the ABM Treaty or its original interpretation, or require the United States to disown SDI—an action that would be inconceivable during the remaining two years of the Reagan Administration. The basic SDI and other issues of principle would remain but would be deferred without prejudice. This would represent a gamble for both sides, but enable START to break out of the current impasse. The prospective initial START agreement would, taken alone, be cast in terms consistent with "strategic equality." If deeper cuts are then sought, as forecast in statements of the two national leaders, or if currently excluded systems (where the United States and its allies have marked advantages) are to be brought under limitations, the two sides will have to resume dialogue on "equality and equal security" and on the principles of strategic equality and the renunciation of pursuit of strategic superiority.

The chances for an initial START agreement in 1987/88 appear low. Whether or not one is signed, further negotiations and U.S.–Soviet cooperation in the strategic arms field will require that the superpowers reexamine, both internally and in their dialogue, the purposes and principles relating to the strategic balance.

These observations are meant to clarify the place of such a START agreement in the strategic arms control process, by no means to object to such a deal. The "deep cuts" in strategic arsenals, which are the stated purpose, must be recognized as less than professed, however, because of the permitted growth of excluded systems or warhead types. But the effect on strategic stability would be clearly beneficent within the field of application. The multiplication of warheads on missiles, and to a lesser extent on bombers, would be halted and reversed. Under SALT II, full MIRVing consistent with treaty constraints could lead to around 15,000 warheads on each side, instead of the present 10 to 12,000. The START ceiling of 6,000 warheads, distributed over 1,600 permitted delivery systems, would give a warhead ratio of less than 4:1. That is a halving of the possible SALT II ratio—a significant improvement in crisis stability, since it sharply reduces the possible payoff and attractiveness of a preemptive strike against opposing MIRVed delivery systems and bases. And if, in adapting force postures to the lower ceilings, preference were to be given to more survivable, less vulnerable systems—SLBMs or mobile ICBMs—crisis stability would be further enhanced.

Whether inadvertent or deliberate, these stabilizing effects would be valuable in themselves, and promising as a base for further negotiations designed to serve the security
interests of both sides by stabilizing the strategic balance and enhancing crisis stability
in the interests of reducing the risk of nuclear war.

The preceding comments suggest that, even though the stated core of initial START
agreement is explicitly cast in numerical terms, the consequences would tend toward
possible common ground on strategic goals which could shape future force postures and
negotiations. If realized, then, a major step would be taken toward restoring a sense of
direction to future negotiations, and a basis for a more principled cooperative approach
in negotiations.

Achieving greater stability in the strategic arms balance is unlikely, however, from
intermittent ad hoc agreements. There has to be some *common ground of goals and
principles* to give structure to negotiations and implementing action. Such basic premises cannot be left to instructed negotiators who are not themselves senior policy officials of cabinet or National Security Council rank. Such exploratory work has often
been done prior to formal negotiations by U.S. senior officials (John Foster Dulles,
Robert McNamara, Henry Kissinger, Cyrus Vance) having presidential confidence.
Sometimes presidents themselves have taken a hand—such as Lyndon Johnson at Glassboro, Gerald Ford at Vladivostok, or Reagan at Geneva and Reykjavik. Summits are
not good occasions for detailed negotiation and bargaining, however, in view of time
and other pressures, and the likelihood that issues will come up on which one or both
leaders are unready to bargain (even if they go ahead and do so). But to get some
common appreciation of intentions and motivations, and some common basis for instructing respective negotiators, summits or other high-level person-to-person exchanges
of view can be invaluable. This is true even when, as at Reykjavik, flawed positions
and crucial misconceptions are exposed. It may be that in no other way can the ultimate
decision makers come to realize what issues and decisions they have to face up to, with
some appreciation of how the comparable leader on the other side views the matter.
Sustained and fruitful pursuit of U.S.–Soviet cooperation is unlikely unless top leaders
have a shared basis for judging what agreements and cooperative relations might prove
viable and useful.

Summit meetings can also serve the important function, particularly in the United
States, of establishing the direction in which negotiations and cooperation will move,
and shaping public expectations and sympathies. This is essential in the U.S. political
system. Public presidential sponsorship and determination are important both for public
understanding and support, and for enforcing discipline within the bureaucracy and even
among senior advisers and agency heads.

Presidential leadership in arms control is not a matter of detailed management of
policy formulation or of negotiations. Some key decisions of course will have to be
taken by the President, but the main need is to insist that a clear policy line be developed, approved by him, and supported by all members of his administration. He will
satisfy himself that it is consistent with his over-all national foreign and defense policy.
He will also have to make the judgment that it is something the Congress and the
interested public can come to understand and support. The President has unique influence on security matters; he has the key role in shaping the view of Congress and the
public as to whether the United States is secure, whether national defense and alliances
are sound, whether particular weapons systems or arms control agreements are of net
benefit to the United States, whether an agreement with the Soviet Union is prudent

given the nature of that state and society, and (for defense programs or arms control agreements) whether acceptable risks are involved. For major arms control agreements, in view of the mixture of yearning and suspicion that characterizes the U.S. attitude, the President can have the decisive voice in shaping public and Congressional understanding and acceptance. If he is seen as wise and firm on the essentials of national security and relations with the Soviet Union, his recommendation of a cooperative arms control agreement can be decisive. If his standing is shaky or his support of arms control agreements and cooperative action with the Soviet Union is equivocal, even sound measures face an uncertain fate.

POTENTIAL PLACE OF ARMS CONTROL IN U.S.–SOVIET SECURITY COOPERATION

For arms control, the decade since 1979 has been a troubled and testing one. Even though there is again a turn toward convergence and agreement, confident prediction of early arms control progress is not possible. Whether or not one or more substantial arms control agreements are signed this year or next, for the first time since 1979 arms control negotiations on central weapons and armed forces are likely to go on.

The hesitations and reservations that are now manifest reflect real problems. Beyond that, they reflect an understandable reaction to a prospect of resumption of movement toward cooperation, and away from the familiar East-West relationship. Arms control of the depth and scope presently in sight would be an "unnatural act," as Paul Warnke used to say. It is nevertheless also a compelling goal, when people (or responsible national leaders) contemplate the tens of thousands of nuclear weapons in the arsenals of each superpower and the grim consequences should they be used, or when they consider the less apocalyptic but hardly less horrible implications of modern chemical and biological technology for warfare. "Unnatural," because for both the Soviet Union and the United States security is a central and emotionally charged preoccupation, and it is identified with strength as the precondition and main guarantor of peace as well as security. The Soviet Union was born, within the memory of some still active, in violent revolution and civil war, with outside involvement of foreign powers, including the United States (as Soviet citizens remember even if few Americans do). It suffered another even more devastating invasion some fifty years ago. It views most of its neighbors as historically and potentially hostile, including those allied with it less by choice than by the presence of the Red Army. It has been trying for decades to match the West and especially the United States in technology and industry, especially that which is relevant to military power and defense of the Soviet Union and of the Soviet system. While the United States lacks such a siege psychology, it retains a fascination of its own with military power, with roots in a frontier history and expansionist first century that culminated in a sense of "manifest destiny" of global as well as continental scope. As the United States assumed the mantle of world leadership after World War II, the role of military power overshadowed that of economic or political leadership. Accepting vulnerability, or the meaninglessness of victory in nuclear war, is hard for us. Sustained engagement in the arduous pursuit of cooperation with an adversary is equally hard, and especially so when limitations on our military power are in prospect.

Nevertheless, when the superpowers turn toward introduction of some measures of cooperation into their security relations, arms control is necessarily one of the first areas to be explored. The dangers and uncertainties and costs of unrestrained military competition and confrontation are a major stimulus to some cooperation to reduce them. Limits on weapons and forces and their respective postures and complex interactions are a logical focus. If cooperation does not affect these, it is superficial and illusory. Cultural exchanges and such commercial relations as are feasible between two such disparate and noncomplementary economies have narrow effect. Political declarations on reducing tensions and seeking cooperation are useful, but transitory unless they have practical consequences. Controlling the substance of their strategic confrontation, primarily through arms control, goes more directly to the heart of the U.S.–Soviet rivalry, and will remain on the active agenda despite frustrations.

The excruciating complexity of strategic arms control negotiations and their implementation leads to the speculation: Why not, once the waste and dangers of the arms race are recognized mutually, simply cease and reverse it by commonsense parallel restraint? This is reasonable in a nonhistorical abstract sense. Indeed, there is a role for informal reciprocal restraint—it will never be possible to negotiate and coordinate every detail of respective force postures even within a nonthreatening relationship. But in the light of prevalent distrust on both sides, some agreed foundation and base is necessary if restraint is to be possible and stable. To see the obstacles to informal restraint, one need only recall the U.S. blindness to actual moderate levels of Soviet arms expenditure and strategic force investment in the late 1970s and early 1980s (as estimated by the CIA), when the official and popular U.S. vision remained one of a malign and unrelenting massive Soviet military buildup; or Soviet suspicions of the President's well-intended SDI program, especially when coupled with the accelerated U.S. strategic modernization program for offensive systems; or reciprocal U.S. and Soviet fears of a first and disarming strike by the other; or suspicions by each of the motives and capabilities of the other in intervening in Third World regions.

Even when motives and goals are not specifically in question, the dynamics of weapons development and the action-reaction cycles that result make sensible restraint and adjustment difficult in the absence of preclusive or limiting accords. Some of this gulf of ignorance and misinterpretation might be bridged by sustained movement toward greater openness on the part of the Soviet Union; there is also an important contribution to be sought from regular high-level meetings. Even then some guidelines and benchmarks of a very specific nature, of the kind embodied in the central commitments of existing and prospective arms control agreements, are essential to begin and sustain movement toward a less threatening military relationship. A more stable relationship in turn would furnish a basis of confidence for supplementary unilateral measures of restraint.

Implicit in what has just been said is that arms control is not an independent or alternate route to common security. If stability is unlikely without arms control, arms control by itself will not do the job. Arms control policy and programs cannot be any better than foreign and defense policy and programs, of which in the United States they are by law an integral part, as specified in the U.S. Arms Control and Disarmament Act of 1961. When over-all foreign and security policy seeks a cooperative component in the U.S. relationship with the Soviet Union, arms control is an important route and element, but one which supplements and moderates, rather than replaces, defense measures. The goal is not to construct a U.S.–Soviet "arms control regime" except in a colloquial sense. Rather, arms control is *part* of the evolving broader security regime, embracing both the respective military postures and the arms control and security policy understandings and resulting patterns of behavior and interaction of the two states. At present only rudimentary and fragile, such a regime is potentially broad and diverse in scope, as is shown not only by Table 1 but also by the even broader range of this volume. But it will not be complete and systematic or regulate the U.S.–Soviet relationship comprehensively in the foreseeable future: the two nations remain two sovereign states pursuing their national interests and security in a mixed cooperative-competitive relationship, with the embedded evolving security regime constituting the core of the cooperative component.

In this context, arms control will be incremental rather than radical. Steps can be cumulative, with failures as well as successes. Measures can complement and reinforce each other, as nuclear and conventional arms postures and arms control should in Europe where the main confrontation and interface is found. But a grand design to be put in place under a pre-agreed over-all plan is unlikely. The uncertainties and complexities of the political context, as well as the constantly evolving weapons technology and military balance, defy such an architectural approach to arms control. Principles and goals can be defined (and from time to time redefined); some interdependencies and sequences can be identified and formally linked, as prudence requires. But experience with grand designs (the Dulles chain of pacts for containment, the Johnson "Great Society," or the Nixon "Generation of Peace"; the Soviet pursuit of absolute security, or its planned economy designed to catch and pass the United States in a generation) should suggest humility and pragmatism—which need not exclude boldness and imagination in important cases.

Radical goals or measures can provide stimulating challenges—elimination of nuclear weapons, general and complete disarmament, replacing deterrence with an assured defense. But realism and prudence are not to be overridden. Nuclear weapons cannot be disinvented, or plutonium and reactors to produce it (even without nuclear power plants) wished away, as President Eisenhower and Soviet leaders agreed as long ago as 1955. General and complete disarmament is for a different world than that of present hostilities and disputes in an imperfect international system. Deterrence is an imperative resulting from the awesome power and destructiveness of nuclear weapons even at levels only a fraction of present arsenals, and from the mutual vulnerability of complex interdependent modern societies. The pursuit of an impregnable defense and the achievement of invulnerability must be appraised for its costs and destabilizing consequences as well as for its ideal hopes; wisdom may then be on the side of more modest but attainable cooperative goals and measures.

The phrase the "arms control process" reflects this practical wisdom. The process cannot be automatic, or have a life of its own. But in a sustained and incremental approach, individual measures can have a reinforcing and cumulative value, yet still be manageable and concrete enough to permit a reasonable estimate of value and risk and ways of balancing them. Allowance can be made for intrinsic linkage with other military programs or arms control possibilities. Experience can be gained in applying limits, interpreting texts, verifying fulfillment of obligations, consulting or adjusting to unforeseen issues and problems, building on successes or accepting failures without disrupting the ongoing enterprise. Such a gradual process is particularly important for verification, both for gaining experience, and for maintaining confidence that dilemmas or uncertainties in the learning period will not be attended by the security perils that could flow from over-bold and sudden reductions. The continuing military balance and retained defense capabilities of the parties can serve as insurance and reassurance against the risk of ineffectiveness or even violation of agreements.

Note

1. "The Law of the Sea: Crossroads for U.S. Policy," *Foreign Affairs,* vol. 60, no. 5 (Summer 1982), pp. 1007, 1011.

26

Incentives for U.S.–Soviet Security Cooperation and Mutual Adjustment

ALEXANDER L. GEORGE

This chapter has the ambitious task of providing an analytical framework and some hypotheses that will enable us to understand better the nature, scope, and likely consequences of incentives for U.S.–Soviet cooperation in security matters. For this purpose, in this as well as in subsequent chapters, relevant historical experience is drawn on, as well as elements of a nascent general theory of cooperation that is being developed by specialists in international relations for possible application to U.S.–Soviet relations.

MUTUALITY OF INTERESTS

Cooperation theory as well as common sense tells us that egoistic, competitive actors are not likely to cooperate unless both perceive that their interests will be served better by cooperation than through unilateral, self-serving actions. It is tempting, therefore, to conclude that "mutuality of interests" is a necessary condition for U.S.–Soviet security cooperation. To the extent that this proposition is valid, however, it is somewhat empty for it does not enable us to predict when actors themselves will experience mutuality of interests on a particular issue, or perceive the possibility of offsetting interests and trade-offs on several issues, of sufficient magnitude to motivate attempts to explore and work out cooperative arrangements. Nor does it tell us when such efforts will be successful.

A number of important theoretical and practical questions need to be addressed. First, what is meant by "mutuality of interests" and is this concept sufficiently clear and sufficiently refined to be useful in the further development of cooperation theory and its practical application? As will be noted, "mutuality of interests" obscures the fact that actors can agree on a cooperative arrangement for different reasons. It is sometimes the case, to be sure, that exactly the same interests on both sides lead to a cooperative arrangement—for example, the agreement to establish the Hotline. But it is also possible, as John Maresca shows in his study of the Helsinki Accord of 1975, that somewhat different, even divergent interests may be accommodated to make possible a cooperative arrangement. Other cooperative arrangements may emerge, as Kurt Steiner notes in the case of the Austrian State Treaty of 1955, from a combination of shared and divergent interests; or as Sean Lynn-Jones finds in the case of the Incidents at Sea Agreement, from a combination of shared and complementary interests. Finally, as will be noted in Chapter 29, Moscow and Washington are sometimes motivated to cooperate on a particular security matter in order to improve their over-all relationship.

Second, if something like "mutuality of interests" is a necessary condition for the emergence of cooperation, is it also a sufficient condition? Clearly it is not and, therefore, we must inquire what else in addition to mutual interests may be required for mutually beneficial, mutually acceptable forms of security cooperation to emerge and be effectively implemented. Even when strong shared and/or diverse interests converge on a particular issue a cooperative outcome may be blocked by various obstacles which the two sides simply cannot overcome or do not deal with adequately. Various obstacles of this kind are discussed in Chapter 27. In the face of such obstacles some cooperative arrangements that would be of mutual interest in principle to both sides may be extremely difficult to achieve; other agreements that could perhaps have been realized ("missed opportunities") may be the victim of domestic constraints, psychological burdens, flaws in superpower negotiations, or other obstacles.

Third, the concept of "cooperation," which has a relatively simple meaning in game theory, needs considerable refinement if its significance and role in U.S.–Soviet security relations are to be better understood. In relations between adversaries cooperation occurs in the context of continuing competition, and for a cooperative agreement to be acceptable it must not be judged by either side as seriously handicapping it in the continuing competition. Thus, "cooperation" has a special meaning when it refers to an agreement, quite useful to both sides, that changes the ground rules and channels, rather than eliminates, continuing competition in a particular security issue-area. Similarly, we encounter the anomaly that some cooperative agreements are possible only because both sides have been effective in competing with each other in that particular issue-area. Thus, in Chapter 12 Condoleezza Rice called our attention to the paradox that U.S.–Soviet cooperation in strategic arms control has been possible *"because* unilateral measures have been taken (by both sides) and could be taken again in order to preserve parity." Thus, "unilateral strength and cooperative measures go hand in hand," and strategic arms control is premised on a shared expectation that each side will respond effectively should the other side be perceived as attempting to significantly exceed parity.

More generally, theory that addresses the role of cooperation in regulating adversary relations must identify different types of cooperative relationships and arrangements, as will be noted later in this chapter, and attempt to clarify the conditions under which each type of cooperative behavior is likely to be considered feasible as well as desirable by the actors in question.

A fourth theoretical and practical question also needs to be considered: is cooperation itself always necessary for the realization of mutual security benefits? Can the interests of both parties be served, without any form of cooperative interaction, through the adoption by one of the parties of unilateral policies that promote its own security interests without posing threats to the interests of the adversary? Such unilateral policies would necessarily be based on a broader, longer-range conception of self-interest that takes into account the reality of mutual interdependence for security. When, on the other hand, is some form of cooperative interaction needed to enhance the security of both? More broadly, is there a combination or mix of unilateral policies and cooperative arrangements that is most likely to enhance over-all security? As Rice suggests, one can usefully regard the history of U.S.–Soviet strategic arms control as the search for an optimal or satisfactory combination of unilateral and cooperative efforts to provide for each side's security. The purpose of many of the strategic arms control provisions was, indeed, to provide rules to constrain the unilateral policies of the two sides that threaten mutual security.

While the present study addresses these four questions and, we hope, makes some progress in answering them, a comprehensive and definitive elaboration of a policy-relevant cooperation theory in the realm of security lies beyond our reach.

Before proceeding to a more detailed analysis of these questions we must remind ourselves of the fundamental distinction between *interests* and *expected payoffs*. An actor's conception of interests may provide incentives for considering the desirability of some kind of cooperation. But any particular cooperative arrangement is judged to be acceptable or not depending on whether its expected results will indeed further the actor's security and foreign policy interests. The actor's assessment of expected payoffs, therefore, is critical, and it becomes a question of comparing the expected payoff from pursuing unilateral policies with the expected payoff from particular cooperative arrangements.

The estimate of an expected payoff from an agreement may depend critically on the actor's expectations regarding *implementation* of its provisions: whether compliance can be effectively monitored, whether ambiguities in the agreement and unexpected developments affecting its interpretation can be adequately resolved, and whether one side will be able to deter violations by the other or exert effective persuasion and pressure to correct such violations as may occur. These are important questions, some of which are discussed by Gloria Duffy in her chapter on compliance issues, and are taken up also by Philip Farley in the chapter on "Managing the Risks of Cooperation."

In the world of international politics, the players themselves must determine expected payoffs. Such assessments are subject to multiple uncertainties and domestic controversy, although there are hedges that can be utilized. (In contrast, in the basic Prisoner's Dilemma game, which has done so much to stimulate interest in and ideas for cooperation theory, the players know the payoff matrix for "cooperation" and "defection" and the only uncertainty is what choice between these two options the other side will make.) Finally, we must recognize that in international politics it is often by no means clear that cooperation is objectively feasible, let alone the best solution to every security problem for both players.

THE IMPORTANCE OF PERCEPTIONS OF MUTUAL DEPENDENCE

If it is true, as Realist theory argues, that in the anarchic international system in which we live—that is, one that lacks a central government—states are forced to rely on self-help and alliances to provide for their security and well-being, then why would powerful antagonists such as the United States and the Soviet Union, who would seem to have ample resources for self-help, seriously consider and occasionally enter into cooperative arrangements to enhance their security and well-being? It is one of the limitations of Realist theory that it does not adequately deal with this apparent paradox. Similarly, if it is true that the two superpowers, like all great powers in the past, often compete for relative advantage and greater influence throughout the world at each other's expense, how does one explain the anomaly of their interest in developing cooperation in the security area?

This paradox and anomaly can be better understood and explained if we recognize that even antagonists as powerful as the United States and the Soviet Union experience significant mutual dependence on each other for their security and well-being. One might say that they do experience an incentive to see whether they can make international politics safe—or safer—for their competition and rivalry. Great powers have always attempted to find ways of regulating their rivalry in order to control its costs and risks.[1] In the modern era it is particularly the specter of thermonuclear holocaust that has forced the superpowers to recognize that outcomes of vital importance to each are influenced not merely by one's own policies and actions nor merely by the other's behavior, but also by the nature of the interaction between them. Not only the ultimate issue of war or peace, but outcomes affecting each side's security and well-being in peacetime as well are influenced by how they manage and adjust to the reality of mutual dependence. For, in fact, outcomes of major importance to each are determined by the *interdependent* decisionmaking of the two superpowers.[2] Each side realizes that it has to take into account, however imperfectly and at times incorrectly, the impact its own policies and actions are likely to have on the other side.[3]

Two factors, therefore, seem particularly important in generating incentives for security cooperation. They are (1) the perception by a superpower that it is dependent to some extent on the other superpower's behavior to assure or improve some aspect of its over-all security; and (2) the judgment that strictly unilateral measures, however important and necessary, will either not suffice to deal adequately with a particular threat to its security that the other side can pose or are too expensive or risky. When both sides experience these perceptions their awareness of mutual dependence on each other for security is accompanied by feelings of vulnerability. This, in turn, arouses incentives for exploring cooperative arrangements.

General awareness of their interdependence and vulnerability is only a starting point; by itself it gives Soviet and American leaders no guidance for policy on specific matters. The full scope of that interdependence and its specific manifestations may remain unclear to one or both sides. The implications of interdependence for policy may be cloudy and controversial within each country. Furthermore, substantial disagreements arise between the superpowers as to what adjustments of policy and behavior each should make to reduce the possibility of outcomes damaging, if not disastrous, to both. The United States and the Soviet Union may agree, as they already have on many occasions, that mutual restraint and reciprocity are called for, but disagree on the specific implications of these general principles or over the distribution of the benefits of cooperation between them. As Keohane and Nye note, there is no guarantee that interdependence will yield mutual benefits. One reason for this is that relations of mutual dependence "always involve costs, since interdependence restricts autonomy . . ."[4] Nations particularly value unfettered freedom of action in matters affecting their fundamental security interests. Hence, it is not surprising that in these circumstances each looks to the other to exercise restraint.

One of the consequences of mutual dependence, as we have noted, is vulnerability to the actions and policies of the other side, vulnerabilities that one can perhaps moderate to some extent through unilateral actions (self-help) but which can be better minimized and controlled perhaps only through some kind of mutual adjustment or cooperation with the adversary. Two aspects of security issues contribute to mutual dependency and vulnerability and we must examine them more closely in order to understand how they contribute to incentives for cooperation and affect the strength of such incentives. The two factors are the "tightness" of mutual dependence in any particular security issue-area and the "centrality" of that issue-area, that is, its importance for fundamental security interests.[5]

THE "TIGHTNESS" OR "LOOSENESS" OF MUTUAL DEPENDENCE

We must examine the nature of mutual dependence more closely in order to understand the challenge it poses to the superpowers and the difficulties they encounter in dealing with it. Perceptions of mutual dependence vary greatly in different components of the over-all U.S.–Soviet security relationship. In some activities that affect security the two superpowers may believe that their dependence and vulnerability to each other's action is very "tight"—that the magnitude of potential damage they are capable of inflicting on each other's interests in that security issue-area is substantial. In other issues-areas, however, they may believe that their mutual dependence and vulnerability are much "looser"—that the magnitude of damage they can inflict on each other's interests is more modest.

The tightness or looseness of one's perceived vulnerability in a particular issue-area will influence the severity of risk that is perceived and hence the strength of incentives to cooperate to avoid it. Thus, for example, when the superpowers are faced with the need to manage their tense, war-threatening crises—as in Cuba, Berlin, the Middle East—they tend to share a perception that their mutual dependency and vulnerability to each other's behavior is very tight. Therefore, the need for cooperation and for coordination of decisions and actions to avoid a possible catastrophe is judged to be particularly acute in crisis management. In dealing with each other in tense confrontations such as occurred over the missiles in Cuba, both sides believe they must behave with restraint lest they trigger unwanted escalation. As a matter of fact, quite early in the Cold War the danger that confrontations might erupt into warfare forced leaders on both sides to grasp the requirements for crisis management and to regulate their behavior accordingly. Indeed, in no other dimension of their competition have the superpowers been more successful thus far in adjusting to their mutual dependence, so acutely has it been experienced in diplomatic confrontations in Berlin, the Middle East, and Asia, as well as in Cuba.

In other dimensions of their security relationship, on the other hand, the superpowers regard their mutual dependence and degree of vulnerability to each other's actions as being of a looser nature. In cases of loose mutual dependency and lower vulnerability both sides believe they have the time and resources as well as the necessary will to undertake appropriate and effective remedial measures should the opponent act to gain an advantage. These remedies may take the form of making credible and potent threats to persuade the opponent to forego, curtail, or call off a damaging initiative, or of mobilizing new capabilities in time to neutralize or moderate the harmful effects of the opponent's initiative. Looser mutual dependence characterizes much though not all of the strategic arms competition. That is, most of the new arms initiatives the other side may undertake can be discovered and countered by unilateral actions of one's own before they can significantly alter the military balance.[6]

In those aspects of their relationship characterized by looser forms of mutual dependence the incentives for moderating competition are weaker and perhaps different than in areas of tight mutual dependence such as crisis management. Accordingly, the superpowers may have greater difficulty deciding whether cooperative strategies and policies are really desirable or necessary for this purpose. This is certainly the case, for example, in the area of crisis avoidance, where, as was noted in Chapter 23, the record of cooperation and mutual adjustment on the part of the superpowers is much less impressive than it is in the area of crisis managment.[7] Paradoxically, however, loose dependence may make cooperative agreement easier sometimes insofar as the risks of flawed agreement and noncompliance are lower and more acceptable in such cases.

THE DEGREE OF "CENTRALITY" OF ISSUES FOR SECURITY

Incentives for cooperation are influenced not only by the tightness of mutual dependency in a particular security issue-area but also by how "central" (and hence how important) that issue-area is for fundamental security interests. Different aspects of the two superpowers' security relationship vary greatly in centrality. Some affect the most fundamental security interests; other activities and interactions between the two superpowers affect more peripheral security interests.

Examples of issues of relatively central security importance to Moscow and Washington include the task of crisis management, the inviolability of peacetime satellite reconnaissance, acceptance of each other's geographic areas of dominant security interests (or spheres of influence), the maintenance of an assured strategic retaliatory capability, maintenance of the strategic balance, and parity. Issues of less central (that is, relatively peripheral) importance include underground nuclear testing, demilitarization of Antarctica, the Hotline, neutralization of Austria and Laos, avoidance of incidents at sea, avoidance of crises in Third Areas, and many activities that contribute to confidence-building.

Generally speaking, one would expect that the more central to fundamental security a particular issue is, the stronger the incentive to work out a cooperative arrangement to reduce vulnerability. Conversely, the less central the security importance of an issue, the weaker the incentive to seek a cooperative arrangement to reduce vulnerability.

"TIGHTNESS OF DEPENDENCY" AND "CENTRALITY": A TYPOLOGY

We have seen that two aspects of a security issue contribute to a perception of mutual dependency and the ensuing feeling of vulnerability—the "tightness" of the dependency that is perceived and the "centrality" the issue-area is judged to have for one's fundamental security interests. Together, the tightness of dependency and centrality of a given security issue determine the strength of the incentive to seek a cooperative arrangement to reduce the feeling of vulnerability aroused by that issue. Since tightness of dependency and centrality are variables that differ for different security issues, several combinations are possible. If to simplify the analysis we regard each of these two aspects of a security issue as dichotomous attributes—that is, tightness *or* looseness, and centrality *or* peripherality—then four types of security issues can be identified:

Type 1: issues of central security importance for which, in addition, the mutual dependence of the superpowers is tight;

Type 2: issues of peripheral security importance for which, however, the mutual dependence of the superpowers is tight;

Type 3: issues of central security importance for which, however, the mutual dependence of the superpowers is loose;

Type 4: issues of peripheral security importance for which, in addition, the mutual dependence of the superpowers is loose.

Type 1 issues clearly engage the most important security interests of the two sides and should arouse the strongest incentive for finding a way to achieve mutual benefits, either through cooperative agreements *or* coordinated unilateral moves. One may hypothesize that for Type 1 issues the incentive for seeking a cooperative arrangement will increase to the extent that the two sides become dissatisfied with relying on unilateral actions to safeguard their security. However, there is no assurance that efforts to deal with Type 1 issues in a cooperative manner will be successful or will produce arrangements that are fully effective.

Type 4 issues, on the other hand, generate the weakest incentives for cooperation since they engage peripheral dimensions of security in which, moreover, the degree of mutual dependence is quite loose. Type 2 and Type 3 issues are intermediate in these respects; the strength of incentives for cooperation they generate are somewhere in between the strong incentives aroused by Type 1 issues and the weak incentives generated by Type 4 issues.

Success and failures of cooperation are possible for each of the four types of security issues. It is obvious that factors other than the degree of centrality and tightness of dependence of an issue influence the willingness and ability of the two superpowers to work together to develop a cooperative agreement for that issue. While the incentives to cooperate may be strong for Type 1 issues, the centrality of these issues may raise the requirements for an acceptable agreement. Thus there is no assurance even for Type 1 issues, which generate the strongest incentives, that the superpowers will be able to develop a cooperative arrangement. Instances of successful cooperation on Type 1 issues are to be found in the ability of Moscow and Washington thus far to manage and terminate crises over Berlin, Cuba, and the Middle East without war. Other Type 1 successes include the ABM Treaty and the emergence of a tacit peacetime satellite reconnaissance regime.

As examples of a Type 2 success we may cite the Austrian State Treaty and the Incidents at Sea Agreement. In these matters mutual dependence was indeed tight but hardly of central security import.

Instances of Type 3 successes include the numerical limitations on categories of strategic forces established by SALT I and II, and the superpowers' respect for each other's geographical sphere of dominant interests (sometimes loosely referred to as sphere of influence). Both issues can be characterized as having central security importance but for which mutual dependence is loose.

The fact that incentives to cooperate are relatively weak in Type 4 issues does not necessarily prevent Moscow and Washington from reaching cooperative agreements on some of these issues. In fact, the low centrality and loose degree of mutual dependence in what was at stake in Laos and in the Antarctic may have actually facilitated those agreements. Similarly, confidence-building measures of modest import may be the more easily agreed upon insofar as such options do not pose risks to central security concerns and are not much constrained by tight mutual dependence. Other instances of successful cooperation that benefited from the fact that the issues in question did not place at risk the fundamental security of either superpower include the partial test ban treaty (which, with the assurance of continued underground testing, did not pose a threat to vital security needs), the Hotline, the Outer Space Treaty of 1967, the nuclear nonproliferation treaty, the Helsinki Accord, the Quadripartite Agreement on Berlin, and the Incidents at Sea Agreement. On the other hand, precisely because Type 4 issues typically generate weak incentives for cooperation, the inducement to do so may not suffice to overcome obstacles to cooperation.

THE INSTABILITY OF INCENTIVES

Incentives for security cooperation—and the scope and consequences of such incentives—change over time for a variety of reasons. Incentives depend essentially upon *perceptions* of interests and of threats to those interests. There is often considerable disagreement on these fundamental questions and their implications for policy among political leaders and influential elites in the United States and the Soviet Union. Outcomes of such disagreements in Moscow and Washington are not necessarily stable over time but subject to challenge and reassessment. Moreover, the perception of interest in cooperation on specific security matters is influenced by changing technological, military, political, and economic factors. There is also the possibility that the perception of one's interest in security cooperation can also change over time as a result of learning, however imperfect and slow it may be, and the cumulation of "consensual knowledge" about complex security matters that may facilitate U.S.–Soviet efforts to cooperate.[8] Finally, incentives for security cooperation are not determined by conditions over which the superpowers have no influence; such incentives can be strengthened (or weakened) as a result of the policies and action of the two sides. We need not exaggerate the leverage potentially available to each side for increasing the other side's incentives to work out cooperative security arrangements in order to call attention to this possibility; both superpowers have attempted to use positive and negative inducements to influence each other's incentives to behave in a cooperative manner.

WAYS OF ADJUSTING TO THE REALITY OF MUTUAL DEPENDENCE

There are a variety of ways in which adversaries such as the Soviet Union and the United States can adjust to the perception of their mutual security dependence. Collaboration to this end is *not* limited to formal and tacit agreements; it may also take the form of adherence to patterns of cooperation and of conflict avoidance that have emerged from earlier experience. Alternatives to cooperative agreements include *mutual adjustment* to each other's power and interests; *reciprocal coordination* of unilateral policies in ways that reduce both sides' insecurity; and *unilateral* actions taken by either side, without expectation of reciprocity, that either contribute directly to that side's own security without increasing the insecurity of the other, or contribute indirectly to its security by reducing the other side's insecurity and incentives to compensate for it.

To simplify the discussion let us distinguish merely between (1) cooperative agreements of one kind or another, and (2) mutual adjustment through unilateral actions that may or may not involve an element of coordination but which involve no agreement.

TYPES OF COOPERATIVE AGREEMENTS

At least three types of cooperative agreements can be identified depending on their purpose and payoff. Each type of agreement represents a collaborative effort to limit in some way and to some degree the harmful effects (either already experienced or anticipated) of unrestrained competition for enhanced security and influence in the face of some degree of mutual dependence.[9] A typology of this kind should be useful in developing a *differentiated* theory of security cooperation. Thus, different circumstances and different objectives pursued by the two superpowers lead to different kinds of agreements. This fact, as noted in Chapter 1, should discourage investigators from assuming that all instances of successful security cooperation must have a similar explanation.

1. Agreements that seek to avoid or reduce competition in a given dimension/area of the security relationship by removing an existing or potential source of conflict.

There are many examples of U.S.–Soviet agreements, successful or unsuccessful, that typify this kind of agreement, some of which are presented as case studies in this volume. Such a list includes the World War II agreement on joint occupation and administration of Germany, the Austrian State Treaty of 1955, the Antarctic Treaty of 1959, the Laos Neutralization Agreement in 1962, the 1971 Quadripartite Agreement on Berlin, and the evolution in the 1960s of a tacit agreement not to interfere (at least in peacetime) with each other's satellite reconnaissance activities.

2. Agreements that delimit competition which, if unrestrained, entails mutual disadvantages or harmful consequences that both sides prefer to minimize.

Many arms control agreements are of this nature. Some (such as the ABM Treaty, SALT I and SALT II) establish some parameters or rules within which unilateral efforts to provide for one's security will continue. As Rice notes, the predictability and "transparency" provided by the agreed-on data exchange and numerical limits on certain strategic weapons helped to reduce the "worst" that had to be taken into account in "worst-case" planning. Similarly, as John Lewis Gaddis suggests, Soviet acceptance of American satellite reconnaissance in the early 1960s may have been influenced by the Kremlin's realization that its earlier policy of secrecy had abetted the American proclivity for "worst-case" analysis. By providing early warning and safeguards against surprise attack, satellite reconnaissance has also contributed importantly to strategic and political stability.

3. Agreements that reduce costs, risks, and uncertainties associated with continuing competition or with failure to cooperate to avoid a common danger.

Examples of agreements intended to avoid or lower some of the costs, risks, and uncertainties of certain aspects of superpower competition include the Hotline agreement, the Incidents at Sea Agreement of 1972, some confidence-building measures (CBMs), efforts to discourage nuclear proliferation, provisions for dealing with events that might trigger accidental war, and nuclear terrorist contingencies.

There are various obstacles to achieving cooperative agreements, many of which are noted in the case studies and will be discussed in Chapter 27. It is all the more fortunate, therefore, that cooperative agreements by no means exhaust the ways in which the superpowers can make constructive, mutually beneficial adjustments to some of the dangers inherent in an unrestrained competition for power and influence, and to other threats to security inherent in the international system.

"PARTISAN MUTUAL ADJUSTMENT"

Cooperation theory has not yet given systematic attention to how states in the international system regulate and moderate the risks of competition through unilateral actions and through processes that lead to "partisan mutual adjustment."[10]

In considering how to pursue egoistic goals states often take into account the impact their actions may have on others and how others may then respond. Through such interactions of this kind some coordination of interdependent decisions takes place and this, in turn, can facilitate mutual adjustment in some aspects of relations between adversaries. Coordination of expectations and behavior may occur in the absence of, as well as through, verbal communication between the two sides.

It is easy to underestimate the extent to which states adjust to each other's power and interests *without* benefit of formal or even tacit agreements. States are sensitive to, and influenced by, the general logic of power and the general logic of relative interests. However imperfectly these logics manifest themselves in specific situations and despite the fact that they can be misread and misinterpreted, they do facilitate mutual adjustment. The process of partisan mutual adjustment generates certain norms, "rules of prudence," practices, and restraints that provide some degree of predictability, order, and stability to an adversarial relationship. These "rules" and norms build upon but go well beyond the conventions and modalities of diplomacy, that is, the code and "rules of accommodation" that underpin diplomacy and contribute to its effectiveness.[11]

THREE UNILATERAL STRATEGIES FOR IMPROVING MUTUAL ADAPTATION WITHOUT COMMUNICATION, NEGOTIATION, OR BARGAINING

It is useful at the outset of this discussion to remind ourselves that there is a deep-seated preference on the part of both the United States and the Soviet Union to rely on unilateral rather than bilateral solutions to their security needs. As Jervis notes, in an "anarchic" international system it has to be expected that states will attempt to maintain autonomy and control over their own fate.[12] Even when recognizing their interdependence in the security realm, therefore, U.S. and Soviet leaders are likely to prefer unilateral rather than bilateral solutions whenever possible.

Let us briefly consider three types of unilateral actions that one or the other side may take to facilitate mutual adaptation without engaging in communication, negotiation, or bargaining with its adversary.[13]

First, one side may undertake actions that are considered necessary for its own security and welfare, and hope that the adversary will accept them without responding in a way that heightens distrust and competition. Examples of unilateral actions of this kind that can contribute to mutual adaptation include measures regarded as necessary to safeguard one's assured retaliatory capability and actions regarded as necessary to promote the internal stability and defense of important allies.

Second, one side may undertake actions to improve mutual adjustment that are "deferential" in that the actions in question are carefully chosen so as to avoid any significant adverse consequences for the adversary. In other words, one actor takes on the entire burden for achieving a mutually satisfactory adjustment to the reality of mutual dependence. There is no expectation or requirement of reciprocity on the adversary's part; the contribution to mutual adjustment the action will make is not dependent on changes in the adversary's behavior. The adversary is expected to realize that the unilateral action will result in mutual advantages. Examples of such unilateral actions include the introduction of permissive action links to avoid accidental or unauthorized firing of one's nuclear weapons.

Third, one side may undertake actions that do impose some damage or threat to the adversary's interests and position but it attempts to minimize the adverse impact on the adversary. In other words, in choosing his action the actor tries to take into account the gains and losses for the adversary and hopes that the adversary will conclude that the resulting contribution to mutual adaptation outweighs the costs to him. For example, the Soviet Union correctly anticipated that the Western powers probably would not attempt to demolish the Berlin wall it began to construct during the 1961 crisis but, rather, that the Western powers would conclude that on balance this unilateral Soviet action contributed to mutual adaptation in a situation fraught with danger to both sides.[14]

Several observations need to be made about the utility of unilateral actions taken with the goal of improving the state of mutual adaptation. First, there are ample possibilities for misperception, miscalculation, and misjudgment on the part of the actor undertaking unilateral actions of this kind. The adversary may judge the actions in question to be hostile and damaging rather than conferring mutual advantage. Second, however, deterioration of the relationship is not an inevitable consequence of miscalculation and misjudgment; what may then ensue is a process of interaction between the two sides that provides opportunities for remedial actions. Third, at any point when reliance on unilateral actions proves unsatisfactory to one or both sides, they may initiate communication, negotiation, and bargaining (topics that are discussed in Chapter 29, "Strategies for Facilitating Cooperation). These activities provide the opportunity for a more explicit, controllable mode of coordination for improving mutual adaptation.

It is possible that the superpowers may learn from experience that unilateral policies for dealing with an important security issue are not effective and be motivated as a result to turn to cooperative procedures to achieve national and mutual interests engaged by that issue. Thus as Nye notes, after their unilateral efforts to deal with nuclear proliferation failed the United States and the Soviet Union placed greater emphasis on cooperating to slow the spread of nuclear weapons. Nye's analysis is important, too, in calling attention to the fact that how the superpowers define their national interests in an important security matter such as nuclear proliferation can change over time.

We must be careful, however, not to overgeneralize from the learning experience in the nuclear proliferation area. There are probably many more instances of failure to learn in time, such as, for example, in the case of MIRV. Moreover, "learning" can occur in the opposite direction as well; that is, one or both sides can conclude from abortive or disappointing experience with cooperative efforts that it is necessary or preferable to place more reliance on unilateral efforts in certain security issue-areas.

We cannot conclude, therefore, that joint efforts to develop coordination and cooperative arrangements are always superior to unilateral strategies. It is also possible that some mixture and sequencing of unilateral strategies and negotiation may succeed in facilitating mutual adjustment. This has implications for strategy that are discussed in a later chapter.

Thus far we have discussed the possibility of cooperation between the United States and the Soviet Union only with reference to specific components of their security relationship. We have focused on incentives for security cooperation that arise from, and in a sense are forced on Moscow and Washington by, their mutual dependence and vulnerability. But interdependence may also be a freely chosen goal; interdependence in nonsecurity areas such as trade may be cultivated as part of a strategy for improving U.S.–Soviet relations. Both security cooperation and other types of interdependence may be facilitated if the superpowers can achieve some understanding regarding a framework for their over-all relationship. (See the discussion of ''The Importance of a Basic Political Framework,'' in Chapter 27.)

This chapter has provided an analytical framework and some hypotheses that help to clarify the nature, scope, and likely consequences of the incentives that American and Soviet leaders experience for developing cooperative arrangements or, in the absence of formal or tacit agreement, for achieving mutual adjustment in security matters.

How, under what circumstances, do incentives for security cooperation arise? Two factors seem particularly important in generating such incentives. They are (1) the emergence of a shared U.S.–Soviet perception that each is dependent on the other's behavior to assure or improve its own security or to lighten the burden of protecting it; and (2) an additional shared judgment that the strictly unilateral measures one side can take, however important and necessary, will not suffice or are not optimal for dealing with a particular threat to its security interests and that, therefore, something may be gained by seriously exploring bilateral (or multilateral) arrangements to this end.

However, the degree to which one side feels it is dependent for its security, and the extent to which it perceives its security to be vulnerable to the policies and actions of the other side, vary greatly in different segments or components of the over-all U.S.–Soviet security relationship. For this reason we introduced into our analytical framework two ways of refining and differentiating perceptions of dependency and vulnerability. One of these analytical refinements is ''tightness or looseness'' of perceived dependency and vulnerability on a particular security issue. The other analytical refinement concerns how ''central'' or ''peripheral'' a particular matter or issue-area is judged to be for one's fundamental security. Obviously, issues of central security importance for which, in addition, dependence is judged to be very tight—for example, crisis management of war-threatening U.S.–Soviet confrontations—differ greatly from issues of peripheral security importance for which, in addition, dependence is perceived to be very loose— such as the Laos situation prior to neutralization in 1962.

Taken together the perceived ''tightness-looseness'' of dependency and the ''centrality or non-centrality'' for security of a given issue determine how strong an incentive to cooperate that issue will generate. But, as was noted, factors other than strength of incentives also influence whether cooperative arrangements can be worked out.

Cooperative agreements having to do with security are not an end in themselves; rather they are a means—and only one means—for achieving various objectives extending all the way from reduction of the risk of war to the development of a more constructive, orderly, and stable U.S.–Soviet relationship. There are bound to be serious limits on promoting these objectives solely through cooperative U.S.–Soviet agreements. Therefore, the scope of inquiry and the policy agenda need to be broadened to include attention to alternative ways in which Moscow and Washington can expect to make progress towards these objectives.

Alternatives to cooperative agreements include *mutual adjustment* to each other's power and interest, *reciprocal coordination* of unilateral U.S. and Soviet policies and behaviors in ways that reduce both sides' insecurity, and *unilateral actions* that either side can take, without expectation of reciprocity, that contribute (a) directly to its own security without increasing the insecurity of the other side, or (b) contribute indirectly to its own security by reducing the other side's insecurity and its incentives to escalate the arms competition.

In sum, cooperative agreements are neither always possible nor always necessary for the realization of mutual security benefits. Rather, some combination or mix of unilateral policies and cooperative arrangements will be necessary to optimize mutual security.

Notes

1. See, for example, the discussion provided by Paul Gordon Lauren, "Crisis Prevention in Nineteenth-Century Diplomacy," in A. L. George, *Managing U.S.–Soviet Rivalry: Problems of Crisis Prevention* (Boulder, Colo.: Westview Press, 1983), pp. 31–64.

2. This point was emphasized by Thomas Schelling and incorporated into his discussion of strategy in his seminal work, *The Strategy of Conflict* (Cambridge: Harvard University Press, 1960). In such "non-zero sum" (or "mixed-motive") games, Schelling observes, "mutual dependence is part of the logical structure and demands some kind of collaboration or mutual accommodation—tacit, if not explicit—even if only in the avoidance of mutual disaster" (p. 83).

3. The significance of interdependence as a major constraint on power as a determinant of outcomes in international relations was emphasized in the pioneering book by Robert O. Keohane and Joseph S. Nye, *Power and Interdependence: World Politics in Transition* (Boston: Little, Brown, 1977). Despite the lead given by these two scholars (cf., e.g., p. 9), the implications of U.S.–Soviet interdependence for cooperation in security matters has not yet been systematically studied.

4. Ibid., p. 9.

5. Readers familiar with international relations theory will recognize that this discussion of mutual dependency in security affairs reformulates and refines the familiar distinction between "sensitivity" and "vulnerability." For our purposes, it is divided into two dimensions: "tightness-looseness" (which captures the distinction between vulnerability and sensitivity, but treats it as a continuum rather than as a dichotomous attribute) and the "centrality-peripherality" of any particular component of security. In addition, both of these dimensions of mutual dependency are regarded here as subjective, perceptual variables at the decision-making level of analysis, not as objective, structural variables.

6. There are, of course, some important exceptions to this generalization. One of these is the possibility of covert preparations for altering the strategic balance after "breakout" from an arms control agreement. Another exception is the kind of sudden, covert deployment of substantial forces, which significantly alters the balance, that was undertaken by Nikita Khrushchev in deploying missiles into Cuba.

7. To be sure, factors other than the "looseness" of mutual dependence help to explain limited superpower cooperation in crisis avoidance and other security matters—for example, the diffuseness and complexity of superpower interests and competition in Third Areas, and the greater complexity of achieving superpower cooperation in nonbilateral security issues.

8. Ernst Haas, "Why Collaborate? Issue-linkages and International Regimes," *World Politics,* vol. 32, no. 1 (October 1980): 357–405; Robert L. Rothstein, "Consensual Knowledge and International Collaboration: Some Lessons from Commodity Negotiations," *International Organization,* vol. 38, no. 4 (Autumn 1984): 733–762.

9. These agreements are similar to what Arthur Stein has referred to as "regimes of mutual aversion" rather than of positive benefits. As Steven Weber has indicated (private communication), it is easier for Moscow and Washington to cooperate to avoid outcomes to which both are averse than to achieve mutual benefits of a positive character.

10. The concept "partisan mutual adjustment" was developed by Charles E. Lindblom, in

The Intelligence of Democracy (New York: Free Press, 1965) to refer to processes by means of which actors "coordinate" their behavior and interactions out of self-interest, in the absence of a central decision-making body that legislates rules for this purpose and enforces them. Lindblom's discussion and examples focus largely on political and economic relations within a given polity, although he also occasionally indicates that his concepts and analysis are relevant also to interstate relations, which indeed they are. The importance and relevance of Lindblom's analysis is briefly noted by Robert O. Keohane, in *After Hegemony* (Princeton N.J.: Princeton University Press, 1984), pp. 51–2.

11. See, for example, R. F. Feltham, *Diplomatic Handbook,* 2nd edition (London: Longman, 1977); Raymond Cohen, *International Politics: The Rules of The Game* (London: Longman, 1981); Fred C. Ikle, *How Nations Negotiate* (New York: Harper & Row, 1964).

12. Robert Jervis, "Cooperation Under Anarchy: Problems and Limitations," draft manuscript, Columbia University, July 1986.

13. This discussion of unilateral strategies has benefited from Lindblom's stimulating conceptualization of methods of partisan mutual adjustment. I have dropped the terms ("parametric," "deferential," and "calculated") he employs to differentiate between three types of unilateral methods, and I have adapted and added to his discussion in order to enhance its relevance for U.S.–Soviet relations.

14. The Soviet expectation that a Berlin wall would be accepted by the Western powers was not entirely speculative or based on wishful thinking. Various indications of this were given by the Kennedy Administration, some of them possibly subtle signals. See Honoré M. Catudal, *Kennedy and the Berlin Wall Crisis* (Berlin: Berlin Verlag, 1980).

27

Factors Influencing Security Cooperation

ALEXANDER L. GEORGE

In the preceding chapter we discussed incentives that the superpowers may have in giving serious consideration to one or another form of security cooperation. Incentives for cooperation may be a necessary condition but certainly not a sufficient one for achieving a specific type of security cooperation. Various obstacles may stand in the way of recognizing mutual interests for security cooperation in general or with respect to any particular security problem. These same obstacles, moreover, can make it difficult to act on the shared perception of mutual interests in order to develop an acceptable cooperative arrangement. The first section of this chapter identifies and discusses these obstacles, and draws on our case studies for specific examples of such obstacles.

Cooperation in specific security matters may also be hindered or facilitated by the over-all relationship that exists between the United States and the Soviet Union at any given time or by the type of relationship they are attempting to create. In the past both American and Soviet leaders have recognized the importance of developing a basic political framework for improving their over-all relationship, which might both facilitate and be supported by cooperation in security matters and in issue-areas such as trade and cultural and scientific exchanges. The second section of this chapter examines the experience thus far in efforts to establish and work within a basic political framework of relations.

Finally, if there are often serious obstacles in the way of developing security cooperation, it is also the case that in other instances there have been conditions that favor cooperation on a specific matter. These favorable conditions are discussed and illustrated in the third section of this chapter.

OBSTACLES TO SECURITY COOPERATION

The problem of security cooperation between the Soviet Union and the United States is rendered more complex and difficult by the fact that security is but one of the principal national interests that the leaders of each country seek to preserve and enhance. The security and physical survival of one's country and people may indeed be the most important of these interests, particularly in an era of thermonuclear weapons. But national leaders and their peoples have always attached great importance also to assuring their country's economic vitality and well-being, and to developing an international system in which it will be easier to maintain their country's freedom and political way of life. Thus, the avoidance of a thermonuclear holocaust may be the dominant concern but it is not the only compelling national interest that foreign policy attempts to protect and enhance. There has been substantial agreement within the United States since the end of World War II that all three of these fundamental national interests should shape the basic purposes and objectives of American foreign policy. At the same time, there has been sharp disagreement over the substance of foreign policy. Quite obviously, the implications of even these fundamental national interests for foreign policy are not self-evident.

One reason for disagreements over national policy has to do with the difficulties experienced in attempts to integrate all three interests in an over-all foreign policy.[1] The accumulation of power, influence, and resources is motivated not only by a desire to achieve security but also to make it easier to maintain political autonomy and economic well-being. Both the United States and the Soviet Union are global powers with world-wide interests and ambitions. Their efforts to maintain prestige and extend influence, often at each other's expense, complicate the search for security, either on a unilateral or cooperative basis.

At the same time, however, it may well be that the competition between the United States and the Soviet Union is, if anything, less in the security area—insofar as the two superpowers come to realize that the security threat they pose to each other is manage-able—than between their economic and political systems. How well the Soviet Union and the United States do in the economic and political realm is important for their internal stability and vitality. The necessity to maintain political and economic viability has already constrained expenditures for enhancing military security, and this tension between competing national interests is likely to become more severe for both super-powers in the future.

We shall discuss six factors that constrain the ability of Soviet and American lead-ers to perceive mutual interests in security cooperation or, when such recognition exists in a particular aspect of their relationship, that complicate efforts to achieve a coopera-tive agreement. These six factors are (1) the security dilemma embedded in the "anar-chic" international system, (2) the role of ideology in exacerbating U.S.–Soviet con-flicts of interests, (3) various asymmetries between the United States and the Soviet Union that complicate the search for security cooperation, (4) the impact of imperfect information and various uncertainties, (5) the role of technology in stimulating the qual-itative dimension of arms competition, and finally (6) the influence of domestic and alliance constraints.

It will be noted that some of these obstacles to security cooperation—the security dilemma, ideology, asymmetries, technology—tend to be fundamental and pervasive. These constraints are ever present and affect to a degree just about all aspects of the over-all U.S.–Soviet security relationship. Domestic and alliance constraints, on the other hand, are less pervasive and much more variable in their impact on security co-operation. Besides, domestic and alliance factors are not always obstacles; on important occasions they may generate pressure for security cooperation.

The Security Dilemma

Any discussion of difficulties in achieving U.S.–Soviet security cooperation should be-gin by recognizing an obstacle that is rooted in the "anarchic" nature of the interna-tional system. "Anarchy" in this context refers to the absence of a supranational authority, with the consequence that individual states are forced to provide for their own survival and welfare by accumulating power resources and participating in alliances. There is no world government to legislate and enforce rules that would serve to moderate and regulate the competition for resources and influence, to mediate disputes, or to facilitate appropriate cooperative arrangements between states that do have some common or complementary interests.

In consequence, states experiencing a conflict of interests easily become victims of the "security dilemma." This term is employed in international relations theory to refer to a familiar phenomenon that exacerbates conflicts of interest: thus, the measures one state adopts to increase its sense of security, to deter and defend against possible encroachments by a hostile (or potentially hostile) state may be viewed by the second state as a threat to its own security that requires it to take additional defense measures of its own. These, in turn, can have a similar effect on the first state, which may respond with additional defense measures, and so on. Thus, unless this vicious cycle is checked, states interact in ways that accentuate distrust, feed the arms race, and exacerbate the security problem for each side.

The security dilemma can operate even when both states genuinely pursue defensive objectives in their policies towards each other. However, the intentions behind an adversary's acquisition of military capabilities may appear ambiguous, and this perception will be heightened, as Robert Jervis has noted,[2] if the adversary acquires weapons that have possible offensive as well as defensive uses and adopts an offense-oriented military doctrine that emphasizes seizing the initiative in the event a war occurs or appears to be inevitable during a diplomatic crisis. The impact of the security dilemma is greater, of course, when one or both sides give evidence of pursuing or contemplating expansionist foreign policy objectives. Such an impression is all too easily conveyed by global powers that develop worldwide interests and ambitions and, in order to pursue them, gradually expand the concept of their "security requirements," thereby making it more difficult for the superpowers to manage their global rivalry.

Nor can the action-reaction dynamics of the security dilemma be easily curbed by arms control agreements. In U.S.–Soviet strategic arms control, as Condoleezza Rice reminds us, maintenance of strategic parity, on which the two sides have agreed, is in the final analysis a unilateral responsibility. Since force modernization is permissible under certain (not entirely unambiguous rules) and the technological dimension of the arms race continues, parity requires a dynamic equilibrium that must be maintained over time in response to real or expected changes in force postures. "Hence," as Rice notes, "unilateral steps to maintain parity over time can be viewed by the other side as threatening parity at best and as a bad faith search for superiority at worst. This leads to exacerbation of the security dilemma."

Three types of malignant consequences ensue when a vicious interaction is set into motion by the security dilemma. First, additional suspicion and distrust develops between states, thereby exacerbating and rigidifying the real conflicts of interests. Besides, as Realist theory reminds us, states in the anarchic international system engaged in competition with each other seek not only to provide for their security, but also to achieve relative advantage over each other. Even a state that is a satisfied, status-quo power is compelled to behave in this way in order to prevent possible deterioration of its security position. And the quest for security and the striving for relative advantage tend to merge into one, thus further exacerbating the security dilemma.

Second, the dynamics of the security dilemma often (though not always) encourage the arms race and severely complicate efforts at arms controls. Motivation for more ambitious arms control agreements is diluted by concern over their possible security disadvantages. It is particularly difficult to reach agreements that effectively control the technological component of arms competition insofar as one or both sides believe that sacrifice of certain promising technological opportunities for achieving better military capabilities may have damaging consequences for their relative security position in the future.

Third, the dynamics of the security dilemma can manifest themselves in a particularly dangerous way during tense diplomatic crises. Thus, the measures one side takes in a crisis to reduce the vulnerability of its military forces, to increase their readiness in case war breaks out, or to signal resolution in order to energize its crisis diplomacy may be viewed by the other side as preparations to initiate or to escalate military operations, thereby requiring it to increase the alert status and readiness of its own forces. As a result, a vicious cycle of interaction and escalation may occur during a crisis that neither side anticipated or wanted, and which can contribute to a breakdown of crisis management and lead to an inadvertent war.

The Role of Ideology

The security dilemma can have malignant consequences of this kind even in the absence of ideological influences on foreign policy. Ideology severely exacerbates these difficulties by creating among political leaders and their publics an idealized self-image and an invidious image of the opponent. Ideology also exacerbates cognitive and affective biases that all individuals are prone to.[3]

That such perceptions of the self and the adversary can severely exacerbate conflicts of interest between two individuals was aptly conveyed in the observation many years ago by the famous American jurist, Oliver Wendell Holmes. In any argument between two persons, Holmes remarked, six persons are actually involved: two persons as they actually are; each of the two as he sees himself, a self-image that may bear little relationship to reality; and each of the two as he is seen by the other, a perception that may be quite different from his image of himself. No wonder, Holmes exclaimed, that two persons engaged in a dispute talk past each other and the argument becomes so heated. Idealized images of the self and invidious images of the adversary are common in conflicts between states; the result is to exacerbate disputes and to make conflict mediation all the more difficult.

In the anarchic international system each state strives to enhance its security, safeguard its way of life, and ensure its basic economic needs. Relations among states would in any case tend to be competitive, but the contentious nature of world politics is much accentuated when states, viewing each other through the prism of their ideologies, regard each other as enemies. An "enemy," in contrast to a "limited adversary," symbolizes the antithesis of one's own core values and threatens one's preferred political and international order.

The image of an opponent is multidimensional and it is useful to consider some of its components and consequences that have particular relevance for foreign policy and interstate relations. In the first place, one side's perception and assessment of threats posed by an adversary are influenced by its general image of that opponent. Intelligence indicators of an opponent's intentions, both his immediate and long-range intentions, tend to be interpreted through the prism of the image of that opponent. Explanations of an adversary's actions can be similarly distorted by the general image of that opponent. Modern attribution theory, a branch of cognitive psychology, reminds us that even under the best of circumstances a person who strives to make objective, scientific judgments is prone to make errors in assessing the character and behavior of others. The "fundamental attribution error" is of particular interest: thus, when one's opponent takes a tough action one tends to explain that behavior as stemming from the adversary's innate hostility rather than as a reasonable response to the situation or to one's own behavior. On the other hand, when the opponent behaves in a conciliatory fashion, one tends to explain that behavior as forced on the adversary by the situation or by one's own behavior rather than as an expression of his character and general disposition. An ideologically inspired image of the opponent can accentuate attribution biases of this kind and complicate efforts at accommodation. A policy-maker's bad-faith image of the opponent can distort his assessment of incoming information about the adversary; operating with such an image the policy-maker all too readily ignores or explains away "discrepant" behavior of a conciliatory kind that, at least on the face of it, logically contradicts the bad faith image of the opponent.[4]

From what had been said it is obvious that a critical dimension of the image one holds of an opponent is the degree of hostility towards oneself attributed to the opponent. In other words, is the opponent perceived to be a limited adversary or an implacable foe? Similarly, does one assume that the nature of the conflict with a particular opponent approximates a zero-sum or a mixed-sum game? In principle, to be sure, such questions are susceptible to rigorous, factual analysis before they are answered, and it is possible, of course, that the results of such an analysis would lead one to conclude that the adversary is indeed implacably hostile and that the contest is a grim zero-sum conflict. But insofar as objective, factual analysis of such fundamental questions is laden with uncertainty, one's ideology can easily tip the balance in one direction or another. One of the functions of ideology generally in decision-making is to help policy-makers cope with critical uncertainties that stem from the well-known "cognitive limits" on rationality.[5]

Another critical dimension in the image of an opponent is how one explains the opponent's animosity and whether one regards his hostility as permanent or subject to change. This aspect of the opponent's image has a significant bearing on judgments of fundamental questions of foreign policy, such as the following: What are the sources of the opponent's hostility and can one do anything to alter them so as to reduce his hostility? Is it realistic to try to develop a more constructive type of relationship with the opponent that includes cooperative as well as competitive elements? How is the opponent likely to respond to conciliatory actions? And how is the opponent likely to respond to policies of firmness?

What these observations suggest is that an ideologically shaped image of an opponent has important implications for one's most fundamental policy decisions concerning that adversary: what kind of relationship with the opponent should one strive for in the long-run that is both desirable and feasible, and what strategy and specific tactics should one adopt for dealing with him?

These questions are difficult to answer with confidence in any event, but the difficulties they pose for U.S. foreign policy toward the Soviet Union are severely exacerbated by fundamental disagreements among U.S. policy-makers as to what is the correct image of the Soviet Union's character and intentions. In fact, ever since the World War II alliance gave way to the Cold War, a fundamental disagreement as to the correct image of the Soviet Union has been at the heart of the many important policy disagreements within the United States as to how to deal with the rival superpower. Policy disagreement on specific issues, or on the best strategy and tactics for dealing with the Soviet Union in general or in concrete situations, can often be traced to rival policy-makers' underlying assumptions as to the nature of Soviet long-range objectives and its strategy for eventually achieving them. American and Western specialists on the Soviet Union themselves have profound disagreements on this issue, and so policy-makers who lack expertise on the Soviet Union are subjected to divergent estimates of the Soviet threat and how best to respond. The disagreement on the correct image of the Soviet Union is not only fundamental, but it does not lend itself to intellectual resolution through scientific methods of weighing evidence on behalf of rival theories. As a result, this unresolved but critically important matter easily becomes involved in the politics of the continuing struggle over American policy towards the Soviet Union.

Finally, the fact that this fundamental issue remains unresolved and subject to the pull-and-tug of intellectual and political controversy has contributed to the difficulty every administration has had since Truman's presidency to develop a coherent long-range policy towards the Soviet Union and to pursue it in a consistent, purposeful manner. The requirements for a coherent, consistent foreign policy are especially difficult to meet in a highly pluralistic democratic system such as that of the United States.[6] Presidential invocations of the "national interest" and "national security" to gain sufficient support for foreign policy have long since declined in their efficiency for this purpose. Instead, the president is faced with the more complex task of developing "legitimacy" for his policy.[7]

How do these manifestations of ideology, centered on the critical question of the image of the opponent, affect the possibility of U.S.–Soviet cooperation in security affairs more concretely? At least seven possible constraints on cooperation can be identified which manifest themselves particularly, but not exclusively, in the arms control field. First, disagreements over the correct image of the Soviet Union can call into question the scope as well as the desirability of cooperative arrangements with the Soviets and reinforce a preference for relying on unilateral policies for assuring U.S. security interests. Second, ideologically inspired distrust of the adversary strengthens the tendency to regard cooperation with the other side as fundamentally unstable, desired by the opponent only for tactical purposes. Third, it reinforces tendencies to favor unilateral policies that yield short-term advantages over alternative policies, including self-restraint and cooperative arrangements, that might yield more important longer-term payoffs. Fourth, it constrains and reduces the attractiveness of reciprocity as a means of developing better relations. Fifth, it encourages and legitimizes more extreme forms of worst-case analysis in force-planning, procurement, and deployment decisions. Sixth, concern over the basic character and long-range intentions of the adversary throws into doubt Soviet compliance with agreements, invokes the possibility of Soviet break-out from existing agreements, and tends to raise requirements for information and verification. Seventh, if agreements are reached, a distrustful image of the adversary encourages the tendency to regard as clear-cut, deliberate Soviet violations what may be compliance issues stemming from ambiguities and loop-holes in the agreement.

Many of these constraints on cooperation that the U.S. image of the Soviets reinforces are evident in the accounts of arms control efforts by Philip Farley and Gloria Duffy. Farley points to the heart of the matter when he notes that, implicit in the willingness to enter into serious arms control negotiations is the "acceptance of the other side as a worthy negotiating partner—a nation with compatible even if not identical security goals and standards, thus making it conceivable that a fair and balanced agreement which could be verified might be arrived at, complied with, and effective. This premise, implicit during the initial phases of the SALT process, came to be highly contentious—especially in the United States—with the decline of détente during the latter half of the 1970s and in the 1980s.''

Moreover, each side can point to efforts it has made to operate with restraint, to forgo short-term advantages in favor of longer-term payoffs, to encourage reciprocity that proved to be abortive. The failure of such well-intentioned efforts can be blamed on the adversary, thereby reinforcing a bad-faith image of the opponent. Americans maintain that it was the Soviet Union which in 1961 broke the long-standing moratorium on nuclear testing.[8] When the United States reduced military expenditures and moderated its global policies after Vietnam, the Soviet Union continued its military build-up and engaged in a more assertive competition for influence in the Third World. And, as Steven Weber and Sidney Drell note, when the United States adopted a strategy of ''contingent restraint'' on ASAT testing to induce reciprocity, the Soviets, seemingly disinterested, resumed testing of an anti-satellite system.

We know less about the role that the Soviet image of the United States has played in Soviet arms control policy. However, there is some reason to believe that Soviet leaders regard the U.S. military build-up in recent years as offering disquieting indications that the Reagan Administration is aiming at military superiority and is not seriously interested in arms control that attempts to maintain a military balance. It would appear, therefore, that the increasingly strong disposition in the United States to view the Soviet Union as bent on eventual world domination has been matched by a growing Soviet disposition to see the United States as a resurgent and hostile imperialist power with dangerous goals. (For additional discussion of Soviet attitudes, see Chapter 24.)

The Role of Asymmetries

The case studies call attention to a variety of asymmetries between the United States and the Soviet Union that have constrained cooperation in security matters. Particularly Farley in his assessment of the strategic arms control experience and Alan Neidle in his analysis of test ban negotiations discuss the impact of these asymmetries in some detail. Many other analysts of U.S.–Soviet relations have also emphasized the important parameters and constraints that various asymmetries impose on U.S.–Soviet relations. A brief summary will suffice for present purposes.

Their different geopolitical positions and historical experience with warfare in the past have shaped U.S. and Soviet military doctrines and force structures in different ways. Given its advantageous geographical isolation, the United States developed an emphasis on naval and air power that continues in the present day. The Soviet Union, in contrast, is a land-locked country that has had many bitter experiences with ground invasion by strong and hostile powers. Not surprisingly, the Soviet Union has placed emphasis on ground and artillery forces and resorts to forward deployment of powerful forces along its borders in Europe and Asia. As Farley notes, the composition of the respective strategic forces of the United States and the Soviet Union also reflects these factors, and ''fitting these asymmetries into formulas for limitation of strategic forces has been a taxing challenge for negotiators. . . . ''

John Steinbruner, too, emphasizes that as a result of geography and history the respective security requirements of the United States and the Soviet Union are strikingly different. Although the principles of "equality" and "equal security" were accepted in SALT I as providing the only realistic basis for stable regulation of the U.S.–Soviet relationship, these principles have not been effectively operationalized in concrete terms nor have they been firmly established within the U.S. political system.[9]

Neidle perceives an important difference between the two superpowers in their receptivity to test bans, with the Soviet Union frequently prepared to accept agreements that have been to its relative military and technical disadvantage. The explanation he offers is that the two sides differ in the way in which they view the purpose of arms control and the risks of nuclear war. The Soviets place more stress on the prevention of war by political means whereas the United States places more emphasis on deterrence of war by military means. Similarly, whereas the United States views the primary danger of war arising from the failure to deter (Soviet) aggression, the Soviets see the primary danger as that of an unintended or inadvertent war arising from loss of control in a crisis. A similar observation is made by Barry Blechman regarding the asymmetry in the ways in which the United States and the USSR view *technical* agreements to reduce the risk of accidental and inadvertent war. Soviet leaders evidently attribute far less importance than would many Americans to the technical risks that might lead to a war.

The difficulty of bridging the disparity in U.S.–Soviet security perspectives is accentuated by differences between the political systems of the two sides. Notwithstanding the development of remarkable national technical means of intelligence, attempts at strategic cooperation between a closed and an open society encounter severe difficulties.

Asymmetries in strategic doctrines may generate requirements for weapon systems that can severely constrain unilateral and joint efforts to stabilize the military balance. NATO's reliance on extended deterrence, for example, requires the United States to provide concrete and visible assurances that it is willing to accept the risk of nuclear war with the Soviet Union in order to discharge its commitment to its Western European allies. To this end, and to counter the political-psychological as well as the military threat posed by Soviet SS-20s against Western Europe, the United States deployed Pershing IIs and cruise missiles into Western Europe. While this move may have reinforced extended deterrence, it also contributes to apprehension about crisis instability. The NATO threat to initiate tactical use of nuclear weapons if confronted by a large-scale Soviet conventional attack, which lies at the core of the extended deterrence strategy, exemplifies the "dilemma of deterrence"—namely, that in order to deter the opponent one is forced to threaten actions that one would much prefer not to carry out. This raises the question of the credibility of extended deterrence and whether political approval for initial use of nuclear weapons to thwart a Soviet conventional onslaught would be forthcoming. To a considerable extent the efficacy of extended deterrence rests on the Soviet leadership's uncertainty as to whether it would be implemented. So long as NATO continues to rely on the strategy of extended deterrence, therefore, it will be reluctant to accept arms control measures that would reduce that uncertainty and create the conviction that nuclear weapons will not in fact be used. This constraint also applies to some of the confidence-building measures that have been suggested.[10]

Another asymmetry in strategic doctrines that complicates cooperation in security matters is the emphasis on the importance of preemption in Soviet military doctrine vis-à-vis NATO. Certainly this is a matter of concern for NATO, but surveillance and other confidence-building measures adopted in the Stockholm Conference of 1986, as noted by James Goodby, may give experience with cooperative measures that will reduce the grounds for such fears.

Finally, as has often been noted, an imbalance between the two superpowers in their military capabilities may be an obstacle to arms control agreements. Thus, the Soviets became amenable to strategic arms control agreements only when they attained parity with the United States. And, as John Lewis Gaddis suggests, Soviet policy shifted towards acceptance of satellite reconnaissance after Moscow, too, achieved a significant, valued capability in this area. And, as he as well as Steven Weber and Sidney Drell suggest, the asymmetries between the ASAT capabilities of the United States and the Soviet Union added to the difficulties of reaching an agreement in that weapons area.

The Role of Uncertainty

The superpowers' pursuit of cooperation in security matters is heavily constrained by a variety of pervasive uncertainties. In stark contrast to the assumption of perfect information in the standard Prisoner's Dilemma game, which is often used as a starting point for the development of cooperation theory, uncertainty plays a major role in exacerbating U.S.–Soviet military competition. As noted in our discussion of the role of ideology, fundamental uncertainties arise for each side concerning the real intentions and future behavior of the adversary. For example, is the adversary really prepared to cooperate on a particular security matter or is his interest in an agreement a tactical move for short-term advantage to be followed by abandonment of the agreement when it becomes advantageous to do so? Is the adversary deliberately and knowingly violating a particular agreement or is he merely exploiting what he perceives to be ambiguities in the agreement? And hedging may be necessary, by such means as major research and development (R & D), to insure against uncertain futures, but such measures may be observed and matched by the rival in enhanced competition.

Uncertainty as to whether one will be able to ascertain in a reliable and timely manner whether the adversary is engaged in significant violations of an agreement under consideration may sway one's judgment against making that agreement. This concern leads, particularly in certain types of arms control agreements, to emphasis on the critical importance of adequate monitoring and verification of compliance. Washington's uncertainty as to the Soviet ABM program played an important role in getting the American MIRV program started and encouraged worst-case analyses of the threat a Soviet ABM might pose.[11]

Uncertainty operates also with reference to the reliability of existing weapons and their eventual obsolescence. Opponents of the comprehensive test ban in the United States, as Neidle notes in his chapter, argue that testing of nuclear weapons is necessary to ascertain the reliability of the stockpile.

The Role of Technology

Technology with potential military applications influences policy in several ways that provide motivation for, but at the same time complicate and constrain cooperation in security matters. To be sure, technology sometimes facilitates cooperation by providing capabilities that can be employed to overcome obstacles to cooperation. A well-known example is the development of satellite technology and other national technical means for verification which have made certain arms control agreements possible. Quite different is the possibility that a new technology that is regarded as extremely dangerous or highly destabilizing by both sides may generate incentives for cooperation to close off competition in that area. Here, however, we will focus on technological developments that hamper security cooperation.

Since World War II, science and technology have provided an increasingly rich menu from which military planners can choose options for research and development. Available options have become too numerous and costly to permit R & D on all technological fronts. Despite the fact that policy-makers bow to resource constraints on the number of R & D options that are pursued, the technological aspect of arms development has a dynamism and momentum that both demands and complicates efforts at arms control. Technology—particularly in the United States—offers seemingly irresistible opportunities to both superpowers to improve their security in the future, to keep up with or outdistance the adversary. However, sometimes military programs predicated on technology improvements do not work out as hoped, which may lead defense officials to scramble for either (a) substantial program changes designed to make up the losses, or (b) ways of fogging over the current deficiencies to keep a program going without essential change.

For other reasons as well, the qualitative, technological component of arms competition is even more difficult to control than its quantitative dimensions. It is difficult to predict with confidence the eventual success of R & D options or their net military value. The additional difficulty of estimating the military payoff the adversary will derive from research on R & D options makes it hard to forgo pursuing one's own. As the history of ASAT development summarized by Weber and Drell indicates, when the expected rewards for exploiting technology are quite modest or unpromising, an opportunity exists for tacit or explicit arms control. But when a shift occurs from poor to more promising technology, as took place later with respect to ASAT, pressures to continue R & D unfettered by arms control considerations may prevail. Similarly, the unpromising technology of the late 1960s facilitated agreement on the AMB Treaty in 1972, but improved technological prospects since then have been used by the United States as arguments for abandoning or substantially modifying that treaty.

The complexity of some technologies adds to the burdens uncertainty imposes on unilateral and cooperative efforts to slow the arms race and to avoid new challenges to strategic stability. Some technologies—most conspicuously, nuclear and space technology—and military systems in R & D programs potentially have multiple military uses that have quite different implications for the military balance. While one might be willing to forgo those uses of an emerging technology that offer quite limited, nonessential military payoffs, the same complex technology may offer the promise of other significant applications. The result is to make control of military technology more difficult, as Weber and Drell note in their discussion of the problem that emerged in trying to decouple the ASAT capability of a complex technology from MILSAT systems that could have significant military payoffs.

The long lead times that have become typical for moving new technology through R & D, should it prove successful, into production and deployment of military systems add further constraints on unilateral or cooperative efforts to manage military competition. Failure by one side to pursue a particular R & D option may give its adversary an opportunity to complete development and to deploy a new weapon system, thereby gaining a political-psychological if not also a substantial military advantage. At the same time, however, long lead times mean that neither side is likely to gain an important or lasting advantage, as the postwar history of the arms race shows.

If one side has successfully tested a new weapon before its adversary has, as in the case of MIRV, the latter may be reluctant or unwilling to enter into an agreement until it, too, has achieved such a capability. Otherwise it would be vulnerable should its adversary decide later to break out of the agreement and deploy the weapon. The challenge to arms control in such cases is to recognize and act on the premise that the best or only opportunity for an acceptable, verifiable arms control agreement exists before development of the weapon. In such cases, proof-testing of the new weapon rather than its deployment may be the watershed.

The dynamics of technology can defeat arms control goals and strategy also when development of new weapons is justified as a "bargaining chip" but leads to a technical race that blocks agreement. (For a fuller discussion of bargaining chips see Chapter 29.)

Finally, an important asymmetry in the over-all U.S.–Soviet relationship—American technological superiority—can also hamper security cooperation. Influential political, military, and scientific elites in the United States—and, indeed, important elements of the public—believe that the general technological superiority of the United States is one of the few advantages we have in the over-all competition with the Soviet Union. Further, they believe that this is an advantage that should not be sacrificed in any arms control agreement. While agreements that impose numerical ceilings on force levels may be acceptable, indeed sometimes desirable from the standpoint of U.S. security interests, the United States should remain free to pursue those aspects of the arms competition in which its technological superiority can be expected to keep it ahead. The fact that, as has often been the case, the Soviet Union eventually catches up and the U.S. advantage proves only temporary may lead some advocates of this point of view to have second thoughts. For them the learning experience is that exploiting U.S. technological superiority to achieve temporary advantages is counterproductive; not only does it stimulate an increasingly costly arms race but it may lead to military developments that are destabilizing and dangerous. Others, however, believe that notwithstanding the fact that the Soviet Union eventually removes the temporary advantage enjoyed by the United States in a particular weapons system, the United States must continue to exploit its over-all technological superiority in order to keep ahead in some new weapons area. From this point of view, therefore, the qualitative arms race is not only inevitable but necessary to insure U.S. security interests. Some adherents of this view believe that the United States must strive to obtain a margin of strategic superiority over the Soviet Union in order to insure superpower political stability or, alternatively, to destabilize the USSR. This reflects a long-standing, deeply rooted belief that as a world power interested in maintaining the status quo the United States needs some degree of military superiority to discourage the Soviet Union, an expansionist power, from expanding its global influence.

Technological and political change requires us to recognize that "strategic stability" cannot be viewed statically. At the very least, with qualitative-technological competition unchecked, strategic stability is not a static state of affairs which, once achieved, can be frozen; rather, it is affected by a dynamic process of continued efforts by both sides either to improve their relative strategic postures or to maintain a balance. While both superpowers in the 1970s accepted in principle the concept of strategic parity as a design point for cooperative security efforts, there are always important elites on both sides that doubt whether this goal is feasible or even desirable.

Domestic and Alliance Constraints

Various domestic factors can present obstacles to security cooperation. We referred earlier to the necessity for political leaders to develop understanding and support for unilateral restraint or cooperative arrangements they believe to be desirable. In the United States, obtaining support for such arms control options within the administration, Congress, and the public by explaining why they are in the nation's interest can be so difficult that political leaders may fail or even be unwilling to try. Alliance constraints may operate in a similar way; weapons may be deployed (such as the Pershing II) and arms restraints avoided in deference to the strong views of one's allies. Changes in military strategy and in weapons deployments may also be constrained by allied opinion. Similarly, as Joseph Nye notes, progress in U.S.–Soviet cooperation to avoid nuclear proliferation may have been held back to some extent during the period of tight polarity in the 1950s and early 1960s by the need experienced by both superpowers to maintain their alliance structures, although this may have been mostly a matter of getting policy priorities straight in Moscow and Washington.

Domestic political considerations may hamper security cooperation in other ways as well. On occasion, U.S. political leaders became concerned about overloading the domestic political agenda with too many arms control or détente issues. This may lead to a decision to push only one arms control option at any given time, putting aside other options that also appear to be desirable. As Neidle notes, President Carter was under some pressure not to take on the struggle to gain domestic support for a comprehensive test ban treaty while engaged in an already difficult effort on behalf of SALT II. And as Weber and Drell note, when the Carter Administration was struggling to muster support for SALT II it thought it best not to overload the domestic political agenda by pursuing an ASAT agreement as well, although the latter was probably stymied for other reasons. Earlier, President Nixon had experienced some pressure not to dilute domestic support for an ABM treaty by a simultaneous struggle to constrain the development of MIRV. To gain support for a particular arms control measure within his own administration a president often must give assurances that other military programs will not be curtailed or, even, that they will be expedited. And, as Blechman notes, there are bureaucratic obstacles in the governments of both superpowers to the conclusion of technical measures for reducing the risk of accidental war when such measures might limit the flexibility of military operations.

Political uncertainties having to do with one's allies may stimulate or constrain consideration of certain measures that could contribute to improvement in the over-all security relationship. As Kurt Steiner notes, the Austrian State Treaty was delayed for a number of years because both the Soviet Union and the United States were concerned over the adverse consequences their withdrawal from Austria might have for the alliances they were attempting to create in Europe. Since then, and into the foreseeable future, the possibility of a truly substantial withdrawal of Soviet forces from Eastern Europe and any negotiations geared to that objective would require Moscow to judge what level of Soviet forces are required to ensure continued control over the area.

On the other hand, domestic and alliance forces can exert constructive pressures on political leaders to explore opportunities for security cooperation more energetically.

THE IMPORTANCE OF A BASIC
POLITICAL FRAMEWORK OF RELATIONS

Cooperation in security matters may be hindered or facilitated by the nature of the over-all political relationship that exists between the United States and the Soviet Union at any given time or by the type of relationship they seek to develop. Thus, we may recall that the Cuban missile crisis created a mutual desire among Soviet and American leaders to move away from the dangerous confrontational policies of the Cold War. Since then halting efforts have been made to define and to move towards a more constructive, stable relationship. Such a goal requires that those responsible for conducting foreign policy in Moscow and Washington address several interrelated questions. The first task is to formulate a conception of a more satisfactory superpower relationship that is to be created. This is necessarily a long-term objective with which short-term policies and actions must be consistent. Moreover, the superpower relationship that policy seeks to develop must be not merely desirable but also feasible. That is, U.S. leaders must have reason to believe that the Soviet Union is capable of, and willing, to enter into or to accept the kind of relationship Washington would like to develop. Soviet leaders must arrive at a similar judgment regarding U.S. acceptance of the type of superpower relationship they wish to create. In addition,, each side must have some reason to believe that situational factors on balance favor the development of the relationship it has in mind and that, indeed, it has sufficient resources and appropriate political skills to bring it about.

The critical question remains, of course, whether the conceptions of a desirable superpower relationship held in Washington and Moscow have sufficient elements in common to facilitate cooperation in achieving it. If Soviet and American leaders believe they do, then they may decide, as Richard Nixon and Leonid Brezhnev did in 1972, to formulate and agree on a basic political framework for their evolving relationship.

Agreement on a basic framework for the over-all relationship is important insofar as it indicates how the two sides view each other, how they wish to see their relationship develop over a longer period of time, and how they identify common or parallel interests in various issue-areas that they wish to pursue. If the two sides can agree on a basic framework, it provides guidelines and an element of political stability to their relationship, at least for the time being. The importance of a viable political framework for the superpower relationship need not be exaggerated in order to convey the significant contribution it can make. Security for both sides in the anarchic international system is affected by the quality of their over-all relationship, its political as well as its military dimensions. Arms control or trade cannot be expected to prosper in the face of fundamental problems in the relationship. The political relationship is at least as important as the strategic relationship and the two are interrelated. Political cooperation, arms control, lowered military confrontation, trade, and other constructive contacts both presuppose and contribute to a viable basic framework for the U.S.–Soviet relationship.

Formal definition of a basic framework of relations should help define the longer-range objectives and payoffs the two sides believe to be worth pursuing. A basic framework could strengthen the role that the ''shadow of the future'' can play in increasing

U.S. and Soviet incentives to find cooperative, mutually acceptable solutions to more immediate problems.[12] In the absence of a basic political framework that holds out the promise of important mutual benefits in the long-run, it is less likely that a superpower will be willing to pass up opportunities for short-term gains at the expense of its adversary.

These, then, are the advantages that, in principle, an agreement on a basic political framework can provide for the development of the relationship. In practice, of course, as the unique experience with the Nixon-Brezhnev détente demonstrated, various difficulties can arise in attempting to formulate and carry out a workable basic framework. The two leaders attempted to provide just such a framework at their first summit meeting in Moscow in May 1972. This was expressed in the Basic Principles Agreement (BPA) which, in effect, constituted a sort of charter defining the basis for the further development of détente. In this document the two leaders expressed agreement that in the nuclear age "there is no alternative to conducting their relations on the basis of peaceful coexistence." They agreed, further, that "differences in ideology and in the social systems of the U.S.A. and the U.S.S.R. are not obstacles to the bilateral development of normal relations based on the principles of sovereignty, equality, noninterference in internal affairs and mutual advantage." Continuing, they agreed that "the prerequisites for maintaining and strengthening peaceful relations between the U.S.A. and the U.S.S.R. are the recognition of the security interests of the parties based on the principle of equality and the renunciation of the use or threat of force." And, more specifically, the two leaders agreed to "attach major importance to preventing the development of situations capable of causing a dangerous exacerbation of their relations." Accordingly, they pledged to "do their utmost to avoid military confrontations and to prevent the outbreak of nuclear wars," to "to exercise restraint in their mutual relations," and to "be prepared to negotiate and settle differences by peaceful means." U.S.–Soviet discussions and negotiations in the future were to be conducted "in a spirit of reciprocity, mutual accommodation and mutual benefit." And in this connection, they agreed that "efforts to obtain unilateral advantages at the expense of the other, directly or indirectly, are inconsistent with these objectives."

Nixon and Brezhnev made a bow in this statement of goals and desiderata for the development of their bilateral relationship to the larger framework of strengthening the international system. They recognized their special responsibility as permanent members of the U.N. Security Council to reduce international tensions and "to promote conditions in which all countries will live in peace and security and will not be subject to outside interference in their internal affairs."

In the BPA, Nixon and Brezhnev also identified the specific issue-areas in which they would seek to promote their mutual interests. Thus, they agreed to continue efforts to limit armaments, and to develop economic, scientific, and cultural ties between their two countries on a long-term basis in order to strengthen their relationship.

It should be noted that the basic framework depicted in the BPA was, at best, a joint declaratory policy of a very loose and general character; the specifics remained to be clarified and filled in over time. In the parlance of nineteenth-century European diplomacy, the BPA was in the nature of a "rapprochement"—that is, an agreement to go beyond a mere relaxation of tensions in their relations to search for specific agreements on various issues. In fact, the BPA also went beyond mere rapprochement to an entente, which in classical diplomacy refers to a recognition of a similarity of views and interests on certain (though not all) issues.

While the BPA registered a mutual desire to develop a relationship of what might be called "collaborative competition" (as against the "confrontational competition" of the Cold War), such a relationship would require the development of norms of cooperation and competition that would be sufficiently clear, mutually understood and accepted. However, as many observers have noted, important ambiguities and divergent interpretations of key elements of the BPA—with respect to "equality," "equal security," "restraint," "reciprocity," "no unilateral advantage"—and the persistence of conflicting interests left the basic framework highly vulnerable to future developments. It was not long before mutually inconsistent hopes and expectations from détente surfaced in Moscow and Washington that resulted in disappointment and recriminations. Although important progress was achieved in arms control, in scientific and cultural exchanges, in movement towards political stabilization in Europe, Nixon was unable to overcome Congressional constraints that blocked fulfillment of his commitment to improve trading arrangements with the Soviets.[13] Soviet military programs and assertive Soviet behavior in Africa raised doubts in the United States regarding the value of détente. And, in general, a variety of domestic constraints complicated the halting efforts of Nixon, Ford, and Carter to formulate and pursue a consistent, coherent policy of détente towards the Soviet Union.

As a result, the political stability and framework that the BPA was supposed to articulate for the further development of the relationship gradually eroded. For all practical purposes détente was dead in the United States after the Soviet invasion of Afghanistan, to be replaced by a revival of Cold War rhetoric, greater reliance on unilateral efforts to strengthen security, and confrontational posturing.

Whereas President Carter and Brezhnev had formally reaffirmed adherence to the Basic Principles Agreement when they signed the Salt II agreement in 1979, it was quite clear that Carter's successor in the White House considered the BPA as no longer operative and that he would not follow Carter's example of reaffirming adherence to it. Moreover, during President Reagan's first term and into the second term, his Administration displayed little interest in improving relations with the USSR, let alone in formulating a new basic framework of relations. Rather, the Reagan Administration's policy towards the Soviet Union was strongly influenced by the desire to develop a "position of strength" from which to deal more effectively with the Soviet Union.

The question of a basic framework was not addressed at the ice-breaking summit meeting of Mikhail Gorbachev and Reagan in November 1985. Statements by the two leaders and their joint communiqué made no mention or allusion to the Basic Principles Agreement of 1972. Neither side accepted the other's draft proposal for a joint communiqué (the contents of the drafts have not been disclosed). For a while during the summit there was even considerable doubt as to whether the two leaders would issue any joint statement at the conclusion of their meeting. Finally, as a result of a last minute compromise, a joint statement was issued. Notably absent in it were any references to "peaceful coexistence," "equality," and other symbols associated with the BPA. However, the Gorbachev-Reagan statement did contain a few points of agreement. The paragraph on "Security" in the joint statement contained three important declarations:

1. The two leaders "have agreed that a nuclear war cannot be won and must never be fought."
2. "Recognizing that any conflict between the U.S.S.R. and the U.S. could have cat-

astrophic consequences, they emphasized the importance of preventing any war between them, whether nuclear or conventional.''
3. ''They will not seek to achieve military superiority.''

A fourth declaration elsewhere in the joint statement reaffirmed a cosmetic formula: ''the tasks set down in the Joint U.S.–Soviet Agreement of January 8, 1985, [are] namely to prevent an arms race in space and to terminate it on earth, to limit and reduce nuclear arms and enhance strategic stability.'' The two leaders also reaffirmed adherence to a procedure that the United States and the Soviet Union had hesitantly tried during the year preceding the summit. Thus, the two leaders agreed to continue ''exchanges of views on regional issues on the expert level,'' which were said to have been useful. However, as noted in Chapter 23, these discussions had been narrow and their function for the Reagan Administration appears to have been limited largely to restating and pressing objections to Soviet foreign policy in various parts of the world.

The long-range relationship the Reagan Administration wishes to develop with the Soviet Union is unclear. This is not surprising since fundamental disagreements persist within the Administration regarding the correct image of the Soviets, whether and to what extent the United States should ''squeeze'' the Soviet Union, and whether and in what ways to ''deal'' with it. While there is strong agreement within the Administration as to the necessity for developing a ''position of strength,'' this ambiguous concept is after all a means to an end, and there has been substantial disagreement and uncertainty as to the objectives to be served by a ''position of strength.'' Left unsettled, too, is the mix of cooperation and competition in the relationship with the Soviets that the Administration envisages. What has been clear is that the Administration prefers to place greater reliance on unilateral efforts to enhance its most important security and foreign policy objectives rather than enter into what it views as risky arms control agreements that might prove to be defective and damaging.

At the same time, the absence of a broader political framework of relations has not kept the superpowers from holding talks on a variety of subjects. In 1986 arms control discussions took place on a variety of issues—nuclear arms, confidence-building measures, mutual and balanced force reductions, chemical weapons, nuclear testing, nuclear risk reduction centers, incidents at sea. Subjects other than arms control under at least pro forma discussion included nuclear energy, regional problems, cultural and scientific exchanges, trade, human rights, people-to-people exchanges. (For a discussion of the pre-summit meeting of Reagan and Gorbachev in Iceland in October 1986, see Chapter 9.)

FACTORS FAVORING SECURITY COOPERATION

Mutuality of interests, we noted in the preceding chapter, may be a necessary condition for security cooperation but hardly sufficient to ensure that it will occur. Various obstacles to cooperation have been noted. When such obstacles are absent or exercise only weak influence on U.S. and Soviet policy-making and on the interaction between the two superpowers, there is greater likelihood of their reaching cooperative arrangements on security issues. There are still other factors and conditions which, if present in a given situation, favor cooperative efforts. Five such factors will be discussed. It should be noted that they operate quite unevenly in influencing the process of exploring and achieving security cooperation, being more important in some situations than in others.

Decomposability of the Issue

The ability to decompose or disaggregate a complex security problem into smaller components may make it possible to deal with at least some of them in a cooperative way. Modest initial successes, in turn, may create incentives, conditions, and procedures for tackling more difficult components later on. The enormously complex and important issue of strategic arms control was dealt with in this way. As arms control specialists put it, the important achievement of the early 1970s was to develop a "process" for dealing with a series of strategic arms controls issues over a period of time.[14]

Cooperation theorists make a similar observation regarding the usefulness of "tactics of decomposition over time to lengthen the shadow of the future. . . . Cooperation in arms reduction or in territorial disengagement may be difficult if the reduction or disengagement must be achieved in one jump. If a reduction or disengagement can be sliced into increments, the problem of cooperation may be rendered more tractable."[15]

Desire to Curb the Security Dilemma

Awareness on the part of the policymakers and influential elites that the dynamics of the security dilemma (discussed earlier in this chapter) pose the danger of a runaway arms race may strengthen incentives to ameliorate its impact on security policy and encourage efforts at cooperation. Concerns of this kind played a role in getting strategic arms control started in the late 1960s and early 1970s. Awareness of the action-reaction dynamics of arms competition also occasionally encourages policy-makers to choose military force options that improve their own security without increasing the adversary's perception of threat. As Weber and Drell note, the United States chose to counter the threat posed by Soviet space activities in late 1966 in a nonescalatory fashion by improving its over-the-horizon radar and other early warning capabilities. More generally, they note, both sides observed reciprocal restraint regarding militarization of space during the period 1963–1968. U.S. defense analysts recommended "unilateral cooperative measures" to cope with a possible Soviet ASAT capability, measures that could increase the security of the United States without posing any threat to the Soviet Union. Such recommendations were generally followed for several years. (see Chapter 16)

The escalatory dynamics of the security dilemma can also be checked on occasion by one side deliberately taking unilateral measures designed to reduce critical uncertainties for the other side regarding its own actions, for example by either supplying or permitting the other side's intelligence arm to obtain relevant information. Provisions to this end have also been included in arms control agreements and are the focal point for some confidence-building measures.

Time Urgency

Time urgency for reaching agreement sometimes facilitates the process of negotiation and compromise. As the end of World War II approached this factor played a role, as David Schoenbaum's case study indicates, in expediting Allied agreement on the essential provisions for joint occupation and administration of Germany. Later, the trend towards international acceptance of East Germany placed the Western powers under some time pressure, Jonathan Dean recalls, to negotiate the Quadripartite Agreement on Berlin. Time urgency played a constructive role also in the negotiations leading to the

Helsinki Accord. As John Maresca notes, Brezhnev needed an agreement that would register acceptance by the Western powers of the status quo in Eastern Europe before the 25th Party Congress convened in 1976. And according to James Goodby, the Stockholm Conference faced a target date that many delegations saw as a deadline that eventually moved them into more intensive negotiations.

Time urgency was also a factor in moving along negotiations of the Peaceful Nuclear Explosions Treaty (PNET) of 1976. In negotiating the earlier Threshold Test Ban Treaty (TTBT) of 1974 both sides accepted an operative obligation to establish an agreement to govern underground nuclear explosions for peaceful purposes by the time—March 15, 1976—the TTBT provisions were to go into effect. The deadline was missed by about a week. This considerable accomplishment rested on good homework on both sides, cooperation among all relevant parts of the executive branch bureaucracy, and acceptance by both the United States and the Soviet Union that the negotiations for the PNET had to be a cooperative effort if the deadline was to be met.[16]

The fixing of a date for summit meetings serves something of the same function as a deadline; it energizes the bureaucratic and political decision-making processes on both sides and increases pressure on those ongoing negotiations that might be successfully concluded in time for approval at the summit by the top political leaders. Sometimes, as in the case of the first Nixon-Brezhnev summit in Moscow in May 1972, some important negotiating issues are finally resolved by the two leaders only at the summit itself. It is, of course, not the deadline alone but its coupling with a political desire for some U.S.–Soviet accords that operates in this way to facilitate agreement. Whether the agreements reached under this special type of political deadline are good agreements is another matter. And it is also possible, as Janne Nolan emphasizes in her study of the Conventional Arms Transfer talks, that the pressure within the Administration for early signs of progress contributed to the failure of these talks.

In the MBFR case, on the other hand, there has been little sense of time urgency or a deadline to expedite negotiations and conclude an agreement. Coit Blacker notes that as a result of domestic pressures to cut back American forces in Europe the Administration did experience some urgency at the outset to initiate the MBFR talks and this may have encouraged the Soviet Union to believe that the asymmetry in this respect would yield it some bargaining advantages. But the time pressure on Washington dissipated rather quickly once negotiations were under way.

Fiscal Constraints

Concern over the mounting costs of security, of course, can also encourage unilateral and/or joint efforts to control the arms race and limit the investment of resources in the competition for global influence. Neither superpower can ignore indefinitely the necessity to make cost-benefit assessments of available options and to estimate the opportunity costs of investing in projects and enterprises not considered essential or of high priority from an over-all security standpoint.

Decisions to limit investment in security may be taken exclusively out of self-interest with no thought or expectation of encouraging moderation on the part of the adversary. But such decisions can also be part of a strategy of attempting to induce reciprocal restraint. Weber and Drell see evidence of this strategy in the policies Washington followed during the late 1960s and early 1970s in an effort to avoid or limit the militarization of space. More generally, the heavy costs of the Vietnam War and the threat of inflation undoubtedly not only contributed to decisions to limit military expenditures but also gave added incentive for strategic arms control as a means of curbing the costly arms race. Interest in arms control for the Indian Ocean, too, as Richard Haass notes, can be traced back to mounting concerns in Congress that a costly arms race might well occur in that region if some action were not taken to avoid it.

Fiscal constraints on Soviet policy differ in some important respects from the U.S. case. Soviet leaders are interested in shifting resources (and particularly scientists and technology and management) from the military sector to the civilian. (On the importance of fiscal constraints on Soviet policy, see Chapter 24.)

Presidential-Level Leadership

White House leadership is often critical for serious exploration of cooperative security arrangements. The presence or absence of presidential commitment and skillful leadership can sometimes make the difference between success or failure. The importance of this variable is strongly emphasized in many of the case studies presented earlier in this study. (See the chapters by Neidle, Nolan, David Hall, Blechman, Harold Saunders, Goodby, Maresca, Weber and Drell, Blacker, and Joseph Nye). A similar observation can be made regarding the importance of top-level Soviet political leadership. Neidle, for example, calls attention to the role that Soviet political leaders have played in setting aside concerns of their military leaders in order to seek test ban agreements with the United States.

Presidential leadership encompasses a number of functions which, depending on how well they are performed, may make the difference between success or failure in achieving a cooperative security arrangement with the Soviet Union. Since these executive functions are well known, it will suffice merely to list them:

1. Set agenda priorities, select Administration policy initiatives, and deal with trade-offs among competing policy goals, interests, and values.
2. Ensure adequate management of the policy-making process within the Administration; control and discipline advisers and bureaucratic actors; force resolution of interagency policy disagreements and break log-jams.
3. Decide what will be a desirable or acceptable agreement or unilateral cooperative policy; decide what level of verification and assurance of compliance is acceptable.
4. Find ways of strengthening the adversary's incentives to reach an acceptable agreement.
5. Develop consensus and an adequate policy coalition in support of decisions.
6. Develop policy legitimacy and support for decisions within the Administration itself, in Congress, and with the public.

The second of the executive functions listed above deserves additional comment. Adequate management of the policy-making process requires not only effective resolution of interagency disagreements but procedures for producing and utilizing high quality analysis of policy options on a timely basis. A number of observers have deplored the erratic performance of this critical function in recent administrations. Interagency homework and policy coordination are all too often incomplete, strongly influenced by personalities, and fall short of producing well-designed, coherent policies that can be pursued consistently over time. The highly centralized "formal options" system devised by President Nixon and Henry Kissinger was designed to meet this need by providing for orderly analysis of key foreign policy issues in ways that reduced the impact of bureaucratic policies. This variant of a strong and dominant NSC system complemented well Nixon's desire to exercise direct personal control over the most important foreign policy issues with which his Administration had to deal.[17]

Like any other model for policy making, the formal options system had its own peculiar limitations which led to considerable criticism of the high degree of centralization of policy making in the White House. The Carter Administration opted for a less centralized model that lodged more responsibility in the operating departments and agencies. At the same time, however, Carter selected as his National Security Adviser a self-confident, assertive specialist on foreign policy, Zbigniew Brzezinski. In time, significant substantive policy differences between the National Security Adviser and Secretary of State Cyrus Vance revealed that Carter's NSC model was not working well. Reflecting on the experiences of the Nixon and Carter administrations, specialists on the NSC system drew the conclusion that the National Security Adviser should be restricted largely to performing the role of custodian-manager of the policy-making process rather than also exercising, as Kissinger and Brzezinski had, the functions of a major independent adviser, spokesman, or implementor of foreign policy. This advice[18] was followed by Ronald Reagan when he became President in 1981.

Reagan deliberately weakened the stature and power of the National Security Adviser as well as restricting his role; and he relied for policy analysis and formulation even more than Carter had on the operating departments and cabinet committees. Coupled with Reagan's management style of broad delegation of responsibility to subordinates, the weakened National Security Adviser was unable to perform effectively the difficult task of interagency coordination. In consequence, what emerged and persisted during the first six years of Reagan's presidency was a fragmented, competitive, inadequately managed system of foreign policy-making in which distrust and rivalry were ever present, giving rise repeatedly to damaging intra-administration conflicts over policy. Symptomatic of this failure was the unprecedented rapid turnover of persons serving as National Security Adviser—five different ones in six years. Dissatisfaction with the workings of the NSC in particular and with Reagan's foreign policy-making system reached a peak in late 1986 with widespread criticism of the Administration's handling of the Reagan-Gorbachev summit at Reykjavik and the Iran-Contra disclosures.

There is, to be sure, no easy way of utilizing procedures for obtaining high quality security policies that command support within and outside an administration. Examples of flawed procedures and results can be cited from any administration and appear in some of our case studies.

As Nolan notes, the sheer number of competing arms control initiatives undertaken at the outset of the Carter Administration overloaded the political process and made it difficult for top-level officials to give concerted attention to each effort. As for the Conventional Arms Transfers (CAT) talks, poor policy conceptualization and inadequate interagency planning and coordination as well as divided views within the State Department itself resulted in confused objectives and an ineffectual strategy for negotiating with the Soviets. On the other hand, as Sean Lynn-Jones observed in his study of the Incidents at Sea Agreement, careful interagency study and the intensive involvement of the U.S. Navy in the preparation of a negotiating position and during the conduct of the negotiations facilitated achievement of a successful though very narrow cooperative arrangement.

In the Incidents at Sea case the policy coalition within the Administration favoring an agreement maintained its cohesion during the course of the negotiations. This was not to be the case during the Indian Ocean talks for, as Haass notes, the Navy and the Joint Chiefs of Staff had reservations from the beginning regarding the military consequences of any ambitious arms control regime for that area although for political reasons they did not oppose the Carter Administration's initiative at the outset. Indeed, Haass sees in the Administration's approach to the Indian Ocean talks something of the same flawed policy conceptualization that Nolan detected in the CAT talks, and he argues persuasively that this was an excessively ambitious, misguided initiative that reflected President Carter's overly optimistic views as to what arms control could achieve. Finally, both Haass and Nolan believe that the Administration's pursuit of overly ambitious objectives in these two initiatives may have resulted in "missed opportunities" to achieve more modest but still useful results.

Finally, we should note the importance of the interaction between the different policy-making styles of the two superpowers. Robert Buchheim calls attention to this factor that complicates U.S.–Soviet efforts to search for cooperative agreements. Drawing on his rich experience in dealing with Soviet representatives in the Standing Consultative Commission, Buchheim notes that Soviet homework all too often tends to be very slow, albeit rather thorough. He adds that Soviet slowness makes it possible for initial U.S. policy positions to be subject to incremental adjustment and that this, in turn, allows legislative and interest groups in the United States to exert pressure for change. More generally, lack of synchronization in the evolution of well thought out U.S. and Soviet negotiating positions on specific cooperation possibilities can result in missed opportunities for agreement. Buchheim concludes that "defects in homework performance—quality or timeliness—can have negative effects on cooperation because of their direct effect on substance. They also can have the negative effect of giving each party reasons (all too often readily seized) to doubt the practicality of coming to desirable agreement with the other party."[19]

Other Favorable Conditions

A particular agreement and its effective implementation can be facilitated, as one might expect, by a variety of idiosyncratic factors that seem to be peculiar to the issue in question or fortuitously embedded in the circumstances surrounding that issue at the time. An unusual concatenation of many favorable factors is well illustrated in Lynn-Jones' account of the Incidents at Sea Agreement. His analysis suggests that a number of factors that contributed to the success of this agreement, *if* present also in other security issues to be negotiated, might be helpful on those occasions as well. These include the fact that the Incidents at Sea Agreement was not a treaty and, therefore, not subject to the often demanding requirements of Senate ratification. Absence of publicity helped in reaching the Incidents at Sea Agreement and in its implementation, as did the unusual ease of monitoring its performance. Unusual, too, is the fact that the criteria of successful implementation of the Incidents at Sea Agreement are permissive and flexible; the agreement is not vulnerable to a few violations (either deliberate or inadvertent) of the "rules of the road" that have been agreed to. It is also relatively easy to enforce in that if deliberate violations occur, the other side can respond with tit-for-tat retaliation. The Incidents at Sea Agreement has included not only regime-type institutionalization of norms and procedures, but there is evidence that both the U.S. and Soviet navies have internalized the new rules of the road into their own operational doctrines.

Finally, implementation of the Incidents at Sea Agreement has been successful partly because it deals with unnecessary and easily avoidable operational causes of instability in one particular kind of military activity, and not with the more complex and controversial questions of fixing the level and types of armament. For all these reasons, Lynn-Jones concludes, this agreement has been more easily shielded from political considerations and the ups-and-downs of the over-all U.S.–Soviet relationship. Both navies evidently value the agreement and have made effective use of periodical meetings to discuss in a constructive manner such incidents as do occur from time to time.

This chapter has discussed a variety of factors that influence the superpowers' perception of mutual interests in some form of security cooperation, and that affect the ability of Soviet and American leaders to act on a shared perception of such mutual interests in order to develop an appropriate cooperative agreement. It was noted that most of the obstacles to security cooperation—the security dilemma, ideology, asymmetries, technology—are fundamental and pervasive; they are ever present and affect just about all aspects of the over-all Soviet-American security relationship. Domestic and alliance constraints, on the other hand, are less pervasive and much more variable in their impact on security cooperation. Besides, domestic and alliance factors are not always obstacles to cooperation on a particular issue; on important occasions they may generate considerable pressure on leaders for security cooperation.

Emphasis was also given to the role that a well-defined basic political framework of relations can play in encouraging and facilitating U.S.–Soviet security cooperation. However, the difficulties of developing a sufficiently unambiguous and stable basic framework are substantial, as the analysis of the Nixon-Brezhnev effort indicates. A related question is the role that the over-all U.S.–Soviet relationship plays in linkage strategies, which is discussed in Chapter 29.

Finally, this chapter also discussed five factors that, from time to time, can importantly favor and facilitate security cooperation. These five factors are the decomposability of a complex security problem, a desire to curb the impact of the security dilemma on U.S.–Soviet relations, a sense of time urgency for reaching a particular agreement, the pressure of fiscal constraints, and presidential leadership. We also called attention to the fact that these factors operate unevenly. The two most important factors favoring security cooperation remain, as was noted in Chapter 26, the emergence of a shared perception that the two superpowers are mutually dependent on each other for their security; and the additional shared perception that unilateral efforts to deal with a particular security problem do not suffice or are too costly or risky and that therefore something may be gained by seriously exploring bilateral (and multilateral) arrangements to enhance each side's security.

Notes

1. For a fuller discussion see Alexander L. George and Robert O. Keohane, "The Concept of National Interests: Uses and Limitations," in A. L. George, *Presidential Decisionmaking in Foreign Policy: The Effective Use of Information and Advice* (Boulder, Colo.: Westview Press, 1980), pp. 217–237.

2. Robert Jervis, "Cooperation Under the Security Dilemma," *World Politics*, vol. 30, no. 2 (January 1978).

3. These cognitive and affective biases, identified by cognitive psychologists, are receiving increasing attention from specialists in international relations. They have been incisively discussed and illustrated in a number of works by Robert Jervis, most recently in his draft manuscript, "Cooperation Under Anarchy: Problems and Limitations," Columbia University, July 1986.

4. For a well-documented study of how the bad-faith model operates in a policy-maker's information processing, see the classic study by Ole R. Holsti, "Cognitive Dynamics and Images of the Enemy: Dulles and Russia," in D. J. Finlay, O. R. Holsti, and R. R. Fagen, *Enemies in Politics* (Chicago: Rand McNally, 1967).

5. For useful discussions of cognitive limits on rational choice see, for example, James G. March and Herbert A. Simon, *Organizations* (New York: Wiley, 1958) and Charles E. Lindblom, "The Science of 'Muddling Through,'" *Public Administration Quarterly* (Spring 1959). For a discussion of various ways of coping with, or avoiding, psychological stress generated by having to make important decisions that are constrained by cognitive limits on rational choice, see A. L. George, *Presidential Decisionmaking in Foreign Policy,* ch. 2.

6. For a detailed discussion see Joseph S. Nye, Jr., ed., *The Making of America's Soviet Policy* (New Haven: Yale University Press, 1984).

7. For a discussion of the concept of "policy legitimacy" and the difficulty of achieving it, see Alexander L. George, "Domestic Constraints in U.S. Foreign Policy: The Need for Policy Legitimacy," in O. R. Holsti, R. M. Siverson, and A. L. George, eds., *Changes in the International System* (Boulder, Colo.: Westview Press, 1980), pp. 233–262.

8. Actually, from a technical standpoint, there was no moratorium in effect at the time. President Eisenhower had earlier terminated the one-year moratorium he had proclaimed in August 1958 but stated that the United States would announce any resumption in advance. Nonetheless, the resumption of testing by the Soviet Union in August 1961 came as a shock and the concern deepened as Moscow proceeded to carry out an unprecedented series of tests. See *Nuclear Arms Control: Background and Issues* (Washington, D.C.: National Academy Press, 1985), p. 191.

9. John Steinbruner, "U.S. and Soviet Security Perspectives," *Bulletin of the Atomic Scientists* (August 1985): 89–93.

10. See Alan J. Vick and James A. Thomson, "Military Significance of Restrictions on the Operations of Strategic Nuclear Forces," in Barry M. Blechman, ed., *Preventing Nuclear War* (Bloomington, Ind.: Indiana University Press, 1985), pp. 99–125.

11. Cf. Steven Weber, "Cooperation and Discord in Security Relationships: The Case of MIRV," manuscript, Stanford University, August 1985.
See also the important theoretical and historical analysis of how uncertainty affects arms control cooperation in George W. Downs, David M. Rocke, and Randolph M. Siverson, "Arms Races and Cooperation," *World Politics,* vol. 37, no. 1 (October 1985): 118–146.

12. The term "shadow of the future" was introduced by Robert Axelrod in his important game-theoretic contribution to cooperation theory, *The Evolution of Cooperation* (New York: Basic Books, 1984), pp. 126–132. The concept calls attention to the fact that concern about future interactions with an adversary can help promote cooperation on more immediate issues. The more the outcome of future interactions are valued relative to the payoff of current interactions, the less the incentive to behave in an uncooperative manner in the present.

13. For a more detailed discussion see especially chapters, 2, 5, 6, 7, 13, and 15 in A. L. George, *Managing U.S.–Soviet Rivalry* (Boulder, Colo.: Westview Press, 1983); also ch. 23 of the present study.

14. This is analogous to the "functional" definition of regimes in international political economy suggested by Robert O. Keohane in *After Hegemony* (Princeton, N.J.: Princeton University Press, 1984).

15. Kenneth A. Oye, "Explaining Cooperation Under Anarchy: Hypotheses and Strategies," *World Politics,* vol. 38, no. 1 (October 1985): 17. Oye cites Thomas Schelling and Robert Axelrod as theorists who have called attention to the possible utility of the tactics of decomposition

over time. See also Roger Fisher, "Fractionating Conflict," in Fisher, ed., *International Conflict and Behavioral Science: The Craigville Papers* (New York: Basic Books, 1964).

16. Personal communication from Robert Buchheim, June 4, 1987.

17. For a discussion of the workings of the formal options system see Alexander L. George, *Presidential Decisionmaking in Foreign Policy*, ch. 10.

18. A strong concensus on behalf of a more restrictive conception of the National Security Adviser's role was registered in hearings held in Spring 1980 by a subcommittee of the Senate Committee on Foreign Relations chaired by Senator Edward Zorinsky. See *The National Security Adviser: Role and Accountability*, Hearings before the Committee on Foreign Relations, U.S. Senate, 96th Congress, 2nd Session, April 17, 1980 (Washington, D.C.: U.S. Government Printing Office, 1980).

19. Personal communication from Robert Buchheim, June 4, 1987.

28

Managing the Risks of Cooperation

PHILIP J. FARLEY

Uncertainties and risk are inherent in relations among sovereign states. An important purpose and prospective reward of efforts to negotiate agreements for mutually beneficial cooperation in economic, political, and even security affairs is to provide a framework for reducing uncertainties and managing risks. Unless they are dealt with effectively, risks and uncertainty occasion tension and instability in cooperative activities, and can result in the collapse of contracts or agreements and the cooperative relationship they aim to establish.

Risk is of course part of the human condition and also present in domestic commercial, industrial, community, and personal relations. Laws, contracts, the establishment of informal relationships, and even trust are brought into play to deal with them. Here however there are recognized state and local authorities, with a structure of laws, courts, police, and complementary nongovernmental means, to deal with disputes over interpretation and application of contracts, and to enforce laws and agreements. In international relations there is no comparable set of authorities.

In reaching and carrying out international agreements, this lack of authoritative means for enforcing agreements and settling disputes accentuates risks. It also makes for greater difficulty in getting the facts needed to assess risks accurately and define a fair and equitable agreement. Differences in the legal, political, and social systems of the parties further complicate the process.

Among international cooperative efforts, arms control and other accords relating to international security involve especially grave risks and uncertainties. Even where risk and uncertainty and their consequences are in fact limited, sensitivity to them tends to be high, and perceptions of security risk weigh heavily in negotiation and implementation.

There is a considerable body of experience and practice concerning the management and reduction of risk in international economic, commercial, and political relations.[1] Many of the techniques developed are applicable to security arrangements. Among these, for example, are provisions for:

— limiting the duration of an agreement;
— withdrawal or release of a party in event of specified intrinsic or extrinsic developments, or of nonperformance or noncompliance by other parties;
— phased carrying out of specific reciprocal obligations;
— standards and measures of performance;
— methods of ascertaining performance by other parties; and
— amendment and dispute consultation or adjudication.

Such measures must face especially testing conditions when applied to arms control or other security cooperation. The parties are often adversaries in many respects, or even (like the United States and the Soviet Union) states with differing political systems and conflicting worldwide interests—and one of them a closed secretive society, particularly when it comes to military affairs.

RISKS AND POLITICAL COOPERATION

The main U.S.–Soviet postwar interface has been in Europe. Most of the cases described in this volume, other than arms control, deal with European security relations.

Cooperation was only a small component of East-West relations in Europe until the second half of the 1970s, following the Helsinki Accords of 1975. Rather, the relationship was an uneasy and often ill-defined modus vivendi, accompanied by uncertainty, risk, and tension. The wartime alliance did as one final act produce an immediate postwar agreement on joint occupation and administration of Germany. But differences in the political and economic systems and strategies of the occupying powers quickly made it evident that there was no common ground that would enable cooperative administration to work. The reality (except in Berlin and Austria) soon became the separate zones of occupation. Conferences and negotiations over the following years produced no formal settlement. Recollection of the devastation of the recent war kept suspicions and rivalries within some bounds.

Other than avoiding war, the one common goal of the former allies was a form of "risk management": prevention of the reemergence of Germany as the major military power in Central Europe, and with it perhaps the revival of some form of Naziism. This goal, however, could be achieved separately. The Federal Republic was, after the occupation regime ended, embedded militarily in the Western European Union and NATO, with allied troops from the United States, United Kingdom, Canada, and several neighboring European nations stationed there alongside reconstituted German forces, under an integrated strategy and command and planning structure. Politically and economically, the Federal Republic was no less embedded, formally and informally, in the European communities and the international economic system dominated by the states of the Atlantic Alliance. In East Europe, Soviet forces, first as occupying troops and then under cover of the Warsaw Pact, insured political control by the local communist regimes in the German Democratic Republic and other East European states.

The risk of a revived Germany military threat was thus dealt with in parallel within these separate and competitive security arrangements. These opposing alliances were also the main elements of the prevailing modus vivendi after 1955. Risk management was not a cooperative effort but was carried out separately. Each side relied on its military power, and its voluntary or coerced political solidarity, to cope with the risks and perceived threat attending the division of Europe and the heavily armed confrontation.

When the period of détente gradually emerged in the late 1960s, and a de facto postwar settlement took shape as described in the chapters by Jonathan Dean, John Maresca, and James Goodby, the alliance (and offsetting American and Soviet military power) remained the protection against the risks and uncertainties attending the pursuit of a European system in which confrontation would be reduced and cooperation gradually extended.

Some specific understandings did have to be arrived at in the interim, particularly on Berlin and Austria. In achieving these agreements and carrying them out, the main risks involved the possibility of unexpected and unwanted developments that could not later be reversed.

In the case of Berlin, a joint occupation arrangement survived the breakdown of the postwar Potsdam agreement. But the isolation and consequent vulnerability of the city led to an attempted fait accompli, the Berlin blockade. The Soviet Union and the East German regime sought to exploit their position by blocking road and rail access, thereby forcing the the Western powers to resort to military action if they were to protect their rights and provision West Berlin. The Western powers, however, with their superior logistical capability, devised the Berlin air lift to maintain the supply link and shift to the Soviets the onus of having recourse to naked military force. This is perhaps the most clearcut instance of exercise of military power, in a nonviolent way, to cope with the risk attending a cooperative arrangement in a difficult environment.

As another example, one of the controlling concerns for the United States regarding the ending of the occupation regime in Austria was that a power vacuum would follow, into which it would be relatively easy for the Soviet Union to find an excuse to intervene and bring Austria into its orbit; the Western powers, once out, would find it difficult if not impossible to react effectively. Once a de facto solution for the German problem was found in 1955, and a degree of military and political stability emerged in Europe, the risk of Soviet violation of Austrian neutrality faded. Political developments also made the risk more tolerable. A stable Austria with no sizable communist party that might call in the Soviets, and a Federal Republic linked to both NATO and the emerging European communities, removed the fear that a neutral Austria might be the precedent for a reunified and neutral Germany, vulnerable to Soviet threats or blandishments.

Apprehensions over an adverse fait accompli in Central Europe has also been a factor in the MBFR impasse. For the West, any substantial withdrawal to the United States of U.S. forces, even if matched initially by Soviet withdrawals, poses the risk that the U.S. troops will either be demobilized or, even if retained at full strength in the United States, be difficult to redeploy for both operational and political reasons. Soviet redeployment would involve less operational difficulty, shorter distances, and fewer political constraints. On the other hand, the Soviet Union has its own risk calculations, since its troops in Eastern Europe have a major function of underwriting Soviet political control; reduction of troop levels would carry the risk of encouraging popular or regime illusions of freedom of action and political choice among East European states. The process of stabilization in Europe now moving ahead slowly pursuant to the Helsinki Accords, as discussed by Maresca and Goodby, may come to make these respective risks of a conventional force reduction tolerable to the NATO countries on the one hand and the Soviet Union on the other.

From the point of view of the United States and the Soviet Union, there has been a special risk in the European détente that has prevailed since the late 1960s and was reflected in the treaty between the two Germanies, the Berlin Quadripartite Agreement, and the Helsinki Accords and their implementation. Many problems of political status and interstate relations have been resolved and a process of improving relations and enhancing stability has been set in train. Although the United States and the Soviet Union have participated fully in the various multilateral negotiations and agreements, increasingly, the states of Western and Eastern Europe have become major, even principal actors in this process. The two superpowers have their own national security interests to consider, however, as well as their shared interests with their allies, and have seen some risk that the process might reduce their ability to shape future developments in Europe. Thus in both the Helsinki Accords and in the Berlin Quadripartite Agreement of 1971, they acted to reaffirm and protect their retained rights growing out of the World War II victory.

Another way of offsetting risks in political agreements is a guarantee of assistance from a protecting power. The U.S. security guarantee was a major factor, for example, in persuading Israel to enter the Camp David Accords. Other risk management measures provide Israel with continuing assurance during implementation of the accords: for example, U.S. supply of advanced weapons to maintain Israeli military superiority in the region, and the U.S. surveillance mission in the Sinai.

The Antarctica Treaty offers another example of a strategy for risk management. Like many other agreements, the treaty seeks to establish a cooperative framework to reduce the risk of economic or military rivalry. It internationalizes Antarctica, demilitarizes it, and reserves it for peaceful purposes, without prejudice to claims to territorial sovereignty, which are thus in effect suspended. In this situation, there is latent risk that enhanced possibilities of economic exploitation, presently unforeseen geopolitical factors leading to interest in bases, or political interests might lead one nation to assert claims or conduct activities that would challenge the interest of other parties.

The parties protect themselves by: reserving their own claims (some of which overlap); maintaining a physical presence through exploration and other activities; consultation to maximize cooperation, especially regarding potential economic exploitation; and exercising their observation rights to keep informed of what others are doing. Such actions serve in the first instance to deter defection by showing that its advantages would be doubtful or limited. They serve also to reduce the chance of surprise, and to enable other parties to assert their own claims if necessary, and to do so effectively. While taking these prudent measures to safeguard their position, the parties to the treaty have so far primarily worked together to make the treaty regime serve their joint and several interests, both in implementing ongoing exploration and other scientific activities, and in anticipating and consulting on emerging issues or potential new areas of cooperation. If the treaty is to continue to be viable and serve its basic purposes, this cooperative and constructive effort to make it of net advantage to the parties as they make their separate risk/benefit calculations is an essential part of risk management.

In some cases, foreseen risks may be judged so unmanageable as to prevent reaching a cooperative agreement. In the conventional arms transfer talks (CAT), the United States and the Soviet Union explored the possibility of agreement on limiting the levels or types or degree of sophistication of conventional arms transfers in Third World regions. The United States decided not to pursue the talks because of risks that arms supplies necessary for the security of key allies (Israel, South Korea, Pakistan, et al.) might be hindered, and also because of fear the U.S.–Soviet cooperation or its prospect might be attended by destabilizing suspicions and loss of confidence on the part of U.S. friends in important regions.

Similarly, U.S.–Soviet talks concerning a possible agreement to limit naval deployments in the Indian Ocean area identified risks as well as technical and drafting problems. The United States was concerned that limits on naval deployments might put at risk U.S. ability to deal with security contingencies in important areas on the periphery of the Indian Ocean—the Horn of Africa, the Suez Canal and adjacent countries, the Persian Gulf—and that the deterrent effect of U.S. security commitments might be undermined by constraints on the exercise of U.S. naval power to back them up.

ARMS CONTROL: RISKS AND RISK MANAGEMENT

Arms control deals with, and is part of, the central security equation. Its purposes include helping to reduce the risk of war and to increase predictability in force planning and in the evolution of the strategic balance. The risks attending U.S.–Soviet arms control negotiations and agreements are only particular forms of the risks and uncertainties involved in the U.S.–Soviet and NATO-Warsaw Pact arms race and military-political interaction. Assessing and dealing with the risks and uncertainties of prospective or operating arms control arrangements thus require assessing the bilateral and interalliance security relationship with and without the arms control measure in question.

These are not abstract observations. They are integral to the procedure more or less explicitly and systematically followed within the U.S. government in deciding whether to pursue a particular agreement, what the requisite provisions should be, and how well an agreement is working out after it has come into effect. Such assessments underlie the presentation of these matters to the Congress and the public. While the process was most clearly articulated in the Nixon policy structure, it applied in other administrations also. It is reflected throughout this volume in chapters on test bans, strategic arms control, MBFR, weapons and military activities in space, incidents at sea, and other topics of negotiation.

When exploratory discussions indicate the possibility of a useful arms control agreement, the United States has to make a national decision regarding the arms control arrangements it will seek or agree to, and the conditions (especially on verification) it will insist on. Such decisions require a calculation of risks as well as potential benefits, for both of which uncertainties are always present. What are the interests of our negotiating partner (usually the Soviet Union)? Will we be better off if the agreement works than if we simply continue to rest our security solely on the military power and other sources of influence of ourselves and our allies? Are the risks calculable and acceptable, or will we be endangered (as distinct from simply disappointed) if the agreement does not work out or is disregarded by other parties?

These questions suggest criteria that should be (and have been) applied before the United States enters into a negotiation, or signs and ratifies the resulting agreement. In summary:

1. We do not rely on *trust* in international agreements—any more than in domestic commercial agreements. For arms control this means that whenever the limitations involved would affect our own military strength, we must be able to satisfy ourselves that other parties are living up to their reciprocal commitments; we rely, not on trust, but on *verification*. Much of the effort of negotiating and formulating agreements goes into establishing verification standards and procedures.

2. While we do not rely on trust, we do not want to enter into agreements that are simply pieces of paper. We must assess carefully, and make a positive answer to, the question: Does the other party (in the case of SALT/START, the Soviet Union) appear to have a substantial interest in the effective working of the agreement, and thus in living up to it? On no other basis can we expect an agreement to be stable and to work.

3. When we have an interest in the success of an agreement, verification must serve positive as well as negative functions. While it must detect violations or questionable activities, it must also provide comprehensive information to enable a confident judg-

ment as to the over-all compliance record and the effectiveness of the agreement in promoting security and stability.

4. The agreement must specify in sufficiently precise and concrete form what is permitted and what is not permitted, so that compliance and noncompliance can be distinguished.

5. There must be a mechanism for raising and resolving issues and taking other cooperative measures to maintain the viability of the agreement.

6. We must be confident that if the agreement were to be violated, or in other ways not work out as expected, our security would not be imperiled. The means of verification should be dependable enough to give us sufficient timely notice to take offsetting measures.

7. Our current and prospective defense posture (including research and modernization consistent with arms control restrictions) should provide us with the means to respond to substantive violations or to destabilizing technical or other developments. Given the size and diversity of the armed forces in existence, the strategic balance is not quickly or easily shaken and ongoing programs may provide adequate hedges. Careful appraisal is called for, and additional hedges may be needed—for example, added research and development, standby production lines.

A risk assessment along these lines does not always result in separate or joint conclusions that cooperation is preferable to continuing independent and even competing activities. In the case of the Incidents at Sea agreement, as Sean Lynn-Jones has described it in his chapter, the assessment was positive: "Both the United States and the Soviet Union eventually recognized that the risks of naval harassment undermine any justification for its continued unconstrained practice. The 1972 agreement was the result of this mutual recognition." Similarly, John Gaddis shows the role of anticipated risk in the Soviets' initial suspicion of reconnaissance satellites, not simply out of general preoccupation with secrecy but in recognition of the role of enemy satellites in strategic targeting and support of military operations. But if these were risks for the Soviet Union caused by the operation of American satellites, they represented practical gains once the Soviets' own satellites came into operation. Thus on balance the risks were offset not only by operational benefits, but by a general perception that reconnaissance satellites might promote détente and peaceful coexistence by providing the means for mutual reassurance and verification.

A similar net risk/benefit assessment presumably underlies the Soviet interest in a treaty banning space arms, including ASATs. Proponents of an ASAT ban or limitation in the United States have based their arguments on such an assessment. The assessment can reach other conclusions, however, as the study by Sidney Drell and Steven Weber reports and as is reflected in the position of the Reagan Administration. The opposing argument runs that some ASAT capability exists on both sides, and indeed is inherent in ICBM launch capabilities or maneuvering satellites. Verification will be difficult once testing has been successful. Thus, it is argued, the prudent course is to obtain and possess an ASAT capability. So long as both sides recognize the costs and disadvantages of attacking satellites, it will not be done; and possession of an ASAT capability may provide a useful deterrent against one side's being tempted to gain advantage by attacking the satellites of the other. The analogy here is to the case for retention of some chemical-warfare capability, even though the Geneva Protocol bans the first use of chemical weapons in war. In actual conflict, such pledges can be weak if one combatant can use a weapon system—CW or ASATS—with impunity, undeterred by the retaliatory capability of its opponent. The analogy is not strong in view of the role of satellites (and potentially ASATs) in promoting strategic stability and crisis management, but it has weight, and currently prevails in the United States, where the conclusion is currently that the risks of an ASAT agreement would not be acceptable.

A negative risk assessment has also been reached by the Reagan Administration with regard to a comprehensive test ban (CTB). The main risk there is defined as the possible unreliability of the nuclear arsenal unless a regular program of testing of stockpile weapons can be carried out. This is not a new argument, nor is the argument (also given much weight currently) that the United States must continue to exploit its technological superiority—including in nuclear weapons design—to offset other Soviet military advantages. Even if an agreement could be negotiated that would be balanced and fully verifiable, then, U.S. policy makers consider the risks unacceptable in their impact on the United States, which they believe requires technical strategic superiority even if not overall military superiority. In such circumstances, risk is judged unacceptable per se, and risk management techniques cannot compensate for them.

One other kind of risk deserves notice. Some agreements have as their explicit purpose the reduction of a recognized risk. One such is the Incidents at Sea agreement. Another is the 1971 agreement on certain measures to reduce the risk of outbreak of nuclear war. It includes various provisions for notifications of ambiguous or threatening circumstances, for consultation, for restraint. One of the concerns of the United States in reaching the decision to propose and agree to such measures was the risk that they could be used for deception or confusion in a crisis. After careful interagency examination of possible scenarios it was concluded that, while attempts at such misuse could not be ruled out, they would be possible in the absence of a treaty and the procedures and data exchanges provided by the agreement offered on balance a useful increase in the chances for mutual clarification and restraint in event of crisis. The measures proposed or accepted by the United States were selected in accordance with this additional risk consideration.

When nations decide that an agreement is worth pursuing, there will usually be some degree of risk and uncertainty to be countered. In the light of these, decisions will be made, for example, as to the duration of the agreement, and the appropriate escape hatches in event security is endangered. Where the case for a ban or limitation appears clearcut, the preference will be for an agreement of indefinite duration, such as the ABM Treaty, the Limited Test Ban Treaty, the Outer Space Treaty. Even where technical or other uncertainties cannot be excluded, negotiators may choose to specify indefinite duration, and place special reliance on provisions regarding withdrawal if circumstances change. A standard clause in arms control agreements—those of limited as well as indefinite duration—provides that any party has the right to withdraw on suitable notice (usually six months) if relevant "extraordinary events" occur "jeopardizing its supreme interests."

Where the subject matter is extremely complex, as is the case for SALT/START, it may not be feasible to work out a comprehensive agreement, or at least to do so without unduly delaying desirable limited measures. Consequently, an agreement of limited duration (five years for SALT I Interim Agreement, seven years for SALT II) may provide an acceptable way to introduce some elements of predictability into the arms race while matters of great complexity, risk, and uncertainty are explored further in an incremental process. Such a procedure may introduce its own complications, however; deployment by one side of omitted systems might in the eyes of the other party undermine the viability of even a short-term agreement. Thus in SALT II, Soviet uneasiness about the omission of limits on cruise missiles other than ALCMs, and U.S. concern about mobile ICBMs, were reflected in a protocol of two-year duration calling for further negotiations explicitly on these weapons systems, with, in effect, a moratorium on their deployment for that period. Such commitments only to negotiate of course have their own uncertainties, but may be judged preferable to complete omission of an issue.

Another standard device for dealing with uncertainty and risk arising from unforeseen changes and developments is an amendment provision. This has its own dilemmas: Should a majority of parties be able to amend a multilateral agreement for all? Should an amendment apply only to those ratifying it? Should a right of withdrawal accrue to a party not favoring and ratifying an amendment? The answers, in a particular agreement, will depend on the salience of the security issues that seem likely to arise.

The risks and uncertainties relating to agreements can be either *intrinsic* or *extrinsic*. The intrinsic ones are clearcut. The basic one is: Will it be clear that the parties are complying? Here, the clarity, precision, and adequacy of the drafting of the agreement are of the first importance, coupled with the effectiveness of the verification provisions and means of carrying them out. These two requirements are closely related; a large part of the text of arms control agreements (especially SALT agreements) relates to verification means, and corollary provisions (such as functionally related observable dimensions [FRODS] and counting rules in SALT II, and radar provisions in the ABM Treaty) to facilitate verification.

Risks and uncertainties must be viewed realistically, of course. They cannot be completely anticipated and can never be eliminated. In the face of technological change (but also political developments), every eventuality cannot be anticipated and every precaution taken. Trying to do so produces agreements of forbidding complexity (such as SALT II). Overly precise language may be premature and prove to be ill-judged or unwise, as was some radar-related language in the ABM Treaty or the use of ''percentage changes'' in ill-defined quantities in SALT I and II. Consultation procedures and supplementary understandings or amendments, as the need and feasibility of greater detail and precision become clear, is the wiser and more practical approach—if the arms control process is alive and there is an element of mutual respect and accommodation. Verification can never yield 100 percent confidence, but where over-all compliance with the main limitation provisions is clear, uncertainties or suspicions on ancillary activities can safely be dealt with by seeking clarification or correction through consultative channels, before considering direct counter-action or withdrawal.

Some *extrinsic* risks or uncertainties of agreements can be at least partially dealt with in the text; others may be a matter for national action, with the withdrawal provision the ultimate protection. The Non-Proliferation Treaty seeks to block the spread of nuclear weapons. For nonnuclear states, however, it carried the risk of interference with their nuclear power programs, on grounds that they might be covers for or precursors of weapons programs. They were also concerned that under the treaty the world might remain indefinitely divided into nuclear haves and have-nots—a nuclear caste system. Articles IV and VI deal with these concerns, providing for assured access to nuclear power materials and technology, and for superpower pursuit of nuclear arms reduction. Here again, the withdrawal clause is the ultimate safeguard for nations not willing to accept permanent ''have-not'' status, as many stated formally in ratifying the treaty.

Japan and West Germany for their part were only willing to adhere to the NPT because their security was underwritten by the U.S. alliance and nuclear guarantee. They could not get specific treaty language reflecting their concern; instead, on ratifying the treaty they made and deposited formal declarations that their acceptance of nonnuclear status was conditional on their alliance ties with the United States, dissolution of which would give them grounds for withdrawal.

A different kind of extrinsic risk has occasioned expressions of concern in the United States. This is the fear that conclusion of agreements such as SALT or the Helsinki Accords, or even engaging in such negotiations, might lead to "euphoria" or a "lulling effect," and a relaxation of necessary defense efforts.[2] As criteria (5) and (6) above reflect, there is a valid concern here. The Joint Chiefs consistently supported the SALT I and II agreements in the 1970s, as modestly useful agreements, but warned that they should not be an excuse for eliminating permitted defense measures. They conditioned their support on pursuit of appropriate weapons modernization and maintenance of an adequate over-all military posture. Arms control activists and opponents of particular weapons programs do use the existence of negotiations and agreements as an argument against weapons systems or budgets. It is less clear that they have had more than isolated victories, or that there has been any general euphoria or lulling. Indeed, there can be an opposite effect. For example, at the time of the Limited Test Ban Treaty a major "safeguards" program (providing for continued weapons research and underground testing, and standby preparations for renewed atmospheric testing if the treaty failed) was an integral part of the U.S. ratification process, and was carried out at considerable expense for many years. Both SALT I and II were accompanied by explicit U.S. programs of related research and development on new or potential weapons systems—Trident submarines and missiles, cruise missiles, ABM research—to the vocal discontent of some arms control proponents. To the extent there was a shrinkage in U.S. military budget and programs in the mid-1970s (a greatly exaggerated phenomenon) it is more traceable to immediate post-Vietnam disenchantment with things military, and an adjustment period within the armed forces, than to arms control. Indeed, the case seems if anything stronger for the opposite effect—that progress on arms control or détente leads to some uneasiness and to support of weapons programs either as bargaining chips or as hedges. In some cases, arms control negotiations have served to ward off Congressional defense limitations; MBFR negotiations, for example, played a role in deflating the Senate push for bringing troops home from Europe.

Another extrinsic risk of arms control is asserted to be disruption of alliance solidarity. Voices of concern have indeed been raised in NATO—and Israel or South Korea—whenever the United States and the Soviet Union negotiate on security matters or appear to be concluding an arms control agreement. But for over twenty years, the combination of NATO commitment to détente in conjunction with defense, and the good U.S. record on consultation within NATO, has helped allay these concerns. Indeed, NATO is in recent years more disposed to urge pursuit of arms control and détente, prudently of course, and adherence to SALT commitments, than to become uneasy over U.S. negotiations. Both the INF negotiations and MBFR would require adjustments in NATO force planning, but not of undue difficulty.

The impasse in MBFR talks on reductions in conventional forces serves to recall another way in which arms control accords relate to risk. Several "arms control" agreements do not actually limit arms or armed forces, but provide for information exchanges, observations, and consultation procedures to reduce uncertainty, risk, and tension. In Europe, one of the concerns associated with the military confrontation is the fear of surprise or overwhelming attack; the fear is fed by uncertainty regarding the size and character and disposition of opposing forces. Despite the MBFR impasse, representatives of both NATO and the Warsaw Pact protest that their forces are not superior or threatening and are defensive in purpose. In this situation, both the 1975 Helsinki Accords, and the Stockholm agreement on more extensive measures, include "confidence-building measures" for the provision to the other side of information on maneuvers and exercises (which can be, or be suspected of being, a cover for surprise attack) and other troop dispositions, together with opportunities for ground and air surveillance. If regular advance information on troop movements and activities, and regular observation of what is reported and done, prove to be consistent with each side's claim as to the character of its troops, some reassurance and reduced tension might follow. And greater confidence regarding the opposing forces in place might also facilitate the Vienna negotiations, by reducing uncertainty about the actual situation before an agreement on limitations and reductions comes come into effect.

Both within the United States and within NATO, there is reason for attention to the over-all adequacy of defense postures, with arms control or without it. The case is weak, however, that this task, inherently difficult and at times contentious, has been or need be put at risk or made more difficult by arms control.

Special problems of risk management are associated with the agreements under which the parties renounce the use in war of chemical weapons (the Geneva Protocol of 1925); of biological weapons (the Protocol, and the Biological Weapons Convention of 1972, which also bans development and possession); and of some types of inhumane or indiscriminate conventional weapons (Convention of 1980). Limitations on the *use* of weapons, as distinct from their *possession,* are best viewed as extensions of the laws of war, rather than as arms control. They represent efforts to establish norms of international conduct, rather than limits on military forces. Uncertainty and risk are involved. All of the listed categories of weapons have been used in war, and there are charges of post-World War II violations by the Soviet Union and the United States, though in Third World conflicts rather than against each other.

For chemical weapons, the United States has pursued risk management by stipulating that its renunciation of use would not apply in event of first use by another state, and by maintaining deterrent stocks of CW munitions for retaliation in kind. CW was not used in World War II, in contrast to extensive use in World War I. Both the Protocol and the existence of retaliatory capabilities no doubt contributed to this outcome. Negotiations are currently underway in the U.N. Committee on Disarmament, with the United States and the Soviet Union taking lead roles, on a treaty to eliminate chemical weapons—a true disarmament measure. The task is difficult, particularly because the materials for chemical weapons are chemicals in common industrial use, even in some developing countries. (Iraq recently used such weapons against Iranian troops.) The problem is thus not just to destroy existing CW stocks and production facilities, which would be relatively easy to verify, but to assure that production is not resumed at basic chemical plants or specialized facilities by some parties after others have disarmed. It is not hopeless, but it would call for phased destruction of existing stocks (estimated to take some ten years at best for practical reasons), with the final stages carried out only if sufficient openness and access by inspectors to nationwide chemical industry facilities have been established, and well-grounded political confidence warranted such a radical step.

Risk calculations are different—and unique—for biological weapons, which are renounced under the 1972 Convention. In 1969–70, the United States, after thorough study, formally and unilaterally renounced BW weapons and even research on any aspect except countermeasures. The rationale was essentially that they were so unreliable and unpredictable as to have no military value, and so risky to the user or even the developer, that they could best be abandoned. The Convention was subsequently proposed and negotiated as a supplementary international step. Allegations have subsequently been made of Soviet BW development activities at Sverdlovsk, where there was an anthrax outbreak in the late 1970s, as well as of Soviet provision of BW agents to Vietnam and their use in Kampuchea. The evidence is substantial but inconclusive. History does not, on reflection, give cause to reconsider the Convention or the U.S. unilateral renunciation. No important military result was accomplished by the BW use in Southeast Asia, if it indeed occurred; the Soviet population was the victim of their BW research program, if the Sverdlovsk anthrax outbreak was indeed not due to natural causes. Widespread protests and inquiries, in the United Nations and elsewhere, were followed by the dwindling away of suspect activity. International norms cannot be firmly established by fiat; they require both adherence in practice by the great majority of states, and effective political protest when there are apparent contraventions. The history of the past decade or so follows that evolutionary pattern.

It is essential, even though difficult, to keep perspective in talking about the ''risks and uncertainties'' of arms control agreements. The very words carry an implication that much is at stake, that the nation's safety may be teetering in the balance. This is far from the case—although concern might be more plausible if radical reductions in strategic deterrent forces were attempted in a brief period of time. As discussed in Part III of this volume, few of the 23 arms control agreements negotiated in the past few decades have had marked effect on levels of weapons and forces, or on the military balance. Most are efforts either to stabilize existing levels, to preclude new or destabilizing developments, or to reduce risks of war and to improve communications and understanding. Presumably the risk we fear is a ''breakout''—massive clandestine activities that would enable a rival to suddenly renounce or ignore an agreement and mount overwhelming new military power undermining the strategic balance. Nothing that has been charged or speculated about alleged or hypothetical Soviet noncompliance approximates such a traumatic scenario. The nearest thing is Soviet ABM activity, about which the Department of Defense in November 1985 asserted:

> The current and future Soviet violations pose real risks to our security and to the process of arms control itself.

> The Krasnoyarsk radar together with other indications suggesting a possible future territorial defense could have a profound impact on our strategic deterrent forces. Even a *probable* territorial defense would require us to increase the number of our offensive forces and their ability to penetrate Soviet defenses to assure that our operational plans could be executed. The deployment in significant numbers of the SS-25 (which is now well underway) will erode deterrence by allowing the Soviets to contemplate a first-strike using their fixed ICBMs, while retaining intact a reserve force of mobile systems resilient to counter-attack.[3]

The Soviet SS-25 deployments referred to are so far proceeding within SALT restrictions, whereby they are offset by dismantling of existing ICBMs; they would become an addition to Soviet power only if the United States carries out its current threat to stop adherence to these limits, thereby freeing the Soviets. Note the contrast with U.S. SLCMs (sea-launched cruise missiles). Several hundred of these are now in the process of being deployed *outside and above SALT limits.* The stated rationale for them is indeed to serve as a strategic reserve.

As for Soviet ABM activities, even if there were (as is highly debatable) the purposeful pattern suggested, the strategic balance could not be quickly undermined. To get a sense of time scale, note that the Krasnoyarsk radar—an early warning radar of limited ABM operational value—has been under construction for six or more years and is still perhaps two years from completion. Many more even more complex radars would have to be built before the radar infrastructure for a territorial ABM defense would take shape. And the quotation carries its own answer to such an eventuality: increasing the number of U.S. missile warheads and penetration aids, which could be done much more quickly and inexpensively and with greater confidence in their performance. Resumption of unilateral or competitive construction programs for territorial ABM defenses would be highly destabilizing, but would not soon blunt the strategic deterrent, and the responses would be various and obvious. The situation is an interactive and reciprocal one. But even if the fears expressed in the Weinberger letter are exaggerated, they are representative of how defense planners can react to uncertainty about the forces and weapons developments of an opposing state. Planners contemplate signs of nascent weapons programs which may not take definite shape for years, and will then take further years to reach deployment. In response, even without necessarily engaging in worst case planning, it will be prudent to be conservative and begin research and other preparations for matching or counterbalancing programs. These will be seen by the other side, and be used for further justification of its own contingent programs. In the absence of dialogue and agreed limits, formal or informal, the action-reaction process goes ahead, sometimes simply raising or reshaping the balance, sometimes with more destabilizing effects.

Such a reciprocal reaction with its attendant suspicions and risks is one instance of the ''security dilemma'' (discussed by Condoleezza Rice) whereby the forces and weapons that one country considers just adequate to meet the threat from its rival, are seen by the other as themselves threatening and calling for increased responsive military power. The resulting action by the rival power confirms and reinforces the fears of the first. In such circumstances, armed forces are shaped by rivalry rather than by the requirements of their primary function—providing assurance to a nation and its people that they can face the risks of a disorderly world. Where a combination of cooperative agreements and reciprocal military restraint provides a stable military balance, lessening suspicions between rival but not hostile nations, there is a basis for improved political relations as well as further arms reductions and risk reduction measures.

Defense measures and arms control are often spoken of as alternative approaches to risk reduction and management. In detail they can be. More basically, they need not be. Arms control can be a way (1) of reducing the risks accompanying the action-reaction cycle just described; (2) of directing weapons development and deployment into stabilizing and nonthreatening rather than destabilizing forms; and (3) of reducing unwarranted threat perceptions on the part of military rivals. This is not all that arms control can do, but it is the commonest set of functions to which it has been directed so far, and remains a useful one. Under an arms control regime, defense postures and arms control cooperative arrangements become complementary, reducing and making more tolerable the risks and uncertainties associated with either opposing military forces or attempted cooperation.

One further kind of extrinsic arms control risk remains—the risk that arms control negotiations, or implementation of agreements, will not succeed, and that the failure will be accompanied by disillusionment with the possibility of even modest peaceful coexistence and security cooperation between the United States and the Soviet Union. Disillusionment can then prevail even as to the prudence of moderate defense postures and of pursuit of improved political relations. These costs can be considerable. They have arisen in the past in the cyclic U.S.–Soviet relationship, however, and need be only temporary. They are at worst far different in kind and scale from the risk of nuclear war; averting this ultimate risk remains the fundamental motivation for the tenacious pursuit of arms control.

Notes

1. For example, see Richard B. Bilder, *Managing the Risks of International Agreement* (Madison: University of Wisconsin Press, 1981). Pages 219–21 contain a useful "Checklist of Risk-Management Techniques."

2. See the thorough examination of this issue in Sean Lynn-Jones' chapter on the Incidents at Sea Agreement.

3. Letter of November 13, 1985, from Secretary of Defense Caspar Weinberger to President Reagan, processed, page 10 of attached "Memorandum for President: Responding to Soviet Violations Policy (RSVP) Study."

29

Strategies for Facilitating Cooperation

ALEXANDER L. GEORGE

We noted in Chapter 26 that "mutual interests" may be necessary for a cooperative arrangement to take place but that such shared and/or converging interests are not sufficient in and of themselves to ensure cooperation. The strategies that actors utilize for influencing each other may be of critical importance if mutual interests are to be recognized and converted into cooperative behavior. The function of strategy in this respect is to overcome, neutralize, or simply bypass obstacles to cooperation and to make use of favorable factors and conditions latent in the situation. At the same time, however, we must recognize that there are important limits on what strategies can be expected to accomplish.

This chapter does not discuss strategies of negotiation per se, however important they are for reaching an agreement that requires the two sides to balance and compromise among the various components of a particular issue—what we may call "within-issue linkage." This chapter deals, rather, with bargaining strategies that cut across several issue-areas and therefore involve "cross-issue linkage." We also discuss strategies that utilize the principle of reciprocity in an effort to develop cooperation.

Professional diplomacy has had rich experience in utilizing strategies of cross-issue bargaining and reciprocity. Although the terms "linkage," "de-linkage," "tit-for-tat," and "GRIT" may not have been employed in traditional diplomacy, the practices they refer to have often been used in the conduct of foreign policy. Diplomats and students of diplomacy, however, have not articulated these practices in abstract, conceptual terms. They have employed an intuitive form of know-how in determining when and how to employ strategies of bargaining and reciprocity and have not attempted to codify their working knowledge of these strategies or to systematically analyze the conditions favoring their successful employment.

Political scientists and other students of international relations who undertake to conceptualize these strategies and to incorporate them into cooperation theory encounter a different set of problems. Game theory is useful but has limited applicability; it must be supplemented with analytical study of relevant historical experience. However, many game theorists interested in cooperation have limited knowledge of history; they and others recognize the relevance of studying strategies of bargaining and reciprocity in real life historical contexts, but to accomplish this task is a slow and uncertain process. Unfortunately, diplomatic historians have not as yet been drawn into the process of utilizing relevant historical case studies to enrich, elaborate, and refine cooperation theory. The empirical case studies in the *World Politics* study referred to in Chapter 1 were important first steps in this direction and the historical case studies presented in this book greatly enrich the data base.

In pursuing this inquiry we found it useful to distinguish between strategies that employ *bargaining* in a specific negotiating context and strategies that make other uses of the principle of *reciprocity*. Robert Keohane correctly notes that the principle and expectation of reciprocity is present in both of these strategies and that the objective of both strategies is to bring about a mutually acceptable exchange.[1] However, following the distinction proposed by Deborah Larson[2] we will employ the term "bargaining strategy" here to refer to an effort to achieve through negotiation an *explicit, specific* exchange that is usually carried out by the two parties *simultaneously*. The term "strategy of reciprocity," on the other hand, will be used to refer to a unilateral initiative taken by one side in the hope that it will encourage the other side to take a conciliatory action in return. The terms of the exchange are not negotiated and are left somewhat *diffuse,* and the action that constitutes the reciprocation comes later, *not simultaneously*.

While this distinction between bargaining and reciprocity is useful for formal analytical purposes, it is not always easily applied to actual behavior. There are several reasons for this. First, as we shall note, cross-issue linkage can be utilized either in bargaining strategy to achieve a specific agreement or in reciprocity strategy to bring about a more diffuse exchange. Either of these two uses of cross-issue linkage can be made with the "bargaining chip" and "tit-for-tat" strategies that will be discussed later in this chapter. The analytical distinction between bargaining and reciprocity encounters an additional real-life complexity in that sometimes the strategy of reciprocity is resorted to in the initial phase of an effort to develop cooperation which, if successful, may then lead to a specific negotiated agreement. We do not have as yet a comprehensive analytical terminology that captures the many nuances and variants of the highly flexible strategy of linkage.

Two types of cross-issue linkage occur in U.S.–Soviet relations. One variant of the strategy seeks to couple two specific issues: for example, an agreement to grant most-favored nation status and credits to the Soviet Union in return for a commitment to allow increased emigration of Soviet Jews. Another version of cross-issue linkage couples a specific issue and the over-all U.S.–Soviet relationship. We will discuss both types of cross-issue linkage. It should be noted at the outset that resort to linkage, if serious, can either help or block agreement, a fact that has to be considered in deciding to employ this strategy.

THE STRATEGY OF CROSS-LINKAGE

Bargaining strategy that makes use of cross-issue linkage to influence the adversary is deliberate and purposeful. As such, therefore, it needs to be distinguished from "inadvertent linkage,"[3] which refers to the unintended effects that developments in one issue-area have on the possibilities of agreement and cooperation in another issue-area.

Cross-issue linkage can indeed create new possibilities for mutual beneficial bargaining. However, as James Sebenius notes,[4] although many analysts recognize that issue linkage is "a prominent and venerable practice," the experience with efforts to employ linkage strategy is not easily evaluated. As a result we lack a general theory that would enable us to make confident predictions as to when cross-issue linkage will and will not work. Still, it may be useful to draw on our case studies and the work of other scholars to sketch a theoretical framework and some hypotheses regarding the conditions under which cross-issue linkage is and is not likely to contribute to an agreement.

Linkage strategy is quite flexible and can take any of several different forms. Thus, the linkage attempted by one side may be very direct and specific: it may tie a particular action or agreement in one issue area explicitly to a particular action or agreement in another issue-area. Or the linkage may be more diffuse: an action that one proposes to take in one issue-area may be tied in more general terms to a change in the adversary's behavior in another issue-area. Thus, as already noted, cross-issue linkage can be part of either a bargaining or reciprocity strategy.

Examples of both forms of the linkage strategy are present in our case studies. As Jonathan Dean notes, direct linkage was effectively employed by both the United States and the Soviet Union in working out a complex package of agreements having to do with several European issues associated with the emergence of détente in the early 1970s. The Federal Republic of Germany (FRG) signed a treaty with the Soviet Union accepting the postwar borders of Poland, the German Democratic Republic, and the Soviet Union on August 12, 1970. The FRG signed a similar treaty with Poland. But the FRG and the Western allies, employing the strategy of linkage, stipulated to the Soviet Union that the FRG Bundestag would not ratify those two treaties prior to the conclusion of a quadripartite agreement on Berlin. Moscow, in turn, applied "reverse linkage," declining to put the quadripartite agreement on Berlin into effect until the Bundestag ratified the two treaties. In the end, the Western powers and the Soviet Union agreed that the entire package of three treaties should go into effect on the same day, June 3, 1972.

As Dean notes, the Soviets also wanted a Western commitment to participate in a Conference on Security and Cooperation in Europe (CSCE), but NATO made it clear that Western participation was dependent on the conclusion of an acceptable agreement on Berlin. John Maresca makes a similar observation, adding that the United States and its allies linked their acceptance of CSCE not only to a Berlin accord but also to Soviet agreement on a CSCE agenda which would include key human rights topics of free movement of people and ideas, and—as Coit Blacker also notes—to Soviet agreement on the opening date for the Mutual Balanced Force Reduction talks (MBFR).

These are instances of "positive" linkage: agreement in one issue-area is coupled with and made contingent upon agreement in another issue-area. Richard Haass in his case study provides an example of what may be termed "negative" linkage. The Carter Administration, he reports, broke off the Indian Ocean talks because of assertive Soviet behavior in Africa.

While cross-issue linkage is often employed, as the preceding examples indicate, to attain short-term objectives of a specific character, it can also be used to achieve longer-term objectives of a more general nature. Thus we may recall that Nixon and Kissinger employed cross-issue linkage (both of a "positive" and "negative" character) in implementing their long-range grand strategy of attempting to alter Soviet attitudes and behavior in the international system. To this end Nixon and Kissinger employed a mixed strategy of carrots and sticks in order to create a web of incentives in Soviet leaders that would induce them to moderate Moscow's foreign policy behavior. The Nixon Administration also attempted to use linkage on behalf of more specific, immediate goals. Its effort to make the opening of SALT I talks conditional on Soviet assistance in bringing about a settlement in Vietnam proved to be abortive. On the other hand, Kissinger claims that the Nixon Administration successfully withheld granting Most Favored Nation trading status to the Soviets until Moscow demonstrated "a commitment to restrained international conduct and willingness to help settle concrete issues, including Vietnam and Berlin."[5]

As for Soviet leaders, while they generally denounce the idea of linkage when the United States attempts it, they try to make use of it themselves when it might serve their interests. In addition to historical examples of Soviet use of linkage already noted, we may recall that Moscow agreed to President Johnson's proposal for strategic arms talks only after the signing of the Nuclear Non-Proliferation Treaty, and that Gorbachev repeatedly tied a second summit meeting with Reagan to progress in arms control. And, Barry Blechman notes, the Soviets have tried to trade movement on technical arrangements to reduce the risk of accidental or inadvertent war for American concessions on subjects of greater interest to Moscow.

Linkage is a flexible strategy. It can be used to induce the adversary to avoid, or desist from, uncooperative behavior in another issue-area (negative linkage) as well as in an effort to induce the adversary to take positive cooperative actions, either of a unilateral kind or jointly. On several occasions U.S. administrations attempted negative linkage on behalf of diffuse objectives, for example by warning on one occasion that general progress in U.S.–Soviet relations would be affected adversely by Soviet support for India in its conflict with Pakistan in 1971 and, on other occasions, that SALT negotiations would be jeopardized by Soviet involvement in Angola in 1975–76, and in Ethiopia in 1978.

Other things being equal, negative linkage of this kind, taken on behalf of diffuse and unrelated objectives, tends to generate weaker bargaining leverage than intrinsic linkage among related objectives such as characterized the package of agreements on European issues put together in the development of détente in the early 1970s. But, of course, other things are not always "equal" and what is probably of critical importance in most cases is the *credibility* of the threat to engage in negative linkage and whether the *potency* of the threat is perceived by the recipient as weighty enough to lead it to do something it would rather not do. Negative linkage, therefore, bears a resemblance to compellance and coercive diplomacy; in efforts to employ such strategies, the diffuseness of what is demanded of the opponent may weaken their effectiveness. Moreover, the more that is demanded of the opponent in negative linkage, as in coercive diplomacy, the stronger his motivation to refuse compliance and, hence, the stronger the coercive threat must be to overcome his resistance.[6]

Linkage strategy may also take the form of initiating self-serving behavior in one issue-area that *threatens* the interests of the adversary in order to induce him into more cooperative behavior in other issue-areas. Thus, the Nixon Administration hoped to use the opening to China and all that portended to generate bargaining leverage in its relations with the Soviet Union. Similarly, the Carter Administration tried to use normalization of relations with China to the same end but, as Kiron Skinner notes, Moscow responded with "reverse-linkage," delaying the signing of SALT II for six months.

What some of the historical experience reviewed here suggests, more generally, is that an attempt at cross-issue linkage by one side may trigger reverse-linkage by the other side and this, in turn, may result in agreement or disagreement. We noted earlier, citing Dean's case study, that both the United States and the Soviet Union effectively employed direct linkage in working out the package of agreements on European issues. Another possible example of resort to reverse-linkage in response to a linkage attempt is the interaction that developed between the two superpowers during the Nixon Admin- istration over the issue of Jewish emigration from the Soviet Union. The U.S. strategy of linking progress in trade and credits to increased emigration of Soviet Jews enjoyed considerable success initially, but when the United States continued to press for more emigration the Soviet Union finally responded by drawing the line: no further progress in emigration without satisfactory progress in arrangements for trade and credits. The outcome of mutual use of linkage in this case, unlike that in the case of the package of agreements on European issues, was a collapse of efforts to work out a cooperative solution to the linked issues.

What, then, can we conclude from this assessment of some past efforts at cross-issue linkage? The effectiveness of a particular use of linkage strategy is not always easy to predict. Moreover, the contribution linkage strategy per se made to an agreement is not always easy to determine because it raises a difficult methodological problem: the fact that linkage was attempted and the outcome was successful does not necessarily mean that linkage was the most important contributor to success. Obviously other factors contributing to the successful outcome must also be considered. This is not to say that linkage does not sometimes contribute importantly to the achievement of a resoundingly successful outcome, such as the package of agreements on Europe in the early 1970s. Linkage worked in this case in part because both sides recognized that the security issues in question were indeed interrelated and could not easily be decoupled from one another. This, then, may be regarded as an example of "systemic" (or intrinsic) link- age, as against "artifical" and arbitrary linkage in which one side attempts to link two unrelated issues simply for bargaining purposes. But even systemic linkage cannot work if the respective interests of the two sides are not accommodated in some way, and this may depend as much if not more on skillful negotiation of each of the specific issues as on the framework provided by cross-issue linkage.

Similarly, care must be taken not to assume that the failure of attempted linkage must be due to its presumed irrelevance in the instant case or to a naively optimistic expectation by policy-makers of what it could accomplish. Such explanations of failed linkage strategy may be justified in some cases but not in others. As Blacker emphasizes in his case study of the prolonged MBFR negotiations, failure to achieve an agreement thus far cannot be attributed to the inability of the two sides to see the contribution it would make to favorable developments in other issue-areas. Rather, the critical factor has been the lack of a mutuality of interest between NATO and the Warsaw Pact on reduction of forces that is strong enough to lead to a specific MBFR agreement accept- able to both sides.

Moreover, as Kiron Skinner persuasively argues in her forthcoming dissertation, the potential efficacy of linkage (as well as "de-linkage") strategy can be thwarted by domestic political constraints.[7] Ethnic-nationalist and ideological groups hampered the ability of several administrations to use trade as leverage to influence Soviet policies. Nixon's and Kissinger's effort to delay initiation of strategic arms negotiations in order to obtain leverage for dealing with other issues was defeated, as Kissinger complains in his memoirs, because of "the cumulative impact of all the bureaucratic indiscipline, with media and Congressional pressures. . . ."[8] On the other hand, it must be recog- nized that under different conditions domestic political constraints can force policymakers to attempt to link an issue that is important domestically with another issue that is under negotiation.

LINKAGE WITH THE OVER-ALL U.S.–SOVIET RELATIONSHIP

One can distinguish three dimensions in the over-all U.S.–Soviet relationship: (1) the basic political framework of relations, if any, on which the two sides have agreed (which was discussed in Chapter 27); (2) the various cooperative arrangements they have already created and the specific issues on which they are attempting to reach new agreements; and (3) the current tone and political-psychological atmospherics of their relations. The state of the over-all relationship at any given time reflects the level of satisfaction or dissatisfaction with each other's behavior in these three dimensions of the relationship. For example, one side may feel that the other is not behaving in accordance with important principles and guidelines contained in the basic political framework; or that it is failing to comply with agreements already in place; or that it is blocking the achievement of new agreements; or that it has introduced a harsh tone into the conduct of relations and has deliberately taken hostile actions that have created tensions and discord.

The state of the over-all U.S.–Soviet relationship is always part of the context in which the two sides deal with a specific issue in their relations. Satisfaction or dissatisfaction with some aspects of the over-all relationship may influence how a specific issue is handled even though neither side attempts for bargaining purposes to make a linkage between that issue and the over-all relationship. The term "inadvertent linkage" has been coined by cooperation theorists to refer to the possible effect dissatisfaction with the handling of one issue can have on another issue even in the absence of an effort to link the two. An example of inadvertent linkage that is often cited by U.S. officials and analysts is the damaging effect assertive Soviet behavior in Africa and the Middle East in the late 1970s had on the over-all détente relationship.

A linkage attempt can be made in either direction: one side could invoke the over-all relationship in order to persuade the other to behave more cooperatively on a specific issue; or one side could use its willingness to cooperate on a specific issue in an effort to get the adversary to join in improving the over-all relationship.

Sometimes one side is more interested than the other in the implications the handling of a specific issue will have on the over-all relationship. Thus, U.S. leaders experienced much greater concern than did Soviet leaders as to the negative impact Soviet behavior in Africa would have on détente generally (as well as on specific issues such as SALT II and the Indian Ocean talks). At other times the linkage is clearly relevant for both sides. Thus, in the Arab-Israeli war of October 1973 both Nixon and Brezhnev wished to minimize the damage that the war between their regional clients would do to détente and they seem in retrospect to have felt that their positive relationship enabled them to cooperate more effectively than would otherwise have been the case in bringing the war to an end. Finally, in still other cases the over-all relationship is hardly relevant at all in influencing U.S. and Soviet attitudes towards cooperation on a specific issue. As Deborah Shapley points out, the Antarctica Treaty was successfully concluded in 1959 despite the Cold War relationship at the time. And David Hall makes a similar observation regarding the Laos neutralization agreement in 1962.

Sometimes a deliberate effort is made to de-couple a specific issue from the over-all relationship, as for example in the Carter Administration's early efforts to shield SALT II from the impact of an eroding détente. De-linkage efforts of this kind have been difficult, as Condoleezza Rice notes, because of the tendency within influential American circles to regard the Soviet Union's assertive foreign policy behavior in the Third World as a consequence of the limits placed on American power by SALT and détente. De-linkage has fared better in other cases. Thus, Sean Lynn-Jones concludes, the willingness of the two sides to separate the problem of avoiding incidents at sea from broader political considerations and to deal with this issue through unpublicized navy-to-navy channels has been important for the successful implementation of the Incidents at Sea agreement. Similarly, after the dangerous Berlin crisis of 1961 and the Cuban missile crisis the following year, something approximating a tacit understanding may have emerged between the two superpowers to cool the Berlin issue and defer efforts to deal with it until more propitious circumstances should emerge. If such a tacit understanding existed, it was converted into a formal agreement some years later, as Dean conveys in his case study: "Through the 1971 Quadripartite Agreement, the Berlin issue, which has been both product and cause of the East-West confrontation, was deliberately decoupled from the continuing worldwide U.S.–Soviet political and military competition. In the course of decades of confrontation over Berlin, the potential costs of East-West war had grown so great that both sides were willing to insulate the Berlin issue with a new modus vivendi. . . . no final solution was possible at the time, only a modus vivendi or regime to administer an unresolved problem."

Having recognized the important role de-linkage sometimes can play in protecting a specific issue from being influenced by a poor over-all relationship, let us now consider efforts to use a specific issue to enhance the over-all relationship. Agreement on a particular issue may be motivated in part by the hope that it will contribute to improving the over-all relationship. Thus, in his study of U.S.–Soviet agreements to reduce the danger of accidental or inadvertent war Barry Blechman finds that after each of three periods of tension in U.S.–Soviet relations, "the political leaders' desire to impart some momentum to improving the relationship, and also to provide tangible evidence of its benefits to domestic and foreign audiences, may have added to the likelihood of success in reaching agreement on the measure under consideration."

Similarly, James Goodby notes that the Stockholm Conference "began in a time of trouble [in U.S.–Soviet relations], but the adverse political climate acted as a positive factor since it provided a strong motivation to use the Conference to improve the East-West relationship. The United States viewed the Conference that way and, to an extent, a desire to establish a more constructive relationship with the Soviet Union prompted the initiatives taken by the U.S. government . . . and enabled the U.S. delegation to exercise a positive and constructive leadership role."

A similar motivation to conclude a specific agreement in order to improve the over-all relationship can be attributed to Soviet leaders as well. Kurt Steiner believes this played some role in Nikita Khrushchev's initiative in 1955 to push for a quick agreement on a neutral Austria. And Dean believes that a similar motivation for improved relations with the West reinforced Soviet interest in defusing the Berlin issue in the early 1970s.

Whether or not linkage is explicitly attempted, the general climate of the superpowers' relationship has often exercised some influence on the outcome of negotiations on a specific issue or on the implementation of existing cooperative arrangements. Alan Neidle emphasizes as the main theme of his case study that the health of test ban projects has depended to a considerable extent on the direction of U.S.–Soviet relations. The impasse in the comprehensive test ban negotiations in the early 1980s, he feels, can be attributed in part to the deterioration of over-all relations. And, more generally, Philip Farley in his review of strategic arms control concludes that arms control in particular is closely linked to the political relationships between the U.S. and Soviet Union, which are the crucial cement.

In a number of our case studies the author finds that the positive state of U.S.–Soviet relations at the time was a contributing factor to the achievement, sometimes short-lived to be sure, of a cooperative arrangement on a specific security issue. Certainly this was the case, as David Schoenbaum reports, when the Allies during World War II experienced little difficulty in reaching an agreement on postwar occupation and administration of Germany, although more important was the imperative need for such an agreement since the end of the war was approaching. John Lewis Gaddis feels that the over-all improvement in superpower relations following the Cuban missile crisis is one of the factors, though certainly not the most important one, that helps explain the Soviet decision to tolerate U.S. satellite reconnaissance activities. Joseph Nye suggests that détente was probably "a necessary condition" for progress on nuclear nonproliferation. Lynn-Jones, too, feels that the movement toward détente in the early 1970s facilitated the Incidents at Sea Agreement. So, too, do Steven Weber and Sidney Drell credit détente with having been conducive to development of limited tacit cooperation to avoid militarization of space in the late 1960s and early 1970s. As for the Helsinki Accord, Maresca emphatically states that not only would an agreement to start the Conference on Security and Cooperation in Europe have been "unthinkable" if over-all relations were not improving but the final summit conference in 1975 at which the agreement was signed, just as support for détente was unravelling in the United States, "would not have been possible later" when détente had become even more controversial.

In other cases involving specific security issues our authors conclude that the negative state of U.S.–Soviet relations contributed at times to the failure of cooperative efforts. The failure for many years to make progress in negotiations over Austria, as Steiner shows, can be explained by the thicket of more fundamental Cold War conflicts and suspicions, and fear on the part of both Moscow and Washington that the solution of the German problem would be prejudiced by an agreement on Austria. Blacker finds that although the improvement in U.S.–Soviet relations in the early 1970s helped to get the MBFR negotiations started, the deterioration in the over-all relationship soon became a constraint on their negotiations. Efforts to avoid militarization of space, Weber and Drell report, became more difficult as the over-all U.S.–Soviet relationship turned sour and a more invidious image of Soviet behavior and intentions began to influence U.S. policy. At the same time, U.S. leaders moved from a policy of contingent restraint to contingent threat of escalation, and then to one of competition in developing space-related weaponry. Similarly, as Robert Buchheim and Philip Farley, and Gloria Duffy indicate in separate essays, the advent of U.S. leaders who never accepted détente or thought it discredited, and the shift towards dealing with the Soviet Union from "a position of strength," contributed to the Reagan Administration's criticism of the Standing Consultative Commission and charges of Soviet noncompliance with arms control agreements.

We should note, however, that the effects of even a sharp deterioration of the over-all relationship on specific forms of cooperation that have already been established may be cushioned by various factors. As Maresca notes, Soviet leaders have displayed a strong interest in holding on to basic agreements made during the détente era and to the détente philosophy itself. In particular, they (as well as U.S. leaders) have displayed a degree of flexibility in accepting and adapting to the Helsinki process set into motion by the 1975 accord. When arrangements to cooperate have been embedded in *formal agreements*, particularly multilateral ones with diverse parties, it helps to preserve them when over-all relations worsen. This has even been true to a limited extent in the case of major arms control agreements—SALT I and SALT II and the ABM treaty—as well as in the continued implementation of the Incidents at Sea Agreement. As Nye empha-sizes in his study of nuclear proliferation, the *institutionalization* of agreements "in which there are explicit norms and multiple opportunities for contact may help to pre-serve an area of cooperation when the overall climate turns sour." Of considerable importance was the fact that nonproliferation was not a bilateral U.S.–Soviet issue but an interest shared with the rest of the world. Nye adds that, for various reasons, with the passage of time the tendency to link cooperation on nonproliferation to the state of over-all U.S.–Soviet relations has declined: "when the sea of hostility rose again, it did not submerge this island of cooperation."

CREATION AND USE OF "BARGAINING CHIPS"

The term "bargaining chip" is often employed very loosely to refer to any contingent concession one side professes it is willing to make in return for something of value from the other side. So defined, "bargaining chip" is no different from any offer of a quid pro quo in bargaining or negotiation. A more useful definition of "bargaining chip" restricts the term to the deliberate creation of an asset not for its contribution to one's capabilities but rather for its exchange value. In other words, the bargaining chip is created with the expectation and hope that it can be given up in return for an appropriate concession from the adversary. Ideally, therefore, the bargaining chip should create leverage to induce the opponent to bargain and make concessions for its removal.[9] As noted earlier in this chapter, a bargaining chip may be created either in the hope that it will assist in achieving a specific agreement or as part of a diffuse reciprocity strategy which leaves open what concession will be accepted in return for the bargaining chip.

While much has been heard in the United States in recent years characterizing the Administration's development of new or improved weapons as intended to serve in some way as bargaining chips, such statements probably do not reflect the stricter definition noted above. Creation of bargaining chips in this sense of the word is not necessarily the same thing as strengthening one's military posture in order to negotiate from a "position of strength." Similarly, the bargaining chip strategy as defined here is not necessarily the same thing as the strategy Secretary of Defense Caspar Weinberger seemed to have in mind when he stated that the Administration's military programs are intended to give the Soviets added incentives to negotiate arms control. What distinguishes such statements from bargaining chips proper is the lack of any indication that a particular military weapons program is being created in order to be given up in return for conces-sions. Creating a position of strength by strengthening one's military posture and doing so to increase the Soviet incentive to negotiate may be useful and necessary policies, but the weapons developed or acquired for these purposes are not necessarily acquired with the expectation or hope that they can be given up in return for appropriate conces-sions from the adversary.

A similar problem arises in labelling certain foreign policy initiatives as ''bargaining chips.'' Thus, for example, Nixon's opening to China was indeed motivated in part by a desire to acquire leverage in dealings with the Soviets, but the move towards détente with the P.R.C. cannot properly be regarded as a bargaining chip since it was not an asset Nixon was prepared to give up in return for Soviet concessions.

It is true that existing military weapons, originally created for their contribution to one's over-all capabilities, may come to be regarded as expendable in negotiations in return for appropriate reductions by the other side. Such expendable assets are also often loosely referred to as having acquired the status of possible ''bargaining chips.'' The difference remains that they were not created for that purpose. This observation applies also to strategic weapons that have been dismantled by the superpowers in accord with the ceiling on numbers agreed to in SALT I and II.

It is indeed possible, on the other hand, that a potential bargaining-chip rationale is among the reasons, though not the sole reason, for creating new military assets. The weapons in question may be desired for their military value as well and may be useful for strengthening one's over-all posture if not given up as bargaining chips in a negotiation. A good example of this was the NATO Euromissile deployment of Pershing IIs and cruise missiles on the ''two-track'' strategy.

Still another possibility is that advocates of a military build-up which is controversial domestically may attempt to gain Congressional and public support for new programs by cloaking them with a spurious bargaining-chip rationale.

Enough has been said to indicate some of the difficulties of ascertaining when assets have been created solely or largely for their intended use as bargaining chips. It is difficult to obtain valid historical data needed to assess the utility of the strategy of creating bargaining chips and using them effectively for that purpose. It seems probable that one reason why Presidents Johnson and Nixon initiated deployment of a limited ABM system was their desire to demonstrate to the Soviets that the United States could move in this direction, thereby strengthening Moscow's incentives to agree to an ABM Treaty. If so, then the creation of the U.S. ABM was a bargaining chip and it may have played a role in facilitating the ABM Treaty. (On the other hand, one may ask whether a vigorous U.S. ABM research program per se would have sufficed to motivate the Soviets to accept an ABM treaty.) Other possible examples of the creation of genuine bargaining chips are harder to identify. It would appear that at one time Kissinger had hoped to use cruise missiles as a bargaining chip and may have urged the Defense Department to procure such weapons for this purpose.[10] Given the difficulty of obtaining data on such matters, we are forced to review arguments for and against the bargaining chip strategy without strong empirical evidence.[11]

Let us consider, first, a major desideratum said to apply in choosing an ideal bargaining chip. This proposition, articulated by George Rathjens, holds that one should procure for use as bargaining chips weapons ''of a kind that would do us little good in terms of improved military capabilities but might be very worrisome to the Soviet Union.''[12] A bargaining chip of this kind would presumably exert strong leverage on the Soviets to make concessions in order to get us to remove it. But the question remains: what price would we demand and what would the Soviets be prepared to offer; in other words, could a bargain then be struck to secure removal of the weapons in question?

We must take note of a fundamental ambiguity in Rathjens' proposition: it does not address the question of the value to the Soviets of the concession they are expected to make in order for the United States to remove the bargaining chip that is so worrisome to them. Rathjens fails to address this important question and thus his proposition is not the same as one of the central propositions of George Homans' social exchange theory: "The open secret of human exchange is to give the other person behavior (on your part) that is more valuable to him or her than it is costly to you and to get behavior in return that is more valuable to you than it is costly to the other."[13] If Homans' principle were to be followed, the United States should be prepared in return for giving up its bargaining chip to accept a Soviet offer to give up something less valuable to itself than to the United States. Homans' principle requires *symmetry:* what each side gives up is less valuable to itself than to the other side.

The simple logic of the bargaining chip strategy encounters real-life complications, the result of which may be an inadvertent, unexpected, unwanted acceleration of the arms race. First, as Rathjens notes, negotiations needed to cash in the bargaining chip are likely to move slowly and meanwhile weapons technology moves forward, opening new options. Therefore, technological developments may provide the country targeted by this strategy with a new military option for neutralizing or markedly reducing the threat posed by the weapons system serving as a bargaining chip, thereby markedly reducing its exchange value. Given this possibility, the side employing the bargaining chip strategy must decide *when* is the optimal time for cashing it in since timing may govern its cash value.

Second, parts of the bureaucracy, Congress, and industry may develop vested interests in the military program intended to serve as a bargaining chip. The program thereby takes on a momentum of its own in generating opposition to efforts to give it up in a negotiation. As a result, the "value" a bargaining chip unexpectedly acquires may increase substantially the price tag for giving it up, so much so that a deal is no longer possible. Hence, as Rathjens notes, "a chip, once acquired, may not be expendable."[14]

A related, third possibility is that the expense required to create the bargaining chip may soar unexpectedly to a level that makes it difficult to scrap it unless the adversary is willing to make substantial concessions, which he may prefer not to.

Fourth, the adversary may choose the alternative of strengthening his own forces or developing bargaining chips of his own. The result in time may be that both sides end up "hoarding" useless (or only marginally useful) and costly bargaining chips which, in addition, may increase insecurity, mutual distrust, and the danger of war.

Finally, we should note that the bargaining chip strategy is the opposite of the strategy of "unilateral cooperative actions" (referred to in Chapter 26) that one side takes to enhance its own security *without* adding a threat to the opponent's security.

STRATEGIES OF TIT-FOR-TAT AND "GRADUATED RECIPROCATION IN TENSION-REDUCTION" (GRIT)[15]

We distinguished at the beginning of this chapter between bargaining strategies and other strategies that make use of the principle of reciprocity in a different way. As was noted, in contrast to agreements achieved through bargaining, the terms of the exchange aimed at through the strategy of reciprocity may be somewhat diffuse rather than specific/explicit, and the exchange takes place sequentially rather than simultaneously. That is, the side employing the strategy of reciprocity acts first, choosing to behave in a way that it hopes will elicit some kind of appropriate conciliatory response. But the initiator of the strategy does not specify what the reciprocated action should be—hence, the terms of the exchange are characterized as "diffuse." Both "tit-for-tat" and "GRIT" can qualify as examples of strategies of reciprocity, as defined here. (But, as noted earlier in this chapter, tit-for-tat can also be employed in a bargaining strategy that attempts to achieve a specific negotiated agreement.)

The initiator of the strategy cannot be certain that his action will be reciprocated. Hence the the strategy, if it is to work at all, is based on the initiator's trust that the other side will respond appropriately and/or his hopes that the other side will regard it as it its own self-interest to make a reciprocating response.

It is in this way, therefore, that the strategy of reciprocity attempts to facilitate cooperation. In some realms of social life, use of the reciprocity strategy is said to be more likely to achieve cooperation if it creates a sense of obligation. But adversaries in international politics are not likely to feel obliged to respond to each other's conciliatory moves; if they do respond positively it is more likely to be because they believe it is in their interest to do so. In the absence of perceived self-interest on the part of the side that is the target of reciprocity strategy, the strategy may well fail to elicit the hoped-for response. Thus, Khrushchev's sustained efforts to employ a strategy of reciprocity, via a series of conciliatory actions,[16] failed to evoke a reciprocal response from President Eisenhower and Secretary of State John Foster Dulles, or to dissipate their distrust of the Soviets, until developments in Europe, as Steiner notes in his case study, removed obstacles delaying an agreement on neutralization of Austria.

When, as in the case of the emergence of the Sino-American détente in 1971, both sides are already predisposed out of self-interest for the amelioration of existing hostility and distrust, the initiation of a reciprocating strategy by one side is likely to elicit a positive response, and a cycle of reciprocating moves may be set into motion easily and quickly to bring about the relaxation of tensions both sides desire. Mutual interests in détente existed prior to the use of the strategy of reciprocity, which served as a trigger and a facilitator rather than as an important causal agent for the Sino-American détente.

A strategy of reciprocity may achieve some results even when the leaders of the target country are not eager for a relaxation of tensions. This can occur when the conciliatory actions of the side initiating the strategy make a favorable impression on public opinion in the target country, thereby generating pressure on its leaders to make some kind of reciprocal gesture. Thus, on one occasion Khrushchev quite appropriately referred to his use of the strategy of reciprocity as "waging peace" and there are elements of this also in some of the actions and announcements that Gorbachev has made in order to generate indirect pressure on U.S. leaders by means of Western European and domestic American opinion.

There are, however, rather severe limits on the efficacy of the strategy of reciprocity in relations between adversaries such as the United States and the Soviet Union. The strategy is much more likely to be successful in helping to bring about a relaxation of tensions, in improving the atmospherics of relations rather than in facilitating an accommodation on issues that engage fundamental security interests or in which serious conflicts of interest are imbedded. For issues of this degree of gravity, bargaining and negotiation rather than diffuse reciprocity are more likely to be necessary if a cooperative solution or modus vivendi is to be reached. Most of the successes in security co-

operation between the United States and the Soviet Union were reached through bargaining involving either explicit or tacit negotiation. As Robert Keohane observes, "Stable
patterns of specific reciprocity [i.e., agreements arrived at through bargaining] are often
the most one can expect in world politics: genuine diffuse reciprocity is rare." [17]

Nonetheless, a brief discussion of the strategies of reciprocity known as tit-for-tat
and GRIT are needed. We should make clear at the outset that the following discussion
of tit-for-tat is confined to its employment in the conduct of foreign policy for purposes
of eliciting a positive, cooperative response. (Tit-for-tat is also often used for punishing
an adversary who has encroached on one's interests. This type of retaliation, permissible
under international law, is usefully distinguished from the initiation of an accommodative, conciliatory action in the hope that it will be reciprocated.) In one variant of
tit-for-tat in experimental games Robert Axelrod found that this strategy did best in
inducing cooperation in iterated rounds of the Prisoner's Dilemma game.[18] In this game
tit-for-tat makes use of a quite simple, primitive variant of the principle of reciprocity.
A player employing this strategy "cooperates" on the first move of a sequence, then he
does on subsequent moves what the other player did on the previous one—that is, if the
response to his conciliatory move is conciliatory, he undertakes another accommodative
move; but if the response to his conciliatory move is antagonistic his next move will be
an appropriately antagonistic one. The two players do not communicate with each other
(this is not possible in the Prisoner's Dilemma); they "learn" to cooperate solely through
responses to each other's moves.

The "solution" to the Prisoner's Dilemma, however, is not the solution to the
security dilemma in international politics. The tit-for-tat strategy may have internal validity within the structure of the experimental game but, not surprisingly, serious questions arise regarding the external validity of the theory if one tries to employ it in more
complex settings such as the adversarial relations between nations.[19] We need not be-
labor the limitations and risks of efforts to employ a tit-for-tat strategy in U.S.–Soviet
relations for the purpose of encouraging the adversary to reciprocate with positive moves
of his own and to move on to a cooperative arrangement in a particular issue-area. In
the first place, a genuinely conciliatory move may not be understood as such and may
not be credited by the recipient who, instead, may either dismiss it as cloaking more
fundamental hostile intentions or discount it as forced upon the side initiating the conciliatory action by circumstances beyond its control. Another constraint on tit-for-tat in
U.S.–Soviet relations is the considerable uncertainly either side is likely to experience
in trying to estimate the expected payoffs, either short-term or longer-term, from "cooperating" with the other's seemingly, or even genuinely, conciliatory moves. (In contrast, in the typical Prisoner's Dilemma, the possible payoffs from different moves are
known; the only uncertainty is whether the other side will choose to cooperate or defect.)

Also, domestic political constraints of one kind or another may limit the willingness and ability of one state to respond to the conciliatory moves of the other side. Still
another risk the strategy encounters arises from the fact that since tit-for-tat calls for
retaliating to each other's refractory actions, it may institute a cycle of retaliatory interaction that worsens the relationship, at least temporarily, instead of improving cooperation. (This is the danger of "feuding," to which cooperation theorists have called
attention.[20])

Another obstacle may arise if the two sides disagree on what constitutes an "equivalent" response—whether of a conciliatory or refractory nature. In international politics

(unlike the Prisoner's Dilemma) the actors playing the game of *realpolitik* are constantly looking for ways of gaining a relative advantage over each other. Such motivations complicate and may vitiate agreement on what constitutes reciprocity and equivalence.

Still another obstacle to tit-for-tat challenges the very assumption of reciprocity on which it is based. Thus, as Weber and Drell suggest, some U.S. leaders may hold an image of the Soviet opponent that leads to the conviction that tit-for-tat will not work with the Soviets. They may believe that returning tit-for-tat provides insufficient incentive to influence the Soviets and that one must act on the principle of many tits for a tat, threatening to escalate the competition to the disadvantage of the Soviets in order to make an impression.

Finally, whereas in the Prisoner's Dilemma a clear-cut, latent mutuality of interest in cooperating is built into the structure of the game, this assumption does not hold for U.S.–Soviet relations, which are characterized instead by a complex mix of conflicting, divergent but possibly converging, and mutual interests.

These reservations regarding the tit-for-tat strategy notwithstanding, it does play a role in regulating relations between adversaries in international politics. When mutuality of interests clearly exists in a particular issue-area and is recognized by the two sides, a conciliatory move by one side may encourage the other side to make a positive response, thereby possibly leading to a tacit or explicit agreement to cooperate on a specific matter. In situations of this kind it may be more appropriate to refer to tit-for-tat as a tactic for activating *pre-existing* mutual interests rather than as a strategy for *creating* mutual interests in cooperation—an objective that lies beyond the ability of tit-for-tat to accomplish.

Furthermore, since communication and negotiation are possible in international relations (as they are not in the Prisoner's Dilemma game), they may be relied upon and be necessary to reduce some of the limitations and risks of the primitive tit-for-tat strategy employed in that game.

Under these special circumstances tit-for-tat may play a role not only in initiating the process of cooperation but in enforcing an agreement already made. In fact, as Lynn-Jones notes in his case study of the Incidents at Sea Agreement, the possibility of enforcing such an agreement through tit-for-tat responses to incidents caused by either side made the agreement more acceptable. (The problem of risk in implementation is discussed in greater detail in Chapter 28, "Managing the Risks of Cooperation.") In the anarchic international system, which lacks a centralized authority to enforce contracts between the actors or to press for observance of the norms and rules of the game to which the actors ostensibly subscribe, adherence to agreements must rest on trust, on the awareness that one has an interest in developing and maintaining a reputation for reliability, or on the credible threat of unilateral or community responses to noncompliance. Retaliation for an act of noncompliance is a variant of the tit-for-tat strategy whether the intention behind the retaliation is to restore compliance in the instant case or, by demonstrating that violation of an agreement will not be cost-free, to deter further violations. Of course, use of the tit-for-tat principle to enforce an existing agreement or norm may not work in practice. The aggrieved party may have difficulty finding an appropriate retaliatory act that will be effective. The offending party may be unmoved by the retaliation or, as noted in the discussion of the danger of "feuding," it may engage in counter-retaliation.[21]

A more complex strategy for reducing tensions in the Cold War was suggested almost thirty years ago by Charles Osgood, a distinguished experimental psychologist.

"Graduated Reciprocation in Tension-Reduction," or GRIT, as Osgood called it, is in many ways a more sophisticated strategy than tit-for-tat for employing the principle of reciprocity in international relations. GRIT employs essentially the same logic of reciprocity as tit-for-tat but avoids some of the latter's limitations and risks. It is all the more regrettable therefore, that cooperation theorists who derive encouragement from tit-for-tat as a solution to the Prisoner's Dilemma and seek to adapt it to the problem of cooperation in the anarchic international system by and large have overlooked Osgood's earlier strategy of reciprocity.[22] An important exception is the recent work of Deborah Larson, who argues persuasively the advantages of GRIT over tit-for-tat.[23]

As conceived and presented by Osgood, GRIT is a strategy based on the principle of reciprocity that is designed for setting into motion a spiral of tension reduction.[24] Each side, when the strategy works, makes increasingly more significant accommodative moves. The key points of the strategy may be summarized as follows: (1) The side initiating GRIT announces in advance that it is beginning a series of accommodations and concessions as part of a policy aimed at replacing distrust with trust and thereby reducing tensions. (2) The specific accommodative moves in the GRIT series are carried out on schedule whether or not the other side reciprocates. (3) When announcing each of its accommodative moves the side employing GRIT invites the other side to reciprocate but does not demand or specify a quid pro quo. (4) The series of accommodative moves is continued over a period of time, even in the absence of reciprocity. (5) The accommodative moves must be unambiguously conciliatory and verifiable. (6) The accommodative moves, while significant, should not impair the GRIT strategist's ability to defend himself. (7) Should the other side respond in a hostile manner or attempt to exploit the accommodative moves of the GRIT strategist, he should retaliate immediately with an appropriately graded response but only in the degree necessary to restore the status quo. (8) Any act of reciprocation by the other side to GRIT moves should be rewarded by a slightly more conciliatory action. (9) The sequence of GRIT moves should cover different spheres of action and geographic locations.

A strategy similar in essentials to GRIT was expounded at about the same time by Amitai Etzioni in *The Hard Way to Peace*[25] Interestingly, both Osgood and Etzioni claimed that the Kennedy-Khrushchev détente accompanying the partial test ban treaty in 1963 was an illustration of the strategy they had advocated earlier.[26] In addition, Osgood recalled that a member of the Kennedy Administration informed him that GRIT principles had been used by Kennedy during the Cuban missile crisis.

GRIT, too, has limitations. As originally expounded by Osgood, its objective is limited to replacing mutual distrust with a measure of mutual trust. The implicit (though vague) assumption of GRIT is that much of the Cold War was essentially a psychological phenomenon, that important mutual U.S.–Soviet interests in security cooperation (or in a much less conflictful relationship) exist but are prevented from being actualized by the psychological overlay of distrust that contaminates the relationship. Strictly speaking, therefore, as formulated by Osgood GRIT is a strategy for tension reduction or, in the language of diplomacy, for bringing about a "détente" which in its strict definition refers only to a "relaxation of tensions" between powers experiencing an acute conflict of interests and hostility. GRIT, in its pure form, does not address the question of whether and how a strategy of reciprocity can facilitate the accommodation of outstanding conflicts of interest. GRIT is a strategy of reciprocity for tension reduction, not a strategy of bargaining for achieving cooperative agreements. Moreover, contrary to GRIT's assumption, trust is not always required for an agreement.

Despite its limitations, GRIT is not without relevance and utility in dealing with some aspects of international conflict. In fact, experienced diplomats and some policymakers are familiar with its essentials and, as noted earlier in this chapter, employ it from time to time, though not always successfully.

Finally, we must distinguish these two strategies of reciprocity—tit-for-tat and GRIT—from unilateral offers of *conditional reciprocity*. In tit-for-tat the initial conciliatory action by the side employing the strategy is not made conditional on the adversary making an adequate reciprocating response; that is, the initial conciliatory action (or the promise of it) is not withdrawn if reciprocity does not follow. What is contingent in tit-for-tat is a willingness to act *again* in a conciliatory fashion should the adversary reciprocate properly to the first conciliatory action. GRIT is even less insistent on immediate reciprocity than tit-for-tat; the strategy of GRIT calls for repeating conciliatory actions several times, even if not reciprocated, in order to make the desired impression on a distrustful adversary. In contrast to both tit-for-tat and GRIT, the strategy of conditional reciprocity offers to undertake or to continue a concession only if it is reciprocated in a stipulated manner. Conditional reciprocity, therefore, is really more of a bargaining technique than a strategy of reciprocity as defined in this chapter.

One of the many examples of conditional reciprocity moves in U.S.–Soviet relations was Gorbachev's unilateral moratorium on nuclear testing. Similarly, in 1968 and 1969 Congressional leaders and some Administration officials urged that President Johnson announce a contingent moratorium on MIRV testing pending talks with the Soviets on banning the weapon altogether, a proposal that came to naught in its original version. What the Administration did eventually propose to the Soviets in April 1970, *after* the United States had developed an operational and reliable MIRV, was a treaty ban on MIRV testing and deployment, but not on MIRV procurement. The Soviets immediately rejected this proposal since it would have frozen an American advantage.[27]

In sum, this chapter has distinguished a number of strategies that can be and have been employed to facilitate security cooperation. We did not discuss the familiar, often critically important, bargaining strategies and tactics associated with "within-issue" linkage whereby the negotiators trade concessions on different components of a single complex issue in order to achieve an agreement. Instead we focused on various strategies of "cross-issue" linkage that attempt to couple two or more different issues with the objective of striking a more inclusive agreement. In cross-issue linkage one side may insist on coupling two specific issues, in effect saying to the other side that it cannot have an agreement on one issue that it values without reaching agreement also on another issue. An important variant of cross-issue linkage strategy in U.S.–Soviet negotiations is the effort to couple a specific security issue with the over-all relationship. This can be, and has been, done in two ways: either the United States or the Soviet Union can argue that an agreement on a specific issue is needed not only because of its intrinsic importance but also because it will help improve the over-all relationship, or, similarly, either side can argue that the other must cooperate in improving the over-all relationship in order to facilitate agreement on a specific security issue.

Cross-issue linkage may indeed create new possibilities for mutually beneficial bargaining that results in improved security cooperation. Examples of successful and unsuccessful efforts of this kind, drawn from our case studies, were cited in this chapter. However, the experience with efforts to employ cross-issue linkage strategy is not easily evaluated and we still lack a general theory that would describe the conditions under which it is likely to be successful. What this chapter contributes is not such a general theory but rather a theoretical framework and some hypotheses as to when cross-linkage is likely to be a viable strategy. We suggest, for example, that cross-linkage is more likely to be effective when both sides recognize that the two security issues in question are indeed interrelated so closely that a solution to one cannot be easily worked out without arriving at a simultaneous, coordinated solution to the other issue as well. This type of systemic (or intrinsic) linkage is well illustrated by the package of agreements having to do with different aspects of security in Europe arrived at in the early 1970s. This contrasts with artificial (or arbitrary) linkage in which one side attempts to link two unrelated security issues simply for bargaining purposes. A caution must be added: even systemic linkage of two or more issues cannot work if the respective interests of each negotiating partner in each of the two issues are not adequately accommodated in the proposed over-all agreement.

More generally, it is probably best not to regard cross-issue linkage per se as a robust strategy but, rather, as providing a possibly useful framework for broadening the agenda for negotiation. In the last analysis, the effectiveness of cross-issue linkage will probably depend more on skillful negotiation of each of the specific issues in question than on the framework provided by cross-issue linkage. On occasion, however, the cross-issue linkage strategy may well provide negotiators with additional flexibility and needed leverage to work out an agreement.

An important finding in the chapter is that the state of over-all U.S.–Soviet relations at certain times helped determine whether efforts to achieve security cooperation succeeded or failed. Equally important is the observation that certain well-established cooperative arrangements have survived even a sharp deterioration of the over-all relationship.

In addition to cross-linkage, we also considered the utility of creating bargaining chips as a strategy for facilitating security cooperation. Empirical analysis of this problem is difficult, however, because the term "bargaining chip" has been employed very loosely and because there are relatively few examples of the creation of new capabilities exclusively or largely for the purpose of using them as bargaining chips. Accordingly, the chapter could do little more than to provide a general and rather sober analysis of the utility of the bargaining chip strategy.

The chapter distinguished between strategies that employ *bargaining* to achieve a specific agreement and strategies that make use of the principle of *reciprocity*. While both bargaining and reciprocity strategies have the objective of facilitating an agreement or a mutually acceptable exchange, they do so in different ways. Bargaining refers to negotiations aimed at achieving an explicit, specific exchange that is to be carried out by the two parties simultaneously. In contrast, in reciprocity one side initiates an action designed to influence the behavior of another party but without specifying what its response should be—that is, the terms of the exchange are not negotiated and the reciprocating response comes later, not simultaneously with the initiation of the interaction. Strategies of reciprocity may be employed in international relations in order to facilitate cooperation or mutual adjustment. Our analysis suggests that there are rather severe limits on the efficacy of two strategies employing the principle of reciprocity—tit-for-tat and Graduated Reciprocation in Tension-Reduction (GRIT)—in U.S.–Soviet relations. Such strategies are much more likely to be successful, if at all, in helping to bring about a relaxation of tensions, in improving the atmospherics of relations rather than in facilitating an accommodation on issues that involve serious conflicts of interest. For issues which engage fundamental security interests, bargaining and negotiation leading to a specific agreement rather than reliance on reciprocity are likely to be necessary if a cooperative solution or modus vivendi is to be reached. Still, tit-for-tat and GRIT-type strategies can play a useful, if limited, role in improving relations between adversaries. When a predisposition to improve relations or a latent mutuality of interests already exists on a particular issue, a conciliatory move by one side may encourage the other side to make a positive response, thereby initiating a process that could lead to a relaxation of tensions and an agreement to try to find mutually satisfactory solutions to one or more outstanding issues.

Notes

1. Robert O. Keohane, "Reciprocity in International Relations," *International Organization,* vol. 40, no. 1 (Winter 1986): 1–27. Professor Keohane also offered useful comments on an earlier draft of this chapter.

2. It may be noted that Deborah Larson relabels as "bargaining" what Keohane calls "specific reciprocity" and restricts "reciprocity" to what Keohane calls "diffuse reciprocity." See particularly her "Detente and Reciprocity," unpublished manuscript, Columbia University, July 23, 1986.

3. In this section we adopt some of the useful distinctions and analytical observations made by Kiron Skinner in her forthcoming Ph.D dissertation in the Department of Government, Harvard University. In addition, she provided incisive comments on an earlier draft of this chapter (personal communication, July 8, 1987).

4. James K. Sebenius, *Negotiating the Law of the Sea* (Cambridge: Harvard University Press, 1984), p. 183. See also Arthur Stein, "The Politics of Linkage," *World Politics,* vol. 33, no. 1 (October 1980); and Robert O. Keohane and Joseph S. Nye, Jr., *"Power and Interdependence* Revisited," draft manuscript, 1986, p. 36.

5. Henry Kissinger, *Years of Upheaval* (Boston: Little, Brown, 1982), pp. 985–86. For Kissinger's views on different forms of linkage and his judgment that linkage is an essential aspect of a coherent foreign policy when issue-areas are inevitably related, see *The White House Years* (Boston: Little, Brown, 1979), pp. 129–30.

6. For further discussion see A. L. George, D. K. Hall, and W. E. Simons, *The Limits of Coercive Diplomacy* (Boston: Little, Brown, 1971).

7. The term "de-linkage" is used to describe the deliberate strategy of attempting to insulate a priority matter in one issue-area (e.g., strategic arms control) from the damaging effects of the adversary's behavior in another issue-area (e.g., Soviet policy in Africa). De-linkage strategy is highly relevant and needs to be incorporated into cooperation theory and practice.

8. Kissinger, *White House Years,* p. 138.

9. For useful discussions of the concept of "bargaining chip" see George Rathjens, "Unilateral Initiatives for Limiting and Reducing Arms," in William Epstein and Bernard T. Feld, eds., *New Directions in Disarmament* (New York: Praeger, 1981), 174 ff.; and Thomas C. Schelling, "A Framework for the Evaluation of Arms Control Proposals," in Franklin A. Long and George Rathjens, eds., *Arms, Defense Policy, and Arms Control* (New York: Norton, 1976).

10. Kissinger, *Years of Upheaval,* p. 271.

11. George Rathjens observes that some new military programs that might not otherwise have had much support may be carried forward, in part at least, because of bargaining chip arguments. He adds, however, that "we have precious little evidence" that weapons procured with this in mind were scrapped ("Unilateral Initiatives," pp. 174–75).

12. Ibid., p. 177.

13. George Homans, *Social Behavior: Its Elementary Forms* (New York: Harcourt, Brace and World, 1961), p. 62.

14. Rathjens, "Unilateral Initiatives," p. 174.

15. It should be clear that the discussion here focuses on the *strategy* of what Robert Keohane, as noted earlier, refers to as "diffuse" reciprocity. As Steven Weber has noted (personal communication), the concept of reciprocity requires additional refinement if its contribution to a theory of cooperation is to be fully realized. Analytical clarity requires that a sharper distinction be drawn between (1) reciprocity as a *strategy* for developing cooperative arrangements; (2) reciprocity as a *process* that may occur through coordination or "partisan mutual adjustment" (see Chapter 26) quite independently of either side employing it as a strategy; (3) reciprocity as an *outcome* in which mutual benefits have been exchanged and/or norms or tacit rules have emerged; and (4) reciprocity as a strategy for *enforcement* of cooperative agreements. Failure to make these distinctions explicitly introduces ambiguities that hamper efforts to develop cooperation theory.

16. These are described as an example of Khrushchev's use of Osgood's GRIT strategy by Deborah Larson in "Crisis Prevention and the Austrian State Treaty," *International Organization*, vol. 41, no. 1 (Winter 1987): 27–61.

17. Keohane, "Reciprocity," p. 23.

18. Robert Axelrod, *The Evolution of Cooperation* (New York: Basic Books, 1984).

19. For constructive, balanced critical evaluations of the relevance and applicability of the tit-for-tat strategy derived by Axelrod for international politics, see for example, Joanne Gowa, "Anarchy, Egoism, and Third Images: *The Evolution of Cooperation* and International Relations," *International Organization*, vol. 40, no. 1 (Winter 1986): 167–186; Francis A. Beer, "Games and Metaphors," *Journal of Conflict Resolution*, vol. 30, no. 1 (March 1986): 171–191; Robert O. Keohane, "Reciprocity in International Relations"; Deborah Larson, "Crisis Prevention and the Austrian State Treaty"; Robert Jervis, "Cooperation Under Anarchy: Problems and Limitations," draft manuscript, July 1986; Duncan Snidal, "Cooperation versus Prisoners' Dilemma: Implications for International Cooperation and Regimes," *American Political Science Review*, vol. 79, no. 4 (December 1985): 923–942; Robert Axelrod and Robert O. Keohane, "Achieving Cooperation Under Anarchy: Strategies and Institutions," *World Politics*, vol. 38, no. 1 (October 1985): 226–254.

20. This was clearly recognized by Robert Axelrod in *The Evolution of Cooperation*, in which he calls attention to the possible "echo effects" of the strategy: "The trouble with TIT-FOR-TAT is that once a feud gets started, it can continue indefinitely" (p. 138). Fortunately, most of the "feuds" initiated by retaliation for a malign action by the opponent in U.S.–Soviet relations do not escalate indefinitely.

21. Recognizing these difficulties, Axelrod and Keohane observe that nonetheless "reciprocity remains a valuable strategy for decentralized enforcement of cooperative agreements. Players who are aware of the problems of echo effects (feuding), bargaining deadlocks, and issue interdependence can compensate for these pitfalls." Continuing, Axelrod and Keohane emphasize that these difficulties also illustrate the importance of developing institutions and regimes within which reciprocity is practiced ("Achieving Cooperation," p. 246).

22. There is no mention of GRIT in Axelrod's *Evolution of Cooperation*, in Keohane's "Reciprocity in International Relations," or in their joint article "Achieving Cooperation Under Anarchy: Strategies and Institutions" in the special issue of *World Politics* (October 1985) devoted to the theme "Cooperation Under Anarchy." Neither does the excellent introductory essay for this special issue of *World Politics* by Kenneth A. Oye, "Explaining Cooperation Under Anarchy: Hypotheses and Strategies," make reference to GRIT.

23. See Larson, "Crisis Prevention" and "Detente and Reciprocity."

24. Cf. Charles E. Osgood, "Suggestions for Winning the Real War with Communism," *Journal of Conflict Resolution*, vol. 3, no. 4 (December 1959): 295–325; *An Alternative to War or Surrender* (Urbana: University of Illinois Press, 1962); and *Perspective in Foreign Policy* (Palo

Alto: Pacific Books, 1966). See also Svenn Linkskold, "Trust Development and the Effects of Conciliatory Acts on Conflict and Cooperation," *Psychological Bulletin,* vol. 85, no. 4 (July 1978): 772–793.

25. (New York: Crowell-Collier, 1962).

26. Elizabeth Hall, "A Conversation with Charles Osgood," *Psychology Today* (November 1973), pp. 54–70; Amitai Etzioni, "The Kennedy Experiment," *Western Political Quarterly,* vol. 20, no. 2 (June 1967): 361–380.

27. For this example I am indebted to Steven Weber, "Cooperation and Discord in Security Relationships: The Case of MIRV," draft manuscript, Stanford University, August 1985, pp. 48–51.

Epilogue: Perspectives

Achievements and Limitations

Efforts to evaluate the record of superpower cooperation in security matters can easily encounter the familiar dilemma of whether to describe the bottle as being half empty or half full. A more appropriate way to evaluate the record requires historical perspective: the bottle that was virtually empty at the outset of the Cold War over forty years ago is now perhaps half full.

Indeed, as our case studies have shown, much *has* been accomplished since the beginning of the Cold War. John Lewis Gaddis provides valuable historical perspective when he reminds us that few students of international affairs in the late 1940s were confident that a war between the Soviet Union and the United States could be avoided; indeed, many observers were entirely pessimistic on that score. Yet, there has gradually emerged since the end of World War II a surprisingly stable U.S.–Soviet relationship. Around the polar Soviet-American relationship there has evolved an international system which, in Gaddis' words, "nobody designed or even thought could last for very long, which was based not on the dictates of morality and justice, but rather upon an arbitrary and strikingly artificial division of the world into spheres of influence and which incorporated within it some of the most bitter and persistent antagonisms short of war in modern history . . ."[1]

Much of the explanation for the absence of war between the superpowers derives from the fear of Armegeddon that has contributed to the stability of the polar relationship. But fear of nuclear war could not, and still does not, guarantee a peaceful and stable relationship between the United States and the Soviet Union. Appropriate behavior, learning, and adaptation on the part of the superpowers have been necessary to keep the peace between them and to create elements of political and military stability in their relationship. Despite the dynamics of mutual distrust, sharp ideological differences, and acute rivalry, and despite the many obstacles to cooperation in security matters, the two superpowers have made considerable progress in developing patterns of restraint, tacit "rules," and even partial regimes in support of an uneasy coexistence.

As we noted in Chapter 26, mutual adaptation and cooperation have been forced on leaders of the superpowers by their recognition of the limits of their ability to assure the security of their country by strictly unilateral policies and by their awareness that each superpower's security is inevitably influenced by the other superpower's policies and behavior. It is an ironic fact that in an otherwise highly competitive relationship the superpowers have been forced by their mutual dependence on each other for security to engage in a complex, continuing process of "partisan mutual adjustment." Moscow and Washington have been obliged, each in pursuit of its own self-interest in security matters, to respect and adapt, however imperfectly, to each other's interests and power.

There have also been important cooperative agreements. To be sure, they fall well short of comprising a *comprehensive* U.S.–Soviet security regime, one that covers all aspects of their security interface. Such an ambitious objective remains unrealistic in the foreseeable future. At the same time, as we have shown in this study, explicit and tacit partial regimes embracing norms, agreed-upon rules, evolving patterns of behavior, and even institutionalized procedures have emerged within the bilateral security relationship or more broadly in a multilateral context. Therefore, in addition to the need for historical perspective in assessing the record, it is also necessary to examine the progress or lack thereof in different parts of the over-all security relationship.

Let us begin by discussing two aspects of the relationship in which relatively little progress has been made. Least progress has been made in formally structuring and regulating the over-all Soviet-American relationship. As noted in Chapter 27, if Moscow and Washington could agree on an unambiguous and stable political framework for their relationship, it could make an important contribution to this goal; but thus far the two sides have found such agreement difficult to achieve. Although both superpowers have evinced a desire to replace the "confrontational competition" of the Cold War with a relationship that might be described as a mixed "competitive-collaborative" relationship, efforts to move in this direction during the détente of the 1970s proved to be abortive. Little progress was made then, or since, in developing norms of competition and norms of collaboration that were sufficiently clear, mutually understood, and accepted. Instead, as George Breslauer has noted, the Nixon-Brezhnev effort to define a competitive-collaborative relationship failed "because each side tried to define the terms of competition and the terms of collaboration in ways more geared to maximizing unilateral advantage than to expanding the mutual interest in institutionalizing the relationship."[2] It remains to be seen whether more progress in this direction will be possible in the future.

Moreover, in the absence of agreed-upon norms the creation of effective institutionalized procedures for managing and developing the over-all U.S.–Soviet relationship has lagged. Nixon and Brezhnev failed to establish procedures for implementing and clarifying the general norms they subscribed to in the Basic Principles Agreement of 1972. Their agreement to hold annual summits was abandoned by their successors. Impetus in strategic arms negotiations tailed off in the mid-1970s; and, though SALT II was later negotiated it could not be ratified. Traditional diplomatic modalities, too, have worked unevenly since the high point of détente in the early 1970s, often being dwarfed by energetic "public diplomacy" conducted from Moscow and Washington more to influence opinion than to facilitate serious discussion of outstanding issues.

At the same time, although the over-all relationship remains highly competitive and is not regulated by a clearly defined set of norms and "rules," for reasons of self-interest both sides do operate with significant restraint in important areas of their competition, such as in respecting each other's vital interests and in crisis management. Undergirding such restraints are patterns of behavior that have become established over time, and tacit "rules of prudence" of the kind discussed in Chapter 23. While such prudential restraints fall well short of well-defined norms of competition and cooperation, they do contribute significantly to the stability of the relationship and to the avoidance of war between the superpowers.

The superpowers have also failed to make much progress in developing norms, rules, and institutionalized procedures for regulating their involvement in Third Areas. Apart from respecting (with some qualifications) each other's sphere of dominant interests, Moscow and Washington have not developed norms for limiting efforts to influence internal processes of political-economic change in Third World countries. Although they pay lip-service to the principle of nonintervention and respect for the sovereignty of all states, the superpowers attempt at times to steer or to check such changes in line with their own perceived interest and ideological preferences. To be sure, a procedural mechanism for frequent bilateral discussion of regional issues has nominally been in place since early 1986 but, as noted in Chapter 23, these U.S.–Soviet talks, while of symbolic importance, have been slow to evolve beyond mutual exhortations and restatements by each side of its familiar position on the regional issue in question.

In contrast to limited progress in defining their over-all relationship and regulating their involvement in Third Areas, significant developments have taken place in structuring other matters of security interest to both superpowers. Notable is the emergence of a modus vivendi and a partial security regime for Europe that has substantially enhanced political stability on the continent. Significantly, security measures have been part of an organized multilateral effort to develop a regime for East-West relations in Europe that extends beyond security to political and other aspects of intercourse between West Europe and East Europe. As our case studies in Part Two have documented, the question of who would fill the power vacuum in Europe created by the defeat of Nazi Germany, which played a prominent role in the origins and development of the Cold War, has been gradually resolved through reluctant but realistic recognition by the superpowers of each other's security interests in Europe and respect for each other's power and resolution to protect those interests. Mutual recognition of the "division of Europe," as noted in the chapters by John Maresca, Jonathan Dean and James Goodby, preceded formal agreements that lend it stability and open the way to further constructive developments and peaceful change. We must also recognize that, as in the strategic arms area, unilateral measures taken by both sides in Europe—for example, the creation and maintenance of NATO and the Warsaw Treaty Organization—made possible the cooperative agreements that eventually emerged and, indeed, undergird the regime that has evolved. One can argue, as Gaddis and Joseph Nye do,[3] that this quasi-regime reflects certain underlying principles and norms that rest on acceptance of the role of the United States and the Soviet Union in European security, the status quo of the division of Europe, the division of Germany, the neutral status of Austria, the special status of Finland, the independence of Yugoslavia, and the anomalous status of West Berlin. Institutionalized procedures have been created for the implementation of access to West Berlin and of the Final Act of the Conference on Security and Cooperation in Europe. As a result, it is possible to say that both Moscow and Washington as well as the West European and East European states have developed a longer-run interest in maintaining and building on the gains in security and in normalizing East-West relations in Europe.

However, the achievement of "political détente" in Europe has not been followed by arms reductions. The prolonged MBFR negotiations have fallen short of agreement, and may soon be superseded by a new forum and mandate. Arms competition in both theater nuclear weapons and conventional forces in Europe has continued between East and West. Efforts to reach an agreement on limitation or reduction of intermediate-range nuclear missiles in the theater, and to decouple the issue from negotiations regarding the levels of U.S. and Soviet strategic capabilities remained deadlocked until recently. Progress on additional confidence-building measures was slow until the recent, surprisingly detailed Stockholm agreement on CBMs. To be sure, the possibility of a major upheaval in Eastern Europe that threatens Soviet control at some point in the future cannot be excluded. The consequences of such a development for the partial security regime that has emerged on the continent cannot be easily forecast since it would depend on the Soviet response and how the turbulence in Eastern Europe would be resolved.

Turning now to developments in arms control, we should emphasize first, as in Chapter 25, that arms control is *not* an independent or alternate route to common security. Arms control provisions cannot by themselves create stability or resolve perceived conflicts of interest and tensions in U.S.–Soviet relations. Indeed, arms control policy and programs cannot be any better than the foreign and defense policies and programs of which they are a part.

Progress of a limited, fragile character has been made in developing regimes for managing strategic arms competition and for avoiding accidental war. Thus, the SALT and ABM agreements contributed to a partial regime for regulating and delimiting strategic arms competition. As Condoleezza Rice pointed out in Chapter 12, the limited strategic arms regime was clearly based on several important norms and principles to which both sides subscribed, namely: (1) recognition of parity as a criterion for regulating the level of U.S. and Soviet strategic forces; (2) recognition and acceptance of mutual vulnerability; and (3) acceptance of the link between offense and defense. These three principles and norms emerged during the SALT negotiations and were indispensable in facilitating, structuring, and rationalizing the agreements on quantitative and qualitative aspects of strategic forces. Moreover, an institution—the Standing Consultative Commission—was created to assist in implementing the agreements. Principles for continuing negotiations were defined and formalized. Important restructuring of the respective strategic forces was carried out pursuant to the agreements.

On the other hand, developments in the late 1970s and 1980s challenged the SALT premises. The belief that the United States has a long-range self-interest in maintaining the strategic arms regime appreciably weakened during the years of the Reagan Administration and the issue became a highly divisive one within the influential political elite in the United States. As of this writing the future of the regime and its various components is clouded with uncertainty; but if the United States and the Soviet Union should reach a new arms control agreement stipulating reductions in strategic nuclear weapons and in intermediate range missiles in Europe, and some limits on SDI development, it would radically and reciprocally affect strategic force postures and restore the regime. It would require monitoring and verification procedures that might breathe new life into the Standing Consultative Commission or require the creation of new joint U.S.–Soviet institutions to fulfill similar functions for the new arms control agreement. It would give renewed impetus to subsequent negotiations to extend and buttress the regime.

The evolving strategic arms regime has had as one of its components the step-by-step development of a sub-regime that implements the superpowers' shared interest in avoiding accidental war. How effective the agreements and arrangements that have been made for this purpose (described by Barry Blechman in Chapter 18) would be, should untoward events create a sudden danger of accidental war, is a matter that cannot be easily judged. Still, Moscow and Washington have continued to explore the usefulness of additional machinery to aid in dealing with various possible triggers of an accidental nuclear war. The "hotline" was upgraded in 1984, and discussions initiated in 1986 to study the proposal for nuclear risk reduction centers of some kind in Moscow and Washington resulted in the announcement in early May 1987 that a draft agreement had been reached to establish a limited variant of the original concept of the centers.[4]

Progress has been made in reducing the likelihood of incidents at sea involving the navies of the superpowers. While the danger that such incidents could lead to a major military clash between the United States and the Soviet Union is perhaps remote, as Sean Lynn-Jones indicates in his chapter on the Incidents at Sea Agreement, this development provides an encouraging example of the ability of the two superpowers to moderate friction. Although many of the factors that favored this success are perhaps unique to the case, some observers believe that it is worthwhile to consider whether a similar opportunity exists to develop "rules of the road" to avoid certain kinds of incidents in space.[5]

Nuclear nonproliferation is another security issue-area in which the two superpowers have succeeded, together with other states, in establishing a regime. A number of specific rules and institutions were established to implement the objective of nonproliferation, including the Nuclear Non-Proliferation Treaty, the International Atomic Energy Agency, and the Nuclear Suppliers Group. As Nye notes, these multilateral arrangements have been supplemented by regular bilateral talks between the two superpowers. And the two superpowers have continued to cooperate within the framework of the nonproliferation regime even when over-all political relations deteriorated and arms control negotiations stagnated.

Other regimes and agreements have served to remove certain areas from over-all Soviet-American competition in the course of filling gaps in the international system. Typically these arrangements have to do with geographical areas or types of activities that lie outside of, or transcend, boundaries of national sovereignty. Thus, as noted in Chapter 25, these regimes have a broader significance for international security and world order, and the fact that the Soviet Union cooperates in developing and adhering to them has significance that goes beyond immediate implications for bilateral U.S.–Soviet relations. Included among these regimes and agreements are the multilateral agreement on Antarctica, the Outer Space Treaty with its provisions relating both to military and to civilian utilization of space, the agreement prohibiting placement of nuclear devices on the seabed, and the agreement for neutralizing Austria. Particularly interesting in this respect, as Deborah Shapley notes in her chapter, is the way in which the Antarctica regime operated to reshape some inchoate initial positions of the participating states into conceptions of a longer-range interest in cooperation.

Whether these various cooperative arrangements add up to a "bottle that is half full" can be left for each reader to judge. In any case perhaps more appropriate analogies can be suggested to characterize the situation. The results of U.S.–Soviet security cooperation can be likened to a jig-saw puzzle only parts of which are in place, or a quite incomplete mosaic which contains pieces that vary in significance and in the contribution they make to the whole.[6] However, all three analogies are misleading if they imply that the bottle can ever be filled, the jig-saw puzzle solved, or the mosaic completed. As we stressed at the outset of the study in Chapter 1, we think it most unlikely that the two superpowers will ever want to or will achieve anything like a comprehensive security regime that deals adequately with all of the many dimensions of their security interface.

Incentives and Mutual Interests for Security Cooperation

We posed at the outset of this study a central research question: "How, under what circumstances, and why do incentives for security cooperation emerge?" Given the fundamentally competitive, conflictful relationship between the United States and the

Soviet Union, each superpower understandably has a strong preference for relying on its own efforts to assure its security rather than to depend on cooperative arrangements with a powerful, distrusted adversary. What incentives, we are obliged to ask, springing from what conditions, lead Moscow and Washington to perceive mutual interests in cooperation that suffice to enable them to overcome their reluctance to cooperate in security matters?

Our study points to two factors that seem particularly important in generating the perception of mutual interests in cooperation and the incentives for achieving it. There is, first, the emergence of a belief among American and Soviet leaders that their countries are inescapably vulnerable in modern war and therefore dependent on each other's behavior to assure or to improve security or to lighten the burden of providing for it. Second, there is the additional belief on both sides that strictly unilateral measures to promote security, however important and necessary, will not suffice and indeed may exacerbate competition and instability; therefore, something may be gained by seriously exploring the possibility of bilateral (or, sometimes, multilateral) arrangements. Together these two beliefs create a sense of mutual dependence on each other for security, and a sense that the superpower's own efforts must be supplemented by cooperation. Just how vulnerable the United States and the Soviet Union consider themselves to be varies greatly in different components of their security interface. Generally speaking, the greater the perceived sense of vulnerablity the stronger the incentive to seriously explore a cooperative arrangement. But other factors also influence the outcome of such efforts. This important issue was discussed and illustrated in Chapter 26.

Security Cooperation: Its Uses and Limitations for the Superpowers

Another fundamental question may be posed: how much and what types of cooperation in which security matters can one expect adversarial powers such as the United States and the Soviet Union to seek and to achieve? Part of the answer to this question was given in the preceding discussion of the special conditions under which incentives to cooperate may arise. These are, indeed, important limiting conditions and they suggest at first glance rather limited possibilities for security cooperation. However, a different picture emerges if we regard incentives as a variable that may be strong enough, for example, to support limited forms of cooperation in quite important security matters and substantial cooperation in security issues of a less fundamental character.

Our study has identified a variety of contributions that cooperative arrangements have made to alleviating different security concerns. Thus, one agreement (the Austrian State Treaty) may entirely or largely remove a particular source of security concern whereas another agreement (on avoiding accidental war) may only partly alleviate another type of security concern. Many agreements make limited but still quite useful contributions.

Leaving aside the importance of the contribution an agreement makes, which varies greatly from one case to another, three types of contributions can be identified:

1. Some agreements seek to *avoid or reduce competition* in a given security matter by removing an existing or potential source of conflict. Examples of this type of contribution are those made by the World War II agreement on joint occupation and administration of Germany, the Austrian State Treaty of 1955, the Antarctica Treaty of 1959, the Laos neutralization agreement in 1962, the 1971 Quadripartite Agreement on Berlin, and the evolution of a tacit agree-

ment not to interfere (at least in peacetime) with each other's satellite reconnaissance activities. Not all of these agreements turned out to be successful in
the long run and there can be no guarantee that the others will remain operative
in the future.

2. Other agreements have attempted to *delimit competition* that, if unrestrained,
would entail mutual disadvantages or harmful consequences that both Moscow
and Washington would prefer to minimize. Many arms control agreements
attempt to make this kind of contribution. The ABM Treaty and SALT established some parameters or rules within which both sides were expected to
continue unilateral efforts to provide for their security. That is, these agreements not only restrain competition in the strategic arms area but they do so
in a way that leads to a degree of reciprocal force planning and postures within
defined limits. Moreover, the elements of "transparency" and predictability
provided by agreed-upon data exchanges (in the 1986 Stockholm agreement as
well as SALT) and limits on certain strategic weapons help to reduce the "worst"
that has to be taken into account in worst-case planning of force posture development.

3. Other agreements (as well as SALT) attempt to *reduce the costs, risks, and
uncertainties* associated with continuing competition or with failure to cooperate to avoid a common danger. Examples of agreements that have attempted
to make this type of contribution include the Hotline agreements, the Incidents
at Sea Agreement, the Antarctica Treaty, efforts to discourage nuclear proliferation, the adoption of confidence-building measures, and agreements on provisions for dealing with events that might trigger accidental war and with nuclear terrorist activities.

As the preceding observations indicate, the concept of "cooperation," which has
a simple meaning in game theory, needs considerable refinement and differentiation if
its limited but still quite important role in U.S.–Soviet security relations is to be better
understood.

As is well known, the acceptability to Washington and Moscow of cooperative
agreements depends on their assessment of the risks of a particular agreement and their
ability to devise joint or unilateral measures to reduce such risks to an acceptable level.
Some ways of reducing and managing the risks of agreements were discussed in Chapter
28. What is an acceptable risk, however, varies tremendously for different security
issues and different types of agreements; and in any case such judgments are sensitive
to a variety of changes affecting the operation of an agreement over time. Most broadly,
when the two states reach agreements to limit or reduce their respective military forces
and power, the substantial forces they retain can usefully be viewed as in effect "risk
insurance." A test of a stabilizing arms control agreement, indeed, will be whether each
party can separately judge its security to be enhanced by the combination of effective
limitations on the rival's military power together with their own retained forces and the
resultant military balance, so that such risks as will unavoidably accompany such an
agreement will be at least as tolerable as those accompanying an unrestricted arms race
and military confrontation.

Prospects

The record of what Moscow and Washington have already accomplished in security
cooperation gives no clear basis for forecasting future developments. Still, by providing

a better general understanding of the incentives for cooperation, the obstacles to cooperation, the factors that favor it, and strategies that may be useful, our analysis offers some relevant knowledge for assessing prospects for cooperation. Such general knowledge, however, must always be applied to the special characteristics of each new possibility of cooperation.

In concluding, we want to emphasize again, as at the outset of the study in Chapter 1, that cooperative agreements in security matters are not an end in themselves; rather they are a means—and only one means—for achieving various objectives extending all the way from reducing the risk of war to the development of a more constructive, orderly, and stable U.S.–Soviet relationship. There are bound to be serious limits on promoting these objectives solely through U.S.–Soviet agreements (or multilateral agreements in which the two superpowers participate). Therefore, the scope of inquiry and the policy agenda need to be broadened to include ways other than cooperative agreements by means of which Moscow and Washington can make progress towards these objectives.

Alternatives to cooperative agreements that have been utilized in the past and must continue to be utilized in the future, as was noted in Chapter 26, include *mutual adjustment* stemming from respect for each other's power and interests, *reciprocal coordination* of unilateral American and Soviet policies and actions in ways that reduce both sides' insecurity, and *unilateral actions* that either side can take, without expectation of reciprocity, that (a) contribute directly to its own security without increasing the other side's insecurity, or (b) contribute indirectly to its own security by reducing the other side's insecurity and, therefore, also the pressure it feels to escalate the arms race and the competition for influence.

In sum, not only are cooperative security agreements not always possible; they are also not always necessary for the realization of mutual security benefits. Rather, some combination or mix of unilateral policies and cooperative arrangements will continue to be necessary to strengthen mutual security. The over-all U.S.–Soviet relationship itself will continue to be a mixed competitive-cooperative one, provided that Moscow and Washington do not stumble into a major crisis in an area such as Europe or the Middle East where it would be less controllable than the Cuban missile crisis. The search for security—through some combination of cooperative arrangements and unilateral efforts—must be expected to continue in a broader context of competition and rivalry. The real choices have to do with whether the dangerous and costly confrontational potential of the rivalry can be avoided or at least substantially muted. We see no reason to assume that U.S. and Soviet incentives for useful, workable cooperative measures to enhance mutual security and to reduce the costs and risks of relying solely on unilateral policies for each side's security will decline in the future. Indeed, viewed historically from the outset of the Cold War, and if we disregard the inevitable ups and downs, the trend has been in the other direction. The challenge will remain, as it has been, to find ways of strengthening these incentives and transforming them into workable cooperative arrangements. This is likely to depend in the future, as in the past, on the quality of leadership in Washington and Moscow and the way in which U.S. and Soviet leaders wish to shape their relationship. It makes a great deal of difference whether there is a Gorbachev or a Stalinist-type leader in Moscow; and, similarly, what the mindset and ideological assumptions are in Washington and in U.S. public opinion regarding the other superpower. We place particular emphasis on this factor because our study has shown and illustrated in so many ways that cooperation in security matters can be facilitated or hindered by the state of the over-all relationship that exists between the two superpowers at a particular time and by the type of improved relationship they may be attempting to facilitate through specific agreements and understandings.

The United States and the Soviet Union can be expected to continue to have a strong interest in managing their rivalry in order to control its costs and risks. This shared interest is coupled with a much more diffuse recognition of the importance of working towards two other goals as well: namely, developing over time a more cooperative, orderly, and stable U.S.–Soviet relationship, and contributing together with other countries to the development of regional and global patterns of behavior and even institutions that create some additional order in the international system from which the two superpowers benefit at least indirectly.

Some progress has been made in both of these respects. As we said at the beginning of this chapter, important progress has been made since the beginning of the Cold War in stabilizing the U.S.–Soviet relationship. And, as noted in Chapter 25, the Soviet Union has demonstrated by its participation in some "preclusive" and regulatory international regimes, such as Antarctica, outer space, and nuclear nonproliferation, that it can on occasion be a reliable partner and work with the rest of the world in establishing institutional arrangements for international order. Significantly, too, as Alexander Dallin pointed out in Chapter 24, the Soviet view of international security has changed since the days of Stalin. Though the sense of Moscow's proclaimed "interdependence" with the outside world is still fragile and, in some sense, perhaps largely rhetorical, the confrontational assumptions have begun to slip, not irreversibly to be sure, and there is unmistakable evidence of learning and adaptation.

In the United States, stabilizing the U.S.–Soviet relationship has been hampered by the lack of continuity in U.S. defense and foreign policy and by the underlying controversy over the nature and extent of the Soviet threat and the soundness of "détente," or a policy of measured cooperation with the Soviet Union.

Thus, convergence of interests remains problematical; for both superpowers "security" is the dominant concern and "cooperation" is at best instrumental or marginal. As noted in chapters 23 and 27, the security dimension of U.S.–Soviet competition is exacerbated under the impact of the security dilemma, the distortions introduced into the relationship by ideological differences, and the influence of geopolitics. Both superpowers—like all great powers in the past—tend to expand geographically their conception of their "security requirements."

Yet security is not the only dimension of the U.S.–Soviet relationship or of the national interests of the two states. Indeed, some of the most important roots of U.S.–Soviet competition and rivalry lie outside the security and military considerations that emerged after World War II. Fortunately, the U.S.–Soviet relationship lacks the element of historical or geographic confrontation, which weighs heavily on many neighboring states that have fought each other over centuries. Instead, insofar as the two superpowers come to realize that the security threat they pose to each other is manageable, it will become clearer that the rivalry is basically between economic and social systems, ideologies, and political systems, with their implicit visions of the proper relationship between the individual and the state. Nonetheless, the United States and the Soviet Union are engaged in a competition for world leadership and with such roots it can be intense, as shown during Cold War periods over the past four decades and reflected in the arms race.

But in recent years both Moscow and Washington have tended to turn away from pursuit of strategic and military superiority, in fact as well as in declaratory policy, and the systemic rivalry may be becoming less tense and threatening. Phrases such as "peaceful coexistence" or "constructive engagement" begin to take on practical meaning, not only in arms control but in economic and even political interaction and selective cooperation. Whether these trends continue, at what pace, and how far they will go, of course, is subject to considerable uncertainty. In contrast to historic regional rivalries, the competition between Moscow and Washington can stay within some constraints (as their success in avoiding armed conflict shows), and remains more responsive to the lessons of experience and reflection. Two such lessons are especially pertinent here.

The first lesson is that neither of the superpowers, nor its economic/social system, can realistically aspire to be the role model, let alone the unchallenged leader, for the rest of the world. The Soviet system, and Marxist-Leninism, found a considerable clientele among leaders of new states during the postwar period of decolonization. Once new states established their independence and took on the formidable task of nation-building, the Soviet model proved of little relevance, and, with a few conspicuous exceptions, Soviet aid was negligible. The United States, along with its allies and the neutral market-economy nations, had much more to offer in the way of aid and technology and markets, as well as the fostering of a hospitable international environment. But U.S. and West European democracy and free market economies, however appealing, turned out to be at best long-term ideals rather than practical immediate models.

The second and related lesson is that competition between rival systems can take the form of an effort to show the excellence and dynamism of each system. This would mean diverting attention and resources to enhancing the economic growth and vitality, the vigor and richness of the competing societies and cultures, and the well-being of their citizens. Such impulses would take quite different forms in the two nations, as befits the very different systems and weaknesses to be corrected. Nevertheless, such an effort can be seen in Gorbachev's calls for economic reform and modernization and for *glasnost'*, as well as in his arms control campaign. In the United States, public and Congressional sentiment increasingly sees defense programs and budgets as about at the right levels, with controlling the fiscal deficit and the arms race having priority over further military buildup. The United States and the Soviet Union could be moving into a form of rivalry in which security becomes a relative goal, calling for as much effort, and no more, as is required for pursuing these other national interests in safety and with confidence.

Notes

1. John Lewis Gaddis, "The Long Peace: Elements of Stability in the Postwar International System," *International Security,* vol. 10, no. 4 (Spring 1986): 99–100.

2. George W. Breslauer, "Why Detente Failed: An Interpretation," in Alexander L. George, *Managing U.S.–Soviet Rivalry: Problems of Crisis Prevention* (Boulder, Colo.: Westview Press, 1983), p. 320.

3. Gaddis, "The Long Peace"; Joseph S. Nye, Jr., "Nuclear Learning and U.S.–Soviet Security Regimes," paper delivered to the 1986 annual meeting of the American Political Science Association, Washington, D.C. (revised draft of September 17, 1986).

4. *New York Times* (May 6, 1987).

5. See for example, Michael M. May, "Safeguarding Our Military Space Systems," *Science,* vol. 232 (April 18, 1986), pp. 336–340.

6. The argument that an incomplete mosaic of security regimes exists and that the various norms and rules imbedded in these regimes and quasi-regimes do constrain the behavior of the two superpowers has also been made by Joseph S. Nye, Jr., in his "Nuclear Learning and U.S.–Security Regimes."

Appendix

As noted in Chapter 1, the plan for this study was described in a detailed prospectus which provided the starting point, framework, and focus for all of the case studies. The most important part of the prospectus was the set of detailed questions developed by the editors to guide the case studies. Each author used these questions, insofar as they were appropriate and relevant, in writing his or her case study. There are two sets of questions, one for analyzing efforts to reach agreements and the other for analyzing efforts to implement agreements.

Questions for Analyzing Efforts to Reach Agreements

1. What was the general political relationship between the United States and the Soviet Union at the time and how did it affect the development of the case in question? How did each of the superpowers view the case at hand in relationship to the development of their long-term security and political relationship?
2. How did each side define its interests and objectives in exploring an agreement? Was there internal disagreement in this respect within the U.S. and Soviet elites? Were other interests perceived to be involved that conflicted with or complicated the utility of an agreement in the matter at hand?
3. Did both sides have much the same interests, incentives, hoped-for benefits in an agreement; or different interests and expectations that might be satisfied by an agreement (that is, did the two sides agree, at least in part, for different reasons)?
4. What value did each side place on securing the cooperative arrangement; how important was it to each side? Was it more important to one side than to the other; if so, how did this perceived asymmetry affect the negotiations and bargaining? What "price" was each prepared—or not prepared—to pay for an agreement that satisfied its interests? To what extent were there internal disagreements on this matter within U.S. and Soviet elites; how did it affect the search for a U.S.–Soviet agreement?
5. What were the perceived risks of an agreement on each side? Were there disagreements on this question within the U.S. and/or Soviet elite? To what extent did such internal disagreements complicate or prevent the search for an agreement? If such internal disagreements were overcome, how did this occur and how did the process of securing sufficient internal support affect the shape and content of the agreement?
6. To what extent were top-level political leaders in the United States and Soviet Union personally committed to, and actively engaged in, the effort to work out an agreement if possible?
   (a) How skillful were top leaders in forming an effective internal policy coalition in support of an agreement? How skillful in mobilizing public (and, where necessary, allied) support for an agreement?

(b) What modifications and compromises in the shape of the agreement and what side-payments and commitments did top political leaders feel it necessary to make in order to gain sufficient internal support?

(c) In the case of "missed opportunities" to achieve an agreement, to what extent was this due to the lack of commitment on the part of top political leaders and/or lack of leadership skill in creating support?

7. Was there a sense of urgency for achieving an agreement? Equally for both sides, significantly more urgent for one side, not urgent for either side? Did one or both sides believe there was a temporary "window of opportunity" for a useful agreement? What role did this variable play in facilitating or reducing incentives for an agreement? In giving a bargaining advantage to the side not experiencing a sense of urgency? How did a sense of urgency, lack of a sense of urgency, disagreement as to sense of urgency influence internal bargaining within the U.S. and Soviet leadership groups?

8. What were each side's expectations regarding the costs and/or risks of no agreement? Was this symmetrical or asymmetrical for the two sides? Was there internal disagreement over this on the U.S. or Soviet side?

9. Did one side believe that the other side had strong incentives to achieve an agreement? Stronger or weaker than its own? If the leaders of one side perceived the other side as lacking strong incentives for the type of agreement they favored, how did they believe these incentives could be strengthened—by positive and/or negative inducements? Linkage?

10. How did the image of the opponent influence each side's judgment of the utility and risks of the type of agreement in question? To what extent did important members of each side operate with a "bad faith" image of the opponent, attributing to it hegemonic goals and lack of trustworthiness? How salient was this type of image for the issue in question and in what general or specific ways did it affect judgments regarding the desirability and feasibility of an agreement for the issue in question? For example:

(a) Did it exacerbate concern that the proposed agreement contained "loopholes" or "break-out" possibilities which the opponent would exploit in the future to gain an important advantage before one's own side would become aware and respond effectively? Did worst-case analysis of this type substantially raise verification requirements? What other ways of managing such risks were considered and/or utilized, or might have been?

(b) Did the image of the opponent encourage the belief that the undoubted short-term advantages of a possible agreement were outweighed by the middle-range or long-range risks and disadvantages? Does a "bad faith" image of the opponent contribute to a self-confirming prophecy: that is, does hedging against uncertainty and risk, for instance, by continued weapons R&D, by both sides "confirm" each side's suspicion and distrust of the other?

(c) Did adherence to a "bad faith" image of the Soviets encourage among U.S. leaders the view that the short-term advantages of a possible agreement could be devalued and rejected because the technological superiority of the United States would in any case enable it to stay ahead in the qualitative arms race? Did this belief make it more acceptable for the United States to accept or favor quantitative limits?

11. In which cases and under what circumstances were the short-term payoffs of an agreement deemed so important that its longer-term risks were not considered potent enough to forego an agreement?

Questions for Analyzing Efforts to Implement Agreements

1. To what extent has the agreement (or less formal arrangement) in practice served the initial common stated or implicit purposes? Has one side turned out to be significantly disadvantaged? Have compliance issues arisen which bring into question the value or viability of the agreement?
2. Where agreements have fallen short of expectations, or proven unsatisfactory or ineffective, what factors are responsible:
   — Texts which were ambiguously drafted, or incomplete or inadequate, or prematurely rigorous and precise.
   — Divergent interests of the parties emerging during implementation period.
   — Changing circumstances (such as international political trends, technological change, domestic factional or policy changes).
   — Circumvention of purposes or key provisions in ways not literally forbidden in the agreement (such as exploitation of loopholes, dramatic increase of underground testing under LTB or of MIRVs under SALT; exploitation of national law or standards to vitiate Helsinki principles on emigration or freedom of the press).
3. Many agreements are explicitly designed to lead to subsequent broader or more intensive agreements as part of a continuing process or expanding "regime": the LTB was to lead to a CTB; SALT II was to lead to further agreements in accordance with the "Joint Principles for Subsequent Negotiations"; the Camp David accords were to lead to negotiations on the Palestine problem; the Outer Space Treaty was to lead to further measures on the militarization of space. Has failure to move on progressively brought the viability of such agreements into doubt? Has the failure to progress reflected excessive expectations; if so, for what reasons? Does a wider regime still appear worth active pursuit?
4. Where there is disillusionment on one side or the other (such as the United States with Soviet interpretation of Helsinki principles of national self-determination and freedom of international intercourse; the Soviets with U.S. commitment to premises of the ABM Treaty) does this throw into question the viability of the relevant regime, or do dialogue and accommodation still offer a route to salvage?
5. If the cases studied are looked at as experiments or test cases as to the feasibility and conditions for U.S.–Soviet cooperation in reducing instability and stabilizing security relations, have they been attended with sufficient risk or penalty to suggest that such efforts should only be undertaken with greater selectivity and prior assurance of success?
6. To what extent have norms or objectives in the agreement been internalized and institutionalized within the United States or the Soviet Union (such as the publicly expressed appreciation by the Joint Chiefs of Staff for SALT understandings as providing useful planning parameters; predisposition to use "Hotline" in time of crisis)?
7. In some multilateral agreements the United States and USSR are parties on a relatively equal footing with other states (NPT, Antarctica Treaty) or even in secondary status (Latin American Nuclear Free Zone; the recently signed Pacific Nuclear Free

Zone). What special implications do such arrangements have for U.S.–Soviet security relations (cooperative or competitive)? (Note that boundaries of the South Pacific Nuclear Free Zone are deliberately defined to extend eastwards to the Latin American Nuclear Free Zone, and southwards to Antarctica—itself a nuclear free zone—thus constituting a major de facto cumulative nuclear free zone negotiated by others to which the United States and the USSR were subsequently asked to adhere by protocol.) Note also that the NPT, which is the core of a multi-faceted ''nonproliferation regime,'' involves a mixed cooperative and adversary relationship between the USSR and the United States on the one hand, and other countries wishing to protect their nuclear power or weapons options on the other.

8. Several arrangements (Antarctica Treaty, Outer Space Treaty, Helsinki accords) more or less explictly promulgate ''security regimes.'' What elements of strength or weakness have appeared that point to characteristics and conditions for successful regimes?

Contributors

COIT D. BLACKER

Coit Dennis Blacker is associate director of the Center for International Security and Arms Control and acting associate professor of political science at Stanford University. His fields of specialization include international security and arms control and Soviet foreign and military policies. He is the author of *Reluctant Warriors: The United States, the Soviet Union, and Arms Control* (1987), and numerous articles. In 1982, while on leave from Stanford, he served as special assistant for national security issues to Senator Gary Hart (D.-Colo). He is a member of the Council on Foreign Relations.

BARRY M. BLECHMAN

Barry M. Blechman is the founder and, since 1984, president of Defense Forecasts, Inc.—a research and analysis enterprise in Washington, D.C. During the Carter Administration he served as assistant director of the Arms Control and Disarmament Agency. He has taught at the Johns Hopkins University, Georgetown University, and the University of Michigan, and is currently a fellow at both the Center for Strategic and International Studies and the Foreign Policy Institute at the Johns Hopkins University. His publications include *Force Without War, International Security Yearbook, Rethinking the U.S. Strategic Posture, A Guide to Far Eastern Navies,* and *Preventing Nuclear War.* Dr. Blechman received a Ph.D. degree in international relations from Georgetown University in 1971.

ROBERT W. BUCHHEIM

Robert Buchheim received a Ph.D. in electrical engineering from Yale University in 1953. He served as chairman of the Inter-agency Working Group at the U.S.–USSR TTBT negotiations in 1974; chairman of the Inter-agency Working Group and delegation manager at the U.S.–USSR PNET negotiations in 1974–1976; U.S. commissioner with ambassadorial rank on the U.S.–USSR Standing Consultative Commission, 1976–1981; and head of the U.S. delegation to the U.S.–USSR ASAT negotiations, 1978–1981.

ALEXANDER DALLIN

Alexander Dallin, Spruance Professor of International History, is director of the Center for Russian and East European Studies at Stanford University. He currently serves as president of the International Committee for Soviet and East European Studies. He is the author of a number of books and articles on Soviet affairs and Soviet-American relations, including *Black Box: KAL 007 and the Superpowers* (1985); ''Reagan and the Russians'' (with Gail W. Lapidus), in Oye, et al., eds., *Eagle Defiant* (1983, rev. ed., 1987); and ''Some Lessons of the Past,'' in Garrison and Gleason, eds., *Shared Destiny; 50 Years of Soviet-American Relations* (1985).

JONATHAN DEAN

Jonathan Dean was deputy U.S. negotiator for the 1971 quadripartite agreement on Berlin. Between 1973 and 1981, he was deputy U.S. representative and then U.S. representative to NATO-Warsaw Pact force reduction negotiations in Vienna, a post that carried the rank of ambassador. After leaving the Foreign Service in 1984, Ambassador Dean became Arms Control Advisor of the Union of Concerned Scientists. He is the author of *Watershed in Europe* (1987) on the future of the NATO-Warsaw Pact military confrontation.

SIDNEY D. DRELL

Sidney D. Drell is Lewis M. Terman Professor, deputy director, and executive head of theoretical physics at the Stanford Linear Accelerator Center. He is also co-director of the Center for International Security and Arms Control at Stanford University. He has been intimately involved for over twenty years with technical issues of American military and arms control policies. He has served on the President's Science Advisory Committee and as a consultant to the National Security Council, the Arms Control and Disarmament Agency, and the Office of Technology Assessment. From 1978 to 1980 he headed studies on MX missile basing for the Pentagon. Dr. Drell is the author of numerous technical publications, and of *Facing the Threat of Nuclear Weapons*. Together with Philip Farley and David Holloway, he edited *The Reagan Strategic Defense Initiative: A Technical, Political and Arms Control Assessment*. A recipient of a MacArthur Foundation Award, he is well-known for his work on human rights in the Soviet Union.

GLORIA DUFFY

Gloria Duffy, a Soviet specialist, received her Ph.D. degree from Columbia University. She is president of Global Outlook, an organization in Palo Alto which does research and consulting on international security issues. She directed the Project on Compliance and the Future of Arms Control, a joint study of arms control compliance by Stanford University and Global Outlook. She was formerly with the RAND Corporation, assistant director of the Arms Control Association, and director of Ploughshares Fund.

PHILIP J. FARLEY

Philip J. Farley is a senior research associate at the Stanford Center for International Security and Arms Control. Beginning with military service in 1943, he was in government service for thirty-five years—in the Army Air Force, as an analyst in Air Force Intelligence after the war, in the U.S. Atomic Energy Commission, the Department of State, and the Arms Control and Disarmament Agency (ACDA). He dealt mainly with international security policy and programs, alliance relations, international science cooperation in military-related fields, and arms control. From 1969 to 1973 he was deputy director of ACDA, alternate chairman of the U.S. SALT I delegation with personal rank of ambassador, and chairman of the SALT Backstopping Committee.

JOHN LEWIS GADDIS

John Lewis Gaddis is Distinguished Professor of History at Ohio University, where he has taught since 1969. A graduate of the University of Texas at Austin, Professor Gaddis has also been Visiting Professor of Strategy at the United States Naval War College (1975–77) and Bicentennial Professor of American History at the University of Helsinki (1980–81). He is the author of *The United States and the Origins of the Cold War, 1941–1947* (1972), *Russia, the Soviet Union, and the United States* (1978), and *Strategies of Containment* (1982). He is at present working on an interpretive history of American foreign relations and a biography of George F. Kennan.

ALEXANDER L. GEORGE

Alexander George is Graham H. Stuart Professor of International Relations at Stanford University. He received a Ph.D. degree in political science from the University of Chicago. His first book, *Woodrow Wilson and Colonel House* (1956), written with his wife, Juliette L. George, is widely regarded as a classic study of the role of personality in politics. He is also the author of *Deterrence in Foreign Policy* (with Richard Smoke, 1974), which won the 1975 Bancroft Prize; *The Limits of Coercive Diplomacy* (with David K. Hall and William E. Simons, 1971); *Propaganda Analysis* (1959); *The Chinese Communist Army in Action* (1967); *Presidential Decisionmaking in Foreign Policy* (1980); *Force and Statecraft* (with Gordon A. Craig, 1983); and *Managing U.S.–Soviet Rivalry* (1983). He is currently a member of the National Academy of Sciences Committee on Contributions of Behavioral and Social Science to the Prevention of Nuclear War.

JAMES E. GOODBY

James Goodby graduated from Harvard College in 1951 and entered the Foreign Service in 1952. Subsequently he served in the U.S. Air Force and on the U.S. Atomic Energy Commission. In the Department of State he was a member of the staff of Special Assistant to the Secretary of State for Atomic Energy, and a member of the Policy Planning Council. In the U.S. Arms Control and Disarmament Agency he served as officer-in-charge of the nuclear test ban negotiations. In his European diplomatic assignments he was concerned with the nuclear nonproliferation treaty, U.S. relations with Euratom (the atomic energy component of the European Community), the Conference on Security and Cooperation in Europe (CSCE), and negotiations on Mutual and Balanced Force Reductions (MBFR). He subsequently served in the State Department as principal deputy director of the Bureau of Political-Military Affairs and as deputy assistant secretary of state for European Affairs. He was ambassador to Finland from 1980 to 1981. From 1981 to 1983 Ambassador Goodby served as vice chairman of the U.S. delegation to the strategic nuclear arms negotiations with the USSR. From 1983 through 1985, he was head of the U.S. delegation to the Conference on Confidence and Security Building Measures and Disarmament in Europe in Stockholm.

RICHARD N. HAASS

Richard Haass is lecturer in public policy at Harvard University's John F. Kennedy School of Government and senior research associate of Harvard University's Center for Science and International Affairs. He is also a consultant to the Department of State. Previously, Richard Haass was deputy (for policy) in the Bureau of European and Canadian Affairs and Special Cyprus Coordinator, Department of State; director of the Office of Regional Security Affairs in the Bureau of Political-Military Affairs, Department of State; special assistant to the deputy undersecretary (policy review), Department of Defense; and a legislative assistant in the U.S Senate. A Rhodes Scholar, Richard Haass holds a B.A. degree from Oberlin College and the Master of Philosophy and Doctor of Philosophy degrees from Oxford University. Dr. Haass is the author of *Congressional Power: Implications for American Security Policy* (1979), co-editor of *Superpower Arms Control: Setting the Record Straight* (1987), and numerous articles on U.S. foreign policy and national security issues.

DAVID K. HALL

David K. Hall is Forrest Sherman Professor of Public Diplomacy at the U.S. Naval War College, Newport, R.I., where he also serves as coordinator of the Policymaking and Implementation Program. He has served as a consultant to the Secretary of the Navy, the Chief of Naval Operations, and the National Security Council staff on national security organizational issues. Earlier he taught political science at Brown University and the U.S. Air Force Academy, and served as a consultant to the Brookings Institution and the RAND Corporation. Dr. Hall is the author of *The Past and Future of the NSC Staff, The DOD Reorganization Act of 1986,* and various articles on national security organization, and is co-author of *The Limits of Coercive Diplomacy.* He received his Ph.D. in political science from Stanford University.

SEAN M. LYNN-JONES

Sean M. Lynn-Jones is a Ph.D. candidate in the Department of Government at Harvard University. He is also managing editor of the journal *International Security* and a research fellow of the Avoiding Nuclear War Project at Harvard's Center for Science and International Affairs. His previous work on the 1972 Incidents at Sea Agreement has appeared in *International Security* (Spring 1985) and in John Borawski, ed., *Avoiding War in the Nuclear Age: Confidence-Building Measures for Crisis Stability* (1986). In addition to his dissertation research, he is the author of a chapter on the so-called "lulling effect" of arms control agreements in Albert Carnesale and Richard N. Haass (eds.), *Superpower Arms Control: Setting the Record Straight* (1987).

JOHN J. MARESCA

John Maresca is a career Foreign Service officer. After serving as a visiting fellow at Georgetown University's Institute for the Study of Diplomacy he was appointed Deputy Assistant Secretary of Defense for European and NATO Policy in August 1986. A graduate of Yale, he spent six years as a naval officer before joining the Foreign Service. Since then he has concentrated on European, political-military, and East-West issues. He has been deputy director of the staffs of two Secretaries General of NATO, deputy chief of the U.S. delegation to the Conference on Security and Cooperation in Europe (CSCE), director of West European Affairs in the State Department, and minister and deputy chief of mission at the U.S. embassy in Paris. Maresca is the author of *To Helsinki: The Conference on Security and Cooperation in Europe, 1973–75* (1985).

ALAN NEIDLE

Alan Neidle served in the U.S. Department of State and the Arms Control and Disarmament Agency from 1957 to 1981. He participated in negotiations on preventing militarization of Antarctica, the partial test ban treaty of 1963, the nonproliferation of nuclear weapons, and the ban on biological weapons. In 1977–1978 he was a U.S. representative to the U.S.–U.K.–USSR negotiations in Geneva on a comprehensive nuclear test ban. Neidle was visiting Tom Slick Professor of World Peace at the Lyndon B. Johnson School of Public Affairs of the University of Texas in 1981–82. In addition to writing numerous articles on arms control and international security, he is the author of a forthcoming book of political satire tentatively titled "Fables For The Nuclear Age." Neidle graduated from Yale in 1950 and received an LL.B. from the University of Michigan in 1956.

JANNE E. NOLAN

Janne Nolan has extensive government and academic expertise in national security affairs. She served as an official in the U.S. Arms Control and Disarmament Agency during the Carter Administration and was a delegate to the U.S.–USSR negotiations on the limitation of conventional armaments. She has previously been affiliated with the Stanford University Center for International Security and Arms Control, the Georgetown Center for Strategic and International Studies, and Harvard University; and has also worked as a consultant to the Defense Department and as national security adviser to Senator Gary Hart. She is currently a guest scholar at the Brookings Institution. Dr. Nolan holds a Ph.D. degree from the Fletcher School of Law and Diplomacy and has published articles on arms control and defense policy in publications such as *Foreign Affairs* and *Foreign Policy*. She is the author of *Defense Industries in Taiwan and South Korea* (1986).

JOSEPH S. NYE, JR.

Joseph S. Nye, Jr., is the director of the Center for Science and International Affairs at the John F. Kennedy School of Government and Ford Foundation Professor of International Security at Harvard University. A graduate of Princeton University, he studied at Oxford University on a Rhodes scholarship and received a Ph.D. degree in political science from Harvard University. In 1977–79 he served as deputy to the under secretary of state for security assistance, science and technology, and chaired the National Security Council Group on Non-Proliferation of Nuclear Weapons. He served on the Commission on International Relations of the National Academy of Sciences and on advisory committees for the Department of State and the Department of Energy. The author of many articles in professional journals, his most recent books are *Living with Nuclear Weapons* (co-authored, 1983); *The Making of America's Soviet Policy* (1984); *Hawks,*

Doves and Owls: An Agenda for Avoiding Nuclear War (co-edited, 1985); and *Nuclear Ethics* (1986).

CONDOLEEZZA RICE

Condoleezza Rice is associate professor of political science and member of the Center for International Security and Arms Control at Stanford University. She received a Ph.D. from the Graduate School of International Studies, University of Denver, and has been a National Fellow at the Hoover Institution. As a Council on Foreign Relations International Affairs Fellow she served in 1986–87 with the Joint Chiefs of Staff. A specialist on Soviet foreign and defense policy and comparative military organization, Dr. Rice is the author of *The Soviet Union and the Czechoslovak Army 1948–83: Uncertain Allegiance* (1984), and numerous articles.

HAROLD H. SAUNDERS

Harold H. Saunders, currently a fellow at the Brookings Institution, participated in the mediation of five Arab-Israeli agreements during 1973–1979. He served on the National Security Council staff, 1961–1974. In the State Department from 1974 to 1981, he served as deputy assistant secretary of state, director of intelligence and research, and assistant secretary for Near Eastern and South Asian affairs, 1978–1981. Since then, he has served as chairman of the American team for the Dartmouth Conference Task Force on Regional Conflicts. His publications include: *The Middle East Problem in the 1980's* (1982); *The Other Walls: The Politics of the Arab-Israeli Peace Process* (1985); and *American Hostages in Iran* (co-author, 1985). He received a Ph.D. in American studies from Yale in 1956.

DAVID SCHOENBAUM

David Schoenbaum is professor of history at the University of Iowa. He studied at the universities of Wisconsin, Bonn and Oxford (St. Antony's College), and has also taught at Kent State University, the University of Freiburg, and the U.S. Naval War College. He is the author of *Hitler's Social Revolution* (1966), *The Spiegel Affair* (1968), and *Zabern 1913* (1982), as well as numerous articles. Among his current projects is a study of American policy on Germany between 1945 and 1949. He serves on the academic advisory board of the American Institute for Contemporary German Studies.

DEBORAH SHAPLEY

Deborah Shapley is a writer on science, foreign affairs, and defense topics. Her book, *The Seventh Continent: Antarctica in a Resource Age,* was published in 1986. Her research and writing on Antarctica were supported by the Carnegie Endowment for International Peace and the Ford Foundation. Her other books are *Lost at the Frontier,* co-authored with Rustum Ray (1985), and a biography of Robert S. McNamara, forthcoming. In addition, she is the author of numerous articles published in the *Technology Review, Science Magazine, Bulletin of the Atomic Scientists,* and other journals, and she has served as Washington editor of the British journal, *Nature.* She received a B.A. from Radcliffe College.

KURT STEINER

Kurt Steiner is professor of political science (Emeritus) at Stanford University. He received the degree of Doctor of Jurisprudence from the University of Vienna and emigrated to the United States in 1938. At the end of World War II he served in Japan and, later, was appointed prosecuting attorney in the war crimes trials before the International Military Tribunal for the Far East. He is the author of *Local Government in Japan* (1965) and *Politics in Austria* (1972), co-editor and co-author of *Modern Austria* and *Political Opposition and Local Politics in Japan* (both 1981), and of *Tradition and Innovation in Contemporary Austria* (1982). He also has published articles on Japanese politics and law in various professional journals.

STEVEN WEBER

Steven Weber is a Ph.D. candidate in the Department of Political Science at Stanford University. He received a B.A. in history from Washington University, and an M.A. in political science from Stanford University. The title of his Ph.D. dissertation is "Cooperation and Discord in Security Relationships: Towards a Theory of U.S.–Soviet Arms Control." He holds a National Graduate Fellowship in Political Science from the U.S. Department of Education, and is currently an Arms Control Fellow at the Center for International Security and Arms Control at Stanford.

INDEX

Anti-satellite weapons (*continued*)
American, 357, 362–64
risk assessment, 684–85
Soviet, 363
Soviet moratorium on, 415–16
APNW. *See* Agreement on the Prevention of Nuclear War
Arab-Israeli conflict, 584, 589–90
and U.S.–Soviet competition, 546–50, 552–54, 574–80
Arab-Israeli peace process, 565, 570
Arab-Israeli settlement
and U.S.–Soviet dialog, 554–56, 558–59, 573
Arab-Israeli War (1967), 547, 550–51
Arab-Israeli War (1973), 562–63
Arab summit (1964), 548
Arab summit (1974), 566
Arms control, 146
compliance, 270–71, 276. *See also* Compliance crisis
and internal U.S. politics, 277–79
and self-interest, 288–89
and Soviet policies, 279–81
and unilateral measures, 270, 290
verifiability of, 276, 282, 287
and détente, 630
negotiations, 629–37
risk management, 688–91
risks of, 683–90. *See also* Cooperation, risks of
theories of, 387
violations of
Soviet, 277–81
U.S., 281
Arms control agreements, 715
Arms Control and Disarmament Act (1961), 638
Arms Control and Disarmament Agency, 388
Arms control process, decline of, 285–87
Arms sales, 510–12
Arms transfer restraint. *See* Conventional Arms Transfer Talks
ASAT. *See* Anti-satellite weapons
ASBM. *See* Air-to-surface ballistic missiles
ASW. *See* Warfare, antisubmarine
Asymmetries, U.S.–Soviet, 661
in military doctrines, 661–63
ATC. *See* Austrian Treaty Commission
Atlantic Charter (1941), 27, 29
Atomic Energy Act, 339
Atoms for Peace, 336, 338, 620, 630
Attlee, Clement R., 21
Attribution theory, 659
Austria
and security risks, 681
and Soviet security interests, 51, 56
and U.S. security interests, 50–53
Austrian Treaty Commission, 50
Axelrod, Robert, 7–10, 12, 704

Ballistic missile defense. *See* Space-based ballistic missile defense
Bargaining chips strategy, 297, 665, 770–702, 708
Baruch Plan, 221, 629
Basic Law of the German Federal Republic, 89, 100
Basic Principles Agreement, 217, 220, 223, 304, 567, 588–90, 610, 668–70, 713
Basic Principles of Relations. *See* Basic Principles Agreement
Begin, Menachem, 569
Belgrade meeting, 111, 117, 118
Berlin
access by Allies, 85–104
access by civilians, 85–104
as the capital of GDR, 88
and Federal German role, 92, 98
occupation sectors, 85
and security risks, 681
as West Berlin, 88
Berlin Air Corridor Agreement, 469
Berlin airlift, 87
Berlin Air Safety Center, 85, 88
Berlin Air Space Center, 469
Berlin blockade (1948), 87
Berlin Conference (1954), 58–61
Berlin crisis (1948), 583
Berlin regime, 83–98
collapse of (1948), 86–87
crisis of, 90–96
Germanization of, 88–90, 92
post-blockade, 88–90
quadripartite negotiations, 96–98
Western draft agreement, 97–98
Berlin status. *See* Berlin regime
Berlin Wall, 91–92
Biological Weapons Convention (1972), 271, 276, 628
Black September, 554, 557
Blechman, Barry, 517
BMD. *See* Space-based ballistic missile defense
Boun Oum, 437, 452
Boun Oum-Phoumi regime, 438–41, 444–45, 449
BPA. *See* Basic Principles Agreement
Brezhnev, Leonid, 108–9, 125, 154, 527, 589
Brezhnev Doctrine, 116
Brezhnev-Ford summit (1974), 566
Brown, Harold, 518–19
Brzezinski, Zbigniew, 518–19, 532–33, 674
Buchsbaum Panel, 399
Budapest Appeal, 157
Bundeswehr, 41
Buzzing. *See* Close air surveillance
BW. *See* Weapons, biological
Byrd, Richard E., 311
Byrnes, James F., 23, 28, 37